International Business Transactions

International Business Transactions

Text, Cases, and Materials

SECOND EDITION

Prof. Dr. Frank Emmert, LL.M., FCIArb

JOHN S. GRIMES PROFESSOR OF LAW AND
EXECUTIVE DIRECTOR OF THE
CENTER FOR INTERNATIONAL AND COMPARATIVE LAW
AT INDIANA UNIVERSITY
ROBERT H. McKINNEY SCHOOL OF LAW
FELLOW OF THE CHARTERED INSTITUTE OF ARBITRATORS

CAROLINA ACADEMIC PRESS
Durham, North Carolina

ISBN   978-1-5310-0567-2
e-ISBN   978-1-5310-0568-9
LCCN   2020942174

Carolina Academic Press
700 Kent Street
Durham, NC 27701
Telephone (919) 489-7486
Fax (919) 493-5668
www.caplaw.com

Printed in the United States of America

Contents

Preface and Acknowledgments

This book is the culmination of several years of work and incorporates more than 25 years of experience in teaching, consulting and arbitration. To justify the expenditure of time and resources, and the trees that will die for this book, I have made great efforts at distinguishing the work from those already on the market. Every part of the book is written from the perspective of a practitioner and for the benefit of future practitioners. As a lawyer, in-house counsel, consultant or arbitrator, you don't need theories and you don't need to know about every case that discussed a particular theory or solution or even the latest case to do so. What you need are hands-on tools, model contracts with explanations, checklists, and practical tips, for example how to find high quality yet affordable legal counsel in a foreign country. To this end, in addition to instructive cases, the book includes 26 charts, 15 checklists, and 15 model contracts and other documents, all with step-by-step explanations. Most of this material is my own and not available anywhere else. Even the index at the end is conceived as a glossary, essentially a mini-dictionary of international business law, finance, shipping and insurance terms, and almost 100 pages long.

The Text, Cases and Materials are accompanied by two volumes of documents. Volume I on Transactional Documents covers Parts One to Five and contains the most important international conventions, treaties, codes, and some national statutes like the UCC, for contracts of sale, payment and financing contracts, shipping contracts, and insurance contracts (ISBN 978-1-950137-99-2, ca. 810 pp.).Volume II on Dispute Settlement Documents covers Part Six with the most important documents on transnational litigation, as well as international commercial mediation and arbitration (ISBN 978-1-950137-01-5, ca. 570 pp.). As a package, the books are intended for advanced JD and LL.M. students but equally for younger practitioners, to be kept close at hand for frequent consultation. As your tools of trade, they will become better and more valuable with use and age.

Naturally, a project like this is not a one-person achievement. I am greatly indebted to my own teachers and mentors, in particular Professors Bruno Simma, Joseph Weiler, Eric Stein, John Jackson, Ingeborg Schwenzer, Frank Vischer, Talia Einhorn, George Bermann and Mohamed Abd El Wahab, who have influenced my thinking in more ways than I can count. I hope the book will live up to their expectations and look forward to their comments and critique. At the Indiana University Robert H. McKinney School of Law, I have enjoyed tremendous institutional support and want to thank, in particular, Deans Andy Klein and Karen Bravo, as well as my colleagues Frank Sullivan, Jim Nehf, Max Huffman, Cynthia Adams and

Xuan-Thao Nguyen, who have helped and inspired me in many ways. My faculty assistants Brooke Merry, Judy Ann Kirkpatrick and Katherine Lundblade deserve much more than just this expression of my gratitude for their support.

At Carolina Academic Press, I was met with enthusiastic support—and endless patience—from a fantastic team of editors, production professionals and designers. Special thanks go to Ryland Bowman, Elisabeth ("Biz") Ebben, and Jennifer Hill. Without their hard work, there would be no book and certainly none on this level of quality.

Most importantly, however, I want to thank generations of my students in the U.S., in Europe, the Middle East, Asia and other parts of the world, who have endured early drafts of the chapters in this book, less complete and less sophisticated charts and checklists, and overall more chaos in the text, cases and materials, and helped me with their comments and questions through one round of improvements after another. By now, I believe that the book is good but I am also counting on future generations of students to help me make it even better. Several former students who are now colleagues and professionals in their own right deserve special mention and thanks: Menachem Kaplan, Heather Grimstad, Kari Morrigan, Aakshita Bansal, Andraea Reed, David Wemhoff, Delainey Burnett and Se Young Jung have all done valuable research that went into the book.

Finally, I want to thank my family for their never ending support and encouragement. This book is dedicated to you.

FE

International Business Transactions

Part One

The General Framework for International Business Transactions

Section 1. Definition of IBT and Scope of the Book

The goal of this book is to enable advanced students of the law, as well as younger practitioners, to understand the specific legal issues related to international business transactions (IBTs) and to provide qualified guidance and advice to large and small enterprises engaged in such transactions, both at the stage of planning a transaction and drafting the relevant contracts, and/or at the stage of subsequently enforcing them. By contrast to more traditional works, the approach taken here is distinctly practice-oriented. I will neither try to cover every case that has ever been decided in this subject area, nor will I discuss every theory that has been advanced to explain the particular problems related to international business transactions. Instead, I provide model contracts and checklists for every step in the implementation of the most common IBTs. These models will be explained in detail to enable readers to adapt and apply them to a great variety of client issues that may be brought before them. In this way, I want to instill the knowledge and with it the confidence it takes to provide qualified advice in the planning stages, to prepare or review all of the relevant documents, and, if necessary, to take charge of the settlement of any disputes and the enforcement of any claims in the international arena. Since virtually all business has become international, I believe that this skill set is indispensable for any lawyer in the twenty-first century who by choice or default will be involved with business of any size or type.

Section 1 of this Introduction is an overview of what the reader can expect in the different parts of the book. It provides the setting of the modern IBT—a transaction between parties in different countries who often don't know each other and never actually meet in person—and the specific challenges this creates for lawyers. Section 2 provides a brief discussion of the economics of international trade, i.e., why so much business has become international and why countries shutting themselves off from international business and trade pay a high price for doing so. However, we must also acknowledge that international trade is not always a force for good and needs to be harnessed to provide the greatest possible benefits for the largest possible number of people. Otherwise, anticompetitive practices, selective protectionism, a race to the bottom for the lowest level of labor and environmental

3

protection, international tax evasion, and other abusive business and trade strategies can do great harm. Sections 3 and 4 continue by introducing the different legal regimes that affect IBTs, including the question what is international law and why and how it matters.

Section 5 concludes with a very brief but important exploration of how lawyers should analyze a case in an exam and in practice. Although this should be something taught in the first year of law school, I meet many lawyers in advanced law classes and even in private practice struggling with this issue. Thus, I decided to dedicate Section 5 of this Part to the problem.

The Landscape of International Trade

From 1960 to 2018, the share of international trade in goods as a percentage of U.S. GDP has more than tripled and stands at around 28% today (Worldbank). In other words, 28 cents of every dollar earned in the U.S. is earned via IBTs. This share is even higher for many other countries. And these numbers have been rising and continue to rise. Global trade in goods and services more than tripled from 2000 to 2018 (WTO) and today exceeds 25 trillion USD per annum. Just for trade in goods, some 2.5 billion tons of sea cargo arrive in the U.S. every year, in addition to some four million tons of air cargo. Around 12 million containers enter and exit the U.S. per year, equivalent to about 70,000 containers every day. On the global scale, almost one million containers cross an international border every day. Fewer in number but greater in volume are so-called bulk shipments in specialized vessels, such as crude oil, liquefied natural gas, iron ore, grain, coffee, orange juice concentrate, etc. By comparison, so-called break bulk freight on pallets and in nonstandard sizes and units contributes only a relatively minor share to modern trade but often requires sui generis contracts and arrangements.

This gigantic business is by no means the prerogative of large multinational corporations. When I began advising enterprises regarding IBTs, the typical customer was a Fortune 500 company. Just 25 years later, the typical company seeking help with IBTs has fewer than 50 employees and a turnover of just a few million U.S. dollars. In 2018, some 300,000 companies exported from the U.S. more than 290,000 of them were small and medium-sized enterprises (SMEs) with less than 500 employees. This was a 30% increase over 2005. The total value of exports in 2018 was more than US$2.5 trillion (Department of Commerce).

Whether in the U.S. or around the world, every international business transaction, and every shipment of goods and transfer of services is subject to several contracts, every one of which should be drafted with an eye on the law. In fact, much grief could be avoided and much money could be saved if more of these contracts would be negotiated, drafted, and enforced, if necessary, by better qualified lawyers.

An international business transaction (IBT) is usually a commercial contract entered into between two or more private parties who have their principal place of business *in different nation-states or countries*. The most common of these IBTs is a *sales* transaction where a seller in one country enters into a sales contract with a buyer in another country. Even if seller and buyer are in the same country, an international dimension is brought in if the contract concerns goods or services to be imported from or exported to another country. The legal issues raised by international sales agreements and their implementation are the main focus of our book. Although our examples are mostly taken from contracts for the sale of goods, *sales* should be broadly interpreted and the explanations and examples given in this book can be adapted to a great variety of individual transactions, including services and even software or other IP licensing agreements. By contrast, if a transaction is more than a one-off sales transaction and involves the establishment of a commercial presence in another country, the necessary contracts go beyond the scope of the present text and require additional skills and expertise.

Part One provides a general overview of the history of and driving forces behind international commerce, the legal framework for IBTs, the scope and sources of international law relevant for IBTs; the impact of the WTO and other international trade laws; regional integration systems like the European Union, NAFTA, ASEAN and Mercosur, and their impact on trade and commerce; the impact of national law on international business transactions, conflicts of (national) laws and their resolution via private international law; as well as additional sources of law, in particular model codes and other optional rules.

Part Two covers in detail the contracts for an international sale of goods as the most common and most basic form of IBT, starting with an overview of the so-called *documentary sale*, continuing with some important pre-contractual documents and a model contract of sale, and then dealing in a comparative manner with the most commonly used international sales laws, in particular the UN Convention on Contracts for the International Sale of Goods (CISG), the UNIDROIT Principles of International Commercial Contracts (PICC), and the European Common Frame of Reference (CFR), as representations of the continental European legal tradition, as well as the Uniform Commercial Code (UCC) of the United States.

Part Three explains the most important contracts for *financing* of international trade, i.e., the various forms of documentary credit. Letters of Credit (L/Cs) are analyzed in detail, including typical problems that occur in practice when L/Cs are the intended form of payment. We also deal with documentary credit as security where it is not intended to be the primary form of payment, i.e., with standby letters of credit, and bank guarantees, as well as common payment arrangements like documentary collection.

Part Four is dedicated to the next step in the implementation of an international sale, the *shipping* contract for the carriage of the goods from seller to buyer. We analyze the International Chamber of Commerce (ICC) Rules for the Use of Domestic and International Trade Terms (INCOTERMS 2020®) as an easy way of determining the distribution of risk and responsibility in international shipping, i.e., who has to organize and pay for shipping and insurance and where does the risk of loss or deterioration of the goods pass from the seller to the buyer. Subsequently, we look at the Bill of Lading (BoL) as the standard shipping contract for maritime transport, as well as a variety of other waybills for other modes of transport.

Part Five deals with the *insurance* contract, the fourth and last of the contracts typically included in a documentary sale. We continue to focus on maritime transport since it accounts for about 90% of international transport. We learn the difference between hull insurance and cargo insurance and analyze the typical terms of a cargo insurance policy.

Finally, **Part Six** focuses on the enforcement of IBT contracts, both via *international litigation* and/or via *international commercial arbitration*. Since rights are largely meaningless unless they can be enforced, if necessary, this part is quite extensive and strongly recommended for anyone practicing or wanting to practice in the area of IBT.

In addition to a **List of Cases** and **Index**, there is also a **Glossary** at the end of the book with short definitions and explanations of key concepts.

Finally, reference should be made to the **Documents Collection** that accompanies this Textbook/Casebook. It has all important international conventions, agreements, model laws, and rules, and some of the most frequently used national laws, for the IBT lawyer.

───────────

When Marco Polo traveled from the Venetian Republic to China in the thirteenth century to bring silk, gunpowder, porcelain, and tea to Europe, or when Portuguese and Arab traders were looking for gold, slaves, and other treasures around the coasts of Africa, IBTs were done rather differently from today. First, the traders usually had to undertake the perilous journeys themselves, with a trip to India or China easily taking a year or two, even if the winds were favorable. Second, they had to take with them the gold or other currency, or the goods they wanted to barter, which attracted not only customs and tax collectors along the way, but all sorts of pirates, thieves, and robbers. Third, once at their destination, the traders had little or no way of knowing whether the goods they were about to buy would survive the voyage home, or even whether the purchase price was competitive enough to make a good profit back home.

In many ways, international business in those days was hopelessly inefficient and ludicrously dangerous. A single storm could mean the difference between riches and ruins for an entire trading family or town. Unsurprisingly, the York Antwerp Rules, one of the foundations of maritime insurance, even in their 2004 edition, speak of such voyages as "maritime adventures." The only reasons why traders were willing to face such perils were the general sense of adventure and discovery and the huge profits that could be made by someone who had, at least for a while, a monopoly over a certain imported good.

By contrast, international business is done very differently today. Anybody with internet access and a credit card can go on Alibaba.com and, within minutes, compare the prices of dozens of potential suppliers in China with wholesalers or retailers in the local market and place an order for a designer handbag or for 100,000 of them. Shipment can be arranged by boat or by air and payment will be made electronically. The goods will arrive within two weeks—or a mere two days if the buyer is willing to pay extra—and can be returned for a full refund if need be. Most important, neither seller nor buyer ever have to leave their home or business, let alone travel abroad to meet.[1]

However, even though more than 90% of all IBTs today are initiated and implemented smoothly and without a glitch, not all of the adventure has been taken out of international sales agreements. Many things can and do still go wrong in such transactions:

- multiple communications, purchase orders, general and specific terms, and pro forma invoices may be exchanged, making it potentially difficult to pin down *when* the contract was concluded and *which terms* made it into the final version;

- seller and buyer may have contributed different terms to the contract that turn out to be ambiguous or even contradictory;

- although the buyer paid, the seller never ships;

- by mistake or negligence, the seller ships a different product or a product of different quality;

- although the seller ships as promised, the goods are lost or damaged on the way;

- although the seller ships as promised, the buyer does not accept the merchandise, with or without reason;

- although the buyer initially accepted the goods, she now refuses to pay, claiming, for example, that the quantity or quality was not as agreed or some other defect of the merchandise;

- by the time the goods arrive, the buyer has fallen into insolvency and the seller never gets paid.

These are just some examples of what can go wrong in international sales and we know all these issues and more from Contracts 101. However, by contrast to

---

1. For a practical example, see Pietra Rivoli, *The Travels of a T-Shirt in the Global Economy—An Economist Examines the Markets, Power, and Politics of World Trade,* John Wiley & Sons 2005.

See also William Bernstein: *A Splendid Exchange: How Trade Shaped the World,* Grove Atlantic 2008; Robert Feenstra: *Advanced International Trade—Theory and Evidence,* Princeton 2004; Elhanan Helpman: *Understanding Global Trade,* Harvard Univ. Press 2011; Kenneth Pomeranz & Steven Topik: *The World that Trade Created—Society, Culture, and the World Economy 1400 to the Present,* Routledge 2nd ed. 2005.

comparable domestic or national business transactions, IBTs raise several additional questions, for example:

- Since seller and buyer never meet, how can they trust each other? How can they even be sure of each other's identity, ability, and solvency? More specifically:
- Since the parties speak different languages and come from different business cultures and legal systems, they may say the same thing in their contract but have very different understandings of the terms.
- How should the seller know whether the buyer is willing and able to pay once the goods are on their way?
- How can a buyer be sure of the quality of the goods before making payment? How does she know whether the promised goods and quantities have indeed been shipped?
- Which contract law should govern the transaction and any remedies for an injured party: seller's law or buyer's law or even a (neutral) third party/country law?
- Even if an injured party has the law on her side, where should a claim be brought to court and how do we know whether a foreign court will be impartial?
- Even if an injured party has obtained a favorable judgment or award, how and where can this be enforced against a foreign party?

These issues will be the focus of Part Two on the international contract of sale, Part Three on payment and financing of international business transactions, Part Four on shipping, Part Five on insurance, and Part Six on dispute settlement. Understanding all of these elements will be required whether a lawyer is shepherding a one-off export-import transaction to its successful completion, is helping with the initial setup or the restructuring of a global supply chain, or is supporting her client in a more substantial and lasting investment abroad.

Section 2. The History and Motors of International Commerce

While many histories of world trade tend to start out somewhere in the fifteenth century,[2] the history of trade actually goes back as far as the earliest human settlements. Due to differences in climate, soil, flora, and fauna, and other natural factors and resources, each localized group of humans typically had or was able to produce

---

2. The key event being the discovery of open ocean navigation by the Portuguese, and therefore the birth of systematic long-distance maritime trade; see, for example, Peter Hugill, *World Trade Since 1431: Geography, Technology, and Capitalism*, Johns Hopkins Univ. Press 1993; John McCusker (ed.), *History of World Trade Since 1450*, Macmillan 2005; Kenneth Pomeranz & Steven Topik, *The World That Trade Created—Society, Culture, and the World Economy 1400 to the Present*, Routledge 1999; for a more comprehensive approach, starting around 3,000 B.C., see William Bernstein, *A Splendid Exchange—How Trade Shaped the World*, Grove Atlantic 2008.

only certain types of food, clothing, tools, etc. By barter trading with other groups who had other resources and goods, each group could overcome, at least to an extent, its own limitations of resources and hence increase its wealth as expressed in chance of survival and quality of life.[3]

This image of early human societies already introduces the first two of the three most important motors of international commerce: absolute advantage/disadvantage and relative advantage/disadvantage. We may speak of an absolute advantage and disadvantage if a society or country has plenty of a given resource or good, while another society or country has none of it at all. For example, Saudi Arabia has a lot more oil than it can consume on its own in a very long time frame, while Germany has virtually no oil at all. Therefore, if Germany needs petroleum for transportation or production or any other purposes, it has to import. Conversely, if Saudi Arabia wants to make use of its abundance, it has to export. Bringing the two together in a trade relationship should benefit both of them.

By contrast, we may speak of a relative advantage or disadvantage if a society or country is able to produce a certain good but only at great cost and effort, while another society or country with different resources or skills can do it much more easily and cheaply. For example, it is certainly possible to grow bananas in Canada or Scandinavia, provided one is willing to grow them in a greenhouse with lots of heating energy—and indeed Iceland is doing exactly this because it has inexpensive geothermal energy in the form of volcanic hot springs—but it probably makes more sense to import the bananas from Central America or Africa, where they basically grow on their own. Thus, we may say that the Nordic countries have a relative disadvantage in producing tropical fruit, while the tropical countries have a relative advantage. Again, bringing the two together in a trade relationship should benefit both of them.

Advantages and disadvantages are not only based on climatic factors and natural resources, but can also be developed or squandered in the form of *skills* by human effort or the lack of it, as some individuals or groups become better at making certain things than other individuals or groups. For example, the Swiss have a relative advantage at selling expensive watches around the world after they have spent centuries developing their watchmaking skills, as well as a reputation for uncompromising quality.

Absolute and relative advantages and disadvantages work nicely to fuel international business and trade, as long as each society can figure out a few things it is good at making, so that it can export some goods and services, and then use the export revenue to import those goods and services the society is not so good at making. To the extent advantages are lasting, they can provide the revenue for sustainable trade relationships. To the extent advantages are more fleeting, a society has to constantly

---

3. For an analysis of the economies of primitive societies, see Marshall Sahlins, *Stone Age Economics*, Routledge 1974. The idea that wealth should be measured by the access to a great many goods and services by average citizens was formulated by Adam Smith in his book *An Inquiry into the Nature and Causes of the Wealth of Nations* in 1776.

reinvent itself to find something else it is good at making if an earlier advantage is no longer valid. To give an example, Colombia has excellent climatic conditions and many years of experience in growing high-quality coffee. Potentially, the country should be able to count on sustainable export revenue from this important commodity. However, political instability or the plant disease leaf rust could put at risk what essentially looked like a safe bet without an end date. Unfortunately, countries and societies rarely prepare for the fading away of their advantages while times are still good and resources flush. By the time change has become imminent, resources may already be scarce and adjustments correspondingly harder. Saudi Arabia may become a case on point when its oil riches run out.

Compared to absolute and relative advantages, the third motor of international commerce is a little harder to understand but quite probably even more important today. The concept of *comparative advantage and disadvantage* was first formulated by the British economist David Ricardo in 1817.[4] To illustrate the idea, we shall look at Country A and Country B and their respective production of cars and bicycles. We shall assume that both countries have to purchase the material and energy and other input factors on the international markets at the same prices. Therefore, the only production factor that will be different in the two countries is the cost of labor and we can disregard the rest:

	Country A	Country B
labor cost	US$20/hour	US$15/hour
productivity in bike manufacturing	12.5 hours/bike	20 hours/bike
productivity in car manufacturing	250 hours/car	500 hours/car
unit cost of bikes	US$250/bike	US$300/bike
unit cost of cars	US$5,000/car	US$7,500/car

Based on these numbers, it would seem that A and B cannot possibly have a profitable long-term trade relationship. Country A is better at making cars *and* bicycles, and both products are more expensive when made by Country B. While Country B would probably like to import cars and bicycles from Country A to get their lower prices, such a one-sided trade relationship is unsustainable since B will soon run out of money if it only imports and cannot export.

However, what Ricardo explained for the first time is that every individual, every company, and even a national economy, always has to work with limited resources.

4. See David Ricardo, *On the Principles of Political Economy and Taxation*, John Murray 1817. For an accessible introduction to the economics of international trade, see William Baumol & Alan Blinder, *Microeconomics: Principles and Policy*, Cengage Learning 13th ed. 2016, Chapter 21, or William Baumol & Alan Blinder, *Macroeconomics: Principles and Policy*, Cengage Learning 13th ed. 2015, Chapter 18; Alan Stockman, *Introduction to Microeconomics*, The Dryden Press/Harcourt Brace College Publishers 1995, Chapter 23. For more detailed analysis, see Paul Krugman, Maurice Obstfeld & Marc Melitz, *International Economics: Theory and Policy*, Pearson 11th ed. 2017.

Even if I am better than my secretary not only at teaching but also at typing, does that mean that I should do my own typing? Probably not, because my day has only 24 hours and I should focus on the higher value activity or, in other words, I should focus on what I am *comparatively* better at, versus what I am *comparatively* less good at. In our two-country two-product model, this can be shown as follows:

	Country A	Country B
available resources	US$10 mio for labor/day	US$10 mio for labor/day
primary need	1,000 cars/day	1,000 cars/day

We shall assume that each country has 10 mio $ available resources to pay for labor in the combined manufacture of cars and bicycles per day. We shall further assume that one of the products is more important to the country than the other, i.e., that the needs for the one product—the cars—have to be satisfied before any leftover resources can be dedicated to making the other product, the bikes. If each country has 10 mio $ available and needs 1,000 cars per day, the overall production looks like this:

Scenario 1: independent manufacturing without specialization and/or trade		
	Country A	Country B
cost of 1,000 cars	US$5 mio	US$7.5 mio
available resources for bikes	US$5 mio	US$2.5 mio
total output	1,000 cars 20,000 bikes	1,000 cars 8,333 bikes

In Scenario 1, each country satisfies its own needs and there is no trade in cars or bicycles between the two. We can see a total output—both countries combined— of 2,000 cars and 28,333 bicycles.

Next, we will assume that the two countries combine their resources and that each specializes on one product, some of which it trades with the other country in exchange for the other product:

Scenario 2: international cooperation with specialization and trade: A makes cars and B makes bicycles, joint resources US$20 mio		
	Country A	Country B
resources needed to make 2,000 cars	US$10 mio	
funds available for bikes		US$10 mio
output	2,000 cars	33,333 bikes
surplus/deficit		+ 5,000 bikes

Scenario 2 shows very nicely an unchanged total output of 2,000 cars, to satisfy the primary needs of both countries. However, with the same amount of total resources we can now produce 33,333 bikes, which translates into a net gain of 5,000 bicycles per day or whatever unit of time we apply. The reader should appreciate that these additional 5,000 bicycles are solely the result of specialization and trade and essentially free. If the trade relationship can be implemented in this way, both countries can share the surplus 5,000 bicycles and both countries will be more wealthy as a result.[5]

Of course, the transition from the first scenario to the second scenario is not free, since the car industry has to shut down in B and it is unlikely that all workers who used to make cars in B can now find equally good employment in the expanding bicycle industry in B, and vice versa in A. However, the transition is a one-time event, while the added surplus occurs every day and potentially forever. Thus, some of the early surplus could be used to support relocation, retraining, or early retirement of the workers who lose their jobs in the transition. Whether this is happening, or whether the surplus will largely be pocketed by the shareholders of the expanding industries, is a question of social and tax policies in the respective countries.

Furthermore, the surplus of 5,000 bicycles per day will be diminished not only during a limited transition period, but continuously by the costs involved with the trading transactions themselves. International transport costs will have to come out of the 5,000 bicycles because they did not occur when all production was domestic. Similarly, customs duties and the cost imposed by non-tariff barriers, such as different product standards or bureaucratic red tape, will also reduce the benefits to be shared between the different participating countries. By contrast to the *transition costs*, these *transaction costs* occur on a continuing basis and with each transaction. If we want to maximize the gains from an open and globalized economy, it is imperative that we minimize the transaction costs and prevent them from eating up the bulk of the 5,000 bicycles. Readers should consider different options for customs and trade laws aimed at keeping the transaction costs under control without compromising product safety, environmental standards, and other bona fide interests of society. In Part Four, we will dedicate some of the discussion to the inefficiency of transport through the middle of the twentieth century and the efficiency revolution in transport since then.

---

5. The model with just two countries and two products is highly simplified, of course. However, if we used 200 countries and tens of thousands of products and services that can be traded, the model would become more complicated but not substantially different. For further reading, see, for example, Paul Krugman, Maurice Obstfeld & Marc Melitz, *International Economics: Theory and Practice*, Pearson 11th ed. 2018, in particular Chapter 3. Readers who are not afraid of numbers and mathematical equations are invited to read up on the Heckscher-Ohlin theory of trade, New Trade Theory, as well as the Ricardo-Sraffa Trade Theory.

Just for fun, we shall also look at what would happen if the two countries would specialize "the other way around," i.e., if B would end up making the cars and A would be making the bicycles:

Scenario 3: B makes cars and A makes bicycles, joint resources US$20 mio		
	Country A	Country B
resources needed to make 2,000 cars		US$15 mio
funds available for bikes	US$5 mio	
output	20,000 bikes	2,000 cars
surplus / deficit	− 8,333 bikes	

As can be seen, we still get 2,000 cars because we have to satisfy the primary needs of both countries, but now we only get a total of 20,000 bikes, which is 8,333 less than if both countries would be working independently and there would be no trade between them. The question is, therefore, how can we make sure that both countries understand their comparative advantages and disadvantages and don't try to specialize in the wrong products. The answer to this question depends on who makes the decisions about the allocation of limited resources. In our example, this is the question of which industries should be shrinking or closing while others are growing and expanding. In open economies, decisions of this kind are taken by the market. Conversely, in state controlled economies, decisions of this kind are taken by bureaucrats somewhere in the state administration. For example, in the COMECON, the Council for Mutual Economic Assistance, which was the regional integration system used by the Soviet Union to impose its centralized model of state communism on its satellite states, the decisions which of the many factories in the automotive sector across the vast Soviet empire would be making the small cars, the medium-sized cars, the large cars, the trucks, the buses, etc. were all taken at the Communist Party headquarters in Moscow.[6] We know from history that the market economy model of the West prevailed over the communist economic model of the East, but it is useful to understand why this is so. Moreover, as we see Washington and other political centers increasingly beleaguered by lobbyists and other special interests, we need to remember that a country does not have to adopt a communist system to succumb to inefficient allocation of resources.

An obvious difference between decision making in a state-controlled economy and a market economy is the degree of centralization. In a perfect market economy, an infinite number of individually small sellers meet with an infinite number of individually small buyers to negotiate production and prices. None of the sellers/producers or buyers/consumers are large enough to dominate the market and dictate

---

6. For further analysis, see János Kornai, *The Socialist System: The Political Economy of Communism*, Princeton Univ. Press 1992; and Alec Nove, *An Economic History of the USSR: 1917–1991*, Penguin Books 3rd ed. 1993.

the prices. All of them are "price takers" and the market is the "price maker." By contrast, in a state-controlled economy, there is only one decision-maker, which is the government, and it controls both production and prices. In both economies, the challenge is to make smart decisions about who should produce what in which way and who gets to buy it at what price, i.e., the optimal allocation of limited resources for greatest overall benefit. At least from a theoretical perspective, it is not immediately obvious why a large number of individually small sellers and buyers should be inherently better at making these decisions than the government. After all, with its superior resources and knowledge, the government will outmatch each of the small producers and consumers, at least individually. Furthermore, the players in the market economy are in the game for their personal benefit more than anything, while the bureaucrats in the government should be disinterested on the personal level and pursue only the common good. Thus, the planned economy should have the advantage. Finally, the idea of a perfect market economy is largely theoretical while in practice many geographic and product markets are characterized by just a handful of powerful economic and/or political players or even outright monopoly, which means that the crucial decisions are controlled by very few decision-makers, similar to the state economy, except that they are openly pursuing their personal benefit and nobody is there to protect the smaller players and promote the common good. How can it be explained, therefore, that the communist model of state controlled economy failed so spectacularly wherever it was systematically employed?

Frank Emmert

The Argument for Robust Competition Supervision in Developing and Transition Economies

Journal of Governance and Regulation, Vol. 5, No. 3, 2016, pp. 67–89

1. The Economics of Competition

It has been said that there is no end to human greed. Pretty much everything else in the world, in particular those things that we consider positive and/or desirable, are in short supply. When something is in short supply, it means that there is not enough of it available to satisfy everyone who would like to have it. We may be able to produce more of one thing but only at the expense of another thing. For example, we may be able to satisfy more people who desire clean air by closing a factory that causes pollution or by forcing it to install expensive filter equipment. However, both of these measures, while increasing the supply of one thing, clean air, decrease the supply of one or more other things, in this case some or all of the jobs in the factory and some or all of the goods it is producing. One of the most important problems facing human societies, therefore, is the need to make decisions about how much to produce of everything and how to distribute the limited production among the many who want to have a share of it. This is called the problem of allocation of limited resources.

Economists[42] have long argued, and 20th century history has ultimately proven, that market economies are more efficient than non-market economies at making these decisions.[43] In a non-market economy, decisions about allocation of scarce resources (capital, labor, goods, etc.) are either made by the state or by a small number of private actors. If these decisions are made by the state, we speak of a planned economy, sometimes also called a socialist or communist economy. If the decisions are made by a small number of private actors, they have to be in a position of monopoly or dominance or they have to collude in the form of cartels in order to have impact. By contrast, the allocation of scarce resources in a market economy is based on large numbers of decisions made by large numbers of buyers and sellers, who

---

42. Many lawyers—and at least some of my readers—very quickly get uncomfortable with any form of economic analysis, in particular if it includes charts, let alone numbers. All too often, the very reason why we went to law school in the first place is that it seemed the furthest from anything that could require mathematics. The reality is not quite like that, however. Whether in tax law, when we have to understand the financial implications of different ways of structuring a corporation or international business transaction, or in the calculation of damages in tort law, a good lawyer will always think about the economic implications of his or her advice for the client. This is all the more true in competition law, where economic analysis has become very important for the way regulatory authorities and courts will analyze conduct or practices of corporations potentially restricting competition [E. Cavanagh, *Antitrust Law and Economic Theory: Finding a Balance*, Loyola University Chicago Law Journal 2013, Vol. 45 No. 1, pp. 123-171]. As Morgan has pointed out, "whether or not one personally likes the implications toward which economic analysis points, a lawyer needs to understand the analysis in order to assess what the purpose and effect of a practice might be, whether the practice is likely to be challenged, and if so, how most courts today will react to it." See [Morgan, T.D., *Cases and Materials on Modern Antitrust Law and Its Origins*, Thomson/West, St. Paul MN, 3rd ed. 2005, at p. 5]. Fortunately, there are a number of relatively accessible books for lawyers seeking to understand economic analysis of law and more particularly competition law. These include [D.W. Barnes & L.A. Stout, *Economic Foundations of Regulation and Antitrust Law*, West Publishing, St. Paul MN, 1992; Simon Bishop & Mike Walker, *The Economics of EC Competition Law: Concepts, Application and Measurement*, Sweet & Maxwell, London UK 2010; T. Calvani & J. Siegfried, *Economic Analysis and Antitrust Law*, Little Brown & Co., Boston MA, 1988; E. Gellhorn, W.E. Kovacic & S. Calkins, *Antitrust Law and Economics in a Nutshell*, West Academic Publishing, St. Paul MN, 5th ed. 2004; D. Hildebrand, *The Role of Economic Analysis in the EC Competition Rules*, Kluwer Law International, Alphen aan den Rijn NL, 3rd ed. 2009; K.N. Hylton, *Antitrust Law and Economics*, Edward Elgar Publishing, Cheltenham UK, 2nd ed. 2010; as well as E.T. Sullivan & J.L. Harrison, *Understanding Antitrust and Its Economic Implications*, Lexis-Nexis, New York NY, 6th ed. 2014].

43. The goal would be to come as close as possible to the so-called "Pareto-optimal allocation of goods and resources." See [Dennis C. Mueller, *Public Choice III*, Cambridge University Press, Cambridge, U.K., 3rd ed. 2003]. A Pareto-optimum is achieved when all production factors, such as resources and other goods, know-how, labor, and capital, are allocated in such a way that any re-allocation making at least one person better off would also leave at least one person worse off.

It should be noted, however, that Pareto-optimal allocation considers only the overall benefits to society. There may be many variations of Pareto-optimal allocation, each one benefitting *society equally* but *individuals differently*. For example, a certain level of employment at a factory may be the Pareto-optimum. Employing *more* workers would reduce overall efficiency. However, employing *different* workers could well be the same from society's point of view while making a huge difference for those who now have jobs and those who do no longer.

meet in the marketplace every day to negotiate deals, each of which individually does not significantly influence the overall economy.[44]

The problem with all of these decisions—market economy or not—is that the decision-makers do not necessarily pursue the public good, that they have limited information, and that the parameters in the market place change all the time. Thus, from a point of view of economic efficiency, we can say that the problem is that a certain number of decisions will inevitably be *wrong*. Either those decisions will promote private benefit at the expense of public good, or they will try to promote the public good but fail to do so in the best possible way because of insufficient factual information or insufficient understanding of the optimal solution for the respective problem. Insufficient understanding may be an objective problem of *predicting the future* or a subjective problem of *not understanding the present*. For the purposes of this article, both types of decisions shall be defined as *mistakes*, namely those that promote short term and/or limited private gain over long term and/or larger public gain, and those that may pursue the best overall result but turn out to be inferior at doing that. Both types of mistakes cause overall loss to society.

In our globalizing world, national economies are no longer predominantly about the allocation of resources on the national level. They are also competing for resources on the global level, for example for profitable sales opportunities in foreign markets, for deals to buy natural or other resources abroad, and for decisions about foreign direct investment. At the same time, countries have become more interdependent, and decisions in one country may directly affect the availability and allocation of resources, hence ultimately the level of prosperity, in another country. This magnifies the impact of good or bad decisions and the importance of making as few mistakes as possible. To illustrate the point, compare the strategic decisions taken by Nissan and General Motors towards the first generation of electric automobile. While the Nissan Leaf runs entirely on electricity, which limits its range to the life of the battery, the Chevy Volt comes with a back-up engine running on gasoline so that it can operate beyond the life of its battery. However, the second engine in the Volt comes at the steep price of an additional $8,000 on the sticker price. The next couple of years will show who made the better bet and either Nissan or General Motors will sell large numbers of automobiles not only in their respective domestic markets but potentially in many countries. Although it is possible

---

44. Relatively small firms in competitive markets are also called *price takers* because they do not make the prices by restricting or increasing their output. Rather, the prices are made by the market, i.e., the aggregate of all buying and selling transactions by all buyers and sellers meeting in the marketplace. If one firm would reduce its output, it would not be able to sell less for more. Instead, it would just lose sales at the market price to another firm. Only if many firms would agree to lower their output and not to pick up customers turned away by their "competitors", prices would go up. The latter, however, would be a cartel and not any more a competitive market. Very nearly every decent book on competition or antitrust law contains a discussion of price theory and competitive markets in its introductory chapters. For examples see note 42. Similar results can also be found in the public choice literature, for example in [Maxwell L. Stearns, *Public Choice and Public Law: Readings and Commentary*, LexisNexis, New York NY, 2003, at pp. 111–117].

that the one type of car may appeal to one type of user and the other to another and that both companies come out as winners, it is also possible that one of them will have sunk billions of dollars in development costs into a product that does not sell (enough) and does not recover this investment. Given the low prices of gasoline and the glut of crude oil in the market in recent [years], it is equally possible that neither of the cars will ever recover its development cost. Needless to say, even large automobile manufacturers with deep pockets can only afford so many of these kinds of mistakes.

It is important to understand that the problem of wrong decision-making is inherent in all economic activities, whether in a market economy or a non-market economy. As long as decisions are taken by humans, we will encounter selfish pursuit of short term private benefit at the expense of society, and we will encounter problems of incompetence and of predicting future developments. One may even argue that a state actor should be less incompetent, on average, than a private actor and that governments should come up with fewer wrong decisions than companies or private investors, simply because of the larger information base and other resources available to the government. However, this may be countered by the problem of ownership. While private actors and investors are using their own money and usually have to bear the consequences of their wrong decisions themselves, civil servants in the government are usually insulated from the consequences of their decisions and thus less motivated to do their best at avoiding mistakes.[45] Whether one believes that private individuals and investors are generally better than government officials at making the kind of decisions we are talking about, is a question of ideology.[46] However, what is beyond doubt and ideology is the fact that both types of actors will make mistakes. Furthermore, while the future has always been uncertain, change comes ever more quickly today, which requires that decisions are adjusted all the time to match the needs of a changing environment and prevent a good decision from becoming a mistake. The crucial question, therefore, is how different economic models deal with their mistakes and how they deal with the change that is imposed on them.

---

45. This is one important reason why larger companies that are run by salaried CEOs rather than owners tend to tie the compensation of their leaders to the overall performance of the company via annual bonuses and longer term stock options. For in-depth analysis see [M. Jensen & K. Murphy, *CEO Incentives — It's Not How Much You Pay, But How*, Harvard Business Review, May–June 1990, No. 3, pp. 138–153].

46. Until recently, the answer seemed pretty obvious. After all, the Soviet Union had proven unable to compete with the West and collapsed and even China had turned to market economy for its remarkable growth. However, the current financial crisis has somewhat discredited Western claims of superiority and indeed, those countries that have suffered less from the crisis seem to be the ones with more government intervention in markets. Nevertheless, there has yet to be a planned economy or an economy with heavy government intervention that reaches, let alone surpasses the level of general prosperity in the Western market economies of the EU and North America. In this context, in can also be instructive to compare different schools of antitrust analysis. See, for example, [Richard A. Posner, *The Chicago School of Antitrust Analysis*, University of Pennsylvania Law Review 1979, Vol. 127 No. 4, pp. 925–948].

The worst model at correcting its mistakes is the economy dominated by a small number of private individuals via monopoly, dominance, or cartels. Such an economy actually *rewards* mistakes as defined above. In the absence of constraints, the private individuals can and usually will pursue their personal self-interest at the expense of public good and will prosper while society as a whole has to pay the price. In the most extreme example of monopoly, the monopolist can and will charge super-competitive prices for its goods or services and become extremely rich. Each individual customer and society at large not only pay too much to satisfy their needs, but chances are that the absence of choice, hence competitive pressure, also results in inferior quality of the goods and services. Change, for example, in the form of technological progress, does not have to be accounted for by the monopolist, unless the very monopoly comes under threat.[47] The situation is only marginally less extreme where an individual enterprise merely has a dominant position and not a full monopoly. The case where several enterprises could compete but rather collude in the form of a cartel may be the worst possible scenario because the monopolist at least benefits from economies of scale even if they are not passed on to the customers. The bottom line is in each of these cases that everybody pays a higher price for lower quality, and the economic loss of the many far outweighs the economic gains of the few.

The planned or state controlled economy is only marginally less bad at correcting its mistakes. While this economy does not actually *reward* the decision-makers for their mistakes, unless there is also corruption, it fails to adequately *punish* the mistakes. To the extent bureaucrats may be held accountable for wrong decisions, this gives them an incentive to hide those decisions, for example by deferring to committees or by suppressing data. It also gives them an incentive to avoid taking decisions in the first place, which makes governmental structures rigid and inflexible in the face of new data and/or external change. Simply speaking, planned economies will be slow to adopt decisions and even slower to correct them once they turn out to be inferior. The Soviet Union was full of examples.

This brings us to the market economy and the question why large numbers of individually small sellers negotiating with large numbers of individually small buyers should be inherently better at understanding how best to allocate resources in the present environment and how best to deal with change in the future. One could even argue that the very fact that none of the buyers or sellers is individually large naturally limits their ability to research and process today's data and to hire the most competent experts at predicting future trends. However, this would completely misunderstand the power of the market. Much like a match between a grandmaster of chess and a supercomputer, the invincible power of the market

---

47. A good example was the supply of end-user telephone equipment in Germany in the 1970s and early 1980s. Since Siemens was the sole—and therefore monopoly—provider licensed by the state telephone company, Germans had to deal with large mouse-grey rotary dial phones at high prices while sleek and colorful dial tone phones were already available in many more competitive markets at much lower prices. For background reading see [K. Morgan & D. Webber, *Divergent Paths: Political Strategies for Telecommunications in Britain, France and West Germany*, West European Politics 1986, Vol. 9 No. 4, pp. 56–74].

relies on its ability simply to try out every possible alternative. We may go as far as saying that the market, compared to the experts, is not very smart at all and makes lots of inferior choices. However, while the expert has to rely on his or her expertise to come up with the best possible solution, one move at a time, the market relies on an infinite number of trial and error moves to find the best possible solution. While individual buying and selling decisions in an open market place may not look very smart at all, the aggregate result of all buying and selling decisions in that market has proven superior to any other form or method of allocating scarce resources today and accounting for change tomorrow.

> "Throughout recorded history, there has never been a serious practical alternative to free competitive markets as a mechanism for delivering the right goods and services to the right people at the lowest possible cost."
>
> (Alan S. Blinder, Princeton)

Market economies have their own problems, however. Two of the most important shortcomings of the market are the failure to account for *externalities* and the trend towards *concentration*.[48] Both of them have to be accounted for by a country that seeks to improve its economic performance, and to promote sustainable growth, overall prosperity, and the gradual reduction of income disparities.

Externalities are sometimes also called *spillover effects.* They occur when some of the costs or benefits of a decision or a deal affect natural or legal persons other than the decision-maker(s) or the partners of the deal [Don Cole, *Encyclopedic Dictionary of Economics*, 4th ed. 1991]. For example, if a company is trying to reduce the cost of production by keeping the wages of the workers low, it may experience high turnover in the form of workers leaving for better paid positions elsewhere, as well as difficulty in recruiting skilled and motivated replacements. This would be an *internality*, as it affects the situation of the decision-maker itself. By contrast, if the same company reduces the cost of production by releasing waste water unfiltered into a nearby stream, this may have no impact on the decision-maker itself as long as there are no governmental or other sanctions. The pollution would be a *negative externality,* as it negatively affects the situation of the neighbors and other downstream users of the water.[49] As the example shows, the problem with externalities is the disconnect between those who take the decisions and those who suffer the consequences. In an unregulated market economy, there is an incentive for

---

48. Externalities as well as monopoly or market power are typically among the key market failures discussed in economics and public choice literature. See, for example, [Robert D. Cooter & Thomas Ulen, *Law and Economics*, Pearson, New York NY, 5th ed. 2007, at pp. 43–45.]

49. Krugman and Wells . . . dedicate an entire chapter of their well-known textbook to negative externalities using the example of acid rain caused by coal burning power plants and other polluters. [See Paul Krugman & Robin Wells, *Economics*, Worth Publishers, New York NY, 2006, at pp. 455–474.]

decision-makers to ignore negative externalities for private profit. This, in turn, creates a justification for government interference in the market. If there are negative externalities, corrective action should be taken in the form of financial disincentives (taxation) and/or regulation and enforcement. Conversely, positive externalities, i.e., benefits to third parties other than the decision-maker(s) or partners of a deal, can be a justification for government subsidies.[50] [Unfortunately, taxation, regulation and/or subsidies in a country trying to take care of externalities can create unwanted incentives to trade, for example if companies from that country seek to re-locate production facilities abroad in order to benefit from lower levels of taxation and/or regulation. Thus, international trade liberalization may have to be combined with a minimum level of international harmonization of environmental and other regulation, and taxation, to prevent the proverbial *race to the bottom*.]

Concentration is the problem of individuals who prefer to cooperate rather than compete. The ideal market is one of perfect competition,[51] characterized by an infinite number of small sellers constantly negotiating deals with an infinite number of small buyers (see [Chart 1-1]), where transactions costs tend towards zero and full information transparency prevails.

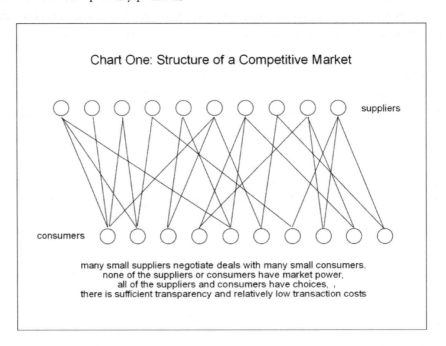

Chart One: Structure of a Competitive Market

suppliers

consumers

many small suppliers negotiate deals with many small consumers,
none of the suppliers or consumers have market power,
all of the suppliers and consumers have choices,
there is sufficient transparency and relatively low transaction costs

---

50. An example of positive externalities could be the social benefits of education or the environmental benefits of the installation of solar panels by homeowners. For discussion see, for example, [Paul R. Krugman & Maurice Obstfeld, *International Economics: Theory and Policy*, Pearson, Boston MA, 8th ed. 2008, pp. 267 et seq.].

51. Bob Lane defines competition as "the struggle by firms to achieve superiority over other firms in the marketplace" and competition law as "the rules limiting the freedom by which they may do so". See [Robert Lane, *EC Competition Law*, Longman, Harlow UK, 2000, at p. 6].

In such a market,[52] each individual producer/seller is in direct and open competition with every other producer/seller and additional sales will go to those who offer the highest quality product at the lowest price. Since transparency is a given, consumers can actually identify the highest quality and lowest price and since transactions costs are negligible, they can then go and contract with the supplier who offers that quality and price, regardless of distance.

Perfect competition is rarely found in reality, of course. The number of producers or sellers and the number of consumers or buyers is rarely infinite. More importantly, transparency is limited since products may not be entirely comparable and consumer time for price and quality research is limited.[53] Finally, transaction costs usually go up when transactions are done over a distance and involve credit financing and other complications. More realistically, therefore, is to speak of *workable* competition or *effective competition*[54] in markets where there are more than a few producers or sellers and more than a few consumers or buyers, where there is a reasonably good level of transparency, and where the transaction costs have little or no influence on purchasing decisions. The terms workable or effective competition signal that competition in these markets may not be perfect but it is generally working or effective enough to secure the general push for producers and sellers to offer the highest possible quality at the lowest possible price today and in the foreseeable future. . . .

While perfect or even just workable competition is the most beneficial situation for society as a whole, it is sub-optimal for the producers and sellers. The only way to grow in such a market is by working harder, longer, faster and/or better/smarter than the others. Since this is hard, some producers or sellers will seek to avoid the

---

52. Markets are defined in terms of products, including essentially all those products that are interchangeable from the consumer's point of view, and in terms of geography, covering the largest possible territory that is sufficiently homogenous and not subject to significant barriers to trade or transaction costs. For example, the market for fresh bread is rarely larger than what can be reached within a 10 minute drive from the consumer's home and may be as small as walking distance. Consequently, it may only include two or three bakers or shops which sell bread. Also having a fast food outlet in the area will not be a useful substitute for consumers trying to buy bread for their breakfast at home. By contrast, the market for large passenger airplanes is a global market and includes Boeing and Airbus as the only producers/sellers. Military transport aircraft and their producers are not in that market because the airlines cannot avoid high prices of Boeing or Airbus by purchasing transport aircraft. As we will see later, makers of military aircraft may nevertheless curb the market power of Boeing and Airbus to charge super-competitive prices because they can be potential entrants into the passenger aircraft market. . . .

53. Indeed, there is an opinion that a certain level of misinformation of consumers is tolerable or even desirable, see [M.R. Darby & E. Karni, *Free Competition and the Optimal Amount of Fraud*, The Journal of Law & Economics 1973, Vol. 16 No. 1, pp. 67–88].

54. For more detailed analysis, see [Phillip E. Areeda, Louis Kaplow & Aaron Edlin, *Antitrust Analysis: Problems, Text, Cases*, Aspen Publishers, New York NY, 6th ed. 2004, pp. 15-32; Bishop & Walker, *supra* note 42, at pp. 15–50; and Eleanor M. Fox, Lawrence A. Sullivan & Rudolph J.R. Peritz, *Cases and Materials on U.S. Antitrust in Global Context*, West Academic Publishing, St. Paul MN, 2nd ed. 2004, pp. 56–76].

competitive pressures of the market place. First, they may seek to merge with competitors to reduce the number of producers or sellers and obtain a stronger position in a smaller crowd (see [**Chart 1-2**]).

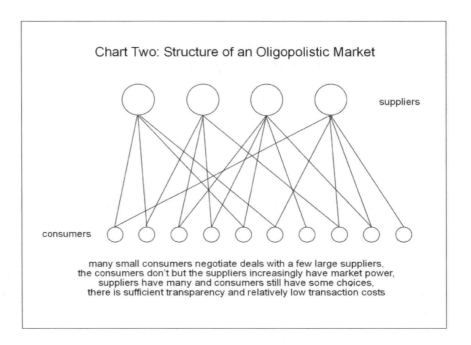

Chart Two: Structure of an Oligopolistic Market

suppliers

consumers

many small consumers negotiate deals with a few large suppliers,
the consumers don't but the suppliers increasingly have market power,
suppliers have many and consumers still have some choices,
there is sufficient transparency and relatively low transaction costs

Once a process of consolidation begins, others come under pressure to follow suit lest their smaller size becomes a disadvantage in negotiating with suppliers or a real or perceived disadvantage regarding economies of scale.[55] In this way, a first mover can trigger an avalanche and, as a result, a structural shift from many competitors to an *oligopoly* of just a few competitors. Second, once the number of players in a market is no longer infinite,[56] the remaining companies may try to form a cartel to fix prices, limit output, or agree on some other form of anti-competitive conduct (see [**Chart 1-3**]). [As a consequence, no matter where the consumer goes, she will get the same mediocre quality at the same inflated price.]

---

55. For a recent example see Los Angeles Times, *Marriott's Plan to Buy Starwood for $12.2 Billion Could Trigger More Hotel Mergers*, Business News, Friday, March 11, 2016.

56. Cartels tend not to work well if the number of players in the respective market is too large. Either some firms will not participate in the cartel for fear of sanctions. Or some participants may begin to cheat, i.e., try to gain market share at the expense of other participants by undercutting the agreed upon prices or conditions. Smaller cartels can detect cheating firms and apply their own sanctions against them. Large cartels are rarely able to detect who is cheating. For more elaborate discussion see [A.R. Dick, *When Are Cartels Stable Contracts?*, The Journal of Law & Economics 1996, Vol. 39 No. 1, pp. 241–283].

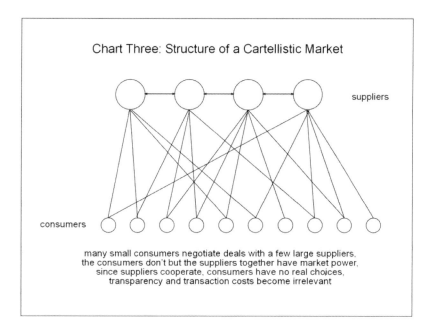

Chart Three: Structure of a Cartellistic Market

suppliers

consumers

many small consumers negotiate deals with a few large suppliers,
the consumers don't but the suppliers together have market power,
since suppliers cooperate, consumers have no real choices,
transparency and transaction costs become irrelevant

In an extreme case, a single company may become so dominant that it is essentially the only remaining significant player in a market and, hence, a *monopoly* (see [**Chart 1-4**]).[57]

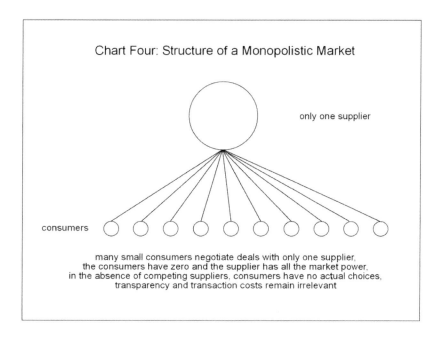

Chart Four: Structure of a Monopolistic Market

only one supplier

consumers

many small consumers negotiate deals with only one supplier,
the consumers have zero and the supplier has all the market power,
in the absence of competing suppliers, consumers have no actual choices,
transparency and transaction costs remain irrelevant

---

57. Since there are several paths to dominance or monopoly, including natural growth of the most innovative and competitive company, mergers, as well as natural monopolies, in particular in network-based industries such as railroads and utilities, *size* alone should not necessarily be condemned. [Instead, the focus should be on *abuse* by a dominant firm.]

Even a country that is blessed with near perfect or at least workable or effective competition in a given geographic and product market, therefore, has to undertake steps to ensure that this competition is not gradually undermined and disappearing. This is where competition law comes into the picture.[58] Unsurprisingly, economists can demonstrate that sustainable economic growth, overall prosperity, and gradual reduction of income disparities, are all supported by the adoption and implementation of robust competition[59] oversight. Even more important, whenever a certain product and geographic market is not sufficiently competitive, let alone when a whole country is characterized by the existence of dominant firms or monopolies in many markets and/or heavy government intervention that is not justified as a measured reaction to correct externalities, there is much to be gained from the introduction of robust competition oversight. Furthermore, robust competition oversight should ideally be paired with measures to promote transparency in the market and measures to reduce transaction costs. . . .

Notes and Questions

1. Although robust competition rules and their enforcement will be in the best interest of society as a whole, it is often opposed by powerful economic interests who have more to gain from the exploitation of their dominant market position. Open borders and liberal trade regimes can overcome some of these problems by opening relatively small and parochial domestic markets controlled by few and powerful economic interests to global competition. Does this mean that smaller countries should be more open to international trade and that a large economy like the U.S. has little or nothing to gain from free trade? Who in the U.S. gains and who loses if trade is (further) liberalized? What about society at large?

2. As explained above, international trade liberalization may have to be combined with a certain level of international regulatory and tax harmonization, to avoid the proverbial race to the bottom. What is meant by this and how can it be accomplished? To what extent have we been successful at this on a global scale? In the Americas? NAFTA?

---

58. The literature on antitrust—or competition—law fills many shelves in our libraries. Books I have personally found particularly informative are, for example, [Areeda, Kaplow & Edlin, supra note 54; Einer R. Elhauge & Damien Geradin, *Global Antitrust Law and Economics*, Hart Publishing, Portland, OR, 3rd ed. 2018; Jonathan Faull & Ali Nikpay eds., *The EU Law of Competition*, Oxford University Press, Oxford UK, 3rd ed. 2014; Andrew I. Gavil, William E. Kovacic & Jonathan B. Baker, Antitrust Law in Perspective: Cases, *Concepts and Problems in Competition Policy*, 3rd ed. 2016; as well as Peter Roth & Vivien Rose eds., *Bellamy & Child: European Union Law of Competition*, Oxford University Press, Oxford UK, 8th ed. 2019].

59. Although in the United States of America, the subject is more commonly referred to as "antitrust law". I prefer to use the European terminology because "competition law" is wider, capturing not only the combat against trusts or cartels but also several other components of the fight against anti-competitive practices implemented or attempted by private parties and even public authorities. . . .

3. Ever since antitrust enforcement was defanged under President Reagan as of 1986, the U.S. economy has been going down a path of decreased competition and increased concentration of market power.[7] As I am writing this book in 2020, ever more sectors of the U.S. economy are dominated by just a handful of enterprises that are either not competing with each other at all or at least not very vigorously. The results are painfully obvious. While average wages have stagnated, exchange-rate adjusted prices in the U.S. across a wide range of goods and services, including food, housing, transportation, telecommunication, education, health care, and many more, are today higher than in comparable economies in Europe and other parts of the world. At the same time, these higher prices typically cannot be justified by better quality and may indeed be charged for inferior quality, compared to other advanced economies. As a result, the average American household today is worse off than 20 or 30 years ago, and certainly worse off than the average household in countries like France or Germany.

Moreover, the U.S. is today characterized by unprecedented levels of inequality, which means that the "average" is distorted by the ultra rich. To illustrate the point, let's assume that we have 99 out of 100 people earning US$100,000/year and 1 person earning US$100 million/year. The average income in such a society would be just short of US$1.1 million/year. One single ultra-rich person is distorting the picture to the point of ridicule. By contrast, the median income in the country would be exactly US$100,000/year,[8] a much more realistic number. Let's not be fooled, therefore, by politicians telling us that our system is better than others because "the average" income is higher or going up faster than elsewhere. Nobel Prize winner Joseph Stiglitz introduces a recent book by diagnosing that "Ninety-one percent of all increases of income from 2009 to 2012 went to the wealthiest 1 percent of Americans—the epitome of unequal growth. . . . This combination of growth for the very wealthy and economic stasis and anxiety for the rest of Americans is politically volatile. . . . [U]nless we change course, we will be a country with slower growth, ever more inequality, and ever less equality of opportunity."[9] For further analysis, see also Robert B. Reich, *Saving Capitalism for the Many, Not the Few*, Vintage Books 2015.

---

7. Admittedly, this was not a linear path. For detailed analysis, see Robert A. Sitkol, *The Shifting Sands of Antitrust Policy: Where It Has Been, Where It Is Now, Where It Will Be in Its Third Century*, 9 Cornell J.L. & Pub. Pol'y 239, Fall 1999; as well as Thomas Philippon, *The Great Reversal—How America Gave Up on Free Markets*, Belknap Press 2019.

8. The median is obtained by dividing the population into two equal halves and identifying the status of the person in the middle, who has half of the country earning less and half of the country earning more than herself.

9. Joseph E. Stiglitz, *Rewriting the Rules of the American Economy—An Agenda for Growth and Shared Prosperity*, W.W. Norton & Co. 2016, at pp. viii, xii and 5. A recent study by the OECD supports the notion that increasing levels of inequality will eventually undermine economic growth and overall wealth, see F. Cingano, *Trends in Income Inequality and Its Impact on Economic Growth*, OECD Social, Employment and Migration Working Paper No. 163, 9 December 2014. See also Simon Reid-Henry, *The Political Origins of Inequality—Why a More Equal World Is Better for Us All*, Univ. Chicago Press 2015.

4. Although competition supervision and enforcement within the U.S. may have declined over the last 30 years, the same time period saw an unprecedented liberalization in international trade. Why does increasing competition from abroad apparently not fill in the gaps produced by decreasing domestic competition, to curb market power of certain enterprises or industries in the U.S.? Does this mean we should not have liberalized trade (to the same extent) or even that we should roll back some of the trade liberalization as suggested by the Trump administration?

5. In the above-mentioned book, Stiglitz postulates that "... [T]he standard model, which assumes perfect information, perfect competition, perfect risk markets, and perfect rationality, fails to provide an accurate description of how various markets in our economy really work. [Recent research] on information asymmetries and imperfections, bargaining theory and imperfections of competition, behavioral economics, and institutional analysis [provides] a whole new perspective on the functioning of labor, product, and financial markets, and essentially show[s] that *institutions and rules are required to force markets to behave competitively, for the benefit of all.*"[10] What kind of institutions and rules could Stiglitz have in mind?

6. Anyone interested in understanding how our economies really work and what is and what is not good for society at large as well as individuals and their households, should read at least one or two of the leading works on behavioral economics. In a nutshell, this subgenre of economics accepts that individuals and firms are not rational actors and often do things they know are not good for them. In other cases, we are too busy or too lazy to seek the information and overcome other transaction costs involved in making optimal decisions for ourselves. In the end, we eat food that is not healthy, overpay at the nearest store, and stick to overpriced phone contracts, to give just a few examples. Behavioral economics tries to understand the reasons for such irrational behavior and also provide solutions how regulators and individual actors can do better. Personally, I found the following books to be both illuminating and eminently readable: Daniel Kahneman, *Thinking, Fast and Slow,* Farrar, Straus and Giroux 2013; Richard H. Thaler, *Misbehaving: The Making of Behavioral Economics*, W.W. Norton & Co. 2016; as well as Richard H. Thaler & Cass R. Sunstein, *Nudge — Improving Decisions About Health, Wealth, and Happiness* Penguin, 2009.

Section 3. The Legal Framework for IBTs — A To-Do List

We just learned in Section 2 that international trade is good for many reasons, as long as it is backed up by certain basic rules to prevent the circumvention of human rights, labor and environmental standards, intellectual property rights, and other

---

10. Joseph E. Stiglitz, *Rewriting the Rules of the American Economy — An Agenda for Growth and Shared Prosperity,* W.W. Norton & Co. 2016, at pp. 10–11 (emphasis added).

achievements of more highly developed societies and countries, via relocating production to less regulated—that is, usually less developed—countries. Therefore, adequate and efficient legal rules, including their implementation and enforcement in practice, are needed on multiple levels if we want to maximize the benefits and minimize the harm of our globalizing economy:

To begin with, we need to have the kind of basic economic constitution that protects and promotes private ownership of factors of production and private enterprise. This goes far beyond a mere guarantee of the right to private property. At the national level, it requires a wide range of suitable legal rules, for example efficient contract law, as well as government institutions for their application and enforcement, in particular a well-functioning system of courts. In addition to private and criminal laws and institutions, it also requires a system of effective administrative laws and courts to limit the power of the state, maintain taxes at reasonable levels, and manage public borrowing and spending. These topics have been competently treated elsewhere[11] and would go far beyond the scope of the present work.

To counterbalance the forces of private, hence egotistical, capitalism, and to manage externalities of economic activity, we need adequate and effective rules and institutions to protect "the commons" at the national and international levels.[12] This includes various forms of environmental protection. To ensure a level playing field between the economic actors, we also need rules and institutions for the protection of employees and consumers, who tend to be the weaker parties in transactions with larger enterprises.[13] Additionally, we need adequate and effective rules and institutions for the prevention of anti-competitive behavior by dominant firms, as well as anti-competitive collusion by multiple firms.[14] An economic system without robust

---

11. The ideological battle over more versus less government involvement in the economy has been fought for more than a century. Among the promoters of a laissez-faire approach with minimal government regulation and intervention were F.A. Hayek and Milton Friedman (see, in particular, F.A. Hayek, *The Constitution of Liberty*, Univ. Chicago Press 1960; and Milton Friedman, *Capitalism and Freedom*, Univ. Chicago Press 1962). By contrast, the case for a more active involvement of the state, and indeed the notion of counter-cyclical government spending, was chiefly promoted by John Maynard Keynes (John Maynard Keynes, *The General Theory of Employment, Interest, and Money*, Palgrave Macmillan 1936). For a modern introduction to the subject, see, for example, Thomas Piketty, *Capital in the Twenty-First Century*, Harvard Univ. Press, 2014.

12. For the basic concepts, see, for example, Richard Cornes & Todd Sandler, *The Theory of Externalities, Public Goods and Club Goods*, Cambridge Univ. Press, 2nd ed. 1996. The definitive work on the global commons is Elinor Ostrom, *Governing the Commons: The Evolution of Institutions for Collective Action* (Political Economy of Institutions and Decisions), Cambridge Univ. Press 1990.

13. For a discussion of the global implications see, *inter alia*, Frank Emmert, *Labor, Environmental Standards and World Trade Law*, U.C. Davis J. Int'l Law & Pol'y, 2003, Vol. 10, No. 1, pp. 75–167.

14. The importance of robust antitrust or pro-competition rules and institutions has recently been highlighted by Robert Reich, who shows that the situation in the U.S. at the beginning of the twenty-first century was characterized by severely constrained competition in many areas of economic activity. The results include a shift of investment away from technological innovation toward political influence in an effort to protect market power. The pollution of the political process, in

antitrust or pro-competition rules and institutions, like a political system without checks and balances, is subject to the tyranny of the few over the many.

Finally, since the parties to an international business transaction are, by definition, located in different countries, and therefore subject to different national rules and institutions, we need rules and possibly institutions to take care of the inherent conflicts between the application of one set of national rules versus another. In other words, we need to determine in each case whether an IBT will be subject to seller's or to buyer's contract laws—or maybe a third and neutral country's rules or an international set of rules (private law conflict rules)—and to what extent the respective home countries of the parties to the transaction can or should apply their other legal rules, for example regarding the protection of intellectual property rights, health and safety standards, environmental protection, etc., and have authority over the parties to enforce them (public law conflict or regulatory jurisdiction rules). Further, we need rules that tell us how and where dispute settlements between the parties about their respective contractual rights and obligations should take place (court jurisdiction rules). All of these subjects will be treated in this book, although some in more detail than others.

Conflicts between *public law rules* of different countries are only touched upon where necessary. They are resolved by recourse to international principles dealing with national sovereignty and jurisdiction.[15] Pursuant to the *territoriality principle*, a country can regulate all activities that take place within its borders, which include embassies in foreign countries, as well as ships and aircraft flying the flag of the respective country. Hence, anybody driving on U.S. roads has to observe the posted speed limits, regardless of their nationality. Along the same lines, anybody manufacturing *or selling* goods inside the U.S. has to observe U.S. federal and/or state standards for health and safety and the protection of the environment, regardless of where the goods were made. Finally, U.S. federal law can prohibit smoking on commercial aircraft registered in the U.S., regardless of where they may be at any given time around the globe.

On the basis of the *active personality principle*, countries can also regulate activities of their citizens/nationals wherever they take place. For example, the U.S., in

---

turn, has fueled the highest level of inequality and a sharp right turn in the political discourse. See Robert Reich, *Saving Capitalism: For the Many, Not the Few*, Vintage Books 2015. The importance of robust antitrust or pro-competition rules and institutions, moreover, is acknowledged on the left and right of the political spectrum. Even Milton Friedman, the poster boy of the laissez-faire and small government camp, understood that only one kind of economic organization "provides economic freedom directly, namely, *competitive* capitalism" and is indispensable for "political freedom because it separates economic power from political power and in this way enables the one to offset the other." Milton Friedman, *Capitalism and Freedom*, Univ. Chicago Press 1962, at p. 9 (emphasis added); see also p. 16.

15. The classic study on the subject is by F.A. Mann, *The Doctrine of Jurisdiction in International Law*, Martinus Nijhoff 1964. For a more recent analysis, see Cedric Ryngaert, *Jurisdiction in International Law*, Oxford Univ. Press 2008.

principle, applies its tax laws to U.S. citizens wherever the taxable revenue is made and regardless of the place of residence of the taxpayer. By contrast, many other countries only tax the worldwide income of individuals or corporations that have their place of residence or incorporation within their territory, as well as any income that is earned within their borders. Hence, Germans living abroad do not pay taxes to the German authorities, unless they have some income source in Germany. However, Germany does make use of the active personality principle in criminal law by subjecting criminal activities of German citizens to its penal code, regardless of where they are committed.

Next is the so-called *passive personality principle*, which allows countries to apply their laws in cases where something is done to one of their citizens, even if the act is committed abroad. To illustrate the application of these first three principles of jurisdiction—and the potential conflicts—we could imagine a German and a British citizen getting into a fight in a bar in Australia. If the German causes injury to the Briton, Australia can apply its criminal law based on the territoriality principle. However, Germany can also prosecute the offender based on the active personality principle. Finally, the United Kingdom could exercise jurisdiction on the basis of the passive personality principle.

In this context, we should distinguish three types of jurisdiction of a country. What we have been talking about is the so-called *prescriptive or regulatory jurisdiction*, allowing a country to regulate a matter. If a country regulates a matter that does not fall under the territoriality principle or the active personality principle, we sometimes speak of an exercise of extraterritorial jurisdiction, which is often frowned upon by the other countries concerned. For example, the U.S. applies its antitrust laws to the conduct of foreign companies if "such conduct has a direct, substantial, and reasonably foreseeable effect" on U.S. domestic or international trade and "such effect gives rise to a claim under the [Sherman Act]."[16] This is more readily justifiable if the foreign companies are colluding to fix prices in the U.S. market. But how about an agreement between a Canadian and a Mexican firm that the one shall supply only the northern states and the other only the southern states of the U.S.? Or an agreement between a Canadian and a European firm about pricing in Canada?[17]

---

16. See Foreign Trade Antitrust Improvements Act of 1982, 15 U.S. Code §6a—Conduct involving trade or commerce with foreign nations, Pub. L. 97-290, title IV, §402, Oct. 8, 1982, 96 Stat. 1246. For discussion, see Russell J. Weintraub, *The Extraterritorial Application of Antitrust and Securities Laws: An Inquiry into the Utility of a Choice-of-Law Approach*, 70 Tex. L. Rev. 1799 (1991–1992); and Richard W. Beckler & Matthew H. Kirtland, *Extraterritorial Application of U.S. Antitrust Law: What Is a "Direct, Substantial, and Reasonably Foreseeable Effect" under the Foreign Trade Antitrust Improvements Act?*, 38 Tex. Int'l L.J. 11 (2003).

17. In 2009, the International Bar Association (IBA) published a *Report of the Task Force on Extraterritorial Jurisdiction*, including chapters on antitrust, tort, criminal, bribery and corruption, securities, and insolvency. See www.ibanet.org.

Having (prescriptive) jurisdiction over an issue is only the first step, however. Being able to exercise it is the next required step and cannot be taken for granted. In our bar fight example, the perpetrator, presumably, would be in the hands of the Australian authorities and without cooperation of these authorities neither the German nor the British prosecutors would be able to get their hands on him. Should Australia decline to intervene, it is conceivable that the crime would go unpunished, lest the perpetrator have the urge to relocate to Germany or the UK. To minimize such cases, the international principle of *aut punire aut dedere*, sometimes also called *aut dedere aut judicare*, was developed, which requires a country either to prosecute or to extradite a person, if so requested.[18]

Similarly, in the antitrust example, the question becomes one of *enforcement jurisdiction*. Large markets like the U.S. or the EU can usually enforce their business and trade rules by denying access to companies if they don't comply. In this way, the extraterritorial application of U.S. antitrust laws is something foreign companies can only avoid if they are willing to forsake access to the U.S. market.

Finally, we distinguish the notion of *judicial* or *adjudicative jurisdiction*, which deals with the question whether the courts of a particular country have jurisdiction over a particular dispute and, if so, which specific court(s) in that country need(s) to be approached. This will be discussed in some detail in Part Six.

The principles on prescriptive and enforcement jurisdiction primarily determine whether a country has a legitimate basis for the exercise of national sovereignty in the form of legislative and/or executive powers. The other side of the same coin is the goal not to leave any geographic spaces or activities anywhere in the world entirely outside of any country's jurisdiction. Such lawless spaces are undesirable because they might become safe havens for wanted individuals and illegal activities.

Although the rules on the exercise of prescriptive and enforcement jurisdiction are reasonably well developed and widely accepted, at least two problems can and do occur in practice. First, there are many instances in which more than one country wishes to exercise its jurisdiction and apply its rules, which may very well be incompatible with the rules applied by one or more other countries to the same activity. In our tax example above, if an American lives and works in Germany, she would be subject to income tax applied both by Germany and by the United States. Fortunately for her, these two countries have concluded a so-called double taxation agreement pursuant to which the jurisdictional conflict is resolved and the income is not taxed twice.[19]

---

18. See, for example, Cherif Bassiouni & Edward Wise, *Aut Dedere Aut Judicare: The Duty to Extradite or Prosecute in International Law*, Martinus Nijhoff 1995.

19. To be precise, the typical DTA provides for the country where the income is procured to tax it first, according to its applicable tax rules. The other country, typically the country of residence, nationality, or incorporation, will then add its own taxes only if the tax rate in the first country is lower. The effect is that the income is always taxed at the higher of the two applicable rates but not actually twice. For example, if country A has a tax rate for the income in question of 25% and

The opposite problem occurs when neither of the countries who can potentially exercise their jurisdiction is interested in doing so. This could result in an activity being entirely unregulated. A well-known example is the original tuna-dolphin dispute between the U.S. on the one side and Mexico, as well as Thailand, on the other. Fishing vessels from Mexico and Thailand were using the so-called "purse seine" fishing method to catch yellowfin tuna in the high seas of the Eastern Pacific. Essentially, this involves encircling a large school of tuna with a huge net and roping in everything that gets caught. Since dolphins feed on tuna, the fishermen were actually using the dolphins swimming at the surface to find the tuna, and many dolphins ended up in the nets together with the tuna. While the fishermen would discard the unwanted bycatch, including the dolphins, the latter had typically drowned by the time the nets were roped in. This resulted in hundreds of thousands of incidental dolphin killings every year. Since the tuna industry provided jobs and export revenue, neither the flag state(s) of the vessels, nor the home countries of the fishermen were interested in regulating the activity. Therefore, in 1972, on the basis of the Marine Mammal Protection Act, the U.S. initiated a ban on the importation of tuna and tuna products from Mexico and Thailand. Both countries then initiated the dispute settlement procedure under the General Agreement on Tariffs and Trade (GATT) with the argument that there was nothing wrong with the tuna itself and that the dolphins caught in the high seas did not come under the jurisdiction of the U.S. As a consequence, the incidental killing of the dolphins was none of the U.S.'s business. This stance was initially confirmed by the GATT dispute settlement panel. In response, the U.S. initiated "dolphin-safe" labeling to enable consumers to shun the products that did not obtain this label. After the entry into force of the WTO Agreements and the creation of the Appellate Body under the WTO Dispute Settlement Understanding, which replaced anonymous experts with well-known "judges," a second tuna-dolphin case resulted in the recognition that the dolphins in the high seas, instead of being nobody's business, were everybody's business because they qualified as "exhaustible natural resources" under Article XX of the GATT.[20] The second tuna-dolphin decision thus became an example of the recognition of universal jurisdiction in exceptional cases that are either such gross violations of international norms owed to all countries and peoples that it is for every country to prosecute them (this applies, in particular, to crimes against humanity,

---

country B has an applicable tax rate of 35%, country A would charge its full tax of 25% and country B would add another 10% of tax to bring the total tax burden up to its higher rate of 35%. Without a DTA, the taxpayer in such a case would be subject to a total tax of 60%. For further analysis, see Roy Rohatgi, *Basic International Taxation*, Vols. I and II, IBFD 2nd ed. 2007.

20. For detailed analysis, see John H. Jackson, *Dolphins and Hormones: GATT and the Legal Environment for International Trade After the Uruguay Round*, 14 UALR L.J. 429 (1991–1992). For further reading, see also Robert Howse, *The Appellate Body Rulings in the Shrimp/Turtle Case: A New Legal Baseline for the Trade and Environment Debate*, 27 Colum. J. Envtl. L. 491 (2002); and Joanne Scott, *On Kith and Kine (and Crustaceans): Trade and Environment in the EU and WTO*, in Joseph Weiler (ed.), *The EU, the WTO and the NAFTA — Towards a Common Law of International Trade*, Oxford Univ. Press 2000, at pp. 125–167.

such as genocide, torture, apartheid, etc.), or that would otherwise fall outside of proper regulation and supervision altogether.

In the next Section, we will pull together all (potential) sources of law of relevance in the context of international business and trade to see whether and where we might find the basic economic constitution, including the most suitable contract laws and enforcement mechanisms, the rules on antitrust or competition oversight and protection of the commons, and the rules on conflicts of laws and conflicts of jurisdiction in case more than one set of rules could or should be applied to a given case.

Section 4. Different Levels of Legal Rules Governing IBTs

A. International Law — Its Scope and Applicability

Literally speaking, "*international*" law refers to the law "*between* nations," i.e., the law governing the relations between different nation-states. The earliest emanations of international law can be traced back almost 5000 years in the form of border agreements, peace agreements, and, soon afterward, agreements dealing with trade. Since then, hundreds of thousands of agreements have been concluded between different nation states on subjects ranging from war and peace, diplomacy, trade and development, human rights, natural resources, food, the environment, science and technology, to the use of outer space.[21]

The reader should note the use of the term "agreements" rather than "laws." Indeed, since there is no international legislature, international law, by and large, does not consist of laws in the traditional sense. The principal sources of international law are defined in Article 38 of the Statute of the International Court of Justice:

    a. international conventions, whether general or particular, establishing rules expressly *recognized* by the contesting states;

    b. international custom, as evidence of a general practice *accepted* as law;

    c. the general principles of law *recognized* by civilized nations; (emphasis added)

As can be seen, all three principal sources are characterized by voluntary acceptance by the respective states. The very notion of state sovereignty implies that states generally do *not* accept a higher authority or higher norms to bind them. As the name

---

21. For information on who can make treaties (in addition to states), how they are made, to whom they apply, how they should be interpreted, and how they can be avoided or terminated, see, for example, Duncan Hollis (ed.), *The Oxford Guide to Treaties*, Oxford Univ. Press, 2012.

suggests, "*international*" law is, therefore, not only the law applicable "*between*" nations or states, but the law applicable on the basis of *voluntary agreement between them*.

To be sure, there are exceptions to the principle of voluntary acceptance or submission. A small but growing subgroup of international law that is binding on states even without or against their will has been referred to as "*supranational*" law, with "supra" or "above" indicating some higher level of law. This term is normally used for the law that is adopted by an international organization, regional or global, in some form of majority voting, and becomes binding upon all member states, including those that voted against it or abstained from voting. The exception to the principle of state sovereignty is justified on the basis of the voluntary accession of the state to the international organization and its acceptance of the decision-making procedures and other rules of that organization.[22] Importantly, even if states delegate far-reaching powers to an international organization, they do not forfeit their sovereignty—their statehood—under international law, as long as they retain the right to (jointly) reverse (some of) the delegations of powers or leave the organization altogether.

International and supranational law have in common that they are as such only binding *upon* a state, i.e., for its government. The question whether or not a rule of international or supranational law is also binding *in* a state, i.e., for its citizens, public authorities, and ordinary courts, is not a question of international law but one of national (constitutional) law. At least in theory, states around the world fall into two groups when it comes to the method applied in this respect. A few countries generally do not distinguish between domestic and international law, as long as both have been properly adopted or approved by the respective branch(es) of the national government. These states are called "monist" states. By contrast, the majority of states around the world follow a "dualist" tradition. For them, rules of international law that have been approved (ratified) by the respective branch(es) of government require an additional act of transformation in order to become part of the law of the land and thus able to create rights and obligations for natural and legal persons that have to be respected by the administrative authorities and enforced by the domestic courts. Charts 1-5 and 1-6 illustrate the monist and dualist traditions.

---

22. Outside of this, there are very few norms of international law that are binding upon all states, regardless of their consent. These are commonly referred to as "ius cogens." They include the prohibition of the use of force in international relations, the prohibition of torture, the prohibition of genocide, and the prohibition of apartheid. For further analysis, see Maarten den Heijer & Harmen van der Wilt (eds.), *Netherlands Yearbook of International Law 2015—Jus Cogens: Quo Vadis*, Asser Press 2016, with contributions by den Heijer & van der Wilt, Shelton, Linderfalk, d'Aspremont, Orakhelashvili, Kadelbach, Kleinlein, Santalla Vargas, Kotzé, Costello & Foster, Cottier, Vadi, Ryngaert, Schutgens & Sillen, and Krommendijk.

Chart 1-5 The Monist State

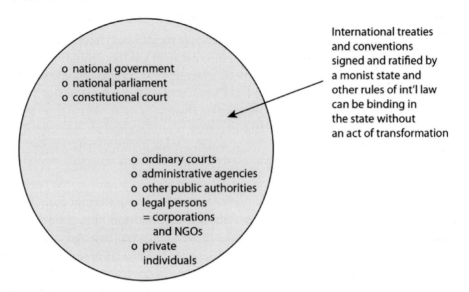

o national government
o national parliament
o constitutional court

o ordinary courts
o administrative agencies
o other public authorities
o legal persons
    = corporations
       and NGOs
o private
   individuals

International treaties
and conventions
signed and ratified by
a monist state and
other rules of int'l law
can be binding in
the state without
an act of transformation

All public and private entities and persons are subject to the same rules; there is only one sphere, "the law of the land".

Chart 1-6 The Dualist State

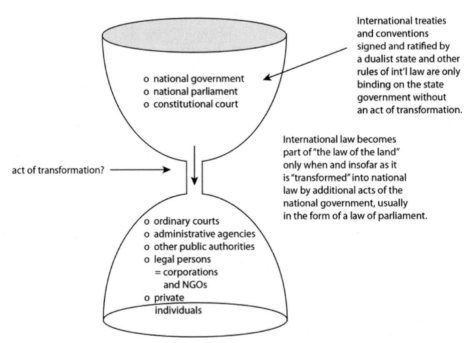

o national government
o national parliament
o constitutional court

act of transformation? →

o ordinary courts
o administrative agencies
o other public authorities
o legal persons
    = corporations
       and NGOs
o private
   individuals

International treaties
and conventions
signed and ratified by
a dualist state and other
rules of int'l law are only
binding on the state
government without
an act of transformation.

International law becomes
part of "the law of the land"
only when and insofar as it
is "transformed" into national
law by additional acts of the
national government, usually
in the form of a law of parliament.

Legal subjects have rights and obligations and conduct transactions between each other only on the basis of national law. "The law of the land" is the lower sphere only.

The importation of a rule of international or supranational law into the national legal order—i.e., into the "law of the land"—either by a general constitutional provision (monist tradition) or by a specific act of transformation (dualist tradition) is only the first step, however, toward the creation of enforceable rights and obligations of individuals. The importation creates merely a *potential* or possibility for the legal rules to create such rights and obligations, which is called "direct applicability" in the European legal tradition. In addition, the rule(s) have to be *suitable*—in their substantive provisions and choice of language—to create these rights and obligations. This is called "direct effect" in Europe. More specifically, the rules have to be: (I) unconditional, (ii) clear and precise, and (iii) objectively suitable to be applied by national administrations or courts without a need for (additional) legislative intervention.[23]

Most countries around the world, including virtually all Member States of the European Union, as well as Russia and the countries of the former Soviet bloc, Japan, China, and most countries in Africa and Central and Latin America, follow the dualist tradition. For them, an international convention, agreement, or other rule of international or supranational law first has to be accepted or ratified *as a document* to have any relevance. Second, there needs to be an act of transformation to bring that document or the specific rules in it from the sphere of politics with rules that are only binding *upon* the state into the sphere of the law of the land, i.e., the rules that are binding *in* the state. Once this is accomplished, *the document* or specific rule is considered to have "direct applicability" in the respective state. However, rights and obligations for individuals are created only if the specific language of a *specific provision*—and/or the language in the act of transformation—is also unconditional, clear, and precise, and suitable to be applied by national authorities or courts without further legislative intervention. If this is the case, that article, paragraph, or part of the rule is considered to have "direct effect" for and against individuals and can be invoked in court and before other public authorities.

By contrast, the United States of America, in principle, follows the monist tradition. For the U.S., a rule of international or supranational law also has to be accepted or ratified to have any relevance. However, in principle, the rule automatically gains direct applicability with its acceptance or ratification[24] and the only remaining

---

23. Sometimes it has been argued that the rules of an international agreement also have to be "intended" to create rights and obligations directly for individuals. However, this would introduce a subjective element and allow states to avoid obligations retroactively by claiming that they never intended to create certain rights for individuals. Unless the intention of the state was clearly manifested one way or the other at the time the agreement was signed and ratified, the objective standard of suitability should be applied. For an excellent analysis of U.S. constitutional law on the matter, see Jordan J. Paust, *Self-Executing Treaties*, Am. J. Int'l L., Vol. 82, 1988, pp. 760–783. The European approach is best explained by J.A. Winter, *Direct Applicability and Direct Effect—Two Distinct and Different Concepts in Community Law*, Common Market L. Rev., Vol. 9, 1972, pp. 425–438.

24. This is evident from the Supremacy Clause in Article VI(2) of the U.S. Constitution: "This Constitution, and the Laws of the United States which shall be made in Pursuance thereof; and all Treaties made, or which shall be made, under the Authority of the United States, shall be the

question is whether the rule is unconditional, clear and precise, and suitable to be applied by national authorities or courts without further legislative intervention. If a rule is both applicable and suitable to create rights and obligations for and against individuals, it is considered to be "self-executing."

The monist and dualist traditions create a tension whenever one or more monist states enter into an international agreement with one or more dualist states. If the agreement contains unconditional and clear and precise obligations that are suitable to create rights and obligations for and against individuals in the national legal orders, these rules become part of the law of the land in the monist state automatically and create enforceable rights and obligations with the ratification of the agreement. By contrast, the mere act of ratification does not create direct applicability in the dualist states and, therefore, no enforceable rights and obligations for individuals. Only when and to the extent the national parliaments of the dualist states adopt the necessary transformation acts, will these rights and obligations become effective. A good illustration of the problem can be found in the practice of the former Soviet Union to ratify numerous international human rights agreements without ever adopting the domestic legislation that would have effectively provided democratic and other rights for its citizens. To the outside world, the Soviet government played the role of the constructive international partner without having to face the music domestically.

Unfortunately, international law is poorly suited to remedy this imbalance and the hypocrisy of states that ratify international agreements but subsequently do not implement them at all into domestic law, or do so only in part or with considerable delay. The tools available to the other states—i.e., the monist states, where the new rules are automatically applicable and the dualist states, which have duly implemented them—are limited to the crude instruments of international law. Besides certain diplomatic measures and "naming and shaming," they mainly consist of tit for tat, i.e., reciprocal denial of the rights and obligations. This works better in some areas of law than in others. Not much is gained, for example, if one state threatens another by saying, "If you torture your citizens, I'll torture mine!" And even in trade law, where retaliation by suspension of trading rights usually works for a quick resolution of disputes between the U.S. and the EU, it is less impressive for the U.S. to be threatened with a trade embargo by New Zealand than the other way around.

For these reasons, ever fewer states are today following truly monist principles. In particular, the U.S. is almost systematically adding a provision to its congressional ratification laws pursuant to which the rules of the respective agreements can only be self-executing if reciprocity is ensured, i.e., if the other signatory states also

---

supreme Law of the Land; and the Judges in every State shall be bound thereby, any Thing in the Constitution or Laws of any State to the Contrary notwithstanding." See also Justice Marshall in *Foster v. Neilson*, 27 U.S. (2 Pet.) 253, 314 (1829) and the discussion in Louis Henkin, *Foreign Affairs and the US Constitution*, Clarendon Press 2nd ed. 1997, pp. 199 et seq.; see also Curtis Bradley, *International Law and the U.S. Legal System*, Oxford Univ. Press 2nd ed. 2015.

grant self-executing status or hold the provisions directly applicable and directly effective. Since this is very nearly never the case,[25] some are already considering the U.S. to have joined the club of dualist states.

As a result, international agreements today rely in almost every state around the world on an act of transformation before they can have any effect in domestic law. This act of transformation can take different forms. An authoritarian dictator may just need to sign an executive order. However, democratic states usually require an additional act of parliament, i.e., the adoption of a piece of domestic legislation. Such legislation can follow one of the three following basic models:

> *First*, the national legislation can be limited to a short statement pursuant to which the international agreement itself, *as attached* in the original form and language, becomes part of the law of the land.

> *Second*, the national legislation can refer to the international agreement but then proceed to *restate* the (translated) language of that agreement in more or less precise terms with additional provisions about national procedures, etc.

> *Third*, the national legislation can proceed to bring about the required changes in different national laws *without ever referring* to the international agreement.

As can be seen quite easily, only the first format of transformation ensures that different administrators and judges in different signatory states have at least the same text in front of them when asked to enforce rights or obligations on the basis of the international agreement. The fact that different administrators and judges in different states have different legal educations and traditions in their work and, therefore, may approach identical legal language differently, is exacerbated with the second and third formats of transformation, where they are not even given the original text of the agreement or where they may not even know that a change in the national laws was made in response to an international obligation.

Furthermore, the rights of natural or legal persons in a state will be impaired in different ways if the state is *late* in adopting the act of transformation or if the act is *incomplete* or *incorrect* in the implementation of the international agreement. Differences between an international agreement and an act of implementation are usually not the result of negligent or incompetent translators. Rather, they are the

---

25. The one country that consistently follows the monist tradition is Switzerland, where even the WTO Agreements, to the extent they contain clear, precise, and unconditional obligations, are deemed to provide directly enforceable rights for individuals and companies. The same is true, at least in theory, for most of the Muslim countries, on the basis of the principle of *pacta sunt servanda* (contractual promises must be honored) enshrined in the Quran, the supreme source of Islamic law (there are, in fact, numerous references in the Quran, for example in Surah 23:8). By contrast, the majority of other countries follow the European dualist tradition, either as former colonies of the European powers or by adoption of major principles of European law.

result of domestic politics. For example, if an international obligation would be widely unpopular in a state, or would cost significant amounts of money or jobs, or would conflict with the interests of powerful lobbies. However, such differences also mean that a private individual or company who relies on the rights provided by the international agreement, for example the right not to be discriminated against, may find those rights unavailable on the basis of the faulty transformation act. In a monist state, at least in theory, the individual and her lawyer should be able to make a direct reference to the actual agreement and overcome the defects in any acts of transformation. However, in a dualist state, it may be difficult or even impossible to persuade a judge to look at the agreement behind a legislative act of transformation to understand that the rights should be understood in ways that are not clear in the transformation act, not mentioned in it at all, or are inconsistent with the language of the transformation act.

These issues need to be kept in mind as we proceed to analyze the application of various international agreements and principles of international law in different countries in the context of international business transactions. In particular, we must never take it for granted that a particular rule of international law is going to be automatically and uniformly applicable in different countries where the parties to an IBT may be located.

B. Public International Trade Law versus Private International Business Law

While international *trade* law regulates the rights and obligations of states and their respective public authorities, international *business* law deals with the rights and obligations of corporations and other private entities engaged in international business transactions. Although our focus will be on international business law, some discussion of international trade law is important since obligations put on states, for example to provide duty free access to certain goods or to refrain from discriminatory taxation, can create rights for private individuals and corporations doing business in or with these states.

International trade law consists of three major levels of agreements: global, regional, and bilateral.

First, on the global scale, the most important originator of trade law is the World Trade Organization (WTO). All major trading nations are among its 164 contracting parties. The most important treaty administered by the WTO is the General Agreement on Tariffs and Trade (GATT). This Agreement has brought average import duty rates for manufactured goods down to almost negligible levels, puts some limits on non-tariff barriers that could substitute tariff or duty barriers, and protects against many forms of discrimination with the principles of most-favored-nation treatment (MFN, GATT Article I) and national treatment (GATT Article III). The WTO also administers the General Agreement on Trade in Services (GATS), the Agreement on Trade-Related Intellectual Property Rights (TRIPS), and a number of other important international sets of rules. The United Nations Conference on Trade and Development (UNCTAD), with its focus on the needs of developing countries, has mostly generated research and technical assistance documents and activities. By contrast, the United Nations Commission on International Trade Law (UNCITRAL) is an active producer of international agreements, albeit more in the field of international business law. The most important example of the latter is the United Nations Convention on Contracts for the International Sale of Goods (CISG), the centerpiece of our explorations in Part Two.

Second, on the regional scale, several organizations are extremely active in generating trade laws, either via agreements or via decisions of the organizations themselves. The most important is the European Union (EU), which represents its 27 member states in external trade relations, both multilateral (in particular at the WTO) and bilateral (for example, the free trade area between the EU and South Korea or the customs union between the EU and Turkey). Examples of other regional trade organizations with less expansive powers are the Economic Community of West African States (ECOWAS), the Association of Southeast Asian Nations (ASEAN), the Mercado Común del Sur (Mercosur) of five Latin American states, as well as the North American Free Trade Area (NAFTA), recently replaced with the new United States-Mexico-Canada Agreement (USMCA). Much of EU law enjoys direct applicability and direct effect with supremacy over (conflicting) national laws and, therefore, can generate direct rights and obligations for individuals trading in and with the EU. By contrast, trade laws generated by other regional trade organizations usually require transformation into national law and only apply to the extent and in the form they have been implemented domestically.

Third, a large and rapidly growing number of *bilateral* trade agreements have to be taken into account by anyone engaged in international business transactions. For example, the U.S. currently has free trade agreements in force with 20 countries, including Australia, Chile, Colombia, Costa Rica, Israel, Korea, Panama, and Peru. Such FTAs typically provide for duty-free trade for a broad range of goods originating in either of the two countries. Businesses wishing to benefit from these advantages typically have to follow certain procedures, for example regarding certificates of origin.

A *fourth* category of rules does not, strictly speaking, come under the rubric of *international* trade laws. These are the national rules about external trade, for example customs codes, export restrictions, and the like. For the U.S., the most important statutes regulating foreign trade are listed on the website of the U.S. Trade Representative (USTR) at https://ustr.gov/about-us/ trade-tool-box/trade-laws. Another page on this website has the current information about free trade agreements ratified by the U.S.: https://ustr.gov/trade-agreements/free-trade-agreements. The EU has similar listings at http://eur-lex.europa.eu/browse/directories/legislation.html.

C. Private International Law

The term "private international law" is somewhat of a misnomer for the issues dealt with by the rules generally associated with this area of law. The rules are not part of traditional *private* law, such as contracts or torts. Nor are they separate *international* rules for relations between nations. Rather, private international law provides national rules to settle conflicts of laws between different states, i.e., whether the national substantive law rules of one country—for example, German contract law—should apply to an international business transaction, or the corresponding substantive law rules of another country—for example, U.S. contract law. In addition to conflicts of laws, private international law also deals with conflicts of jurisdiction, in particular whether a dispute between an individual or a corporation located in one country with an individual or a corporation located in another country should be brought to the courts of the former or the latter. The only thing "private" about these rules is the fact that they deal with legal relationships between private parties, i.e., natural or legal persons other than government entities or international organizations.[26]

The private legal relationships covered by private international law can be classified into three types:

  i.   the relationship is noncommercial for both sides, such as disputes related to family law or trusts and estates;

  ii. the relationship is noncommercial for one but commercial for the other side, also known as business-to-consumer or B2C contracts;

  iii. the relationship is commercial for both sides, also known as business-to-business or B2B contracts.

Governments tend to have relatively far-reaching rules to regulate private relationships in the first two categories, partly to protect the weaker side, for example the consumer in a B2C relationship or the children in family law, and partly to ensure that certain procedures are followed, for example with regard to marriage and divorce. By contrast, governments tend to leave wide discretion to the parties of the third type of relationship. To say it differently, the freedom of contract is very broad in B2B transactions and includes, for example, the right to choose the applicable substantive law and to choose the courts or arbitration services for settlement of any disputes. This is why the area of law is sometimes also referred to as *choice of laws*.

---

26. For further analysis, see, for example, Talia Einhorn, *Private International Law in Israel*, Kluwer Law International 2nd ed. 2012; James Fawcett & Janeen Carruthers, Cheshire, *North & Fawcett: Private International Law*, Oxford Univ. Press 14th ed. 2008; James Fawcett, Maire Ni Shuilleabhain & Sangeeta Shah, *Human Rights and Private International Law*, Oxford Univ. Press 2014; Alex Mills, *The Confluence of Public and Private International Law: Justice, Pluralism and Subsidiarity in the International Constitutional Ordering of Private Law*, Cambridge Univ. Press 2009; Jan L. Neels, *The Nature, Objective and Purposes of the Hague Principles on Choice of Law in International Contracts*, Yearbook of Private International Law, Vol. XV 2013/14, pp. 45–56; Symeon Symeonides, *American Private International Law*, Kluwer Law International 2008.

However, the most accurate label for the entire body of rules would still be *conflicts of laws*.

The most important producer of rules in the field of private international law is the Hague Conference on Private International Law (HCCH), also called the World Organisation for Cross-Border Co-Operation in Civil and Commercial Matters. Eighty countries and the EU are members and another 68 countries have signed and ratified at least some of the conventions developed by the HCCH. Among the agreements or conventions the HCCH has developed are, for example, the 1978 Convention on the Law Applicable to Matrimonial Property Regimes, the 1973 Convention on the Law Applicable to Maintenance Obligations, and the 1973 Convention on the Recognition and Enforcement of Decisions Relating to Maintenance Obligations. Of interest in the context of international business transactions and international commercial litigation are, in particular, the 2005 Conventions on Choice of Court Agreements, the 1986 Convention on the Law Applicable to Contracts for the International Sale of Goods, the 1978 Convention on the Law Applicable to Agency, the 1965 Convention on the Service Abroad of Judicial and Extrajudicial Documents in Civil and Commercial Matters, the 1970 Convention on the Taking of Evidence Abroad in Civil and Commercial Matters, and the 1971 Convention on the Recognition and Enforcement of Foreign Judgments in Civil and Commercial Matters.[27]

The problem with HCCH conventions, as with all sources of international law, is the fact that states are in no way obliged to ratify them, even if they are members of the HCCH and have participated in the drafting of the conventions. Naturally, without ratification, states have no legal obligation, let alone any kind of enforceable obligation, to follow the rules enshrined in a given convention. Although its language may not be particularly controversial, a convention like the 1986 Hague Convention on the Law Applicable to Contracts for the International Sale of Goods, as of May 2018, has only attracted ratifications by Argentina and Moldova. Since its entry into force requires at least five ratifications, it has not even entered into force although it has been open for signature and ratification for 30 years.[28]

However, it would be quite unintelligent to dismiss the work of the HCCH merely because some if its conventions have attracted little formal support. For example, the 1971 Hague Convention for the Recognition and Enforcement of Foreign Judgments in Civil and Commercial Matters (Documents, p. II-43) has been ratified only by Albania, Cyprus, Kuwait, the Netherlands, and Portugal. Notably absent, as with many HCCH conventions, is a ratification by the United States. However, Sections of the 1962 Uniform Foreign-Country Money Judgments Recognition Act, as

27. All HCCH Conventions and the countries having ratified them are accessible on the website of the organization at https://www.hcch.net/en/instruments/conventions.

28. On the specific subject, the member states of the HCCH recently adopted the 2019 Hague Convention on the Recognition and Enforcement of Foreign Judgments in Civil and Commercial Matters (Documents, p. II-54). Whether this Convention can do for transnational litigation what the New York Convention has done for international commercial arbitration will depend on the number of ratifications and the practical implementation in the member states, however.

revised in 2005 and implemented in many U.S. jurisdictions (Documents, p. II-68) are largely congruent with the 1971 Convention.

Thus, the significance of some HCCH conventions derives from their broad support as evidenced by a large number of ratifications (the 1965 Hague Convention on the Service Abroad of Judicial and Extrajudicial Documents in Civil or Commercial Matters, Documents p. II-23, is a case on point). By contrast, the significance of other HCCH conventions derives from the fact that they codify general principles of law as recognized in their national law by a large number of states in different parts of the world and with different legal systems. Unfortunately, it can be quite difficult to determine whether a convention with limited formal support is nevertheless reflective of widely recognized principles. In practice, this question can become relevant in two distinct settings. First, in case of international commercial litigation, the court where a case is brought will look at its own national law to determine whether it has jurisdiction and, if the answer is in the affirmative, whether its national procedural rules on service abroad, taking of evidence, etc., have been observed and which substantive law should be applied to the case based either on an effective choice by the parties or, if there is no such choice or the choice is ineffective, based on the national rules of private international law. We will discuss in Part Six that public courts in any country around the world will always apply their national rules of procedure and will always have a preference for the application of their national substantive law rules. Nevertheless, they may sometimes come to the conclusion that party choice or private international law rules force them to apply some other substantive law. The outcome of such a procedure may then become quite unpredictable and significant additional costs and delays may be incurred.

The second setting, if there is a valid arbitration clause or agreement between the private parties to a transaction and dispute, would be international commercial arbitration. In this alternative to litigation abroad, the parties can designate the applicable *substantive and procedural* rules quite freely. Furthermore, in the absence of specific party designations, the arbitrators will often look at widely accepted or particularly equitable principles of law and these may very well be found in Hague conventions, in spite of limited numbers of ratifications.

The most dynamic entity producing rules of private international law, for several decades already, has been the European Union. Initially, the EU itself did not have legislative powers in this area and the Member States of the EU generated their common private international law rules via agreements or conventions that required ratification and implementation like other agreements of international law and also created the problems outlined above in cases of late, incomplete, or incorrect implementation by individual Member States. However, as of 1999, the EU itself took over the legislative powers in this area from its Member States.[29] As a result, the former agreements have been recast into EU regulations and now enjoy supremacy over

---

29. The respective powers were first created by the Treaty of Amsterdam, signed on October 2, 1997, and entered into force on May 1, 1999, see Articles 61(c), 65 and 67 of the consolidated EC

national Member State law, as well as direct applicability and—if the conditions of clarity, unconditionality and suitability of specific provisions are met—direct effect in the Member States.[30] Important examples are:

- Regulation 593/2008 of the European Parliament and of the Council of 17 June 2008 on the Law Applicable to Contractual Obligations, the so-called "Rome I Regulation" (OJ 2008 L 177, pp. 6-16, Documents, p. I-53);[31]

- Regulation 864/2007 of the European Parliament and of the Council of 11 July 2007 on the Law Applicable to Non-Contractual Obligations, the so-called "Rome II Regulation" (OJ 2007 L 199, pp. 40-49, Documents, p. I-67);[32]

- Regulation 1393/2007 of the European Parliament and of the Council of 13 November 2007 on the Service in the Member States of Judicial and Extra-Judicial Documents in Civil or Commercial Matters (OJ 2007 L 324, pp. 79-120, Documents, p. II-71);

- Regulation 1206/2001 of the Council of 28 May 2001 on Cooperation Between the Courts of the Member States in the Taking of Evidence in Civil and Commercial Matters (OJ 2001 L 174, pp. 1-24, Documents, p. II-82);

- Regulation 1215/2012 of the European Parliament and of the Council of 12 December 2012 on Jurisdiction and the Recognition of Judgments in Civil and Commercial Matters, the so-called "Brussels I bis Regulation" (OJ 2012 L 351, pp. 1-32, Documents, p. II-92).[33]

For individuals and corporations outside the EU, in particular those domiciled in the U.S., these EU rules are of interest in two kinds of situations: First, whenever a party from a third country like the U.S. brings a lawsuit against a party domiciled in the EU, the Regulations have to be applied just as if the lawsuit was brought by a

---

Treaty. After the reforms brought about by the Treaty of Nice, the respective powers are now contained in Article 81 of the Treaty on the Functioning of the European Union (TFEU).

30. For further discussion, see Peter Stone & Youseph Farah (ed.), *Research Handbook on EU Private International Law,* Edward Elgar Publishing 2015.

31. For detailed analysis, see Ulrich Magnus & Peter Mankowski (eds.), *European Commentaries on Private International Law—Rome I Regulation*, Sellier European Law Publishers 2017.

32. While Rome I deals with contracts, Rome II determines the applicable law for "non-contractual obligations in civil and commercial matters" (Article 1(1) of the Regulation). These are defined as "tort/delict, unjust enrichment, *negotiorum gestio* or *culpa in contrahendo*" (Article 2(1) of the Regulation). Together with property claims, these are the five possible claim bases we will revisit in Section 5: pre-contractual obligations (here referred to as *negotiorium gestio* or *culpa in contrahendo*), contractual obligations, as well as claims based on unjust enrichment, tort, and property.

33. This Regulation replaces Regulation 44/2001 which, in turn, replaced the well-known 1968 Brussels Convention. It applies to the 27 Member States of the EU except for Denmark. For details, see Ulrich Magnus & Peter Mankowski (eds.), *European Commentaries on Private International Law—Brussels I Regulation*, Sellier European Law Publishers 3rd ed. 2016.

There is a parallel document, the 2007 Lugano Convention, successor to the 1988 Lugano Convention, that extends many of the same principles to Denmark, as well as the member states of the European Free Trade Area (EFTA), namely Iceland, Norway, and Switzerland (OJ 2009 L 147, pp. 5–43).

party domiciled in one Member State against a party domiciled in another Member State. The scope of application is determined by the territoriality principle and attaches to domicile of the defendant.[34] The nationality of the parties is irrelevant.

Second, if a U.S. corporation operates a subsidiary inside the EU or if a corporation that is incorporated, say, in the U.S. Virgin Islands, has its principal place of business in a Member State, it has a domicile in the EU for the purposes of the Brussels I bis Regulation (see note 34 below) and can be sued there pursuant to these rules by parties from other Member States and by third-country parties.

The Organization of American States (OAS) is also an active player in the development of private international law at the regional level. Every four to six years, the OAS convenes a Specialized Conference on Private International Law (Conferencia de Derecho Internacional Privado—CIDIP) and, since 1975, these conferences have resulted in the drafting of 26 conventions. These include the 1994 Inter-American Convention on the Law Applicable to International Contracts, the so-called "Mexico Convention" (Documents, p. I-48), and the 1979 Inter-American Convention on Conflicts of Laws Concerning Commercial Companies. Unfortunately, similar to the conventions produced by the Hague Conference, the record of ratifications by the OAS Member States is somewhat patchy and, in particular, the U.S. has usually not signed, let alone ratified, these conventions. Nevertheless, they can be an expression of regionally recognized principles of private international law.

Another regional player active in the development of private international law is the Mercado Común del Sur (Mercosur). This trade bloc, composed of Argentina, Bolivia, Brazil, Paraguay, Uruguay, and Venezuela, has generated a number of agreements on choice of law in international contracts, as well as conflicts of jurisdiction, providing rules for IBTs between companies located in the member countries. Argentina, Brazil, Paraguay, and Uruguay have generally ratified these agreements. However, they are not self-executing or directly applicable and will only be applied by courts in the member countries to the extent they have been implemented by domestic legislation.

Many of the issues at the heart of private international law will reappear in our discussion of dispute settlement in Part Six.

---

34. For natural persons, Article 62 of the Regulation refers to the internal law of "the Member State whose courts are seised of a matter" for the determination of domicile. This can lead to jurisdictional conflicts if more than one Member State considers that a person is domiciled within its territory. Most EU Member States refer to "habitual residence" in this regard, i.e., where a person de facto lives and, if a person has more than one residence, the place where she spends most of her time and is most integrated socially.

For companies and legal persons, Article 63 of the Regulation provides an autonomous standard, namely domicile at the place where it has (i) its statutory seat; or (ii) its central administration; or (iii) its principal place of business. If a company is incorporated in one Member State, has its central administration in another Member State, and its principal place of business in a third Member State, it is domiciled and can be sued in all three Member States, see Paul Vlas, in Magnus & Mankowski (eds.), *Brussels I Regulation*, Sellier European Law Publishers 2012 at p. 811.

D. National Law

Contrary to what the foregoing discussion may suggest, national law remains the most important source of law for international business transactions. In this context, we should consistently distinguish three types of national law: substantive law, for example the law on contracts, procedural law, for example the civil procedure code, and mandatory rules of public law, such as customs laws or health and safety regulations.

In business-to-business (B2B) transactions, the parties are generally free to choose the applicable substantive law. They could choose the substantive law applicable in seller's country or the substantive law applicable in buyer's country. They could also choose a neutral third country for the applicable substantive law, or even one of several international codifications, for example the United Nations Convention on Contracts for the International Sale of Goods (CISG). Such a choice of law, as long as it meets certain standards of effectiveness, will normally be respected by any court and any arbitration tribunal around the world.

If the parties to the IBT have not made a choice of law or the choice is deemed ineffective or if they have chosen a body of law like the CISG and the legal dispute falls outside of the scope of the convention, the applicable substantive national law will be determined by the rules of private international law, i.e., the rules on conflicts of laws. However, since private international law is by and large national law on conflicts, different courts in different countries will apply different rules to resolve the conflicts. A notable exception is the European Union, where many conflicts rules have already been harmonized for the entire trading bloc, as outlined above. To illustrate the point, if a dispute should arise between a seller in Switzerland and a buyer in the U.S., the applicable private international law would depend on the place where the dispute is brought. If the Swiss seller should sue the U.S. buyer in the U.S. for payment, the American court would apply American private international law or conflicts rules to determine the applicable law. That is easier said than done, however. There is no actual code of conflicts of laws or private international law in the U.S. Therefore, questions of choice of law, as they are called here, are determined by common law, and common law is normally state law. Thus, if the case is brought at the buyer's domicile in Texas state court, the court will apply Texas common law to determine the applicable substantive law. If, for some reason, the case is brought in California state court, the Texas buyer can either allow the case to proceed and the California state court will apply California common law to determine the applicable substantive law, or the Texas buyer can have the case removed to federal court on diversity grounds; but the federal court located in California will, under the *Erie* doctrine,[35] still have to apply California state common law to determine the applicable substantive law. The good news is that state common law throughout the U.S. tends to refer to the law of the state where the transaction

---

35. Erie Railroad Company v. Tompkins, 58 S. Ct. 817, 304 U.S. 674, 82 L. Ed. 1188 (1938).

took place, the so-called *lex loci,* or the place with the *most significant relationship* to or *center of gravity* of the transaction. The bad news is not only that these places may be uncertain, but also that a court may want to apply its own law, the *lex fori.*[36] In any case, the relevant references to precedent differ from state to state and typically require local counsel even if the case is pending in federal court. However, this situation explains, at least to some extent, the significance of the work undertaken by the American Law Institute and the National Conference of Commissioners on Uniform State Laws in the development of the Uniform Commercial Code (UCC), which has achieved a level of harmonization of state laws and, thereby, reduced the importance and complexity of conflict of laws analysis in the U.S. We will deal with the UCC in some detail in Part Two. Of course, the UCC only reduces conflicts between the laws of different states in the U.S. and does not address the conflict between itself and Swiss law. Interestingly, foreign parties before American courts are largely treated the same as out-of-state American parties, i.e., the system often does not distinguish between interstate and international cases. Through this back door, the elaborate construct of conflict theory comes back to haunt us.

The situation regarding the conflict of laws is much simpler in Switzerland, although it is also a country with a strong federal tradition. If the American buyer should sue the Swiss seller for nonperformance, any court in Switzerland with jurisdiction over the defendant, usually the cantonal court at her domicile, would simply refer to the Swiss Federal Code on Private International Law of 1987, where any questions of jurisdiction of judicial and administrative authorities, questions of applicable law, as well as conditions for the recognition and enforcement of foreign judgments, are clearly regulated.[37]

---

36. For a classical treatment of the issue, see Walter Wheeler Cook, *The Logical and Legal Bases of the Conflict of Laws,* Yale L.J., Vol. 33, No. 5, 1924, pp. 457–88; as well as Elliott E. Cheatham, *American Theories of Conflict of Laws: Their Role and Utility,* Harvard L. Rev. Vol. 58, No. 3 (1945), pp. 361–394; and the three-volume work by Joseph H. Beale, *A Treatise on the Conflict of Laws,* Baker, Voohis & Co. 1935. The "American conflicts revolution" (Hartley) was spearheaded by Currie and his "balance of interest analysis"; see Brainerd Currie, *Notes on Methods and Objectives in the Conflict of Laws,* Duke L.J. 1959, No. 2, pp. 171–181. At the bottom line, this method asks whether the forum state has an interest in the outcome of the case, for example to protect consumers, and would this interest be better served if it was applying its own law to the case? An alternative approach was taken by Ehrenzweig, who postulated the "primacy of forum law" according to which a court should always apply its own substantive law (*lex fori*) unless the court had a really good reason to apply the substantive law of another state, let alone another country; see Albert Ehrenzweig, *A Treatise on the Conflict of Laws,* West Publishing 1962. Finally, there is the "better law theory," promoted by Leflar and others, according to which the courts should undertake a comparative analysis of the outcome of the case under both or all potentially applicable laws and then select the laws that provide the better or best solution for the dispute; see Robert A. Leflar, *Choice-Influencing Considerations in Conflicts Law,* 41 N.Y.U. L. Rev. 1966, pp. 267–327.

37. The Swiss Code is considered a model of clear and concise legislative drafting and is largely the brainchild of the famous private international lawyer Professor Frank Vischer. For some reflections on the drafting project, see Frank Vischer, *Drafting National Legislation on Conflict of Laws: The Swiss Experience,* in L. & Contemp. Problems, Vol. 41, Spring 1977, pp. 131–145. An English translation of the act is available at http://www.rwi.uzh.ch/dam/jcr:00000000-14c0-11a6-0000

While the question of the applicable substantive law may cause some headaches in the absence of a clear and effective choice by the parties, the question of the applicable procedural law is generally more easily answered. Choice of law rules generally do not apply to procedural law and each forum generally applies its own procedural law, the *lex fori*. This is invariably true for public courts and it is increasingly even true for arbitration institutions, unless the parties to an arbitration unambiguously selected the application of different procedural rules. Since procedural law regulates questions of available remedies, accessible evidence, deadlines, preemption of claims, etc., as well as enforcement, it can be decisive for the outcome of a case *where* it is brought, even if the parties have chosen the substantive law they like best.

Naturally, any mandatory rules of public law have to be applied, whether or not the parties like it. This includes tax laws, customs laws, rules on competition or antitrust, environmental, health, and safety regulations, consumer protection laws, labor laws, etc. Problems may nevertheless arise if more than one country wants to apply its mandatory laws to one issue and the rules cannot be reconciled.

E. Subnational Law

As we have seen in the preceding section, sub-national law can play a role for IBTs if there are differences in the contract law of the different states or provinces or cantons that make up a federal state. This is the case primarily in the U.S. Even strongly federal systems, like Switzerland, Germany, or Brazil, have federal codes of civil or contract law that apply uniformly in all constituent states. The same is true for India. Although India inherited the common law tradition from its former colonial masters, the British themselves imposed the Indian Contract Act on the entire country as early as 1872, a kind of codification of the common law on contracts. A country that comes close to the U.S. model is Canada, where contract law remains common law and the Sale of Goods Act serves a function similar to the UCC in the U.S. A bit like Louisiana, which does not follow the UCC and instead applies a contract law modeled on the French *Code Civil*, in the Canadian province of Quebec has the Quebec Civil Code, which follows the continental European tradition. Finally, Australia also uses common law in contract law and does not even have a modern uniform model for the states to follow. However, Australia has developed a kind of uniform common law via the jurisprudence of the High Court of Australia, which has appellate jurisdiction over all state and federal courts. Finally, New Zealand follows the common law tradition but is not a federal system and, therefore, also does not have sub-national differences in its contract law.

The problem of sub-national differences is more pronounced in administrative law. While this does not usually affect the kind of IBTs we will be discussing in this

---

-0000115fcc32/PILA.pdf. Since Article 1(2) of the Act gives precedence to international treaties, the Act does not apply in cases coming under the Lugano Convention, i.e., disputes between a Swiss party and a party in the EU or in Iceland or Norway, see also above, note 33.

book, investors seeking to establish durable business organizations abroad will need to carefully evaluate regional and local laws and ordinances in areas such as taxation, environmental protection, land-use and zoning law, as well as labor law and health and safety regulations.

F. Model Laws and Private Codes

As we will analyze different aspects of international business transactions, we will come across a number of unconventional rules. We have already encountered the Uniform Commercial Code or UCC, which is a kind of model law developed by experts on behalf of the American Law Institute (ALI) and the National Conference of Commissioners on Uniform State Laws. These are not really public bodies and certainly not legislatures. Therefore, "the UCC" as such does not have the force of law. There are two ways, however, in which the UCC can become the substantive law applicable to a given IBT. First, and most important, the UCC, as adopted by the ALI and the Uniform Law Commissioners, is recommended for adoption by the several states in the U.S. Although the state legislatures often make some changes,[38] by and large, the UCC has been enacted via state statutes in all 50 states, the District of Columbia, Puerto Rico, and the U.S. Virgin Islands. One notable exception is Louisiana, where Article 2 has not been implemented and, instead, the Louisiana Civil Code of 1948 applies. The latter is more similar to the French *Code Civil* than the American contract law regimes of the other states. The second way the UCC can become the substantive law governing an IBT is via a valid choice of law by the parties to the contract. In B2B transactions, the parties are not limited to choosing the law of a country or state; they can also choose a model code or even write their own.

The United Nations Commission on International Trade Law (UNCITRAL) has already been mentioned above. It gathers experts from around the world into six working groups, each of which is charged with the development of international conventions and other instruments aimed at the regulation and facilitation of business and trade transactions. The most important convention developed by UNCITRAL[39] is the 1980 United Nations Convention on Contracts for the International Sale of Goods or CISG, also called the Vienna Convention. As of June 2020, the CISG has been ratified by 93 countries, including the U.S. and virtually all other major trading nations. We will discuss at length in Part Two how it becomes the default substantive law for many international sales contracts and what this means for the rights and obligations of the parties. Even if the CISG does not apply by force of law

---

38. WestlawNext, in its database Uniform Commercial Code Local Codes Variation, provides information about variations in different states. Volume I of the Documents Collection contains several Articles of the UCC that are relevant to international business transactions.

39. The text—in multiple languages—and the ratification status of all UNCITRAL Conventions and information about the national adoption of legislation based on its Model Laws, can be accessed on the website of UNCITRAL at http://www.uncitral.org/uncitral/en/uncitral_texts.html. The English version of the CISG is included in the Documents Collection at p. I-79.

(Article 1(1)), parties to a B2B transaction can choose it as the substantive law governing the rights and obligations under their contract.

As the representative of the UN in this area of law, UNCITRAL is today also the sponsor of the 1958 Convention on the Recognition and Enforcement of Foreign Arbitral Awards, the so-called New York Convention (Documents, p. II-500). Supported by 164 countries from around the world as of June 2020, this convention is the cornerstone of the international commercial arbitration system.

UNCITRAL is in charge of a number of additional conventions, but it has also ventured into the territory of model laws. One important document is the 1985 Model Law on International Commercial Arbitration, as amended (Documents, p. II-185). Like with the UCC, the idea is to provide a well-balanced and comprehensive model that can be enacted via national legislation. Indeed, more than 80 states have adopted national laws based on and largely congruent with the Model Law. Another example is the 2001 Model Law on Electronic Signatures, which has been implemented by 33 states from around the world as of June 2020.

Finally, UNCITRAL also develops so-called "contractual texts" that are not intended for adoption via national legislation but for incorporation into private contracts. The most important examples are the UNCITRAL Arbitration Rules, first adopted in 1976 and last updated in 2013 (Documents, p. I-199).

The next institution worth mentioning is the International Institute for the Unification of Private Law, better known as UNIDROIT. This is an intergovernmental organization with 63 member countries, seated in Rome, Italy. It relies on experts, not unlike the Uniform Law Commission, to analyze private law differences and similarities around the world and propose model codes that promote the harmonization of national laws. Its most successful product is called the UNIDROIT Principles of International Commercial Contracts (PICC).[40] Again, they can become relevant for an IBT either via adoption by a state into their national law or by party choice. Since the UNIDROIT Principles are also recognized as a codification of the so-called *lex mercatoria*, they are often cited when judges or arbitrators have to fill gaps in contracts via general principles of law.

Another prolific producer of rules for IBTs is the International Chamber of Commerce (ICC).[41] Created in 1919 by private businessmen from different continents, it has its seat in Paris and today counts hundreds of thousands of individuals and companies among its members. In addition to lobbying at the national and international level on behalf of private enterprise, the ICC is active in developing rules for commerce and in providing arbitration services. One of the first sets of rules we

---

40. See https://www.unidroit.org/instruments/commercial-contracts/unidroit-principles-2016. The Principles will be discussed in some detail in Part 2. They are included in the Documents Collection on p. I-101.

41. Information about the ICC, the texts of its various codes, and access to its dispute settlement rules and services are all available at https://iccwbo.org/.

will come across are the so-called INCOTERMS®, which are regularly incorporated in international sales contracts to determine whether and how far seller or buyer have to take care of transport and insurance and where the risk of loss or damage will pass. Another important document is the Uniform Customs and Practice for Documentary Credits (UCP600) (Documents, p. I-500), which is the standard for letter of credit transactions around the world. Although we will encounter several other ICC codes and documents, the last to be mentioned here are the ICC Rules of Arbitration, which can be relied upon not only in arbitration proceedings organized by the ICC, but also in other institutional and ad hoc arbitrations (Documents, p. II-294). All ICC documents have in common that they are not enacted via national legislation but are adopted voluntarily by the parties to a private contract or arbitration agreement.

Finally, it is also worth mentioning at this time the International Bar Association.[42] The IBA was founded in 1947 as a global representation of lawyers and national bar associations. It has a membership of more than 80,000 individual lawyers and almost 200 bar associations and law societies from more than 160 countries. Among the goals of the IBA are the promotion of professional ethics and freedoms of lawyers, as well as the independence of courts and judges around the world. Among the documents produced by the IBA that we will come across are the 2014 Guidelines on Conflicts of Interest in International Arbitration (Documents, p. II-269) and the 2010 Rules on the Taking of Evidence in International Arbitration (Documents, p. II-239). IBA rules can be incorporated into private contracts or arbitration agreements. Guidelines can also play an important role as expressions of general principles recognized by lawyers from around the world and from all different legal systems. We will return to this function shortly, when we discuss the resolution of conflicts and the filling of gaps in the set of rules that can or must apply to an IBT.

G. Private Contracts

As we have already mentioned, the freedom of contract is generally broad in B2B transactions. The parties can choose to play within the rules that apply by the force of law, and merely determine the type and quantity of the goods, the price, and the time and place of delivery. The various rights and obligations of the parties, as well as the applicable law and the forum for the settlement of any disputes, will then be determined on the basis of standard legal rules. For example, if the seller is located in New York and the buyer in the United Kingdom, chances are that the applicable law will be the contract laws of New York and they will determine the rights and obligations in case of problems with the performance of either side. Any claims would have to be brought in the defendant's forum, i.e., if the buyer is unhappy with the goods, she would sue the seller at her home in New York. Conversely, if the seller

---

42. See https://www.ibanet.org/.

does not get paid in full, he would have to pursue the buyer in the UK. Litigating in front of English courts under New York state law may not be the best idea, however.

Alternatively, the parties to a B2B transaction can take more control of the rules they want to abide by. They can do so first, by explicitly selecting the applicable substantive law. In our example, the parties could opt for English law or Scottish law instead of New York law, or they could agree on a neutral set of rules, such as the CISG. They can go much further than that, however. As long as the parties are in agreement with each other, they could select a set of rules like the CISG and then start deviating from it for specific questions or issues. One example would be liquidated damages for certain types of performance problems that are not otherwise provided by statutory law. Finally, the parties are perfectly entitled to write up a comprehensive set of rules by themselves that would leave little or no scope of application to any default or back-up legal system.

In short, the private contract concluded by the parties can provide anywhere from almost 0% to almost 100% of the applicable contract rules or laws. Which choices of existing laws and which party-drafted alternatives make the most sense has to be determined on a case-by-case basis. In Part Two we discuss the options and provide some advice.

H. How to Resolve Conflicts and Gaps in the Rules Governing IBTs

It should be easy to see by now that many rules from many sources on many levels are potentially applicable to an IBT. This poses a number of problems for lawyers and legal advisors, namely:

- finding all applicable rules, on all relevant levels;
- correctly interpreting all applicable rules to understand their impact in a given case and their relevance for the rights, obligations, and remedies of the parties to an IBT;
- correctly resolving potential conflicts between simultaneously applicable rules, either on the basis of hierarchy, where a mandatory higher order rule displaces a discretionary and/or lower order rule, or on the basis of other conflicts or choice of law rules; and
- filling any gaps between different sets of rules to come up with solutions for problems or questions for which none of the applicable rules seems to provide an answer.

These encompass the themes of the entire book. After working through this book, anyone should be able to handle all of the elements of shepherding an IBT from the first negotiations, to the contract drafting and conclusion, to the contract implementation, all the way to the contract enforcement, if necessary.

As a general or rule of thumb, in B2B transactions, the party agreements in the contract — or after a dispute has arisen — override any other rules, except for mandatory rules, such as tax and antitrust. Optional rules in the respective sales and contract laws are next in line. The following pyramid illustrates the hierarchy of norms within a legal system.

Chart 1-7 Hierarchy of Norms

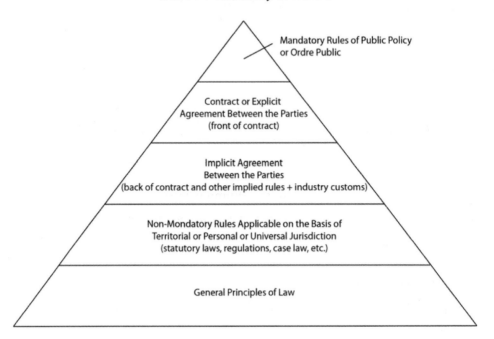

Mandatory Rules of Public Policy or Ordre Public

Contract or Explicit Agreement Between the Parties (front of contract)

Implicit Agreement Between the Parties (back of contract and other implied rules + industry customs)

Non-Mondatory Rules Applicable on the Basis of Territorial or Personal or Universal Jurisdiction (statutory laws, regulations, case law, etc.)

General Principles of Law

For IBT, there is the added problem that we are usually dealing with more than one legal system, namely seller's country and laws, and buyer's country and laws. To the extent the parties have not agreed or cannot agree, private international law, or the rules on conflicts of laws, determine the applicable substantive law and the forum for the settlement of any disputes. The problem in this regard is that private international law or conflicts rules are national rules and they are not necessarily harmonized internationally. Thus, each party to an international contract may think of her own rules without necessarily understanding that they are different from the assumptions of the other side. When push comes to shove, the court first called upon — if it affirms its adjudicative jurisdiction over the parties and the dispute — will apply its *lex fori* conflicts rules. This can create an incentive for a party to race to the courthouse at a time when negotiations for a friendly settlement might otherwise still have been possible.

If the parties write their own rules or refer to an international set of rules, like the CISG, there is a risk that the chosen law(s) do not cover all elements of a dispute. This leaves a gap and an open question in the rights and duties of the parties and for the settlement of any disputes between them. Such a gap can be filled by one of two methods. First, the incomplete international or contractual regime can be supplemented by a comprehensive national legal system, which can be agreed upon by the parties or found via the application of conflicts rules. Second, if this method is not possible or leads to undesirable outcomes, the gaps can be filled via reference to general principles of law. This is not really different in international contexts from national settings, where courts also have to resort quite frequently to general principles of law if a new type of situation has never before been resolved by statutory or case law rules. As always, mandatory public laws of the country or countries with prescriptive jurisdiction provide the outer guardrails, certainly if the parties also have to fear enforcement jurisdiction.

Section 5. Putting It All Together: How to Analyze a Case in an Exam and in Practice

---

Checklist 1-1
8 Steps to a Winning Brief

Step 1:   Gathering and Understanding the Facts of the Case

Step 2:   Identifying Binary Claims: Who Wants What from Whom and Why? ("5Ws")

Step 3:   Finding All Applicable Rules for the Case

Step 4:   Identifying the Claim Bases in the Applicable Rule(s)

Step 5:   Isolating the Conditions for a Claim to Have Arisen, Not to Be Extinguished, and to Be Enforceable

Step 6:   Presenting a Persuasive Argument (1)—Road Map

Step 7:   Presenting a Persuasive Argument (2)—Subsumption of the Facts under the Law and the Four Levels of Analysis

Step 8:   Presenting a Persuasive Argument (3)—Conclusions

Explanations

For those accustomed to the so-called *IRAC Method*, Steps 1 and 2 fall into category I—identification of the issues; Steps 3, 4, and 5 are part of category R—identification of the applicable rule(s); Steps 6 and 7 form core category A—application of the rule(s) to the case at hand; and Step 8 is equivalent to category C—conclusions.

Step 1: Gathering and Understanding the Facts of the Case

In addition to the fact that students work with hypothetical cases and any triumphs and mistakes do not affect real clients, the biggest difference between the work of a student in an exam and the work of a lawyer in practice is that the student is working in a controlled and self-contained environment. The student only has to deal with the information provided in the exam and has to take that information at face value. She does not have to search for additional facts and she normally does not have to worry about the accuracy of information, trustworthiness of witnesses, etc. One would think that this would make Step 1 very easy for the student—gathering and understanding all relevant facts. However, experience teaches that students struggle with Step 1 and often overlook important pieces of information although the entire hypothetical provided for an exam may be no longer than a page or two. This is unacceptable and also entirely unnecessary. The following method can teach anyone to gather all relevant facts and to organize them in such a way that their correct interpretation and understanding is virtually guaranteed.

Learning and practicing this method is all the more important since the facts in the real world are not delivered to the lawyer on a silver platter. Real cases may present dozens of different sources and hundreds or even thousands of pages of information to be analyzed in a limited time. Naturally, the information is not presented in a logical manner, at least not the way we would need it for the legal analysis. Furthermore, even though the amount of information may be vast, critical pieces of the puzzle may be missing and have to be obtained via additional factual research, or via interviews with clients, witnesses, or experts. Some critical information may remain elusive. Other pieces of information seem to or may actually contradict each other. This makes it all the more important that students learn early and learn well how to digest and dissect information. However, in a textbook, we can only address this issue up to a point, since we cannot include information sources such as witnesses to be interviewed. The method presented on the following pages focuses on the analysis of *documents*, such as an exam hypothetical, business correspondence and contracts in a moot court case or in a real case, written witness statements and expert opinions, and of course judicial decisions and statutory provisions of any kind. On its own, the method does not teach students how to deal with *people*, such as clients, witnesses, jurors, judges, or arbitrators. Moot court competitions can teach a certain measure of these skills. The rest has to be acquired by working in legal clinics or externships as students, and by working as lawyers under a supervisor or mentor on the job itself.

The challenge in Step 1 is to get a comprehensive and correct understanding of all relevant facts. This begins with the extraction and logical rearrangement of the information. It continues with the identification of missing information and how it may be obtained, and the identification of contradictory facts or statements and how they may be resolved. It also includes the question of who has the bear the consequences if certain information cannot be found, or if some contradictions or disputed facts cannot be conclusively resolved.

Surveying the Information and Making an Inventory

Challenge: Gather and organize all relevant documents; understand the basics of the case

The first step is gathering, reading, and organizing all available information. Which documents and materials are there? Who are the authors, who are the addressees, and what was the title or purpose of each communication? What is the underlying story? What is the problem? Which areas of law does it concern? What is your role and what are the expectations of your client or boss?

At this stage, you just want to understand the general idea and direction of the assignment. If there are many different documents or pieces of information, an inventory or table of contents should be produced. The entries in the inventory should be nontechnical, for example, "letter of January 15," "draft contract of January 30," "draft letter of credit of February 3," "witness statement of Mr. X of April 20," etc. Unless a different arrangement seems indicated, for example, a breakdown into different relationships (A and B, B and C), we can already sort the documents in chronological order. Another way could be grouping communications by sender or by the party who submitted them to the court or arbitral tribunal (for example, "submissions by the applicant").

Once we know what kind of sources of information we have, the next step is a fairly superficial reading to get the main ideas and understand what was going on, who are the parties to the dispute, and what caused the problem between them. Importantly, at this stage we also need to find out the role we are expected to play: counsel to the seller or the buyer? Clerk or assistant to the judge or arbitrator? From the outset, we need to avoid any actions or statements that are incompatible with this role.

Since the analysis is still proceeding on a superficial level, qualifications should be avoided at this stage. For example, if it is not clear when a number of offers and counteroffers actually led to the formation of a contract, a designation such as "the contract of February 5" or "the acceptance of March 4" should be avoided, even if the parties used those qualifications. Instead, neutral classifications should be used, such as "buyer's e-mail of February 16." At a later stage, the communications will have to be analyzed to see whether the fax or e-mail called "acceptance" by the buyer was in effect an acceptance, or maybe another counteroffer.

Careful Reading with a Ruler and a Red Pen

Challenge: Mark all potentially relevant facts, arguments, claims, etc. in all available documents; understand the details of the case; make sure that nothing is overlooked

Having understood on a superficial level what went on and what the case or dispute is about, the second step is a comprehensive and careful analysis of the facts as they are currently presented or presenting themselves. To this end, all available information must be analyzed in great detail. Not one relevant piece of information should be overlooked. For example, if you rely on the fact that a particular communication was sent on February 16 to conclude that a contract was formed, you cannot overlook the information that Friday, February 16, was a public holiday in the seller's country and nobody saw the communication until several days later. Did the parties modify the written contract orally during their phone call of April 30? What about the fact that process was served on an office assistant, rather than an authorized representative of the company? We don't know at this early stage whether these facts make a difference in law but we absolutely must not overlook them later in our analysis.

A good method for comprehensive information extraction is to read each document very closely. Every piece of information that potentially has any legal significance should be underlined separately in this process. It is recommended that this be done very meticulously, with a ruler and a red pen. Subsequently, when the facts are subsumed under the law and integrated into our analysis and arguments (Step 7), each underlined piece of information is then ticked off with a green pen when it has been evaluated or when you have decided that it is ultimately irrelevant. By tracking our progress in this way, we can always see any facts or claims that have not yet been fully dealt with in our analysis. The Red-and-Green Method enables us to verify, before we finish our analysis, whether every potentially relevant piece of information has indeed been taken care of and nothing has been overlooked.[43] As long as any information is still red and not green, you are not done.

Making a Time Line

Challenge: Make a comprehensive time line with all potentially relevant elements of the story

Now that we know in detail what happened, we need to organize the facts in a logical manner. In almost all cases, we need a **chronological organization** because we need to understand exactly how the story unfolded that ultimately led to the dispute between the parties. The importance of this job should not be underestimated, in particular if there are several story lines told by several parties or witnesses, or in cases where deadlines had to be met or where the parties are arguing whether or not certain communications were sent or received on time or were received before others. To give just one illustration of the importance of careful organization, the author has been involved in more than a few cases where the question whether or not something was done before the deadline depended on the time zones where seller and buyer were located. What was on time in one time zone does not mean that it was on time in another.

As always in legal analysis, *precision* is important here. Claims of many millions of dollars may turn on the question whether an offer was revoked before it was accepted or whether a claim was presented within the statute of limitations. Even in cases where there are no tight deadlines that may or may not have been missed, the organization of the information in chronological order requires us to undertake a

---

43. In practice, at least in complex cases where tens or hundreds of thousands of pages of business communications may have to be reviewed, this system has its limitations. Almost invariably, it is not possible for the lawyers to read each and every page very carefully. Instead, it is common practice today to scan all documents that are still on paper and add them to the electronic documents and e-mails and then run keyword and name searches via computer to find the documents that actually need careful review. Once those are identified, however, we can go back to printing them out and reading them carefully with the Red-and-Green Method.

third reading of the facts and, in turn, promotes complete and correct understanding of the underlying story.

Making a Relationship Chart

Challenge: Make a relationship chart with all potential players; understand exactly how each of the players is connected to any other parties and who may have claims against whom

In particular in cases where more than two actors are involved, it is important that we include everybody in the analysis of whose statements, actions, or omissions may be of relevance, and to understand correctly their relationship to each other. Who are the parties to the dispute? If there are other individuals or entities, what is their relationship to the parties? We need to understand exactly the claims company A is bringing against company B and company C, whether counterclaims by C are going to be presented only against A or also against B, whether A and B would potentially be joint and severally liable for those counterclaims, and whether D, E, and F were representing A, B, or C in the negotiations. If Mr. X was the managing director of subsidiary S, are his statements also binding on the mother company M? If subsidiary S is wholly owned by M, does it mean that Buyer B can bring claims against both S and M? Although it is too early to answer the questions at this stage, we need to be aware of all actual and potential relationships. If subsidiary S is in liquidation, it would be professional malpractice if the buyer's lawyers did not try to bring their claims also against M.

Another important point, as we begin to classify facts as to their relevance in law, is an understanding of what is and what is not (potentially) in dispute. For example, if it is not clear whether Agent A acted on behalf of Seller S or Buyer B, we may have to make a reasoned argument for one option or the other. This raises two points: which of two or more solutions do we advocate? And how detailed and sophisticated should the argument for that solution be? The question of detail, which is ultimately a question of dedicating time and resources to make an argument more forceful, will be discussed below when we talk about the Four Levels of Analysis. The question of which position to take is related but also somewhat different. On the one hand, if the answer is not very important because it does not really matter one way or another for the final outcome whether Agent A acted on behalf of Seller S or Buyer B, this is an indication that we will need only a low level of analysis and may even leave the answer open. On the other hand, and this is much more common, if our argument on the question at hand may potentially affect the overall outcome of the dispute, this is an indication that we will need a higher level of analysis and that we need to carefully consider which side we should take on the issue to best advance the interests of our client. Finally, if we are advising a judge or arbitrator, we should analyze both sides of the argument and simply recommend the answer that seems more logical or better supported by the facts.

A useful rule of thumb has always been: if there are more than two dates, make a time line; if there are more than two persons, make a relationship chart.

Telling an Organized Story

Challenge: Tell an organized story that is convincing and supportive of your position in law

Now that we have essentially analyzed the factual information already four times (superficially, carefully, chronologically, relationally), we should be able to summarize the facts in an organized way for our brief. This is a particularly tricky part of the work of a lawyer and requires different approaches depending on the position we have in the dispute at hand. If we are advising the seller who wants to get paid in spite of some problems with his performance, we will emphasize different parts of the story than if we are advising the buyer who does not want to pay although she does want to keep the somewhat imperfect goods. There are important ethical considerations here: as a partisan attorney, we do not have an obligation to point out factual elements that work against the interests of our client but may have been overlooked by the other side. At the same time, however, we must never misrepresent the facts or actively suppress evidence.

That being said, for our internal analysis, we always want to have _the full story_, with all details and all evidentiary elements, whether friendly or hostile to the position of our client. In our brief we may not need to say that seller's acceptance of buyer's terms was sent out late or that requesting a letter of credit from the bank could be interpreted as an acceptance of the terms of the contract of sale. However, we still need to be aware of these possibilities because they may be brought up by the other side in their reply to our claims and we may need to warn our client in advance of certain weaknesses in our position that, in turn, may suggest that a settlement is preferable to litigation or arbitration.

Thus, you should put together a comprehensive story for yourself and then pick out from it the elements that are common ground, those that need to be communicated to make the story coherent, and those that are supportive of your client's position and not in conflict with the truth, and put them into the summary of the facts in your brief.

Finally, when telling the story of what happened, we need to include references to the documents and other pieces of evidence that support our story. If the material has not already been provided in a particular manner, for example, a common record of 60 or 600 or 60,000 pages with consecutive page numbering, we have to produce the file or files ourselves. For the other side, references may have to be to particular dated or named documents and perhaps a particular page or paragraph in those. For our own purposes, we may want to have one master file with consecutive page numbering to make it easy and quick to find any particular document and information. Your test of whether your system is working is a hypothetical question by a judge or arbitrator in a hearing where you are making a particular claim: "What is the source of that information?" If you cannot find the document within a couple of seconds, your system is not working.

Highlighting Contradictions, Missing Information, Additional Research Needs, and Other Questions

Challenge: Identify facts that are missing or disputed and need to be obtained or clarified via discovery

In particular, if a story is quite complex and at least some elements in it may not be common ground between the different parties, we need to go over the facts again—and during this fifth round of analysis we focus on the identification of any logical breaks in the narrative, and any contradictions or gaps. Along the way, we also highlight any information, data points, or statements of fact that have already been disputed by one side or the other and mark them accordingly (for example "disputed by seller, see fax of March 15/p. 63 of the record").

Identifying How Any Contradictions, Missing Information or Open Questions May Be Resolved and What Happens If They Are Not

Challenge: Come up with solutions how missing or disputed facts may be clarified and how you will adjust your strategy and arguments if they are not

If information, data points, or statements are disputed or missing, this will usually have consequences. Occasionally, it may turn out that it does not actually matter whether a fax was received on a particular day or whether a witness statement is credible or supported by other evidence. In such a case, we still need to explain why we believe that the discrepancy does not matter and say so using one of the four levels of analysis. For example, we might say "buyer disputes seller's claim that the revocation of the offer arrived before or at the same time as the offer itself; however, the question is ultimately moot because _____"

More likely than not, however, discrepancies, gaps, and disputed facts will be of relevance. This raises the question who has the burden of proof, i.e., whose position in the dispute will be affected negatively if the particular discrepancy or gap cannot be resolved. For example, if the seller wants to collect the purchase price from the buyer, he will need to demonstrate that a contract was concluded accordingly. If the formation of the contract is in dispute, seller's demand for payment is in jeopardy. If our client has the weaker position, we need to think about possible research, discovery, or fact-finding options that could clarify the situation and strengthen our position in the dispute. And we need to think about alternative legal strategies, as a contingency plan, if we should ultimately not be able to prove our position in fact.

Step 2: Identifying Binary Claims: Who Wants What from Whom and Why?

Breaking Down a Complex Case into Manageable Pieces Corresponding to Legal Claims

In an exam, as in real life, the question may be quite clear:

1. A may say something like "I want my money back from B." or

2. "I want damages from B for the failure to perform."

On the other hand, the question may be far less obvious, along the lines of:

3. "What are the rights and obligations of the parties?" or

4. "Who can get what from whom?" or

5. "What can you do for this client?"

Even if the questions seem straightforward, some additional thought should be invested before we narrowly focus on the answers. In example 1, there seems to be a reference to a payment made by A to B that should be recovered. But recovery in full may not be available if A cannot return all the goods or property received from B in exchange for the money. On the other hand, recovery of monies paid may not be enough if A has incurred additional damages on account of a breach of contract or other obligations by B. Any claims for damages, like in example 2, require not only persuasive justification in law, but also a persuasive calculation of the claimed amount. Finally, there is always the question whether costs (for example, for legal representation) and interest may be recoverable on top of items or monies claimed. Thus, we should always go about a systematic analysis of all possible claims along the 5Ws Formula: Who Wants What from Whom and Why?

Challenge: Formulate all actual and/or potential claims—primary claims, secondary claims, costs, and interest—for all possible binary relationships

If there are more than two actors in the story, consider all possible binary claims, for example "A from B" and "B from A," but also "A from C" and "B from C" and, of course, "C from A" and "C from B."

In each binary relationship, consider:

I. Primary claims: These are intended to put the parties in the position they would have been in had there been no breach of law or promise. For example, the primary claims of the seller against the buyer are for taking of delivery and payment of the purchase price. The primary claims of the buyer against the seller are for delivery of conforming goods and transfer of ownership or title. However, there are also primary claims outside of contractual relationships, for example, for the customer and potential buyer not to be harmed during pre-contractual negotiations (see Part Two on pp. 71), or the claim of the property owner to recover possession from the wrongful possessor. Finally, special contracts may involve special primary obligations, for example the claim of the beneficiary named in a letter of credit against the issuing and/or the confirming bank to honor a complying presentation (see Part Three on pp. 409).

If primary claims can be brought, they should be brought. Alternatively, an explanation should be provided why the claimant is no longer interested in the primary claim and what the claimant wants instead. Certain (additional) conditions may need to be met before a shift from the primary to one or more secondary claims can be made. For example, if there was a contract of sale, it may have to be avoided before the parties are released from their primary obligations and can claim damages instead.

ii. Damages as secondary claims: These can be claimed instead of primary claims or in addition to them. For example, if there was a contract of sale and the seller fails to deliver or tenders non-conforming goods, the buyer may be entitled to specific performance (primary claim) *plus* damages for delay and/or loss of profit (secondary claims). If a contract was never concluded or it was concluded but also successfully avoided, contractual or primary claims do not exist but damage claims may remain. In general, damages may be due if the primary claim never came about or if it was extinguished (the goods were destroyed; the contract was avoided), or if performance of the primary claim alone does not put the claimant in the same position she would be in had there been no breach of law or promise.

In some cases damages may be available only for the negative interest — putting a party in the position it would be if she had never met the other party — or they may be available for the positive interest — putting a party in the position as if the other party had performed as promised. The extent of damages available is determined by the legal basis, which may be statutory law with case law interpreting it, or case law alone.

In some cases, damages may be claimed above and beyond what is necessary to put the claimant in the same position she would be in had there been no breach of law or promise. These are usually referred to as punitive damages. However, punitive damages are only available if they are specifically mentioned in law. In all other cases, the party claiming damages has to prove that it actually suffered these damages. A limited exception can apply if the contract provides for liquidated damages that do not have to be proven.

Excessive and/or poorly substantiated damage claims can lead a court or tribunal to reject all damage claims instead of reducing them to a realistic level.

iii. Cost: The *commercial* losses and expenses caused by a breach of contract or other obligation are in general recoverable as damages. By contrast, the *legal* expenses have to be claimed as cost. In principle, they include attorney fees and expenses, as well as the cost of the actual dispute settlement procedures, such as court fees, fees of an arbitration tribunal and honoraria of arbitrators, travel expenses, and administrative expenses related to the procedure (conference rooms, translation and interpretation expenses, secretarial services, etc.). A thorough listing of costs incurred as a consequence of a breach of law or contract may go beyond these, however, and also include in-house counsel expenses, in-house administrative expenses such as courier services, and even extra work done by nonlegal employees of the claimant.

Whether or not a particular cost item will be recoverable depends on a number of factors. First, the parties may have entered into an agreement in the context of the initiation of litigation or arbitration pursuant to which each side has to bear her own cost or only certain costs will be recoverable. In such a case, it is usually not necessary to track other expenses very carefully and try to claim them (except to claim them as business expenses for tax purposes). However, in the absence of a party agreement or a statutory provision[44] limiting claims for cost recovery, costs imposed on one party by the breach of law or contract of the other will often be recoverable, provided they are well-documented and reasonable.

iv. Interest: This can often be claimed from the time when a payment became due to the time when the payment is actually made. An award of interest accounts for the fact that money later is worth less than money sooner, in terms of purchasing power—the so-called time value of money—and in terms of opportunity cost. We sometimes distinguish between prejudgment interest,[45] for the time from when a payment was due until the court confirms the payment obligation, and post-judgment interest,[46] until payment is effected. In such cases, the court will typically specify the amount of prejudgment interest as a lump sum and specify the amount of post-judgment interest as a daily sum or based on an average interest rate to encourage the obligated party to make payment sooner rather than later. In many cases, interest will not be awarded *ex officio,* but must be specifically claimed. If this is the case, it would amount to malpractice for an attorney to "forget" to claim interest on behalf of her client. If the court or tribunal does not follow specific rules regarding the calculation of interest, the claim has to specify in a persuasive way the amount of interest that should be awarded. Typically, such a claim can be for a certain percentage above the prime rate, depending on the actual borrowing cost of the claimant. Excessive or unpersuasively high interest claims can lead to a rejection of any interest instead of a reduction to a reasonable level.

Even when you are only representing one party in a dispute, you need to identify the actual or potential claims of all parties in all binary relationships because claims available to other parties can come back to you as counterclaims. Being aware of them—and their respective strengths and weaknesses—can be crucial when deciding whether or not to seek a settlement and/or how much time and money to expend in litigation or arbitration.

Step 3: Finding All Applicable Rules for the Case

Making Sure That All Relevant Rules at All Levels Are Identified:
International, Regional, Bilateral, Federal, State, Statutory,
Case Law, Customary, Contractual, and Other

While the responsibility for the identification of all relevant *facts* is shared between the client and the attorney, the identification of all applicable legal rules is

---

44. In Germany, for example, recoverable attorney and court fees are stipulated by law as a function of the amount in dispute. Even if a party can demonstrate that they had higher attorney expenses, these will normally not be recoverable.

45. For a useful discussion, see Michael S. Knoll, *A Primer on Prejudgment Interest,* Tex. L. Rev. 1996, Vol. 75, No. 2, pp. 293–374; as well as Anthony E. Rothschild, *Prejudgment Interest: Survey and Suggestion,* Nw. U.L. Rev. 77 (1982-1983), pp. 192–222; and John C. Keir & Robin C. Keir, *Opportunity Cost: A Measure of Prejudgment Interest,* Bus. Law. 1983, Vol. 39, No. 1, pp. 129–152.

46. See, *inter alia,* Susan Margaret Payor, *Post-Judgment Interest in Federal Courts,* 37 Emory L.J. 495 (1988).

entirely the attorney's job. If it turns out during or after a dispute settlement procedure that the client's outcome was negatively affected because some factual information was not brought (or not brought in time) to the attention of the court or tribunal, the attorney will not be liable if she generally gathered all available information, and asked the client and any witnesses or other sources of information for specific missing information and any other relevant information. By contrast, if it turns out that the client's outcome was negatively affected because the attorney *overlooked an applicable rule*, there is normally no way the attorney can escape responsibility because she did not know, did not have time, or did not have access to the particular rule.

Challenge: Find all applicable rules (statutory rules, case law, and contractual provisions), understand what they say about the rights and obligations of the parties and, if necessary, identify a hierarchy between potentially contradictory rules

Rules generally come in the form of statutory law (in the broadest sense of the word, including applicable international conventions, applicable industry codes such as the UCP 600, domestic legislation, domestic regulations, etc.), case law, and contractual stipulations. The contract itself is usually the most important source of rules and the easiest to identify. Based on the freedom of contract between private parties, contractual clauses can deviate from and even comprehensively displace most other rules that might otherwise apply. However, to the extent that a contract does not comprehensively regulate a particular situation and/or that there are mandatory public rules (both statutory and case law-based), several types of rules will have to be applied simultaneously and questions of hierarchy may have to be resolved.

Thus, the attorney first has to identify to what extent a particular legal relationship—for example, the rights and obligations of buyer and seller in a given transaction—is comprehensively regulated in the contract that was validly concluded between the parties and not validly avoided or terminated. Contractual terms are the individually negotiated terms on the front of the contract. By reference in the negotiated terms, general terms on the back of the contract may be elevated to the status of contractual terms, but generally only to supplement and not to contradict the individually negotiated terms. Second, the attorney has to identify to what extent mandatory laws (*ordre public*, public policy) may apply to the legal relationship and require a reinterpretation or non-application of some contractual provisions or even cause the entire contract to be illegal and therefore null and void. Third, the attorney has to identify to what extent optional rules of statutory law may be applicable and regulate or at least affect some of the rights or obligations of the parties in the absence of valid contractual rules on a given question or if the contractual rules about the particular issue are unclear or otherwise in need of interpretation. Optional statutory rules may be found in international conventions, national or subnational laws, and even in industry codes such as the UCP 600. They may apply by law for questions not comprehensively dealt with in the contract between the parties, or they may apply by party agreement, i.e., by reference in the contract. Fourth, the attorney needs to fill any remaining gaps with case law, especially if there are neither contractual stipulations nor applicable statutory rules, or if the contractual stipulations and/or any applicable statutory provisions are unclear and, therefore, in need of interpretation.

Comprehensive research, the identification of *all* applicable rules, and a correct understanding of the hierarchy of these rules in relation to each other are of crucial importance. The three biggest mistakes in this respect are:

- *overlooking an applicable rule,* either a statutory rule or an exception in a different part of the statute or in another applicable piece of legislation or regulation; *or overlooking an important precedent* of persuasive, binding character;

- *reliance on an outdated rule,* either a statutory rule that had been amended or repealed at the time the facts occurred, or a precedent that has already been overruled; and

- *reliance on a lower-ranked provision* of the law that is incompatible with a higher-ranked provision of the law; for example, reliance on a contractual provision that is incompatible with a mandatory rule in the respective jurisdiction, or reliance on an optional law that is incompatible with a contractual provision.

Step 4: Identifying the Claim Bases
Finding the Rules That Give Rights or Claims

After all applicable rules have been identified and ranked in a general manner (for example, the contract, the CISG, cases x, y, and z), the analysis has to home in on specific provisions in these different sets of rules. In statutory law this requires analysis of specific articles, or even paragraphs or sub-paragraphs of these articles. In case law the equivalent may be a reference to a specific passage or paragraph in a judgment.

Challenge: Identify and isolate the claim bases that support the binary claims found in Step 2. A claim basis is a clear and unambiguous provision in a legal rule providing *a right* to bring a primary claim, and/or a secondary claim (damages), and/or cost, and/or interest, if certain specified conditions are met. A claim basis typically takes the form of "if *X*, then *Y* is entitled to/may demand/claim/require *Z*."

Example 1   "The seller must deliver the goods, hand over any documents relating to them and transfer the property in the goods, as required by the contract . . ." (Art. 30 CISG)

Example 2   "If the seller fails to perform any of his obligations under the contract or this Convention, the buyer may (a) require performance . . ." (Art. 45(1)(a) with Art. 46(1) CISG)

The provision in example 1 is *not* a claim basis. It merely stipulates obligations of the seller but does not stipulate rights of the buyer. By contrast, the provision in example 2 is a claim basis. The passage in example 2 "obligations under . . . this Convention" actually refers to Art. 30, where the primary obligations of the seller are spelled out. Thus, Arts. 45(1)(a) and 46(1) provide the claim basis for the buyer to receive the goods and the relating documents and the ownership or title in the goods and anything else that may have been stipulated in the contract, such as qualities of the goods, time and place of delivery, etc. Provisions such as Art. 31 CISG about the place of delivery only become relevant if the contract itself does not provide a rule for the place of delivery.

In particular, if a statutory provision or the relevant passages in a judgment are longer, it is important to refer to the exact paragraph, sub-paragraph, sentence, and/or alternative in the statute or judicial decision. Sloppy, imprecise references do not show mastery of the subject and make your brief less persuasive.

Step 5: Isolating the Conditions for a Claim to Have Arisen, Not to Be Extinguished, and to Be Enforceable

Enumerating the Conditions in the Rules That Give Rights or Claims

Since claim bases provide rights or claims only if certain conditions are met, the next step is to identify all applicable conditions and exceptions. These may be directly contained in the claim basis itself, i.e., in the same article or paragraph, or they may be identifiable via references in the claim basis, or via provisions in the chapter of the law or the surrounding passages of the judgment, where the claim basis is provided.

Challenge: Identify all conditions that have to be met for every claim basis to be successfully invoked

Again, it is of crucial importance that we identify *all* applicable conditions as well as any relevant exceptions. It is simply unforgivable for an attorney to present an elaborate argument why her client should be entitled to x, y, and z, and then be schooled by a judge or arbitrator about having overlooked a relevant exception that invalidates most or all of her claims. Since conditions and, in particular, exceptions, are not always provided in the immediate vicinity of the claim basis itself, it is important to read all relevant parts of contracts, statutory materials, and cases. Sometimes an exception or a bar against enforceability, such as a statute of limitations, may be found at the end of a piece of legislation or in a different piece of legislation altogether.

Once the facts, parties, claims, applicable rules, claim bases, conditions, and exceptions have been identified and understood for our internal analysis, we can finally proceed to the presentation of our case.

Step 6: Presenting a Persuasive Argument (1) — the Road Map

Outlining a Written Brief or Oral Presentation

Persuasive speaking and writing is often related to saying everything three times: "Tell them what you will tell them, tell them what you want to tell them, and tell them what you just told them." Translated to legal writing, we need a road map of our arguments, the actual arguments, and a summary of these arguments.

Challenge: Present an outline of the legal arguments you are making on behalf of your client in short, clear, and affirmative style.

The road map should generally be kept short and affirmative. Thus, it may sound something like this: "The buyer is entitled to delivery of conforming goods. Seller's obligation arises from the contract of January 15, as well as Articles x, y, and z CISG. Conditions a, b, and c are fulfilled in the present case. At the same time, the seller cannot rely on exception d."

Lacking confidence, students often avoid concrete and affirmative language and use phrases such as "the question is whether ___" or "if this then that, however, if not then not" and the like. They may introduce their presentation with "I think ___," which has never been a strong legal basis because the attorney on the other side will probably think the opposite. It should be obvious to anyone that none of this is conducive to making a persuasive argument and students should diligently avoid this kind of language. If at a loss for models, students may want to consult the Restatements of the Law, for example, the Restatement (Second) of Contracts (Documents, p. I-199), for good examples of the kind of clear, straightforward, and affirmative language that makes for persuasive writing.[47]

Step 7: Presenting a Persuasive Argument (2) — Subsumption of the Facts under the Law and the Four Levels of Analysis

Showing How the Facts Correspond to the Conditions in the Rules That Give Rights or Claims

The main part of the presentation should follow the outline presented in the road map. Each point in the outline now needs to be taken up and discussed in a way that merges the facts and the law, or, better, draws the facts under the law (subsumption). This is best done in the following steps:

I. **Leading statement:** "The buyer is entitled to delivery of conforming goods." This should be formulated affirmatively. The use of questions, such as "whether the buyer is entitled" introduces the possibility of alternative outcomes and reduces persuasiveness.

ii. **Applicable rules for the claim to arise:** "The right of the buyer to demand delivery of conforming goods is based on Articles x, y, and z of the CISG. The CISG is applicable because _____ Articles x, y, and z are conditional upon a, b, and c."

iii. **Subsumption of the facts, part 1 (positive conditions):** "In the present case, condition a is met because _____; condition b is met because _____; condition c is met because _____"

---

47. The best and most accessible book on the subject may well be Antonin Scalia & Bryan A. Garner, *Making Your Case — The Art of Persuading Judges*, Thomson West 2008.

iv. Negation of exceptions and other factors that might extinguish a claim or bar its enforceability: "The seller cannot rely on exception d because its conditions e and f are not met in the present case."

v. Subsumption of the facts, part 2 (negation of exceptions or other extinguishing factors): "Condition e is not met because _____; condition f is not met because_____ "

vi. Statement of interim result: "Therefore, buyer's claim to delivery of conforming goods based on the contract of January 15 and Articles x, y, and z of the CISG is valid and seller cannot rely on the exception d."

This procedure needs to be repeated for every primary claim, secondary claim, alternative claims if the court or tribunal should not agree with any of the main claims, as well as claims for costs and/or interest.

Challenge: Make a persuasive argument for each claim by drawing the facts of the case under the applicable rules to show how the facts meet the conditions of the rules; defeat obvious counterarguments against your claims by showing that the facts do not meet the conditions of the counterarguments; use the Four Levels of Analysis to determine your priorities and how much to say with regard to each argument or condition.

In addition to the correct identification of the facts, the parties, and their respective claims, as well as the correct interpretation and application of all applicable rules and exceptions, mastery of the subject also requires the correct allocation of time and effort to the different parts of the analysis. This question of priorities is dictated in practice by the fact that the client has to pay several hundreds of dollars per hour of her attorney's time and would not want to pay for work that is unnecessary. Also, if an attorney does not clearly distinguish the important from the unimportant arguments, the issues that really matter for a successful presentation of her client's claims may get buried in irrelevant elaborations. In an exam, correct prioritization is required by the fact that time (and sometimes space) is limited. Thus, the student, just like the attorney, cannot spend an unlimited amount of time and effort on the case and cannot afford to discuss at length issues that are either not controversial, or not conducive to the realization of the client's claims. Misallocation of time and effort leads to overcharging of the client in practice and to underperformance in both exams and practice. The problem is that as human beings, we are not naturally inclined to allocate our time and effort correctly in these cases. Thus, students have to unlearn their natural inclinations and consciously learn a system called the *Four Levels of Analysis.*

As we work our way through Step 7, or the equivalent to part A of the IRAC Method, our natural inclination is to write more where we are confident and believe that we know the answers and where our position is strong. By contrast, we will be inclined to avoid writing much with regard to points that are difficult, controversial, or weak in our arguments. However, this natural inclination is diametrically opposed to what is required from a good lawyer because it is simply not necessary to spend much time or effort on issues that are obvious or that the other side will concede. By contrast, we have to invest our time and effort where the other side will try to exploit weaknesses in our legal or factual position to deny the claims we are making on behalf of our client.

Thus, once the road map and outline are clear *and before we start the actual writing of the brief*, we need to consciously allocate one of the four levels of analysis to each point or question in the outline. In particular, in exams where time is limited, we should do this early, when we still have time to think clearly.

Level 1 = So irrelevant that readers would be surprised to see the point even mentioned:

> "What does this have to do with that?" → Don't even mention it.

Level 2 = Relevant but uncontroversial:

> "Everybody knows that." → Mention the point, without explaining or justifying it, if it is necessary to understand the progression of thought, the connection between different and more important points.

Level 3 = Important and potentially controversial:

> "I am not so sure about that." → Elaborate the point with your supportive arguments, which should end the doubt or controversy, since you have the stronger position on this point.

Level 4 = The crux of the matter:

> "I don't believe that." → Elaborate the point with your supportive arguments *as well as* obvious counter-arguments and how and why those can be disproven; try to deliver the triple punch: (i) state your main arguments in favor and add persuasive reasoning "because ____"; (ii) name the obvious or previously stated counter-arguments and explain why they are not relevant or persuasive; (iii) state your supportive or alternative arguments in favor, in case your first and second points have not fully persuaded the court or tribunal. Conclude by summarizing why your arguments win, although it may look as if the other side has the stronger position on this point.

> One problem on this level is deciding which counterarguments to anticipate and deal with before the other side has actually made or substantiated them. On the one hand, we don't want to wake up sleeping dogs by alerting the other side to weaknesses in our position they may not be aware of. On the other hand, we don't want to write a beautiful brief that is then easily destroyed by an obvious counterargument of the other side and leaves us at a distinct disadvantage and in an uphill battle for our reply or rebuttal. The distinction should be made along the lines of what is obvious and what every halfway decent lawyer would understand and what the judges or arbitrators will also think of immediately. Those points definitely need

to be anticipated and dealt with before the other side can even develop them very forcefully. To the extent possible, you never want the judges or arbitrators to doubt your arguments because you did not deal with obvious counterarguments right away.

Finally, how do you decide which level to apply? Put yourself in the shoes of your opposing counsel or a critic of your paper. Which points would the other side concede? And where would they put in their greatest effort to prove you wrong?

Step 8: Presenting a Persuasive Argument (3) — Conclusions
Closing the Circle

In the overall conclusions, the brief should summarize or restate the outcome of the analysis of each primary, secondary, and alternative claim, as well as any claims for costs and interest: "In summarizing, as we have shown, our clients are entitled to _____ (primary claims), as well as _____ (damages), and _____ (costs), and _____ (interest)." The summary should correspond to the Road Map at the beginning.

Challenge: Wrap up by summarizing your claims, as they have been proven in your brief, in clear, concise, and neutral style; avoid triumphant or emotional language or ill-suited metaphors.

Checklist 1-2
Bryan Garner's "10 Tips for Better Legal Writing"

1. Be sure you understand the client's problem.

2. Don't rely exclusively on computer research.

3. Never turn in a preliminary version of a work in progress.

4. Summarize your conclusions up front.

5. Make your summary understandable to outsiders.

6. Don't be tentative in your conclusions, but don't be overconfident, either.

7. Strike the right professional tone: natural but not chatty.

8. Master the approved citation form.

9. Cut every unnecessary sentence; then go back through and cut every unnecessary word.

10. Proofread one more time than you think necessary.

Bryan Garner, *10 Tips for Better Legal Writing — You'll Be Glad You Found Your Mistakes Before Your Readers Do*, ABA Journal, Vol. 100, No. 10, October 2014, pp. 24–25, with additional details. For more information, see Bryan Garner, *Legal Writing in Plain English*, Univ. Chicago Press 2nd ed. 2013.

Part Two

The Documentary Sale 1 of 4:
Sales Contracts

In most cases, lawyers get involved in business transactions either at the beginning, when the transaction is being planned and the necessary contracts and other documents are being drafted, or at the end, after the transactions have gone wrong and the parties are going after each other for performance and/or damages. It is much to be preferred for the lawyers to review the relevant contracts and documents before they are signed and changes cannot be made. In Parts Two through Five of the book, we will review step by step the planning of the business transaction and the drafting or reviewing of the corresponding documents—the contract of sale (Part Two), the payment or finance contract (Part Three), the shipping contract (Part Four), and the insurance contract (Part Five). Issues related to the enforcement of rights and obligations after a breach of contract and a breakdown of friendly negotiations will be the subject of Part Six.

Section 1. The Documentary Sale—An Overview

The archetypical transaction we will use to explain the majority of legal issues recurring in the context of IBTs is the documentary sale. Rather than just the contract of sale, this analysis involves all major steps required to execute an international sale of goods or export-import business transaction. In addition to the four main contracts themselves, we will look step by step at how the negotiations unfold and how the transaction is planned and implemented, including the performance of the seller (transfer of goods, documents, and title) and the performance of the buyer (acceptance of the goods and payment). The example we will be working from assumes the use of INCOTERM® CIF, where the seller has to arrange for shipping and insurance. If the contract of sale stipulates FOB, the buyer herself has to take care of shipping and insurance, which changes the picture only marginally but is important for the passing of risk and the question of who may have to bear any loss or damage (see below, p. 240 et seq.).

In addition to the four main contracts, a number of ancillary contracts may have to be concluded to complete a documentary sale. These include a nondisclosure agreement between seller and buyer, and an agreement with an independent inspection company for pre-shipment inspection. If the seller does not bring the

goods himself to the port for the maritime voyage and if the buyer does not collect the goods herself at the port after the maritime voyage, contracts with local
shipping companies for truck or rail transport to and from the ports may have to
be concluded. Alternatively, the parties can use an integrated logistics company
that will collect the goods at the seller's premises and deliver them at the buyer's
premises while also handling all required customs and other procedures along the
way. Obviously, the latter alternative is convenient for the parties but comes at a
price.

The documentary sale can be broken down into 25 typical steps as follows.
Depending on the particulars of a given transaction, the picture may vary in some
of the details—for example, who has to contract and pay for shipping and insurance and who has to take care of export and import formalities. Much of this will
be discussed in the context of drafting the Contract of Sale and when we analyze the
different INCOTERMS®.

#1   The first step is the communication of Marketing Material or other product
information from the seller to the buyer. This could be at a trade fair, via
catalogs and other print media, or simply via the website of the seller. On
the basis of the material or information, the buyer becomes interested in the
goods offered by the seller. However, she may still want to compare the quality and price of the seller's goods with those of other sellers.

#2   To understand in more detail what an offer from the seller might look like,
to compare the quality and pricing details with those of competitors, and
to check whether the bank will be willing to provide financing, the buyer
requests a Pro-Forma Invoice from the seller. As the name suggests, this is
not a real invoice but a quote of what the seller is potentially willing to provide with regard to the kind and quantity of the goods, their weight, packaging and transportation charges, other services such as the procurement of
insurance, inspections, export licenses, customs clearance, etc., and the price
with and without tax.

#3   If the intended use of the goods on the side of the buyer contains propri-
etary information, the buyer will also ask the seller to sign a nondisclosure
agreement. If the buyer has already requested a Nondisclosure Agreement
(NDA), the seller signs and returns it with the pro-forma invoice. If the buyer
has not requested one but the seller wants to protect proprietary information
related to the goods, the seller will now ask the buyer to sign a nondisclosure
agreement.

#4   The seller prepares the pro-forma invoice, potentially with several alterna-
tives with regard to quantity, ancillary services, and price, and transmits it to
the buyer.

#5   Once the buyer is reasonably sure that she wants to purchase the goods from
the seller, she contacts her bank and submits an application for a Letter of

Credit (L/C) to be issued for the benefit of the seller. Only after the bank has issued the L/C can the buyer proceed to close the contract with the seller. Otherwise she might be stuck with a binding agreement to purchase the goods but have no way of paying for them. If the buyer is confident about her ability to get the L/C, she may want to delay this step until after the contract has been concluded and all details regarding pricing and other terms of the purchase are known. The position of the seller is different, however, and he should ask to see a draft of the L/C before the contract is finalized to ensure that the terms of the L/C are acceptable to him. Once the L/C is issued, the terms cannot easily be changed.

#6 Now that the buyer has the assurance that the bank will finance the transaction and she has at least a draft of the L/C, she can submit a **Purchase Order** (**PO**) to the seller, ideally together with the draft L/C, which is the offer to enter into a contract of sale (§ 2-206 UCC; Article 14 CISG). The purchase order moves the negotiations from the level of nonspecific inquiries and/ or negotiations with multiple potential suppliers to the contract formation stage.

It may have been preceded by the exchange of specific offers and counter-offers of a less formal kind, in particular in a series of letters or faxes or oral conversations, that may already have led to a binding agreement, which is only being formalized now.

#7 In response to the purchase order, the seller produces a formal **Contract of Sale** and submits it to the buyer. If the contract conforms to the purchase order, it is an acceptance. If the contract contains additional or different clauses, which is often the case because it is more detailed than the previous negotiations, it is a counteroffer. Similarly, if the seller asks for changes before the final L/C is issued, the response is usually not an acceptance but a counteroffer.

acceptance

#8 Acceptance by the buyer, expressed as signature on the contract, must be communicated to the seller to become effective. Since most contracts contain a **merger clause** (see below, p. 350), acceptance by the buyer not only seals the deal, but also ensures that the final written contract — sometimes referred to as a completely or **Fully Integrated Agreement** (see, for example, Restatement (Second) of Contracts, § 210) — supersedes all prior promises made and agreements reached in less formal communications.

#9 Depending on the payment arrangements agreed upon in the contract of sale, the buyer now requests her bank, also referred to as the Issuing Bank, to issue the L/C and send it to a suitable bank in the seller's country.

L/C

#10 Buyer's Bank identifies a bank in seller's country with which it has a business relationship and asks it to advise the L/C. If the Advising Bank is conveniently located for the seller, Buyer's Bank will nominate it to process the

Chart 2-1 The Documentary Sale

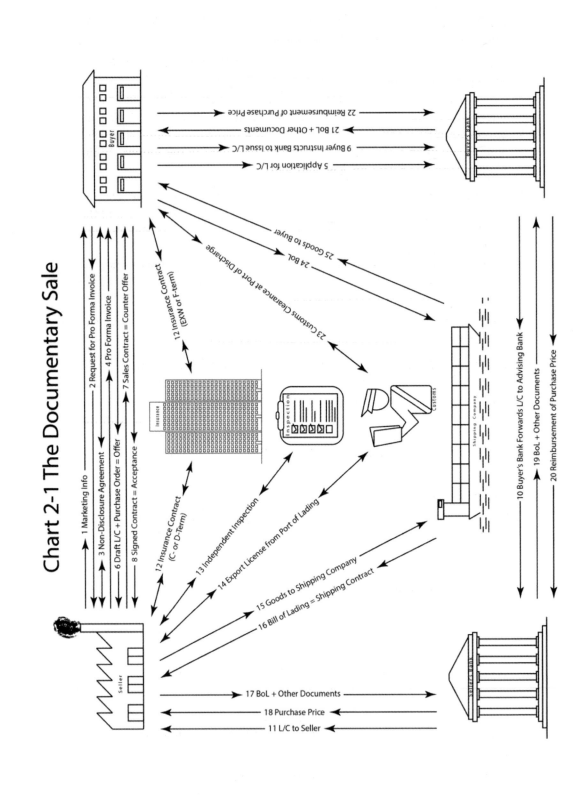

payment upon a complying presentation. If not, another bank or any bank can be nominated to process the payment.

#11 Seller's Bank as the advising bank authenticates the L/C and forwards it to the seller. If Seller's Bank is not merely an advising bank but also a Nominated Bank, the seller can later present his documents to this bank rather than having to make the presentation with the Issuing Bank/Buyer's Bank in buyer's country. If Seller's Bank is additionally a Confirming Bank, the seller will be paid upon a complying presentation regardless of the approval of the Issuing Bank (see below, pp. 439–440, 446).

#12 Depending on the INCOTERM® agreed upon in the Contract of Sale, the seller or the buyer now purchase insurance coverage for the shipment of the goods. The Insurance Contract is concluded by the party bearing the risk during the voyage. **If the INCOTERM® is EXW or an F-term like FOB, the risk during the maritime voyage is borne by the buyer.** If the INCOTERM® is a C-term like CIF, the seller has to purchase the insurance with the buyer as beneficiary. If the INCOTERM® is a D-term, the risk does not pass until the goods have arrived and the seller will purchase insurance with himself as beneficiary (see below, pp. 240 et seq. and 631 et seq.).

#13 In many cases, the goods also have to be inspected by a specialized third party to ensure that the quality and quantity corresponds to the Contract of Sale. The **Inspection Contract** is made by the seller with the Inspection Company, if the L/C requires him to submit an **Inspection Certificate** with the other documents to get paid. Alternatively, the inspection can be organized by the buyer. Usually, it is easier and more efficient if each side is responsible for whatever has to happen is his or her country.

#14 Depending on the distribution of responsibilities agreed upon in the Contract of Sale, the list of requirements in the Letter of Credit, and the legal requirements in the country of exportation, the seller may also have to procure an Export License from the customs authorities.

#15 Once all pre-shipment procedures are completed and all other documents required by the L/C have been procured, the seller takes the goods to the shipping company/carrier.

#16 In exchange for the goods, the Shipping Company issues a **Bill of Lading (BoL). The BoL is a form contract prepared by the carrier representing at the same time a Receipt for the goods, the Contract of Carriage, and a Title Document** (see below, pp. 553 et seq.).

#17 Having completed all required tasks, the seller now goes to the Nominated Bank, which may be a Confirming Bank, and makes a Presentation of the L/C with all required documents to get paid.

#18 If the Nominated and Confirming Bank deems the Presentation complying, it will release the funds secured by the L/C and the seller gets paid. If the bank is merely advising, it will pass complying documents to the Issuing Bank and seller has to wait until the money arrives from there. In any case, the seller is done as soon as he has made a Complying Presentation to the Bank. This happens after the goods have been shipped but before and independent of their arrival and approval by the buyer.

#19   Having purchased the documents from the seller, Seller's Bank now presents them to the Issuing Bank, which is Buyer's Bank, for reimbursement.

#20   If the Issuing Bank deems the presentation complying, it will release the funds secured by the L/C to Seller's Bank.

#21   Having purchased the documents from Seller's Bank, Buyer's Bank forwards them to the buyer, who needs the BoL to get the goods from the carrier upon arrival.

#22   In exchange for the documents, the buyer has to pay up on the L/C, either by transferring cash to Buyer's Bank, having money debited from her account with Buyer's Bank, or via another financing agreement to defer actual payment until the goods have been received and processed and/or re-sold. Typically, Buyer's Bank will require some lien on the goods, a real estate mortgage, or a security interest in other assets, if a financing agreement is concluded. If the buyer is a trader, the goods are for re-sale, and buyer's country allows nonpossessory security interests, Buyer's Bank may even use a floating charge on buyer's inventory as collateral for the loan.

#23   As soon as the buyer is in possession of all controlling documents, she can proceed to get Customs Clearance for the goods. This may involve payment of import duties, as well as other formalities.

#24   With the BoL and the Customs Clearance, buyer meets carrier on arrival.

#25   In exchange for the Bill of Lading, the carrier hands over the goods to the buyer.

What we can see from this arrangement is that it protects the interests of both the seller and the buyer. On the one hand, the seller does not have to ship the goods merely hoping that the buyer will pay. The seller has the L/C in hand and can work down the list of required documents. Once all conditions of the L/C are met, the seller is confident that he will be paid. Importantly, this happens as soon as the seller has fulfilled his part of the deal, typically as soon as the goods have been handed over to the carrier. In particular, the seller does not have to wait for the goods to arrive safely at the buyer's place and to be approved by the buyer.

At the same time, the buyer is also protected to a large degree. First, the buyer does not have to pay in advance, merely hoping that the seller will keep up his end of the bargain and ship the goods. In order for the seller being able to make a draft on the L/C, the seller has to meet a number of conditions. These often include an inspection of the goods by an independent company to verify that they match with the contractual obligations. In addition, no money will be withdrawn before the goods are shipped to the buyer. While in transit, the goods are insured against damage or loss, which also protects the buyer against surprises.

Nevertheless, **problems can still arise**, for example if the different agreements are not drafted well, or if there are gaps or mishaps when the goods are handed over from the responsibility of one party to the next. It is not uncommon for the local trucking company to arrive at the port before the ship arrives or for the goods to have to be stored temporarily. What if they get damaged while in storage? Finally, the buyer may not be happy with the quality of the goods in a way that the inspection company was not able to detect. It is one thing for an inspector to assess the quality of, for example, corn, wheat, or crude oil, and quite another to determine whether an injection molding machine will indeed produce 1500 units per hour. Therefore, **the different contracts mentioned above not only have to be drafted well and work seamlessly together, they also need suitable choice of law and dispute settlement clauses.** All of these issues will be discussed in the coming Parts.

Section 2. Common Pre-Contractual Documents: Pro-Forma Invoice, Purchase Order and Nondisclosure Agreement

Our basic assumption is that obligations between sellers and buyers arise from voluntary agreements between them and that, in the absence of a contract, such obligations do not exist. This is not entirely true, however, as Sections 2 and 3 will show. Therefore, the actual contract of sale is not the first document we need to consider. Legal issues can arise as soon as two parties meet. What is the legal nature of their early communication? Can a website or a marketing brochure be interpreted as an offer, meaning that a buyer can create contractual obligations simply by sending an acceptance, maybe in the form of a purchase order? What other documents are often drawn up and maybe even signed before an actual contract of sale is agreed upon? To what extent may we return to these if the interpretation of the subsequent contract is unclear or in dispute?

The first document we will be looking at a bit more closely is a **Pro-Forma Invoice. The purpose is somewhere between a nonbinding price quotation and a binding offer.** Typically, it is used by the potential buyer to compare competing offers from different sellers on the basis of real prices, including packaging, sales commissions, shipping, and tax. Once the potential buyer has decided upon the best supplier and secured financing from her bank, she will finalize negotiations with this supplier/seller based on the earlier pro-forma invoice. Although the seller might still decline to enter into a contract of sale, for example if he has meanwhile sold the goods to another buyer, he can normally not increase the price beyond the pro-forma invoice without good reason. Therefore, the document has also been called a good faith estimate of the total sale price. On the other hand, the buyer can still try to negotiate a discount, for example, for volume purchases or for favorable payment terms.

Sometimes the invoice traveling with the goods and used for customs processing is also referred to as a "pro-forma invoice." In contrast to the abovementioned document, this document has to be an accurate reflection of the actual goods being shipped and their customs value. For purposes of distinction, this should be called a "commercial invoice."

Pro-Forma Invoices Explained (see Sample Document 2-1)

#1   The document should be clearly marked as a "pro-forma" invoice to indicate that it is neither a binding offer nor an effective demand for payment.

#2   Whenever the seller or buyer is identified in a document or contract, there should also be the name, phone number, and e-mail address of the person authorized to send or receive any communication regarding the transaction. This avoids disputes over messages sent to the other party but not received in time by the right person.

#3   If an expiration date is provided, it indicates that the seller is promising to have the goods available at the quoted price until this date. If no such promise is intended, the space should not just be left blank, but the entire entry should be deleted to make it clear that there is no promise for any time frame made beyond the general good faith estimate.

#4   The customer reference would be to the letter or e-mail address or phone number of the potential buyer from which the pro-forma invoice was requested.

#5   "Buyer" and "Destination" can differ in two ways. First, the buyer may have more than one location and it should be made clear where the goods have to be shipped. Second, the buyer may not purchase the goods for herself but rather for a customer. Thus, it never hurts to specify the destination name and address separately, even if it is the same as the name and address of the company identified as the buyer.

#6   There are four main modes of transport: air, rail, road, and sea. There is also a combination of two or more of these, usually referred to as "multimodal." While the mode of transport may not be of interest to the buyer, as long as a certain arrival date is guaranteed, it may be a significant cost factor and require different paperwork and insurance coverage.

In particular, if the seller only promises a certain date for departure of the shipment, the mode of transport will also affect the date of arrival. In general, therefore, it is better to include the mode of transport in the quote and in the final contract.

#7   Different INCOTERMS® lead to different distributions of responsibilities for shipping and insurance charges and possibly other expenses, see below,

p. 247. To be a meaningful quote, therefore, it is essential that seller and buyer understand and agree on the INCOTERM® suggested.

#8 The unit of measure will depend on the customary way of describing the goods in question in a given industry. This may refer to units or pieces, gallons, bushels, barrels, and many other units of measure. In international sales, additional care is often required because different units or customs may prevail in other countries. For example, a reference to "gallons" is not necessarily clear because the U.S. gallon (3.7854 liters) differs significantly from the UK or imperial gallon (4.546 liters); similarly, a U.S. pound or lb (0.4536 kg) differs from a metric pound (0.5 kg); even a ton is different in the UK (1,016 kg) from the rest of the world (1,000 kg). In general, metric measures are safer because they have no differences between countries. When in doubt, the unit of measure should be supplemented with a reference to the country. The goal is to prevent any ambiguity. The motto should be "better safe than sorry."

#9 Regarding the description of the goods, there is an essential conflict of interest between seller and buyer. The seller's interest is to keep the description rather basic, while the buyer would want to see additional information—for example, regarding suitability and performance of the goods. We will return to this discussion as we home in on the final sales contract (below, pp. 332 et seq.). For the purposes of the pro-forma invoice, on the one hand, the description has to be detailed, including the country of origin and the customs code in the Harmonized Schedule system (see below, p. 86) to enable the potential buyer to understand exactly what she is negotiating for. On the other hand, the description does not need to include assurances as to performance, suitability, marketability, warranty, etc., unless they are important elements of price.

#10 The subtotal reflects the net price of the goods and is composed of all units multiplied by quantity. It generally includes standard packaging. However, unless there is a well-established custom in a particular industry, it does not include any special packaging or other uncommon services such as inspections, certificates of origin for customs clearance, and the like, as well as the cost of carriage/freight and insurance, which will depend on the destination.

#11 The pro-forma invoice should only include freight, shipping, or carriage charges if the seller is offering to organize and pay for at least some of the carriage. With an INCOTERM® of EXW, this entry should be zero. We will discuss below when a seller should offer to organize and pay for carriage and roll the expenses over to the buyer in the contract price, versus leaving it to the buyer to organize and pay for carriage directly (see p. 247–248).

#12 In the same way, the pro-forma invoice should only include insurance charges if the seller is offering to organize and pay for insurance, expressed via the INCOTERM®. We will also discuss below when a seller should offer

Sample Document 2-1: Pro Forma Invoice

Company Name & Logo of Seller
Contact Person[2]
Street Address
City, Zip Code & Country
Phone, Fax and e-mail

Pro Forma Invoice [1]
Expiration Date ....[3]
Customer Reference ....[4]

Customer/Buyer
Company Name
Contact Person
Street Address
City, Zip Code & Country
Phone, Fax and e-mail

Destination for Shipping
Company Name[5]
Contact Person
Street Address
City, Zip Code & Country
Phone, Fax and e-mail

Shipping Details
Mode of Transport ....[6]
INCOTERM® ....[7]
Port of Departure ....
Port of Arrival ....
Estimated Ship Date ....

Description of Goods

Part #	Unit of Measure[8]	Description[9]	Unit Price	x Quantity	= Net Price

Total # of Pieces:	Subtotal[10]	
	x Tax Rate =	
Estimated Net Weight and/or Volume:[17]	+ Total Tax	
	+ Freight[11]	
Packaging Specifics:[18]	+ Insurance[12]	
	+ Customs & Legal Fees[13]	
Estimated Gross Weight and/or Volume:[19]	+ Inspection[14]	
	+ Other (specify!)[15]	
	= Total w/Currency[16]	

Payment Terms[20]

☐   Payment on Open Account, Bank ...., Account # ...., SWIFT # ....
     by .... Date[21]

☐   Letter of Credit ☐ confirmed   ☐ unconfirmed

☐   Other

Signature of Seller Representative and Date

to organize and pay for insurance and roll the expenses over to the buyer in the contract price, versus leaving it to the buyer to organize and pay for insurance directly (see p. 247).

#13 An entry like "Customs and Legal" would cover a number of other services required for the implementation of the export/import transaction. The scope of services to be included here would again depend on the INCO-TERM®. For example, both FOB and CIF require that the goods are cleared for export and loaded onto the ship agreed upon among seller, buyer, and carrier. Thus, any procedures and dealings with the authorities of the exporting country would be the seller's responsibility and the seller would want to enter his expected cost or compensation here. If the INCOTERM® requires delivery in buyer's country, additional procedures and dealings with the authorities of the importing country will become the seller's responsibility and the corresponding expenditure of time and money would have to be reflected here.

#14 A reference to an "inspection" would be to separate services of a private inspection company, not to the customs inspection by the authorities of the exporting or importing country. An inspection by an independent third party is usually done if the buyer wants to verify that a certain quantity and quality of goods has indeed been shipped before the seller can go to the bank with the L/C and collect his money.

#15 Depending on the specifics of the goods and the transaction being negotiated, other costs may be incurred and have to be distributed, for example special packaging, quarantine charges, or the cost of warehousing, brokerage fees, etc.

#16 The total amount should reflect all elements supplied by the seller until the risk and responsibility for the goods passes to the buyer.

#17 The net weight is for the goods themselves, in their standard packaging, if applicable.

#18 Packaging other than the standard packaging and the shipping container should be specified here. The general understanding is that normal packaging for the selected mode of transport and destination is included in the price for the goods and only special and/or additional packaging should be mentioned here and can be billed separately.

#19 The gross weight is for the shipping containers including dunnage, if applicable.

#20 Payment terms will be discussed in detail in Part Three. In the pro-forma invoice, the seller needs to indicate the payment terms he would expect in order to be able to offer the quoted price. The default time of payment pursuant to Article 58 CISG and §2-310 UCC is the time when the seller "delivers" in accordance with the contract and the INCOTERM®, for example when the seller hands over the goods to the buyer or her designated representative (EXW) or when the seller hands over the controlling documents, including the BoL, to the bank as the buyer's designated representative to get paid at sight (FOB or CIF). Less favorable terms, such as 30, 60, or even 90 days after sight or even delivery (time draft), may entitle the seller to ask for a higher price for the goods.

#21 Most prices will be quoted for payment by L/C "at sight" or for payment on open account around the time of shipping. If the seller accepts payment by term draft, he effectively extends a credit line to the buyer and may want a higher price for the goods. Conversely, if the seller requires advance payment, for example full or at least partial payment at the time the contract is signed or within a few days thereof or in installments during the production of the goods, the buyer may be able to negotiate a discount off the regular or list price.

The next document to consider is a standard Purchase Order, typically used by a buyer after a pro-forma invoice was received and found satisfactory. By contrast to most pro-forma invoices that still leave certain options open, the average purchase order is sufficiently specific to qualify as an offer. From the point of view of the buyer, therefore, it is very important that the purchase order is carefully drafted and contains all elements the buyer would want to see in the final contract of sale in case the seller accepts without further ado. If the buyer does not want the purchase order to be an offer, she has to indicate this clearly, for example by requesting that the seller send a draft contract for acceptance and signature by both parties.

Sample Document 2-2: Purchase Order

Company Name & Logo of Buyer
Contact Person[2]
Street Address
City, Zip Code & Country
Phone, Fax and e-mail

Purchase Order [1]
Date .... [3]
PO Number .... [4]
Vendor Reference .... [5]

Addressee / Vendor
Company Name
Contact Person
Street Address
City, Zip Code & Country
Phone, Fax and e-mail

Destination for Shipping
Company Name[6]
Contact Person
Street Address
City, Zip Code & Country
Phone, Fax and e-mail

Shipping Details
Mode of Transport .... [7]
INCOTERM®................................. [8]
Port of Departure ....
Port of Arrival .... [9]
Shipping Date .... [10]

Description of Goods

Part #	Unit of Measure[11]	Description[12]	Unit Price	x Quantity	= Net Price

Total # of Pieces:	= Subtotal[13]
Estimated Net Weight and/or Volume:[17]	- Discount[14]
Packaging Specifics:[18]	+ Tax, Carriage, Insurance and any other costs[15]
Estimated Gross Weight and/or Volume:[19]	= Total w/Currency[16]

Payment Terms[20]
....

Other Terms and Conditions[21]
....
Please contact us immediately, if you should be unable to ship the goods as requested.
We enclose our general terms, which form an integral part of this PO.

Signature of Buyer Representative and Date

Purchase Orders Explained (see Sample Document 2-2)

#1 By marking the document as "purchase order" the buyer signals that she is now ready to commit and that the agreement would be acceptable to her as reflected in the PO. A binding contract would be concluded if the seller simply accepts the PO without further details or conditions. At least under the CISG (Article 18(1)) and in the common law of contracts (§ 50 Restatement (Second) of Contracts) the acceptance of the PO and formation of the contract is possible via declaration or promise and also via performance, in particular if the seller ships the goods.

In electronic commerce, placing an order on a website is generally considered a purchase order, hence an offer, because it specifies all essential elements of a contract of sale (seller, buyer, goods, quantity, and price). The seller typically confirms by e-mail before shipping the goods. The confirmation is the acceptance and finalizes the contract.

#2 Whenever the seller or buyer is identified in a document or contract, there should also be the name, phone number, and e-mail address of the person authorized to send or receive any communication regarding the transaction. This avoids disputes over messages sent to the other party but not received in time by the right person.

#3 In business communications, where several offers and counteroffers may be exchanged within a short time, it is essential that all documents are clearly dated. Sometimes they may need to be identified further to avoid any confusion about which document is the last one in a series and supersedes all earlier ones.

#4 A unique identifier number should be provided and used as a reference in all further communications referring to this PO.

#5 In particular, if the PO is sent in response to a particular pro-forma invoice or an offer by the seller, a clear reference to the respective document should be included.

#6 Every contract or draft contract should always specify who is bound by it (the seller and the buyer are the principals), where the goods are to be sent, and, if necessary, who should be invoiced. Even if several of these names and addresses are the same, it does not hurt to list them separately.

#7 All contracts should specify the mode(s) of transport. As we have seen, there are four main modes of transport: air, rail, road, and sea. A combination of two or more of these is usually referred to as "multimodal" transport. While the mode of transport may not be of interest to the buyer, as long as a certain arrival date is guaranteed, it may be a significant cost factor and require different paperwork and insurance coverage. In particular, if the seller only promises a certain date for departure of the shipment, the mode of transport will also affect the date of arrival. In general, therefore, it is better to include the mode of transport in the PO and in the final contract.

#8   Different INCOTERMS® lead to different distributions of responsibilities for shipping and insurance charges and possibly other expenses; see below, pp. 240 et seq. Any contract should absolutely ensure that seller and buyer agree on the INCOTERM®. As an offer, therefore, the PO needs to be unambiguous in this regard.

#9   The port of arrival matters primarily if the seller, per INCOTERM®, is expected to organize and pay for carriage and insurance (C-terms), or even carry the risk until delivery at the port of arrival (D-terms). It is irrelevant if the buyer has to pick up the goods at the seller's premises (EXW), and it is less important if the seller merely has to bring the goods to the port of departure and a specific vessel (F-terms). In the latter case, the buyer will still want to include the port of arrival because the seller has to clear the goods through customs at the port of origin or departure, often also called the port of lading. This may require an export license for some destination countries and ports.

#10 The important date is usually the date when the risk will pass from the seller to the buyer. With F and C terms, this will be at the port of origin or departure when the goods are handed over to the carrier for the marine voyage. If the parties include a D-term, the date to be entered here should be the arrival date. If the parties should agree on EXW, the date should be the date when the goods have to be handed over to the buyer or buyer's representative at the seller's premises. Instead of "shipping date," the parties may specify "delivery date" in these cases and the place or port of delivery, i.e., where the goods are handed over and the risk passes to the buyer. In many industries it is still customary not to specify a particular day, but a calendar week for the agreed-upon delivery. This gives a measure of flexibility to the seller but requires notification of the final date to ensure a seamless handover.

#11 Again, the unit of measure will depend on the customary way of describing the goods in question in a given industry. This may refer to units or pieces, gallons, bushels, barrels, and many other units of measure. In international sales, additional care is often required because different units or customs may prevail in other countries. For example, a reference to "gallons" is not necessarily clear because the U.S. gallon (3.7854 liters) differs significantly from the UK or imperial gallon (4.546 liters); similarly, a U.S. pound or lb (0.4536 kg) differs from a metric pound (0.5 kg); even a ton is different in the UK (1,016 kg) from the rest of the world (1,000 kg). In general, metric measures are safer because they have no differences between countries. When in doubt, the unit of measure should be supplemented with a reference to the country. The goal is to prevent any ambiguity. The motto should be "better safe than sorry."

#12 Regarding the description of the goods, there is an essential conflict of interest between seller and buyer. The seller's interest is to keep the description rather basic, while the buyer would want to see additional information — for example, regarding suitability and performance of the goods. We will return to this discussion as we home in on the final sales contract. For the purposes of the PO, the description has to be detailed, including the country of origin and the customs code in the Harmonized Schedule system[1] to make clear what the buyer and seller are talking about. Since the PO is drafted by the buyer, she may additionally want to include requirements as to performance, suitability, marketability, warranty, etc., in particular if they are important elements of price.

#13   The subtotal reflects the net price of the goods and is composed of all units multiplied by quantity. It generally includes standard packaging. However, unless there is a well-established custom in a particular industry, it does not include any special packaging and other uncommon services such as inspections, certificates of origin for customs clearance, and the like, as well as the cost of carriage/freight and insurance, which will depend on the destination. All of those should be included in #15.

#14   In particular, if the seller at some point in the negotiations mentioned any possibility of discounts for new customers, volume purchases, up-front payment, or the like, the buyer should try to get them into the contract here.

#15   The buyer should list agreed-upon services of the seller at this point, in particular if the contract is for a C-term and the seller has to organize and pay for carriage and insurance. However, the buyer should also include a clause such as "and any other costs and expenses" to prevent the seller from claiming, at a later stage, expenses for export licenses, origin receiving charges, and the like. The buyer wants to ensure that the total price will remain as stated in #16 and any surprises will not be at her expense.

#16   The total amount should reflect all elements supplied by the seller until the risk and responsibility for the goods passes to the buyer.

#17   The net weight is for the goods themselves, in their standard packaging, if applicable. Since the buyer may not know the weight of the goods, this would have to refer to information supplied by the seller in the pro-forma invoice or other documentation.

#18   Packaging other than the standard packaging and the shipping container should be specified here. The general understanding is that normal packaging for the selected mode of transport and destination is included in the price

---

1. The Harmonized Tariff Schedule (HTS or HS) was developed by the World Customs Organization and has been in use since 1988. It classifies all tradeable goods in 99 chapters with 1,244 headings and 5,224 subheadings. The HS is applied by more than 200 countries and customs territories. The goods have 8- to 10- digit numbers, the first six of which are harmonized. Thus, traders can easily look up the applicable import duties for their products in all countries where they may want to export goods.

for the goods and only special and/or additional packaging, if required by the buyer, should be mentioned here.

#19   The gross weight is for the shipping container(s) including dunnage, if applicable. Again, since the buyer may not know the weight of the goods, this would have to refer to information supplied by the seller in the pro-forma invoice or other documentation. Even if the buyer does not know the weight, it is not irrelevant for her and should be part of the contract. If the actual weight should deviate significantly from the contractual weight, the buyer may hold the seller accountable for additional expenses.

#20   Payment terms will be discussed in detail in Part Three. In the PO, the buyer needs to indicate the payment terms she is expecting at the quoted price. Less favorable terms, such as payment in advance on an open account, would either be unacceptable to the buyer or at least entitle her to ask for a lower price for the goods.

#21   If they were not included earlier in the description of the goods, any assurances sought by the buyer on issues such as suitability of the goods for a specific purpose, marketability, performance targets, warranties, etc. should be clearly spelled out here. In addition, the buyer may want to specify the choice of law and forum.

Many buyers don't invest a lot of time when generating a PO and send more or less just a list of the goods they are seeking to buy and the price agreed upon in earlier communications. This is a grave mistake, since the seller can simply accept the PO and there would be no clear record of many of the terms that should be included in the contract of sale, which we will discuss below.

––––––––––

Finally, we turn to a document that is becoming increasingly widely used, often without real need. This is the Confidentiality Agreement or Nondisclosure Agreement (NDA) for the protection of proprietary information of the seller and/or the buyer. The seller will ask for an NDA to be signed before revealing proprietary information related to the goods to be sold, for example secret methods or processes used in the production of the goods or certain of their features or performance characteristics. The buyer may ask for an NDA to be signed before revealing proprietary information related to the intended use of the goods, for example pricing strategies, production or sales targets, marketing strategies, client lists and other information about clients, and also how parts might be integrated into a larger unit, etc.

In some companies, it is now a general requirement that anyone who enters into negotiations with the company and, in the course of such negotiations, may receive any kind of proprietary information, first has to sign an NDA. This may include all vendors and customers (sellers and buyers). However, with the exception of NDAs used by employers with their employees, it is not so obvious that these agreements are worth the trouble and ultimately serve more than psychological purposes. Here are some of the concerns:

- NDAs have to be sufficiently broad to cover all intended aspects of a business relationship, but also sufficiently specific to identify the proprietary information they are protecting. Aggressive use of overly broad NDAs can expose a company to antitrust liability based on attempted restraint of competition.

- Identifying the proprietary information and who owns it is important so that the other side cannot later say they already knew the information or obtained it from elsewhere.

- Only confidential information can be protected via an NDA. If a party has already disclosed the information in marketing materials or otherwise publicly available technical product specifications, in a patent filing, or during public hearings in an antitrust case or lawsuit, the information is no longer confidential and cannot be protected via an NDA.

- Many trade secrets are already protected at common law (misappropriation, breach of confidentiality, and unfair competition can trigger liability) and in statutory law. The U.S. Federal Trade Commission Act, and various state-level legislation implementing the Uniform Trade Secrets Act, provides protection and a range of remedies including injunctions and damages. The 27 Member States of the EU had to adopt national legislation for the implementation of EU Directive 2016/943 of the European Parliament and the Council of 8 June 2016 on the Protection of Undisclosed Know-How and Business Information (Trade Secrets) Against their Unlawful Acquisition, Use and Disclosure (OJ 2016 L 157, pp. 1–18) by 9 June 2018. The national implementation acts supersede any prior national laws. An NDA is not needed in areas covered by these rules, but may still facilitate proof of misappropriation or misuse of confidential information.

The following is a classic example of an overly broad NDA clause that will be hard to enforce and could easily be interpreted as an illegal restraint of competition:[2]

---

2. Cf. Sage Languages Pte Ltd — Standard Confidentiality Agreement, available at http://www. sagelanguages.com/wp-content/uploads/2013/09/Confidentiality-Agreement.pdf (last visited September 8, 2016).

> The Confidential Information to be disclosed can be described as and includes: Invention description(s), technical and business information relating to proprietary ideas and inventions, ideas, patentable ideas, trade secrets, drawings and/or illustrations, patent searches, existing and/or contemplated products and services, research and development, production, costs, profit and margin information, finances and financial projections, customers, clients, marketing, and current or future business plans and models, regardless of whether such information is designated as "Confidential Information" at the time of its disclosure.

By contrast, if an NDA is well crafted, it can be a life-saver for a company if proprietary information is misappropriated. An illustration is provided by *RRK Holding Co. v. Sears, Roebuck, & Co.,* 563 F. Supp. 2d 832 (N.D. Ill. 2008). In the 1990s, RRK manufactured and sold a spiral saw under the brand name "Roto Zip" with some success. Sears contacted RRK in 1997 about manufacturing an updated model to be distributed under the "Craftsman" brand owned by Sears. The two companies entered into an NDA and RRK disclosed information about its next-generation model to Sears. The two companies eventually could not agree about the pricing of the device and terminated their cooperation before a single saw was produced by RRK for Sears. Shortly thereafter, Sears introduced its own new spiral saw under the Craftsman label, which incorporated the technology RRK had disclosed to it. RRK sued and was able to show that all key documents handed over to Sears had been marked as confidential. Although Sears claimed that the respective technology was by then public knowledge in the power-tool industry, a jury agreed with RRK that the technology was innovative and returned a verdict finding Sears liable for breach of the NDA and for misappropriating RRK's trade secret. A judgment granted RRK US$11,665,105 for actual losses, US$1,688,136 for unjust enrichment, and US$8,011,344 for punitive damages. Defendant then moved for a judgment as a matter of law, claiming that there was no legally sufficient evidentiary basis for a reasonable jury to find for the other side. RRK moved for prejudgment and post-judgment interest. In the end, the court denied defendant's motion and granted plaintiff's motion ordering Sears to pay US$21,363,585 in total damages, US$3,715,479 in prejudgment interest, and US$1,931.50 per day in post-judgment interest until the damages were paid as awarded.

Against this background, we can now draft a model that can be adapted to most IBT relationships of the kind discussed in this book. We have to distinguish unilateral NDAs where one company is the "disclosing party" and the other is the "receiving party," and mutual NDAs, where both parties are disclosing information and both are sworn to secrecy.

NDAs Explained (see Sample Document 2-3)

In some industries or settings the name "confidentiality agreement" is more commonly used (for example in employment contexts), in others the name "nondisclosure agreement"; there is no material difference between the two, as long as the other terms are clear.

#1 The entry on "purpose" clarifies several things: i) there will be a transfer of information that is currently not publicly available, i.e., it is confidential; ii) the information is considered valuable by both parties and is, therefore, "consideration" (see also #9); iii) the information has to remain confidential; iv) the present agreement does not affect the ownership of the disclosing party and does not constitute a license or permission for the receiving party to do anything with the information other than the purpose for which it is being disclosed.

#2 There are generally three ways of determining the scope of the NDA or CDA: (i) The information can be broadly described with reference to the IBT in question (see the example on p. 89); (ii) the information can be specifically described; and (iii) the information can be marked. The present NDA or CDA uses a combination of (ii) and (iii) (see also #3). To the extent that existing information is disclosed, it needs to be described quite clearly. In practice, very general NDAs and CDAs have often proven unenforceable. To this end compare below, *Magellan International Corporation v Salzgitter Handel GmbH*, pp. 200–208, in particular paragraphs 36–46.

#3 The proposal specifies that future information will be marked if it is to fall under the NDA. This ensures a high level of enforceability and also puts a significant burden on the disclosing party. They may want to have a stamp made and place it on every piece of paper and other information that is being transmitted by mail, fax, or e-mail attachment and contains confidential information. They may also want to include a rider in all e-mails and delete it when it is not needed versus adding it when it is needed.

#4 The obligations of the receiving party are spelled out clearly in this model. They cover both voluntary and involuntary disclosure by the receiving party. The obligation to maintain a high level of computer security is increasingly important in practice.

Clause #4(c) is of particular importance. By way of the NDA, the receiving party acknowledges that existing information described under #2 falls under the NDA; by way of clause (c), the receiving party also acknowledges that future information falls under the NDA if it is so marked by the disclosing party and not contradicted by the receiving party. This prevents the receiving party from claiming that some information was already in the public domain when received or that they had already independently arrived at the same research results (see also #6).

#5 The exclusions are important because it is always possible that confidential information becomes publicly known without an act or fault of the receiving party. For example, the disclosing party may have transferred it to third parties with or without an obligation to keep it confidential. Third parties may

Sample Document 2-3: Unilateral Nondisclosure or Confidentiality Agreement

Confidentiality Agreement

entered into between

Company Name & Logo of Disclosing Party and	**Company Name of Receiving Party**
Contact Person	Contact Person
Street Address	Street Address
City, Zip Code & Country	City, Zip Code & Country
Phone, Fax & E-mail	Phone, Fax & E-mail

1. Purpose

In the course of their business dealings, the disclosing party has transmitted or will transmit valuable information to the receiving party. This information currently is and needs to be kept confidential. It is and remains the property of the disclosing party. Neither its disclosure nor the present agreement imply that a license is granted or rights are transferred to the receiving party, unless otherwise agreed between the parties in writing.

2. Existing Trade Secrets Being Disclosed

The parties agree that the following specific information is proprietary information of the disclosing party and falls under the nondisclosure obligations of the receiving party.

(1) ....

(2) ....

3. Future Confidential Information

Any communication in any medium transmitted in future from the disclosing party to the receiving party will be marked as "Confidential — Subject to NDA of .... [date]" if it contains trade secrets and other information falling under the scope of this agreement.

4. Obligations of the Receiving Party

The receiving party agrees to protect the proprietary information of the disclosing party identified pursuant to this agreement with all lawful means, in particular

(a)   to not disclose the information to any third party unless required by law;

(b)   to maintain the confidentiality of the information in its internal procedures, to limit access to the information among its staff to those who need to know, to maintain binding legal agreements with all employees and independent contractors who have been given or may gain access to the information, and to safeguard against unauthorized third party access to facilities and computers;

(c)   to notify immediately if it disagrees with the designation of information pursuant to #3 because it has already received the information from a third party, considers the information to be part of the public domain and can name the sources to back up this claim, or is able to prove that it has already independently developed the same information itself;

(d)   not to use the information in any way in competition with the disclosing party, including but not limited to the acquisition of patents or trademarks, the registration of domain names, the solicitation of employees, customers or suppliers, or the development of products or services;

(e)   to delete the information from all electronic media and destroy any documents containing such information, when the business relationship ends or the information is otherwise no longer needed, whichever comes first;

(f)   to take any other measures reasonably required to protect the confidentiality of the information.

Nondisclosure or Confidentiality Agreement, Page 2

5. Exclusions

The obligations of the receiving party do not extend to information that has become part of the public domain by action of the disclosing party or a third party. If the receiving party has disclosed or wishes to disclose information covered by this agreement based on this exclusion, the receiving party bears the burden of proof that the information has become part of the public domain before its disclosure. If a lawsuit or other procedure is started against the receiving party that might require disclosure of protected information, the receiving party shall notify the disclosing party in a timely manner to enable it to intervene and protect its rights if necessary.

6. No Implied Warranties

The fact that the information is classified as valuable in this agreement does not imply any warranties on behalf of the disclosing party, for example that the information is accurate, that it will be of use for the receiving party, or that it will never be disclosed to third parties or otherwise become known or available to them.

7. Assignability

The rights and obligations under this agreement are binding on the parties and not assignable to third persons without mutual consent of the parties to this agreement in writing.

8. Term

The agreement is valid for the duration of the negotiations and business dealings of the parties and for a period of five years beyond. It can be extended by mutual consent in writing.

9. Consideration

The parties agree that the disclosure of the confidential information is of sufficient value for the receiving party to constitute consideration.

10. Remedies

Any breach of this agreement that entails access of third parties to the protected information can cause irreparable harm to the disclosing party. Therefore, the receiving party agrees to compensate the disclosing party for proven loss or a minimum amount of liquidated damages of US$.........., whichever is higher. The receiving party will also compensate the disclosing party for the cost of any legal remedies against itself and against any third party that gained access to the information as a result of the breach by the receiving party.

11. Governing Law and Forum

This agreement shall be subject to the laws of .... Any disputes about the agreement or a breach of the agreement shall be settled in arbitration administered by the International Centre for Dispute Resolution of the AAA in accordance with its international arbitration rules. The place of arbitration shall be .... and the proceedings shall be conducted in English. The number of arbitrators shall be one/three.

12. Final Clauses

This is the entire agreement between the parties and supersedes any earlier communications, negotiations, and agreements with respect to its subject matter. Any modifications or subsequent agreements on the subject matter must be in writing and duly signed by both parties. Should any part of this agreement be found to be invalid, the remaining parts shall remain binding and enforceable between the parties.

Date and Signatures

On behalf of the disclosing party   On behalf of the receiving party have violated their NDAs. Third parties may have independently arrived at the same research results. Clause #5 accounts for these possibilities. However, it also puts the burden of proof on the receiving party that it has not and will not disclose information in breach of the NDA.

The last sentence refers to Clause #4(a) and the possibility that the receiving party may be required by law to disclose information protected under the NDA. In such a case, the disclosing party needs to be informed and may seek to protect the confidentiality of the information.

#6   This clause protects the disclosing party from any claims by the receiving party about the quality and/or the continued confidentiality of the information. The disclosing party owns the information and can basically do with it as it pleases.

#7   Assignment implies disclosure. Even if a third party agrees to step into the position of the receiving party and be equally bound by the NDA, assignment requires permission by the disclosing party.

#8   In many cases, the disclosing party would like the receiving party to honor the NDA indefinitely. However, very long protection terms have caused problems with enforcement in practice. Five years beyond the business dealings of the parties would seem a reasonable compromise. Still, the ideal term would depend on the information and the nature of the business. Parties should opt for a shorter term if the value of the information is very time-sensitive and tends to decline rapidly. On the other hand, disclosing parties can justify a longer term if the information is likely to remain confidential and valuable for a long time.

Disclosing parties should remember that the effects of the NDA not only end at the end of the protection term, but also if the information becomes known to third parties and/or the general public at an earlier time (see #6).

#9   Common law jurisdictions generally require consideration for a contract to be binding (see § 17(1) of the Restatement (Second) of Contracts). This can be a problem if the receiving party has to protect the confidentiality of information of the disclosing party without getting paid or receiving some other form of compensation. With this clause, the receiving party acknowledges that the information is of value to it and, therefore, constitutes consideration. The language in Clause #6 is somewhat problematic in this regard, since the disclosing party refuses to guarantee via that clause that the information is in fact objectively valuable and of subjective value to the receiving party. Theoretically, the disclosing party could pay the receiving party a nominal sum, say US$25, for keeping the information confidential. This would certainly qualify as consideration, but the cost of making an international bank transfer would exceed the amount in question. Thus, the present clause should be a good compromise.

#10   The problem with remedies is that the loss to the disclosing party is usually hard to quantify. At the same time, a very large sum in "liquidated damages" will often be considered unreasonable by a court asked to enforce it. Again, we need to find a compromise that provides a deterrent against disclosure in breach of the NDA, a sum that would seem adequate compensation for the disclosing party, and a reasonable amount for a court or arbitration tribunal. In the end, the amount to be entered here will depend on the transaction in question and the objective or subjective value of the information in question. If the parties are negotiating a multibillion-dollar investment, liquidated damages of several million dollars would probably not seem unreasonable to an arbitration tribunal. However, a court or arbitration tribunal will probably not enforce an amount similar to or higher than the envisaged transaction as such.

The situation is quite different if the value of the information can be proven, for example if the receiving party, armed with the confidential information of the disclosing party, decides to go into business with a third party instead and generates considerable profits based on this breach of the NDA. An arbitration tribunal and probably even a court would in such a case at least consider a full disgorgement of the respective profits.

#11 Like every contract between parties in different countries, it is highly recommended that a choice of law clause and a choice of forum should be included. The benefits have been discussed elsewhere. Parties should never assume that the choice of law and forum clauses agreed upon in the main contract would also apply to ancillary agreements such as an NDA. Furthermore, the NDA is often concluded before the main contract and the latter may never come together. However, if both an NDA and a main contract and maybe other ancillary agreements are concluded between the same parties, it makes sense to include the same choice of law and forum clauses in all agreements that refer to the same business transaction(s). In this way, the parties could avoid having to litigate or arbitrate related questions in different fora, with different lawyers, under different and potentially incompatible laws, and with potentially conflicting outcomes.

#12 The severability clause is standard and should always be included in international and domestic contracts.

The question whether or not an NDA or CDA is enforceable depends more than anything on the reasonableness of its terms. Many models otherwise available may provide broader protection for the disclosing party on paper. However, if they should be considered unreasonably broad when push comes to shove, they won't be worth the paper they are written on. The present model should be reasonable overall and thus enforceable in most cases.

Notes and Questions

1. On the basis of Articles 14 and 18 CISG and §2-206 UCC, explain when a pro-forma invoice might be construed as an offer and when a purchase order might

be construed as an acceptance (compare also Restatement (Second) of Contracts, Chapter 3, Formation of Contracts). How should these documents be formulated by the seller and the buyer to indicate clearly that the negotiations are ongoing and that neither an offer nor an acceptance has yet been declared? What is a pro-forma invoice if it is not an offer? Are the CISG, UCC, and Restatement coming to the same results in this regard?

2. At the bottom, the purchase order contains a request that the seller should get in touch if he does not accept or is not able to fulfill the order as requested. Does this mean that the seller has an obligation to act if he does not want to be bound by the contract? Could silence be interpreted as consent and trigger obligations for the seller and, potentially, damages for the buyer? If so, on what conditions? In this respect, is there a difference between the CISG and the UCC?

3. If a purchase order is sent and either qualifies as an offer or as an invitation to make an offer, does the PO alone trigger obligations, even if there is no acceptance or final contract? Are there obligations on the buyer? Let's assume the seller receives the PO and proceeds to manufacture the goods. Simultaneously, he sends a contract draft but the buyer never returns it or informs the seller after a while that she is no longer interested in the goods. What are the rights of the seller? (Check Section 3 below for further discussion.)

4. When is an NDA too narrow for its purpose? When is it too broad? Discuss the sample clause on p. 89 and explain why this is too broad.

5. How would a *mutual* NDA or CDA have to be formulated differently from Sample Document 2-3?

Section 3. Pre-Contractual Obligations and Pre-Contractual Liability

In commercial law, claims from one party against another can generally be based in one or more of five different areas of law:

- **contract law**, if a contract was concluded between the parties and not all mutual obligations were correctly met;

- **pre-contractual liability**, sometimes referred to as *culpa in contrahendo* and/ or *negotiorum gestio* (see p. 96, note 4 and discussion on p. 105), if the parties entered into contract negotiations and one or both sides suffered losses although a contract was never concluded;

- **tort liability**, if one party suffers a loss as a consequence of unlawful conduct of the other;

- **unjust enrichment**, if a party somehow acquires assets at the expense of another party without having a contract or another legal basis for the acquisition of the assets; this may include cases where a contract was avoided and, therefore, no longer provides a legal basis for the buyer to have the goods and the seller to have the money; and

- **property**, if a party is in possession of or otherwise benefiting from material or immaterial goods (including intellectual property rights) owned by another party.

All five areas of claim bases will appear and reappear in different sections of this book. In the present section, we will focus on pre-contractual liability.[3] The concept is not well established in the U.S., UK, and other common law countries. However, depending on the applicable law, parties to IBTs and their legal counsel may find themselves exposed to this kind of liability whether they are aware of it or not.[4]

In the European legal tradition, the concept of pre-contractual obligations and pre-contractual liability, in cases of breach of such obligations, is well-established. However, the legal basis varies from one country to another. In some countries, pre-contractual liability is part of tort liability. This can be problematic because tort liability typically requires a level of culpability—an unlawful act—on the side of the tortfeasor. If a party merely breaks off negotiations with another party or otherwise changes its mind before a contract is finalized, an unlawful act will rarely be committed. This is a corollary of the freedom of contract, which includes the freedom *not* to contract. Therefore, other European jurisdictions, like Germany, have developed the concept of pre-contractual liability as distinct from tort liability.

The dichotomy and some of the ramifications are illustrated in the case that led to the judgment of the European Court of Justice of September 17, 2002, in *Case C-334/00, Tacconi*.[5] In 1996, the Italian company Tacconi had entered into negotiations with German supplier HWS for the sale of a moulding plant. With knowledge of HWS, Tacconi concluded a leasing contract for the plant with a third party before the contract of sale with HWS was finalized. After HWS broke off the contract negotiations, Tacconi claimed damages of some US$2 million, alleging a breach of

---

3. For detailed discussion, see Ingeborg Schwenzer, Pascal Hachem & Christopher Kee, *Global Sales and Contract Law*, Oxford Univ. Press 2012, pp. 275–287.

4. See Larry A. DiMatteo, *An International Contract Law Formula: The Informality of International Business Transactions Plus the Internationalization of Contract Law Equals Unexpected Contractual Liability, L=(ii)²*, Syracuse J. Int'l L. & Com. 1997, Vol. 23, pp. 67–111.

See also Gregory S. Crespi, *Recovering Pre-Contractual Expenditures as an Element of Reliance Damages*, SMU L. Rev. 1995/96, Vol. 49, pp. 43–72, with comparative analysis of U.S. and Commonwealth case law. Essentially, in the common law systems, the issue is dealt with either under the notion of misrepresentation, unconscionability, or under promissory estoppel. For further analysis of U.S. case law, see also Violeta Solonova Foreman, *Non-Binding Preliminary Agreements: The Duty to Negotiate in Good Faith and the Award of Expectation Damages*, 72 U.T. Fac. L. Rev. 12 (2014). An attempt at a unified solution for the U.S. legal system—the concept of "no-retraction" pursuant to which a party can at some point no longer walk away from contract negotiations without incurring some form of liability—was advanced in Omri Ben-Shahar, *Contracts Without Consent: Exploring a New Basis for Contractual Liability*, U Penn. L. Rev. 2004, Vol. 152, No. 6, pp. 1829–1872.

5. *Case C-334/00, Fonderie Officine Meccaniche Tacconi SpA v. Heinrich Wagner Sinto Maschinenfabrik GmbH*, 2002 ECR I-7383 (see p. 97).

the duty to act honestly and in good faith. Tacconi brought the case not in defendant court in Germany, but in its own court in Italy based on its conviction that HWS had committed a tort. HWS, by contrast, claimed that any case by Tacconi should either be brought via arbitration, as envisaged in the draft contract, or in defendant court in Germany. Matters of jurisdiction between EU Member States are subject to the mandatory rules of *EU Regulation 1215/2012 on Jurisdiction and the Recognition and Enforcement of Judgments in Civil and Commercial Matters.*[6] The Italian court was unsure how this Regulation should be interpreted in a case involving pre-contractual liability and requested an authoritative interpretation of the Regulation from the European Court of Justice. If pre-contractual liability was akin to tort, it would be covered by Article 7(2) of the Regulation and the injured party could bring the case "where the harmful event occurred," i.e., her own court (see *Mines de Potasse d'Alsace*, below, p. 703). By contrast, if pre-contractual liability was covered by contract law, it would be subject to Article 7(1) of the Regulation and the case would have to be brought "in the courts for the place of performance," here the defendant court. To find out about the legal nature of pre-contractual liability and the applicable provision of the Regulation, the Italian court referred the following questions to the European Court of Justice pursuant to Article 267 TFEU:

1. Does an action against a defendant seeking to establish pre-contractual liability fall within the scope of matters relating to tort, delict or quasi-delict (Article [7(2) of the Regulation 1215/2012])?

2. If not, does it fall within the scope of matters relating to a contract (Article [7(1) of the Regulation]), and if it does, what is "the obligation in question"?

3. If not, is the general criterion of the domicile of the defendant the only criterion applicable?

The European Court answered as follows:

Case 2-1

Fonderie Officine Meccaniche Tacconi v. Heinrich Wagner Sinto Maschinenfabrik (HWS)

European Court of Justice, Case C-334/00, 2002 ECR I-7383

(Footnotes omitted.)

---

6. OJ 2012 L 351, pp. 1–32. Regulation 1215/2012 is the successor to *Regulation 44/2001 on Jurisdiction and the Recognition and Enforcement of Judgments in Civil and Commercial Matters*, which, in turn, is the successor to the *1968 Brussels Convention on Jurisdiction and the Enforcement of Judgments in Civil and Commercial Matters*. Although the applicable law at the pertinent time was the 1968 Convention, references here are to the current 2012 Regulation, since the relevant provisions—at least in substance—have remained unchanged since 1968 and the interpretations given by the ECJ to the older versions are applicable to the current version.

Opinion of Advocate General Geelhoed of 31 January 2002

... V—Observations submitted

⁴⁶ Tacconi contends that pre-contractual liability must be regarded as non-contractual and therefore constitutes a delict or quasi-delict. ...

⁴⁷ Tacconi construes the case-law of the Court as meaning that the concept 'matters relating to a contract' [in Article 7(1)(a) of the Regulation] cannot cover a situation in which there is no obligation freely assumed by one party towards another. Tacconi contends that at the pre-contractual stage there is no contractual link between the parties and if no agreement results from the negotiations no contractual obligation can arise therefrom in respect of the parties. ...

VI—Pre-contractual liability

⁵⁵ It follows from the principle of freedom of contract that each person is free to choose with whom and on what matter he wishes to enter into negotiations and the point to which he wishes to continue negotiations. Therefore, in principle persons are free to break off negotiations whenever they wish to so without incurring liability in that regard. However, the freedom to break off negotiations is not absolute. Article 2.15 of the UNIDROIT principles provide that 'a party who ... breaks off negotiations in bad faith is liable for losses caused to the other party'. According to the explanatory note to this article, negotiations can reach a point after which they may no longer be broken off abruptly and without justification. When such a point is reached depends firstly on the extent to which the other party, as a result of the conduct of the first party, had reason to rely on the positive outcome. Secondly, it depends on the number of issues on which the parties had already reached agreement. However, where a party breaks off negotiations abruptly and without justification, it must compensate for the loss incurred by the other party.

⁵⁶ Thus, pre-contractual liability arises where negotiations on a contract are broken off without justification.

⁵⁷ This is the first time that the Court has had to deal, in connection with the [1968 Convention and/or its subsequent reiterations as Regulations 44/2001 and 1215/2012], with the legal nature of the liability which can arise between two potential contracting parties during negotiations over a contract. [Neither the original Convention nor the Regulation now in force] lays down [any] rules on liability arising from pre-contractual relations per se. The clearest indication is still to be found in the Evrigenis Report which provided clarification on the Convention on the occasion of the accession of Greece. This report states that pre-contractual relations can fall within the scope of Article [7(1)]. However, the report does not state the foundation on which this view is based. Furthermore, there are extensive academic writings on pre-contractual liability in the Member States and also in connection with international private law. The academic writings do not follow the same lines in all the Member States.

⁵⁸ In most legal systems a party which breaks off negotiations without just cause, having created an expectation on the part of the other party that a contract will be

entered into, is liable for the negative contractual interest. In general, such interest includes not only the expenses but also the lost opportunities to conclude another contract with a third party. Negotiations which are broken off dash an expectation that they will lead to a result. In this respect I will briefly examine some of these legal systems below. This brief account of the law relating to pre-contractual liability is certainly not intended to provide an exhaustive picture of the law in the Member States as it now stands, but merely serves as an illustration. The Court may use national law as a source of inspiration when answering the questions referred to it.

59 In Italian law Article 1337 of the Codice Civile contains a specific provision governing pre-contractual liability. Parties must act in good faith during negotiations over and the formation of a contract. A party who breaks off negotiations without just cause, having created an expectation that a contract will be entered into, is liable for the negative contractual interest. Such negative interest specifically includes lost opportunities in addition to expenses. The positive interest is not compensated for, that is to say the other party need not be placed in the situation in which it would have been had the contract actually been concluded. The legal requirement which is not observed when negotiations are broken off abruptly is intended to prevent the other party suffering harm as a result of the fact that it is involved in negotiations and not because the negotiations did not ultimately result in a contract. Fault is not required.

60 In German law a party who culpably breaks off negotiations without just cause or on irrelevant grounds, having created an expectation on the part of another party that a contract will certainly be entered into, is liable for the negative contractual interest. Usually the liability is based on the doctrine of *culpa in contrahendo*: a party who suddenly breaks of negotiations is liable for the culpable non-fulfilment of the obligation to take account of the other party's interests. Therefore, in German law almost the same criterion applies as in Italy, except that the requirement relating to fault has a role to play.

61 French law does not lay down provisions on pre-contractual negotiations and entering into contracts. Pre-contractual liability is based on the doctrine of abuse of rights in conjunction with reasonableness and equity. It arises wherever a party suddenly breaks off negotiations without just cause at a time when the other party could legitimately expect that a contract would be entered into. As long as no contract has been entered into, the harm which results from the pre-contractual stage is regarded as covered by the law governing tort, delict or quasi-delict. The loss suffered by the other party must be compensated for. It is uncertain whether this also covers lost opportunities ('perte d'une chance') because it is not established that a contract with a third party has actually been entered into. Furthermore, the French courts appear reluctant to declare that pre-contractual liability exists as they do not wish to curb the principle of freedom of contract.

62 Netherlands law is different. Liability is possible before the other party can legitimately expect that the contract will be entered into. Under Netherlands law, a stage can be reached in negotiations at which they may no longer be broken off. However,

where this occurs, liability for positive contractual interest is possible. Three stages in the negotiations are identified. In the first stage negotiations may be broken off without liability being incurred. This is followed by a stage during which negotiations may be broken off, but the costs incurred by the other party must be compensated for. Finally, there is the concluding stage at which negotiations may no longer be broken off. This is reached when the other party can legitimately expect that a contract will be entered into or there are no other circumstances which justify the negotiations being broken off. If a party breaks off negotiations at this stage, it can even be liable for lost profit. In Netherlands academic writings it is argued that at this stage actions may be subsumed under Article [7(1)] on account of the 'closeness of the links' which [have] developed between the parties.

[63] Liability arising from negotiations which have been broken off has not been recognised in United Kingdom law since time immemorial. The risk that a party will break off negotiations before a contract has been entered into is regarded as a 'business loss'. The continental notion of pre-contractual good faith per se is unknown in the United Kingdom. There is no obligation to negotiate in conformity with the requirements of reasonableness and equity. However, neither of these facts mean that there are no rules governing conduct during the pre-contractual stage. For example, liability can be based of the doctrine of 'misrepresentation'. However, I consider that the legal concept of 'estoppel by representation' is more important. In accordance with this legal concept, a party may not withdraw a previous statement if the other party has suffered harm as a result of that statement. Thus, this legal concept is—albeit not identical—comparable with notions in continental law such as the protection of good faith and legitimate expectations. Finally, it should be noted that in so far as liability arises as a result of negotiations which have been broken off, this is based on actions which constitute a 'tort'. A clear distinction must be drawn between such liability and liability in connection with failure to fulfil contractual obligations.

[64] I now turn to the relevance of the abovementioned legal principles to the answer to the question which has been referred in the light of the [Regulation].

[65] To that end, I will divide the negotiation process into two stages. During the first stage freedom of contract is paramount. The parties may break off negotiations. However, during the second stage the parties may no longer break off negotiations. The expectation which been created on the part of the other party and the harm which it suffers because negotiations are broken off can give rise to liability. In any event, that liability includes the negative contractual interest, that is to say the expenses incurred and the opportunities lost. In general this liability does not go so far as to enable the other party to demand that the contract nevertheless be concluded.

[66] It is possible that a further, third stage should be identified—which I deduce from the legal principles in the Netherlands. It is possible that the links between the parties are so close that a positive contractual interest can also be claimed. This involves either an action for the contract nevertheless to be concluded or compensation which is the equivalent thereto. . . .

The relationship between Article [7(1) Jurisdiction in Matters Relating to a Contract] and Article [7(2) Matters Relating to Tort, Delict or Quasi-Delict]

[71] As I have said, in matters of liability under civil law the [Regulation] provides for a closed scheme: whatever the case, either Article [7(1)] or Article [7(2)] applies. The provisions can never apply simultaneously.

[72] As regards this closed scheme, I concur with the Commission's assessment of the relationship between Article [7(1)] and Article [7(2)]. The Commission contends that, unlike the concept of 'matters relating to tort, delict or quasi-delict', the concept of 'matters of contract' is open to a literal interpretation.

[73] In brief, according to the case-law of the Court, the scope of Article [7(1)] is precisely defined. Where a matter does not fall within the scope of Article [7(1)], Article [7(2)] applies. In this sense Article [7(2)] is a residual category. Thus, it is necessary to establish in which cases a matter falls within the scope of Article [7(1)]. In that respect the aspect of freedom is central. According to [Case C-26/91] *Handte*, the phrase 'matters relating to a contract' is not 'to be understood as covering a situation in which there is no obligation freely assumed by one party towards another'. Whether an obligation is freely assumed is determined primarily by the principle of legal certainty as applied inter alia in *Handte*. Must a normally well-informed individual foresee that he has assumed an obligation?

[74] The precise definition of the scope of Article [7(1)] is important for another reason. Article [7(1)] includes the possibility of choice of forum. Under Article [25 of the Regulation], the parties to a contract may confer jurisdiction on another court or even a forum which has exclusive jurisdiction to settle a possible dispute. The parties thereby freely renounce the jurisdiction of the court which would be competent in their case. The decision to waive such a fundamental right can be made only on the basis of a well-considered choice.

The importance of pre-contractual relations

[75] As the national court emphasises, the pre-contractual liability derives from the failure to observe a legal requirement and not from the failure to fulfil a contractual obligation. That is because there. is no contract. In the present case the legal requirement derives from Article 1337 of the Italian Codice Civile under which parties must act in good faith during negotiations over a contract.

[76] I consider that this requirement is a generally applicable rule of conduct enshrined in law which does not differ from other rules of conduct derived from law. Under certain circumstances failure to comply with such rules of conduct can constitute a delict or quasi-delict. Consequently, Article [7(2)] of the [Regulation] should apply.

[77] That would make it possible to give a simple answer to the question referred by the national court. However, I consider that the issue of pre-contractual liability is more complex in nature. In my view, the decisive factor as regards the application of the [Regulation] is whether an agreement has been entered into between the parties. Have the parties assumed obligations towards one another? Where an obligation

has been freely assumed, Article [7(1)] applies. I would draw a distinction between obligations and expectations—legitimate or otherwise—which the parties have in relation to one another. Such expectation can consist in the negotiations not being broken off suddenly or, for example, negotiations being held at the same time—but not openly—with a competitor. I consider that the dashing of such expectations constitutes a delict or quasi-delict.

[78] The obligation referred to in the above paragraph need not relate to the actual contract on which negotiations are being held. It can also relate to a preformation contract under which one of the parties makes a start on performance. By way of illustration, I refer to the case in the main proceedings. Even before there is a complete contract for delivery of the moulding plant by HWS, which also lays down all the financing terms and conditions, for example, an agreement may possibly exist between the parties under which HWS is to make a start on performance by, for example, reserving production capacity or ordering materials. Disputes which subsequently arise could, possibly, fall within the scope of Article [7(1) of the Regulation].

[79] The criteria laid down in Article [25 of the Regulation] could also be relevant in answering the question concerning the time at which an obligation arises. This relates in particular to the criteria referred to at Article [25(b) and (c)]. Where there is no agreement in writing (or evidenced in writing), the existence of an obligation can be inferred from:

> "— the practices which the parties have established between themselves, or,
>
> — in international trade or commerce, the usage of which the parties are or ought to have been aware and which in such trade or commerce is widely known to, and regularly observed by, parties to contracts of the type involved in the particular trade or commerce concerned."

[80] I will clarify my view by reference to the various stages in the negotiating process which I identified in Section VI of this Opinion.

[81] During the first stage of the negotiating process the parties may break off negotiations without incurring liability. At this stage Article [7] of the Convention is irrelevant. There is no delict or quasi-delict, or an agreement.

[82] During the second stage an expectation has been created which can result in harm. At this point a party may no longer break off negotiations suddenly. If it nevertheless does so, it commits, under certain circumstances, a delict or quasi-delict. It can then be ordered to compensate for the expenses incurred by the other party or to compensate for the opportunities lost by the other party.

[83] The third stage is the stage at which there is still no (signed) contract, but at which it can be inferred from the circumstances that an obligation has been assumed between the parties. At this stage Article [7(1) of the Regulation] can apply. Such circumstances might lie in the fact that agreement has been reached on the main

aspects of a contract—the draft of the contract and the price—but negotiations are still under way on the other terms and conditions. It is also possible that one of the party has already made a start on performing the contract since it was able to deduce from the conduct of the other party that it intended to conclude a contract. Finally, I refer to the circumstances set out in Article [25 of the Regulation].

[84] I am aware that at the third staged described here there is almost a complete contract. The extent to which this stage is regarded as pre-contractual depends on the content of national private law.

[85] I conclude that an action for pre-contractual liability can be regarded as falling within the scope of matters relating to delict or quasi-delict within the meaning of Article [7(2) of the Regulation]. Where such action relates to an obligation which the other party has assumed towards the claimant, it must also be regarded as falling within the scope of matters relating to a contract within the meaning of Article [7(1) of the Regulation].

Judgment of the European Court of Justice of 17 September 2002

. . . Question 1 . . .

[19] It should be observed at the outset that the Court has consistently held (see Case 34/82 *Martin Peters Bauunternehmung* [1983] ECR 987, paragraphs 9 and 10, [Case C-261/90] *Reichert and Kockler* [[1992] ECR I-2149], paragraph 15, and [Case C-26/91] *Handte* [[1992] ECR I-3967], paragraph 10) that the expressions 'matters relating to a contract' and 'matters relating to tort, delict or quasi-delict' in Article [7(1) and (2) of Regulation 1215/2012] are to be interpreted independently, having regard primarily to the objectives and general scheme of the [Regulation]. Those expressions cannot therefore be taken as simple references to the national law of one or the other of the [Member] States concerned.

[20] Only such an interpretation is capable of ensuring the uniform application of the [Regulation], which is intended in particular to lay down common rules on jurisdiction for the courts of the [Member] States and to strengthen the legal protection of persons established in the Community by enabling the claimant to identify easily the court in which he may sue and the defendant reasonably to foresee in which court he may be sued (see Case C-295/95 *Farrell* [1997] ECR I-1683, paragraph 13, and Case C-256/00 *Besix* [2002] ECR I-1737, paragraphs 25 and 26).

[21] As the Court has held, the concept of 'matters relating to tort, delict or quasi-delict' within the meaning of Article [7(2) of the Regulation] covers all actions which seek to establish the liability of a defendant and which are not related to a 'contract' within the meaning of Article [7(1) of the Regulation] ([Case 189/87] *Kalfelis* [[1988] ECR 5565], paragraph 18, *Reichert and Kockler*, paragraph 16, and Case C-51/97 *Réunion Européenne and Others* [1998] ECR I-6511, paragraph 22).

[22] Moreover, while Article [7(1) of the Regulation] does not require a contract to have been concluded, it is nevertheless essential, for that provision to apply, to identify an obligation, since the jurisdiction of the national court is determined, in matters relating to a contract, by the place of performance of the obligation in question.

[23] Furthermore, it should be noted that, according to the Court's case-law, the expression 'matters relating to contract' within the meaning of Article [7(1) of the Regulation] is not to be understood as covering a situation in which there is no obligation freely assumed by one party towards another (*Handte*, paragraph 15, and *Réunion Européenne and Others*, paragraph 17).

[24] It does not appear from the documents in the case that there was any obligation freely assumed by HWS towards Tacconi.

[25] In view of the circumstances of the main proceedings, the obligation to make good the damage allegedly caused by the unjustified breaking off of negotiations could derive only from breach of rules of law, in particular the rule which requires the parties to act in good faith in negotiations with a view to the formation of a contract.

[26] In those circumstances, it is clear that any liability which may follow from the failure to conclude the contract referred to in the main proceedings cannot be contractual.

[27] In the light of all the foregoing, the answer to the first question must be that, in circumstances such as those of the main proceedings, characterised by the absence of obligations freely assumed by one party towards another on the occasion of negotiations with a view to the formation of a contract and by a possible breach of rules of law, in particular the rule which requires the parties to act in good faith in such negotiations, an action founded on the pre-contractual liability of the defendant is a matter relating to tort, delict or quasi-delict within the meaning of Article [7(2) of Regulation 1215/2012].

Questions 2 and 3

[28] As the first question has been answered in the affirmative, there is no need to answer the other questions put by the national court.

Notes and Questions

1. While Tacconi suggests a straightforward solution, the Advocate General compares different Member State solutions and opts for a differentiated solution to be adopted by the EU. What does the Court do and why? In your opinion, what would be the best solution? Why?

2. What is the legal basis for the pre-contractual liability in the present case? Surely not the Regulation 1215/2012 on Jurisdiction and the Recognition and Enforcement of Judgments in Civil and Commercial Matters? More generally, what is the applicable contract law when the parties did not conclude a contract? The CISG, for example, does not contain any provisions about pre-contractual liability.

3. As a result of the judgment, where should Tacconi go to sue for damages? How likely are they to succeed? If anything, will Tacconi be compensated only for the "negative interest" (to put them in the same position as if they had never met with HWS) or also the "positive interest" (to put them in the position as if HWS had not walked away but concluded the contract with Tacconi)?

4. If two parties conclude an NDA at an early stage of contract negotiations and one side later breaks off the negotiations, just before the main contract of sale is finalized, would the existence of the NDA influence the analysis of the European Court of Justice and potentially change the outcome?

5. *Tacconi* was decided in 2002. By 2007, the European Parliament and Council explicitly included "*culpa in contrahendo*" in Regulation 864/2007 of the European Parliament and of the Council of 11 July 2007 on the Law Applicable to Non-Contractual Obligations, the so-called "Rome II Regulation" (Documents, pp. I-67). According to the Preamble of the Regulation, "Culpa in contrahendo for the purposes of this Regulation is an autonomous concept and should not necessarily be interpreted within the meaning of national law. It should include the violation of the duty of disclosure and the breakdown of contractual negotiations" (recital 30). Article 2(1) provides that "damage shall cover any consequences arising out of tort/delict, unjust enrichment, negotiorum gestio or culpa in contrahendo." On the basis of this language, does the Regulation provide an autonomous legal basis in EU law for a damage claim based on pre-contractual liability? Compare Articles 12 and 15 of the Regulation when pondering your answer to this question. If the Regulation does not provide a legal basis, where might such a legal basis be found? Would it provide for compensation of the negative interest only? The positive interest as well? Always? What does "any consequences" mean in Article 2(1) in this regard? Go back to question 1 and reconsider your answer in light of these new statutory provisions.

6. What is the legal situation in the U.S. with regard to pre-contractual liability? Is there a legal basis in the UCC for such a liability? In common law? In the United Nations Convention on Contracts for the International Sale of Goods (CISG)? In the UNIDROIT Principles of International Commercial Contracts (PICC)? Or in the European Union Common Frame of Reference (CFR)? If so, what is the extent of any compensation that can be claimed as damages in a case similar to *Tacconi*? Consider the following explanations before giving your answer. How would these explanations influence your answer to question 5?

7. How could a doctrine of good faith dealing be formulated based on the discussion in this case?[7]

The CISG does not contain any specific rules about pre-contractual obligations and liabilities. Indeed, a proposal to include such rules was rejected by the drafters.[8] In principle, this means that pre-contractual liability or *culpa in contrahendo* joins

---

7. For further analysis, see, in particular, Reinhard Zimmermann & Simon Whittaker (eds.), *Good Faith in European Contract Law*, Cambridge Univ. Press 2000, in particular the contributions by Whittaker & Zimmermann on European contract law (pp. 7–62), and Robert S. Summers on American contract law (pp. 118–141).

8. See Schroeter in Ingeborg Schwenzer (ed.), *Schlechtriem & Schwenzer Commentary on the UN Convention on the International Sale of Goods (CISG)*, Oxford Univ. Press 4th ed. 2016, at p. 255.

issues such as mistake or fraud in the formation of a contract—issues not covered by the CISG to which the rules of the national legal system have to be applied that were chosen as back-up by the parties, or that applies pursuant to private international law. This outcome is less than ideal because it diminishes the harmonizing and simplifying effects of the CISG. Therefore, some commentators argue that a universal and uniform requirement of good faith and fair dealing in contract negotiations could be introduced into the CISG via Article 7(2).[9] If such proposals gain traction, they could lead to similar results as in the U.S. (see below).

The UNIDROIT Principles (PICC) contain a provision about "negotiations in bad faith" in Article 2.1.15:

> (1) A party is free to negotiate and is not liable for failure to reach an agreement.
>
> (2) However, a party who negotiates or breaks off negotiations in bad faith is liable for the losses caused to the other party.
>
> (3) It is bad faith, in particular, for a party to enter into or continue negotiations when intending not to reach an agreement with the other party.

Given the nature of the PICC as a reflection of the global law merchant (see below, p. 126–132), one could argue that this is a universal principle applicable to contract negotiations unless specifically excluded or regulated differently by an applicable contract law or by agreement of the parties. However, several questions remain unanswered: is this liability contractual, tort-based, or *sui generis*? The consequences extend not only to possible questions of jurisdiction, as in *Tacconi*, but also to statutes of limitations, etc. And what would be the extent of the liability? Does it provide only for the reliance or negative interest, to put the injured party in the position it would be in if she had never met the other party? Or could the injured party claim also the positive interest, i.e., any gains it would have made from the conclusion and proper implementation of the contract?

The Common Frame of Reference of the EU (CFR) has similar and, if anything, even more detailed rules compared to the PICC. First, Article II-3:301(1) establishes the principle that "[a] person is free to negotiate and is not liable for failure to reach an agreement." Then the provision continues:

> (2) A person who is engaged in negotiations has a duty to negotiate in accordance with good faith and fair dealing and not to break off negotiations contrary to good faith and fair dealing. This duty may not be excluded or limited by contract.
>
> (3) A person who is in breach of the duty is liable for any loss caused to the other party by the breach.

---

9. Ibid.

(4) It is contrary to good faith and fair dealing, in particular, for a person to enter into or continue negotiations with no real intention of reaching an agreement with the other party.

Compared to the PICC, it is remarkable that the CFR specifies liability *for any loss*. Presumably, this would include not only the negative interest but any positive interest as well. Does it mean, however, that the PICC would only reimburse the negative interest?[10]

The CFR further establishes quite detailed rules about the duty to disclose information pertinent to the parties and the goods or services subject to negotiation, as well as the corresponding duty to maintain the confidentiality of information versus third parties, and provides remedies for breach of these pre-contractual duties (Articles II-3:101 to II-3:109, as well as Article II-3:302). Again, the PICC are shorter but they do contain the provision of Article 2.1.16 regarding the duty of confidentiality.

The UCC, like the CISG, does not contain an express provision regarding pre-contractual liability. There is some case law, however,[11] and the Restatement (Second) of Contracts provides in §90 under the title "Promise Reasonably Inducing Action or Forbearance" that:

(1) A promise with the promisor should reasonably expect to induce action or forbearance on the part of the promisee or a third person and which does induce such action or forbearance is binding if injustice can be avoided only by enforcement of the promise. The remedy granted for breach may be limited as justice requires. . . .

Which of the options outlined by AG Geelhoed in *Tacconi* would the Restatement seem to support? Contractual liability? Tort? Or *sui generis*? And what is the remedy prescribed or awarded by the Restatement? Negative interest only? Or even the positive interest, if justice so requires? Finally, do you see a sufficient trend toward global harmonization of pre-contractual liability that would allow us to formulate a universal rule in the making?[12]

---

10. The latter is the view of Kleinheisterkamp in Stefan Vogenauer & Jan Kleinheisterkamp (eds.), *Commentary on the UNIDROIT Principles of International Commercial Contracts (PICC)*, Oxford Univ. Press 2009, at p. 306, and consistent with the official commentary to the PICC.

11. UCC §1-103(2) provides that "[u]nless displaced by the particular provisions of this Act, the principles of law and equity, including the law merchant and the law relative to capacity to contract, principal and agent, estoppel, fraud, misrepresentation, duress, coercion, mistake, bankruptcy, or other validating or invalidating cause shall supplement its provisions." It was applied, for example, in *Corestar v. LPB Communications*, 513 F. Supp. 2d 107, and in *Kolber v. Body Cent. Corp.*, 2012 WL 3095324.

12. See also Stathis Banakas, *Liability for Contractual Negotiations in English Law: Looking for the Litmus Test*, InDret 2009, Vol. 1, available at https://papers.ssrn.com/sol3/papers.cfm?abstract_id=1368208.

Section 4. The Contract for the Sale of Goods

A. The Principle of Party Autonomy and the Freedom of Contract

If seller and buyer are located in different countries, a number of potential problems are added to those we potentially encounter in contracts of sale on the domestic level. First, the legal system in seller's country will be different from the legal system in buyer's country and this may affect anything from the formation of the contract to the different rights and obligations and how they should be interpreted and applied in a given case. The seller will be familiar with his own legal system but rarely with buyer's legal system and vice versa. Thus, the natural inclination of the seller will be to insist that his own legal system or law should be applied to the contract while the buyer will insist on her legal system or law. Without compromise, there will be no contract. Second, each party will be more familiar with her own court system and will be more or less distrustful of the court system and the chances of enforcing a claim against a local party in the other country. Against this background, we now have to examine to what extent and by what means parties can choose the law that should govern their transaction and to what extent they can choose the forum where any disputes should be settled. As we will see, the parties have many options in this regard and many opportunities to make mistakes or at least less-than-optimal choices.[13]

In Business-to-Business (B2B) transactions, the principle of party autonomy and freedom of contract are universally respected to a great degree. This is confirmed, first of all, by all international conventions and agreements dealing with the law applicable to international sales and similar contracts. For example, the 1955 Hague Convention on the Law Applicable to International Sale of Goods (Documents, p. I-30) stipulates in Article 2 that "[a] sale shall be governed by the domestic law of the country *designated by the contracting parties*" (emphasis added). Only then does it proceed to provide for the case where the parties have not made a choice of law or where the party choice turns out to be invalid. Similarly, the 1986 Hague Convention on the Law Applicable to Contracts for the International Sale of Goods (Documents, p. I-32) provides in Article 7, as the default rule, that "[a] contract of sale is governed by the law chosen by the parties." The same is true for the 1994 Inter-American Convention on the Law Applicable to International Contracts (Article 7, Documents, p. I-48), and even the broader EU Regulation 593/2008 on the Law Applicable to Contractual Obligations (Rome I) (Article 3(1), Documents p. I-53). While the U.S. is not party to any of these conventions and agreements, the principle is inherent to U.S. law and can be found, for example, in UCC § 1-301, which reads in paragraph (c): "(1) an agreement by parties to a domestic transaction that

---

13. For useful analysis, see, for example, Ingeborg Schwenzer, *Who Needs a Uniform Contract Law, and Why?*, 58 Vill. L. Rev. 723 (2013).

any or all of their rights and obligations are to be determined by the law of this State or of another State is effective, whether or not the transaction bears a relation to the State designated; and (2) an agreement by the parties to an international transaction that any or all of their rights and obligations are to be determined by the law of this State or another State or country is effective, whether or not the transaction bears a relation to the State or country designated" (Documents, pp. I-145). A good summary of the internationally recognized standards can also be found in the 2015 Hague Principles on Choice of Law in International Commercial Contracts (Documents, p. I-38). Although the Principles are non-binding, they have been widely endorsed and approved.[14]

In a similar way, the international conventions and national laws dealing with the question of jurisdiction respect the choice of the parties as the primary criterion for determining which courts are competent to hear any disputes between the parties to an international business transaction. For example, the 2005 Hague Convention on Choice of Court Agreements (COCA) (Documents, p. II-11), which applies to "international cases . . . in civil or commercial matters" (Article 1) provides that "[t]he court or courts of a Contracting State designated in an exclusive choice of court agreement [between two or more parties to a contract] shall have jurisdiction to decide a dispute to which the agreement applies, unless the agreement is null and void under the law of that State" (Article 5(1)).[15]

---

14. The Principles are available online on the website of the Hague Conference on Private International Law, see https://www.hcch.net/en/instruments/conventions/full-text/?cid=135. For further reading, see, *inter alia*, Jonathan Levin, *The Hague Principles on Choice of Law in International Commercial Contracts: Enhancing Party Autonomy in a Globalized Market*, 13 N.Y.U. J.L. & Bus. 271 (2016); Daniel Girsberger & Neil B. Cohen, *Key Features of the Hague Principles on Choice of Law in International Commercial Contracts*, Unif. L. Rev. 2017, Vol. 22, No. 2, pp. 316–335; Jan L. Neels, *The Nature, Objective and Purposes of the Hague Principles on Choice of Law in International Contracts*, in Petar Šarčević et al. (eds.), Yearbook of Private International Law, Vol. XV, 2013/2014, pp. 45–56; Marta Pertegás & Brooke Adele Marshall, *Party Autonomy and its Limits: Convergence Through the New Hague Principles on Choice of Law in International Commercial Contracts*, 39 Brook. J. Int'l L. 975 (2014); Geneviève Saumier, *The Hague Principles and the Choice of Non-State "Rules of Law" to Govern an International Commercial Contract*, 40 Brook. J. Int'l L. 1 (2014); Andreas Schwartze, *New Trends in Parties' Options to Select the Applicable Law? The Hague Principles on Choice of Law in International Contracts in a Comparative Perspective*, 12 U. St. Thomas L.J. 87 (2015); S.I. Strong, *Limits of Procedural Choice of Law*, 39 Brook. J. Int'l L. 1027 (2014); as well as Symeon C. Symeonides, *Choice of Law*, Oxford Univ. Press 2016.

For further reading, see also James J. Fawcett, Jonathan M. Harris & Michael Bridge: *International Sale of Goods in the Conflict of Laws*, Oxford Univ. Press 2005; and Henry Deeb Gabriel, *Contracts for the Sale of Goods—A Comparison of U.S. and International Law*, Oxford Univ. Press, 2nd ed. 2009.

15. Like the 2015 Hague Principles on Choice of Law in International Commercial Contracts, the 2005 Hague Convention is more widely supported than the actual number of ratifications would indicate. As of January 2020, it has been ratified by 32 countries. While this number is impressive, it includes all 28 Member States of the EU. Outside of the EU, the 2005 Hague Convention has only been ratified by Mexico, Montenegro, and Singapore. Nevertheless, China and the United States are signatories and may ratify in the foreseeable future.

Similarly, the EU Regulation 1215/2012 on Jurisdiction and the Recognition and Enforcement of Judgments in Civil and Commercial Matters (Brussels Ia or I bis), which is the relevant law in the 27 Member States of the EU, provides in Article 25(1) "[i]f the parties, regardless of their domicile, have agreed that a court or the courts of a Member State are to have jurisdiction to settle any disputes which have arisen or which may arise in connection with a particular legal relationship, that court or those courts shall have jurisdiction. . . . Such jurisdiction shall be exclusive unless the parties have agreed otherwise." (Documents, p. II-92).

In the United States, jurisdiction and recognition of foreign judgments are matters of state law. To the extent that these rules are part of state common law, they are usually applied equally for the recognition and enforcement of a judgment from a sister state in the U.S. and for judgments from foreign countries. To facilitate access for lawyers who are unfamiliar with the (common) law of a particular state of the Union and to achieve a level of harmonization, the Uniform Law Commission first adopted the 1948 Uniform Enforcement of Foreign Judgments Act and then the 1962 Uniform Foreign Money-Judgments Recognition Act. The former covers the enforcement of sister state judgment in implementation of the Full Faith and Credit Clause of the U.S. Constitution. The latter deals specifically with the recognition and enforcement of judgments from foreign countries. It was recast recently in the form of the 2005 Uniform Foreign-Country Money Judgments Recognition Act (UFCMJRA) (Documents, p. II-68). The 1962 version of the Act was implemented by 31 States plus the District of Columbia and the U.S. Virgin Islands. The 2005 version of the Act has been implemented by 24 states and the District of Columbia and is pending—as of January 2020—in Wisconsin and Massachusetts.[16] The 2005 UFCMJRA provides in Sec. 5(a) that "[a] foreign-country judgment may not be refused recognition for personal jurisdiction if: . . . (3) the defendant, before the commencement of the proceeding, had agreed to submit to the jurisdiction of the foreign court with respect to the subject matter involved."

Finally, some 159 countries, by ratifying the 1958 New York Convention on the Recognition and Enforcement of Foreign Arbitral Awards (Documents, p. II-500), have accepted that parties to a B2B transaction can choose not to take their disputes to a public court at all.

Choice of forum options and clauses will be examined in detail in Part Six, Section 2, on International Commercial Litigation, and Section 3 on International Commercial Arbitration.

However, party autonomy and freedom of contract goes beyond the mere choice of law and forum in international B2B transactions. In general, the parties cannot merely choose the contract or sales law they wish to abide by from a range of

---

16. For up-to-date information on the enactment status, visit the website of the Uniform Law Commission at http://www.uniformlaws.org/Act.aspx. Since some states have enacted first the 1962 and then the 2005 version, about a dozen states, including Utah, Kansas, Arkansas, Louisiana, Kentucky, Mississippi, New Hampshire, and Vermont, have not enacted either version.

different national laws—they can also select contract or sales rules that are not part of any national legal system or make up their own rules entirely. One example is Article 6 of the United Nations Convention for the International Sale of Goods (CISG), which reads: "The parties may exclude the application of this Convention or . . . derogate from or vary the effects *of any of its provisions*" (emphasis added). Pursuant to this provision and within the scope of application of the CISG, parties are literally able to write up their own contract law. The same deference can be found in the Uniform Commercial Code (UCC), beginning with § 2-301, pursuant to which the obligations of the seller and buyer are determined "in accordance with the contract." The same notion is reflected in § 2-303 on the Allocation or Division of Risk ("unless otherwise agreed") and numerous other provisions of the UCC.

Of course, the freedom of the parties to a contract is not unlimited. First, there are structural limits in most national legal systems, such as the prohibitions provided by criminal law (fraudulent contracts or contracts dealing in illegal goods), administrative law (contracts violating antitrust laws, trade sanctions against a foreign country, or provisions of environmental or food and drug laws), human rights and labor law, etc. Second, there are limitations for Business-to-Consumer (B2C) contracts. Finally, there are limitations for contracts where one party takes advantage of its superior bargaining power and/or the inexperience or lack of information of the other party to achieve a contract that is so grossly unfair that it violates fundamental principles of justice and equity. The latter set of rules can be found in public interest/public order/*ordre public* provisions in many countries, although they generally kick in only in extreme cases when B2B contracts are concerned.[17] Compare the provisions of the UCC, which talks in § 2-302 about "unconscionable" contracts or terms, but also assumes in § 2-104 that "merchants" have the "knowledge or skill peculiar to the practices or goods involved in the transaction," i.e., they know what they are doing.

As a result of these various provisions relating to the freedom of contract and providing a very large measure of party autonomy for B2B transactions, we can conclude that within the outer guardrails of the law, in 95% of all international business transactions, the parties have broad discretion to determine the scope of their mutual rights and obligations, as well as the applicable law and forum for any disputes over these rights and obligations. Naturally, a wide freedom to design virtually all provisions of a contract includes also many opportunities for making mistakes. In other words, the freedom of contract includes the freedom to draft or to accept unfavorable contracts and to be bound by them, for better or worse.

A particular problem arises because many attorneys, in particular in the U.S., use the freedom of contract in B2B transactions to produce very lengthy and highly detailed contracts for each individual transaction, including many substantive rules

---

17. For further discussion, see Alexander Bělohlávek, *Public Policy and Public Interest in International Law and EU Law*, Czech Yearbook of International Law, 2012, pp. 117–147.

of contract law. In a way, these attorneys rewrite the rules of contract law each time they prepare a contract, instead of simply subjecting their contract to a preexisting contract law like the UCC or the CISG. The question is, of course, whether this effort makes sense, in particular since it inevitably costs the clients a lot of money.

Theoretically, it can indeed be in the client's interest to rely on a set of preexisting rules, such as the UCC or CISG, and then to make extensive modifications to those rules for any aspects of them that are less than favorable for the client in her role as buyer or seller. However, this would require that the attorneys not only do a careful study of the particular transaction to determine how and why the general rules of contract law should be modified, it would also require the ability to impose such modifications, which presumably tilt the balance of the contract in favor of the respective party and—consequently—against the other party. The reality is usually quite different. First, very few attorneys will go to the trouble of examining carefully what may go wrong in a particular type of transaction. For example, the present author frequently meets with the engineers rather than just the in-house counsel and the sales executives who negotiate the contracts. By asking the engineers "if something would go wrong with this sale, most likely, what would it be?" we can get a better understanding whether any problems may have to be anticipated with the performance of the goods—for example, because they are highly innovative and potentially unproven—or whether the main issues may be with timely delivery, safe transport, export or import licenses, intellectual property rights, or payment modalities. Unfortunately, the majority of our colleagues, while billing for time as if they had done such a detailed background investigation, mainly cobble a lengthy contract together from contracts used in other cases and circulating on the law firm computers. More than a few times, when we asked a colleague why he or she used a particular phrase or formula in a contract, the answer we would get is that they did not know but that this is what was usually done at the firm.

More importantly, contract laws like the CISG or the UCC were drafted by teams of the most highly respected experts from the respective countries and legal systems and often took years to create and multiple updates to refine. One could be forgiven for saying that it is somewhat preposterous for an attorney to think that he or she can do better for each transaction or at least for a particular type of transaction. Among the distinguishing features of the CISG and UCC are that they are well-balanced and fair for both sides, which we consider essential, not only because it is often hard to predict whether one's client will be sued or may have to sue or even where such a suit may have to be brought. What matters most in the end is to provide a good contract that ideally avoids any disputes from arising in the first place, enables the parties to settle most of their disagreements amicably, and even if litigation or arbitration becomes inevitable, leaves the parties with the feeling that the outcome of any such dispute settlement was fair and that the business relationship can be continued. This will rarely happen, however, if a contract is deliberately tilted to favor one side over the other and to carve exceptions out of contract law systems that have not foreseen them precisely because they would render the rights and obligations of the parties unbalanced and potentially unfair. Finally, we have seen more than a few contracts that say one thing on page 17 and quite the opposite on page 53 because it is very hard and—given the legalese favored by many attorneys to create the impression of highly specialized know-how—probably quite impossible to avoid such contradictions in a document of 80 or 100 pages that is largely a cut-and-paste product from multiple earlier contracts with input from many different individuals. Ken Adams elaborates on this point in his excellent book A Manual of Style for Contract Drafting (ABA Publishing, 4th ed. 2017).

For these reasons, and because we constantly encounter poorly drafted contracts in our international consulting practice and as international arbitrators, we will put significant emphasis on the development of fair and efficient contracts and intelligent choices for law and forum in the coming Parts.

B. Planning for Disputes—Choice of Law and Choice of Forum

As outlined above, parties to B2B transactions are generally free to choose the applicable law and the forum where any disputes must be settled. This raises the following questions:

- What are sensible choices for law and forum in a given case? What kind of guidance can we provide for businesses and their legal counsel when planning for disputes?
- How should a choice of law and a choice of forum be implemented in order to be valid and—if necessary—enforceable?
- What happens if the parties to a B2B transaction fail to make a choice of law and/or a choice of forum? What happens if the parties make a choice of law and forum but the choice turns out to be invalid or ineffective?

The first rule with regard to making wise choices for law and forum is that the two are always related. There is no such thing as "the right" law for a particular commercial relationship without knowing where any disputes would have to be settled. Similarly, there is no "right court" as long as we don't know which legal system or set of rules the forum would have to apply. Simply speaking, a wonderful legal system or set of rules won't work in the wrong forum; and an otherwise good and trustworthy forum won't be a good choice if it has to apply the wrong legal system.

Since there is no "one size fits all" solution and different combinations of law and forum will work best for different types of transactions and different sellers and buyers, rather than recommending "a solution," we have to think about the criteria that determine whether a particular choice is good or not so good in a particular context.

We have already learned that parties to B2B transactions can literally choose from among about 200 national legal systems[18]—assuming about 200 sovereign

---

18. See UCC § 1-301(c)(2): "an agreement by parties to an international transaction that any or all of their rights and obligations are to be determined by the law of this State or of another State

countries around the world—plus at least three international legal systems (CISG, UNIDROIT Principles, and European Common Frame of Reference) as the contract law to govern the transaction. Fortunately, even the best and most diligent lawyer will not have to compare all of them before recommending the contract law that should govern a particular transaction. First, we can sort the 203 or so contract laws around the world into a far smaller number of families of legal systems. Within each family, the difference between national legal systems will be quite small and other considerations, such as language, will become more important.

1. *The Family Trees of National Legal Systems Around the World*[19]

The common law countries are the United States of America (with the exception of Louisiana), the United Kingdom of Great Britain and Northern Ireland (with the exception of Scotland), Canada (with the exception of Quebec), Australia, and New Zealand. Although the basic idea of "common law" is the predominance of case law as the source of law, rather than statutory law, in modern times, none of these countries relies exclusively on case law and in many areas of law they have adopted as many statutory provisions as one might expect in civil law countries.[20] Importantly, however, Australian, New Zealand, Canadian, and English *contract* law remain largely case law-based.[21] In Australia, a level of harmonization is accom-

---

or country is effective, whether or not the transaction bears a relation to the State or country designated." By contrast, § 187(2)(a) of the Restatement (Second) of Conflict of Laws requires that the law chosen by the parties has a "substantial relationship to the parties or the transactions" or that there is "[an]other reasonable basis" for the parties' choice.

Courts in the European Union will apply Regulation 593/2008 on the Law Applicable to Contractual Obligations ("the Rome I Regulation") to disputes between parties from different countries (Documents, p. I-53). Pursuant to Article 3(1) of the Rome I Regulation, "a contract shall be governed by the law chosen by the parties." As van Calster elaborates, "[t]he choice . . . is absolutely free: the law chosen need not have any connection with the parties or the contract." See Geert van Calster, *European Private International Law*, Oxford Univ. Press 2nd ed. 2016, at p. 203.

19. For further analysis, see René David & Camille Jauffret-Spinosi, *Les Grandes Systèmes de Droit Contemporains*, 11th ed, Editions Dalloz-Sirey 2002; and Konrad Zweigert & Hein Kötz, *An Introduction to Comparative Law*, Oxford Univ. Press 3rd ed. 1998; for a critique, see Mariana Pargendler, *The Rise and Decline of Legal Families*, Am. J. Comp. L. 2012, Vol. 60, No. 4, pp. 1043–1074. A mediating approach can be found in Uwe Kischel, *Rechtsvergleichung*, Beck Verlag 2015, in particular pp. 217–228. Kischel also provides a discussion of the important idea of *legal cultures*, see id. p. 229.

20. Indeed, Professor Glenn comments that "[t]oday, jurisprudence or case law has grown in importance in civil law jurisdictions while common law jurisdictions are filled with legislation. . . . There are no longer major differences in sources of law; there are only more minor differences in the specific content of rules." See Patrick H. Glenn, *Conciliation of Laws in the NAFTA Countries*, La. L. Rev. 2000, Vol. 60, No. 4, pp. 1103–1112, at p. 1106.

21. But see the UK Sale of Goods Act 1979, which governs contracts of sale, in particular those between commercial parties (B2B), while other contracts remain largely within the realm of common law/case law. As Professor Bridge points out, however, "gaps that appear in a code over time," and the fact that "the Sale of Goods Act is largely presumptive and rarely mandatory," i.e., party choices in the contract can override its provisions, render the Act like any other "aging statute" which—*nolens volens*—"increasingly defers to case law responsive to changes in commercial

plished by the fact that the High Court of Australia has the final say over all other courts and thus provides the one authoritative source of common law;[22] a similar situation exists in New Zealand and in England. By contrast, Canada, with the Sale of Goods Act, and the U.S., with the Uniform Commercial Code and the respective state-level statutory implementations for commercial contracts, have achieved a degree of harmonization and simplification in spite of the dualism between federal and state law. Furthermore, in the U.S., we have the Restatement (Second) of Contracts, a kind of codification, albeit nonbinding, of the common law of contracts that does not fall under the UCC, and its state-level implementation.

The civil law tradition traces its roots back to Roman law and, in particular, the Codex Justinianus and the Corpus Juris Civilis. In many ways, these sixth-century AD codifications from the Byzantine or East Roman Empire were the first modern law books. After being largely forgotten for centuries, the codes were rediscovered in Bologna, Italy, in the twelfth century and became the foundation of modern civil law. In our day and age, civil law can be divided into two distinct but similar streams, the French legal tradition (largely followed also by Italy, Greece, Spain, Portugal, the Central- and Latin American countries, including Mexico,[23] the US State of Louisiana, the Canadian province of Quebec, as well as Egypt and—via the reception of the Egyptian civil code—in much of the rest of the Middle East and North Africa), as well as the German legal tradition (largely followed also by Austria, Switzerland, Turkey, Central and Eastern Europe, as well as Japan and China). Some commentators see the legal systems of the Scandinavian or Nordic countries as distinct (e.g., Zweigert & Kötz), others put them into the German group. The Russian civil code—to the extent that it is applied at all[24]—is based on Dutch law,

practice" (Michael Bridge, *The Sale of Goods*, Oxford Univ. Press 3rd ed. 2014, paras. 1-01 and 1-05). When compared with the CISG, let alone the CFR, the UK Act does indeed have many gaps and provides relatively little by way of codification. For further analysis, see Michael Whincup, *Contract Law and Practice—The English System, with Scottish, Commonwealth, and Continental Comparisons*, Kluwer Law International 5th ed. 2006.

22. This system has been so successful that at least some commentators reject a need for codification; see, for example, Warren Swain, *Contract Codification in Australia: Is It Necessary, Desirable and Possible?*, 36 Sydney L. Rev. 131 (2014).

23. For more information, see Stephen Zamora et al., *Mexican Law*, Oxford Univ. Press 2005.

24. On the one hand, ordinary Russians settle their divorce proceedings, contract disputes, personal injury disputes etc. quite normally in the courts and "the law" is applied largely without difficulties (see Kathryn Hendley, *Everyday Law in Russia*, Cornell Univ. Press 2017). On the other hand, large commercial disputes involving politically connected oligarchs and their corporate and commercial interests are settled in backroom deals and, if they come to the courts at all, via blackmail or bribery. For our purposes, therefore, in IBTs, we can neither count on Russian law nor on Russian courts for the enforcement of legitimate claims. For further analysis, see, for example, Anders Åslund, *Russia's Crony Capitalism: The Path from Market Economy to Kleptocracy*, Yale Univ. Press 2019; Karen Dawisha, *Putin's Kleptocracy—Who Owns Russia?*, Simon & Schuster 2014; Jordan Gans-Morse, *Property Rights in Post-Soviet Russia: Violence, Corruption, and the Demand for Law*, Cambridge Univ. Press 2017; David E. Hoffman, *The Oligarchs—Wealth and Power in the New Russia*, Public Affairs 2011; William Pomeranz, *Law and the Russian State: Russia's Legal Evolution from Peter the Great to Vladimir Putin*, Bloomsbury Academic 2018.

which in turn was close to the French family or sub-group until the reforms of 1992 and today is closer to the German legal tradition.

The socialist legal systems played an important role in the Soviet bloc countries and in China, Vietnam, and Cuba during the cold war. In many ways, socialist law is a merger of civil law traditions with Marxist-Leninist ideology, in particular the rejection of private ownership of factors of production like land, factories, large amounts of capital, corporations, intellectual property rights, etc. This has far-reaching consequences for contract and property law, corporate and securities law, etc., which were underdeveloped or abolished. After the fall of the Soviet Union, and the market economy reforms in China, some forms of socialist law today remain only in a handful of countries like Cuba and Vietnam. Everywhere else, the socialist laws were replaced with civil law codes rather than common law because the jurists were used to detailed blackletter rules and found themselves quite unable to switch to case law approaches.[25]

Among the original families of legal systems, we should also acknowledge the religious legal systems, which have to be broken down into Jewish law, Canon law, Muslim law, and Hindu law,[26] as well as the Confucian legal tradition.[27] However, even the Vatican and Iran, respectively the most conservative religious jurisdictions, today do not rely exclusively on religious law. Therefore, it is more useful to think of two branches of mixed legal systems.[28] The first branch would be a mix of one religious legal system with one secular legal system. Thus, in many of the Arab countries, family and inheritance matters are governed by Muslim law (Sharia), while commercial and contract law is largely governed by civil law. There may be some inroads, however, of Islamic principles into commercial and contract law that make certain types of contracts or certain contract clauses invalid. An example would be the unenforceability of contracts for the sale of alcohol in Saudi Arabia or the problems that can arise if a contract specifically provides for interest, which is prohibited by many Islamic countries.[29] Pakistan and Malaysia are different examples, with a mix of the English Common law tradition and Islamic law. In India, we have a mix of common law and Hindu law. In China, some Confucian principles and traditions continue to coexist with an otherwise modern civil law

---

25. Very instructive in this regard is the excellent article by Zdenek Kühn, *European Law in the Empires of Mechanical Jurisprudence*, Croatian Yearbook of European Law & Policy 2005, pp. 55–73, explaining the strictly positivist interpretation and application of blackletter law by the public administration and the courts in Central and Eastern Europe. See also Frank Emmert, *Rule of Law in Central and Eastern Europe*, Fordham Int'l L.J. 2009, Vol. 32, No. 2, pp. 551–586.

26. See, for example, Werner F. Menski, *Hindu Law Beyond Tradition and Modernity*, Oxford Univ. Press 2009.

27. Tibet had a distinctly Buddhist legal system from 1940 to 1959. Today, some remnants can still be found there, as well as in Laos, Myanmar, Thailand, and Sri Lanka.

28. In general, see Reinhard Zimmermann, Daniel Visser & Kenneth Reid, *Mixed Legal Systems in Comparative Perspective*, Oxford Univ. Press 2005.

29. For additional examples, see Ahmed A. Altawyan, *International Commercial Arbitration in Saudi Arabia*, Council on Int'l L. & Politics 2018, at pp. 189–218.

following the German legal tradition. In Japan, Buddhist and Confucian traditions were largely replaced in the nineteenth century with Western-style codifications using German and French civil law systems as models. In more recent times, Anglo-American law has had a stronger influence.[30] Israel has a mix of Common law and Jewish law, but there are also remnants of Ottoman or Muslim law, as well as some German legal traditions.[31]

The other branch of mixed legal systems **combines customary or tribal law with one of the modern secular systems or presents a mix of two such secular systems**. The legal systems of the African countries are usually a mix of pre-colonial customs, rules inherited from the former colonial powers, and more recent reforms and developments. Thus, an influence of English common law can be detected in most countries that were once British colonies, while the countries that were at some point French colonies often still show a noticeable influence of the French Code Civil. Finally, South African law is a mix of Roman-Dutch Civil law and English common law.

2. *Choosing the Best Law for an IBT*

Although both the **French Code Civil** (Code Napoléon) of 1804, and the **German Bürgerliches Gesetzbuch** (BGB) of 1900 have their roots in the *Corpus Juris Civilis* enacted by the Eastern Roman Emperor Justinian in the year 529 AD, they were the first truly modern codifications of civil law or the law of obligations in the world. Among their many strengths are the comprehensive coverage of the all issues related to contractual and non-contractual obligations, as well as their clear language and systematic organization, which greatly facilitated their study and application by lawyers and judges. These are also the main reasons why both the French Code Civil and the German BGB became the models for the civil codes of many other countries around the world (see above, p. 115).

Why is it the position of this author that neither of these eminent codifications is to be recommended as the basis for an international business transaction today, even if at least one of the parties to the transaction is based in France or Germany respectively? Why would this author argue that the CISG of 1980, the Dutch Wetboek of 1992, and in particular the CFR of 2012, are better codifications?

At the outset, we may safely assume that none of the legal systems mentioned above are inherently unfair or unbalanced. In this regard, there are no clear winners or losers. However, **other important qualities of a legal system are clarity, predictability, and ease of application**. These criteria are particularly important for international business transactions where at least one party is by definition trying to understand the scope of her rights and obligations from an outsider's perspective.

---

30. See Hiroshi Oda, *Japanese Law*, Oxford Univ. Press 3rd ed. 2011.

31. For further analysis, see, for example, Menachem Mautner, *Law and Culture of Israel*, Oxford Univ. Press 2011; Eyal Zamir, *Private Law Codification in a Mixed Legal System — the Israeli Successful Experience*, 32 IUS Gentium 233 (2013).

From the point of view of clarity, predictability, and ease of application of different national laws belonging to different legal families, we may indeed find some winners and some losers and a few that are in the middle. In a nutshell, case law systems will always be more cumbersome to research and come up with more ambiguous results simply on account of the many voices that have a say in the development and interpretation of the law. By contrast, statutory law systems, often referred to as civil law systems or Continental European legal systems, rely on one relatively compact source of rules. That being said, older legislation will have experienced more evolutionary changes in practice, which means that a lot of case law may have to be taken into account to understand and interpret how the antiquated statutory language should be applied today. As a result, the most recent codifications generally provide the easiest and quickest results and require few if any updates via case law.[32]

In the author's opinion, and this is certainly somewhat subjective, the mixed legal systems are the least suitable for international business transactions. Typically, even the lawyers in the respective countries will not easily agree on the solution to cases that are just a bit more complicated than the average. This makes it hard, if not impossible, for lawyers in other countries to understand and predict how an issue should be resolved and how a lawsuit might end in such a legal system.

Whenever lawyers from mixed legal systems draft contracts, they have a tendency to select English law, if their country was once an English colony and/or their legal system still carries some of the marks of English common law. However, many English lawyers who are also trained in other legal systems confirm that English law is bulky and unwieldy and time-consuming to work with.[33] The same would be true, by the way, for the U.S. common law of contract, i.e., outside of the scope of application of the UCC, unless the parties make an express choice of law in favor of the Restatement (Second) of Contracts.

---

32. This is why "[c]odification . . . has increasingly become the preferred method of shaping the development of commercial law." See David Frisch, *Commercial Common Law, the United Nations Convention on the International Sale of Goods, and the Inertia of Habit*, Tulane L. Rev. 1999–2000, Vol. 74, No. 2, pp. 495–559.

33. Similar to the situation in the United States, English law is characterized by the duality between the common law of contract—based entirely on case law; and commercial law of contract—based on the 1979 Sale of Goods Act and the case law interpreting and applying the Act. Although the 1979 Act is a decent piece of legislation, it hews close to the structure of the original 1893 Sale of Goods Act, which makes it "an archaic statute, essentially Victorian" (Michael Bridge, *The Sale of Goods*, at p. 3). Among the common law, the statute, more recent amendments of the statute, and the case law interpreting the statute, one cannot say that the English law of contract is straightforward and readily understood by lawyers from other parts of the world. It is, therefore, somewhat of a marvel that "English law" is quite frequently chosen as the law applicable to an international business transaction, in particular by lawyers who actually don't know much about it. It shares this distinction with "Swiss Law," another domestic legal system chosen far more frequently as the basis of an IBT than the size of the country and its import and export business would suggest.

If the mixed legal systems had originally experienced an influence from French law, as it is the case, for example, in the Middle East,[34] the lawyers like to select French law as the governing law for their international contracts. Unfortunately, the French Civil Code dates back to the year 1804 and, although a stroke of genius at the time, has become rather outdated and somewhat of a quilt of frequent amendments and judicial interpretations.[35] Much the same has to be said about the German BGB from the year 1900[36] and the Swiss Civil Code of 1907.[37]

This leaves us with just a handful of truly modern codifications, three on the national level and three on the international level. The **Dutch Civil Code** (Wetboek) is the most modern comprehensive codification in force anywhere. It was substantially reformed and recast in 1992. Although the official language is Dutch, a semi-official translation into English is available online.[38] However, for lawyers and researchers unfamiliar with the Dutch language, the practice of the courts in the interpretation of the Wetboek is not accessible.

The second national codification of good quality and relatively recent vintage is the **Restatement (Second) of Contracts** in the U.S. (Documents, p. I-199). Interestingly, this is a private effort by the American Law Institute with the help of distinguished experts from around the U.S. and the world. Begun in 1962 and finalized in 1981, the experts developed not a treatise on the common law of contracts, nor a commentary on its principles and rules, but an actual code with sections and paragraphs that could be enacted as statutory law without further ado. Although no one has actually enacted it as law, the Restatement could be chosen as the law governing a contract by the parties in a B2B transaction. However, while the Restatement has many strengths, for example its relatively clear and modern language and its extensive coverage of topics such as fraud and mistake (which are poorly covered in several other codifications, most notably the CISG), the Restatement is not really all that modern as a codification. Rather than a forward-looking contract law for the

---

34. The French Code Civil was translated and adapted for Egyptian needs by Abd El-Razzak El Sanhuri (1895–1971). Also referred to as the **Sanhuri Code** of 1948, the contract law is virtually the same as in the French Code Civil. Differences pertain, for example, to property law, where the more socialist system of Egypt at the time shines through. The Sanhuri Code, in turn, stood model for the civil codes of Syria, Libya, Saudi Arabia, and many of the remaining countries of the Middle East. For more information see, *inter alia*, Chibli Mallat, *Introduction to Middle Eastern Law*, Oxford Univ. Press 2007.

35. For further analysis, see Eva Steiner, *French Law — A Comparative Approach*, Oxford Univ. Press 2010.

36. More information can be found in Nigel Foster & Satish Sule, *German Legal System and Laws*, Oxford Univ. Press 4th ed. 2010.

37. It may be of interest to some that the Turkish Civil Code is by and large a translation of the Swiss Civil Code.

38. Several parts of the Russian Civil Code of 1996, including the second part on the law of obligations, are essentially translations of the Dutch Wetboek. The Russian Civil Code, in turn, is the model for the codes applicable in many of the CIS States. For more information, see William E. Butler: *Civil Code of the Russian Federation,* Oxford Univ. Press 2003; and more generally William Butler: *Russian Law,* Oxford Univ. Press 3rd ed. 2009. See also note 24 above.

twenty-first century, the Restatement is backward-looking and "restates" what the courts have said about the common law of contracts over the decades and centuries preceding it.

The third codification on the national level and the other rulebook in the common law tradition is the **Uniform Commercial Code (UCC)** in the U.S. From 1942 to 1952, experts engaged by the National Conference of Commissioners on Uniform State Laws (NCCUSL) and the American Law Institute (ALI) produced the first edition of this model law. Since then, there have been a number of supplementations and revisions. The UCC has several strengths, but also a number of weaknesses when it comes to its use in IBTs. First, it should be remembered that there is really not one UCC in the sense of one and the same codification that would apply all across the U.S. Commercial law in the U.S. is state law. Therefore, the UCC is merely a model for voluntary adoption by the 50 states. Although the large majority of the states did enact legislation based on the UCC, many of them made non-uniform amendments at the time of first enactment or at later stages.[39] In addition, since the UCC does not provide definitions for important terms like "offer" or "acceptance," these have to be supplemented by common law (see § 1-103(b)), which is again different in different states. Furthermore, after relatively uniform commercial laws were adopted on the state level, they are now evolving via case law and they are doing so in different directions since there is no one court that plays the role of final arbiter when it comes to the interpretation of the commercial laws based on the UCC.[40] Another major weakness of the UCC is its rather convoluted language, certainly when compared with the Restatement (Second) of Contracts or a codification like the CISG or the CFR. All of this makes it relatively difficult (even more so for foreign lawyers) to determine with some degree of certainty the precise content of the UCC rules, as applicable, for example, in New York, dealing with a particular issue.[41]

The three international codifications are the **1980 United Nations Convention on Contracts for the International Sale of Goods (CISG), the UNIDROIT Principles of International Commercial Contracts (PICC)**, as last updated in 2010, and the **Common Frame of Reference (CFR)** of the European Union, as finalized in 2012. All three of these follow the civil or Continental European legal tradition. Most recently, another international codification, also following the civil or Continental European traditions, has been produced by academics and other experts specifically

---

39. In 2003, NCCUSL and ALI proposed updates to Articles 2, 2A, and 7, and a new Article 2B for online transactions. While sensible as such, a pattern of slow and potentially modified adoption by the states would have added to the overall nonuniformity of the uniform act. By 2011, there had been no adoptions of the revised UCC and it was withdrawn.

40. See Gerald T. McLaughlin, *The Evolving Uniform Commercial Code: From Infancy to Maturity to Old Age*, 26 Loy. L.A. L. Rev. 691 (1993).

41. For anyone having to work with and seeking to understand the UCC, the most recommended work is James J. White & Robert S. Summers, *Uniform Commercial Code*, West Publishing 6th ed. 2010. For a comparative analysis, see Henry Deeb Gabriel, *Contracts for the Sale of Goods — A Comparison of U.S. and International Law*, Oxford Univ. Press 2nd ed. 2009.

for Latin America. At present, it is hard to predict whether the Principles of Latin American Contract Law (PLACL) will primarily trigger academic discussions or also become a relevant code for practitioners.[42]

The **United Nations Convention on Contracts for the International Sale of Goods (CISG)** is the most important of the three, because it is actually law in force in about 91 countries, including major trading nations such as the U.S., Canada, Mexico, China, Russia, and the majority of EU Member States.[43] Theoretically, it would cover around 80% of all international sales transactions since it is automatically applicable on the basis of Article 1(1)(a) CISG when seller and buyer have their place of business in different Contracting States. Unfortunately, law schools have done a poor job at making this fact widely known. Therefore, in many of the countries that have ratified the CISG, even today, only a small percentage of law graduates is able and willing to work with this set of rules. As a consequence, the CISG is often excluded by lawyers drafting contracts for international sales transactions via Article 6 CISG, even if that may work to the detriment of their clients.[44] In other cases, even if the CISG is not excluded, many briefs and judgments are written that ignore its applicability.[45]

Professor Dodge of the U.C. Davis School of Law made a passionate appeal in favor of teaching the CISG in first-year Contracts. Referring to it as "[the other] body of U.S. contract law," he argues that:

> [t]he failure to teach the CISG in first-year Contracts is problematic. As
> a treaty the CISG is federal law, which preempts state common law and

---

42. For more information, see Rodrigo Momberg & Stefan Vogenauer (eds.), *The Future of Contract Law in Latin America — The Principles of Latin American Contract Law*, Hart Publishing 2017; as well as Rodrigo Momberg & Stefan Vogenauer, *The Principles of Latin American Contract Law: Text, Translation, and Introduction*, Unif. L. Rev. 2018, Vol. 23, No. 1, pp. 144–170.

43. The current list of signatories can be found on the website of UNCITRAL at http://www.uncitral.org/uncitral/en/uncitral_texts/sale_goods/1980CISG.html. See also Documents, p. I-98.

The roots of the CISG can be traced back to the Uniform Law on the International Sale of Goods (ULIS) and the Uniform Law on the Formation of Contracts for the International Sale of Goods (ULF), drafted as early as 1935 at the International Institute for the Unification of Private Law — better known as UNIDROIT — in Rome. The model laws were adopted in 1964 as the Hague Convention Relating to a Uniform Law on the International Sale of Goods (ULIS) and the Hague Convention Relating to a Uniform Law on the Formation of Contracts for the International Sale of Goods (ULFC). While ratifications were few and only from European countries, the two conventions were very influential in the drafting of the UNIDROIT Principles of International Commercial Contracts (PICC, see below, pp. 126–132) and the CISG. For more information, see Schwenzer, *Introduction*, in Peter Schlechtriem & Ingeborg Schwenzer (eds.), *Commentary on the UN Convention on the International Sale of Goods (CISG)*, Oxford Univ. Press, 4th ed. 2016, p. 1. For details on the working methods of UNIDROIT, see the website of the organization at www.unidroit.org.

44. On that subject, see William P. Johnson, *Understanding Exclusion of the CISG: A New Paradigm of Determining Party Intent*, 59 Buff. L. Rev. 213 (2011).

45. See David Frisch, *Commercial Common Law, the United Nations Convention on the International Sale of Goods, and the Inertia of Habit*, Tulane L. Rev. 1999, Vol. 74, No. 2, pp. 495–559. Along the same lines, see Qiao Liu & Xiang Ren, *CISG in Chinese Courts: The Issue of Applicability*, Am. J. Comp. L. 2017, Vol. 65, No. 4, pp. 873–918.

the UCC. Whenever a party whose place of business is in the United States contracts for the sale of goods with a party whose place of business is in another country that has joined the CISG, it is the CISG and not the UCC or the common law that governs the formation of their contract and their respective rights and obligations under it. This means that the CISG is potentially applicable to an enormous number of contracts. As of [January 2020, 91 countries] are parties to the CISG, including Canada, Mexico, Germany, France, China. . . . The lawyers who draft these contracts and litigate disputes arising under them will not necessarily have taken International Business Transactions in law school, which means that if they are not exposed to the CISG in Contracts, they will probably not be exposed to the CISG at all. Thus, by failing to teach the CISG in Contracts, American law schools are producing lawyers who are ill equipped to represent their clients competently.[46]

One way of fixing the problem, as suggested by Kina Grbic, would be to insert explicit language into the UCC "that Article 2 does not apply to a sale of goods contract when a buyer and seller have their principal place of business in two different contracting states under the CISG."[47] At least for the time being, however, neither the suggested change of the UCC nor the more widespread teaching of the CISG in American law schools is likely to happen. The situation is not always better in other Contracting States.

The willful ignorance of many lawyers, including in the U.S., is unfortunate.[48] The CISG actually has many strengths and few weaknesses. The most important

---

46. William S. Dodge, *Teaching the CISG in Contracts*, 50 J. Legal Educ. 72 (March 2000), at pp. 72–73.

47. Kina Grbic, *Putting the CISG Where It Belongs: In the Uniform Commercial Code*, 29 Touro L. Rev. 173 (2012), at p. 175. The underlying idea is supported, *inter alia*, by John F. Coyle, *The Case for Writing International Law into the U.S. Code*, 56 B.C. L. Rev. 433 (2015).

48. Professor Fitzgerald conducted an empirical study on the usefulness—or lack thereof—of the CISG and the UNIDROIT Principles for American practitioners. In the introduction, he writes that "[i]n an era of globalization it is perplexing that so many U.S. practitioners, jurists, and legal academics continue to view contract issues as governed exclusively by state common law and the Uniform Commercial Code. In essence, a significant number of lawyers may be defaulting to the wrong law, in the absence of an effective choice of law clause, when trying to determine the rights and responsibilities arising out of international commercial transactions." The results of his study are summarized as follows: "In sum, while the CISG and UNIDROIT Principles provide numerous concepts and rules that could be of use in serving client interests, they are being underutilized. Moreover, they are being underutilized not because of a conscious selection of a 'better' rule or approach found in the common law or the UCC. Rather, they are being ignored either because of outright ignorance or because these instruments are simply unfamiliar and perceived—correctly (in the case of the UNIDROIT Principles) or quite incorrectly (in the case of the CISG)—as 'foreign' law. The CISG is, and should be recognized as, the default law for a vast number international commercial transactions involving U.S. parties. The persistent failure to do so is neither professional nor good lawyering, and may well constitute malpractice. In the era of globalization, an era that international trade helped foster and create, legal ethnocentricity has no legitimate role. American lawyers, be they practitioners, jurists, or academics, need to be more aware of the CISG

strength is that it is a universal code with universal application.[49] Businesses around the world and their legal counsel can all look at the same set of rules and no one has to submit to someone else's laws. Second, it is available in all official languages of the UN: Arabic, Chinese, English, French, Russian, and Spanish, and in many additional official and unofficial translations, including Dutch, German, Hebrew, Italian, Korean, Polish, Portuguese, Turkish, and many others.[50] It is also well-crafted, easy to read and understand, and short. Furthermore, there is a rapidly growing body of case law and academic literature that we can call on to clarify how the CISG should be applied to a particular situation.[51] Another crucial factor for the

---

and the UNIDROIT Principles." See Peter L. Fitzgerald, *The International Contracting Practices Survey Project: an Empirical Study of the Value and Utility of the United Nations Convention on the International Sale of Goods (CISG) and the UNIDROIT Principles of International Commercial Contracts to Practitioners, Jurists, and Legal Academics in the United States*, 27 J.L. & Com. 1 (2008).

For an example where an American court tries to bend the applicable CISG to conform to the familiar UCC see below, Case 2-7, *Hanwha Corporation v. Cedar Petrochemicals.*

49. When the United Nations Commission on International Trade Law (UNCITRAL) launched its project for the harmonization of international sales law in 1968, it made sure that all regions of the world and all legal systems were represented. Nevertheless, initial support for the Convention on Contracts for the International Sale of Goods (CISG) was slow to build. While 62 States participated in the drafting, only 42 voted in favor of the final result in April 1980. The required first 10 ratifications for entry into force did not emerge until December 1986 and the CISG finally entered into force on January 1, 1988. Since then, however, the success of the CISG has been unstoppable. As of June 2020, the CISG has been ratified by 93 countries, including the United States, Canada, Mexico, Russia, China, Japan, Australia, New Zealand, most of the member states of the European Union, and many of the more important emerging trading nations like Brazil, Turkey, and Vietnam.

50. A full list with links is available at http://www.cisg.law.pace.edu/cisg/text/text.html. Although all official languages are officially equal and every user should be looking at the same text, sometimes concepts in law are hard to translate into another language where the same concept may not even exist. This is rarely a problem in practice but still has to be kept in mind when using the CISG—or, for that matter, any multilingual international convention. For discussion, see Claire M. Germain, *Language and Translation Issues*, in Larry DiMatteo, Andre Janssen, Ulrich Magnus & Reiner Schulze (eds.), *International Sales Law*, Chapter 2, Hart Publishing 2016.

51. The United Nations Commission on International Trade Law (UNCITRAL) publishes a Digest of Case Law on the CISG. The 2012 edition is freely available online at http://www.uncitral.org/pdf/english/clout/CISG-digest-2012-e.pdf. Even more useful is the electronic library of case law maintained by Pace Law School. It can be searched in various ways, including by relevant article of the CISG, country, case name, goods involved, or keyword. There are more than 3,000 decisions reported in the database, with summaries in English of decisions that are not originally in English. Pace maintains this collection with the explicit purpose of "debunking the myth" that "there are hardly any cases on the CISG."

As far as literature in English is concerned, there are numerous treatises and two very good commentaries. The work, which stands head and shoulders above the rest and should be in the library of every good international law firm, is Ingeborg Schwenzer (ed.), *Schlechtriem & Schwenzer Commentary on the UN Convention on the International Sale of Goods (CISG)*, Oxford Univ. Press 4th ed. 2016. Not as comprehensive is Stefan Kröll, Loukas Mistelis & Pilar Perales Viscasillas (eds.), *UN Convention on Contracts for the International Sale of Goods (CISG)—A Commentary*, Beck 2nd ed. 2018. Other works worth mentioning include Peter Huber & Alastair Mullis, *The CISG—A New Textbook for Students and Practitioners*, Sellier European Law Publishers 2nd ed. 2014; as well as Joseph Lookofsky, *Understanding the CISG in the USA*, Kluwer 5th ed. 2017.

success of the CISG is its direct and horizontal applicability in the legal systems of the Contracting States. American lawyers might call it a "self-executing" convention. This means that the CISG itself, and not some national law implementing it more or less faithfully, becomes part of the law of the land in the Contracting States. The CISG itself creates the rights and obligations of the contractual parties, and not some national laws that will invariable differ from one country to another. The CISG itself is what lawyers, traders, judges, and arbitrators across the world are looking at.

Two features of the CISG have been criticized and have been used as arguments to reject its application. One of them, however, is probably a strength and not a weakness: The CISG contains many rules that are open to interpretation and thus more easily acceptable to lawyers coming from different legal systems and traditions. An example is the concept of "fundamental breach," which is defined as "[a] breach of contract by one of the parties [resulting] in such detriment to the other party as substantially to deprive him of what he is entitled to expect under the contract" (Article 25 CISG). Obviously, provisions such as this one leave significant discretion to judges and arbitrators when hearing breach of contract claims. The uninitiated may find this frustrating when trying to predict whether particular conduct will be classified as a minor breach or a fundamental breach, with quite different consequences in law. For more experienced lawyers, however, there are not only tools that outline practice from around the world as guidance, there are also strategies for building arguments that a particular case does or does not present a fundamental breach. We will discuss both the tools and the strategies in this Part. Importantly, the absence of too many hard-and-fast rules enables the CISG — via its dynamic interpretation by courts and tribunals — to evolve in step with the realities of business. For example, the CISG can be applied without further ado to electronic contracts, although these were clearly not foreseen when the CISG was drafted in the 1970s.

Articles in law reviews and other academic publications are far too numerous to mention here. Some particularly readable examples shall suffice: Villy de Luca, *The Conformity of the Goods to the Contract in International Sales*, 27 Pace Int'l L. Rev. 165 (2015); Sarah Howard Jenkins, *Rejection, Revocation of Acceptance, and Avoidance: a Comparative Assessment of UCC and CISG Goods Oriented Remedies*, 22 Minn. J. Int'l L. 152 (2013); Larry A. DiMatteo, *Contractual Excuse Under the CISG: Impediment, Hardship, and the Excuse Doctrines*, 27 Pace Int'l L. Rev. 261 (2015); Bruno Zeller, *Damages Under the Convention on Contracts for the International Sale of Goods*, Oxford Univ. Press 2nd ed. 2009.

Finally, also worth mentioning is the work of the CISG Advisory Council, a private group of experts with observer status at UNCITRAL and UNIDROIT. The Advisory Council publishes opinions about the interpretation of specific articles of the CISG and, more broadly, the way the Convention should be applied to certain problems, such as electronic communications (Opinion No. 1), or the calculation of damages under Article 74 (Opinion No. 6) as well as 75 and 76 (Opinion No. 8). The opinions, references to case law citing them, as well as bibliographic references, can be accessed at http://www.cisgac.com.

The only noticeable downside, other than the fact that many lawyers are still too poorly trained to apply it, **is the limited coverage of the CISG.**[52] Pursuant to Article 4 CISG:

> This Convention governs only the formation of the contract of sale and the rights and obligations of the seller and the buyer arising from such contract. In particular, except as otherwise expressly provided in this Convention, it is not concerned with:
>
> (a) the validity of the contract or of any of its provisions or of any usage;
>
> (b) the effect which the contract may have on the property in the goods sold.

Thus, the CISG does not deal with questions such as invalidity on account of mistake or fraud,[53] issues of party capacity, or the rights of third parties — for example, if the seller has to make delivery to a third party. As Article 4(b) clarifies, the CISG also does not deal with the transfer of title and related issues, in particular the retention of title and its consequences.[54] Logically, tort actions are not covered, either.[55] In this regard, the CISG is an incomplete regulatory framework[56] and the parties should specify which national legal system they wish to apply if a question should arise that is not covered by the CISG. In the absence of party agreement on the issue, the applicable backup system has to be determined pursuant to the rules of private international law, respectively the rules on international conflicts of laws, applicable where the forum is located. By contrast, questions that are covered by the CISG but not expressly resolved should be answered by recourse to general principles of international contract law before any recourse to national laws. In practice, however, the incompleteness of the CISG has not prevented it from successfully harmonizing the most important issues related to international sales transactions. In this way,

---

52. For a more skeptical view of unification and harmonization in general, see Paul B. Stephan, *The Futility of Unification and Harmonization in International Commercial Law*, 39 Va. J. Int'l L. 743 (1999).

53. For a useful discussion of misrepresentation versus fraud and the scope of application of the CISG, see Ulrich G. Schroeter, *Defining the Borders of Uniform International Contract Law: the CISG and Remedies for Innocent, Negligent, or Fraudulent Misrepresentation*, 58 Vill. L. Rev. 553 (2013).

54. See below, p. 344.

55. For further discussion, see Allison E. Butler, *A Practical Guide to the CISG: Negotiations Through Litigation*, Aspen Publishers 2007, at pp. 14–16.

56. At the same time, Professors Schwenzer and Hachem point out that "[t]he phrase 'governs only' is misleading and should be read as 'governs without doubt,' as the Convention also governs the interpretation of statements, conduct, and contracts (Article 8), the relevance of practices established between the parties and usages (Article 9), formal aspects by establishing the principle of freedom of form (Article 11), the modification and termination of contracts by agreement (Article 29), and furthermore establishes rules for the interpretation of its own provisions and gap filling (Article 7)." Ingeborg Schwenzer & Pascal Hachem, Article 4, in Ingeborg Schwenzer (ed.), *Schlechtriem & Schwenzer Commentary on the UN Convention on the International Sale of Goods (CISG)*, Oxford Univ. Press 4th ed. 2016, para. 2 at p. 74.

the CISG is today, and every day a little more, the global sales law for business-to-business transactions across borders.[57]

The **UNIDROIT Principles of International Commercial Contracts (PICC)** (Documents, p. I-101) have been called "an international restatement of contract law" by Michael Bonell, one of its authors and most ardent supporters.[58] While the CISG could still be called a predominantly continental European codification because of its closeness in style and method to the French Code Civil and the German BGB, the UNIDROIT Principles have strong roots also in the English common law of contracts and represent the most universal of contract law codifications.[59] The Principles themselves are available in English, French, German, Italian, and Spanish as official languages, as well as semi-official translations into Arabic, Chinese, Greek, Hungarian, Japanese, Persian, Portuguese, Romanian, Russian, Turkish, and Ukrainian from the website of the Institute. There is also Unilex, a database with case law organized by date, court, arbitral tribunal, and issue, freely available for everyone. Furthermore, there is a rapidly growing body of literature discussing the PICC and their interpretation from a variety of national and international perspectives—enabling both academics and practitioners to understand how the Principles should be and are being applied in practice.[60] Given the fact that the PICC are also broader in scope and coverage than the CISG, it is not obvious that they have remained in the shadow of the CISG and are rarely selected specifically as the applicable law in international business transactions. The importance of the PICC, therefore, lies elsewhere and can be best explained in the historic context.

In parallel to the evolution of the common law applicable to private individuals in England, which relied essentially on court decisions, English and other merchants developed their own customary law applicable to their trades. Like the common law, it was mostly not codified. In contrast to the common law, it developed largely outside of the public system of courts and government. The origins of this "law merchant" or *lex mercatoria* were in the trade usages and customs already applied

---

57. See also Peter L. Fitzgerald, *The International Contracting Practices Survey Project: An Empirical Study of the Value and Utility of the United Nations Convention on the International Sale of Goods (CISG) and the UNIDROIT Principles of International Commercial Contracts to Practitioners, Jurists, and Legal Academics in the United States*, 27 J. L. & Com. 1 (2008).

58. See Michael J. Bonell, *An International Restatement of Contract Law—The UNIDROIT Principles of International Commercial Contracts*, Transnational Publishers Inc. 3rd ed. 2005.

59. See, for example, Henry Deeb Gabriel, *UNIDROIT Principles as a Source of Global Sales Law*, 58 Vill. L. Rev. 661 (2013).

60. While not a "commentary" in the strict sense, extensive "comments" on the PICC in an article-by-article format can be downloaded free of charge from the website of the Institute at http://www.unidroit.org/english/principles/contracts/principles2010/integralversionprinciples2010-e.pdf.

A commercial commentary is available from Oxford University Press, Stefan Vogenauer (ed.), *Commentary on the UNIDROIT Principles of International Commercial Contracts (PICC)*, 2nd ed. 2015. While nowhere near the level of sophistication of the Schlechtriem/Schwenzer Commentary on the CISG (see above, note 51), this is a very useful work for anyone seeking to understand the PICC and work with them in practice.

in ancient Greece and Rome. They were updated and occasionally even codified in the Middle Ages by various trading nations and ports. An important recognition happened in 1759, when Lord Mansfield, as Chief Justice of the English King's Bench, defined a kind of *lex mercatoria maritima* as not being "the law of any particular country, but the general law of nations."[61] For example, in some trades it may have been customary that a contract need not be in writing but could be concluded with a handshake. Under the *lex mercatoria*, such a rule, once established, could be imposed on anyone participating in the respective trade and, if necessary, enforced via special tribunals of the guilds and trades. If a person did not respect the rules and did not comply with a dispute settlement, he or she would simply be excluded from the trade or would lose trust and have to pay up front in future.[62]

Among the key features of the *lex mercatoria* were the following:

- development by industry insiders without reliance on lawyers or government offices;
- evolution without codification, allowing constant fine-tuning, as needed;
- emphasis on independence from authority and wide-ranging party autonomy;
- gradual establishment of common core principles applicable to everyone plus more special rules applicable only to certain trades or transactions;
- dispute settlement by industry insiders following principles of equity (*ex aequo et bono*) where rules did not yet exist or did not clearly cover the dispute;
- swift, confidential, and efficient settlement of disputes; and
- effective enforcement via trade sanctions.

Although the English traders pioneered this system in many ways, parallel and important development also took place in Germany (for example, in the framework of the Hanse), France, and Italy. Among the legal instruments invented by the traders were the power of attorney and the letter of credit.

While the *lex mercatoria* was initially extremely successful and paved the way for a massive expansion and internationalization of trade, it eventually declined in the face of two simultaneous developments. On the one hand, the *lex mercatoria* itself had become too complex and expansive and the number of participants too great for everyone to know and understand the rules and be effectively sanctioned in case of noncompliance. On the other hand, the commercial laws adopted by the parliaments and governments of the larger trading nations became more sophisticated and the judiciary better trained to apply them, reducing the need for an independent law merchant.

---

61. For more historic background, see Klaus Peter Berger at https://www.trans-lex.org/the-lex-mercatoria-and-the-translex-principles_ID8.

62. For comprehensive analysis, see Orsolya Toth, *The Lex Mercatoria in Theory and Practice*, Oxford Univ. Press 2017. See also Roy Goode, *Usage and its Reception in Transnational Commercial Law*, Int'l & Com. L. Q. 1997, Vol. 46, No. 1, pp. 1–36.

Two features survive to this day, however: (i) the notion of virtually unlimited party autonomy in B2B transactions, including the freedom to select or even make up the rules that should govern a transaction; and (ii) the option to seek dispute settlement from experts rather than judges, in private and confidential procedures, where the "jurisdiction" of the tribunal is determined entirely by the consensus of the parties, i.e., which questions to submit, which evidence to present, etc. The first feature is a central fixture of international business transactions today. The second feature is the foundation of international commercial arbitration.

Given the increasing sophistication of national legal systems to deal with commercial transactions, including international transactions, and the emergence of common and codified international rules for such transactions in the form of the CISG, there is today not much room or need for the survival of the *lex mercatoria* as a set of contract laws. Indeed, given the difficulty of determining what is the *lex mercatoria* for any given question or dispute, the entire set of rules would have probably fallen into disuse.[63] However, since merchants continue to put *lex mercatoria* into their contracts as the applicable law, and since the emerging CISG had two major shortcomings from a global business perspective—it is somewhat limited in scope and does not, for example, cover such issues as fraud and mistake in the formation of contracts; and it is rather heavily influenced by continental European approaches to contract law—the Istituto Internazionale per l'Unificazione del Diritto Privato (UNIDROIT) in Rome started in 1971 to develop a kind of "international restatement of general principles of contract law."[64]

The first edition of the UNIDROIT Principles of International Commercial Contracts (PICC) was finally published in 1994. It was expanded and updated in 2004, 2010, and most recently in 2016.[65] Strictly speaking, it is neither a Model Law,

---

63. Indeed, Professor Cuniberti argues that the main beneficiaries of the *lex mercatoria* today are the international arbitrators who resort to the *lex mercatoria* if the parties have not made a valid choice of law or have chosen a legal system that is incomplete, hard to understand, or might lead to unsatisfactory outcomes. While Cuniberti concludes that this approach by the arbitrators can put them in conflict with the interests of the parties who appointed them, I disagree, having more faith in the common sense and fairness of my fellow arbitrators who are certainly more interested in their reputation and future appointments than in taking the easy way out in a difficult choice of law situation. See Giles Cuniberti, *Three Theories of Lex Mercatoria*, 52 Colum. J. Transnat'l L. 369 (2014). See also Christopher R. Drahozal, *Contracting Out of National Law: An Empirical Look at the New Law Merchant*, 80 Notre Dame L. Rev. 523 (2005).

64. Governing Council of UNIDROIT, *UNIDROIT Principles of International Commercial Contracts*, Rome 1994, at p. vii. The idea, however, goes back to 1928, when Ernst Rabel suggested to Vittorio Scialoja, then President of the newly founded Istituto, that he would start working on the unification of international sales law; see Ingeborg Schwenzer, *Introduction*, in Ingeborg Schwenzer (ed.), *Schlechtriem & Schwenzer Commentary on the UN Convention on the International Sale of Goods (CISG)*, Oxford Univ. Press 4th ed. 2016, at p. 1; see also Vanessa M. Johnson, *Codification of the Lex Mercatoria: Friend or Foe?*, 21 L. & Bus. Rev. Am. 151 (2015).

65. The 2016 edition of the PICC, together comments/explanations is available online at http://www.unidroit.org/unidroit-principles-2016/official-languages/english-integral. The PICC without comments are also included in the Documents, p. I-101.

although it could inspire legislators seeking to reform their national contract laws, nor a Restatement in the traditional sense, since it does not merely "restate" or reproduce what the law is. On many levels, it ventures into the territory of "what the law ought to be." The reason is simple. Given the fact that the UNIDROIT Principles draw inspiration from all major legal systems around the world, choices had to be made to arrive at a single rule for each question, or, as Professor Vogenauer has put it,

> a pure 'restatement' of contract rules from different legal systems on a given issue in a single provision is only possible if these rules produce similar outcomes — as is frequently the case between the contract laws of the states of the USA. Where such a commonality does not exist — as is frequently the case between the contract laws of the different jurisdictions around the world — the elaboration of a single rule on the issue in question necessarily involves policy decisions and departures from the existing law in at least one of these jurisdictions and therefore promotes changes in the law.[66]

Similarly, the Governing Council of UNIDROIT admits that "[f]or the most part the UNIDROIT Principles reflect *concepts to be found in many, if not all, legal systems.* Since however the Principles are intended to provide a system of rules especially tailored to the needs of international commercial transactions, they also embody what are perceived as *the best solutions,* even if still not yet generally adopted."[67]

In the end, the practical importance of the UNIDROIT Principles for IBTs is threefold: They can be chosen by the parties to an international contract of sale; they can be applied when the parties have chosen "general principles of law" or the *lex mercatoria* as the law to govern their agreement;[68] finally, they can be used to fill gaps in transnational codes like the CISG.

First, the relative merit of the PICC as an explicit party choice to govern their contract can be summarized as follows:

---

66. Stefan Vogenauer, *Introduction*, in Stefan Vogenauer & Jan Kleinheisterkamp (eds.), *Commentary on the UNIDROIT Principles of International Commercial Contracts (PICC)*, Oxford Univ. Press 2009, at p. 6.

67. Governing Council of UNIDROIT, *UNIDROIT Principles of International Commercial Contracts*, Rome 1994, at p. viii, emphasis added.

68. To distinguish the original and by now antiquated *lex mercatoria* from its contemporary use, some writers have coined the phrase "New Lex Mercatoria"; see, for example, Klaus Peter Berger, *The Relationship Between the UNIDROIT Principles of International Commercial Contracts and the New Lex Mercatoria*, Unif. L. Rev. 2000, Vol. 5, No. 1, pp. 153–170; as well as Bernardo M. Cremades & Steven L. Plehn, *The New Lex Mercatoria and the Harmonization of the Laws of International Commercial Transactions*, Boston Univ. Int'l L.J. 1984, Vol. 2, No. 3, pp. 317–348. I tend to agree with others, however, who have determined that there is a continuous evolution of the *lex mercatoria*, rather than a cessation of the old and a new beginning; see, for example, Vanessa L.D. Wilkinson, *The New Lex Mercatoria — Reality or Academic Fantasy?*, J. Int'l Arb. 1995, Vol. 12, No. 2, pp. 103–118. Therefore, there is no need to come up with a new label and the "good old" *lex mercatoria* continues to survive and thrive on the margins of transnational contract law.

- while the CICL and, in particular, the Common Frame of Reference, are rather heavily influenced by the continental European legal traditions, the UNIDROIT Principles are truly global;

- they are available in five official language versions (English, French, German, Italian, and Spanish) and have been translated into many more languages, including Arabic, Chinese, Japanese, and Russian (see above, p. 126);

- they are more comprehensive than the CISG, covering important issues like agency in the formation of contracts, mistake, fraud, and other grounds of avoidance, as well as assignment of rights, transfer of obligations, pluralities of parties, and other third-party rights, as well as limitation periods;

- they are as well-crafted and comprehensible as the CISG and the Restatement (Second) of Contracts, almost as clear as the CFR, and definitely superior to the UCC;

- they are more widely known and more widely discussed in literature and case law than the CFR, although not as widely as the CISG, since they never apply by force of law.

Second, in the absence of an explicit choice by the parties, the PICC may be applied as an implicit choice. As the Preamble points out, "[t]hey may be applied when the parties have agreed that their contract be governed by general principles of law, the *lex mercatoria* or the like." In practice, this function of the Principles may be more important than their application by explicit choice. Arbitrators and even judges around the world have generally been happy to apply the Principles as a kind of codification of general principles of law and/or the *lex mercatoria*, vastly simplifying their determination of what rules should be applied to the dispute in front of them.[69]

Third, the UNIDROIT Principles, as a reflection of the customs and usages that built the *lex mercatoria*, are the fallback option of choice if a selected or otherwise applicable set of rules does not provide an answer for a specific question. The Preamble states that the PICC "may be used to interpret or supplement international uniform law instruments" like the CISG, and "[t]hey may be used to interpret or

---

69. An example would be Arbitral Award No. 12040 of 2003 of the ICC International Court of Arbitration. The parties to the underlying business transaction had elected "international trade usages" as the law applicable to the merits of the dispute. The arbitral tribunal decided to apply the UNIDROIT Principles. A similar choice was made in Arbitral Award No. 11575 of 2003, where the parties had referred to the lex mercatoria. In Arbitral Award No. 12111 of 2003, an ICC tribunal applied the PICC after the parties had chosen "international law" as governing their contract.

An interesting discussion can also be found in Arbitral Award No. 13012 of 2004 of the ICC. The parties had not made an explicit choice of law in their contract. In the arbitration, one side was arguing for the application of French law and the other side for the application of Illinois law. The tribunal held that neither of the two domestic laws had compelling connecting factors to the case and instead relied on general principles of law and the lex mercatoria, with the PICC coming in as the generally accepted codification of the latter.

supplement domestic law."[70] Any need of supplementation or interpretation of the chosen law needs to be clearly demonstrated, however. Specifically, a judge or arbitrator first needs to analyze pertinent case law to check whether a gap or an ambiguity has already been clarified or filled from within the chosen legal system.

Fourth, the Preamble stipulates that the PICC "may be applied when the parties have not chosen any law to govern their contract." Again, this statement requires qualification. As pointed out above, whenever the parties to an IBT do not make a choice of law or whenever a choice is invalid or ineffective, the applicable law needs to be determined via the rules of private international law, respectively the rules of international conflict of laws. The outcome of this determination can be somewhat arbitrary. Private international law or conflict rules differ from one jurisdiction to another and each forum applies its own rules. Thus, if the seller sues the buyer in her court, a different set of conflict rules will be applied than if the buyer sues the seller in his court.[71] While judges may not be too concerned about this problem and proceed to apply their own conflict rules and—most likely—their own contract law, arbitrators may decide that the application of one contract law versus another, with potentially far-reaching consequences for substantive claims, should not be determined based on who brings the dispute first to court. In such cases, and in other situations where the conflict rules are inconclusive, the PICC could provide a neutral system to be applied instead of any of the potentially applicable national laws.[72]

With the 2016 edition, the PICC now cover the following subjects and generally present a more global and more comprehensive set of rules than the CISG:

Chapter 1: General Provisions

Chapter 2: Formation and Authority of Agents

Chapter 3: Validity

---

70. See, in particular, Ralf Michaels, *The UNIDROIT Principles as a Global Background Law*, Unif. L. Rev. 2014, Vol. 19, pp. 643–668. Michaels, on p. 655, names a few rules that are applied quite often. By contrast, the entire PICC are rarely used in practice. See also Juraj Kotrusz, *Gap-Filling of the CISG by the UNIDROIT Principles of International Commercial Contracts*, Unif. L. Rev. 2009, Vol. 14, No. 1-2, pp. 119–163; Pilar P. Viscasillas, *Interpretation and Gap-Filling Under the CISG: Contrast and Convergence with the UNIDROIT Principles*, Unif. L. Rev. 2017, Vol. 22, No. 1, pp. 4–28.

71. The outcome can be manipulated by the party who anticipates a lawsuit from the other side and preempts it with a lawsuit of her own. For example, if the seller is faced with claims from the buyer that the goods did not conform and expects to be sued for performance and/or damages, he could bring a preemptive strike, sometimes referred to as a "torpedo action," for a declaration that performance was rendered and no damages are owed. This will be elaborated on in more detail in Part 6.

72. The literature on the UNIDROIT Principles is vast. Many good contributions are published every year in the Uniform Law Review by Oxford Univ. Press. For a recent contribution supporting a broader role of the PICC, see Michael J. Bonell, *The Law Governing International Commercial Contracts and the Actual Role of the UNIDROIT Principles*, Unif. L. Rev. 2018, Vol. 23, No. 1, pp. 15–41.

The **Common Frame of Reference (CFR)** is the most recent, the most comprehensive, and the most ambitious codification of transnational contract law (Documents, p. I-280). Although essentially an academic exercise, it was funded by the EU Commission and many, including the present author, would like to see it evolve into a pan-European civil code. The following article elaborates on its history and scope.[73]

Frank Emmert

The Draft Common Frame of Reference (DCFR) — the Most Interesting Development in Contract Law since the Code Civil and the BGB

Cuadernos de la Maestría en Derecho, Universidad Sergio Arboleda,
Edición anual No. 2, Bogotá 2012, pp. 1–25
(footnotes in the original)

I. What Is the "Draft Common Frame of Reference"?

After the horrors of World War II, European integration was conceived by Jean Monnet, and the great statesmen who understood and picked up his ideas, as a radically new way of securing long term peace and prosperity in Europe. Integration instead of exclusion, cooperation instead of discrimination, community instead of nationalism. In 1953, an initial six European states, including the "arch enemies" France and Germany, tied their fates together in the European Coal and Steel Community, designed to remove control over key industries for military buildup from nationalist politicians and giving it to dispassionate European bureaucrats.[1] The European Economic Community and the European Atomic Energy Community followed in 1957. Since then, membership in the greatest experiment in voluntary

---

73. For in-depth analysis, see Christian von Bar & Eric Clive (eds.), *Principles, Definitions and Model Rules of European Private Law — Draft Common Frame of Reference (DCFR)*, Oxford Univ. Press, Oxford, 2010. For an early reference in case law, see the decision of the Scottish Outer House, Court of Session, in *Phil Wills v. Strategic Procurement (UK) Ltd.*, [2013] CSOH 26.

1. For more information, see, for example, Dinan, D. (2004). *Europe Recast — A History of European Union*. Basingstoke: Palgrave Macmillan.

integration of sovereign states has grown to 27, with several more countries currently negotiating entry to the club. Among the many accomplishments of European integration is a period of peace between its Member States that is unprecedented in European history, as well as a general level of prosperity that has never been seen before in this part of the world. Although these accomplishments have recently been cast in a less favorable light due to the economic crisis in Europe, the appeal of membership may well be greater than ever, which is evidenced, for example, by the application of Iceland in the wake of its economic meltdown. As more and more countries are coming to realize, being part of the European Union and having partners that are not only fair-weather friends but that are contractually obligated to stand together, is even more precious in times of hardship and crisis. For this reason, the doomsday sayers, who have been predicting the end of European integration as we know it, will be proven wrong once again and it is more likely than not that the EU will accelerate its integration program because of the crisis, rather than slow it down, let alone abandon it altogether.

One of the key components of European integration is the development of the "internal market" of the EU, which is defined as "an area without internal frontiers in which the free movement of goods, persons, services and capital is ensured".[2] Merging the relatively small national markets of the Member States into one large European market yields numerous economic benefits. The ability to buy and sell to and from all Member States greatly increases trade and competitive pressures in the EU, resulting in vastly increased choices for consumers in combination with lower prices for higher quality goods and services.[3]

The free movement of goods, services, people, companies, and capital, however, has presented and continues to present various challenges to European regulators and law makers. To give but one example, if goods can move freely from one Member State to another under the Cassis de Dijon principle that what is good enough in one Member State has to be good enough for the other Member States,[4] a formidable race to the bottom could ensue. To ensure that Member States are not tempted to attract investment and jobs by waiving standards for product safety, environmental and workplace protection, etc., the EU has embarked on a massive program of

---

2. See Article 26(2), formerly Article 14(2), of the Treaty on the Functioning of the European Union TFEU.

3. Good books on the subject include: Artis, M. & Nixson, F. (Eds., 2007). *The Economics of the European Union — Policy Analysis* (4.th ed.). Oxford: Oxford University Press; Jørgen Drud Hansen, J. D. (2001). *European Integration — an Economic Perspective.* Oxford: Oxford University Press; McDonald, F. & Dearden, S. (2005). *European Economic Integration* (4.th ed.). Harlow: Financial Times/Prentice Hall; Molle, W. (2006). *The Economics of European Integration — Theory, Practice, Policy* (5th ed.). Aldershot: Ashgate ; Neal, L. & Barbezat, D. (1998). *The Economics of the European Union and the Economics of Europe.* Oxford: Oxford University Press; and in particular Pelkmans, J. (2006). *European Integration — Methods and Economic Analysis* (3rd ed.). Harlow: Prentice Hall/Financial Times.

4. See the Judgment of the European Court of Justice of 20 February 1979 in Rewe-Zentral AG v Bundesmonopolverwaltung für Branntwein ("Cassis de Dijon"), 1979 ECR 649, in particular Rec. 14.

harmonization of these rules across the Member States, essentially replacing diverging national legislation with common European rules.

Intensive trade between Member States with different legal rules and systems also creates challenges in the area of private international law. Every time a contract is made between parties in different Member States, the law governing the contract has to be determined. At least if the parties are both merchants, they have numerous choices regarding the applicable law. These choices include seller's law, buyer's law, the law of pretty much any other country, as well as certain international contract law regimes, such as the United Nations Convention on Contracts for the International Sale of Goods (CISG),[5] or the infamous "lex mercatoria".[6] And if the parties did not make a choice of law at all, or if their choice was ineffective, the applicable law has to be determined on the basis of private international law, which may in turn differ from one forum to another, potentially causing significant uncertainty and even an incentive for a race to the courthouse.

Against this background, harmonization of contract law across all Member States of the EU has long been an attractive idea. However, while the EU was explicitly given powers to pursue legal harmonization in areas such as environmental

---

5. The literature on the CISG is vast. An easy introduction is supplied by: Ferrari, F. (2011). *Contracts for the International Sale of Goods—Applicability and Applications of the 1980 United Nations Sales Convention*. The Hague: Martinus Nijhoff; see also Huber, P. & Mullis, A. (2007). *The CISG—a New Textbook for Students and Practitioners*. München: Sellier; and Lookofsky, J. (2008). *Understanding the CISG in the USA* (3rd ed.). The Hague: Wolters Kluwer Law International. For comprehensive analysis, see Kröll, S., Mistelis, L. & Perales, P. (Eds., 2011). *UN Convention on Contracts for the International Sale of Goods (CISG)—Commentary*. München: Verlag C. H. Beck; and, in particular, Schlechtriem, P. & Schwenzer, I. (Eds., [2016]). *Commentary on the UN Convention on the International Sale of Goods-CISG* ([4th] ed.). Oxford: Oxford University Press.

6. Literally translated, "lex mercatoria" means "law of merchants". Commonly, the reference is to the customs and unwritten rules applied within a certain circle of traders. Essentially, these were self-enforced: if you didn't play by the rules, your former business partners would shun you and/or you could not get deals or credit on the same good terms (any more). On the one hand, the *lex mercatoria* could differ from one trade or industry to another, on the other hand, it was never written down, let alone adopted as law, in any coherent and systematic fashion. Entirely wrong is, therefore, the definition provided by "The Free Dictionary by Farlex", which says that LEX MERCATORIA is "[t]hat system of laws which is adopted by all commercial nations, and which, therefore, constitutes a part of the law of the land." (see http://legal-dictionary.thefree-dictionary.com/Lex+mercatoria). Fortunately, the core of the *lex mercatoria* was eventually codified and is now available to us in multiple languages in the form of the UNIDROIT Principles of International Commercial Contracts adopted by the International Institute for the Unification of Private Law UNIDROIT in Rome in 1994 and revised in 2004, 2010 and 2016, available online at http://www.unidroit.org/unidroit-principles-2016/official-languages/english-integral. Even these, however, are not part of the law of the land anywhere in the world and only become applicable if merchants agree to use them as (part of) the law to govern their contract by explicit reference to the UNIDROIT Principles or the lex mercatoria. For comprehensive analysis of the UNIDROIT Principles see: Vogenauer, S. & Kleinheisterkamp, J. (Eds., 2009). *Commentary on the UNIDROIT Principles of International Commercial Contracts (PICC)*. Oxford: Oxford University Press.

[For further discussion of the UNIDROIT Principles and the *lex mercatoria*, see above, pp. 126–132.]

protection (Article 192 TFEU), free movement of services (Article 59 TFEU), the right to establishment for self-employed natural and legal persons (Article 50 TFEU), and the free movement of employed persons (Article 46 TFEU), a power to replace Member State contract laws with a common European system is not explicitly provided in the Treaties.[7] Nevertheless, the European Commission, with encouragement and support from the European Parliament, started as early as 1974, to play with the idea of a "European Code of Obligations".[8] By 1980, a group of experts from all Member States, most of them academics, had been composed and by 1995, this group, on the basis of extensive comparative analysis of the legal systems of all Member States of the EU and the CISG and even the American Uniform Commercial Code (UCC), had completed the first phase of its work: "The Principles of European Contract Law (PECL), Part I, Performance, Non Performance and Remedies."(Lando & Beale, 2000, p. xi)

As the name suggests, these "Principles" were no code at all, certainly not in the form of binding legislation. They were, however, formulated in such a way that they could be adopted as legislation, much like the well known model codes in the American system, with the UCC just the best known example. And although not a single country has as yet adopted the Principles as domestic law, and they remain, therefore, really just a good idea, these European Principles quickly became immensely popular among comparativists and private international lawyers. This popularity is based on two grounds. First, the team around Professor Ole Lando had accomplished a genuine synthesis of all European contract laws, to the extent that they found broad support in every single Member State. Second, and even more importantly, the Principles are crafted in elegant, simple, and efficient language, much easier to understand than any other contract law around the world.

This explains why the Lando Group continued, and in 1999 presented the second phase of its work, this time covering rules on formation of contracts, authority of agents to bind their principal, validity of contracts, interpretation, content, and effects.[9] A third part followed in 2003.[10] It also explains why other groups have

---

7. To retain their sovereignty, the Member States have clearly established the principle of enumerated powers codified in Article 5 TEU: "(1) The limits of Union competences are governed by the principle of conferral. . . . (2) Under the principle of conferral, the Union shall act only within the limits of the competences conferred upon it by the Member States in the Treaties. . . . Competences not conferred upon the Union in the Treaties remain with the Member States."

8. Ole Lando tells the story "How It Started" in the Preface Lando, O. & Beale, H. (Eds., 2000), *Principles of European Contract Law* (p. xi). The Hague: Wolters Kluwer Law International.

9. Lando, O. & Beale, H. (Eds., 1999). *Principles of European Contract Law, Parts I and II.* The Hague: Wolters Kluwer Law International.

10. Lando, O., Clive, E., Prüm, A. & Zimmermann, R. (Eds., 2003). *Principles of European Contract Law Part III.* The Hague: Wolters Kluwer Law International. This third part covers plurality of parties, assignment of claims, substitution of new debtor: transfer of contract, set-off, prescription, illegality, conditions, and capitalization of interest.

become busy[11] and have been working, with the same or similar methods,[12] in other areas of civil law. After broad consultations with Member State governments, enterprises, legal professionals, consumer organizations, and other stakeholders, the EU Commission, in its *2003 Action Plan for European Contract Law*,[13] announced the concept of a *Common Frame of Reference* (CFR), envisioned as a collection of the "best solutions" for definitions, terminology, and substantive rules in European private law. To this end, the various academic groups were brought together, the pre-existing Principles were united, and the remaining gaps were filled. Although the Commission and the academic study groups today avoid the politically sensitive language of a "European Civil Code", the *2009 Draft Common Frame of Reference*, as the preliminary end result of the comparative study and drafting process, retains the format of a model code and, fortunately, also retains the elegance, efficiency, and comprehensibility that were the hallmark of the original European Principles.[14]

The DCFR is organized by "books" in the following manner:

- Book I covers "General Provisions", such as the "intended field of application", the principle of "good faith and fair dealing", and rules about "computation of time".

- Book II covers "Contracts and Other Juridical Acts" in a general manner, with chapters on "general provisions", "non-discrimination", "marketing and pre-contractual duties", "formation", "right of withdrawal", "representation", "grounds of invalidity", "interpretation", as well as "contents and effects of contracts".

---

11. To name just a few, the Lando Commission was succeeded by the Study Group on a European Civil Code in 1998 and from 1992 to 2005, the European Group on Tort Law produced the Principles of European Tort Law (PETL). For much more detail on these initiatives and a comprehensive bibliography see: Antoniolli, L. & Fiorentini, F. (2011). *A Factual Assessment of the Draft Common Frame of Reference*. (pp. 3-7 and 419 et seq). Munich: Sellier.

12. An interesting approach was also pioneered by former Advocate General Walter van Gerven with the Ius Commune Casebook series. The editors collect national court judgments from across the Member States of the EU and show that comparable fact scenarios result in comparable judicial decisions, which in turn proves the common core or common heritage of law in Europe. For examples in the Ius Commune Casebooks for the Common Law of Europe series by Hart Publishing see: Beale, H., Hartkamp, A., Kötz, H. & Tallon, D. (Eds., 2002). *Cases, Materials and Text on Contract Law*. Oxford: Hart Publishing; Beatson, J. & Schrage, E. (Eds., 2003). *Cases, Materials and Texts on Unjustified Enrichment*. Oxford: Hart Publishing; Micklitz, H., Stuyck, J. & Terryn, E. (Eds., 2010). *Cases, Materials and Text on Consumer Law*. Oxford: Hart Publishing; Schiek, D., Waddington, L. & Bell, M. (Eds., 2007). *Cases, Materials and Text on National, Supranational and International Non-Discrimination Law*. Oxford: Hart Publishing; and Van Gerven, W. (2001). *Tort Law*. Oxford: Hart Publishing [as well as van Erp, S. & Akkermans, B. (Eds., 2012). *Cases, Materials and Text on Property Law*, Oxford: Hart Publishing].

13. EU Commission (Ed.). Action Plan on a More Coherent European Contract Law, 12 February 2003, COM/2003/68 fin.

14. The full text of the Outline Edition of the Principles, Definitions and Model Rules of European Private Law—Draft Common Frame of Reference (DCFR) can be downloaded for free at https://www.law.kuleuven.be/web/mstorme/2009_02_DCFR_OutlineEdition.pdf (Von Bar, Clive, & Schulte-Nölk, 2009). [See also Documents, pp. I-280.]

- Book III covers "Obligations and Corresponding Rights", in particular "performance", "remedies for non-performance", problems related to "plurality of debtors and creditors", "change of parties", "set-off and merger" of contracts, and "prescription".

- Book IV, in many ways the heart of the code, covers "Specific Contracts and the Rights and Obligations Arising from Them", with chapters on "sales", "lease of goods", "services", "mandate contracts",[15] "commercial agency, franchise and distributorship", "loan contracts", "personal security", and "donation" agreements.

- Book V deals with "Benevolent Intervention in Another's Affairs".

- Book VI covers "Non-Contractual Liability Arising out of Damage Caused to Another", i.e., tort law.

- Book VII deals with "Unjust Enrichment".

- Book VIII is about "Acquisition and Loss of Ownership of Goods".

- Book IX covers "Proprietary Security in Movable Assets".

- Book X is about "Trusts".

- Finally, there is an extensive annex with definitions and an index, bringing the entire document to a good 600+ pages.

As can been seen even from this extremely brief introduction, considerable time and money has been expended for the development of this *Draft* and this begs the question: What is the point, what is the purpose, beyond mere academic curiosity, what is the usefulness of the Draft Common Frame of Reference? This shall now be addressed in the second part of the article.

II. What the Draft Common Frame of Reference Can and Cannot Do Today

The declared purposes of the DCFR are actually quite modest. First, and consistent with the mandate given to the drafters by the EU Commission, the DCFR is "a possible model for a political CFR" (Von Bar, Clive & Schulte-Nölk, 2009, para. 6 p. 7) a proposal for what could eventually evolve into a European Code of Obligations. Along this path, the DCFR is more likely to be used as a quarry, from which precious stones are mined to be used in other constructs,[16] although it could just as well form a blueprint to be adopted, lock stock and barrel, as binding European legislation.[17]

---

15. These are essentially personal agency contracts.

16. The Outline Edition of the DCFR itself refers to a European directive on consumer contractual rights as an example, see paras. 59 et seq., in particular para. 62, of the Introduction (on p. 37) (Von Bar, Clive, & Schulte-Nölk, 2009).

17. Cf. According to the European Commission (2011). Proposal for a Regulation of the European Parliament and of the Council on a Common European Sales Law, 635 final, Brussels 11 October 2011, from: http://eur-lex.europa.eu/LexUriServ/LexUriServ.do?uri=COM:2011:0635:FIN:EN:PDF, 27.3.2012.

The second purpose is for "legal science, research and education" (Von Bar, Clive & Schulte-Nölk, 2009, para. 7 p. 7), to show to students, researchers and professors the vast areas of private law that are indeed very similar across Europe, or at least typically lead to similar, if not identical, outcomes, and "the relatively small number of cases in which the different legal systems produce substantially different answers to common problems." (Von Bar, Clive & Schulte-Nölk, 2009, para. 7 p. 7). Indeed, when I was Dean of an international law school in the Baltics in the early 2000s, where we delivered a law program in English to students from a number of different countries, I taught Contract Law on the basis of the PECL instead of any one of the national contracts laws, which were still in flux in the early years of transition from Communism, and in any case where not available in English or any one other language accessible to all of our students. What surprised me most about this experiment was how easy it was to communicate not only the basics but also the intricacies of this field of law on the basis of the PECL. With my German background, I had previously thought of the German Bürgerliches Gesetzbuch *(BGB)* as the pinnacle of wisdom and had greatly enjoyed my studies under giants like Dieter Medicus in Munich. While I had already heard that the Dutch *Wetbook* was a much more modern and easier code than the BGB and the French *Code Civil*, it is one thing to hear such claims and quite another to experience that, indeed, there could be such a thing as legislation more logical and systematic and ultimately more accessible than *German* legislation.

The third declared purpose of the DCFR is to provide "a possible source of inspiration" (Von Bar, Clive & Schulte-Nölk, 2009, para. 8 p. 7–9) for legislative drafters. This is different from the first purpose because it is aimed primarily at the Member State level, as well as any other countries around the world, where efforts are undertaken at modernization of contract law, independent from the motive of harmonization in the EU internal market.

The purpose of inspiring lawyers to pursue a "modernization" of their respective contract laws does not have to be limited to legislative drafting projects, however. The freedom of contract, at least for commercial agreements between merchants, is virtually unlimited. It not only allows merchants to design their substantive contract terms any way they see fit. It also extends to the choice of law and forum for the settlement of any disputes. And, as already stated above, the choices for the applicable law and forum are many, including some that make sense and some that don't. Among the considerations that should go into a well drafted contract are the following:

1) The applicable law has to be *predictable.* This requires an explicit and effective choice of law. Avoiding a choice altogether or trying to make a choice that turns out to be ineffective, creates unnecessary problems in case of a dispute over correct performance of the contractual obligations. Even before substantive issues can be addressed, the parties may have to spend time and money fighting over the applicable law as a preliminary question. Depending on where such a fight may be taken, the court (= forum) will apply its own private international law to determine the

applicable substantive law. And this can be unpredictable. Some countries simply refer to seller's law as the applicable law. Others refer to the law of the country with the closest connection to the contract. This, in turn, may be seller's law if it is defined as the country where the party that has to effect the characteristic performance is *domiciled*. However, it can also be a reference to the place *where* the characteristic performance has to be effected, which in turn can depend on the chosen INCOTERM®.

2) The choice of law and forum also has to be *efficient.* This may require considerations about speediness of a particular venue, travel and translation expenses, other costs and their distribution between the parties, and the enforceability of the decision(s) of the dispute settlement body.

3) Finally, the choice of law and forum has to be *fair.* Unfortunately, the lawyers like to forget that for their clients it is often more important to continue a business relationship than to win a particular dispute. A settlement on reasonable terms may be more advantageous in the long term than the extraction of maximum benefits in the short term.

With regard to consumer contracts, most national legal systems provide safeguards to assure that the professional party cannot take advantage of the lack of experience and specialized knowledge of the private party. For business-to-business contracts, by contrast, no such safeguards are provided since it is assumed that merchants know what they are doing. In practice, however, this is by no means always the case and the majority of agreements for the sale of goods, let alone agreements for more complex business dealings, are drafted by in-house lawyers or external attorneys. And this is where the DCFR could and should come in, as inspiration to the lawyers drafting the international sales agreements and—ideally—as the chosen legal system for such agreements. In spite of many obvious advantages, however, our lawyers are rarely inspired and generally opt for their own legal system as the applicable law. Unfortunately, they do this primarily in their own best interest— because that happens to be the legal system they know best and often the only legal system they know at all—and not necessarily in their client's best interest. This will be illustrated in Part III with an example.

III. Application of the DCFR in Contemporary Commercial Practice

In our hypothetical, Botellas PET SA in Bogotà wants to buy a new injection molding machine for the production of plastic bottles for non-alcoholic carbonated beverages. B has identified Shure Robotics Inc in Indianapolis as the manufacturer offering the fastest machines at the lowest prices. According to S's website, their model TX1500 can make 30 bottles per cycle and 50 cycles per hour, adding up to 1,500 bottles every hour. The purchase price of the machine is USD 2.4 million EXW, which makes it the largest single acquisition in the history of B. Therefore, they need to make absolutely sure that all required elements of the documentary sale are carefully drafted to ensure smooth implementation of this important transaction.

The typical documentary sale consist of four separate contracts, all of which have
to be drafted and negotiated between the parties. The most important is the contract for the sale of the machine. In addition, there will be a financing contract for
the payment of the purchase price, typically in the form of a letter of credit. Then
there will be a shipping contract, typically in the form of a bill of lading. Finally, the
party or parties bearing the risk of loss or damage during transport will enter into
an insurance contract. The second, third and fourth are usually pre-formulated
by the bank, shipping and insurance company respectively. Nevertheless, the merchants have to make certain choices in them and have to do so in a way that is both
fair and efficient.[18] The contract for the sale of the goods, by contrast, is in no way
pre-determined and can be anything from a very superficial oral agreement to a
very sophisticated document of 50-100 pages.

Although all elements of the contract of sale can usually be written down in clear
and unambiguous language on about 6-10 pages, the average law firm, certainly
in the United States, typically comes up with a multiple of this. They will claim
that their lengthy elaborations are necessary to cover all eventualities and yet, they
accomplish often the exact opposite. The large majority of these contracts are copy-
pasted patchwork from previously drafted agreements that have been sitting on
computer hard-drives at the firm. As a consequence, verbose language and generally poor drafting, including ambiguous language and even mutually contradictory
terms in different parts of a contract, are perpetuated. Individual provisions are not
individually thought through and may indeed be bad for the client. One example is
the choice of law and forum. Few and far between are the attorneys that will even
consider a choice of law other than their own or a forum outside of their own bai-
liwick. After all, if a dispute should arise, the attorneys would not get to handle it if
they are not familiar with the applicable law and/or are not admitted to the bar in
the country where the court will be hearing the case.

In our hypothetical, if the seller S is providing the first draft of the sales agreement, chances are that her lawyers will choose the law of Indiana as the applicable
law and the courts of Indiana as the chosen forum. Under no circumstances will
they consent to buyer's law (Columbia) and buyer's courts. If the buyer refuses to
litigate in US courts, seller will probably accept to go to arbitration but will probably
continue to insist on the application of the UCC. Let's consider the consequences of
such a choice of law and forum. The most common problems of performance are
a) buyer does not pay, and b) seller's machine does not perform. If there should be
a problem for the seller to get paid, she would be very poorly served if she now had

---

18. It would go beyond the scope of the present article to try to outline even just the most
important elements and the most common mistakes in all of these agreements. It usually takes me
anywhere from a couple of weeks to an entire semester to teach all of these. While my own textbook on International Business Transactions [was] still being written, I [recommended] Chow, D.
(2010). *International Business Transactions.* (2.nd ed.). New York: Wolters Kluwer Law & Business;
and Moens, G. & Gillies, P.(2006). *International Trade & Business — Law, Policy and Ethics.* Oxford:
Routledge/Cavendish.

to go to court in Indiana. While application of Indiana law or UCC would not be a problem, a judgment from a U.S. court will not easily be enforceable in Columbia, where buyer's assets are located. This would already be quite different if the parties had agreed to arbitration because Columbia is a signatory to the New York Convention on the Recognition and Enforcement of Foreign Arbitral Awards. Pursuant to Article III et seq. of that Convention, Columbian courts will enforce an international arbitral award without further complications. . . .

The issue gets even more interesting if there is a problem with seller's performance, i.e., if the machine does not produce 1,500 bottles per hour. If the seller insisted on application of the UCC, she will be bound by the so-called "perfect tender" rule in § 2-601. This would entitle the buyer to reject the entire performance if "the goods or the tender fail *in any respect* to conform to the contract" (emphasis added). In practice, an injection molding machine will require several days for installation, potentially up to several weeks of running-in and training, and only then it will become apparent whether or not the machine is capable of producing the contractually promised number of units. Let's assume the machine, after the required preparations, simply does not get up to the promised 1,500 bottles. On a good day, it may come close, say 1,400 or even 1,450, but on a bad day it barely produces 1,300 bottles in an hour. My clients in the industry assure me that this is a fairly common type of issue with these kind of machines.

Under the perfect tender rule of the UCC, as originally conceived and phrased, a buyer could potentially reject the seller's performance if the machines fell short by even just a single bottle. Fortunately, no court in the U.S., let alone the rest of the world, today applies a strictly literal interpretation of the perfect tender rule. However, once a performance of the type here in question falls short, on average, by more than 5-10%, the UCC kicks in and the buyer can indeed reject the performance. What this means in practice can be nicely illustrated by our case. Once the buyer reject's the seller's performance, the seller has just two choices: she can send another machine to Columbia in the hope that it will do better and that the buyer will eventually have to pay the contracted price, minus damages for delay, lost profit, etc. Or she can give up on the transaction, waive her claim to the contracted price and refund any money that has already been paid, plus any damages for delay, lost profit, etc. In both cases, the imperfect machine sitting in Colombia has probably become a very expensive piece of scrap metal, much more of a liability for the seller than an asset.[19]

The situation for the seller changes dramatically if the contract is not subject to the UCC but to any of the laws in the continental European tradition. These legal systems do not have a similarly strict standard for the performance of the seller. Instead, they usually apply the test whether there was a "fundamental breach" of the

---

19. The perfect tender rule is by no means the only problem with the application of the UCC to international commercial contracts. Several other important rules differ from the standards used in most other countries and do so often to the disadvantage of (American) exporters.

contractual obligations, which means that the buyer can only reject the performance of the seller if there is a "fundamental breach". In the practice of the courts, a fundamental breach is found either if the performance objectively deviates so significantly from what had been promised and expected that a mere compensation for damages is inadequate. A deviation of 5 or 10% from the expected performance will normally not fulfill this test. A stricter standard is applied only if the seller knew that strict compliance with the contractual promises was of essential importance to the buyer. In our hypothetical, this would only be the case if the buyer had clearly communicated that an output of 1,500 bottles per hour was the very reason for choosing this machine and that anything less would be basically useless to the buyer.

As a consequence, if Dutch, French, German, or Swiss law, to name just a few, would be applied to the contract in our example, the buyer would not be entitled to reject the performance altogether. Instead, the buyer would have to keep the machine and pay for it, however, with a set-off equivalent to damages for the lower output.

Of course, a choice of a particular national European legal system would be inefficient for the parties in the example. Neither of them probably knows much about these legal systems and in most likelihood, neither speaks the respective language (well enough). Furthermore, the chosen forum has to be considered. State courts, whether in Indiana or anywhere else, should never be made to apply a foreign law. They would ask for extensive expert opinions and translations, which creates unnecessary costs. Arbitrators, of course, can be selected to have any required expertise, but they may be more expensive if they are not from the country or region where the dispute has to be settled. Much better, therefore, would be the choice of one of the international contract regimes. The best known and most widely used is the CISG. In fact, this regime would become the applicable law of its own motion in a contract between an American and a Colombian party on the basis of its Article 1(1)(a), unless it is specifically excluded. However, if the parties are making a conscious choice of an international contract law regime, the CISG is not necessarily the best choice they can make. For the most part, the provisions of the CISG, the UNIDROIT Principles, and the DCFR should lead to the same result, certainly with regard to the problem in our hypothetical. That being said, there are differences in detail between the three regimes. First, there is the question whether the regime is well known to whichever forum is selected by the parties. The CISG has the advantage here and the DCFR is probably the least well known, although it is catching up. Second, there is the question of comprehensiveness. All three regimes do not cover every possible question and need to be accompanied with a backup choice of law, for example "the contract shall be governed by the CISG; for any questions not covered therein, Swiss law shall apply".[20] In this respect, the advantage is with

---

20. Anything else would be an incomplete choice of law and would require, in case such a problem did arise, that the backup is determined by the forum on the basis of its private international law.

the DCFR, which is the most comprehensive and leaves the fewest questions unresolved. Finally, the third question is about comprehensibility and efficiency. Once
again, the DCFR has the advantage here. Even a superficial reading of the three texts
shows right away that the DCFR is more easily understandable, better organized,
and generally more clear and straightforward than the other two.

In concluding, I would advise the American seller to make a choice for the DCFR
and arbitration.[21] As for the Colombian buyer, the best choices would probably be for
the UCC with litigation in Indiana. Although the latter would be expensive, Indiana courts would happily apply the perfect tender rule and any decisions could be
easily enforced against the American seller. Ironically, UCC and Indiana courts are
most likely also the recommendation of the attorneys retained by Shure Robotics at
considerable expense.

———————

While the CFR is of considerable interest to professional traders and their
lawyers, it does not contain specific protections for consumers or small businesses.
Therefore, having identified differences in the contract law regimes of the different Member States of the European Union as one of "the top barriers in business-
to-consumer transactions," the EU Commission, building on the work done by
UNIDROIT and in the context of the CFR, presented in 2011 a Proposal for a Regulation of the European Parliament and of the Council on a Common European
Sales Law (CESL).[74] Pursuant to its Article 1, the CESL "can be used for cross-border
transactions for the sale of goods, for the supply of digital content and for related
services where the parties to a contract agree to do so."[75] By contrast to a number
of other contract law regimes, the CESL specifically includes elaborate consumer
protection rules, and offers itself: "1. . . . only if the seller of goods or the supplier of
digital content is a trader. Where all the parties to a contract are traders, the Common European Sales Law may be used if at least one of those parties is a small or
medium-sized enterprise ('SME'). 2. For the purposes of this Regulation, an SME
is a trader which (a) employs fewer than 250 persons; and (b) has an annual turnover not exceeding EUR 50 million . . ." (Article 7). In practice, of course, it is not

———————

21. I would not advise any party at this time to bring the DCFR to a regular court, since the
outcome is still too unpredictable, given the limited experience of most courts with this regime.

74. Preamble (1), COM(2011) 635 final, Brussels, 11 October 2011, available at http://eur-lex.
europa.eu/LexUriServ/LexUriServ.do?uri=COM:2011:0635:FIN:en:PDF. For detailed analysis,
see Reiner Schulze (ed), *Common European Sales Law (CESL)—Commentary*, C.H. Beck/Hart/
Nomos 2012; see also Stefan Grundmann, *Costs and Benefits of an Optional European Sales Law
(CESL)*, Common Mkt. L. Rev. 2013, Vol. 50, No. 1/2, pp. 225–242; Martijn W. Hesselink, *How to
Opt into the Common European Sales Law? Brief Comments on the Commission's Proposal for a Regulation*, European Review of Private Law 2012, Vol. 20, No. 1, pp. 195–212; Ole Lando, *Comments
and Questions Relating to the European Commission's Proposal for a Regulation on a Common European Sales Law*, European Rev. Priv. L. 2011, Vol. 19, No. 6, pp. 717–725.

75. Article 13 makes it clear, however, that EU Member States can allow the use of the CESL also
for purely domestic B2C transactions.

likely that an SME, let alone a consumer, would know about the CESL and have the negotiating power to get it as the governing law of a contract. At the same time, a larger business contracting with an SME or a consumer is not likely to propose the CESL or agree to it, not least because in actual B2C transactions, the CESL "may not be chosen partially, but only in its entirety" (Article 8(3)). This begs a bit the question of the usefulness of the CESL, unless it is eventually adopted as mandatory for cross-border consumer contracts in Europe. Because of this unclear mission, the proposal was widely misunderstood as an attempt at replacing the national contract laws and enforcing a uniform European contract law regime from the top down, rather than an additional and entirely voluntary option for cross-border contracts in the internal market of the EU. As a consequence, there was considerable resistance in a number of Member States, most notably the UK. Therefore, in 2014, the Commission withdrew the Proposal to take account of criticism and suggestions by the European Parliament, and to work on a revision that will include more advanced rules on e-commerce.

The resistance of the EU Member States against the CESL should also serve as a warning for anyone dreaming about the enactment of the CFR, in the foreseeable future, as a pan-European civil code. In practice, these transnational codifications will remain model codes available for sophisticated lawyers and businesses as voluntary choices of law. The only one applicable by law, unless explicitly excluded, is and will be the CISG.

———————

After this discussion of the relative strengths and weaknesses of the modern contract laws available to parties in B2B transactions, we can see that the choice will usually boil down to the CISG as representative of the civil law tradition versus the UCC as representative of the common law tradition. Therefore, our analysis of the rights and obligations of parties to an IBT will focus on these two sets of rules. However, parties still make a selection in favor of the "lex mercatoria" quite regularly, which justifies some comparative analysis of the UNIDROIT Principles. Similarly, some remarks about the Restatement (Second) of Contracts are warranted since it is used for the interpretation of terms and if there are gaps in the UCC. In particular in commodities trade, "English law" is another frequent choice and since many of those making it probably know little or nothing about it, some explanations are in order here as well. Finally, the author considers the CFR to be a brilliant and forward-looking code, standing head and shoulders above all other contract laws. This is why a comparison to the CISG, UCC, and UNIDROIT Principles is also included below, [76] a kind of marketing stint for the CFR. However, before we explore the rights and duties of the parties under these different legal regimes, a brief discussion of the mechanics of making a valid choice of law and forum — and the question what happens if the parties did not make an effective choice — is necessary.

———————

76. A similarly broad approach is also taken in Henry Deeb Gabriel: *Contracts for the Sale of Goods — A Comparison of U.S. and International Law*, Oxford Univ. Press 2nd ed. 2008.

3. How Do Choice of Law and Choice of Forum Have to Be Made to Be Valid and Enforceable?

In commercial contracts, the freedom of choice of the parties with regard to the applicable law is largely unlimited. However, a few exceptions do apply:

- almost all legal systems impose limitations if one of the parties to the contract is a consumer (e.g., § 1-301(e) UCC; Article 6 Rome I Regulation);

- some legal systems also impose limitations in employment contracts (e.g., Article 8 Rome I Regulation);

- furthermore, almost all legal systems have a safeguard provision for *ordre public* or public order considerations. (Pursuant to § 1-301(f) UCC, the parties cannot make a choice in favor of another legal system if that "would be contrary to a fundamental policy" of the country whose legal system would apply pursuant to the rules of private international law, or international conflicts of law; similarly, Article 9 Rome I Regulation allows a forum to apply any "overriding mandatory provisions" applicable at its seat and/or those that apply where the contract has been or should be performed).

In typical B2B transactions, these exceptions will rarely be a problem for the validity of a choice of law made by the parties. We just need to remember that choice of law and choice of forum are related because a particular forum should normally not be made to apply a law with which it is unfamiliar, if it can be avoided. Thus, when drafting or reviewing contracts, careful consideration should be given to the most desirable forum, including courts of the seller or buyer, third-country courts, and arbitration. The choice of forum and the choice of the preferred substantive law have to be taken together, i.e., whether the preferred or required forum will be competent to handle the preferred substantive law. Ideally, these considerations will be made during the negotiations of a contract and will be included via valid choice of law and choice of forum clauses when the contract is finalized. If a contract does not include valid clauses for choice of law and forum or if the choices turn out to be less than ideal, the parties can make new or different choices at a later stage, in particular when a dispute arises. However, this requires an agreement between the parties that may no longer be forthcoming when problems with the contract or the business relationship have already materialized and litigation or arbitration is imminent.

If there are no valid choices in the original agreement and the parties are unable to agree later, the applicable law and forum have to be determined via the rules of private international law, or international conflict of laws. This will be discussed in the next section. At the present time, we will focus on the drafting of valid choice of law clauses to be included in a contract for an IBT. Choice of forum will be discussed at length in Part Six on Dispute Settlement (below, pp. 699 et seq.).

The relative strengths and weaknesses of different substantive contract laws were discussed earlier. However, a dispute may go beyond contract law in the narrow sense and include pre-contractual issues such as capacity and agency, as well as ancillary or consequential issues such as tort liability. Thus, a narrow choice of law clause along the lines of "*this contract* shall be governed by the law of X" should be avoided.

Against this background one may find recommendations such as this one:

> This contract shall be governed and construed in accordance with the laws of [selected State], excluding that State's choice-of-law principles, and all claims relating to or arising out of this contract, or the breach thereof, whether sounding in contract, tort or otherwise, shall likewise be governed by the laws of [selected State], excluding that State's choice-of-law principles.[77]

While such a clause is probably suitable to achieve the desired result, it is also verbose, inelegant, and violates fundamental principles of good legal writing and drafting. We suggest the following two models instead:

> 1. With CISG: "This contract and all related aspects of the business relationship between the parties shall be governed by the CISG. Any questions not covered by the CISG shall be governed by the domestic law of [selected country]."

> 2. Without CISG: "This contract and all related aspects of the business relationship between the parties shall be governed by the domestic law of [selected country] without CISG."

If dispute settlement takes place via arbitration, the parties can also choose the CFR as the governing law:

> The Parties agree that this contract and all related aspects of the business relationship between them shall be subject to equitable rules and customs as expressed in the Common Frame of Reference of the European Union. Any disagreements between the Parties will be resolved amicably. If either side feels that negotiations cannot achieve an amicable resolution, it may call upon independent mediators or arbitrators to settle the dispute pursuant to the MedArb Rules of the International Smart Mediation and Arbitration Institute. (For more examples see below, Part Six, pp. 948 et seq.)

4. *What Happens in the Absence of a Valid Choice of Law or Choice of Forum?*

Two scenarios usually lead to the same result, the absence of valid choices for law and forum. Sometimes the parties did not make a choice of law and/or a choice of forum in the first place. This can happen if they use poorly drafted contract models

---

77. See http://www.lexology.com/library/detail.aspx?g=19184c3b-3d68-427a-87f5-c7e3ef3e 60f5, last visited June 27, 2017. 2017. See also the review of this clause by Ken Adams, Adams on Contract Drafting, https://www.adamsdrafting.com/examining-a-recommended-governing-law-provision/, last visited 21 July 2020.

that do not remind them that a choice of law and forum should be included or if they do not have a written contract at all and have not discussed the issues of law and forum in the contractual negotiations. More likely, however, the parties thought of and tried to include choice of law and forum but they were unable to agree which law and which forum to select. In the end, they decided to drop the issue from the contract in order to be able to move forward with the business transaction.

Alternatively, the parties may have included a choice of law and a choice of forum in their contract, but either one or both of the choices turn out to be invalid or ineffective. A choice may be invalid, for example, if it is not in writing and written form is required. A choice may be ineffective if the chosen forum does not accept jurisdiction over the dispute. If the parties have chosen arbitration, the choice can be invalid if the arbitral institution is not clearly identified.[78]

The consequences of the absence of a valid choice for law and forum depend a bit on where a case is brought. In the European tradition, verifying that the court where a case is brought actually has jurisdiction over the dispute and the parties will be done ex officio. The parties can neither trigger nor prevent this step in the procedure. Once the court has determined that it has subject matter and personal jurisdiction over the parties, it will proceed with an examination of the applicable law. If the court concludes that it does not have jurisdiction, the case is thrown out and the procedure terminated. The plaintiff may have to pay court fees and expenses of the defendant if she brought her case in the wrong court. If the court concludes that it does have jurisdiction, it will apply the substantive law chosen by the parties or determined via application of the forum's conflict rules (the rare case that a forum might apply a different set of conflict rules is discussed in the next sub-section). If the court concludes that the substantive law of the forum has to be applied, the case will proceed without further ado. However, if the court concludes that because of party choice or specific conflicts rules, a foreign substantive law has to be applied, the parties will be asked to provide and pay for experts to instruct the court on this foreign law.

The traditional common law approach is different. The potential relevance and impact of foreign law is a matter of fact rather than law, i.e., it will not be examined ex officio but only if raised and proven by one party and not successfully disproven by the other. As a matter of fact, foreign law was traditionally subject to the appreciation of the judge or jury and not subject to appellate review. This is still the approach generally taken by the several States in the U.S., including Louisiana.[79] By contrast, the Federal Rules of Civil Procedure now follow the continental European approach. Although the applicability of foreign law still has to be brought up by a

---

78. On issues related to choice of law, see also the discussion above, p. 109, regarding the 2015 Hague Principles on Choice of Law in International Commercial Contracts, available at https://www.hcch.net/en/instruments/conventions/full-text/?cid=135.

79. The same is true in Canada for the provinces, including Quebec, see § 2809 of the Quebec Civil Code.

party, it will then be examined by the court as a matter of law and, thus, removed from the appreciation of a jury, and subject to appellate review.[80]

As stated earlier, it is almost never a good idea to force a public court to apply a law that is foreign to it. At best, the procedure will be slower and more expensive. At worst, the outcome may be unpredictable and potentially unfair. Since choices of law and forum cannot only be made at the beginning of a transaction (ex ante) but also when a dispute arises during or after the performance (ex post), parties acting in good faith and interested in continuing the business relationship should be able to overcome an unfortunate result of a poor choice or unexpected conflict rules. However, inefficient and/or unpredictable procedures are sometimes in the interest of a defendant party who would not stand a chance of winning in fair and efficient procedures. Such a party may try to use the leverage it is gaining from the unfortunate choices to push for a poorly balanced settlement or even discourage the other side from pursuing her rights altogether. This is why it is so important to *always* include sensible and valid choice of law and forum clauses in IBT contracts.

The situation is somewhat better if the parties have agreed to arbitration in their contract or do so when the dispute has arisen. Since the parties can select the arbitrator or arbitrators themselves, they can select neutrals with proficiency in the chosen legal system. Even if the parties are no longer able to agree, once the dispute has arisen, arbitrators are generally more willing to make themselves knowledgeable in a particular area of business or law and/or resort to general principles of law to overcome rules that might lead to unfair or unintended outcomes. However, even the most experienced arbitrators will have their hands tied if a contract clearly stipulates that a particular legal system has to be applied and the respective provisions lead to an outcome that is quite different from the outcome that most other legal systems would provide. After all, the freedom of contract includes the freedom to make stupid choices and become bound to unfavorable contracts and it is not the job of the arbitrators to override clear contractual provisions to provide for more equitable outcomes.

5. The Problem of "Renvoi"

"Renvoi" is French and literally means "to send back" or "to return unopened." It describes a particular scenario where a national court does not accept jurisdiction over a case and sends it back to where it came from. In the first alternative, the parties to an IBT may have a valid choice of law in favor of a particular national legal system, for example, "French law." However, the French court approached by one of the parties as the defendant court applies not only its substantive contract law but

---

80. See 28 U.S.C. Rule 44.1. "Determining Foreign Law: A party who intends to raise an issue about a foreign country's law must give notice by a pleading or other writing. In determining foreign law, the court may consider any relevant material or source, including testimony, whether or not submitted by a party or admissible under the Federal Rules of Evidence. The court's determination must be treated as a ruling on a question of law."

also the French rules on conflict of laws or private international law. And the latter might provide, for a case like the one at hand, that the applicable law should be the seller's law and any disputes should be decided in the seller's courts. If the seller is in the U.S. and the French court does not want the case, it can "renvoi" the case based on the argument that the choice of French law was also a choice of French conflict rules. However, the American court may then find that it does not have jurisdiction because the parties have, after all, chosen French law and, according to American conflict rules, the case needs to be brought in defendant courts, i.e., French courts.

In a variation, the parties may not have a choice of law and forum in their contract at all. When the plaintiff approaches the courts in country A, they decide on the basis of their conflict rules that the courts and legal system of country B should be in charge. However, when the plaintiff then approaches the courts in country B, they send the case back because, under their own conflict rules, the courts and legal system in country A should be called upon.

In another variation, a court in country A decides that the law of country B should be applied to a case before it, including the conflict rules of B. The conflict rules of B, however, suggest that the law of country A should apply, including the conflict rules of country A, which send the question of the applicable law right back again to B. After a while the judges will just get dizzy. However, the question is no longer purely theoretical if the plaintiff should prevail under the laws of A, while the defendant should prevail under the laws of B.

Academics have written extensively about the problem, although its relevance in practice is probably quite small. However, given the fact that all courts today are overloaded and judges don't get anything extra for doing extra work, the issue is not merely academic.[81] The best way to avoid the problem, in my view, is a choice of arbitration, rather than a convoluted choice of law and forum.

6. Practical Examples

Our first case is a good example of issues arising from unclear procedures at the contract formation stage. Although both parties are experienced commercial operators, they fail to integrate all terms and conditions into one mutually acceptable contract of sale. As a result, there is now argument about what was the offer and when or how was it accepted. The consequences are far reaching, potentially including the applicable law, forum, and whether the seller has a lien on unpaid merchandise. As you are reading the decision, consider how the problems could have been avoided from the seller's point of view. In addition, ask yourself how the contract would have to be formulated to allow for the application of the Michigan Special Tools Lien Act.

---

81. For further analysis, see Kermit Roosevelt III, *Resolving Renvoi: The Bewitchment of Our Intelligence by Means of Language*, Notre Dame L. Rev. 2005, Vol. 80, No. 5, pp. 1821–1891, with many more references.

Case 2-2

Easom Automation Systems v. Thyssenkrupp Fabco, Corp.

2007 WL 2875256 (E.D. Mich. 2007)
(Paragraph numbers added, footnotes omitted.)
ORDER DENYING PLAINTIFF'S MOTION FOR IMMEDIATE POSSESSION
Denise Page Hood, United States District Judge

I. Introduction

[1] This matter is before the Court on Plaintiff Easom Automation Systems, Inc.'s Motion for Immediate Possession, filed on January 30, 2007. Defendant Thyssen-Krupp Fabco, Corp. filed its Response to Plaintiff's Motion for Immediate Possession on March 2, 2007.

[2] On October 17, 2006, Plaintiff filed the instant action pursuant to 28 U.S.C. § 1332 alleging the following against Defendant: Count I, Breach of Contract; Count II, Breach of Implied Contract; Count III, Unjust Enrichment; and Count IV, Enforcement of Michigan Special Tool Lien.

II. Statement of Facts

[3] Plaintiff is a Michigan Corporation with its principal place of business in Madison Heights, Michigan. Plaintiff designs, builds, integrates and installs automation equipment and systems for the auto industry. Defendant is a Nova Scotia Corporation headquartered in Ontario, and it is in the business of supplying medium and heavy metal stampings and systems to automotive customers. The present matter arises out of an "agreement" between the parties where Plaintiff was to design, fabricate and install the Sport Bar Assembly System (SBA) for Defendant.

[4] Plaintiff asserts that on July 19, 2005, it issued a Quote to Defendant for the SBA, which specified a price of $5,400,000.00 and a delivery date of March 30, 2006. According to Plaintiff, that same day, Defendant orally instructed Plaintiff to commence work on the SBA. Plaintiff commenced work on the SBA. Plaintiff asserts that Defendant issued a written purchase order on August 30, 2005, which included the following choice of law/forum selection clause:

> 25. *Jurisdiction/Governing law.* The contract created by Seller's acceptance of Buyer's offer as set out in Paragraph 3 hereof shall be deemed in all respects to be a contract made under, and shall for all purposes be governed by and construed in accordance, with, the laws of the Province where the registered head office of Buyer is located and the laws of Canada applicable therein. Any legal action or proceeding with respect to such contract may be brought in the courts of the Province where the registered head office of buyer is located and the parties hereto attorn to the non-exclusive jurisdiction of the aforesaid courts.

[5] Between August and October 2005, during the design and engineering phase of the SBA, Plaintiff asserts that Defendant's representatives regularly met for weekly meetings at Plaintiff's Madison Heights facility.

[6] Plaintiff alleges that on October 21, 2005, Defendant's Vice-President, Gary Herman, instructed Plaintiff to begin delivery of the SBA in an "as is" condition by December 31, 2005, with the remainder of the installation to occur on Defendant's facility floor in Dresden, Ontario. Plaintiff permanently affixed its name and address to the SBA's component parts before shipment. Plaintiff began to ship the SBA in an "as is" condition on December 31, 2005. Plaintiff further alleges that it agreed to deliver the SBA on this expedited basis because of Defendant's agreements to do certain things to assist in the expedited installation of the SBA. Plaintiff asserts that Defendant failed to follow through on these agreements. Plaintiff's employees worked on the installation, and testing of the SBA at Defendant's facility.

[7] On March 9, 2006, Plaintiff filed a Financing Statement with the Ontario Ministry of Consumer and Industry Services. On November 4, 2006, after this suit was already filed, Defendant filed an Application in the Ontario Superior Court of Justice seeking discharge of Plaintiff's financing statement. Plaintiff also alleges that Defendant has failed to pay Plaintiff $1,484,498.05, plus interest, while Defendant continues to operate the SBA.

III. Procedural Posture

[8] On December 29, 2006, Defendant filed a Motion to Dismiss on Grounds of *Forum Non Conveniens,* asserting, among other things, that the Choice of Law/Forum Selection Clause governs the agreement between the parties. On August 1, 2007, this Court denied Defendant's Motions to Dismiss on Grounds of *Forum Non Conveniens,* holding, without definitively answering the question of what law governs this action, that Defendant's failure to demonstrate that the "balance of hardships" or trial of this matter in this Court would be "oppressive and vexatious" to Defendant.

IV. Applicable Law & Analysis

[9] Plaintiff argues that pursuant to Michigan's Special Tools Lien Act, MICH. COMP. LAWS § 570. 563 *et seq.,* it is entitled to immediate possession of the SBA, currently in Defendant's possession in Canada. Plaintiff asserts that because it complied with the requirements of the Act to perfect the lien on the SBA, specifically affixed its name and address to the SBA, filed a financing statement with the Province of Ontario, sent notification and a demand for payment letter to Defendant, and waited ninety days without receiving payment, Plaintiff is entitled to immediate possession of the SBA.

[10] Defendant's argument mainly rests upon the assumption that the purchase orders it issued to Plaintiff constituted Defendant's offer, not the quote issued by Plaintiff. By accepting Defendant's offer to build the SBA pursuant to the terms and conditions set forth in the purchase orders, specifically the Choice of Law/Forum

Selection Clause, Defendant claims Plaintiff agreed the contract was governed by Ontario law. Defendant argues that since the parties expressly agreed that Ontario law would govern their agreement, the Michigan Special Tools Lien Act is inapplicable, and Plaintiff has no right to immediate possession. Alternatively, Defendant argues that if the Act does apply to this action, Plaintiff expressly waived its right to enforce the lien, and, in any event, Plaintiff did not comply with the financing statement filing requirements, as such, the lien is invalid.

[11] It is Plaintiff's contention that the United Nations Convention on Contracts for the International Sale of Goods, or the CISG . . . controls this matter based upon the fact that on July 19, 2005, Plaintiff sent Defendant a series of quotes, which constitutes Plaintiff's offer to manufacture and assemble the SBA. According to Plaintiff, Defendant verbally accepted this offer on July 19, 2005 (the very same day), and Plaintiff began work on the SBA shortly thereafter.

[12] The CISG governs only the formation of the contract of sale, and the rights and obligations of the seller and the buyer arising from such a contract. See CISG, Art. 4. The CISG governs contracts for the sale of goods between parties whose places of business are in different nations, if the nations are Contracting States, unless the subject contract contains a choice-of-law provision. See CISG, Art. 1, 6; See also American Biophysics Corp. v. DuBois Marine Specialities, 411 F.Supp.2d 61, 63–64 (D.R.I.2006); See also BP Oil Int'l, Ltd. v. Empresa Estatal Petroleos de Ecuador, 332 F.3d 333, 337 (5th Cir.2003). Both the United States and Canada are signatory nations.

[13] Under the CISG, the July 19, 2005 quote issued by Plaintiff could constitute Plaintiff's offer because the quote was "sufficiently definite and indicate[d] the intention of the offeror to be bound in case of acceptance." See CISG, Art. 14. Article 14 indicates that "[a] proposal is sufficiently definite if it indicates the goods and expressly or implicitly fixes or makes provisions for determining the quantity and the price." Id. Plaintiff's quote specifically indicates that Plaintiff would design and build the SBA in the amount of $5,400,000.00.

[14] Defendant's oral acceptance of the quote is recognized as a valid form of acceptance under the CISG. See CISG, Art. 18. The CISG specifically states that "[a] statement made by or other conduct of the offerree indicating assent to an offer is acceptance." See CISG, Art. 18(1). Additionally, "[a]n acceptance of an offer becomes effective at the moment the indication of assent reaches the offeror. . . ." See CISG, Art. 18(2).

[15] The CISG makes provision for the parties to a contract to opt out of the CISG as the governing law and agree that their contract be governed by another law. See CISG, Art. 6. "The parties may exclude the application of this Convention, or . . . derogate from or vary the effect of any of its provisions." CISG, Art. 6. Courts that have reviewed this provision have held that the parties must expressly opt out of applying the CISG to their agreement. See BP Oil Int'l, 332 F.3d at 337; Asante Techs., Inc. v. PMC-Sierra, Inc., 164 F.Supp.2d 1142, 1150 (N.D.Cal.2001)[see

p. 155] ("A signatory's assent to the CISG necessarily incorporates the treaty as part of that nation's domestic law."); *See also Ajax Tools Works, Inc. v. Can-Eng Manu. Ltd.,* 2003 U.S. Dist. LEXIS 1306, at *8 (holding that since Germany is a contracting state, "the CISG is an integral part of German law. Where parties designate a choice of law clause in their contract, selecting the law of a contracting state without expressly excluding application of the CISG, German courts uphold application of the Convention as the law of the designated Contracting state. To hold otherwise would undermine the objectives of the Convention which Germany has agreed to uphold").

[16] Under either the Plaintiff's quote or Defendant's purchase orders, the CISG applies as neither the quote nor the purchase orders expressly indicated that the CISG did not apply. Further, stating that the law of Canada applied to the agreement indicates that the CISG applied as well, as the Convention is the law of Canada.

[17] The CISG governs only the formation of the contract of sale, and the rights and obligations of the seller and the buyer arising from such a contract. As such, if the Plaintiff's quote constitutes the contract in this case, as opposed to Defendant's purchase orders, the Michigan Special Tools Lien Act may apply to the parties' agreement.

[18] If Defendant's purchase orders govern, Plaintiff has no right to immediate possession because the purchase orders contain a waiver of liens provision. Specifically, the purchase orders contain the following language: "Seller hereby waives all mechanic liens and claims and agrees that none shall be filed or maintained against Buyer or the Product on account of any Product stored by or on behalf of Seller. . . ."

[19] Even if the Special Tools Lien Act applies, Defendant argues that Plaintiff failed to file its financing statement with Michigan's Secretary of State as the Act requires. *See* Mich. Comp. Laws §§ 440.9501 and 9502. Plaintiff instead filed its financing statement with the Ontario Ministry of Consumer and Business Services. As such, the lien is invalid. . . .

[20] At this juncture, there remain issues of fact as to which document constitutes the contract in this case—the quotes prepared by Plaintiff or the purchase orders prepared by Defendant. Until this issue is resolved, the Court is unable to determine whether Michigan law applies and whether the Michigan's Special Tools Lien Act applies. Plaintiff is correct that under M.C.L.A. § 570.567(a), a special tool builder may take possession without judicial process if it can be done without breach of the peace. However, Plaintiff has not chosen this alternative since Plaintiff involved the judiciary by filing the instant action in this Court.

V. Conclusion

For the reasons set forth above,

IT IS ORDERED that Plaintiff Easom Automation System, Inc.'s Motion for Immediate Possession is DENIED without prejudice.

Notes and Questions

1. What does *Easom Automation* tell us about the CISG as the law applicable to an international contract of sale? Can you formulate a rule in just a few sentences?

2. Neither the contract terms suggested or claimed by the plaintiff, nor the contract terms suggested or claimed by the defendant provided for an exclusion of the CISG. So it would seem that the CISG applies regardless of whether the contract draft of one party or the other is endorsed by the court. How can the success or failure of plaintiff's motion depend on whether the quote issued by the plaintiff was the offer or the purchase order placed by the defendant?

3. How can or will the court go about determining whether the quote or the purchase order was the offer and, therefore, what are the terms of the contract?

4. What should the plaintiff do if the court should ultimately decide that Michigan law does not apply?

5. Defendant, in reliance on the forum selection clause quoted in the decision, did not want to litigate in Michigan, where the court might decide to apply the Michigan Special Tools Lien Act. How did the case nevertheless come before the U.S. Federal District Court for Eastern Michigan? On what basis would this court potentially have jurisdiction? Do you think it was wise for the defendant to claim that trial in the present court would be "oppressive and vexatious" to it? Can you suggest what kind of cases might qualify for such a claim?

———————

Our next case is similar in the sense that it also does not have a properly drawn-up contract of sale as the one and only document determining the rights and obligations of the parties. As a consequence, there is no clear and unambiguous choice of law and forum. Given that the defendant operates facilities both in the U.S. and in Canada, it is not even clear whether the seller is a domestic or a foreign party. The unfortunate result is, once again, a round of litigation over the applicable law and forum as a precursor to the actual battle over performance, damages, and other consequences of the alleged breach of contract.

The U.S. ratified the CISG in November 1986 and the Convention entered into force for the U.S. on January 1, 1988. The present case, decided in 2001, finds that the question "whether or not the CISG preempts state law is a matter of first impression" (para. 24). How can it be that for more than a decade, not a single attorney in the U.S. argued before an American court that the CISG displaces not just federal but also state law, where applicable? Professor Frisch may be providing the sad but true response. His 1999 article in the *Tulane Law Review* was titled "The United Nations Convention on the International Sale of Goods, and the Inertia of Habit" (74 Tul. L. Rev. 495). It seems that many of our attorneys, in spite of rather widespread CLE requirements, are stuck in certain habits instead of delivering state-of-the-art services, at least when it comes to international law aspects of their work.

Case 2-3

Asante Technologies, Inc. v. PMC-Sierra, Inc.

164 F. Supp. 2d 1142 (N.D. Cal. 2001)
(Paragraph numbers added, some footnotes and details omitted.)
Order Denying Motion to Remand and Request for Attorneys'
Fees WARE, District Judge

I. Introduction

[1] This lawsuit arises out of a dispute involving the sale of electronic components. Plaintiff, Asante Technologies Inc., filed the action in the Superior Court for the State of California, Santa Clara County, on February 13, 2001. Defendant, PMC-Sierra, Inc., removed the action to this Court, asserting federal question jurisdiction pursuant to 28 U.S.C. section 1331. Specifically, Defendant asserts that Plaintiff's claims for breach of contract and breach of express warranty are governed by the United Nations Convention on Contracts for the International Sale of Goods ("CISG"). Plaintiff disputes jurisdiction and filed this Motion to Remand and for Attorneys' Fees. The Court conducted a hearing on June 18, 2001. Based upon the submitted papers and oral arguments of the parties, the Court DENIES the motion to remand and the associated request for attorneys' fees.

II. Background

[2] The Complaint in this action alleges claims based in tort and contract. Plaintiff contends that Defendant failed to provide it with electronic components meeting certain designated technical specifications. Defendant timely removed the action to this Court on March 16, 2001.

[3] Plaintiff is a Delaware corporation having its primary place of business in Santa Clara County, California. Plaintiff produces network switchers, a type of electronic component used to connect multiple computers to one another and to the Internet. Plaintiff purchases component parts from a number of manufacturers. In particular, Plaintiff purchases application-specific integrated circuits ("ASICs"), which are considered the control center of its network switchers, from Defendant.

[4] Defendant is also a Delaware corporation. Defendant asserts that, at all relevant times, its corporate headquarters, inside sales and marketing office, public relations department, principal warehouse, and most design and engineering functions were located in Burnaby, British Columbia, Canada. Defendant also maintains an office in Portland, Oregon, where many of its engineers are based. Defendant's products are sold in California through Unique Technologies, which is an authorized distributor of Defendant's products in North America. It is undisputed that Defendant directed Plaintiff to purchase Defendant's products through Unique, and that Defendant honored purchase orders solicited by Unique. Unique is located in California. Determining Defendant's "place of business" with respect to its contract with Plaintiff is critical to the question of whether the Court has jurisdiction in this case.

[5] Plaintiff's Complaint focuses on five purchase orders.[1] Four of the five purchase orders were submitted to Defendant through Unique as directed by Defendant. However, Plaintiff does not dispute that one of the purchase orders, dated January 28, 2000, was sent by fax directly to Defendant in British Columbia, and that Defendant processed the order in British Columbia. Defendant shipped all orders to Plaintiff's headquarters in California.[2] Upon delivery of the goods, Unique sent invoices to Plaintiff, at which time Plaintiff tendered payment to Unique either in California or in Nevada.

[6] The Parties do not identify any single contract embodying the agreement pertaining to the sale. Instead, Plaintiff asserts that acceptance of each of its purchase orders was expressly conditioned upon acceptance by Defendant of Plaintiff's "Terms and Conditions," which were included with each Purchase Order. Paragraph 20 of Plaintiff's Terms and Conditions provides "APPLICABLE LAW. The validity [and] performance of this [purchase] order shall be governed by the laws of the state shown on Buyer's address on this order." . . . The buyer's address as shown on each of the Purchase Orders is in San Jose, California. Alternatively, Defendant suggests that the terms of shipment are governed by a document entitled "PMC-Sierra TERMS AND CONDITIONS OF SALE." Paragraph 19 of Defendant's Terms and conditions provides "APPLICABLE LAW: The contract between the parties is made, governed by, and shall be construed in accordance with the laws of the Province of British Columbia and the laws of Canada applicable therein, which shall be deemed to be the proper law hereof. . . ."

[7] Plaintiff's Complaint alleges that Defendant promised in writing that the chips would meet certain technical specifications. . . . Defendant asserts that the following documents upon which Plaintiff relies emanated from Defendant's office in British Columbia: (1) Defendant's August 24, 1998 press release that it would be making chips available for general sampling . . . ; (2) Defendant's periodic updates of technical specifications . . . ; and (3) correspondence from Defendant to Plaintiff, including a letter dated October 25, 1999. It is furthermore undisputed that the Prototype Product Limited Warranty Agreements relating to some or all of Plaintiff's purchases were executed with Defendant's British Columbia facility. . . .

[8] Defendant does not deny that Plaintiff maintained extensive contacts with Defendant's facilities in Portland Oregon during the "development and engineering" of the ASICs. . . . These contacts included daily email and telephone correspondence and frequent in-person collaborations between Plaintiff's engineers and Defendant's engineers in Portland. . . . Plaintiff contends that this litigation concerns the inability of Defendant's engineers in Portland to develop an ASIC meeting the agreed-upon specifications. . . .

---

2. Plaintiff contends in this suit that the delivered ASICs did not comply with required technical specifications.

[9] Plaintiff now requests this Court to remand this action back to the Superior Court of the County of Santa Clara pursuant to 28 U.S.C. section 1447(c), asserting lack of subject matter jurisdiction. In addition, Plaintiff requests award of attorneys fees and costs for the expense of bringing this motion.

III. Standards

[10] A defendant may remove to federal court any civil action brought in a state court that originally could have been filed in federal court. 28 U.S.C. § 1441(a); *Caterpillar, Inc. v. Williams*, 482 U.S. 386, 107 S.Ct. 2425, 96 L.Ed.2d 318 (1987). When a case originally filed in state court contains separate and independent federal and state law claims, the entire case may be removed to federal court. 28 U.S.C. 1441(c).

[11] The determination of whether an action arises under federal law is guided by the "well-pleaded complaint" rule. *Franchise Tax Board v. Construction Laborers Vacation Trust*, 463 U.S. 1, 10, 103 S.Ct. 2841, 77 L.Ed.2d 420 (1983). The rule provides that removal is proper when a federal question is presented on the face of the Complaint. *Id.* at 9, 103 S.Ct. 2841. However, in areas where federal law completely preempts state law, even if the claims are purportedly based on state law, the claims are considered to have arisen under federal law. *Ramirez v. Fox Television Station, Inc.*, 998 F.2d 743 (9th Cir.1993). Defendant has the burden of establishing that removal is proper. *Gaus v. Miles*, Inc., 980 F.2d 564 (9th Cir.1992). If, at any time before judgment, the district court determines that the case was removed from state court improperly and without jurisdiction, the district court must remand the case. 28 U.S.C. § 1447(c).

[12] The Convention on Contracts for the International Sale of Goods ("CISG") is an international treaty which has been signed and ratified by the United States and Canada, among other countries. The CISG was adopted for the purpose of establishing "substantive provisions of law to govern the formation of international sales contracts and the rights and obligations of the buyer and the seller." U.S. Ratification of 1980 United Nations Convention on Contracts for the International Sale of Goods: Official English Text, 15 U.S.C.App. at 52 (1997). The CISG applies "to contracts of sale of goods between parties whose places of business are in different States . . . when the States are Contracting States." 15 U.S.C.App., Art. 1(1)(a). Article 10 of the CISG provides that "if a party has more than one place of business, the place of business is that which has the closest relationship to the contract and its performance." 15 U.S.C.App. Art. 10.

IV. Discussion

[13] Defendant asserts that this Court has jurisdiction to hear this case pursuant to 28 U.S.C. section 1331, which dictates that the "district courts shall have original jurisdiction of all civil actions arising under the Constitution, laws, or treaties of the United States." Specifically, Defendant contends that the contract claims at issue necessarily implicate the CISG, because the contract is between parties having their places of business in two nations which have adopted the CISG treaty. The Court concludes that Defendant's place of business for the purposes of the contract at issue

and its performance is Burnaby, British Columbia, Canada. Accordingly, the CISG applies. Moreover, the parties did not effectuate an "opt out" of application of the CISG. Finally, because the Court concludes that the CISG preempts state laws that address the formation of a contract of sale and the rights and obligations of the seller and buyer arising from such a contract, the well-pleaded complaint rule does not preclude removal in this case.

A. Federal Jurisdiction Attaches to Claims Governed By the CISG

[14] Although the general federal question statute, 28 U.S.C. § 1331(a), gives district courts original jurisdiction over every civil action that "arises under the . . . treaties of the United States," an individual may only enforce a treaty's provisions when the treaty is self-executing, that is, when it expressly or impliedly creates a private right of action. See *Tel-Oren v. Libyan Arab Republic*, 726 F.2d 774, 808 (D.C.Cir.1984) (Bork, J., concurring); *Handel v. Artukovic*, 601 F.Supp. 1421, 1425 (C.D.Cal.1985). The parties do not dispute that the CISG properly creates a private right of action. See *Delchi Carrier v. Rotorex Corp.*, 71 F.3d 1024, 1027–28 (2d Cir.1995); *Filanto, S.p.A. v. Chilewich Int'l Corp.*, 789 F.Supp. 1229, 1237 (S.D.N.Y.1992) [see p. 882]; U.S. Ratification of 1980 United Nations Convention on Contracts for the International Sale of Goods: Official English Text, 15 U.S.C.App. at 52 (1997) ("The Convention sets out substantive provisions of law to govern the formation of international sales contracts and the rights and obligations of the buyer and seller. It will apply to sales contracts between parties with their places of business in different countries bound by Convention, provided the parties have left their contracts silent as to applicable law."). Therefore, if the CISG properly applies to this action, federal jurisdiction exists.[3]

B. The Contract in Question Is Between Parties from Two Different Contracting States

[15] The CISG only applies when a contract is "between parties whose places of business are in different States."[4] 15 U.S.C.App., Art. 1(1)(a). If this requirement is not satisfied, Defendant cannot claim jurisdiction under the CISG. It is undisputed that Plaintiff's place of business is Santa Clara County, California, U.S.A. It is further undisputed that during the relevant time period, Defendant's corporate headquarters, inside sales and marketing office, public relations department, principal warehouse, and most of its design and engineering functions were located in Burnaby, British Columbia, Canada. However, Plaintiff contends that, pursuant to Article 10

---

3. Diversity cannot serve as a basis for jurisdiction in this case, because both parties are incorporated in the state of Delaware. See *Bank of California Nat'l Ass'n v. Twin Harbors Lumber Co.*, 465 F.2d 489, 491–92 (9th Cir.1972).

4. In the context of the CISG, "different States" refers to different countries. U.S. Ratification of 1980 United Nations Convention on Contracts for the International Sale of Goods: Official English Text, 15 U.S.C.App. at 52 (1997).

of the CISG, Defendant's "place of business" having the closest relationship to the contract at issue is the United States.[5]

[16] The Complaint asserts inter alia two claims for breach of contract and a claim for breach of express warranty based on the failure of the delivered ASICS to conform to the agreed upon technical specifications. . . . In support of these claims, Plaintiff relies on multiple representations allegedly made by Defendant regarding the technical specifications of the ASICS products at issue. Among the representations are: (1) an August 24, 1998 press release . . . ; (2) "materials" released by Defendant in September, 1998 . . . ; (3) "revised materials" released by Defendant in November 1998 . . . ; (4) "revised materials" released by Defendant in January, 1999 . . . ; (5) "revised materials" released by Defendant in April, 1999 . . . ; (6) a September, 1999 statement by Defendant which included revised specifications indicating that its ASICS would comply with 802.1q VLAN specifications . . . ; (7) a statement made by Defendant's President and Chief Executive Officer on October 25, 1999 . . . ; (8) a communication of December, 1999 . . . ; and (9) "revised materials" released by Defendant in January, 2000 . . . . It appears undisputed that each of these alleged representations regarding the technical specifications of the product was issued from Defendant's headquarters in British Columbia, Canada. . . .

[17] Rather than challenge the Canadian source of these documents, Plaintiff shifts its emphasis to the purchase orders submitted by Plaintiff to Unique Technologies, a nonexclusive distributor of Defendant's products. Plaintiff asserts that Unique acted in the United States as an agent of Defendant, and that Plaintiff's contacts with Unique establish Defendant's place of business in the U.S. for the purposes of this contract.

[18] Plaintiff has failed to persuade the Court that Unique acted as the agent of Defendant. Plaintiff provides no legal support for this proposition. To the contrary, a distributor of goods for resale is normally not treated as an agent of the manufacturer. Restatement of the Law of Agency, 2d § 14J (1957) ("One who receives goods from another for resale to a third person is not thereby the other's agent in the transaction."); *Stansifer v. Chrysler Motors Corp.*, 487 F.2d 59, 64–65 (9th Cir.1973) (holding that nonexclusive distributor was not agent of manufacturer where distributorship agreement expressly stated "distributor is not an agent"). Agency results "from the manifestation of consent by one person to another that the other shall act on his behalf and subject to his control, and consent by the other so to act." Restatement of the Law of Agency, 2d, § 1 (1957). Plaintiff has produced no evidence of consent by Defendant to be bound by the acts of Unique. To the contrary, Defendant cites the distributorship agreement with Unique, which expressly states that the contract does not "allow Distributor to create or assume any obligation on

---

5. Article 10 of the CISG states inter alia: "For the purposes of this Convention: (a) If a party has more than one place of business, the place of business is that which has the closest relationship to the contract and its performance, having regard to the circumstances known to or contemplated by the parties at any time before or at the conclusion of the contract."

behalf of [Defendant] for any purpose whatsoever." . . . Furthermore, while Unique may distribute Defendant's products, Plaintiff does not allege that Unique made any representations regarding technical specifications on behalf of Defendant. Indeed, Unique is not even mentioned in the Complaint. To the extent that representations were made regarding the technical specifications of the ASICs, and those specifications were not satisfied by the delivered goods, the relevant agreement is that between Plaintiff and Defendant. Accordingly, the Court finds that Unique is not an agent of Defendant in this dispute. Plaintiff's dealings with Unique do not establish Defendant's place of business in the United States.

[19] Plaintiff's claims concern breaches of representations made by Defendant from Canada. Moreover, the products in question are manufactured in Canada, and Plaintiff knew that Defendant was Canadian, having sent one purchase order directly to Defendant in Canada by fax. Plaintiff supports its position with the declaration of Anthony Contos, Plaintiff's Vice President of Finance and Administration, who states that Plaintiff's primary contact with Defendant "during the development and engineering of the ASICs at issue . . . was with [Defendant's] facilities in Portland, Oregon." . . . The Court concludes that these contacts are not sufficient to override the fact that most if not all of Defendant's alleged representations regarding the technical specifications of the products emanated from Canada. . . . Moreover, Plaintiff directly corresponded with Defendant at Defendant's Canadian address. . . . Plaintiff relies on all of these alleged representations at length in its Complaint. . . . In contrast, Plaintiff has not identified any specific representation or correspondence emanating from Defendant's Oregon branch. For these reasons, the Court finds that Defendant's place of business that has the closest relationship to the contract and its performance is British Columbia, Canada. Consequently, the contract at issue in this litigation is between parties from two different Contracting States, Canada and the United States. This contract therefore implicates the CISG.

C. The Effect of the Choice of Law Clauses

[20] Plaintiff next argues that, even if the Parties are from two nations that have adopted the CISG, the choice of law provisions in the "Terms and Conditions" set forth by both Parties reflect the Parties' intent to "opt out" of application of the treaty.[6] Article 6 of the CISG provides that "[t]he parties may exclude the application of the Convention or, subject to Article 12, derogate from or vary the effect of any of its provisions." 15 U.S.C.App., Art. 6. Defendant asserts that merely choosing the

---

6. Plaintiff's Terms and Conditions provides "APPLICABLE LAW. The validity [and] performance of this [purchase] order shall be governed by the laws of the state shown on Buyer's address on this order." The buyer's address as shown on each of the Purchase Orders is San Jose, California.

Defendant's Terms and Conditions provides "APPLICABLE LAW: The contract between the parties is made, governed by, and shall be construed in accordance with the laws of the Province of British Columbia and the laws of Canada applicable therein, which shall be deemed to be the proper law hereof. . . ." It is undisputed that British Columbia has adopted the CISG.

law of a jurisdiction is insufficient to opt out of the CISG, absent express exclusion of the CISG. The Court finds that the particular choice of law provisions in the "Terms and Conditions" of both parties are inadequate to effectuate an opt out of the CISG.

[21] Although selection of a particular choice of law, such as "the California Commercial Code" or the "Uniform Commercial Code" could amount to implied exclusion of the CISG, the choice of law clauses at issue here do not evince a clear intent to opt out of the CISG. For example, Defendant's choice of applicable law adopts the law of British Columbia, and it is undisputed that the CISG is the law of British Columbia. (International Sale of Goods Act ch. 236, 1996 S.B.C. 1 et seq. (B.C.).) Furthermore, even Plaintiff's choice of applicable law generally adopts the "laws of" the State of California, and California is bound by the Supremacy Clause to the treaties of the United States. U.S. Const. art. VI, cl. 2 ("This Constitution, and the laws of the United States which shall be made in pursuance thereof; and all treaties made, or which shall be made, under the authority of the United States, shall be the supreme law of the land.") Thus, under general California law, the CISG is applicable to contracts where the contracting parties are from different countries that have adopted the CISG. In the absence of clear language indicating that both contracting parties intended to opt out of the CISG, and in view of Defendant's Terms and Conditions which would apply the CISG, the Court rejects Plaintiff's contention that the choice of law provisions preclude the applicability of the CISG.

D. Federal Jurisdiction Based Upon the CISG Does Not Violate the Well-Pleaded Complaint Rule

[22] The Court rejects Plaintiff's argument that removal is improper because of the well-pleaded complaint rule. The rule states that a cause of action arises under federal law only when the plaintiff's well-pleaded complaint raises issues of federal law. *Gully v. First National Bank*, 299 U.S. 109, 112, 57 S.Ct. 96, 81 L.Ed. 70 (1936); *Louisville & Nashville R. Co. v. Mottley*, 211 U.S. 149, 29 S.Ct. 42, 53 L.Ed. 126 (1908). Anticipation of a federal preemption defense, such as the defense that federal law prohibits the state claims, is insufficient to establish federal jurisdiction. *Gully*, 299 U.S. at 116, 57 S.Ct. 96. Even where both parties concede that determination of a federal question is the only issue in the case, removal is improper unless the plaintiff's complaint establishes that the case "arises under" federal law. *Caterpillar, Inc. v. Williams*, 482 U.S. 386, 393, 107 S.Ct. 2425, 96 L.Ed.2d 318 (1987).

[23] It is undisputed that the Complaint on its face does not refer to the CISG. However, Defendants argue that the preemptive force of the CISG converts the state breach of contract claim into a federal claim. Indeed, Congress may establish a federal law that so completely preempts a particular area of law that any civil complaint raising that select group of claims is necessarily federal in character. *Metropolitan Life Ins. Co. v. Taylor*, 481 U.S. 58, 62, 107 S.Ct. 1542, 95 L.Ed.2d 55 (1987) (holding that Employee Retirement Income Security Act (ERISA) preempts an employee's common-law contract and tort claims arising from employer's insurer's termination

of disability benefits, establishing federal jurisdiction); *Avco Corp. v. Aero Lodge No. 735, Int'l Ass'n. of Machinists*, 390 U.S. 557, 560, 88 S.Ct. 1235, 20 L.Ed.2d 126 (1968) (holding that section 301 of Labor Management Relations Act (LMRA) preempts any state cause of action for violation of contracts between an employer and a labor organization).

[24] It appears that the issue of whether or not the CISG preempts state law is a matter of first impression. In the case of federal statutes, "[t]he question of whether a certain action is preempted by federal law is one of congressional intent. The purpose of Congress is the ultimate touchstone." *Pilot Life Ins. Co. v. Dedeaux*, 481 U.S. 41, 45, 107 S.Ct. 1549, 95 L.Ed.2d 39 (1987) (internal quotations and citations omitted). Transferring this analysis to the question of preemption by a treaty, the Court focuses on the intent of the treaty's contracting parties. See *Husmann v. Trans World Airlines, Inc.*, 169 F.3d 1151, 1153 (8th Cir.1999) (finding Warsaw Convention preempts state law personal injury claim); *Jack v. Trans World Airlines, Inc.*, 820 F.Supp. 1218, 1220 (N.D.Cal.1993) (finding removal proper because Warsaw Convention preempts state law causes of action).

[25] In the case of the CISG treaty, this intent can be discerned from the introductory text, which states that "the adoption of uniform rules which govern contracts for the international sale of goods and take into account the different social, economic and legal systems would contribute to the removal of legal barriers in international trade and promote the development of international trade." 15 U.S.C.App. at 53. The CISG further recognizes the importance of "the development of international trade on the basis of equality and mutual benefit." Id. These objectives are reiterated in the President's Letter of Transmittal of the CISG to the Senate as well as the Secretary of State's Letter of Submittal of the CISG to the President. Id. at 70–72. The Secretary of State, George P. Shultz, noted:

> Sales transactions that cross international boundaries are subject to legal uncertainty—doubt as to which legal system will apply and the difficulty of coping with unfamiliar foreign law. The sales contract may specify which law will apply, but our sellers and buyers cannot expect that foreign trading partners will always agree on the applicability of United States law. . . . The Convention's approach provides an effective solution for this difficult problem. When a contract for an international sale of goods does not make clear what rule of law applies, the Convention provides uniform rules to govern the questions that arise in making and performance of the contract. (Id. at 71.)

[26] The Court concludes that the expressly stated goal of developing uniform international contract law to promote international trade indicates the intent of the parties to the treaty to have the treaty preempt state law causes of action.

[27] The availability of independent state contract law causes of action would frustrate the goals of uniformity and certainty embraced by the CISG. Allowing such avenues for potential liability would subject contracting parties to different states'

laws and the very same ambiguities regarding international contracts that the CISG was designed to avoid. As a consequence, parties to international contracts would be unable to predict the applicable law, and the fundamental purpose of the CISG would be undermined. Based on very similar rationale, courts have concluded that the Warsaw Convention preempts state law causes of action. *Husmann,* 169 F.3d at 1153; *Shah v. Pan American World Services, Inc.,* 148 F.3d 84, 97–98 (2d Cir.1998); *Potter v. Delta Air Lines*, 98 F.3d 881, 885 (5th Cir.1996); *Boehringer-Mannheim Diagnostics v. Pan Am. World*, 737 F.2d 456, 459 (5th Cir.1984). The conclusion that the CISG preempts state law also comports with the view of academic commentators on the subject. See William S. Dodge, Teaching the CISG in Contracts, 50 J. Legal Educ. 72, 72 (March 2000) ("As a treaty the CISG is federal law, which preempts state common law and the UCC."); David Frisch, Commercial Common Law, The United Nations Convention on the International Sale of Goods, and the Inertia of Habit, 74 Tul. L.Rev. 495, 503–04 (1999) ("Since the CISG has the preemptive force of federal law, it will preempt article 2 when applicable.").

[28] Furthermore, the Court has considered Plaintiff's arguments and finds them unpersuasive. Plaintiff argues that the CISG is incomparable to preemption under the Warsaw Convention, because "the CISG leaves open the possibility of other, concurrent causes of action." (Reply Brief at 9.) This argument merely begs the question by assuming that the state law causes of action asserted by Plaintiff are properly brought. Based on the proper applicable legal analysis discussed above, the Court concludes that the pleaded state law claims are preempted.

[29] Plaintiff next claims that the CISG does not completely supplant state law, because the CISG is limited in scope to the formation of the contract and the rights and obligations of the seller and buyer arising from the contract. (Id.) Plaintiff's correct observation that the CISG does not concern the validity of the contract or the effect which the contract may have on the property in the goods sold fails to support Plaintiff's conclusion that the CISG does not supplant any area of state contract law. Although the CISG is plainly limited in its scope (15 U.S.C.App., Art. 4.), the CISG nevertheless can and does preempt state contract law to the extent that the state causes of action fall within the scope of the CISG. . . .

[30] Finally, Plaintiff appears to confuse the matter of exclusive federal jurisdiction with preemption. Plaintiff first asserts that "[i]f . . . the CISG is 'state law' . . . then the California courts have jurisdiction to adjudicate a case arising under these laws." (Reply Brief at 9.) The matter of whether California courts may have jurisdiction to interpret the CISG is irrelevant to the determination of whether the CISG preempts state law and establishes federal jurisdiction over the case. Even where federal law completely preempts state law, state courts may have concurrent jurisdiction over the federal claim if the defendant does not remove the case to federal court. *Teamsters v. Lucas Flour Co.,* 369 U.S. 95, 103–04, 82 S.Ct. 571, 7 L.Ed.2d 593 (1962). This Court does not hold that it has exclusive jurisdiction over CISG claims. Hence, the Court's conclusion that the CISG preempts state claims is not inconsistent with Plaintiff's examples of the adjudication of CISG-based claims in

state court. Plaintiff further asserts that "if the CISG so completely supplants state law as to deny the California courts the opportunity to rule on a CISG cause of action, then the reference to 'state law' in Asante's choice-of-law provision is unambiguous, and the CISG also does not apply." . . . The Court also rejects this claim, as the determination of CISG preemption is wholly independent of the question of whether a choice-of-law clause in a particular contract is ambiguous or not.

[31] The Court concludes that the well-pleaded complaint rule does not preclude federal jurisdiction in this case, because the CISG preempts state law causes of action falling within the scope of the CISG.

V. Conclusion

[32] For the foregoing reasons, Plaintiff's Motion to Remand is DENIED. Accordingly, the Request for Attorney's Fees is also DENIED.

Notes and Questions

1. *Asante* is a classic in many respects. Both parties first incorporate in Delaware, although neither of them has any actual business there. Next, they do not sign a proper sales agreement but work from purchase orders that do not include choice of law or choice of forum clauses in the negotiated front of the contract. Instead, each side relies on its own "General Terms and Conditions," which naturally designate different applicable laws and are either silent or inconclusive about forum. As a consequence, a first round of litigation is entirely about the applicable law and the appropriate forum for the actual dispute, to be conducted later. The demand for attorney fees for this preliminary litigation is a reminder that such an exercise is not only an enormous waste of time but also money.

2. What were the consequences of the party choices—or the failure to make effective choices—for the applicable law and the jurisdiction of the court?

3. What do you think of the court's discussion of the question of agency, i.e., whether Unique Technologies in the U.S. was an agent for PMC-Sierra or just a distributor? Since when and under which rules does the domicile of an agent determine the law applicable to the contract concluded by the principal?

4. What about the fact that both parties were Delaware corporations? Shouldn't this fact alone make the case a domestic case, rather than one involving parties from different countries? Why or why not?

5. As a rule, does applicability of the CISG displace state law in the U.S.? Comprehensively? What about the issues where the CISG has gaps?

6. If there is a need to apply the contract law of one of the several states of the U.S., does this lead to the application of that state's version of the UCC? Or to the common law of contract, as evidenced by the case law of the courts of that state?

7. If there ever should be a need to apply the common law of contract of one of the several states of the U.S. to an IBT, how can an out-of-state party or lawyer, let alone

a foreign party or lawyer, gain a reasonably good idea of that contract law without studying dozens or even hundreds of individual judgments, many of which may be hard to understand and potentially incoherent?

––––––––––

The next case is an example of how far lawyers and even judges will go in order to *not* apply the CISG. When reading the judgment, consider what the judge is doing wrong. Wouldn't it make more sense to expend this kind of energy and effort to study the CISG, rather than the incorrect ways of how to hopefully avoid it?

Case 2-4

Barbara Berry v. Ken M. Spooner Farms

2009 WL 927704 (W.D. Wash. 2006)
(Paragraph numbers added, some footnotes and details omitted.)
ORDER GRANTING DEFENDANT'S MOTION FOR SUMMARY JUDGMENT
FRANKLIN D. BURGESS, District Judge.

Introduction

[1] The case summary provided in the Joint Status Report states that this is a case involving a contract between the parties whereby Spooner Farms agreed to provide viable raspberry roots to Berry for the Purpose of planting and producing commercial quality raspberry fruit in Mexico. Berry alleged breach of contract in that the product sold by Spooner Farms was defective and caused Berry to incur damages.

[2] Plaintiff Barbara Berry S.A. de C.V. (Barbara Berry or Berry) is a corporation formed under the laws of Mexico with its principal place of business located in Los Reyes, Michoacan, Mexico. Defendant Ken M. Spooner Farms, Inc. (Spooner Farms) is a Washington corporation with its principal place of business located in Puyallup, Washington.

[3] Defendant Spooner Farms moves for summary judgment based on a written exclusionary clause that excludes Spooner Farms from all liability for Barbara Berry's Claim. Berry disputes this claim contending that what is involved is an oral contract for the sale of raspberry roots, that the warranty disclaimer was not negotiated, was unknown to Berry at the time the contract was formed, and was not delivered to Berry until after the roots were paid for and delivered to Mexico. Berry also contends that the contract is governed by the United Nations Convention on Contracts for the International Sale of Goods (CISG) rather than the Uniform Commercial Code (UCC).

Summary Judgment Standard

[4] Summary judgment is proper if the moving party establishes that there are no genuine issues of material fact and it is entitled to judgment as a matter of law. Fed.R.Civ.P. 56(c). If the moving party shows that there are no genuine issues of material fact, the non-moving party must go beyond the pleadings and designate

facts showing an issue for trial. *Celotex Corp. v. Catrett*, 477 U.S. 317, 322-323 (1986). Inferences drawn from the facts are viewed in favor of the non-moving party. *T.W. Elec. Service v. Pacific Elec. Contractors*, 809 F.2d 626, 630-31 (9th Cir.1987).

[5] Summary judgment is proper if a defendant shows that there is no evidence supporting an element essential to a plaintiff's claim. *Celotex Corp. v. Catrett*, 477 U.S. 317 (1986). Failure of proof as to any essential element of plaintiff's claims means that no genuine issue of material fact can exist and summary judgment is mandated. *Celotex*, 477 U.S. 317, 322-23 (1986). The nonmoving party "must do more than show there is some metaphysical doubt as to the material facts." *Matsushita Elec. Indus. Co. v. Zenith Radio Corp.*, 475 U.S. 574, 586 (1986).

Applicable Law

[6] The CISG does not govern the enforceability of the exclusionary clause pursuant to an express provision in the CISG. The CISG provides at Article 4 in pertinent part:

> This Convention governs only the formation of the contract of sale and the rights and obligations of the seller and the buyer arising from such a contract. In particular, except as otherwise expressly provided in this Convention, it is not concerned with:
>
> (a) the validity of the contract or of any of its provisions or of any usage;

[7] Whether a clause in a contract is valid and enforceable is decided under domestic law, not the CISG. *Geneva Pharmaceuticals Technology Corp. v. Barr Laboratories, Inc.*, 201 F.Supp.2d 236 S.D.N.Y. (2002), reversed on other grounds, 386 F.3d 485 (2004). The Geneva Court stated:

> Under the CISG, the validity of an alleged contract is decided under domestic law. By validity, CISG refers to any issue by which the "domestic law would render the contract void, voidable, unenforceable." *Geneva Pharmaceuticals* at 282.

[8] In Washington, the consistent rule has been that the exchange of purchase orders or invoices between merchants forms a written contract, and the terms contained therein are enforceable. *M.A. Mortenson Co., Inc. v. Timberline Software Corp.*, 140 Wn.2d 568, 580-85 (2000) . . . ; *Puget Sound Financial, L.L.C. v. Unisearch, Inc.*, 146 Wn.2d 437 (2002), . . . ; *Smith v. Skone & Connors Produce, Ins.*, 107 Wn.App. 199, 207 (2001). . . .

[9] A limitation of liability clause is enforceable unless it is unconscionable. *Puget Sound Financial*, 146 Wn.2d at 440. Whether an exclusionary clause is unconscionable is determined as a matter of law. Id. at 438. *Mortenson*, 140 Wn.2d at 586. In a commercial transaction, exclusionary clauses are prima facie conscionable, and the burden of establishing unconscionability is on the party attacking the clause. *Mortenson*, 140 Wn.2d at 585-86.

[10] There are two types of unconscionability in contracts in Washington: (1) substantive unconscionability, involving those cases where a clause in the contract is

"shocking to the conscience." and (2) procedural unconscionability, which relates to impropriety during the process of forming the contract. Id. at 586.

[11] With regard to "substantive unconscionability," the Washington Supreme Court stated: "As an initial matter, it is questionable whether clauses excluding consequential damages in a commercial contract can ever be substantively unconscionable." *Mortenson*. 140 Wn.2d at 586. The Court in Mortenson cited *Tacoma Boatbuilding Co. v. Delta Fishing Co.*, 28 U.C.C. Rep. Serv. 26, 35 (W.D. Wash 1980) where the District Court stated in rejecting an argument that the limitation clause therein was unconscionable:

> Comment 3 to [U.C.C.] § 2-719 generally approves consequential damage exclusions as "merely an allocation of unknown or undeterminable risks." Thus, the presence of latent defects in the goods cannot render these clauses unconscionable. The need for certainty in risk-allocation is especially compelling where, as here, the goods are experimental and their performance by nature less predictable.

[12] With regard to "procedural unconscionability" in commercial transactions, the concern is that there is no "unfair surprise" to the detriment of one of the parties. *Puget Sound Financial*, 146 Wn.2d at 439-41. The Washington Supreme Court uses a "totality of the circumstances" approach to making the determination of procedural unconscionability. *Mortenson*, 140 Wn.2d at 588. There is a non-exclusive list of factors for assessing the totality of the circumstances, which include: (1) the conspicuousness of the clause in the agreement, which includes whether the important terms were "hidden in a maze of fine print"; (2) the manner in which the parties entered into the contract, which includes whether the parties had reasonable opportunity to understand the terms of the contract; (3) the custom and usage of the trade; and (4) the course of dealing between the parties. *Puget Sound Financial*, 146 Wn.2d at 442-44.

Analysis and Conclusion

[13] For the following reasons, the Court concludes that the exclusionary clause at issue herein is valid and precludes Plaintiff's claim.

[14] The Warranty and Limitation of Liability at issue is set forth in full in the Defendant's Motion for Summary Judgment. While Ken M. Spooner Farms, Inc. does warrant that "the product variety will be true to name" and that it will "replace, free of charge, nursery stock that is proven to be untrue to name, or refund the original amount paid, at our option," the limitation states in capital letters:

> Buyer, and Any Purchaser from Buyer, Acknowledges and Agrees That Seller Makes No Warranty as to the Productivity or Performance of the Nursery Stock and Buyer, and Any Purchaser from Buyer, Further Acknowledges and Agrees to Accept the Entire Risk as to Quality, Performance and Viability of Nursery Stock and That All Items Are Sold "As Is" and with All Faults. . . . in No Event Shall Seller Be Liable for Any Direct, Indirect, Special or Incidental or Consequential Damages (Including Loss of Profits

and Recovery for Attorney's Fees) Whether Based on Contract, Tort or Any Other Legal Theory.

[15] . . . Plaintiff Berry had more than one opportunity to read the terms of the exclusionary clause. On February 17, 2004, the original documents were delivered to DHL/Danzas in Guadalajara, where the raspberry stock was delivered, and Berry admits by email that it was notified of this delivery. . . .

[16] On February 25, 2004, a second delivery of the original invoice before shipment of the product was sent to Sun Belle Berries, designated by Plaintiff Berry. . . . Plaintiff Berry's contention that its agent Sun Belle did not provide it with the documents is unavailing under basic agency principles, acknowledged by the UCC. . . . "The general rule is that "the principal is bound by the act of his agent when he has placed the agent in such position that persons of ordinary prudence, reasonably conversant with business usages and customs, are thereby led to believe and assume that the agent is possessed of certain authority, and to deal with him in reliance upon such assumption." E.g., *Schoonover v. Carpet World, Inc.*, 91 Wn.2d 173, 176-77 (1978).

[17] A third delivery of the documents was made by fax on February 25, 2004 to Plaintiff Berry's agent Sun Belle. Spooner Farms notes that Berry's contentions that it did not receive the original invoices fails because (1) the raspberry stock could not be released from customs unless the original invoice — not a copy — was provided, and this is why Spooner Farms sends multiple original invoices approximately a week prior to shipment of the product . . . , and (2) Plaintiff Berry produced in its initial disclosure the entire terms of sale containing the exclusionary clause, in a font different from that printed on the boxes of the raspberry roots.

[18] Finally, the exclusionary clause was printed in bright red on top of all 63 boxes of raspberry planting stock, and there is no dispute that Plaintiff Berry received and opened these boxes. Even if this were the only notice of the exclusionary clause, similar to the case in *Mortenson*, the clause is conscionable and enforceable.

[19] Even if the CISG did apply, the exclusionary clause is still enforceable because Plaintiff paid the price for the goods and opened the package where the exclusionary clause was prominently displayed on top in red. (Article 18(3): "assent by performing an act, such as one relating to the dispatch of the goods or payment of the price . . ."; Article 18(1): an additional term can be accepted by "conduct by the offeree indicating assent.") Also, under Article 9(2), "the parties are considered, unless otherwise agreed, to have impliedly made applicable to their contract or its formation a usage of which the parties knew or ought to have known and which in international trade is widely known to, and regularly observed by, parties to contracts of the type involved in the particular trade concerned." It appears that the placement of oral orders for goods followed by invoices with sales terms is commonplace, and while every term of the contract is not usually part of the oral discussion, subsequent written confirmation containing additional terms are binding unless timely objected to. See, e.g., *W.T. GmbH v. P. AG*, No. P4 1991/238 (ZG Basel, Switz. Dec. 21, 1992).

[20] Spooner Farms' exclusionary clause is valid, it is not unconscionable, it is of a type commonly used in the nursery stock trade, and Plaintiff had ample opportunity to read the exclusion, which was prominently displayed in the invoices and on the shipping crates. Acceptance of Plaintiff's argument would result in sellers of nursery stock being virtual insurers of the crop regardless of the vagaries of the weather or the individual farmer's practices or other influences over which the nursery has no control.

ACCORDINGLY, IT IS ORDERED:

1. Defendant's Motion for Summary Judgment . . . is GRANTED. . . .

Notes and Questions

1. Judge Burgess relies on the fact that the CISG supposedly does not deal with questions of validity of the contract (CISG Art. 4(a)) to decide that it does not apply to the question whether a limitation of liability was validly included in a contract. What kind of validity issues are excluded from the scope of application of the CISG by its Article 4(a)?

2. The plaintiff claims that the contract was concluded orally and that limitations of liability were not discussed or disclosed at the contract formation stage. Why does the Judge not discuss questions of contract formation?

3. The Judge goes to significant lengths to show that the plaintiff was given the relevant provisions excluding seller's liability in the documents shipped for customs clearance and also "printed in bright red on top of all 63 boxes of raspberry planting stock." What is the relevance of limitation clauses made available after a contract was already concluded without them?

4. What do you think of the passage in paragraph 19 of the judgment, "[e]ven if the CISG did apply, the exclusionary clause is still enforceable because the plaintiff paid the price for the goods and opened the packages where the exclusionary clause was prominently displayed on top in red"?

———————

Our preliminary conclusion from these cases is that competence in the correct application of the rules on conflict of laws, choice of law and forum, and any questions related to the CISG cannot be taken for granted. Attorneys and judges should have had plenty of time to integrate the CISG and various other international law rules into their practice—but, if the truth be told, many of them still don't. Other than working only with counsel able to show a proven track record in these areas of business and law, parties can best protect themselves with unambiguous contracts along the model we shall discuss on pp. 331–354.

After having determined the applicable law, the next major step is a careful analysis of contract formation, validity, and interpretation. It is impossible to determine the rights and obligations of the parties without a careful analysis of which terms made it into the contract, whether they are valid, and how they have to be interpreted.

7. Summary: What to Do and What Not to Do about Choice of Law and Choice of Forum

- When drafting a contract for an international business transaction, whether a sales contract, a services contract, a loan contract, or a larger investment contract, *always* include a choice of law and a choice of forum clause covering the entire business relationship between the parties initiated or expanded by the contract at issue, not just the rights and obligations under the present contract itself.

- Any time more than one contract or more than two parties are involved in the same IBT, it is highly desirable to have *the same choice of law and choice of forum clauses* across the entire IBT. Otherwise it may well happen that disputes over different aspects of one and the same IBT or between different parties to one and the same IBT have to be taken to different fora and/or decided under different legal regimes. This is wasteful and can lead to conflicting outcomes.

- While arbitrators can be selected to be competent to handle pretty much any set of rules, *never* force regular judges to apply a legal system other than their own.[82] In many countries, the CISG may be the applicable contract law if both parties to a sale are domiciled in Contracting States, but for the average judge the CISG may still be a foreign legal system.

- *Every time* a choice of law is made in favor of a transnational set of rules, in particular the CISG, be sure to also make a choice for a backup system, i.e., a national law that applies to any questions not covered by the transnational law.

- Remember that the CISG is the default contract law whenever both parties to a contract of sale are domiciled in Contracting States unless it is explicitly excluded. *Never* exclude the CISG, however, without thinking about the specific consequences this will have for the client.

- *Never* make a choice in favor of a neutral third-country law without very good reasons for doing so. The mere fact that the chosen law is foreign for both parties and their lawyers is not a good enough reason.

- The CISG and, even more so, the CFR, are much better choices for a *neutral* system that is equally accessible and familiar or unfamiliar to both sides than a neutral third-country law.

- Whenever a dispute arises and it becomes apparent that the underlying contract or contracts were drafted without any choice of law or choice of forum clauses or with less than ideal clauses, *try to get the parties to agree retrospectively* to better choice of law and choice of forum clauses. To this end, use economic

---

82. For more information, see Sofie Geeroms, *Foreign Law in Civil Litigation—A Comparative and Functional Analysis*, Oxford Univ. Press 2004; and Michael James, *Litigation with a Foreign Aspect—A Practical Guide*, Oxford Univ. Press 2009.

arguments and the desire of the parties to put the dispute behind them and get back to business.

- In sum, make *a choice for national courts* only if they meet the criteria we will discuss at length in Part Six, in particular that presenting the case to them can be done in an economically efficient way and that they will normally provide a fair and well-reasoned decision within a year or so. Furthermore, make a choice for these same national courts only if you are willing to subject the IBT to the normal contract law applicable in that jurisdiction.

- Although *arbitration* can be more expensive than litigation, there are ways to contain the cost of arbitration. In any case, once there is an appeal against a trial court judgment, not only the time, but also the money spent in litigation, is likely to exceed the cost of arbitration. Thus, do not disregard arbitration on account of its actual or perceived cost. Make the choice for or against arbitration after careful analysis of its pros and cons as outlined in detail in Part Six.

Section 5. Contract Formation, Validity, and Interpretation

A. Introduction

Contractual claims are by far the most important claims resulting from B2B transactions. The other types of claims discussed on p. 43, note 32, and pp. 95–96 play a relatively minor role.

As the name suggests, contractual claims are based on the contract concluded between the parties to a transaction. We have already seen above that the statutory provisions of the CISG or the UCC or any other applicable contract law yield in most cases to the specific agreement between the parties. It is therefore of paramount importance that we establish exactly what the parties have agreed between themselves. This is often easier said than done. In an ideal scenario, the parties will have only one written contract and it will contain only clear and straightforward rights and obligations for the seller and buyer. In such a case, it should be quite easy to establish whether each side has fulfilled its obligations and is entitled to the goods or services, or to get paid. Lawyers might only be required to determine the consequences of a breach or potential breach by either side. We will discuss issues related to performance, nonperformance, and related remedies below in Section 7.

However, the ideal scenario of only one written contract with perfectly clear provisions is rare in practice. More likely than not, the parties exchanged an entire series of written and oral communications, possibly sent back and forth a number of contract drafts, and continued to negotiate changes or exceptions or waivers regarding product qualities or delivery dates even after a formal contract was signed. Unless every communication is properly qualified, it will be impossible to determine exactly what the parties have agreed. Was the request for a pro-forma invoice an offer? Did the seller accept the buyer's terms during the phone call of March 20? Were the general terms from the website of the seller effectively incorporated into the contract? Was the delivery date modified when the seller gave notice of the delay in shipping and the buyer did not protest?

Since students and less experienced lawyers often struggle with issues related to contract formation, I am including a chart with most types of communications that may have been exchanged between the parties and their meaning in law. Readers should carefully consider these options and their impact on contract formation and interpretation and then check the case law reproduced further below to see how the courts are handling the issues in practice.

In line with the recommendations on pp. 53 et seq. on how to analyze a case and write a persuasive brief or exam, we need to draw up a time line of events that happened in the context of contract formation—from the first contacts between the parties about the IBT in question to the last communication about performance. Then we have to classify these events—written and oral communications and even nonverbal acts and omissions—to understand their possible relevance in law:

Checklist 2-1
Legal Classification of Verbal Communication and Nonverbal Acts
Related to Formation and Interpretation of Contracts

A. Verbal communication and nonverbal acts *before/until the contract* is formed

#1 General communication or acts *not specific enough* to constitute an offer or acceptance but relevant to the formation or interpretation of a subsequently concluded contract, e.g., exchange of marketing material, personal or product related information.

#2 Invitation to make an offer (Art. 14(2) CISG; §§ 2-202–206 UCC)

#3 Offer (Art. 14(1) CISG; §§ 2-202–206 UCC)

#4 Acceptance with or without modifications (Art. 18(1) CISG; §§ 2-202–206 UCC)

#5 Rejection or rejection with counteroffer (Arts. 17, 19 CISG; §§ 2-202–206 UCC)

#6 Other communication or acts *not relevant* to the formation or interpretation of the contract, e.g., communication with third parties

B. Verbal communication and nonverbal acts *after the contract* is formed

#7 Offer to modify or cancel all or part of the contractual obligations

#8 Rejection of #7 or rejection with counteroffer

#9 Acceptance to modify or cancel all or part of the contractual obligations

#10 Other communication or act *relevant* to the interpretation of the contractual obligations, e.g., clarifications of earlier communications or acts (Art. 65 CISG)

#11 Other communication or acts *not relevant* to the interpretation of the contractual obligations, e.g., communication with third parties

#12 Communication or act in partial or full *performance* of the contractual obligation, e.g., timely delivery, delivery of conforming goods, taking delivery, payment of price, but also notification of changes in time or place of delivery that do not amount to a breach (Arts. 31–37, 41 CISG; §§ 2-313, 2-314 UCC)

#13 Communication or act in partial or full *breach* of the contractual obligation, e.g., notification that delivery will be late, or non-conforming delivery, failure to take delivery, or failure to pay

#14 Suspension of performance and/or preventive avoidance for anticipated breach by other side (Arts. 71, 72 CISG; §§ 2-609, 2-610 UCC)

C. Verbal communication and nonverbal acts *after a breach* of the contract

#15 Notification of nonconformity of performance (Arts. 38, 39 CISG; §§ 2-607(3), 2-508 UCC)

#16 Notification of third party claims (Art. 43 CISG; § 2-607(3)(b) UCC)

#17 Communication setting additional time limit for performance (Arts. 47, 63 CISG)

#18 Communication of claim seeking first performance or cure after partial or nonconforming performance (CISG Arts. 46 (buyer), 62 (seller); UCC §§ 2-711, 2-716 (buyer), 2-709 (seller))

#19 Acceptance of nonconforming goods for reduced price (Art. 50 CISG)

#20 Declaration of avoidance of the contract (Arts. 26, 49, 64, 25, 81, 82, 84 CISG; R § 378 et seq.)

#21 Communication or act effecting cover transaction (Art. 75 CISG; §§ 2-706, 2-712 UCC) or other measures to mitigate damages (Arts. 77, 85–88 CISG; § 2-715(2)(a) UCC and R § 347)

#22 Communication of claim for damages and interest (Art. 74 CISG; §§ 2-703, 2-711 UCC)

#23 Initiation of litigation or arbitration to enforce claims

#24 Communication of claim for attorney fees and cost of legal procedures

Checklist 2-1 Explained

#1 In general, communications not addressed to specific persons, such as websites and sales brochures, are at best invitations to make an offer. Even if legally relevant documents are exchanged, they do not amount to offer and acceptance if they are about other matters. For example, even if two traders conclude a nondisclosure agreement (see above, pp. 87–95), this generally does not compel them to also enter into a contract of sale or other IBT. However, business communications and agreements related to an IBT—or even unrelated communications and agreements—may play a role if ambiguous statements or clauses in a subsequent contract need to be interpreted.

#2 The line between a mere invitation and an actual offer is not always clear and may have to be drawn by partisan attorneys in the best interest of their clients with persuasive arguments. Whenever there could be a dispute over contract formation, i.e., *when* a contract has been concluded via offer and acceptance and *what terms* made it into that contract, lawyers should analyze each communication between the parties in chronological order and assign labels such as "mere preliminary communication," "invitation to make an offer," "offer," "acceptance," "acceptance with modifications," "rejection," "rejection with counteroffer," etc. The labels have to be supported with persuasive arguments pursuant to the four levels of analysis (above, pp. 66, 68).

The most important difference between an offer and a mere invitation to make an offer is the number of potential parties addressed. A website can be accessed by an unlimited number of potential buyers or sellers. Unless the owner of the website is willing and able to buy or sell to all of them, the website cannot be an offer.

#3 Another difference between a mere invitation and an actual offer is the degree of specificity with regard to the goods. A communication amounts to an offer, if it provides the necessary information for the determination of the five essential elements of a contract of sale (compare Art. 14(1) CISG):

i.   identity of the seller,

ii.   identity of the buyer,

iii. the goods to be sold,

iv.   the quantity of the goods to be sold, and

v.   the price.

The litmus test is whether the other side can simply say "I accept" and, thereby, nail down an agreement about all five essential elements of the sale. If the other side has to ask questions such as "yes, but how many do you want?" the contract has not been formed and the communications are still only on the level of invitations.

A problem occurring rather frequently in practice is implied terms. For example, the parties to an IBT may not talk at all about the price to be paid, if it is customary in the industry to pay whatever is the current market price for the goods (compare Art. 55 CISG).

We should also note that certain information, such as time and place of performance, is not essential for a contract to be formed, in particular if it can be supplied by law (e.g., Arts. 31 and 33 CISG; §§ 2-308 and 2-309 UCC) or industry custom.

Once we have identified an offer, there are six possible responses from the other side:

i.   simple acceptance, essentially a "yes," communicated verbally or by conduct;

ii.   acceptance with minor modifications;

iii. "acceptance" with major modifications is equivalent to rejection plus counteroffer;

iv.   simple rejection, essentially a "no";

v.   rejection plus counteroffer;

vi.   no response at all equates to rejection.

From a legal perspective, since silence or inactivity on its own does not amount to an acceptance (Art. 18(1)[2] CISG),[83] these can be condensed into just two main categories with two subcategories each, namely:

i.   acceptance, with or without minor modifications or

ii.   rejection, with or without counteroffer.

We will discuss these in turn.

#4   Both the CISG and the UCC provide for acceptance to be communicated verbally or by conduct, in particular by shipping of the goods (seller) or making payment (buyer) (cf. Art. 18(1)[1] CISG; § 2-206(1)(a) and (2) UCC).

If there is a straightforward acceptance of an offer, without modifications, one or both of the following issues may still need to be discussed:[84]

---

83. The UCC does not explicitly state that silence does not amount to acceptance. The Restatement (Second) of Contracts, in § 69, provides a more comprehensive and differentiated answer: In general, silence does not amount to acceptance. There are three exceptions, however: (a) if the offeree "*takes the benefit* of offered services" although he could have rejected them and had "reason to know that they were offered with the expectation of compensation"; (b) if the offeror stated that "assent may be manifested by silence or inaction" and the offeree, "in remaining silent and inactive *intends* to accept the offer"; and (c) where it is reasonable, on the basis of *previous dealings* between the parties "that the offeree should notify the offeror if he does not intend to accept" (emphasis added).

84. We are assuming that any form requirements are respected and that the intended transaction is not illegal or otherwise invalid.

— whether the person expressing acceptance has legal capacity to make the declaration on behalf of herself or the principal she is representing;

— whether the acceptance was timely.

As always, these questions have to be answered on the basis of the applicable law. The CISG does not deal with questions of legal capacity or agency. Recourse should be made to the backup legal system selected by the parties or, in the absence of such a choice, to the legal system applicable on the basis of conflict of laws rules/private international law. The UCC, like the CISG, does not cover legal capacity and agency. In the absence of federal law, these questions belong to the domain of state law in the U.S. Fortunately, at least for issues of agency, the Restatement (Third) of Agency provides comprehensive and straightforward answers. International arbitrators are also known to refer to Article 2.2 of the UNIDROIT PICC as an international instrument providing equitable solutions removed from any one side's domestic legal system.

Whether an acceptance was timely is dealt with in the CISG but not in the UCC. Section 41 of the Restatement stipulates that "[a]n offeree's power of acceptance is terminated at the time specified in the offer, or, if no time is specified, at the end of a reasonable time." The same language is used in Article 18(2) of the CISG: "An acceptance is not effective if the indication of assent does not reach the offeror within the time he has fixed or, if no time is fixed, within a reasonable time." What is "a reasonable time" has been dealt with in case law. Among the factors to be taken into consideration are the complexity of the offer and transaction, and the means of communication applied by the parties. Complex offers require more time to be studied and understood. The time for communications to run back and forth has to be added. In an oral negotiation, there may be an expectation of immediate response. When fax or e-mail is used, there will also be an expectation of rather swift communication. By contrast, if regular mail is being used in international negotiations, the offeror will not reasonably expect an answer for several days or even weeks. Another set of factors to be taken into consideration are the customs in the respective industry and the likelihood that changes of outside circumstances—such as price fluctuations in the marketplace—affect the balance of rights and obligations. In rapidly changing markets, it is highly unlikely that an offeror wants to keep his offer open for any extended period.

If an acceptance is communicated with additional and/or different terms, several scenarios have to be distinguished. Under § 2-207(1) UCC, an acceptance may contain additional and different terms. Whether they make it into the contract is determined under § 2-207(2) UCC.

An earlier version of the UCC, in line with older common law, provided the so-called mirror image rule. At common law, only a response mirroring precisely the terms of the offer was an acceptance. Any deviation caused the response to be a rejection with a counteroffer and no contract was made unless that counteroffer was accepted. The UCC was just a little bit less strict. Pursuant to the old § 2-207, a contract could be formed even if the parties had not agreed on all the details. In such a case, the terms of the contract were "(a) terms that appear in the records of both parties; (b) terms, whether in a record or not, to which both parties agree; and (c) terms supplied [by law]". In practice, this meant that the parties still had to be in agreement about the five essentials of the contract (the front of the contract) but not about all the details in the other terms (the back of the contract). Specifically, in the battle of forms only the terms that were contained or mirrored in both sets made it into the contract. Any terms found only in the seller's or only in the buyer's terms were simply ignored (cf. the decision in *Hanwha v. Cedar Petrochemicals*, below, p. 210, at para. 14).

The current version of the UCC has abandoned this mirror image rule and replaced it with the following language in § 2-207 (see also the discussion in *Northrop v. Litronic Industries*, below, p. 230):

(1) A definite and seasonable expression of acceptance or a written confirmation which is sent within a reasonable time operates as an acceptance even though it states terms additional to or different from those offered or agreed upon, unless acceptance is expressly made conditional on assent to the additional or different terms.

(2) The additional terms are to be construed as proposals for addition to the contract. Between merchants such terms become part of the contract unless:

(a) the offer expressly limits acceptance to the terms of the offer;

(b) they materially alter it; or

(c) notification of objection to them has already been given or is given within a reasonable time after notice of them is received.

(3) Conduct by both parties which recognizes the existence of a contract is sufficient to establish a contract for sale although the writings of the parties do not otherwise establish a contract. In such case the terms of the particular contract consist of those terms on which the writings of the parties agree, together with any supplementary terms incorporated under any other provisions of this Act.

This gives us several options:

(i) Before performance or equivalent conduct:

1 if the offer expressly limits acceptance to the terms of the offer, an acceptance with different or additional terms is a rejection with a counteroffer; if nothing else happens, there is *no contract*;

2   if the offer did not expressly limit acceptance to the terms of the offer, an acceptance with different or additional terms is an acceptance with a proposal to modify the contract; if nothing else happens, *the contract is formed without the different or additional terms.*

(ii)   If the negotiations are "between merchants":

3   if the offer expressly limits acceptance to the terms of the offer, an acceptance with different or additional terms is a rejection with a counteroffer; if nothing else happens, *no contract* is formed;

4   if the offer did not expressly limit acceptance to the terms of the offer, an acceptance with different or additional terms is an acceptance and *the contract is formed with the different or additional terms,* unless

5   they "materially alter" the contract, or the offeree sends an objection. If either of those two conditions are met, *the contract is formed without the different or additional rules.*

(iii)   If the writings of the parties do not amount to an offer and an acceptance, of if we otherwise don't have a contract (our cases 1 and 3), yet the parties have proceeded with performance, indicating their opinion that a contract was formed, it would be very inconvenient, in most cases, to come to a conclusion that there was no contract and that everything has to be undone. Therefore, subsection (3) creates yet another solution:

6   if conduct by both parties "recognizes the existence of a contract . . . although the writings . . . do not otherwise establish a contract . . . the terms of the particular contract *consist of those terms on which the writings of the parties agree* . . ." (emphasis added).

The latter has been called the knock-out rule because inconsistent terms knock each other out and are replaced with statutory language and general principles, where necessary.

Now compare the language in the CISG. Under Article 19(1) CISG, a reply with additional and/or different terms is generally a rejection with a counteroffer. However, Article 19(2) makes an exception for different and/or additional terms, "which do not materially alter the terms of the offer," i.e., constitute only minor differences. Those become part of the contract, unless the offeror objects to them and notifies the offeree accordingly. This is called the last shot rule, since the last communication—unless objected to—determines the terms of the contract. Importantly, the last shot rule is limited by Article 19(3). Pursuant to this rule, additional and/or different terms "relating, among other things, to the price, payment, quality and quantity of the goods, place and time of delivery, extent of one party's liability to the other or the settlement of disputes *are considered to alter the terms of the offer materially*" (emphasis added) in the sense of Article 19(2) and, therefore, turn the purported acceptance into a rejection with a counteroffer.

Can you now explain what happens under the UCC if the parties trade inconsistent contract language for a while and then proceed with performance? And under the CISG? Which solution is more equitable? Why?[85]

#5   The communication of an unambiguous rejection terminates the offer. This is clear from Article 17 CISG. The UCC does not contain an explicit rule, but R § 38 is even clearer than the CISG—the offeree cannot accept after having rejected. If the offeree changes her mind, she has to make a new offer.

This is the same if the reply to the offer is intended and/or labeled as an "acceptance" but is so different from the offer that it cannot be understood as an acceptance (UCC/Restatement), or if it contains material alterations (CISG).

A rejection beyond a "no" is a counteroffer if it meets the standards for an offer, i.e., allows the determination of the five essentials of a contract. Since the counteroffer comes in the context of ongoing business negotiations, some of the essentials may be ascertainable from the earlier offers and counteroffers, provided it is clear which terms are intended to remain on the table and which are being changed.

#6   "Other communications" can be classified into two groups: First, there are possible communications between the parties to the IBT that do not amount to offers and acceptances or counteroffers or offers to modify an already existing contract. For example, if the seller sends additional information, like brochures, to the buyer, these will not be considered counteroffers or modifications on their own, even if they demonstrate potentially different qualities of the product. Second, there may be communications between one party to the IBT and a third party. Again, these will not be considered offers, acceptances, or counteroffers unless the other party is notified. For example, if the buyer applies for a letter of credit, this cannot be considered acceptance by conduct (payment) unless the seller is officially advised of

---

85. An interesting proposal was made by Professor Goldberg, namely to introduce the best shot rule. Goldberg wants to incentivize parties to draw up clear and fair standard form contracts, rather than increasingly self-serving forms, hoping that their last shot will be unopposed or accepted by conduct. Under his proposal, if there is a battle of forms, the court or arbitral tribunal would have to choose "the fairer of the two—the one closest to the "center." The court looks not to the first shot, nor the last shot; it looks to the *best shot*." See Victor P. Goldberg, *The "Battle of the Forms": Fairness, Efficiency, and the Best-Shot Rule,* 76 Or. L. Rev. 155 (1997), in particular p. 166. The problem in practice would be the assessment of what is fairer. Should the court or tribunal look at the entire package? But how would a limitation of liability in one form and a vote for arbitration in the other stack up? Or should the court or tribunal cherry-pick the best options for each subject, a little bit from this side and a little bit from that? Since this would not only be inefficient but also unpredictable, Goldberg advocates "the all-or-nothing approach" as "essential." "The more terms that are considered at the same time, the easier it will be to judge the overall reasonableness of the package." (Id., p. 166).

the L/C. Similarly, if the seller places an order for components with a third-party supplier, this alone does not mean that she is accepting the contract with the buyer, even if she intends to use the components to fulfill that contract if it does materialize.

Statements and conduct can generally only be relevant for the formation of a contract if they are directed at the other party or otherwise intentionally brought to their attention.

#7   Once a contract is formed, the parties are bound and cannot unilaterally change the terms. If one of the parties continues to send additional communications or engages in other conduct that indicates a desire to negotiate or change the terms, these are offers to modify the existing contract, whether the party realizes and agrees that there is already a contract in place or not. Importantly, the other side is under no obligation to accept these offers. While it would be practically advisable to notify rejection, silence must not be interpreted as acceptance unless the contract or a well-established custom indicate otherwise.

Along the same lines, a request to cancel the contract or be released from its obligations is merely an offer to enter into an agreement that revokes the earlier contract. Unless provided in that earlier contract, a right to unilaterally rescind or avoid the contract exists only under very specific conditions:

> CISG Articles 45, 49, 25, 26 and 81 (for the buyer), or Articles 61, 64, 25, 26 and 81 (for the seller), or Articles 72, 25, 26, and 81 (for either side), i.e., the requirement of a fundamental breach; or

> UCC §§ 2-601, 2-602, 2-711 UCC for the buyer, i.e., the perfect tender rule (but see limitations in § 1-304 if buyer acts in bad faith; § 2-504, minor delay; § 2-508, right to cure, and § 2-612, installment contracts require "substantial impairment"); or UCC §§ 2-702, 2-703 UCC for the seller.[86]

#8   If one side proposes to change or cancel the existing contract per #7, the other side is free to accept, reject, or ignore those proposals. Obviously, it is almost always better to communicate than to ignore such requests, even if silence will rarely be interpreted as acceptance. If the other side rejects, it can add a counteroffer of its own, for example, along the lines of "we can only accept your request to modify or cancel the existing contract if you pay us damages, under the following conditions. . . ."

Silence or rejection of the request discussed in #7 leaves the original contract in place.

If the #7 request is rejected with a counteroffer, the original contract may be modified if the counteroffer is accepted by the #7 proposer.

---

86. The Restatement deals with these issues in much greater detail, see in particular Chapters 10 and 16.

#9 If the #7 proposal is accepted, the original contract is modified accordingly (§ 2-209 UCC). This can range from minor changes—a later shipping date, for example—to the complete cancellation of the transaction. Unless the accepted #7 proposal included a change of the dispute settlement clauses (applicable law and forum), the original clauses remain in place even if the contract is modified without new clauses or canceled altogether.

#10 "Other communications" after conclusion of a contract can be important for the rights and obligations of the parties, e.g., related to qualities of the goods (Art. 65 CISG; § 2-311 UCC), **or** they are merely relevant for general interpretation of the contract without reaching the level of promises to be kept (e.g., informal inquiries about suitability of the goods for certain purposes, or requests for help/guidance with unpacking and installation).

relevant

#11 Besides the #10 communications, there are yet other communications that should not have any impact on the interpretation of the contract and/or the contractual rights and obligations of the parties. They may, however, play a role if there is a claim of fraud or other non-contractual claim. For example, if the seller expresses to third parties her intention not to honor the contract with the buyer or her opinion that the price was unfair or the goods unsuitable for buyer's purposes, this is not relevant from a contract law point of view, but it can be relevant from a tort perspective.

not relevant

#12 While #7 to #11 communications are less common, there will almost always be communications and actions of the parties in partial or complete fulfillment of their contractual obligations. Those amounting to partial or full performance generally do not raise concerns. Potentially problematic are unilateral acts that deviate from the contractual course of action or at least from the reasonable expectations of the other party. For example, if the seller notifies a delay with shipment, this could be a mere courtesy, a minor deviation that does not entitle the buyer to anything, a deviation that entitles the buyer to damages, or a fundamental breach that entitles the buyer to avoid the contract and procure the goods in a cover transaction and bill the extra cost to the original seller. Lawyers have to determine which is which on the basis of the original contract (e.g., whether timely delivery was of the essence), the significance of the delay, given the contractual and known intentions of the buyer (a day late may be insignificant for the delivery of a boat load of scrap metal but it can make all the difference for a wedding cake), and the cause for the delay and who is responsible for it (if shipping is delayed by a storm, the INCOTERM® will determine whether the risk has already passed from seller to buyer; even if the seller still bears the risk, she may not be liable for force majeure, cf. Art. 79 CISG).

#13 Communications or actions/omissions that are incompatible with the contract, the law, and/or reasonable expectations of the other side have to be classified in several ways:

- Importance (Fundamental breach under Art. 25 CISG? Material breach as required in some cases under the UCC? Any other breach with limited consequences?)

- Responsibility (Did the risk pass? Is anybody at fault?)

- Consequences (Which primary and/or secondary remedies are available?)

- Procedure (Which steps are needed or have already been taken, e.g., a declaration of avoidance, and what do they mean for available remedies?)

Nota bene: In most cases, the parties have the following claims after a breach: (i) contractual (or primary) remedies, (ii) damages (secondary remedies), (iii) costs, and (iv) interest. The primary remedies, such as making/repeating (specific) performance, getting paid under the contract, curing an imperfect performance, or reducing the price for an imperfect performance, are eliminated if the contract is avoided. Thus, a contract should not be avoided if contractual remedies are still of interest. Additional damages are available with or without the contract to compensate for other consequences of the breach.

#14 Under both CISG (Arts. 71, 72, 73) and UCC (§§ 2-609, 2-610), if a party has reasons to be insecure whether the other side is willing and able to perform, she can ask for adequate assurances of performance and, if those are not provided, suspend her own performance until such assurances are given or the other side performs. However, if the first party does not have sufficient reasons for making these demands, she will herself be held in breach.

#15 The buyer has to inspect the goods and notify the seller of any issues with conformity. If the buyer fails to inspect and notify within a reasonable time, he may lose various rights. What is considered a reasonable time for the inspection has to be determined based on the circumstances of the case — in particular, what the parties have agreed upon, the time and place where the risk passed, the type of goods, the packaging, and when the buyer had access to the goods.

#16 To protect the buyer against third-party claims based on contract or property, including intellectual property, the seller has to deliver goods free from any third-party rights, unless otherwise agreed between the seller and the buyer (Arts. 41, 42 CISG; § 2-312(2) and (3) UCC). If third parties should have rights or present claims against the goods, the seller has to notify the buyer accordingly (Art. 43 CISG; § 607(3)(b) UCC).

#17 If there is a delay with the delivery of the goods (Art. 47 CISG) or payment (Art. 63 CISG), the other side can initially set a new deadline for performance before taking other steps. In some cases this will be inevitable before the buyer can avoid the contract for late delivery (Art. 49(1)(b) CISG). The UCC and the Restatement do not have corresponding options or obligations.

#18 If there is a problem with the primary performance of the seller (delivery of conforming goods, transfer of documents and title) or the buyer (taking of delivery, payment of the price), the first remedy is a demand for specific performance or cure. The goal is to put the parties in the position they would be in if the contract had been properly performed. Cf. Arts. 46 and 62 CISG; §§ 2-711, 2-716, 2-709 UCC. Additional damages can compensate for the lateness or other remaining problems with the performance, see #22.

#19   If the buyer is willing to accept non-conforming goods, she may have a right to reduce the price (Art. 50 CISG).

#20   In some cases, the performance of the seller is no longer of interest to the buyer. Therefore, both the CISG and the UCC give the buyer the choice to go directly for damages. Under the UCC, this choice exists, in principle, with any breach (perfect tender rule). Under the CISG, however, this choice only exists if the breach of the seller is fundamental (Arts. 49, 25 CISG). In the absence of a fundamental breach, the CISG buyer can only demand performance, cure or repair, price reduction, and damages. Under the CISG, if performance was rendered or is still possible, the buyer will not be released from the contract unless the seller has committed a fundamental breach.

#21   If the buyer has successfully canceled or avoided the original contract, she is still left without the goods she needs. Article 75 CISG and § 2-712 UCC provide an explicit remedy to the buyer to procure the goods elsewhere, a so-called cover transaction, and charge the original seller for the additional expenses plus any incidental and consequential damages.

     If the buyer is in breach by failing to take delivery of the goods, the right to cover is also given to the seller who has to find an alternate buyer and potentially sell the goods for a lower price (Art. 75 CISG; § 2-706 UCC).

     Under the explicit language of the UCC, and the obligation to mitigate damages in Art. 77 CISG, the parties have to act in good faith and keep the expenses for the cover transaction and incidental or consequential damages within reasonable limits (see also § 2-715 UCC).

#22   In general, damage claims can be presented pursuant to Article 74 of the CISG, or §§ 2-703 and 2-711 UCC. As with the preference for performance, the main goal of the provisions on damages is to put the injured party as close as possible to the position she would be in had there been no breach (cf. § 1-305 UCC). The general damage provisions can accomplish this goal in addition to other remedies, taking care only of remaining problems and losses, or they can be the sole or main remedy.

     In principle, any kind of damages can be claimed after a breach of contract. This includes direct losses, such as the lower value of the non-conforming goods (#19) or the reasonable costs of a cover transaction (#21), and also incidental damages for inspection, repair, storage, return shipment, expedited shipment of substitute goods, financing costs, etc., as well as consequential damages, in particular lost profits. These kinds of damages need to be well documented to be awarded. Immaterial losses such as personal time, reputation of a business, or future business opportunities are problematic because they are hard to quantify. They also clash with the requirement, common to CISG and UCC, that damages have to be foreseeable.

Personal injury and resulting tort claims are not covered by the CISG and may be brought under the applicable backup law. The UCC does allow for personal injury claims (§ 2-715(2)(b)).[87]

Punitive damages are not provided for in either UCC or CISG. They may be agreed upon between the parties, however.

Attorney fees can be claimed as damages under the CISG but not necessarily under the UCC, at least when claimed in front of U.S. courts.[88] In arbitration, if the English Rule does not apply, reasonable attorney fees should always be recoverable (see below, pp. 786, 791–792, and 1036–1038).

The provisions on damages in the CISG and UCC can be modified by party agreement. In the original contract or a subsequent agreement, the parties may have excluded certain types of damages and/or provided specific limits and/or simplified calculations bases for damages, waiving the documentation requirement (liquidated damages).

#23 In almost all cases, litigation or arbitration should aim at recovery of (i) contractual claims, *and* (ii) damages, *and*

#24 (iii) costs, *and* (iv) interest.

We will discuss in Part Six how these have to be calculated and presented to maximize chances of success.

---

87. Professor Eisenberg points out that the UCC distinguishes between "general or direct damages on the one hand and special or consequential damages on the other. General or direct damages are the damages that flow from a given type of breach without regard to the buyer's particular circumstances . . . for example . . . the difference between the contract price and the market or cover price." These kind of damages are generally *foreseeable* even at the time when the contract was made and, therefore, compensated. By contrast, "[s]pecial or consequential damages are the damages above and beyond general damages that flow from a breach as a result of the buyer's particular circumstances." These include, in particular, "the profits [the buyer] would have made if the seller had performed." For special and consequential damages, *Hadley v. Baxendale* (9 Exch. 341 (1854)) has established a higher level requirement of foreseeability. While general and direct damages merely have to be reasonably foreseeable, special and consequential losses have to be *highly probable* to occur in order to be compensated. This means that many foreseeable damages are excluded and the liability of the seller is unduly limited. Given that § 2-715(2)(b) introduces a third standard for the case of injury to person or other property, Professor Eisenberg argues for a general application of the proximate cause test, which refers to the time when the breach occurred. To the extent that such a test would be wider than the current practice because it would include some losses that were not foreseeable at the time the contract was made, the sellers can insert limitations of liability into their contracts, which would have to meet fair disclosure standards. See Melvin Aron Eisenberg, *The Principle of Hadley v. Baxendale*, Cal. L. Rev. 1992, Vol. 80, pp. 563–613, at pp. 565–568.

88. See Henry Deeb Gabriel: *Contracts for the Sale of Goods — A Comparison of U.S. and International Law*, Oxford Univ. Press 2nd ed. 2008, at p. 226, fn. 1149.

B. Contract Formation and Interpretation Under the CISG

Before the CISG can be applied to a specific IBT, two questions have to be answered separately. First, does the CISG as such apply and on what basis? Second, is the specific legal problem covered by the CISG, and if not, what happens next?

1. Applicability of the CISG

a. Applicability by Party Agreement

In general, party autonomy in B2B transactions is far reaching and includes the possibility to choose the applicable contract law. A valid choice of law by the parties, therefore, has to be respected. As a matter of fact, as an alternative to seller's, buyer's, or a third-country law, the CISG is not a bad choice at all because it is international, hence neutral, and well developed in literature and practice. On pp. 117 et seq. there is a more detailed discussion of the pros and cons of different choices of contract laws and the respective strengths and weaknesses of the CISG as a choice. At this point, it may suffice to say that if the parties have made a valid choice in favor of the CISG, a court or arbitration tribunal should honor this choice and determine the respective rights and obligations of the parties on the basis of the CISG. The choice of law in this regard is no different from any other contract clause—and should be respected just as a court or tribunal would respect an obligation to deliver a certain quantity and quality of goods in exchange for a certain amount of money on the basis of an offer and its timely acceptance. The choice of law makes the sales agreement somewhat more specific, not unlike a delivery date or a limitation of liability does.

b. Applicability of the CISG Pursuant to Article 1 of the CISG

By far the most common reason for the application of the CISG to a given contract is the fact that seller and buyer have their place of business in different states, *both of which* are Contracting States of the CISG (Article 1(1)(a) CISG). In such a case, the CISG automatically and without further ado becomes the primary source of law to determine the rights and obligations of the parties under the contract—after the contractual clauses themselves—*unless* the parties have explicitly excluded the application of the CISG pursuant to Article 6 CISG.[89] In light of the fact that the United States and many of its most important trading partners have indeed become Contracting States, the CISG is the default law to be applied to thousands of international sales transactions every day. It is, therefore, both disappointing and disheartening to see that a large majority of American attorneys and judges seem completely oblivious to this fact and instead continue to default to the common law and the UCC in the absence of an explicit and effective choice of law

---

89. On that subject, see William P. Johnson, *Understanding Exclusion of the CISG: A New Paradigm of Determining Party Intent*, 59 Buff. L. Rev. 213 (2011).

clause in a contract.[90] Attorneys who are aware of the CISG, by majority, usually try to exclude its application. For a discussion whether this is good for their clients or not, see pp. 140–143.

By contrast, if *neither* of the parties has their place of business in a Contracting State of the CISG, and other special circumstances do not exist (see below), the CISG can only become the governing law of the contract by explicit party agreement, as discussed in subsection a. above.

The situation is slightly more complicated if *only one* of the parties has their place of business in a Contracting State of the CISG—for example, in a sale between a party in Canada and a party in England.[91] This situation is covered by Article 1(1)(b) CISG. In such a case, the question is *which* national legal system is applicable pursuant to the rules of private international law. In a standard export/import sales transaction, the rules of private international law of most countries—absent a valid choice of law by the parties—would lead to the application of the seller's law.[92] As a consequence of Article 1(1)(b), if the seller's country is the one that has ratified the CISG (e.g., Canada), the application of the seller's law means the application of the CISG. By contrast, if the seller's country is the one that has not ratified the CISG (e.g., England), the application of the seller's law would be the domestic law (i.e., English law), without the CISG.

Yet another variation applies for the United States and a few other countries that have made a reservation against Article 1(1)(b) under Article 95 of the CISG. Pursuant to the reservation, the U.S. rejects the application of the CISG in the preceding situation. Therefore, if an American seller enters into a contract with an English buyer, then U.S. law would apply without the CISG. As we have discussed on pp. 140–143., this makes little sense because it subjects U.S. sellers to the stricter standards of performance under the UCC.

Finally, in a very small number of cases, Article 1(1)(b) could also apply if neither of the parties has their place of business in a Contracting State of the CISG, but the rules of private international law lead to the application of the legal system of a third country that is a Contracting State of the CISG. This is possible, in particular, when the entire transaction is more closely connected to the third country than to the seller's or buyer's country, namely because it is where the contract was concluded

---

90. See Peter L. Fitzgerald, *The International Contracting Practices Survey Project: An Empirical Study of the Value and Utility of the United Nations Convention on the International Sale of Goods (CISG) and the UNIDROIT Principles of International Commercial Contracts to Practitioners, Jurists, and Legal Academics in the United States*, 27 J. L. & Com. 1 (2008).

91. For discussion, see Sally Moss, *Why the United Kingdom Has Not Ratified the CISG*, 25 J. L. & Com. 2006, pp. 483–485.

92. The rules might explicitly refer to "seller's law," or they might refer to the law of the party "who has to make the characteristic performance" under the contract. Since the primary obligation of the buyer is the payment of the purchase price and money is generally fungible, the characteristic performance in a sales contract is typically the obligation of the seller to deliver the goods. Thus, this formulation also leads to the application of seller's law.

and/or has to be performed. The reservation under Article 95, however, would also apply in this case.

c. Applicability of the CISG by Party Disagreement?

Finally, in some cases it has to be determined whether a disagreement between the parties could lead to the application of the CISG. First, such a disagreement could occur explicitly, although this would be quite unlikely. For example, the offeror might propose her legal system, and the offeree accepts on condition that the applicable law should be his legal system. Prima facie, this would seem to be a rejection with a counteroffer and much would depend on what happens next. Are the parties proceeding with performance, showing that they assume the contract has been formed? Or is at least one of them walking away, showing an assumption that the negotiations have failed? If both of the legal systems mentioned in the negotiations are signatories of the CISG, the disagreement would be much smaller than it would seem. In such a case, both sides would have opted for the CISG—as part of the legal system chosen—and would have disagreed only on the rules to be applied to questions *not* covered by the CISG.

In practice, the disagreement as here described is most likely to occur in oral negotiations or in case of exchange of contradictory general terms. Oral contracts are generally permitted and, therefore also oral choice of law clauses as components of a contract, as long as there is other evidence for the agreement, for example in the form of business correspondence or witnesses to phone conversations (see Art. 11 CISG).[93] Similarly, choice of law clauses can be part of general terms and get drawn into a "battle of the forms," namely if each side wants to incorporate its own general terms into the agreement. The general solution to the disagreement can be found in Article 19 CISG. As such, **conflicting choice of law clauses are "material" alterations and would prevent contract formation.** However, should this be the same if both systems chosen have incorporated the CISG? Would there still be a "material" alteration if the disagreement is limited to the rights and duties of the parties that are not covered by the CISG? We would suggest a somewhat nuanced approach: **At least in the cases where the two legal systems also happen to belong to the same legal family,** for example the continental European legal systems, **the differences between the rules outside the CISG, if they have to come into play at all, are usually not so important that a "material" alteration would be called for.** A different approach might be required if the parties are located in countries applying different legal systems, such as common law in Canada and civil or statutory law on the European Continent. Nevertheless, one could ask whether the differences have to

---

93. Certain jurisdictions, in particular the former socialist countries, do require written form for the types of contracts here at issue. A partial list can be found in the form of the countries that have made a reservation pursuant to Article 96 CISG. If the private international law rules would lead to the application of the legal system of such a country and the parties to an IBT had only an oral agreement to apply the CISG, such choice of law would not be valid. Of course, the contract as such would have to be in writing, otherwise there would be no binding agreement at all.

be considered material if all important questions in the particular case are falling within the coverage of the CISG.

Next, we will examine the actual coverage of the CISG in substantive terms.

2. Substantive Coverage of the CISG

It is very important to understand that, unlike modern national legal systems, the CISG does not contain a comprehensive contract law regime that covers every conceivable problem related to international sales. Certain subjects — for example, the transfer of property in the goods sold — were not included either because they were not considered central to the sale of goods or because they were considered too controversial and, therefore, likely to jeopardize broad global support of the Convention.[94] This is why a choice of law in favor of the CISG should always be phrased along the following lines: "This contract of sale shall be governed by the CISG. Any questions not covered by the CISG shall be governed by the domestic law of _____" (see the Model Contract, below pp. 332 et seq.).

Why on earth would the parties to an IBT voluntarily choose an incomplete legal system to govern their contract, you may ask. However, since the CISG covers the most important issues and the most common problems that may occur in sales transactions, it is not such a big problem in practice that certain ancillary issues have to be referred to a backup legal system. What matters is threefold. First, we need to understand exactly what is and what is not covered by the CISG. Second, we need to make a sensible choice of law for the backup legal system. Third, we need to understand how to fill the gaps in the CISG when the parties have not made a backup choice.

a. Substantive Coverage of the CISG

Article 4 CISG is the point of departure for any analysis of substantive coverage. It must not be narrowly interpreted, however, since it is clear that the Convention goes beyond formation and rights and obligations under a contract. As *Schlechtriem* has pointed out, the Convention also covers the "interpretation of statements, conduct, and contracts (Article 8), the applicability of usage and custom (Article 9), (freedom of) form (Article 11 . . .), termination or modification of contracts by agreement (Article 29(1)), interpretation of the Convention, and gap filling ([Article 7, see below])."[95]

Nevertheless, certain matters remain outside the scope of coverage of the CISG. First, there are the two matters specifically cited in Article 4, namely questions of validity of contracts (mistake, fraud, issues falling under *ordre public* and other

94. For more information, see Schwenzer & Hachem, above, p. 125, note 56.
95. Ibid., para. 3.

elements of public law, such as consequences of bankruptcy, etc.),[96] and questions related to property rights in the goods sold. Another matter outside of the CISG are the rights and obligations of any third parties, although rights of third parties can be created by the seller and buyer pursuant to Article 6.

Finally, some matters are in dispute. Some commentators want to apply a broad interpretation of the "rights and obligations of the seller and the buyer" to include even tort claims, if they are the result of a breach of contract. The exception would be Article 5 CISG.

As will be shown below, this author would support an interpretation according to the principle *in dubio pro uniformitatem* or, when in doubt, **try to apply the CISG or at least some international uniform principles of law,** and stay away from recourse to national laws that will necessarily differ.

b. Selecting a Backup Legal System

The very reason for the creation of the CISG was the problem that parties from different countries engaging in international business transactions have to make painful choices. Either seller's law will apply and buyer will not really know what that means or the other way around. The choice of a neutral country's law, such as Swiss law, would only mean that both parties don't really know the applicable rules. By contrast, an international system like the CISG is readily available to everyone and thus—at least in theory—familiar to both parties to the transaction.

Unfortunately, the CISG is an incomplete system and does not cover all potential problems. This requires the selection of a backup system that would only come into play if an issue arises that is not covered by the CISG. National legal systems are by definition complete legal systems. At least the more developed systems will have statutory or case law rules for every conceivable problem. Therefore, selecting a national legal system as the backup, along the lines of "This contract of sale shall be governed by the CISG. Any questions not covered by the CISG shall be governed by the domestic law of _____" will provide a solution for every conceivable problem. However, the choice of either seller's law or buyer's law or a neutral country's legal system will bring back, to an extent, the problem that at least one party will not really know the rules it is subjecting itself to.

While the backup system will be far less significant for the parties to the contract because most of the important issues are already taken care of in the CISG, there is at least one international system that is mostly complete—**the Common Frame of Reference** (Documents, p. I-280). A selection of the CFR as the backup system would, therefore, be the most equitable solution for both sides. Another option would be the selection of "general principles of law as codified, in particular, in

---

96. For a useful discussion of misrepresentation versus fraud and the scope of application of the CISG, see Ulrich G. Schroeter, *Defining the Borders of Uniform International Contract Law: the CISG and Remedies for Innocent, Negligent, or Fraudulent Misrepresentation*, 58 Vill. L. Rev. 553 (2013).

the UNIDROIT Principles of International Commercial Contracts (PICC)" (Documents, p. I-101). Although the PICC are far less comprehensive than the CFR, they are generally understood as a codification of customary rules of business and trade law. In combination, the codification and the custom can provide answers to every conceivable problem. However, custom can be hard to determine and outcomes, therefore, somewhat unpredictable.

In light of the many choices for the backup system, what should parties to an IBT do in practice? To give a meaningful answer, we have to revert to the question of the forum for dispute resolution:

- If disputes are to be resolved by arbitration, the CFR is a safe choice and the PICC is also feasible, in particular if the parties are fine with a higher dose of equity in the analysis.

- If disputes are to be resolved in front of national courts, the backup system should be the legal system of the respective country.

- If it is not clear which national courts would be called upon because the parties have not made an unambiguous choice, the parties need to worry more about the problem of going to a first round of litigation over choice of forum and choice of law than about the backup system.

c. Filling Gaps in the CISG

Opinions are divided about what should happen between parties to an international sale of goods if an issue arises that is not covered by the CISG. For clarification, this question can only present itself if:

- the sale is subject to the CISG either on the basis of party choice or on the basis of Article 1 CISG; *and*

- a dispute arises between the parties that requires a legal solution not explicitly provided within the CISG; *and*

- the parties have not agreed upon a backup legal system when entering into their agreement, nor at any later time, and they cannot agree on such a backup now.

A strict interpretation of the CISG would require the following two-step analysis: First, is the matter "governed" by the CISG pursuant to Article 4, even though the specific question does not find an answer in the CISG, even if broadly interpreted pursuant to Article 7(1)? If yes, then, second, Article 7(2) CISG directs us to find a solution in "the general principles on which [the CISG] is based." Only if no such solution can be found, recourse may be had to the national law that would be applicable pursuant to the rules of private international law. However, if the matter is already not governed by the CISG pursuant to Article 4, then we should move to the national law that would be applicable pursuant to the rules of private international law.

While in line with a literal or strict interpretation of the CISG, this approach is problematic in several ways:

- it is by no means obvious and universally agreed what is and what is not "governed" by the CISG;

- once the CISG is held *not* to govern a particular question, different rules of private international law applicable in different fora can lead to the application of different national legal systems to fill the gap;

- thus, whether or not something is governed by the CISG will depend on who gets to answer the question and there is a risk, in particular, that a national court will try to quickly eliminate the CISG in order to return to the better known and presumably safer waters of its national legal system; and

- different national courts applying different national rules of private international law will each arrive at different conclusions, usually in favor of their own national legal system; this creates an element of arbitrariness and a potential incentive for a race to the courthouse, the exact result the CISG wanted to prevent in the first place.

To avoid or at least reduce the incidents where such unfortunate results occur, we suggest that step one and step two, namely Articles 4 and 7(2) CISG, should be read together. This is supported by the mandate in Article 7(1) CISG that the Convention should be interpreted in an international manner and with a view toward promoting uniformity as far as possible.[97] It is also supported by the inclusion of recourse to national law only as a last resort in Article 7(2). Consequently, we would argue that the scope of application of the CISG (Article 4^1) should be interpreted broadly and the elements that are not governed by the CISG (Article 4^2) should be interpreted narrowly. As a consequence, *unless a question is clearly outside the scope of application of the CISG*, the text of the Convention should first be given a broad interpretation in good faith (Article 7(1)); if this does not yield an answer, reference should be made to general principles of law to fill any gaps (Article 7(2^1)), and reference to any national legal systems (Article 7(2^2)) should be avoided as much as possible.

The question remaining is how to determine the general principles that can be relied upon to fill gaps in the CISG. By now it should be obvious that the goal must be to find uniform principles, i.e., principles common to most, if not all, legal systems, and in particular the systems that may be involved. One way to achieve this goal would be a comparative study of case law from around the world, which would yield, for example, the rule that parties have to act in good faith, the principle of estoppel, or the principle that unjust enrichment must be restituted. Fortunately, such comparative analysis has already been done and we can refer to commentaries and other academic literature for a variety of lists. Another way of pursuing the same goal would be to refer to the UNIDROIT Principles of International Commercial Contracts, which are widely recognized as the codification of general principles of

---

97. See, for example, Susanne Cook, *The Need for Uniform Interpretation of the 1980 United Nations Convention on Contracts for the International Sale of Goods (1988)*, 50 U. Pitt. L. Rev. 197, 197 (Fall 1988).

contract law common to all major legal systems of the world.[98] Pursuant to the same logic, if both parties are located in Europe, one might look at the Common Frame of Reference, which does the job of the UNIDROIT Principles on a higher level of detail but for a smaller geographic area with fewer differences in legal systems.

3. Application of the CISG in Practice

Having clarified the cases *when* the CISG has to be applied, we will now turn to the question *how* the CISG has to be applied, starting with the creation of contractual obligations, i.e., the problems related to contract formation and interpretation.

Checklist 2-2
Provisions on Contract Formation and Interpretation in the CISG

Issue	Rule(s)
Pre-Contractual Obligations	not explicitly covered in CISG → resort to general principles under Art. 7(2), except - duty not to break off negotiations, Art. 16(2)(b) - duties to inform under Arts. 35(2)(b) and 71
Form Requirements?	Arts. 11–13
Capacity	not explicitly covered in CISG → resort to general principles under Art. 7(2)
Offer or Invitation?	Art. 14
Rejection	Art. 17
Acceptance	Arts. 18–23
Modified Acceptance or Counteroffer?	Arts. 18, 19
Incorporation of General Terms and Conditions	Art. 19
Relevance of Previous Negotiations or Dealings between the Parties and other Outside (Parol) Evidence Prior to or Simultaneous to Contract Conclusion	Arts. 8, 9
Consideration	N/A
Conditions	Art. 20(1) + general principles under Art. 7(2)
Mistake	explicitly not covered in CISG → resort to backup legal system

---

98. The Preamble of the UNIDROIT Principles specifically suggests that they "may be used to interpret or *supplement international uniform law instruments*" (emphasis added). For further analysis, see Alejandro M. Garro, *The Gap-Filling Role of the UNIDROIT Principles in International Sales Law: Some Comments on the Interplay Between the Principles and the CISG*, 69 Tul. L. Rev. 1149 (1994–1995).

Issue	Rule(s)
Misrepresentation, Duress, Undue Influence	explicitly not covered in CISG → resort to backup legal system
Relevance of Subsequent Negotiations or Communications	Art. 29
Public Policy Considerations	not explicitly covered in CISG → resort to general principles under Art. 7(2)
Other Methods to Fill Gaps in Contracts:Implied Warranties, Usages	Arts. 8, 9
Other Tools of Interpretation	Arts. 8, 9
Involvement of Agents	not explicitly covered in CISG → resort to general principles under Art. 7(2)
Validity	explicitly not covered in CISG → resort to backup legal system

In *Solae v. Hershey* and *Magellan v. Salzgitter*, we will be looking at contract formation, or modification, by offer and acceptance. As is often the case in business, the parties exchanged a number of communications and among the questions before the court was the formation and substance of a contract. Note how the parties agreed on many things—but did they agree on the inclusion of the seller's general terms?[99]

At issue in *Solae v. Hershey* was a substantial recall of Hershey chocolate products, exposing it to some US$20 million in losses. Hershey was pursuing damages for these losses in court in Canada, but Solae wanted to preempt the case by a torpedo action in Delaware. Observe how Solae tries to establish Delaware jurisdiction first via an alleged contractual choice of forum clause and then via Delaware's long-arm statute.

Case 2-5

Solae v. Hershey Canada

557 F. Supp. 2d 452 (D. Del. 2008)
(Paragraph numbers added, footnotes omitted.)

Farnan, District Judge.

Background

[Solae USA filed a complaint in court in Delaware against Hershey Canada for a declaratory judgment that it did not owe damages to Hershey, together with a breach

---

99. A good comparative overview of contract formation is provided by Sarah Howard Jenkins, *Contract Resurrected! Contract Formation: Common Law—UCC—CISG*, 40 N.C. J. Int'l L. & Com. Reg. 245 (2015).

of contract action against Hershey. The decision focuses on questions of choice of forum and jurisdiction.]

[3] Solae is a Delaware limited liability company with its principal place of business in St. Louis, Missouri. . . . Hershey Canada is a Canadian corporation with its principal place of business in Mississauga, Ontario. . . . For the past several years, Solae has supplied soy lecithin to Hershey Canada. . . . In late 2005, Laurie Cradick ("Ms. Cradick"), Solae's account manager responsible for sales of soy lecithin products to, and the customer relationship with The Hershey Company ("Hershey"), and Kim McLucas ("Ms. McLucas"), of Hershey's commodities department, began negotiating the projected volume of soy lecithin products that Hershey and Hershey Canada would be ordering in 2006, and the sale price that would apply during that period. . . . In December 2005, Ms. Cradick and Ms. McLucas reached agreement that "for the period from January 1, 2006 to December 31, 2006 Hershey Canada would order up to 250,000 pounds of [soy lecithin] at a price of US $1.2565 per pound." . . . The parties dispute whether the terms of this agreement were reduced to writing. Ms. McLucas then notified James Kuehl ("Mr. Kuehl"), a materials analyst for Hershey Canada at its Smith Falls, Ontario manufacturing plant ("the Smith Falls plant"), of this agreement, which she referred to as contract "46044618," by e-mail on January 20, 2006.

[4] Under the 2006 agreement, as under agreements reached in previous years, Mr. Kuehl would fax a purchase order to Solae's customer service department, indicating, among other things, that the quantity ordered should be "release[d] against contract 46044618." . . . After faxing Mr. Kuehl an order confirmation, Solae would ship the soy lecithin. Following shipment, Solae would send an invoice to the Smith Falls Plant. Solae's standard order confirmations and invoices refer to attached "Conditions of Sale." The parties do not dispute that these Conditions of Sale were not mentioned during negotiations between Ms. McLucas and Ms. Cradick.

[5] This action arises largely out of Solae's September 27, 2006 shipment of 40,000 pounds of soy lecithin allegedly contaminated with Salmonella to Hershey Canada for use in chocolate products at its Smith Falls, Ontario manufacturing plant. . . . The shipment was made pursuant to Mr. Kuehl's faxed purchase order on June 21, 2006, requesting delivery on September 29, 2006. Solae's order confirmation, sent June 23, 2006, did not include its Conditions of Sale, but did refer to them. The invoice sent to the Smith Falls Plant following shipment did contain the Conditions of Sale.

[6] The contamination was discovered by Hershey Canada in October 2006 while conducting routine testing. Before the contamination was realized, Hershey Canada had incorporated this allegedly-contaminated soy lecithin into over two million units of Hershey Canada product shipped throughout Canada. . . . This contamination resulted in a large-scale recall of Hershey Canada chocolate products, the temporary closure of the Smith Falls plant, and an extensive investigation by the

Canadian Food Inspection Agency ("CFIA") and the Office of Food Safety and Recall ("OFSR"). . . . Subsequently, Hershey Canada notified Solae of the contaminated soy lecithin, and informed Solae that it would hold Solae responsible for damages incurred as a result of the incident. . . . Hershey Canada also refused to accept delivery or pay for any additional lots of soy lecithin, including a lot for which an order had been placed on October 17, 2006. . . .

Parties' Contentions

[8] Hershey Canada contends, first, that the Court should exercise its discretion and dismiss Solae's declaratory judgment action because it was motivated by bad faith and forum shopping. Next, Hershey Canada contends that the Court should dismiss this case on *forum non conveniens* grounds because it has no connection to the State of Delaware and a comparable case is pending in Ontario, Canada, which Hershey Canada contends is the proper forum for this action. Finally, Hershey Canada contends that the Court should dismiss the action under Federal Rule of Civil Procedure 12(b)(2) because it lacks personal jurisdiction over Hershey Canada. . . .

Analysis

I. Forum Selection Clause

[10] The parties dispute the relevant contract governing this dispute. If the relevant contract contains a forum-selection clause, Hershey Canada's contentions regarding personal jurisdiction are largely irrelevant. When a party is bound by a forum selection clause, the party is considered to have expressly consented to personal jurisdiction. *Res. Ventures, Inc. v. Res. Mgmt. Int'l, Inc.*, 42 F.Supp.2d 423, 431 . . . . An express consent to jurisdiction, in and of itself, satisfies the requirements of Due Process. *Sternberg v. O'Neil*, 550 A.2d 1105, 1116. . . . Such consent is deemed to be a waiver of any objection on Due Process grounds and an analysis of minimum contacts becomes unnecessary. See *Hornberger Mgmt. Co. v. Haws & Tingle General Contractors, Inc.*, 768 A.2d 983, 987 (Del.Super.Ct.2000) (stating "[a] party may expressly consent to jurisdiction by agreeing to a forum selection clause . . . If a party consents to jurisdiction, a minimum contacts analysis is not required."); *USH Ventures v. Global Telesystems Group, Inc.* C.A. No. 97C-08-086, 1998 WL 281250, at *7 . . . . Accordingly, the Court must determine whether Hershey Canada is bound by a forum selection clause.

[11] According to Solae, the relevant contract is the invoice and "Conditions of Sale," mailed to Hershey Canada on or about September 27, 2006, concurrent with Solae's shipment of the allegedly-contaminated soy lecithin. . . . Solae contends these Conditions of Sale set forth terms governing the transaction, and have been "included in invoices from Solae to Hershey for soy lecithin and other soy-based products since approximately 2003." . . . The Conditions of Sale provide:

> This Agreement is to be construed and the respective rights of Buyer and seller are to be determined according to the laws of the State of Delaware,

USA, without regard to choice of law or conflict principles of Delaware or any other jurisdiction, and the courts of Delaware shall exclusive jurisdiction over any disputes or issues arising under this Agreement. . . .

[12] Solae contends that Hershey Canada accepted the September 2006 shipment of soy lecithin and rendered payment in full, without objecting to or rejecting the Conditions of Sale, and therefore the forum selection clause governs the transactions at issue.

[13] Hershey Canada contends that a "Quantity Contract" entered in January 2006 governed Solae's sale of soy lecithin to Hershey Canada for the year 2006, which contains no provision identifying Delaware as either a proper forum, or the source of governing law. Under the terms of the 2006 Quantity Contract, the parties agreed to the total volume of soy lecithin that Hershey Canada was obligated to purchase before December 31, 2006, the price at which Solae was obligated to sell such volume, and the freight terms of "FOB Destination." Hershey Canada contends that no modifications to the Quantity Contract were proposed after January 2006.

[14] Hershey Canada points out that the Conditions of Sale that Solae contends govern the dispute arrived after the shipment of the allegedly-contaminated soy lecithin had been delivered, and were received by individuals with no authority to modify the existing 2006 Quantity Contract. Hershey Canada further contends that there was never an affirmative assent to modify the parties' existing contract, and that, under the United Nations Convention of Contracts for the International Sale of Goods, Solae's "unilateral attempt to add terms through an invoice did not modify the parties' contract." . . .

[15] In response, Solae contends that the Conditions of Sale were familiar to Hershey Canada through Solae and Hershey Canada's "long history of dealing under Solae's terms." . . . Solae contends that the discussions between the parties regarding 2006 shipments to Hershey Canada did not give rise to a binding contract, and that the parties' course of dealing as to these shipments confirm that the annual volume discussions did not create binding agreements. Solae contends that it never received Hershey Canada's 2006 Quantity Contract, pointing to the incorrect address and fax number listed for Solae on the face of the contract, and that Solae's representative had not seen a document akin to the 2006 Quantity Contract prior to this litigation. . . .

[16] The parties agree that the United Nations Convention of Contracts for the International Sale of Goods ("CISG") governs contract formation here. Under the terms of the CISG, "a contract is concluded at the moment when an acceptance of an offer becomes effective in accordance with the provisions of this Convention." CISG, Art. 23. An offer must be "sufficiently definite," and "demonstrate an intention by the offerer to be bound if the proposal is accepted." *Id.*, Art. 14. An offer is accepted, and a contract is formed when the offeree makes a statement or other conduct, "indicating assent to an offer." *Id.*, Art. 18. The CISG does not contain a statute of frauds, stating that "a contract of sale need not be concluded in or evidenced by writing and

is not subject to any other requirement as to form." *Id.*, Art. 11. Courts have held that a binding contract exists when the parties sufficiently agree to the goods, the quantity and the price. See, e.g., *Chateau des Charmes Wines Ltd. v. Sabate U.S.A., Inc.*, 328 F.3d 528, 531 (9th Cir.2003).

[17] Having reviewed the record in light of the applicable legal standard, the Court is not persuaded by Solae's contention that its Conditions of Sale control the disputed transaction. . . .

[18] The record is clear that Ms. Cradick and Ms. McLucas had reached agreement as to the amount of soy lecithin Solae was obligated to sell Hershey Canada during the calendar year 2006, and the price at which Solae was obligated to sell. Under this agreement, Hershey Canada was obligated to purchase a substantial quantity of soy lecithin from Solae at the price agreed upon. The Court concludes that this is sufficient to create a complete and binding contract under the CISG (the "2006 Contract").

[19] Because the 2006 Contract did not include a forum-selection clause, the Court must now determine if the forum-selection clause contained in the Conditions of Sale subsequently became part of the 2006 Contract under the CISG. As Hershey Canada points out, this issue was addressed by the Ninth Circuit in *Chateau des Charmes Wines Ltd.*, 328 F.3d 528:

> Under the Convention, a "contract may be modified or terminated by the mere agreement of the parties." [CISG], art. 29(1). However, the Convention clearly states that "[a]dditional or different terms relating, among other things, to . . . the settlement of disputes are considered to alter the terms of the offer materially." Id., art. 19(3). There is no indication that [the buyer] conducted itself in a manner that evidenced any affirmative assent to the forum selection clauses in the invoices. Rather, [the buyer] merely performed its obligations under the oral contracts. Nothing in the Convention suggests that the failure to object to a party's unilateral attempt to alter materially the terms of an otherwise valid agreement is an "agreement" within the terms of Article 29. *Id.* at 531.

[20] Here, as in *Chateau,* Solae has set forth no substantive evidence indicating that Hershey Canada agreed to a modification of the terms of the 2006 Contract, beyond Hershey Canada's receipt of the Conditions of Sale. Solae has not set forth evidence refuting Mr. Kuehl's statement that he was not authorized to negotiate contractual terms or to commit Hershey Canada to Solae's Conditions of Sale, and the Court does not agree with Solae's contention that because multiple invoices and pre-shipment confirmations containing these Conditions of Sale were sent to Hershey Canada over "years of sales and dozens of transactions," these terms necessarily became part of the 2006 Contract. "[A] parties' multiple attempts to alter an agreement unilaterally do not so effect." *Chateau*, 328 F.3d at 531. In sum, the Court concludes that Hershey Canada's continued performance of its duties under the 2006 Contract did not demonstrate its acceptance of the terms contained in the

Condition of Sales, and the Court further concludes that Solae's Conditions of Sale did not modify the 2006 Contract to add a forum-selection clause.

II. Whether the Court Can Properly Assert Jurisdiction Over Hershey Canada

[21] Having determined that Hershey Canada did not consent to this Court's jurisdiction, the Court will now determine whether personal jurisdiction exists over Hershey Canada.

[22] In support of its motion, Hershey Canada contends that its contacts with Delaware "do not even arguably subject it to personal jurisdiction, either as a statutory or constitutional matter," since Hershey Canada has no business operations in Delaware, does not regularly solicit business or engage in persistent conduct in Delaware, and does not derive any significant revenue from the State of Delaware. (D.I. 27 at 27.) Hershey Canada further contends that, in connection with its relationship with Solae and the events giving rise to this dispute, it has not transacted business or performed work or services in Delaware, contracted to supply services or goods or to act as a surety in Delaware, caused tortious injury in Delaware, nor maintained an interest in real property in Delaware. . . .

[24] For personal jurisdiction to exist over a non-resident defendant, two requirements must be met, one statutory and one constitutional. *Merck & Co., Inc. v. Barr Laboratories, Inc.*, 179 F.Supp.2d 368, 371 . . . With regard to the statutory requirement, the Court must determine whether there is a statutory basis for jurisdiction under the forum state's long arm statute. . . . As for the constitutional basis, the Court must determine whether the exercise of jurisdiction comports with the defendant's right to Due Process. . . .

[25] "When a non-resident [defendant] challenges personal jurisdiction, the burden is on the plaintiff to show that the defendant purposefully availed itself of the privilege of conducting activities within the forum State, thus invoking the benefits [and] protections of its laws." *Virgin Wireless, Inc. v. Virgin Enterprises Ltd.*, 201 F.Supp.2d 294, 298 . . . As such, the plaintiff may not rely on the pleadings alone to withstand a motion to dismiss for lack of personal jurisdiction. . . . Rather, "the plaintiff must come forward with facts to establish by a preponderance of the evidence that the court can exercise personal jurisdiction over the defendant." *Id.* . . .

[26] The Delaware Supreme Court has construed its long-arm statute, Del.Code Ann. tit. 10 § 3104 liberally to confer jurisdiction to the maximum extent possible in order "to provide residents a means of redress against those not subject to personal service within the State." *Kloth v. Southern Christian University*, 494 F.Supp.2d 273, 278 (D.Del.2007) (quoting *Boone v. Oy Partek Ab*, 724 A.2d 1150, 1156-1157 (Del. Super.Ct.1997)).

[27] Delaware state courts have interpreted section 3104(c)(1)-(3) as specific jurisdiction provisions of the Delaware long-arm statute. *Outokumpu Eng'g, Enters., Inc. v. Kvaerner Enviropower, Inc.*, 685 A.2d 724, 729 (Del.Super.Ct.1996). Specific jurisdiction exists when the defendant has purposefully directed his activities toward the

forum, and the litigation arises out of or is related to the defendant's contacts with the forum. *Helicopteros Nacionales de Colombia, S.A. v. Hall et al.,* 466 U.S. 408, 414-16, 104 S.Ct. 1868, 80 L.Ed.2d 404 (1984). Specific jurisdiction requires that there be a "nexus" between the plaintiff's cause of action and the conduct of the defendant that is used as a basis for jurisdiction. *See id.* at 414 at n. 8, 104 S.Ct. 1868; Boone, 724 A.2d at 1155.

[28] In this case, the only contact with the State of Delaware that Solae alleges is Hershey Canada's filing of the UCC financing statement. However, Solae has not asserted that there is any nexus between this act in Delaware and the conduct which is the basis of this lawsuit. Accordingly, **the Court concludes that this contact is insufficient to give rise to specific jurisdiction over Hershey Canada.**

[29] Subsection (c)(4) of the Delaware long-arm statute provides for general jurisdiction. While this section authorizes jurisdiction even when the tortious acts and the injury occurred outside the State of Delaware, the defendant must still be "generally present" in the state. *TriStrata Tech., Inc. v. Neoteric Cosmetics, Inc.,* 961 F.Supp. 686, 691 . . . Under the statute, a "general presence" requires that the defendant "regularly does or solicits business, engages in any other persistent course of conduct in the State or derives substantial revenue from services, or things used or consumed in the State." Del.Code Ann. tit. 10 § 3104(c)(4). **The Court concludes that the filing of a UCC financing statement is not sufficient to establish "continuous and substantial" activity within the forum necessary to subject Hershey Canada to general personal jurisdiction.** *Intel Corp. v. Silicon Storage Technology, Inc.,* 20 F.Supp.2d 690, 699. . . .

[34] Having concluded that personal jurisdiction does not exist over Hershey Canada, the Court declines to address Hershey Canada's remaining arguments concerning the Court's equitable discretion to decline jurisdiction, and *forum non conveniens.* Accordingly, Hershey Canada's Motion to Dismiss . . . will granted. . . .

Notes and Questions

1. Do you agree with the court's decision that Solae's General Terms were not incorporated into the contract at issue? What about the long history of dealings between the parties and the claim that Solae's General Terms were well known to Hershey? Do you think parol evidence under the CISG could have been more forcefully argued by counsel on behalf of Solae? Maybe with reference to some persuasive precedents from other jurisdictions, if none existed in the U.S.?

2. In the absence of a valid choice of forum, the default place for litigation should be the defendant's court. Why didn't Solae (for its attempt to get a declaratory judgment in Delaware) or Hershey (with its damage suit in Canada) go to the defendant's court? Review the rules on jurisdiction on pp. 699–787 if you are in any doubt about your answer.

———————

The next case, *Magellan*, takes the question of contract formation to a higher level, including questions of anticipatory repudiation.

Case 2-6

Magellan International Corporation v. Salzgitter Handel GmbH

76 F. Supp. 2d 919 (N.D. Ill. 1999)
(Paragraph numbers added, some footnotes and details omitted.)
MEMORANDUM OPINION AND ORDER
SHADUR, Senior District Judge.

[1] Salzgitter Handel GmbH ("Salzgitter") has filed a motion pursuant to Fed.R.Civ.P. ("Rule") 12(b)(6) ("Motion"), seeking to dismiss this action brought against it by Magellan International Corporation ("Magellan"). Because the allegations in Complaint Counts I and II state claims that are sufficient under Rule 8(a), Salzgitter's Motion must be and is denied as to those claims. Count III, however, is deficient and is therefore dismissed without prejudice.

Facts

[2] In considering a Rule 12(b)(6) motion to dismiss for failure to state a claim, this Court accepts all of Magellan's well-pleaded factual allegations as true, as well as drawing all reasonable inferences from those facts in Magellan's favor (*Travel All Over the World, Inc. v. Kingdom of Saudi Arabia*, 73 F.3d 1423, 1429 (7th Cir.1996)). What follows is the version of events set out in the Complaint, when read in that light.

Offers, Counteroffers and Acceptance

[3] Magellan is an Illinois-based distributor of steel products. Salzgitter is a steel trader that is headquartered in Dusseldorf, Germany and maintains an Illinois sales office. In January 1999[1] Magellan's Robert Arthur ("Arthur") and Salzgitter's Thomas Riess ("Riess") commenced negotiations on a potential deal under which Salzgitter would begin to act as middleman in Magellan's purchase of steel bars — manufactured according to Magellan's specifications — from a Ukrainian steel mill, Dneprospetsstal of Ukraine ("DSS").

[4] By letter dated January 28, Magellan provided Salzgitter with written specifications for 5,585 metric tons of steel bars, with proposed pricing, and with an agreement to issue a letter of credit ("LC") to Salzgitter as Magellan's method of payment. Salzgitter responded two weeks later (on February 12 and 13) by proposing prices $5 to $20 per ton higher than those Magellan had specified.

[5] On February 15 Magellan accepted Salzgitter's price increases, agreed on 4,000 tons as the quantity being purchased, and added $5 per ton over Salzgitter's numbers to effect shipping from Magellan's preferred port (Ventspills, Latvia). Magellan memorialized those terms, as well as the other material terms previously discussed by the parties,[2] in two February 15 purchase orders. Salzgitter then responded on

---

1. Because all the relevant events took place this year, all further date references will omit "1999."
2. Price, quantity, delivery date, delivery method and payment method had all been negotiated and agreed to by the parties.

February 17, apparently accepting Magellan's memorialized terms except for two "amendments" as to prices. Riess asked for Magellan's "acceptance" of those two price increases by return fax and promised to send its already-drawn-up order confirmations as soon as they were countersigned by DSS. Arthur consented, signing and returning the approved price amendments to Riess the same day.

[6] On February 19 Salzgitter sent its pro forma order confirmations to Magellan. But the general terms and conditions that were attached to those confirmations differed in some respects from those that had been attached to Magellan's purchase orders, mainly with respect to vessel loading conditions, dispute resolution and choice of law.

[7] Contemplating an ongoing business relationship, Magellan and Salzgitter continued to negotiate in an effort to resolve the remaining conflicts between their respective forms. While those fine-tuning negotiations were under way, Salzgitter began to press Magellan to open its LC for the transaction in Salzgitter's favor. On March 4 Magellan sent Salzgitter a draft LC for review.[3] Salzgitter wrote back on March 8 proposing minor amendments to the LC and stating that "all other terms are acceptable." Although Magellan preferred to wait until all of the minor details (the remaining conflicting terms) were ironed out before issuing the LC, Salzgitter continued to press for its immediate issuance.

[8] On March 22 Salzgitter sent amended order confirmations to Magellan. Riess visited Arthur four days later on March 26 and threatened to cancel the steel orders if Magellan did not open the LC in Salzgitter's favor that day. They then came to agreement as to the remaining contractual issues.[4] Accordingly, relying on Riess's assurances that all remaining details of the deal were settled, Arthur had the $1.2 million LC issued later that same day.

Post-Acceptance Events

[9] Three days later (on March 29) Arthur and Riess engaged in an extended game of "fax tag" initiated by the latter. Essentially Salzgitter demanded that the LC be amended to permit the unconditional substitution of FCRs for bills of lading—even for partial orders—and Magellan refused to amend the LC, also pointing out the need to conform Salzgitter's March 22 amended order confirmations to the terms of the parties' ultimate March 26 agreement. At the same time, Magellan requested minor modifications in some of the steel specifications. Salzgitter replied that it was too late to modify the specifications: DSS had already manufactured 60% of the order, and the rest was under production.

---

3. One of the LC terms—also included in Magellan's purchase orders—required ocean bills of lading to be presented as a condition precedent to Salzgitter's right to draw on the LC. But Salzgitter was permitted to substitute Forwarder's Certificates of Receipt ("FCR") for bills of lading as to the full order if Magellan were to be more than 20 days late in providing a vessel for shipment.

4. For example, the parties agreed that the contract would be governed by the United Nations Convention on the International Sale of Goods (the "Convention").

[10] Perhaps unsurprisingly in light of what has been recited up to now, on the very next day (March 30) Magellan's and Salzgitter's friendly fine-tuning went flat. Salzgitter screeched an ultimatum to Magellan: Amend the LC by noon the following day or Salzgitter would "no longer feel obligated" to perform and would "sell the material elsewhere." On April 1 Magellan requested that the LC be canceled because of what it considered to be Saltzgitter's breach. Salzgitter returned the LC and has since been attempting to sell the manufactured steel to Magellan's customers in the United States.

Magellan's Claims

[11] Complaint Count I posits that—pursuant to the Convention—a valid contract existed between Magellan and Salzgitter before Salzgitter's March 30 ultimatum. Hence that attempted ukase is said to have amounted to an anticipatory repudiation of that contract, entitling Magellan to relief for its breach.

[12] Count II seeks specific performance of the contract or replevin of the manufactured steel. That relief is invoked under the Illinois version of the Uniform Commercial Code ("UCC," specifically 810 ILCS 5/2-716)[5] because Magellan is "unable to 'cover' its delivery commitments to its customers without [un]reasonable delay" . . .

[13] Finally, Count III asserts that specifications given to Salzgitter for transmittal to DSS constitute "trade secrets" pursuant to the Illinois Trade Secrets Act ("Secrets Act," which defines the term "trade secret" at 765 ILCS 1065/2(d)). Salzgitter is charged with misappropriation of those trade secrets in attempting to sell the manufactured steel embodying those secrets to Magellan's customers. . . . Magellan relatedly claims that the threat of future disclosure and use of those asserted trade secrets by Salzgitter causes Magellan irreparable harm. . . .

Documentary Grist for the Motion Mill . . .

[16] . . . When parties engage in a chain of correspondence relating to a transaction within a short period of time, and then one party detaches and presents only certain links of the chain in its effort to state a claim for relief, the party against whom such an incomplete picture is painted is entitled to fill in the skeletal outline thus presented by the complaining party by adding the missing links (see Fed.R.Evid. ("Evid.Rule") 106).

[17] In this instance Magellan and Salzgitter corresponded no fewer than 16 times within a two-month time span (January 28 to March 31). Magellan asks this Court to take into account the 5th, 6th, 7th, 10th, 11th, 12th and 15th items in that sequence, while ignoring the 1st through 4th, 8th, 9th, 14th, and 16th items. Though this Court is duty-bound at this stage of the game to look at the picture of

---

5. Although Magellan's contention that Illinois law governs its specific performance claim seems at odds with the framing of its breach of contract claim under the Convention, any presumed conflict in that regard would not pose a problem, because Rule 8(e) expressly permits inconsistency in pleading. But as it turns out, in light of the appropriate analysis of the Convention's terms discussed below, Magellan's contention is on the mark anyway.

the parties' transaction (as framed by their correspondence) through a lens most favorable to Magellan, it cannot do so by examining only half of that picture in that light.

[18] Evid.Rule 106's embodiment of the evidentiary rule of completeness seeks to avoid the "misleading impression created by taking matters out of context" (see 1972 Advisory Committee Note to Evid.Rule 106). And it is no less important to insist on a complete picture in ruling on the current motion to dismiss than to do so on a motion to admit evidence at trial. Even to a greater extent than the rule of completeness in the latter context recognizes the "inadequacy of repair work when delayed to a point later in the trial" (id.), it would be totally wasteful to uphold a claim on the false premise created by less than complete documentation when the delayed consideration of the remaining documents would lead to dismissal of that claim.

Rule 12(b)(6) Standard

[19] This opinion began by citing *Travel All Over the World*, 73 F.3d at 1429–30 for the rule applicable to Rule 12(b)(6) scrutiny of a complaint (and see also such cases as *Sanner v. Board of Trade*, 62 F.3d 918, 925 (7th Cir.1995)). *Scott v. City of Chicago*, 195 F.3d 950, 951 (7th Cir.1999) (internal quotation marks and numerous citations omitted) has described the threshold notice pleading standard:

> Federal notice pleading requires the plaintiff to set out in her complaint a short and plain statement of the claim that will provide the defendant with fair notice of the claim. However, a complaint need not spell out every element of a legal theory to provide notice. . . . A pleading need contain only enough to allow the defendant to understand the gravamen of the plaintiff's complaint.

[20] Thus no claim will be dismissed unless "it is clear that no relief could be granted under any set of facts that could be proved consistent with the allegations" (*Hishon v. King & Spalding*, 467 U.S. 69, 73 . . . (1984), quoting *Conley v. Gibson*, 355 U.S. 41, 45–46 . . . (1957)).

Count I: Breach of Contract

Choice of Law

[21] As stated earlier, Magellan first claims entitlement to relief for breach of contract. Because the transaction involves the sale and purchase of steel—"goods"—the parties acknowledge that the governing law is either the Convention or the UCC.[10] Under the facts alleged by Magellan, the parties agreed that Convention law would

---

10. Salzgitter seeks to rely upon several cases decided pursuant to the Illinois common law of contracts. As Magellan correctly points out, such reliance is misplaced in sales-of-goods cases such as this one. Instead the UCC would apply if the Convention did not and if Illinois choice of law rules pointed to the application of Illinois law (*Klaxon Co. v. Stentor Elec. Mfg. Co.*, 313 U.S. 487, 491, 61 S.Ct. 1020, 85 L.Ed. 1477 (1941)).

apply to the transaction, and Salzgitter does not now dispute that contention. That being the case, this opinion looks to Convention law.[11]

Pleading Requirements

[22] As n. 11 reflects, the specification of the pleading requirements to state a claim for breach of contract under the Convention truly poses a question of first impression. Despite that clean slate, even a brief glance at the Convention's structure confirms what common sense (and the common law) dictate as the universal elements of any such action: formation, performance, breach and damages. Hence under the Convention, as under Illinois law (or the common law generally), the components essential to a cause of action for breach of contract are (1) the existence of a valid and enforceable contract containing both definite and certain terms, (2) performance by plaintiff, (3) breach by defendant and (4) resultant injury to plaintiff. In those terms it is equally clear that Magellan's allegations provide adequate notice to Salzgitter that such an action is being asserted. . . .

[23] Formation of a contract under either UCC or the Convention requires an offer followed by an acceptance (see Convention Pt. II). Although analysis of offer and acceptance typically involves complicated factual issues of intent—issues not appropriately addressed on a motion to dismiss—this Court need not engage in such mental gymnastics here. It is enough that Magellan has alleged facts that a factfinder could call an offer on the one hand and an acceptance on the other.

[24] Under Convention Art. 14(1) a "proposal for concluding a contract addressed to one or more specific persons constitutes an offer if it is sufficiently definite and indicates the intention of the offeror to be bound in case of acceptance." So, if the indications of the proposer are sufficiently definite and justify the addressee in understanding that its acceptance will form a contract, the proposal constitutes an offer (id. Art. 8(2)). For that purpose "[a] proposal is sufficiently definite if it

---

11. As of the date of this opinion, only seven United States courts' opinions available in published opinions or via Westlaw have interpreted substantive provisions of the Convention, and none of those opinions has addressed the pleading requirements for a breach of contract action. See *MCC-Marble Ceramic Ctr., Inc. v. Ceramica Nuova d'Agostino, S.p.A.*, 144 F.3d 1384 (11th Cir.1998), holding the parol evidence rule inapplicable under the Convention; *Delchi Carrier SpA v. Rotorex Corp.*, 71 F.3d 1024 (2d Cir.1995), calculating the damages available to a buyer under the Convention when the seller delivered nonconforming goods; *Medical Marketing Int'l, Inc. v. Internazionale Medico Scientifica, S.R.L.*, No. CIV.A. 99-0380, 1999 WL 311945 (E.D. La. May 17, 1999), interpreting the Convention's Art. 35 public laws and regulations provision; *Mitchell Aircraft Spares, Inc. v. European Aircraft Serv. AB*, 23 F.Supp.2d 915 (N.D.Ill.1998), following *MCC-Marble*; *Calzaturificio Claudia s.n.c. v. Olivieri Footwear Ltd.*, No. 96 Civ. 8052(HB) (THK), 1998 WL 164824 (S.D.N.Y. Apr. 7, 1998), applying the Convention rules eliminating statute of frauds and the parol evidence rule; *Helen Kaminski Pty. Ltd. v. Marketing Australian Prods., Inc.*, Nos. M-47 (DLC), 96B46519, 97-8072A, 1997 WL 414137 (S.D.N.Y. July 23, 1997), holding that the Convention's scope did not extend to a distributorship agreement; *Filanto, S.p.A. v. Chilewich Int'l Corp.*, 789 F.Supp. 1229 (S.D.N.Y.1992), interpreting the battle-of-forms provision of Convention Art. 19 and noting the Convention's lack of statute of frauds and parol evidence rules.

indicates the goods and expressly or implicitly makes provision for determining the quantity and the price" (id. Art. 14(1)).

[25] In this instance Magellan alleges that it sent purchase orders to Salzgitter on February 15 that contained the material terms upon which the parties had agreed. Those terms included identification of the goods, quantity and price. Certainly an offer could be found consistently with those facts.

[26] But Convention Art. 19(1) goes on to state that "[a] reply to an offer which purports to be an acceptance but contains additions, limitations or other modifications is a rejection of the offer and constitutes a counter-offer." That provision reflects the common law's "mirror image" rule that the UCC has rejected (see *Filanto*, 789 F.Supp. at 1238). And Salzgitter's February 17 response to the purchase orders did propose price changes. Hence that response can be seen as a counteroffer that justified Magellan's belief that its acceptance of those new prices would form a contract.

[27] Although that expectation was then frustrated by the later events in February and then in March, which in contract terms equated to further offers and counteroffers, the requisite contractual joinder could reasonably be viewed by a factfinder as having jelled on March 26. In that respect Convention Art. 18(a) requires an indication of assent to an offer (or counteroffer) to constitute its acceptance. Such an "indication" may occur through "a statement made by or other conduct of the offeree" (id.). And at the very least, a jury could find consistently with Magellan's allegations that the required indication of complete (mirrored) assent occurred when Magellan issued its LC on March 26. So much, then, for the first element of a contract: offer and acceptance.

[28] Next, the second pleading requirement for a breach of contract claim—performance by plaintiff—was not only specifically addressed by Magellan . . . but can also be inferred from the facts alleged in Complaint ¶ 43 and from Magellan's prayer for specific performance. Magellan's performance obligation as the buyer is simple: payment of the price for the goods. Magellan issued its LC in satisfaction of that obligation, later requesting the LC's cancellation only after Salzgitter's alleged breach. . . . Moreover, Magellan's request for specific performance implicitly confirms that it remains ready and willing to pay the price if such relief were granted.

[29] As for the third pleading element—Salzgitter's breach—Complaint ¶ 38 alleges:

> Salzgitter's March 30 letter (Exhibit G) demanding that the bill of lading provision be removed from the letter of credit and threatening to cancel the contract constitutes an anticipatory repudiation and fundamental breach of the contract.

It would be difficult to imagine an allegation that more clearly fulfills the notice function of pleading.

[30] Convention Art. 72 addresses the concept of anticipatory breach:

(1) If prior to the date for performance of the contract it is clear that one of the parties will commit a fundamental breach of contract, the other party may declare the contract avoided.

(2) If time allows, the party intending to declare the contract avoided must give reasonable notice to the other party in order to permit him to provide adequate assurance of his performance.

(3) The requirements of the preceding paragraph do not apply if the other party has declared that he will not perform his obligations.

And Convention Art. 25 states in relevant part:

A breach of contract committed by one of the parties is fundamental if it results in such detriment to the other party as substantially to deprive him of what he is entitled to expect under the contract. . . .

[31] That plain language reveals that under the Convention an anticipatory repudiation pleader need simply allege (1) that the defendant intended to breach the contract before the contract's performance date and (2) that such breach was fundamental. Here Magellan has pleaded that Salzgitter's March 29 letter indicated its pre-performance intention not to perform the contract, coupled with Magellan's allegation that the bill of lading requirement was an essential part of the parties' bargain. That being the case, Salzgitter's insistence upon an amendment of that requirement would indeed be a fundamental breach.

[32] Lastly, Magellan has easily jumped the fourth pleading hurdle—resultant injury. Complaint ¶ 40 alleges that the breach "has caused damages to Magellan."

Count II: Specific Performance or Replevin

[33] Convention Art. 46(1) provides that a buyer may require the seller to perform its obligations unless the buyer has resorted to a remedy inconsistent with that requirement. As such, that provision would appear to make specific performance routinely available under the Convention. But Convention Art. 28 conditions the availability of specific performance:

If, in accordance with the provisions of this Convention, one party is entitled to require performance of any obligation by the other party, a court is not bound to enter judgment for specific performance unless the court would do so under its own law in respect of similar contracts of sale not governed by this Convention.

Simply put, that looks to the availability of such relief under the UCC. And in pleading terms, any complaint adequate to provide notice under the UCC is equally sufficient under the Convention.

[34] Under UCC § 2-716(1) a court may decree specific performance "where the goods are unique or in other proper circumstances."[16] That provision's Official

---

16. Because the Convention does not have a replevin provision similar to UCC § 2-716(3), Convention Art. 28 renders such relief unavailable under Complaint Count II.

Commentary instructs that inability to cover should be considered "strong evidence" of "other proper circumstances." UCC § 2-716 was designed to liberalize the common law, which rarely allowed specific performance (see, e.g., 4A Ronald A. Anderson, Uniform Commercial Code § 2-716: 11 (3d ed.1997)). Basically courts now determine whether goods are replaceable as a practical matter—for example, whether it would be difficult to obtain similar goods on the open market (see generally Andrea G. Nadel, Annotation, Specific Performance of Sale of Goods Under UCC § 2-716, 26 A.L.R.4th 294 (1983)).

[35] Given the centrality of the replaceability issue in determining the availability of specific relief under the UCC, a pleader need allege only the difficulty of cover to state a claim under that section. Magellan has done that. . . .

Count III: Trade Secret Misappropriation

[36] Magellan finally advances a claim for violation of the Secrets Act. By definition a trade secret is information that (765 ILCS 1065/2(d)):

> (1) is sufficiently secret to derive economic value, actual or potential, from not being generally known to other persons who can obtain economic value from its disclosure or use; and

> (2) is the subject of efforts that are reasonable under the circumstances to maintain its secrecy or confidentiality. . . .

[38] To state a claim of the type sought to be advanced in Count III, Magellan must provide appropriate allegations that the information at issue (1) was indeed a trade secret, (2) was misappropriated and (3) was used in defendant's business (*Composite Marine Propellers, Inc. v. Van Der Woude*, 962 F.2d 1263, 1265–66 (7th Cir.1992) (per curiam)). Here Magellan alleges only that its purported trade secrets are "sufficiently secret" and "the subject of reasonable efforts to maintain their secrecy" . . . .

[39] But even though the federal notice pleading regime makes conclusory allegations permissible . . . such mere rote repetition of the statutory language does not suffice. Those references to "sufficiently secret" and to "reasonable efforts" say nothing at all about what Magellan assertedly did to assure the confidentiality of its alleged trade secrets. Complaint ¶ 9 stands alone with its reference to a statement in Magellan's February 3 letter that the "requirements have not been given by us to any other company or individual for submittal to the subject supplier." But that statement was totally lacking in any warning to Salzgitter that it could not sell the goods embodying Magellan's specifications, as contrasted with its not revealing the specifications themselves to anyone (other than to fabricator DSS, of course).

[40] In that regard, Magellan's entire trade secret presentation has really muddied the waters. Its Complaint did not provide the necessary identification of just what it claimed to be its "trade secrets" entitled to judicial protection.

[41] What has since emerged from the parties' briefing is that those claimed secrets are Magellan's specifications for the steel that it was purchasing from Salzgitter— yet Magellan is somehow seeking protection for the manufactured steel itself. By

doing that Magellan has clarified itself right out of court, for it is obvious that the steel as such cannot be the subject of trade secret protection. After all, Magellan of course contemplates no effort to keep the steel under lock and key—instead it has ordered the steel so it can in turn sell the steel to its customers. And if the information that it really seeks to be kept secret (the specifications) were to be apparent or readily derivable from the product said to embody the secret (the steel itself), it would not be a "secret" at all.

[42] For much the same reason, Magellan's allegation as to claimed misappropriation is equally deficient. Although Magellan claims its trade secrets have been or will be misappropriated by Salzgitter, again the only specific acts to which the Complaint refers are Salzgitter's attempts to sell the manufactured steel to Magellan's customers. That does not state a claim of threatened (much less actual) misappropriation, for it does not say that Salzgitter has in fact used or threatened to use the asserted trade secrets themselves, or even that it will inevitably do so (*Teradyne, Inc. v. Clear Communications Corp.*, 707 F.Supp. 353, 357 (N.D.Ill.1989)). On the contrary, what Magellan says is essentially "that defendant[ ] could misuse plaintiff's secrets, and plaintiff [ ] fear[s it] will" (id.) But even when a defendant is in possession of secret information, disclosure or use of that information is not inevitable (*PepsiCo, Inc. v. Redmond*, 54 F.3d 1262, 1269 (7th Cir.1995), quoting *AMP Inc. v. Fleischhacker*, 823 F.2d 1199, 1207 (7th Cir.1987)). . . .

Conclusion

[47] It may perhaps be that when the facts are further fleshed out through discovery, Magellan's claims against Salzgitter will indeed succumb either for lack of proof or as the consequence of some legal deficiency. But in the current Rule 12(b)(6) context, Salzgitter's motion as to Counts I and II is denied, and it is ordered to file its Answer to the Complaint on or before December 20, 1999. As to the Count III trade secret claim, however, Salzgitter's motion to dismiss is granted without prejudice.

Notes and Questions

1. This is obviously not the final judgment on the matter, just a decision on Salzgitter's motion to dismiss for failure to state a claim. After the major part of the motion was denied, Salzgitter filed an "Answer and Affirmative Defenses" to the complaint brought against it by Magellan. The response of the court is worth reading:

> This memorandum order is issued sua sponte, triggered by a pervasive violation of Fed.R.Civ.P. ("Rule") 8(b) that taints virtually all of Salzgitter's Answer.

> Rule 8(b) is extraordinarily clear and straightforward in permitting only three alternatives by which a responding party may address each of the allegations (referred to there as "averments") in a complaint: either an admission or a denial or an assertion in the form set out in Rule 8(b)'s second sentence as the predicate for getting the benefit of a deemed denial. But

[handwritten annotation: "wlo order from judge" above "sua sponte"]

despite that plain roadmap, by far the majority of Salzgitter's responses . . . repeat this formulation:

> To the extent that this paragraph purports to characterize a specific document, such document speaks for itself and, accordingly, Salzgitter neither admits or denies the allegations relating thereto.

This Court has been attempting to listen to such written materials for years (in the forlorn hope that one will indeed give voice) — but until some such writing does break its silence, this Court will continue to require pleaders to employ one of the three alternatives that are permitted by Rule 8(b) in response to all allegations about the contents of documents. Because the Answer is so chock full of such impermissible refusals to plead, Salzgitter's entire responsive pleading is stricken. It is of course granted leave to file an appropriate Amended Answer and Affirmative Defenses in this Court's chambers on or before January 10, 2000 (with a copy transmitted to Magellan's counsel), failing which all of the corresponding allegations of Magellan's Complaint will be deemed to have been admitted.

Salzgitter was subsequently unable or unwilling to file a proper Answer. →Magellan gets what they want.

2. The fact scenario shows a pretty standard pattern of communications sent back and forth without ever being memorialized properly into one final and binding contract of sale. Readers should be reminded that it is imperative in cases such as this to clearly establish the sequence of offers and counteroffers until an acceptance and the terms of the agreement are identified. Here we also have a series of post-acceptance communications seeking to change the original contract. These also have to be classified as offers to amend and counsel has to determine whether or not they were accepted.

3. An interesting feature of the case is the involvement of a Letter of Credit (L/C). As is usually the case, a draft was first presented and, after approval, the actual L/C was issued. However, in an unusual turn, the seller then demanded amendments to the L/C, namely an authorization that "FCRs" could be used instead of "BoLs." Transport documents will be discussed in Part Four. You will then be asked about the difference between the two and whether Magellan was justified in refusing to amend the L/C.

4. Can you explain what exactly Magellan wants (and ultimately gets) from Salzgitter in this case (paras. 11–13)? And why was each of the three claims based on a different legal basis even though the parties were in agreement that the CISG was the governing law?

5. With regard to a claim for specific performance, the court seems to use Article 28 CISG as a welcome exit and then proceeds with discussion of specific performance under the UCC (para. 33). The correct application of Article 28 is different, however. If specific performance would be available under the CISG — in our case Article 46(1) — a national court can check whether specific performance would also be available in a parallel case under national law. If that is the case — for example

under § 2-716(1) UCC—then the claim has to be granted not on the basis of national law but on the basis of the CISG, which remains the governing law.

6. In paragraph 22 and footnote 11, the court says that "the pleading requirements to state a claim for breach of contract under the [CISG] [are] a question of first impression." Note 11 cites all seven cases that came before American courts in the first decade of the applicability of the Convention. Seven cases arising over an entire decade, of thousands of contracts concluded every day, millions every year, between companies in the U.S. and companies in other CISG Contracting States. Professor Reimann of the University of Michigan picked up on this in 2007—eight years later—by showing that out of some 1,800 judicial decisions reported in the CISG database operated by Pace Law School, only 87 "or less than 5%" originated in the U.S., although it is by far the largest of the Contracting States and certainly does not lack in litigation otherwise. Even the tiny country of Switzerland, with its seven million people, had already produced 137 decisions by 2007. It gets worse, however. Out of the 87 American decisions, about half do not apply the CISG, let alone interpret its provisions. They just mention it in passing or declare it inapplicable. Professor Reimann calls this record "shockingly low," and examines the following possible explanations: fundamental ignorance, illicit avoidance, and conscious exclusion. He does admit that conscious exclusion would explain why the CISG does not come up in litigation but also asks the necessary follow-up question: Why do American attorneys prefer to exclude the CISG? To this, he provides three answers: real or perceived legal uncertainties, mere parochialism, and/or irrational hostility toward international law.[100] Unfortunately, the cross section of all the explanations does not shed a favorable light on the American legal profession. See also my remarks above, on pp. 121–126.

The next case is about a classic problem in contract formation, the so-called battle of forms.

Case 2-7

Hanwha Corporation v. Cedar Petrochemicals, Inc.

760 F. Supp. 2d 426 (S.D.N.Y. 2011)
Alvin K. Hellerstein, District Judge
(Paragraph numbers added, footnotes and some details omitted.)

Opinion and Order

[1] Plaintiff Hanwha Corporation ("Hanwha") has sued Defendant Cedar Petrochemicals, Inc. ("Cedar") in a two-count complaint alleging breach of contract. The

---

100. See Mathias Reimann, *The CISG in the United States: Why It Has Been Neglected and Why Europeans Should Care*, Rabels Zeitschrift für Ausländisches und internationales Privatrecht 2007, Vol. 71, pp. 115–129, at pp. 116–125.

complaint arises from the parties' disagreement about the choice of law to govern their contract for the sale and purchase of an amount of the petrochemical Toluene. Cedar now moves under Federal Rule of Civil Procedure 56 for summary judgment dismissing the complaint, contending the parties never formed a final contract; Hanwha cross-moves for summary judgment in its own favor. For the reasons that follow, I hold that because the parties could not agree on a choice of law, they did not form a contract. I therefore grant Cedar's motion for summary judgment dismissing the complaint, and I deny Hanwha's cross-motion.

I. Background

[2] From January 2003 to April 2009, Cedar, a New York corporation, and Hanwha, a Korean corporation, entered into twenty discrete transactions for the purchase and sale of various petrochemicals. In each of the twenty transactions, the parties formed contracts under the same procedure. First, Hanwha would submit a bid to Cedar for a given petrochemical at a given quantity and at a given price. Cedar would accept Hanwha's bid, forming what the parties describe as a "firm bid," or an agreement regarding product, quantity, and price. Following formation of the firm bid, Cedar would transmit a package of contract documents to Hanwha, meant to incorporate and finalize all the terms of the contract. The package of documents contained two items: (I) a "contract sheet" that embodied the terms of the firm bid and a choice of law to govern the contract, and (ii) a set of "standard" terms and conditions incorporated by reference in the contract sheet. Cedar always signed the contract sheet when submitting these documents to Hanwha.

[3] The contract sheets drafted by Cedar for the twenty contracts provide the same substantive information, which can be described in three parts. First, at the top, Cedar provided a provision stating, "We hereby confirm the following transaction between Hanwha Corp. and . . . Cedar Petrochemicals. [The] [f]ollowing sets forth the entire agreement of the parties." . . . Second, in the body of the contract sheets, Cedar would identify the product, quantity, and price contemplated by the firm bid. Third, at the bottom, Cedar would provide a provision incorporating the standard terms and conditions by reference. This final provision also identified the laws Cedar chose to govern the contracts, and typically provided that New York law, the Uniform Commercial Code ("UCC"), and Incoterms 2000 governed the contract. This choice of law was reinforced by a provision in Cedar's standard terms and conditions, which also provided that New York law was to govern.

[4] After Cedar would send these signed contract documents to Hanwha, Hanwha would do one of three things: it would countersign and return the contract sheet, accepting Cedar's terms; or modify the contract sheet, and then sign and return it for Cedar's consideration; or not sign at all. On three occasions, Hanwha modified the contract sheets by providing its own choice of law to govern the contracts. Whenever Hanwha modified the contract sheets and sent them back to Cedar, Cedar did not object to the changes—including Hanwha's choices of law—but did not countersign Hanwha's version. On all twenty occasions, upon completion of this process, Cedar and Hanwha both performed their obligations under their contracts.

[5] The present case concerns the parties' efforts to form a twenty-first contract. On May 27, 2009, Hanwha submitted a bid for the purchase of 1,000 metric tons of the petrochemical Toluene at $640 per metric ton, the market rate at the time. Cedar accepted the bid, thus creating a firm bid for the purchase and sale of the Toluene. Cedar followed up its acceptance of the bid by sending Hanwha, via email, a signed contract sheet and a document setting forth Cedar's usual standard terms and conditions. As per usual, Cedar provided in the contract sheet that New York law, the UCC, and Incoterms 2000 would govern the contract, and also provided in the standard terms and conditions that New York law would govern. Hanwha did not immediately respond to the contract documents, but engaged with Cedar in preparing a bill of lading and nominating a vessel for the ocean carriage.

[6] Approximately a week after Cedar had sent Hanwha the contract documents for the Toluene sale, Hanwha returned them in modified form. On the contract sheet, Hanwha had modified the provision providing for governing law, crossing out New York law and the UCC, leaving only the provision that Incoterms 2000 was to govern the contract. Hanwha also provided a new set of "standard" terms and conditions; in relevant part, Hanwha's new set of conditions provided that Singapore law would govern the contract, rather than New York law. In summary, Hanwha struck Cedar's nomination of New York law, the UCC, and Incoterms 2000 to govern the contract, substituting instead Singapore law and Incoterms 2000.

[7] When Hanwha returned the amended contract documents, it added an additional term, stated in the body of the email transmitting the amended documents. In the email, Hanwha provided that no contract would "enter into force" unless Cedar countersigned Hanwha's proposed version of the contract documents. . . . Cedar refused to accept Hanwha's terms, and sent Hanwha an email explaining that the contract would be finalized only if Hanwha accepted Cedar's original terms. The email asked Hanwha to sign and return an unaltered version of the contract documents.

[8] While Cedar waited for a response to this last request, the parties worked out the necessary letter of credit for the transaction. Hanwha submitted a letter of credit unsatisfactory to Cedar on June 8, 2009, and an acceptable letter of credit on June 10, 2009. However, the next day, June 11, 2009, Cedar advised Hanwha that because of its failure to sign the version of the contract tendered by Cedar, there was no contract between the parties, and Cedar had the right to sell the Toluene to another party. The price of Toluene as of that date, June 11, 2009, had risen from $640 per metric ton to $790.50.

[9] In November 2009, Hanwha filed a two-count complaint in Supreme Court, New York County, alleging (I) breach of contract by Cedar for failing to deliver the Toluene at the agreed-upon price and (ii) anticipatory breach of contract for Cedar's statement of June 11, 2009 that the deal was void and it was free to sell the Toluene to another buyer. The complaint also stated that the dispute arose under United Nations Convention on Contracts for the International Sale of Goods ("CISG"), . . . thus creating federal subject-matter jurisdiction under 28 U.S.C. § 1331. Cedar

removed the case to this court, and Hanwha thereafter moved unsuccessfully to remand. . . . The parties now move and cross-move for summary judgment.

II. Standard of Review

[10] Summary judgment is appropriate if "the pleadings, the discovery and disclosure materials on file, and any affidavits show that there is no genuine issue as to any material fact and that the movant is entitled to judgment as a matter of law." Fed. R. Civ. P. 56(c)(2). On cross motions for summary judgment, the district court is obligated to consider each motion on its own merits, "taking care in each instance to draw all reasonable inferences against the party whose motion is under consideration." *Byrne v. Rutledge,* 623 F.3d 46, 52–53 (2d Cir. 2010) . . . . In considering a motion for summary judgment, "the mere possibility that a factual dispute may exist, without more, is not sufficient to overcome a convincing presentation by the moving party." *Quinn v. Syracuse Model Neighborhood Corp.,* 613 F.2d 438, 445 (2d Cir. 1980). Further, "to defeat summary judgment . . . nonmoving parties must do more than simply show that there is some metaphysical doubt as to the material facts . . . and they may not rely on conclusory allegations or unsubstantiated speculation." *Jeffreys v. City of N.Y.,* 426 F.3d 549, 554 (2d Cir. 2005) . . . .

III. Discussion

a. Choice of Law

[11] Before deciding whether the parties formed a contract, I must establish which law governs the analysis. Here, both parties are members of CISG signatory nations, but they have attempted to opt out of the CISG's substantive terms by designating other choices of substantive law. The question therefore arises whether the CISG, some other law, or both, governs the question of contract formation.

[12] The CISG is a self-executing treaty, binding on all signatory nations, that creates a private right of action in federal court under federal law. *Delchi Carrier SpA v. Rotorex Corp.,* 71 F.3d 1024, 1027–28 (2d Cir. 1995). As a treaty, the CISG is a source of federal law. See 28 U.S.C. § 1331(a); *Usinor Industeel v. Leeco Steel Prods., Inc.,* 209 F. Supp. 2d 880, 884 (N.D. Ill. 2002); *Asante Techs, Inc. v. PMC-Sierra, Inc.,* 164 F. Supp. 2d 1142, 1147 (N.D. Cal. 2001)[see p. 155]; *Riccitelli v. Elemar New England Marble and Granite, LLC,* 08 Civ. 1783, 2010 U.S. Dist. LEXIS 95086, 2010 WL 3767111, at *4 (D. Conn. 2010). Because caselaw interpreting the CISG is relatively sparse, this Court is authorized to interpret it in accordance with its general principles, "with a view towards the need to promote uniformity in its application and the observance of good faith in international trade." *Delchi Carrier,* 71 F.3d at 1028 (internal quotations omitted). "Caselaw interpreting analogous provisions of Article 2 of the Uniform Commercial Code ('UCC') may also inform a court where the language of the relevant CISG provisions track that of the UCC." *Id.* at 1028.

[13] The intent to opt out of the CISG must be set forth in the contract clearly and unequivocally. See *St. Paul Guardian Ins. Co. v. Neuromed Med. Sys. & Support,* [see p. 250]; *Asante Techs.,* 164 F. Supp. 2d at 1149–50 (declining to apply a choice-of-law clause that did not "evince a clear intent to opt out of the CISG") [see pp. 185 et seq.];

see also *Delchi Carrier*, 71 F.3d at 1027 n.1 (where the contract is silent on a choice of law, the CISG governs). Absent a clear choice of law, "the Convention governs *all* contracts between parties with places of business in different nations, so long as both nations are signatories to the Convention." *Filanto, S.p.A. v. Chilewich Intern. Corp.*, 789 F. Supp. 1229, 1237 (S.D.N.Y. 1992)[see p. 882] (emphasis in original).

[14] In this case, the parties each attempted to opt out of the CISG, but could not agree on the law to displace it, Cedar preferring New York law and the UCC, and Hanwha preferring Singapore law. This situation is not unlike the one contemplated by UCC § 2-207(b), which notes that terms upon which contracting parties do not agree are not part of the contract. In such a situation, the extraneous terms "fall away" and typically leave the Court with the obligation to provide a term of its own crafting. See, e.g., *Cloud Corp. v. Hasbro, Inc.*, 314 F.3d 289, 294–95 (7th Cir. 2002) (Posner, J.). Here, the parties never agreed to a substantive law to displace the CISG, and their competing choices must fall away, leaving the CISG to fill the void by its own self-executing force.

[15] Accordingly, in resolving these motions for summary judgment, I apply the terms of the CISG without regard to the law either party attempted to select when bargaining over the terms of the last contract.

b. The Merits

[16] The issue in this case is whether Hanwha made a binding offer within the meaning of the CISG when it bid on the 1,000 metric tons of Toluene. Several articles of the CISG bear upon this issue. First, Article 14 of the CISG states, "[a] proposal for concluding a contract addressed to one or more specific persons constitutes an offer if it is sufficiently definite *and* indicates the intention of the offeror to be bound in case of acceptance. CISG art. 14(1) (emphasis added). Second, in complementary fashion, Article 8 of the CISG sets out the relevant considerations for finding an offeror's intent. It states in full:

> (1) For the purposes of this Convention statements made by and other conduct of a party are to be interpreted according to his intent where the other party knew or could not have been unaware what the intent was.

> (2) If the preceding paragraph is not applicable, statements made by and other conduct of a party are to be interpreted according to the understanding that a reasonable person of the same kind as the other party would have had in the same circumstances.

> (3) In determining the intent of a party or the understanding a reasonable person would have had, due consideration is to be given to all relevant circumstances of the case including the negotiations, any practices which the parties have established between themselves, usages and any subsequent conduct of the parties.

[17] Finally, Article 19(1) modifies the analysis by providing that "[a] reply to an offer which purports to be an acceptance, but contains additions, limitations or other

modifications is a rejection of the offer and constitutes a counter-offer." Even if the additional or altered terms are not "material" to the contract, the offeree's amendments constitute a counter-offer if the offeror objects to them "without undue delay." *Id.* art. 19(2).

[18] In this case, it is clear that Hanwha made, and Cedar accepted, a "sufficiently definite" offer within the meaning of Article 14(1), for Hanwha's bid was for a specific product, at a specific price, and for a specific quantity. Beyond this, however, Article 14 requires that Hanwha must also have intended to be bound when it made the bid. *Id.* On this latter point, the undisputed facts make clear Hanwha did not possess this intent. Rather, the course of dealing between the parties makes clear that neither party was to be bound until they agreed on other material terms and conditions, namely the choice of law and forum-disputes provisions.

[19] As a threshold point, although the CISG expresses a preference that the offeror's intent be considered subjectively, that consideration is not possible in this case since neither party submitted any competent evidence of their subjective intentions. *See* id. art. 8(1). The parties have submitted only self-serving declarations of how they respectively viewed the other side's offers and counter-offers, from the hindsight of their dispute. Such declarations do nothing more than make out "the mere possibility of a factual dispute," *Quinn,* 613 F.2d at 445, and can be neither a basis to grant or deny either party's motion, see *Jeffreys,* 426 F.3d at 554.

[20] Turning to the objective analysis called for by Article 8(2), it is clear from all the relevant circumstances that Hanwha did not intend to be bound by making its bid for the 1,000 metric tons of Toluene. Id. art. 8(3). In the twenty prior transactions, these parties had engaged in a familiar two-step process, whereby they first formed their firm bid and then negotiated the final terms and conditions of the contracts. On each of these twenty prior occasions, the parties did not perform until after they had achieved agreement, explicit or implicit, on all the final terms of the contract. The contract sheets reflect this, for each bears a provision stating, "[The] [f]ollowing sets forth the entire agreement of the parties." . . . From this, it is clear that these parties did not enter into a final contract until they agreed to the final terms embodied in the contract documents, and not when they agreed Hanwha's bids on product, quantity, and price.

[21] On this occasion, the undisputed facts show that the parties never worked out the final terms of the contract because they never formed an agreement on a term they deemed material, a choice of governing law. Previously, Hanwha had on several occasions proposed a different choice of law and Cedar had accepted the proposal, either implicitly or explicitly. The parties thereafter performed under the various contracts. But here, after Hanwha modified Cedar's contract documents and proposed a different choice of law, Cedar rejected the change. These activities constitute a counter-offer, and a rejection of the counter-offer, within the meaning of Article 19(1).

[22] Further evidence that the parties failed to contract can be seen by the way they treated Hanwha's modification of Cedar's choice of law. Beyond simply modifying

Cedar's choice of law, Hanwha insisted that Cedar accept the modification explicitly, by advising Cedar that the contract could "enter into force" only if Cedar explicitly countersigned Hanwha's version of the contract documents. . . . By objecting immediately and insisting on its own nomination, Cedar made clear that it regarded the change as material, thus rendering the different choice of law a material term under Article 19(2). As the parties thereafter failed to reconcile their views, it is apparent that they never formed a final contract.

[23] Finally, I note that Hanwha's alternative argument that summary judgment is inappropriate at this time is unavailing. Hanwha argues that issues of fact exist regarding the norms of contracting practices in the Korean petrochemicals industry. Where the parties have established a course of dealing between themselves, industry norms that might otherwise apply are irrelevant.

IV. Conclusion

[24] For the foregoing reasons, Cedar's motion for summary judgment is granted, and the case is dismissed. Hanwha's cross-motion for summary judgment is denied. The Clerk shall terminate the motions . . . and close the case.

SO ORDERED.

Notes and Questions

1. What do you think of the idea that "analogous provisions" of UCC Article 2 should be relied upon for the interpretation of the CISG? (para. 12) *Hanwha* is by no means the only case where an American court is trying to put a square peg into a round hole by interpreting the CISG in the way it is used to interpreting the UCC. The *Hanwha* judge cited *Delchi*. There is also *Chicago Prime Packers*,[101] and there is the even more egregious decision in *Raw Materials Inc. v. Manfred Forberich GmbH & Co. KG (RMI)*.[102] In *RMI*, there was a question whether seller Forberich could rely on force majeure to excuse late delivery of the goods. The court had to interpret Article 79 CISG and proceeded as follows:

> The parties agree that their contract is governed by the Convention on Contracts for the International Sale of Goods ('CISG'). . . . Although the contract does not contain an express force majeure provision, the CISG provides that: 'A party is not liable for failure to perform any of his obligations if he proves that failure was due to an impediment beyond his control and that he could not reasonably be expected to have taken the impediment into account at the time of the conclusion of the contract or to have avoided or overcome its consequences.' CISG Art. 79. RMI asserts that '[w]hile no American court has specifically interpreted or applied Article 79 of the

---

101. *Chicago Prime Packers, Inc. v. Northam Food Trading Co.*, 01 C 4447, 2003 U.S. Dist. LEXIS 9122 (N.D. Ill. May 25, 2003), available at http:// cisgw3.law.pace.edu/cases/030529u1.html.

102. *Raw Materials Inc. v. Manfred Forberich GmbH & Co., KG*, U.S. Dist. 2004 WL 1535839, 53 UCC Rep. Serv 2d 878 (N.D. Ill., July 7, 2004) No. 03 C 1154.

CISG, caselaw interpreting the Uniform Commercial Code's . . . provision on excuse provides guidance for interpreting the CISG's excuse provision since it contains similar requirements as those set forth in Article 79.' This approach of looking to caselaw interpreting analogous provisions of the UCC has been used by other federal courts. See, e.g., *Delchi* . . . ; *Chicago Prime Packers*. . . . Furthermore, *Forberich does not dispute that this is proper* and, in fact, also points to caselaw interpreting the UCC. . . . Accordingly, in applying Article 79 of the CISG, the Court will use as a guide caselaw interpreting a similar provision of § 2-615 of the UCC. (at p. 3, emphasis added)

So it would seem to be up to the parties to object to a court simply using the traditional UCC interpretation when looking at the CISG. What happened to the time-honored maxim that *iura novit curia?*[103]

2. Given the history of the parties' dealings with each other, do you think the judge was right in concluding that a contract had not been formed? Concerning the application of the "last shot rule" versus the "knock-out rule" in the battle of forms under the CISG, Professor Leandro Tripodi of the University of São Paolo wrote instructive comments about this judgment. As you read the comments, consider whether the solution proposed by Prof. Tripodi would bring the CISG closer to the UCC or move it further away. Do you agree or disagree with the conclusions of Prof. Tripodi about the formation of the contract? Why?

"In a transaction governed by the CISG, the *Hanwha* court found that the parties did not conclude a contract of sale. Such finding was based on two different grounds:

1) no final agreement was reached on a modification of the offer that qualifies as material according to the parties' intentions and to the CISG;

2) no intent of being bound could be extracted from the parties' exchange in light of their course of dealing.

#1 Recent developments in CISG contract formation place decreasing importance on a disagreement of the parties where such disagreement refers only to standard terms and conditions. These developments point to the application of the *knock-out rule* to those cases, as opposed to the *last shot rule*, which is in line with the plain wording of Article 19.

Under the *knock-out rule*, where the parties have agreed on essential features of the contract (the *essentialia negotii*), such as nature of the goods, quantity and price, their failure to come to terms as regards other, non-essential, terms should not be understood as a failure to enter into the contract. In other words, a disagreement

---

103. For comments, see the excellent article by Francesco G. Mazzotta, *Why Do Some American Courts Fail to Get It Right?*, 3 Loy. U. Chi. Int'l L. Rev. 85 (2005). See also Franco Ferrari, *The Relationship Between the UCC and the CISG and the Construction of Uniform Law*, 29 Loy. L.A. L. Rev. 1021 (1996).

merely referring to standard terms is in principle not an obstacle to contract forma-tion, provided that the parties have agreed on essential terms.

According to a commentator (MAGNUS, Ulrich, *Last shot vs. Knock-out: still battle over battle of forms under the CISG*, <http://www.cisg.law.pace.edu/cisg/biblio/magnus4.html>, at V), in order to determine whether the *knock-out rule* applies, one should estimate how far the parties went through the performance of their deal. While little doubt remains in instances where complete performance was achieved, partial performance has to be analyzed on a case-by-case basis.

In *Hanwha*, it was noted by the court that both plaintiff and defendant "engaged . . . in preparing a bill of lading and nominating a vessel for the ocean carriage" and "worked out" two letters of credit. One, issued on June 8, 2009, was unsatisfactory, but an acceptable letter of credit was opened on June 10, 2009. This means that, besides reaching an agreement on the nature of the goods (Toluene), the quantity (1,000 metric tons) and the price (US $640,00 per ton), the parties effec-tively commenced performance. It was only due to a disagreement over "second-class" contractual terms, however Article 19(3) may indicate them as material, that one of the parties unilaterally unwound the transaction.

Among the terms that were never settled there was a choice of law clause. The court's finding that competing terms (including a choice of law clause) must "fall away," giving rise to application of the CISG under its Article 1(1)(a) is sufficient to overcome any difficulty arising from a negative choice of law. Good for the CISG, since one of its goals is to "fill the void" where no governing law was agreed.

#2 In the court's words, evidence supports that: "[a]fter [defendant] would send these signed contract documents to [plaintiff], [plaintiff] would do one of three things: it would countersign and return the contract sheet, accepting [defendant]'s terms; or modify the contract sheet, and then sign and return it for [defendant]'s consideration; or not sign at all. On three occasions, [plaintiff] modified the con-tract sheets by providing its own choice of law to govern the contracts. Whenever [plaintiff] modified the contract sheets and sent them back to [defendant], [defen-dant] did not object to the changes—including [plaintiff]'s choices of law—but did not countersign [plaintiff]'s version. On all twenty occasions, upon completion of this process, [defendant] and [plaintiff] both performed their obligations under their contracts."

What emerges from these facts is that terms and conditions attached to the bid have, actually, always been immaterial in the eyes of the parties. In any of three sce-narios, the parties went forward irrespectively of which standard terms had eventu-ally prevailed. Therefore, in the transaction before the court, either the course of dealing was overturned, as modifications that had so far been immaterial became material, or, as a matter of fact, these modifications became only purportedly material.

The significant rise of over US $150 per ton in Toluene price between May 27, 2009 (date of submission of bid) and June 11, 2009 (day on which defendant advised plaintiff that no contract existed between the parties) made it considerably attractive for the defendant to bail out from the deal and look to sell the product off. Unexpected price fluctuations are inherent to the commodity market. Had Toluene price plummeted by 23% in those fifteen days and the plaintiff would be the one looking good to walk away.

According to the standard of Article 7(1) CISG, the text of the Convention has to be interpreted with due regard for the observance of good faith in international trade. While one should not resort to the good faith requirement as a source of new obligations not created by CISG drafters, Article 7(1) is an adequate bar to prevent a party from raising an interpretation which violates good faith.

In *Hanwha*, the contention that a contract was not concluded is inconsistent with a good faith interpretation of Article 14(1), Article 18(1) and (3) and Article 19 of the CISG. A good faith interpretation of these articles cannot lead to a finding that a party is allowed to baffle contract formation only because the deal is no longer interesting or a different one would pay off better.

Both parties issued statements insisting that the other party accept the unaltered standard terms, which clearly shows their intent to be bound. Furthermore, they engaged in acts of performance, which corroborates that intent. The defendant's intent disappeared, however, once Toluene was struck by an international price rise of more than 20%. All of a sudden, disagreements that had been tolerated during a course comprising no less than 20 prior transactions between the parties became material in the sense of Article 19(2) CISG.

A party cannot have it both ways. On June 10, 2009, the defendant was insisting that plaintiff accept its terms and even engaging in acts of performance. One day later, the same party was advising the other party that no contract was made and they would sell the product off. In fact, either the defendant was, or was not, intended to be bound, and, on the basis of the information provided by the court, one can see that it was.[104]

3. If you agree with Professor Tripodi, does this mean that the rules in the CISG about battle of forms have evolved for all such cases and that the knock-out rule should now be applied instead of the last shot rule? What would be the legal basis for such a re-interpretation of Art. 19 of the CISG?

4. Do you think the judge's application of the reasonable person test in Article 8(2) CISG was reasonable?[105]

---

104. Professor Leandro Tripodi, Editorial Remarks, CISG Case Presentation, available at http://www.cisg.law.pace.edu/cisg/wais/db/cases2/110118u1.html; reproduced with permission.

105. For more information, see Aleksanders Fillers, *Concept of the Reasonable Person Under Article 8 of the United Nations Convention on Contracts for the International Sale of Goods*, 17 Vindobona J. Int'l Comm. L. & Arb. 171 (2013).

The following case elaborates on the interpretation of the CISG.[106]

Case 2-8   Can skip.

R J & A M Smallmon v. Transport Sales Ltd and Grant Alan Miller

Court of Appeal of New Zealand
C A 545/2010 [2010] N Z C A 340
22 July 2011
(Footnotes and some details omitted.)
JUDGMENT OF THE COURT

The appeal is dismissed.

The Appellants must pay to the Respondents costs on a standard appeal on a band A basis and usual disbursements. We certify for second counsel.

Reasons of the Court

An international sale of trucks

[1] The appellants, [Buyers], operate a road transport, water and earthmoving business in Queensland, Australia. [Buyers] decided to purchase four trucks for use in their business from a New Zealand company, the first respondent, [Seller]. The owner of TSL is the second respondent, [Owner].

[2] The four trucks were Volvo model FM12 and were originally assembled in Australia to comply with the Australian Design Rules (ADRs). At the time of assembly, the compliance plate (certifying that the vehicle was manufactured to comply with the ADRs) was not attached to each truck, as the vehicles were intended for export to New Zealand and required some minor modifications for that market. The trucks were brought to New Zealand and operated [there]. [Seller]'s role was as sales agent of the used trucks on behalf of the owner. . . .

[3] The four trucks were purchased in New Zealand by [Buyers] and shipped to Queensland. After the trucks arrived, [Buyers] experienced a series of problems with the Queensland regulatory authorities. Despite the trucks being roadworthy, [Buyers] were not able to have the trucks registered by Queensland Transport because they did not have a compliance plate attached and because [Buyers] had not obtained an authority to import from the National Transport Department. Eventually, these regulatory authorities agreed to issue exemption permits allowing [Buyers] to use the trucks on a limited basis.

[4] The contract between [Seller] and [Buyers] did not contain an express term as to the registerability of the trucks in Queensland. At trial, a key issue was whether, and in what circumstances, a seller of goods can be liable for breach of an implied term

---

106. On this subject, see, *inter alia*, Sarah Howard Jenkins, *Construing Laws Governing International and U.S. Domestic Contracts for the Sale of Goods: a Comparative Evaluation of the CISG and UCC Rules of Interpretation*, 26 Temp. Int'l & Comp. L.J. 181 (2012).

as to fitness for purpose when the alleged lack of fitness arises not from the physical features of the goods, but as a result of the alleged non-compliance with regulatory requirements in the buyer's country.

[5] In the High Court, French J held that this issue was determined by the application of the provisions of the United Nations Convention on Contracts for the International Sale of Goods (the Convention), notably art 35. This article sets out the primary requirement that a seller in an international transaction deliver to the buyer goods which are of the quantity, quality and description required by the contract. Relevant to this case, art 35(2) establishes that the goods do not conform with the contract (except where the parties have agreed otherwise) unless the goods are fit for the purposes for which goods of the same description would ordinarily be used or fit for any particular purpose expressly or impliedly made known to the seller.

[6] The Judge found that [Buyers] had failed to establish that [Seller] was liable for breach of an implied term as to fitness for purpose. The seller was not responsible for compliance with the regulatory requirements of the importing country and there was no basis for finding that TSL knew or ought to have known about the applicable regulatory requirements for trucks in Queensland.

[7] [Buyers] appeal against this aspect of the decision. . . .

High Court Judgment

[25] The Judge was required to determine [Buyers]'s claim that there had been a breach by [Seller] of art 35(2) of the Convention on the basis that the trucks were not fit for purposes for which they would ordinarily be used or a particular purpose made known to the seller at the time of contracting. The Judge held that there was no express warranty in the contract between [Seller] and [Buyers] relating to registrability of the trucks in Queensland. Thus the standards set out in art 35(2), including the requirement that goods be fit for the purposes for which they are ordinarily used, were implied terms that formed part of the contract. The Judge reasoned that trucks are ordinarily used for the cartage of goods on the road. The trucks purchased by [Buyers] were mechanically capable of being driven on the road. [Buyers] contention was that "because the trucks were not registerable at the point of sale, and could never be fully registered, they could not be driven and were therefore not fit for the ordinary purpose".

[26] The Judge considered a number of overseas decisions and academic articles. In particular, she referred to the leading cases, including the *New Zealand Mussels Case*" in the Bundesgerichtshof (German Supreme Court), the *"Italian Cheese Case*" (Court of Appeal, Grenoble, France), and *Medical Marketing v Internazionale Medico Scientifica* (Federal District Court, Louisiana, United States). The Judge concluded that the following principles emerged from the authorities:

> As a general rule, the seller is not responsible for compliance with the regulatory provisions or standards of the importing country even if he or she knows the destination of the goods unless:

a. The same regulations exist in the seller's country.

b. The buyer drew the seller's attention to the regulatory provisions and relied on the seller's expertise.

c. The seller knew or should have known of the requirements because of special circumstances.

Special circumstances may include:

i. The fact the seller has maintained a branch in the importing country.

ii. The existence of a long-standing connection between the parties.

iii. The fact the seller has often exported into the buyer's country.

iv. The fact the seller has promoted its products in the buyer's country.

[27] In terms of interpretation of the Convention, the Judge held that under art 7 recourse to domestic law is prohibited. This conclusion was not challenged by [Buyers] on appeal.

[28] In the High Court it was common ground that the registration requirements in Queensland are different to those prevailing in New Zealand. It was also common ground that at no stage did [Buyers] ever raise the issue of registration requirements with Mr. Miller. Further, there was no evidence that Mr. Miller knew what the registration requirements were in Queensland. Accordingly, for [Buyers] to establish a breach of art 35(2)(a), it could only be on the grounds that Mr. Miller and [Seller] ought to have known about such requirements because of special circumstances.

[29] On this issue the Judge held:

> [94] What is alleged to amount to special circumstances are the facts that [Seller] advertised in Australia and that [Seller] had exported trucks previously into Australia. The evidence established that prior to the [Buyer] transaction, [Seller] had exported seven Volvo trucks into Australia.
>
> [95] As the authorities make clear, these are circumstances capable of amounting to special circumstances.
>
> [96] However, in my view, they are outweighed by two other considerations. The first is the terms of the advertisement which stated "landed" at Brisbane. The second is that Mr. Miller expressly recommended Australian contractors who would be able to assist [Buyers] with importation and ADR compliance. He was thereby delineating the parties' respective responsibilities, as well as delineating his own field of expertise and knowledge, and in my view in those circumstances it would be wrong to say that Mr. Miller or [Seller] ought to have known. . . .

[32] As a result the Judge concluded that [Buyers] had failed to establish a breach of art 35(2) of the Convention on the part of Mr. Miller or [Seller].

The issues on appeal

[33] The central issue is the application of art 35 of the Convention to the sale of the four trucks by [Seller] to [Buyers]. There was no express provision in the contract

that the trucks would in fact be registrable in Queensland. Hence there was no question of breach of art 35(1). So the first question is: was there an implied term of the contract that the trucks met the requirements for registration in the buyer's home state, when the seller was located in a different country? The second question is: which of the parties had responsibility for obtaining registration of the four trucks in Queensland?

[34] These questions involve the application of the provisions of art 35(2) of the Convention to the facts of the case as outlined above. Accordingly, we will first consider the principles arising from art 35(2) as derived from the international jurisprudence in the form of cases and articles. We will then provide our evaluation of the facts in the light of those principles.

Applicable legal principles

Convention articles

[35] There are three relevant articles: arts 7, 8 and 35(2). Article 7 provides:

(1) In the interpretation of this Convention, regard is to be had to its international character and to the need to promote uniformity in its application and the observance of good faith in international trade.

(2) Questions concerning matters governed by this Convention which are not expressly settled in it are to be settled in conformity with the general principles on which it is based or, in the absence of such principles, in conformity with the law applicable by virtue of the rules of private international law.

[36] Because the intent and conduct of the parties to the contract is in issue, art 8 is also relevant. Article 8 states:

(1) For the purposes of this Convention statements made by and other conduct of a party are to be interpreted according to his intent where the other party knew or could not have been unaware what that intent was.

(2) If the preceding paragraph is not applicable, statements made by and other conduct of a party are to be interpreted according to the understanding that a reasonable person of the same kind as the other party would have had in the same circumstances.

(3) In determining the intent of a party or the understanding a reasonable person would have had, due consideration is to be given to all relevant circumstances of the case including the negotiations, any practices which the parties have established between themselves, usages and any subsequent conduct of the parties.

[37] The key articles are arts 35(2) and 35(3), which provide:

(2) Except where the parties have agreed otherwise, the goods do not conform with the contract unless they:

(a) are fit for the purposes for which goods of the same description would ordinarily be used;

(b) are fit for any particular purpose expressly or impliedly made known to the seller at the time of the conclusion of the contract, except where the circumstances show that the buyer did not rely, or that it was unreasonable for him to rely, on the seller's skill and judgement;

(c) possess the qualities of goods which the seller has held out to the buyer as a sample or model;

(d) are contained or packaged in the manner usual for such goods or, where there is no such manner, in a manner adequate to preserve and protect the goods.

(3) The seller is not liable under subparagraphs (a) to (d) of the preceding paragraph for any lack of conformity of the goods if at the time of the conclusion of the contract the buyer knew or could not have been unaware of such lack of conformity.

Interpreting the Convention

[38] New Zealand acceded to the Convention, which opened for signature on 11 April 1980 and entered into force on 1 January 1988, on 22 September 1994. As noted, the Convention was enacted for New Zealand by the Sale of Goods (United Nations Convention) Act 1994. The aim of the Convention was to seek to achieve the harmonisation and unification of trade law regarding international sales of goods.

[39] Counsel for [Buyers] properly acknowledged that resort to authorities dealing with domestic law is not permissible. This follows from the requirement in art 7, dealing with the interpretation of the Convention, to have regard to "its international character and to the need to promote uniformity in its application and the observance of good faith in international trade". Thus the Convention is to be given an autonomous interpretation requiring the Convention to be interpreted exclusively on its own terms and applying Convention-related decisions in overseas jurisdictions.

[40] As urged by the late Professor Peter Schlechtriem, recourse to domestic law must be avoided:

> In reading and understanding the provisions, concepts and words of the Convention, recourse to the understanding of these words and the like in domestic systems, in particular the domestic legal system of the reader, must be avoided. This seems to be self-evident, but experience shows that practitioners and scholars tend to understand words and concepts of the Convention according to their familiar domestic law.

[41] We therefore propose to consider only the international authorities and articles in interpreting art 35(2).

Principles to be distilled from art 35(2)

[42] ... The international jurisprudence concerning art 35(2) has established that, generally, the seller is not responsible for compliance with the regulatory provisions or standards of the importing country. The seminal case is the New Zealand mussels case, where the Supreme Court of Germany stated that a buyer cannot expect compliance with the specialised public law provisions of the buyer's own country. More recently, case law emanating from the Oberster Gerichtshof (the Supreme Court of Austria) confirms that a seller cannot be expected to know all of the rules of the buyer's country or the country of usage, and that the standards of the seller's country specify the standard of ordinary usage. Just because the seller knows generally of the buyer's country or the country where the goods are destined, that does not place upon the buyer an obligation to comply with the regulations of that country.

[43] The German Supreme Court did, however, identify certain situations where the requirements of the buyer's country can be taken into account. These are when the relevant regulatory standards of the buyer's country:

(a) exist in the seller's country as well; or

(b) the buyer has pointed them out to the seller and thereby relied on and was allowed to rely on the seller's expertise; or

(c) the relevant provisions in the anticipated export country are known or should be known to the seller due to the particular circumstances of the case.

[44] The German Supreme Court went on, in statements not directly necessary to the reasoning, to list different circumstances in which a court might find that the seller knew or ought to have known the relevant public law provisions of the buyer's country. These circumstances included that the seller had a branch in the buyer's country; the seller already had a business connection with the buyer for some time; the seller often exports to the buyer's country; or the seller has promoted his or her products in that country.

[45] In the United States, the District Court for the Eastern District of Louisiana essentially adopted the reasoning of the *New Zealand Mussels Case*. The Court stated that the decision of the German Supreme Court was authority for the proposition that the seller was not obligated to supply goods that conformed to public law provisions of the buyer's country. The exception was when, due to special circumstances, "such as the existence of a seller's branch office in the buyer's state", the seller knew or ought to have known of the regulations at issue. Case law in France has also shown that the business relations of the parties may be important in determining non-conformity pursuant to art 35. These cases encourage the conclusion that the existence of such "special circumstances" may lead to the seller being liable for breach of public law and regulatory requirements in the buyer's country.

[46] The international authorities and articles support the proposition that the seller will not be liable for goods that do not conform to the regulatory provisions or

standards of the buyer's country unless the seller knew or ought to have known of the requirements because of special circumstances. It seems that this principle can apply to the provisions of both art 35(2)(a) and 35(2)(b).

[47] With respect to proof of particular circumstances, the examples identified in the cases and the literature include the seller maintaining a branch in the buyer's country, a long-standing business connection between the parties, the seller making regular exports to the buyer's country and the provision of goods in the buyer's country. These are illustrative of the factors that may enable a buyer to establish liability on the seller, despite the general principle to the contrary. Where the reasonableness of the buyer's reliance on the seller's skill and judgment is in issue under art 35(2)(b), the seller may be able to point to proof of such special circumstances.

[48] Finally, we note that the existence of an opportunity by the buyer to inspect the goods before the contract is entered into may be relevant to the analysis. In the "Frozen Chicken Legs Case", the Audiencia Provincial de Granada (an appellate court in Spain) seemed to uphold the principle that the seller is not expected to know the public law provisions of the buyer's country or the ultimate destination of the goods. It was also material in this case that the buyer had had an opportunity to inspect the frozen chicken legs, further pushing responsibility for non-conformity with regulatory provisions towards the buyer. Hence the fact of inspecting the goods may well be relevant to the particular circumstances of the case.

Appellants' submissions

[49] For the appellants, Mr. Dale emphasises that the problems with registration in Australia were unforeseen by both the buyers and the seller, and are the result of "unusual rulings" by the regulatory authorities in Australia. But counsel submits that art 35(2) of the Convention places the risk of non-registration with the seller.

[50] Counsel submits that the seller is liable under art 35(2)(a) because the inability to register the trucks means that they are not fit for purpose. He submits that it is sufficient for [Buyers] to prove that the trucks could not be registered, as was the case. It is not necessary for the buyers to go on and prove that the seller ought to have known of the unusual circumstances in Queensland that prevented registration. This is because art 35(2)(a) itself puts the seller at risk. Any principle from the international jurisprudence that the seller is not responsible for compliance with regulatory requirements in the buyer's country is a general one only and open to proof to the contrary. . . .

Our evaluation

Article 35(2)(a)

[58] Article 35(2) is premised on the fact that the parties have not agreed otherwise. As stated in the text by Schlechtriem and Butler: Article 35(2) . . . sets out what reasonable parties would have agreed upon had they put their mind to it. This is important since it means that the first inquiry has to be what the parties agreed upon and only if that inquiry is not satisfactory is Article 35(2) . . . applicable.

[59] With respect to the first inquiry, the Judge found that there was no express term in the contract relating to the registrability of the trucks in Queensland. This finding was not challenged on appeal. The next question concerns any terms to be implied under art 35(2). Here the starting point is that the goods must be fit for purpose.

[60] Then there is the principle that, under art 35(2) of the Convention, in an international sale of goods generally the seller is not responsible for compliance with the regulatory provisions or standards of the buyer's country. Here, it was common ground that the registration requirements for trucks in Queensland were different to those applicable in New Zealand. Further, at no stage prior to contracting with [Seller] did [Buyers] raise the issue of registration requirements with Mr. Miller. The Judge found (and this was not challenged on appeal) that there was no evidence that Mr. Miller knew what the registration requirements were in Queensland. . . .

[62] On the question of whether he ought to have known about them, the particular circumstances identified by the Judge as relevant to the analysis are: first, the advertising of trucks for sale in Australia by [Seller] and, second, the fact that, prior to the sale to [Buyers], [Seller] had sold seven used Volvo trucks to buyers in Australia. The Judge correctly observed that these factors are "capable of amounting to special circumstances". But, like the Judge, we are satisfied that neither of these circumstances, nor any other factor, is sufficient to justify a departure from the general principle under art 35(2) because [Seller] ought to have known about the regulation provisions or requirements governing registration of the trucks in Australia.

[63] With respect to the promotion by [Seller] of trucks for sale in the Australian trade magazine, we do not consider much weight, if any, can be placed on this factor. In the advertisement the seller made no promises about registration or the provision of services to achieve registration in Queensland. As noted by the Judge, the advertisement offered shipping prices ex New Zealand or landed at Brisbane (or elsewhere), indicating that the seller's role ceased at the latest upon delivery by ship onto the wharf at Brisbane.

[64] The fact that [Seller] had previously exported seven Volvo trucks to Australia likewise can have little weight as a particular circumstance in overcoming the general principle. First, in all previous sales to Australia, Mr. Miller was not aware that the buyers had encountered any problems with the import regulations, or in achieving registration in Queensland. The regulatory authorities had facilitated the registration process, despite the trucks not having compliance plates attached and the owners not having an authority to import.

[65] It was against this background and state of Mr. Miller's knowledge that the sale to [Buyers] took place. Mr. Miller expressly recommended to the buyers two expert Australian contractors, Messrs Walsh and Tucker, who could assist with the importation, ADR compliance and registration processes. We agree with the Judge's view that Mr. Miller was thereby delineating the respective responsibilities of the parties to the contract. At the same time, Mr. Miller was informing the buyers about the

limits of his own expertise and knowledge about regulatory requirements within Australia.

[66] Another circumstance that we consider to be material is the knowledge and experience of [Buyers]. As the Judge found, they were experienced transport operators. Hence they were in a much better position than Mr. Miller to know the registration requirements of their own country. Moreover, having received preliminary expert advice from Mr. Walsh about matters to watch out for, they had the opportunity to (and did) inspect the four trucks in New Zealand. The fact that the trucks did not have compliance plates on them was not kept from them. It was there for them (and anyone else) to see. The Judge was satisfied that, given their experience, they could be expected to be able to identify the presence or absence of a compliance plate. We agree. . . .

[70] For all of the above reasons, we are satisfied that there is no proper basis upon which [Buyers] establish that the general principle does not apply on the ground that Mr. Miller ought to have known about the regulatory standards or requirements of Australia. . . .

Result

[84] The appeal is dismissed. . . .

Notes and Questions

1. How and why is a case from New Zealand applicable to what we have studied so far?

2. The main question in this case was whether certain standards for the conformity of the goods could be implied in the absence of specific provisions in a contract, more specifically whether the goods were "fit for the purposes" for which such goods are ordinarily used pursuant to Article 35(2) of the CISG. What is the method applied by the courts in New Zealand for the interpretation of the language of Article 35? How easy or how difficult would it be for a judge in the United States to apply this method? Can you find cases where a judge in the United States actually did so?

3. Why did Professor Schlechtriem advocate that recourse to domestic law should be avoided in the interpretation of the CISG (para. 40)?

C. Contract Formation and Interpretation Under the Uniform Commercial Code (UCC) and the Restatement (Second) of Contracts

In this section, we will examine the provisions on contract formation and interpretation applicable in the U.S. if the CISG is excluded or otherwise not applicable. Readers should look for differences and similarities with the CISG rules.

☆Checklist 2-3
Provisions on Contract Formation and Interpretation in UCC and Restatement

Issue	UCC Rule(s)	Restatement
Pre-Contractual Obligations		
Form Requirements	§§ 1-206, 2-201, 8-319	§§ 6, 19, 27, 30, 65, 110–123, 131–137, 138–150
Capacity		§§ 12–16
Offer or Invitation	§§ 2-204–2-206	§§ 24, 26, 33, 34
Rejection		§ 38
Acceptance	§ 2-206	§§ 22, 29, 30, 35–70
Modified Acceptance or Counteroffer?	§§ 2-207, 2-209	§§ 39, 40, 58–61
Incorp. of General Terms and Conditions	§ 2-207	
Relevance of Previous Negotiations or Dealings between the Parties and other Outside (Parol) Evidence Prior to or Simultaneous to Contract Conclusion	§ 2-202	§ 213
Consideration	N/A	§§ 71–94
Conditions		§§ 224–230
Mistake		§§ 20, 151–158
Misrepresentation, Duress, Undue Influence		§§ 159–177
Relevance of Subsequent Negotiations or Communications		§ 61
Public Policy Considerations		§§ 178–185, 186–188, 192–196
Other Methods to Fill Gaps in Contracts:Implied Warranties Usages	§§ 2-308, 309 §§ 2-314–318 §§ 1-303, 1-307	§ 204 §§ 219–223
Other Tools of Interpretation		§§ 200–208, 209–218, 231–234
Involvement of Agents		Restatement (Third) of Agency
Validity		§§ 78, 178–185, 186–188, 192–196

We will look at one frequently cited decision that beautifully illustrates the problem of the battle of forms under the UCC.

Case 2-9

Northrop Corporation v. Litronic Industries

29 F.3d 1173 (7th Cir. 1994)
(Paragraph numbers added, footnotes and some details omitted.)
POSNER, Chief Judge

[1] "Battle of the forms" refers to the not uncommon situation in which one business firm makes an offer in the form of a preprinted form contract and the offeree responds with its own form contract. At common law, any discrepancy between the forms would prevent the offeree's response from operating as an acceptance. See *Poel v. Brunswick-Balke-Collender Co.*, 216 N.Y. 310, 110 N.E. 619, 621–22 (1915). So there would be no contract in such a case. This was the "mirror image" rule, which Article 2 of the Uniform Commercial Code jettisoned by providing that "a definite and seasonable expression of acceptance or a written confirmation which is sent within a reasonable time operates as an acceptance even though it states terms additional to or different from those offered or agreed upon, unless acceptance is made conditional on assent to the additional or different terms." UCC § 2-207(1). See *Union Carbide Corp. v. Oscar Mayer Foods Corp.*, 947 F.2d 1333, 1335–36 (7th Cir.1991). Mischief lurks in the words "additional to or different from." The next subsection of 2-207 provides that if additional terms in the acceptance are not materially different from those in the offer, then, subject to certain other qualifications (*id.* at 1335–37), they become part of the contract, § 2-207(2), while if the additional terms are materially different they operate as proposals and so have no effect unless the offeror agrees to them, UCC § 2-207, comment 3; if the offeror does not agree to them, therefore, the terms of the contract are those in the offer. A clause providing for interest at normal rates on overdue invoices, or limiting the right to reject goods because of defects falling within customary trade tolerances for acceptance with adjustment, would be the sort of additional term that is not deemed material, and hence it would become a part of the contract even if the offeror never signified acceptance of it. *Id.*, comment 5.

[2] The Code does not explain, however, what happens if the offeree's response contains *different* terms (rather than additional ones) within the meaning of section 2-207(1). There is no consensus on that question. See James J. White & Robert S. Summers, *Uniform Commercial Code* 33–36 (3d ed. 1988); John E. Murray, Jr., "The Chaos of the 'Battle of the Forms': Solutions," 39 *Vand.L.Rev.* 1307, 1354–65 (1986). We know there is a contract because an acceptance is effective even though it contains different terms; but what are the terms of the contract that is brought into being by the offer and acceptance? One view is that the discrepant terms in both the nonidentical offer and the acceptance drop out, and default terms found elsewhere in the Code fill the resulting gap. Another view is that the offeree's discrepant terms drop out and the offeror's become part of the contract. A third view, possibly the most sensible, equates "different" with "additional" and makes the outcome turn on

whether the new terms in the acceptance are materially different from the terms in the offer—in which event they operate as proposals, so that the offeror's terms prevail unless he agrees to the variant terms in the acceptance—or not materially different from the terms in the offer, in which event they become part of the contract. John L. Utz, "More on the Battle of the Forms: The Treatment of 'Different' Terms Under the Uniform Commercial Code," 16 *U.C.C.L.J.* 103 (1983). This interpretation equating "different" to "additional," bolstered by drafting history which shows that the omission of "or different" from section 2-207(2) was a drafting error, . . . because all different terms are additional and all additional terms are different.

[3] Unfortunately, the Illinois courts—whose understanding of Article 2 of the UCC is binding on us because this is a diversity suit governed, all agree, by Illinois law—have had no occasion to choose among the different positions on the consequences of an acceptance that contains "different" terms from the offer. We shall have to choose.

[4] The battle of the forms in this case takes the form of something very like a badminton game, but we can simplify it a bit without distorting the issues. The players are Northrop, the giant defense firm, and Litronic, which manufactures electronic components, including "printed wire boards" that are incorporated into defense weapon systems. In 1987 Northrop sent several manufacturers, including Litronic, a request to submit offers to sell Northrop a customized printed wire board designated by Northrop as a "1714 Board." The request stated that any purchase would be made by means of a purchase order that would set forth terms and conditions that would override any inconsistent terms in the offer. In response, Litronic mailed an offer to sell Northrop four boards for $19,000 apiece, to be delivered within six weeks. The offer contained a 90-day warranty stated to be in lieu of any other warranties, and provided that the terms of the offer would take precedence over any terms proposed by the buyer. Lynch, a purchasing officer of Northrop, responded to the offer in a phone conversation in which he told Litronic's man, Lair, that he was accepting the offer up to the limit of his authority, which was $24,999, and that a formal purchase order for all four boards would follow. Litronic was familiar with Northrop's purchase order form, having previously done business with Northrop, which had been using the same form for some time. Had Lair referred to any of the previous orders, he would have discovered that Northrop's order form provided for a warranty that contained no time limit.

[5] Lynch followed up the phone conversation a month later with a "turn on" letter, authorizing Litronic to begin production of all four boards (it had done so already) and repeating that a purchase order would follow. The record is unclear when the actual purchase order was mailed; it may have been as much as four months after the phone conversation and three months after the turn-on letter. The purchase order required the seller to send a written acknowledgment to Northrop. Litronic never did so, however, and Northrop did not complain; it does not bother to follow up on its requirement of a signed acknowledgment.

[6] Although Litronic had begun manufacturing the boards immediately after the telephone call from Lynch, for reasons that are unknown but that Northrop does not contend are culpable Litronic did not deliver the first three boards until more than a year later, in July of 1988. Northrop tested the boards for conformity to its specifications. The testing was protracted, either because the boards were highly complex or because Northrop's inspectors were busy, or perhaps for both reasons. At all events it was not until December and January, five or six months after delivery, that Northrop returned the three boards (the fourth had not been delivered), claiming that they were defective. Litronic refused to accept the return of the boards, on the ground that its 90-day warranty had lapsed. Northrop's position of course is that it had an unlimited warranty, as stated in the purchase order.

[7] As an original matter one might suppose that this dispute is not over the terms of the warranty but over whether Northrop waited more than the "reasonable time" that the Uniform Commercial Code allows the buyer of nonconforming goods to reject them. UCC § 2-602(1). That in fact is how the magistrate judge framed the issue, as we shall see. But the parties continue to treat it as a "warranty" case. Their implicit view is that Litronic's 90-day warranty, if a term of the contract, not only barred Northrop from complaining about defects that showed up more than 90 days after the delivery of the boards but also limited to 90 days the time within which Northrop was permitted to reject the boards because of defects that rendered them nonconforming. We accept this view for purposes of deciding these appeals.

[8] The parties have an unrelated dispute, over a different specification of printed wire boards, which Northrop claims were also defective. Northrop filed this suit to recover the money that it had paid for both types of board. The magistrate judge gave judgment for Northrop in the amount of $58,000, representing the money it had paid for the three No. 1714 boards that it had taken delivery of, but denied it recovery for the other boards on the ground that Northrop had failed to return them to Litronic. Both parties appeal.

[9] Northrop in its appeal argues that it was entitled to retain the other boards as security for its claim of breach of contract. UCC § 2-711(3). The purchaser of defective goods by paying for them obtains a security interest, which he is entitled to enforce, as by reselling the goods in a reasonable manner and deducting his damages from the resale price, remitting the balance to the seller. § 2-711(1). The Code says resell or "hold" them, § 2-711(3), and if the goods are worthless, or (what is really the same thing) their storage costs or other costs of retention exceed their value, the buyer is free to throw them away without liability, *Smith v. Watson*, 406 N.W.2d 685 (N.D.1987); cf. UCC § 2-608 comment 6—and might in some cases even be required to do so, in order to mitigate his damages. See *Smith v. Watson, supra,* 406 N.W.2d at 688; cf. *Ford Motor Credit Co. v. Caiazzo*, 387 Pa.Super. 561, 564 A.2d 931, 935 n. 2 (App.1989); *Walter E. Heller & Co. v. Hammond Appliance Co.*, 29 N.J.

589, 151 A.2d 537, 539 (1959) (per curiam). But what he cannot do is fail to account for the goods, cf. UCC §§ 9-207, 9-506, as happened here.

[10] Northrop's main argument at trial was that it had returned the boards, but the magistrate judge disbelieved it and did not commit clear error in doing so. Northrop's trial brief asserted as an alternative argument that the company had not been required to return the boards. . . . Even if . . . Northrop was not required to return the goods, it cannot prevail in its appeal. If the buyer does not return the defective goods, it must explain why (that it sold them, or that they were unsalable, or whatever), to scotch any inference that it is seeking a double recovery. For suppose Northrop had resold the boards at a price equal to what it had paid for them. Then it would not be entitled to any damages, for it would not have sustained any loss. For aught that appears this is what happened; or at least Northrop's failure to offer an explanation of what happened to the boards precludes its denying in this court that it sold or otherwise disposed of them to its advantage. Maybe it used them in some other product.

[11] Litronic's appeal concerns the breach of its warranty on the No. 1714 boards. It wins if the warranty really did expire after only 90 days. The parties agree that Litronic's offer to sell the No. 1714 boards to Northrop, the offer made in response to Northrop's request for bids, was the offer. So far, so good. If Northrop's Mr. Lynch accepted the offer over the phone, the parties had a contract then and there, but the question would still be on what terms. Regarding the first question, whether there was a contract, we may assume to begin with that the acceptance was sufficiently "definite" to satisfy the requirement of definiteness in section 2-207(1); after all, it impelled Litronic to begin production immediately, and there is no suggestion that it acted precipitately in doing so. We do not know whether Lynch in his conversation with Lair made acceptance of the complete contract expressly conditional on approval by Lynch's superiors at Northrop. We know that he had authority to contract only up to $24,999, but we do not know whether he told Lair what the exact limitation on his authority was or whether Litronic knew it without being told. It does not matter. The condition, if it was a condition, was satisfied and so drops out.

[12] We do not think that Northrop's acceptance, via Lynch, of Litronic's offer could be thought conditional on Litronic's yielding to Northrop's demand for an open-ended warranty. For while Lynch's reference to the purchase order might have alerted Litronic to Northrop's desire for a warranty not limited to 90 days, Lynch did not purport to make the more extensive warranty a condition of acceptance. So the condition, if there was one, was not an express condition, as the cases insist it be. . . .

[13] There was a contract, therefore; further, and, as we shall note, decisive, evidence being that the parties acted as if they had a contract—the boards were shipped and paid for. The question is then what the terms of the warranty in the contract were.

Lynch's reference in the phone conversation to the forthcoming purchase order shows that Northrop's acceptance contained different terms from the offer, namely the discrepant terms in the purchase order, in particular the warranty—for it is plain that the Northrop warranty was intended to be indefinite in length, so that, at least in the absence of some industry custom setting a limit on warranties that do not specify a duration (cf. UCC § 2-207, comments 4 and 5), a point not raised, any limitation on the length of the warranty in the offer would be a materially different term. *Daitom, Inc. v. Pennwalt Corp.*, 741 F.2d 1569, 1577 (10th Cir.1984); cf. *Owens-Corning Fiberglas Corp. v. Sonic Development Corp.*, 546 F.Supp. 533, 538 (D.Kan. 1982). Of course the fact that Northrop preferred a longer warranty than Litronic was offering does not by itself establish that Northrop's acceptance contained different terms. But Lynch did not accept Litronic's offer and leave it at that. He said that he would issue a Northrop purchase order, and both he and Lair knew (or at least should have known) that the Northrop purchase order form contained a different warranty from Litronic's sale order form. And we have already said that Lynch did not, by his oral reference to the purchase order, condition Northrop's purchase on Litronic's agreeing to comply with all the terms in the purchase order form, given the courts' insistence that any such condition be explicit. (Judges are skeptical that even businesspeople read boilerplate, so they are reluctant, rightly or wrongly, to make a contract fail on the basis of a printed condition in a form contract.) But Lynch said enough to make clear to Lair that the acceptance contained different terms from the offer.

[14] The Uniform Commercial Code, as we have said, does not say what the terms of the contract are if the offer and acceptance contain different terms, as distinct from cases in which the acceptance merely contains additional terms to those in the offer. The majority view is that the discrepant terms fall out and are replaced by a suitable UCC gap-filler. E.g., *Daitom, Inc. v. Pennwalt Corp., supra,* 741 F.2d at 1578–80; *St. Paul Structural Steel Co. v. ABI Contracting, Inc.,* 364 N.W.2d 83 (N.D.1985); *Challenge Machinery Co. v. Mattison Machine Works,* 138 Mich.App. 15, 359 N.W.2d 232, 236–38 (1984) (per curiam). The magistrate judge followed this approach and proceeded to section 2-309, which provides that nonconforming goods may be rejected within a "reasonable" time (see also § 2-601(1)), and she held that the six months that Northrop took to reject Litronic's boards was a reasonable time because of the complexity of the required testing. The leading minority view is that the discrepant terms *in the acceptance* are to be ignored, *Valtrol, Inc. v. General Connectors Corp.,* 884 F.2d 149, 155 (4th Cir.1989); *Reaction Molding Technologies, Inc. v. General Electric Co.,* 588 F.Supp. 1280, 1289 (E.D.Pa.1984), and that would give the palm to Litronic. Our own preferred view—the view that assimilates "different" to "additional," so that the terms in the offer prevail over the different terms in the acceptance only if the latter are materially different, has as yet been adopted by only one state, California. *Steiner v. Mobil Oil Corp.,* 20 Cal.3d 90, 141 Cal.Rptr. 157, 569 P.2d 751, 759 n. 5 (1977). Under that view, as under what we are calling the "leading" minority view, the warranty in Litronic's offer, the 90-day warranty, was

the contractual warranty, because the unlimited warranty contained in Northrop's acceptance was materially different.

[15] Because Illinois in other UCC cases has tended to adopt majority rules, e.g., *Rebaque v. Forsythe Racing, Inc.,* 134 Ill.App.3d 778, 89 Ill.Dec. 595, 598, 480 N.E.2d 1338, 1341 (1985), and because the interest in the uniform nationwide application of the Code—an interest asserted in the Code itself (see § 1-102)—argues for nudging majority views, even if imperfect (but not downright bad), toward unanimity, we start with a presumption that Illinois, whose position we are trying to predict, would adopt the majority view. We do not find the presumption rebutted. The idea behind the majority view is that the presence of different terms in the acceptance suggests that the offeree didn't *really* accede to the offeror's terms, yet both parties wanted to contract, so why not find a neutral term to govern the dispute that has arisen between them? Of course the offeree may not have had any serious objection to the terms in the offer at the time of contracting; he may have mailed a boilerplated form without giving any thought to its contents or to its suitability for the particular contract in question. But it is just as likely that the discrepant terms *in the offer* itself were the product of a thoughtless use of a boilerplate form rather than a considered condition of contracting. And if the offeror doesn't want to do business other than on the terms in the offer, he can protect himself by specifying that the offeree must accept all those terms for the parties to have a contract. UCC § 2-207(2)(a); *Tecumseh International Corp. v. City of Springfield,* 70 Ill.App.3d 101, 26 Ill.Dec. 745, 748, 388 N.E.2d 460, 463 (1979). Now as it happens Litronic did state in its offer that the terms in the offer "take precedence over terms and conditions of the buyer, unless specifically negotiated otherwise." But, for reasons that we do not and need not fathom, Litronic does not argue that this language conditioned the existence of the contract on Northrop's acceding to the 90-day warranty in the offer; any such argument is therefore waived.

[16] It is true that the offeree likewise can protect himself by making his acceptance of the offer conditional on the offeror's acceding to any different terms in the acceptance. But so many acceptances are made over the phone by relatively junior employees, as in this case, that it may be unrealistic to expect offerees to protect themselves in this way. The offeror goes first and therefore has a little more time for careful specification of the terms on which he is willing to make a contract. What we are calling the leading minority view may tempt the offeror to spring a surprise on the offeree, hoping the latter won't read the fine print. Under the majority view, if the offeree tries to spring a surprise (the offeror can't, since his terms won't prevail if the acceptance contains different terms), the parties move to neutral ground; and the offeror can, we have suggested, more easily protect himself against being surprised than the offeree can protect *himself* against being surprised. The California rule dissolves all these problems, but has too little support to make it a plausible candidate for Illinois, or at least a plausible candidate for our guess as to Illinois's position.

[17] There is a further wrinkle, however. The third subsection of section 2-207 provides that even if no contract is established under either of the first two subsections, it may be established by the "conduct of the parties," and in that event (as subsection (3) expressly provides) the discrepant terms vanish and are replaced by UCC gap fillers. This may seem to make it impossible for the offeror to protect himself from being contractually bound by specifying that the acceptance must mirror his offer. But subsection (3) comes into play only when the parties have by their conduct manifested the existence of a contract, as where the offeror, having specified that the acceptance must mirror the offer yet having received an acceptance that deviates from the offer, nonetheless goes ahead and performs as if there were a contract. That is one way to interpret what happened here but it leads to the same result as applying subsection (2) interpreted as the majority of states do, so we need not consider it separately.

[18] Given the intricacy of the No. 1714 boards, it is unlikely that Northrop would have acceded to a 90-day limitation on its warranty protection. Litronic at argument stressed that it is a much smaller firm, hence presumably unwilling to assume burdensome warranty obligations; but it is a curious suggestion that little fellows are more likely than big ones to get their way in negotiations between firms of disparate size. And Northrop actually got only half its way, though enough for victory here; for by virtue of accepting Litronic's offer without expressly conditioning its acceptance on Litronic's acceding to Northrop's terms, Northrop got not a warranty unlimited in duration, as its purchase order provides, but (pursuant to the majority understanding of UCC § 2-207(2)) a warranty of "reasonable" duration, courtesy the court. If special circumstances made a 90-day warranty reasonable, Litronic was free to argue for it in the district court.

[19] On the view we take, the purchase order has no significance beyond showing that Northrop's acceptance contained (albeit by reference) different terms. The fact that Litronic never signed the order, and the fact that Northrop never called this omission to Litronic's attention, also drop out of the case, along with Northrop's argument that to enforce the 90-day limitation in Litronic's warranty would be unconscionable. But for future reference we remind Northrop and companies like it that the defense of unconscionability was not invented to protect multi-billion dollar corporations against mistakes committed by their employees, and indeed has rarely succeeded outside the area of consumer contracts. . . .

Affirmed.

RIPPLE, Circuit Judge, concurring.

. . . As I have on other similar occasions, I respectfully decline to express, by way of an opinion of this court, a view on whether the majority interpretation of § 2-207 is preferable to the other interpretations. Federal courts sitting in diversity must, from time to time, determine the content of state law in order to decide the cases before them. It is, however, the constitutional prerogative of the states to determine the course of their jurisprudence and, in my view, our respect for that prerogative counsels that we refrain from taking an *institutional* position as a court on such matters. The National Conference of Commissioners on Uniform State Laws has appointed a drafting committee to revise Article 2 of the Uniform Commercial Code and that body is considering changes to § 2-207 with the hope that it will not only eliminate the "battle of the forms" but also make the section more responsive to the technological changes that are taking place in the manner in which commercial agreements are made. During that process, I am sure that the Commissioners welcome the perspective of all who have an expertise and interest in the question, and I would hope that my colleagues on the federal bench who have views on the matter would join all other members of the profession in the dialogue currently underway on the future shape of § 2-207. However, I believe that, as an institution, we should stay within the confines of our constitutional role and make the best "Erie guess" that we can. The principal opinion adopts a principled approach to that task and I am pleased to join in its adoption.

Notes and Questions

1. To begin, please re-read the analysis of contract formation under the UCC and the CISG above, on p. 171 et seq.

2. How could Litronic have won this dispute? Could it be argued that Litronic's lawyer committed malpractice? How and why? Check paragraphs 15 and 18 for your answer.

3. How would you summarize "the majority view" on determining the substance of a contract where a "battle of forms" has occurred versus Chief Judge Posner's "leading minority view"? If you could ignore the goal of uniform application throughout the United States, which view is to be preferred and why?

4. What would the substance of the contract be in this case, if contract formation were subject to the CISG? Is the approach of the CISG closer to "the majority view" or the "leading minority view" referred to in question 3?

D. The Provisions in UNIDROIT Principles and CFR Regarding Contract Formation and Interpretation

Although they play a much smaller role in practice, we are going to briefly look at the provisions in the PICC and in the CFR on contract formation and interpretation. The purpose of the comparative study is twofold: First, the rules in the CISG with regard to contract formation and, in particular, the battle of forms, might be thought of as less than ideal when it comes to equity, and the rules in the UCC might be thought of as less than ideal when it comes to clarity. Together with other reasons, this should make it attractive to look for alternative solutions; the CFR may just be the answer to many of these problems. Second, choice of law provisions in contracts referring to the PICC or—more likely—to the *lex mercatoria* are out there and we may just have to apply them, like it or not. Fortunately, we may discover that they are not so bad after all.

☆ Checklist 2-4

Provisions on Contract Formation and Interpretation in UNIDROIT Principles and Common Frame of Reference

Issue	PICC	CFR
Pre-Contractual Obligations		Arts. II-3:101–109 Arts. II-3:201–202 Arts. II-3:301–302 Arts. II-3:401, 3:501 Art. II-9:102
Form Requirements	Arts. 1.2, 2.1.1, 2.1.18	Art. II-1:106
Capacity	Art. 3.1.1 → via Art. 1.6(2) resort to general principles	
Offer or Invitation	Art. 2.1.2	Art. II-4:201–203
Rejection	Art. 2.1.5	
Acceptance	Arts. 2.1.6–2.1.10	Art. II-4:204–207, II-4:211
Modified Acceptance or Counteroffer?	Art. 2.1.11, 2.1.12	Art. II-4:208
Incorporation of General Terms and Conditions	Arts. 2.1.12, 2.1.19–2.1.22	Arts. II-1:109 + 110 Art. II-4:209 Art. II-9:102
Relevance of Previous Negotiations or Dealings between the Parties and other Outside (Parol) Evidence Prior to or Simultaneous to Contract Conclusion	Art. 4.3	Art. II-8:102
Consideration	N/A	N/A
Conditions	Arts. 5.3.1–5.3.5	
Mistake	Arts. 3.2.1–3.2.4	Arts. II-7:201–204, 208
Misrepresentation, Duress, Undue Influence	Arts. 3.2.5, 3.2.6	Arts. II-7:205–208
Relevance of Subsequent Negotiations or Communications	Art. 2.1.14	Art. II-8:102
Public Policy Considerations	Arts. 1.4, 3.2.7	Arts. II-2:101, II-9:401–409
Other Methods to Fill Gaps in Contracts:	Arts. 1.6, 1.7, 1.8, 2.1.14–2.1.21	Art. I-1.103 + 104,
Implied Warranties Usages	Art. 1.9	Art. II-1.104
Other Tools of Interpretation	Arts. 4.1–4.8, 5.1.1–5.1.7	Arts. II-8:101–9:303
Involvement of Agents	Arts. 2.2.1–2.2.10	Arts. II-6:101–112
Validity	Arts. 3.1.2–3.1.4, 3.3.1	Arts. II-7:101 + 102

A comparative analysis of the different contract laws we have been discussing—starting with the U.S. common law as reflected in the Restatement and the UCC, and then the international UNIDROIT Principles, to the more European CISG and CFR—demonstrates time and again that differences between the different rules are smaller than we may think. This is good news, indeed, because contract problems are similar regardless of the country or legal system the parties are located in, and if the solutions to these problems would differ widely, we would have to ask whether at least one of the systems is unfair. As an international arbitrator, I have applied all of these contract laws to disputes at different times and I have always found ways of interpreting them in such a way that the outcome seemed just, fair, and communicable. The differences, therefore, are more in the way a legal system presents itself, whether the language is more or less accessible, and how it is organized. To be sure, there are some differences in the details, but they will rarely justify very different outcomes when a specific dispute over a specific transaction needs to be resolved.

From a practitioner's point of view, therefore, the real question is rarely whether the client would fare better under this or that contract law. The real question is whether we want to enable or disable our clients. If we resort to legalese instead of straightforward rules, if we go for common law instead of statutory law, if we draft bulky contracts instead of slim and transparent ones, we serve ourselves instead of our clients—who are paying for our time. As a result, legal services have become too expensive and alternative providers—who get at least some of the work done by computer and by foreign contract lawyers—are eating an ever-larger slice of our pie. Unsurprisingly, "lawyer" is no longer among the 10 most prestigious professions in America (*Forbes*), and a majority of clients today do not trust their lawyers anymore.[107]

I would like to challenge my readers, therefore, to become truly global lawyers, always looking after the best interest of the clients, and moving easily between different legal systems and legal cultures to that effect. What matters, more than anything else, is to find solutions that are simple, fair, elegant, and transparent. Ideally, our contracts will be drafted in such a way that they don't cause any disputes in the first place. And if there should be a problem, we should be proud if our clients can resolve it on their own, without having to come back to us at all. The more we seek to eliminate ourselves from our clients' business, by teaching them how to draw up their contracts without asking every time, and how to resolve any differences without having to resort to formal and expensive legal procedures, the more we will win back the trust and appreciation of these clients. In the short term, we may have fewer hours to bill to the same clients. In the medium and long term, they will come to us with more interesting questions and they will bring other business and businesses along.

---

107. https://www.forbes.com/sites/niallmccarthy/2019/01/11/americas-most-least-trusted-professions-infographic/#36605fef7e94.

Section 6. INCOTERMS 2020®

A. Introduction

Whenever a contract is made for the sale of goods across an international border, a number of issues related to the transfer of the goods from seller to buyer have to be agreed upon. These include, in particular, the time and place where the buyer should take delivery and the extent, if any, to which the seller or the buyer should engage third parties for the carriage of the goods and possibly their insurance while in transit. Any misunderstandings between seller and buyer are bound to create problems, for example if the seller wants to deliver the goods to a particular carrier at a particular place and time but the carrier does not show up, or if the buyer assumes that the goods are insured while in transit but after they are damaged or lost it turns out they were not. Given the fact that the parties to an IBT are usually located in different countries, speak different languages, and are used to different legal rules and industry customs, the opportunities for misunderstandings are multiplied compared to purely domestic transactions.

To provide a global standard for the settlement of a number of typical questions related to the transfer of goods from seller to buyer, the International Chamber of Commerce (ICC) introduced a set of International Commercial Terms or "INCOTERMS" for the first time in 1936. Since then, the INCOTERMS® have been updated regularly and have established themselves as a truly global standard used in thousands of contracts around the world every day. The latest edition is the ninth edition, generally referred to as INCOTERMS 2020®.[108]

Via fewer than a dozen three-letter terms, the INCOTERMS® provide a clear and universal way for seller and buyer to agree upon the distribution of tasks, risk, and cost in the transfer of the goods. The INCOTERMS® marked with an asterisk (*) are recommended only for maritime transport, while the other INCOTERMS® have been specifically developed with a view toward other modes and multimodal transport. One very important common feature of all INCOTERMS® is the need to add the place where delivery is to be made, for example "FOB Norfolk VA." Since the time and place of delivery usually determine the time and place when the risk of loss or damage and the other responsibilities for the goods pass from seller to buyer, the parties have an interest in stipulating as precisely as possible where and when this should be.

By way of legal nature, the INCOTERMS® are part of the specially agreed-upon terms in the front of the contract and take precedence over general terms in the back of the contract and any default clauses in the applicable sales law, such as Article 31

---

108. The information on the following pages is based on the booklet International Chamber of Commerce (ed.), *INCOTERMS 2020 by the International Chamber of Commerce—ICC Rules for the Use of Domestic and International Trade Terms*, ICC Services Publications 2019.

CISG.[109] The more detailed definitions published by the ICC—which are the basis for the subsequent explanations—should be considered usages of trade and become part of the binding obligations between the parties via Article 9 CISG and similar provisions in other sales laws.[110]

For any discussion of INCOTERMS®, it is imperative to visualize the path a product takes from the manufacturer or seller to the importer or buyer in another country. In most international transactions, three different carriers are involved: the local or first carrier in the seller's country, the maritime carrier, and the local delivery carrier in the buyer's country. INCOTERMS® determine the distribution of risks and responsibilities between seller and buyer. Depending on the place where the risk passes, namely where the goods are "delivered," the carriers will either be the seller's agents or buyer's agents.

1. EXW (Ex Works) *3rd most commonly used.*

Under EXW, the seller merely makes the goods available to the buyer, usually by putting them out the door at the seller's own premises, although a different location could be stipulated. EXW puts minimal obligations on the seller, while the buyer has to organize and pay for the entire transfer of the goods. The seller does not even need to load the goods onto the vessel sent by the buyer, although he is often in a better position to do so at his own factory or premises. If the seller volunteers his help in loading the goods, he does so at buyer's risk. If the buyer wants the seller to take charge of the loading and is willing to pay for this service, the INCOTERM® FCA (Free Carrier) should be used. In addition, the seller has no obligation to provide documents for export clearance, etc. If the buyer needs more than an invoice, she has to make a separate agreement with the seller to that effect, for example via specific stipulation in the contract of sale. The seller does have to provide customary packaging. If special packaging is required, for example for an extended maritime voyage, an agreement to that end has to be made in the contract of sale or otherwise.

Delivery and thus transfer of risk and responsibilities takes place when the seller makes the goods available to the buyer at the stipulated time and place, whether or not the buyer or her representative actually shows up to take delivery.

2. FCA (Free Carrier)

Under FCA, the seller delivers the goods to a carrier or other person nominated by the buyer. The place of delivery could be the seller's premises, carrier's premises, or any other mutually agreed-upon location—for example, a ship in a specified port. Beyond the obligations placed upon the seller under EXW (Ex Works), the

---

109. See, for example, Juana Coetzee, *The Interplay Between INCOTERMS® and the CISG*, 32 J.L. & Com. 1 (2013).

110. So argued persuasively, *inter alia*, in William P. Johnson, *Analysis of INCOTERMS as Usage Under Article 9 of the CISG*, 35 U. Pa. J. Int'l L. 379 (2013).

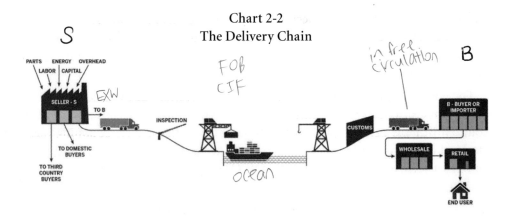

Chart 2-2
The Delivery Chain

seller now—and in all subsequent INCOTERMS®—has to package the goods in the manner that is required by the agreed-upon means of transport. The seller then has to take the goods to the agreed-upon place of delivery and load them onto the carrier's means of transport. This could be a truck at the seller's loading dock, a storage area (terminal), or even a ship in a port halfway across the seller's country.

If export licenses, pre-shipment inspections, or the like are required by the exporting country's authorities for the goods to be delivered at the agreed-upon place, the seller is responsible for obtaining these documents and clearances. The seller is also responsible for the costs of export formalities, export duties, and other mandatory charges payable upon export.

Delivery (and thus transfer of risk and responsibilities) takes place when the seller makes the goods available to the carrier or another person nominated by the buyer at the appointed time and place and loads the goods onto the nominated means of transport or otherwise places them in the nominated storage area or terminal. If the goods are loaded onto a ship or other means of transport, the carrier can issue a Bill of Lading or corresponding transport document, which the seller can then take to the bank to get paid under a Letter of Credit.

If the buyer or her representative fails to take delivery, the risk nevertheless passes at the end of the appointed time unless the buyer successfully avoids the contract and thus the obligation to take delivery.

3. FAS (Free Alongside Ship)*

This INCOTERM® is recommended exclusively for contracts of sale where the only agreed-upon transport is by ship. The fact that the seller may need other means of transport to get the goods to the nominated port of delivery, or that the buyer may need other means of transport to pick up the goods from her port, is irrelevant since it is not reflected in the contract of sale.

Under Free Alongside Ship (FAS), delivery takes place when the seller places the goods on the quay or on a barge within reach of the ship's lifting tackle or any other means of loading used at the specific port. The INCOTERM® is not recommended for containerized goods that have to be delivered to a holding area (terminal) in the port that is not located immediately adjacent to the vessel. In these cases, FCA should be used instead.

As in FCA, if export licenses or pre-shipment inspections or the like are required by the exporting country's authorities for the goods to be loaded onto the carrier's ship at the agreed-upon place, the seller is responsible for obtaining these documents and clearances. As in FCA, the seller is also responsible for the costs of export formalities, export duties, and other mandatory charges payable upon export.

Delivery (and thus transfer of risk and responsibilities) takes place when the seller makes the goods available to the carrier or another person nominated by the buyer on the quay or on a barge at the appointed time and place. If the buyer or her representative fails to take delivery, the risk nevertheless passes at the end of the appointed time unless the buyer successfully avoids the contract and thus the obligation to take delivery.

4. FOB (Free on Board)* → seller is done, buyer has to organize

This INCOTERM® is recommended exclusively for contracts of sale where the only agreed-upon transport is by ship. The fact that the seller may need other means of transport to get the goods to the nominated port of delivery, or that the buyer may need other means of transport to pick up the goods from her port, is irrelevant since it is not reflected in the contract of sale.

Under Free on Board (FOB), delivery takes place when the seller places the goods on the ship provided by the carrier and/or nominated by the buyer. The INCOTERM® is not recommended for containerized goods that have to be delivered to a holding area (terminal) in the port and cannot be immediately loaded onto the vessel. In these cases, FCA should be used instead.

As in FCA and FAS, if export licenses or pre-shipment inspections or the like are required by the exporting country's authorities for the goods to be loaded onto the carrier's ship at the agreed-upon place, the seller is responsible for obtaining these documents and clearances. As in FCA and FAS, the seller is also responsible for the costs of export formalities, export duties, and other mandatory charges payable upon export.

Delivery—and thus transfer of risk and responsibilities—takes place when the goods are being loaded and cross the rail of the appointed ship.

5. CIF (Cost, Insurance, and Freight)* → seller is done

This INCOTERM® is recommended exclusively for contracts of sale where the only agreed-upon transport is by ship. The fact that the seller may need other means of transport to get the goods to the nominated port of delivery, or that the buyer may need other means of transport to pick up the goods from her port, is irrelevant since it is not reflected in the contract of sale.

Seller's obligations, delivery and passing of risk, are the same as in FOB, except that the seller additionally agrees to procure the shipping contract and the insurance contract to the agreed-upon foreign destination. Thus, under CIF and the other C-terms, there is a split between the place where the risk of loss or damage is transferred from seller to buyer (when the goods cross the ship's rail or otherwise arrive at the delivery point in the seller's country) and the place where the seller's other responsibilities end (usually buyer's port).

Under Cost, Insurance, and Freight (CIF), delivery takes place when the seller places the goods on the ship provided by the carrier and/or nominated by the buyer. However, this is not the location stipulated in the INCOTERM®. Since the seller's port is where the risk of loss or damage passes to the buyer, the location should be separately stipulated in the contract of sale. The INCOTERM® is not recommended for containerized goods that have to be delivered to a holding area (terminal) in the port and cannot be immediately loaded onto the vessel. In these cases, CIP should be used instead.

As in FCA, FAS, and FOB, if export licenses or pre-shipment inspections or the like are required by the exporting country's authorities for the goods to be loaded onto carrier's ship at the agreed-upon place, the seller is responsible for obtaining these documents and clearances. As above, the seller is also responsible for the costs of export formalities, export duties, and other mandatory charges payable upon export.

In addition to the delivery of the goods onto the vessel at the port of shipment and any formalities for export clearance, the seller under CIF has to procure and pay for the contract of carriage, usually in the form of a prepaid Bill of Lading.

Furthermore, the seller also has to procure and pay for cargo insurance (at the level of Institute Cargo Clauses A or "all risk" or equivalent, unless agreed otherwise). The insurance contract has to be made out with the buyer as beneficiary, since the risk of loss or damage has passed to her. If the buyer intends to sell the goods while in transit, she should request an insurance policy for the benefit of any person with an insurable interest in the cargo, to be demonstrated typically by presenting the original Bill of Lading. Insurance has to be purchased for 110% of the CIF value of the goods unless otherwise stipulated in the contract of sale. The goods have to be covered from the moment they are loaded onto the vessel (passing of risk) at least until they are discharged at the port of destination named in the INCOTERM®.

6. CFR (Cost and Freight)*

This INCOTERM® is recommended exclusively for contracts of sale where the only agreed-upon transport is by ship. The fact that the seller may need other means of transport to get the goods to the nominated port of delivery, or that the buyer may need other means of transport to pick up the goods from her port, is irrelevant since it is not reflected in the contract of sale.

CFR is equivalent to CIF, except that the seller only procures and pays for the contract of carriage. The buyer has the choice whether or not to buy cargo insurance and at what level.

7. CIP (Carriage and Insurance Paid to)

CIP is equivalent to CIF, but suitable for multimodal transport. Delivery (and thus transfer of risk) takes place when the seller makes the goods available to the carrier or another person nominated by the buyer at the appointed time and place and loads the goods onto the nominated means of transport or otherwise places them in the nominated storage area or terminal. If the buyer or her representative fails to take delivery, the risk nevertheless passes at the end of the appointed time unless the buyer successfully avoids the contract and thus the obligation to take delivery.

As in CIF, in addition to the delivery of the goods at the nominated place and any formalities for export clearance, the seller under CIP has to procure and pay for the contract of carriage and the seller has to procure and pay for "all risk" cargo insurance to the named place or port of destination.

8. CPT (Carriage Paid to)

CPT is equivalent to CIP, except that the seller only procures and pays for the contract of carriage. The buyer has the choice whether or not to buy cargo insurance and at what level.

9. DAP (Delivered at Place)

D-terms are "delivery" terms. In general, the seller has to bring the goods to the buyer's country. Under Delivered at Place (DAP), the seller delivers the goods when they are ready to be unloaded from the transport vessel at the appointed place. The place of delivery could be a quay, warehouse, terminal, container yard, or other type of storage area, or any other mutually agreed-upon location in the specified port or place.

Beyond the obligations placed upon the seller under previous INCOTERMS®, the seller is now responsible for the entire voyage to the named terminal or place. The risk of loss or damage and all other responsibilities of the seller end only upon delivery at the terminal (usually in the buyer's country or port).

If export licenses, pre-shipment inspections, or the like are required by the exporting country's authorities for the goods to be delivered at the agreed-upon place, the seller is responsible for obtaining these documents and clearances. The seller is also responsible for the costs of export formalities, export duties, and other mandatory charges payable upon export. In order to get the goods to the nominated terminal, the seller also has to procure and pay for the contract of carriage. Since the seller bears the risk until delivery, he has the choice whether or not to procure and pay for cargo insurance and at what level.

The seller is not responsible for the cost and formalities of customs upon importation, however. If the nominated place of delivery cannot be reached without clearing customs in the country of destination, DDP should be used instead.

10. DPU (Delivered at Place Unloaded)

DPU is equivalent to DAP, except that the seller only delivers when the goods are unloaded from the transport vessel at the appointed place and made available to the buyer or a person nominated by the buyer.

The seller is still not responsible for the cost and formalities of customs upon importation, however. If the nominated place of delivery cannot be reached without clearing customs in the country of destination, DDP should be used instead.

11. DDP (Delivered Duty Paid)

Under Delivered Duty Paid (DDP) the seller is fully responsible for the delivery of the goods, including clearing the goods through customs upon importation and paying any related duties and fees. Thus, DDP puts maximal obligations on the seller, while the buyer has minimal obligations, cost, and risk. Delivery takes place when the goods are made available to the buyer or a person nominated by the buyer at the appointed time and place, ready for unloading from the transport vehicle or vessel. The seller bears all cost and risk until delivery. The buyer only has to organize and pay for unloading at the final destination.

Chart 2-3
Illustration of the Distribution of Tasks, Risk, and Cost

	EXW	FCA	FAS*	FOB*	CIF*	CFR*	CIP	CPT	DAP	DPU	DDP
Packaging	S	S	S	S	S	S	S	S	S	S	S
Packing list & invoice	S	S	S	S	S	S	S	S	S	S	S
Marking & labeling	S	S	S	S	S	S	S	S	S	S	S
Loading onto first carrier	B	S	S	S	S	S	S	S	S	S	S
Transport to port of departure	B	S / B	S	S	S	S	S	S	S	S	S
Export clearance	B	S / B	S	S	S	S	S	S	S	S	S
Loading onto main vessel	B	S / B	B	S	S	S	S	S	S	S	S
Freight charges	B	B	B	B	S	S	S	S	S	S	S
Insurance	B	B	B	B	S	B	S	B	S	S	S
Unloading at destination port	B	B	B	B	B	B	B / S	B / S	B / S	S	S
Terminal charges	B	B	B	B	B	B	B / S	B / S	B / S	B	S
Import duties & clearance	B	B	B	B	B	B	B	B	B	B	S
Delivery to final destination	B	B	B	B	B	B	B	B	B	B	S
Unloading at final destination	B	B	B	B	B	B	B	B	B	B	B

B. How to Determine the INCOTERM® to Be Used

The natural inclination of the seller would be to keep his obligations as minimal as possible and offer only EXW. By contrast, the buyer would usually prefer to get comprehensive service, i.e., delivery of the goods to her place of business under DDP. Obviously, if both parties would insist on their positions, a contract of sale could not be concluded.

One logical compromise—and certainly one of the most frequently used in practice—is for each side to take care of the transport logistics and associated costs in his or her own country. The seller in country S will usually be in a much better position to organize transport from his premises to the port of departure in country S than the buyer who may be located halfway around the world in country B, not speak the language of country S, and not have any experience with domestic carriers that could be hired in country S to pick up the goods at the factory of the seller and take them to the port of departure. Conversely, the buyer in country B will usually be in a much better position to organize the final leg of the transport from the port of destination to her premises in country B. This means that the most extreme divisions of responsibilities, EXW on the one side and DDP on the other, are quite rare in practice. However, this leaves a number of options in between and the question of which INCOTERM® should be used in each particular situation.

Several considerations should be weighed in the determination of the most suitable INCOTERM®: The willingness of the parties to take on more obligations, costs and/or the risk of loss or damage may depend on the nature of the goods, the experience of the parties with the kind of international transactions in question, and the eagerness of each side to conclude the deal. The latter will depend in large measure on the competitive situation in the respective market. If the seller operates in a highly competitive environment, i.e., the buyer has many alternative sources of supply, the seller may have to offer more comprehensive service to get the deal. In particular, if the buyer is a powerful player—for example, Walmart in the retail sector, or General Motors in the automotive sector—the buyer can largely set the terms of trade for his or her suppliers (see also the example of BMW cited on page 542). By contrast, if the seller has a very strong market position, the seller may not be very hungry to get a particular deal and the buyer may have to accept broader responsibilities with regard to organizing the carriage of the goods. This could be the case, for example, if the seller has exclusive rights to manufacture or distribute the goods based on patents or other forms of legal monopoly, or because seller's goods are highly regarded and coveted in the market for their quality and reputation. The same may happen if the seller is very large and used to sell in bulk, while the buyer is a small or medium-sized company looking for a relatively small quantity or the buyer is otherwise unlikely to become a repeat customer for the seller.

The selected form of payment will also play a role. As we will see in Part Three, the most common form of payment in international sales transactions is the Letter of Credit (L/C). For the seller to get paid under an L/C, he has to gather a number of documents and take them to the bank. This is why these transactions are often referred to as "documentary sales." The documents confirm to the bank—and ultimately to the buyer, who has to reimburse the bank—that the seller has delivered the goods. Thus, it is relatively easy for the seller to document delivery in his own country by presenting a Bill of Lading (see Part Four) from the carrier confirming that the goods have been received for shipment. By contrast, if the seller has to document arrival of the goods in the buyer's country (D-terms), he not only has to wait for the ship to make the voyage halfway around the world, he also has to wait for the arrival documents to be sent back to him.

In most cases, therefore, the choice is between FOB and CIF for maritime transport, or between FCA and CIP for multimodal transport. In all four cases, delivery takes place when the seller hands over the goods to the main carrier at the port, rail terminal, airport, or other agreed-upon place in his own country. Whether or not the goods arrive on time and in good shape halfway around the world is no longer of concern to the seller. More importantly, the seller does not have to wait and is not at the mercy of any foreign authorities or companies that are supposed to issue arrival or other documents required by the bank.

The remaining question is whether the seller should procure and pay for the contract of carriage and/or the contract of insurance (C-terms) or whether this burden should be upon the buyer (F-terms). If the market is competitive, i.e., neither side has a powerful position that would allow it to impose its preferred terms of trade on the other side, the question should be answered based on economic efficiency. At the end of the day, the cost of carriage and insurance will have to be included in the price of the goods one way or another. Neither the seller nor the buyer will be willing or able to cover these expenses from profits, in particular since the profit margin will be slim on either side if the market is indeed competitive. Thus, if the seller offers CIF or CIP, he will raise his overall price accordingly, and if the buyer can only get FOB or FCA, she will expect a lower price because she will now have to pay for the carriage and insurance herself. In the end, the question boils down to which of the two parties can procure the carriage and insurance more easily and on better terms than the other, based on experience, business connections, and volume. If the seller is a large manufacturer in China who regularly ships his goods to different buyers in the United States, he is probably in a better position to procure carriage and insurance across the Pacific Ocean than any of his relatively less experienced and smaller buyers. On the other hand, if the buyer is a large distributer in the United States, like Walmart, she can almost certainly get better deals from different carriers and insurance companies than any of her smaller and less powerful suppliers.

In the end, efficient supply chain management will consider all the options and make an informed choice in full knowledge of the economic and legal consequences. Unfortunately, this is not self-evident in practice, where too many traders and in-house legal counsel seem to remember only FOB and CIF and continue to use them even in multimodal situations where they are poorly suited and in situations where a different INCOTERM® would yield economic advantages for all those involved.

C. Practical Examples from Case Law

As we have learned, contract clauses FOB and CIF both provide for a passing of the risk when the merchandise is loaded onto the vessel (when they cross the ship's rail). Take a look at the following case for an exception to this rule.

Case 2-10

St. Paul Guardian Insurance Company v. Neuromed Medical Systems & Support, GmbH

2002 WL 465312 (S.D.N.Y. 2002)
(Paragraph numbers added.)
STEIN, District J.

[1] Plaintiffs St. Paul Guardian Insurance Company and Travelers Property Casualty Insurance Company have brought this action as subrogrees of Shared Imaging, Inc., to recover $285,000 they paid to Shared Imaging for damage to a mobile magnetic resonance imaging system ("MRI") purchased by Shared Imaging from defendant Neuromed Medical Systems & Support GmbH ("Neuromed"). Neuromed has moved to dismiss the complaint on two grounds, namely that (1) the forum selection clause of the underlying contract requires the litigation to take place in Germany and (2) pursuant to Fed.R.Civ.P. 12(b)(6), the complaint fails to state a claim for relief. In an Order dated December 3, 2001, this Court first found that the contractual forum selection clause did not mandate that the action proceed in Germany and second, held the rest of the motion in abeyance pending submissions by the parties on German law, which, pursuant to the underlying contract, is the applicable law. The parties have now submitted affidavits from German legal experts.

[2] The crux of Neuromed's argument is that it had no further obligations regarding the risk of loss once it delivered the MRI to the vessel at the port of shipment due to a "CIF" clause included in the underlying contract. Plaintiffs respond that (1) the generally understood definition of the "CIF" term as defined by the International Chamber of Commerce's publication, Incoterms 1990, is inapplicable here and (2) the "CIF" term was effectively superceded by other contract terms such that the risk of loss remained on Neuromed.

[3] Pursuant to the applicable German law—the U.N. Convention on Contracts for the International Sale of Goods—the "CIF" term in the contract operated to pass the risk of loss to Shared Imaging at the port of shipment, at which time, the parties agree, the MRI was undamaged and in good working order. Accordingly, Neuromed's motion to dismiss the complaint should be granted and the complaint dismissed.

Background

[4] Shared Imaging, an American corporation, and Neuromed, a German corporation, entered into a contract of sale for a Siemens Harmony 1.0 Tesla mobile MRI. Thereafter, both parties engaged various entities to transport, insure and provide customs entry service for the MRI. Plaintiffs originally named those entities as defendants, but the action has been discontinued against them by agreement of the parties. . . . Neuromed is the sole remaining defendant.

[5] According to the complaint, the MRI was loaded aboard the vessel "Atlantic Carrier" undamaged and in good working order.... When it reached its destination of Calmut City, Illinois, it had been damaged and was in need of extensive repair, which led plaintiffs to conclude that the MRI had been damaged in transit....

[6] The one page contract of sale contains nine headings, including: "Product;" "Delivery Terms;" "Payment Terms;" "Disclaimer;" and "Applicable Law." ... Under "Product" the contract provides, the "system will be delivered cold and fully functional." ... Under "Delivery Terms" it provides, "CIF New York Seaport, the buyer will arrange and pay for customs clearance as well as transport to Calmut City." ...

[7] Under "Payment Terms" it states, "By money transfer to one of our accounts, with following payment terms: US $93,000—downpayment to secure the system; US $744,000—prior to shipping; US $93,000—upon acceptance by Siemens of the MRI system within 3 business days after arrival in Calmut City." ... In addition, under "Disclaimer" it states, "system including all accessories and options remain the property of Neuromed till complete payment has been received." ... Preceding this clause is a handwritten note, allegedly initialed by Raymond Stachowiak of Shared Imaging, stating, "Acceptance subject to Inspection." ...

Discussion

[8] Neuromed contends that because the delivery terms were "CIF New York Seaport," its contractual obligation, with regard to risk of loss or damage, ended when it delivered the MRI to the vessel at the port of shipment and therefore the action must be dismissed because plaintiffs have failed to state a claim for which relief can be granted. Plaintiffs respond that the generally accepted definition of the "CIF" term as defined in Incoterms 1990, is inapplicable. Moreover, plaintiffs suggest that other provisions of the contract are inconsistent with the "CIF" term because Neuromed, pursuant to the contract, retained title subsequent to delivery to the vessel at the port of shipment and thus, Neuromed manifestly retained the risk of loss.

A. Legal Standards

[9] In reviewing a motion to dismiss pursuant to Fed.R.Civ.P. 12(b)(6), a district court's role is to assess the legal feasibility of the complaint; it is not to weigh the evidence which might be offered at trial.... A motion to dismiss should not be granted unless "it appears beyond doubt that the plaintiff can prove no set of facts in support of the claim which would entitle him to relief." *Staron v. McDonald's Corp.*, 51 F.3d 353, 355 (2d Cir.1995) (quoting *Conley v. Gibson*, 355 U.S. 41, 45–46 (1957)); ...

B. Applicable Law

1. Rule 44.1

[10] Pursuant to Fed.R.Civ.P. 44.1, determinations of foreign law are questions of law. The Court "may consider any relevant material or source" to determine foreign

law, whether or not submitted by a party or admissible under the Federal Rules of Evidence." Fed.R.Civ.P. 44.1. In short, under Rule 44.1, the court may "consider any material that is relevant to a foreign law issue, whether submitted by counsel or unearthed by the court's own research." . . .

[11] The parties have each submitted relevant opinions of German legal experts (Werkmeister Op.; Strube Op.; Werkmeister Reply Op.) and the Court has independently researched the applicable foreign law. On the basis of those submissions and analysis, the Court finds the expert opinion of Karl-Ulrich Werkmeister for the defendants to be an accurate statement of German law.

2. Applicable German Law

[12] The parties concede that pursuant to German law, the U.N. Convention on Contracts for the International Sale of Goods ("CISG") governs this transaction because (1) both the U.S. and Germany are Contracting States to that Convention, and (2) neither party chose, by express provision in the contract, to opt out of the application of the CISG. . . .

[13] The CISG aims to bring uniformity to international business transactions, using simple, non-nation specific language. . . . To that end, it is comprised of rules applicable to the conclusion of contracts of sale of international goods. . . . In its application regard is to be paid to comity and interpretations grounded in its underlying principles rather than in specific national conventions. See CISG art. 7(1), (2); see also *Delchi Carrier SpA v. Rotorex Corp.*, 71 F.3d 1024, 1028 (2d Cir.1995).

[14] Germany has been a Contracting State since 1991, and the CISG is an integral part of German law. . . . Where parties, as here, designate a choice of law clause in their contract — selecting the law of a Contracting State without expressly excluding application of the CISG — German courts uphold application of the Convention as the law of the designated Contracting state. . . . To hold otherwise would undermine the objectives of the Convention which Germany has agreed to uphold.

C. CISG, INCOTERMS and "CIF"

[15] "CIF," which stands for "cost, insurance and freight," is a commercial trade term that is defined in *Incoterms 1990*, published by the International Chamber of Commerce ("ICC"). The aim of INCOTERMS, which stands for international commercial terms, is "to provide a set of international rules for the interpretation of the most commonly used trade terms in foreign trade." (Werkmeister Op. Ex. *Incoterms 1990*, at 106.) These "trade terms are used to allocate the costs of freight and insurance" in addition to designating the point in time when the risk of loss passes to the purchaser. DiMatteo, *supra*, Contracting at 188. INCOTERMS are incorporated into the CISG through Article 9(2) which provides that,

> The parties are considered, unless otherwise agreed, to have impliedly made applicable to their contract or its formation a usage of which the

parties knew or ought to have known and which in international trade is widely known to, and regularly observed by, parties to contracts of the type involved in the particular trade concerned. (CISG, art. 9(2), *reprinted* in 15 U.S.C.A.App.)

[16] At the time the contract was entered into, *Incoterms 1990* was applicable.... INCOTERMS define "CIF" (named port of destination) to mean the seller delivers when the goods pass "the ship's rail in the port of shipment." (Werkmeister Op. Ex. *Incoterms 1990* at 152.) The seller is responsible for paying the cost, freight and insurance coverage necessary to bring the goods to the named port of destination, but the risk of loss or damage to the goods passes from seller to buyer upon delivery to the port of shipment....

[17] Plaintiffs' legal expert contends that INCOTERMS are inapplicable here because the contract fails to specifically incorporate them.... Nonetheless, he cites and acknowledges that the German Supreme Court (Bundesgerichtshof [BGH]—the court of last resort in the Federal Republic of Germany for civil matters,... concluded that a clause "fob" without specific reference to INCOTERMS was to be interpreted according to INCOTERMS "simply because the [INCOTERMS] include a clause 'fob'."...

[18] Conceding that commercial practice attains the force of law under section 346 of the German Commercial Code (Handelsgesetzbuch [HGB], plaintiffs' expert concludes that the opinion of the BGH "amounts to saying that the [INCOTERMS] definitions in Germany have the force of law as trade custom." (*Id.* at 9.) As encapsulated by defendant's legal expert, "It is accepted under German law that in case a contract refers to CIF-delivery, the parties refer to the INCOTERMS rules...." (Werkmeister Op. at 7.)

[19] The use of the "CIF" term in the contract demonstrates that the parties "agreed to the detailed oriented [INCOTERMS] in order to enhance the Convention." Neil Gary Oberman, *Transfer of Risk From Seller to Buyer in International Commercial Contracts: A Comparative Analysis of Risk Allocation Under CISG, UCC and Incoterms*, at http:// www.cisg.law.pace.edu/cisg/thesis/Oberman.html. Thus, pursuant to CISG art. 9(2), INCOTERMS definitions should be applied to the contract despite the lack of an explicit INCOTERMS reference in the contract.

D. INCOTERMS, the CISG, and the Passage of Risk of Loss and Title

[20] Plaintiffs argue that Neuromed's explicit retention of title in the contract to the MRI machine modified the "CIF" term, such that Neuromed retained title and assumed the risk of loss. INCOTERMS, however, only address passage of risk, not transfer of title.... Under the CISG, the passage of risk is likewise independent of the transfer of title. See CISG art. 67(1). Plaintiffs' legal expert mistakenly asserts that the moment of 'passing of risk' has not been defined in the CISG. (Strube Op. at 4.) Chapter IV of that Convention, entitled "Passing of Risk," explicitly defines the time at which risk passes from seller to buyer pursuant to Article 67(1),

If the contract of sale involves carriage of the goods and seller is not bound to hand them over at a particular place, the risk passes to the buyer when the goods are handed over to the first carrier for transmission to the buyer in accordance with the contract of sale. If the seller is bound to hand the goods over to a carrier at a particular place, the risk does not pass to the buyer until the goods are handed over to the carrier at that place. (CISG, art 67(1), *reprinted* in 15 U.S.C.A.App.)

[21] Pursuant to the CISG, "[t]he risk passes without taking into account who owns the goods. The passing of ownership is not regulated by the CISG according to art. 4(b)." . . . Article 4(b) provides that the Convention is not concerned with "the effect which the contract may have on the property in the goods sold." CISG art. 4(b). Moreover, according to Article 67(1), the passage of risk and transfer of title need not occur at the same time, as the seller's retention of "documents controlling the disposition of the goods does not affect the passage of risk." CISG art. 67(1).

[22] Had the CISG been silent, as plaintiffs' expert claimed, the Court would have been required to turn to German law as a "gap filler." . . . There again, plaintiffs' assertions falter. German law also recognizes passage of risk and transfer of title as two independent legal acts. (Werkmeister Reply Op. at 3.) In fact, it is standard "practice under German law to agree that the transfer of title will only occur upon payment of the entire purchase price, well after the date of passing of risk and after receipt of the goods by the buyer." (Id . at 7.) Support for this proposition of German law is cited by both experts. They each refer to section 447 of the German Civil Code (Bügerliches Gesetzbuch [BGB], a provision dealing with long distance sales, providing in part—as translated by plaintiff's expert—that "the risk of loss passes to the buyer at the moment when the seller has handed the matter to the forwarder, the carrier or to the otherwise determined person or institution for the transport." (Strube Op. at 5; see also Werkmeister Op. at 7 .)

[23] Accordingly, pursuant to INCOTERMS, the CISG, and specific German law, Neuromed's retention of title did not thereby implicate retention of the risk of loss or damage.

E. The Contract Terms

[24] Plaintiffs next contend that even if the "CIF" term did not mandate that title and risk of loss pass together, the other terms in the contract are evidence that the parties' intention to supercede and replace the "CIF" term such that Neuromed retained title and the risk of loss. That is incorrect.

1. "Delivery Terms"

[25] Citing the "Delivery Terms" clause in the contract, plaintiffs posit that had the parties intended to abide by the strictures of INCOTERMS there would have been no need to define the buyer's obligations to pay customs and arrange further

transport. . . . Plaintiffs' argument, however, is undermined by Incoterms 1990, which provides that "[i]t is normally desirable that customs clearance is arranged by the party domiciled in the country where such clearance should take place." (See Werkmeister Op. Ex. *Incoterms 1990* at 109.) The "CIF" term as defined by INCOTERMS only requires the seller to "clear the goods for export" and is silent as to which party bears the obligation to arrange for customs clearance. . . . The parties are therefore left to negotiate these obligations. As such, a clause defining the terms of customs clearance neither alters nor affects the "CIF" clause in the contract.

2. "Payment Terms"

[26] Plaintiffs also cite to the "Payment Terms" clause of the contract, which specified that final payment was not to be made upon seller's delivery of the machine to the port of shipment, but rather, upon buyer's acceptance of the machine in Calumet City. These terms speak to the final disposition of the property, not to the risk for loss or damage. INCOTERMS do not mandate a payment structure, but rather simply establish that the buyer bears an obligation to "[p]ay the price as provided in the contract of sale." (Id. at 151.) Inclusion of the terms of payment in the contract does not modify the "CIF" clause.

3. The Handwritten Note

[27] Finally, plaintiffs emphasize the handwritten note, "Acceptance upon inspection." . . . Based upon its placement within the contract and express terms, the note must serve to qualify the final clauses of the "Payment Terms," obliging buyer to effect final payment upon acceptance of the machine. . . . As defendant's expert correctly depicts, "A reasonable recipient, acting in good faith, would understand that the buyer wanted to make sure that receipt of the GOOD should not be construed as the acceptance of the buyer that the GOOD is free of defects of design or workmanship and that the GOOD is performing as specified. This addition does not relate to the place of delivery." (Werkmeister Reply Op. at 3.) Accordingly, despite plaintiffs' arguments to the contrary, the handwritten note does not modify the "CIF" clause; it instead serves to qualify the terms of the transfer of title.

[28] The terms of the contract do not modify the "CIF" clause in the contract such that the risk of loss remained with Neuromed. The fact remains that the CISG, INCOTERMS, and German law all distinguish between the passage of the risk of loss and the transfer of title. Thus, because (1) Neuromed's risk of loss of, or damage to, the MRI machine under the contract passed to Shared Imaging upon delivery of the machine to the carrier at the port of shipment and (2) it is undisputed that the MRI machine was delivered to the carrier undamaged and in good working order, Neuromed's motion to dismiss for failure to state a claim is hereby granted. . . .

SO ORDERED:

Notes and Questions

1. What do you think of the fact that the court needed two German lawyers to explain "German" law, even though the relevant provisions of "German" law were those of the CISG? Could or should the U.S. court have been able to understand the applicable law without foreign experts? Why or why not?

2. How would the case have come out under the UCC?

3. Why is there a somewhat lengthy argument over the question whether or not INCOTERMS® are incorporated into the contract? Wasn't there a clear reference to CIF in the contract?

4. Summarize in a few sentences what is regulated by CIF and what is not.

Section 7. Performance Requirements and Remedies for Nonperformance

The contract between the parties is the main, but not the only, source of rights and obligations. To determine whether each side to an IBT has met her obligations, or whether there was a breach of some or all of these obligations, we need to review all sources of law that may become sources of rights and obligations. Per our **pyramid depicting the hierarchy of norms** (see Chart 1–7 on p. 52), this potentially includes mandatory rules of public policy, the individually negotiated contract clauses (front of the contract), any implicit agreements between the parties such as general terms (back of the contract), industry customs, the non-mandatory rules of the applicable contract law, and other non-mandatory rules of the applicable national law, as well as general principles of law. The pyramid is not just a random collection, but depicts a hierarchy. Mandatory rules, such as consumer protection or antitrust laws, always have to be respected where applicable. Other than that, we only move from the front of the contract to the next lower levels to the extent a particular issue is not already covered. In practice, this usually means that we determine the terms that made it into the party agreement (front and back) and fill any gaps with the applicable contract law. Reference to lower-level rules will often not even be required.

Having compiled and interpreted the rules that govern a specific IBT, it is always a good idea to summarize the obligations of both parties. Then we compare these obligations to the fact pattern to identify for each obligation whether it has been complied with in full, in part, or not at all. In this context, post-contractual communications of the parties have to be taken into account. For example, if the contract required delivery of the goods in calendar week 42 and the seller was unable to meet that deadline, we have to evaluate the legal relevance of the notification of delay by the seller and the response, if any, from the buyer.

Next, we should clearly identify the performance elements that did not comply with the respective obligations of the party. This should be done as precisely as possible because we will then have to determine whether the breach was material (UCC) or fundamental (CISG). Context matters in this regard. For example, a delay of one day may not make much of a difference for the delivery of a machine but it may be essential for a wedding cake. Similarly, it may be a minor problem if five percent of a shipment of light bulbs is broken on arrival, whereas an entire nuclear reactor cannot be started up if 5 out of 100 fuel rods are damaged on arrival. Another example would be the just-in-sequence supply chain agreement BMW had with Autoliv (below, p. 542).

In practice, just like in a good exam, it may not be obvious whether a particular breach is material/fundamental or not. The party in default may argue that it is not while the other side may argue that it is. To represent our clients effectively, we will need to deliver **Level 4 Analysis** on such a point (above, pp. 66 and 68).

After any breaches have been identified, we need to consider **possible justifications or exceptions**. They may eliminate any responsibility of the defaulting party (e.g., force majeure, Art. 79 CISG), or they may affect the remedies available to the other side (e.g., restitution, Art. 82 CISG).

Finally, to the extent we have breaches that are not justified or excused, the other side may have a choice between one or more **primary remedies** (performance), secondary remedies (**damages**), as well as **costs** and **interest**. Again, this should be done as precisely as possible, including a clear and transparent—and mathematical—analysis of monetary claims at each level, any counterclaims, set-offs, reductions for unforeseeable damages or losses, shared responsibility, etc. Excessive or unjustified claims, as well as double-dipping, must be strictly avoided, in particular in arbitration or litigation where the so-called English Rule applies (see below, pp. 786, 791–792, and 1036–1038).

In this section, we will first look at case law examples on the CISG and then the UCC. The cases show how the claim bases are applied by courts and tribunals. At the end, there is a checklist for your analysis of claims, summarizing what courts and tribunals should but don't always do in practice.

A. Contracts Subject to the CISG

With more than 90 ratifications, the CISG already covers, at least potentially, more than 80% of all international sales of goods. If a recent proposal finds broader acceptance, the scope of application may be extended to service contracts very soon.[111]

---

111. See Ingeborg Schwenzer, Julian Ranetunge & Fernando Tafur, *Service Contracts and the CISG*, Indian J. Int'l Econ. L. 2019, pp. 170–193.

Checklist 2-5
Claim Bases in the CISG

(handwritten margin notes:)
4 claims:

1. primary remedies: specific performance

2. secondary remedies: damages

3. costs

4. interest

Seller → Buyer		
Claim	**Legal Bases**	**Exceptions**
1. Right to Performance/ Contractual Claims		
a. Take Delivery	Arts. 61, 62, 53, 60	49, 81 et seq.; 77; 79
b. Pay Purchase Price	Arts. 61, 62, 53, 54, 57 66–70	49, 81 et seq.; 77; 79
c. Restitution of Goods after Avoidance	Arts. 81(2), 82, 84(2), 49	
2. Damages	Arts. 61, 74 et seq.	77; 79
3. Interest	Art. 78	77; 79

Seller ⇄ Buyer		
Claim	**Legal Bases**	**Exceptions**
1. Right to Performance/ Contractual Claims		
a. Delivery of Conforming Goods	Arts. 45, 46, 47, 30–36	39(1) (but see 40 and 44) 64, 81 et seq. 77, 79
b. Transfer of Documents	Arts. 45, 46, 47, 30, 34	64, 81 et seq.; 77, 79
		43(1) (but see 43(2) and 44) 64, 81 et seq. 77, 79
c. Transfer of Ownership	Arts. 45, 46, 47, 30, 41	
d. Carriage & Insurance	Arts. 45, 46, 47, 30, 32	64, 81 et seq.; 77, 79
e. Price Reduction	Arts. 46, 46, 47, 50	64, 81 et seq.; 77, 79
f. Repair, Replacement or Cure	Art. 37	82, 83
g. Restitution of Price after Avoidance	Arts. 81(2), 84(1), 49	
2. Damages	Arts. 45, 74 et seq.	77; 79
3. Interest	78	77; 79

We will now look at examples of practical application of the CISG and the UCC. Our first case is a good example where they are actually applied together.

Case 2-11

U.S. Nonwovens v. Pack Line Corp. and Nuspark Engineering

4 N.Y.S.3d 868 (2015)

(Paragraph numbers added, footnotes and some details omitted.)

Factual and Procedural Background

[2] In March 2009, the plaintiff U.S. Nonwovens Corp. ("Plaintiff") entered into separate agreements with defendant Pack Line Corp. ("Pack Line") and defendant Nuspark Engineering Corp. ("Nuspark") for the purchase of a custom automatic filling and sealing machine ("Auto Tubber") for use in its business of producing non-woven products including sanitary disposables and wipes. The Auto Tubber was to be comprised of several distinct components, with a conveyor system designed and manufactured by Nuspark. Plaintiff agreed to pay Nuspark $150,000 for the conveyor and installation and commissioning of the integrated machine.

[3] On May 21, 2014, Plaintiff commenced this action against Pack Line and Nuspark. Plaintiff alleges, among other things, that "[b]etween in or around December 2009 and August 2010, the Auto Tubber was delivered, set up, installed and tested in [Plaintiff's] facility." Plaintiff also alleges that "[u]pon completion of installation, Pack Line tested the Auto Tubber, and it was immediately apparent that the machine was completely defective and unsatisfactorily manufactured." Plaintiff further alleges that "[i]mmediately upon delivery, [Plaintiff] made numerous complaints about the defective Auto Tubber to Pack Line and Nuspark." Plaintiff asserts causes of action for breach of contract, breach of the implied covenant of good faith, breach of express warranty, breach of the implied warranty of merchantability, breach of the implied warranty of fitness, and unjust enrichment.

[4] Nuspark now moves to dismiss the Verified Complaint as asserted against it. Nuspark initially contends that Plaintiff's claims against it pursuant to New York State law fail to state causes of action because they are preempted by the United Nations Convention on Contracts for the International Sale of Goods ("CISG"). Additionally, Nuspark argues that Plaintiff's claims are barred under the CISG because Plaintiff failed to notify Nuspark of any alleged nonconformity of the conveyor designed and manufactured by Nuspark prior to the commencement of this action. Finally, Nuspark contends that Plaintiff's contractual claims are barred by the statute of limitations.

[5] In opposition, Plaintiff concedes that the CISG applies to its contract with Nuspark and that it preempts its state law contract claims. However, Plaintiff argues that dismissal is not warranted because valid substantive claims for breach of contract, breach of implied covenant of good faith, and breach of implied and express warranty have been stated under New York law and the UCC, which satisfies the similar substantive requirements under the CISG for such claims. Plaintiff contends that its Verified Complaint sufficiently alleges that it provided the requisite notice to Nuspark of the lack of conformity of the conveyor by alleging that "[i]mmediately

upon delivery [Plaintiff] made numerous complaints about the defective Auto Tubber to . . . Nuspark." Finally, Plaintiff argues that its claims were commenced within
the applicable four-year statute of limitations as its claims did not accrue under tender of delivery was complete which, Plaintiff alleges, occurred in August 2010 when
the contractually required delivery, installation, integration and testing of the Auto
Tubber were completed.

Discussion

[6] As summarized by United States Senior District Judge Walls in *Beth Schiffer Fine
Photographic Arts, Inc. v. Colex Imaging, Inc.*, 2012 WL 924380 (U.S. Dist. Ct., N.J.,
March 19, 2012, Walls, J.):

> "Ratified by the United States on December 11, 1986, the CISG 'applies to
> contracts of sale of goods between parties whose places of business are in
> different States . . . when the States are Contracting States.' CISG Art. 1(1)
> (a). See *Forestal Guarani S.A. v. Daros International, Inc.*, 613 F.3d 395, 397
> (3d Cir.2010) . . . The CISG is a self-executing treaty that preempts contrary
> provisions of Article 2 of the UCC and other state contract law to the extent
> that those causes of action fall within the scope of the CISG. U.S. Const.,
> Art. VI; *Medellin v. Texas*, 552 U.S. 491, 504–05, 128 S.Ct. 1346, 170 L.
> Ed.2d 190 (2008). See *American Mint LLC v. GOSoftware, Inc.*, No. 1:05-
> cv-650, 2005 WL 2021248, at *2–3 (M.D.Pa. Aug. 16, 2005) (noting that 'if
> the CISG applies to the contract at issue, it will preempt domestic sale laws
> that otherwise would govern the contract.'). Outside the scope of the CISG,
> otherwise applicable state law governs the dispute. See *Caterpillar Inc. v.
> Usinor Industeel*, 393 F.Supp.2d 659, 676 (N.D.Ill.2005)."

[7] In considering a motion to dismiss a complaint pursuant to CPLR 3211(a)(7):

> The complaint must be liberally construed and the plaintiff given the ben-
> efit of every favorable inference (citations omitted). The court must also
> accept as true all of the facts alleged in the complaint and any factual sub-
> missions made in opposition to the motion (citations omitted). If the court
> can determine that the plaintiff is entitled to relief on any view of the facts
> stated, its inquiry is complete and the complaint must be declared legally
> sufficient (citations omitted). While factual allegations contained in the
> complaint are deemed true, bare legal conclusions and facts flatly contra-
> dicted on the record are not entitled to a presumption of truth (citations
> omitted). (*Symbol Tech., Inc. v. Deloitte & Touche, LLP*, 69 A.D.3d 191, 193–
> 195, 888 N.Y.S.2d 538 [2d Dept.2009].

[8] Here, as mentioned above, Plaintiff concedes that the CISG applies and preempts
its state law contract claims. Thus, the issue is whether the claims as asserted in the
Verified Complaint should be dismissed because they fail to state causes of action.
The Court agrees with Plaintiff that dismissal of the claims for breach of contract
and breach of express and implied warranties is not warranted. "The elements of a

breach of contract claim are the same [under the CISG and the UCC]; a [plaintiff] must show: '(1) the existence of a valid and enforceable contract containing both definite and certain terms, (2) performance by plaintiff, (3) breach by defendant and (4) resultant injury to plaintiff.'" (*Maxxsonics USA, Inc. v. Fengshun Peiying Electro Acoustic Co., Ltd.*, 2012 WL 962698, U.S. Dist. Ct., N.D.IL., March 21, 2012, Leinenweber, J., quoting *Magellan Intern. Corp. v. Salzgitter Handel GmbH*, [see above, p. 200]. Under New York law, "[t]he elements of a cause of action for breach of contract are (1) formation of a contract between plaintiff and defendant, (2) performance by plaintiff, (3) defendant's failure to perform, (4) resulting damage" (2 N.Y. PJI2d 4:1, at 676 [2013]). Additionally, although the CISG does not specifically include the implied warranties of fitness and merchantability, CISG Article 35 may properly be read to suggest them (*Norfolk Southern Railway Co. v. Power Source Supply, Inc.*, 2008 WL 2884102, U.S. Dist. Ct., W.D.Pa., July 25, 2008, Gibson, J.; *Electrocraft Arkansas, Inc. v. Super Elec. Motors, Ltd.*, 2009 WL 5181854, U.S. Dist. Ct., E.D.Ark., Dec. 23, 2009, Wright, J.). The fact that the Verified Complaint does not mention the CISG is not fatal to Plaintiff's claims for breach of contract and breach of express and implied warranties (see *Citgo Petroleum Corp. v. Odfjell Seachem*, 2013 WL 2289951, U.S. Dist. Ct., S.D.Tex., May 23, 2013, Miller, J.), as the Verified Complaint sufficiently alleges breach of contract and breach of warranty claims under the CISG (Id.; *Electrocraft Arkansas, Inc. v. Super Elec. Motors, Ltd.*, 2009 WL 5181854, U.S. Dist. Ct., E.D.Ark., Dec. 23, 2009, Wright, J.). Accordingly, to the extent that Nuspark's seeks dismissal, pursuant to CPLR 3211(a)(7), of the claims for breach of contract, breach of express warranty, breach of the implied warranty of merchantability, and breach of the implied warranty of fitness, the motion is denied.

[9] However, because an express contract exists between Plaintiff and Nuspark, the CISG preempts Plaintiff's claim for unjust enrichment and such is dismissed (see *Semi-Materials Co., Ltd. v. MEMC Elec. Materials, Inc.*, U.S. Dist. Ct., E.D.Mo., Jan. 10, 2011, Buckles, M.J.). Similarly, Plaintiff's claim for breach of the implied covenant of good faith is also dismissed because it is duplicative of the claim for breach of contract as it is based on the same underlying facts (see *Weihai Textile Group Import & Export Co., Ltd. v. Level 8 Apparel, LLC*, 2014 WL 1494327, U.S. Dist. Ct., S.D.N.Y., March 28, 2014, Carter, J.).

[10] Although Nuspark cites no authority in support of its contention that a plaintiff must plead compliance with the notice requirement of Article 39 of the CISG, the Verified Complaint sufficiently alleges notice of lack of conformity to Nuspark as Plaintiff alleges that immediately upon delivery it made numerous complaints about the defective Auto Tubber to Nuspark. Thus, that branch of Nuspark's motion which seeks to dismiss the claims as asserted against it pursuant to CPLR 3211(a)(7) because Plaintiff failed plead that it gave notice of lack of conformity to Nuspark is denied.

> "In moving to dismiss a cause of action as barred by the applicable statute
> of limitations, a defendant bears the initial burden of demonstrating, prima

facie, that the time within which to commence the action has expired (see *Jalayer v. Stigliano*, 94 A.D.3d 702, 703, 941 N.Y.S.2d 243; *Fleetwood Agency, Inc. v. Verde Elec. Corp.*, 85 A.D.3d 850, 925 N.Y.S.2d 576; *Rakusin v. Miano*, 84 A.D.3d 1051, 923 N.Y.S.2d 334). The burden then shifts to the plaintiff to raise a question of fact as to whether the statute of limitations was tolled or was otherwise inapplicable, or whether the action was actually commenced within the applicable limitations period (see *Jalayer v. Stigliano*, 94 A.D.3d at 703, 941 N.Y.S.2d 243; *Williams v. New York City Health & Hosps. Corp.*, 84 A.D.3d 1358, 923 N.Y.S.2d 908). To make a prima facie showing, the defendant must establish, inter alia, when the plaintiff's cause of action accrued (see *Swift v. New York Med. Coll.*, 25 A.D.3d 686, 687, 808 N.Y.S.2d 731)." (*Loiodice v. BMW of N. America, LLC*, 125 A.D.3d 723, 4 N.Y.S.3d 102 [2d Dept.2015]).

[11] Here, the parties agree that because the CISG does not provide a statute of limitations, the four-year statute of limitations set forth in UCC 2-275 applies in this case. That section provides, in relevant part:

> (1) An action for breach of any contract for sale must be commenced within four years after the cause of action has accrued.

> (2) A cause of action accrues when the breach occurs, regardless of the aggrieved party's lack of knowledge of the breach. A breach of warranty occurs when tender of delivery is made, except that where a warranty explicitly extends to future performance of the goods and discovery of the breach must await the time of such performance the cause of action accrues when the breach is or should have been discovered.

[12] Plaintiff claims that the breach of contract cause of action against Nuspark accrued in August 2010 when, as alleged in the Verified Complaint, the installation, integration and testing of the Auto Tubber machine was complete. Nuspark claims that Plaintiff's claims accrued in December 2009 upon delivery of the Auto Tubber. However, Nuspark's agreement with Plaintiff clearly and unequivocally obligated Nuspark to perform the installation and commissioning of the integrated machine. As such, the Plaintiff's causes of action accrued when installation of the unit was complete (see Franklin Nursing Home v. Power Cooling, Inc., 227 A.D.2d 374, 375, 642 N.Y.S.2d 80 [2d Dept.1996]). Accepting Plaintiff's allegation that installation was not completed until August 2010 as true, as the Court must do, Nuspark has not met its burden of demonstrating that the time within which to commence the action expired before the action was commenced in May 2014. Although Nuspark may ultimately prevail on this defense, it has not demonstrated entitlement to dismissal under CPLR 3211(a)(5) on this pre-answer motion. Accordingly, it is

ORDERED that Nuspark's motion is granted to the extent that the second and sixth causes of action as asserted against it are dismissed, and the motion is otherwise denied; . . .

Notes and Questions

1. In paragraph 8, we have a nice summary of what it takes to present a valid claim: "(1) the existence of a valid and enforceable contract containing both definite and certain terms, (2) performance by plaintiff, (3) breach by defendant and (4) resultant injury to plaintiff." Unsurprisingly, as the court affirms, this is the same under the UCC, the CISG, and New York State common law. Readers will not be surprised that the same is true for pretty much any other system of contract laws.

2. In paragraph 6, the court also reminds us how the interplay between the CISG and national law should work. Please re-read the respective passages and remember them well. You will need them in practice.

3. An interesting argument is discussed in paragraph 8, namely that Nonwovens' claim might fail because it "does not mention the CISG." The plaintiff did present "causes of action for breach of contract, breach of the implied covenant of good faith, breach of express warranty, breach of the implied warranty of merchantability, breach of the implied warranty of fitness, and unjust enrichment." Which of these elements are covered by the CISG and which are not? How does the CISG work with domestic or national law? Which domestic law will a court apply to fill any gaps in the CISG? Did this court get it right (see, *inter alia*, para. 9)?

4. At the end, the case turns on the question whether or not the plaintiff was barred from her claims because of the statute of limitations. The court simply says "the parties agree that because the CISG does not provide a statute of limitations, the four-year statute of limitations set forth in UCC 2-275 applies in this case." Why do you think the court did not apply the 1974 UN Convention on the Limitation Period in the International Sale of Goods, ratified by the United States and in force since 1994? (See Documents, p. I-132.) Which rule should be applied in such a case? Would the outcome have been different under the Convention?

Our next case shows a different choice of law problem, namely between the CISG and a domestic consumer protection statute. In addition, it is not clear whether the defendant was a seller or an agent for the seller and can be held responsible for nonperformance.

Case 2-12

2P Commercial Agency v. Len Familant

2013 WL 246650 (M.D. Fla. 2013)
(Paragraph numbers added, some footnotes and some details omitted.)

Opinion And Order

I.

[2] The following facts are undisputed. Plaintiff 2P Commercial Agency S.R.O. (2P Commercial or plaintiff) is an entity existing under the laws of the Czech Republic,

with its principal place of business in Prague, Czech Republic. 2P Commercial is engaged in the business of the wholesale trade of mobile telephones on the global market. Prior to the transaction at issue, 2P Commercial and SRT USA, Inc. (SRT)[2] and Len Familant (Familant or defendant) had never conducted any business together. Michael Bocchino (Bocchino)[3] introduced Familant to a corporate representative for 2P Commercial, Alexander Roshal (Roshal).

[3] Familant advised Roshal that he could obtain Apple iPhones with European specifications at a price that was lower than the then-current price on the market for such iPhones. Ultimately, a Purchase Order was drafted for the purchase of 400 iPhones. The Purchase Order lists the supplier as "SRT USA, Inc." and the "Good Sender" as "SRT USA, Inc." The Purchase Order is dated July 13, 2011, listed the date for delivery to Prague as July 19, 2011, and was signed by both Roshal and Familant. On the same day, a Purchase Invoice was prepared on SRT letterhead which listed bank information for making an initial deposit of $55,360.00. On July 14, 2011, 2P Commercial initiated a wire transfer to the bank account listed on the Purchase Invoice. The deposit was not consummated, however, because the banking information listed on the Purchase Invoice was incorrect. On July 19, 2011, the deposit was consummated in the correct bank account.

[4] The iPhones were not delivered on the July 19, 2011, date for delivery listed in the Purchase Order. The parties agree that 2P Commercial did not object to accepting the goods if they were delivered on July 26, July 27, July 29, 2011, or the week of August 1, 2011. No delivery was made and on either August 8, 2011, or August 10, 2011, 2P Commercial notified the defendants that the original order was being cancelled. Nonetheless, 2P Commercial again agreed to accept shipment between August 13, and August 15, 2011. Ultimately, the goods were never received by 2P Commercial. SRT returned $5,000.00 of the deposit to 2P Commercial, but has not returned the remaining deposit.

[5] Around the time that the parties entered into the purchase agreement, Familant executed a personal guarantee. The document provided a guarantee up to $300,000.00 if SRT failed to deliver the goods or make payment. Although the iPhones were never delivered to 2P Commercial, Familant has not honored the personal guarantee (he asserts that it is invalid).

[6] 2P Commercial initiated this action asserting a claim for: breach of contract under the United Nations Convention on Contracts for the International Sale of Goods (CISG) (Count I); violation of the Florida Deceptive and Unfair Trade Practices Act (FDUTPA) (Count II); and breach of personal guarantee (Count III). Familant seeks summary judgment in his favor on all three counts. 2P Commercial opposes the motion.

---

2. SRT was also a named defendant in this matter. However, on August 13, 2012, a default judgement was entered against this defendant.

3. Whether or not Michael Bocchino was a business partner of 2P Commercial is disputed by the parties.

[7] II. Summary judgment is appropriate only when the Court is satisfied that "there is no genuine issue as to any material fact and that the moving party is entitled to judgment as a matter of law." . . . An issue is "genuine" if there is sufficient evidence such that a reasonable jury could return a verdict for either party. . . . A fact is "material" if it may affect the outcome of the suit under governing law. . . .

[8] The moving party bears the burden of identifying those portions of the pleadings, depositions, answers to interrogatories, admissions, and/or affidavits which it believes demonstrate the absence of a genuine issue of material fact. . . . In order to avoid the entry of summary judgment, a party faced with a properly supported summary judgment motion must come forward with extrinsic evidence, i.e., affidavits, depositions, answers to interrogatories, and/or admissions, which are sufficient to establish the existence of the essential elements to that party's case, and the elements on which that party will bear the burden of proof at trial. . . .

[9] In ruling on a motion for summary judgment, the Court is required to consider the evidence in the light most favorable to the nonmoving party. . . . The Court does not weigh conflicting evidence or make credibility determinations. . . . "If the record presents factual issues, the court must not decide them; it must deny the motion and proceed to trial." *Tullius v. Albright*, 240 F.3d 1317, 1320 (11th Cir. 2001) (citing *Clemons v. Dougherty Cnty.*, 684 F.2d 1365, 1369 (11th Cir. 1982)). However, "[t]he mere existence of some factual dispute will not defeat summary judgment unless that factual dispute is material to an issue affecting the outcome of the case." *McCormick v. City of Fort Lauderdale*, 333 F.3d 1234, 1243 (11th Cir. 2003). A genuine issue of material fact exists only if there is sufficient evidence favoring the nonmoving party for a reasonable jury to return a verdict in its favor. . . .

III. A. Count I

[10] Count I asserts a claim for breach of contract under the CISG. Familant asserts that summary judgment is appropriate because: (1) the CISG is not applicable to him because he was not a buyer or seller in the contested transaction; (2) the contract is not enforceable under the CISG because it lacks the requisite specificity; and (3) 2P Commercial is precluded from bringing their claim because it breached the terms of the CISG upon breach of the underlying contract. 2P Commercial argues to the contrary.

1. Whether Familant was a "Seller" for Purposes of the CISG

[11] Familant asserts that he was not a buyer or a seller in this transaction and that "[t]he contract was between SRT and the Plaintiff, and any conduct of Mr. Familant was on behalf of, or as an agent of, SRT, the seller." Familant asserts that because 2P Commercial has admitted that SRT was a seller in the transaction, he cannot also be a seller. 2P Commercial asserts that there are genuine issues of material fact as to whether SRT was the only seller in the transaction, and whether Familant was the principal seller in the transaction and SRT was the agent of Familant.

[12] As the Court has previously found, although plaintiff has both pled, and conceded, that SRT was a seller in this transaction, this does not preclude a finding that

Familant, too, was a seller. Therefore, defendant's contention that because SRT is a seller in the transaction, Familant could not have been a seller, is without merit.

[13] The Court further finds that there is a genuine issue of material fact as to whether or not Familant was a seller, or at least held himself out to be a seller, in the contested transaction. Familant's role in the contested transaction, as well as his relationship with SRT, is unclear from the evidence. For example, some evidence provided to the Court suggests that Familant attempted to sell the iPhones to 2P Commercial personally through his own company. Other evidence suggests that both Familant and SRT were the seller. As such, there is a genuine issue of material fact as to Familant's role in the contested transaction. Summary judgment on this basis is denied.

2. Whether the Contract is Enforceable Under the CISG

[14] Familant further avers that Count I fails because it is unenforceable under the CISG. Specifically, Familant contends that although the original Purchase Order and Purchase Invoice obligated delivery in Prague by July 19, 2011, the actual deposit in SRT's account was not made until July 19, 2011, the date of mandated delivery. Familant asserts that because plaintiff did not cancel the contract on July 19, and subsequently agreed to later delivery, there was no definite date for delivery under the contract. Familant asserts that delivery is an essential term of a contract under Article 19(3) of the CISG, and without it, the contract is not enforceable.

[15] Defendant's reliance on Section 19(3) is misplaced. Section 19(3) falls under Part II of the CISG, which is concerned with formation of the contract. Section 19(3) provides that:

> "Additional or different terms relating, among other things, to the price, payment, quality and quantity of the goods, place and time of delivery, extent of one party's ability to the other or the settlement of disputes are considered to alter the terms of the *offer* materially." (Emphasis added).

[16] There is no dispute between the parties in relation to the formation of the contract. Indeed, Familant concedes that the contract entered into by the parties provided for delivery on July 19, 2011, and he makes no argument that there was any dispute as to this date. He also does not dispute that the goods were not delivered on July 19, 2011. Rather, Familant argues that plaintiff's agreement to accept late delivery materially altered an essential term of the contract. This contention is without merit as plaintiff's willingness to accept untimely delivery of the goods was an exercise of 2P Commercial's rights under the CISG upon breach of the contract. Section III of the CISG relates to a buyer's remedies for breach of contract by the seller. Section III, Article 47 provides in relevant part, "(1) The buyer may fix an additional period of time of reasonable length for performance by the seller of his obligations." Accordingly, the fact that 2P Commercial was willing to accept delivery of the purchased goods after July 19, 2011, does not demonstrate that there were any issues relating to contract formation, and therefore plaintiff's assertion that defendant violated Article 19(3) of the CISG is without merit. Summary Judgment on this basis is denied.

3. Whether 2P Commercial Breached the Contract Under the CISG

[17] Familant recognizes that Article 47 provides 2P Commercial with a remedy for breach by permitting an additional period of time for performance, but asserts that 2P Commercial did not strictly comply with the provisions of this Article, and therefore cannot maintain its claim for breach of contract. Specifically, Familant argues that Article 47 requires a fixed date for untimely performance and that "precatory language" concerning untimely delivery is insufficient.

[18] Familant's contention is without merit. Familant cites to no "precatory language" among the parties regarding late delivery. Furthermore, in his motion for summary judgment, Familant provides specific dates that 2P Commercial was willing to accept the goods, including July 26, 27, and 29, 2011. Familant makes no argument that this time frame was unreasonable under the CISG. Summary judgment on this basis is denied.

B. Count II

[19] Count II asserts a claim for violation of FDUTPA. Familant asserts that summary judgment is appropriate because: (1) FDUTPA is not applicable to plaintiffs who are not United States citizens; (2) 2P Commercial has impermissibly attempted to convert a breach of contract claim into an alleged violation of FDUTPA; and (3) there is no evidence of any deceptive statements or conduct by Familant that caused any damages.

1. Whether FDUTPA Applies to Plaintiff's Claims

[20] In its Opinion and Order on Familant's Motion to Dismiss, the Court addressed Familant's assertion that FDUTPA does not apply to 2P Commercial because it is a foreign entity. The Court determined that FDUTPA's protections extend to out of state plaintiffs.[112] Nothing has changed. Accordingly, summary judgment on this basis is denied.

---

112. The decision of 19 December 2012 reads in this regard as follows: "Florida courts are split on whether the protections of FDUTPA extend to out-of-state consumers. Compare *OCE Printing Sys. USA v. Mailers Data Serv., Inc.*, 760 So.2d 1037, 1042 (Fla. 2d DCA 2000) ('Other states can protect their own residents. . . . [O]nly in-state consumers can pursue a valid claim under [FDUTPA].') with *Millennium Commc'n & Fulfillment, Inc. v. Office of Attorney Gen., Dept. of Legal Affairs, State of Fla.*, 761 So.2d 1256, 1262 (Fla. 3d DCA 2000) ('[W]here the allegations . . . reflect that the offending conduct occurred entirely within this state, we can discern no legislative intent for the Department to be precluded from taking corrective measures under FDUTPA even where those persons affected by the conduct reside outside of the state.') There is no Florida Supreme Court decision resolving this divergence of authority. At least one federal district court has held that a foreign corporation could maintain a FDUTPA claim. See *Barnext Offshore, Ltd. v. Ferretti Group, USA, Inc.*, No. 10-23869-CIV, 2012 WL 1570057 at *5 (S.D.Fla. May 2, 2011).

The Court finds that *Millennium Commc'n & Fulfillment, Inc.* more appropriately reflects both the text of FDUTPA and its enumerated purpose. The express language of FDUTPA does not include any "geographical or residential restrictions." *Barnext Offshore, Ltd.*, 2012 WL 1570057 (S.D.Fla. May 2, 2011) quoting *Millennium Commc'n & Fulfillment, Inc.*, 761 So.3d at 1262. In addition, one of the three enumerated purposes of FDUTPA is '[t]o protect the consuming public and legitimate business enterprises from those who engage in unfair methods of competition, or

2. Whether 2P Commercial Has Impermissibly Converted a Breach of Contract Claim for Violations of FDUTPA

[21] Familant asserts that Count II alleges a cause of action for breach of contract under the disguise of a claim under FDUTPA. Familant asserts that this is improper, and therefore summary judgment should be granted in his favor.

[22] The Florida Deceptive and Unfair Trade Practices Act (FDUTPA) provides a civil cause of action for "[u]nfair methods of competition, unconscionable acts or practices, and unfair or deceptive acts or practices in the conduct of any trade or commerce." Fla. Stat. § 501.204(1). "A consumer claim for damages under FDUTPA has three elements: (1) a deceptive act or unfair practice; (2) causation; and (3) actual damages." *City First Mortg. Corp. v. Barton*, 988 So. 2d 82, 86 (Fla. 4th DCA 2008) (internal citations and quotation omitted). See also *KC Leisure, Inc. v. Haber*, 972 So. 2d 1069, 1073–74 (Fla. 5th DCA 2008). A "deceptive act" is "one that is likely to mislead consumers and an unfair practice is one that offends established public policy and one that is immoral, unethical, oppressive, unscrupulous, or substantially injurious to consumers." *Washington v. LaSalle Bank Nat'l Ass'n.*, 817 F. Supp. 2d 1345, 1350 (S.D. Fla. 2011). Further, causation must be direct, rather than remote or speculative. See e.g., Fla. Stat. § 501.211(2) ("In any action brought by a person who has suffered a loss as a result of a violation of this part . . . may recover actual damages.") "Actual damages" under the statute must directly "flow from the recovery of nominal damages, speculative losses, or compensation for subjective feelings of disappointment." *City First Mortg. Corp.*, 988 So. 2d at 86 (internal citations omitted).

[23] Although Familant styles his argument as one in favor of summary judgment, his argument is essentially that plaintiff has failed to state a claim for FDUTPA. In any event, the Court finds that Familant's contention that 2P Commercial has not set forth a claim under FDUTPA is without merit. Count II makes specific allegations that Familant induced 2P into making a contract for the purchase of goods although he had no intention of delivering the goods. Further, Count II alleges that Familant made written and oral promises that he could deliver the promised

---

unconscionable, deceptive, or unfair acts or practices in the conduct of any trade or commerce.' Fla. Stat. § 501.202(2). FDUTPA does not specifically limit 'consuming public' or 'legitimate business enterprises' to citizens or residents of Florida. Indeed, that statute defines 'consumer' as 'an individual; child, by and through its parent or legal guardian; business; firm; association; joint venture; partnership; estate; trust; business trust; syndicate; fiduciary; corporation; any commercial entity, however denominated; or any other group or combination.' Fla Stat. § 501.203(7). 'Trade or commerce' is defined as 'the advertising, soliciting, providing, offering, or distributing, whether by sale, rental, or otherwise, of any good or service or any property, whether tangible or intangible, or any other article, commodity, or thing of value, wherever situated.' Fla. Stat. § 501.203(8). Neither of these definitions provide any residential or citizen limitations. Importantly, defendant makes no allegations that the alleged fraudulent conduct alleged in Count II occurred anywhere other than Florida. Accordingly, the motion to dismiss on this ground is denied." No. 2:11-cv-652-FtM-29SPC, 2012 WL 6615889.

goods although he never had the capacity to do so. Certainly, if true, this is behavior that is likely to mislead consumers within the meaning of FDUTPA. Count II further alleges that plaintiff entered into a contract for the goods, paid a deposit for the goods, and the goods were not delivered, resulting in a financial loss of over $55,000.00. Accordingly, 2P Commercial has pled a deceptive act or unfair practice, causation, and actual damages.

3. Whether 2P Has Presented Evidence of Deceptive Statements Causing Damages

[24] Familant further asserts that there is no evidence of any deceptive statements made by Familant that resulted in damages to 2P Commercial. The Court disagrees. Plaintiff has produced evidence of false representations by Familant, including that he was part of the Apple distribution system, which defendant later admitted to be false. Further, plaintiff provided evidence of statements by Familant to 2P Commercial that defendant was actively engaged in overseas trade, although it was later discovered that the contested transaction was Familant's first overseas mobile phones sale. This evidence could give rise to a finding that Familant made fraudulent statements to 2P Commercial to induce it to contract for the sale of iPhones although Familant lacked the capacity to deliver on the contract. Accordingly, summary judgment is denied.

C. Count III

[25] Count III asserts a claim for breach of personal guarantee. The parties agree that Familant signed a Letter of Guarantee which guaranteed that in the event SRT failed to deliver the purchased goods, he would compensate 2P Commercial up to $300,000.00. The signed letter of guarantee is attached to the Complaint. Familant asserts that the personal guarantee is not enforceable and summary judgment is appropriate because: (1) the guarantee suffers from lack of consideration; (2) the guarantee was fraudulently induced, and (3) the guarantee fails due to ambiguity and indefiniteness. . . .

[34] Accordingly, it is now ORDERED:

Defendant, Len A. Familant's Dispositive Motion for Summary Judgment and Incorporated Memorandum of Law (Doc. #55) is DENIED.

Notes and Questions

1. In its discussion, the court finds that Familant's claims are not sufficiently supported by evidence to justify summary judgment. On October 24, 2012, the court had already ruled against SRT and in favor of 2P Commercial, awarding US$72,760 in damages plus US$10,627.50 in attorney fees. However, 2P Commercial had not been able to execute a Writ of Execution. Whether or not Familant had issued a valid personal guarantee remained unresolved.

2. The first point of contention is about the role of Familant in the matter. The court discusses whether Familant was "the seller" or at least "a seller." In our

discussion on pp. 171 et seq., we determined that the identity of seller and buyer, together with the identification of the goods, the quantity, and the price, were "essentials" of a valid contract. How can there be a claim under the CISG if the defendant is not necessarily a seller? Can there be more than one seller in an IBT? What is the definition of a seller?

3. In paragraphs 14–16, the court has to deal with the defendant's argument that there was no valid contract or that a valid contract became unenforceable because the plaintiff agreed to reschedule the delivery date after SRT failed to deliver as promised. Defendant literally argued that "plaintiff's agreement to accept late delivery materially altered an essential term of the contract." Why is this argument, as the court puts it diplomatically, "without merit"?

4. From paragraph 20 onward, the court discusses the application and impact of the Florida Deceptive and Unfair Trade Practices Act (FDUTPA). On our pyramid showing the hierarchy of potentially applicable rules (above, p. 52), where does the FDUTPA come in?

5. In paragraph 22, the court outlines the elements of a claim under the FDUTPA: "A consumer claim for damages under FDUTPA has three elements: (1) a deceptive act or unfair practice; (2) causation; and (3) actual damages." While "consumer" usually refers to someone making a purchase "for personal, family, or household use" (CISG Art. 2(a)), the Florida Deceptive and Unfair Trade Practices Act is notably wider in its scope of application and stipulates that "consumer" can include a "business; firm; association; joint venture; partnership; estate; trust; business trust; syndicate; fiduciary; corporation; any commercial entity, however denominated; or any other group or combination" (see above, fn. 112 on p. 267).

While the FDUTPA protects consumers, the CISG is for "parties whose places of *business* are in different states" (Art. 1(1) CISG, emphasis added) and is *not applicable* to "goods bought for personal, family or household use" (Art. 2(a) CISG). Can a party be at the same time a business and a consumer? Can the FDUTPA be applied next to the CISG? Or does the FDUTPA displace the CISG within its scope of application? Or the other way around? Who gets to decide? On what basis?

———————

Our next case concerns questions of breach and foreseeability of damages.

Case 2-13

Barbara Berry v. Ken M. Spooner Farms

2009 WL 927704 (W.D. Wash. 2009)
(Paragraph numbers added, some footnotes and details omitted.)
April 3, 2009

ORDER GRANTING DEFENDANT'S MOTION FOR SUMMARY JUDGMENT
FRANKLIN D. BURGESS, District Judge.

Introduction

[The facts of the case are explained in the context of an earlier order regarding defendant's first motion for summary judgment, above p. 165. At this point, we will take a look at the discussion of damages under the CISG.]

[1] This cause of action concerns raspberry plants sold by Defendant Spooner Farms to Plaintiff Barbara Berry. Plaintiff Barbara Berry is a commercial berry grower in the Michoacan area of Mexico and Defendant Spooner Farms, Puyallup, Washington, sells certified root stock for raspberry plants. Barbara Berry purchased 3,150 pounds of raspberry root stock (Summit variety) from Spooner Farms in December 2003, and this root stock was shipped to Mexico in February/March 2004. With this root stock, Barbara Berry intended to plant 74 acres, but since there was not enough root stock to plant this many acres, Barbara Berry explained that it propagated the root stock through a method known as "etiolation," which Barbara Berry asserts is commonly done in Mexico and can be considered industry standard. Barbara Berry asserts that the plants propagated from the Spooner Farms root stock were planted but these plants produced fruit that was malformed and crumbly.

[2] Spooner Farms moves for summary judgment on the basis that Barbara Berry did not use Spooner Farms certified root stock to grow raspberries. Rather, Barbara Berry used Spooner Farms certified root stock to produce a new generation of raspberry plants contrary to the standards of the industry, and that the "new plants" produced the fruit complained of, not the certified roots supplied by Spooner Farms. As such, any express warranty contained in the contract or any warranty implied by law does not extend to a product Spooner Farms did not manufacture. Alternatively, Spooner Farms moves for partial summary judgment limiting the number of acres that Barbara Berry can claim as the basis of damages to 11 acres and not 74.

[3] The instant motion assumes that the invoice terms are not part of the contract; thus Barbara Berry must rely on an implied warranty as the basis of its breach of contract claim. The issue of whether the invoice terms are part of the contract will continue to proceed to trial because if they are part of the contract, Spooner Farms contends that it will be entitled to its attorney fees and costs as the prevailing party as the invoice contains an attorney fees clause. . . .

Parties' Contentions

Spooner Farms' Motion

[6] Spooner Farms specializes in growing certified nursery stock for the commercial production of rapberries[sic] . . . in Western Washington, which has an ideal raspberry-growing climate and is the center of raspberry production in North America. Spooner Farms describes the propagation process in detail. . . .

[7] Spooner Farms contends that the standard practice in commercial raspberry farming is to plant certified nursery stock directly into the production fields. In Mexico, when using certified root stock, the standard practice is to plant 300 pounds

per acre. Spooner Farms contends that Barbara Berry used the 3,150 pounds of root stock from Spooner Farms to plant approximately 69 acres of land rather than approximately 11 acres of land. Furthermore, Spooner Farms contends that Barbara Berry created this nearly seven-fold increase in planting material by embarking on its own propagation program.

[8] Barbara Berry alleges that the fruit produced from the Spooner Farms plants was malformed, but that this problem was not present as to the plants obtained from the roots from Sakuma Nursery. . . .

[10] In its order, the Ninth Circuit held that the U.N. Convention on Contracts for the International Sale of Goods (CISG) applies in this matter. The burden of proof is on the buyer to prove that the product was defective at the time of delivery. Spooner Farms contends that Barbara Berry cannot prove that the Spooner Farms root stock was defective at the time of delivery because of two undisputed facts: (1) the allegedly defective fruit came from a new generation of plants created by Barbara Berry; and (2) the same generation of root stock was sold to another farmer and performed as expected.

[11] Spooner Farms contends that it is undisputed that the fruit complained of was grown on "new plants" propagated from the certified roots and not the certified roots themselves. Thus, Spooner Farms argues that any implied warranties do not extend to a product that Spooner Farms did not manufacture. . . .

[12] Spooner Farms contends that its certified root stock was merchantable at the time of delivery. Moreover, the same certified stock was also delivered to another buyer, Liepold Farms, which planted the root stock in its production fields to grow berries that were then sold to customers at market rates.

[13] Spooner Farms also argues that even if there were a breach of warranty, the evidence is insufficient as a matter of law to prove that the breach caused the alleged damage, because there are so many potential causes of the damaged fruit that are beyond the control of Spooner Farms.

[14] Alternatively, Spooner Farms argues that even if the implied warranty were extended to Barbara Berry's "new plants" and there were facts to demonstrate that the certified stock was defective at delivery, Barbara Berry's damages should be limited as a matter of law because they were not foreseeable, because under the CISG, Article 74, a buyer may only recover those damages that were foreseen or reasonably foreseeable by the seller as a probable consequence of breach. In this case, Spooner Farms argues that in assessing foreseeability, "the usual or intended use by the buyer should be the decisive factor." Peter Schlechtriem, Uniform Sales Law-The UN-Convention on contracts for the International Sale of Goods 97 (1986); see also, *Skibs A/S Gylfe v. Hyman-Michaels Co.*, 438 F.2d 803, 808 (6th Cir.1971) (stating that loss due to breach of contract is unrecoverable where the damage is unforeseeable at the time of contracting). Thus, Spooner Farms argues that damages are foreseeable only if they flow from standard commercial practice in the industry, and it violates the industry standard for a buyer of certified root stock to propagate.

[15] Additionally, Spooner Farms argues that Article 74 of CISG states that damages, including loss of profit, "may not exceed the loss which the party in breach foresaw or ought to have foreseen. . . ." Under industry standard planting practices, Spooner Farms sold Barbara Berry enough root stock for 11 acres, and even if it is found that Spooner Farms should have foreseen Barbara Berry's type of damages arising from the propagated plants, damages should be limited to those resulting from 11 acres of plants. . . .

[17] . . . Barbara Berry argues that if summary judgment is not denied as premature, it should be denied because there are numerous issues of material fact. First, Barbara Berry contends that the propagated plants were exact copies of the plants provided by Spooner Farms and cites to Spooner Farms' Motion at page 3 where it states that "each new generation of a propagated plant is a genetic copy of the prior generation."

[18] Second, Barbara Berry contends that it is common industry practice in Mexico and Chile to use certified root stock to propagate additional plants for planting, and that the etiolation method is the standard practice in the raspberry production industry in Mexico. . . .

[21] Fifth, Barbara Berry contends that it made it clear to Spooner Farms that it intended to plant approximately 74 acres and that it was, therefore, foreseeable that Barbara Berry would use the root stock to propagate additional root stock for planting substantially more than 11 acres. Moreover, it is likely that Spooner Farms was aware that it was standard practice to use certified root stock to propagate plants.

[22] Sixth, and finally, Barbara Berry argues that the lost profit damages claimed from being unable to market malformed, crumbly fruit were foreseeable. Barbara Berry contends that damages should not be limited to 11 acres because Barbara Berry made it clear to Spooner Farms that it intended to plant approximate 74 acres, and thus the amount of damages claimed was foreseeable. . . .

[26] Spooner Farms argues that the parties are in agreement that Article 74 of the CISG limits damages to "the loss which the party in breach foresaw or ought to have foreseen at the time of the conclusion of the contract, in light of the facts and matters of which he then knew or ought to have known, as a possible consequence of the breach." Spooner Farms argues that Barbara Berry does not claim that it told Spooner Farms it intended to propagate—it said it intended to plant 75 acres—and the inference should not be drawn that the 11 acres' worth of roots Spooner Farms sold would be propagated by Barbara Berry. The email exchanges between Spooner Farms and Barbara Berry indicate that Barbara Berry was seeking additional roots; Barbara Casillas emailed Andrea Spooner (Exhibit A to Casillas Decl.): "I want to know when your other clients get you a cancelation [sic] because I am interested in buying the roots." This was confirmed in the Casillas and Gonzalez declarations as well, where they state their desire to obtain more roots if any other orders are cancelled, as Barbara Berry wanted to cover approximately 75 acres. Thus, Spooner Farms contends that in light of the express statements by Barbara

Berry to Spooner Farms indicating Barbara Berry would be planting rather than propagating, there is no basis for asserting that Spooner Farms should have foreseen propagation due to the existence of any alleged industry standard in Mexico. Spooner Farms argues that the extent of damages was not foreseeable in excess of 11 acres, and the type of damages arising from fruit grown from propagated plants was also not foreseeable.

[27] Spooner Farms argues that the implied warranty does not extend to the propagated plants, *citing Wittkamp v. United States*, 343 F.Supp. 1075, 1078–79 (1972) holding that implied warranties do not extend to a new product created by the purchaser. . . .

Discussion and Conclusion . . .

[31] Having considered the parties' arguments and authorities and their submissions accompanying their memoranda, the Court concludes that Spooner Farms' Second Motion for Summary Judgment must be granted. Barbara Berry produced new plants from the certified root stock that it purchased from Spooner Farms; there are no implied warranties attached to these new plants that Spooner Farms did not sell. Moreover, there is no showing that the certified root stock supplied by Barbara Berry was defective at the time of delivery, and there is contrary evidence that Rod Liepold planted Summit certified root stock that was genetically identical to the Summit certified root stock received by Barbara Berry, and which certified root stock grew as expected and did not produce crumbly fruit. Additionally, Barbara Berry has not established proximate cause, as it has not identified the alleged genetic defect nor explained how it caused crumbly fruit when there are many reasons why a farmer may not be able to grow a good crop of fruit (soil conditions, bee activity, farming methods, diseases, etc.), which are outside the control of the nursery stock provider. . . .

NOW, THEREFORE, IT IS ORDERED: Spooner Farms' Second Motion for Summary Judgment . . . is GRANTED. . . .

Notes and Questions

1. What kind of damages can be claimed under Article 74 CISG? What does the claimant have to show in order to get those damages? How could a rule be formulated for "forseeability"? If parties do business in other countries, does this affect the question whether they foresaw or should have foreseen a particular loss? If so, how?

2. Where does the standard of "proximate cause" come from that the court applies in paragraph 31? What language is used in the CISG? What is the difference, if any?

3. At the end, Barbara Berry lost her case. Review the history of the litigation (above, pp. 165 and 271) and explain whether you agree with the outcome or not and why.

Another case involving a breach of contract also discussed the question of mitigation of losses pursuant to Article 77 of the CISG:

Case 2-14

Treibacher Industrie v. Allegheny Tech and TDY Industries

464 F.3d 1235 (11th Cir. 2006)
(Paragraph numbers added, some footnotes and details omitted.)
Appeal from the United States District Court for the
Northern District of Alabama.
TJOFLAT, Circuit Judge

I. A.

[1] This lawsuit arises out of two contracts, executed in November and December of
2000, respectively, whereby Treibacher Industrie, AG ("Treibacher"), an Austrian
vendor of hard metal powders, agreed to sell specified quantities of tantalum carbide
("TaC"), a hard metal powder, to TDY Industries, Inc. ("TDY")[1] for delivery to "consignment." TDY planned to use the TaC in manufacturing tungsten-graded carbide
powders[2] at its plant in Gurney, Alabama. After it had received some of the amount
of TaC specified in the November 2000 contract, TDY refused to take delivery of the
balance of the TaC specified in both contracts, and, in a letter to Treibacher dated
August 23, 2001, denied that it had a binding obligation to take delivery of or pay
for any TaC that it did not wish to use. Unbeknownst to Treibacher, TDY had purchased the TaC it needed from another vendor at lower prices than those specified
in its contracts with Treibacher. Treibacher eventually sold the quantities of TaC of
which TDY refused to take delivery, but at lower prices than those specified in its
contracts with TDY. Treibacher then filed suit against TDY, seeking to recover the
balance of the amount Treibacher would have received had TDY paid for all of the
TaC specified in the November and December 2000 contracts.[3]

---

1. TDY, a California corporation, is a subsidiary of Allegheny Technologies, Inc., a Pennsylvania corporation, which produces various metals and metal-based products.

2. TaC is a component of tungsten-graded carbide powder, which is used to harden other metals.

3. Treibacher's complaint contains six counts. Count I is a claim for "Breach of Contract under
the United Nations Convention on Contracts for the International Sale of Goods." Count II is a
claim for "Anticipatory Breach of Contract" under the same United Nations convention. Count III
is a claim for "Breach of Contract" under Alabama law. Count IV is a claim for "Moneys Owed and
Unjust Enrichment" under Alabama law. Count V is a claim for "Conversion" under Alabama law.
Count VI is a claim for "Misrepresentation," alleging that TDY misrepresented that it would accept
and pay for the goods Treibacher shipped to it. Counts II through VI incorporate by reference the
allegations of all previous counts.
On TDY's motion for summary judgment, the district court isolated Treibacher's claims from the
complaint and granted the motion on all counts but Counts I and VI. The court, following a bench
trial, gave Treibacher judgment on Counts I and VI, awarding Treibacher $5,327,042.85. Since we
affirm the court's judgment on Count I, we need not review the court's disposition of Count VI.

[2] The case proceeded to a bench trial, where TDY and Treibacher disputed the meaning of the term "consignment"—the delivery term contained in both contracts. TDY introduced experts in the metal industry who testified that the term "consignment," according to its common usage in the trade, meant that no sale occurred unless and until TDY actually used the TaC. Treibacher introduced evidence of the parties' prior dealings to show that the parties, in their course of dealings (extending over a seven-year period), understood the term "consignment" to mean that TDY had a binding obligation to pay for all of the TaC specified in each contract but that Treibacher would delay billing TDY for the materials until TDY had actually used them. The district court ruled that, under the United Nations Convention on Contracts for the International Sale of Goods ("CISG"), . . . evidence of the parties' interpretation of the term in their course of dealings trumped evidence of the term's customary usage in the industry, and found that Treibacher and TDY, in their course of dealings, understood the term to mean "that a sale had occurred, but that invoices would be delayed until the materials were withdrawn."[4] The court therefore entered judgment against TDY, awarding Treibacher $5,327,042.85 in compensatory damages (including interest).

B.

[3] TDY now appeals. TDY contends that, under the CISG, a contract term should be construed according to its customary usage in the industry unless the parties have expressly agreed to another usage. TDY argues, in the alternative, that the district court erred in finding that, in their course of dealings, Treibacher and TDY understood the term "consignment" to require TDY to use and pay for all of the TaC specified in each contract. Finally, TDY contends that, if we uphold the district court's ruling that TDY breached its contracts with Treibacher, we should remand the case for a new trial on damages on the ground that the district court erroneously found that Treibacher reasonably mitigated its damages.

[4] Reviewing the district court's legal conclusions de novo and factual findings for clear error, *Newell v. Prudential Ins. Co.,* 904 F.2d 644, 649 (11th Cir.1990), we hold that the district court properly construed the contract under the CISG—according to the parties' course of dealings—and did not commit clear error in finding that the parties understood the contracts to require TDY to use all of the TaC specified in the contracts. As to the mitigation of damages issue, which we review for clear error, *Bunge Corp. v. Freeport Marine Repair, Inc.,* 240 F.3d 919, 923 (11th Cir.2001), we find that the evidence before the district court supported its finding that Treibacher's mitigation efforts were reasonable under the circumstances. We therefore affirm the judgment of the district court.

---

4. Although the parties presented conflicting evidence regarding the customary usage in the industry of the term "consignment," the district court did not make a finding regarding the customary usage of the term because it found that the parties had established a meaning for the term in their course of dealings, thus rendering customary usage irrelevant.

II. A.

[5] We begin our analysis by discussing the CISG, which governs the formation of and rights and obligations under contracts for the international sale of goods. CISG, arts. 1, 4.[5] Article 9 of the CISG provides the rules for interpreting the terms of contracts. Article 9(1) states that, "parties are bound by any usage to which they have agreed and by any practices which they have established between themselves." Article 9(2) then states that, "parties are considered, unless otherwise agreed, to have impliedly made applicable to their contract . . . a usage of which the parties knew or ought to have known and which in international trade is widely known to . . . parties to contracts of the type involved in the particular trade concerned." Article 8 of the CISG governs the interpretation of the parties' statements and conduct. A party's statements and conduct are interpreted according to that party's actual intent "where the other party knew . . . what that intent was," CISG, art. 8(1), but, if the other party was unaware of that party's actual intent, then "according to the understanding that a reasonable person . . . would have had in the same circumstances," CISG, art. 8(2). To determine a party's actual intent, or a reasonable interpretation thereof, "due consideration is to be given to all relevant circumstances of the case including the negotiations, any practices which the parties have established between themselves, usages and any subsequent conduct of the parties." CISG, art. 8(3).

[6] In arguing that a term's customary usage takes precedence over the parties' understanding of that term in their course of dealings, TDY seizes upon the language of article 9(2), which states that, "parties are considered, unless otherwise agreed, to have made applicable to their contract" customary trade usages. TDY contends that article 9(2) should be read to mean that, unless parties to a contract expressly agree to the meaning of a term, the customary trade usage applies. In support of its argument, TDY points to the language of article (9)(1), which binds parties to "any usage to which they have agreed and by any practices which they have established between themselves." According to TDY, the drafters of the CISG, by separating the phrase "usages to which they have agreed" from the phrase "practices which they have established between themselves," intended the word "agreed," in article 9, to mean express agreement, as opposed to tacit agreement by course of conduct. Applying this definition to the language of article 9(2), TDY contends that contract terms should, in the absence of express agreement to their usage, be interpreted according to customary usage, instead of the usage established between the parties through their course of conduct.

---

5. The parties do not dispute that the CISG governs their dispute. Article 1 of the CISG provides, in relevant part, that it "applies to contracts of sale of goods between parties whose places of business are in different States . . . when the States are Contracting States." The United States and Austria are Contracting States. Article 4 of the CISG provides, in relevant part, that it "governs . . . the formation of the contract and the rights and obligations of the seller and buyer arising from such a contract." The parties dispute their respective "rights and obligations" under the contracts at issue in this case.

[7] TDY's construction of article 9 would, however, render article 8(3) superfluous and the latter portion of article 9(1) a nullity. The inclusion in article 8(3) of "any practices which the parties have established between themselves," as a factor in interpreting the parties' statements and conduct, would be meaningless if a term's customary usage controlled that term's meaning in the face of a conflicting usage in the parties' course of dealings. The latter portion of article 9(1) would be void because the parties would no longer be "bound by any practices which they have established between themselves." Instead, in the absence of an express agreement as to a term's meaning, the parties would be bound by that term's customary usage, even if they had established a contrary usage in their course of dealings. We therefore reject TDY's interpretation of article 9(2), and, like the district court, adopt a reading that gives force to articles 8(3) and 9(1), namely, that the parties' usage of a term in their course of dealings controls that term's meaning in the face of a conflicting customary usage of the term. . . .

B.

[8] The district court did not commit clear error in finding that, in their course of dealings, TDY and Treibacher defined the term "consignment" to require TDY to accept and pay for all of the TaC specified in each contract. The parties do not dispute that they executed, between 1993 and 2000, a series of contracts in which Treibacher agreed to sell certain hard metal powders, such as TaC, to TDY. In each instance, TDY discussed its needs with Treibacher, after which Treibacher and TDY executed a contract whereby Treibacher agreed to sell a fixed quantity of materials at a fixed price for delivery to "consignment." Treibacher then delivered to TDY the specified quantity of materials—sometimes in installments, depending upon TDY's needs.[6] TDY kept the materials it received from Treibacher in a "consignment store," where the materials were labeled as being from Treibacher and segregated from other vendors' materials. As it withdrew the materials from the consignment store for use, TDY published "usage reports," which documented the amounts of materials withdrawn. TDY sent the usage reports to Treibacher, and Treibacher, in turn, sent TDY invoices for the amounts of materials withdrawn at the price specified in the relevant contract. TDY then paid the invoices when they came due. In each instance, TDY ultimately withdrew and paid for the full quantity of materials specified in each contract.

[9] A particularly telling interaction, the existence of which the parties do not dispute, occurred in February 2000, when a TDY employee, Conrad Atchley, sent an email to his counterpart at Treibacher, Peter Hinterhofer, expressing TDY's desire to return unused portions of a hard metal powder, titanium carbonitride ("TiCN"), which Treibacher had delivered. Hinterhofer telephoned Atchley in response and explained that TDY could not return the TiCN because TDY was contractually

---

6. TDY would notify Treibacher as to when it wanted to take delivery of portions of the quantity of materials provided for in each contract.

obligated to purchase the materials; Treibacher had delivered the TiCN as part of a quantity of TiCN that it was obligated to provide TDY under a contract executed in December 1999. Atchley told Hinterhofer that TDY would keep the TiCN. TDY subsequently used the TiCN and sent a usage report to Treibacher, for which Treibacher sent TDY an invoice, which TDY paid. This interaction—evidencing TDY's acquiescence in Treibacher's interpretation of the contract—along with TDY's practice, between 1993 and 2000, of using and paying for all of the TaC specified in each contract amply support the district court's finding that the parties, in their course of dealings, construed their contracts to require TDY to use and pay for all of the TaC specified in each contract.

C.

[10] With respect to damages, the district court did not commit clear error in finding that Treibacher reasonably mitigated its damages. Article 77 of the CISG requires a party claiming breach of contract to "take such measures as are reasonable in the circumstances to mitigate the loss." Article 77, however, places the burden on the breaching party to "claim a reduction in the damages in the amount by which the loss should have been mitigated." Treibacher's Commercial Director, Ulf Strumberger, and Hinterhofer testified that Treibacher sought to mitigate damages as soon as possible and ultimately obtained the highest prices possible for the quantity of TaC that TDY refused; their first sale in mitigation occurred on September 9, 2001, seventeen days after the date of TDY's letter denying its obligation to purchase all of the TaC. TDY, the party carrying the burden of proving Treibacher's failure to mitigate, presented no evidence showing that Treibacher did not act reasonably. The district court therefore had no basis upon which to find that Treibacher did not take reasonable steps to mitigate its losses.

III.

[11] In sum, the district court properly determined that, under the CISG, the meaning the parties ascribe to a contractual term in their course of dealings establishes the meaning of that term in the face of a conflicting customary usage of the term. The district court was not clearly erroneous in finding that Treibacher and TDY understood their contracts to require TDY to purchase all of the TaC specified in each contract and that Treibacher took reasonable measures to mitigate its losses after TDY breached. Accordingly, the judgment of the district court is AFFIRMED.

Notes and Questions

1. The judgment reminds us that there can be no meaningful discussion whether there was a breach and what the remedies might be, before the exact scope of the rights and obligations of the parties under the contract has been determined. In the present case, this required an interpretation of the contract in light of contractual language, industry usages, and specific prior dealings between the parties.

2. Paragraph 6 of the judgment presents the opposing arguments about party-specific or agreed-upon usages and general usages in the industry. TDY argues that

in the absence of an explicit agreement to the contrary, parties are bound to industry customs even if they do not reflect their prior practice or understanding. To that effect, TDY makes a textual or grammatical argument about Article 9(1) of the CISG, seeking to distinguish general usages "to which they have [tacitly] agreed" from specific practices "which they have [explicitly] established between themselves." At first glance, the argument does not seem outright untenable. However, in light of Article 8(3) and the clear position taken by commentators such as Professor Schmidt-Kessel,[113] chances of success of TDY with this argument were literally zero. Why do you think TDY's lawyers brought an appeal centrally based on this point anyway?

3. What can we learn about the obligation to mitigate damages under Article 77 of the CISG after a breach of contract?

––––––––––––

In the next case, we will take a look at the Article 79 exemption for unforeseen circumstances, often colloquially referred to as "the force majeure defense."

Case 2-15

Macromex Srl. v. Globex International Inc.

American Arbitration Association
International Centre for Dispute Resolution
Case No. 50181T 0036406, Award of October 23, 2007
(Paragraph numbers added.)

Interim Award

[1] I, the Undersigned Arbitrator, having been designated by the International Centre for Dispute Resolution ("ICDR") pursuant to an arbitration clause contained in each of the purchase orders dated April 14, 2006 (the "Contracts") between the above-noted parties; having been duly sworn; and having duly heard the allegations, proofs and arguments of the parties; do hereby award on an interim basis as follows with respect to the issues arising in this proceeding:

I. Facts

[2] Globex International ("Seller") is an American company engaged in the export of food products to multiple countries globally, including in Eastern Europe. Seller has contracts containing exclusivity agreements with companies in certain locales. In the ordinary course of business Seller developed a non-exclusive relationship with Macromex Srl. ("Buyer"), a Romanian company, and to ship, among other things, chicken leg quarters to Buyer.

[3] The Contracts in question involved order confirmation/sales agreements dated April 14, 2006 for chicken leg quarters to be shipped to Buyer, which had an address

––––––––––––

113. Martin Schmidt-Kessel, *Commentary on Article 9*, in Schwenzer (ed.), *Schlechtriem & Schwenzer Commentary on the UN Convention on the International Sale of Goods (CISG)*, Oxford Univ. Press 4th ed. 2016, pp. 181 et seq.

in Bucharest, Romania. The shipment dates were expressly established in each order as follows:

No. 38268-38297: 4/24/06 + 1–2 weeks

No. 38298-30297: 5/1/06 + 1–2 weeks

No. 38328-38353: 5/8/06 + 1–2 weeks

No. 38354,38379: 5/15/06 + 1–2 weeks

[4] As such, all product was to be shipped no later than May 29, 2006. No particular supplier of the chicken products was specified in the Contracts. The Contracts are governed by the U.N. Convention on International Sale of Goods ("CISG").

[5] Evidence at hearing established that in the normal course of dealing within the industry, as well as between the two parties to this proceeding, some flexibility in delivery was allowed at times, albeit with industry players utilizing somewhat different (rather than uniform) purchase order language on shipment terms. After the conclusion of the Contracts between the parties, the price of chicken increased very substantially, and Seller's supplier failed to ship to it in a timely manner. Seller impacted this supply situation—unknowingly perhaps, at least initially—by allocating such product to two breakbulk shipments for itself, rather than to container sales for customers like Buyer. While Buyer did become more insistent regarding prompt delivery as the month of May progressed, Buyer did not formally claim breach; nor did Buyer set another delivery date prior to the issuance of a decree by the Romanian government, which established a chicken product importation ban with virtually no notice.

[6] To explain, an avian flu outbreak prompted the Romanian government to bar all chicken imports not certified as of June 7, 2006. The Romanian Bulletin addressing the restriction stated that: "Transports loaded within 5 days of June 2, 2006 will be allowed to be imported into Romania." An extension of one day was subsequently granted. Had Seller loaded the chicken within the two week window expressly provided for in the Contracts, or even within a week thereafter, the chicken would have been allowed into Romania. However, Seller was unable to certify all the remaining chicken in the order in time, so the final delivery was deficient. Buyer then proposed that Seller ship the balance of the chicken order to it at a location outside of Romania, suggesting certain ports. Another supplier to Buyer provided such alternative performance following implementation of the ban with respect to shipments on which it too was late. Seller ultimately refused the proposal, maintaining that the unfilled portions of the Contracts were voided by the Romanian government's action, which constituted a force majeure event. Seller thereafter sold the undelivered chicken to another buyer at a substantial profit. Buyer now seeks a damages remedy with respect to the undelivered product under the Contracts.

II. The Merits and Applicable Law

[7] The facts of this case are less complicated than the applicable law. Seller's defense to the claim is grounded in a legal exemption provided by Article 79 of the CISG.

Its ability to invoke the defense is dependent on whether the initial delay in delivery constituted a fundamental breach. This issue, in turn, potentially impacts whether Seller's tardiness under the Contracts prevents a finding that the governmental ban impediment caused the fundamental breach. The second basic legal issue is whether Buyer's proposed alternative of a different destination was a commercially reasonable alternative such that Seller was obligated to comply. This issue, in turn, is impacted by whether resort to private law, and specifically the UCC (to define what is "commercially reasonable" in the circumstances), is appropriate under Article 7(2) of the CISG. As explained below in detail, I hold in Buyer's favor and award damages, as the weightier facts and more persuasive precedent/scholarly commentary all support that result.

A. Breach of Contract under the CISG

[8] The CISG states that the "seller must deliver the goods . . . if a period of time is fixed by or determinable from the contract, at any time within that period." CISG Article 33. The goods delivered must be "of the quantity, quality and description required by the contract and . . . contained or packaged in the manner required by the contract." CISG Article 35. In the event that "seller delivers only a part of the goods . . . [buyer's rights] apply in respect [to] the part which is missing. . . ." CISG Art. 51(1).

[9] It is also worth noting that the language of the CISG concerning damages is very broad: it states that: "[i]f the seller fails to perform *any* of his obligations under the contract or this Convention, the buyer may" either "exercise the rights provided in arts. 46–52;" or "claim damages as provided in arts. 74–77." CISG Art. 45(1) (emphasis added). However, there is nothing in the Convention provisions to suggest that a failure to perform a minor contractual obligation would trigger the full amount of damages sought herein. While it is unclear on the existing record reflected in the evidentiary record what damages would be available for an immaterial breach if sought, it is clear that for the Buyer to be entitled to the full damages sought in this proceeding, the Seller would have to have been in fundamental breach of the Contracts.

[10] Under a strict reading of the CISG provisions above and the language on the face of the Contracts, Seller breached the Contracts upon the expiration of the additional two weeks expressly granted in the Contracts beyond the fixed delivery date. The lapse in time between the contractual shipment periods and the Romanian government's blockage of imports was a matter of weeks or days, depending upon the particular Contract. However, this delay in performance did not amount to a fundamental breach for several reasons. As explained below, first, the parties' prior course of dealing and industry practice allowed for some flexibility in the delivery date—a flexibility that was shown in Buyer's responses here, at least at the onset of the delivery delay. Second, the Buyer and Seller appear to have revised the contract as to shipment dates as a matter of law under the CISG, at least for a limited period, through their continued dealing, based on the email chains reflected in the evidentiary record. Third, even if the breach could have been considered fundamental,

Buyer failed to notify Seller of Buyer's avoidance, which is legally significant as explained below.

[11] While there is no "bright-line" rule for what constitutes a reasonable delay, if the delay was within the parties' and/or industry's definition of "reasonable" it would not be sufficient to find a fundamental breach under Article 49. *See Valero Marketing & Supply Co. v. Greeni Oy*, No. Civ. 0l-5254 at *7-8, 2006 WL 891196 (D.N.J. Apr. 4 , 2006) (finding two day delay did not amount to fundamental breach under Article 49 because it was reasonable within industry). Provided that the delay here was within the scope of the course of business of the Seller and Buyer and/or their industry, then Seller's actions could not be found to constitute a fundamental breach. However, the evidence does not permit a specific finding in this regard, as only general latitude was referenced in postponement practice testimony, rather than specific temporal parameters. The absence of specificity cuts against the Seller since it is seeking to invoke it as an excuse, and therefore had the burden of proof on industry practice. At the same time though, the parties behaved until June 2, 2006 — the date of the Romanian government ban — in a manner that did not rise to the level of Buyer either declaring or acting upon a fundamental breach.

[12] Second, "[a] contract may be modified or terminated by the mere agreement of the parties." CISG Article 29(1). Modifications or terminations are only required to be in writing when the contract contains a provision requiring such. CISG Article 29(2). The failure to object to a unilateral attempt to modify a contract is not an agreement to modify a contract. *See Chateau des Charmes v. Sabate USA, Inc.*, 328 F.3d 528, 531 (9th Cir. 2003). However, "[f]ollowing arts. 29(1) and 11 CISG, any agreement, regardless of the form in which it came about, can in principle be changed or ended by the mere agreement of the parties, which may be proved by any means, including the behavior of the parties themselves." Belgium, 15 May 2002 Appellate Court Ghent (*NV A.R. v. NV I.*) (*Design of radio phone case*) <http://cisgw3.law.pace.edu/cases/020515b1.html> (finding a "positive meaning attached in trade to silence when receiving all kinds of documents, correspondence and so on."). Here, Buyer acquiesced for a time to the shipment delay, albeit while pressing for action to be taken and status information provided by Seller.

[13] Third, "according to Article 26 CISG, a contract is not avoided automatically when a fundamental breach of contract occurs; the Buyer must explicitly declare the avoidance." Evelien Visser, *Gaps in the CISG: In General and with Specific Emphasis on the Interpretation of the Remedial Provisions of the Convention in the Light of the General Principles of the CISG*, § 2.3 (1998) <http://www.cisg.law.pace.edu/cisg/biblio/visser.html> [hereinafter *Gaps in the CISG*]. There is nothing in the record to indicate that Buyer provided such notice, written or otherwise, to Seller of any intent to avoid the contract in the circumstances, which occurred during a steep increase in poultry prices in the global marketplace between April and June, 2006.

[14] Finally, even if Seller were found liable for damages, Seller potentially could avoid this liability if the Romanian government's decision to block chicken imports

constituted a force majeure event, such that Seller qualified for an "exemption" under CISG Article 79. Force majeure, of course, is an event or effect that can be neither anticipated nor controlled. The CISG codified an "exemption" in Article 79, which states in relevant part that:

> "A party is not liable for a failure to perform any of his obligations if he proves that the failure was due to an impediment beyond his control and that he could not reasonably be expected to have taken the impediment into account at the time of the conclusion of the contract or to have avoided or overcome it or its consequences."

[15] The term "exemption" was purposefully used in lieu of the more common term "force majeure" in an effort to avoid unintentional reference to private law, Catherine Kessedjian, *Competing Approaches to Force Majeure and Hardship*, in 25 International Review of Law and Economics 64I, § l.l.l. (Sept. 2005) available at< http:www.cisg.law.pace.edu/cisg/biblio/ kessedjian.html>. Although the Contracts contained no "force majeure" clause, the CISG helps to fill the "gap" in the Contracts in this regard; there is no legal significance here to the differing practice of Seller evident in at least one of its agreements with another entity in the evidentiary record regarding inclusion of a force majeure clause.

[16] Irrespective of whether Seller's delay prior to the Romanian government's ban on chicken imports constituted a fundamental breach, Seller's ultimate failure to deliver all of the contracted for chicken would be a fundamental breach, unless Seller can claim the "exemption" under Article 79.

B. Qualification for an "Exemption" under the CISG

[17] If successfully proven, an Article 79 "exemption" bars the party from "liability for failure to perform any of his obligations." CISG Article 79. "The effect . . . is to exempt the non-performing party only from liability for damages. All of the other remedies are available to the other party." Secretariat Commentary, Guide to CISG Article 79, §§ 7, 8. Article 79 only exempts from certain liabilities, and does not "address other types of relief, such as a buyer's right to reduction on price (Article 50), the right of compel performance [sic] (Articles 46, 62), the right to avoid the contract (Articles 49, 64), the right to collect interest (Article 78), or the right to collect penalties or liquidated damages if local law permits. Indeed, it specifically reserves a party's right to these remedies." Carla Spivack, *Of Shrinking Sweatsuits and Poison Vine Wax: A Comparison of Basis for Excuse under U.C.C. § 2-615 and CISG Article 79*, in 27 Pennsylvania Journal of International Economic Law 757, 799 (Fall 2006) available at <http://cisgw3.law.pace.edu/cisg/biblio/ spivack.html> [hereinafter *Of Shrinking Sweatsuits*].

[18] Article 79 contains four factors a party must meet to qualify for the exemption. First, there must be "an impediment beyond the defaulting party's control." CISG Article 79; see also Chengwei Liu, *Force Majeure: Perspectives from the CISG, UNIDROIT Principles, PECL and Case Law*, § 4 (2d ed. Apr. 2005) available at <http://www.cisg.law.pace.edu/cisg/biblio/liu6.html> [hereinafter *Force Majeure*].

Second, the impediment "could not have been reasonably taken into account by the defaulting party at the conclusion of the contract." *Id*. Third, the impediment or the consequences of the impediment "could not have been reasonably avoided or overcome." *Id*. Fourth, the "defaulting party proves that the challenged non-performance was due to such an impediment." *Id*. The burden of proof is on the party failing to perform. Germany, 9 January 2002 Supreme Court (*Powdered milk case*) <http://cisgw3.law.pace.edu/cases/020109g1.html>.

[19] The Romanian government's decision to stop all chicken imports on virtually no notice to the industry was certainly beyond Seller's control, and it would not have been reasonably contemplated as a risk assigned to the Seller at the conclusion of the contract, as no prior ban experienced by either party was taken as precipitously. The third and fourth factors are closer questions, and are addressed in greater detail below (in reverse order) because of their ultimate importance to the determination of the merits.

i. Meeting the Fourth Factor of Causality

[20] This requirement essentially requires a showing of causality between the impediment and the non-performance. "The non-performance of the contract must be 'due to' the impediment." Chengwei Liu, *Force Majeure* §4. Causality exists here between Seller's inability to deliver the chicken and the Romanian government's ban on imports. The question is whether Seller's delay in performance beyond the shipment "window" expressly provided for in the Contracts and/or by industry practice bars the Seller from claiming protection of the exemption by precluding Seller's ability to show causation.

[21] Two cases have addressed whether a party can claim an exemption under Article 79 when it is in breach of the terms of the contract. In one case where the Buyer was supposed to have paid for a caviar delivery prior to the imposition of U.N. sanctions that made payment impossible, the court held that when "Buyer was in default before the sanctions [the force majeure] became effective, he could have and should have paid at a date when payment was possible and his status of being a defaulting party cannot be changed by a later force majeure." Hungary, 10 December 1996 Budapest Arbitration Vb 96074 (*Caviar case*) <http://cisgw3.law.pace.edu/cases/961210h1.html> ("Buyer was supposed to pay US $15,000 before delivery, while the balance was due 'within two weeks after delivery'."). A second court found that a party to a contract could not claim that a strike was an impediment because it occurred after the seller was already in arrears. Bulgaria, 24 April 1996 Arbitration Case 56/1995 (*Coal case*) <http://cisgw3.law.pace.edu/cases/960424bu.html> However, these cases can be distinguished here since the Seller is found not to be in fundamental breach prior to the occurrence of the impediment, and no CISG case was found directly addressing a fact pattern involving immaterial breach.

[22] Two scholarly approaches to access the ability of a seller to raise a force majeure exemption when the seller has already failed to perform some portion of the

contractual obligations are also available and to be considered. Compare, e.g., Denis Tallon, Article 79, in Commentary on the International Sales Law: the 1980 Vienna Sale Convention, 581–82 (Bianca & Bonell, eds.) (Milan 1987) available at <http://www.cisg.law.pace.edu/cisg/biblio/tallon-bb79.html>, with Chengwei Liu, *Force Majeure* (citing Enderlein & Maskow, International Sales Law: United Nations Convention on Contracts for the International Sale of Goods 322 (1992)). Tallon argues that "the exempting event must necessarily be the exclusive cause of the failure to perform. If goods not properly packaged are damaged following an unforeseeable and unavoidable accident, the seller remains nonetheless liable. . . . The judge cannot reduce, even partly, the damages owed by the seller on account of that latter accident. The loss is attributable to the seller's failure to provide adequate accident-proof packaging." Denis Tallon, *Article 79*. Chengwei Liu adopts the position of *Enderlein & Maskow*, that "on the contrary . . . 'it cannot be required that the impediment is the exclusive cause of a breach of contract;' . . . the impediment should also be accepted when a cause overtakes another cause . . . 'It is decisive . . . whether the impediment lastly has caused the breach of contract. If this is so, it consumes other breaches of contract for which there are no grounds for exemption insofar as those no longer appear independently." Chengwei Liu, *Force Majeure* 4.6.

[23] However, Chengwei Liu also stresses that "[t]he force majeure must have come about without the fault of either party. There will be no excuse if an unforeseeable event impedes performance of the contract when the event would not have affected the contract if the party had not been late in performing." *Id*. Chengwei Liu goes on to state that it is a general rule that "a change in circumstances will not be taken into account if it occurred during a delay in performance of the person alleging application of the doctrine" due to the good faith requirements of the CISG, and that when "the impediment occurs during the delay, its causality for the breach of contract is given only if it had an effect in the case of delivery within the period prescribed'." Chengwei Liu, *Force Majeure*.

[24] Seller has argued that its failure to ship the chicken within the time period set by the contract did not constitute fundamental breach, and was within acceptable commercial norms of the industry. The logical implication is that it is distinguishable from the cases and commentary above because the Romanian government's action overtook its prior minor breach. Seller's argument may be frustrated, however, as the intent of this rule is that "[t]he obligor is always responsible for impediments when he could have prevented them but, despite his control over preparation, organization, and execution, failed to do so." Germany, 24 March 1999 Supreme Court (*Vine wax case*) <http://cisgw3.law.pace.edu/cases/990324g1.html>. Still, the CISG case law and commentary on it does not expressly address the issue of whether a seller in non-fundamental breach is barred from proving causation when the impediment would not have resulted in fundamental breach had the non-fundamental breach not occurred. As such, persuasive precedent and related commentary is of limited import on this potentially dispositive factor.

ii. Meeting the Third Factor that Impediment Could Not
Reasonably Be Overcome

[25] The remaining key legal issue is whether the Seller should have complied with the Buyer's proposed alternative shipment to a location outside of Romania. Article 79 states that party will be exempted from liability if it "could not reasonably be expected to . . . have avoided or overcome it or its consequences." Article 79(1). There is very little case law under Article 79 defining what the Secretariat Commentary to the CISG terms a "commercially reasonable substitute." Secretariat Commentary, Guide to CISG Article 79, §7. As such, there is no clear answer to this question under the CISG. Given the paucity of CISG case law, it is necessary to draw from private law to explicate "commercially reasonable substitute" in the circumstances of this case; and I conclude I am able to do so under CISG Article 7(2).

(a) Interpretation of CISG Provisions Generally

[26] Material "for interpretation of the Convention unless CISG expressly provides otherwise, [must] be taken from the convention itself . . . CISG is not a law complementary to national laws but is meant to be an exhaustive regulation." Gyula Eörsi, *General Provisions*, in International Sales: the United Nations Convention on Contracts for the International Sale of Goods, 2-1 to 2-36 (Galston & Smit eds.) (1984), available at <http://www.cisg.law.pace.edu/cisg/biblio/eorsi1.html>. In order to determine what material outside of the Convention may be used to define commercially reasonable substitute, Article 7(2) requires the determination of two issues. First, "[i]s the matter governed by the Convention? If not, that is the end of the inquiry as a gap can only exist in relation to matters that are governed by the Convention." Mark N. Rosenberg, *The Vienna Convention: Uniformity in Interpretation for Gap-filling—An Analysis and Application*, 445–46 available at <http://www.cisg.law.pace.edu/cisg/ biblio/rosenberg.html> [hereinafter *The Vienna Convention*]. Second, "[i]f the matter is governed by the Convention, the next question is whether it is expressly settled under it. If so, a gap cannot exist as the Convention already deals with the matter." *Id*. There is scholarly commentary about provisions of Article 79 supporting the conclusion that the provision is not settled. See, e.g., Joseph Lookofsky, Walking the Article 7(2) Tightrope Between CISG and Domestic Law, 25 Journal of Law and Commerce 87, 99–105 (2005–6) (considering the matters governed, but not settled by the CISG and specifically whether Article 79 preempts private law regarding hardship).

(b) Interpretation within the Case Law and CISG

[27] First, the actual language and relevant case law requires a preliminary determination of the meaning of the relevant CISG's provisions. Following this initial inquiry the "[c]onvention permits three methods which should be applied subsidiarily." Nives Povrzenic, *Interpretation and Gap-Filling under the United Nations Convention on Contracts for the international Sale of Goods*, <http://www.cisg.law. pace.edu/cisg/text/gap-fill.html>. First, "specific provisions by analogy[,]" second,

"general principles on which the Convention is based[,]" and finally, "private international law." *Id.*

[28] The four corners of the CISG provide little guidance as to what constitutes a commercially reasonable substitute. CISG Article 79. The general principles of the CISG provide a preference for performance and the international character and promotion of good faith. *See* CISG Article 7(1); Evelien Visser, *Gaps in the CISG* ("Overall, the aim of the CISG is to give preference to the performance remedies."). These principles do little to advance the definition of commercially reasonable substitute in present circumstances. The Secretariat Commentary to the CISG provides some illuminating guidance, stating in pertinent part that:

> "Even if the non-performing party can prove that he could not reasonably have been expected to take the impediment into account at the time of the conclusion of the contract, he must also prove that he could neither have avoided the impediment nor overcome it nor avoided or overcome the consequences of the impediment. This rule reflects the policy that a party who is under an obligation to act must do all in his power to carry out his obligation and may not await events, which might later justify his non-performance. This rule also indicates that a party may be required to perform by providing what is in all the circumstances of the transaction a commercially reasonable substitute for the performance, which was required under the contract." (Secretariat Commentary, Guide to CISG Article 79, § 7.)

[29] The case law only provides limited assistance in defining "commercially reasonable substitute" under Article 79. One court held that there was no exemption where "[t]he two parties did not stipulate in the contract that the contract goods must be Hunan oranges; therefore, even though there was flood in Hunan Province, which caused a shortage of canned mandarin oranges production, it should not be a barrier for the [Seller] to get contract goods from other provinces." China, 30 November 1997 CIETAC Arbitration proceeding (*Canned oranges case*) <http://cisgw3.law.pace.edu/cases/971130c1.html>.

[30] In order to determine if there is an applicable general principle "a uniform rule based on general principles, on which the Convention is based, should be searched for and formulated." Peter Schlechtriem, Requirements of Application and Sphere of Applicability of the CISG, 790 available at <http://www.cisg.law.pace.edu/cisg/biblio/schlechtriem9.html> [hereinafter *Requirements of Application*]. The problem with this formulation is that "the Convention . . . does not state [the rules] explicitly. Therefore, they have to be derived from an analysis of concrete provision so to unearth the general principles underlying them." *Id.*

[31] The scholarly discussion provides somewhat more guidance. Chengwei Liu recommends the following approach:

> "Thus, even an unforeseeable impediment exempts the non-performing party only if he can prove that he could neither avoid the impediment, nor

by taking reasonable steps, overcome its consequences. . . . To 'overcome' means to take the necessary steps to preclude the consequences of the impediment. It is closely associated with the condition of the external character of the impending event. In no event, however should the promisor be expected to risk his own existence by performing his obligations at all costs. What is required here is that a party who is under an obligation to act must do all in his power to carry out his obligation. . . . Again the yardstick used to measure the efforts of the party concerned is what can reasonably be expected from him. And that is what is customary, or what similar individuals would do in a similar situation. The exemption is thus granted when efforts would have been necessary that go beyond the former. Thus, the basis of reference is the same as for unforeseeability, i.e., the reasonable person. In this context, with both the foreseeability condition and the unavoidability condition read together, the concept of CISG Art. 79 may be referred to as, 'exonerations for events which a reasonable person in the same situation was not bound (could not be expected) to take into account or to avoid or to overcome.' This reasonable criterion regarding the unavoidability requirement is, however, to a degree uncertain, because whether an event could have been reasonably avoided or its consequences overcome depends on the facts. Here again a case-by-case analysis is required. If an object is lost at sea and can be fished out in good condition although at great cost, the final solution will not be the same if the object were a highly valuable sculpture or merely a machine tool. Thus, *everything is a question of measure.*" (Chengwei Liu, *Force Majeure* § 4.5. (emphasis added))

[32] The facts of the instant case cut against the Seller in that another supplier to Buyer, Tyson, did deliver the chicken leg quarters to the Buyer in another locale. Even applying "commercial practicability" as a test for excuse (uniform comment 10 to § 2-615) the shipment term was treated in fact as incidental aspect of performance despite the ban; an alternative unloading port was substituted as the destination consistent with U.C.C. § 2-614(1). While Seller raised the prospect that its agreements with other parties made substitute performance impossible without harm to Seller through breach of its other contracts, the Seller admitted that not all markets were covered by exclusive arrangements. Thus, under this approach Seller should have explored possible alternatives in this regard with Buyer, but failed to do so to Buyer's detriment and Seller's enrichment.

(c) Interpretation Aided by Sources Outside the Convention

[33] If the CISG and its case law fail to provide the necessary information the next step is to look beyond that to private law. Mark N. Rosenberg, The Vienna Convention, 445–46. However, the CISG allows recourse to the rules of private international law "only as a last resort." John O. Honnold, Uniform Law for International Sales under the 1980 United Nations Convention, 472–495 (3d ed. 1999) available at <http://www.cisg.law.pace.edu/cisg/biblio/ho79.html>. The analysis reaches that point.

[34] Analytic approaches of American courts have certainly included analogizing to the UCC to clarify Article 79 of the CISG. *See Delchi Carrier S.p.A. v. Rotorex Corp.*, 71 F.3d 1024, 1028 (2d Cir. 1995); *Raw Materials Inc. v. Manfred Forberich GmbH*, No. 03 C 1154, 2004 WL 1535839 (N.D. Ill., July 7, 2004); *Chicago Prime Packers, Inc. v. Northam Food Trading Co.*, No. 01-4447, 2004 WL 116628, at *4 (N.D. Ill. May 21, 2004). One court stated: "that '[w]hile no American court has specifically interpreted or applied Article 79 of the CISG, caselaw interpreting the Uniform Commercial Code's ("U.C.C.") provision on excuse provides guidance for interpreting the CISG's excuse provision since it contains similar requirements as those set forth in Article 79'." That court then concluded that "[t]his approach of looking to caselaw interpreting analogous provisions of the UCC has been used by other federal courts". Thus, in applying the CISG, the court used "caselaw interpreting a similar provision of § 2-615 of the UCC." *Raw Materials Inc. v. Manfred Forberich GmbH*, 2004 WL 1535839 (N.D. Ill., July 7, 2004). This approach is persuasive as the UCC contains a provision on commercially reasonable substitutes, stating in pertinent part: "[i]f without fault of either party the agreed berthing, loading, or unloading facilities fail or an agreed type of carrier becomes unavailable or the agreed manner of performance otherwise becomes commercially impracticable but a commercially reasonable substitute is available, the substitute performance must be tendered and accepted." UCC § 2-614(1).

[35] While there are differences between the exemption provisions under CISG Article 79 and UCC § 2-615, the provisions governing substitute performance are quite similar. Carla Spivack, *Of Shrinking Sweatsuits*, 769–70. "The third requirement of Article 79, that the impediment be one that the party could not have overcome or avoided, does not appear in the text of UCC § 2-615, but finds expression in U.C.C. § 2-615 case law." *Id.* Both of the "regimes apply the reasonable person standard to determine what actions must be taken." *Id.* The relevance of using the UCC to interpret the CISG depends on whether the UCC has been interpreted in such a way that would provide more guidance than the CISG and its provisions. As one scholar put it: "where no principle can be found, gap-filling by uniform rules is impossible, and one has to revert to domestic law. [Thus], recourse to domestic law is unavoidable in most cases." Peter Schlechtriem, *Requirements of Application*.

[36] The general approach of utilizing the UCC by analogy justifies invoking American case law interpreting the UCC § 2-614(1) to help give substance to the CISG mandate of avoiding or overcoming consequences by performing, as the Secretariat's commentary reflects, a commercially reasonable substitute. Such language is found in U.C.C. § 2-614(1), to which U.C.C. § 2-615 is expressly subject. A search for U.S. cases interpreting U.C.C. § 2-614 revealed a fairly small number of relevant cases. *See Jon-T Chemicals, Inc. v. Freeport Chemical Co.*, 704 F.2d 1412, 1416–17 (5th Cir. 1983) (finding that substitute performance through 2-614 had no relevance where the parties provided for "the action to be taken if the agreed type carrier became unavailable."); *Fabrica Italiana Lavorazione Materie Organiche, S.A.S v. Kaiser Aluminum & Chemical Corp.*, 684 F.2d 776, 778–79 (11th Cir. 1982) (holding that

Seller could not avoid the application of U.C.C. § 2-614(1) by reformulating its claim into one of proximate cause when "agreed manner of delivery otherwise becomes commercially impracticable but a commercially reasonable substitute is available, such substitute performance must be tendered and accepted"); *Eastern Air Lines, Inc. v. McDonnell Douglas Corp.*, 532 F.2d 957 (5th Cir. 1976); *American Trading & Production Corp. v. Shell International Marine, Ltd.*, 453 F.2d 939, 942–43 (2d Cir. 1972) (finding a commercially reasonable substitute to shipping); *Camden Iron & Metal, Inc. v. Bomar Resources, Inc.*, 719 F.Supp. 297, 309 (D.N.J. 1989) (concluding that a certain condition "rendered Camden Iron's obligation to load the vessel 'commercially impracticable'."); *United Equities Co. v. First National City Bank*, 52 A.D. 2d 154 (N.Y. App. Div. 1976).

[37] The evidentiary record concerning what alternative steps were commercially reasonable in the limited time availability prior to the Romanian ban taking effect focused in substantial part on: (I) the Herculean effort to load as much product as possible from the supplier Seller had been using; (ii) the labeling requirements of the Romanian market as a factor limiting the ability to divert shipments at sea to Romanian customers; (iii) the logistical challenges attendant to identifying port docking space and refrigerated container availability if alternative manufacturers with product could even be found, particularly given the limited resources and time available to search for such alternatives instead of maximizing what could be loaded in timely fashion. The record in this regard reflects a commercially reasonable effort by Seller.

[38] However, the inquiry does not end here in searching for commercially reasonable alternatives. Buyer raised the prospect of accepting delivery of the product elsewhere to make subsequent shipment possible. Another American supplier facing the same Romanian ban as Seller shipped to another port. While that particular port may not have been a viable alternative for Seller, the evidence made clear there were ports where exclusivity arrangements would not have precluded such delivery. It was Seller's duty to do so here and it failed to do so, preferring to pocket the profit available in a market experiencing a dramatic rise in prices. In doing so Seller misappropriated a profit that should have been made available to Buyer through an alternative shipment destination. The law does not countenance such a result. Accordingly, Buyer is entitled to damages as a remedy.

[39] Article 74 of the CISG provides the applicable standard for the damages claim asserted by Buyer. Basically, under it Buyer is entitled to lost profits caused by Seller that were foreseeable at the time of entry into the Contracts. The damages requested by Buyer meet the Article 74 standard and are adequately evidenced (See, e.g., Ex. 7). Seller's challenge to the damages sought, apart from a force majeure defense, is largely grounded upon the premise that market loss should not take into account a commercially reasonable phased release of product for sale. As such, Seller seeks to blur receipt of product with release of it into the market. However, there was no credible evidence on which to base that inference or to support such a finding. Seller's position is unpersuasive, and is divorced from commercial reality.

III. Award

A. Damages

[40] Accordingly, damages in the full amount requested of $608,323.00 are awarded.

[41] Pre and post-judgment interest issues relating to such damages shall be addressed in the Final Award per the Scheduling and Procedural Order that shall be made a part of this Interim Award.

B. Cost Shifting

[42] I find that Buyer has prevailed on claims and; in accordance with the terms of the ICDR Rules, is entitled to award of the costs (including reasonable attorneys' fees) that it incurred in connection with the prosecution of its claims in this proceeding. Such award of costs, as well as an allocation of the ICDR's administrative fees and the sole arbitrator's compensation, shall be made in the Final Award upon consideration of further written submissions by the parties pursuant to the Scheduling and Procedural Order that shall be made a part of this Interim Award.

C. Resolution of All Issues

[43] All of the parties' claims, counterclaims and arguments have been considered and, except as expressly granted in this Interim Award, which is in full settlement of all claims and counterclaims submitted to this arbitration, are hereby denied.

SO ORDERED

Notes and Questions

1. With costs of the arbitration proceedings and attorney fees, the final award for Macromex came to a total of $876,310.58. When buyer Macromex petitioned the court for confirmation of the award pursuant to §9 of the FAA, seller Globex cross-petitioned to have the award vacated pursuant to §10 of the FAA. The U.S. District Court for the Southern District of New York confirmed the arbitration award and denied the cross-petition to vacate. Judge Scheindlin wrote:

B. Vacatur of Award

The confirmation of an arbitration award is a summary proceeding that converts a final arbitration award into a judgment of the court.[24] "Arbitration awards are subject to very limited review in order to avoid undermining the twin goals of arbitration, namely, settling disputes efficiently and avoiding long and expensive litigation."[25] "A court is required to confirm the

---

24. See *Yusef Ahmed Algahanim & Sons v. Toys "R" Us*, 126 F.3d 15, 23 (2d Cir.1997) (citing *Florasynth, Inc. v. Pickholz*, 750 F.2d 171, 176 (2d Cir.1984)).

25. *Willemijn Houdstermaatschappij, BV v. Standard Microsystems Corp.*, 103 F.3d 9, 12 (2d Cir.1997) (quotation marks omitted). *Accord Ono Pharm. Co. v. Cortech, Inc.*, No. 03 Civ. 5840, 2003 WL 22481379, at *2 (S.D.N.Y. Nov. 3, 2003).

award unless a basis for modification or vacatur exists."[26] The Federal Arbitration Act ("FAA") lists specific instances where an award may be vacated.[27] In addition, the Second Circuit has recognized that a court may vacate an arbitration award that was rendered in "manifest disregard of the law."[28] However, "review for manifest error is severely limited."[29]

Although "its precise boundaries are ill defined . . . its rough contours are well known."[30] To find manifest disregard, the Second Circuit held in *Duferco Int'l Steel Trading v. T. Klaveness Shipping A/S* that the court must conduct a three step analysis. *First,* the court must find that the arbitrator ignored a law that was clearly and explicitly applicable to the case.[31] *Second,* the court must find that the law was improperly applied, leading to an erroneous outcome.[32] *Third,* the court must find that the arbitrator acted with the subjective knowledge that she was overlooking or misapplying the law.

"A federal court cannot vacate an arbitral award merely because it is convinced that the arbitration panel made the wrong call on the law. On the contrary, the award 'should be enforced, despite a court's disagreement with it on the merits, if there is a barely colorable justification for the outcome reached.'"[33] In deciding whether to confirm an arbitration award, the court "should not conduct an independent review of the factual record" to check if facts support the panel's conclusion. Rather, "[t]o the extent that a federal court may look upon the evidentiary record of an arbitration proceeding at all, it may do so only for the purpose of discerning whether a colorable basis

---

26. *Insurance Co. of N. Am. v. Ssangyong Eng'g & Const. Co.,* No. 02 Civ. 1484, 2002 WL 377538, at *4 (S.D.N.Y. Mar. 11, 2002).

27. The statutory grounds for vacatur listed in the FAA are: (1) the award was procured by corruption, fraud or undue means; (2) the arbitrators exceeded their powers or "so imperfectly executed [their powers] that a mutual, final, and definite award upon the . . . matter submitted was not made;" (3) the arbitrator was guilty of "misconduct in . . . refusing to hear evidence pertinent and material to the controversy;" (4) the arbitrators exhibited "evident partiality" or "corruption;" or (5) the arbitrators were guilty of "misconduct in refusing to postpone the hearing, upon sufficient cause shown," or guilty of "any other misbehavior" that prejudiced the rights of any party. *Ono,* 2003 WL 22481379, at *2 n. 24; 9 U.S.C. § 10(a). Globex does not argue that any of these provisions apply.

28. *Wallace v. Buttar,* 378 F.3d 182, 189 (2d Cir.2004) (quoting *DiRussa v. Dean Witter Reynolds, Inc.,* 121 F.3d 818, 821 (2d Cir.1997)).

29. *Id.* (quoting *Government of India v. Cargill Inc.,* 867 F.2d 130, 133 (2d Cir.1989)). In *Duferco Int'l Steel Trading v. T. Klaveness Shipping A/S,* 333 F.3d 383, 389 (2d Cir.2003), the court noted that "since 1960 we have vacated some part or all of an arbitral award for manifest disregard in . . . four out of at least 48 cases where we applied the standard."

30. *Duferco,* 333 F.3d at 389.

31. *See id.* at 389–90.

32. *See id.*

33. *Wallace,* 378 F.3d at 190 (emphasis in original) (quoting *Banco de Seguros del Estado v. Mutual Marine Office, Inc.,* 344 F .3d 255, 260 (2d Cir.2003)).

exists for the panel's award so as to assure that the award cannot be said to be the result of the panel's manifest disregard of the law."[34]

Macromex Srl, Plaintiff, v. Globex International, Inc., Defendant, U.S. District Court, S.D. New York, No. 08 Civ. 114(SAS), April 16, 2008, 2008 WL 1752530. Footnotes in the original.

In spite of the high bar for vacatur of an arbitral award, Judge Scheindlin went on to discuss Globex's argument that the arbitrator had misinterpreted the UCC when filling the gaps in the CISG. He concluded that case law differed on the interpretation of § 2-614 but that at least some decisions also required the seller "to arrange substituted performance." Hence, "the arbitrator correctly applied section 2-614." Subsequently, the Judge examined at some length whether the arbitrator had miscalculated the damages and, again, concluded that "the arbitrator's calculation of damages was correct."

Globex appealed, but the U.S. Court of Appeals affirmed the District Court judgment. Circuit Judges Walker, Sotomayor, and Wallace referred *inter alia* to *Stolt-Nielsen SA v. AnimalFeeds Int'l Corp.,* 548 F.3d 85, 92 (2d Cir. 2008) ("In the context of contract interpretation, we are required to confirm arbitration awards [even if we have] serious reservations about the soundness of the arbitrator's reading of the contract." (internal quotation marks and brackets omitted)); and to *Merrill Lynch, Pierce, Fenner & Smith, Inc. v. Bobker,* 808 F.2d 930, 933 (2d Cir. 1986) ("Manifest disregard of the law . . . clearly means more than error or misunderstanding with respect to the law." (internal quotation marks omitted)); as well as *Wallace,* 378 F.3d at 190 ("Our cases demonstrate that we have used the manifest disregard of law doctrine to vacate arbitral awards only in the most egregious instances of misapplication of legal principles."). (See *Macromex SRL, Petitioner-Appellee, v. Globex International Inc., Respondent-Appellant,* U.S. Court of Appeals, Second Circuit, No. 08-2255-cv. May 26, 2009, 330 Fed. App'x 241.)

Why would the District Court Judge first say that an arbitral award is only reviewable on the merits if there is "manifest disregard of the law" and then proceed to review the award on the merits? Do you see weaknesses in the analysis of the arbitrator that suggest an erroneous decision, one that could at least potentially amount to a "manifest disregard of the law"?

Similar to the District Court, the Court of Appeals talks about "being required to confirm arbitration awards [even if the Court has] serious reservations about the soundness of the arbitrator's reading of the contract" and how even manifest disregard of the law by the arbitrator would only lead to a vacatur "in the most egregious instances of misapplication of legal principles."

On the assumption that the U.S. courts are not seriously suggesting that *any* deviation by an arbitral tribunal in an international commercial arbitration from

---

34. *Id.*

well-established U.S. court practice can be reason for a review on the merits to see whether vacatur may be merited, was there anything in the arbitral award that would suggest grave injustice being inflicted on an American company? More specifically, were there *any* plausible arguments for Globex to challenge the award, or were the lawyers of Globex just out to make some more money?

If the arbitral award came under the New York Convention, would the reading of the FAA by the District Court (fn. 27 and accompanying text), as affirmed by the Court of Appeals, be in conformity with Article V of the New York Convention? In other words, if the award was rendered outside of the U.S., and thus a "foreign" award, do the U.S. courts have the rights of review they are exercising in the present case? For more information, see below, Part Six, pp. 691 et seq., in particular pp. 922 and 1014 et seq.

2. The case is interesting not only because it is our first arbitral award and there were court proceedings to prevent its recognition and enforcement. The case also provides a thorough discussion of breach of contract and when a breach is a fundamental breach. More importantly, the case is one of relatively few to provide a differentiated analysis of the Article 79 exemption, the concept of *force majeure*, and how and when the *force majeure* defense can be successfully invoked.[114]

When looking at the positions of Tallon and Chengwei Liu respectively (para. 22), who is right and who is wrong? Why?

3. Finally, the award goes into some detail about the question of what a party to an IBT has to do in order to try to overcome an impediment that potentially falls under Article 79. The arbitrator reminds us that "the aim of the CISG is to give preference to the performance remedies" (para. 28), that is, the primary remedies, over secondary remedies (damages).

In this context, once again, the question of a gap in the CISG arises and how it can be resolved. Can you summarize in one sentence the arbitrator's conclusions in paragraph 26? Does paragraph 27 provide the answer?

4. Do you believe the arbitrator ultimately "got it right"? Consider the summary in paragraph 38 *in fine*.

B. Contracts Subject to the UCC or the Restatement (Second) of Contracts

Although not the main focus of our inquiry, it makes sense to do some comparative analysis into the provisions and the case law dealing with breach of contracts and available remedies under the UCC and state common law, as reflected in the Restatement. Checklist 2-6 provides a list of the relevant provisions. Several cases follow, with notes and questions.

---

114. See also Christoph Brunner: *Force Majeure Under General Contract Principles—Exemption for Non-Performance in International Arbitration*, Wolters Kluwer 2008.

Checklist 2-6
Claim Bases in UCC and Restatement

Seller → Buyer				
Claim	Legal Bases UCC	Restatement	Exceptions UCC	Restatement
1. Right to Performance/ Contractual Claims	§ 2-703	§§ 235, 250– 253, 255–257	§ 2-725	§§ 261–272 §§ 273–287
a. Take Delivery	§§ 2-301, 2-507 2-606			
b. Pay Purchase Price	§§ 2-301, 2-507 2-607			
c. Restitution of Goods after Avoidance				
2. Damages	§§ 2-706, 718, 719	§§ 236, 243–249, 254	§ 2-725	
3. Interest				

Buyer → Seller				
Claim	Legal Bases UCC	Restatement	Exceptions UCC	Restatement
1. Right to Performance/ Contractual Claims	§ 2-711	§§ 235, 250– 253, 255–257	§ 2-725	§§ 261–272 §§ 273–287
a. Delivery of Conforming Goods	§§ 2-503, 2-716			
b. Transfer of Documents	§§ 2-503, 504			
c. Transfer of Ownership	§§ 2-711, 714, 717			
d. Carriage & Insurance	§§ 2-614, 2-712		§ 2-508	
e. Price Reduction				
f. Repair, Replacement or Cure				
g. Restitution of Price after Avoidance		§ 241		
2. Damages	§§ 2-713, 714, 715, 718, 719	§§ 236, 243–249, 254	§ 2-725	
3. Interest				

Our first example deals with an important difference between the UCC and the CISG, namely the standard of performance. § 2-601 UCC on Buyer's Rights on Improper Delivery provides certain remedies for buyers "if the goods or the tender of delivery *fail in any respect* to conform to the contract" (emphasis added). The buyer is given the choice to "reject the whole." This is commonly referred to as the "perfect tender" rule.

Under the CISG, the buyer also has remedies "[i]f the seller *fails to perform any of his obligations* under the contract or this Convention" (Art. 45(1), emphasis added). However, the CISG makes a distinction depending on the severity of the breach. A right to avoid, i.e., to reject the whole, is given only if there is "a fundamental breach" (Arts. 49(1), 25).

Case 2-16

Practical Products Corporation v. Paul W. Brightmire

864 P.2d 330 (Okla. 1993)
(Paragraph numbers added, some details and some footnotes omitted.)

WATT, Justice:

Facts

[1] On December 25, 1987, a severe ice storm knocked out electric service to the Tulsa home of defendant, Paul W. Brightmire. The electricity remained off for several days. . . .

[2] On December 28, 1987, defendant telephoned plaintiff, Practical Products Corporation, and spoke with its vice-president, Gary Dundee, regarding the availability of a 5000 watt portable generator. Although plaintiff did not have any generators in stock, Dundee stated that he could obtain one from its distributor, Brown Engine and Equipment in Oklahoma City. Defendant testified that he and Dundee specifically discussed generators manufactured by Kawasaki during their conversation. He claimed that Dundee described the proposed unit as a deluxe 5000 watt Kawasaki generator. Dundee denied defendant's claim and insisted that he told defendant that the available unit was a generator set assembled by Brown and powered by a Kawasaki engine. Testimony revealed that generator sets normally have two main components, an alternator and an engine. The sets are generally named after the company that assembled the unit or the one that manufactured the alternator component. A *Kawasaki* generator is one that was manufactured by Kawasaki Motors Corporation and not simply one that is driven by a Kawasaki engine. Dundee quoted a price of $1,129.00 for the unit discussed and defendant said that he would think about the offer.

[3] Between the 28th and the 30th of December, defendant continued to shop around for generators. After talking with several distributors, defendant concluded that Kawasaki generator sets were among the best in the industry and that plaintiff's offer of $1,129.00 was a good price. On December 30th, defendant called Dundee and ordered the generator they had previously talked about. The parties did not discuss or otherwise clarify their earlier conversation regarding the brand of generator to be ordered. Defendant also asked that wheels and a handle be added to the unit, which Dundee said could be done at a cost of about $50.00.

[4] A Brown generator set powered by a Kawasaki engine was delivered to plaintiff's place of business on the morning of December 31st. The wheels and handle

were installed and defendant was notified that the unit was ready to be picked up. When defendant arrived, an employee handed him a bill for the generator. The bill included a charge for freight, which defendant claimed had not been agreed to. He then inspected the generator and maintained that it was not what he ordered. Finally, defendant asked to see a user's manual. Plaintiff's employee searched for a manual, but surmised that the vendor failed to include one when it shipped the generator. Thereupon, defendant rejected the tendered unit.

[5] On January 8, 1988, Gary Dundee telephoned defendant and told him that plaintiff had obtained a user's manual for the generator. Dundee also offered to lower the price of the generator, agreed to deduct the freight charge from defendant's bill, and offered to deliver the generator to defendant's home. The conversation ended without defendant agreeing to purchase the generator.

[6] Several days later, defendant received a bill from plaintiff for $261.55. The total included a fifteen percent restocking fee, a charge for modification of the generator and charges for both inbound and outbound freight. Defendant had not responded to the bill by February 5th.

Procedural History

[7] On February 5, 1988, plaintiff sued defendant in small claims court for breach of contract. Plaintiff sought damages of $261.00, which included restocking, modification and freight charges for the rejected generator. Defendant counterclaimed alleging fraud in the inducement and breach of contract. His petition prayed for $1,500.00 compensatory damages and in excess of $10,000.00 punitive damages. The case was then transferred to the District Court of Tulsa County, where it was tried to a jury on October 2nd and 3rd, 1989.

[8] At the close of evidence, both parties moved for a directed verdict on the other's cause of action. Defendant's motion for a directed verdict was overruled. The court granted plaintiff's motion to dismiss defendant's fraud claim, but overruled its motion with respect to defendant's contract claim and submitted that issue to the jury. The jury returned verdicts for plaintiff on both remaining claims and awarded plaintiff $267.00.

[9] Defendant's motion for judgment notwithstanding the verdict or new trial was overruled. Plaintiff filed a motion to tax fees and costs in the amount of $3,667.10. After a hearing, the court ruled that 60% of plaintiff's fees were attributable to prosecuting plaintiff's claim, while 40% were attributable to defending against defendant's counterclaims. Therefore, the court assessed defendant $2,200.00 (60% of $3,667.10) for plaintiff's attorney fees and costs.

Issues

[10] On appeal, defendant asserts that the trial court erred in refusing to direct a verdict in his favor with regard to plaintiff's claim. Correspondingly, defendant argues that the court erred in denying his motion for judgment notwithstanding the verdict or new trial. He also contends that the jury was erroneously instructed

regarding plaintiff's claim and his defense. Finally, defendant maintains that the trial court erred in dismissing his fraud claim. In its cross-appeal, plaintiff claims that the trial court erred in its calculation of attorney's fees. We hold that the trial court erred in denying defendant's motion for a directed verdict on plaintiff's claim. Consequently, plaintiff's award of attorney fees and costs is vacated. We hold that the trial court did not err in dismissing defendant's cause of action for fraud.

I.

[11] Defendant first contends, with respect to plaintiff's cause of action, that the trial court erred in refusing to direct a verdict in his favor. He also asserts that the trial court erred in denying his motion for judgment notwithstanding the verdict or new trial regarding plaintiff's claim. These arguments are based upon defendant's claimed right to reject the generator because plaintiff failed to provide a user's manual at the time of tender.

> It is well established that a motion for directed verdict or motion for judgment N.O.V. raises the question of whether there is any evidence to support a judgment for the party against whom the motion is made. In ruling on such a motion the trial court must consider as true all the evidence and all the inferences reasonably drawn therefrom favorable to the party against whom the motion is made and any conflicting evidence favorable to the movant must be disregarded. (*Woods v. Fruehauf Trailer Corp.*, 765 P.2d 770, 773 (Okla.1988) (citations omitted)).

[12] Defendant argues that the contract for the purchase of the generator contained an implied requirement that plaintiff provide a user's manual. The undisputed evidence showed that plaintiff did not produce, either before or after defendant's specific request, a user's manual when it tendered the generator unit. Defendant therefore asserts that the evidence presented at trial will not, as a matter of law, support a judgment for plaintiff because defendant rightfully rejected the generator. We agree.

[13] Oklahoma's Uniform Commercial Code defines an agreement as "the bargain of the parties in fact as found in their language or by implication from other circumstances including course of dealing or usage of trade or course of performance. . . ." 12A O.S.Supp.1984 § 1-201(3). "Whether an agreement has legal consequences is determined by the provisions of the Uniform Commercial Code, if applicable; otherwise by the law of contracts." Id. The term "contract" is defined as "the total legal obligation which results from the parties' agreement as affected by the provisions of the Uniform Commercial Code and any other applicable rules of law." 12A O.S.Supp.1984 § 1-201(11).

[14] Defendant contends, and we agree, that usage of trade required plaintiff to supply a user's manual with the tendered generator. "A usage of trade is any practice or method of dealing having such regularity of observance in a place, vocation, or trade as to justify an expectation that it will be observed with respect to the transaction in question." 12A O.S.1981 § 1-205(2). Section 1-205(2) provides that the existence

and scope of a trade usage are to be proven as facts. In the present case, Michael Bryant, an employee of plaintiff's business, testified that purchasers of most major appliances are ordinarily supplied with an operator's manual. Gary Dundee, plaintiff's vice-president, agreed that it was not unreasonable for defendant to expect an operator's manual with the generator. Dundee apparently sought and claimed that he had received a user's manual within eight days of defendant's rejection of the generator. He then telephoned defendant and informed him that a manual had been obtained. Thus, it is reasonable to assume that Dundee also considered a manual to be an important aspect of the agreement. More extensive arguments and authority concerning trade usage were presented to the trial court in defendant's post-trial motion.

[15] Notwithstanding § 1-205(2), courts may take judicial notice of a general trade usage or a generally known fact. *United States v. Stanolind Crude Oil Purchasing Co.,* 113 F.2d 194, 200 (10th Cir.1940); *Bd. of Educ. of Indep. School Dist. No. 20 v. Adams,* 465 P.2d 464, 467 (Okla.1970). See also 12 O.S.1981 § 2202(c), which states that a court may take judicial notice of a fact, "whether requested or not." It is a matter of common knowledge that manufacturers and suppliers of consumer equipment, machines and appliances generally provide use and care instructions with their products. Manufacturers advise purchasers to read manuals and become familiar with the proper and safe way to maintain and operate their equipment. Such advice is of paramount importance where, as here, the product poses a serious risk of danger to life and property if improperly used. It is difficult to imagine a consumer buying any new piece of equipment, machine or appliance without being supplied operational and care instructions. Defendant had a reasonable expectation that a user's manual would accompany his purchase of a powerful and potentially dangerous 5000 watt generator.

[16] In the present case, the trade usage in question was both proven to the trial court and so commonly known as to have permitted the court to take judicial notice of its existence. Thus, we find that general trade usage supplemented the terms of the agreement to require that plaintiff supply a user's manual with the generator unit. See 12A O.S.1981 § 1-205(3). Because no user's manual was produced at the time of tender, the delivery failed to conform to the contract and defendant rightfully rejected the generator. 12A O.S.1981 § 2-601. Accordingly, we hold that the evidence did not support the judgment in favor of plaintiff. The judgment in favor of plaintiff on plaintiff's claim is therefore REVERSED.

[17] As a consequence of this decision, we need not address defendant's proposition that the jury was erroneously instructed regarding plaintiff's claim or his defense. Finally, because defendant is the prevailing party on plaintiff's cause of action, the award to plaintiff of attorney fees and costs is VACATED. . . .

Conclusion

[20] The judgment for plaintiff on plaintiff's cause of action is REVERSED and the trial court is instructed to enter judgment in favor of defendant. Consequently, the

award of attorney fees and costs to plaintiff arising from that judgment is VACATED. The judgment for plaintiff on defendant's counterclaim for fraud in the inducement is AFFIRMED. Because neither party appeals the judgment for plaintiff on defendant's counterclaim for breach of contract, that judgment remains undisturbed. . . .

Notes and Questions

1. This decision is an example of a very strict application of the perfect tender rule. Although a user's manual was not specifically mentioned in the sales agreement, the court held that it was a "usage of trade" to supply a user's manual for goods such as electric generators. However, "[b]ecause no user's manual was produced at the time of tender, the delivery failed to conform to the contract and defendant rightfully rejected the generator" pursuant to § 2-601. The fact that the plaintiff/seller was able to produce a user's manual a few days later and offered free delivery to defendant/buyer's home did not move the court. Do you think the decision is correct? Fair? Do you see any indication that the court was influenced by the fact that the defendant was a consumer rather than a professional buyer? Do you think the court should have taken into account that the buyer was not as eager to conclude the deal after the ice storm was over and the power was back on?

2. The default standard for seller's liability in case of problems with the time, place, or quality of the delivered goods can be summarized as follows:

English Common Law	Continental European Codes	Restatement (Second) of Contracts	American UCC
caveat emptor (buyer beware)	fundamental breach	material breach or substantial performance	perfect tender rule
no protection for buyers	medium protection for buyers	medium protection for buyers	highest protection for buyers

In practice, the courts have sometimes softened their stance on the *perfect* tender rule, in particular when the performance of the seller is *almost* perfect. United States common law developed the standard of *substantial performance* or, as an alternative, the requirement of a material breach. This doctrine "allows a party that has substantially complied with a contract to recover for its performance despite the fact that it has breached the contract by failing to comply fully with its terms."[115] Pursuant to this principle, the buyer cannot avoid the contract as long as the seller's performance is *substantially similar* to the contractual promise. In such cases, it is deemed unreasonable for the buyer to avoid the contract and deny any payment. As a consequence, the buyer would have to accept the performance and would be limited to reducing her payment and/or claiming damages in compensation for the

---

115. Cf. *Bear Peak Res., LLC v. Peak Powder River Res., LLC*, 2017 WY 124, ¶ 40, 403 P.3d 1033, 1047 (Wyo. 2017), reh'g denied (Nov. 7, 2017) (quoting 15 Williston on Contracts § 44:58 (4th ed. 2017)).

shortfall of the seller's performance. However, there is disagreement about whether this limitation of seller liability can be applied under the UCC, in light of its perfect tender rule. Most courts and commentators seem to insist that the UCC "does not rely on concepts of substantial performance, but instead requires that the seller make a perfect tender, meaning that the seller must tender goods that conform in all respects to those specified in the parties' agreement."[116] This can have the extreme effect that "the buyer may reject a seller's tender for any trivial defect, whether it be in the quality of the goods, the timing of performance, or the manner of delivery."[117]

Courts have tried to mitigate the more extreme scenarios by relying on the buyer's obligation to act in good faith. As Professor William Lawrence has pointed out, "[t]he perfect tender rule does not give buyers the power to seize upon the slightest contract deviation, even though it is not important to the buyer, as a pretext for discontinuing the contract. A buyer acts in bad faith by feigning dissatisfaction with the seller's performance when the real motive for rejecting the goods is some other consideration, such as avoiding the contract obligation during a falling market. The good faith requirement of the Code effectively prevents such improper strategic behavior, and thus assures that application of the perfect tender rule will occur only in those instances when it is invoked honestly."[118]

We may ask whether it makes sense first to insist on perfect tender but then to exclude insistence on perfect tender by reliance on good faith obligations.

The Restatement (Second) of Contracts, in Section 241, shows the more flexible approach in common law and brings American and European solutions closer together:

§ 241. Circumstances Significant in Determining Whether a Failure Is Material[119]

In determining whether a failure to render or to offer performance is material, the following circumstances are significant:

(a) the extent to which the injured party will be deprived of the benefit which he reasonably expected;

(b) the extent to which the injured party can be adequately compensated for the part of that benefit of which he will be deprived;

---

116. Cf. *Pomerantz Paper Corp. v. New Cmty. Corp.*, 207 N.J. 344, 25 A.3d 221, 231–32 (2011).

117. Cf. *Midwest Mobile Diagnostic Imaging, L.L.C. v. Dynamics Corp. of Am.*, 965 F. Supp. 1003, 1011 (W.D. Mich. 1997), *aff'd*, 165 F.3d 27 (6th Cir. 1998) (unpublished opinion).

118. See William H. Lawrence, *Appropriate Standards for a Buyer's Refusal to Keep Goods Tendered by a Seller*, 35 Wm. & Mary L. Rev. 1994, pp. 1635–1690, at p. 1651 (footnotes omitted). See also *Printing Ctr. of Texas, Inc. v. Supermind Pub. Co.*, 669 S.W.2d 779, 784 (Tex. App. 1984); *Y & N Furniture, Inc. v. Nwabuoku*, 190 Misc. 2d 402, 734 N.Y.S.2d 382, 385 (N.Y. Civ. Ct. 2001); *Hubbard v. UTZ Quality Foods, Inc.*, 903 F. Supp. 444, 451 (W.D.N.Y. 1995); *Clark v. Zaid, Inc.*, 263 Md. 127, 282 A.2d 483, 484 n.1 (1971).

119. *Restatement of the Law Second, Contracts*, copyright © 1981 by the American Law Institute. All rights reserved. Reprinted with permission.

(c) the extent to which the party failing to perform or to offer to perform will suffer forfeiture;

(d) the likelihood that the party failing to perform or to offer to perform will cure his failure, taking account of all the circumstances including any reasonable assurances;

(e) the extent to which the behavior of the party failing to perform or to offer to perform comports with standards of good faith and fair dealing.

3. If we ignore for a moment the option of modifying the provisions of a chosen legal system, which of the four systems discussed in question 2 would seem most buyer-friendly? And which one would seem most seller-friendly? What, therefore, should be the default choice of American parties to international business transactions?

The next case is an example of a court weighing the perfect tender rule against the substantial performance rule.

Case 2-17

D.P. Technology Corp. v. Sherwood Tool

751 F. Supp. 1038 (D. Conn. 1990)
(Paragraph numbers added, some details and footnotes omitted.)
RULING ON dEFENDANT'S MOTION TO DISMISS

NEVAS, District Judge.

[1] In this action based on diversity jurisdiction, the plaintiff seller, D.P. Technology ("DPT"), a California corporation, sues the defendant buyer, Sherwood Tool, Inc. ("Sherwood") a Connecticut corporation, alleging a breach of contract for the purchase and sale of a computer system. . . .

[2] The facts of this case can be easily summarized. On January 24, 1989, the defendant entered into a written contract to purchase a computer system, including hardware, software, installation and training, from the plaintiff. The complaint alleges that the computer system was "specifically" designed for the defendant and is not readily marketable. The contract, executed on January 24, 1989, incorporates the delivery term set forth in the seller's Amended Letter of January 17, 1989 stating that the computer system would be delivered within ten to twelve weeks. The delivery period specified in the contract ended on April 18, 1989. The software was delivered on April 12, 1989 and the hardware was delivered on May 4, 1989. On May 9, 1989, the defendant returned the merchandise to the plaintiff, and has since refused payment for both the software and the hardware. Thus, the plaintiff alleges that the defendant breached the contract by refusing to accept delivery of the goods covered by the contract while the defendant argues that it was rather the plaintiff who breached the contract by failing to make a timely delivery. . . .

[4] A federal court sitting in diversity must be mindful that it follow the law determined by the highest court of the state whose law is applicable to resolution of the

dispute. *Plummer v. Lederle Laboratories,* 819 F.2d 349, 355 (2d Cir.), cert. denied, 484 U.S. 898 . . . (1987). When that state court has not directly ruled on the issue under consideration, the federal court "'must make an estimate of what the state's highest court would rule to be its law.'" *Carpentino v. Transp. Ins. Co.,* 609 F.Supp. 556, 560 (D.Conn.1985) (Zampano, J.) (quoting *Cunninghame v. Equitable Life Assurance Soc'y of United States,* 652 F.2d 306, 308 (2d Cir.1981)). See also *Plummer,* 819 F.2d at 355. In calculating this estimate, the federal court may consider all data the high court would use in reaching its decision. *Doyle v. St. Paul Fire & Marine Ins. Co.,* 583 F.Supp. 554, 555 (D.Conn.1984) (Dorsey, J.). Thus, the federal court may discern the forum state's law by examining relevant decisions from the forum state's inferior courts, decisions from sister states, federal decisions, and the general weight and trend of authority.

[5] Because the contract between the parties was a contract for the sale of goods, the law governing this transaction is to be found in Article 2 of the Uniform Commercial Code ("UCC") . . . . In its motion to dismiss, the defendant argues that the plaintiff fails to state a claim upon which relief can be granted because the plaintiff breached the contract which provided for a delivery period of ten to twelve weeks from the date of the order, January 24, 1989. Since the delivery period ended on April 18, 1989, the May 4 hardware delivery was 16 days late. The defendant contends that because the plaintiff delivered the hardware after the contractual deadline, the late delivery entitled the defendant to reject delivery, since a seller is required to tender goods in conformance with the terms set forth in a contract. U.C.C. § 2-301 . . . .

[8] . . . [T]he plaintiff argues that the defendant relies on the perfect tender rule, allowing buyers to reject for any nonconformity with the contract. Plaintiff points out that the defendant has not cited one case in which a buyer rejected goods solely because of a late delivery, and that the doctrine of "perfect tender" has been roundly criticized. While it is true that the perfect tender rule has been criticized by scholars principally because it allowed a dishonest buyer to avoid an unfavorable contract on the basis of an insubstantial defect in the seller's tender, *Ramirez v. Autosport,* 88 N.J. 277, 283–85, 440 A.2d 1345, 1348–49 (1982); *Moulton Cavity & Mold, Inc. v. Lyn-Flex Indus., Inc.,* 396 A.2d 1024, 1027 (Me.1979); E. Peters, *Commercial Transactions* 33–37 (1971) (even before enactment of the UCC, the perfect tender rule was in decline), the basic tender provision of the Uniform Commercial Code continued the perfect tender policy developed by the common law and embodied in the Uniform Sales Act. Section 2-601 states that with certain exceptions, the buyer has the right to reject "if the goods or the tender of delivery fail in any respect to conform to the contract." (emphasis supplied). . . . The courts that have considered the issue have agreed that the perfect tender rule has survived the enactment of the Code. See, e.g., *Intermeat, Inc. v. American Poultry, Inc.,* 575 F.2d 1017, 1024 (2d Cir.1978) ("There is no doubt that the perfect tender rule applies to measure the buyer's right of initial rejection of goods under UCC section 2-601."); *Capitol Dodge Sales, Inc. v. Northern Concrete Pipe, Inc.,* 131 Mich.App. 149, 158, 346 N.W.2d 535, 539 (1983) (adoption of 2-601 creates a perfect tender rule replacing pre-Code cases defining

performance of a sales contract in terms of substantial compliance); *Texas Imports v. Allday*, 649 S.W.2d 730, 737 (Tex.App.1983) (doctrine of substantial performance is not applicable under 2-601); *Ramirez*, 440 A.2d at 1349 (before acceptance, the buyer may reject goods for any nonconformity); *Sudol v. Rudy Papa Motors*, 175 N.J.Super. 238, 240–241, 417 A.2d 1133, 1134 (1980) (section 2-601 contains perfect tender rule); see also *Bowen v. Young*, 507 S.W.2d 600, 602 (Tex.Civ.App.1974) (where goods fail in any respect to conform to the contract the buyer may, under 2-601, reject the entire unit); *Maas v. Scoboda*, 188 Neb. 189, 193, 195 N.W.2d 491, 494 (1972) (under the UCC a buyer is given the right to reject the whole if the goods fail in any respect to conform to the contract); *Ingle v. Marked Tree Equip. Co.*, 244 Ark. 1166, 1173, 428 S.W.2d 286, 289 (1968) (a buyer may accept or reject goods which fail to conform to the contract in any respect). Similarly, courts interpreting 2-601 have strictly interpreted it to mean any nonconformity, thus excluding the doctrine of substantial performance. *Printing Center of Texas, Inc. v. Supermind Pub. Co. Inc.*, 669 S.W.2d 779, 783 (Tex.App.1984) (the term conform within 2-601 authorizing the buyer to reject the whole if the goods or tender of delivery fail in any respect to conform to the contract does not mean substantial performance but complete performance); *Astor v. Boulos, Inc.*, 451 A.2d 903, 906 (Me.1982) (the generally disfavored "perfect tender rule" survives enactment of the UCC as respects a contract for sale of goods but does not control in the area of service contracts which are governed by the standard of substantial performance); *Moulton Cavity & Mold, Inc. v. Lyn-Flex Indus., Inc.*, 396 A.2d 1024, 1027–28 (1979) (holding that the doctrine of substantial performance "has no application to a contract for the sale of goods"); *Jakowski v. Carole Chevrolet, Inc.*, 180 N.J.Super. 122, 125, 433 A.2d 841, 843 (1981) (degree of nonconformity of goods is irrelevant in assessing buyer's concomitant right to reject them). These courts have thus found that the tender must be perfect in the context of the perfect tender rule in the sense that the proffered goods must conform to the contract in every respect.

[9] Connecticut, however, appears in this regard to be the exception. Indeed, in the one Connecticut case interpreting 2-601, *Franklin Quilting Co., Inc. v. Orfaly*, 1 Conn.App. 249, 251, 470 A.2d 1228, 1229 (1984), in a footnote, the Appellate Court stated that "the 'perfect tender rule' requires a substantial nonconformity to the contract before a buyer may rightfully reject the goods." *Id.* at 1229 n. 3, citing White & Summers, *Uniform Commercial Code* (2d Ed.), section 8-3 (emphasis supplied). Thus, the Connecticut Appellate Court has adopted "the White and Summers construction of 2-601 as in substance a rule that does not allow rejection for insubstantial breach such as a short delay causing no damage." *Id.* (3rd Ed.) section 8-3. See also *National Fleet Supply, Inc. v. Fairchild*, 450 N.E.2d 1015, 1019 n. 4 (Ind.App.1983) (despite UCC's apparent insistence on perfect tender, it is generally understood that rejection is not available in circumstances where the goods or delivery fail in some small respect to conform to the terms of the sales contract (citing White and Summers)); *McKenzie v. Alla-Ohio Coals, Inc.*, 29 U.C.C.Rep.Serv. (Callaghan) 852, 856–57 (D.D.C.1979) (there is substantial authority that where a

buyer has suffered no damage, he should not be allowed to reject goods because of an insubstantial nonconformity).

[10] As noted above, a federal court sitting in diversity must apply the law of the highest court of the state whose law applies. Since this court has determined that Connecticut law governs, the next task is to estimate whether the Connecticut Supreme Court would affirm the doctrine of substantial nonconformity, as stated in *Orfaly*, an opinion of the Connecticut Appellate Court. When the highest state court has not spoken on an issue, the federal court must look to the inferior courts of the state and to decisions of sister courts as well as federal courts. As noted, the weight of authority is that the doctrine of substantial performance does not apply to the sale of goods. However, as noted by White and Summers, in none of the cases approving of perfect rather than substantial tender was the nonconformity insubstantial, such as a short delay of time where no damage is caused to the buyer. White and Summers, *Uniform Commercial Code* (3rd Ed.), section 8-3 n. 8. In the instant case, there is no claim that the goods failed to conform to the contract. Nor is there a claim that the buyer was injured by the 16-day delay. There is, however, a claim that the goods were specially made, which might affect the buyer's ability to resell. Thus Connecticut's interpretation of 2-601 so as to mitigate the harshness of the perfect tender rule reflects the consensus of scholars that the rule is harsh and needs to be mitigated.[8] Indeed, Summers and White state that the rule has been so "eroded" by the exceptions in the Code that "relatively little is left of it; the law would be little changed if 2-601 gave the right to reject only upon 'substantial' non-conformity," especially since the Code requires a buyer or seller to act in good faith. R. Summers and J. White, *Uniform Commercial Code* (3rd Ed. 1988), 8-3, at 357. See also *Alden Press Inc. v. Block & Co., Inc.*, 123 Ill.Dec. 26, 30, 173 Ill.App.3d 251, 527 N.E.2d 489, 493 (1988) (notwithstanding the perfect tender rule, the reasonableness of buyer's rejection of goods and whether such rejection of goods is in good faith are ultimately matters for the trier of fact); *Printing Center of Texas v. Supermind Pub. Co., Inc.*, 669 S.W.2d 779, 784 (Tex. App.1984) (if the evidence establishes any nonconformity, the buyer is entitled to reject the goods as long as it is in good faith); *Neumiller Farms, Inc. v. Cornett*, 368 So.2d 272, 275 (Ala.1979) (claim of dissatisfaction with delivery of goods so as to warrant their rejection must be made in good faith, rather than in an effort to escape a bad bargain). A rejection of goods that have been specially manufactured for an insubstantial delay where no damage is caused is arguably not in good faith.

[11] Although the Connecticut Supreme Court has not yet addressed the issue of substantial nonconformity, it has stated, in a precode case, *Bradford Novelty Co.*

---

8. This was the concern of Karl Llewellyn, which led the Code's drafters to carve out exceptions to the perfect tender rule. See, e.g., *Leitchfield Dev't Corp. v. Clark*, 757 S.W.2d 207 (Ky.App.1988) (perfect tender rule of UCC is modified and limited by Code language that seller has reasonable opportunity to cure improper tender); *T.W. Oil, Inc. v. Consolidated Edison Co. of New York, Inc.*, 457 N.Y.S.2d 458, 463, 57 N.Y.2d 574, 443 N.E.2d 932, 937 (1982) (seller's right to cure defective tender, Section 2-508, was intended to act as a meaningful limitation on the absolutism of the perfect tender rule under which no leeway was allowed for any imperfections.)

v. Technomatic, 142 Conn. 166, 170, 112 A.2d 214, 216 (1955), that although "[t]he time fixed by the parties for performance is, at law, deemed of the essence of the contract," where, as here, goods have been specially manufactured, "the time specified for delivery is less likely to be considered of the essence . . . [since] in such a situation there is a probability of delay, and the loss to the manufacturer is likely to be great if the buyer refuses to accept and pay because of noncompliance with strict performance." *Id*. But see *Marlowe v. Argentine Naval Com'n*, 808 F.2d 120, 124 (D.C.Cir.1986) (buyer within its rights to cancel a contract for 6-day delay in delivery since "time is of the essence in contracts for the sale of goods") (citing *Norrington v. Wright*, 115 U.S. 188, 203 . . . (1885) ("In the contracts of merchants, time is of the essence.")

[12] After reviewing the case law in Connecticut, this court finds that in cases where the nonconformity involves a delay in the delivery of specially manufactured goods, the law in Connecticut requires substantial nonconformity for a buyer's rejection under 2-601, and precludes a dismissal for failure to state a claim on the grounds that the perfect tender rule, codified at 2-601, demands complete performance. Rather, Connecticut law requires a determination at trial as to whether a 16-day delay under these facts constituted a substantial nonconformity.

Conclusion

For the foregoing reasons, the defendant's rule 12(b)(6) motion to dismiss this one count complaint is denied.

SO ORDERED.

Notes and Questions

1. From the perspective of private business, i.e., our clients, the situation described in these cases cannot be satisfactory. What transpires is a fundamental disagreement about the liability of the seller with regard to her performance. Within the sphere of application of state common law, it seems that an older preference for the perfect tender rule has given way to a more moderated approach looking for a substantial nonconformity or material failure before a buyer is entitled to reject delivery and avoid or cancel the contract. The older and stricter approach, however, has been codified in the UCC and today informs the majority of courts within the sphere of application of the Code. Unsatisfactory outcomes under the UCC are supposedly mitigated via the application of the good faith doctrine, however unpredictable its scope and requirements may be. And then there are states like Connecticut that bend the language of the UCC to make room for the more flexible approach taken in the Restatement. Do we even realize the huge burden we are imposing on commercial operators trying to adjust their business practices to the requirements of the law and make sensible decisions when a dispute over contractual rights and remedies arises? In politics, the U.S. is widely seen as preferring candidates promoting lower taxes and smaller government. In law, we seem to be doing exactly the opposite, namely holding on to and promoting solutions that impose huge financial burdens

on individuals and companies and require substantial government resources and operations to implement. Who is being served by all of this? And who pays the price? More importantly, what could and should be done about it?

2. In paragraph 8, the court cites a precedent pursuant to which the perfect tender rule does not apply in the area of service contracts. Instead, the standard of substantial performance is applied. Why would that be the case? Should service contracts be treated differently from contracts for the sale of goods? Why?

3. What do you think of a general doctrine that time is of the essence in contracts of sale between merchants (para. 11 *in fine*)?

The next case is concerned with the obligations of the parties after a breach of contract was committed by the seller and specifically the rights of the buyer to receive damages for various kinds of losses and expenses.

Case 2-18

Carbontek Trading v. Phibro Energy

910 F.2d 302 (5th Cir. 1990)
(Paragraph numbers added, some details and footnotes omitted.)
THORNBERRY, Circuit Judge:

[1] This appeal involves a dispute over the amount of damages a seller, Carbontek Trading Company, Ltd. ("Carbontek"), owes to a buyer, Phibro Energy, Inc. ("Phibro"), as a consequence of Carbontek's delivery of a shipment of coal that did not conform to contract specifications. We find that the district court erred in holding Carbontek liable for less than the full amount of damages suffered by Phibro and in denying recovery to Phibro for delay expenses.

Facts and Procedural History

[2] Carbontek and Phibro are both corporations engaged in selling and trading coal in bulk. In March 1987, Carbontek and Phibro entered into a contract in which Carbontek agreed to sell and Phibro agreed to buy approximately 70,000 metric tons of steam coal at a price of $25 per ton. Phibro contracted to sell the cargo of steam coal to Elkraft Power Company, Ltd. ("Elkraft"), a Danish utility, for $31.95 per ton. Both contracts provided that the steam coal was to comply with certain listed specifications. Phibro chartered a vessel, the M/V SENECA, and was responsible for shipping the coal from its loading point at Davant, Louisiana, to Elkraft in Denmark.

[3] The coal that Carbontek delivered at Davant had approximately 6,500 tons of petroleum coke ("pet coke") combined with it. Pet coke is a by-product of petroleum refining. Carbontek added the pet coke to the coal to meet its interpretation of the specifications of the contract. Many utility companies consider pet coke undesirable for burning because it contains less volatile matter than coal, and many coal-burning plants are not set up to burn low-volatility fuels. Pet coke can also create

dust problems. Elkraft's labor contracts provided that Elkraft would not buy any pet coke.

[4] On Wednesday, April 8, 1987, Carbontek, Phibro, and Elkraft each had a representative present at Davant to inspect the coal piles intended for Phibro and to observe loading of the coal aboard the M/V SENECA. Upon inspection of the cargo, Elkraft and Phibro discovered that it contained some pet coke. Carbontek began loading the cargo that evening, as scheduled. The next morning Phibro notified Carbontek by telex that Elkraft intended to reject the coal because of the presence of pet coke, and that Phibro was therefore rejecting the coal and holding Carbontek liable for any damages. Carbontek then stopped loading at 7:40 p.m. on April 9. On April 10 Phibro called upon Carbontek to discharge the blended coal and replace it with steam coal. Carbontek did not discharge the coal.

[5] On Saturday, April 11, the M/V SENECA resumed loading. It is unclear who ordered the resumption of loading; it may have occurred because of a breakdown in communications over the weekend. Loading of a total cargo weight of 64,797.283 metric tons was completed at 6:00 a.m. on April 12.

[6] The M/V SENECA left the dock on Sunday morning, April 12, and proceeded to a point off the Louisiana coast, seaward of the Southwest Pass. There it remained anchored until 5:46 p.m. on April 14, when it departed toward Asnaes, Denmark, upon Phibro's instructions. At that time Phibro did not communicate with Carbontek other than to inform Carbontek that it should try to find an alternate buyer for the coal.

[7] On April 15, 1987, Carbontek brought this action against Phibro in the United States District Court for the Eastern District of Louisiana, complaining that Phibro and its agent violated their duty to issue a bill of lading for the coal and that Phibro converted the coal to its own use.[1] Carbontek sought to recover the full contract price of the coal from Phibro, because Phibro had not paid for the coal at the time Carbontek filed suit.

[8] Meanwhile, Phibro was negotiating with Elkraft to accept the cargo of steam coal and pet coke for a discounted price. On April 14, Phibro and Elkraft agreed that Elkraft would accept the full load for a reduction of $192,000 in the contract price, subject to final inspection in Denmark. On April 21, Phibro informed Carbontek of its tentative arrangement with Elkraft and indicated it would welcome any lower cost alternatives that Carbontek might have. Carbontek requested information as

---

1. Carbontek also named as defendants Tradax Ocean Transport, S.A. (time charterer of the M/V SENECA), Hall-Buck Marine, Inc. (agent for Phibro and Tradax in dealings with the vessel), and Shipping Management S.A.M. (owner of the vessel), in personam, and the M/V SENECA and the coal, in rem. The district court found that Hall-Buck Marine's delay in issuing a corrected bill of lading did not violate 46 U.S.C. App. § 193, which requires the owner of a vessel transporting merchandise to issue a bill of lading to the shipper. The court then dismissed all defendants other than Phibro as not properly part of the litigation over the contractual dispute. These aspects of the district court's judgment are not challenged on appeal.

to the position, direction, and speed of the vessel so that it could locate an alternate buyer at a location to which the vessel could be diverted. On April 23 and again on May 1, Phibro informed Carbontek that the coal was scheduled to arrive at Asnaes, Denmark, on May 2. The M/V SENECA arrived at Asnaes on schedule.

[9] While the vessel was sailing toward Denmark, Carbontek continued to negotiate with potential purchasers. On May 1, Carbontek received an offer of $33.25 per ton through a broker in the United Kingdom for delivery in the eastern Mediterranean. Phibro never learned of this offer. On May 4, Carbontek asked Phibro to hold up discharge of the coal for 24 hours so it could confirm an offer of $32.50 per ton from a consignee in Hamburg, Germany. Phibro responded that it would hold up discharge only if Carbontek agreed to be responsible for any delay expenses and for cancellation of its agreement with Elkraft. Carbontek did not agree to take responsibility for the delay.

[10] Elkraft took delivery of the coal on May 5 and thereafter paid Phibro the original contract price less $192,000. Phibro then paid Carbontek its contractually agreed price, less a deduction of $219,555.49: $192,000 for the reduction in Elkraft's price and $27,555.49 for expenses incidental to difficulties in loading the vessel and delays caused by the dispute over the pet coke.[2] . . .

[12] The district court held a nonjury trial in March 1989, and thereafter entered findings of fact and conclusions of law. The court found that Carbontek violated the perfect tender rule of New York Uniform Commercial Code ("UCC") section 2-601(a) by tendering contaminated coal to Phibro. The court found that Phibro initially rejected the coal, but later accepted it on May 5, when it consummated the sale to Elkraft. The court found that Phibro's acceptance was subject to its right to claim damages for the inclusion of approximately 10% pet coke, under UCC section 2-714. The damages would be the difference between the value of the goods delivered and their value had the cargo not been controverted, and under UCC section 2-717, Phibro could deduct such damages from the price due under the contract.

[13] The court found, however, that the amount Phibro deducted was excessive. The court concluded that, because Carbontek "apparently received offers" close to the original Elkraft contract price from other buyers relatively near Denmark, a reasonable deduction would be $50,000. The court disallowed the delay expenses of $27,555.49, saying that those damages were the result of Phibro's own delay. Therefore, the court awarded Carbontek damages in the amount of $169,555.49 plus interest. Phibro appeals the damage award.

Discussion

[14] On appeal, the only issue is the amount of damages that Phibro should recover for Carbontek's breach. Carbontek does not dispute the district court's conclusion that Carbontek breached the contract when it violated the perfect tender rule.

---

2. In fact, the record shows Phibro withheld $229,555.49 from its payment to Carbontek, or $10,000 more than it should have withheld according to its damages calculation.

[15] Phibro urges that the district court should have awarded it the full $219,555.49 in damages. Carbontek agrees with the district court's award. Both parties agree that New York law applies to their dispute, in accordance with a provision in the Carbontek/Phibro contract.

A. Damages for the Reduced Value of the Coal as Delivered

[16] New York UCC section 2-714 determines the manner in which a buyer who accepts defective goods and gives notice is entitled to recover damages:

> (1) Where the buyer has accepted goods and given notification (subsection (3) of Section 2-607) he may recover as damages for any non-conformity of tender the loss resulting in the ordinary course of events from the seller's breach as determined in any manner which is reasonable.

> (2) The measure of damages for breach of warranty is the difference at the time and place of acceptance between the value of the goods accepted and the value they would have had if they had been as warranted, unless special circumstances show proximate damages of a different amount.

> (3) In a proper case any incidental and consequential damages under the next section may also be recovered. (N.Y.U.C.C. Law §2-714 (McKinney 1964))

[17] The buyer is entitled to deduct the damages from the price due under the contract. N.Y.U.C.C. Law §2-717; *Created Gemstones, Inc. v. Union Carbide Corp.*, 47 N.Y.2d 250, 391 N.E.2d 987, 989, 417 N.Y.S.2d 905, 907–08 (1979). Phibro deducted its alleged damages from the price due to Carbontek under the contract in accordance with section 2-717.

[18] Phibro argues that $192,000 is a reasonable calculation of the difference in fair market value between the conforming and nonconforming coal, because that is the reduction in Elkraft's price that Elkraft required in return for accepting the nonconforming coal. Under New York law, "when a seller delivers nonconforming goods to ultimate buyers, the intermediate buyer may claim as damages the amount it had to pay the ultimate buyers to compensate them for the delivery of the defective goods." *Happy Dack Trading Co. v. Agro-Industries, Inc.*, 602 F.Supp. 986, 994 (S.D.N.Y.1984) (citing *Rite Fabrics, Inc. v. Stafford-Higgins Co.*, 366 F.Supp. 1 (S.D.N.Y.1973)). In *Happy Dack*, the court accepted as a reasonable measure of damages a specified amount of compensation that an intermediate buyer of resin agreed to pay the ultimate buyer in exchange for the ultimate buyer's agreement to keep the defective resin. Because the parties fixed the amount of compensation pursuant to arm's length bargaining, the court concluded that that amount could be considered the difference in fair market value between conforming and nonconforming resin. *Happy Dack*, 602 F.Supp. at 994. Phibro argues that the district court should have applied the same principle in this case.

[19] The district court found that the terms of the arrangement between Phibro and Elkraft did not indicate that Elkraft's deduction was considered to be a measure

of damages. Carbontek also disputes the relevance of the arrangement as evidence of the coal's value, and argues that Phibro never showed any correlation between the discounted price paid by Elkraft and any actual damage sustained by Phibro or Elkraft. But the telex dated April 15 from Phibro's agent in Stockholm to Elkraft, confirming Phibro's agreement with Elkraft, says, "As full compensation for the contamination of petcoke we will from the invoice value deduct a lump sum of USD 192,000." According to Phibro, the district court erred in overlooking this sentence, which indicates that the $192,000 deduction was intended to represent the difference in value between the coal as warranted and the coal as accepted. A previous telex dated April 14 from Phibro's agent in Stockholm to Phibro's main office in Greenwich, Connecticut, indicates that the $192,000 figure was calculated by multiplying $32 per ton (an approximation of the contract price Elkraft was to pay) by 6,000 tons of pet coke.

[20] The district court relied on Phibro's telex of April 15 for its factual finding that Elkraft agreed to accept the contaminated coal "as full performance under [the] contract," but seems to have ignored the subsequent language of the telex describing the deduction as compensation for contamination. We think the telex is competent evidence that the $192,000 deduction was intended to compensate for the contamination. The testimony of John Dallin, a director of Phibro, also indicates that the deduction was compensation for contamination. Carbontek did not offer any evidence indicating that the agreement between Phibro and Elkraft was anything other than an arm's length agreement. In accordance with *Happy Dack*, therefore, we think $192,000 is a reasonable measure of Phibro's damages. See *Happy Dack*, 602 F.Supp. at 994. The district court's finding that no evidence showed Elkraft and Phibro considered the $192,000 to be a measure of damages is clearly erroneous.

[21] As a breaching seller, Carbontek had the burden to show that Phibro could have mitigated its damages in a commercially reasonable manner. See *City of New York v. Pullman Inc.*, 662 F.2d 910, 917 (2d Cir.1981), cert. denied, 454 U.S. 1164 . . . (1982) (although an injured buyer is under a duty to mitigate damages, the burden is on the breaching seller to show that its alternative option "was a viable means of reducing damages"); *Larsen v. A.C. Carpenter, Inc.*, 620 F.Supp. 1084, 1132 (E.D.N.Y.1985), aff'd, 800 F.2d 1128 (2d Cir.1986) (the burden of showing failure to mitigate is on the wrongdoer). Carbontek did not meet this burden. Carbontek did not offer any evidence showing that the Phibro/Elkraft agreement was not commercially reasonable or that a less expensive option was available to Phibro.

[22] Carbontek argues that a less expensive solution, such as replacing the coal at the loading dock, might have been feasible if Phibro had remained in contact with Carbontek all along. Phibro did not communicate with Carbontek between April 10 and April 21 about the efforts Phibro was making to replace the coal or find alternate buyers, and only contacted Carbontek after Phibro had already tentatively settled with Elkraft. However, one of Phibro's witnesses, John Dallin, testified that discharging the contaminated coal alone would have cost $120,000. Additional costs mentioned by Phibro's witness included $6,000 per day for the ship's delay and

dead freight of $6 per ton. Carbontek did not contradict any of this evidence. The only evidence Carbontek contradicted involved the timing of replacement: Phibro's witness estimated it would have taken two to three months to replace the cargo; Carbontek's witness testified it would have taken two weeks. There was some evidence that the market price of coal was rising and that ocean freight for a replacement cargo would have cost $1.50 per ton more than ocean freight under the M/V SENECA charter. Because the price of coal was higher than the price of pet coke, the price of coal was rising, and replacement coal probably would have cost more than any price received for the SENECA's blended cargo, it seems likely that discharging and replacing the cargo would have cost more than $192,000. We find nothing in the record to suggest otherwise.

[23] Carbontek insists that it had two alternate offers at prices comparable to the Elkraft contract price, and that Phibro never gave Carbontek a chance to confirm an alternate offer because Phibro never notified it of the ship's speed and estimated time of arrival in Denmark. Without such information, Carbontek says it could not have provided a potential buyer with certainty as to delivery time. However, Carbontek's telex to a potential alternate buyer indicates that on April 28 Carbontek knew the M/V SENECA was five days from its destination. The two alternate offers came in after April 28.

[24] Carbontek never showed that if Phibro had accepted one of the last-minute alternate offers, Phibro could have covered its obligation to Elkraft in a time frame acceptable to Elkraft and at a price that would have resulted in a mitigation of damages. Moreover, Phibro conditionally assented to delay unloading at Asnaes so that Carbontek could confirm an offer if Carbontek would take responsibility for any delay costs; when Carbontek failed to respond, Phibro allowed discharging to begin.

[25] The district court found that a "reasonable deduction" would be $50,000 because Carbontek "apparently received" other offers for the coal similar to the original Elkraft price. However, the record does not support the $50,000 figure. Since the deduction of $192,000 from Elkraft's contract price is the only measure of damages for which there is any real evidence, and that amount seems commercially reasonable in these circumstances, we think $192,000 is a more appropriate measure of damages than the arbitrary figure of $50,000.

B. Delay Expenses

[26] The district court denied the recovery of incidental damages for delay that Phibro sought in the amount of $27,555.49, on the ground that these expenses were "the result of Phibro's own delay," not the result of the initial rejection of the cargo.

[27] Under UCC section 2-714(3), a buyer who has accepted goods and given notification may recover, inter alia, any incidental damages caused by a nonconformity of tender. Section 2-715(1) provides a description of incidental damages:

Incidental damages resulting from the seller's breach include expenses reasonably incurred in inspection, receipt, transportation and care and custody of goods rightfully rejected, any commercially reasonable charges, expenses or commissions in connection with effecting cover and any other reasonable expense incident to the delay or other breach. (N.Y.U.C.C. § 2-715(1) (McKinney 1964))

[28] The official comment indicates that this list of enumerated expenses is not exhaustive. N.Y.U.C.C. § 2-715(1) comment 1. Incidental damages can include all reasonable expenses the buyer incurred "in inspecting, shipping, handling and storing" the defective goods. *Consolidated Data Terminals v. Applied Digital Data Systems,* 708 F.2d 385, 393–94 (9th Cir.1983); see also *Happy Dack,* 602 F.Supp. at 994 (intermediate buyer could recover travel and testing expenses incurred after ultimate buyer rejected the goods).

[29] Specifically, Phibro requests (1) $9,000.00 of demurrage, which is compensation to the vessel owner for any delay exceeding the loading time allowed by the contract—in this case, for the lapse in loading time at Davant caused by the dispute over cargo quality; (2) $635.42 for lost dispatch, which is the contractual bonus Phibro would have earned for loading the vessel faster than scheduled but for the delays caused by the dispute; (3) $1,337.42 for lost interest on ocean freight that Phibro would have earned had it delivered the cargo as scheduled; (4) $14,766.40 in demurrage and additional costs to the vessel owners while the vessel waited at the Southwest Pass for sailing orders; (5) $554.25 for the cost of extra sampling and chemical analysis performed on the coal that was loaded on the vessel; and (6) $1,262.00 for extra pilotage and harbor expenses at Davant incurred because the vessel had to be moved between the loading dock and anchorage. These expenses incurred by Phibro are supported by documentary evidence and testimony. John Dallin, a director of Phibro, testified that Phibro paid all of these charges.

[30] Carbontek does not dispute the validity of Phibro's expenses, but asserts that the delay causing the expenses to accrue was Phibro's fault. The district court accepted Carbontek's argument. Again, we disagree with the district court. Phibro incurred the enumerated expenses only because Carbontek's coal was nonconforming. The initial delay from April 9 to April 11 began when Carbontek stopped loading the ship in response to Phibro's initial exercise of its right to reject the cargo. Clearly, that delay resulted from Carbontek's breach of contract in delivering nonconforming coal.

[31] The delay at the Southwest Pass from April 12 to April 14 occurred while Phibro was trying to mitigate damages by finding other buyers or concluding a settlement with Elkraft. The telex of April 14 from Phibro's agent in Stockholm to Phibro's main office in Greenwich, Connecticut, describes Phibro's unsuccessful attempts to find other buyers for the coal. The ship sailed as soon as Phibro concluded an agreement with Elkraft. Contrary to the district court's conclusion, the delay at the Southwest Pass resulted from the initial rejection of the cargo, and

occurred only because Phibro was trying to mitigate damages. It was only because Carbontek delivered nonconforming coal that Phibro had to attempt to mitigate damages.

[32] In its brief Carbontek notes that the contract excluded claims for consequential damages. The damages for delay claimed by Phibro, however, are not consequential damages, but incidental damages similar to those described in UCC section 2-715(1). Incidental damages may be recovered even when consequential damages are excluded. See, e.g., *Carbo Industries v. Becker Chevrolet*, 112 A.D.2d 336, 491 N.Y.S.2d 786, 790 (N.Y.App.Div.), appeal dismissed, 66 N.Y.2d 1035, 499 N.Y.S.2d 1030, 489 N.E.2d 1303 (1985) (towing costs and costs of diagnosing the problem were compensable incidental damages).

Conclusion

[33] Phibro's agreement with Elkraft for a discount of $192,000 as compensation for the contamination of the coal with pet coke does not seem commercially unreasonable. The record shows that Phibro unsuccessfully attempted to mitigate damages by finding other buyers. Moreover, Carbontek did not meet its burden to show that a less expensive option was viable, considering Phibro's obligation to Elkraft. The deduction of $192,000 from Elkraft's contract price is the only measure of Phibro's damages for which there is any real evidence. Therefore, we hold that Phibro is entitled to damages of $192,000.

[34] Furthermore, Phibro's delay expenses of $27,555.49 were reasonable and should be awarded as incidental damages. The district court erred in finding that the expenses resulted from Phibro's own delay, since the delay occurred only because Phibro was trying to mitigate damages caused by Carbontek's breach.

[35] Because the amount Phibro withheld from its payment to Carbontek was $229,555.49, or $10,000 more than it should have withheld, our modification of the district court's award of damages to Phibro does not result in a judgment that Carbontek take nothing. Carbontek is entitled to the difference between the full contract price and the damages recovered by Phibro. Therefore, we render a judgment in favor of Carbontek for $10,000 plus prejudgment interest as described in the district court's judgment below, i.e., at the rate of 6.30% from April 12, 1987 to entry of the district court's judgment, and postjudgment interest thereafter until paid. The judgment is AFFIRMED AS MODIFIED.

Notes and Questions

1. What kind of primary claims (performance) and/or damage claims can be brought by a buyer and on what legal basis, if:

   a. the seller refuses to honor the contract, although the buyer wishes to proceed?

   b. the seller is late in delivering?

   c. the seller's goods do not entirely conform but buyer accepts them anyway?

    d. the seller's goods do not conform and buyer rejects them?

    e. there are any other problems with the seller's performance?

2. What kind of primary claims (performance) and/or damage claims can be brought by a seller and on what legal basis, if:

    a. the buyer refuses to take delivery, although the tender of performance by the seller is conforming?

    b. the buyer is late with payment?

    c. the buyer, after delivery, avoids or cancels the contract for lack of conformity?

    d. there are any other problems with buyer's performance?

3. What is the difference between *incidental* damages and *consequential* damages?

4. What can we learn from this case about persuasive presentation of damage claims?

5. How does a calculation of prejudgment and post-judgment interest work?

C. Claim Bases in UNIDROIT Principles and Common Frame of Reference

While it is hardly justifiable to present court decisions and/or arbitral awards that rely primarily on the UNIDROIT Principles of International Commercial Contracts (PICC) or the EU Common Frame of Reference (CFR), the following chart should make comparative studies a bit easier. It will also come in handy where a contract has to be analyzed under the PICC or CFR because of party choice, or where provisions in the CISG do not answer all questions related to the rights and obligations under a contract and reference is made to the PICC as the codification of general principles and/or *lex mercatoria* (see above, pp. 126–132).

Checklist 2-7

Claim Bases in the PICC and CFR

Seller → Buyer				
Claim	Legal Bases UNIDROIT	CFR	Exceptions UNIDROIT	CFR
1. Right to Performance/ Contractual Claims a. Take Delivery b. Pay Purchase Price c. Restitution of Goods after Avoidance	Art. 7.2.1 Art. 7.3.6		Art. 6.2.3 (Hardship) Art. 7.1.7 (Force Majeure) Arts. 10.1–10.11 (Statute of Limitations) Art. 7.3.6 limitations	
2. Damages	Arts. 7.4.1–7.4.6 and 7.4.11–7.4.13		Arts. 7.4.7, 7.4.8	
3. Interest	Arts. 7.4.9, 7.4.10			

Buyer → Seller				
Claim	Legal Bases UNIDROIT	CFR	Exceptions UNIDROIT	CFR
1. Right to Performance/ Contractual Claims a. Delivery of Conforming Goods b. Transfer of Documents c. Transfer of Ownership d. Carriage & Insurance e. Price Reduction f. Repair, Replacement, or Cure g. Restitution of Price after Avoidance	Art. 7.2.2 Art. 7.2.3 + case law Art. 7.2.3 Arts. 7.3.1, 7.3.2, 7.3.5, 7.3.6		Art. 7.2.2 limitations Art. 6.2.3 (Hardship) Art. 7.1.7 (Force Majeure) Arts. 10.1–10.11 (Statute of Limitations)	
2. Damages	Arts. 7.4.1–7.4.6 and 7.4.11–7.4.13		Arts. 7.4.7, 7.4.8	
3. Interest	Art. 7.4.9, 7.4.10			

D. Practical Exercises

In practice, at least in the Western hemisphere, the majority of IBTs are either subject to the CISG—representative of the Continental European legal systems—or to the UCC—representative of the U.S. and common law systems. Therefore, we shall now turn to a comparison of outcomes with the help of a number of hypotheticals. In the process, we shall also develop a number of checklists for the analysis of contractual claims. These should be employed in the answers to the hypotheticals. The examples start with issues of contract formation, then move into contract interpretation, and finally into breaches, justifications, and remedies.

1. Overview and Checklists

A specific problem at the outset of any analysis of contractual obligations and ensuing claims is the precise determination when and on what terms a contract was concluded. In the context of IBTs, it is common that the parties exchange a series of communications, declarations, and documents, in the contract formation stage. Review Checklist 2-1 on p. 172 for all possible verbal communications and nonverbal acts and their meaning with regard to contract formation and interpretation. **Nota bene:** contractual rights and obligations can only be correctly determined after the formation and interpretation of the contract has been clarified.

The applicable law can be one of the problems subject to contract formation and interpretation, namely when it is not clear whether a choice of law clause made it into the contract or how the parties wanted their choice of law to be understood.

This can pose the famous chicken or egg question: Under what law should contract formation and interpretation be assessed to find out what law the parties have chosen to govern their contract?

Our general overview table will include relevant provisions of other contract laws. However, once we look closer at the step-by-step analysis of contractual claims, we will focus only on UCC and CISG.

Those are also the only provisions we will take into account when we work through a number of practical exercises and hypotheticals.

Chart 2-4
Comparison Table UCC — R2C — UK Sales Act — CFR — PICC — CISG

Subject Matter	UCC	US Restatement	CFR	PICC	CISG
Offer / acceptance (mirror image rule)	2-207	§§ 17-94 §§ 39, 59	II 4:101 et seq II 4:201 + II 4:208 (materially alter)	2.1.11	19 (2) 14
Revocable / irrevocable offers	2-205	§§ 35 et seq.	II 4:202	2.1.4	16 (2)
Unwritten terms and conditions	2-201	§§ 4, 18, 19, 27, 53, 54, 110 et seq.	II 1:106	1.2, 1.3	11
Battle of forms	2-207		II 4:209; II 9:103; II 9:402	2.1.22, 2.1.20	
Necessity of clear price term	2-305	§§ 33, 34, 204	II 9:104	5.7, 2.1.14	55
Time of contract formation	2-206, 2-204	§§ 63 et seq.	II 4:205		18 (1) and (2)
Relevance of outside circumstances (parol evidence)	2-202	§§ 213, 214 §§ 219 et seq.	II 4:104	2.1.17	8 (3)
Consequences of non-conforming goods	perfect tender rule, 2-601	§§ 231 et seq. §§ 344 et seq.	III 3:502	7.3.1, 7.1.1 et seq	49 + 25 "fundamental breach"
Seller's right to cure; assurances	2-609, 2-508		III 3:201 et seq		72 (1), 34, 37, 48
Force majeure as an excuse for non-performance	2-615	§§ 261 et seq.	III 1:110 see also III 3:104	6.2.1 hardship 7.1.7 force majeure	79

Subject Matter	UCC	US Restatement	CFR	PICC	CISG
Gross disparity, excessive advantage	2-302		II 7:207	3.10	
Consequences of warranties given	2-313, 2-314, 2-315				36
Buyer's right to reduce price (set-off)	2-711, 2-714 (2) damages		III 3:601	8.1, 7.4.1 price reduction	50 price reduction / set-off
Buyer's right to specific performance	2-716 2-709	§§ 357 et seq.	III 3:301 III 3:302	7.2.2 7.2.1	46, 62, 28
Calculation & scope of damages		§§ 346 et seq.	III 3:701 et seq	7.4.2, 7.4.3	74-78

Checklist 2-8
Step-by-Step Analysis for Contractual Claims of the Buyer

#1   Contractual obligations of the seller were created

— contract formed via offer and acceptance (Arts. 14-24 CISG; § 2-206 UCC) (see Checklist 2-12 for the interpretation of verbal communications and nonverbal acts of the parties at the contract formation stage)

— the terms of the contract contain relevant obligations of the seller, e.g., delivery of conforming goods (§ 2-213 UCC)

— if not, a persuasive interpretation of the contract implies relevant obligations of the seller (Arts. 8, 9 CISG; §§ 2-202, 305, 308, 309, 310, 314, 315 UCC)

#2   The contractual obligations of the seller are valid and due (§§ 2-201, 302 UCC)

#3   The contractual obligations of the seller have not ended

— no initial impossibility of performance by the seller (§ 2-302 UCC)

— no termination of the contract by agreement of the parties (Art. 29 CISG; §§ 2-209, 309 UCC)

— no unilateral rescission of the contract for incapacity, mistake, or fraud (§ 2-209 UCC, but see § 2-721 UCC)

— no successful avoidance of the contract by either side (Arts. 49, 64 CISG; § 2-209 UCC)

— no expiration on account of statute of limitations (§ 2-725 UCC)

#4 The seller is in breach of at least some of his contractual obligations

— no complete and conforming performance by the seller, in particular not timely delivery of conforming goods (Arts. 30–44 CISG; §§ 2-503, 504, 507, 508 UCC)

#5 The breach was neither justified nor excused

— justification because of anticipated breach by buyer (Arts. 71, 72 CISG; § 2-610(c) UCC)

— excuse based on force majeure (Art. 79 CISG; § 2-615 UCC)

#6 Therefore, the buyer has the following primary remedies

— require performance pursuant to the obligation (Art. 46 CISG; § 2-711, 716 UCC)

— require late performance or cure of defective performance (Arts. 48, 51, 52 CISG)

— accept defective performance and reduce price (Art. 50 CISG; § 2-217 UCC)

#7 To the extent that primary remedies are no longer possible, no longer of interest to the buyer, or insufficient to make up for the breach, the buyer also has the following secondary remedies

— damages for cover transaction (Art. 75 CISG; § 2-711, 712 UCC)

— expectation damages for other losses directly related to the IBT, including lost profit (Art. 74 CISG; §§ 2-713, 2-714, 715 UCC)

— consequential damages for other losses caused by the breach (Art. 74 CISG; § 2-715 UCC)

— liquidated damages (Art. 6 CISG; § 2-718 UCC)

— but consider limitation of damages by foreseeability or agreement(Art. 74 CISG, § 2-719 UCC)

— and limitation to reasonable damages? (§§ 2-715, 718 UCC

— and the obligation to mitigate damages (Art. 77 CISG; § 2-715(2)(a) UCC)

— interest (Art. 78 CISG)

— attorney fees and costs of legal procedures? (Art. 74 CISG)

Checklist 2-9
Step-by-Step Analysis for Contractual Claims of the Seller

#1 Contractual obligations of the buyer were created

— contract formed via offer and acceptance (Arts. 14–24 CISG; § 2-206 UCC) (see Checklist 2-12 for the interpretation of verbal communications and nonverbal acts of the parties at the contract formation stage)

— the terms of the contract contain relevant obligations of the buyer, e.g., payment of the purchase price and taking delivery of the goods (§ 2-313 UCC)

— if not, a persuasive interpretation of the contract implies relevant obligations of the buyer (Arts. 8, 9 CISG; §§ 2-202, 305, 308, 309, 310, 314, 315 UCC)

#2 The contractual obligations of the buyer are valid and due (§§ 2-201, 302 UCC)

#3 The contractual obligations of the buyer have not ended

— no initial impossibility of performance by the seller (§ 2-302 UCC)

— no termination of the contract by agreement of the parties (Art. 29 CISG; §§ 2-209, 309 UCC)

— no unilateral rescission of the contract for incapacity, mistake or fraud (§ 2-209 UCC, but see § 2-721 UCC)

— no successful avoidance of the contract by either side (Arts. 49, 64 CISG; § 2-209 UCC)

— no expiration on account of statute of limitations (§ 2-725 UCC)

#4 The buyer is in breach of at least some of her contractual obligations

— no complete and conforming performance by the buyer, in particular no complete and timely payment of the purchase price (Arts. 53–60 CISG; §§ 2-511, 512, 513, 514 UCC)

#5 The breach was neither justified nor excused

— justification because of anticipated breach by seller (Arts. 71, 72 CISG; § 2-610(c) UCC)

— excuse based on force majeure (Art. 79 CISG; § 2-615 UCC)

#6 Therefore, the seller has the following primary remedies:

— require performance pursuant to the obligation (Art. 62 CISG; § 2-709 UCC)

— require late performance or cure of defective performance (Arts. 63, 65 CISG)

#7   To the extent that primary remedies are no longer possible, no longer of interest to the seller, or insufficient to make up for the breach, the seller also has the following secondary remedies:

— damages for breach of contract (Art. 74 CISG; § 2-708 UCC)

— expectation damages for other losses directly related to the IBT, including lost profit (Art. 74 CISG; §§ 2-710 UCC)

— consequential damages for other losses caused by the breach (Art. 74 CISG; § 2-710 UCC)

— liquidated damages (Art. 6 CISG; § 2-718 UCC)

— but consider limitation of damages by foreseeability or agreement (Art. 74 CISG; § 2-719 UCC)

— and limitation to reasonable damages? (§ 2-710 UCC)

— and the obligation to mitigate damages (Art. 77 CISG; § 2-708 UCC)

— interest (Art. 78 CISG)

— attorney fees and costs of legal procedures? (Art. 74 CISG)

2. Hypotheticals for the Comparison of CISG and UCC Rights and Obligations

Outline the rights and obligations of Company A and Company B using Checklists 2-8 and 2-9 under both CISG and UCC.

(1) Company A in Indianapolis has a website that "offers" the following machine: PremierTool at $y_____ Company B in London sends a fax "We hereby accept your offer and request shipment of 5 units of machine PremierTool at 5 x $y_____, to be delivered fob M/S Equator, Norfolk VA, July 15." Company A does not respond.

(2) Same as (1) but Company A responds as follows "We have received your offer and accept. The contract shall be subject to our general terms, as attached."

(3) Same as (2) but Company A also adds "The contract shall be subject to Indiana law. Any dispute between the parties shall be settled in court in Indianapolis."

(4) Same as (1) Company A replies: "Thank you for your order. We accept but have to inform you that due to market developments the new prices shall be $y+__"

(5) Same as (1) except that Company B is located not in London but in Amsterdam.

(6) Company A in Indianapolis has a website that "offers" the following machine: PremierTool at $y. . . . Company B in London sends a fax "We hereby accept your offer and request shipment of 5 units of machine PremierTool at 5 x $y_____, to be delivered fob M/S Equator, Norfolk VA, July 15, 2012. Our general terms are attached."

Company A does not respond.

(7) Same as (6) but Company A responds as follows "We have received your offer and accept. The contract shall be subject to our general terms, as attached."

(8) Same as (7). In the general terms of A there is a clause subjecting any contract to Indiana law. In the general terms of B there is a parallel clause subjecting any contract to UK law. After the exchange of communication outlined in (6), both companies proceed with performance.

(9) Company A in Indianapolis sends an e-mail to its usual clients stating "We offer overstock at rock bottom prices . . . prices good through September 30."

Company B in London sends a fax "We hereby accept your offer and request shipment of 5 units of machine PremierTool at 5 x $y_____, to be delivered fob M/S Equator, Norfolk VA, July 15, 2012." Company A does not respond.

(10) Same as (9) but Company A sent the e-mail explicitly addressed to Company B.

(11) Company A in Indianapolis has a website that "offers" the following machine: PremierTool at $y . . .

The purchasing manager of Company B in London calls and orders "5 units of machine PremierTool at 5 x $y____, to be delivered fob M/S Equator, Norfolk VA, July 15, 2012."

(a) the call is received by the switchboard operator at Company A and since the sales manager is out to lunch, she takes the call and promises to pass on the message;

(b) the call is received by the sales manager of Company A who responds by saying that "A is pleased to accept the order."

(c) since nobody picks up at Company A because of the time difference, the call goes to voicemail. Later that day, the sales manager of Company A calls back to London—where everyone has gone home by now, and leaves an acceptance message on the voicemail of B.

(12) Company A in Indianapolis has a website that "offers" the following machine tools: PremierTool at $y_____

Company B in London sends a fax "We hereby accept your offer and request shipment of 5 units of machine PremierTool at 5 x $y___, to be delivered fob M/S Equator, Norfolk VA, July 15, 2012."

(a) A responds by fax "We have received your offer and accept." The fax arrives in London after hours. Before anybody reads it there, A sends another fax to cancel the acceptance and also leaves a voicemail to that effect.

(b) A responds by airmail "We have received your offer and accept." Before the letter arrives in London, A calls to cancel the acceptance.

(13) Company A in Indianapolis has a website that "offers" the following machine: PremierTool at $y . . .

Company B in London sends a fax "We hereby accept your offer and request shipment of 5 units of machine PremierTool at 5 x $y_____, to be delivered FOB

M/S Equator, Norfolk VA, July 15, 2012." Company A responds as follows "We have received your offer and accept."

(a) The machines are scheduled to leave the factory in Indianapolis on July 10. The night before the departure, a tornado damages the building and the machines; the shipment is delayed by several days.

(b) Same as (a) except that A knows that B needs the machines up and running by August 15 to meet a major contract.

(c) Same as (a) except that the damage to the machines is caused by a truck driver employed by A who hit the container with the packaged machines. Consequently, they had to be unpacked, tested, and re-packed.

(d) Same as (a) except that the machines get damaged on board M/S Equator because of heavy weather during the passage across the Atlantic.

(e) Same as (d) except the damage on board M/S Equator is caused by the ship's crew.

(14) Company A in Indianapolis has a website that "offers" the following machine: PremierTool at $y . . .

Company B in London sends a fax "We hereby accept your offer and request shipment of 5 units of machine PremierTool at 5 x $y____, to be delivered CIF M/S Equator, Norfolk VA, July 15, 2012." Company A responds as follows "We have received your offer and accept. Shipment shall be made FOB M/S Equator, Norfolk VA, July 15, 2012. Our general terms shall apply."

Subsequently, both parties proceed with performance. Problems?

What are the rights and obligations of the parties under the following circumstances?

(15) Company D in Indianapolis is a coffee roasting and distribution center. On July 3, they receive a large order from a hotel chain and promptly need to order additional quantities of dried coffee beans. The purchasing manager calls Company C in Colombia and leaves the following message on the voice mail: "Dear _____ We just received a large order from a new client and need to increase our purchase of your quality xyz. Please ship 7,500 kg by the end of next week at the usual price."

(a) C calls back, confirms orally, and proceeds to ship at $4.90 per kg. When D receives the coffee and invoice, they don't want to pay $4.90. Previously, they had bought some quantities at $4.90 but most recently they had paid only $4.75.

(b) Same as (a) except that prices had always fluctuated somewhere between $4.50 and $5.00.

(c) Same as (b) except that the reference in the original order was to a "market price" and the market price is fluctuating on a daily basis. Which date should be used?

(d) Same as (b) except that Company C had the prices of $4.90 clearly visible on its website.

(e) Same as (c) except that D has several witnesses who participated in a conference call with C a few weeks earlier where both sides discussed the price of $4.75 as a special offer for long-standing clients.

(16) Company A in Indianapolis offers die casting machines to make various types of metal objects, *inter alia* Matchbox cars. On their website they have a machine type 405 and claim that it will turn out 1,200 cars/hour. Company E in Shantou (China) wants to upgrade its toy manufacturing facilities and wants to acquire several 405s. This machine is about the size of an average delivery truck, consists of several hundred moving parts and a computer control center. It can be packaged into a 20-foot container when totally disassembled. Assembly and start-up at the final location has to be done by specialists of Company A, who will also train the operators at the client's facility until they can handle the machine properly.

Pursuant to A's website and brochures, the list prices include packaging and shipping fob to any U.S. port, unpacking and assembly at the destination, as well as up to two weeks of training of client's operators. The machines come with a five-year warranty. Any contracts are to be subject to Indiana law and dispute settlement shall be by arbitration.

(a) E sends an order to A for two machines type 405, per the advertisement on the website of A. The order stipulates that the contract shall be subject to E's general terms. *Inter alia*, those terms foresee the application of the CISG and arbitration at China International Economic and Trade Arbitration Commission (CIETAC). A responds with an acceptance "pursuant to our general terms," which are the same as on the website. Neither of the communications discusses price. Nevertheless, A proceeds to manufacture and ship the merchandise. Before the containers leave the factory, A contacts E about payment but E replies that they do not feel bound by a contract since A's response was a rejection with a counteroffer.

(b) Same as (a) except that the companies did agree on the price of $426,000 for the two machines.

(c) Same as (a) except that when contacted by A the Chinese buyer insists on making payment only once the machines are up and running in Shantou. A nevertheless proceeds with shipping.

(d) Same as (a) except that E negotiates and A accepts delivery duty paid (DDP) Shantou. What is the law applicable to the contract?

(e) The machines arrive in Shantou and a crew from A flies out to set them up. The assembly takes a week because the factory space needs modifications. In the remaining week covered under the contract terms of A, the machines barely get going and the Chinese staff is clearly not yet sufficiently trained to operate them. What are the rights and obligations of the parties?

(f) Same as (e) except that the machines are up and running and occasionally, when operated by the team from A, they get close to an output of 1,200 units/hour, but most of the time—and at all times when operated by the team of E—they fall significantly short of that goal. What are the rights and obligations of the parties?

(g) Same as (f) except that the machines are running smoothly with an hourly output of 1,150 units. What are the rights and obligations of the parties?

(h) Same as (g) except that one machine achieves 1,200 units/hour and the other only gets to 1,000. E does not want to pay anything.

(i) Same as (h) except that E accepts the first machine, gives A another two weeks to get the second machine up to the promised level of performance, and then, when that is unsuccessful, proceeds to buy a replacement machine from a competitor of A. In the end, E rejects the second machine and deducts the higher cost of the replacement machine and the loss of output during the setup period, during the additional two weeks, and during the time until the replacement machine arrives and reaches full capacity, with the result of paying nothing to A.

(j) Same as (I) except that E gives A a month to ship a new machine and get it up to speed and threatens major damage claims if this should not happen.

(17) Seller is located in Germany, buyer is located in Sweden. On July 1, S faxes a letter to G, inviting the latter "to make an offer for specified merchandise of quality A." G responds by fax on July 2, providing prices and delivery times. On July 3, S "orders" 3,400 units of the specified merchandise at the given price and also adds an order of 290 units of six different other items not previously mentioned. On July 4, G replies by thanking S for the order and requests a draft letter of credit. On July 5, S requests a pro-forma invoice from G and G replies with a document that lists all ordered items, but they are of quality B. S immediately responds by objecting and insisting on delivery of the items of quality A "as ordered." G replies that pursuant to their catalog and website only quality B could be delivered by the time and at the prices desired by S. The higher quality A would need more time to manufacture and would be more expensive. Several days later, S replies and insists on delivery of goods of quality A at the prices discussed earlier and threatens to file a claim for breach of contract.

(18) Seller has a fish wholesale business in the Netherlands. buyer is a retail chain in Switzerland. Parties agreed to a transaction involving several hundred kg of fresh mussels. At importation, Swiss authorities check a small sample of the mussels and detect levels of cadmium above the advisory level. They inform N that further samples have to be checked. N passes this information on to S to explain the delay. S responds with notice of avoidance. N replies and refuses to take the merchandise back. After further examination of the mussels, it is clear that the cadmium level is elevated but not to an extent that is harmful to human health. Meanwhile, the mussels are spoiled.

(19) Seller is located in Poland and buyer is located in France. Buyer acquires 100 tons of apple juice concentrate from the seller. Upon arrival in several rail wagons, buyer does a superficial inspection and then proceeds to mix the concentrate with similar concentrate from other suppliers and to dilute it to juice level and to pack it into tetra pack bricks. When the juice is delivered to F's customers they complain

about sugar and it is discovered that P had added sugar to the concentrate in contravention of the contract that stipulated pure fruit concentrate. It is undisputed that F cannot sell the juice in the existing packaging but could sell it as lower-priced fruit nectar, where the addition of sugar is permitted.

(20) An Italian meat producer and a Greek distributor entered into a contract for delivery of beef of a certain quality. After the meat arrived in Greece, the buyer discovered that the fat content was too high and, therefore, that the meat did not conform to the contracted quality. Consequently, G declared the contract terminated but also offered to purchase the meat at a lower price. When I did not accept the lower price offer and G did not pay the full price, I initiated proceedings against G for nonperformance. G responded with a counterclaim of nonperformance and various claims for damages.

(21) Korean seller K entered into a contract with U.S. buyer U for a supply of compressors to be used in air-conditioning units. K shipped a sample to U in January and, after approval of the sample, U ordered 10,800 units to be delivered in three shipments by May. K sent the first shipment in March and U paid for it. Subsequently, when U installed the compressors into it's a/C units, it was discovered that a majority of the compressors used more energy and produced less cooling capacity than specified in the contract. Meanwhile, a second shipment had been dispatched by K. When U notified K of the inconsistency and demanded supply of conforming quality goods, K responded that the performance specifications had been miscommunicated in the contract negotiations. Eventually, it turned out that 93% of the goods delivered deviated between 5% and 15% from the promised standards. U made a cover transaction to purchase conforming goods from another supplier in Korea, but had to pay more for rush delivery and still lost part of its business in the summer season of that year.

(22) Your New York-based client manufactured a sophisticated machine for the cleaning and canning of sprats, a variety of fish common in the Baltic Sea, for a customer in Russia.

The sales agreement, subject to the CISG, stipulates payment of the purchase price of $1,750,000 DAT St. Petersburg (Russia) by irrevocable letter of credit drawn on a Russian bank and confirmed by Chase Bank in the U.S. upon presentation of an invoice, a certificate from inspection company CERT, the bill of lading and an arrival notice issued by the carrier after the off-loading of the equipment at the port of St. Petersburg.

The Russian buyer emphasized that the time of delivery is important in order to have the machine operational for the very short harvest season in November/December.

The equipment was shipped aboard MS Sonja, which got caught in a storm on the North Atlantic and as a result had to stop in Liverpool (UK) for repairs. The cargo finally arrived in St. Petersburg on October 15, i.e., five days behind schedule.

The buyer had been notified of the delay together with a request to alter the terms of the letter of credit but the buyer refused to do so. When your client presented the unamended documents to Chase, the bank refused payment because the letter of credit required arrival on or before October 10. Your client then offered to the buyer to send a team of technicians to help with the installation, but the buyer refused to take delivery and announced a claim for damages, including at least $100,000 for the acquisition of a more expensive competitor's machine, which cannot possibly arrive before October 30, as well as loss of production in the amount of $75,000 and lost profits of $100,000.

Since there is no general market in Europe for the kind of machine at issue, your client cannot sell it to another buyer without major alterations.

(a) Was the buyer entitled to avoid the contract and was Chase entitled to refuse payment? (See the discussion of letters of credit in Part Three.) What course of action do you recommend to your client?

(b) How would the situation be different, if the INCOTERM® had been CIF St. Petersburg instead of DAT St. Petersburg?

(23) You are an attorney based in Indianapolis. On March 22, you receive an e-mail from Jack Lennox, executive vice president of Industrial Robotics Inc., a long-term client of your firm. Jack has finally managed to reach an agreement with Fiat Motors of Torino, Italy, about delivery of 14 specialized welding robots for automobile assembly lines, to be manufactured by IR according to Fiat specifications, essentially a number of modifications to IR's type WR1520. Fiat has so far always dealt with IR's chief competitor and the deal is of great importance to IR. Jack asks you to draft the contracts for the transaction. Since you are working for IR, the draft has to be in the best interests of IR. However, it also has to include the following terms, which were conditions of Fiat in the negotiations, and it has to avoid any one-sided provisions that might make Fiat change its mind. Jack wants you to explain what you are proposing and to include backup clauses for any conditions that might be unacceptable to Fiat.

(a) IR needs US$890,000 per robot to break even. Fiat has accepted that all expenses necessary for shipping etc. will be added, but insists that these remain as low as possible.

(b) The robots are to be delivered in pairs. Each shipment of two will be in one 20-foot container. IR takes care of loading the robots into the container and of packaging them in a way that will protect them from damage during transit. This is included in the sales price.

(c) On-time delivery is of paramount importance for Fiat, since they will be opening a new production line. The first container with two robots has to be at the factory gate in Torino on the first Monday in May, at the beginning of the 8:00 shift. Subsequent shipments have to arrive in intervals of two to three weeks in sets of two robots in one container.

(d) IR had to agree to arrange shipping all the way to the doorstep of Fiat. However, they would like to keep their risk as low as possible once the robots leave their own factory.

(e) IR has good experience using DFDS, the Danish liner shipping company. DFDS has a container ship leaving Elizabeth, New Jersey, every Tuesday evening and arriving in Rotterdam, the Netherlands, the following Tuesday morning. In order to be on the ship, a container has to be cleared by U.S. customs by Tuesday, 9.45 a.m.

(f) The customs office in Elizabeth works every day, except Sundays, from 6:30 a.m. to 7:30 p.m. The average processing time is four hours, except when there is a line. The robots have to obtain an export license because they might fall under federal restrictions on exportation of high technology.

(g) Storage of containers at the Elizabeth seaport is US$50/day prior to customs clearance and US$450/day in the free zone after customs clearance. The port does not provide insurance.

(h) IR wants to use Eastern Standard Trucking (EST) to pick up the containers at the factory in Ft. Wayne, Indiana, and take them to the port in Elizabeth. EST has a customs agent to deal with the procedures at the customs office. EST charges US$480 for the transport from Ft. Wayne to Elizabeth plus US$140 per hour of waiting on either side, as well as US$500 for the customs clearance.

(i) Fiat suggested that the containers be picked up at the port in Rotterdam by Transalpina Inc., a Swiss trucking company, which also has an agent in Rotterdam for customs clearance for the EU. Transalpina can take care of transit procedures through Switzerland and is obviously aware of restrictions against truck traffic from Saturday 10:00 p.m. to Monday 4:00 a.m. in Europe. Transalpina will charge US$2,900 for the transport of each container from Rotterdam (port) to Torino (factory) plus US$150 per hour of waiting time on either side, as well as US$500 for import clearance into the EU.

(j) After arrival of the first pair of robots, Fiat will notify the date when it requires the next pair. After the arrival of the second pair, it will notify the date when it requires the third pair, etc. Due to space constraints and safety considerations, Fiat does not want the containers to arrive at its facilities more than an hour prior to the required time.

(k) American Insurance Group (AIG) charges between 0.3% and 1% of the insured value for container cargo (Institute Cargo Clauses, All Risk), depending on the vulnerability of the cargo and other risk factors.

(l) Jack hopes you will suggest the best way for the payment to be handled and explain it to him.

Jack's worst-case scenario is as follows: A container misses the boat or otherwise is delayed, or a robot arrives damaged after a rough voyage. Fiat might reject the shipment and cancel the entire contract. IR might not get paid and have to take back a custom-built robot from Italy that is hard to sell to anyone else. IR would also have to bury the hope of selling a further 10–20 robots/year to Fiat. *This must not happen*, if at all possible.

Jack would like drafts for the contract of sale, the financing or payment contract, the shipping contract, and the insurance contract, all with explanations of any clauses that are not self-explanatory. Your payment will be US$40,000 for the four contracts.

9116 .*3. Practical Exercises for INCOTERMS 2020®*

(1) Seller S is located in Durham, North Carolina (USA) and Buyer B in Cairo (Egypt). S and B enter into a contract of sale for textbooks for American University Cairo (AUC). S arranges for inland transport to the port of Elizabeth, New Jersey, where the books are to be loaded onto a ship bound for Alexandria, Egypt. When the books get to Elizabeth at the appointed time, the ship is not there yet and the inland carrier hired by S arranges for storage at the port of Elizabeth and notifies both S and B of the storage location where the books should be picked up for loading onto the ship. Before the ship arrives and before S or B can make alternate arrangements, the books are destroyed at the storage facility. S demands payment of the purchase price, payment for inland shipping from Durham to Elizabeth, and payment for the storage at the port of Elizabeth. B does not want to pay anything, since she will now not get the books, and furthermore demands the higher cost of a cover transaction. The books were not insured at the storage facility. What are the rights and obligations of S and B:

(a) with INCOTERM® EXW?

(b) with INCOTERM® FAS?

(c) with INCOTERM® FOB?

(d) with INCOTERM® CIF?

(e) with INCOTERM® CFR?

(f) with INCOTERM® DAP Alexandria?

(g) with INCOTERM® DDP Cairo?

(2) The same scenario as above, with the following modification: the books are loaded and the ship leaves Elizabeth as planned. However, when it arrives in Alexandria, there is no one to receive the goods and they are put into storage in Alexandria and notifications are sent to S and B. Before the truck arrives that is supposed to take the books to Cairo and before S or B can make alternative arrangements, the books are destroyed at the storage facility in Alexandria. What are the rights and obligations of S and B:

(a) with INCOTERM® EXW?

(b) with INCOTERM® FAS?

(c) with INCOTERM® FOB?

(d) with INCOTERM® CIF?

(e) with INCOTERM® CFR?

(f) with INCOTERM® DPU Alexandria?

(g) with INCOTERM® DDP Cairo?

Section 8. Drafting an Actual Contract of Sale

Having discussed the important considerations that are specific to *international* business transactions, we shall now put together an entire contract of sale with all required elements. This is intended as a model contract, to be modified and adapted in each individual case. Together with the explanations provided, the reader should be able to make intelligent choices for every contract term in standard international sales or export/import transaction. Obviously, one model cannot possibly capture every possible variation, in particular if an IBT no longer follows the four corner model we have outlined at the outset of this Part (p. 74). However, even for nonstandard transactions, the model provides many useful tips and suggestions for contract terms.

Some further remarks before we get going:

• First, whenever drafting or reviewing a contract, remember the goals of brevity, clarity, and fairness. This model is brief, clear, and fair. The 85-page sample on the server at your law firm probably meets none of these criteria. As a rule, if you don't know exactly what a particular provision in a contract is supposed to do, rephrase or delete it.

• Second, the model is just that: a model. Success comes from the intelligent adaptation of the model to the specifics of the IBT you are working on. Never cut and paste without knowing exactly what you are doing.

• Third, the model is primarily intended for sellers as the drafting party. However, it is also intended for review by buyers. Furthermore, it can easily be adapted if the buyer is not just reviewing and partly rewriting a seller draft but coming up with a comprehensive draft of her own. Depending on who is doing the drafting, some sections may need to be expanded. For example, the buyer may want more specific descriptions of the goods, as well as statements as to suitability for purpose and/or specific metrics of performance, output, and the like. On the other hand, the seller may want to include limited or unlimited warranties, etc. As always, each side should know exactly what it is doing and delete any promises it does not intend to make and any provisions that are not needed and may be misunderstood.

Sample Document 2-4

International Sales Contract for Manufactured Goods [1]　　page 1 of 8

©Prof. Dr. Frank Emmert, LL.M., FCIArb

Part A: INDIVIDUALLY NEGOTIATED TERMS [2]　　　　Date ....[3]

1. SELLER Company Name & Logo

Authorized Representative ....[4]	Contact Person [5] ....
Street Address	Seller's Contract Number ....[6]
City, Zip Code & Country	
Phone, Fax and e-mail	PO or other Buyer Reference ....[7]

2. BUYER

Principal Buyer [8]　　　　　　　　　　　　　**Destination for Shipping [9]**

Company Name	Company Name ....
Contact Person	Contact Person ....
Street Address	Street Address ....
City, Zip Code & Country	City, Zip Code & Country ....
Phone, Fax and e-mail	Phone, Fax and e-mail ....

3. DESCRIPTION OF GOODS SOLD

Part #	Unit of Measure [10]	Description [11]	Unit Price	x Quantity	= Net Price

Total # of Pieces / Packages / Containers / Pallets: [16]	= Subtotal [12]	
Estimated Net Weight and/or Volume: [17]	- Discount [13] (current transaction only)	
Packaging Specifics: [18]	+ Tax, Carriage, Insurance and any other costs [14]	
Estimated Gross Weight and/or Volume: [19]	= Total Payable by Buyer w/Currency [15]	
	in words	

4. PLACE OF DELIVERY & PASSING OF RISK

Shipping Details

Mode of Transport ....[20]	Place or Port of Departure ....[21]
INCOTERM 2020® ....[22]	Place or Port of Arrival ....[23]
Shipping Date ....[24]	Delivery Date&Time at Place or Port of Arrival ....[25]

Time and Place of Passing of Risk [26]

Time of Delivery (Month, Calendar Week, Exact Date, Exact Time) ....
Agreed Place of Delivery ....
☐ Timely Delivery is Essential to Buyer [27]

First Carrier in Seller's Country [28]

Company Name	Contact Person ....
Street Address	City, Zip Code & Country ....
Phone, Fax and e-mail	

Main or International or Maritime Carrier [29]
Company Name ....   Contact Person ....
Street Address ....   City, Zip Code & Country ....
Phone, Fax and e-mail ....

Final or Delivering Carrier in Buyer's Country [30]
Company Name ....   Contact Person ....
Street Address ....   City, Zip Code & Country ....
Phone, Fax and e-mail ....

5. INSPECTION OF THE GOODS (depending on the type of goods and customs in the industry, a standard for the inspection may have to be provided or referred to) [31]

☐ by the Buyer [32]
     ☐ Before Shipment   Time and Place . . . .
     ☐ Other   Time and Place . . . .
☐ by the Following Third Party [33]

     at the Expense of . . . .
. . . .   Time and Place . . . .

6. RETENTION OF TITLE [34]

☐ Yes   until. . . . .
☐ No

7. REQUIRED DOCUMENTS (this should conform to the selected INCOTERM® and Letter of Credit) [35]

a) Documents to Be Provided by the **Seller** [36]
☐ Transport Documents, namely . . . .
☐ Commercial Invoice   ☐ Packing List
☐ Certificate of Origin   ☐ Certificate of Quality Inspection by . . . .
☐ Health or Sanitary or Phytosanitary Inspection Certificate
☐ Export License   ☐ Import License
☐ Insurance Document   ☐ Other . . . .

b) Documents to Be Provided by the **Buyer** [37]
☐ Transport Documents, namely . . . .
☐ Certificate of Origin   ☐ Certificate of Quality Inspection by . . . .
☐ Health or Sanitary or Phytosanitary Inspection Certificate
☐ Export License   ☐ Import License
☐ Insurance Document   ☐ Other . . . .

8. PAYMENT TERMS [38]

☐ **Payment in Advance** by Electronic Funds Transfer EFT before controlling documents are sent to buyer
     by Date ....   ☐ Total price   ☐ .... % of total price
     Account No. ....   Bank Name ....
     Acc. Holder ....   Bank Address ....   SWIFT ....

☐ **Irrevocable Documentary Credit**   ☐ confirmed   ☐ unconfirmed
     Bank & Place of Issue . . . .
     Bank & Place of Confirmation (if applicable) . . . .
     Credit Available
          ☐ by Payment at Sight
          ☐ by Deferred Payment, ... days
          ☐ by Acceptance of Drafts, ... days
          ☐ by Negotiation

Partial shipments   □ allowed   □ not allowed
Transhipment   □ allowed   □ not allowed
Date on which the documentary credit must be notified to seller ....
[unless otherwise specified, 30 days before the beginning of the delivery period]

□ **Documentary Collection**
      □ D/P Documents Against Payment   □ D/A Documents Against Acceptance
      Collection Instructions ....
      Other Details ....

□ **Payment on Open Account** by Electronic Funds Transfer EFT after controlling documents are sent to and received by buyer
      Time for Payment ....   days from Date of Invoice   Other ....
      Account No. .... Bank Name ....
      Acc. Holder .... Bank Address .... SWIFT ....
      □ Open Account Backed by Demand Guarantee or Standby Letter of Credit

9. WARRANTIES AND LIABILITIES

Seller Warranties [39]

Seller warrants that the goods are merchantable, shall pass without objection in the trade under contract, and fit for the ordinary purposes for which goods of that description are used. The goods are of the quantity and quality described in this contract and any variations are within permitted or customary tolerances. The goods will be adequately contained, packaged, and labeled as required by this contract and the stipulated mode of transport. The goods will conform to any affirmations of fact made on the container or label, if any. Seller makes no express or implied warranties beyond these affirmations, unless explicitly stipulated here: ....

Liability for Late Payment by Buyer [40]

□   In case of delayed payment by buyer, interest shall be payable at a rate of .... % above the average bank short-term lending rate for prime borrowers prevailing for the currency of payment at the place of payment.
□   Other ....

Liability for Late Delivery by Seller [41]

Liquidated damages for delay in delivery shall be
□   .... % of price of delayed goods per week,
with a maximum of .... % of delayed goods
□   specific amount .... currency ....
In case of termination for delay, seller's liability for damages for delay shall be limited to
□   .... % of price of delayed goods
□   specific amount .... currency ....

Liability for Non-Conforming Goods [42]

Seller's aggregate liability for damages, including loss of profit, any and all consequential damages, court and attorney fees, and other costs of enforcement of rights and obligations, etc., arising from lack of conformity of the goods shall be
□   limited to proven loss (incl. consequential loss, loss of profit etc.) and not exceeding ....% of the contract price;
□   limited to insurance coverage available at the time of settlement or judgment;
□   determined as follows ....

Limitation of Liability Where Non-Conforming Goods Are Retained by the Buyer [43]

Any price abatement for retained non-conforming goods shall
□   not exceed .... % of the price of such goods
□   be determined as follows ....

Time-Bar [44]

☐   Buyer has to inspect goods immediately upon arrival and notify any lack of conformity in the time and place of delivery, quality or quantity of the goods, or any accompanying documents within .... [hours/days] **of arrival**. Any non-conformity that was undetectable upon arrival has to be notified within .... [hours/days] **of discovery** and in any case no later than .... [weeks/months/years] of arrival.

☐   Any action for non-conformity of the goods must be taken by the buyer not later than ....[days] from the date of arrival of the goods at the destination.

☐   Before any action for non-conformity of the goods is taken, the buyer has to notify the seller and provide an opportunity for the seller to cure the lack of conformity.

Cancellation Date [45]

If the goods are not delivered for any reason whatsoever (including force majeure) by ....[date] the buyer is entitled to cancel the contract immediately by notification to the seller.

10. CHOICE OF LAW AND FORUM

Resolution of Disputes [46]

☐ Any disputes arising out of this contract or the underlying business transaction shall be resolved exclusively by arbitration

        ☐   Institutional arbitration under the rules and auspices of .... institution

        ☐   ad hoc arbitration under UNCITRAL Rules

If the parties can agree on a sole arbitrator, the arbitration shall proceed accordingly. If agreement is not forthcoming within 14 days, each side nominates one arbitrator and the two shall then agree on the presiding arbitrator.

The seat of the arbitration shall be ....

The language of the arbitration shall be ....

        ☐   The parties shall not resort to arbitration unless good faith attempts to resolve the dispute with the help of a mediator have not produced a satisfactory result within 45 / 60 / 90 days.

☐ Any disputes arising out of this contract or the underlying business transaction shall be subject to litigation in the ordinary courts of . . . .

Applicable Law [47]

This sales contract and all related aspects of the business relationship between the parties shall be

☐   governed by the CISG. Any questions not covered by the CISG shall be governed by the domestic law of .... *→ not federal law in US*

☐   governed by the domestic law of .... without CISG *exclude expressly*

☐   governed by .... Any questions not covered by this international set of rules shall be governed by the domestic law of . . . .

11. ADDITIONAL TERMS AGREED UPON BETWEEN THE SELLER AND THE BUYER [48]

☐   Applicability of our General Conditions of Sale (see below pp. 5-8) to the extent they are compatible with the specific agreements on pp. 1-4.

☐   The following Annexes are an integral part of this Contract . . . .

☐   other . . . .

12. MERGER CLAUSE [49]

☐   This is the entire agreement between the parties and supersedes any communications, negotiations, and agreements with respect to its subject matter prior to its conclusion. Any subsequent agreements and modifications must be in writing and signed by duly authorized representatives of both parties.

☐   other . . . .

ex. email, communication

For the Seller   **For the Buyer**
Authorized Signature [50]   Authorized signature

. . . .
Name and Title   Name and Title

. . . .
Date and Place   Date and Place

. . . .

Part B: GENERAL CONDITIONS
Based on ICC General Conditions of Sale (Manufactured Goods Intended for Resale) [51]

Art. 1 General
1.1 These General Conditions are intended to supplement the Specific Conditions (pages 1-4 of the present contract). In case of contradiction between these General Conditions and any Specific Conditions agreed upon between the parties, the specific conditions shall prevail.
1.2 Any questions relating to this contract which are not expressly or implicitly settled by the provisions contained in the contract itself (i.e. these General Conditions and any specific conditions agreed upon by the parties) shall be governed: [52]
A.   by the United Nations Convention on Contracts for the International Sale of Goods (Vienna Convention of 1980, hereafter referred to as CISG), and
B.   to the extent that such questions are not covered by CISG, by reference to the law of the country where the Seller has his place of business.
1.3 Any reference made to trade terms (such as EXW, FCA, etc.) is deemed to be made to the relevant term of the INCOTERMS® published by the International Chamber of Commerce.
1.4 Any reference made to a publication of the International Chamber of Commerce is deemed to be made to the version current at the date of conclusion of the Contract.
1.5 No modification of the Contract is valid unless agreed or evidenced in writing. However, a party may be precluded by his conduct from asserting this provision to the extent that the other party has relied on that conduct. [53]

Art. 2 Characteristics of the Goods
2.1 It is agreed that any information relating to the goods and their use, such as weights, dimensions, capacities, prices, colors and other data contained in catalogues, prospectuses, circulars, websites, advertisements, illustrations, price-lists of the Seller, shall not take effect as terms of the contract unless expressly referred to in the Contract. [54]
2.2 Unless otherwise agreed, the Buyer does not acquire any property rights in software, drawings, etc. which may have been made available to him. The Seller also remains the exclusive owner of any intellectual or industrial property rights relating to the goods. [55]

Art. 3 Inspection of the Goods Before Shipment [56]
If the parties have agreed that the Buyer is entitled to inspect the goods before shipment, the Seller must notify the Buyer within a reasonable time before the shipment that the goods are ready for inspection at the agreed place.

Art. 4 Price [57]
4.1 If no price has been agreed, the Seller's current list price at the time of the conclusion of the Contract shall apply. In the absence of such a current price, the price generally charged for such goods at the time of the conclusion of the Contract shall apply.
4.2 Unless otherwise agreed in writing, the price does not include VAT, and is not subject to price adjustment.
4.3 The price indicated under [20] (contract price) includes any costs which are at the Seller's charge according to this Contract. However, should the Seller bear any costs which, according to this Contract, are for the Buyer's account (e.g. for transportation or insurance under EXW or FCA), such sums shall not be considered as having been included in the price under [20] and shall be reimbursed separately by the Buyer.

Art. 5 Payment Conditions

5.1 Unless otherwise agreed in writing, or implied from a prior course of dealing between the parties, payment of the price and of any other sums due by the Buyer to the Seller shall be on open account and time of payment shall be 30 days from the date of invoice. The amounts due shall be transferred, unless otherwise agreed, by teletransmission to the Seller's bank in the sellers country for the account of the Seller and the Buyer shall be deemed to have performed his payment obligations when the respective sums due have been received by the Seller's bank in immediately available funds. [58]

5.2 If the parties have agreed on payment in advance, without further indication, it will be assumed that such advance payment, unless otherwise agreed, refers to the full price, and that the advance payment must be received by the Seller's bank in immediately available funds at least 30 days before the agreed date of delivery or the earliest date within the agreed delivery period. If advance payment has been agreed only for a part of the contract price, the payment conditions of the remaining amount will be determined according to the rules set forth in this article.[59]

5.3 If the parties have agreed on payment by documentary credit, then, unless otherwise agreed, the Buyer must arrange for a documentary credit in favor of the Seller to be issued by a reputable bank, subject to the Uniform Customs and Practice for Documentary Credits published by the International Chamber of Commerce (UCP600), and to be notified at least 30 days before the agreed date of delivery or at least 30 days before the earliest date within the agreed delivery period. Unless otherwise agreed, the documentary credit shall be payable at sight and allow partial shipments and transshipments. [60]

5.4 If the parties have agreed on payment by documentary collection, then unless otherwise agreed, documents will be tendered against payment (D/P) and the tender will in any case be subject to the Uniform Rules for Collections published by the International Chamber of Commerce (URC522). [61]

5.5 To the extent that the parties have agreed that payment is to be backed by a bank guarantee, the Buyer is to provide, at least 30 days before the agreed date of delivery or at least 30 days before the earliest date within the agreed delivery period, a first demand bank guarantee subject to the Uniform Rules for Demand Guarantees published by the International Chamber of Commerce (URDG758), or a standby letter of credit subject either to such Rules or to the Uniform Customs and Practice for Documentary Credits published by the International Chamber of Commerce, in either case issued by a reputable bank. [62]

Art. 6 Interest in Case of Delayed Payment [63]

6.1 If a party does not pay a sum of money when it falls due the other party is entitled to interest upon that sum from the time when payment is due to the time of payment.

6.2 Unless otherwise agreed, the rate of interest shall be 2% above the average bank short-term lending rate to prime borrowers prevailing for the currency of payment at the place of payment, or where no such rate exists at that place, then the same rate in the State of the currency of payment. In the absence of such a rate at either place the rate of interest shall be the appropriate rate fixed by the law of the State of the currency of payment.

Art. 7 Retention of Title [64]

If the parties have validly agreed on retention of title, the goods shall remain the property of the Seller until the complete payment of the price, or as otherwise agreed.

Art. 8 Contractual Term of Delivery [65]

Unless otherwise agreed, delivery shall be "Ex Works" (EXW).

Art. 9 Documents [66]

Unless otherwise agreed, the Seller must provide the documents (if any) indicated in the applicable INCOTERM® or, if no INCOTERM® is applicable, according to any previous course of dealing.

Art. 10 Late-Delivery, Non-Delivery and Remedies Therefor [67]

10.1 When there is delay in delivery of any goods, the Buyer is entitled to claim liquidated damages equal to 0.5% or such other percentage as may be agreed of the price of those goods for each complete week of delay, provided the Buyer notifies the Seller of the delay. Where the Buyer so notifies the Seller within 15 days from the agreed date of delivery, damages will run from the agreed date of delivery or from the last day within the agreed period of delivery. Where the Buyer so notifies the Seller after 15 days of the agreed date of delivery, damages will run from the date of the notice. Liquidated damages for delay shall not exceed 5% of the price of the delayed goods or such other maximum amount as may be agreed.

10.2 If the parties have agreed upon a cancellation date in [44], the Buyer may terminate the contract by notification to the Seller as regards goods which have not been delivered by such cancellation date for any reason whatsoever (including a force majeure event).

10.3 When article 10.2 does not apply and the Seller has not delivered the goods by the date on which the Buyer has become entitled to the maximum amount of liquidated damages under article 10.1, the Buyer may give notice in writing to terminate the contract as regards such goods, if they have not been delivered to the Buyer within 5 days of receipt of such notice by the Seller.

10.4 In case of termination of the contract under article 10.2 or 10.3 then in addition to any amount paid or payable under article 10.1 the Buyer is entitled to claim damages for any additional loss not exceeding 10% of the price of the nondelivered goods.

10.5 The remedies under this article are exclusive of any other remedy for delay in delivery or nondelivery.

Art. 11 Nonconformity of the Goods [68]

11.1 The Buyer shall examine the goods as soon as possible after their arrival at destination and shall notify the Seller in writing of any lack of conformity of the goods within 15 days from the date when the Buyer discovers or ought to have discovered the lack of conformity. In any case the Buyer shall nave no remedy for lack of conformity if he fails to notify the Seller thereof within 12 months from the date of arrival of the goods at the agreed destination.

11.2 Goods will be deemed to conform to the contract despite minor discrepancies which are usual in the particular trade or through course of dealing between the parties but the Buyer will be entitled to any abatement of the price usual in the trade or through course of dealing for such discrepancies.

11.3 Where goods are nonconforming (and provided the Buyer, having given notice of the lack of conformity in compliance with article 11.1, does not elect in the notice to retain them), the Seller shall at his option:

(a)   replace the goods with conforming goods, without any additional expense to the Buyer, or

(b)   repair the goods, without any additional expense to the Buyer, or

(c)   reimburse to the Buyer the price paid for the nonconforming goods and thereby terminate the contract as regards those goods.

The Buyer will be entitled to liquidated damages as quantified under article 10.1 for each complete week of delay between the date of notification of the nonconformity according to article 11.1 and the supply of substitute goods under article 11.3 (a) or repair under article 11.3 (b) above. Such damages may be accumulated with damages (if any) payable under article 10.1, but can in no case exceed in the aggregate 5% of the price of those goods.

11.4 If the Seller has failed to perform his duties under 11.3 by the date on which the Buyer becomes entitled to the maximum amount of liquidated damages according to that article, the Buyer may give notice in writing to terminate the contract as regards the nonconforming goods unless the supply of replacement goods or the repair is effected within 5 days of receipt of such notice by the Seller.

11.5 Where the Contract is terminated under article 11.3 (c) or article 11.4, then in addition to any amount paid or payable under art.11.3 as reimbursement of the price and damages for any delay, the Buyer is entitled to damages for any additional loss not exceeding 10% of the price of the nonconforming goods.

11.6 Where the Buyer elects to retain nonconforming goods, he shall be entitled to a sum equal to the difference between the value of the goods at the agreed place of destination if they had conformed with the Contract and their value at the same place as delivered, such sum not to exceed 15% of the price of those goods.

11.7 Unless otherwise agreed in writing, the remedies under this article 11 are exclusive of any other remedy for nonconformity.

11.8 Unless otherwise agreed in writing, no action for lack of conformity can be taken by the Buyer, whether before judicial or arbitral tribunals, after 2 years from the date of arrival of the goods. It is expressly agreed that after the expiration of such term, the Buyer will not plead nonconformity of the goods, or make a counterclaim thereon, in defense to any action taken by the Seller against the Buyer for nonperformance of this Contract.

Art. 12 Cooperation between the Parties [69]

12.1 The Buyer shall promptly inform the Seller of any claim made against the Buyer by his customers or third parties concerning the goods delivered or intellectual property rights related thereto.

12.2 The Seller will promptly inform the Buyer of any claim which may involve the product liability of the Buyer.

Art. 13 Force Majeure [70]

13.1 A party is not liable for a failure to perform any of his obligations in so far as he proves

(a)   that the failure was due to an impediment beyond his control, and

(b)   that he could not reasonable be expected to have taken the impediment and its effects upon his ability to perform into account at the time of the conclusion of the contract, and

(c)   that he could not reasonably have avoided or overcome it or its effects.

13.2 A party seeking relief shall, as soon as practicable after the impediment and its effects upon his ability to perform become known to him, give notice to the other party of such impediment and its effects on his ability to perform. Notice shall also be given when the ground of relief ceases.

Failure to give either notice makes the party thus failing liable in damages for loss which otherwise could have been avoided.

13.3 Without prejudice to article 10.2, a ground of relief under this clause relieves the party failing to perform from liability in damages, from penalties and other contractual sanctions, and from the duty to pay interest on money owing, as long as and to the extent that the ground subsists.

13.4 If the grounds of relief subsist for more than six months, either party shall be entitled to terminate the contract without notice.

Art. 14 Resolution of Disputes [71]

14.1 Unless otherwise agreed in writing, all disputes arising in connection with the present contract shall be finally settled under the Rules of Arbitration of the International Chamber of Commerce by one or more arbitrators appointed in accordance with the said Rules.

14.2 An arbitration clause does not prevent any party from requesting interim or conservatory measures from the courts.

Sales Contract Explained: (see Sample Document 2-4)

Suitability of this model contract: The model was designed for one-off contracts for the sale of manufactured goods [1]. It has to be suitably adjusted for sales transactions involving significant service components, for example, the installation of equipment at buyer's premises or the training of buyer's operators. The same is true for contracts envisaging a long-term business relationship, including repeat delivery or subscription contracts and, in particular, if an exclusive supplier or distributor relationship is intended.

A. Individually Negotiated Terms: The individually negotiated terms [2], sometimes casually referred to as the "front of the contract," have to be modified for each IBT. They are distinguished from general terms or conditions, sometimes referred to as the small print on "the back of the contract," which a company will often include in each IBT without review or adjustment. If there is an inconsistency between the front and the back, individually negotiated terms overrule inconsistent general terms.

Sustainable business relationships based on win-win interactions require general terms without surprises and individually negotiated terms reflecting, to the greatest possible extent, the real requirements and intentions of the parties. In particular, if there is an imbalance of power, information, or experience between the parties, it is important to communicate clearly and negotiate fairly to ensure genuine and unforced agreement. An imbalance may result from one party having a monopoly on the goods or services based on intellectual property rights, or because the other party has little or no experience in international business, or because one side works in her native English, while the other struggles with English as her third or fourth language. The party drafting the contract or proposing certain clauses should also remember the principle of *contra proferentem*, pursuant to which an ambiguous provision in a contract, in case of a dispute, will be interpreted against the drafter, see, e.g., § 206 of the Restatement.

Date: Every contract needs to be dated [3]. The date is important for many reasons, including references to "the contract of May 15," deadlines to be set in motion, as well as the exclusion of prior communications from influencing the rights and obligations of the parties per the merger clause in #12. The date at the top will be the relevant date, even if the signatures at the bottom are dated differently, because the parties, by signing, agree on the date stipulated here.

1. Seller's Name and Contact Information: The seller is the natural or legal person who is bound by the contract. In particular, if negotiations are conducted by representatives of the parent company and a subsidiary, or if more than two parties are otherwise involved, it is important to identify the seller in unambiguous terms. Whenever the seller is a corporate entity, there should also be the name, phone number, and e-mail address of the person authorized to sign [4] and the contact person [5] to send or receive any communication regarding the transaction. This avoids disputes over messages sent by one party but not received in time by the right person at the other. If the person conducting the negotiations (authorized representative) is not a high-ranking employee of the seller, he or she should present a power of attorney or other proof of authority to be negotiating on behalf of the seller. In the absence of actual or apparent authority, the principal is not bound unless she ratifies the actions of the agent.

Identifiers for seller and buyer: Most companies today use numeric identifiers for every contract and other forms sent out to potential business partners. It is useful not only to add the identifiers of the party drafting the agreement [6], but also the reference number of any prior orders or offers it responds to [7].

2. Buyer's Name and Contact Information: Same as [4]. Additional ambiguity can arise if the goods are purchased by one natural or legal person [8] for delivery to another [9]. The entity identified as the buyer is the one who pays the purchase price. It may make sense in such a case to mention here that the goods are "for delivery to [third party]." Ambiguous language such as "x on behalf of y" is to be avoided.

3. Description of Goods Sold: The contract of sale supersedes all prior communications between the parties, see below [49]. This includes any indicators of suitability of the goods for particular purposes or promises of performance, whether made on the website or in other marketing materials, or even in letters, faxes, e-mails, or phone conversations between the parties. Thus, both sides have a strong interest in incorporating in the description of the goods [10] and/or the warranties [39] everything the seller is promising to deliver and everything the buyer is expecting for the successful execution of the IBT. The buyer, in particular, should ensure that any promises made earlier regarding qualities of the goods, quantity, suitability, performance, durability, etc. are incorporated here. The seller, on the other hand, should ensure that he does not promise anything he cannot or does not plan to deliver and that any promises regarding ancillary services, such as special packaging [17], extended warranties [39], etc. are reflected in the overall contract price.

The interests of the parties are not identical with regard to the description of the goods. While the buyer will often want more specific descriptions, including affirmations of suitability for a given purpose, as well as performance metrics or standards, the seller will prefer to avoid detailed descriptions and affirmations that may increase the risk of less-than-perfect tender of performance.

To avoid disappointment on either side, let alone a dispute between the parties, it is imperative that the parties understand all expenses involved in the transaction, in particular for the shipping of the goods on the one side and the transfer of payment on the other. Once the parties have a clear understanding of all performance elements and their respective costs, they have to agree: (i) which performance elements are the seller's responsibility and compensated within the price of the goods, (ii) which performance elements are the seller's responsibility, but to be compensated by the buyer in addition to the price of the goods, and (iii) which performance elements are the buyer's responsibility and neither compensated by seller nor deductible from the price of the goods. The contract price is the total price payable by the buyer [15] and should include full compensation for all obligations of the seller (a and b above). To avoid ambiguities, it is recommended that the price be broken down into key elements such as price per unit, number of units [10], corresponding total price of the goods [12], any discounts granted on the current purchase [13], any payments to be made in addition by the buyer for packing and handling, freight and/or insurance, as well as any sales or other taxes to be paid by the buyer separately from the list price per unit [14]. Unless otherwise specified, the parties should understand that the contract price also covers the cost of any warranties given by the seller [39], inspection by a third party [33], whenever the seller has agreed to organize and pay for this, any costs incurred by the seller with regard to payment conditions, in particular incoming wire fees of seller's bank and/or the fees of seller's bank or another bank in seller's country for advising or confirming a letter of credit [38], as well as the cost of procuring any documents for which the seller is responsible [36].

4. Place of Delivery and Passing of Risk: A majority of problems related to shipping of the goods occur at the time and place when responsibilities are handed over from one party to another. For example, if the seller is supposed to deliver FOB on a certain vessel at a certain place and time, the truck may get stuck in traffic and the ship may be gone when the truck finally arrives at the port. Conversely, when the truck arrives on time, the ship may not be there yet and the driver may have to unload and store the cargo. To ensure that responsibilities can be allocated correctly and fairly and without having to go to dispute settlement, it is important to specify those responsibilities, and when and where they switch from the seller to the buyer, as far as possible. This includes the anticipated mode(s) of transport [20], the place or port of departure/origin [21], the INCOTERM® [22], the agreed-upon place or port of arrival/destination [23], the date when the goods are supposed to be sent out by the seller [24], and the calendar week, day, or time of day when they are supposed to arrive [25].

Once again, the interests of the parties are not identical with regard to the time and place of delivery of the goods. While the buyer will often have a preference for a very specific (and early) time of delivery, tight deadlines and a high level of specificity can be problematic for a seller who still has to acquire or manufacture the goods and bring them to the place of delivery. In some industries, it is still customary to specify only the calendar week when delivery has to be made and leave the detailed arrangements to the parties for subsequent specification. In other industries, where "just in time" delivery is required to minimize buyer's need to hold inventory, the time of delivery may be specified down to the hour and the minute. Also, if the seller has to organize and pay for shipping, he may want flexibility with regard to carriers and routes to be able to negotiate a favorable deal. By contrast, the buyer will want only reputable carriers involved without having to pay extra. Who gets what will depend on the sophistication of the negotiators and their respective bargaining power.

The responsibilities of the parties and the time and place when the risk of loss or damage passes from the seller to the buyer are determined by the selected

INCOTERM® [22]. At this point, you should review Chart 2-2 on p. 242, the Delivery Chain, to be reminded about all the steps it takes to get the goods from the seller's premises to the buyer's premises. If there is a problem, in particular if there is a delay during shipping, or the goods are damaged or lost, be sure to identify on this Chart exactly where the problem occurred. This will make it easier to decide who bears responsibility for the problem.

Under the CISG and in most Continental European legal systems, a relatively minor delay is not considered a fundamental breach by the seller and entitles the buyer only to damages but not to avoidance of the contract. This is different, however, if the buyer indicates and the seller accepts that timely delivery is essential [27].

The standard under the UCC is generally stricter on account of the perfect tender rule in §2-601 pursuant to which the seller's tender of delivery must not "fail in any respect to conform to the contract." This includes the time of delivery and potentially entitles the buyer to avoid the contract for delay. However, the provision is moderated by §2-504, pursuant to which the buyer can often reject the contract only "if material delay or loss ensues." As with the CISG, buyers can insist on and sellers can accept a stricter standard. This will be binding and entitle the buyer to additional damages and/or avoidance, as long as it is clearly reflected in the contract.

Not all details of the shipping need to be specified in every contract. However, it is highly advisable that at least the parties that have to make the handshake at the time and place when the risk passes are clearly identified [25], [26]. For example, if the INCOTERM® is FOB, the responsibilities and risk pass when the goods are loaded onto the ship in the seller's port. This is where "delivery" in conformity with the contract should happen. However, the parties themselves are rarely present when the goods are loaded at the port. They rely on agents, namely the local or first carrier [28], who takes the goods to the port (seller's agent under FOB), and the maritime or main carrier [29], who takes the goods across the international border (buyer's agent under FOB). By contrast, the identity of the final or delivering carrier, who receives the goods at the buyer's port and delivers them to the buyer's premises [30], is of little or no interest to the seller under FOB.

5. Inspection of the Goods: The seller will always inspect the goods to protect himself and his reputation. However, for the buyer this may not be enough, in particular if payment has to be made in advance or if collection against documents or credit is foreseen before the goods arrive at the buyer's premises. The buyer has several options to protect her interests. First, she can inspect the goods herself or send an agent or trusted business partner to do so [32]. Second, she may bring in a professional inspection company [33]. For practical matters, it also has to be decided where and when the inspection will take place and who has to pay for it. Since the inspection is in the interests of the buyer, the basic assumption is that the buyer will bear the costs of the inspection unless the contract specifically stipulates otherwise. The parties should consider the options carefully to avoid delays and extra expenses—for example, if the goods have to be unloaded and unpacked en route for the inspection.

In certain industries and for certain types of goods or commodities, there are customary or international standards or procedures for the inspection [31]. Companies such as Intertek or SGS provide so-called "Q and Q" inspections (quantity and quality) pursuant to whatever the parties may require and/or relevant international standards.[120] Certain countries also require pre-shipment inspections regardless of the agreement between the parties to safeguard against substandard, let alone dangerous, goods arriving at their ports.

6. Retention of Title: Provision [34] creates a kind of conditional sale. The seller retains title or ownership of the goods until full and timely payment is made by the buyer. Upon full payment, the seller's title disappears (resolving condition), and the buyer automatically obtains title and ownership. Prior to full payment, the buyer is not without rights either, since the seller cannot easily transfer the goods to a third party. Dalhuisen, for example, argues that the buyer initially obtains a kind of title, too, however, pending full payment (suspending condition).[121] The question whether the buyer can pay early to complete his rights and deal with the goods like an owner depends on the applicable sales law; see, for example, Article III.-2:103 CFR. Of greater importance in practice is the question what happens when the buyer is late with payment. Contractual rights must be sought in the applicable sales law, for example Articles 61–64, 25, 81, 84 CISG. As owner, the seller can additionally pursue rights based on property.

In international transactions, the reservation of title is not always of much use, even if the buyer does not pay at all or pays so late or so little that it entitles the seller to recover the goods. In addition to the problems this may cause in a domestic setting, if the goods have been processed or commingled in buyer's business or sold onward by the buyer (compare Article 82 CISG; §§ 2-403, 7-205 and 9-320 UCC), any property rights in the goods would have to be pursued wherever the goods are now located, most likely in buyer's country. Whether this will be promising, in particular whether the goods can be seized via a prejudgment writ of attachment or a temporary restraining order or similar interim or conservatory measures, depends on the method of dispute settlement agreed upon by the parties and the applicable law (for details, see Part Six).

7. Required Documents: By definition, an IBT results in the movement of goods across an international border. This has always necessitated additional documents that are not needed for domestic transport, in particular for customs processing. Trade embargoes on certain goods and countries for political reasons, as well as restrictions on the movement of certain goods for security reasons, have added to the

---

120. See, for example, https://www.sgs.com/-/media/global/documents/brochures/sgs-gis-psi-guidelines-for-exporters-09-en-a4.pdf.

121. See Jan H. Dalhuisen: *Dalhuisen on Transnational Comparative, Commercial, Financial and Trade Law, Vol. II Contract and Movable Property Law,* Hart Publishing 4th ed. 2010, p. 457.

bureaucratic complexity of these kinds of transactions. In practice, if certain documents are missing or incomplete, goods are likely going to be held up at the border, either upon exportation or importation, or both. If this happens, it invariably causes delays, extra work, and extra expenses. In extreme cases, the goods may be so much delayed that they are no longer of interest to the buyer or they may never arrive. It is, therefore, of great importance that the parties be aware of all required documents and come to a clear understanding of who has to provide what. Ideally, they should also divide the responsibilities in a way that corresponds to practical and economic realities, i.e., charge the seller with the provision of documents that only the seller [36] can provide (commercial invoice, packing list), and documents that are much easier for the seller to obtain (in general, documents to be procured from the authorities in the seller's country, such as certificates of origin and export licenses).

By contrast, the buyer [37] should be charged with the procurement of documents that are much easier for her to obtain (in general, documents to be procured from the authorities in the buyer's country, such as import licenses).

If one of the parties is much more experienced in the field of international business transactions and international shipping of goods, she may agree to a different distribution of responsibilities and handle even some of the formalities in the other country by relying on established practices and contacts. This would generally be considered a concession and may need to be reflected in the price.

Importantly, the distribution of responsibilities agreed upon by the parties here should correspond to the distribution of responsibilities agreed upon elsewhere. Every commercial Letter of Credit also contains a list of documents to be presented by the seller at the bank in order to get paid. If the list in the contract of sale is different from the list in the L/C, the seller will have to procure one set of documents to get paid and a different set to meet his contractual obligations. Another issue to pay attention to is the INCOTERM® and the distribution of responsibilities and risks it provides. All of these should be in harmony.

8. Payment Terms: The parties have numerous options on how and when payment should be made from the buyer to the seller. These are outlined and compared in Chart 3-1 on p. 412 and explained in detail in Part Three. The most suitable option depends on many factors, including the level of trust between the parties, the importance of the amount at issue relative to the size of the companies involved, i.e., whether a significant delay or a default by the buyer could become a major or even existential issue for the seller, whether the seller or a third party grant extra time for payment by the buyer, i.e., provide credit, and the cost of a particular mode of payment. As a rule of thumb, the higher the level of security for the seller and/or the longer the credit until the buyer has to pay, the more expensive the transaction will be. Four options are most commonly used in practice:

• **Payment or cash in advance** requires the buyer to wire the money or send a check or bank draft (certified check) *before* the seller does anything. While this method is inexpensive, it provides no security to the buyer. Since the buyer has to advance her performance, she is essentially financing the transaction. In practice, this method is used mainly if the seller needs advance payment to be able to acquire or manufacture the goods. Most often, only a percentage of the purchase price is paid in advance. Unless there is a high level of trust between the parties, the buyer who is advancing the payment may want to get a bank guarantee ("performance guarantee") to get her money back in case the seller never performs.

• **Documentary credit** involves a Letter of Credit (L/C) issued by the buyer's bank, to be confirmed by a bank in the seller's country. Payment is made by the advising or confirming bank in the seller's country as soon as the seller presents the controlling documents. By contrast to documentary collection, the L/C is an irrevocable payment promise by the issuing bank, independent of the buyer's willingness and ability to make payment at the time of delivery. The seller has a high level of security, as long as he can procure all documents required under the credit. Details will be discussed in Part Three.

• **Documentary collection** involves a bank in the buyer's country. After the seller ships the goods and receives the controlling documents (Bill of Lading, etc.), he sends the documents to a bank in the buyer's country, which collects payment from the buyer in exchange for handing over the controlling documents. This provides a relatively high level of security for the buyer because the seller cannot get paid until he has performed. However, it does not provide much or any security for the seller because the only party promising to pay when the documents are presented is the buyer. The bank is just a facilitator and neither provides credit nor undertakes a payment obligation. Thus, if the buyer is no longer willing or able to pay when the documents are presented, the seller does not get paid. The only protection for the seller at this point is that the bank is not supposed to hand over the documents without getting paid. Thus, the seller can recover the goods from the carrier because he still has the Bill of Lading. Details will be discussed in Part Three.

• **Payment on open account** is largely the opposite of payment or cash in advance. It requires the buyer to wire the money or send a check or bank draft *after* the goods have been delivered. Again, this method is inexpensive, but in this situation the risk is on the seller, who gets no security. Since the seller now has to advance his performance, he is essentially financing the transaction. In practice, this method is used primarily if the seller is willing and able to wait for payment, for example 30, 45, 60, or even 90 days after the invoice is drawn up and delivery is made.

The seller's risk can be mitigated if he also receives a standby letter of credit or a demand guarantee. These are backup payment options not intended to be used. They will only be activated if the buyer does not pay at the agreed-upon time. Naturally, the transaction becomes more expensive if such backup options are included. However, since the demand guarantee or the standby are not intended to be used, they may cost less than a regular letter of credit. In practice, inclusion of a standby or a demand guarantee is used mostly for installment contracts or other repeat transactions where it would be too expensive to provide a regular letter of credit for each payment. This will be discussed in detail in Part Three.

9. Warranties and Liabilities:

Seller warranties: Basic warranties such as the formula in **[39]** (taken almost verbatim from the UCC) can rarely be avoided by sellers of goods. What is important, by contrast, is a clear statement that further warranties are not provided unless explicitly stated here.

Liability for late payment by buyer: **[40]** is a provision for liquidated damages, i.e., a contractual agreement that the buyer will pay a certain percentage of interest if payment is late. In general, if there is no such clause for late payment, the seller can still ask for interest and enforce it in court or arbitration, if necessary. In practice, however, it will be easier to get damages for late payment if they have been specifically agreed upon. For example, if the contract provides for interest of two to four percent above the prime lending rate, a court or tribunal will normally enforce this without asking questions. If the contract does not stipulate an interest rate, the seller would have to prove his cost of borrowing. In addition, if the seller was eventually paid the contract price, he is unlikely to start proceedings over an unmet demand for unspecified interest. But if an actual dollar amount can easily be calculated based on the inclusion of a specific rate in the contract, the seller is much more likely to ask for and get this compensation. The importance of this should not be underestimated in a day and age where the majority of all international contract payments are late, often by months.

A different approach has to be taken in contracts with parties based in certain Muslim countries. For example, in Iran and Saudi Arabia, many judges refuse to award interest as a matter of principle and may even refuse to enforce an entire contract or an arbitral award if it includes provisions for interest (among others). Thus, in these situations, the contract should provide for liquidated damages without mentioning the word "interest" and without a clear connection to the passing of time.

Liability for late delivery by seller: **[41]** is a provision for liquidated damages in parallel to **[40]**, i.e., a contractual agreement that the seller will pay a certain amount of damages if delivery is late. In general, if there is no such clause for late delivery, the buyer can still ask for damages and enforce them in court or arbitration, if necessary. In practice, however, it will be easier to get damages for late delivery if they have been specifically agreed upon. If the contract does not stipulate an amount for the damages, the buyer would have to prove his damages on a case-by-case basis in order to get any compensation. This can be quite difficult. In addition, if the seller eventually delivered conforming goods, the buyer is unlikely to start proceedings unless she had specific, clearly identifiable, and significant losses. But if an actual dollar amount can easily be calculated based on the inclusion of a specific rate in the contract, the buyer is much more likely to ask for and receive this compensation. Incidentally, the perspective of having to pay significant amounts in liquidated damages can also motivate the seller to make special efforts in order to meet the delivery date.

Liability for nonconforming goods: While [39] works in favor of the buyer, [42] is a limitation of liability in favor of the seller. Without a limitation of liability, the supplier of a minor component that fails and causes significant damages to much larger and more expensive things and their users could be on the line for virtually unlimited consequential losses. The suggested clause would limit all payments, including the expenses for dispute settlement, to a percentage of the contract price or to the available insurance coverage. Even if the percentage is set at 100% of the contract price, the seller should be able to survive a conformity problem, regardless of the actual losses incurred by the buyer.

The clause cannot protect the seller against claims by third parties, for example, employees or customers of his buyer, and any other damaged parties or interests, since they are not parties to the contract and did not consent to the limitation of liability. However, in most cases, a tort liability in favor of third parties will only exist if some kind of fault of the seller can be proven.

Limitation of liability where nonconforming goods are retained by the buyer: In case of nonconformity of the goods, the buyer may have a choice between avoidance of the contract and price abatement (cf. Articles 49 and 25 CISG versus Article 50 CISG, as well as UCC §§ 2-711 and 2-714). [43] limits the right of the buyer to reduce the price. If the reduction is too restrictive, however, it may create an incentive for the buyer to avoid the contract and ask for all of her money back.

Time bar: The purpose of [44] is to provide legal certainty to the seller that there will be no claims of nonconformity after a specified amount of time has passed. The provision contains three elements. First, it requires that the buyer inspect the goods immediately upon arrival and notify any lack of conformity within a specified amount of time. The default pursuant to CISG Article 38(1) is that buyer must inspect the goods "within as short a period as is practicable in the circumstances." CISG Article 39(1) provides that the buyer has to notify nonconformity "within a reasonable time" after he has become aware or ought to have become aware. The time when the buyer ought to have become aware is the time provided in CISG Article 38, unless the defects are hidden (see also CFR III-3:107). The UCC provides in § 2-606 "a reasonable opportunity" for the buyer to inspect the goods. If the non-conformity was not immediately discoverable, § 2-608 provides the buyer with "a reasonable time" after discovery of the nonconformity to revoke her acceptance of the goods. The suggested contract clause makes both the time for inspection and the time for notification more specific. Second, the clause also suggests a definitive cut-off point for any claims of non-conformity, even if they were not detectable before. Since CISG Article 39(2) provides an upper limit for such cases, this clause only makes sense if it provides for less than two years of time. Note, however, that CISG Article 40 provides an exception to CISG Article 39(2) if the seller acted in bad faith. Although the clause here suggested could be interpreted as overriding both CISG Article 39(2) and CISG Article 40 and impose a definitive cutoff even if the seller knew of or could not have been unaware of the defect, it is likely that a court or arbitration tribunal would set aside an absolute time-bar in cases where the seller acted in bad faith. Of course, the fact that the seller knew or could not have been unaware would have to be proven by the buyer. In the case of the UCC, the absolute cutoff is four years, see § 2-725. Finally, [44] offers a procedural requirement, namely that the buyer has to give the seller an opportunity to cure the lack of conformity before taking decisive action, in particular before avoiding the contract.

Cancellation in case of late delivery: In general, minor delays in delivery do not entitle the buyer to avoid or cancel the contract, although the details depend on the applicable sales law (CISG: fundamental breach; UCC: perfect tender rule). Even in case of major delays, the buyer's rights may be limited if the seller is not responsible for the delays (see, for example, § 2-615 UCC and Article 79 CISG). The suggested contractual provision [45] enables the buyer to free herself from the contract after a reasonable time, regardless of the cause or causes of delay.

10. Choice of Law and Forum: Every contract for an IBT should have clear and unambiguous choice of law and forum provisions. The goal is to avoid a first round of litigation over the question which forum has jurisdiction and which law should apply. The parties do not only want to avoid such a waste of time and resources, they want suitable dispute settlement mechanisms, i.e., procedures that will yield fair, efficient, and enforceable outcomes with a reasonable investment of time and money. To achieve this goal, they have to choose the right law for the right forum. While arbitrators can be chosen and appropriate experts for any law and industry are available, judges should never be forced to apply a foreign law.

Resolution of disputes: The considerations for choice of forum [46], for the pros and cons of arbitration versus litigation, and for the drafting of arbitration clauses are discussed in detail below, pp. 699 et seq, 898, 948 et seq., and 951. They should be reviewed at this time.

Applicable law: The considerations for choice of law [47] are discussed in detail above, pp. 117 et seq., and 170. They should be reviewed at this time.

11. Additional Terms Agreed Upon between the Parties: Whenever the parties want to include general terms into their agreement, a reference like [48] must be included in the specifically negotiated clauses on the front of the contract. Unfortunately, unreflected references by each side to its own general clauses in communications sent back and forth — the proverbial "battle of the forms" — leads to a lot of uncertainty and ultimately frustration, in particular if the general clauses contain "material alterations" to the agreement in the sense of Article 19 CISG. The problem can be minimized if both parties ultimately sign on to one written version of the contract (front and back) and this final version contains a merger clause per [49]. By contrast, if the formation of the contract is determined on the basis of multiple drafts sent back and forth, and the final acceptance is in the form of initiation of performance, the inclusion of the general terms may cause more harm than good under the CISG. The UCC has a better solution in this regard, but it is also not without problems. The reader should look out for this problem in the context of our discussions on contract formation (pp. 171 et seq.).

12. Merger Clause: Article 11 CISG allows "any means, including witnesses" to be used in the determination whether a contract has been formed and what it says. In a similar way, § 2-202 UCC allows "parol or extrinsic evidence" to be used, under certain conditions, to clarify or supplement contract provisions. The merger clause largely cuts this off and prevents a party from claiming that statements made or allegedly made in one form or the other during the negotiations are binding even if they did not make it into the final written agreement. This facilitates the determination of the rights and obligations of the parties and avoids lengthy depositions of witnesses, invariably tainted by their association with either of the parties, and other fact-finding missions during dispute settlement.

Signatures: Each party should ensure that the person signing the contract for the other side has signing authority for the amounts and commitments in question [50]. *Actual authority* is either based on the position in the company or a specific power of attorney. When in doubt, corporate statutes, corporate resolutions, employment agreements, or express authorizations should be examined. Even if actual authority was not established and may not exist, a contract binding on the principal can also be made on the basis of *apparent authority.* This may have to be established in case a party should claim that it is not bound by the signature on the contract because the person in question did not act on its behalf. Apparent authority can be based on the way the agent acted with knowledge of the principal, his or her title or function in the principal's organization, previous contract negotiations involving the same agent and principal, and many other factors. Since disputes over authority can be tedious and unpredictable, establishment of actual authority is highly recommended.

Part B: ICC General Conditions for Sale of Manufactured Goods for Resale: The general terms reproduced here are largely based on the general terms suggested by the International Chamber of Commerce (ICC) for international contracts of sale [51]. They are not entirely neutral—for example, the default dispute settlement clause is in favor of arbitration administered by the ICC—but as a set they are very good and suitable for most of these kind of contracts. Importantly, Article 1.1 of the General Terms is a reflection of [48] of our contract, namely that the general terms of pp. 5–8 only become relevant to the extent an issue is not clearly elaborated in the individually negotiated terms of pages 1–4.

Article 1.2 Choice of law clause: Clause [52] provides a default choice of law in favor of the CISG and, as a backup system, seller's law. If the parties include a specifically negotiated clause, as suggested in Contract Clause [47], the provision in the general terms is superseded. Its function is, primarily, to have an unambiguous choice of law even if the parties, for whatever reasons, do not otherwise make or include such a choice in their agreement.

Article 1.5 Subsequent amendments of the contract: Clause [53] is a modified version of the second part of the merger clause suggested in [49]. The latter seeks to exclude *any* subsequent modifications of contractual rights and obligations unless agreed upon in writing and duly signed by both parties. By contrast, Article 1.5 of the general terms is qualified. Pursuant to the second sentence, a party may have to acknowledge a modification of the contract if its conduct led the other side to presume consent and was relied upon. Article 1.5 can be problematic from an evidentiary perspective and [49] would provide a clearer rule. However, a complete exclusion as suggested by Clause [49] may not always be acceptable in court or arbitration.

Article 2.1 Exclusion of various forms of parol evidence: Provision [54] is a milder version of the first part of the merger clause suggested in [49]. It stipulates that general informational materials of the seller do not amount to contractual and enforceable promises. However, by contrast to [49], this provision does not exclude earlier offers and counteroffers and/or various elements of the contract negotiations to be relied upon in the *interpretation* of the contract and the determination of the rights and obligations of the parties. Clause [49] would provide a clearer rule. However, a complete exclusion as suggested by [49] may not always be acceptable in court.

Article 2.2 Intellectual property rights: [55] clarifies that any IP does not get transferred with the contract of sale unless specifically agreed upon. This should be self-evident but it is a good reminder. If IP intensive goods are sold, it is advisable to include this provision in the main parts (front) of the contract.

Article 3 Inspection: Pre-shipment inspection is common, although usually not done by the buyer herself. Instead, the buyer will usually involve an inspection company or agent in the seller's country with specific knowledge of the contracted goods. Since the inspection should be done before the goods are packaged and shipped, it is important for the seller to notify the buyer of the most suitable time for the inspection [56].

Article 4 Price: Since agreement on price, or at least a way in which the price can be determined, is an essential element of a valid contract of sale, Article 4 [57] provides just that, in case the parties did not include a clear provision in the main part of the contract. Article 4.3 reflects the principle that each side has to cover its own obligations: the seller is responsible for expenses incurred up to the point of delivery; the buyer is responsible from the point of delivery. The point of delivery is generally the place where the risk passes from the seller to the buyer. For example, under INCOTERMS® FOB or FCA, this would be when the goods are loaded onto the ship or handed over to the carrier. An exception applies under C-terms, as was discussed above, pp. 240 et seq.

Article 5 Payment terms: Article 5 provides backup provisions for payment terms, as well as specifics for each of the five options. Article 5.1 refers to payment by wire transfer into an open account *after* the goods have been shipped [58]. Making this the default in the absence of party agreement on different payment terms is very buyer-friendly, as is explained above, pp. 345 and 346, and below, pp. 409 et seq. Sellers should not include this provision in their general terms without full understanding of its potential impact. Article 5.2 refers to payment by wire transfer into an open account *before* the goods are shipped [59]. This is by and large the opposite of the arrangement under 5.1 and very seller-friendly. Buyers should not include this provision in their general terms without fully understanding its potential impact.

Article 5.3 refers to payment by documentary credit [60], the most common form of, and most secure, payment term—although not the cheapest way of handling payment. In contracts where the seller and buyer do not know each other and have no particular reasons to trust that the other side will perform as promised, this should be the default payment term. The payment terms referred to in Article 5.4 and 5.5—documentary collection [61] and payment by wire transfer backed up with a bank guarantee or a standby letter of credit [62]—have various advantages and disadvantages that will be discussed below, pp. 409 et seq. In general, neither sellers nor buyers should include these provisions in their general terms without full understanding of their potential impact.

Article 6 Interest for late payment: Clause [63] is a more general version of the contract clause suggested in [40]. Two percent above prime is a relatively low level for the interest obligation, which is adequate for general contract terms that should not contain surprises. However, with a clear and specifically agreed-upon clause such as [40], sellers can generally get a higher level of interest more adequately reflecting their actual borrowing and opportunity costs.

Article 7 Retention of title: [64] is a more general version of the contract clause suggested in [34]. The default is "complete payment of the price," which is the most common condition. For a general contract clause, the following might be even better: "Unless otherwise agreed in writing, the goods shall remain the property of the seller until the complete payment of the price. Complete payment shall be understood as receipt of any sums due by seller's bank in immediately available funds."

Article 8 Default delivery term/INCOTERM®: This provision reflects the customary rule that goods have to be picked up, while money has to be sent, unless the parties have agreed otherwise [65]. Thus, the default delivery term, in the absence of a specific agreement suggested in Contract Clause [22], is EX WORKS. The seller only promises to make the goods available at his facility for the buyer, or her agent, to pick them up. This clause is seller-friendly because the seller has minimal responsibilities.

Buyers might want to put "FOB" or "FCA" as default into their general terms as it makes sense that each party should be responsible for the documents and services that need to be provided or procured in her country. For further discussion, see above, p. 247.

Article 9 Documents to be supplied by seller: Clause [66] is redundant because the agreed-upon INCOTERM® will impose the same requirement. It is also a waste of opportunity for an efficient arrangement of responsibilities. Since the default INCOTERM®, pursuant to the ICC General Terms, is EX WORKS, the buyer may find herself in the difficult position of having to procure various documents for export processing in the seller's country. At the very least, the seller should be obliged to support the buyer by providing his documents, such as invoices and packing lists, in the format required for export.

Article 10 Buyer's remedies for late delivery and nondelivery: [67] is a more general version of the contract clause suggested in [41]. One-half percent per week of delay and a cap of five percent is very seller-friendly. An individually negotiated contract clause such as Clause [**41**] could easily provide for significantly higher percentages, in particular if the buyer could show that the liquidated damages are not entirely disconnected from actual business losses. Even if a modest percentage per week is agreed upon, it may be worthwhile for the buyer to insist on a minimum compensation amount if the goods are more than a few days or a week late.

Article 11 Buyer's obligations and remedies in case of nonconformity of the goods: Clause [**68**] contains seller-friendly elements, in particular Articles 11.2 and 11.3, but also buyer-friendly elements, since Article 11.1 is more generous than our Clause [**42**]. In general, limitations of liability like these have to be used with caution. The CISG, via Articles 49, 25, 74, and 75, does not limit the amount of damages if the seller commits a fundamental breach. The only limits under the CISG are the foreseeability rule in Article 74, the obligation to mitigate damages under Article 77, and the exemptions under Article 79, force majeure, and Article 80, contributory fault. Article 11.7 of the general terms cuts off recourse to these other provisions, i.e., it limits the buyer to the liquidated damages even if she could easily prove more extensive losses caused by the seller's breach. Thus, overall the clause favors the seller. A contract drafted by the buyer might provide for similar levels of liquidated damages regardless of foreseeability and leave the option open for the buyer to seek larger amounts of damages if these can be specifically proven and were foreseeable.

Article 12 Cooperation between the parties in case of third-party claims: Clause [**69**] provides for a useful information exchange in case of third-party claims. It does not obligate the parties to support each other in litigation or arbitration against third parties.

Article 13 Force majeure: Article 13.1 [**70**] is a verbatim reproduction of Article 79(1) of the CISG. Article 13.2 is largely a reflection of Article 79(4) of the CISG. The innovation of the general terms is tucked away in Articles 13.3 and 13.4. Under the CISG, force majeure only exempts from damages "under this Convention" (Article 79(5)), i.e., under Articles 74 to 77. This does not cover contractual or liquidated damages, any contractual penalties (as suggested in [**41**]), or interest. The general terms overrule the limitations in the CISG and also provide a right of termination after six months, unless otherwise agreed upon specifically in [**45**].

Article 14 Choice of forum / dispute resolution: The dispute resolution clause is general and does not specify the number of arbitrators, nor the seat or the language of the arbitration. While all these can be determined by the ICC pursuant to its Arbitration Rules, the parties to the contract should agree on the most appropriate arrangements before a dispute arises and such agreement may become elusive. In Part Six, we will discuss not only better options for dispute settlement clauses, but also suggestions for cost control in arbitration.

Notes and Questions

1. Can you list and explain all possible cases in which the UCC will be the substantive law governing an international sales contract? Can you do the same for all possible cases in which the CISG will be the substantive law?

2. If you have successfully worked your way through question 1, it should now be quite easy for you to list and explain all possible cases in which German, French, Japanese, or Australian contract law will govern a particular contract of sale.

3. Can you explain what the U.S. has done with the reservation under Article 95 CISG and when and how this reservation affects the applicability of the CISG to a particular contract?

4. Why is the CISG not a complete set of rules for international contracts of sale? What do we do about that?

5. Is the UCC a complete set of rules for (international) contracts of sale? If not, what do we do about that?

6. Is English law, French law, or Chinese law a complete set of rules for (international) contracts of sale? Explain why or why not.

7. Is New York law a complete set of rules for (international) contracts of sale? What are its components?

8. Other than the applicable contract law, which other rules of law can the parties to an IBT select in their initial agreement or at a later time, e.g., when a dispute arises?

9. Which rules can the parties to an IBT *not* avoid or unselect?

Section 9. Specifics of Electronic Contracts and Documents

Until about the turn of the millennium, the method of choice for communication between businesses in different countries was the fax machine. As many of us will remember, this involved the production of a document on the computer, the printing of the document on a printer, and the transmission of the document, one page at a time, with a fax machine, a device somewhere between a scanner and a photocopier connected to a phone line. The method had the advantage of transmitting an exact, albeit black and white, copy of the original in seconds, and for the price of a short phone call. This was a major improvement over regular mail and courier services, and even the telex system,[122] when first introduced toward the end of the 1980s. An added benefit was the ability of the two fax machines to "handshake," which gave the sender a confirmation of receipt (or, for that matter, an error message if the message had been scrambled due to a bad signal or other reasons). While it was not entirely foolproof—an "OK" message might have been sent although the receiving fax was out of paper and merely recorded the incoming

---

122. The telex system is an electronic method of communication that is even less well known today but still in use in certain industries. See the description in the context of SWIFT communications between banks on pp. 416–418 and 495–497.

message in memory, and at some point a real person would still have to look at the "in" tray for the message to be genuinely received—fax machines brought about a revolution in business communication: enormous acceleration and cost savings, and with that the ability to send offers, counteroffers, and entire contracts back and forth multiple times and within hours or even minutes of each other. Naturally, this was not without legal problems, but they were largely dealt with by treating faxes essentially like regular mail that had to be sent and received. Since the fax machines printed a time stamp and the phone numbers of the two parties, and the document itself had the original signatures, the problems were not overly complex.

Today, e-mail and e-mail attachments have become the dominant method for business communication, even if some businesses and industries still use fax for certain documents and as a backup. Electronic communication raises a plethora of new legal issues, however. First, hacking a phone line is certainly possible but it is quite difficult, in particular if the hacker is physically not close to the line. Thus, the armies of hackers sitting in North Korea, Russia, China, and other countries may be able to generate millions of fake e-mails per day, but they have never been interested in fax or telex technology. Second, even the sender of a genuine e-mail typically does not get a confirmation that her message was received at the other end. Therefore, claims that a notice or a draft or an acceptance of a contract were never received by the other side are daily occurrences in business. Third, certain cultures, such as Japan, still perceive electronic communication as impersonal and potentially rude and prefer the more personalized style encompassed in a fax; although this can be overcome, to an extent, by attaching a pdf of an actual document to an e-mail. Corporations have been sometimes slow to discover and resolve new training needs to ensure that staff members are sufficiently cautious with their e-mail, keeping access codes safe and confidential, but also maintaining a level of propriety in what may often be perceived as a more casual form of communication. Finally, not everyone in a firm used to sign documents that got faxed and there was a certain level of awareness of doing something significant and potentially legally binding when writing on the company letterhead. Today every person in an organization with access to a computer is probably sending dozens of e-mails a day, often without thinking at all that some of these could result in legal consequences for the firm.

While most people by now are used to online transactions on consumer sites and have no problem with sending contracts and other kinds of documents as e-mail attachments, a number of providers are developing more sophisticated and more integrated digital document management systems that are less prone to unauthorized third-party access.

The best known example for digital transaction management or DTM may be DocuSign, a company widely recognized as a global leader for the electronic exchange and signing of documents. DocuSign enables users to create or choose a form contract and highlight fields that need to be signed by the other party. The documents are transmitted by e-mail and signed on screen with a stylized "signature" in the requested fields. Once all parties to a contract have duly signed, the finalized version of the contract is converted from the xDTM standard and sent to everyone in pdf format. Important competitors for DocuSign are PandaDoc, Adobe Sign, eSignLive, SignNow, and HelloSign.[123] In addition to the option of uploading preexisting contracts, these platforms are offering, or at least developing, some form of contract drafting tool. The system works well for highly standardized transactions and not so well for contracts that are highly customized and negotiated between the parties. In addition, transmission by e-mail remains subject to hacking risks and mechanisms to ensure the identity of the parties are sometimes weak.

Another useful tool for DTM is Box, a cloud-based storage app that allows sharing of documents between users in different locations. Box, and its competitor, Dropbox, invite users to save all their documents in the cloud, where they are protected better than on individual desktop and laptop computers. DocuSigned documents can be stored directly in Box as well. Similar to DocuSign, these document-sharing apps have good security features while the documents are under their control, but the weak link is the verification of the identity of the users and the communication with the users, which goes via regular internet and e-mail channels.

A number of companies are currently working in two important directions. One is the generation of certain types of contracts with the help of artificial intelligence systems, i.e., semi-automatic translation of layman's terms into professional contracts. The other is the replacement of conventional internet and e-mail transmission with distributed ledger technology (DLT), commonly known as the Blockchain. DLT saves information on a multitude of servers and, thereby, makes it practically impossible for anyone, authorized or not, to change the data after it has been created. This promises to be a game changer for digital transactions because it will ensure the authenticity of stored information. By combining AI-enabled contracts with Blockchain technology, so-called Smart Contracts can be created. Strictly speaking, these are not contracts, but computer programs designed to automatically implement contracts. This means that parties negotiate a contract as before but then activate it using an app on their desktop, laptop, tablet, or phone. The activation sets a program in motion that will automatically execute if certain conditions are met. For example, the purchase price for a consignment of goods can be uploaded with the Smart Contract onto the Blockchain and will be automatically released to the seller after she uploads the necessary documents, including the Bill of Lading, documenting that the goods have been shipped to the buyer. Since the Blockchain secures the immutability of the Smart Contract, neither the buyer, nor a bank providing the funds, or any other party, can tamper with the agreed-upon terms or stop the disbursement of the purchase price. More complex Smart Contracts can even provide for exceptions, for example, that the money does not get released but is returned to the buyer, if the seller fails to meet certain deadlines or cannot procure a "clean" Bill of Lading or a required Inspection Certificate.

---

123. HubSpot, in a review dated February 8, 2020, presented the strengths and weaknesses of 14 of the best electronic signature apps. See https://blog.hubspot.com/sales/electronic-signature.

The Corda Blockchain (https://www.corda.net/) was used in February 2018 to issue the first letter of credit on the Blockchain. The transaction time was brought down from an average of about 10 days to less than 24 hours. Corda developers are working on Smart Contracts for a variety of transactions commonly used in IBTs.

Specifically for payment transactions, IBM has introduced an app called World-Wire (https://www.ibm.com/blockchain/solutions/world-wire), which runs on the Stellar Blockchain and enables users to transfer funds within seconds and directly competes with the much slower SWIFT network.

PrepayWay is working on Smart Contracts for international real estate transactions and also for certain types of export/import transactions we are discussing in this book (https://prepayway.com/).

The problem with these kind of systems, for the time being, is that all participants in a transaction have to be linked on the platform, i.e., they have to be willing and able to make transactions on the Blockchain. This is still largely not the case. Huffington Post contributor Nicholas Cole declared in January 2018, "[i]f 2017 was the year of Bitcoin, then 2018 is going to be the year blockchain technology disrupts the technology world forever."[124] At the beginning of 2020, it is safe to say that this has not happened yet. However, as more and more enterprises are developing capabilities in this field, it is only a question of time until a tipping point is reached and many small pockets of activity connect to form a network that will indeed change the world, or at least the way the most efficient companies do IBTs. When that moment comes, laggards will pay a high price for their inability to connect and compete.

In this Section we will highlight some of the more common legal issues related to electronic document transfers, contracts, and signatures, and introduce legislative measures taken by the U.S. and the EU to reduce these concerns.

A. The Evolving Rules for Electronic Documents and Signatures in the U.S.[125]

The Uniform Computer Information Transaction Act (UCITA)[126] and the Uniform Electronic Transaction Act (UETA)[127] were developed by the National Conference of Commissioners on Uniform State Laws (NCCUSL) for adoption by the several States. The respective state implementation acts, along with the federal Electronic Signatures in Global and National Commerce Act 2000 (E-SIGN),[128]

---

124. https://www.huffingtonpost.com/entry/why-2018-will-be-the-year-of-the-blockchain_us_5a4b1b72e4b0df0de8b06c91.

125. I am grateful to Aakshita Bansal for drafting the subsection on the U.S.

126. https://www.uniformlaws.org/viewdocument/final-act-with-comments-14?CommunityKey=92b2978d-585f-4ab6-b8a1-53860fbb43b5&tab=librarydocuments.

127. https://www.uniformlaws.org/viewdocument/final-act-with-comments-29?CommunityKey=2c04b76c-2b7d-4399-977e-d5876ba7e034&tab=librarydocuments.

128. https://uscode.house.gov/view.xhtml?path=/prelim@title15/chapter96&edition=prelim.

provide legal validity to interstate and international electronic transactions. As of spring 2020, 47 states have adopted the UETA, except for New York, Illinois, and Washington;[129] whereas only two states—Virginia and Maryland—have adopted the UCITA. The two model laws and the federal law are discussed in some detail below, highlighting the enforceability of e-commerce transactions. It is important to keep in mind that the fundamentals of contract law remain applicable for the recognition of e-contracts in the courts. In other words, every e-contract must have an offer, acceptance, and consideration—the three basic elements of any contract formation. In the same way, defenses such as lack of legal capacity to enter into a contract, public policy, unconscionability, and the like also apply.

1. The Uniform Computer Information Transaction Act of 2001 (UCITA)

UCITA is an ambitious statute that aims to create a uniform commercial code for contracts involving computer information, like a software license agreement or an online access contract, whether entered electronically or by other means. UCITA does not apply to financial services transactions or insurance contracts. If a sale involves hardware and software, UCITA does not apply to the hardware elements of the contract. UCITA explicitly states that "[a] record or authentication may not be denied legal effect or enforceability solely because it is in electronic form." UCITA replaces the concept of "in writing" with that of "a record," and requires contracts valued at US$5,000 or above to be enforceable only when "the party against which enforcement is sought authenticated a record sufficient to indicate that a contract has been formed and which reasonably identifies the copy or subject matter to which the contract refers." The term "record" is defined to include an electronic record, and "authenticate" replaces the terms "signature" and "signed." As the commentary clarifies, "authentication includes qualifying use of any identifier, such as a personal identification number (PIN) or a typed or otherwise signed name." UCITA itself does not require parties to retain an authenticated record.

UCITA contains several substantive contracting provisions. For example, it provides that "a contract may be formed in any manner sufficient to show agreement, including offer and acceptance or conduct of both parties or operation of electronic agents which recognizes the existence of a contract." UCITA resembles the UCC with respect to the manifestation of mutual assent and contract formation, and the fact that it "invites acceptance in any manner and by any medium reasonable under the circumstances," unless otherwise specified by the offeror. However, there are also interesting differences:

SECTION 206. OFFER AND ACCEPTANCE: ELECTRONIC AGENTS.

(a) [Formation by interaction of electronic agents.] A contract may be formed by the interaction of electronic agents. If the interaction results in

---

129. The Act was introduced in the Washington State legislature in early 2020.

the electronic agents' engaging in operations that under the circumstances indicate acceptance of an offer, a contract is formed, but a court may grant appropriate relief if the operations resulted from fraud, electronic mistake, or the like. . . .

(c) [Terms of the contract.] The terms of a contract formed under subsection (b) . . . do not include a term provided by the individual if the individual had reason to know that the electronic agent could not react to the term.

UCITA attempts to clarify the time when an e-contract is formed by stating that in case of a "computer information transaction . . . a contract is formed when an electronic acceptance is received." (Sec. 102(a)(11)).

UCITA is a very controversial piece of legislation. It is backed by software publishers and computer manufacturers and opposed by consumers, librarians, and various copyright industries like associations representing broadcasters, music publishers, motion picture studios, etc.[130]

2. The Uniform Electronic Transaction Act of 1999 (UETA)

Compared to UCITA, UETA has a wider scope of application, covering all types of online transactions, with a few exceptions (Documents, p. I-467). UETA was enacted to "remove barriers to electronic commerce by validating and effectuating electronic records and signatures." Section 7(a) and (b) of the act provide that "[a] record or signature may not be denied legal effect or enforceability solely because it is in electronic form;" and "[a] contract may not be denied legal effect or enforceability solely because an electronic record was used in its formation." In other words, whether information (a record, contract, or signature) is in paper or electronic form does not affect its legal validity. Subsection (c) further states that "[i]f a law requires a record to be in writing, an electronic record satisfies the law," thus equating an electronic record to a writing. In addition to validating electronic records, UETA permits electronic storage of records.

Under the UETA, contract formation or an "agreement" means the "bargain of the parties in fact, as found in their language or inferred from other circumstances and from rules, regulations, and procedures given the effect of agreements under laws otherwise applicable to a particular transaction." (Sec. 2(1)). The term "contract" is defined as "the total legal obligation resulting from the parties' agreement as affected by this Act and other applicable law." (Sec. 2(4)). The official comment to Section 2 of the act talks about "manifestation of mutual assent" between the contracting parties, relevance of "usage and conduct of other party" to infer an agreement, etc., to emphasize the fact that UETA does not intend to affect the existing relevant substantive contract law. According to Prefatory Note B of UETA, the

---

130. See Cem Kaner, *e-Commerce Provisions in the UCITA and UETA*, available at http://kaner.com/pdfs/kanereta.pdf.

existing substantive laws of contract would still apply to the electronic transactions and UETA only validates the electronic format of the contract, signature, or record.

UETA is more detailed with regard to the time of contract formation:

SECTION 15. TIME AND PLACE OF SENDING AND RECEIPT.

(a) Unless otherwise agreed between the sender and the recipient, an electronic record is sent when it:

(1) is addressed properly or otherwise directed properly to an information processing system that the recipient has designated or uses for the purpose of receiving electronic records or information of the type sent and from which the recipient is able to retrieve the electronic record;

(2) is in a form capable of being processed by that system; and

(3) enters an information processing system outside the control of the sender or of a person that sent the electronic record on behalf of the sender or enters a region of the information processing system designated or used by the recipient which is under the control of the recipient.

(b) Unless otherwise agreed between a sender and the recipient, an electronic record is received when:

(1) it enters an information processing system that the recipient has designated or uses for the purpose of receiving electronic records or information of the type sent and from which the recipient is able to retrieve the electronic record; and

(2) it is in a form capable of being processed by that system.

(c) Subsection (b) applies even if the place the information processing system is located is different from the place the electronic record is deemed to be received under subsection (d).

(d) Unless otherwise expressly provided in the electronic record or agreed between the sender and the recipient, an electronic record is deemed to be sent from the sender's place of business and to be received at the recipient's place of business. . . .

(e) An electronic record is received under subsection (b) even if no individual is aware of its receipt.

(f) Receipt of an electronic acknowledgment from an information processing system described in subsection (b) establishes that a record was received but, by itself, does not establish that the content sent corresponds to the content received.

(g) If a person is aware that an electronic record purportedly sent under subsection (a), or purportedly received under subsection (b), was not actually sent or received, the legal effect of the sending or receipt is determined by other applicable law. Except to the extent permitted by the other law, the requirements of this subsection may not be varied by agreement.

An e-signature includes a "digital signature using public key encryption technology," "the standard webpage click through process," inclusion of "one's name as part of an electronic mail communication," and the like (Sec. 2(8)).

The act is silent on invitations to make an offer and on the effects of revocation of an offer. As discussed above, matters on which UETA is silent are intended to be governed by otherwise existing laws, i.e., the UCC or state contract laws.

3. The Electronic Signatures in Global and National Commerce Act of 2000 (E-SIGN)

E-SIGN is a federal law that came into effect on October 1, 2000, and provides for broad enforceability of e-signatures, e-contracts, and e-records in internet transactions affecting interstate or foreign commerce (Documents, p. I-475). The act sets forth the national uniform standard, that is, the "floor" for all internet-based transactions. E-SIGN does not automatically preempt all state laws. If a state law uniformly incorporates Sections 1 through 16 of UETA it is not preempted by E-SIGN. However, a state that has enacted a non-uniform statute is preempted and governed by section 7002(a)(2) of E-SIGN unless the law provides for an alternative method for the acceptance of electronic records, consistent with E-SIGN, or makes specific references to E-SIGN, and does not give greater legal status to any specific technology designed for the use of electronic signatures or records.

Similar to the UETA, E-SIGN does not intend to alter the existing substantive contract laws and regulations with respect to the parties' contractual rights and obligations, whether there was mutual assent between the parties, the timing and effect of sending and receiving an acceptance, and the actual effect of the electronic signature. It only validates electronic contracts by stating that "a signature, contract, or other record relating to such transaction may not be denied legal effect, validity, or enforceability solely because it is in electronic form" and that "a contract cannot be denied legal effect [. . .] solely because an electronic signature or electronic record was used in its formation." An "electronic signature" is defined as "an electronic sound, symbol, or process attached to or logically associated with a contract or other record and executed or adopted by a person with the intent to sign the record." This definition is the same as the one provided under UETA. As explained by PandaDoc, the following requirements need to be fulfilled before an "electronic signature" is upheld in a court of law, both under UETA and E-SIGN:[131]

> **Parties' mutual consent to transact business electronically:** E-SIGN allows parties to engage in business transactions electronically but does not compel them to do so. Mutual consent of all the parties to do business online is required. This could be demonstrated via a clause in the contract. For B2C

transactions, E-SIGN provides a detailed set of rules regarding consumer consent.

Intent to execute the contract: Each party must clearly indicate their intent to sign the contract. Such intent can be inferred from clicking an "I Agree" button, typing their respective names, placing initials on the document, or drawing their signature.

E-signatures associated with the record: The electronic signature or symbol used to execute an electronic contract must in some way be associated with the electronic record being signed. For example, e-signature software like PandaDoc or DocuSign can produce a simultaneous "textual or graphic" statement when the record is being signed or when it is being amended, expressly stating that the record was executed with an e-signature and then attach the statement to the signed record. In other words, an audit trail must be maintained.

Record retention: An electronic record can be denied legal effect if it is not retainable and is not capable of being accurately reproduced.

While broad in coverage, E-SIGN is not applicable to wills or testamentary trusts; laws governing divorce, adoption, and other family matters; UCC transactions (other than Articles 2 and 2A); and notices of cancellation or termination of utility services or notices of default, acceleration, repossession, foreclosure, and eviction under a credit card agreement secured by the "primary residence of an individual." With respect to transactions falling under UCC Articles 3 through 9, the UCC itself determines the legal effect of e-signatures and electronic contracts.

4. *Choice of Law Clauses in Electronic Contracts*

UCITA, as a general rule, enforces a choice of law clause mutually agreed by the parties in their electronic commercial contract, except in cases of unconscionability or superseding public policy of the forum state. In the absence of a choice of law agreement, the act specifies a number of rules that govern in such a scenario. For miscellaneous situations, other than access contracts, electronic delivery contracts, and consumer contracts, UCITA adopts a "most significant relationship" test.[132]

As noted above, UCITA has been adopted in only two States and thus, in the absence of a uniform choice of law statute for contracts that are entered electronically,

---

132. Per comment 4 on Section 109(b)(3): "Applying [the most significant relationship] test requires consideration of factors including the: (a) place of contracting, (b) place of negotiation, (c) place of performance, (d) location of the subject matter of the contract, (e) domicile, residence, nationality, place of incorporation and place of business of one or both parties, (f) needs of the interstate and international systems, (g) relative interests of the forum and other interested states in the determination of the particular issue, (h) protection of justified expectations of the parties, and (i) promotion of certainty, predictability and uniformity of result."

the UCC and the Restatement (Second) of Conflict of Laws must be relied upon to determine the applicable substantive law.

5. Dispute Resolution

The U.S. does not have any particular legislation to determine internet jurisdiction in disputes arising out of electronic commercial transactions. Therefore, the procedural law issue remains in the hands of the U.S. courts, which have not yet articulated a uniform set of rules to determine personal jurisdiction for e-commerce-related disputes. Nonetheless, the U.S. courts have provided us with three internet-adapted and heavily used tests that provide legal guidance for deciphering personal jurisdiction issues in e-contracts.

First, a Sliding Scale Test originated in *Zippo Manufacturing Co. v. Zippo Dot Com.*[133] The issue in Zippo was whether the World Wide Web provides sufficient "minimum contacts" to establish personal jurisdiction over the defendant. The Zippo court introduced a "sliding scale" to evaluate contacts formed via their websites by potential defendants. The court concentrated on the "nature and quality of commercial activity that an entity conducts over the Internet," to determine whether personal jurisdiction could be exercised constitutionally. The scale divided internet activity into three categories:

I. Active Websites, which constitute one extreme end of the scale, where a defendant clearly transacts business over the internet. In other words, a defendant "enter[s] into contracts with residents of foreign jurisdiction that involve the knowing and repeated transmission of computer files." In such a case, jurisdiction is proper.

ii. Passive Websites, which constitute the other extreme end of the scale, and only make certain information (advertisements, etc.) available to the website visitors or internet browsers in foreign jurisdictions but do not allow any interaction between the website host and the visitor. Such websites do not conduct any sale-purchase transactions, and hence are not a proper ground for the exercise of personal jurisdiction.

iii. Interactive Websites, which constitute the middle portion of the scale, and provide a platform for the website users to interact or exchange information with the host computer. Here, proper jurisdiction depends on the "level of interactivity and commercial nature of the exchange of information that occurs on their website between the forum resident and non-forum resident." Determination of personal jurisdiction in this case involves a fact-specific inquiry taking into consideration the totality of circumstances of each case. If the level of interactivity tilts toward the passive side of the scale, personal jurisdiction will not be upheld; if it tilts toward the active side of the scale (e.g., conclusion of contracts online), personal jurisdiction will likely be upheld.

---

133. 952 F. Supp. 1119 (W.D. Pa. 1997).

Originally, *Zippo's* Sliding Scale Test was one of most developed and applied doctrines of U.S. law for resolution of personal jurisdiction disputes involving internet contacts. However, due to the lack of guidance from the *Zippo* court to ascertain the "sufficiency of interactions" required for personal jurisdiction, and because of an increasing number of websites being inherently interactive in nature, the *Zippo* test is slowly losing its relevance in solving today's web-based jurisdiction questions.

The Effects Test developed by the Supreme Court in *Calder v. Jones*, a pre-internet case, has been adapted to internet contacts. This test focuses on the actual effects that the nonresident defendant's online activity intentionally caused within the forum state rather than calculating the level of contact between the parties over the website. Courts have noted that this Effects Test is better suited for torts like defamation, and might be difficult to apply to corporations and other non-natural persons, because it can be challenging to connect harm caused to a corporation to a single forum or a particular geographic location.

Finally, a Targeting Test was developed, which requires that a defendant, who is "alleged to have engaged in wrongful conduct[,] *targeted* at a plaintiff whom the defendant knows to be a resident of the forum state," before permitting a finding of "purposeful availment" by the defendant of the forum state. A "deliberate action" directed at the forum state consisting of "transactions between the defendant and residents of the forum or conduct of the defendant purposefully directed at residents of the forum state," is required under this approach.[134] *ALS Scan v. Digital Service Consultants*, adopted the targeting approach, ruling that:

> [A] State may, consistent with due process, exercise judicial power over a person outside of the State when that person (1) directs electronic activity into the State, (2) with the manifested intent of engaging in business or other interactions within the State, and (3) that activity creates, in a person within the State, a potential cause of action cognizable in the State's courts.[135]

In other words, "deliberate action" is required regardless of whether a website is passive or interactive in nature.

---

134. Cf. *Millenium Enters. v. Millennium Music,* 33 F. Supp. 2d 907, 921 (D. Or. 1999), holding that although defendant's website was interactive in nature allowing for purchase of CDs from it from different states, no one from Oregon had actually purchased from the defendant's website. The defendant made no contact with the residents of Oregon through their website. Therefore, there is no evidence that defendant's activities were directed or targeted at the residents of Oregon. Mere foreseeability that Oregon residents might purchase CDs from the defendant's website is not sufficient to establish personal jurisdiction. "[T]he foreseeability that is critical to due process analysis is not the mere likelihood that a product will find its way into the forum state. Rather, it is that the defendant's conduct and connection with the forum state are such that he should reasonably anticipate being haled into court there." *World-Wide Volkswagen Corp. v. Woodson,* 444 U.S. 286, 297, 100 S. Ct. 559, 62 L. Ed. 2d 490 (1980).

135. 293 F.3d 707, 714 (4th Cir. 2002).

In practice, courts often ping-pong among the three tests discussed above to determine jurisdiction on the basis of internet contacts. Sometimes they apply a looser version of one approach and a stricter of another, and sometimes a combination.

B. The International Legal Framework for Electronic Contracts

Recognizing that different national rules and regulations about the use of electronic communications in international business transactions are bound to create problems, the United Nations Commission on International Trade Law (UNCITRAL) prepared a convention to harmonize the rules on a global scale. A second purpose of the initiative was the goal of establishing the equivalence of electronic and written form whenever a written document is required, as it is the case, for example, in Article 13 of the CISG or in Article II of the 1958 UN Convention on the Recognition and Enforcement of Foreign Arbitral Awards (the "New York Convention"). The 2005 United Nations Convention on the Use of Electronic Communications in International Contracts entered into force on 1 March 2013 and has attracted 14 ratifications as of June 2020, including from Russia and Singapore. China, the Philippines, Korea, Saudi Arabia, and several more countries have signed and are presumably in the process of ratification (Documents, p. I-460). The Convention applies to "the use of electronic communications in connection with the formation or performance of a contract between parties whose places of business are in different States." (Art. 1(1)). It does not apply to B2C transactions, nor to inter-bank payment or clearance agreements, bills of exchange, promissory notes, consignment notes, bills of lading, warehouse receipts, and the like (Art. 2). Its application can be excluded by the parties to an IBT (Art. 3).

Pursuant to Article 8 of the Convention, "[a] communication or a contract shall not be denied validity or enforcement on the sole ground that it is in the form of an electronic communication" (para. 1). Articles 9–13 are of particular importance for our purposes:

Article 9. Form Requirements

1. Nothing in this Convention requires a communication or a contract to be made or evidenced in any particular form.

2. Where the law requires that a communication or a contract should be in writing, or provides consequences for the absence of a writing, that requirement is met by an electronic communication if the information contained therein is accessible so as to be usable for subsequent reference.

3. Where the law requires that a communication or a contract should be signed by a party, or provides consequences for the absence of a signature, that requirement is met in relation to an electronic communication if:

(a) A method is used to identify the party and to indicate that party's intention in respect of the information contained in the electronic communication; and

(b) The method used is either:

(i) As reliable as appropriate for the purpose for which the electronic communication was generated or communicated, in the light of all the circumstances, including any relevant agreement; or

(ii) Proven in fact to have fulfilled the functions described in subparagraph (a) above, by itself or together with further evidence.

4. Where the law requires that a communication or a contract should be made available or retained in its original form, or provides consequences for the absence of an original, that requirement is met in relation to an electronic communication if:

(a) There exists a reliable assurance as to the integrity of the information it contains from the time when it was first generated in its final form, as an electronic communication or otherwise; and

(b) Where it is required that the information it contains be made available, that information is capable of being displayed to the person to whom it is to be made available.

5. For the purposes of paragraph 4 (a):

(a) The criteria for assessing integrity shall be whether the information has remained complete and unaltered, apart from the addition of any endorsement and any change that arises in the normal course of communication, storage and display; and

(b) The standard of reliability required shall be assessed in the light of the purpose for which the information was generated and in the light of all the relevant circumstances.

Article 10. Time and Place of Dispatch and Receipt of Electronic Communications

1. The time of dispatch of an electronic communication is the time when it leaves an information system under the control of the originator or of the party who sent it on behalf of the originator or, if the electronic communication has not left an information system under the control of the originator or of the party who sent it on behalf of the originator, the time when the electronic communication is received.

2. The time of receipt of an electronic communication is the time when it becomes capable of being retrieved by the addressee at an electronic address designated by the addressee. The time of receipt of an electronic communication at another electronic address of the addressee is the time when it becomes capable of being retrieved by the addressee at that address and the

addressee becomes aware that the electronic communication has been sent to that address. An electronic communication is presumed to be capable of being retrieved by the addressee when it reaches the addressee's electronic address.

3. An electronic communication is deemed to be dispatched at the place where the originator has its place of business and is deemed to be received at the place where the addressee has its place of business, as determined in accordance with article 6.

4. Paragraph 2 of this article applies notwithstanding that the place where the information system supporting an electronic address is located may be different from the place where the electronic communication is deemed to be received under paragraph 3 of this article. . . .

Article 13. Availability of Contract Terms

Nothing in this Convention affects the application of any rule of law that may require a party that negotiates some or all of the terms of a contract through the exchange of electronic communications to make available to the other party those electronic communications which contain the contractual terms in a particular manner, or relieves a party from the legal consequences of its failure to do so.[136]

While it may not answer all questions related to the use of electronic communications in the formation of contracts, the Convention does provide a clear set of rules for many of the most common issues. However, the small number of ratifications and the notable absence of the U.S. and the Member States of the EU make it impossible, for the time being, to suggest that the rules embodied in the Convention reflect a global standard. Since it is unlikely that the parties to an IBT specifically choose to submit their electronic contract formation to the Convention, the scope of application is currently as follows: The rules of the Convention are part of the legal systems of the countries that have ratified it. Thus, if an IBT is subject to the law of a country that has ratified the Convention ("Contracting State"), either by choice of the parties or via the application of the rules of private international law of the forum, the Convention applies as part of the law of that Contracting State and governs the formation of a contract by electronic communications, regardless of the location of the court or tribunal that hears the dispute between the parties.

While the direct application of the rules of the 2005 Convention remains limited on account of the limited number of ratifications, UNCITRAL also developed the 1996 Model Law on Electronic Commerce (as amended in 1998), and the 2001 Model Law on Electronic Signatures.[137] Much like the UCC, these Model Laws are

---

136. The Convention is available in the official languages of the UN on the website of UNCITRAL, http://www.uncitral.org/uncitral/en/uncitral texts/electronic_commerce/2005Convention.html.

137. Available at http://www.uncitral.org/uncitral/en/uncitral_texts/electronic_commerce.html.

not intended to be ratified like international conventions, but to be emulated via the adoption of national laws on electronic commerce and electronic signatures. The difference is important in two respects. First, the procedure for the ratification of an international convention differs in many countries from the procedure for the adoption of regular legislation. It may well be easier to implement certain rules on electronic commerce and electronic signature in the form of ordinary legislation without the expression of an international commitment. Second, the implementation of domestic legislation can deviate from some of the provisions of the model law or some amendments to the domestic legislation can be made at a later stage even if they are incompatible with the model law, and yet there would not be a breach of any international obligations in either case. Unsurprisingly, therefore, both Model Laws were vastly more successful than the 2005 Convention. As of June 2020, the 1996 Model Law on Electronic Commerce has seen the implementation of legislation based on or influenced by it in no less than 74 countries, including Australia, Canada, China, France, India, Mexico, Korea, Saudi Arabia, Thailand, the United Kingdom, 47 of the states in the U.S. and the District of Columbia, as well as Vietnam.[138] Even the more recent 2001 Model Law on Electronic Signatures has already seen the adoption of legislation based on or influenced by it in some 33 countries, including China, India, Mexico, Saudi Arabia, Thailand, the United Kingdom, and Vietnam.[139] Both Model Laws, therefore, deserve a closer look.

The 1996 UNCITRAL Model Law on Electronic Commerce (as amended in 1998) is supposed to inspire the adoption of national laws applicable "to any kind of information in the form of a data message used in the context of commercial activities" (Art. 1 Sphere of Application). Pursuant to Article 2, a "data message" is any "information generated, sent, received or stored by electronic, optical or similar means." Article 5 stipulates that "[i]nformation shall not be denied legal effect, validity or enforceability solely on the grounds that it is in the form of a data message" and Article 5*bis* expands this principle to information that is referred to in a data message. Similar to the U.S. codifications, Article 6(1) clarifies that "[w]here the law requires information to be in writing, that requirement is met by a data message if the information contained therein is accessible so as to be useable for subsequent reference" and Article 7(1) provides the same for the validity of signatures, provided "(a) a method is used to identify that person and to indicate that person's approval of the information contained in the data message; and (b) that method is as reliable as was appropriate for the purpose for which the data message was generated or communicated, in the light of all the circumstances, including any relevant agreement."

---

138. See http://www.uncitral.org/uncitral/en/uncitral_texts/electronic_commerce/1996Model_status.html.

139. See http://www.uncitral.org/uncitral/en/uncitral_texts/electronic_commerce/2001Model_status.html.

Several provisions are of particular interest and expand on principles already found and cited above:

Article 8. Original

(1) Where the law requires information to be presented or retained in its original form, that requirement is met by a data message if:

(a) there exists a reliable assurance as to the integrity of the information from the time when it was first generated in its final form, as a data message or otherwise; and

(b) where it is required that information be presented, that information is capable of being displayed to the person to whom it is to be presented. . . .

(3) For the purposes of subparagraph (a) of paragraph (1):

(a) the criteria for assessing integrity shall be whether the information has remained complete and unaltered, apart from the addition of any endorsement and any change which arises in the normal course of communication, storage and display; and

(b) the standard of reliability required shall be assessed in the light of the purpose for which the information was generated and in the light of all the relevant circumstances. . . .

Article 11. Formation and Validity of Contracts

(1) In the context of contract formation, unless otherwise agreed by the parties, an offer and the acceptance of an offer may be expressed by means of data messages. Where a data message is used in the formation of a contract, that contract shall not be denied validity or enforceability on the sole ground that a data message was used for that purpose. . . .

Article 13. Attribution of Data Messages

(1) A data message is that of the originator if it was sent by the originator itself.

(2) As between the originator and the addressee, a data message is deemed to be that of the originator if it was sent:

(a) by a person who had the authority to act on behalf of the originator in respect of that data message; or

(b) by an information system programmed by, or on behalf of, the originator to operate automatically.

(3) As between the originator and the addressee, an addressee is entitled to regard a data message as being that of the originator, and to act on that assumption, if:

(a) in order to ascertain whether the data message was that of the originator, the addressee properly applied a procedure previously agreed to by the originator for that purpose; or

(b) the data message as received by the addressee resulted from the actions of a person whose relationship with the originator or with any agent of the originator enabled that person to gain access to a method used by the originator to identify data messages as its own.

(4) Paragraph (3) does not apply:

(a) as of the time when the addressee has both received notice from the originator that the data message is not that of the originator, and had reasonable time to act accordingly; or

(b) in a case within paragraph (3)(b), at any time when the addressee knew or should have known, had it exercised reasonable care or used any agreed procedure, that the data message was not that of the originator.

(5) Where a data message is that of the originator or is deemed to be that of the originator, or the addressee is entitled to act on that assumption, then, as between the originator and the addressee, the addressee is entitled to regard the data message as received as being what the originator intended to send, and to act on that assumption. The addressee is not so entitled when it knew or should have known, had it exercised reasonable care or used any agreed procedure, that the transmission resulted in any error in the data message as received.

(6) The addressee is entitled to regard each data message received as a separate data message and to act on that assumption, except to the extent that it duplicates another data message and the addressee knew or should have known, had it exercised reasonable care or used any agreed procedure, that the data message was a duplicate.

Article 14. Acknowledgement of Receipt

(1) Paragraphs (2) to (4) of this article apply where, on or before sending a data message, or by means of that data message, the originator has requested or has agreed with the addressee that receipt of the data message be acknowledged.

(2) Where the originator has not agreed with the addressee that the acknowledgement be given in a particular form or by a particular method, an acknowledgement may be given by (a) any communication by the addressee, automated or otherwise, or

(b) any conduct of the addressee sufficient to indicate to the originator that the data message has been received.

(3) Where the originator has stated that the data message is conditional on receipt of the acknowledgement, the data message is treated as though it has never been sent, until the acknowledgement is received.

(4) Where the originator has not stated that the data message is conditional on receipt of the acknowledgement, and the acknowledgement has not been received by the originator within the time specified or agreed or, if no time has been specified or agreed, within a reasonable time, the originator:

(a) may give notice to the addressee stating that no acknowledgement has been received and specifying a reasonable time by which the acknowledgement must be received; and

(b) if the acknowledgement is not received within the time specified in subparagraph (a), may, upon notice to the addressee, treat the data message as though it had never been sent, or exercise any other rights it may have.

(5) Where the originator receives the addressee's acknowledgement of receipt, it is presumed that the related data message was received by the addressee. That presumption does not imply that the data message corresponds to the message received.

(6) Where the received acknowledgement states that the related data message met technical requirements, either agreed upon or set forth in applicable standards, it is presumed that those requirements have been met.

(7) Except in so far as it relates to the sending or receipt of the data message, this article is not intended to deal with the legal consequences that may flow either from that data message or from the acknowledgement of its receipt.

Article 15. Time and Place of Dispatch and Receipt of Data Messages

(1) Unless otherwise agreed between the originator and the addressee, the dispatch of a data message occurs when it enters an information system outside the control of the originator or of the person who sent the data message on behalf of the originator.

(2) Unless otherwise agreed between the originator and the addressee, the time of receipt of a data message is determined as follows:

(a) if the addressee has designated an information system for the purpose of receiving data messages, receipt occurs:

  (I) at the time when the data message enters the designated information system; or

  (ii) if the data message is sent to an information system of the addressee that is not the designated information system, at the time when the data message is retrieved by the addressee;

(b) if the addressee has not designated an information system, receipt occurs when the data message enters an information system of the addressee.

(3) Paragraph (2) applies notwithstanding that the place where the information system is located may be different from the place where the data message is deemed to be received under paragraph (4).

(4) Unless otherwise agreed between the originator and the addressee, a data message is deemed to be dispatched at the place where the originator has its place of business, and is deemed to be received at the place where the addressee has its place of business. For the purposes of this paragraph:

(a) if the originator or the addressee has more than one place of business, the place of business is that which has the closest relationship to the underlying transaction or, where there is no underlying transaction, the principal place of business;

(b) if the originator or the addressee does not have a place of business, reference is to be made to its habitual residence. . . .

Pursuant to Articles 16 and 17, laws based upon the 1996 Model Law can also extend to Bills of Lading and other contracts of carriage of goods, as well as various transport documents.

The 2001 UNCITRAL Model Law on Electronic Signatures defines "electronic signatures" as "data in electronic form in, affixed to or logically associated with, a data message, which may be used to identify the signatory in relation to the data message and to indicate the signatory's approval of the information contained in the data message" (Art. 2(a)). In addition to stipulating that electronic signatures have the same legal effects as traditional written signatures (Art. 3), the Model Law provides useful clarifications:

Article 6. Compliance with a Requirement for a Signature

1. Where the law requires a signature of a person, that requirement is met in relation to a data message if an electronic signature is used that is as reliable as was appropriate for the purpose for which the data message was generated or communicated, in the light of all the circumstances, including any relevant agreement.

2. Paragraph 1 applies whether the requirement referred to therein is in the form of an obligation or whether the law simply provides consequences for the absence of a signature.

3. An electronic signature is considered to be reliable for the purpose of satisfying the requirement referred to in paragraph 1 if:

(a) The signature creation data are, within the context in which they are used, linked to the signatory and to no other person;

(b) The signature creation data were, at the time of signing, under the control of the signatory and of no other person;

(c) Any alteration to the electronic signature, made after the time of signing, is detectable; and

(d) Where a purpose of the legal requirement for a signature is to provide assurance as to the integrity of the information to which it relates, any alteration made to that information after the time of signing is detectable.

4. Paragraph 3 does not limit the ability of any person:

(a) To establish in any other way, for the purpose of satisfying the requirement referred to in paragraph 1, the reliability of an electronic signature; or

(b) To adduce evidence of the non-reliability of an electronic signature. . . .

Article 8. Conduct of the Signatory

1. Where signature creation data can be used to create a signature that has legal effect, each signatory shall:

(a) Exercise reasonable care to avoid unauthorized use of its signature creation data;

(b) Without undue delay, utilize means made available by the certification service provider pursuant to article 9 of this Law, or otherwise use reasonable efforts, to notify any person that may reasonably be expected by the signatory to rely on or to provide services in support of the electronic signature if:

> (I) The signatory knows that the signature creation data have been compromised; or

> (ii) The circumstances known to the signatory give rise to a substantial risk that the signature creation data may have been compromised;

(c) Where a certificate is used to support the electronic signature, exercise reasonable care to ensure the accuracy and completeness of all material representations made by the signatory that are relevant to the certificate throughout its life cycle or that are to be included in the certificate.

2. A signatory shall bear the legal consequences of its failure to satisfy the requirements of paragraph 1.

Article 9. Conduct of the Certification Service Provider

1. Where a certification service provider provides services to support an electronic signature that may be used for legal effect as a signature, that certification service provider shall:

(a) Act in accordance with representations made by it with respect to its policies and practices;

(b) Exercise reasonable care to ensure the accuracy and completeness of all material representations made by it that are relevant to the certificate throughout its life cycle or that are included in the certificate;

(c) Provide reasonably accessible means that enable a relying party to ascertain from the certificate:

> (I) The identity of the certification service provider;

> (ii) That the signatory that is identified in the certificate had control of the signature creation data at the time when the certificate was issued;

(iii) That signature creation data were valid at or before the time when the certificate was issued;

(d) Provide reasonably accessible means that enable a relying party to ascertain, where relevant, from the certificate or otherwise:

(I) The method used to identify the signatory;

(ii) Any limitation on the purpose or value for which the signature creation data or the certificate may be used;

(iii) That the signature creation data are valid and have not been compromised;

(iv) Any limitation on the scope or extent of liability stipulated by the certification service provider;

(v) Whether means exist for the signatory to give notice pursuant to article 8, paragraph 1 (b), of this Law;

(vi) Whether a timely revocation service is offered;

(e) Where services under subparagraph (d) (v) are offered, provide a means for a signatory to give notice pursuant to article 8, paragraph 1 (b), of this Law and, where services under subparagraph (d) (vi) are offered, ensure the availability of a timely revocation service;

(f) Utilize trustworthy systems, procedures and human resources in performing its services.

2. A certification service provider shall bear the legal consequences of its failure to satisfy the requirements of paragraph 1.

Article 10. Trustworthiness

For the purposes of article 9, paragraph 1 (f), of this Law in determining whether, or to what extent, any systems, procedures and human resources utilized by a certification service provider are trustworthy, regard may be had to the following factors:

(a) Financial and human resources, including existence of assets;

(b) Quality of hardware and software systems;

(c) Procedures for processing of certificates and applications for certificates and retention of records;

(d) Availability of information to signatories identified in certificates and to potential relying parties;

(e) Regularity and extent of audit by an independent body;

(f) The existence of a declaration by the State, an accreditation body or the certification service provider regarding compliance with or existence of the foregoing; or

(g) Any other relevant factor.

Article 11. Conduct of the Relying Party

A relying party shall bear the legal consequences of its failure:

(a) To take reasonable steps to verify the reliability of an electronic signature; or

(b) Where an electronic signature is supported by a certificate, to take reasonable steps:

> (I) To verify the validity, suspension or revocation of the certificate; and

> (ii) To observe any limitation with respect to the certificate. . . .

What emerges from a comparison of the language of the UNCITRAL Model Laws and the various U.S. acts is a qualitative difference when it comes to clarity and coverage (qualitative expectations on the parties, liability etc.). It would be nice to see greater consideration given to international model laws in future U.S. legislative drafting efforts.

C. European Union Law

The Digital Single Market Strategy of the European Union is primarily aimed at the protection of consumers, as they are making use of the internet in the internal market of the EU for the purchase of goods and services. Member States are bound by *Regulation 2017/2394 on Cooperation Between National Authorities Responsible for the Enforcement of Consumer Protection Laws* (Regulation on Consumer Protection Cooperation),[140] which includes consumer protection in online transactions. The system is triggered, *inter alia*, if a trader in one Member State targets consumers in another Member State with misleading or fraudulent information or harmful or illegal products or services. *Directive 2019/771 on Certain Aspects Concerning Contracts for the Sale of Goods*[141] specifically provides "common rules on certain requirements concerning sales contracts concluded between sellers and consumers, in particular rules on the conformity of goods with the contract, remedies in the event of a lack of such conformity, the modalities for the exercise of those remedies, and on commercial guarantees" (Art. 1) and has to be implemented by the Member States into national law by January 1, 2022. For the protection of consumers in general, and in online transactions in particular, there are dozens of additional pieces of legislation in force at the level of the EU. A fuller description of this legislative framework would go beyond the scope of this book.

In the context of electronic commerce, e-privacy is another important factor and the EU has recently updated its data protection rules for the digital economy. *Regulation 2016/679 on the Protection of Natural Persons with Regard to the Processing of Personal Data and on the Free Movement of Such Data* (General Data Protection

---

140. OJ 2017 L 345, pp. 1–26.
141. OJ 2019 L 136, pp. 28–50.

Regulation—commonly known as the "GDPR")[142] became directly applicable law in the Member States on May 25, 2018. By contrast, *Directive 2016/680 on the Protection of Natural Persons with Regard to the Processing of Personal Data by Competent Authorities for the Purposes of the Prevention, Investigation, Detection or Prosecution of Criminal Offences or the Execution of Criminal Penalties, and on the Free Movement of Such Data* provides mostly framework rules and had to be implemented by the Member States into their national legal systems by May 6, 2018. Another *Regulation Concerning the Respect for Private Life and the Protection of Personal Data in Electronic Communications* has been proposed by the EU Commission but has yet to be adopted as law by the Council and the Parliament of the EU.[143]

Providers of goods or services who are based outside the EU are not directly affected by these regulations and directives, although the EU seeks to conclude international agreements with third countries for cooperation and mutual assistance in the protection of its consumers. To the extent third country providers of goods or services have subsidiaries or other assets in the EU, the EU rules can and will be directly enforced against them regardless of the existence of international agreements or the support or lack of support of their home countries.

Beyond the ambit of consumer and data protection, a number of EU regulations and directives deal with electronic signatures and contracts and are important for business-to-business (B2B) transactions.

EU Regulation 910/2014 on Electronic Identification and Trust Services for Electronic Transactions in the Internal Market[144] "seeks to enhance trust in electronic transactions in the internal market by providing a common foundation for secure electronic interaction between citizens, businesses and public authorities" (Preamble (2)). It repeals the earlier *Directive 1999/93 on a Community Framework for Electronic Signatures* and replaces its provisions with expanded and directly applicable rules. The Regulation "(a) lays down the conditions under which Member States recognise electronic identification means of natural and legal persons falling under a notified electronic identification scheme of another Member State; (b) lays down rules for trust services, in particular for electronic transactions; and (c) establishes a legal framework for electronic signatures, electronic seals, electronic time stamps, electronic documents, electronic registered delivery services and certificate services for website authentication" (Art. 1). It "applies to electronic identification schemes that have been notified by a Member State, and to trust service providers that are established in the Union" (Art. 2(1)). It "does not affect national or Union law related to the conclusion and validity of contracts or other legal or procedural obligations relating to form" (Art. 2(3)). EU Member States are expected to create their

---

142. For analysis see, inter alia, Meg Leta Jones & Margot E. Kaminski, *An American's Guide to the GDPR*, 97 Denv. L. Rev. (2020), forthcoming.

143. COM(2017) 10 final of January 10, 2017. The text of the proposal, which may be amended during the deliberations in the Council and the Parliament, is available at https://eur-lex.europa .eu/legal-content/EN/TXT/?uri=CELEX%3A52017PC0010.

144. OJ 2014 L 257, August 28, 2014, p. 73.

own electronic identification means or rely on private sector providers. Trust services are "electronic service[s] normally provided for remuneration which consists of: (a) the creation, verification, and validation of electronic signatures, electronic seals or electronic time stamps, electronic registered delivery services and certificates related to those services; or (b) the creation, verification and validation of certificates for website authentication; or (c) the preservation of electronic signatures, seals or certificates related to those services" (Preamble (16)). Trust service providers from outside the EU "shall be recognised as legally equivalent to . . . qualified trust service providers established in the Union where the trust services originating from the third country are recognised under an agreement concluded between the Union and the third country in question or an international organisation" (Art. 14(1)). The Regulation foresees a system of multiple assurance levels (low, substantial, and high) to correspond to the importance of a particular transaction. Trust service providers "shall verify, by appropriate means and in accordance with national law, the identity and, if applicable, any specific attributes of the natural or legal person" in question (Art. 24(1)).

The Regulation reiterates the familiar principle that electronic signatures are equivalent to traditional written signatures (Art. 25). It also introduces the notion of an "advanced electronic signature" — "(a) it is uniquely linked to the signatory; (b) it is capable of identifying the signatory; (c) it is created using electronic signature creation data that the signatory can, with a high level of confidence, use under his sole control; and (d) it is linked to the data signed therewith in such a way that any subsequent change in the data is detectable" (Art. 26). Section 5 of the Regulation deals with electronic seals, Section 6 covers electronic time stamps, and Section 7 regulates electronic registered delivery services provided by qualified trust service providers. Section 8 and Annex IV are about website authentication. Finally, Annex I identifies the requirements for qualified certificates for electronic signatures and Annex II deals with the requirements for qualified electronic signature creation devices.

Directive 2000/31 on Certain Legal Aspects of Information Society Services, in Particular Electronic Commerce, in the Internal Market,[145] generally referred to as the Directive on Electronic Commerce, establishes the principle that information services provided in one Member State in conformity with its national laws and any applicable EU laws benefit from the freedom to provide information services across all EU Member States. This allows for a limited level of forum shopping for providers who may want to set up shop in the Member State with the friendliest regulatory framework for their specific activities. That being said, other Member States may take measures against particular services or providers as long as those measures are:

(i) necessary for one of the following reasons:

— public policy, in particular the prevention, investigation, detection and prosecution of criminal offences, including the protection of

---

145. OJ 2000 L 178, July 17, 2000, pp. 1–16.

minors and the fight against any incitement to hatred on grounds of race, sex, religion or nationality, and violations of human dignity concerning individual persons,

— the protection of public health,

— public security, including the safeguarding of national security and defence,

— the protection of consumers, including investors;

(ii) taken against a given information society service which prejudices the objectives referred to in point (i) or which presents a serious and grave risk of prejudice to those objectives; [and]

(iii) proportionate to those objectives;[146]

Furthermore, a Member State wishing to restrict the freedom of a service provider from another Member State first has to ask the other Member State to ensure compliance by the service provider with applicable laws and the other Member State did not take effective measures. In addition, a Member State wishing to restrict freedoms provided under the Directive has to notify the EU Commission.

In line with the doctrine that freedoms in the internal market have to be interpreted broadly and restrictions have to be limited to what is objectively necessary, Article 4 requires Member States to "ensure that the taking up and pursuit of the activity of an information society service provider may not be made subject to prior authorisation or any other requirement having equivalent effect."

Other important provisions of the Electronic Commerce Directives are the following:

Article 9 Treatment of Contracts

1. Member States shall ensure that their legal system allows contracts to be concluded by electronic means. Member States shall in particular ensure that the legal requirements applicable to the contractual process neither create obstacles for the use of electronic contracts nor result in such contracts being deprived of legal effectiveness and validity on account of their having been made by electronic means.

2. Member States may lay down that paragraph 1 shall not apply to all or certain contracts falling into one of the following categories:

(a) contracts that create or transfer rights in real estate, except for rental rights;

(b) contracts requiring by law the involvement of courts, public authorities or professions exercising public authority [such as notaries];

---

146. Article 3(4)(a).

(c) contracts of suretyship granted and on collateral securities furnished by persons acting for purposes outside their trade, business or profession;

(d) contracts governed by family law or by the law of succession. . . .

Article 11 Placing of the Order

1. Member States shall ensure, except when otherwise agreed by parties who are not consumers, that in cases where the recipient of the service places his order through technological means, the following principles apply:

— the service provider has to acknowledge the receipt of the recipient's order without undue delay and by electronic means,

— the order and the acknowledgement of receipt are deemed to be received when the parties to whom they are addressed are able to access them.

2. Member States shall ensure that, except when otherwise agreed by parties who are not consumers, the service provider makes available to the recipient of the service appropriate, effective and accessible technical means allowing him to identify and correct input errors, prior to the placing of the order.

3. Paragraph 1, first indent, and paragraph 2 shall not apply to contracts concluded exclusively by exchange of electronic mail or by equivalent individual communications.

Article 9 mainly requires the Member States of the EU to allow the formation of contracts via electronic means. While some contracts, pursuant to paragraph 2, do not fall within the scope of application of the article and, thus, remain subject to the regulatory powers of the Member States themselves, these are rarely of importance in the type of international business transactions we are dealing with.

Article 11 is mainly tailored to the conclusion of contracts via the placing of an order on a website, for example when we purchase something on Amazon.com. Pursuant to its paragraph 3, Article 11 is largely inapplicable if a contract is concluded via an exchange of offer and acceptance by e-mail. There is one provision of the article, however, that is not excluded via its paragraph 3, namely the requirement in paragraph 1, first indent, that electronic communications "are deemed to be received when the parties to whom they are addressed *are able* to access them" (emphasis added). This does not require that a human being at the other end actually received or read the message, as long as the addressee would have been able to access the message. Unsurprisingly, this causes a plethora of difficulties in the realm of contract formation if the trust services dealt with in Regulation 910/2014 are not relied upon—since the moment when an offer or an acceptance is received is not clear from the Directive. As a consequence, and whenever a harmonized rule is not provided in EU law, the formation of electronic contracts is subject to Member State law and the solutions in the different Member States can differ substantially. For example, in Spain, a communication is deemed to be received when it is deposited into the e-mail account of the recipient, regardless of whether or not the recipient is aware of it. By contrast, in the United Kingdom, a communication needs to be acknowledged either by way of an electronic confirmation or by other means, such as making payment. Italy considers a communication to be received if it is sent to an e-mail address previously provided by the addressee for such communications. France seems to allow all of the above methods.[147] Although the harmonization at the level of the EU is a vast improvement over the preexisting patchwork of 27 national sets of rules, Member State laws remain relevant wherever the EU has not dealt comprehensively with an issue.

In addition to the multitude of existing acts, the 2018 Communication from the EU Commission "Completing a Trusted Digital Market for All"[148] lists no fewer than 29 ongoing legislative initiatives for the timeframe 2015–2018. Although the intentions of the EU authorities are certainly laudable, it is doubtful that such a highly detailed regulatory framework is practical and effective in an environment where available technology is evolving rapidly.

D. Case Law Examples for E-Commerce Disputes

The cases deal with different problems related to contract formation. Observe how the courts deal with e-mails and, more recently, digital transaction management (DTM) systems.

Case 2-19

Robert Naldi v. Michael Grunberg and Grunberg 55 LLC

908 N.Y.S.2d 639 (2010)
(Paragraph numbers added, some footnotes omitted.)
OPINION OF THE COURT
Friedman, J.

[1] The complaint in this action seeks enforcement of a right of first refusal that plaintiff claims he held for 30 days while conducting due diligence in contemplation of entering into a contract to purchase real property. Defendant Grunberg 55 LLC, appealing from the denial of its motion to dismiss, argues, among other things, that the alleged right of first refusal is not enforceable under the applicable statute of frauds (General Obligations Law § 5-703) because it was memorialized in an e-mail only. We reject this argument, reaffirming our prior decisions that have held (albeit without extensive discussion) that an e-mail will satisfy the statute of frauds so long as its contents and subscription meet all requirements of the governing statute. In this case, however, the record — including plaintiff's admissions in the complaint,

---

147. See Esperanza Gómez Valenzuela, *Regulation of Electronic Contracts in the European Community: New Challenges*, European Int'l J. Sci. & Tech., Vol. 2, No. 8, 2013, pp. 209–215, with further references.

148. https://ec.europa.eu/digital-single-market/en/news/completing-trusted-digital-single-market-all.

the undisputed documentary evidence of the parties' dealings, and the affidavit of plaintiff's representative in the negotiations—establishes as a matter of law that plaintiff never accepted the right of first refusal proposed in the e-mail. The right to match "any legitimate, better offer" proffered by the e-mail was tied to the asking price of $52 million. Given that the parties did not tentatively agree on the price term linked to the right of first refusal proposed in the e-mail, there was never any meeting of the minds between the parties as to that right of first refusal. Although plaintiff apparently alleges that the parties subsequently reached an oral or implied-in-fact agreement that plaintiff would have a right of first refusal based on a different price term ($50 million), any such unwritten right of first refusal is unenforceable under General Obligations Law § 5-703. Accordingly, defendant's motion to dismiss the complaint should have been granted.

[2] The complaint alleges that, on February 9, 2007, plaintiff, a citizen and resident of Italy, offered, through his broker, to purchase the property owned by defendant at 15-19 West 55th Street in Manhattan for $50 million. Three days later, on February 12, defendant's broker, Mark Spinelli of Massey Knakal Realty Services, responded to plaintiff's broker with an e-mail that stated in pertinent part:

> "Below is a response to your customer's offer for 15-19 West 55th Street. Please review with your customer and let me know how you would like to proceed.
>
> Counteroffer: $52 million
>
> DD: No due diligence period although complete unfettered access and first right of refusal on any legitimate, better offer during a 30 day period[.]
>
> Deposit: 10% deposit hard in escrow in the US upon signing of contract that the ownership will furnish to them forthwith. Negotiations will take place during their due diligence.
>
> The ownership will not take the property off the market for anyone without a signed contract and hard money.
>
> Mark J. Spinelli, Director of Sales, Massey Knakal Realty Services."

[3] The complaint does not allege, and conspicuously omits from its partial quotation of the above e-mail, the price term ($52 million) contained in defendant's counteroffer. Instead, the complaint alleges that Spinelli's February 12 e-mail "duly acknowledged Plaintiff's offer and made a counterproposal, while providing Plaintiff with the subject Right of First Refusal in consideration for his continuing interest in the property." The complaint further alleges: "Based upon the actual, constructive and/or apparent authority of Massey Knakal, the Right of First Refusal was immediately binding and enforceable and provided Plaintiff with specific and definite rights in the Property."

[4] After receiving the above e-mail, plaintiff allegedly began conducting costly due diligence on the property. The record shows that the parties exchanged e-mail concerning this due diligence, which required defendant's cooperation. For example,

an e-mail from plaintiff's counsel to defendant's counsel, dated February 26, 2007, states: "[W]e [plaintiff's counsel] would like to send 2 people on Wednesday to review Seller's records/files in regard to the property. Please advise where the files are located and whether Seller is able to accommodate the Wednesday request."

[5] Despite the $52 million counteroffer set forth in Spinelli's e-mail, on or about February 16, 2007, defendant's attorney forwarded to plaintiff's attorney a draft of a contract for sale of the property for $50 million, the amount of plaintiff's original offer. Notably, far from alleging that the $50 million price term in the draft contract was a mistake, the complaint affirmatively relies on the draft contract as evidence of an alleged tentative agreement in principal that the property would be sold for $50 million. In this regard, the complaint alleges: "Significantly, the contract forwarded by [defendant's attorney] provided for a $50 million purchase price consistent with Plaintiff's offer without any indication that the contract was not to be considered a definitive offer to sell the Property for $50 million." To like effect, plaintiff's representative in this matter, Federico Santini, stated in his affidavit opposing the motion to dismiss:

> Defendants fail to explain why the proposed contract contains a purchase price of $50 million (not $52 million). The dissemination of a $50 million contract, prepared by Defendants' own counsel, not only suggests that the purported $52 million counterproposal was not seriously pursued by Defendants, but also completely undermines Defendants' argument that Plaintiff rejected the counteroffer of $52 million. In view of the subsequent [draft] contract, Massey Knakal's email [*sic*] must be read to simply mean that a counteroffer was potentially under discussion by the parties' [*sic*] subject, of course, to Plaintiff's right of first refusal.

[6] Neither the draft contract nor the cover letter transmitting it (which are in the record) contains any reference to a right of first refusal.

[7] The complaint further alleges that plaintiff subsequently learned that defendant was pursuing a sale with a third party in the amount of $52 million. In March, plaintiff sent defendant a letter purporting to exercise the "first right of refusal" referenced in Spinelli's February 12 e-mail, stating:

> Pursuant to the first right you granted me as per above [*sic*; nothing appears above], I hereby offer to purchase the properties for a cash consideration of $52,000,000 . . . . I am ready to sign the sale contract and to deposit 10% in escrow on [*sic*] your attorney's account within [*sic*] 9:00 p.m. of Monday 12th March, 2007.

[8] Defendant rejected the foregoing offer and went forward with the sale of the property to another purchaser.

[9] The complaint asserts a single cause of action against defendant for breach of contract, based on defendant's refusal to honor the right of first refusal allegedly granted to plaintiff in the February 12 e-mail of defendant's broker. In lieu of answering, defendant moved to dismiss the complaint . . . , arguing: (1) that there

was never any meeting of the minds as to the right of first refusal; (2) that the right of first refusal was barred by the statute of frauds because it was memorialized only in an e-mail; (3) that, even if it is possible for an e-mail to satisfy the applicable statute of frauds, the e-mail in question contained only the automatically generated identification block of the brokerage firm from which it was sent and therefore was not properly subscribed; and (4) that neither Spinelli, the broker for defendant whose e-mail referred to the right of first refusal, nor his firm (Massey Knakal) had authority under the firm's listing agreement to contractually bind defendant. As previously stated, we reverse on the ground that there was no meeting of the minds on the right of first refusal embodied in Spinelli's e-mail counterproposal to sell the property for $52 million, and any oral or implied-in-fact agreement on a right of first refusal with reference to a different price term is barred by the statute of frauds.

[10] At the outset of our analysis, we reject defendant's argument that an e-mail can never constitute a writing that satisfies the statute of frauds of General Obligations Law § 5-703 ("Conveyances and contracts concerning real property required to be in writing").[2] Again, this Court has held in other contexts that e-mails may satisfy the statute of frauds (*see Williamson v Delsener*, 59 AD3d 291 [2009] [stipulation settling litigation]; *Stevens v Publicis S.A.*, 50 AD3d 253, 255–256 [2008], *lv dismissed* 10 NY3d 930 [2008] [modification of written agreement barring oral changes], citing *Rosenfeld v Zerneck*, 4 Misc 3d 193 [Sup Ct, Kings County 2004] [stating, in dicta, that an e-mail reflecting an agreement to sell real property may satisfy the statute of frauds, although the e-mail at issue failed to state all essential terms]; *see also Bazak Intl. Corp. v Tarrant Apparel Group*, 378 F Supp 2d 377, 383–386 [SD NY 2005] [holding that e-mail satisfied the requirement of a "writing in confirmation of the contract" under New York's UCC 2-201 (2)]).[3] We reaffirm the holdings of *Williamson* and *Stevens*.

---

2. Each of the first three subdivisions of General Obligations Law § 5-703 sets forth a writing requirement applicable in specified circumstances. Defendant relies on General Obligations Law § 5-703 (3), which provides:

> "A contract to devise real property or establish a trust of real property, or any interest therein or right with reference thereto, is void unless the contract or some note or memorandum thereof is in writing and subscribed by the party to be charged therewith, or by his lawfully authorized agent."

However, there is authority treating General Obligations Law § 5-703 (2) as the provision applicable to a contract creating a right of first refusal as to real property (*see Pfeil v Cappiello*, 29 AD3d 1187, 1188 [2006]). General Obligations Law § 5-703 (2) provides:

> "A contract for the leasing for a longer period than one year, or for the sale, of any real property, or an interest therein, is void unless the contract or some note or memorandum thereof, expressing the consideration, is in writing, subscribed by the party to be charged, or by his lawful agent thereunto authorized by writing."

Under either subdivision, our analysis of whether the writing requirement may be satisfied by an e-mail would be the same.

3. *Cf. MP Innovations, Inc. v Atlantic Horizon Intl., Inc.*, 72 AD3d 571, 572 (2010) (e-mail did not satisfy the statute of frauds because it failed to "identify a number of material terms" of the alleged agreement); *Page v Muze, Inc.*, 270 AD2d 401, 401 (2000) (e-mail did not satisfy the statute

[11] Somewhat paradoxically, in support of its argument that an e-mail is not a writing for these purposes, defendant relies on a 1994 amendment of the general statute of frauds . . . specifically providing that, as to certain "qualified financial contracts" defined in the legislation . . . , the record of an "electronic communication" . . . , such as a retrieved e-mail, satisfies the statute of frauds (see General Obligations Law § 5-701 [b] [1]; see also General Obligations Law § 5-701 [b] [4] ["For purposes of this subdivision, the tangible written text produced by . . . computer retrieval or other process by which electronic signals are transmitted by telephone or otherwise shall constitute a writing"]). In essence, defendant argues that, since the Legislature specifically amended only General Obligations Law § 5-701 (which does not apply to "contracts concerning real property" covered by General Obligations Law § 5-703) to specify that an e-mail or other electronic communication constitutes a writing—and even then only as to a specifically defined subset of the transactions covered by General Obligations Law § 5-701—the implication is that an electronic communication cannot satisfy the statute of frauds for contracts outside the scope of the amendment. This argument might have had some plausibility as a matter of statutory construction when General Obligations Law § 5-701 (b) was first enacted.[4] Sixteen years later, however, with e-mail omnipresent in both business and personal affairs, it is too late in the day to accept it.[5] . . .

[13] Today, a decade into the twenty-first century, e-mail is no longer a novelty. Although not enacted by New York, the Uniform Electronic Transactions Act . . . [UETA], which was promulgated in 1999 and has been enacted by 47 states, the District of Columbia, and the Virgin Islands . . . , provides, inter alia, that "[a] contract may not be denied legal effect or enforceability solely because an electronic record was used in its formation" (UETA § 7 [b]) and that "[i]f a law requires a record to be in writing, an electronic record satisfies the law" (UETA § 7 [c]).[8] Moreover,

---

of frauds where it "made only an equivocal reference" to the right claimed by plaintiff and "was not shown to have satisfied the subscription requirement").

4. See McKinney's Cons Laws of NY, Book 1, Statutes § 74 ("the failure of the Legislature to include a matter within the scope of an act may be construed as an indication that its exclusion was intended"); § 197, Comment, at 368 ("that two independent statutes contain similar provisions does not require that an amendment of one be incorporated as an amendment to the other," since "[t]he Legislature can amend one or both, in its discretion"); § 240, Comment, at 411 ("the specific mention of one person or thing implies the exclusion of other persons or thing[s]"); but see § 76, Comment, at 169 ("rules of construction for a statute are to be invoked only where its language leaves its purpose and intent uncertain"); § 91, Comment, at 174 ("The object of these [rules of statutory construction] is not to lay down inflexible principles . . . but to render assistance in determining the legislative intent," and "[r]esort is had to the rules . . . only when it is necessary to apply them to ascertain the meaning of a statute").

5. We thus disagree with Vista Developers Corp. v VFP Realty LLC (17 Misc 3d 914 [Sup Ct, Queens County 2007]), which essentially accepted the argument made by defendant here (see id. at 919–921).

8. See also UETA § 7, Official Comment 1 (the "fundamental premise" of the UETA is "that the medium in which a record, signature, or contract is created, presented or retained does not affect [its] legal significance").

in 2000, Congress enacted the Electronic Signatures in Global and National Commerce Act . . . [E-SIGN], which provides in pertinent part:

> Notwithstanding any statute, regulation, or other rule of law . . . , with respect to any transaction in or affecting interstate or foreign commerce —
>
> (1) a signature, contract, or other record relating to such transaction may not be denied legal effect, validity, or enforceability solely because it is in electronic form; and
>
> (2) a contract relating to such transaction may not be denied legal effect, validity, or enforceability solely because an electronic signature or electronic record was used in its formation (15 USC § 7001 [a]).

[14] It could be argued (although plaintiff has not done so) that E-SIGN applies here based on plaintiff's Italian nationality, and perhaps on other grounds as well (*see* 12 Lawrence's Anderson on the Uniform Commercial Code, E-SIGN § 101:2 [3d ed]). However, we need not determine whether the transaction at issue here was one "in or affecting interstate or foreign commerce" for purposes of E-SIGN. Any uncertainty that existed in 1994 as to whether the record of an electronic communication satisfied the statute of frauds under New York state law has long since been resolved.

[15] In 1999, the New York Legislature enacted the Electronic Signatures and Records Act (ESRA) . . . . ESRA does not specifically address whether an "electronic record" constitutes a writing for purposes of the statute of frauds.[9] However, ESRA does provide, in pertinent part:

> In accordance with this section [directing the state Office for Technology to establish rules and regulations governing the use of electronic signatures and authentication] unless specifically provided otherwise by law, an electronic signature may be used by a person in lieu of a signature affixed by hand. The use of an electronic signature shall have the same validity and effect as the use of a signature affixed by hand (ESRA § 304 [2]).[10]

---

9. ESRA defines "electronic record" to mean "information, evidencing any act, transaction, occurrence, event, or other activity, produced or stored by electronic means and capable of being accurately reproduced in forms perceptible by human sensory capabilities" (ESRA § 302 [2]). E-SIGN defines the same term as "a contract or other record created, generated, sent, communicated, received, or stored by electronic means" (15 USC § 7006 [4]).

10. While the applicable statute of frauds requires a signature or other subscription by the party to be charged or its duly authorized agent (*see* General Obligations Law § 5-703 [2], [3]) — a matter apparently addressed by ESRA § 304 (2) — ESRA, as codified, does not directly address whether an electronic record constitutes a writing for purposes of the statute of frauds. ESRA § 305 (3) provides that "[a]n electronic record shall have the same force and effect as those records not produced by electronic means," but, viewed in the context of the remainder of section 305, this provision appears to be addressed to government records. The regulation promulgated by the Office for Technology providing that "[a]n electronic record used by a person shall have the same force and effect as those records not produced by electronic means" (9 NYCRR 540.5 [a]) also appears, in the context of the remainder of section 540.5, to be addressed to documents filed with the government.

[16] In 2002, the Legislature enacted certain amendments to ESRA. Among other things, the 2002 legislation amended ESRA's definition of the term "electronic signature" to conform to E-SIGN's definition of the same term (*see* L 2002, ch 314, § 2).[11] ...

[17] ... New York's lawmakers appear to have chosen to incorporate the substantive terms of E-SIGN into New York state law.[12] Thus, we conclude that E-SIGN's requirement that an electronically memorialized and subscribed contract be given the same legal effect as a contract memorialized and subscribed on paper ... is part of New York law, whether or not the transaction at issue is a matter "in or affecting interstate or foreign commerce."[13]

[18] Even in the absence of E-SIGN and the 2002 statement of legislative intent, given the vast growth in the last decade and a half in the number of people and entities regularly using e-mail, we would conclude that the terms "writing" and "subscribed" in General Obligations Law § 5-703 should now be construed to include, respectively, records of electronic communications and electronic signatures, notwithstanding the limited scope of the 1994 amendment of the general statute of frauds. [14] As one scholar has observed, "In most cases, ... definitions of a 'writing' or a 'signature' are transferable to the electronic context and the primary issue is whether the writing contains the relevant, required content" (Nimmer, Law of Computer Technology § 13:12). As much as a communication originally written or typed on paper, an e-mail retrievable from computer storage serves the purpose of the statute of frauds by providing "'some objective guaranty, other than word of mouth, that there really has been some deal'" (*Bazak Intl. Corp. v Mast Indus.*, 73 NY2d 113, 120 [1989],

---

11. ESRA § 302 (3) now defines "electronic signature" to mean "an electronic sound, symbol, or process, attached to or logically associated with an electronic record and executed or adopted by a person with the intent to sign the record." This substantially conforms to the definition of "electronic signature" set forth in E-SIGN (15 USC § 7006 [5]).

12. An alternative approach, which the Legislature evidently chose not to take, would have been to adopt UETA, as most states have done. E-SIGN permits states to supersede the federal act by enacting UETA (*see* 15 USC § 7002 [a]).

13. In this regard, the legislative memorandum in support of the 2002 amendments to ESRA demonstrates that the bill was motivated by a desire to eliminate possible inconsistencies between ESRA and E-SIGN. The memorandum states: "It is essential ... to the success and promotion of electronic commerce and electronic government for both laws to be interpreted and applied consistently. Determining which law applies to particular transactions has caused confusion in the business community and thereby has an inhibiting effect on the expansion of electronic commerce in New York. Consequently, [the Office for Technology] is proposing that ESRA be amended to eliminate some of the definitional differences between ESRA and [E-SIGN]" (Senate Mem in Support of L 2002, ch 314, 2002 McKinney's Session Laws of NY, at 1881).

14. This approach seems to be consistent with the current weight of authority nationwide (*see* John E. Theuman, Annotation, *Satisfaction of Statute of Frauds by E-Mail*, 110 ALR5th 277, 283, § 2 ["Courts addressing this question have ... determined on a case-by-case basis whether the particular e-mail messages ... satisfy the elements of the applicable Statute of Frauds provision, an approach which may imply acceptance of the general proposition that e-mails can satisfy the Statute of Frauds in a proper case"]).

quoting 1954 Report of NY Law Rev Commn, at 119; *see also Bazak Intl. Corp. v Tarrant Apparel Group*, 378 F Supp 2d at 383–384 ["because '(u)nder any computer storage method, the computer system "remembers" the message even after being turned off,' whether or not the e-mail is eventually printed on paper or saved on the server, it remains an objectively observable and tangible record that such a confirmation exists"], quoting Wilkerson, 41 U Kan L Rev at 412). The writing and subscription requirements of the statute of frauds have been held flexible enough to accommodate earlier innovations in communications technology, such as the telegram, the telex, and the fax (*see* Robertson, 49 SC L Rev at 797–803; Wilkerson, 41 U Kan L Rev at 409–414), and the same logic used to reach those results "justif[ies] a rule that permits e-mail or other electronic media to constitute an acceptable memorandum, so long as the other requirements of a valid memorandum are met" (10 Lord, Williston on Contracts § 29:23, at 592 [4th ed]; *see also Shattuck v Klotzbach*, 14 Mass L Rptr 360, 2001 WL 1839720, *4, 2001 Mass Super LEXIS 642, *9–10 [2001] [decided before state's adoption of UETA]; Maker, *Of Keystrokes and Ballpoints: Real Estate and the Statute of Frauds in the Electronic Age*, 80 NY St BJ [No. 6] 46, 47 [July/Aug. 2008] [the "similarity between telegrams and e-mails cogently argues for the importation of 'telegram jurisprudence' into the world of e-mails"]).

[19] Notwithstanding that an e-mail may satisfy the statute of frauds, we conclude that the motion should have been granted and the complaint dismissed. Even if the e-mail on which plaintiff relies would satisfy General Obligations Law § 5-703, the allegations of the complaint itself, together with plaintiff's admissions and undisputed documentary evidence in the record, establish, as a matter of law, that there was never a meeting of the minds between the parties on the terms of the proposed right of first refusal set forth in the February 12, 2007 e-mail sent by Spinelli, defendant's broker. . . .

[22] Finally, as previously noted, defendant makes two additional arguments. The first of these is that the "signature block" at the bottom of the Spinelli e-mail (identifying the writer and his title, firm, address, and telephone and fax numbers) was automatically generated by the e-mail system rather than deliberately typed and therefore does not qualify as an intentional subscription for purposes of the statute of frauds (*see Parma Tile Mosaic & Marble Co. v Estate of Short*, 87 NY2d 524 [1996]). Defendant's remaining argument is that, even if Spinelli "subscribed" the e-mail within the meaning of General Obligations Law § 5-703, neither he nor his brokerage firm, Massey Knakal, had authority to enter into binding contracts on defendant's behalf. Given that the complaint must be dismissed for the reason already discussed, we need not resolve whether either of these additional arguments would furnish independent grounds for dismissing the complaint on a pre-answer, pre-discovery motion. . . .

Notes and Questions

1. Why did the state of New York not enact a law based on the UETA? What are the rules that apply in New York?

2. What is the scope of application of the federal E-SIGN Act?

3. In paragraph 14, the court suggests that the E-SIGN Act might apply based on "plaintiff's Italian nationality, and perhaps other grounds as well." Can you explain what "other grounds" the court may have been thinking of?

4. The court does not apply the E-SIGN Act, *inter alia*, because the plaintiff did not argue that it should be applied. What are the rules about applicable laws before U.S. courts? Is it the court's job or the parties' job to find the applicable law? What if a party argues applicability of a law that clearly does not apply and the other party does not contradict?

5. Where does the court find a rule that e-mails have to be saved and retrievable to satisfy the requirement of "writing"? Why?

6. Can you point out differences among UETA, E-SIGN and/or New York's ESRA that justify the coexistence of different legal sources? The present court does not seem to care very much about which of the rules it applies.

Case 2-20

Alliance Laundry Systems, LLC v. ThyssenKrupp Materials, NA

570 F. Supp. 2d 1061 (E.D. Wis. 2008)
(Paragraph numbers added, footnotes as in the original.)
DECISION AND ORDER
Lynn Adelman, District Judge

[1] Plaintiff Alliance Laundry Systems, LLC, a Delaware limited liability company whose members are Wisconsin citizens, brings this diversity action against defendant Thyssenkrupp Materials, NA, a Delaware corporation whose principal place of business is Michigan, alleging that defendant, through its distribution division, Ken-Mac Metals, breached a contract to sell stainless steel. Before me now are plaintiff's motion for summary judgment and defendant's motion to compel discovery.

I. Facts[1]

[2] Plaintiff manufactures commercial laundry equipment and defendant, through its KenMac Metals division,[2] sells and distributes various metals, including stainless steel. Plaintiff needs stainless steel to manufacture its products, and in May 2005 plaintiff and defendant entered into a written agreement for the supply of stainless steel. The supply agreement commenced on July 1, 2005 and remained in effect until December 31, 2006. The agreement required defendant to supply steel in the specific sizes and gauges necessary for plaintiff's products, and it established a fixed

---

1. As I am required to do at the summary judgment stage, I state the facts in the light most favorable to defendant, the non-movant, and draw all reasonable inferences from those facts in defendant's favor. Plaintiff has objected to most of defendant's proposed findings of fact as irrelevant. However, for reasons explained later in this decision, such proposed findings are relevant.

2. All references to "defendant" refer to defendant's Ken-Mac Metals division.

base price for the steel as well as a floating surcharge. Usually, when plaintiff wanted to purchase steel pursuant to the supply agreement, it sent a signed purchase order to defendant. Defendant would then also sign the purchase order and either mail it back to plaintiff or send it with the shipment of purchased metal.

[3] Defendant's credit department approves all orders before defendant fills them, and defendant's repeat customers, including plaintiff, have a line of credit. When defendant enters an order for metal into its computer system, the system will run the order against the customer's line of credit. If the customer's account is in good standing, the computer will automatically print the paperwork necessary to fill the order. Defendant will then assemble and ship the order. But if the customer's account is delinquent, someone in defendant's credit department must approve the order before defendant will fill it. Before the credit department will approve such an order, a credit analyst will speak with the customer to obtain assurances that if defendant ships the metal, the customer will pay for it.

[4] During the term of the supply agreement, defendant periodically sent invoices to plaintiff for the metal plaintiff purchased pursuant to the supply agreement. Such invoices requested payment within thirty days. If plaintiff paid the balance due within thirty days, defendant permitted it to discount the amount owed. The backside of every invoice included the following provision:

> 8. CREDIT TERMS. All orders and shipments shall at all times be subject to the approval of the Seller's Credit Department. The Seller reserves the right to decline to make shipment whenever, for any reason, there is doubt as to Buyer's financial responsibility and Seller shall not in such event be liable for breach or nonperformance of this contract in whole or in part. . . .

Defendant issued dozens of invoices to plaintiff containing this language.

[5] In the early months of the supply agreement, plaintiff paid all invoices in a timely fashion. However, beginning in 2006, plaintiff began accumulating past-due balances. Throughout 2006, defendant sent plaintiff a number of e-mails reminding it of these balances. Defendant encouraged plaintiff to pay the past-due balances so that defendant would not need to place a hold on future shipments to plaintiff. In the meantime, plaintiff decided to obtain its metal from a different supplier and therefore did not renew the supply agreement when it expired at the end of 2006. When 2007 commenced, plaintiff had still not paid invoices for metal purchased under the supply agreement.

[6] When the supply agreement expired at the end of 2006, defendant had a significant amount of steel in its inventory that it had earmarked for plaintiff. Defendant had anticipated selling such steel to plaintiff pursuant to the supply agreement. Because defendant had designed it to plaintiff's specifications, the steel had significantly less value to other potential buyers. When plaintiff terminated the supply agreement, defendant attempted to find buyers for the inventory as quickly as possible to avoid taking a loss. Defendant sold some of the inventory to other buyers, but much of it remained unsold. Thus, on February 22, 2007, defendant, through its employee,

Matt Halterman, sent an e-mail to plaintiff's employee, Joel Kuenzli, asking whether plaintiff would submit an offer for the left-over steel. Kuenzli did not immediately respond. On March 5, 2007, another of defendant's employees, Barry Brunner, sent a follow-up e-mail to Kuenzli, inquiring about plaintiff's interest in the steel. Finally, on March 19, 2007, Brunner sent an e-mail to Kuenzli stating that if plaintiff wanted the excess steel, it needed to submit a proposal by the end of the week. The e-mail added that defendant "need[ed] to move this to you by the end of the month." . . .

[7] On March 20, 2007, Kuenzli responded to Brunner's e-mail by sending an e-mail stating that the "attached Excel spreadsheet lists my offer," referring to a spreadsheet attached to the e-mail electronically. . . . The e-mail added that "[t]he 'Pay Price' column is my offer for the base price of the material and the 'Proposed Surcharge' column is my offer for the surcharge rate/lb per item. We can discuss once you've had a chance to review." . . . About two hours later, Brunner sent a reply e-mail instructing Kuenzli to "Give Matt [Halterman] the purchase order number, so we can start shipping this metal to you." . . . On March 23, 2007, Kuenzli sent an e-mail to Halterman stating:

> The po for the remaining inventory is 334364. It's 81 pages long and I'm in the process of checking and signing it as I write. I will mail the hard copy today to your attention. Please coordinate with Scott on the shipments. I know you're planning to ship all material next week.. No problem . . . But. . . . Some material goes to plant 1 while others go to plant 2. Please work that out with Scott. (Halterman Decl. Ex. C.)

[8] The "Scott" to whom Kuenzli referred was Scott Stettbacher, another employee of plaintiff's with whom Halterman had dealt in the past. After writing the e-mail, Kuenzli signed the purchase order, dated it March 23, 2007 and, as promised, mailed a hard copy to defendant.

[9] In accordance with Kuenzli's instructions relating to shipping, on March 23, 2007, Halterman sent an e-mail to Kuenzli and Stettbacher stating:

> Joel, Thank you for the info, I appreciate the heads-up on the ship-to's.

> Scott, what is the address for plant 2? I'm assuming that's the new one and plant 1 is the regular one. Do you have a copy of Joel's PO? Can you let me know which items go to which facility? If it's just a case of "Ripon" parts going to plant 1 and "Marianna" parts going to plant 2 that's easy for me to figure out, but if it isn't that cut and dry please let me know by part number. . . .

[10] The record does not indicate whether Stettbacher ever answered Halterman's questions about where to ship the metal, but on March 26, 2007, Stettbacher sent an e-mail to Halterman providing some additional instructions about how plaintiff wanted to prepare the metal.

[11] At the same time that the parties were negotiating the sale of the left-over metal, defendant's credit department was trying to get plaintiff to pay its overdue invoices.

The credit department was communicating with Kuenzli, who, as discussed, was also involved in the attempt to purchase the left-over steel. The credit department sent e-mails and made phone calls to Kuenzli on January 5, January 8, and February 7. In addition, on March 1, 2007, the credit department sent an e-mail to Kuenzli informing him that although plaintiff had paid some of the past-due invoices, it had improperly taken thirty-day discounts on them. Because plaintiff failed to pay within thirty days, it owed the full balance, not the discounted amount. On March 9, 2007, the credit department sent another e-mail to Kuenzli stating that some invoices were 200 days overdue and demanding immediate payment. . . .

[13] Plaintiff did not dispute the amount of its past-due balance, nor did it complain about defendant's decision to withhold further shipments until plaintiff paid the past-due balance. . . .

[15] In late April, because of plaintiff's failure to pay its outstanding balance, defendant sold the inventory to a steel broker. Although plaintiff offered a higher price, defendant decided that plaintiff was not creditworthy and that therefore it should sell the steel to the broker. . . .

II. Discussion

[17] Summary judgment is required "if the pleadings, depositions, answers to interrogatories, and admissions on file, together with the affidavits, if any, show that there is no genuine issue as to any material fact and that the moving party is entitled to judgment as a matter of law." Fed.R.Civ.P. 56(c). In evaluating plaintiff's motion, I draw all inferences in a light most favorable to defendant. *Matsushita Elec. Indus. Co. v. Zenith Radio Corp.*, 475 U.S. 574, 587, 106 S.Ct. 1348, 89 L.Ed.2d 538 (1986). The parties agree that Wisconsin law governs the substantive issues presented.

[18] The question raised by plaintiff's summary judgment motion can be viewed as one of contract formation (Did the parties form a contract before defendant became insecure about plaintiff's ability to pay and sold the inventory to a broker?) or one of contract interpretation (Assuming a contract, could defendant decline to ship the inventory because of plaintiff's unpaid balance?). As explained below, however I characterize the question, the facts and circumstances surrounding the transaction and the parties' history will determine the answer. These facts and the inferences to be drawn from them are disputed, and I cannot say that a reasonable jury could not find for defendant. Therefore, I will deny plaintiff's motion for summary judgment. Further, the discovery that defendant seeks is relevant to the issues presented, and I will therefore grant defendant's motion to compel.

[19] I first consider the issue as one of contract formation: did defendant agree to sell the inventory to plaintiff? The Uniform Commercial Code ("UCC") governs this issue because the case involves the sale of goods. . . . Article 2 of the UCC provides that "[a] contract for the sale of goods may be made in any manner sufficient to show agreement, including conduct by both parties which recognizes the existence of such a contract." . . . In the present case, defendant invited plaintiff to submit an offer to purchase steel. On March 20, 2007, plaintiff did so by e-mailing defendant

a spreadsheet detailing the items of defendant's inventory that it wished to purchase and the price it would pay. Later that day, defendant e-mailed a response directing plaintiff to supply a purchase order number so that defendant could "start shipping this metal to [plaintiff]." . . . A reasonable jury could find that these e-mail communications formed a contract in which defendant promised to ship steel, and plaintiff promised to pay for it.[3] Cf. *Webster Mfg. Co. v. Montreal River Lumber Co.*, 159 Wis. 456, 150 N.W. 409 (1915) (holding that letters exchanged between parties could constitute a contract if they evidenced an agreement to be bound).

[20] However, in the parties' previous dealings, when defendant received a purchase order from plaintiff, defendant typically signed and returned it, and in the present case, defendant did not do so. Thus, a reasonable jury could conceivably conclude that the parties understood that until defendant signed and returned plaintiff's purchase order, their e-mail agreement was tentative. Cf. *Francis H. Leggett Co. v. W. Salem Canning Co.*, 155 Wis. 462, 144 N.W. 969, 972 (1914) ("It is equally well settled, however, that letters or telegraphic communications between the parties will not be construed as a contract when it is plain that they were intended only as preliminary negotiations to be followed by a formal contract containing material provisions not contained in or to be inferred from the preliminary letters or communications.").

[21] The "conduct by both parties" after the initial exchange of e-mails is also relevant in determining whether the parties recognized the existence of a contract. . . . Although plaintiff contends that on March 20, 2007, the parties formed a binding contract calling for the immediate shipment of steel, it did not object when defendant advised it that it would not ship steel until plaintiff paid its outstanding bill. If

---

3. Although defendant argues that under the Uniform Electronic Transactions Act ("UETA"), Wis. Stat. §§ 137.11-137.26, parties cannot form a contract electronically unless they first agree to do so, defendant is not technically correct. The UCC, not the UETA, provides the substantive law that determines whether parties form contract, and nothing in the UCC prohibits the formation of agreements by electronic means. See UETA Prefatory Note ¶ 3 ("It is important to understand that the purpose of UETA is to remove barriers to electronic commerce by validating and effectuating electronic records and signatures. It is NOT a general contracting statute-the substantive rules of contracts remain unaffected by UETA.") Thus, in the present case, if the jury determines that the parties' e-mails were sufficient to form a contract, the UETA will not prevent its enforcement. However, as explained below, the UCC does require, with certain exceptions, that a contract for the sale of goods priced at $500 or more be evidenced by a writing "signed by the party against whom enforcement is sought." . . . Whether an e-mail signature constitutes the signature called for by the UCC is a question to which the UETA might be relevant. . . . But absent a statute of frauds defense, a contract formed by electronic means will be enforceable under the UCC even if for some reason the UETA does not apply to the transaction. As a practical matter, however, if the parties have formed a contract electronically, they will likely be deemed subject to the UETA because "the context and surrounding circumstances, including the parties' conduct" will indicate that they have "agreed to conduct transactions by electronic means." . . . That is, if the facts show that the parties reached an agreement electronically, they will likely also show that the parties agreed to conduct the transaction by electronic means. Thus, as the parties prepare this case for trial, they are advised to focus on principles of contract formation under the UCC rather than whether and under what circumstances the UETA allows the formation of contracts by electronic means.

plaintiff believed that it had entered into a contract that required defendant to ship steel immediately, it is reasonable to infer that it would have demanded shipment by the end of March. Indeed, on past occasions when defendant did not ship metal on time, plaintiff immediately inquired as to the status of the shipment. A jury might (but need not) infer from plaintiff's failure to complain that it did not recognize that the parties had entered into a contract.[4] Thus, whether the parties formed a contract before defendant sold its inventory to someone other than plaintiff is a question of fact to be resolved by the jury after it considers all of the facts and circumstances surrounding the transaction and the parties' prior history.

[22] Because the jury must determine whether the parties entered into a contract, it is premature to determine the contract's terms. Nevertheless, I will discuss several issues regarding terms because they are relevant to defendant's motion to compel. First however, I will address defendant's argument that the statute of frauds prevents enforcement of any purported contract. Under the UCC, a contract for the sale of goods priced at $500 or more is not enforceable "unless there is some writing sufficient to indicate that a contract for sale has been made between the parties and signed by the party against whom enforcement is sought or by the party's authorized agent or broker." . . . In the present case, the steel at issue was worth more than $500; thus, the UCC required a writing signed by defendant. According to defendant, because the parties conducted the transaction via e-mail and no party physically signed a writing, no writing "signed by the party against whom enforcement is sought" exists. . . . However, the UETA . . . authorizes parties "to agree" to conduct transactions by e-mail and directs courts determining whether parties have so agreed to consider the "surrounding circumstances, including the parties' conduct." . . . If the parties have agreed to do business electronically, an electronic signature will constitute the signature required by the UCC's statute of frauds. . . .

[23] In the present case, the parties dispute whether or not they intended to conduct the transaction by e-mail and whether or not defendant's e-mails constitute a writing signed by defendant. As noted, whether the e-mails were sufficient to form a contract is a question for the jury to decide by applying UCC rather than UETA principles. Further, I need not concern myself about UETA in resolving the statute of frauds issue because if the jury finds that the e-mails formed a contract, the case will fall within an exception to the statute of frauds provided in Wis. Stat. § 402.201(2), which states:

> Between merchants if within a reasonable time a writing in confirmation
> of the contract and sufficient against the sender is received and the party
> receiving it has reason to know its contents, it satisfies the requirements of

---

4. A jury might also conclude that the parties formed a contract that allowed defendant to cancel the transaction if it became insecure about plaintiff's ability to pay. As discussed, whether I characterize the issue as one of contract formation or contract interpretation, the same facts are relevant.

[Wis. Stat. § 402.201(1)] against such party unless written notice of objection to its contents is given within 10 days after it is received.

[24] Here, both parties are merchants. After they exchanged e-mails agreeing to the sale of steel, plaintiff sent defendant a signed purchase order by both e-mail and regular mail. . . . If the jury determines that the parties formed a contract electronically, this purchase order will constitute a "writing in confirmation of the contract." Because plaintiff signed it and it describes the steel to be purchased, it is "sufficient against the sender." 1 James J. White & Robert S. Summers, Uniform Commercial Code § 2-5, at 140 (5th ed.2006) (stating that a confirmatory writing is sufficient against the sender if it is signed by the sender and states a quantity). Further, defendant admits receiving the purchase order and thus had reason to know its contents. Finally, defendant did not object to the contents of the purchase order in writing within ten days. Indeed, defendant admits that such purchase order "sat unsigned and forgotten in a desk drawer at [defendant's] facility in Kenosha." . . . Thus, if the jury determines that the parties formed a contract, the statute of frauds will not prevent its enforcement.

[25] As indicated, if the jury concludes that the parties formed a contract, it must also identify the contract's terms. Specifically, it will have to determine whether the contract allowed defendant to sell the inventory to others if it became insecure about plaintiff's ability to pay for it.[5] However, the parties disagree about what evidence the jury may consider in determining such terms. Plaintiff argues that the two e-mails that constitute the purported "offer" and "acceptance"—its proposal to buy steel and defendant's response that plaintiff should "Give Matt the purchase order number, so we can start shipping this metal to you"—plus the terms in its purchase order establish the terms of the contract and that no other evidence is relevant. Defendant argues that to determine the terms of the purported agreement, the jury must also consider the parties' prior course of dealing, including the terms of defendant's invoices, specifically as they relate to whether defendant could decline to ship steel if it doubted plaintiff's financial responsibility. Plaintiff has thus far declined to produce discovery relating to the parties' history, and defendant has moved to compel it to do so.

---

5. Defendant suggests that § 2-609 of the UCC, Wis. Stat. § 402.609, applies to this question. To oversimplify, § 2-609 allows a seller to terminate a contract when "reasonable grounds for insecurity arise." However, § 2-609 merely provides another lens through which to look at the same factual question that is also dispositive of the issues of contract formation and the meaning of the contract's terms. As some commentators note: "Whether a party has reasonable grounds for insecurity depends upon many factors including the seller's exact words or actions, the course of dealing or performance between the particular parties and the nature of the industry. What constitutes reasonable grounds for insecurity in one case might not in another. Consequently, the trier of fact must normally answer whether grounds for insecurity exist." White & Summers, supra, § 6-2, at 376. For the reasons stated in my discussion of contract formation and terms, whether § 2-609 justifies defendant's decision to terminate the purported contract is a question for the jury, the resolution of which will depend on all the facts and circumstances, including the parties' course of dealing.

[26] As I have explained, the entirety of the parties' business relationship is relevant to determining whether the parties' formed a contract. Under the UCC, the details of such relationship are likewise relevant to determining the meaning of any contract that they may have formed. Wis. Stat. § 402.202 provides:

> **402.202 Final written expression; parol or extrinsic evidence.** Terms with respect to which the confirmatory memoranda of the parties agree or which are otherwise set forth in a writing intended by the parties as a final expression of their agreement with respect to such terms as are included therein may not be contradicted by evidence of any prior agreement or of a contemporaneous oral agreement but may be explained or supplemented:
>
> (1) By course of dealing or usage of trade (s.401.205) or by course of performance (s.402.208);
>
> (2) By evidence of consistent additional terms unless the court finds the writing to have been intended also as a complete and exclusive statement of the terms of the agreement.

[27] Had the parties carefully negotiated a detailed written contract set forth in a single document that each party signed, plaintiff's argument that the contract constituted a "final expression of their agreement" and was intended "as a complete and exclusive statement of the terms of the agreement" might have greater force. However, in the present case, no such document exists. Although the parties' e-mails may constitute a final expression of their agreement with respect to the items to be purchased and the price, nothing in the e-mails indicates that the parties intended them to constitute a complete and exclusive statement of the agreement's terms. Further, although plaintiff sent a signed purchase order confirming the e-mails and containing additional terms and conditions, the facts surrounding the present transaction plus the parties' prior course of dealing, including the fact that defendant normally sent its own invoices containing its own terms and conditions, suggest that the parties did not intend the purchase order itself to be a complete and exclusive statement of their agreement. Thus, contrary to plaintiff's argument, it would be incorrect to exclude everything except the purported "offer" and "acceptance" e-mails. Instead, because in engaging in the present transaction, the parties more or less continued the business relationship established under the supply agreement, the manner in which they conducted business in the past is relevant to determining the meaning of the words used and the conduct involved in the present transaction. See Wis. Stat. § 401.205(3) (stating that a course of dealing "give[s] particular meaning to and supplement[s] or qualif[ies] terms of an agreement"). Accordingly, the UCC does not prevent defendant from introducing at trial parol or extrinsic evidence, including evidence concerning course of dealing, regarding the question of whether, if the parties formed a contract, defendant could cancel the transaction if it became insecure about plaintiff's ability to pay. It follows that plaintiff must cooperate in producing such evidence during discovery.

III. Conclusion

[28] For the reasons stated above, no party is entitled to summary judgment, and I will schedule the matter for trial. Defendant's motion to compel is granted. . . .

Notes and Questions

1. In paragraph 27, the court laments that the parties did not enter into a "carefully negotiated and detailed written contract set forth in a single document that each party signed." The case is a prime example of the problems that come from different people—and pretty much all of them without legal counsel—participating in e-mail exchanges that ultimately turn into offers and counteroffers and acceptances and may be binding on their employers. How can a larger organization contain this problem?

2. The parties did not pursue the matter further and we will never know whether a jury would have decided that a contract was concluded and whether it would have allowed the defendant to sell the inventory to third parties, once it became insecure about plaintiff's ability to pay. What is your opinion on contract formation? Why?

3. In footnote 3, the court elaborates the rules of UETA but also discusses the UCC rules on contract formation. How do these statutes coexist and which elements of a dispute are subject to one or the other or both?

4. In paragraph 20, the court introduces an analysis of the parties' *previous* dealings for the determination whether a contract was presently concluded or not. In paragraph 21, the court refers to conduct of the parties *after* the initial exchange of e-mails. What are the rules about the relevance of prior and subsequent conduct? What can parties do to limit the impact of extra-contractual communications before and after the formation of a contract?

5. When, how, and why do the contractual obligations of a seller change if she becomes insecure about her buyer's willingness or ability to pay?

Case 2-21

Khoury v. Tomlinson

518 S.W.3d 568 (Tex. Ct. App. 2017)
(Paragraph numbers added, some footnotes omitted.)
Laura Carter Higley, Justice . . .

[4] Tomlinson is the president and CEO of PetroGulf, Ltd., a company "formed in August 2008 to be a physical trader of fuel oil and crude oil from Iraq into selective markets in the region." On December 9, 2008, Tomlinson met with Khoury and presented him with an 11-page business plan, seeking investment in PetroGulf. The business plan offered to pay investors 14% interest on their investment along with sharing 10% of net profits. The business plan identified its initial goal was "to build an ongoing business to purchase, transport and sell fuel oil from Iraq initially to Syria and Kurdistan." After that, the goal was to expand into other markets.

[5] The business plan makes repeated reference to a contract in Syria and sale of fuel oil within Syria. It states PetroGulf's business plan begins with "purchas[ing], transport[ing] and sell[ing] fuel oil from Iraq initially to Syria and Kurdistan. The business plan stated, "We intend to complete delivery of 15,000 metric tons [of fuel oil] to Kurdistan by the end of December 2008 and to complete the delivery under our contract to Syria by the end of February 2009." The business plan reported on known needs for oil in Syria. It explicitly asserted PetroGulf had a contract for oil sale in Syria and offered investors 10% of the profits obtained from that contract. It stated that the purpose of the proposed arrangement with investors was to "implement an initial contract for the export of Fuel Oil from Iraq into Syria."

[6] As a result of the meeting and the investment document, Khoury invested $400,000 in PetroGulf. Khoury obtained the money by taking out a loan from Garantia Financiera Vital y Accidentes S.A. When he was asked to whom PetroGulf should send its interest payments, Khoury said to send the payments to Garantia.

[7] As part of the investment, the parties signed a note, and Khoury signed a subscription agreement. In the subscription agreement, Khoury acknowledged that PetroGulf had "made available to him . . . the opportunity to obtain the information necessary to evaluate the merits and risks of the investment." He also represented in the subscription agreement that all of his questions had been satisfactorily answered and that he had "carefully evaluated . . . the risks associated with this investment."

[8] Khoury ultimately became dissatisfied with his investment and the lack of disclosures of PetroGulf's financial information. As a result, Khoury met with Tomlinson on January 9, 2012. During that meeting, Tomlinson agreed to personally repay Khoury the amount loaned to PetroGulf. They agreed that Tomlinson would repay the debt over a four or five year period. Khoury testified at trial that they had agreed that Tomlinson would elect whether to pay over four or five years. A week later, Khoury sent an email to Tomlinson summarizing what agreements they had made. Tomlinson replied, writing, "We are in agreement."

[9] Tomlinson did not make any of the payments he had agreed to make. Khoury brought suit alleging breach of contract, securities violations under the Texas Securities Act, and common-law fraud. In his live answer, Tomlinson asserted that any recovery for breach of contract was barred by the Statute of Frauds.

[10] At trial, Tomlinson was asked about the Syrian contract discussed in the business plan. He admitted that he had declined the Syrian contract before he met with Khoury to solicit his investment. He also admitted that the representations about the Syrian contract "should not have been in" the business plan.

[11] Tomlinson also acknowledged at trial that he had sent the email responding to Khoury's summary of their January 9 meeting. He claimed that his statement in the email of his being in agreement with Khoury referred to an agreement entirely different from the terms identified in the email to which he responded.

[12] The jury found in favor of Khoury on all of his claims, awarding the same amount ($400,000) for each claim. The jury also awarded attorneys' fees. For the

breach of contract claim, the jury found that Tomlinson had obligated himself to repay the investment amount to Khoury. It also found that Tomlinson breached that agreement.

[13] After trial, Tomlinson filed a motion for judgment notwithstanding the verdict, seeking to overturn the jury's findings in favor of Khoury on each of Khoury's claims. For Khoury's breach of contract claim, Tomlinson argued that the jury's findings of liability should be overturned because the contract was barred by the Statute of Frauds and because the contract was too indefinite to be enforceable.

[14] For his Statute of Frauds argument, Tomlinson acknowledged his email constituted a writing but argued the email was not signed. Tomlinson attached a copy of his email . . . to his motion.

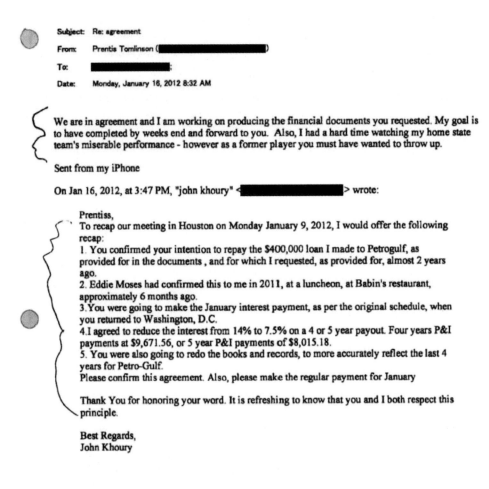

. . .

[20] . . . Khoury argues the trial court erred by granting the judgment notwithstanding the verdict on his breach of contract claim. Tomlinson presented two grounds for why the jury's finding on liability should have been overturned. First,

Tomlinson argued that the contract was barred by the Statute of Frauds. Second, Tomlinson argued that the contract was too indefinite to be enforceable.

A. Statute of Frauds

[21] "[A] promise by one person to answer for the debt . . . of another person" "is not enforceable unless the promise or agreement, or a memorandum of it, is (1) in writing; and (2) signed by the person to be charged with the promise or agreement. . . ." TEX. BUS. & COM. CODE ANN. §26.01(a)(1)–(2), (b)(2) (Vernon 2015). The parties agreed at trial that they met on January 9, 2012, and that they entered into an agreement. The evidence shows that, a week later, Khoury sent Tomlinson an email listing the terms of their agreement and requesting Tomlinson's confirmation of those terms. Tomlinson acknowledged at trial that he received the email and sent the responding email, writing, "We are in agreement."

[22] The email shows that Tomlinson's name does not appear in the body of the email that he wrote. His name and email address do appear, however, in the "from" field for the email. The question before us is whether the name or email address in the "from" field constitutes a signature for purposes of the Statute of Frauds. . . .

[23] It is undisputed by the parties that their email correspondence is governed by the Texas Uniform Electronic Transactions Act ("UETA"). . . . Subject to exceptions not applicable to this case, UETA "applies to electronic records and signatures relating to a transaction." [Sec. 3(a)] "A record or signature may not be denied legal effect or enforceability solely because it is in electronic form." [Sec. 7(a)]. "If a law requires a signature, an electronic signature satisfies the law." [Sec. 7(d)]. We must construe and apply UETA in a manner "to be consistent with reasonable practices concerning electronic transactions and with the continued expansion of those practices." [Sec. 6(2)].

[24] Under UETA, an electronic record is "a record, created, generated, sent, communicated, received, or stored by electronic means." [Sec. 2(7)]. An electronic signature is "an electronic sound, symbol, or process attached to or logically associated with a record and executed or adopted by a person with the intent to sign the record." [Sec. 2(8)].

[25] An email satisfies all of the disjunctive definitions of an electronic record. [Sec. 2(7)]. A name or email address in a "from" field is a symbol logically associated with the email. [Sec. 2(8)]. We are left to determine, then, whether a name or email address in a "from" field can be construed to be "executed or adopted by a person with the intent to sign the record." [*id.*]

[26] While UETA defines "electronic signature," it does not define "sign." This was by design. See TEX. BUS. & COM. CODE ANN. ch. 322 official comment (Vernon 2015) (recognizing UETA "defers to existing substantive law" for "the meaning and effect of 'sign'"). Accordingly, we look to existing law to determine the meaning and effect of "sign." *See id.*

[27] "The signature of the person against whom enforcement is sought [under the Statute of Frauds] authenticates the document as reliable evidence of that person's

agreement to the transaction." *Lone Star Air Sys., Ltd. v. Powers*, 401 S.W.3d 855, 859 (Tex. App.-Houston [14th Dist.] 2013, no pet.). "[F]or the purpose of the Statute of Frauds, the signature of the 'person to be charged' is the act which authenticates the document as reliable evidence of that person's agreement to the transaction." *Capital Bank v. Am. Eyewear, Inc.*, 597 S.W.2d 17, 19 (Tex. Civ. App.-Dallas 1980, no writ). "What is essential [for a signature under the Statute of Frauds] is that the signature of the party to be charged shall authenticate the whole of the writing." *Gruss v. Cummins*, 329 S.W.2d 496, 500 (Tex. Civ. App.-El Paso 1959, writ ref'd n.r.e.); see also *Betts v. Betts*, No. 14-11-00267-CV, 2012 WL 2803750, at *2 (Tex. App.-Houston [14th Dist.] July 10, 2012, pet. denied) (mem. op.) (recognizing Texas law treats documents as signed when they contain any mark sufficient to show intent to be bound by document).

[28] The "from" field in the email authenticated the writing in the email to be Tomlinson's. UETA expressly allows for automated transactions to satisfy the requirements of contract formation. [Sec. 14] The very nature of automated transactions requires the mechanisms for the transaction to be established in advance of the actual transactions. The fact that the name or email address to appear in a "from" field was set up in advance of sending the email in question, then, does not preclude any legal effect of the name or email address. See also [Sec. 6(2)] (requiring UETA to be construed and applied consistently with continued expansion of practices for electronic communications); UNIF. ELEC. TRANSACTIONS ACT § 2 cmt. 7 (UNIF. LAW COMM'N 1999) (recognizing that entering in identifying information into website and later clicking "I agree" button satisfies signature requirement).

[29] Related authority backs up the conclusion that the name or email address in a "from" field functions as a signature in an email. The New Oxford American Dictionary defines sign to mean to "write one's name . . . to identify oneself as the writer or sender." . . . Black's Law Dictionary defines sign as "[t]o identify (a record) by means of a signature, mark, or other symbol with the intent to authenticate it as an act or agreement of the person identifying it." . . . The "from" field functions to identify the sender of the email and authenticate the email as his act. Legal scholarship likewise recognizes this point. . . .

[30] Finally, other states that have adopted the uniform code have reached the same conclusion. . . .

[31] In his motion for rehearing, Tomlinson identifies a case from another state that he argues conflicts with our opinion. See *SN4, LLC v. Anchor Bank*, fsb, 848 N.W.2d 559, 568 (Minn. Ct. App. 2014). Despite Tomlinson's argument, the court in *SN4* held that a "from" field can constitute a signature, but did not, under the facts of the case, extend to sign an attachment to the email. . . . It also held that there was no evidence that the parties agreed to transact electronically, a legal point not at issue in this case.

[32] We recognize that the Fort Worth Court of Appeals has reached a holding in conflict with ours. In *Cunningham v. Zurich American Insurance Co.*, the court

considered whether the signature line within an email constituted a signature and concluded it did not. 352 S.W.3d 519, 529–30 (Tex. App.-Fort Worth 2011, pet. denied). The court held,

> There is nothing to show that the signature block was typed by Grabouski and not generated automatically by her email client. If Grabouski did personally type the signature block at the bottom of the email, nothing in the email suggests that she did so with the intention that the block be her signature, and Cunningham does not direct us to any other place in the record raising a fact issue about her intention. . . . We decline to hold that the mere sending by Grabouski of an email containing a signature block satisfies the signature requirement when no evidence suggests that the information was typed purposefully rather than generated automatically, [or] that Grabouski intended the typing of her name to be her signature. . . . *Id.* at 530.

[33] The court offered no explanation for why physically typing in a signature line at the time of drafting the email should be required for a "signature block" to constitute a signature. See *Cox Eng'g, Inc. v. Funston Mach. & Supply Co.,* 749 S.W.2d 508, 511 (Tex. App.-Fort Worth 1988, no writ) (holding letterhead on invoice satisfied signature requirement under Statute of Frauds).

[34] Another court has criticized this holding. See *Williamson v. Bank of New York Mellon,* 947 F.Supp.2d 704, 710–11 (N.D. Tex. 2013). The court observed that signature blocks with a person's name are created by the account owner, not the email client. *Id.* at 710. "There is no fundamental difference between, on the one hand, manually typing a signature block into a series of emails and, on the other, typing the block once and instructing a computer program to append it to future messages." *Id.* at 711.

[35] The court further noted that UETA was designed to remove barriers to electronic transactions by setting an expansive view of what constitutes electronic records and signatures. Id. The court recognized that UETA requires the act to be construed and applied consistently with reasonable practices for electronic communications. *Id.* (citing [Sec. 6]). "Email communication is a reasonable and legitimate means of reaching a settlement in this day and age." *Id.*

[36] We agree. A signature block in an email performs the same authenticating function as a "from" field. Accordingly, it satisfies the requirement of a signature under UETA. . . .

[37] In his motion for rehearing, Tomlinson points out that UETA requires an "*intent* to sign the record." [Sec. 2(8)] (emphasis added). Tomlinson argues that the intent requirement was not satisfied because, he asserts, there is proof in the record that the parties did not intend to be bound by the email. The statute does not require an intent to be *bound,* however. It requires an intent to sign. See *id.*; see also UNIF. ELEC. TRANSACTIONS ACT § 2 cmt. 7 (recognizing that entering in identifying information into website and later clicking "I agree" button satisfies signature

requirement); *WCT & D, LLC v. City of Kansas City*, 476 S.W.3d 336, 342 (Mo. Ct. App. 2015) (holding party's admission of hitting the send button and sending emails established intent to authenticate and adopt the content of the e-mails as their own writing). We have held that signing the document is an act authenticating the document. The question is, then, whether the party attached a symbol with an intent to authenticate the document. Tomlinson testified that he sent the email and wrote its contents. The evidence reasonably establishes, then, that Tomlinson intended to authenticate the email.

[38] We hold that the email name or address in the "from" field satisfies the definition of a signature under existing law. See *Lone Star Air Sys.*, 401 S.W.3d at 859.

[39] While UETA does not require an intent to be bound, the memorandum as a whole must establish that the parties did more than just agree to make a contract in the future. See *Hartford Fire Ins. Co. v. C. Springs* 300, Ltd., 287 S.W.3d 771, 778 (Tex. App.-Houston [1st Dist.] 2009, pet. denied) (holding writing that contemplates contract or promise to be made in future does not satisfy Statute of Frauds). Here, the evidence establishes that the parties agreed to be bound by the terms described in the email. After Khoury described the essential terms of their deal in his email to Tomlinson, Tomlinson responded, saying, "We are in agreement." We hold that this language clearly and unambiguously expresses the intent to be bound by the terms of their agreement.

[40] Accordingly, we hold that the evidence is sufficient to establish that Tomlinson signed the email and that the signed email satisfies the Statute of Frauds.

B. Indefiniteness

[41] Tomlinson's other ground for overturning the jury's finding of liability is that the contract was too indefinite to be enforceable. To be enforceable, an agreement must contain all of its essential terms. See *Fischer v. CTMI, L.L.C.*, 479 S.W.3d 231, 238 (Tex. 2016). We construe the contract as a whole "'to determine what purposes the parties had in mind at the time they signed' it." *Id.* at 239 (quoting *Kirby Lake Dev., Ltd. v. Clear Lake City Water Auth.*, 320 S.W.3d 829, 841 (Tex. 2010)). . . .

[43] Here, the evidence shows that Tomlinson agreed to pay Khoury $400,000 at 7.5% interest over a period of four or five years. The estimation of payments required under either option establishes that the payments were to have been submitted monthly. Khoury testified that the parties agreed that Tomlinson would elect whether to pay over a four year period or a five year period.

[44] Tomlinson argued to the trial court that the agreement was indefinite because it did not specify whether the loan would be repaid in four or five years. Because the parties agreed that Tomlinson would elect which time period he would prefer, this was not a term requiring further negotiation. See Fischer, 479 S.W.3d at 237 (holding leaving material terms open for future agreement means document is not binding). . . . We hold the contract is sufficiently certain to sustain the jury's finding of liability for breach of contract. . . .

Notes and Questions

The image of the e-mail is reproduced because it is a typical e-mail sent from a phone, a practice that has become ubiquitous. While most businesspeople use more comprehensive signature lines, including titles and contact information, at the bottom of e-mails sent from office computers, a signature line "Sent from my iPhone" is quite typical for e-mails sent from a mobile phone. In the present case, the court struggled with the question whether such an e-mail can be considered to be "signed." The original jury decided in favor of the investor and against the sender of the e-mail. The trial court, however, rendered judgment NOV. On appeal, the jury award was largely reinstated. Regardless of sympathies for the plaintiff and against the defendant, a decision that the "from" field of an e-mail is sufficient as signature is problematic.

1. What are the functions of a traditional handwritten signature? How can all of these functions be replicated in the context of electronic communications?

2. Should the "from" line in the header of an e-mail suffice as a "signature"? In all cases? How about a scenario where an e-mail is sent from a phone or computer by a third party as a prank or as the result of fraudulent activity? Is such a case different from a counterfeit signature on a letter or check? If so, how?

3. What happens if an e-mail is dispatched by the authorized account holder by mistake—for example, while she was still working on a draft and had not yet decided whether or not to send the e-mail at all?

4. How would you summarize the approach taken under the UETA toward the validity of electronic communications and contracts?

Case 2-22

IO Moonwalkers, Inc. v. Banc of America Merchant Services, LLC

814 S.E.2d 583 (N.C. Ct. App. 2018)
(Paragraph numbers added, some footnotes omitted.)
DIETZ, Judge.

[1] This case is one of a growing number of contract cases requiring the courts to fit decades-old (sometimes centuries-old) contract principles to the realities of the digital age.

[2] Banc of America Merchant Services, LLC (BAMS) provided credit card processing services to IO Moonwalkers, Inc., a company that sells hoverboard scooters. BAMS uses a standard contract with its customers and sent that contract to Moonwalkers using an electronic document application called DocuSign. DocuSign transmits the contract in an email and the software records when the contract accompanying that email is viewed and when it is electronically signed.

[3] After a dispute concerning chargebacks for fraudulent purchases, Moonwalkers asserted that it never electronically signed the contract with BAMS and should not

be bound by its terms. The company asserted that a salesperson for BAMS likely signed the contract on behalf of Moonwalkers without permission.

[4] At summary judgment, BAMS produced records showing the exact date and time that someone using the Moonwalkers company email viewed the proposed contract, electronically signed it, and later viewed the final, fully executed version. Moonwalkers does not dispute the accuracy of these DocuSign records, and does not claim that it never viewed the proposed contract, but insists that the contract was not signed by anyone at the company authorized to do so.

[5] BAMS also produced emails and letters sent in the following months in which BAMS referenced the contract and asked Moonwalkers to take action required by the contract, such as providing documentation. Moonwalkers complied with those requests without ever suggesting the parties had no written contract.

[6] As explained below, in light of this evidence, the trial court properly held that, even if Moonwalkers did not sign the contract, the company ratified the contract through its actions. We therefore affirm the trial court's grant of partial summary judgment based on the doctrine of ratification.

Facts and Procedural History . . .

[8] Defendant Banc of America Merchant Services, LLC processes credit card transactions for retail businesses. The company uses an electronic signature service called DocuSign to enter into written contracts with its customers that BAMS calls "merchant services agreements." DocuSign gives each merchant services agreement an identifying number, which then appears on each page of the document. DocuSign sends an email with an electronic link to a copy of the agreement. Through DocuSign, the party viewing the contract can sign it using a digital signature. DocuSign tracks the date and time when the contract is sent, viewed, and signed by each party.

[9] Once a contract between BAMS and a customer is executed, DocuSign sends a "certificate of completion" to BAMS that includes the identifying number for that contract, the email address of the contract recipient, the IP address of the computer that viewed the email and contract, and details of relevant "events" that occurred such as the time and date when the contract was viewed and signed. BAMS maintains these certificates of completion as business records in the ordinary course of its business.

[10] Rilwan Hassan, the owner of Moonwalkers, is familiar with the DocuSign process because he used the service in 2014 to contract with BAMS for credit card processing services for American Coins & Gold, another business he owns. Hassan concedes that he used DocuSign to review and sign the BAMS contract with American Coins & Gold.

[11] In 2015, Hassan met with BAMS employee Robert Kanterman to contract for similar card-processing services for Moonwalkers. Moonwalkers concedes that BAMS sent proposed merchant services agreements to Moonwalkers at the company email address Hassan provided. Those contracts contain various terms concerning

BAMS services as well as a provision permitting the execution of the contract by electronic signatures.

[12] Hassan stated in an affidavit that he "may have glanced at some of those emails" but he could not recall if he looked at all of them. DocuSign's electronic records indicate that someone with access to the Moonwalkers email account viewed the emails and corresponding contracts sent by DocuSign, and then electronically signed the contracts several minutes later. DocuSign later sent copies of the fully executed contracts to the Moonwalkers email account and, again, someone with access to that email account viewed the completed contracts. In an affidavit, Hassan asserts that he believes Robert Kanterman, the BAMS employee with whom he negotiated the contract, electronically signed Hassan's name on the contracts on behalf of Moonwalkers without Hassan's permission. The affidavit provides no explanation of how Kanterman could have accessed the Moonwalkers email account or altered the DocuSign records to make it appear as if someone with access to that account viewed and signed the contracts.

[13] Once BAMS received the certificate of completion for the merchant services agreements with Moonwalkers, it began providing credit card processing services to the company. Several months later, after a series of transactions involving stolen credit card numbers, BAMS issued "chargebacks" to Moonwalkers, which occur when a credit card holder reports that a particular credit card purchase resulted from fraud. Under the terms of BAMS's merchant services agreements, BAMS requires the retail merchant to repay BAMS the funds from the fraudulent purchase. The chargebacks in this case were extensive and posed a significant financial challenge to Moonwalkers. . . .

Analysis . . .

[16] In the trial court, BAMS relied on a number of legal theories to support its motion for partial summary judgment. As explained below, the trial court properly entered judgment based on the doctrine of ratification and we therefore address that legal theory first.

[17] In contract law, ratification is a legal doctrine that binds a principal to certain unauthorized acts of an agent, such as executing a contract. *Carolina Equip. & Parts Co. v. Anders*, 265 N.C. 393, 400, 144 S.E.2d 252, 257 (1965). "In order to establish the act of a principal as a ratification of the unauthorized transactions of an agent, the party claiming ratification must prove (1) that at the time of the act relied upon, the principal had full knowledge of all material facts relative to the unauthorized transaction, and (2) that the principal had signified his assent or his intent to ratify by word or by conduct which was inconsistent with an intent not to ratify." *Id.* at 400–01, 144 S.E.2d at 258 . . . .

[18] "Intent to ratify can be evidenced by a course of conduct on the part of the principal which reasonably tends to show an intention on his part to ratify the agent's unauthorized acts." *Carter v. TD Ameritrade Holding Corp.*, 218 N.C. App. 222, 229, 721 S.E.2d 256, 262 (2012). "[T]o constitute ratification as a matter of law,

the conduct must be consistent with an intent to affirm the unauthorized act and inconsistent with any other purpose." *Id.*

[19] Moonwalkers argues that the trial court could not enter summary judgment on the issue of ratification because there were genuine issues of material facts. Specifically, Moonwalkers argues that it did not sign the contracts and that it believes an employee of BAMS signed the contracts without authorization. Moonwalkers also argues that it did not have knowledge of the terms of the contracts and did not take any action indicating intent to ratify the unauthorized assent.

[20] Were this a more traditional contract negotiation, in which the parties had mailed proposed contracts back and forth, a sworn affidavit stating that Moonwalkers never reviewed or signed the contracts might be sufficient to create a genuine issue of material fact with respect to the knowledge element of ratification. But this case is different because BAMS presented evidence from the DocuSign records indicating that it sent the merchant services agreements to Moonwalkers at the company email address. BAMS also submitted evidence from the DocuSign records that someone with access to that email viewed both the emails and the accompanying contracts, electronically signed them, and later viewed the completed contracts, which were sent to Moonwalkers in a separate email.

[21] Simply put, the electronic trail created by DocuSign provides information that would not have been available before the digital age—the ability to remotely monitor when other parties to a contract actually view it. . . .

[23] In his second affidavit, Hassan . . . states that "the so-called 'signed' contracts that were sent to me came from an email account for 'Contract Management Services' rather than any email for any of the Defendants in this case." He explains that "I received an excessive amount of emails from Bank of America, many of which were not related to this issue. At no point, was I under the impression that any of those emails would create a contract between me and any of the Defendants in this case for merchant services."

[24] Missing from Hassan's two lengthy affidavits is any assertion that the DocuSign records are incorrect or that no one from the company actually viewed the emails and accompanying contracts, as the DocuSign records indicate. To be sure, Hassan's affidavit states that Moonwalkers never *signed* those contracts and that the company never *intended* to be bound by them. But Hassan does not assert that the company never *received* or *reviewed* the contracts. Thus, the trial court properly determined that there was no genuine dispute concerning whether Moonwalkers had knowledge of the terms of the contracts because the undisputed evidence at summary judgment showed that the company had received and reviewed them. . . .

[30] Moonwalkers . . . received services from BAMS covered by those contracts for several months. During that time, BAMS repeatedly asked Moonwalkers to comply with specific terms and conditions of the "merchant card processing contract" and "Merchant Agreement" and Moonwalkers did so, without ever suggesting that the parties were not bound by any written contracts containing specific terms and

conditions. We agree with the trial court that these undisputed facts demonstrate that Moonwalkers "had full knowledge of all material facts relative to the unauthorized transaction and . . . had signified [its] assent or [its] intent to ratify by word or by conduct which was inconsistent with an intent not to ratify." *Carolina Equip. & Parts Co.*, 265 N.C. at 400–01, 144 S.E.2d at 258.

Notes and Questions

1. This case may be the first reported decision on the validity of a DocuSign contract where a party claims not to have understood or not to have intended to enter into a formal agreement. Moonwalkers first asserted that they got so many e-mails from the bank that they were not able to read all of them carefully. Second, they argued that the decisive message(s) did not come from the bank but from "Contract Management Services," making it harder for them to understand the legal significance. Finally, they claimed that an unauthorized outsider — actually a bank employee — signed on their behalf in DocuSign. The court did not have to consider whether these claims were sufficiently substantiated because of the doctrine of ratification. Where does this doctrine come from and when is it applicable? What conditions have to be met?

2. It is only a question of time until a case comes before the courts where a party claims that it did not sign or intend to sign a contract on DocuSign or a similar DTM system and there is no subsequent conduct that would suggest that ratification has occurred. For example, a potential seller and a potential buyer might negotiate an IBT until the seller presents a DocuSign agreement to the buyer. Having received a confirmation via the DTM, the seller then proceeds to purchase supplies and manufacture custom-made goods at great expense, while the buyer satisfies her needs from an alternate source. How would and how should the courts deal with such a case?

Part Three

The Documentary Sale 2 of 4: Payment and Financing Contracts

Section 1. Different Options for IBT Financing and the Basic Terminology

Trade financing—sometimes also called supply chain financing (SCF)—addresses three primary sets of questions. First, it is concerned with the transfer of the purchase price for a given set of goods or services. This secures the seller's right to get paid on time and in full and the buyer's right to receive the promised goods or services. Since buyer and seller generally don't meet face to face to exchange the goods/services for money, there is a question of sequencing for the reciprocal performance. If the buyer has to make payment before the seller will ship or send his performance, the buyer bears the risk of never receiving the goods or services or not receiving what she was entitled to under the contract. Conversely, if the buyer does not have to make payment until she receives the goods or services in the promised condition, the seller bears the risk of never getting paid or getting paid only in part or only with substantial delay. As you are reading this Part, pay attention how and to what extent the different instruments address this question.

Second, trade finance is about the provision of easy and inexpensive credit, in particular if the buyer cannot pay for the goods or services until she resells or processes them. The seller may be willing and able to extend such credit in order to make the sale happen, i.e., wait to get paid until a more or less clearly defined point in time, for example "90 days same as cash." However, more likely than not, the seller needs to recover his own investment and the cost of production as quickly as possible to be able to continue with his own business. Sometimes, the seller may even need to get paid in advance in order to be able to manufacture the goods. Furthermore, the seller may not know the buyer well enough to trust that she will be willing and able to make payment at an agreed-upon later time. This is where third-party financing comes in. Therefore, as you are reading about the different instruments in this Part, pay attention whether they provide for credit, and if so, for how long and at what cost.

Third, trade finance also has to determine the allocation of various forms of risk. The main elements of foreign party or counterparty risk have already been mentioned above under transfer of the purchase price. This would include the risk that not only a foreign party, but also its bank, can become unwilling or unable to honor the contractual obligations and may have to be pursued in foreign courts under a foreign legal system. A potential solution to this problem is evolving rapidly right now: Smart Contracts on the Blockchain. The Blockchain is a new iteration of the internet where all transactions—but not the parties to them—are publicly visible and stored on multiple decentralized computers. Thus, they cannot be modified or tampered with. Smart Contracts on the Blockchain are contracts coded to execute certain functions automatically, once predetermined conditions are fulfilled. For example, a Smart Contract could stipulate that a payment already deposited by a buyer should be released to a seller once the goods have been shipped.

Another question to watch out for in the context of trade financing concerns the currency of payment. In particular, if the payment is made weeks or months after the conclusion of the contract, a different exchange rate between seller's and buyer's currency can significantly alter the fairness and profitability of the transaction. If the transaction price is fixed in seller's currency, he has certainty over the amount he will receive, while the buyer may have to spend more than expected to purchase the agreed-upon amount of the seller's currency, if her currency depreciates, or less than expected, if her currency appreciates in relation to seller's currency. Conversely, if the transaction price is fixed in the buyer's currency, she will know how much to spend in her currency, while the seller will not know how much he can expect to spend in his own currency after the exchange rate has changed. The easiest way to eliminate the *currency risk* would be for the party who has to pay a foreign currency at a later point in time (buyer) to buy the currency in advance. However, this blocks liquidity or credit. Therefore, the party who has to acquire a foreign currency in the future to make a payment (if the buyer has to pay in seller's currency) or the party who will receive a foreign currency in the future (if the seller will get paid in the buyer's currency) can hedge the risk of getting less or having to pay more than anticipated by entering into a foreign exchange or FX future contract with a bank of financing company. An FX future is called a forward contract if the currency conversion is agreed upon today at a given exchange rate but will occur at a given future date. Although this eliminates the risk of unfavorable exchange rate fluctuations, it may itself turn out to be unfavorable if the exchange rate moves in the opposite direction. A compromise solution would be to hedge the currency risk in the form of an options contract, i.e., for the party that has to acquire or dispose of the other currency at some future time, to enter into a futures contract with a third party that allows her—but does not require her—to purchase (call option) or sell (put option) the currency at a given price at that time. Like all forms of insurance, however, hedging is not free and cuts into the profitability of business transactions.

In addition to currency risk, there is the so-called *country risk* associated with political and legal factors, such as unforeseen export or import restrictions, trade embargoes, civil unrest, and even war, only some of which may be subject to insurance coverage.

Finally, there is the *transportation risk,* which is distributed via the INCO-TERMS® discussed above, pp. 240–250. The transportation risk is small for standard manufactured goods shipped along common shipping routes directly between developed and stable countries. The risk increases substantially if the cargo is high in value and/or perishable and/or if the port of origin and the port of destination are not directly connected and/or located in less stable countries. The risk can be mitigated, to an extent, via the acquisition of cargo insurance, further discussed below in Part Five. Shipping and insurance documents play an important role when it comes to the presentation of documents required by a letter of credit.

In the end, any element of risk becomes an element of cost and every element of cost has to be paid by someone. Thus, the third main issue in this Part is about the allocation of risk and costs.

The International Trade Administration (ITA), a branch of the U.S. Department of Commerce tasked with the promotion of trade and investment, summarizes the situation as follows:

> International trade presents a spectrum of risk, which causes uncertainty over the timing of payments between the exporter (seller) and importer (foreign buyer).
>
> For exporters, any sale is a gift until payment is received.
>
> Therefore, exporters want to receive payment as soon as possible, preferably as soon as an order is placed or before the goods are sent to the importer.
>
> For importers, any payment is a donation until the goods are received.
>
> Therefore, importers want to receive the goods as soon as possible but to delay payment as long as possible, preferably until after the goods are resold to generate enough income to pay the exporter.[1]

The following table provides an overview of different options for trade financing, sometimes referred to as terms of payment, and their respective riskiness for seller and buyer. The most important of them will then be discussed in subsequent Sections of this Part. The table is sorted from most secure for the seller to least secure for the seller. All options involve at least one bank as a facilitator of the payment from buyer to seller. In some, but not all of them, the bank provides credit for a certain amount of time. Also, in some, but not all of them, the bank or even several banks add their own creditworthiness to the transaction, essentially insulating the seller from the risk that the buyer might at some point become unwilling or unable to make payment.

Jan Dalhuisen, in his excellent book, *Financial Products, Financial Services and Financial Regulation*, makes an important point about payment:

> It cannot be repeated often enough that promising payment, writing a cheque, giving a payment instruction to the bank, or even tendering

---

1. See https://www.export.gov/article?id=Trade-Finance-Guide-Methods-of-Payment, last visited 10 October 2019.

Chart 3-1
Payment and Financing Options for IBTs

Method of Payment	Time of Payment	Time of Shipment & Release of Goods to Buyer	Risk to Seller	Risk to Buyer	Pros and Cons
Cash in Advance w/ Wire Transfer on Open Account	payment before shipment	shipment only after payment	None	buyer bears full risk for seller's willingness and ability to ship conforming goods	very inexpensive (cost of a wire transfer); requires high level of trust between parties; buyer advances performance & may need to get credit separately
Cash in Advance w/ Check or Bank Draft or Bill of Exchange in the Mail	payment before shipment	shipment only after payment	none, provided seller can wait with any kind of performance related activities and expenses until check clears; moderate penalty if check bounces; no risk with bank draft	buyer bears full risk for seller's willingness and ability to ship conforming goods	inexpensive (cost of mailing & processing check); requires high level of trust between parties; buyer advances performance & may need to get credit separately
Confirmed Letter of Credit	depends on agreement between buyer and issuing bank	shipment before payment; release of goods after payment	goods are only released against payment; seller is secured by issuing bank & confirming bank; any risk depends on terms of L/C	payment only made in exchange for controlling documents; buyer bears nonconformity risk unless comprehensive inspection done	most expensive form of trade financing but also most secure; buyer applies for loan & needs collateral for issuing bank; confirming bank adds security at a price

Un-confirmed Letter of Credit	depends on agreement between buyer and issuing bank	shipment before payment release of goods after payment	goods only released against payment; seller is secured only by issuing bank, may have to pursue claims in buyer's country any other risk depends of terms of L/C	payment only made in exchange for controlling documents; buyer bears nonconformity risk unless comprehensive inspection done	buyer applies for loan & needs collateral for issuing bank advising or nominated bank in seller's country does not add security, only convenience
Standby Letter of Credit	standby is not intended form of payment, only backup	before payment	seller is secured by issuing bank additional security can be added with confirmation any risk depends on terms of L/C	buyer receives goods before payment but cannot (easily) stop payment if seller presents documents required by L/C, even if goods are non-conforming	more expensive than a single L/C because it requires a primary form of payment (usually several wire transfers) and has longer validity suitable as backup for multiple payments (one standby plus multiple wire transfers instead of multiple commercial L/Cs)
Bank Guarantee or Performance Bond	guarantee is not intended form of payment, only backup	before payment	seller is secured by issuing bank confirmation not possible, seller bears risk of insolvency of issuing bank, as well as foreign country risk any other risk depends on terms of guarantee	buyer can also be secured by a guarantee, for example if goods are non-conforming	more expensive than commercial L/C or standby because of additional security for buyer more flexible than L/C if buyer's bank issues counter-guarantee in favor of seller's bank, seller's bank can issue guarantee to seller w/similar effects like confirmation

Chart 3-1

Payment and Financing Options for IBTs

Method of Payment	Time of Payment	Time of Shipment & Release of Goods to Buyer	Risk to Seller	Risk to Buyer	Pros and Cons
Documentary Collection w/ Bill of Exchange, Sight Draft				payment only made in exchange for controlling documents; buyer bears non-conformity risk unless comprehensive inspection done	
Documentary Collection w/ Bill of Exchange, Time Draft				payment only made in exchange for controlling documents; buyer bears non-conformity risk unless comprehensive inspection done	
Open Account Cash After Delivery w/ Wire Transfer on Open Account	after arrival of goods in conformity with invoice	before payment	seller bears full risk for buyer's willingness and ability to make payment per contract	none	very inexpensive (cost of a wire transfer); requires high level of trust between parties; seller advances performance & may need to get credit separately can be combined with deferred payment by 30, 45, 60, 90, or 120 days

Method		before payment		
Cash After Delivery Check, Bank Draft, or Bill of Exchange in the Mail	after arrival of goods in conformity with invoice	before payment	seller bears full risk for buyer's willingness and ability to make payment as per contract; seller bears additional risk/fees if check bounces; unless bank draft is used	none	inexpensive (cost of mailing & processing check); requires high level of trust between parties; seller advances performance & may need to get credit separately; can be combined with deferred payment by 30, 45, 60, 90, or 120 days
Consignment w/ Payment on Open Account, Check, Bank Draft, or Bill of Exchange in the Mail	after goods have been sold by first buyer	before payment	seller not only bears risk for buyer's willingness and ability to make payment but also that goods may not be saleable or at least take a long time to sell	none	very attractive for buyer who does not have to pay seller until goods are sold onward; may be attractive to avoid multiple taxable transactions since first buyer does not become owner

payment is not the same as payment . . . [n]either are credit card imprints or even the use of a debit card . . . as they do not effectively result in the unconditional and complete cash or bank transfers to the creditor (giving him full disposition rights in the money) thereby entitling the payor to a release and a final discharge extinguishing the relevant payment obligation. . . . . A key issue is therefore always to determine when payment has happened, and that is often less clear than it may appear. As has been pointed out . . . , the key is that the payee has acquired the unconditional and immediate disposition right in the money received.[2]

This issue needs to be kept in mind as well, as we are going to examine different payment terms and methods in some detail.

Dalhuisen also distinguishes "push" and "pull" systems for inter-bank payments. A "push" system would be one where the payment is initiated by the debtor — for example, when a buyer instructs her bank to make a wire transfer for the benefit of a seller in another country. By contrast, a "pull" system would be one where the payment is initiated by the creditor — for example, when a seller presents a check from a customer to his bank or forwards a credit or debit card swipe to his bank.[3]

A key practical aspect of trade financing is secure communication between banks and traders. It should be easy to imagine the problems that could arise if banks in different countries, such as the bank issuing a letter of credit in one country and the bank advising or even confirming it in another country, did not have a reliable and standardized way of communicating. Misinterpretation of messages between people working in different languages would be just the beginning and, given the sheer volume of trade financing sent around the world every day, the entire system would be a prime target for hackers and other criminal elements. To address this challenge, the SWIFT system was created and is today owned and operated jointly by some 9,000 banks around the world; the acronym stands for Society for Worldwide Interbank Financial Telecommunications. SWIFT communications use standardized language or terms and run on a secure system based on the old telex net and not connected to the internet. The result is a system where third-party interference is largely excluded and parties from around the world can communicate virtually instantaneously and without ambiguity as to language and interpretation. Larger corporations can also become members of SWIFT and directly send and receive the messages. The standardized messages are organized in categories, namely

| Category 1 | Customer Payments and Cheques (includes, for example, "MT 103 Single Customer Credit Transfer," and the corresponding "MT 107 General Direct Debit Message") |

---

2. Jan H. Dalhuisen: *Dalhuisen on Transnational Comparative, Commercial, Financial and Trade Law, Vol. III Financial Products, Financial Services and Financial Regulations*, Hart Publishing 5th ed. 2013, at p. 303.

3. *Ibid.*, pp. 305–308.

Category 2   Financial Institution Transfers

Category 3   Treasury Markets Foreign Exchange, Money Markets and Derivatives

Category 4   Collections and Cash Letters (includes, for example, "MT 400 Advice of Payment"; and "MT 456 Advice of Dishonour")

Category 5   Securities Markets (includes, for example, "MT 502 Order to Buy or Sell")

Category 6   Treasury Markets Precious Metals

Category 7   Documentary Credits and Guarantees (includes, for example, "MT 700 Issue of a Documentary Credit"; "MT 750 Advice of Discrepancy"; and "MT 752 Authorization to Pay, Accept or Negotiate")

Category 8   Travellers Cheques

Category 9   Cash Management and Customer Status (includes, for example, "MT 900 Confirmation of Debit"; and "MT 910 Confirmation of Credit")

Category n   Common Group Messages (includes, for example, "MT n91 Request for Payment of Charges, Interest and Other Expenses")

Every category also provides an option for a "free format message."[4]

An example of a SWIFT message is reproduced below on p. 496 as Sample Document 3-4. At first glance, the message seems very technical and the reader may ask what this bank-to-bank gibberish has to do with the work of lawyers in international business transactions. Unfortunately, the reality is that despite the harmonization of the communications in SWIFT, there are sometimes misunderstandings or disputes over the interpretation of messages that were sent or should have been sent. As a consequence, SWIFT messages are being considered quite regularly in disputes over the payment obligations of banks or their rights to reimbursement. The above-mentioned Smart Contracts on the Blockchain, however, may make the entire SWIFT system superfluous within the next couple of years.

Since SWIFT only moves messages and does not move money, other systems are required for the actual transfer of the assets. These systems have evolved into highly efficient networks that avoid having to send tens of thousands of payments every day—many of which may be quite small—by setting off the obligations of the different players in the network. For example, if Bank A has to transfer US$ 100,000 to Bank B on behalf of one of its customers, and Bank B has ten payment obligations to Bank C, each in an amount of US$ 10,000, while Bank C has to transfer US$ 110,000 for a client to Bank A, this could require no fewer than 12 transfers if individually executed. However, by using a system of set-off and netting, the banks

---

4. In coming years, SWIFT will replace the MT Categories with the new standard ISO 20022.

adjust the different account balances and only transfer one amount of US$10,000 from Bank C to Bank A.

For domestic payments in the U.S., the Board of Governors of the Federal Reserve System, as a public entity, and The Clearing House, as a privately owned alternative, provide such services via the Automated Clearinghouse (ACH) system. The Federal Reserve also operates the FedWire Funds Service for transfers going via one of the Federal Reserve Banks. The Clearing House operates Clearing House Interbank System (CHIPS) and claims to be able to clear US$1.5 trillion in daily payments via settlements of only about US$85 billions, or only about 6% of the total sum, after setting off and netting all claims at the end of each business day.[5] In the EU, the respective services are TARGET, operated by the European System of Central Banks, as well as Euro-1, operated by the privately owned European Banking Association.

Legal disputes arise when customer instructions to banks turn out to be inaccurate or messages between banks are miscommunicated or misunderstood and funds are transferred to the wrong person or in the wrong amount. Moreover, every now and then, a participant in a set-off and netting system defaults and fails to settle, which also raises the question whether transfers can be recalled. Case law discussed below provides a number of examples and shows why lawyers cannot be oblivious to these interbank communication and transfer systems and the very legal problems that might arise from them.

Section 2. Cash in Advance

A. Introduction

The first thing we need to understand about payments in international settings is that "cash" rarely means a physical transfer of bank notes and coins from one human being to another. The classic movie scene where an attaché case full of cash is handed over basically never happens in legitimate business operations (anymore). It would be too cumbersome, since buyer and seller rarely meet in person and would have to trust couriers or other persons to deliver the cash. It is also too dangerous since the money could be lost or stolen. Finally, it is frowned upon by the authorities because there is no comprehensive paper trail. This means that a transfer of larger amounts of money in actual cash is appealing primarily to people for whom the avoidance of the paper trail outweighs the inconvenience and risk associated with the carriage of cash, such as tax dodgers, drug dealers, money launderers, and other

---

5. See https://www.theclearinghouse.org/payments/chips. For more information on set-offs and netting see, *inter alia*, Jan H. Dalhuisen: *Dalhuisen on Transnational Comparative, Commercial, Financial and Trade Law, Vol. III Financial Products, Financial Services and Financial Regulations*, Hart Publishing 5th ed. 2013, at pp. 313–334.

See also the 2013 UNIDROIT Principles on the Operation of Close-Out Netting Provisions, available at https://www.unidroit.org/english/principles/netting/netting-principles2013-e.pdf.

individuals trying to conceal how much money they have and where it came from. In many cases, these transactions are universally frowned upon. In some cases, they are illegal only in one country but not in the other, for example, when a tax dodger in the U.S. is taking money to a secret account in an offshore tax haven or when a business person in a developing country is trying to circumvent capital controls of her home country in order to purchase supplies or spare parts for her business. For our purposes, however, "cash" shall not mean the physical transfer of bank notes and coins but rather their debiting from one person's account and crediting to another person's account in a bank or wire transfer. Traditional currencies are collectively referred to as "fiat" money in this context. In the very near future, the equivalent will be the debiting and crediting of Bitcoin, Ether, or other cryptocurrencies in the ledgers of buyers and sellers and other business parties. Cryptocurrencies can be exchanged for each other and bought and sold for fiat money in a number of online and physical exchanges.

A payment made by electronic or bank or wire transfer is considered effective if and when it meets the following conditions:

- the credit to the payee's account or ledger gives him the full disposal rights over the money, i.e., the recipient can withdraw all or part of it in fiat money (bank notes and coins) or cryptocurrency, transfer all or part of it onward via electronic or bank or wire transfer, or simply leave it in the account or ledger for later use or to gain interest;

- the money in the account is in the payee's currency or another currency acceptable to the payee or at least convertible to payee's currency or another acceptable currency;

- the money is accessible immediately or by a date agreed upon between the parties to the transaction.

A payment may be effective but not complete if the amount that meets these conditions is less than the amount the payee was entitled to receive, for example, because the exchange rate applied by the bank resulted in a smaller amount credited to recipient's account and he did not have to carry that exchange rate risk, or because banking fees or other transactional costs were deducted that the payee should not have to bear according to the agreement between the parties to the IBT. Since an incomplete payment does not fully discharge the debtor, the creditor may have to pursue the unpaid portion of the payment obligation separately. In practice, this may be futile, however, if the shortfall is relatively small. First, the banking fees to send another wire transfer may exceed the shortfall. Second, under most sales laws, a minor shortfall in the payment by the buyer does not entitle the seller to cancel or avoid the contract and will certainly not warrant the expenses and hassle involved in litigation, arbitration, or another form of dispute settlement. In most cases, this means that parties will simply have to write off any minor shortfalls in the payments they expected through the banks caused by unexpected fees or exchange rate-related losses. In particular, if a seller operates on narrow margins and/or receives many small individual payments in the course of his business, he will need to figure out ways of securing full payment via suitable contractual arrangements and modes of payment.

The most expensive mode of transferring money from one country to another is usually a Western Union transfer. Since the sender and the recipient can go to physical offices of Western Union, this system is particularly popular among low-income people who don't have bank accounts. As a result, those with the least amount of money to spare are being charged the highest percentage of fees, usually between five and 10 percent of the amount to be transferred. At least for larger sums, regular wire transfers between banks are usually cheaper, somewhere in the region of $25 to $50 on each side, regardless of the amount to be transferred. Finally, some new providers like PayPal and Payoneer offer the most cost effective options, with fees in the range of one to two percent. Although it is too soon to tell, it looks as if all of these providers will come under pressure from Smart Contracts on the Blockchain, where fees of one percent or less are already being promoted by providers like Revolut.

Technicalities aside, cash in advance would be the preferred option for most sellers. They would get paid before or during the time when they incur the cost of production and they would never have to worry about the buyer becoming unwilling or unable to pay for the goods once they are manufactured and shipped out. However, for two reasons this rarely happens in reality: First, the option is undesirable for the buyer from the point of view of party risk. Can the buyer trust that the seller, after getting paid in full, is still diligently and honestly pursuing his performance obligations? Second, the option is also economically unfavorable for the buyer because she has to advance the money long before the goods arrive and can be processed or resold. Thus, the buyer has to carry considerable financing costs. Therefore, as long as several potential sellers are competing for the same business, it will be part of the competitive advantage of a particular seller if he can offer better terms to a potential buyer than insisting on cash in advance.

In practice, cash in advance is negotiated primarily in two cases: (i) if the seller has such a strong market position that he can insist on such favorable terms because the buyer really can't go anywhere else to obtain the same goods or services, for example, if the seller has a monopoly in law (the sole license or a patent) or in fact (on the basis or market share or sheer size, the seller is the only company able to offer the quantity and quality required by the buyer); (ii) the seller is unable to finance the production of the goods and/or nobody is willing to produce them without getting paid in advance for at least part of the purchase price, for example, because the goods are so specific that they cannot be sold to anyone else if the buyer should change her mind.

If cash in advance is agreed upon, it is usually only for part of the contract price, more along the lines of a down payment, earnest money, or a number of installment payments as the goods are being produced and shipped out. For example, a contract may foresee a payment of 10% at signing, 30% when the goods are ready, 30% after they are shipped, and a final 30% after they have arrived and are found conforming by the buyer. In this Section, we only consider contracts where the large majority of the payments have to be made in advance, with no payments or only a small percentage coming due later. If a larger percentage of the contract price has to be paid at a later stage, the seller will need to ensure that this actually happens and protect himself against the buyer becoming unwilling or unable to pay that part of the contract price. The options for doing so are discussed in subsequent Sections of this Part.

However, when all or very nearly all of the contract price does indeed get paid before the goods are shipped out, there are still two issues to be taken care of: (i) how and where does the buyer get the money to advance the purchase price? and (ii) how should the money be transferred from the buyer to the seller?

B. Credit Options for the Buyer[6]

Even if goods are sold off the shelf from one country to another, it will usually take several weeks before they can be resold or processed by the buyer. If they have to be manufactured first by the seller, or if the buyer has to process them and/or if it may not be easy for the buyer to find a customer in her country, the time during which the buyer has to advance the purchase price with this payment term will be even longer. Although the buyer's options to obtain financing are not usually international, we shall briefly list the most important options here:

- traditional long-term bank loans or short-term bridge loans using other collateral: Buyer's Bank is funding the purchase of the goods using buyer's other assets, such as real estate, or a floating charge on buyer's inventory, as collateral; the buyer pays interest to her bank at a rate depending on the prevailing interest rates in the country and the buyer's credit rating;

- bank loan using accounts receivable from downstream buyers as collateral; this is an option, if the buyer is merely an intermediary for subsequent buyers and does not otherwise have sufficient collateral or creditworthiness; however, banks will be hesitant to accept receivables if they are still rather vague — the goods are not even manufactured or received by the buyer at this stage — unless they are accompanied by some kind of assurance — for example a Bank Draft — that downstream buyers are expecting the goods and will pay at the appointed time;

- the buyer can try to sell the accounts receivable from downstream buyers instead of borrowing against them; in this option, the buyer has to find a bank or other financier who will purchase her future claims against the downstream buyers at a discount; this kind of transaction is often referred to as factoring, if it includes collection services, and the financier buying the discounted

---

6. This part was inspired by Edward G. Hinkelman: *A Short Course in International Payments*, World Trade Press 2nd ed. 2003, pp. 29–35.

accounts receivable is called a factor; specialized financing companies assess the maturity of the claim, the downstream buyer's creditworthiness, and other risk factors, such as general country risk and enforceability; the discount is rarely less than 10% and can be as high as 50%; buyers can reduce the discount by accepting the financier's recourse in case the downstream buyer does not pay, meaning that the financier can recover what he paid to the buyer and possibly as much as 100% of the claim in case of the downstream buyer's default; buyers should also be aware that collection of accounts receivable by a factor can negatively impact their relations with the downstream buyers because it reveals that the buyer is short of cash;[7]

- if the buyer does not yet have sellable accounts receivable against downstream buyers, she may be able to use purchase order financing; in this option, purchase orders from downstream buyers are assigned to a financier who also assumes the risk and the task of collecting the claims later on; as with factoring, collection of accounts by a financier can negatively impact the relations with the downstream buyers;

- while sellers may also be able to obtain loans or at least loan guarantees from their government via export promotion organizations,[8] governments are generally less eager to finance imports; an exception applies when (developing) countries are investing in larger infrastructure projects or the like with payment terms often extending over several years; in these cases it is not uncommon for the importing country's government to guarantee buyer's payment to the foreign seller; with this guarantee on his medium- to long-term accounts receivable, the foreign seller can then sell the receivables at a discount in a forfaiting transaction.

The main differences between selling accounts receivable in a factoring transaction and selling them in a forfaiting transaction are the following:[9]

---

7. This can be avoided if the factoring transaction is kept confidential and the buyer collects from the downstream buyers as an agent of the factor. However, this reduces the benefits of the factoring transaction.

For more information, in general, on receivable financing and factoring, see Jan H. Dalhuisen: *Dalhuisen on Transnational Comparative, Commercial, Financial and Trade Law, Vol. III Financial Products, Financial Services and Financial Regulations*, Hart Publishing 5th ed. 2013, pp.182–206 et seq.; see also the website of Factors Chain International FCI (https://fci.nl/en/home).

8. For information on the Export-Import Bank of the United States and similar agencies of certain other countries, see below, pp. 430, 489 and 535.

9. Commercial banks will normally base forfaiting transactions on the ICC's URF 800 set of rules (available at http://store.iccwbo.org/Content/uploaded/pdf/ICC-Uniform-Rules-for-Forfaiting-URF-800.pdf); by contrast, the standard set of rules for factoring transactions are the General Rules for International Factoring (GRIF) (developed by the International Factoring Group IFG and Factors Chain International FCI; IFG was integrated into FCI in 2016; the combined group represents more than 400 factoring companies in 90 countries, making it the global representation of the factoring industry; FCI also developed a Model Law for Factoring that can be adopted by countries

- both transactions are more commonly used by sellers who have to wait to get paid by their buyers, for example with Open Account or Cash After Delivery terms (see below); in these cases, the seller can get money faster by selling the receivables from his buyer prior to their maturity; however, both transactions can also be used by buyers who have to pay cash in advance and sell the receivables from their onward buyers to get money faster;

- factoring is generally used for short-term maturities (up to six months), while forfaiting is generally used for medium to long-term maturities;

- factoring is generally used for the purchase of ordinary goods via the types of IBTs discussed in this book, while forfaiting is used for larger investments involving capital goods (construction of airports, highways, power plants, etc.);

- factoring contracts are not negotiable instruments, hence there is no secondary market; by contrast, forfaiting contracts are negotiable instruments and can be sold (and bought) in secondary markets;

- factoring provides financing for up to 80 or 90% of the purchase price, while forfaiting can cover 100% of an investment;

- the fees and other costs involved in factoring have to be borne by the party who wants to get money faster than envisaged in his contract (normally the original seller, and here also the original buyer who uses receivables from onward buyers); by contrast, the cost of forfaiting is always borne by the final buyer, which is usually a foreign public authority.

Whichever financing option the buyer chooses, the overall cost of financing will have to be reflected in the calculation of the profitability of the IBT. In addition to the risk that the seller does not deliver at all or not as promised, this is the main reason why buyers are reluctant to pay in advance.

---

wishing to provide a secure framework for factoring transactions; for more information, see https://fci.nl/en/home).

In addition to the private rule sets, there are two international conventions, namely the 1988 UNIDROIT Convention on International Factoring, also referred to as the Ottawa Convention (http://www.unidroit.org/ instruments/factoring) and the 2001 UN Convention on the Assignment of Receivables in International Trade (https://www.uncitral.org/pdf/english/texts/payments/receivables/ctc-assignment-convention-e.pdf). In spite of their support by the UN, respectively by UNIDROIT, the former has only been ratified by nine countries as of January 2017 (Belgium, France, Germany, Hungary, Italy, Latvia, Nigeria, Russia, and Ukraine), and the latter has only been ratified by Liberia and requires four more ratifications to enter into force. Nevertheless, these Conventions could become important if chosen by parties to a transaction as the governing law. For more information, see Roy Goode, Herbert Kronke & Ewan McKendrick, *Transactional Commercial Law: Text, Cases, and Materials*, Oxford Univ. Press, Oxford, 2nd ed. 2015, in particular Chapter 13, Receivables *Financing: The UNIDROIT Convention on International Factoring and the United Nations Convention on the* Assignment of Receivables in International Trade, pp. 369–424; as well as William Johnston (ed.), *Security over Receivables—An International Handbook*, Oxford Univ. Press 2008, with comparative analysis of 39 jurisdictions.

C. Transfer of Funds from Buyer in Country A to Seller in Country B

International bank or wire transfers involve a payor (usually the buyer) and the payor's bank, both in country B, and a payee (usually the seller) and the payee's bank, both in country S. The transaction is initiated when the payor gives instructions to her bank to transfer a certain sum of money to a specified account of the payee at payee's bank in S. Today, this usually requires provision of the following information:

- payee's name and address;
- payee's account number, usually in the so-called International Bank Account Number (IBAN) format (the IBAN is a unique identifier for every bank account in the world, starting with a country code; it is harmonized pursuant to the ISO 13616:2007 standard);
- payee's bank name and address;
- payee's bank SWIFT or BIC code (BIC stands for "business identifier code"; for banks, this BIC is usually in the SWIFT code format; SWIFT codes are unique identifiers for each bank and allow the banks to communicate via the SWIFT network, see pp. 416-417 and 495-497);
- the amount to be transferred;
- the currency in which the amount is to be transferred;
- and the date when the transfer should be made.

After receiving the instructions from the payor, Bank B will first check whether the required information is complete and then whether the payor has sufficient funds or credit available. Then Bank B will send a message via SWIFT to Bank S announcing the funds transfer. In most cases, the message format will be an *MT103 Single Customer Credit Transfer* (see p. 416). Simultaneously, Bank B will debit the amount plus its transaction fees (typically US$25 to $50) from payor's account. If Banks B and S do not have a direct relationship, they may need to involve one or more correspondent banks because essentially what happens between the banks is a debit/credit transaction in accounts mutually held, so-called "nostro" and "vostro accounts." During the day or business cycle, these accounts run up positive or negative balances and eventually different claims between all participating banks are set off against each other. Even if balances remain to be settled after this clearing procedure, actual money—bank notes and coins—rarely, if ever, physically moving.

Bank B may also have to meet one or more reporting requirements imposed by country B. Examples are a KYC (Know Your Customer) Report, or an AML (Anti-Money Laundering) Report. In the U.S., a report to OFAC, the Office of Foreign Assets Control at the Treasury Department, is required; OFAC monitors transactions that might affect national security, for example, if transactions are made by or to people or organizations on terrorism and other watch lists. In all OECD countries, additional reporting requirements apply for transactions in excess of US$10,000 (so-called Threshold Reporting). The latter are mostly about tax evasion.

After receiving the MT103 or similar notice, Bank S will debit the account of Bank B (or the correspondent bank) and credit the sum to payee's account, minus its own transaction fees for incoming wire transfers (typically US$10 to $25). If one or more correspondent banks have to be involved, additional fees will be deducted along the way, bringing the total cost of the transaction to around US$100. Bank S may have to meet its own reporting requirements imposed by country S upon receipt of the transfer.

Chart 3-2 Structure of an International Wire Transfer Between Banks Without Direct Business Relations

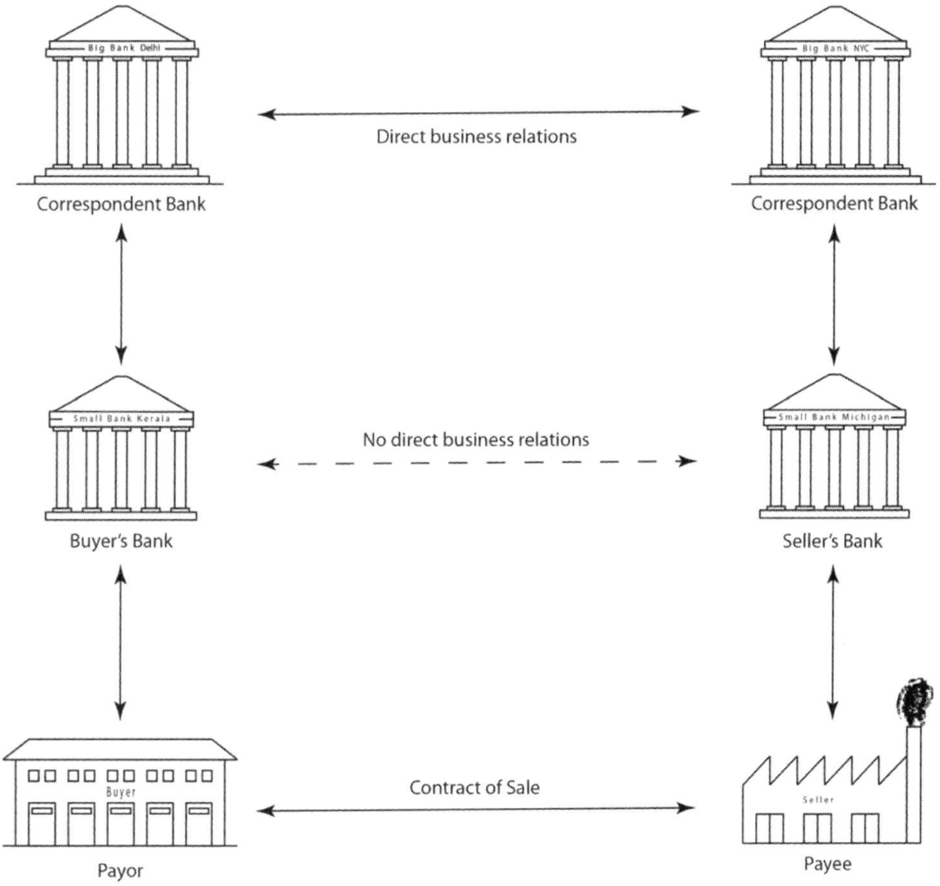

Several things can go wrong in these of kinds of transactions. First, the payor may not have the right to transfer the money, for example, due to internal company ceilings or rules or because there is fraud. Second, the payor may have made the payment to the wrong person or in an amount in excess of her intentions. Third, the banks may make a mistake and credit the wrong amount or the wrong person. Fourth, the payee may not accept the payment because it is too early, too late, too much or too little, or in the wrong currency. Fortunately, all of these are quite rare. Thus, in the normal course of business, it is assumed that a payor acted with intent and sufficient capacity if instructions and funds are provided and that a payee acted with intent and capacity to accept the funds and release the payor from her obligations if the money is withdrawn or knowingly left in the account. Either side will have to promptly protest to prevent finality of the transaction and will have to meet a high standard of proof to contradict appearances.

However, this does not answer the question of what happens if something does go wrong. More precisely, who has to bear the risk for late or non-arrival of the payment? If the buyer gave proper instructions to the banks but the money is sent somewhere else regardless, does it mean that the buyer is now relieved of her payment obligations to the seller? Or does she have to make another transfer to the seller and carry the risk of recovering the first one from the erroneous recipient and/ or the banks? What if timely payment was of the essence and the buyer does not find out that her payment did not arrive on time until it is too late? Can the seller still avoid the contract? If yes, can the buyer then demand additional damages for the lost business opportunity from the banks?

The general principle about the place of delivery of the goods is that the seller, if nothing different is agreed in the contract, merely has to make the goods available to the buyer and the latter is responsible for the carriage; by contrast, the general principle about the place of payment is that the buyer, if nothing different is agreed in the contract, is responsible for the transfer of the payment to the seller (see, for example, §§ 2-308(a) and 2-310(a) UCC; Articles 31, 57(1)(a) CISG; Article 6.1.6 PICC; Article III.-2:101 CFR).

Article 4A UCC provides specific rules for **bank transfers in the U.S.** (Documents, p. I-622). Section 4A-205 UCC provides the rules for payments made to the wrong person or payments made in an amount greater than intended by the sender/buyer, if the mistake is caused by a security system used by the banks and §§ 4A-303 and 305 deal with other mistakes made by the bank(s). Sections 4A-207 and 208 deal with mistakes made by the sender/buyer in the payment order to the bank. The time and extent of payment to the beneficiary is defined in § 4A-405, and § 4A-406 determines whether and to what extent the underlying payment obligation is discharged.

Other countries apply their own rules and these may be quite different from the rules applied in the U.S. Section 4A-507 UCC provides guidance on the applicable law in case of transfers from one state to another within the U.S. Internationally, the applicable law has to be determined pursuant to the rules of private international law, or the private international law rules applicable to a specific relationship or in a specific dispute. For present purposes, § 4A-507 is a good reflection of the rules most likely to be applicable internationally. In a nutshell, the relationship between seller and buyer is determined by the law chosen in their contract of sale and, in the absence of a valid choice of law, usually by seller's law, or by the law of the party that has to make the characteristic performance (seller), or by the law of the place of performance. The relationship between the buyer and her bank, where the payment order is placed, is usually determined by the law applicable at the seat of the buyer's bank, and the relationship between the seller and his bank, where the payment has to be effected, is usually determined by the law applicable at the seat of the seller's bank. On both sides, the banks can stipulate otherwise in the agreement with their clients.

For payments made between Member States of the **European Union**, and to some extent for payments made to and from third countries, special rules have been adopted by the EU that supersede the national laws of the Member States. Member State law, on the other hand, continues to apply to domestic payments within a Member State and to the extent payments to and from third countries are not covered by EU law. Provisions similar to those in Article 4A UCC can be found in *Directive 2015/2366 on Payment Services in the Internal Market* (OJ 2015 L 337, pp. 35–127, also known as *PSD 2*), which includes provisions on the transparency (Articles 52 and 60) and distribution of banking charges between the parties (Articles 62, the default being that each side pays her bank's charges), other rights and obligations of the clients and the payment service providers (Articles 61 et seq.), liability of the payment service provider for unauthorized transactions (Articles 71, 73, 74) and non-execution or defective execution of a payment order (Articles 89, 90), as well as any liability of the sender for incorrectly identifying the beneficiary (Article 88). One of the major innovations of the PSD 2 compared to its 2007 predecessor is the introduction of "strong customer authentication" requirements (Articles 97, 98). *Regulation 924/2009 on Cross-Border Payments in the Community* (OJ 2009 L 266, pp. 11–18, as amended) mandates that the charges for payments sent from one Member State of the EU to another not exceed the charges for corresponding purely domestic transactions (Article 3(1)). The rights and obligations of payment service providers are further elaborated in *Regulation 260/2012 Establishing Technical and Business Requirements for Credit Transfers and Direct Debits in Euro* (OJ 2012 L 94, pp. 22–37). Occasionally, *Directive 2011/7 on Combating Late Payment in Commercial Transactions* (OJ 2011 L 48, pp. 1–10),[10] as well as *Directive 2015/849 on the*

---

10. The European Court of Justice interpreted the earlier version (Directive 2000/35) of this Directive in its judgment of April 3, 2008, in *Case C-306/06, 101051 Telecom v. Deutsche Telekom* (2008 ECR I-1923). The ECJ decided, in line with the American and international approach, that a payment obligation is discharged only when the payment is credited to the account of the payee and that the payor or debtor has the risk of non-payment or insufficient payment until that time. Hence, bank transfers have to be initiated by the payor *before* the payment is due, taking into account "the periods normally necessary for execution of a bank transfer" (Rec. 30). Nevertheless, the payor is not responsible for delays caused by the banks, provided "the late payment is not the result of the debtor's conduct" (ibid.).

The problem of late payments is enormous. As Cara Bilotta reports in her article *Ending the Commercial Siesta: The Shortcomings of European Union Directive 2011/7 on Combating Late Payments in Commercial Transactions*, Brook. J. Int'l L. Vol. 38, No. 2, 2013, p. 699, "[a]t present, the

Prevention of the Use of the Financial System for the Purpose of Money Laundering or Terrorist Financing (OJ 2015 L 141, pp. 73–117), *Regulation 2015/847 on Information Accompanying Transfers of Funds* (OJ 2015 L 141, pp. 1–18), and *Regulation 1889/2005 on Controls of Cash Entering or Leaving the Community* (OJ 2005 L 309, pp. 9–12), may also be of interest.

Notes and Questions

1. During the maternity leave of the CFO, employee Elise was briefly in charge of payments at Crawford & Co. and set up a recurring monthly payment of US$499 to her niece Natalie in Nicaragua. The transfers, although unauthorized and unwarranted, went unnoticed at C for 20 months. What, if anything, can C do now to get the money back?

2. Due to an internal error in Buyer B's bureaucracy, a payment of US$25,000 is wired to third party P instead of Seller S. (i) B has no payment obligation to P; alternatively, (ii) B had a payment obligation of US$5,000 to P; alternatively, (iii) B is going to have a payment obligation to P in the amount of US$50,000 after 90 days for an unrelated transaction. What are the rights and obligations of the parties?

Section 3. Letters of Credit, Confirmed and Unconfirmed[11]

A. Introduction

In this section, we shall discuss commercial letters of credit, or L/Cs. They come in two main forms: confirmed and unconfirmed. Both forms are intended to be the primary form of payment for an IBT, which distinguishes them from Standby-Letters

---

average time for payment of invoices for goods and services in the EU is 56 days for the private sector and 65 days for the public sector. This EU average, however, is skewed by the abysmal average payment periods in many south European countries. Greece and Italy are the slowest with regard to settling invoices. The average payment period in Greece is 110 days for the private sector and 168 days for the public sector, while in Italy the average payment periods are 103 days and 180 days for the private and public sectors, respectively. Spain is in a similar situation, with an average payment period of 99 days for Spanish businesses and 153 days for the government. The consequences of late payment can be dramatic. Late payments cause approximately one in four bankruptcies in the EU, leading to the loss of nearly 450,000 jobs every year. For businesses that manage to stay afloat, late payment can generate substantial additional costs, such as essential external financing or lost investment opportunities. Furthermore, on a regional level, the fear and uncertainty surrounding payment of bills impedes trade among EU Member States" (pp. 699–700, footnotes omitted). However, Bilotta goes on to criticize the approach taken by the Directive and suggests that the EU should have followed the standards already contained in the CISG about when payment is due and liability for interest (ibid., pp. 710 et seq.).

11. For additional background and analysis, see Ebenezer Adodo, *Letters of Credit—The Law and Practice of Compliance*, Oxford Univ. Press 2014; James Byrne, *International Letter of Credit Law and Practice*, Thomson West 2015; Jan H. Dalhuisen, *Dalhuisen on Transnational Comparative,*

of Credit (Section 4) and Bank Guarantees (Section 5), which are only backup security in case the intended primary form of payment fails.

Since L/Cs almost always require the presentation of a number of very specific documents by the beneficiary who wants to get paid, commercial L/Cs are also referred to as documentary credit. Commercial L/Cs are the most widely used tools for trade financing and are suitable for a variety of IBTs. As long as they are well drafted, they provide a high level of security for both buyer and seller. However, in practice, more than 50% of all L/Cs are dishonored by the banks upon first presentation. Careful study of this Section will enable lawyers and their clients to reduce problems with L/Cs and avoid costly and potentially unsuccessful disputes with foreign trade partners and banks.

To begin the analysis of documentary credit, we need to review the mechanics of the documentary sale on pp. 72–76, the so-called four corners model. The reader will recall how seller and buyer enter into the underlying contract of sale and then proceed, with the involvement of the issuing bank (buyer's bank) and an advising bank (seller's bank), to effect payment for the goods via letter of credit. Right after the contract of sale is concluded and before the seller delivers the goods to the carrier for shipment to the buyer, the seller receives the L/C and starts to work down the list of required documents including, for example, a signed invoice, a packing list, a certificate of origin, an inspection or quality certificate from an independent inspection company, an insurance contract (for CIF), and finally, a bill of lading from the carrier to whom the goods have been delivered. As soon as the seller has gathered all required documents, he can proceed to the nominated bank, the advising bank, or any other bank, present his documents, and get paid. A bank not named in the L/C may be chosen for convenience, although it may charge higher fees. The seller who gets an L/C from a reputable foreign bank or, even better, has it confirmed by a reputable local bank, has the assurance of getting paid independent of the solvency or any change of heart of the buyer, as long as he can present all required documents. On the other hand, the buyer has the assurance that no money will be transferred to the seller until the latter has handed over a certified quantity and quality of the goods to an independent carrier for shipment to the buyer.

Some authors still distinguish between revocable and irrevocable letters of credit, although a revocable credit never made much sense because it gives no real security to the beneficiary. Per Article 3 of the Uniform Customs and Practice for Documentary Credit (UCP 600), which is the governing law for virtually all L/Cs issued by

---

Commercial, Financial and Trade Law, Vol. III Financial Products, Financial Services and Financial Regulations, Hart Publishing 5th ed. 2013, pp. 349 et seq.; Peter Ellinger & Dora Neo, *The Law and Practice of Documentary Letters of Credit*, Oxford Univ. Press 2010; E.P. Ellinger, E. Lomnicka & C.V.M. Hare, *Ellinger's Modern Banking Law*, Oxford Univ. Press 5th ed. 2011; Edward G. Hinkelman, *A Short Course in International Payments*, Novato 3rd ed. 2009; Matti S. Kurkela, *Letters of Credit and Bank Guarantees Under International Trade Law*, Oxford Univ. Press 2nd ed. 2008; as well as the somewhat outdated but still useful introduction by Christopher Leon, *Letters of Credit — A Primer*, 45 Md. L. Rev. 1986, pp. 432–464.

major commercial banks (Documents, p. I-500), irrevocable is today the default. This means that once it is issued, neither the applicant (buyer) nor the issuing bank (buyer's bank), nor a confirming bank in seller's country, can revoke or modify the credit without the consent of the beneficiary, see Article 10a. of the UCP 600.

By contrast to a commercial credit, a standby letter of credit is not intended to actually be used for payment of a purchase price or other payment obligation. The standby is more akin to an insurance policy that the payments will be made via other means, for example by wire transfer into an open account. If a seller expects to be paid by wire transfer after the goods are shipped, he can fall back on the standby in case the wire transfer does not materialize. Standbys should be based on the International Standby Practices (ISP98) (Documents, p. I-531) and not the UCP 600. The former was specifically developed for standby letters of credit, whereas the latter was developed for commercial credits. The UCP 600 includes a number of rules that are poorly suited for standbys and may cause confusion. More about this below, at pp. 486-487. As is the case for commercial credits, standbys are today irrevocable by default (Articles 1.06 (a) and (b) and 7.01 of the ISP98, but see also Article 4.10). The conditions for a draw to be made on a standby can be as simple as a demand or a notice of default from the beneficiary in writing (Article 4.16 and 4.17), and they may be as complicated as a court order or arbitration award confirming the payment obligation of the applicant to the beneficiary (Article 4.19).

Another form of protection against nonpayment by a foreign customer is provided by the Export-Import Bank of the United States and similar organizations in other countries. Mainly designed for small and medium-sized exporters, the ExIm Bank offers export credit insurance to cover 85–95% of a loss if a foreign customer is no longer able to pay due to bankruptcy or political or other factors (war, trade restrictions, etc.).[12]

B. The Governing Law for Letters of Credit, in Particular the UCP 600

Although we have statutory law that governs letters of credit, such as UCC Article 5 (Documents, p. I-639), the *principles of party autonomy and freedom of contract* apply here as well. Thus, the parties to an L/C—the applicant (buyer) and her bank (issuing bank)—can agree to terms that differ from any provisions of statutory law. Indeed, they regularly do so by incorporating as governing law the Uniform Customs and Practice for Documentary Credits drawn up by the International Chamber of Commerce, better known in its current form as the UCP 600 (Documents, p. I-500).

On this basis, we can establish the hierarchy of norms governing L/Cs as follows:

- at the top of the pyramid, any documentary credit must not violate mandatory rules of public law, often referred to as *ordre public*, such as protection against

---

12. See https://www.exim.gov/ and discussion below, pp. 489 and 535.

fraud or money laundering, both in the issuing country and in the country where a presentation is made;

- within those outer guardrails, which will rarely become an issue in practice, the most important rules governing a particular L/C are the individually negotiated terms between the parties, i.e., the front of the contract;

- to the extent any rights and obligations or procedures are not individually negotiated between the parties, they are determined by the general terms and conditions agreed upon between the parties, i.e., the back of the contract; the most important of these are the provisions that subject the credit to the UCP 600 as the applicable law;

- only to the extent that an issue is neither agreed upon between the parties nor regulated comprehensively in the UCP 600, we can fall back on specific provisions of statutory law applicable at the place of issue of the L/C or otherwise by choice of law between the parties, for example, UCC Article 5;[13]

- Finally, if none of the specific written rules listed above provides an answer to a question, we can fall back on other elements of contract law applicable by way of party choice or private international law, which may include UCC Article 2 and even the common law of contract, as well as general principles of law.

In practice, the parties do not negotiate a lot of terms and conditions individually for every L/C. The applicant just fills in a pre-printed form made available by her bank, today usually online. To the extent the form allows choices, for example with regard to the amount, the expiration date, the terms of payment, and the list of required documents, these become the individually negotiated terms. For everything else, reference is first made to the UCP 600, which every commercial bank around the world will refer to in its general terms. Beyond that, reference to UCC Article 5, let alone general law of contract, is rarely necessary.

The next important thing to remember about documentary credit is its nature as an *independent mechanism* for payment of a debt owed on the basis of another contract, the contract of sale. The contracts are between different parties and for different purposes.

#1: The contract of sale is *between seller and buyer* about an exchange of goods or services for money. L/Cs are also often used for payments due for commercial real estate or equipment lease, licensing fees, etc.

#2a: The letter of credit is a contract *between the buyer and buyer's bank* to provide the financing for the contract of sale. Rather than a wire transfer into an open account, for which the buyer needs to have cash on hand, the

---

13. For a more detailed analysis of the relationship between Rules of Practice like the UCP 600 and UCC Article 5, see James E. Byrne, *Contracting Out of Revised UCC Article 5 (Letters of Credit)*, 40 Loy. L.A. L. Rev. 2006, pp. 297–400. See also Ramandeep Kaur Chhina, *The Uniform Customs and Practice for Documentary Credit (the UCP): Are They Merely a Set of Contractual Terms?*, 30 B.F.L.R. 245 (2015).

L/C provides credit for a time agreed upon between the parties and specified in the L/C. It also provides a measure of security for the buyer regarding the willingness and ability of the seller to perform on his obligations under contract #1 because buyer's bank promises not to allow draws on the L/C unless certain documents confirming delivery of the goods or services are presented, hence the term "documentary credit."

#2b: In advising the seller of the letter of credit, *a unilateral promise is made by the issuing bank, and potentially a confirming bank, to the seller* who accepts the L/C and starts his performance on contract #1. This part of the financing contract is about an irrevocable promise by the issuing bank, and potentially a confirming bank, to pay up to the amount available under the credit, provided a specified set of documents is presented, irrespective of any changes in the financial position of the buyer or any changes in contract #1.[14]

If, for some reason, the payment contract #2b does not work out as planned, for example because the L/C expires before the seller can meet all conditions, the obligations of seller and buyer on the basis of the contract of sale #1 remain in force. Failure of the L/C is merely a failure of the intended mode of payment. The parties still need to meet their obligations to exchange the goods for money and, typically, now have to work out another mode of payment. This could be a new L/C, a documentary collection, or a wire transfer into an open account. Importantly, a breakdown in the relationship between the buyer and his bank (#2a), for example, because the buyer becomes insolvent, also does not touch upon the commitment made by buyer's bank to the seller/beneficiary under #2b. Similarly, failure of the contract of sale #1, for example because a party avoids the contract for mistake or for breach by the other party, does not automatically invalidate the L/C parts #2a and #2b. In such a case, a valid L/C remains in circulation and the beneficiary or a third-party holder may make a withdrawal on its basis. Without a valid contract of sale as the reason for the transfer of funds, this may constitute a case of unjust enrichment, however. This principle of independence of the credit is reflected in Article 4 of the UCP 600.[15]

The independence of the credit from the underlying business transaction means that the bank, upon presentation of an L/C for payment, will consider only the

---

14. Some authors treat this leg of the transaction as a contract between the issuing bank and/or the confirming bank on the one side and the beneficiary on the other; see, for example, Ellinger & Neo, above note 11, at pp. 109–113. However, since the beneficiary makes no promises or payments in return and, indeed, has no obligation to make use of the L/C, this seems doubtful and unnecessary. What is generally agreed upon is the fact that the undertaking of the issuing and/or the confirming bank is a binding and irrevocable obligation for the benefit of the beneficiary induced by the contract between the applicant and the issuing bank, respectively the contract between the issuing bank and the confirming bank.

15. For in-depth analysis, see Nelson Enonchong, *The Independence Principle of Letters of Credit and Demand Guarantees*, Oxford Univ. Press 2011.

documents presented and required under the L/C. The bank will, in particular, not take into consideration any aspects of the underlying business transaction—the reason for the payment. The bank does not want to see the contract of sale, it does not want to know what kinds of goods or services were sold and whether they conform to the contract of sale, and it does not concern itself with any elements of the business relationship that are not reflected in documents required under the credit, see Articles 4(b) and 5 of the UCP 600.[16] As a corollary, however, the bank will be very careful in reviewing the documents that are required by the L/C and presented by the beneficiary who is seeking to get paid. The principle of strict compliance, as embodied in Article 14 of the UCP 600, reflects the standard applied by the bank when an L/C is presented. In a nutshell, the bank will examine each required document on its face, meaning as presented and without doing any background research. On its face, each required document has to be in strict compliance with the requirements stipulated in the credit. For example, if the L/C requires an "on board bill of lading," a BoL stipulating "received for shipment" is not in compliance because the goods may not be "on board" the vessel yet, meaning that shipment could be delayed. Similarly, if a credit requires a certificate from an inspection company verifying quality "standard A," a certificate verifying "standard 12" will not be in compliance even if the beneficiary presents additional documents, not required under the credit, that show an equivalence of standard A and standard 12. The bank will not concern itself with any documents that are not required by the credit (see Article 14(g) UCP 600) or any information that is not apparent from the face of the required documents. Kurkela summarizes as follows:

> The strict compliance doctrine refers in general to the examination of documents under both stand-by and commercial letters of credit. The documentary conditions precedent must be strictly met in order for the duty to honor to arise. The strict compliance requirement, as applied [to] these instruments means formal or literal compliance, and the reality existing or even known beyond the documents is not relevant at all. The formal test is merciless: discrepancy leads to dishonor regardless of its substance or significance. . . .
>
> The strict compliance rule demonstrates the special character of these instruments: they do not operate as ordinary contracts. Under contract law a breach must in general be material in order to justify cancellation or termination for cause, whereas under these instruments any insignificant deviation or discrepancy entitles the bank to refuse payment.[17]

---

16. Since a draft under an L/C typically requires presentation, *inter alia*, of the relevant transport document, such as a Bill of Lading (BoL), and the seller will not give up the controlling documents without getting paid, it is unlikely that a buyer finds out about non-conformity of the goods in time to try to block payment under the L/C. This issue does present itself, however, in the context of standby letters of credit and will be discussed below at pp. 440 and 486–487.

17. Matti S. Kurkela, *Letters of Credit and Bank Guarantees Under International Trade Law*, Oxford Univ. Press, 2nd ed. 2008, at pp. 120 and 122.

The principle of strict compliance has sometimes produced results that were perceived as problematic, for example, dishonoring of a presentation because of a minor spelling error or a different address of the beneficiary in one of the documents. Therefore, Article 14(d) of the UCP 600 today stipulates that "data in a document . . . *need not be identical* to, but *must not conflict* with, data" required by the credit (emphasis added). However, banks generally approach this matter conservatively for two reasons. First, bankers are used to the principle of strict compliance and it takes time for them to get used to a slightly more flexible approach. Second, and more importantly, if a bank honors a presentation, it takes on a certain amount of risk if there are any discrepancies, however insignificant they may seem, between the requirements under the credit and the documents presented to it. If a bank makes a payment upon a noncomplying presentation, it may lose its right to be reimbursed by the applicant. Simply speaking, there is no reason for the bank to accept the risk that something is wrong. Instead, what the bank will do is to give the presenter a choice: leave the documents with us and we will try to get a waiver from the applicant (for example that standard 12 is fine, although standard A was stipulated) or keep the documents and try to get the waiver from the applicant or a modified document yourself and then come back with a complying presentation (see Article 16(b) of the UCP 600). Importantly, neither of the two approaches to resolve an apparent inconsistency extends the expiration date of the credit and the entire L/C will become worthless if neither the bank nor the beneficiary can procure a waiver or complying documents in time.

Notes and Questions

How would you formulate the difference between "need not be identical" and "must not conflict" from the perspective of a bank? (See also *Bulgrains v. Shinhan Bank*, below, p. 450.)

C. Detailed Analysis of a Typical Commercial Letter of Credit

After a (potential) seller in one country and a (potential) buyer in another find each other and enter into contract negotiations, the usual procedure for the creation of a commercial L/C is for the applicant/buyer to fill in the form provided by her bank, today often online (see Sample Document 3-1), and send a draft to the seller. By sending the draft, the buyer makes an offer to effect payment in this way, provided the contract of sale is actually concluded. If the draft L/C, or a modified version of it, is accepted by the seller and the contract of sale is finalized between buyer and seller as the reason for the payment, the seller begins with his performance, e.g., production of the goods, while the buyer begins with her performance — payment — by submitting the L/C application to her bank. After the buyer's bank satisfies itself that the applicant/buyer has sufficient funds in her account, or that her creditworthiness is sufficient, buyer's bank issues the letter of credit, becoming the issuing bank. Since it is usually not convenient for the seller, who is located in a different country, to pick up the L/C himself, the issuing bank has to involve a correspondent bank in the seller's country. This is done via a SWIFT message from the issuing bank to the correspondent bank about the opening of the credit (*MT700 Issue of a Documentary Credit*; a sample of such a message is included above, pp. 416-417; see also below, p. 496). Ideally, this correspondent bank will be in physical proximity to the seller or even the seller's regular bank and will simultaneously have a standing business relationship with the issuing bank. In such a case, the correspondent bank will happily authenticate the credit and notify the seller, and the correspondent bank would probably also be willing to add its confirmation to the credit at a reasonable fee. Theoretically, a single correspondent bank could be the advising bank (checking the authenticity and notifying the seller), and the nominated bank (authorized to make payment upon presentation of conforming documents), and the confirming bank (adding its own promise to the beneficiary) in one. In practice, however, it is more likely that two or even three banks in the seller's country have to be involved. For example, if the buyer's bank in China only has a business relationship with Bank N in New York but the seller is located in Chicago and usually works with Bank C, it will be more convenient and cheaper if Bank N can be the advising and potentially confirming bank, while Bank C is nominated for the seller's convenience. Indeed, an L/C can stipulate that it is available with "any bank" since nomination does not impose obligations on a bank and merely entitles it to receive the presented documents and forward them to the issuing and/ or the confirming bank (see Article 12 UCP 600).

Sample Doc 3-1: Commercial Letter of Credit

Letter of Credit	[1] Logo of Buyer's Bank = Issuing Bank

□ confirmed [6] □ transferable [7] □ stand-by [8]	expiry date [9]	currency code and amount....................[10]

[2] **Applicant** for the credit (name, address) = buyer	[3] **Beneficiary** (name, address) = seller

[4] Letter of Credit available with
□ Nominated Bank, town, country...   SWIFT code.............[5]
□ Any bank

[11] Buyer's Bank's charges to be paid by	□ Applicant □ Beneficiary
Advising Bank's charges to be paid by	□ Applicant □ Beneficiary
Confirming Bank's charges to be paid by	□ Applicant □ Beneficiary

[12] Credit payable against presentation of required documents:
□ at sight   □ deferred ....days after sight   □ ....days after BoL   □ other...................................

□ by acceptance   □ by negotiation

[13] Brief **Description of the Goods**

[14] **Terms of Delivery** (INCOTERMS 2020)® □ EXW □ FCA □ FAS □ FOB □CFR □ CIF □ CPT □ CIP □ DAP □ DPU □ DDP	Place [15]

[16] **Shipment** departure at the latest from to	[17] Transshipment □ allowed □ not allowed	[18] Partial shipments □ allowed □ not allowed

[19] **Consignee**	[20] Buyer's representative to be notified ....

[21] Required **Documents**
□ full set of clean marine bills of lading	□ signed invoice in .... copies
□ clean "on board" bill of lading	□ packing list
□ combined transport bill of lading	□ movement certificate EUR.1
□ CMR waybill	□ certificate of origin issued by ....
□ duplicate of rail waybill	□ quality certificate issued by ....
□ air waybill, original no. 3	□ insurance policy/certificate for 110% of CIF/CIP value
□ ...	□ ...

[22] Documents to be presented   □ within .... days of shipment   □ within validity of credit

[23] Additional conditions

[24] **Collateral** for the credit
□ transfer cover amount as cash collateral for our obligations under the credit from our account to cover the amount before issuing the credit
□ other collateral (subject to buyer's bank's approval)

[25] We request you to issue an irrevocable documentary credit in accordance with above instructions and UCP 600 terms. We agree with general conditions below.

[26] Applicant account no...	[28] Signatures, stamp and date
[27] Contact person	phone/fax ....

General Conditions[29]
[back of the contract]

Obligations of Buyer's Bank

Buyer's Bank, issuing a documentary credit in accordance with Applicant's instructions on the front of this contract, undertakes to pay to the Beneficiary the Credit Amount (or part of it) in case the Beneficiary complies with these conditions on the reverse. Having effected payment against documents which appear to be in compliance with Credit stipulations, Buyer's Bank is not responsible for genuineness of these documents nor for the shipment of goods or other contractual performance of Beneficiary in accordance with these documents to take place.

Obligations of Applicant

The Applicant undertakes to reimburse Buyer's Bank for any payment effected in accordance with Credit stipulations.

In case the Credit Amount (or part of it) is credited to the Cover Account simultaneously with the issuance of the Credit, Buyer's Bank shall debit the amount of its payment obligation under the Credit to the Cover Account simultaneously with payment (payments) to the Beneficiary. The Applicant can use the funds credited to the Cover Account only upon Buyer's Bank's approval. In case the Credit expires unutilized, Buyer's Bank will return the Credit Amount to Applicant's Account within 15 days after Expiration Date.

In case the Credit Amount is not entirely credited to the Cover Account, Buyer's Bank will debit the amount of its payment obligation under the Credit to Applicant's Account two working days prior to effecting payment to the Beneficiary. Buyer's Bank is entitled to debit the amount of its payment obligation under the Credit without prior notice to Applicant. The Applicant is obliged to maintain sufficient funds on its Account at least one working day before the maturity of Buyer's Bank's payment obligation.

Charges and Expenses

Buyer's Bank is entitled to debit without prior notice to Applicant's Account all its charges and expenses in connection with the Credit, as well as those of other banks involved in handling the Credit, in case these banks should also claim their charges and expenses from Buyer's Bank. In case of insufficient cover on Applicant's Account, the Applicant is obliged to pay the missing amount within two working days after relevant notice by Buyer's Bank.

Collaterals

The Applicant guarantees its obligations under the Credit with all its assets. Pledge and warranty agreements concluded between Buyer's Bank and the Applicant and/or Buyer's Bank and a third party form an undetachable appendix to this Application. The Applicant is obliged to provide Buyer's Bank at any time, within five working days after Buyer's Bank's request, with clear, complete, documented overview of its financial and economic situation, in form acceptable to Buyer's Bank.

The Applicant is also obliged to immediately inform Buyer's Bank of any change in its contact-information and/or any events which might influence the fulfilment of Applicant's obligations under the Credit. In case the Applicant does not fulfil its above-mentioned obligations to provide information, Buyer's Bank is entitled to transfer the Credit amount (or the unutilized part of it) from Applicant's Account to Cover Account. The Applicant is obliged to maintain sufficient balance on its Account within three days after Buyer's Bank's relevant request.

Fine for Delay

In case of inadequate fulfilment of above-mentioned obligations by the Applicant, Buyer's Bank is entitled to claim a cumulative fine of 30% per annum of the corresponding debt amount for every day of delay in adequate fulfilment of Applicant's obligations.

Disputes

All disputes arising in connection with the Credit shall be settled under the Rules of Conciliation and Arbitration of the International Chamber of Commerce.

Commercial Letters of Credit Explained:

#1 **Bank logo:** The Letter of Credit (L/C) is a contract between the applicant (the buyer who has to pay for the goods) and her bank, who becomes the issuing bank. The subject of the contract is the processing of a payment on behalf of the applicant to the beneficiary (the seller who has to get paid). Since there is typically a certain lapse of time between the disbursement of the payment to the beneficiary and the debiting of the amount from the applicant, the bank lends the money, i.e., provides credit, until the transaction is complete. Although it provides for a third-party beneficiary, the contract cannot create *obligations* for any third parties. Since the L/C is prepared as a form contract by the issuing bank, it typically bears the logo and the address of this bank, which serves as the identification of the issuing bank. Pursuant to Article 7 of the UCP 600, the L/C can always be presented to the issuing bank for payment and, as long as the presentation is complying and the credit is not expired, the issuing bank *must* honor the credit.

#2 **Applicant:** The applicant is generally the buyer, but it could also be another party that offers to pay for the goods subject to the contract of sale (or whatever other business transaction may be the reason for the payment) on behalf of the buyer. For example, if the buyer is a relatively small company belonging to a larger group of companies, it is not uncommon for a large payment to be made by the parent company or another bigger company in the group. This means the parties to the contract of sale can be entirely different from the parties to the letter of credit.

#3 **Beneficiary:** The beneficiary is generally the seller but it could also be another party named by the seller as the party to whom payment should be made, for example a supplier of the seller. Since L/Cs are generally "negotiable," the presentation to the issuing bank as the party ultimately obligated under the credit does not have to be made by the beneficiary herself. Much more common is a situation where the named beneficiary presents the credit and the required documents to an advising bank and that bank basically purchases the credit and the documents from the named beneficiary. Then the advising bank presents it to the issuing bank for payment. However, to ensure that the presenter received the credit lawfully, the named beneficiary has to endorse when selling it. In some cases, this allows a bank that has made a payment to have recourse against the beneficiary in case an issuing bank or a confirming bank refuses to pay. Sometimes a credit may be negotiated several times, for example from the named beneficiary to a creditor, from that creditor to her bank, from that bank to the nominated bank (see #4), and from the nominated bank to the issuing bank. There is no problem as long as the chain of endorsements is unbroken and the credit has not expired.

#4 **Availability:** In this field, the parties stipulate *where* the credit can be presented, with the required documents. If only one bank is "nominated," the credit has to be presented either to that bank or to the issuing bank (see Article 6(a) of the UCP 600). However, if the credit is available with "any bank," the beneficiary has a choice of which bank to approach for payment. He can always go to the issuing bank and any nominated bank.

Furthermore, regardless of which bank advised the credit to the beneficiary on behalf of the issuing bank, the beneficiary can choose any bank to advise him on payment under the credit. Even if a bank is not nominated and the credit is not available with "any bank," any bank can purchase the credit with the accompanying documents from the beneficiary and then sell the package to the issuing or confirming bank. In such a case, the bank is negotiating. Obviously, the bank will purchase the credit at a discount from the beneficiary and the rate of discounting depends on the maturity date, i.e., how long it will be until the bank can get reimbursed from the issuing or confirming bank, as well as any perceived riskiness of the transaction.

An exception applies if an L/C is marked as "straight." A straight letter of credit is a transaction between the issuing bank and the beneficiary only. Such an L/C is not negotiable and cannot be presented to any other bank. Since standby letters of credit usually require far fewer documents to be presented and are inherently more risky for the applicant and, to an extent, the issuing bank, standbys are often straight whereas regular commercial credits rarely are.

#5 **SWIFT Code of nominated bank:** The SWIFT Code is determined pursuant to Standard 9362 of the International Organization for Standardization (ISO). It provides a unique identification for each bank or financial institution. In addition to identifying the bank, SWIFT also enables different banks to communicate with each other via the secure telex net (see above, p. 416).

#6 **L/C confirmed?** If the seller wants the credit to be confirmed by a bank in his country, this needs to be marked clearly and has to be accepted by the confirming bank. Confirmation means that the bank undertakes a payment obligation separate from the issuing bank, see Article 8 UCP 600. The advantage for the seller is that in case of problems, in particular the inability or unwillingness of the issuing bank to honor the credit upon presentation, he does not have to pursue the issuing bank in some foreign country, but can insist on payment by the confirming bank in his own country. However, any payment obligation of any bank is always conditional upon a complying presentation and if the seller is unable to present all required documents in full compliance with the conditions marked on the credit before the expiration date, he need not try to pursue the issuing or confirming or any other bank.

#7 **L/C transferable?** Pursuant to Article 38 UCP 600, a credit can be transferable or not. Transfer means substitution of the original or first beneficiary with one or more new or second beneficiaries. While availability terms like negotiation or acceptance (below, #12) affect who gets paid at what time after an L/C has been honored, a transfer of the L/C and change in beneficiary affects who has to gather the required documents to make the complying presentation and get paid.

#8 **L/C stand-by only?** A standby letter of credit fulfils somewhat different purposes from an ordinary commercial letter of credit. This is discussed in some detail below, pp. 486–487. The present model is not ideal to be used for a standby. First, it references the UCP 600 as the governing law, while the International Standby Practices (ISP98) have been specifically developed by the Institute of International Banking Law & Practice for standby letters of credit and have been adopted by the ICC as publication no. 590. Second, a standby rarely references a variety of "live" documents, like waybills or bills of lading. Any such documents have probably become "stale" by the time a standby letter of credit is activated (compare Article 14(c) UCP 600). Nevertheless, many banks give the option of marking an L/C as "standby" on their general forms for commercial L/C applications. This places an additional onus on reviewers to ensure that the information entered into the form makes sense from the point of view of, in particular, the beneficiary.

#9 **Expiration date of the L/C:** Pursuant to Article 6(d) UCP 600, every letter of credit must state an expiration date. This date is strictly enforced, see Article 29 UCP 600, and the credit becomes literally worthless for the beneficiary after it expires.

#10 **Currency code and amount:** In general, the amount stated in the credit is a ceiling and draws for lower amounts are possible. This statement needs to be classified in two ways, however. First, if the credit requires shipment of a certain quantity of goods, say 100 tons of coffee beans for $500,000 USD CIF, the beneficiary can put less money in his draft, for example, if it turns out that the market price has gone down or if the shipping or insurance charges turned out to be lower than anticipated. The amount of money the seller is entitled to would have to be determined on the basis of the underlying business transaction, i.e., the contract of sale or whatever it is in a given case. However, the beneficiary cannot draw $250,000 after shipping half of the goods, unless partial shipments are allowed (see below, #18). Second, the seller may withdraw up to 10% more than the amount stipulated in the credit pursuant to Article 30(a) UCP 600, provided the credit is issued for "about" or "approximately" the sum stipulated in it. This is useful, for example, if the parties do not know, when applying for the credit, the precise cost of some elements of the transaction—for example, the cost of the inspection by an independent third

party, and the seller has agreed to organize the inspection but the buyer has promised to pay for it. What remains crucial in any case is that the seller draws only the
amount he is entitled to under the IBT, even if he could go beyond that amount
under the credit itself.

#11 **Distribution of charges:** Although the default is that the issuing bank is lia-
ble for all fees of any other banks it involves in the transaction (Article 37(c) UCP
600), the standard practice is that the applicant and the beneficiary pay the respective fees in their countries, i.e., applicant pays issuing bank fees and beneficiary
pays advising or confirming bank fees. The level of fees of the issuing bank depends
on the relationship the issuing bank has with the applicant, how credit worthy it
considers the applicant and how much collateral it has for the loan. Similarly, if the
advising bank is also confirming, it undertakes a level of risk and will adjust the fees
to reflect how much it trusts the issuing bank and/or its ability to recover from the
beneficiary if the reimbursement from the issuing bank never arrives.

Overall, there will be the general fee of the issuing bank, usually between about
0.75% and 1.5% of the amount of the credit for an L/C of some four months of
validity, as well as a variety of charges and commissions for postage, courier services, bank-to-bank reimbursements, authentication, and other services. Such
administrative charges typically range from about US$25 to about US$250 each. A
confirming bank will also charge a general fee and certain administrative charges
or commissions. Thus, an L/C for an amount of US$1 million can easily cost
US$10,000 or more, while a simple wire transfer of the same amount into an open
account may cost less than US$100.

#12 **Availability of the credit:** In this field the L/C determines when payments
under the credit will be made. A demand for payment by the beneficiary is called a
"draft." The L/C will either provide for a "sight draft" or for a "time draft." If the
credit is available at sight, the bank has to pay as soon as a complying presentation
is made to it (but see Article 14(b) UCP 600). If the credit specifies a time period
until maturity, i.e., the payment is deferred by a certain number of days after sight,
after the date on a Bill of Lading, or after some other event, the beneficiary should
still make the presentation right after having gathered all required documents.
Although he will not actually get paid until the maturity date of the credit, there
are several benefits for the beneficiary. First, he has to make the presentation within
the validity of the credit anyway. Second, if the required documents include original
transport documents, such as a Bill of Lading, presentation has to be made no later
than 21 days after shipment (Article 14(c) UCP 600). The reason for the 21-day limit
is that the consignee needs to get the original transport documents to receive the
goods from the carrier and if she does not get them in time, the goods will need to
be stored upon arrival. Third, the beneficiary will immediately be told at the time
of presentation whether the bank honors the presentation as complying or not. The
bank honors it by giving a deferred payment undertaking. If the bank dishonors it,
it has to provide a list of reasons (Article 16(c) UCP 600) and the beneficiary may
still be able to obtain a waiver from the applicant or a revised document from the

inspection company or whatever the discrepancy may be, before the expiration of the credit.

Thus, after a complying presentation of a sight draft, the beneficiary goes home with money; and after a complying presentation of a time draft, he still goes home with the certainty of receiving the money at maturity.

In addition, a credit may stipulate that it is available "by acceptance" or "by negotiation." Negotiation is the option of the beneficiary to present the L/C and the required documents before the maturity date and get paid immediately. In essence, the bank buys the L/C and the documents at a discount and holds it until maturity, basically providing credit to the beneficiary. Negotiation can be done with or without recourse, meaning that an advising bank may be allowed to recover the funds from the beneficiary if there should be a problem with the issuing bank upon maturity. Naturally, the fees taken by the bank will be higher if the negotiation is without recourse. An exception applies if the bank is confirming. In that case, it must negotiate without recourse (Article 8(a) ii. UCP). If a credit is available by acceptance, the beneficiary can present the L/C and the required documents before the maturity date and receive a time draft instead of actual cash. Such a bank draft is a negotiable instrument, much like a check, and can be used to make payments or receive a discounted payment. If the time draft provides for maturity like the original L/C, the bank does not actually provide credit.

For the buyer/applicant, an L/C available by negotiation or by acceptance can be slightly more risky because the advising bank will make a payment before the documents are received and reviewed by the issuing bank. If any documents turn out to be falsified, it may be harder or impossible to track down and recover from the beneficiary. On this point, compare also the *Fortis* case, below, p. 455.

(#13) **Description of the goods:** ~~Inconsistencies~~ in the description of the goods are the most common reason for an L/C to fail as the intended mechanism of payment. The bank will insist that the description be perfectly identical in all documents required under the credit. Thus, if the description in the credit differs from the description by the inspection company or in the packing list or in the export license or in the bill of lading, the bank will dishonor and require a waiver from the applicant to be sure that there is no problem with the goods described in the discrepant document.

brief = description

Therefore, the description should generally be kept short and straightforward. Moreover, the seller should review a draft of the L/C before it is issued to make sure that he will be able to procure all required documents with that description. Some documents should be easy since the seller issues them himself, such as the packing list and the invoice. Others can be managed because the seller can take the L/C to the inspection company and the carrier and ask them to use the same description. However, some are not under the control of the seller, for example the export license or the certificate of origin issued by the customs authorities of the exporting country.

#14 INCOTERM: INCOTERMS® were explained in Part 2, Section 6 (see above, pp. 240 et seq.). For the letter of credit, it is important first that the INCOTERM® correspond to the division of obligations agreed upon between seller and buyer in the underlying contract of sale. For example, if the contract of sale stipulates a price "FOB," the seller has not agreed and will not get paid for purchasing insurance and paying for carriage. However, if the letter of credit stipulates "CIF," the seller will not get paid under the credit unless he provides a bill of lading and an insurance contract and both are prepaid. Thus, the seller may have to do more under the credit than he would have to do under the contract of sale and this "more" may not be reflected in the price of the goods per the contract of sale. As outlined above, it may not be cost-effective or even possible to recover this "more" from the buyer. Second, the INCOTERM® should also correspond to the documents the seller is able to and has agreed to procure and submit under #21. Again, it does not make sense to stipulate "FOB" in #14 but then require an insurance policy for 110% of CIF/CIP value under #21. Third, different documents would need to be included for the less common INCOTERMS®. If a D-term is stipulated here, some kind of arrival certificate would need to be added in #21. On the other hand, it would be up to the seller whether he wants to purchase insurance coverage in such a case and an insurance policy or certificate should not be required under #21.

#15 **Place of delivery:** The named place is an integral part of the INCOTERM®. For EXW, F-terms and D-terms, the place is where the risk of loss or damage passes from seller to buyer *and* where the responsibilities for care, carriage, and insurance shift from the seller to the buyer. In the case of C-terms, the place determines how far the seller has to organize and pay for carriage and/or insurance, usually the port of destination, although the risk of loss or damage already passes to the buyer when the goods are handed over to the main carrier at the port of departure.

#16 **Shipment:** Two important pieces of information are included here: *When* the shipment has to be made and *from where to where*. Under a C- or D-term, the applicant/buyer may not care from which port the shipment departs, but she will be very keen to determine the destination port that is most convenient to her. However, the port of departure is important for F-terms because the buyer will have to organize carriage and insurance from this point onward.

The latest acceptable departure date is almost always important to the buyer, who wants to know when she will receive the goods. The date is enforced both via the validity or expiration date of the credit and via the transport document. Thus, if the credit requires a "clean on board bill of lading," the BoL date will be the shipping date and the bank will dishonor the credit if the BoL date is after the latest acceptable departure date. See also #22.

#17 **Transshipment:** If transshipment is allowed, the goods can first go to a different destination and then onward to the final destination. This may be inevitable if there are no direct connections and/or if the means of transport has to be changed.

#18 **Partial shipments:** If partial shipments are not allowed, the seller can only make a complying presentation after shipping all or nearly all of the goods, see Article 30 UCP 600. However, if partial shipments are allowed, the seller has the option of making a partial draw from the L/C after a partial shipment, see Article 31 UCP 600.

#19 **Consignee:** The consignee is the person to whom the goods should be delivered at the other end of the voyage. This could be the buyer, a representative of the buyer, or an importer handling the customs processing for seller and/or buyer (depending whether this processing is seller's responsibility (DDP INCOTERM® and possibly DAP) or buyer's responsibility (all other INCOTERMS®)). For the purposes of receiving the goods and customs processing, the consignee is considered the owner of the goods, primarily because she will hold the Bill of Lading, which is a document of title. However, formal ownership of the goods is usually not conferred upon the consignee if she is not also the buyer, because she is only an agent acting upon instructions by buyer or seller. In particular, if the seller has reserved title to the goods until paid in full, formal ownership at this point may still be in seller's hands. Conversely, if the buyer has paid in full, she will be the formal owner.

#20 **Buyer's representative:** As in all contracts, it is important to always name a person entitled to receive notices for a corporate entity and to make statements on its behalf. Notices sent to general addresses of a company rarely are noticed in time and statements made by people who may not have power of attorney to act on behalf of a company may not be held against it.

#21 **List of documents required for a complying presentation:** This part of a draft L/C should always be very carefully reviewed. As has already been explained above (#13-16), it is important that the list of documents required from the beneficiary for a complying presentation has to be consistent with the obligations of the beneficiary under the contract of sale, in particular the INCOTERMS®. Otherwise there is a risk that the seller will have to do things under the credit to get paid (e.g., provide a prepaid insurance contract and a prepaid BoL (as under CIF) that he would not have to do under the contract of sale (if FOB). Second, it is important for the beneficiary that he can actually obtain all required documents before the expiration of the credit.

In the example, the list is organized with a variety of transport documents on the left and a variety of other documents on the right. Logically, only one of the transport documents on the left can be required while more than one of the other documents on the right can be required.

#22 **Presentation deadline:** If the L/C stipulates that a complying presentation has to be made before the expiration of the credit, this can make it hard for the beneficiary to get all required documents in time. The logic behind such a shorter deadline is the need to send the BoL to the buyer in time for the arrival of the goods. If any original transport documents are required under the credit (the documents in the left column), Article 14(c) UCP 600 requires presentation within 21 days for the same reason.

#23 **Additional conditions:** This field is usually left blank. However, an L/C applicant can ask for additional conditions, such as all documents to be dated and signed, all documents to indicate beneficiary's name, all documents to contain a reference to an L/C number or identifier, or for any additional freight charges (Article 26(c) UCP 600) to be prohibited.

#24 **Collateral:** This field is of no consequence to the beneficiary. It stipulates how the applicant intends to provide security for the L/C.

#25 **Inclusion of the UCP 600 as the governing law:** This is standard practice by almost all commercial banks. Reference to national statutory provisions for letters of credit (e.g., Article 5 UCC) or general provisions of contract law to fill gaps in the UCP 600 is rarely necessary.

#26 **Applicant's account number:** Like #24, this is an internal communication between the applicant and the issuing bank and of no consequence to the beneficiary.

#27 **Applicant's contact person:** While buyer's representative under #20 would be the person to be notified in case of shipping delays and the like, the contact person under #27 can be the person in the accounting department responsible for the financial transaction.

#28 **Signatures and date:** The applicant signs when applying and the representative for the issuing bank signs when the L/C is issued.

#29 **General conditions:** This section is subordinate to the front of the L/C and the UCP 600. It becomes relevant only if an issue is neither regulated by individual agreement between the parties (the front of the L/C), nor by the UCP 600 (the applicable law by choice of the parties).

D. Checklist for the Seller/Beneficiary for Reviewing a Draft L/C[18]

Whenever an international business transaction includes payment via L/C, it is highly recommended that the seller insist on reviewing a draft before the actual L/C is issued by buyer's bank. Experience teaches that it is much easier for the seller/beneficiary to ask for changes before the actual L/C is issued. Conversely, the seller/beneficiary is much more likely to accept an L/C in spite of some unfavorable clauses or terms simply because it is already issued and modifications would be troublesome. The result of the latter situation is predictable: the seller/beneficiary struggles to meet all terms and conditions before the L/C expires. At the very least, such difficulties cause stress and additional expenses. Remember that *more than 50%* of all letter

---

18. This was originally inspired by Chris Lidberg, http://www.shippingsolutions.com/blog/my -checklist-for-reviewing-a-letter-of-credit.

of credit presentations are dishonored upon first presentation to the bank.[19] Unless the beneficiary has time to get a waiver or complying documents, he has to struggle to get his money from the buyer in other ways. The majority of these problems could easily be avoided through careful review of a draft before an L/C is issued and forwarded to the seller.

Checklist 3-1
Ten Points for Reviewing a Draft Letter of Credit

1. The beneficiary's name and address have to be correct and precise. If a company has more than one branch or subsidiary, all documents required by the L/C have to refer to the same address. Please review the *Bulgrains* case on p. 450 to see how far this can go.

2. If the L/C is not confirmed, only the issuing bank has an obligation to honor a complying presentation. If the beneficiary, in case of problems, does not want to pursue the issuing bank because it is far away, may itself become insolvent, and/or is not subject to rule of law and efficient enforcement procedures at its seat, the beneficiary should insist on confirmation of the L/C by a reputable financial institution in his home country that is unrelated to the issuing bank.

3. Are the stipulated amount and currency correct? There are multiple opportunities for mistakes here. First, the overall amount of the credit might be too low — for example, if it covers only the price of the goods without applicable sales taxes or if it covers only the price EXW or FOB but the credit requires "freight prepaid" and a certificate of insurance, i.e., seller has to provide the goods CIF. In case of doubt, an L/C stipulating "about" or "approximately" for the given amount will be a safer choice (see Article 30(a) UCP600).

Second, the overall amount of the credit might be too high, if the seller wants to get paid for part of the total amount but the L/C might not allow partial shipment (see p. 440). In such a case, the seller can only make a compliant presentation of the L/C if all or very nearly all of the goods have indeed been shipped. Shipment of 94% of the goods will not be enough and the bank will call a discrepancy (see Article 30(b) and (c) UCP600). On the other hand, as long as at least 95% of the goods have been shipped, a draft for less than the full amount of the credit is generally acceptable. This problem does not occur if the L/C allows for partial shipments (see clause #12). In such cases, the beneficiary can generally present the documents for shipment of any fraction of the contractual quantity of goods and make a corresponding partial withdrawal under the L/C. If partial shipments are of no interest to the buyer and/or would cause significant additional costs, the buyer/applicant should not allow partial shipments under #12.

---

19. See International Chamber of Commerce, *ICC Moves to Cut Documentary Credit Rejections*, February 3, 2003, cited by James D. Rosener of Pepper Hamilton LLP, available at http://www.pepperlaw.com/publications/recent-developments-letter-of-credit-transactions-2005-07-14/.

4. The time of payment has to be acceptable. If the credit is available *at sight*, the seller can get his money generally within five business days (Article 14(b) UCP 600). If the credit is available *by deferred payment* only, the seller generally has to wait until maturity for his money. The decision whether or not the credit will be honored, i.e., whether the presentation is complying, will be made within five business days, but the payment will only be made at maturity.

However, if the credit is available *by negotiation*, the seller can sell the L/C and accompanying documents to the nominated bank or any bank immediately and does not have to wait for five business days, let alone until a deferred maturity date. In this case, the bank that negotiates (purchases) the credit basically advances the money until maturity. Naturally, such an advance is not free and the seller would not get the full amount available under the credit in the negotiation. Moreover, if the bank negotiates *with recourse*, the seller has to return the money if the issuing bank subsequently refuses to honor the credit. However, if the credit is confirmed, the confirming bank must honor or negotiate *without recourse*, see Article 8(a) UCP 600.

5. The description of the goods should be kept as simple as possible. Unnecessary details greatly increase the risk of discrepancies. For example, if the description in the L/C stipulates a specific weight of the goods, the bank will call a discrepancy if any of the other documents indicate a different weight. In general, banks will compare any description of the goods required by the L/C word for word and letter for letter with the description of the goods contained in any other required document. Article 14(e) UCP 600 has introduced a modicum of flexibility in this regard. A shorter description in some of the documents will not prevent a complying presentation as long as there is no conflict with other documents. To be clear, if the L/C stipulates a weight, the commercial invoice will have to contain exactly the same entry regarding the weight (and every other element of description of the goods). That should not be a problem, since the seller himself issues the commercial invoice and he can always change it if there is a discrepancy, unless he waited until the last minute with his presentation to the bank. Other documents like the certificate of origin could omit information about weight altogether. This would not prevent a complying presentation. However, if any document, such as a BoL, stipulates a different weight, the bank will dishonor the credit.

6. The INCOTERM® in the contract of sale should match the INCOTERM® in the credit. If the credit has a different INCOTERM®, it does not necessarily prevent a complying presentation, since the contract of sale is disregarded by the bank (Articles 4(b) and 14(g) UCP 600). However, if the L/C requires more from the seller than the contract of sale, for example, if the L/C references CIF or CIP and/or stipulates among the required documents an arrival certificate or an insurance policy, the seller will not be able to make a complying presentation without these documents and will not get paid under the credit even if the contract of sale was for EXW or FOB or another F-term. Conversely, if the seller goes the extra mile to match the conditions of the L/C, although that was not agreed in the contract of sale, it is not at all clear that the extra expenses can be collected from the buyer. If the credit

stipulates "about" or "approximately" with regard to the amount of money available under it, the seller can use this flexibility because the advising of a credit for CIF could be seen as an offer to modify the FOB clause in the contract of sale. However, if the credit does not provide for a sufficiently large amount, the seller would have to pursue other ways of getting the extra compensation from the buyer.

In the rare case that the conditions in the credit are fewer than those in the contract of sale, the seller does not stand to benefit, either. Although he may be able to get paid under the credit for merely handing over the goods to the carrier if the credit provides for FAS or FOB and does not require a prepaid Bill of Lading and/or a prepaid insurance policy, the seller may be in breach of the contract of sale if the latter provided for CIF or CIP, let alone a D-term. If the seller wants to comply with the contract of sale and goes beyond his duties under the L/C, his presentation may end up being dishonored by the bank if any of the documents do not comply with the L/C.

7. The requirements for shipment have to be acceptable. As always, they should conform to the contract of sale, if anything was agreed there. Any additional details regarding the port of departure and arrival, departure dates, arrival dates, carriers, consignees, transshipment, partial shipment, etc. have to be acceptable to the seller because there will be problems with the bank if any of the conditions are not precisely met. In practice, the latest day for shipment causes most problems, if the seller cannot produce conforming goods on time. It should be remembered in this regard that banking holidays lead to an extension of banking deadlines (Article 29(a) UCP 600), but weekends and other holidays do not extend shipping deadlines (Article 29(c)).

8. The list of required documents and any information about them has to be acceptable to the seller. If an unexpected document is listed, there will be no payment under the L/C until that document is provided, regardless of what was stipulated in the contract of sale. As for documents that were expected, the seller should check whether the requirements are correct. For example, there is an important difference between an "on board" or "on deck" Bill of Lading and one that is merely confirming "received for shipment." Any requirements for prepaid shipping and/or prepaid insurance documents have to match the INCOTERM® in the credit and, if possible, also the one in the contract of sale.

9. The distribution of banking fees and charges between buyer and seller has to be acceptable to the seller. The customary solution is for each side to pay the fees and charges of the banks in his or her country. Did the seller expect those fees and charges? Is the distribution possibly indicated differently? Is that in conformity with the contract of sale and otherwise acceptable to the seller? Compare the judgment in *Fortis* below, p. 455.

10. Finally, and maybe most importantly, the expiration date of the credit has to be acceptable. The buyer/applicant has an interest in keeping the expiration date relatively tight since a more distant date will increase the fees charged by the issuing bank. However, for the seller it is important that he has enough time not only to

meet the latest shipping date, but also to gather together any other documents and make his way to the bank. Since transport documents have to be "live" and must not be "stale" (compare Article 14(c) UCP 600), an expiration date 21 days after the latest date for shipping should be acceptable, but an earlier expiration date can easily become problematic.

Notes and Questions

1. What are the strengths and weaknesses of documentary credit? What types of risks can it reduce or eliminate and what are the types of risks it cannot?

2. If a letter of credit is primarily intended to protect the buyer against *non-shipment* and the seller against *nonpayment*, what are the options of the buyer to be protected against *nonconformity* of the goods? Keep this question in mind as you ponder the main forms of financing and payment in international business transactions.

3. What are the 10 most important steps the parties to an IBT should take if they intend to use documentary credit as the means of payment for the goods, services, lease, or license (or whatever may be the underlying transaction)?

4. How can the parties to a one-off transaction minimize the cost of the payment arrangements? How does this affect the risk? What about the parties to an ongoing business relationship where regular or repeated payments have to be made?

E. Electronic Letters of Credit[20]

In a traditional documentary sale, a large number of documents were created and moved around between the different parties to the transaction. Transfer by fax or e-mail attachment was an option for evolving drafts of a contract of sale, but for other documents, like letters of credit and bills of lading, original documents were required and often had to be sent by courier from one country to another to ensure authenticity and prevent fraud. This was time-consuming and expensive.

Therefore, there is an ongoing effort in the industry to switch as many documents as possible into electronic format and avoid working with paper altogether. To support the digitization of trade finance and create a set of ground rules for the protection of clients and limits of liability of finance institutions, the ICC Banking Commission has developed a Uniform Customs and Practice for Documentary Credit (UCP 600) Supplement for Electronic Presentation (eUCP). This document will probably be further refined, but Version 2.0 has been published and included in the Documents Collection (pp. I-518).

The eUCP are not fundamentally different rules, but supplement the UCP 600 with some provisions specific for the electronic rather than paper-based presentation of L/Cs.

---

20. See also Part Two, pp. 354 et seq.

In this context, readers should also be aware of the work of the United Nations Centre for Trade Facilitation and e-Business (UN/CEFACT) and its Uniform Rules of Conduct for Interchange of Trade Data by Teletransmission (UNCID). See also Part Two, Section 9 on Electronic Contracts and Documents.

F. Practical Examples from Case Law

As mentioned above, more than 50% of all letters of credit are dishonored upon first presentation. In many cases, the discrepancies can be fixed or waivers can be obtained and the beneficiary does get paid when making a new presentation to the issuing or confirming bank. However, there remain a significant number of cases where the letter of credit as the intended form of payment fails and the beneficiary or seller has to fall back on the original contract of sale and seek payment from the buyer by other means. Obviously, this is not always successful either, in particular if the buyer has meanwhile fallen into insolvency or a pursuit of the claims in the buyer's country is otherwise not promising or excessively cumbersome, for example, because the courts are notoriously slow or biased toward domestic parties. In such cases in particular, the seller may opt for a lawsuit against the bank that issued or confirmed and later dishonored the letter of credit. The following examples illustrate the standards applied by the courts and by various arbitration tribunals for the obligations of the issuing and any confirming banks. The first case, *Bulgrains*, is a pretty straightforward case of alleged discrepancies, although it also includes some issues related to the single notice that has to be given by the bank according to Article 16c of the UCP 600. The reader should pay attention to the interpretation given to the principle of strict compliance, the mechanics of the transmission of the single notice, and who bears the risk of less than perfectly clear communications.

The second case, *Fortis*, is about the way an issuing bank has to provide notice under Article 16 UCP 600 and what happens if the required procedures are not complied with. Particular emphasis is on Article 16(f) UCP 600, which precludes a bank, under certain circumstances, from claiming that a set of documents does *not* constitute a complying presentation.

The third case, *Bayfern*, concerns the distribution of risk between the issuing bank and the confirming bank if some of the documents turn out to be fraudulent.

Case 3-1

Bulgrains & Co Limited v. Shinhan Bank

High Court of Justice, Queen's Bench Division
[2013] EWHC 2498 (QB), Case No: TLQ/13/0593, 24 July 2013

[1] JUDGE GORE: This is the expedited trial ordered by consent intended to determine the liability of the London branch of the defendant Bank to pay the sum of US$825,000 to the claimant, pursuant to the irrevocable letter of credit issued on 13 March 2013. The defendant denies the claim of the claimant in full. . . .

[6] The claimant is a company registered in Bulgaria and registered with BCCI. It trades within and out of Bulgaria primarily in wheat and similar foodstuffs. The sole share-holder is Mr Metodi Nikolov, who also controls the claimant. Mr Nikolov was con-tacted by a Mr Hyun Seung Ju acting on behalf of Heungsung Fee Company Limited by email on 30 March 2012, who was looking to buy approximately 3,000 metric tonnes of wheat bran pellets. Almost a year later, on 15 March 2013, at Heungsung's request, the defendant in Seoul issued a letter of credit No MT42421303NU00300 for the sum of US$825,000 in relation to the supply of 3,000 metric tonnes of grain. . . . I observe, as far as is material to this judgment, that the beneficiary is identified as: "Bulgrains Co Limited, Sofia, Bulgaria 9 Pozitano Str"—presumably the street— "represented by M Nikolov Executive Director." The description of the goods to which the credit relates was:

1. Wheat bran pellets in bulk. Moisture max 13.5PCT—Protein Min 12.0PCT—Ash Max 7.0PCT—Fiber Max 12.0PCT—Free from alive and dead insects—Pellet's diameter 6-12mm—Pellet's length 20-30MM

2. Quantity: 3,000 M/T(10% M/L)".

There is no dispute that "PCT" means per cent, "MT" is metric tonnes and "ML" is "more or less".

[7] Under the letter of credit, the defendant was required to pay the sum of US$825,000 to the claimant once the claimant presented or had presented to the defendant's main office in Korea the documents listed in the letter of credit, which can be sum-marised as being:

1. A signed commercial invoice in quadruplicate;

2. A full set of clean on-board ocean bills of lading made to the order of the defendant in Seoul marked "Freight fee paid and notify applicant";

3. Certificate of origin or "Euro 1" issued by local Chamber of Commerce (one original and three copies;

4. A copy of the phytosanitary certificate;

5. A certificate of quality and quantity issued by independent inspectors (again one original and three copies);

6. A fumigation certificate (again one original and three copies);

7. A veterinary certificate (one original);

8. The hold's Cleanliness certificate issued by independent inspectors;

9. A loading manifest and/or stowage plan issued by the vessel's agent at the loading port.

[8] It is now common ground that documents were presented and received by the defendant on 29 April 2013. The documents received by the defendant's head office are alleged by the defendant to have been discrepant in significant respects, as a result of which it has failed to pay upon the letter of credit, and the claimant claims this to have been wrongful and claims to enforce the letter of credit.

⁹ The defendant submits that the claimant's claim fails on three distinct grounds. Ground 1 asserts that, on the documents alone, the claim cannot succeed because, firstly, the documents for payment under the letter of credit were not in conformity with the letter of credit. Specifically, there was a discrepancy between the name of the beneficiary as it appears on the letter of credit (where it appears as Bulgrains Co Limited), and allegedly it was markedly different, referring to Bulgrains & Co Limited on one of the documents presented. And, in addition, on the commercial invoice the description of the goods does not conform with that in the letter of credit.

¹⁰ The defendant alleges that these discrepancies were notified to the claimant in two substantively identical notices, each of which conformed to the requirements of the ICC's Uniform Customs and Practice for Documentary Credits 2007 Ed (the so-called UCP 600), which there is no dispute were incorporated into and govern the letter of credit. Notification that the letter of credit would not be honoured was sent via SWIFT to the claimant directly on 6 May 2013. A second SWIFT notice allegedly was sent via a relaying bank, ING Sofia, on 7 May 2013. In both cases the notices, if valid, were sent by the defendant within the stipulated period for notification that the documents were being rejected, such that there is now no issue as to timing. It is submitted that, if the defendant's case on ground 1 is proved, that would suffice to deal with the claim in its entirety and the court would not need to consider the other two defences raised by the defendant. There appears to be no dispute on that point. . . .

¹³ So the following matters are to be determined. Firstly, whether the documentation was discrepant. Secondly, whether the defendant complied with inter alia Articles 14(b) and 16(c) of the UCP in purporting to reject. Thirdly, . . .

Documentation

¹⁴ There is no dispute that the letter of credit sent by SWIFT sets out the beneficiary and its address thus:

> "Bulgrains Co Ltd, Sofia, Bulgaria 9 Pozitano Str represented by M Niko-lov—Executive Director." . . .

There is also no dispute that the commercial invoice that was in due course presented sets out the seller and its address thus:

> "Bulgrains & Co Ltd, 9 Pozitano str, 1000 Sofia, Bulgaria."

The invoice is then signed on behalf of the seller "M Nikolov—Executive Director" . . . .

¹⁵ There is a dispute about whether the invoice is discrepant, and also about whether the defendant's reliance upon it is valid. There is no dispute that the description of the goods at line 45A in the letter of credit (trial bundle 2 tab 17 page 500) was in the following terms:

> "Wheat bran pellets in bulk—moisture max 13.5%, protein min 12.0%, hash max 7.0%, fibre max 7.0%, free from alive and dead insects, pellets diameter 6-12 mm, pellets length 20-30 mm."

However, the commercial invoice . . . is in markedly different terms. Under the heading "Description of goods" one finds the following:

"Bulgarian wheat grain pellets."

There is no dispute about this discrepancy, but only about whether the defendant's reliance upon it is valid.

[16] Therefore, the first issue for me to decide is whether the presence or absence of either the ampersand or the word "and" between "Bulgrains" and the word "Co" (for company) makes the documentation discrepant. The defendant submits that the general requirement for conformity between the letter of credit and the documents presented thereunder is well established. In particular, it submits that the rule is that a set of documents which does not precisely meet the terms of the credit should ordinarily be rejected—see *Equitable Trust Company of New York v Dawson Partners Limited* (1926) 27 Ll L Rep 49 at 52, per Viscount Sumner, cited with approval by Lord Diplock in *Gian Singh & Co Ltd v Banque de L'Indochine* [1974] 1 WLR 1234, and in particular at pages 1239 and 1240. The defendant, adds that the concept of strict compliance is the foundation stone of the approach of the English courts to the operation of documentary credits. As Sir Thomas Bingham MR (as he then was) put it in *Glencore International AG v Bank of China* [1996] 1 Lloyd's Rep 135 at 152:

"The duty of the issuing bank is, and is only, to make payment against documents which comply strictly with the terms of the credit."

[17] The only exception, the defendant submits, may be where the discrepancy is insignificant or trivial such that it cannot be regarded as material—see *Astro Exito Navigacion SA v Chase Manhattan Bank NA, The Messiniaki Tolmi* [1986] 1 Lloyd's Rep 455 (a case also cited by the claimant), and also *Bankers Trust Co v State Bank of India* [1991] 2 Lloyd's Rep 443. The defendant submits that materiality is the key, as illustrated by *Bankers Trust*, where the misstatement of a telex number was regarded as trivial. By contrast, in *Seaconsar (Far East) Ltd v Bank Markazi Jomhouri Islami Iran* [1993] 1 Lloyd's Rep 236, in particular page 240 columns 1 and 2, per Lloyd LJ (as he then was), with whom Beldam LJ agreed, the Court of Appeal's judgment being left undisturbed on this point by the House of Lords on appeal, [1993] 3 WLR 756, the Court of Appeal held that the absence of the buyer's name from the presented documents was fatal to a claim for payment, because the letter of credit specifically required that it be stipulated. There is no dispute between the parties that, as the authorities cited above make clear, in determining what is material the court must have regard to the terms of the letter of credit alone.

[18] The test to be applied by the court is best summarised by the editors of Jack: Documentary Credit 4th Ed 2009 at paragraph 8.38 in saying:

"It is suggested that the correct approach is that a document containing an error with a name or similar should be rejected unless the nature of the error is such that it is unmistakeably typographical and the document could not reasonably be referring to a person or organisation different from the one specified in the credit. In assessing this, the bank should look only at the context in which the name appears in the document, but not judge it against the facts of the underlying transaction."

[19] In support of this proposition the defendant cites the United States case of *Beyene v Irving Trust Company* [1985] 762 Fed Rep 2nd series at page 4, in which the name "Sofan" was misspelled in the bills of lading as "Soran". The United States Court of Appeals Second Circuit stated:

"While some variations in a bill of lading might be so insignificant as not to relieve the issuing or confirming bank of its obligation to pay . . . we agree with the district court that the misspelling in the bill of lading of Sofan's name as 'Soran' was a material discrepancy that entitled Irving to refuse to honor the letter of credit. First, this is not a case where the name intended is unmistakably clear despite what is obviously a typographical error, as might be the case if, for example, 'Smith' were misspelled 'Smithh.'"

[20] This approach, that a typographical error is a discrepancy, but anything that *might* be anything *other* than an inadvertent misspelling is not, is exemplified in the decision in *Singapore in United Bank Limited v Banque National de Paris* [1992] 2 SLR 64, in which the court held that the bank was entitled to reject documents in the name of a company called Pan Associated Pte Ltd, when the letter of credit was issued in favour of Pan Associated Ltd, even though there was evidence that under Singaporean company law there could not be two different companies with those names, and even though in the relevant documents the same address was given for each corporation described. . . .

[22] So the claimant submits that because ampersands cannot be transmitted by the SWIFT system (which fact is not disputed), and the correct address and director name had ensured that there could be no doubt as to the entity identified, there was, in its submission, no relevant or material discrepancy.

[23] In my judgment, the ratio and reasoning of Tin J in *United Bank Limited* explains why this cannot be the case, because, having considered a lot of authority, including some of the cases cited to me, he said at page 73I to 74B:

"On these authorities it seems reasonably clear that any discrepancy, other than obviously [his emphasis] typographical errors, will entitle [his word] either the negotiating or the issuing bank to reject. It is tempting to say that whether a bank is entitled to reject must surely depend on whether the discrepancy is really material. But why should a bank assume the responsibility of determining the question of materiality and take the risk of it, if it goes wrong. As is so clearly stated in the UCP, documentary credit transactions are concerned with documents. There cannot be any doubt that the name of the beneficiary is a very significant matter."

He adds at page 75B:

"A negotiating bank can only be certain of the position if it makes a search at the Registry of Companies. But I seriously doubt that the Bank is expected to make such enquiries, bearing in mind that all that should be looked at are the documents."

[24] I agree, and I find therefore, that there was a discrepancy as to name that was not clearly and demonstrably simply a typographical error and was material, and it, together with the discrepancy as to description in the invoice, gave the defendant the right to reject the documents. Even if there was no facility to insert an ampersand in SWIFT, the word "and" could have been used, and, in my judgment, it also should have been used because the name of the company in the Cyrillic alphabet, included the single letter the translation of which means "and" which word therefore should have been used. . . .

Notes and Questions

1. This case became famous because an important issue was whether an ampersand could create a discrepancy that entitles a bank to dishonor a letter of credit. As lawyers, upon reading Article 16(d) UCP 600 ("Data in a document, when read in context with the credit, the document itself and international standard banking practice, *need not be identical, but must not conflict* with, data in that data in that document, any other stipulated document or the credit." (emphasis added)), we might be inclined to think that it should not matter whether a company is referred to as "Bulgrains Co." or as "Bulgrains and Co." or as "Bulgrains & Co." However, this is not the way bankers approach the subject. What arguments are advanced by the parties and on what basis does the judge conclude that the documents were indeed discrepant? Do you find the reasoning of the judge persuasive? Why or why not?

2. Regardless of whether or not you agree with Judge Gore in *Bulgrains*, let this case be a reminder of the principle of strict compliance and the need to review drafts of L/Cs and all documents subsequently generated to avoid problems upon presentation of the L/C to the bank. Compare also how a similar question is treated in the subsequent *Fortis* decision.

Case 3-2

Fortis Bank and Stemcor UK v. Indian Overseas Bank

Court of Appeal [2011] EWHC 538 (Comm), 31 January 2011
Lord Justice Thomas

[1] This appeal raises a number of issues in relation to letters of credit. One of them is of more general importance as it raises an issue under the Uniform Customs and Practice for Documentary Credits, 2007 Revision, ("UCP 600") as to the position which arises when an issuing bank which has rejected the documents gives notice that it is returning the documents, but fails to do so.

The factual background

[2] The second respondents to the appeal (Stemcor), a company carrying on in London an international business of selling steel, entered into five contracts to sell

various quantities of containerised scrap to SESA International Limited ("SESA") CFR CY Haldia (or Haldia/Kolkata) in August 2008. The contracts all provided for the incorporation of Incoterms 2000; and that (I) the law of England was to govern, with arbitration of disputes in London; (ii) payment was to be through a letter of credit opened by a first class bank acceptable to Stemcor in workable form and received in London with the advising bank nominated as the Aldermanbury Square branch of the first respondents (Fortis), an international bank incorporated in Belgium.

³ The contracts were made through MSTC Limited ("MSTC"), an Indian government owned company within the Ministry of Steel, who were described in the letters of credit as the "Facilitator". The appellant, IOB, a bank carrying on business in India with its international business branch in Kolkata, issued the five letters of credit on the application of MSTC in favour of Stemcor in respect of the purchases by SESA. The letters of credit were made available by negotiation with Fortis' London branch each naming Stemcor as beneficiary. The five letters of credit (L/C1 — L/C5) were:

L/C 1, 14 August 2008, US$ 1,160,000

L/C 2, 18 August 2008, US$ 1,440,000

L/C 3, 29 August 2008, US$ 2,625,000

L/C 4, 13 August 2008, US$ 1,800,000

L/C 5, 18 August 2008, US$ 1,240,000

The first three were confirmed at Stemcor's request by Fortis. Each letter of credit was subject to UCP 600.

[The scrap metal under the contract was shipped from Europe to India over several weeks at the end of 2008. Stemcor was listed as "shipper" and the consignee was to be determined by IOB. Between the time the contracts were made and the time the goods were shipped, the market price for scrap metal had fallen considerably and, indeed, below the contract price. Thus, SESA wanted to extract itself from the unfavorable contracts and tried to do so by raising alleged discrepancies in the documents presented by Stemcor with the L/Cs. However, by that time, Fortis Bank had already negotiated and honored the first three L/Cs, and presented the other two to IOB with the documents from Stemcor (factual background added by Steven Fox and Reema Shour, INCE & Co.).]

⁴ Stemcor presented the documents under L/Cs 1–3 which Fortis accepted and paid Stemcor the amount due; the documents were forwarded by Fortis to IOB. The documents presented under L/Cs 4 and 5 were forwarded by Fortis to IOB.

⁵ IOB rejected the documents presented under L/Cs 1–4 on dates between 4 and 19 November 2008 on the basis of discrepancies (as I set out below in more detail). It refused to reimburse Fortis (in respect of the drawings under L/C 1–3) and payment to Stemcor (in respect of L/Cs 4–5) on the basis that the documents contained discrepancies in respect of L/Cs 1–4 and for a different reason in respect of L/C5. It

gave notice under sub-article 16(c)(iii)(c) of UCP 600 stating that it was returning the documents in respect of all the presentations except for 5 presentations under L/C3 where IOB stated that it exercised the option under sub-article 16(c)(iii)(a) to hold pending further instructions from the presenter; those further instructions were given, on terms, by Fortis in January 2009. IOB did not return any of the documents until 16 February 2009.

[6] Stemcor and Fortis commenced proceedings in the Commercial Court against IOB under the letters of credit for a sum in excess of $8m and for damages, including container demurrage and port costs:

> i) Fortis as confirming bank claimed US$5,024,041.80 under L/Cs 1–3;

> ii) Stemcor as beneficiary claimed US$3,033,037.20 under L/Cs 4–5 which Fortis had not confirmed.

Stemcor and Fortis applied for summary judgment on all their pleaded claims (save for Stemcor's claims for container demurrage and port costs).

[7] IOB disputed their entitlement to summary judgment; the application was heard by Hamblen J in September 2009. By that time, IOB accepted that certain payments should have been made; they also abandoned reliance on some of the alleged discrepancies. The four principal issues that arose were:

> i) Whether there were discrepancies in the documents presented;

> ii) Whether Fortis was technically a confirming bank;

> iii) Whether the bill of lading date was the date of issue of the bill of lading or the date of shipment (and subsequently whether IOB would have a counterclaim if it were the latter on the basis that Fortis' presentation was non-compliant because it occurred more than 21 days after that date).

> iv) Whether IOB by reason of its late return of the documents should be precluded under sub-article 16(f) of UCP 600 from claiming that the documents did not constitute a complying presentation.

[8] In a judgment given on 25 September 2009, Hamblen J determined that the only discrepancies in the documents were in the beneficiary's consolidated certificate; he also determined the second and third issues in favour of Stemcor and Fortis. He considered that the fourth issue in relation to preclusion should be determined as a preliminary issue and made directions for the trial of the following issues:

> 1. Does the preclusion in sub-article 16(f) of UCP 600 apply at all (whether by a process of construction of the express words of the Article or by virtue of an implied term) in relation to actions taken or not taken by an issuing bank at the time of and/or subsequent to the issuance of a sub-article 16(c)(iii) notice?

> 2. If the answer to question 1 is "yes"

> a. What is the content of the obligation on the issuing bank in relation to a "return" notice?

b. What is the content of the obligation on the issuing bank in relation to a "hold" notice?

3. Were IOB's actions or inactions following their respective sub-article 16(c)(iii) notices such that IOB were precluded from relying upon the relevant discrepancy?

[9] The preliminary issues were heard by him over three days in January 2010; expert evidence from two bankers was called. In a further judgment given on 28 January 2010, Hamblen J held that IOB, having elected to return the documents under article 16, was under an obligation under that article to return them with reasonable promptness; it also received instructions from Fortis with which it was obliged to comply. As it had failed in breach of its obligation to return the documents, it was precluded under sub-article 16(f) by reason of its breach from relying on the discrepancies in the beneficiary certificate.

[10] IOB appeal with his permission on two issues and Fortis and Stemcor cross appeal on a third issue:

i) Whether IOB was precluded under sub-article 16(f) from relying on the discrepancies;

ii) Whether the Bill of Lading was the date of shipment on board;

iii) Whether there was a discrepancy in the beneficiary's consolidated certificate.

[11] I will consider the third issue first, for if Fortis and Stemcor are correct in their cross appeal on this issue, the preclusion issue does not arise.

I. The Discrepancy in the Beneficiary's Consolidated Certificate

[12] As I have set out at paragraph 8, Hamblen J rejected all of the discrepancies alleged by IOB, save for one in the beneficiary's consolidated certificate. This was required under Field 46A, clause 7D, of each letter of credit:

"BENEFICIARY'S CONSOLIDATED CERTIFICATE CERTIFYING AS FOLLOWS:

WE HEREBY CERTIFY THE FOLLOWING . . .

D) THAT THE NEGOTIATING BANK HAS BEEN ADVISED TO DESPATCH ORIGINAL SHIPPING DOCUMENTS ONLY BY AIR COURIER SERVICE TO THE LC OPENING BANK AT OUR COST. . . ."

[13] The document presented under each of the letters of credit was:

"WE HEREBY CERTIFY THE FOLLOWING: . . .

D) THAT THE NEGOTIATING BANK HAS BEEN ADVISED TO DESPATCH ORIGINAL SHIPPING DOCUMENTS ONLY BY AIR COURIER SERVICE TO THE LC OPENING BANK AT ISSUING BANK'S COST"

[14] The consolidated certificate did not therefore follow the terms of the letters of credit by referring to "OUR" cost and instead replaced it with a reference to the "ISSUING

BANK'S" cost. The judge considered that the terms of Field 46A clause 7D required the documents to be despatched at Stemcor's cost and not IOB's. He rejected the contention that there was any ambiguity, as the "we" in the field was plainly Stemcor and therefore the "our" plainly referred to Stemcor. He also rejected the contention that, as IOB would know that it had not been charged for the air courier service by the time the documents were received by it, the discrepancy was trivial. He held that the bank was not only under no duty to check whether it had been charged (as no enquiry beyond an examination of the documents was required), but also that IOB did not know it would not be charged.

[15] I agree with the decision of the judge on this short point.

[16] The letter of credit on its ordinary reading required the beneficiary's consolidated certificate to certify that the negotiating bank had been advised to despatch the shipping documents by air courier to the opening bank at Stemcor's cost. The word "our" referred back to "we". "We" was plainly the beneficiary — Stemcor. The certificate was plainly discrepant as it certified that the cost was not Stemcor's but that of the issuing bank. It was argued, however, by Stemcor and Fortis that there was a sufficient ambiguity in the language of the letter of credit which would excuse the discrepancy; it is not necessary to consider the extent of any ambiguity or the consequences of any such ambiguity as, in my view there was none. I cannot see how "our" can be read as referring to the issuing bank.

[17] Stemcor and Fortis next contended that, although strict compliance was required, trivial discrepancies could be ignored: *Seaconsar Far East Ltd v Bank Markazi* [1993] 1 Lloyd's Rep 236 at 240. In determining whether there was compliance, the exercise of judgment rather than a mechanistic approach was required: reliance was placed on *Kredietbank Antwerp v Midland Bank plc* [1999] CLC 1108 at paragraph 12 where Evans LJ said:

> ". . . the requirement of strict compliance is not equivalent to a test of exact literal compliance in all circumstances and as regards all documents. To some extent, therefore, the banker must exercise his own judgment whether the requirement is satisfied by the documents presented to him."

[18] I cannot accept that the discrepancy can be regarded as trivial or that a banker in the exercise of judgement would regard the documents as in conformity. Take for example the facts in *Kredietbank* where the letter of credit had specified a "Draft survey report issued by Griffith Inspectorate at port of loading". What was presented was a draft surveyor's report signed by Daniel C Griffith (Holland) BV on that company's notepaper which also bore the notation "Member of the worldwide inspectorate group dedicated to the elimination of risk". This court upheld the judge's conclusion that any banker would know that there were a number of groups which carried out surveys and that what was required was a report issued by a Griffith company; there was an obvious misnomer and the document was compliant.

[19] In contrast in the present case, there was no mistake of name or obvious error discernable from the document; the certificate certified that the charges were to be

paid by the issuing bank. It appears that in fact the charges were paid by the beneficiary; it was therefore submitted that this must have been known by IOB as IOB had not engaged the courier and had not paid a charge on delivery. Even if this were known to someone in IOB, those checking the documents (including management supervising them) would not have known this; they could not have discerned this from the documents and they were under no obligation to make enquiries of others within IOB as to whether IOB had engaged the courier or paid the courier.

[20] I therefore turn to the issue of preclusion which raises issues of more general importance.

II. The Preclusion Issue

[21] The issue on preclusion gave rise to a dispute both as to the law and the application of that law to the facts.

(1) The legal issues

(a) The disputed issue of law

[22] Sub-article 16(c) of UCP 600 makes clear provision as to what an issuing bank must do if, after examination of the documents, it decides to reject them: . . .

Sub-article 16(d) provides for the time within which the notice must be given:

> The notice requirements in sub-article 16(c) must be given . . . no later than the close of the fifth banking day following the date of presentation.

[23] Fortis and Stemcor contended that if the issuing bank gave notice that it would return the documents then, on the proper construction of article 16 it was under an obligation to return them promptly. If it failed to do so, then sub-article 16(f) applied:

> If an issuing bank or a confirming bank fails to act in accordance with the provisions of this article, it shall be precluded from claiming that the documents do not constitute a complying presentation.

In the alternative they contended that, if article 16 could not be construed in this way, then a term to similar effect should be implied into article 16.

[24] IOB disputed this construction. Its primary case was that the issuing bank was under no obligation on a proper construction of article 16 to return the documents; the only obligation of the issuing bank was to give a notice; nor should any term be implied into article 16 of the UCP to that effect. Any obligation to return the documents was outside the scope of the UCP. If, contrary to its primary contention, there was an obligation to return the documents, then that obligation arose under an implied term of the letter of credit and not under article 16; if that were so, then Fortis and Stemcor could not rely on sub-article 16(f) as they could only do so if the issuing bank were in breach of its obligation under article 16.

[25] It is plain that Fortis and Stemcor can only rely on preclusion under article 16(f) if the obligation to return arose under article 16. As it cannot realistically be disputed for the reasons set out below that an issuing bank which rejects documents and

states it is returning them, must return them, the real issue is in fact whether the obligation to return arose under the UCP or outside the UCP.

(b) The approach to the UCP

[26] The generally accepted approach a court should take to the construction of the UCP is set out in the judgment of Sir Thomas Bingham MR in *Glencore v Bank of China* [1996] 1 Lloyd's Rep 135 at 148.

> "Practice is generally governed by . . . the UCP, a code of rules settled by experienced market professionals and kept under review to ensure that the law reflects the best practice and reasonable expectations of experienced market practitioners. When courts, here and abroad, are asked to rule on questions such as the present they seek to give effect to the international consequences underlying the UCP."

[27] In *Schutze and Fontane's Documentary Credit Law throughout the World* (2001, ICC), there is a helpful discussion at paragraph 2.2.4 of the relationship of national law and the UCP where the meaning of the UCP is in dispute or UCP does not contain an express provision for the issue that is before a national court.:

> "While the UCP aim to harmonise worldwide trade practices and aim to safeguard the interests of the international trade and banking community, national laws vary from country to country. The application of national laws to issues not expressly addressed by the UCP can result in a de-internationalisation of the rules and conflict with their purpose. The application of national laws and doctrines needs to be handled carefully. If the UCP generally address an issue in question but do not provide for an explicit solution to a particular aspect of it, there is also the option of considering whether a solution can be found in a general rule contained in the UCP. An interpretation of the UCP in accordance with their aims and evaluations is generally preferable."

[28] Similar views are expressed in *Brindle and Cox on the Law of Bank Payments,* paragraph 8-005:

> "As to the interpretation of the UCP itself, while some courts have tended to construe its provisions according to traditional English cannons of interpretation, a more purposive approach is appropriate to a document which after all does not have its origin in English law, but represents international banking opinion and practice."

and Dr Kurkela's *Letters of Credit and Bank Guarantees under International Trade Law* at paragraph V.I.4

> "The interpretation of such rules should be global and universal and should avoid parochial concepts and meanings."

[29] In my view, a court must recognise the international nature of the UCP and approach its construction in that spirit. It was drafted in English in a manner that it could easily be translated into about 20 different languages and applied by bankers

and traders throughout the world. It is intended to be a self-contained code for those areas of practice which it covers and to reflect good practice and achieve consistency across the world. Courts must therefore interpret it in accordance with its underlying aims and purposes reflecting international practice and the expectations of international bankers and international traders so that it underpins the operation of letters of credit in international trade. A literalistic and national approach must be avoided.

[30] I turn therefore to consider first the commercial practice of international bankers and traders which arises when an issuing bank rejects documents, as that is essential to identify any underlying aim and purpose relevant to the issue.

(c) The practice upon rejection

[31] The evidence of practice was clear. As I have mentioned, the judge heard expert evidence from two bankers; Stemcor and Fortis called Mr Gary Collyer, a technical adviser to the ICC since 1996, a member of the ICC Banking Commission and Chairman of the ICC Drafting Group responsible for the revision of UCP 500 to create UCP 600. IOB called Mr Roger Jones, a retired banker who is chairman of the ICC UK Banking Committee and also a member of the ICC Banking Commission. Their reports contained evidence of practice. They also set out their views on the drafting of the UCP, its scope and other matters to which I refer at paragraph 50. Their oral evidence encompassed the issues raised in the reports.

[32] The judge succinctly summarised their evidence on practice at various paragraphs of his judgment:

> 20. Mr. Collyer stated that where "return" is indicated, the return of documents "should occur immediately or at the very latest during the course of the following working day" and that where "hold" is indicated and the presenter instructs the issuing bank to return documents "it is international banking practice to comply promptly with instructions received from the presenter, especially instructions relating to the disposal of documents".

> 21. Mr. Jones said that "best practice" entails the "speedy" return of documents and, based on his own experience of UK practice, that would normally be "within a day or two unless there is a good reason why not". However, Mr. Jones also said that "there is certainly room for limited divergence in market practice dependent on local conditions" and referred in this context to matters such as weather conditions, religious holidays, the means by which the documents are in fact returned and courier pick-up times.

> 23 . . . . I was referred to a number of ICC Opinions under UCP 500 in which it was recognised that the issuing bank would be liable if it failed to act in accordance with the required statement it had made, although none of them specifically addressed the issue of preclusion. The experts said that that the requirement to act in accordance with the disposal statement made related back to the 1963 revision of UCP, although it was thought that the

consequent preclusion was introduced in the 1970's. It has therefore long been the position under UCP that the issuing bank is required to act in accordance with its disposal statement. . . .

52. It was the evidence of both experts that the reasonable expectation of a presenting bank which received an Article 16 disposal notice would be that the issuing bank would act as stated. That would be not only good practice, but normal and expected practice. . . .

73. . . . The expert evidence in this case is that it is normal and expected international banking practice for documents to be returned and document disposal instructions to be complied with promptly.

[33] It is clear from this evidence that there was no difference in view as to the practice of acting in accordance with the notice and, if there was notification of return, of returning the documents promptly—as Mr Jones put it "within a day or two"; the only difference related to a minor difference as to how the practice of acting promptly was applied.

[34] A clear illustration of this practice is DOCDEX Decision 242; DOCDEX decisions are decisions by experts selected by an ICC committee from a list maintained by the ICC Banking Commission on disputes referred for non-binding resolution according to the ICC DOCDEX Rules. Decision 242 related to UCP 500 article 14(d) and (e) (corresponding to article 16 (c)—(f) of UCP 600). Article 14 of UCP 500 provided:

d. I. If the Issuing Bank . . . decides to refuse the documents, it must give notice to that effect by telecommunication or, if that is not possible, by other expeditious means without delay, but no later than the close of the seventh banking day following the day of receipt of the documents. . . .

ii Such notice must state all discrepancies in respect of which the bank refuses the documents and must also state whether it is holding the documents at the disposal of, or is returning them to, the presenter.

iii The Issuing Bank . . . shall then be entitled to claim from the remitting bank refund, with interest, of any reimbursement which has been made to that bank.

e. If the Issuing Bank . . . fails to act in accordance with the provisions of this Article and/or fails to hold the documents at the disposal of, or return them to the presenter, the Issuing Bank . . . shall be precluded from claiming that the documents are not in compliance with the terms and conditions of the Credit.

Decision 242 pointed out that neither the UCP nor any ICC paper provided a specific time or a time such as "without delay" or a means by which the documents should be returned:

"Notwithstanding the absence of a specific requirement or specific guidance in this regard, there is a market expectation that, consistent with the reading of Articles 13 and 14, international standard banking practice and the importance associated with possession of the documents, especially title documents, the timely return of dishonoured commercial documents requires priority processing, as delay in returning the documents may prejudice the beneficiary's rights and security.

While the Experts do not have the authority to establish such a standard concerning an exact time period to return the documents once notice is sent, the Experts agree that once the notice is sent stating that the documents are being returned, documents should be returned without delay and by expeditious means."

It was common ground that there had been no change in practice since UCP 500.

[35] It therefore seems to me indisputable that the practice of bankers and international traders is that, on rejection, the issuing bank must hold the documents in accordance with the instructions of the presenter or return them promptly and without delay.

(d) Is an obligation to act in accordance with the notice to be found in sub-article 16(c) of UCP 600 as a matter of construction?

[36] In my view construing the UCP in accordance with the approach to construction I have set out at paragraphs 26–29, sub-article 16 (c) contains an obligation to act in accordance with the notice. These are the principal reasons for my view:

[37] First, the issuing bank has no option but to comply with the option it has chosen. It is fundamental to the operation of letters of credit that, when the issuing bank determines that the documents do not conform, it may reject them. If it does, then it cannot be entitled to retain the documents, as it is implicit in rejection that it has refused to accept them. It must either hold them at the disposal of or in accordance with the instructions of the presenter or return them. Therefore once the issuing bank has rejected the documents, it cannot do anything else but act in accordance with its chosen option. Thus, it was not necessary to spell out in the sub-article the issuing bank's obligation to act in accordance with the notice. It was implicit in the wording of the article.

[38] Second, the obligation to act in accordance with the notice is what is required by the standard international banking and trading practice set out at paragraphs 31–35 above. It is necessary to make letters of credit work in practice so that the presenter can deal with the goods which are represented by the documents which the issuing bank has rejected. The consequences of the inability of the presenter to deal with the documents are too well known to need enumeration; illustrations are obvious such as in the case of a perishable cargo, or where the market falls or where the ship arrives and seeks to discharge the cargo.

[39] Submissions were made on behalf of IOB that there was no need for such an obligation, as letters of indemnity might be used to procure delivery. The fact that one consequence might in certain circumstances be overcome by the presenter providing

a letter of indemnity to the carrier cannot be relevant to the existence of the obligation. Another submission made on behalf of IOB was that the presenter would have a remedy by bringing an action for conversion of the documents, if they were not returned. However, that submission implicitly accepts and confirms the position that the issuing bank has no right to retain the documents; if it has no right to retain, it is impossible to understand what the issuing bank is entitled to do other than to return the documents or hold them at the disposal of the presenter in accordance with its instructions or pending instructions.

40 It would make no commercial sense, contrary to the submissions of IOB, if having made an election to return the documents, the issuing bank was not obliged to do anything. It would have the absurd consequence that the documents of title would remain with the bank which had rejected them and the presenter would be unable to deal with them. It was hardly surprising that Mr Jones, the expert called by IOB, could not think of any reason why the issuing bank should not be obliged to act in accordance with the notice given under sub-article 16(c). Furthermore, as the UCP is intended to be a self-contained code for the areas which it covers, it would make no sense to interpret the UCP in such a way that the obligation to act in accordance with the notice was omitted from its scope.

41 It is also clear from the evidence of practice to which I have referred that an issuing bank that elects to return documents is expected to do so promptly and without delay. Taking into consideration the necessity for the presenter to be able to deal with the documents, it is clear in my view that if the issuing bank elects to return the documents, it must do so with reasonable promptness. I accept that the notice under sub-article 16(c) has to be given within the specified time of 5 banking days and what is reasonable promptness does not produce an equivalent exact time. However, I cannot accept that interpreting the provision in this way is likely to give rise to any real uncertainty. It is likely to be very clear whether the issuing bank has acted with reasonable promptness.

42 My third reason for my conclusion that the obligation is contained within article 16 of the UCP is that the provisions of sub-article 16(e) are necessary only if article 16 is construed in this way. The sub-article provides:

> A nominated bank acting on its nomination, a confirming bank if any or
> the issuing bank may, after providing notice required by sub-article 16(c)
> (iii) (a) or (b), return the documents to the presenter at any time.

It was submitted by IOB that sub-article 16(e) was necessary as an exception to the notice provision or simply set out for clarity and convenience a practice on which all were agreed. However, it seems to me clear that sub-article 16(e) is only necessary if an obligation to act in accordance with the notice is imposed by sub-article 16(c); the sub-article permits the issuing bank having given notice under (a) or (b) that it is holding the documents to act in a different manner; this provision would not be necessary if the issuing bank was under no obligation whatsoever.

[43] It was submitted by Miss Cockerill on behalf of IOB that this construction is wrong as all sub-articles 16(c) and (d) require is what is set out on its face, namely:

I) sets out the four available options as to what an issuing bank which refuses to honour can do.

ii) requires the issuing bank to give notice of which of the four options it has elected within 5 days.

[44] The submission that the issuing bank is not required to go any further by article 16 and to carry out what it has elected to do was supported by a number of arguments:

I) First, if the issuing bank was under an obligation under the UCP to act in accordance with the choice it had elected, it would have been easy to express in article 16 the obligations to act in accordance with the elected choice. This was not done. I cannot accept this submission. It is plain from the practice to which I have referred that it was the expectation that an issuing bank would return the documents; such a bank would do what it said it would do. There was no need to spell it out.

ii) Second, there was no uniform practice as to the time content of the obligation; using a term such as "reasonable time" or "promptly" or "with reasonable promptness" would cause uncertainty and be contrary to one of the objectives of the UCP which was to provide for certainty, consistency and ease of application. I cannot accept this; there is nothing to suggest requiring return "promptly" or with "reasonable promptness" would cause any uncertainty.

iii) Third, there were no words in sub-article 16(f) which expressly provided for the sanction of preclusion if there was a failure to act in accordance with the notice. Preclusion would be a harsh sanction where the content of the obligation was not spelt out in the article. I again cannot accept that submission as, for the reasons I have given, there is no uncertainty as to the obligation and the sanction is not uncommercial. The effect of not returning the documents or doing as the presenter instructs has very similar consequences to a delay in making a decision on the documents — the presenter cannot deal with the goods.

[45] In my view, therefore, in agreement with the judge, sub-article 16 (c) can and must be read as expressing an obligation that the issuing bank would act in accordance with the option it elected. Thus, as in most of the presentations in this case, where a bank elects to return the documents, the bank is required to return the documents with reasonable promptness. . . .

(2) The factual issue

(a) The findings made by the judge

[56] In respect of L/C 1, 2 and 4 and one presentation under L/C3 IOB rejected the documents; it sent SWIFT notices stating "Return"; it was common ground that

this was the conventional means of expressing the exercise of the option under sub-article 16(c)(iii)(c) of the UCP. Most were sent on 4 November 2008; some were sent on 11, 15, or 19 November 2008.

[57] The response of Fortis was to tell IOB that it should not return the documents, but to accept them and pay. The response of 4 November 2008 was:

> "Documents must not be returned, but must be paid without further delay."

That of 11 November 2008 was:

> "We insist that you hold the documents at your counters and that you effect payment as per L/C terms."

[58] On 21 November 2008, Fortis sent a further message relating to the rejections and to the presentations under consideration by IOB in these terms:

> "In any event you must continue to hold the documents at your counter. They must not be returned to us, or released to any party, without our further explicit instructions."

[59] On 26 November 2008, IOB rejected five of the presentations under L/C3; it sent a SWIFT message stating "HOLD". It was common ground that this was the conventional means of exercising the option under 16(c)(iii)(a) to hold pending further instructions from the presenter.

[60] On 23 December 2008 IOB stated that it had been trying to obtain the applicant's (i.e. MSTC's) acceptance of the documents and suggested that Fortis use its "good offices" with Stemcor to resolve the matter.

[61] On 1 January 2009 IOB requested Fortis to advise Stemcor

> "to do the needful to protect their interest in respect of the merchandise shipped under the contract/LCs in question".

[62] On 13 January 2009 Fortis requested IOB that the bills of lading be endorsed to Fortis' order and "return them to our office via urgent courier".

[63] On 19 January 2009 Fortis requested IOB to

> "Please urgently confirm that you have acted in accordance with said instructions to endorse bills of lading to our order and return all documents to our counters . . ."

[64] On 9 February 2009 IOB replied to say

> "We are not in position to endorse the bills of lading to your order in the absence of written authority to this effect from the shipper/beneficiary of LC. . . . we continue to hold the documents at your risk and responsibility."

Hitherto there had been no indication to Fortis that there was any difficulty about the endorsing of the bills of lading or about its demand for the return of the documents.

[65] On 9 and then on 11 February 2009 Fortis told IOB that its failure to return the documents constituted an affirmation of the presentations as complying presentations

in accordance with sub-article 16(f) and accordingly that it had no further interest in the documents.

⁶⁶ The documents were returned on 16 February 2009. None had been endorsed.

(b) The contentions

⁶⁷ There were two particular periods of delay relied upon by Stemcor and Fortis: first, the period beginning immediately following the "return" notices in November 2008, and second, in relation to both the "return" and the "hold" notices, the period after 13 January 2009.

⁶⁸ IOB contended that, if it was under an obligation to return, the responses given by Fortis to its "return" notices, namely that IOB was to retain the documents, had the consequence that IOB was not in breach of its obligation. I cannot accept this contention for the reasons given by the judge at paragraph 83 of his judgment on the preliminary issues. It is clear that what Fortis was saying was that IOB had no right to reject the documents and should accept them; Fortis' request that the documents be retained was solely for the purpose of IOB accepting them. As IOB continued to reject the documents, it was not entitled to retain them on the basis that it was holding them pending instructions from Fortis. It was obliged to return them. It did not do so for a substantial period of time and was therefore clearly in breach of the obligation under article 16.

⁶⁹ As set out at paragraph 59 above, IOB's notice on the rejection of five of the presentations under LC/3 was a "hold" notice under Article 16(c)(iii)(a). Fortis submitted that their instruction on 13 January 2009 (set out at paragraph 62) was an instruction to return with which IOB had failed to comply. IOB contended that it was not in breach as the instruction by Fortis was an instruction to return after endorsement and Fortis had no right to insist on an endorsement. The judge concluded that, as Fortis had negotiated the documents and was therefore their owner, it was entitled to give the instruction, but even if it was not, there was no reason why IOB did not return them unendorsed.

⁷⁰ The judge was plainly correct in his conclusion that IOB was obliged to return the documents; on the assumption most favourable to IOB that it was right in its contention that Fortis were not entitled to require endorsement, IOB had, on that assumption, no right to retain the documents. It should simply have returned them unendorsed. IOB was therefore in breach of its obligation to return.

III: The Bill of Lading Date

⁷¹ The final issue was a short issue raised by IOB in relation to L/C3. That letter of credit provided in Field 48 that:

> "Period for presentation: within 21 days from B/L Date but within the validity of L/C"

⁷² At the summary judgment hearing, IOB contended during the course of argument that a presentation made under L/C 3 on 25 November 2008 was more than 21

days after the Bill of Lading Date; this was not a point taken at the time of presentation of the documents or at any time prior to the oral argument.

[73] The facts can be briefly summarised:

i) The Bill of Lading on its face contained the following:

Place and Date of Issue: MSC(UK)Ltd—Ipswich 14 November 2008

Shipped on Board Date: 31 October 2008

ii) Although a presentation under L/C3 was made on 18 November 2008, one of the documents, the Consolidated Certificate was not in an acceptable form. A new presentation with a Consolidated Certificate in proper form was made on 25 November 2008.

iii) If the "Bill of Lading Date" was 31 October 2008, that presentation was more that 21 days after that date; if the "Bill of Lading Date" was 14 November 2008, the presentation was within the 21 days.

[74] The judge in a very short paragraph of his judgment held that the "Bill of Lading date" was the date the bill of lading was issued—14 November 2008.

[75] It was contended on behalf of IOB that the judge was wrong; the bill of lading date was the date of shipment. The judge had failed to give sufficient weight to the provisions of the UCP 600 and that his construction was therefore out of step with the approach of the UCP:

I) Sub-article 14(c) provided

"A presentation including one or more original transport documents. . . . must be made by or on behalf of the beneficiary not later than 21 calendar days after the date of shipment as described in these rules, but in any event not later than the expiry date of the credit."

ii) This mirrored the provision in Field 48 of LC/3 by providing for presentation to be within 21 days of the bill of lading date.

iii) Sub-article 20 (a)(ii) of the UCP provided that:

"The date of issuance of the bill of lading will be deemed to be the date of shipment unless the bill of lading contains an on board notation indicating the date of shipment, in which case the date stated in the on board notation will be deemed to be the date of shipment."

iv) The date of shipment was the date that the goods were "shipped on board" and not the date of issue of the bill of lading; there was a clear obligation under the UCP to present within 21 days of the actual shipment date as recorded in the bill of lading.

v) As LC/3 was subject to the UCP, it should be construed consistently with the UCP unless its terms evidenced a clear intent to vary the provisions of the UCP: *Forestal Mimosa Ltd v Oriental Credit Ltd* [1986] 1 WLR 631, 639.

[76] I cannot accept this submission. It is clear that the judge was right. L/C 3 expressly referred to presentation within 21 days from the date of the bill of lading, not the date of shipment. The date of the bill of lading was, as it stated on its face, 14 November 2008.

[77] There is nothing in the UCP that can displace this clear provision. Sub-article 14(c) which requires presentation to be 21 days from the date of shipment simply makes a provision which is different; the express terms of L/C 3 prevail. Furthermore the definition in sub-article 20 (a) (ii) "The date of issuance of the bill of lading will be deemed to be the date of shipment" is a deeming provision for the date of shipment for the purpose of sub-article 14(c); it is not relevant to the construction of L/C3 which is on its face clear. In any event, even if it were relevant, it is not a provision deeming the date of the bill of lading.

Conclusion

[78] I would therefore dismiss the cross-appeal and the appeal.

Notes and Questions

1. The background scenario is not an uncommon one: The price of the contracted goods falls in the global markets between the time a purchase order is placed and an L/C is issued and the time of delivery. The buyer and her bank now try to get out of the contract or at least the payment obligation by claiming various real or perceived discrepancies of presented documents with the requirements of the L/C. To avoid the problems encountered by Stemcor and Fortis, it is all the more important for attorneys reviewing draft L/Cs to review all documentary requirements and subsequently, upon presentation, to ensure strict compliance of the presented documents.

2. What is the relationship between the UCP 600 and provisions of national law, for example UCC Article 5? What law or laws should be applied for the review of an L/C? (Review paras. 27 et seq. for the answer.)

3. The judge refers multiple times to "DOCDEX" decisions, e.g., paragraph 34. What are these? Where can they be found? What is the precedential value?

4. As in *Bulgrains*, the rule that data in documents need not be identical (Article 14(d) UCP 600) was unable to overcome the principle of strict compliance (paras. 17–19). In this case, the discrepancy was whether payment for courier charges should be made by the issuing bank (IOB) or by the beneficiary (Stemcor), presumably a rather minor amount, compared to the funds secured under the L/Cs. Moreover, it seems that the beneficiary did indeed pay the courier charges as a matter of fact. Note, however, that in the end the judge did not care whether any costs were imposed on or paid by IOB, simply because it could not be expected of one bank employee to always know what another might have done. The judge decided that the presentation of the consolidated certificate was discrepant. In spite of the discrepancies, however, the issuing bank was made to honor the L/Cs. Why?

5. Among other issues, the case also concerns itself with the requirement of Article 14(c) UCP 600 that original transport documents have to be presented within 21 days. This is commonly referred to as the requirement of presenting "live" transport documents instead of "stale" documents. Why is there such a relatively tight time limit for the presentation?

6. IOB argued at some point that Fortis and Stemcor could have provided a "letter of indemnity" to the carrier (para. 39). What does that mean and what could have been accomplished with such a letter?

7. Article 14(c) clearly requires presentation "not later than 21 calendar days after the date of shipment." A strict application of this rule would have meant that L/C 3 was presented late. However, the original judge (confirmed on appeal) interpreted the rule to be no more than 21 days *after the date on the bill of lading*. Did the judges simply not like the refusal of IOB to honor the L/Cs or did they have a good reason for this interpretation? What could be a good reason?

8. After the issuing bank (IOB) indicated that it would not honor the L/Cs, the confirming bank (Fortis) responded that "documents must not be returned, but must be paid without further delay" (paras. 57 and 58). In the end, IOB was told off for having kept the documents. Can you explain how Article 16(f) of the UCP 600 was interpreted in the present case? What is meant by "preclusion" in this context (para. 44)?

9. The claims by Stemcor and Fortis focused on payment in honor of the L/Cs. However, there was also a claim for "damages, including container demurrage and port costs" (para. 6). What is meant by "container demurrage and port costs" and why should IOB pay for these?

10. What is the overall outcome of the case?

Case 3-3

Banco Santander SA v. Banque Paribas, Bayfern et al.

Case No: 1998 folio No. 794
In the High Court of Justice, Queen's Bench Division, Commercial Court
Royal Courts of Justice, 9 June 1999
(Some details omitted, paragraph numbers added.)
THE HON MR JUSTICE LANGLEY

[1] This judgment relates to the trial of certain preliminary issues arising only between the Plaintiff, Banco Santander, and the Third Defendant, Banque Paribas in these proceedings. In a nutshell the question is whether the risk of fraud on the part of the beneficiary of a confirmed deferred payment letter of credit is to be borne by the issuing bank (and so possibly the applicant for the credit) or by the confirming bank where the confirming bank has discounted its own payment obligations to the beneficiary and paid over the discounted sum to it and the fraud

is discovered only after it has done so but before the maturity date of the letter of credit. "Santander" was the Confirming Bank and "Paribas" the Issuing Bank. The applicant was Napa Petroleum Trade Inc and the Beneficiary, Bayfern Limited.

The Letter of Credit

[2] By a telex dated June 5, 1998 Paribas requested Santander to release a letter of credit to Bayfern adding Santander's confirmation. Santander had previously agreed with Bayfern that it would confirm such a credit on certain terms.

The letter of credit (so far as material) provided that:

> We, Banque Paribas, Paris, open our irrevocable confirmed documentary credit NR. 151734G
>
> By order and for account of: Napa Petroleum Trade Inc. . . .
>
> In favour of: Bayfern Limited . . .
>
> Validity: At the counters of Banco Santander London until the 15th September 1998
>
> Amount: USD 18,469,000 + or − 10%.
>
> This documentary credit is available with yourselves in London by deferred payment at 180 days from Bills of Lading date against presentation of the following documents:
>
> 1/ . . . Commercial Invoices . . .
>
> 2/ . . . Bills of Lading . . .
>
> 3/ Original Certificates of Quality and Quantity issued or countersigned by Saybolt . . .
>
> 4/ Cargo Insurance Certificate
>
> Covering: 200,000 Metric Tons + or − 10%
>
> Product: Russian Export Blend Crude Oil . . .
>
> This documentary credit is subject to the UCP for documentary credits (1993 Revision) of the International Chamber of Commerce . . .
>
> Please advise the beneficiaries adding your confirmation by fax or courier of this credit.
>
> At maturity we undertake to cover Banco Santander . . . in accordance with their instructions.

[3] On June 8 Santander duly advised Bayfern of the letter of credit by attaching a copy of it to an advice of that date in which Santander also stated that:

> We confirm this credit and hereby agree that documents presented under and in compliance with the Credit terms and conditions will be duly accepted and honoured at maturity if presented to us on or before the stipulated expiry date. Discounting of bills accepted under this letter of credit may be possible by prior arrangement;

and that:

> ... As previously agreed our Confirmation commission is 1.25% p. a.,
> our Deferred payment or Discount Commission is 1.25% p. a. plus out of
> pocket expenses ...

Discounting

[4] Whilst not intending to suggest that what follows is necessarily agreed, so far as
the issues before the court are concerned the essential facts appear from the documents to be as follows.

[5] By June 15, Bayfern had presented documents to Santander which Santander
had examined and found to be conforming. Santander took up the documents and
under the terms of the letter of credit thereby incurred a liability to pay Bayfern on
November 27, 1998 the sum of US$ 20,315,796.30. November 27 was the date 180
days from the date of the Bills of Lading.

[6] On June 9 Bayfern had confirmed a request to Santander "to discount the full
value of the credit at the agreed rate of 1.25% p.a." asking for payment to be made
directly to "our bankers" Royal Bank of Scotland PLC.

[7] On June 16, Santander replied to Bayfern's letter of June 9 and wrote:

> ... in accordance with the terms of our agreement we have discounted
> amount of documents and credited the sum of USD 19,667,238.84 value
> 17th June 1998 into your account with Royal Bank of Scotland. ...

> Please complete and return to us the attached letter requesting discount
> and assignment of proceeds under the above mentioned Letter of Credit.

[8] The sum of US$ 19,667,238.84 was shown calculated as the sum of US$
20,315,796.30 less LIBOR plus 1.25% for 163 days (ie from 17th June to 27th November) and less a confirmation fee of 1.25% from 8th June to 17th June and a small fee
relating to handling discrepant documents. The amount of the discount, ignoring
the fees, was US$ 641,023.33.

[9] The "attached letter" was duly signed and returned by Bayfern to Santander. It was
also dated June 16. It set out short particulars of the letter of credit and continued:

> We refer to the above-mentioned letter of credit and hereby request you to
> discount your deferred payment/acceptance undertaking to us as follows ...
> (the figures were stated) ...

> In consideration we hereby irrevocably and unconditionally assign to you
> our rights under this letter of credit.

[10] The request for and agreement to an assignment was made in accordance with
Santander's Operational Procedures Manual which included the following under
"Corporate Settlements : Trade Finance":

> Where documents under a usance letter of credit are found to be in strict
> conformity with all the letter of credit terms and conditions, the Bank may

be prepared to offer the Beneficiary a discount of the proceeds due, providing the letter of credit is either:

a) Issued by the Bank; or

b) Confirmed by the Bank.

In most cases agreement to discount, i.e., a 'facility' would have been reached between the Beneficiary and the Bank prior to the presentation of the documents. . . .

Providing the Beneficiary has a facility to discount and remains within the authorised limit, proceed as follows: . . .

6. If the Beneficiary agrees to discount, request that they send to the Bank a Notice of Assignment confirming that the funds due under the letter of credit have been assigned to the Bank in return for the discount. This must be signed by the company officials. . . .

18. If the letter of credit is in a foreign currency and reimbursement must be claimed from a Reimbursing Bank . . . payment instructions must be given three days prior to the value date by telex. . . .

The Issues

[11] By an Order dated February 12, 1999 on an application by Santander for summary judgment against Paribas and an application by Paribas for the determination of certain questions under R.S.C. Order 14A, Rix J ordered that there be a trial of the issues raised in Paribas' order 14A application and in paragraphs 20A, 20B and 20C of Santander's Re-Amended Points of Claim. Those are the issues to which this judgment relates and I should therefore set out the terms of them.

[12] Paribas' Order 14A application sought a determination of the following questions:

1. I. The effect of the "discounting" agreement between the Plaintiff ("Santander") and the first defendant ("Bayfern") contained in the letters dated 8th, 9th and 16th June annexed hereto.

ii. In particular, whether the payment by Santander of US$ 19,667,238.84 to Bayfern on 17th June 1998 was a payment made purportedly under the letter of credit or a payment outside the letter of credit in consideration of an assignment to Santander of Bayfern's rights under the letter of credit.

iii. Whether Santander's rights, if any, against Paribas are limited to such rights, if any, that Bayfern had to claim payment on 27th November 1998 from Paribas under the letter of credit.

2. In the light of the answers to (1) judgment for Paribas together with the costs of the action.

[13] Paragraphs 20A, 20B and 20C read as follows:

20A. In the premises, as between the Plaintiff and the Third Defendant:

(1) The Plaintiff was the Nominated Bank under UCP Article 10(b)(I) and it had the Third Defendant's authority to incur a deferred payment undertaking to the First Defendant against documents which appeared on their face to be in compliance with the terms and conditions of the Letter of Credit.

(2) By UCP Articles 10(d) and 14(a) the Third Defendant undertook and was bound to reimburse the Plaintiff in the event of the Plaintiff incurring such a deferred payment undertaking.

(3) On 15th June 1998 the Plaintiff duly incurred a deferred payment undertaking to the First Defendant to pay the sum of US$ 20,315,796.30 on 27th November 1998.

(4) The Plaintiff duly discharged its deferred payment undertaking to the First Defendant by effecting a payment to the First Defendant of US$ 19,667,238.84 on 17th June 1998.

(5) By reason of the foregoing, the Third Defendant became bound to reimburse the Plaintiff by a payment of US$ 20,315,796.30 on 27th November 1998.

20B. The Plaintiff will if necessary contend that it had the Third Defendant's authority to discharge its deferred payment undertaking by a discounted payment in that:

(1) It is routine banking practice for a bank to discount its own future payment obligation at the request of the party to whom the obligation is owed. This practice operates both generally and in the specific context of deferred payment letters of credit and acceptance letters of credit.

(2) There would be no commercial purpose in a bank's refusal to discount its own future payment obligations because such obligations can be discounted in the market in any event by third parties.

(3) In the specific context of letters of credit, the discounting of deferred payment undertakings and acceptances facilitates international trading by assisting the beneficiary's cash flow while preserving the credit period which such letters of credit give to the applicant.

(4) Accordingly, a Nominated Bank authorised to incur a deferred payment undertaking has implied and/or usual and/or customary authority to discharge any such undertaking by a discounted payment to the beneficiary.

20C. Further or alternatively, authority is to be inferred from the following additional facts and matters:

(1) The Third Defendant was at all material times the issuer of a substantial number of deferred payment letters of credit. It issued such credits intending that Nominated Banks should act on their authority to incur deferred payment undertakings.

(2) At all material times the Third Defendant knew that the potential for earning a profit on discounting is a material inducement to Nominated Banks to act on their authority to incur a deferred payment undertaking under such credits.

(3) It was the likely consequence of issuing the Letter of Credit, and the Third Defendant so intended, that the Plaintiff would incur a deferred payment undertaking and discount the same if so requested by the First Defendant.

Subsequent History

[14] Santander sent to Paribas the documents received from Bayfern under the letter of credit. Santander paid the sum of US$ 19,667,238.84 into Bayfern's account at the Royal Bank of Scotland on June 17. On June 24 Paribas informed Santander of a message received from Saybolt via Napa Petroleum that the Saybolt certificates of quality and quantity "should be considered to be false". Santander obtained asset freezing relief against Bayfern that evening with the consequence that approximately US$ 14m is frozen in Bayfern's account at the Royal Bank of Scotland.

[15] There are several issues in the proceedings (which have been discontinued against Royal Bank of Scotland) including whether there was any fraud, if so when it was known, and as to other alleged discrepancies in the documents. For the purpose of the issues before me it is to be assumed that Santander was not aware of any fraud when it confirmed the letter of credit or on June 17 when it paid the discounted sum to Royal Bank of Scotland but that there was fraud and it was known to both banks prior to November 27, 1998 the maturity date of the letter of credit. . . .

The Uniform Customs and Practice for Documentary Credits (UCP)

[17] The letter of credit was subject to the UCP (1993 Revision). [The 1993 Revision was commonly referred to as the UCP 500. The following analysis, however, has been edited to refer to the UCP 600, i.e., the 2007 Revision, which is currently in use and happens to contain virtually identical language in the provisions at issue.] Articles [4] and [5] of the UCP provide for the well known rules that credits are separate transactions from the sales or other contracts on which they are based and that the parties deal with documents and not the performance of those contracts. Article [4.a] provides in part that:

> Consequently, the undertaking of a bank to [honour, to] negotiate [or] to fulfil any other obligation under the credit, is not subject to claims or defences by the applicant resulting from his relationships with the issuing bank or the beneficiary.

[18] Part of the difficulty in construing this Article and all the provisions of the UCP is that, at least in this jurisdiction, they have to be read subject to or qualified by the exception for *established fraud* to which I shall have to refer further. . . .

[21] [Pursuant to Articles 7 and 8 of the UCP 600]:

> (A) The obligations of the Issuing Bank and the Confirming Bank mirror each other and are cumulative (*in addition to*);

(B) In the case of a deferred payment Credit (as here) the obligation is *to pay on the maturity date* in contrast to payment *at sight*;

(c) In the case of acceptance credits or credits available by negotiation the obligation is to accept and pay drafts or to negotiate documents presented under the credit.

[22] *Negotiation* is defined in Article [2]:

[Negotiation means the purchase by the nominated bank of drafts (drawn on a bank other than the nominated bank) and/or documents under a complying presentation, by advancing or agreeing to advance funds to the beneficiary on or before the banking day on which reimbursement is due to the nominated bank.]

[24] Read in context, the Issuing Bank's authority to the Confirming Bank *to pay* must I think be meant to cover both payment at sight and payment under a deferred payment undertaking at maturity. That is the obligation of the Confirming Bank under a deferred payment credit (Article [7.a.iii and 7.c) and it is the discharge of that obligation which the Issuing Bank is to "reimburse" in accordance with this Article of the UCP. . . .

[26] . . . In this case Santander had the role of both Confirming Bank and Nominated Bank. . . . The consideration for the Confirming or Nominated Banks' undertaking to pay at maturity is that if and when it does so [provided there is a complying presentation,] the Issuing Bank will reimburse it. . . .

Established Fraud

[28] In *United City Merchants v Royal Bank of Canada* [1983] AC 168, the House of Lords considered the question of fraud which would entitle a banker to refuse to pay under a letter of credit notwithstanding the rule requiring payment when the documents were in order on their face. In the course of his speech, with which the other members of the House agreed, Lord Diplock, at page 183, said:

The whole commercial purpose for which the system of confirmed irrevocable documentary credits has been developed in international trade is to give to the seller an assured right to be paid before he parts with control of the goods that does not permit of any dispute with the buyer as to the performance of the contract of sale being used as a ground for non-payment or reduction or deferment of payment.

To this general statement of principle as to the contractual obligations of the confirming bank to the seller, there is one established exception, that is, where the seller, for the purpose of drawing on the credit, fraudulently presents to the confirming bank documents that contain, expressly or by implication, material representations of fact that to his knowledge are untrue. Although there does not appear among the English authorities any case in which this exception has been applied, it is well established in the American cases of which the leading or "landmark" case is *Sztejn v J. Henry Schroder*

Banking Corporation (1941) 31 N.Y.S. 2d 631. . . . The exception for fraud on the part of the beneficiary seeking to avail himself of the credit is a clear application of the maxim *ex turpi causa non oritur actio* or, if plain English is to be preferred, "fraud unravels all". The courts will not allow their process to be used by a dishonest person to carry out a fraud.

[29] In my judgment it must follow on the assumed facts, that had Bayfern in this case sought to enforce the obligation of Santander to pay the letter of credit at maturity Santander would have been entitled and on the present state of law bound to refuse to make that payment or lose its right to reimbursement. The fact that the documents had been taken up before any fraud was notified would not alter the fact that when it was sought to enforce the consequent payment obligation the claimant would be dishonestly seeking to use the process of the courts to carry out a fraud. . . .

[30] In *European Asian Bank A.G. v Punjab and Sind Bank* [1983] 1 LL Rep 611 the Court of Appeal considered a claim by the appellant bank against the issuing bank of a deferred payment letter of credit. The Court decided that on the evidence the issuing bank had unequivocally represented to the appellants that they were entitled to act as negotiating bankers under the credit and that they would be paid as negotiating bankers on the maturity date. The appellants had negotiated the credit by paying its discounted value to the Beneficiary. Between that date and the maturity date fraud, or alleged fraud, on the part of the Beneficiary was discovered and the issuing bank denied liability under the credit. The Court held that there was no arguable defence and entered a summary judgment against the issuing bank. . . .

[31] A submission on behalf of the issuing bank that the appellants were merely agents for collection for the beneficiary (and so fixed with its fraud) was rejected, but at page 619, Robert Goff LJ added:

Even if it were a fact that, as at August 13 (when the appellants had forwarded the documents to the issuing bank to enquire whether they would accept them) the appellants had been appointed agents for collection by (the Beneficiary) it is beyond question that by August 20 the appellants had negotiated the letter of credit, and there is no suggestion that they acted otherwise than in good faith in so doing. Thereafter, in February 1980, they claimed payment from the respondents; and this was refused. In our judgment it is not open to the respondents, on these facts, to say against the appellants that they were justified in refusing payment on the ground that the documents were fraudulent or even forged. In our judgment the relevant time for considering this question is the time when payment falls due and is claimed and refused. If, at that time, the party claiming payment had negotiated the relevant documents in good faith, the issuing bank cannot excuse his refusal to pay on the ground that at some earlier time the negotiating bank was a mere agent for collection on behalf of the seller and allege against him fraud or forgery (if that indeed be the case) on the part of the beneficiary of the letter of credit.

[32] The essential distinction between that case and this is that in the *European Asian Bank* case the appellants were or were to be considered to be negotiating bankers. . . .

[33] As Robert Goff LJ said at page 621:

> After all it was obvious that the appellants as negotiating bankers, would be discounting the letter of credit and so paying out a very large sum of money on the faith of these messages (that is the messages which constituted the representation that the appellants were entitled to act as negotiating bankers under the letter of credit).

[34] Thus the case was one in which it was in effect held that the discounting of the letter of credit was expressly authorised by the issuing bank on terms that it would be liable at the maturity date for the undiscounted sum of the credit. That reflects the meaning of "negotiation" . . . and the express undertaking of the Issuing Bank to reimburse the negotiating bank for doing just that in Article [7.c]. . . .

[35] . . . The difficulty facing Santander is however, that the UCP spells out the extent of express authorisation in a deferred payment credit in terms of payment at maturity. . . .

[36] In this context I should add a word about acceptance credits as Mr Hapgood's submission was that there was no good reason why the effect of established fraud should differ in the case of acceptance credits and deferred payment credits. An acceptance credit, however, expressly involves authority from the Issuing Bank to the Confirming Bank to accept drafts and pay them at maturity. . . . The Issuing Bank's obligation is to reimburse the Confirming Bank for undertaking those obligations. If the Beneficiary discounts the accepted draft to a bona fide third party the third party will be a holder in due course entitled regardless of subsequently discovered fraud to payment on the draft by virtue of the provisions of the Bills of Exchange Act 1882. If the Confirming Bank discounts its own acceptance it will become a holder of the draft and if it holds it at maturity the draft will in law then be discharged: section 61 of the Act. In either case therefore the express obligation of reimbursement of the Issuing Bank is effective. The authorised acceptance of the draft itself carries with it that consequence.

Assignment and Practice

[37] Finally, in the context of fraud by the Beneficiary, it is necessary because of the way the submissions have developed and because of the references to assignment in the documentation to which I have referred, to consider the effects of the assignment from Bayfern to Santander in this case and the evidence relating to the practice of discounting deferred payment credits.

[38] The Beneficiary of a confirmed deferred payment letter of credit has the promise of *both* the Issuing Bank and the Confirming Bank to pay on the maturity date. . . .

[39] If the Confirming Bank agrees to discount the proceeds of the letter of credit it is in effect agreeing to "buy" its own future promise to pay at a current price. Whether it does so and if so on what terms is, as all the witnesses agree, entirely a matter for

its own decision in agreement with the Beneficiary and will be done (as it was done here) without any reference or notice to the Issuing Bank. For example, it could be done with or without recourse to the Beneficiary (in this case it was with recourse). On the evidence, it could also be done with or without taking an assignment and with or without any attempt to assess the credit or character of the Beneficiary to whom the discounted price was to be paid. Mr Turnbull said it was not his practice to ask for an assignment on discounting "his own" confirmation. But he acknowledged some banks would insist on an assignment, which he said was unnecessary as there was nothing to assign once the discounted payment had been made.

[40] Santander did insist on an assignment as their own Manual required. Mr MacNamara described it as "belt and braces". Mr Savage said taking an assignment was the normal practice. Although both experts agreed that market practice would not take account of the credit risk of the beneficiary they also agreed that banks would often assess the integrity of the beneficiary. In this case Santander in fact obtained a bank reference on Bayfern from the Royal Bank of Scotland. It is obvious that any bank contemplating discounting is in a position at least to seek to know who it is dealing with. . . .

[42] Counsel are not agreed on either the utility or effect of an assignment. Mr Hapgood's first submission, indeed, is that the assignment was worthless because there was nothing to assign. He submits that the payment made by Santander to Bayfern on June 17 was "plainly intended by both parties to extinguish all Bayfern's rights under the Credit, both against Santander and against Paribas." He points to the report of *Re Charge Card Services Ltd* [1987] Ch 150 at page 175C/D where it is recorded that counsel conceded that a debt cannot be assigned in whole or in part to the debtor since such an assignment operates wholly or partially as a release. That he submits remains unaffected by the decision in *Re BCCI SA* (No 8) [1997] 4 All ER 568 at pages 575 to 578. Mr Hapgood also submits that in any event an assignee is not affected by the subsequent emergence of fraud *on the principle that the claim of an assignee is not defeated by an unknown fraud which induced the debtor to enter into the relevant contract.* The authority cited for this principle is the decision of the Court of Appeal in *Stoddart v Union Trust Ltd* [1912] 1 KB 181.

[43] One context in which this question could arise directly is the forfaiting market. In simple terms a forfaiter may buy, also at a discounted price, the obligations of the issuing bank and confirming bank (if any) under a deferred payment letter of credit. In other words the forfaiter is an independent party to the Credit itself, albeit frequently a bank, and trades in trade paper by the purchase of the obligations it represents. The experts agree that there is a well established forfaiting market which deals in deferred payment undertakings both in London and elsewhere. They also agree that the documentation in such a case provides for the forfaiter to obtain an assignment from the beneficiary of its own rights under the credit and that the forfaiter will give notice that it has done so to the banks whose obligations it has bought. In such a case the basis in law on which the forfaiter is entitled to the proceeds of the credit must be the assignment as it is not a party to the credit.

[44] Mr Howard, on the other hand, submits that an assignment does involve assigning valuable rights, the rights to a future payment from both the Issuing and Confirming Banks. In other words, that even in a case where the Confirming Bank is discounting or buying its own future obligation the position is the same as for a forfaiter. He also submits, on well known principles (see Chitty on Contracts, Vol. 1, paras 19-039 to 042) that an assignee takes subject to equities against the assignor, and thus that in both cases if the assignor had no right to payment, for example because the documents were forged, then the Confirming Bank and forfaiter cannot recover as they are in no better position than the assignor. . . .

[46] At this stage I would simply record the following:

(1) It is agreed that the forfaiter's legal rights are dependant on the efficacy of the assignment to it of the rights of the beneficiary.

(2) Mr Hapgood submits and it is his primary case that the discounting Confirming Bank's rights are to be found in Article [7.c] of the UCP and only if he is wrong about that does he now seek to find them in the assignment.

(3) There is therefore in Santander's own primary case a material difference in the legal basis for a claim by a forfaiter and a claim by a Confirming Bank which has discounted its own obligation.

(4) On any view the rights of a bona fide assignee of an obligation owed to an assignor who has been guilty of fraud in the context of that obligation are as a matter of law of some nicety. Yet, on the evidence of Mr Turnbull, it seems the forfait market has not appreciated this or, if it has, has chosen to run the risk.

(5) It is not easy to see why a Confirming Bank which discounts its own confirmation should be in any better or different position than the forfaiter, especially so where (as here) the discounting agreement with the Beneficiary is in effect on the same basis as a forfaiter would use.

(6) It is a matter of commercial indifference for the issuing bank whether the Beneficiary is able to or chooses to "discount" its rights under a confirmed deferred payment letter of credit with the confirming bank or a forfaiter. It will also be ignorant whether one or the other has in fact occurred. Thus, if the consequences in law are different, that will be so for no apparent commercial reason and without the knowledge of the Issuing Bank.

(7) There can be no doubt that in a case where no fraud is involved both the discounting Confirming Bank and the forfaiter must have an enforceable right to be "reimbursed" by the Issuing Bank.

(8) It was comforting to hear from both experts that the incidence of fraud in these situations is very rare indeed. Thus the extent of the problem, whilst when it arises no doubt capable of involving very large sums, is such that one might expect it to ameliorate Mr Turnbull's expressed concerns about the effect on the market should Santander not be entitled to recover from Paribas. Moreover, as I have already said, the use of Credits for negotiation is an option and at the least it is agreed that the

forfait market has and has always had, a "problem" in such cases but it has continued to grow and develop nonetheless. If as Mr Turnbull's evidence suggests that was because forfaiters believed they were immune from fraud once they had "bought" the obligations under a deferred payment letter of credit then the belief was wrong.

(9) I accept that it is difficult for a Confirming or any bank to protect itself against fraud and that the UCP looks to the Applicant for the credit to do that. But the law is only that payment is to be refused in cases of established fraud known to the Bank before the due date for payment. That is not harsh. This case concerns the consequences when for its own reasons and without reference to the Issuing Bank or Applicant the Confirming Bank chooses to commit itself to making a payment before it is bound to do so. . . .

Conclusions

[50] . . . The basic authority given by the Issuing Bank to the Confirming Bank in a deferred payment letter of credit is to pay at maturity. The consequent obligation to reimburse is to reimburse on payment being made at maturity. If at that time there is established fraud, there is no obligation on the Confirming Bank to pay nor on the Issuing Bank to reimburse. I cannot construe either Article [7.c nor Articles 12 or 13 of the UCP] as entitling Santander to "reimbursement" for having incurred a deferred payment undertaking as opposed to paying it at maturity, as Mr Hapgood submits I should. That seems to me both to fail to recognise the existence and rationale of the established fraud exception and to be inconsistent with the normal meaning of the word reimbursement. Nor can I accept that the payment of the discounted sum discharged the obligations of Santander and Paribas under the Credit for the reasons stated below. I should make clear that it is no part of Mr Howard's case or my reasoning that "discounting" of the payment obligation under a deferred payment letter of credit is a "breach of mandate" or that for some other reason (in the absence of established fraud) the Issuing Bank's reimbursement obligation cannot be invoked. In my judgment Mr Howard is right in his submissions that:

(I) where the Confirming Bank discounts its own obligation, at maturity either it is to be deemed to make payment at that date or it is entitled to claim as assignee of the claims of the Beneficiary.

(ii) where a forfaiter discounts the Credit it is entitled to claim as assignee.

[51] Assignment. (a) Despite the attraction of Mr Hapgood's submission that an assignment to the debtor of his own obligation to pay extinguishes the debt and discharges it, I am not persuaded. First, the "debt" in question was owed by two parties (Paribas and Santander) not just Santander and was payable only in the future (unlike the existing debts in the *Re Charge Card Services* case). Second, the expressed consideration for the payment of the discounted sum was the irrevocable and unconditional assignment to Santander of Bayfern's rights under the Credit. Third, the agreement to discount and assign cannot be read as Mr Hapgood submits it is to be read as an agreement to discharge or, on payment of the discounted sum, as an actual discharge of the obligations of either Bank under the Credit. Indeed the

agreement is inconsistent with such an outcome. The expressed purpose was to keep the Credit intact. Fourth, I do not see anything objectionable in one (Santander) of two parties (Santander and Paribas) liable for a future payment agreeing with the creditor (Bayfern) to acquire the creditor's rights against the other (Paribas) on terms that his own obligation to make a payment in the future to the creditor is to be preserved so as to be treated as discharged at that future date and thus available then to trigger the obligation on the other debtor to reimburse him. That seems to me to have been the intention of both Santander and Bayfern expressed in the agreement and I do not see why the court should not give effect to it.

[52] (b) The second question in relation to assignment which now arises is whether a claim by Santander as assignee of Bayfern would be sustainable on the assumed facts that Bayfern was guilty of fraud in submitting the documents under the Credit but that fraud was unknown to Santander at the time of assignment but known at the maturity date.

[53] In my judgment the answer to this question is "No". It is no surprise that Santander have not pleaded a claim on this basis. . . . On the assumed facts, Bayfern had no rights under the Credit and so nothing to assign to Santander. Unless (which is in reality the first question) Santander has an independent right to recover from Paribas, I do not think qua assignee Santander could obtain more than Bayfern had to give at the time of the assignment.

[54] Custom and Practice. Mr Turnbull's views are of course entitled to respect and in reaching the conclusions I have I have had them in mind. Essentially, however, I think they come to no more than a reflection of expectations on the part of Banks (or at least discounting banks with London operations) that it is safe to discount Credits and that they are not concerned with the bona fides of the Beneficiary. I cannot spell out from that any relevant custom or practice or the basis for the implication of any relevant contractual term. If I am right in my construction of the UCP it provides for the obligations undertaken in this case and there is nothing in Mr Turnbull's evidence which can alter that. It also establishes what it was that Santander was authorised to do ("pay at maturity") and no wider authorisation is justified on the evidence nor any of the ways in which Santander have sought to express the claim in paragraphs 20B or 20C of the Re-Amended Points of Claim. On the evidence there is no common practice even as regards the documentation where a Confirming Bank discounts its own confirmation and the incidence of fraud has been so slight that no practice in that context could exist. Nor, as I have said, in the related case of the forfait market, would it seem that whatever the expectation it reflects the reality.

[55] It follows that on all the issues before the court in my judgment Paribas are right and Santander wrong.

The Answers to the Issues

[56] . . . My essential conclusion is that on the assumption that Bayfern was guilty of fraud in the manner alleged and that was known to Santander before November 27, 1998 the risk of that fraud falls on Santander and not Paribas.

Notes and Questions

1. What is the difference between "payment at sight" and "payment at maturity"?

2. What is a "deferred payment" L/C and what is its purpose?

3. What are the different options for a beneficiary to access the value secured by an L/C before its maturity date? What are the pros and cons of the different options?

4. What is meant by "discounting" in the present case? How does it work and what does it accomplish?

5. In paragraph 13 20B, the plaintiff states that it does not make sense for a bank to refuse to discount its own future payment obligations because they could "in any event" "be discounted in the market . . . by third parties." What is meant by this?

6. The court concludes that Santander, as confirming bank, loses its right to reimbursement from Parisbas, the issuing bank, if fraud is discovered after it made payment to the beneficiary but before the maturity date. Why would a bank discount its own future payment obligations, i.e., pay before maturity, given the risk of not being reimbursed by the issuing bank? How big is this risk? How does the discounting bank deal with the risk?

7. In paragraphs 39 et seq., the court discusses the question whether "an assignment" should have been taken. What does this mean? See also paragraphs 51 et seq. in this regard.

8. In general, a bank has six defenses or reasons for refusing to honor a letter of credit: fraud, illegality, nullity, unconscionable conduct, non-complying documents, and expiration.[21] Would you argue that the timeline for all six defenses should be the same, i.e., that discovery of the reason after negotiation or some other form of advance payment but before maturity of the credit falls on the nominated or advising bank? If so, why?

G. Hypotheticals for L/C Transactions

Case 1[22]

Pursuant to an application by XinXin Industries in Guangzhou, Swiss Bank B issued a letter of credit in favor of SelTec Industries in Palo Alto to cover the purchase of 100,000 computer chips for use in cellular phones. The L/C was confirmed by California Bank C. Although the L/C specified that the chips should be shipped by sea in such a way as to arrive in Guangzhou on or before July 1, there was a holdup in production and SelTec ended up shipping the chips by air on June 28. Upon presentation of its draft to Bank C, the L/C was dishonored by the bank

---

21. For further discussion, see Deborah Horowitz, *Letters of Credit and Demand Guarantees—Defences to Payment*, Oxford Univ. Press 2010.

22. Adapted from Roger LeRoy Miller, Gaylord A. Jentz, *Business Law Today—The Essentials*, South-Western College/West 8th ed. 2008, p. 784.

because shipment by air did not match the precise terms of the L/C. SelTec tried to get a waiver from XinXin but so far there is no response. Can SelTec successfully compel Bank C to pay?

Case 2 (Alternative to Case 1)

Pursuant to an application by XinXin Industries in Guangzhou, Swiss Bank B issued a letter of credit in favor of SelTec Industries in Palo Alto to cover the purchase of 100,000 computer chips for use in cellular phones. The L/C was confirmed by California Bank C. Although the L/C requires a "full set of clean on-board marine bills of lading," SelTec, on June 10, presented a BoL stating "received for shipment" and Bank C honored the draft. Later it turned out that the chips were forgotten in the warehouse of the shipping company and did not make it to Guangzhou until July 11. How and where can XinXin get damages for delay?

Case 3[23]

On April 1, PRS, a French corporation, entered into a contract for the purchase of US$700,000 worth of goods from GYP, a California corporation. To facilitate the purchase, the parties agreed that PRS would procure the issuance of a letter of credit in GYP's favor in the amount of the purchase price. The contract also specified that the letter was to be confirmed by GYP's bank, Harley National Bank of California. On April 10, PRS negotiated with Parisbas Bank of Paris for the issuance of the letter. Parisbas Bank, in accordance with its agreement with PRS, then engaged Harley Bank to confirm the letter.

On May 27, three days before the letter was to expire, GYP presented documents purporting to conform to the terms of the letter. Upon review, Harley Bank declined to honor the draft because the certificate of origin, a required document, had not been legalized by the French Embassy located in New York. GYP stated that it would return shortly with the certified stamp. At that time GYP authorized the bank to apply the proceeds of the letter to an outstanding loan. One hour later the certificate of origin, purportedly legalized, was again produced. The legalization stamp bore a New York address. Despite the impossibility of GYP's having obtained the required stamp in New York within one hour, Harley Bank honored the draft and applied the proceeds toward GYP's outstanding balance. Harley Bank then debited Parisbas Bank's account for the sum paid to GYP, plus its fee, and forwarded the documents to Parisbas Bank. Satisfied that the documents complied on their face with the terms of the letter, Parisbas Bank sent the documents to PRS and obtained reimbursement. The goods never arrived in France, and consequently, PRS suffered a loss of US$700,000.

Who owes what to whom? How and where — and under which law — can claims be brought?

---

23. Adapted from Diane Furman Dann, *Confirming Bank Liability in Letter of Credit Transactions: Whose Bank Is It Anyway?*, Fordham L. Rev. 1983, Vol. 51, No. 6, pp. 1219–1253.

Section 4. Standby Letters of Credit[24]

The difference between a regular or "commercial" letter of credit and a standby letter of credit is the fact that the regular L/C is intended to be used as the means of payment for the underlying IBT while the standby is not. The standby is basically an insurance policy that will be activated only in case an ongoing business relationship breaks down or a debtor fails to make payments that should be made in other ways. The most sensible way of using standbys is as follows: if the parties to an ongoing commercial relationship would use a regular L/C as the means of payment for every delivery of goods or services agreed between them, the cost would become quite significant (see above, p. 441). Thus, parties planning on implementing repeated transactions in the foreseeable future can agree that the corresponding payments will be made by the buyer each time by wire transfer into an open account. This is cost-efficient, but it does not provide security for the seller, who has to deliver before getting paid. However, if the seller obtains from the buyer a standby credit and keeps it for the duration of the business relationship, he can always ship one or even several installments of the goods and services and rest assured that if for some reason the wire transfers should not arrive (anymore), there is always the standby to fall back on.

To fulfill this function, the standby L/C will differ from the regular L/C in several details: first, the amount should be large enough to cover potential payments for several transactions intended over a period of at least 30 to 45 days. If the seller has to ship, say, on a monthly basis, they will need at least two months before it becomes a certainty that the buyer is no longer making payment for the most recent shipments, further shipments should be suspended, and the standby should be activated. Second, the standby needs to have a longer validity. While regular commercial L/Cs usually expire after about three to four months, a standby is more likely to be valid for an entire year and will often be renewed beyond that. Third, the standby will be less specific with regard to required documents since it is never clear at what point it will need to be activated. In fact, it is not uncommon for a standby to be "clean," i.e., not to require any specific "live" documents, such as bills of lading or other transport documents, before a draft can be made. Instead of a regular draft, they tend to require a demand from the beneficiary that states the reason for the draw. This demand and the reasons to be given are less formal than a draft that would have to be in strict, word-for-word compliance with certain documentary requirements. Fourth, in exchange for the reduced documentary requirements, standby letters of credit are

---

24. For an excellent discussion of standby letters of credit, see Carter H. Klein, *Standby Letter of Credit Rules and Practices Misunderstood or Little Understood by Applicants and Beneficiaries*, UCC L.J. 2007/08, Vol. 40, No. 2, pp. 125–168. A shorter introduction can be found in Matti S. Kurkela, *Letters of Credit and Bank Guarantees Under International Trade Law*, Oxford Univ. Press 2nd ed. 2008, pp. 36–42. See also Jan H. Dalhuisen, *Dalhuisen on Transnational Comparative, Commercial, Financial and Trade Law, Vol. 3, Financial Products, Financial Services and Financial Regulations*, Hart Publishing 5th ed. 2013, pp. 334–365.

usually "straight" L/Cs, meaning that only the beneficiary can present them for payment and do so only at the issuing bank. Straight L/Cs are not negotiable.

Since a single standby can potentially replace dozens of regular L/Cs, it is a cost-efficient way of securing the interests of the seller, even though the banking fees are typically higher for a single standby than for a single regular L/C, mostly on account of its longer validity, which increases the risk for the issuing bank that the financial situation of the applicant may deteriorate.[25]

Although the use of standby L/Cs in regular IBTs is increasing, these forms of documentary credit are even more common in the context of construction contracts, commercial real estate or equipment leases, as well as certain types of insurance arrangements.

The governing law for a standby letter of credit also differs from the regular letter of credit. While the UCP 600 can be and often is selected, a more suitable set of rules can be found in the International Standby Practices (ISP98) developed by the Institute of International Banking Law & Practice, Inc. and subsequently adopted as ICC Publication No. 590 (Documents, p. I-531).

Finally, the distinction between a standby letter of credit and a bank guarantee is not always clear. In fact, the courts have sometimes treated them the same, although there are differences.

Notes and Questions

1. What are the pros and cons of using a standby letter of credit instead of one or more commercial L/Cs? From the perspective of the applicant? From the perspective of the beneficiary? More specifically, what is the distribution of cost and risk under a standby and how does it differ from one or more commercial L/Cs?

2. If goods are sold "90 days same as cash" and the seller is secured via a standby letter of credit, who provides the credit?

3. Can a standby letter of credit issued by the buyer's bank be "confirmed" by a local bank in the seller's country?

Section 5. Bank Guarantees[26]

Bank guarantees fulfill similar purposes as standby letters of credit. In contrast to standard commercial letters of credit, and similar to standby letters of credit, bank guarantees are not intended as the primary method of payment in an IBT.

---

25. Depending on the credit rating of the applicant and the length of validity of the standby, the cost is between 1% and 10% of the secured amount, with an average between 2% and 3%. By contrast, a commercial L/C of US$100,000 and beyond will typically cost 0.75% of the secured amount, although various charges for postage, courier services, authentication, confirmation, etc. will be added.

26. For further analysis, see, for example, Roeland Bertrams, *Bank Guarantees in International Trade*, 4th ed., Kluwer Law International 2013.

Rather, the seller and the buyer may agree upon payment into an open account by wire transfer at some future time and, to provide additional security for the seller, the buyer agrees to provide a bank guarantee. If the buyer fails to make payment as agreed, the beneficiary of the guarantee, i.e., the seller, is entitled to financial compensation from the bank. This form of guarantee would be called a payment guarantee.

Bank guarantees are also used in other contexts. For example, a public entity or a larger private company inviting bids for a contract to deliver goods or services may require a bank guarantee in case a bidder is awarded the contract but does not deliver. In such a case, the principal may need to repeat the tender procedure and stands to lose substantial amounts of time and money. To protect against such losses, many entities require bank guarantees from bidders that can be activated in case a bidder withdraws her bid or fails to enter into an agreement after being awarded the contract. This form of guarantee would be called a tender guarantee.

Buyers and sellers may require from each other a bank guarantee to compensate for losses in case of nonperformance of contractual obligations. Such bank guarantees are often referred to as performance guarantees. They rarely cover the entire contractual amount, however, and are more commonly limited to a percentage of the contract value that is deemed adequate to cover the nonperformance losses.

If a buyer makes one or more advance payments to a seller, for example, for the development and production of machines or for construction services, the buyer may demand a bank guarantee from the seller to secure either the delivery of the goods or services or a return of the advance payment, with or without additional damages. Such a guarantee would be called an advance payment guarantee.

Another common form of bank guarantees can be activated by a buyer who obtained certain warranties from her seller with regard to the performance and/or durability of the contracted goods (or services). If the buyer is unsure of the performance and the seller's willingness and ability to provide compensation if the warranties are not kept, she can demand a guarantee for warranty obligations.

Other purposes of bank guarantees include the provision of security for rent payments, customs duty payments, loan payments, and many more.

All of these guarantees have in common that they back up the willingness and/or ability of a party to an IBT to adhere to her contractual obligations with an unconditional payment obligation by a bank. While the guarantee letter, similar to a letter of credit, will stipulate the requirements for the beneficiary to be able to draw on the guarantee, the terms are generally not very complicated or onerous. This is why bank guarantees of this kind are also referred to as demand guarantees, i.e., they can be activated by a simple demand from the beneficiary.

In international transactions it may be necessary to involve two banks, namely the instructing bank in country A, where the principal is located, and the guarantor bank in country B, where the beneficiary is located. Since the guarantor bank has no direct relationship with the principal, it can obtain a counter-guarantee from the instructing bank to indemnify it for any payments it may have to make to the beneficiary under the guarantee.

Bank guarantees from major commercial banks are almost always regulated by the Uniform Rules for Demand Guarantees URDG 758 (Documents, p. I-552). Since the guarantor, i.e., the bank, enters into a similar risk with a commercial letter of credit, a standby letter of credit, and a bank guarantee, the fees are also comparable and will depend in large part on the solvency or credit rating of the applicant and the period of validity.

A special form of guarantee is mostly used in the construction industry and commonly referred to as a contract bond or construction bond. These are surety bonds that are flexible like bank guarantees but provided by insurance companies or specialized surety companies. A bid bond secures a contractor's willingness and ability to accept a job if her bid is selected. A contractor license bond provides compensation if a contractor fails to follow all applicable licensing laws and regulations. In particular, large developers and government agencies often also require payment bonds, supply bonds, performance bonds, maintenance bonds, and/or subdivision bonds that secure the performance before, during, and after the construction project is completed. The ICC has developed Uniform Rules for Contract Bonds, which can be incorporated by agreement between the principal and the guarantor (URCB 524, Documents, p. I-564).

If an enforceable guarantee or bond is not yet required, a contractor or bidder may also use a comfort letter by a third party, like an auditor or an affiliated company, to assure the recipient that the contractor or bidder is willing and able to meet the respective financial or contractual obligations. Such a letter does not provide an enforceable obligation, however.

In some cases, exporters may benefit from government-backed guarantees available from the Export-Import Bank of the United States and/or the U.S. Small Business Administration.[27]

---

27. See http://www.exim.gov/ and https://www.sba.gov/surety-bonds, and below, p. 535.

Sample Doc 3-2: Application for Bank Guarantee

Demand Guarantee Application Form
(to be completed by applicant/instructing party)
[front of the contract]

[1] **X-Bank Name & Logo**   **Date:** ....

[2] **Instructing Party / Principal** Company Name and Address ....

Contact Person .... Phone .... Fax .... e-mail ....

[3] Please arrange for the issue of a Guarantee, in accordance with these instructions, the Indemnity Terms overleaf, and the ICC URDG 758.

[4] Name of **Applicant** to appear on Guarantee ....

[5] **Beneficiary** Name and Address ....

Contact Person .... Phone .... Fax .... e-mail ....

[6] **Type of Guarantee**

☐ Performance   ☐ Payment   ☐ Warranty   ☐ Tender   ☐ Customs   ☐ Other: ....

[7] **Amount of Guarantee**

In numbers .... In words .... Currency ....

[8] **Validity**   ☐ From date of issue   ☐ from fixed date ....

              ☐ Until fixed date .... ☐ until event ....

              Last day for claims   ☐ same as expiry date   ☐ other ....

[9] **Underlying Business Transaction**

☐ Order .... ☐ Contract # and date ....

Brief description of goods or services ....

Guarantee value as % of contract value ....

[10] **Delivery** to   ☐ Beneficiary   ☐ Applicant   ☐ Agent ....

     Delivery method   ☐ SWIFT   ☐ Courier   ☐ Certified Mail

[11] **Indemnifying Party**, if different from Applicant and/or Instructing Party

Company Name and Address ....

Contact Person .... Phone .... Fax .... e-mail ....

[12] **Account** to be debited for all charges and costs

Account Number .... Account Holder ....

Signatures
For the Applicant ....

For the Indemnifying Party (if different from Applicant) ....

For the Account Holder / Principal (if different from Applicant) ....

Indemnity Terms
Customer Counter-Indemnity to X Bank[13]
[back of the contract]

This Indemnity is given to X-Bank by the Indemnifying Party, referred to as "I/we/us," "my/our,"or "Indemnifying Party" in this Indemnity. In consideration of X-Bank issuing or arranging for the issue by another party (against X- Bank's counter-indemnity) of the Guarantee requested in this Application, the Indemnifying Party and its successors and assigns hereby:

(a) unconditionally and irrevocably agree to indemnify X-Bank against all actions, proceedings, liabilities, claims, damages, losses, costs, and expenses of whatever nature (including reasonable legal costs) in relation to or arising out of the Guarantee, including but not limited to X-Bank's actual or attempted enforcement of its rights under this Indemnity, and to pay to X-Bank on demand all payments, losses, costs, and expenses suffered or arising therefrom in the currency in which the same are incurred or if X-Bank so specifies the equivalent in another currency calculated at X-Bank's spot selling rate prevailing at the time of demand; and

(b) irrevocably authorize X-Bank to make any payments and comply with any demands which may purport or appear to be claimed from or made upon X-Bank under the Guarantee without any further authority or reference and agree that any payment made shall be binding on me/us and shall be accepted as conclusive evidence between us as to X-Bank's liability to make such payment or comply with such demand; and

(c) irrevocably authorize X-Bank to: (i) debit any account I/we may have with X-Bank for all such payments, losses, costs and expenses or provide X-Bank with funds to meet such payments; and (ii) in its sole discretion, with or without prior notice to us, from time to time, set-off, apply or combine any monies from time to time standing to the credit of any of our accounts with X-Bank in and toward satisfaction of any indebtedness to X-Bank in respect of this Indemnity; and

(d) agree the liability hereunder shall apply to: (i) any extension or renewal (whether in the same terms or not) of the Guarantee or any other amendment and this indemnity shall remain valid until notification by X-Bank that X-Bank is satisfied that it has no further liability under the Guarantee; and (ii) X-Bank's payment to or failure to pay (as the case may be) a third party who makes a demand claiming (whether correctly or not) that it is the assignee or transferee of a Guarantee, in circumstances where a Guarantee is issued, at the Applicant's request, without a full prohibition on transferability and assignability; and

(e) agree that if X-Bank uses the services of another party for the purposes of giving effect to the Applicant's instructions, X-Bank shall do so for the Applicant's account and at the Applicant's risk and that X-Bank shall assume no liability or responsibility should any instructions which X-Bank gives to any such other party not be carried out even if the choice of such other party was X-Bank's; and

(f) agree, to the extent that the Indemnifying Party is not also the Applicant and/or the Principal, that your rights hereunder shall not be impaired, discharged, or otherwise affected by any time or indulgence granted by you to the Applicant or any other person or by any liability of the Applicant or any other person or any security therefor being varied or released or by your failure to take or perfect any such security or by any other act, event or omission which would, but for this provision, discharge or otherwise affect any such rights; and

(g) agree, to the extent that the Indemnifying Party is not also the Applicant and/or the Principal, that we will not, prior to your written confirmation that all liabilities of the Applicant to you in relation to the Guarantee have been discharged finally and in full, take any security from the Applicant in respect of any liabilities the Applicant may have to us, nor shall we exercise, without your written consent, any right or make any claim against the Applicant (including any right of subrogation or to prove in any winding up), in each case arising by virtue of any payment made hereunder.

This Indemnity is in addition to and not in substitution for any other indemnity of other security interest now or hereafter held by or available to you.

This Indemnity and any non-contractual obligations arising out of or in connection with it shall be construed and governed in accordance with the laws of England and shall be subject to the non-exclusive jurisdiction of the English courts.

"Guarantee" means a guarantee, bank guarantee, tender, due performance, facility or customs bond, advance payment, hold cover or other similar obligation, to be issued, pursuant to this Application, by X-Bank or at X-Bank's request (supported by counter-indemnity by X-Bank in favor of such issuer), substantially in the wording specified (and, if applicable, incorporating any amendments to such wording which may be advised or are purported to be advised to X-Bank on the Applicant's behalf).

Bank Guarantees Explained:

#1 A guarantee involves at least three parties: (i) the guarantor (the bank), (ii) the applicant or principal (the buyer or other person who owes a specific performance or payment), and (iii) the beneficiary (the seller or other person to whom the applicant owes the performance or payment); the guarantor is usually the applicant's or buyer's bank since it will be easier for the obligated party/applicant to obtain a guarantee from her own bank where a long-term business relationship already exists. If the beneficiary insists on having a guarantor in her own country, it may be necessary to involve two banks, an arrangement often referred to as an indirect guarantee. The guarantor is sometimes also referred to as a surety, in particular if the guarantor is an insurance company. However, if the guarantor is not a bank, the guarantee is usually called a bond or contract bond.

#2   The instructing party/applicant/principal/indemnifying party can all be one and the same entity, which is obligated under an international business transaction to render a certain performance or fulfill other types of obligations that have to be guaranteed. However, they don't have to be the same. It is possible that one party—the instructing party—has the relationship with the bank and acts as principal/applicant. However, a different party, for example a subsidiary of the instructing party, has to provide a guarantee of her performance and is appearing as "Applicant/Principal" under #4, and yet another party promises to indemnify the bank under #12.

#3   The guarantee is governed by several sets of rules, which form a pyramid or hierarchy of norms. At the top are mandatory public laws applicable at the seat of the bank providing the guarantee. These may include provisions against terrorism financing or tax evasion, trade sanctions, and the like. On the second level are the instructions agreed upon in the guarantee. The applicant drafts the front of the contract via the present document. The back of the contract (general terms of the bank for guarantees, here called "indemnity terms") is included via this reference. Both parts become binding if and when the bank accepts the application. On the third level are the URDG 758, via inclusion in the present clause of the application and acceptance by the bank. On the fourth level are the non-mandatory public laws applicable at the seat of the bank, for example Article 5 UCC, to the extent it applies to bank guarantees,[28] as well as common law. Finally, any remaining gaps are filled by reference to general principles of law.

#4   The applicant and the principal appearing on the guarantee do not have to be identical. For example, a parent company could apply for the guarantee to be issued on behalf of a subsidiary.

#5   The beneficiary is the entity authorized to demand payment from the bank. Typically, this is the business partner of the principal/applicant who wants to ensure that she gets paid (seller of goods or services), that the goods or services conform to the underlying contract of sale (buyer or holder of warranties), or that a bidder in a tender procedure will follow through with an offer if selected (developer or government agency).

#6   Guarantees can serve many different purposes. The most common are payment guarantees (for example, if the payment terms are 30/45/60/90/180 days after BoL and the seller carries the risk that the buyer may be unwilling or unable to pay at maturity), and performance guarantees (for example, if the seller is providing goods or services that may or may not conform to the contract and the buyer carries the risk of nonconformity).

---

28. Article 5 of the UCC was drafted for Letters of Credit but applies to all independent promises made by an issuer and documentary in nature. See, e.g., *American Express Bank Ltd. v. Banco Español De Crédito, S.A.*, below p. 511, in particular paragraphs 23–30.

#7   The amount of the guarantee may range from a relatively small percentage of the underlying IBT (for example, 20% of the purchase price for a nonconformity that does not amount to a fundamental breach) to a multiple of the underlying IBT (for example, if consequential damages of a major breach are to be included).

#8   The validity of a bank guarantee is flexible and should be agreed upon in a way that suits its purpose. If the guarantee backs up a warranty or the performance of a larger (construction) contract, it may extend to several years.

#9   The underlying IBT must be identified to link the guarantee to a specific *transaction* rather than a *relationship* between two or more entities. Thus, if a seller and a buyer have a guarantee for one of their contracts but not for another, the beneficiary can only demand payment if the principal is in default of her obligations under that contract. Should a demand be made without sufficient justification or for reasons unrelated to the contract that is being guaranteed, the bank may still have to pay but the beneficiary may be subject to refund and damage claims for unjust enrichment or fraud.

#10 Instructions about the delivery of the guarantee letter cover the entity to whom the letter should be sent (for example, if the applicant wants to add it to a bid in a tender procedure), and the method of delivery (non-banks are usually not members of the SWIFT network).

#11 The indemnifying party has to pay back any monies and expenses the bank incurs when a demand is made under the guarantee.

#12 The account of the instructing party is only used for charges and costs, not for indemnification. However, under clause (c) of the Counter-Indemnity agreement, all accounts and credits of the applicant/principal/instructing party/indemnifying party/account holder are ultimately subject to the indemnification claims of the bank.

#13 These particular Counter-Indemnity Terms (back of the application/contract) are adapted from an application form supplied by HSBC (UK) (https://www .business.hsbc.co.uk/1/PA_esf-ca-app-content/content/pdfs/en/guarantee _application_form.pdf). The main goal of the counter-indemnity is the promise by the indemnifying party to reimburse any payments the bank has to make under the guarantee to the beneficiary, plus any other costs and expenses incurred in the same context. The indemnity or counter-indemnity expresses the unconditional *willingness* of the indemnifying party to pay the bank. However, the bank still holds the risk of the *ability* of the indemnifying party to do so. Note that there is a choice of law clause for English law and a choice of forum clause for settlement of any disputes in English courts. In the absence of a choice of law and forum clause, most countries provide that claims against banks have to be brought in the courts and under the law at the seat of the bank.

The next document shows how the actual guarantee letter issued pursuant to the application is quite simple and straightforward.

Sample Document 3-3: Bank Guarantee Letter

Letter of Guarantee

X-Bank Name & Logo

Bank Guarantee Nr. ....
International Securities Identification Number (ISIN) ....
Issue Date ....
Maturity Date [Expiration Date] ....

We, the undersigned X-Bank [Place] ....
hereby open this ☐ irrevocable, ☐ transferable, ☐ divisible, ☐ assignable and ☐ confirmed Bank Guarantee for
the benefit of [Beneficiary] ....
up to an amount of .... [Currency] .... (in words: ....).

The guarantee secures the obligations of [Applicant/Principal] ....
arising under the contract .... dated ....
for delivery of [Goods / Services] ....

Payment is available by Beneficiary first written Demand submitted via SWIFT. The Demand must be marked
"drawn under the Letter of Guarantee Nr. .... with ISIN .... dated .... [issue date]."

We undertake that the Demand Draft under and in compliance with the terms of this Letter of Guarantee shall be
duly honored on the date of presentation to us. There will be no "stop payment" issued.

This Letter of Guarantee is subject to the Uniform Rules for Demand Guarantees URDG 758 of the ICC.

All charges are for the account of the Applicant/Principal.

This Letter of Guarantee expires on [Date]   ....

On behalf of X-Bank [Place] [Stamp]
Date   ....

Signature of authorized bank representative   ....

In essence, a bank guarantee is more flexible than a commercial L/C or a standby L/C. But it also provides less security for the applicant, since the beneficiary does not have to produce a whole range of documents (BoL etc.) to get paid.

———

Finally, it may be of interest to see the communication exchanged via SWIFT between the different banks. SWIFT messages follow a standard format that reduces misunderstandings by bankers located in different countries and working in different languages, but every now and then they are misunderstood or otherwise incorrectly followed—or not followed at all—and disputes can and do go to court or arbitration.

Sample Document 3-4: Bank Guarantee in MT 760 SWIFT Format[29]

+++++++++++++++++++++++++++ INCOMING MESSAGE ++++++++++++++++++++++++++++
Message Receive Time: 03.08.2014 - 11:00
Message Type: 760 - GUARANTEE / STANDBY LETTER OF CREDIT
Delivery: N
Record Number: 0006000261000
Sender: DEBRDEGGXXX EXPORT BANK AG-FRANKFURT AM MAIN - GERMANY
Receiver: TLHLTRISXXX TURKISH IMPORT BANK A.S.- ISTANBUL - TURKEY
Value Date: 0
Currency:
Amount: ,00
Branch: TUM
Department: MUTUAL
Session Number: 4400
Sequence Number (ISN): 960000

===

27: Sequence of Total 1/1
20: Transaction Reference Number 100BGS1100000
23: Further Identification ISSUE
30: Date 02.08.2014
40C: Applicable Rules URDG
77C: Details of Guarantee
WE HEREBY KINDLY REQUEST YOU TO ADVISE OUR FOLLOWING GUARANTEE TO
BENEFICIARY WITHOUT ANY OBLIGATION ON YOUR PART:

– QUOTE –

PAYMENT GUARANTEE NO. 100BGS1100000
DATED 02 AUGUST 2014
THE GUARANTOR: EXPORT BANK AG-FRANKFURT AM MAIN - GERMANY
THE APPLICANT: A COMPANY, BELARUS, 220000 MINSK, ZAKOVSKAYA STR.10
THE BENEFICIARY: B COMPANY A.S., GUZELYALI MAH. PAZARSUYU MEVKII
BODRUM-MUGLA, TURKEY.

AS GUARANTOR, WE HAVE BEEN INFORMED THAT THE BENEFICIARY AND THE
APPLICANT, HAVE CONCLUDED CONTRACT NO.1 DD JULY 17, 2014, CALLED `THE
CONTRACT`, FOR SUPPLY OF CS-12000 KF (SUNFLOWER SEED, HAZELNUT AND ETC.)
ROASTING LINE, CALLED `THE GOODS` FOR THE TOTAL AMOUNT OF EUR240.000,00.

ACCORDING TO THE CONTRACT TERMS THE APPLICANT`S OBLIGATIONS TO PAY FOR
THE SUPPLIED GOODS MUST BE SECURED BY A BANK GUARANTEE ISSUED IN THE
BENEFICIARY`S FAVOUR IN THE AMOUNT OF EUR180.000,00.

IN CONSIDERATION OF THE AFORESAID, WE, AS GUARANTOR, HEREBY IRREVOCABLY
UNDERTAKE TO PAY TO THE BENEFICIARY ANY AMOUNT(S) IN EURO CLAIMED BY
THE BENEFICIARY UP TO THE MAXIMUM OF EUR180.000,00. (IN WORDS: ONE HUNDRED
EIGHTY THOUSAND EURO) UPON PRESENTATION OF THE ORIGINAL OF THE BENEFI-
CIARY`S COMPLYING DEMAND IN PAPER FORM WITH REFERENCE TO THIS GUARAN-
TEE NUMBER STATING THAT THE BENEFICIARY SUPPLIED THE GOODS TO THE APPLI-
CANT IN CONFORMITY WITH THE CONTRACT TERMS AND THE APPLICANT HAS
FAILED TO MEET A PART OF OR ALL HIS PAYMENT OBLIGATIONS THEREUNDER IN
DUE TIME IN THE AMOUNT CLAIMED BY THE BENEFICIARY UNDER THIS GUARANTEE,
BUT NOT EXCEEDING EUR180.000,00 IN THE AGGREGATE.

29.   Adapted from http://www.letterofcredit.biz/Bank-Guarantee-Sample-in-MT-760-Swift-Format.html.

ANY DEMAND UNDER THIS GUARANTEE WILL BE HONOURED BY THE GUARANTOR
ONLY WHEN:
1. PRESENTED TO THE GUARANTOR AFTER 15 CALENDAR DAYS FROM THE DATE OF
    SHIPMENT INDICATED IN ANY RELEVANT INTERNATIONAL ROAD WAYBILL (CMR)
    (INCLUDING THE DATE OF SHIPMENT IN CALCULATION),
2. SUPPORTED BY COPIES OF THE FOLLOWING DOCUMENTS PRESENTED IN PAPER
    FORM:
    A) BENEFICIARY`S INVOICE INDICATING THE CONTRACT NUMBER AND DATE,
        AND
    B) INTERNATIONAL ROAD WAYBILL (CMR) CONTAINING DATE OF SHIPMENT,
3. PRESENTED THROUGH THE INTERMEDIARY OF TURKISH IMPORT BANK A.S.-
    ISTANBUL - TURKEY WHICH WILL
    A) FORWARD IT TO THE GUARANTOR UNDER THEIR COVER LETTER TOGETHER
        WITH THE DOCUMENTS AS PER POINT 2. OF PRESENT PARAGRAPH, AND
    B) CONFIRM TO THE GUARANTOR BY AUTHENTICATED SWIFT MESSAGE FORMAT
        MT799 TO THE GUARANTOR`S SWIFT ADDRESS DEBRDEGGXXX THE AUTHEN-
        TICITY OF SIGNATURE(S) APPEARING ON THE BENEFICIARY`S DEMAND.
LANGUAGE OF ALL REQUIRED DOCUMENTS UNDER THIS GUARANTEE IS ENGLISH.

THIS GUARANTEE IS VALID UNTIL 26.09.2014, CALLED `THE EXPIRY DATE`.
AFTER THE EXPIRY DATE THE GUARANTOR`S LIABILITIES HEREUNDER WILL EXPIRE
IN FULL AND AUTOMATICALLY. THE ORIGINAL OF THE BENEFICIARY`S DEMAND
TOGETHER WITH REQUIRED DOCUMENTS MUST BE RECEIVED BY THE GUARANTOR
A) ON OR BEFORE THE EXPIRY DATE,
B) AT THE PLACE OF PRESENTATION - EXPORT BANK AG-FRANKFURT AM MAIN -
    GERMANY, EXCEPT FOR DOCUMENT 3B) OF PRESENT GUARANTEE WHICH MUST
    BE PRESENTED IN ELECTRONIC FORM TO GUARANTOR`S SWIFT ADDRESS:
    DEBRDEGGXXX.

ALL CHARGES UNDER THE GUARANTEE ARE FOR THE PRINCIPAL`S ACCOUNT.

THIS GUARANTEE IS SUBJECT TO THE UNIFORM RULES FOR DEMAND GUARANTEES
(URDG) 2010 REVISION, ICC PUBLICATION NO.758.

– UNQUOTE –

THIS IS THE OPERATIVE INSTRUMENT AND NO MAIL CONFIRMATION WILL FOLLOW.

PLEASE CONFIRM EXECUTION. KIND REGARDS

SWIFT Messages Explained (see Sample Document 3-4)

SWIFT stands for Society for Worldwide Interbank Financial Telecommunication and is a member-owned cooperative bringing together more than 11,000 banking and securities organizations, trading platforms, and corporate customers in
some 200 countries around the world. SWIFT itself does not move money or hold
accounts. Its primary function is to enable secure communication of financial messages in a standardized format. Sample Document 3-4 shows a typical SWIFT communication and its essential components.

––––––––––

The following cases illustrate how standby letters of credit, bonds, or guarantees
can be used and how they may be interpreted in court, for better or for worse.

Case 3-4

Kristabel Developments v. Credit Guarantee Insurance Corp. of Africa

High Court of South Africa, Gauteng Local Division, Johannesburg
Case number: 23125/2014, 20 October 2015
Satchwell J:

Introduction

1. Applicant, who was the employer in a [building] contract and the beneficiary under a performance guarantee, has claimed the sum of R 12,438,671.61 [approximately USD 1 million in 2015] premised on a credit guarantee also named the construction guarantee ('the guarantee'). The respondent, the guarantor, has opposed this application . . . on the grounds of claimed non-compliance with the terms of the guarantee.

[Chronology of Events]

2. . . .

   a. Respondent issued the credit guarantee (31st October 2012).

   b. Applicant cancelled the contract with the contractor third party (on 30th April 2014).

   c. Applicant emailed a copy of the letter of cancellation to the respondent of which receipt was acknowledged (20th May 2014).

   d. Applicant sent a letter of demand to respondent (4th June 2014).

   e. Applicant launched motion court proceedings against respondent claiming payment under the guarantee (26th June 2014). . . .

4. The relevant portions of the . . . documents read as follows:

   The Credit Guarantee—clause 5

   "Subject to the Guarantor's maximum liability . . . , the Guarantor undertakes to pay the Employer the Guaranteed Sum or the full outstanding balance upon receipt of a first written demand from the Employer to the Guarantor at the Guarantors physical address calling up this Construction Guarantee. . . .". The Guaranteed Sum is defined to mean "the maximum aggregate amount of R 20,731,119.36". . . .

Compliance with the Guarantee

19. Clause 5 of the credit guarantee requires a first written demand stating that:

   "5.1 The Agreement has been cancelled due to the Contractor's default and that the Construction Guarantee is called up in terms of 5.0. The demand shall enclose a copy of the notice of cancellation; or

   5.2 A provisional sequestration or liquidation court order had been granted against the Contractor and that the Construction Guarantee is called up in terms of 5.0. The demand shall enclose a copy of the court order."

20. The letter of cancellation reads at par 5-6:

> "(5) Your e-mail to the Employer of 9 April 2014 constitutes a clear and unequivocal rejection by you of your obligations imposed in terms of the [building] agreement.

> (6) You are hereby advised that the employer accepts your repudiation of your obligations under the agreement, without prejudice to its rights to claim from you such amounts as are due by you to the Employer, and that the [building] agreement is accordingly terminated with immediate effect".

21. The letter of demand states at par 3-6:

> "(3) On 30 April 2014, and as a result of the contractor's default and repudiation of its obligations arising in terms of the Agreement, we cancelled the Agreement.

> (4) We enclose under cover of this letter, marked as annexure "A", *a copy of our letter of cancellation.* [my underlining].

> (5) Pursuant to clauses 5.0 and 5.1 of the guarantee, we demand payment from you of the amount of the guaranteed sum, R12,438,671.61.

> (6) Pursuant to clause 8 of the guarantee, we accordingly await payment by you of this amount within 7 days of the date of this letter".

22. It is not in dispute that the letter of cancellation, dated 30th April 2014, was sent to respondent on 20th May 2014. Respondent's attorneys were copied on emails on meetings subsequent thereto during May 2014.

23. It is common cause that the letter of cancellation was not attached to the letter of demand dated 4th June 2014.

24. Respondent argues that there has not been 'strict' compliance with the terms of the credit guarantee by reason of the failure to attach the letter of cancellation to the letter of demand and, with such failure to comply with a peremptory provision of the guarantee, the demand is fatally defective. Applicant argues that 'strict' compliance is not a requirement, that the letter of cancellation was delivered prior to the letter of demand which constitutes compliance and that, in any event, respondent has waived any entitlement to require applicant to attach the letter of cancellation to the letter of demand. . . .

Compliance

25. The first issue is whether or not 'prior' compliance rather than 'contemporaneous' compliance in the context of this particular matter means there has not been the required compliance with the credit guarantee.

26. In *Lombard Insurance Holdings (Pty) Ltd v Landmark Holdings (Pty) Ltd and Others* 2010 (2) SA 86 (SCA), the court stated that performance guarantees are "not unlike irrevocable letters of credit where the bank undertakes to pay provided only that the conditions specified in the credit are met". . . .

29. The distinction between performance / construction guarantees and letters of credit has been explained in *Siporex Trade SA v Banque Indosuez* [1986] 2 Lloyd's Rep 146 at 159 where Hirst J said that the "contrast" between a letter of credit and a performance guarantee was "sound", since with the former the bank deals with the documents themselves, whereas with the latter the guarantor can rely on a statement that a "certain event has occurred". This statement was approved by the Court of Appeal in *IE Contractors Ltd v Lloyds Bank plc and Rafidain Bank* ([1990] 2 Lloyd's Rep 496 (CA) at 501 where Staughton LJ said that there is less need for a doctrine of strict compliance in the case of performance bonds. But he said also that 'it is a question of construction of the bond'."

30. Accordingly, the English courts (followed by the South African courts) have, thus far, taken the approach that there is a difference or 'contrast' between a guarantee where the call is simply based on the say-so statement of the one party that an event has occurred and between letters of credit where the bank is in possession of documents (such as bills of lading) establishing the foundation of the call. The courts have indicated that the more 'strict' compliance is required of the banks and of the documents presented to activate letters of credit because the banks themselves are in a position to evaluate the call by perusing the various documents. No mention has been made of the degree of rigour of compliance in the case of performance guarantees.

31. Our courts have not yet found necessary to determine whether or not 'strict' compliance is required of the beneficiary under a performance guarantee. In *Compass Insurance Co Ltd v Hospitality Hotel Developments (Pty) Ltd,* [32.] the terms of the guarantee required (as in this matter) that the letter of cancellation be attached to the letter of demand. In that case, the court found that there had been 'no compliance' at all because there had, in fact, been no letter of cancellation extant at the time that the letter of demand was sent and so the letter of cancellation could therefore never have been attached. In fact, there was only a belief or 'knowledge' that the required condition for breach, i.e., liquidation, had taken place—no one was in possession of the requisite order which was expressly required to be attached to the demand. Absent attachment, there could be no compliance at all.

33. In *Compass . . .* , the [Supreme Court of Appeal] reiterated the need for compliance:

> "It should not be incumbent on the guarantor to ascertain the truth of the assertion made by the beneficiary that the subcontractor had been placed under provisional liquidation. That is why Compass Insurance required a copy of the order itself. Similarly the guarantor should not have to establish whether a contract has in fact been cancelled. That is why a copy of the notice of cancellation, if there has in fact been cancellation, is required to be attached to the demand. . . . The very purpose of a performance bond

is that the guarantor has an independent, autonomous contract with the beneficiary and that the contractual arrangements with the beneficiary and other parties are of no consequence to the guarantor."

34. In the present case, the notice of cancellation did exist. It was sent to the guarantor and received by the guarantor. Guarantor's attorneys were also copied on the correspondence arranging meetings to discuss this cancellation in May 2014. The existence of the cancellation and the reasons therefor were known to the guarantor at the time demand was made.

35. Any quibble about the wording of either the cancellation or the demand is no longer argued by the respondent. The guarantee required the letter of demand to state that "The Agreement has been cancelled due to the Contractor's default and that the Construction Guarantee is called up" while the demand read "On 30 April 2014, and as a result of the contractor's default and repudiation of its obligations arising in terms of the Agreement, we cancelled the Agreement".

36. The only issue is whether or not provision of the notice of cancellation (to the third party) to both the respondent (and its attorneys) independently of and prior to the demand can constitute compliance with the guarantee.

37. The respondent and applicant engaged in discussions by email about this notice of cancellation. The issue was not ignored. Neither was it treated as irrelevant or moot by respondent and applicant. Both guarantor and beneficiary engaged on this cancellation.

38. To require that this notice of cancellation, already received and discussed and engaged upon, be attached to the notice of demand 15 days later is not requiring moonwalking and beneficiary/applicant could certainly have complied therewith. However, to find that failure to attach a written cancellation already received and under discussion, constitutes complete non-compliance with the terms of the guarantee and therefor disentitles the beneficiary/applicant from proceeding with its demand under that guarantee is, I believe, a step too far. The reasons requiring compliance with terms of the guarantee, especially as restated by the Supreme Court of Appeal in Compass supra, are carefully kept in mind in the present instance.

39. According, I find that the prior presentation of the cancellation by applicant to respondent (and to respondent's attorneys) instead of contemporaneous presentation with the demand constitutes, in these circumstances, compliance with the guarantee. . . .

Notes and Questions

How and why is the standard of compliance different in commercial letters of credit, compared to demand guarantees and standby letters of credit?

Case 3-5

Cargill International SA v. Bangladesh Sugar and Food Industries Corporation

Court of Appeal England and Wales, 19 November 1997
The Weekly Law Reports 20 March 1998, p. 461
Staughton, Swinton Thomas, and Potter, L.JJ.
(Paragraph numbers added.)

[1] The plaintiffs, Cargill International . . . brought an action against the defendant, Bangladesh Sugar and Food Industries Corporation, for an injunction restraining the defendant from drawing on a performance bond provided by the plaintiffs as part of a contract for the sale and delivery of sugar, and a declaration that the defendant was not entitled to make any call on the bond or to retain any payment so received. On 2 May 1996 Rix J. ordered two preliminary issues to be heard: (1) whether the defendant was entitled to draw down the whole amount of a performance bond issued in favour of the defendant by Banque Indosuez in any of the alternative events that no loss, a loss less than the bond's amount and a loss equal to or greater than the bond's amount was suffered by the defendant; (2) whether in each of those situations the defendant was entitled to retain the whole of the bond moneys, only such amount as was equal to the loss suffered or some other amount. On 7 June 1996 Morison J. answered the first question "Yes" and the second question that the defendant was obliged to account to the plaintiffs if the sum paid exceeded the damage actually suffered.

[2] By a notice of appeal dated 24 September 1996 the defendant appealed on the grounds that the judge (1) had erred in construing the contract by failing to give the word "forfeited" its natural and true meaning and by reading it to mean "called" or "encashed;" (2) should have held that the defendant, having lawfully called the bond moneys, was entitled to retain the full amount even if it had suffered no loss at all; (3) had erred in concluding that clause 13 of the contract of sale was a penalty clause and that he could give relief from the effect of such a provision; and (4) had erred in failing to construe clause 13 as a forfeiture clause.

[3] The facts are stated in the judgment of Potter L.J.

[4] POTTER L.J. This is an appeal by the defendant, Bangladesh Sugar and Food Industries Corporation, which was, under a contract dated 16 June 1994, the buyer of a quantity of sugar from the plaintiffs, Cargill, under a contract of sale in connection with which the plaintiffs as sellers provided the defendant with a performance bond issued on their behalf by the Banque Indosuez on 4 June 1994, in a sum equivalent to 10 per cent. of the total c. & f. value of the sugar to be supplied.

[5] Disputes have arisen between the parties in respect of alleged contractual breaches arising from of the late arrival and the age of the ship carrying the cargo. The defendant claimed to be entitled to forfeit the bond in respect of the plaintiffs' breaches of contract. The plaintiffs in turn claimed that the breaches were in fact caused by the default of the defendant. The plaintiffs also claimed that, in any event, the defendant

suffered no loss because the market price of the sugar had fallen over the period between the date of contract and the date for delivery. . . .

[10] For the purposes of the arguments raised before us on this appeal it is necessary to refer to three principal documents.

[11] The first is the form of tender invitation issued by the defendant to tenderers in respect of 12,500 metric tons, plus or minus five per cent. of sugar as described. This required tenderers to furnish various documents under various headings. In particular, by clause 10, it required submission of two documents described as "earnest money/bid bond" and "performance guarantee." In that respect clause 10 provided

> "(a) The tenderer/bidder will furnish one per cent, of the total quoted value as earnest money/bid bond in the form of bank draft/ bank guarantee in favour of this corporation as per format given at annexure A . . . (c) The earnest money in respect of the tenderer/ bidder whose offers have been accepted will be released to them only after they have furnished performance guarantee and signed the contract. The corporation reserves the right to forfeit the earnest money if the tenderers/bidders fail to sign the contract or to furnish performance guarantee for performance of the contract within the time stipulated and/or allowed for the purpose . . . (d) In the event of the acceptance of this tender by the corporation, a letter of intent will be issued to the successful tenderer/bidder (hereinafter referred to as the supplier) who shall provide, within seven days from the date of the issue of the letter of intent, the performance guarantee in the form of a bank guarantee in the format given at annexure B. . . . The performance guarantee is liable to be encashed/forfeited (I) if the successful bidder fails/ refuses to sign the formal contract and (ii) if the full cargo in respect of both quality and quantity as per bill of lading and invoice is not received. But such encashment and forfeiture of the performance guarantee shall not limit the consignee to have the right to seek redress of full recovery of short receipt through other means."

[12] Although the tender invitation, which was dated 5 May 1994, provided for signature by the tenderer and was in fact signed to indicate that the plaintiffs as tenderer had understood and accepted the conditions as laid down, it also provided under the heading "Acceptance and Contract" that: "Issuance of a letter of intent shall not mean a formal contract and will be completed in all aspects when the formal contract is signed."

[13] The plaintiffs' firm offer in response to the invitation to tender was dated 28 May 1994. It gave details of the tonnage offered, origin, payment, delivery, price, etc. and ended "all other terms and conditions: as per tender." It was accepted on 30 May. The plaintiffs then procured its bankers, Banque Indosuez, to issue the second important document, namely the performance bond or "performance guarantee" as it was called in the tender invitation. It took the form of a banker's "letter of guarantee" dated 4 June 1994. It provided, inter alia:

"Whereas . . . [the defendant] . . . has accepted the offer . . . [of the plaintiffs] . . . for supply of 12,500 metric tons (5 per cent, more/less at [the plaintiffs'] option) of sugar to be supplied by [the plaintiffs] . . . on the terms and conditions governing the purchase order and whereas the supplier has requested us through the Chase Manhattan Bank, London to issue a guarantee for an amount of U.S.$526,273.15 . . . only being 10 per cent, of the c. & f. (c.) value of the contract, in consideration of aforesaid we, Banque Indosuez, Dhaka hereby undertake and guarantee due signing, acceptance and performance of the contract by the supplier and we unconditionally and absolutely bind ourselves (I) to make payment of U.S.$526,273.15 . . . to [the defendant] or as directed by [the defendant] in writing without any question whatsoever. (II) . . . The guarantee is unconditional and it is expressly understood that the sole judge for deciding whether the suppliers have performed the contract and fulfilled the terms and conditions of the contract will be [the defendant]."

[14] On 16 June 1994 there was completed and dated the third important document: the contract of sale. Under its terms the plaintiffs agreed to sell c. & f. (c.) to the defendant 12,500 metric tons of sugar plus or minus 5 per cent, at the plaintiffs' option. There was an express promise by the plaintiffs to ensure the arrival of the sugar at Chittagong before 15 September 1994 "positively." There was also a stipulation in the contract that the cargo would be shipped in a vessel which was not more than 20 years old.

[15] Clause 13 of the contract of sale provided

"Performance Bond. The seller [plaintiffs] has already submitted a performance bond to the buyer [defendant] in the form of bank guarantee equivalent to 10 per cent, of the total offered c. & f. (c.) value of 12,500 metric tons plus or minus 10 per cent, of sugar. The performance bond is liable to be forfeited by the buyer if the seller fails to fulfil any of the terms or conditions of the contract . . . and also if any loss/damage occurs to the buyer due to any fault of the seller."

[16] Clause 16 of the contract of sale provided:

"Special clause, (I) The arrival period/time is the essence of the contract. Therefore the seller shall strictly adhere to the arrival period/time stipulated in this contract. If the seller fails to do so, the buyer shall be entitled to recover from the seller liquidated damage at 2 per cent. of the contract value, as agreed, of the undelivered goods for each month or part of the month during which the delivery of the goods will be in arrears, or to terminate the contract and call back the letter of credit and also to forfeit the performance bond mentioned at clause 13."

The decision of Morison J.

[17] Morison J. held that it is implicit in the nature of a performance bond that in the absence of clear contractual words to a different effect there will be an accounting

between the parties at some stage after the bond has been called, in the sense that their rights and obligations will be determined at some future date. If the amount of the bond is not sufficient to satisfy the beneficiary's claim for damages he can bring proceedings for his loss, giving credit for the amount received under the bond.

[18] Conversely if the amount received under the bond exceeds the true loss sustained, the party who provided the bond is entitled to recover the overpayment. The judge's reasoning in that respect . . . is not the subject of challenge in this appeal. The issue in this appeal centres upon the reservations expressed by Morison J. that the implicit features set out above must give way to contractual words of contrary effect. It is the contention for the defendant that the use of the word "forfeited" in clause 13, echoed by the word "forfeit" in special clause 16, demonstrates that the parties indeed intended to oust the usual implication as to any subsequent accounting between the parties. In that respect the judge observed [1996] 4 All E.R. 563, 572 in relation to clause 13:

> "It seems to me that on a proper construction of this clause, there is no indication that it was the parties' intention that the bond would either satisfy the whole of the buyer's damages (see above), or prevent the seller from recovering any overpayment. The word 'forfeit' might be apt to suggest that once called, the bond moneys had 'gone' for good. But if it had been the intention of the parties to produce a result whereby the buyer could both call on the bond and sue for damages, whereas the seller forfeited his right to any overpayment, then much plainer words would have been required to take this case away from the general principles as I perceive them to be. That being so, it seems to me that treating the two parts of the clause disjunctively, and treating the right to forfeit as arising if either there was a breach or if any loss or damage occurred to the buyer due to any fault of the seller (which might not be a breach) would make commercial good sense. The buyer is stipulating clearly that, as between himself and the seller, all he needs to show to be entitled to call on the bond as a breach of contact; he need not show damage (although damage will almost always follow); if, on the other hand, say through a misrepresentation by the seller, damage was caused to the buyer then the right to call the bond was conferred by the second half of the clause. But in either event, there will be an 'accounting' at trial or arbitration to ensure the buyer has not been underpaid or overpaid. Further, it seems to me that the more natural reading of the clause is to treat the events giving rise to a right to 'forfeit' the bond as disjunctive. The words 'also if' would otherwise be unnecessary and the words 'due to any fault of the seller' would not lie easily with a construction which treated the only triggering event as a breach of contract ('fails to fulfil any of the terms and conditions of this contract')."

[19] In relation to clause 16 the judge continued:

> "It seems to me that clause 16 clearly provides that if the arrival period/ time stipulated in the contract is not adhered to then the buyer will either

be entitled to liquidated damages or to terminate the contract and call back the letter of credit and forfeit the bond. Again, the right, as between the parties, of the buyer to call on the bond is not conditional upon him showing any damage. On termination he is entitled to receive immediate payment of the bond moneys and sue for damages, and the seller, conversely, is entitled to recover any overpayment."

[20] Given his conclusion on the question of construction, the question of whether or not the terms of the contract of sale as to forfeiture of the bond were penal in effect did not arise for the judge's decision. However it had been argued before him, and in this respect he held, at p. 573:

"Had I been persuaded that there was a term of the contract between the parties which enabled the buyer to call on the bond when he had suffered no damage, and to retain the moneys, I would have held the provision to have been penal." . . .

[25] [Mr. Hossain, counsel for the defendant,] relied upon the principle that no term should be implied into a contract which conflicts with other express terms of the contract. He argued that the meaning of the term "forfeit" is clear. He relied upon the definition of the word in its ordinary and popular sense in the *Shorter Oxford English Dictionary,* that the verb "to forfeit" means to lose, to give up, to render oneself liable to be deprived of, or to have to pay as the penalty of a fault, breach of duty or breach of engagement. He observed that it is implicit within that definition that the party to whom something, whether money or other property, is said to be forfeit is entitled to retain it. Thus, he said, use of the expression "forfeit" in clause 16 and "liable to be forfeited" in clause 13 in respect of a performance bond of this kind carries the plain and inevitable connotation that, once moneys have been paid pursuant to its terms, it is irrevocably lost to the payee. That being so, he relied upon the long established dictum that contractual terms are to be understood in their "plain, ordinary, and popular sense, unless they have generally in respect to the subject matter, as by the known usage of trade, or the like, acquired a peculiar sense distinct from the popular sense:" *Robertson v. French* (1803) 4 East 130, 135.

[26] Thus, submitted Mr. Hossain, the judge was wrong in regarding the use of the words "forfeit" and "forfeited" as insufficiently clear to displace the implied term of ultimate accountability which is the usual incident of a performance bond. In this connection, he rightly made the point that, when construing the effect of particular words in a commercial contract, it is wrong to put a label on the contract in advance and thus to approach the question of construction on the basis of a preconception as to the contract's intended effect, with the result that a strained construction is placed on words, clear in themselves, in order to fit them within such preconception.

Discussion and conclusions

[27] As Saville J. observed in another context in *Palm Shipping Inc. v. Kuwait Petroleum Corporation* [1988] 1 Lloyd's Rep. 500, 502:

"It is not a permissible method of construction to propound a general or generally accepted principle . . . and then . . . to seek to force the provisions of the [contract] into the straitjacket of that principle . . ."

[28] On the other hand, modern principles of construction require the court to have regard to the commercial background, the context of the contract and the circumstances of the parties, and to consider whether, against that background and in that context, to give the words a particular or restricted meaning would lead to an apparently unreasonable and unfair result.

[29] As Lord Reid observed in *Wickman Machine Tool Sales Ltd.* v. *L. Schuler A.G.* [1974] A.C. 235, 251: "The more unreasonable the result the more unlikely it is that the parties can have intended it, and if they do intend it the more necessary it is that they shall make that intention abundantly clear."

[30] That approach may fairly be said to have reached a highwater mark in the recent decision of the House of Lords in *Charter Reinsurance Co. Ltd.* v. *Fagan* [1997] A.C. 313, in which "the landscape of the instrument as a whole," as Lord Mustill put it at p. 384, led the court effectively to construe the words "actually paid" in the ultimate net loss clause of a reinsurance contract as meaning "actually payable."

[31] If questions of reasonableness are taken into account and if the usual characteristics and broad commercial purpose of performance bonds are borne in mind, it seems to me that the following matters are pertinent to the task of construction in the case. First, as Mr. Hossain accepted, such a bond is a guarantee of performance. That is not to say it is a guarantee in the sense that it has all the normal incidents of a contract of surety; it is of course a contract of primary liability so far as the bank that gives it is concerned. However, it has the feature that its purpose is to provide security to the buyer for the fulfilment by the seller of his contractual obligations: see Kerr J. in *R. D. Harbottle (Mercantile) Ltd.* v. *National Westminster Bank Ltd.* [1978] Q.B. 146, 149B. Second, its purpose is also that the buyer may have money in hand to meet any claim he has for damage as a result of the seller's breach. Third, it confers a considerable commercial advantage upon a buyer. Not only does the buyer have an unquestionably solvent source from which to claim compensation for a breach by the seller, at least to the extent of the bond, but payment can be obtained from the seller's bank on demand without proof of damage and without prejudice to any subsequent claim against the seller for a higher sum by way of damages. In these circumstances the obligation to account later to the seller, in respect of what turns out to be an overpayment, is a necessary corrective if a balance of commercial fairness is to be maintained between the parties.

[32] In the light of those considerations, the question arising in this case is whether, by use of the word "forfeit" in relation to the bond, the parties intended to negative any later obligation of the buyers to account, should the sum paid over exceed the damage actually suffered.

[33] Turning to the use of the words "forfeit" and "forfeited" in the context in which they appear, I do not accept that such intention is plain. I start from the position

that the words have not been used with any degree of precision, let alone with any eye to the ultimate position between the parties so far as damage suffered is concerned. In both clause 13 and clause 16 the terms "forfeited" and "forfeit" respectively are applied to the bond, not (as one would expect if Mr. Hossain were right) to the moneys paid under the bond. While Mr. Hossain submitted the point is a technicality and that, by their reference to the bond, the parties must in fact have intended to refer to the moneys paid under it, I consider that the term has simply been used as a shorthand for the exercise of the buyer's right to call for payment under the bond. In other words, it refers to the position as between the defendant and the bank, not the defendant and the plaintiffs. This seems to me to be consistent with a further feature, that the bond is said to be "liable to be forfeited by the buyer," whereas if the clause were intended to convey that the sum paid or payable under the bond would be forfeited, in the sense of irrecoverably lost to the plaintiffs, a reference to forfeiture by the seller would have been more appropriate.

[34] Further, the decision of the judge to read the words "liable to be forfeited," in the context in which they appear, as equivalent to "liable to be called or encashed" accords more with reason, fairness and commercial good sense than does the meaning for which Mr. Hossain contended. The effect of Mr. Hossain's construction would be to provide the defendant with a substantial windfall in any case where it had suffered no loss or relatively nominal loss, and would run counter to the general proposition that compensation for breach of contract depends on proof of loss. Whilst national and international trade is encouraged and enhanced by the role of the performance bond, both as a security and as an incentive for the performance of the parties' contractual obligations, the very fact that such bonds are payable by bankers on demand and without proof of loss seems to me to require that, as between the parties, the circumstances said to justify such demand should remain open to subsequent challenge, and to quantification of damage so that an ultimate balance may be struck between the parties.

[35] For those reasons I do not regard the "dictionary definition" approach of Mr. Hossain as helpful. However, even if that approach is appropriate, I note that one of the definitions of "forfeit" on which he relies is "to render oneself liable to have to pay." Taken on its own, that definition is certainly not one which precludes or excludes any later intention or obligation on the part of the parties to account in respect of the actual loss suffered. I come back to the point that the real purpose of clause 13 is to define as between the parties the circumstances in which the buyer shall be entitled to make a call on the bank, a matter upon which the A bond itself is silent. The use of the words "forfeit" and "forfeited" fall to be considered in that light.

[36] Mr. Hossain referred us also to certain examples of the use of the word "forfeit" and "forfeited" in *Stroud's Judicial Dictionary,* 5th ed. (1986). While it is true that the opinion is expressed in the text that the words seem to involve the idea of permanent loss or liability thereto, the statutory examples given do not afford any real assistance in the present contractual context.

[37] In further support of his argument Mr. Hossain submitted (1) that without the meaning contended for by the defendant the bond would provide no incentive for the sellers to fulfil the terms of the contract and would be commercially worthless to achieve its claimed purpose; (2) . . . ; (3) that clause 13 of the contract should be construed by reference to, and in harmony with, the earlier bid bond required to be provided by way of earnest to the value of 1 per cent, of the contract price, in which respect clause 10 of the invitation to tender provided that the defendant reserved the right to forfeit the earnest money if the tenderers/bidders failed to sign the contract or furnish the performance guarantee.

[38] I find none of those arguments persuasive. (1) I do not think it is right to stigmatise the obligation to provide the bond as commercially worthless simply because the moneys paid over under its terms are not to be regarded as irrecoverable by the seller. I have already touched upon the commercial advantage to the buyer in obtaining a bond. The right to call on the bond at an early stage in respect of any breach or suspected breach by the seller is plainly of value. It acts as an obvious incentive for his performance. It achieves the effect of an early payment against loss or possibility of loss without the need to resort to litigation, and if it is sufficient (or more than sufficient) to compensate the buyer, it places the onus of challenge and recovery upon the seller. (2) . . . . (3) I do not consider that clauses 13 and 16 of the sale contract fall to be construed by reference to the terms of the earlier bid bond. It is plain, from the terms of that bond and from the requirement for the seller to furnish 1 per cent, as earnest money in respect of the signature of the contract and the performance bond, that the bid bond was to be provided as a deposit in the conventional sense. That is to say, as an earnest of good faith prior to signature of a formal contract, the amount of which would be forfeit to the buyer, in the sense that he would be entitled to retain it, if the matter went off through the seller's default.

[39] I consider that the judge was correct in the decision he reached upon the principal point for the reasons which he gave. That being so, the need to consider the argument as to the penal effect of clauses 13 and 16, had he come to a different conclusion, does not fall for decision.

[40] There is one other aspect of this appeal to which I have not yet referred; it concerns costs. The judge ordered that the defendant should pay to the plaintiffs three-quarters of the plaintiffs' costs for the preliminary issues, determined pursuant to the order of Rix J.

[41] Mr. Hossain suggests that there were no good grounds for the judge to make his order in that form because he had answered one issue in favour of the defendant and the other in favour of the plaintiffs; thus honours were at the very least even. The parties are not able to produce a proper note of the judge's reasons or, indeed, to recall them in detail. This court can only speculate that the order was made either on the basis of time spent in argument upon the issues or on the basis of the view the judge took of the overall merits, in the absence of any suggestion that any damage had actually been suffered by the defendant. He may have had both or, indeed, other considerations in mind; however, bearing in mind the width of the judge's

discretion in the matter of costs, I see no reason or warrant to interfere with the order which he made. I would dismiss the appeal. . . .

[45] STAUGHTON L.J. If my heart ruled my head I would award the $526,000 to the state corporation of Bangladesh and not to an arm of the Cargill empire. But I have to decide this appeal according to law. I regard the law as providing that the Bangladesh Sugar and Food Corporation cannot keep the money, except to the extent that it can establish loss from a breach of contract by Cargill.

[46] The general situation as to performance bonds is that they provide that the bank or other party giving the bond has to pay forthwith, usually on demand. But subsequently there has to be an accounting between the parties to the commercial contract.

[47] Mr. Hossain accepts that, and in my judgment he is right to do so. But as Potter L.J. has said, one does not place too much weight on that general approach. It is wrong to apply a label to a contract before one looks at the wording, and then bend the words to meet that label.

[48] Nevertheless it seems to me right to bear in mind that the parties very probably will have known that that is a general feature of performance bonds. Is there then wording in this contract which shows a different intention? In my judgment there is not. The references to forfeiture of the performance bond in clauses 13 and 16 of the sale contract are capable of being read as referring only to the position as between the Bangladesh Sugar and Food Corporation and the bank, and not as between the Bangladesh Sugar and Food Corporation and Cargill. In other words, the bond is to be forfeited when it is called upon in the circumstances described, the bank must pay, and the money must go to the Bangladesh Food and Sugar Corporation. But that does not affect the position which generally applies, as between the Bangladesh Sugar and Food Corporation and Cargill, that there must be an accounting. . . .

Appeal dismissed with costs.
Leave to appeal refused.

Notes and Questions

1. What is the difference between a bank guarantee and a performance bond? What is a bid bond compared to a performance bond?

2. Who are the parties to a performance bond?

3. What is normally required for a beneficiary to get paid under a performance bond or guarantee? What kind of protections are in place for the principal against unmerited claims of the beneficiary?

4. What did Bangladesh Sugar, the beneficiary in the present case, hope to achieve with the guarantee? Compare the contract of sale to answer this question.

5. Why did Bangladesh Sugar think the guarantee would be "worthless" if not interpreted in line with their intentions under #4 (see para. 37)? What was the "worth" attributed by the judge to the guarantee in spite of his refusal to interpret it as claimed by Bangladesh Sugar (see para. 38)?

6. How should Bangladesh Sugar have formulated the tender invitation to achieve the result they failed to achieve before the present court?

7. Is it possible that price fluctuations in the sugar market lead to a result where the buyer does not get any compensation for late delivery by the seller? How so? If so, how can a buyer avoid such a result?

When considering the answers to these questions, also take into account the next case.

Case 3-6

American Express Bank Ltd. v. Banco Español De Crédito, S.A.

597 F. Supp. 2d 394 (S.D.N.Y. 2009)
(Paragraph numbers added, some footnotes omitted.)
Richard J. Holwell, District Judge

Memorandum Opinion and Order

[1] This case is about international demand guaranties, a form of commercial credit used to secure the performance of international construction contracts. In particular, it involves a bank's attempts to enforce another bank's counterguaranties, despite the fact that it has refused to pay the primary guaranties on the ground that demand was made in bad faith.

[2] The banks' dispute originates in two contracts to build power substations in Pakistan. The contractor, a Spanish company, claims that it fully performed the contracts. The purchaser, a semi-autonomous agency of the government of Pakistan, thinks otherwise. A panel of arbitrators appointed by the International Chamber of Commerce ("ICC") sided with the contractor and directed the Pakistani purchaser to cancel guaranties securing the contractor's performance. Instead of abiding by the arbitrators' decision, the purchaser continued to demand payment of the guaranties and initiated an action in Pakistan to set aside the award and enforce the guaranties. Neither the contractor nor the purchaser is a party to this action. . . .

I. Background . . .

A. The Underlying Contracts

[5] In April and July 1995, Isolux Wat S.A. ("Isolux") and the Pakistan Water and Power Development Authority ("WAPDA") entered into two contracts for the construction of electrical substations in Pakistan. . . . Isolux is a Spanish engineering and construction company. . . . WAPDA is a semi-autonomous agency of the government of Pakistan, which is responsible for coordinating infrastructure development schemes in the water and power sectors. . . .

[6] The contracts required Isolux to install two 220/132 KV substations . . . , and to supply and install telecommunication equipment for twenty lower voltage peripheral grid stations. . . . In exchange, WAPDA apparently agreed to pay Isolux about $35 million. . . . In the event of a dispute, the parties agreed to submit their claims

to arbitration at the ICC. . . . The arbitration clause provided that "any difference, dispute or question arising out of or with reference to this agreement which cannot be settled amicably . . . shall within 60 days from the date that either party informs the other in writing that such difference[,] dispute or question exists, be referred to arbitration of three arbitrators." . . . The clause further provided that "[t]he award of the majority of the [arbitrators] shall be final and binding on both parties." . . .

B. The Guaranties and Counterguaranties

[7] To secure Isolux's performance, WAPDA required Isolux to obtain two demand guaranties. Such guaranties, which are common in international construction contracts, provide a simple way for a buyer to obtain cash for substitute performance if a contractor defaults. . . . Isolux asked defendant Banes to arrange the guaranties. . . . Banes to in turn asked AEB, the plaintiff here, to execute guaranties in favor of WAPDA in Lahore, Pakistan. . . . This kind of arrangement is also common, since buyers frequently prefer to work with local banks, such as the AEB branch in Pakistan, instead of unfamiliar foreign institutions. . . . The AEB branch in Pakistan agreed to issue guaranties to WAPDA, provided that Banes to issue counterguaranties in its favor. . . .

[9] Banes to and AEB made arrangements for the guaranties in a series of SWIFT messages sent in November 1995. On November 16, Banes to sent AEB a message asking that it issue two guaranties in WAPDA's favor, both for a total of U.S. $1,778,571.50 and 5,486,500 Pakistani rupees. . . . The critical undertakings in the guaranties provided:

> the surety [i.e., AEB] waiving all objections and defences under the aforesaid contract, hereby irrevocably and independently guarantee[s] to pay to WAPDA without delay upon WAPDA's first written demand any amount claimed by WAPDA upto [sic] the sum named herein, against WAPDA's written declaration that the principal [Isolux] has refused or failed to perform the aforementioned contract. . . .

AEB, in other words, agreed to pay WAPDA under the guaranties based on a written certification that Isolux had failed to perform. For its part, Banes to agreed to repay any liabilities AEB incurred under the guaranties. Specifically, Banes to's messages to AEB promised, in banker's pidgin, that "Our counterguarantee irrevocable unconditional in your favour is valid to receive your eventual claims made under your guarantee that we undertake to pay to you on your first demand notwithstanding any contestation from us or our applicants part [sic] or third party." . . .

[10] On November 30, 1995, AEB executed the guaranties. . . . At Banes to's request, the guaranties' expiration dates were extended from time to time, most recently until September 30, 2004.

C. Contract Disputes

[11] By 2004, disputes arose regarding Isolux's performance of the contracts and WAPDA's concomitant payment obligations, the details of which are unimportant

here. . . . The disputes provoked legal proceedings in four jurisdictions: Switzerland, Spain, Pakistan, and the United States. Since 2004, however, neither AEB nor Banes to has paid anyone a cent. . . .

[12] Legal proceedings began on February 11, 2004, when Isolux submitted a request for arbitration to the ICC International Court of Arbitration. . . . Isolux's request sought money damages and an order requiring WAPDA to return all the guaranties issued in connection with the construction contracts. . . . At the same time that Isolux submitted a request for arbitration, it obtained an injunction from a Spanish court to freeze the status quo. The injunction (1) enjoined WAPDA from demanding payment on the AEB guaranties, and (2) directed Banes to not to honor any requests for payment of any guaranties or counterguaranties related to the construction contracts. . . .

[13] Five months later, WAPDA informed AEB that Isolux had failed to performed the underlying contracts and demanded payment of AEB's guaranties. Without having paid the guaranties, AEB on July 15 and July 16, 2004 sent Banes to SWIFT messages demanding payment of the counterguaranties. . . . Banes to refused, citing the Spanish injunction. . . .

[14] In February 2005, WAPDA filed a lawsuit against AEB in Lahore, Pakistan to recover on the guaranties. . . . The complaint alleged that Isolux failed to perform the construction contracts . . . , that WAPDA had made demand on the guaranties . . . , and that AEB had wrongfully refused to honor them. . . . As relief, WAPDA demanded damages in the amount of the guaranties, plus the costs of suit.

[15] In March 2006, an arbitral hearing was held in Geneva, Switzerland. . . . Both Isolux and WAPDA participated fully in the proceeding.

[16] Before the arbitral panel issued its decision, AEB on May 8, 2006 filed suit against Banes to in the Southern District of New York. In its complaint, AEB alleged that Banes to breached its agreement to pay AEB under its counterguaranties, and that Banes to breached the terms and conditions of an account agreement governing a U.S. dollar account Banes to maintained with AEB. . . . AEB demanded damages in the amount of the counterguaranties, plus the costs of enforcement. . . . On August 16, 2006 AEB moved for summary judgment, and on September 15, 2006 Banes to moved to dismiss the complaint. In light of the pending decision by the ICC arbitral panel, the Court dismissed both motions without prejudice to refiling once a decision had been issued by the ICC panel. . . .

D. The Arbitral Decision and Subsequent Proceedings in Pakistan

[17] While not communicated to this Court in a timely fashion, the ICC tribunal had issued its decision on February 6, 2007. The decision ordered that (1) Isolux pay WAPDA U.S. $196,116.92 and 892,589 rupees; (2) WAPDA pay Isolux 60,632,495.86 rupees; and (3) WAPDA cancel a large number of guaranties and performance bonds, among them the guaranties at issue here. . . . Under the decision, which called for set-offs to be calculated at the exchange rate prevailing on the date of the award, WAPDA owed Isolux approximately $788,066. Isolux owed WAPDA nothing. According to a

report submitted by Banes to and not contested by AEB, the award became final and binding as a matter of Swiss law upon notification to the parties. . . .

[18] Undeterred by the arbitral decision, WAPDA continued its efforts to enforce the guaranties in Pakistan. By letter dated May 29, 2007, AEB informed this Court that "WAPDA . . . is not abiding by the award, including the direction to release the guaranties of American Express Bank, and has filed a proceeding in Pakistan to have the award set aside." . . . In its defense of that action, AEB specifically claims that (1) WAPDA's demands for payment of the guaranties are mala fide (in bad faith), and (2) AEB has no obligation to pay WAPDA. . . .

[19] On May 29, 2007, the parties renewed their motions for summary judgment and dismissal in this Court. . . . In the most recent round of briefing, AEB claims a right to immediate payment of the counterguaranties regardless of whether it has paid WAPDA and despite its refusal to do so. . . . In the alternative, AEB contends it is entitled to a declaration that if a Pakistani court requires it to pay the principal guaranties, Banes to must pay its counterguaranties. . . . Banes to disputes both claims. Thus, the principal issues now before the Court are whether, on the current record, AEB has a right to enforce AEB's counterguaranties even though it has not paid the principal guaranties, or, alternatively, to a declaration that if it is ordered to pay the guaranties by a Pakistani court, it will be entitled to repayment.

II. Discussion

[20] The Court holds that AEB is not entitled to immediate payment of the counterguaranties or a declaration of its future rights. . . .

B. Choice of Substantive Law

[23] . . . [T]he parties dispute whether AEB's guaranties and Banes to's counterguaranties, assuming New York law applies, are subject to letter-of-credit law, particularly Article 5 of the New York Uniform Commercial Code. Banes to contends that AEB's guaranties are "functionally and legally equivalent" to international letters of credit, and thus subject to letter-of-credit law. . . . AEB counters that the instruments are simple contracts, not subject to Article 5. . . . The practical significance of the dispute is that if letter-of-credit law applies, Banes to can take advantage of the "material fraud" exception recognized in Article 5. See N.Y. U.C.C. § 5-109 . . . . The Court agrees with Banes to, and holds that both the guaranties and the counterguaranties are governed by letter-of-credit law.

[24] By way of background, the typical letter-of-credit transaction involves three legal relationships: (1) an underlying contractual relationship between the party that obtains the letter of credit (the "applicant") and the party entitled to draw on it (the "beneficiary"); (2) a relationship between the party that issues the letter of credit (the "issuer") and the applicant concerning the terms and amount of the credit; and (3) a relationship between the issuer and the beneficiary, which "embod[ies] the issuer's commitment to 'honor drafts or other demands for payment presented by the beneficiary or a transfer beneficiary upon compliance with the terms and conditions specified in the credit.' . . .

[25] In a standard "commercial" letter of credit, the issuer undertakes to pay the purchase price of goods upon receiving the seller's invoice and other documents evidencing a right to payment. . . . A "standby" letter of credit differs with respect to the documents necessary to draw on the credit. Unlike a commercial letter, a standby typically does not require the presentation of a negotiable bill of lading or other transport document; instead, the beneficiary may collect simply by certifying that the applicant failed to perform its underlying contractual obligations. . . .

[26] Both standby and commercial letters of credit create "an obligation wholly independent of the underlying commercial transaction." . . . This feature of letters of credit, known as the "independence principle," has been termed a "fundamental principle" of the law of credits. . . . Because of this principle, it is ordinarily enough to present documents that strictly comply with the terms of a letter of credit to draw on it.

[27] The guaranties and counterguaranties at issue in this case share this essential feature of independence from the underlying contractual relationships, and, therefore, are governed by letter-of-credit law. In the guaranties, AEB "irrevocably and independently guarantee[d] to pay to WAPDA without delay upon WAPDA's first written demand any amount claim by WAPDA." . . . In the counterguaranties, Banes to undertook to pay AEB "on [its] first simple demand which shall be final and conclusive." . . . These provisions plainly reflect the parties' expectation that WAPDA would receive money promptly if it submitted a facially valid certification that Isolux failed to perform its obligations—a defining characteristic of standby letters of credit.

[28] Beyond this, a leading treatise on the law of credits favors treating instruments such as the ones at issue here as letters of credit. See [John F. Dolan, *The Law of Letters of Credit: Commercial and Standby Credits* (Rev. Ed. 1996), ¶ 1.05[2], at 1–31]. As the treatise explains, "foreign banks and foreign branches of domestic banks have introduced a product that they call a 'guarantee' (sic) and to which letter of credit law is quite congenial. 'First-demand guarantees,' 'performance guarantees,' and 'simple-demand guarantees' are the foreign bank equivalents of the standby." *Id.*

[29] Lastly, at least one decision of a United States Court of Appeals supports the conclusion that the guaranties and counterguaranties are governed by letter-of-credit law. In *Banque Paribas v. Hamilton Industries International, Inc.*, 767 F.2d 380 (7th Cir.1985), the Seventh Circuit considered a guaranty that, like the ones here, secured performance of a construction contract. Judge Posner's opinion for the court labeled the guaranty an "international letter of credit" and applied letter-of-credit law. . . . As the district court in *Paribas* noted, letter-of-credit law applied because the issuer agreed to pay the beneficiary upon its presentation of a facially valid documentary demand for payment, and described its obligations as "unconditional and irrevocable." *Amer. Nat. Bank & Trust Co. of Chicago v. Hamilton Indus., Intern., Inc.*, 583 F.Supp. 164, 169–170 (N.D.Ill.1984), rev'd on other grounds, 767 F.2d 380 (7th Cir.1985). So too here.

[30] Without citation to judicial authority, AEB contends that the absence of express conditions requiring "documentary presentation" in Banes to's counterguaranties takes the counterguaranties out of letter-of-credit law.... AEB's argument, however, ignores the undertakings in the principal guaranties whereby AEB agreed to pay WAPDA "upon [its] first written demand." ... Since the principal guaranties and the counterguaranties were transmitted to AEB in an integrated document (a SWIFT message), the Court finds it rather obvious that Banes to intended the counterguaranties, like the guaranties, to be nothing more than documentary credits.

C. Merits

[31] Turning to the merits, AEB contends that it is entitled to immediately enforce the counterguaranties, and to a declaration setting out Banes to's liabilities in the event that it pays WAPDA pursuant to a Pakistani court order. Neither contention has merit.

1. AEB Has No Basis To Immediately Enforce the Counterguaranties

[32] Taking a somewhat extreme view of the independence principle, AEB first maintains that it is entitled to draw on the counterguaranties regardless of its obligation to pay WAPDA.... The flaw in this argument is obvious: In view of the ICC award—and as a question of basic contract law, international law, and New York law—WAPDA's continued demands for payment of the guaranties lack any basis in law or fact. Thus, until the award is modified or vacated, neither WAPDA nor AEB has a "colorable right" to demand honor of the guaranties or counterguaranties. See N.Y. U.C.C. § 5-109 official cmt. 1.

[33] First, as for contract: The construction contracts' arbitration clause provides that "[t]he award of the majority of the [arbitrators] shall be final and binding on both parties." ... WAPDA participated fully in the ICC arbitration, and lost. And the parties here have made no suggestion that there is a colorable ground for vacating the award. In short, on the record before the Court, WAPDA's continued demands for payment are flatly inconsistent with its contractual obligations.

[34] Second, as for international law: In 2005, Pakistan ratified the New York Convention on the Recognition and Enforcement Arbitral Awards.... Though the convention does not expressly speak to the res judicata effect of an international arbitral award, Stavros Brekoulakis, *The Effect of an Arbitral Award and Third Parties in International Arbitration: Res Judicata Revisited*, 16 Am. Rev. Int'l Arb. 177, 181 (2005), it reflects the principle that until it is successfully challenged, an arbitral award presumptively establishes the rights and liabilities of the parties to the arbitration. Specifically, the convention provides that subject to its enforcement provisions, "[e]ach Contracting State shall recognize arbitral awards as binding and enforce them in accordance with the rules of procedure of the territory where the award is relied upon." N.Y. Conv. art. 3. WAPDA's continued demands for payment of AEB's guaranties are inconsistent these international law obligations as well.

[35] Finally, as for New York law: Since at least 1980, New York courts have recognized that a final and conclusive international arbitral award is res judicata as to a party

that fully participated in the proceeding. See *Guard-Life Corp. v. S. Parker Hardware Mfg. Corp.*, 50 N.Y.2d 183, 428 N.Y.S.2d 628, 406 N.E.2d 445, 452 (1980). To the extent that the bona fides of WAPDA's and AEB's demands for payment are judged under New York law, the ICC award precludes WAPDA's continuing demands for payment.

[36] Thus, under multiple bodies of law, the ICC award presumptively establishes the rights and liabilities of WAPDA and AEB until such time as WAPDA succeeds in having the award modified or vacated by a court. AEB, moreover, recognizes this. In Pakistan, it has argued that all disputes arising out of the construction contracts are to be settled in arbitration; that WAPDA's demands for payment under the guaranties were made in bad faith; and that it has no obligation to pay WAPDA anything. . . . By demanding immediate payment under the counterguaranties, however, AEB seeks to have things both ways. Refusing to recognize the validity of WAPDA's claims in Pakistan, AEB argues in this Court that those very claims (and the remote possibility that a Pakistani court will recognize them at some point in the indefinite future, see infra § II.C.2) justify its demand for immediate honor of the counterguaranties.

[37] Whether or not AEB is estopped from taking an inconsistent position here, its position in Pakistan better reflects the legal relationships at the heart of this case. AEB has no obligation to pay under its guaranties and, therefore, no good faith basis to demand payment of the counterguaranties issued by Banesto. It follows that, on the current record, Banesto's refusal to honor AEB's demands for honor is proper. . . .

2. AEB Is Not Entitled to Declaratory Relief

[38] Anticipating this conclusion, AEB points out that there is nothing illegitimate about WAPDA's efforts to have the arbitral award vacated in Pakistan. It thus argues that "to avoid possible future circularity of payment," the Court should issue a declaration that AEB will be entitled to payment if it is ordered to pay WAPDA by a Pakistani court. . . . The first half of this argument is sound. Though WAPDA's continued demands for payment are unjustified in view of the ICC award, nothing in the award or the law of judgments precludes WAPDA from undertaking legal efforts to have the award vacated. Indeed, though the question is not yet presented, the Court is preliminarily of the view that if AEB pays WAPDA because it has been ordered to do so by a Pakistani court, Banesto will be under an obligation to reimburse it. In such circumstances, AEB could make a good faith demand for honor of the counterguaranties, as the presumption of validity that attaches to the arbitral award would no longer be conclusive. And even if the counterguaranties could not be enforced because of the Spanish injunction, Banesto likely would have an independent obligation to reimburse AEB by virtue of having procured the guaranties from AEB. Cf. N.Y. U.C.C. § 5-108(i)(1) ("An issuer that has honored a presentation as permitted or required by this article . . . is entitled to be reimbursed by the applicant in immediately available funds not later than the date of its payment of funds. . . .").

[39] It does not follow, however, that AEB currently is entitled to a declaration of its future rights. The Declaratory Judgment Act, 28 U.S.C. § 2201, provides that

"In a case of actual controversy within its jurisdiction . . . any court of the United States . . . may declare the rights and other legal relations of any interested party seeking such declaration. . . ." The act does not expand the constitutional limitations on federal judicial power. *Ashwander v. Tennessee Valley Authority*, 297 U.S. 288, 325, 56 S.Ct. 466, 80 L.Ed. 688 (1936). Instead, an action for a declaratory judgment can be maintained only if a case presents a justiciable controversy under Article III of the Constitution, meaning among other things that "[c]laims based merely upon 'assumed potential invasions' of rights are not enough to warrant judicial intervention." Id. (quoting *Arizona v. California*, 283 U.S. 423, 462, 51 S.Ct. 522, 75 L.Ed. 1154 (1931)).

[40] When a controversy depends on a future or contingent event, these limitations call for careful analysis of whether the dispute presents an "actual controversy." On one hand, the simple fact that a liability is contingent "does not necessarily defeat jurisdiction of a declaratory judgment action." *Associated Indem. Corp. v. Fairchild Indus., Inc.*, 961 F.2d 32, 35 (2d Cir.1992) (dictum). If however "the contingent event upon which the controversy rests is unlikely to occur, the controversy lacks 'sufficient immediacy and reality' to warrant declaratory relief." *In re: Prudential Lines, Inc.*, 158 F.3d 65, 70 (2d Cir.1998). . . .

[42] Dismissal pending further developments is likewise the proper course here. Pakistan's courts have not yet ruled on WAPDA's challenge to the ICC Award. There is no way of telling when—if ever—they will rule.[4] And there is no way of telling what relief they will grant. AEB's request for declaratory relief thus asks the Court to assume that Pakistan's courts will rule in WAPDA's favor in a way that both requires AEB to pay the guaranties, and triggers a corresponding duty on the part of Banesto to pay the counterguaranties. Though the question is close, the Court finds that in view of these multiple contingencies, the disagreement between AEB and Banes to has not yet "taken on [a] fixed and final shape so that [the] court can see what legal issues it is deciding, what effect its decision will have on the adversaries, and some useful purpose to be achieved in deciding them." *Pub. Serv. Comm'n of Utah v. Wycoff Co., Inc.*, 344 U.S. 237, 244, 73 S.Ct. 236, 97 L.Ed. 291 (1952).

[43] Even if there were Article III jurisdiction over AEB's claim, the Court would decline to hear it in the exercise of its discretion. "[A] district court is authorized, in the sound exercise of its discretion, to stay or to dismiss an action seeking a declaratory judgment before trial or after all arguments have drawn to a close," particularly when doing so is consistent with "considerations of practicality and wise judicial administration." *Wilton v. Seven Falls Co.*, 515 U.S. 277, 288, 115 S.Ct. 2137, 132 L. Ed.2d 214 (1995). Because of the uncertainty surrounding proceedings in Pakistan, wise judicial administration counsels in favor of declining to hear AEB's claim now.

---

4. The Court delayed issuing this opinion for more than a year to allow for developments in Pakistan. On October 28, 2008, the parties informed the Court that there were no developments to report.

[44] Undeniably, this decision leaves AEB in a difficult position. If Pakistan's courts order that AEB honor the principal guaranties, AEB honors the guaranties, and Banes to refuses to honor the counterguaranties or otherwise reimburse AEB, AEB will be required to initiate a new action to recoup payment from Banes to. As the Court has already indicated, a demand for honor in the event that AEB was ordered to pay the guaranties would almost certainly be made in good faith. Moreover, Banes to would likely have an independent obligation to repay AEB if AEB paid WAPDA in reliance on a Pakistani court judgment. But this is not the scenario before the Court. And until Pakistan's courts act, this Court cannot, consistent with the Constitution's limits on federal jurisdiction, issue a binding declaration of the future rights of AEB and Banes to.

Notes and Questions

1. In paragraphs 26 and 27, the court emphasizes "the independence" of the guarantee from the underlying business transaction as a "fundamental principle" and uses this commonality to justify the application of letter-of-credit law. However, in paragraph 32, the court calls it a "somewhat extreme view of the independence principle" when AEB tries to draw on the guarantee independently from the underlying business transaction.

While the court's view is understandable in light of the arbitral award, Andrey Kuznetsov wrote that "[t]he district court incorrectly held that the local bank does not have a right to immediate payment under its counterguarantees regardless of whether the local bank has paid the beneficiary under its independent guarantees and despite its refusal to do so. . . . The district court's ruling unduly circumscribed the independence principle by making the ability of local banks to obtain payment under their counter-guarantees/counter-standbys be noticeably sensitive to the status of the underlying construction contract. . . . [R]elying on decisions of arbitral panels concerning the underlying contract as basis for not enforcing payment obligations under independent guarantees/standbys and counter-guarantees/ counter-standbys is not well grounded in contract law, international law, standard international letter of credit practice and New York law. . . . [C]ontrary to the independent nature of the relationship between the local undertaking and the counter-guarantee/counter-standby, the district court effectively treated the two undertakings as dependent, thereby conflating them."[30]

What are the pros and cons of strict independence with regard to commercial L/ Cs? Guarantees? Standby letters of credit? Are there differences and, if so, why?

2. What could or should Banco Español have done to protect itself against an unwarranted draw on the counterguarantee?

---

30. Andrey V. Kuznetsov, *Sacrificing the Utility of Counter-Guarantees and Counter Standby Letters of Credit for International Infrastructure Projects by Neglecting the Virtues of Strict Adherence to the Independence Principle: American Express Bank Ltd. v. Banco Espanol de Credito,* Geo. Mason J .Int'l Comm. L. 2010, Vol. 2, No. 1, pp. 62–99, at p. 68.

3. What do you think of the court's application of letter-of-credit law to the guarantee (paras. 23 et seq.)? Is the court trying to put a square peg into a round hole for lack of a more suitable provision in U.S. law? Why did the court not resort to the URDG 758 instead?

4. The arbitration was administered by the ICC in Switzerland. Where can an arbitral award be challenged in court and on what grounds? Assuming that the Pakistani court called upon by WAPDA decides differently from the ICC tribunal, what does that do to the award? What do you think of the obiter dictum of the present court that a favorable decision in Pakistan would entitle AEB to draw on the counterguarantee? What would that do to the exclusive choice of arbitration in the contracts between the parties? Is it relevant in this context that WAPDA, as a Pakistani public authority, might expect to get a more favorable hearing in a Pakistani court than elsewhere? Should it?

Section 6. Documentary Collection

In a commercial L/C transaction, *the buyer* asks his bank to issue an L/C for the benefit of the seller and send it to a correspondent bank in the seller's country. The seller is advised of the credit, gathers the required documents, takes them to the nominated bank in his own country and trades the documents for payment. The Buyer's Bank is called the "issuing bank" and in seller's country the functions of the "advising" and/or "nominated" and/or "confirming bank" can be split between different banks or handled by the same bank.

In a documentary collection, *the seller* requests his bank, the "remitting bank," to send the documents to a correspondent bank, the "collecting bank," in the buyer's country. The buyer is advised of the availability of the documents, goes to his bank, the "presenting bank," in his own country and trades the documents for payment. The functions of the collecting and presenting banks can be split between different banks or handled by the same bank.

In both procedures, the controlling documents (bill of lading as title document, the insurance policy, etc.) are not released to the buyer unless payment is made (documents against payment D/P) or a guarantee of payment at a later time is provided (documents against acceptance D/A). Eventually, the buyer's bank transfers the money to the seller's bank for release to the seller.

By contrast to letter of credit transactions, documentary collection does not provide credit from the banks and does not create payment obligations on the banks. This makes documentary collection cheaper than commercial credit. The banks only collect the payment on behalf of the seller and only promise not to release the controlling documents unless payment or acceptance is received.

The risk for the buyer is the same as in a letter of credit transaction, namely that the goods may not conform to the sales contract. However, for the seller, the risk is higher because there is no payment guarantee from the side of the banks. The seller has to ship in order to gather the controlling documents. If the buyer turns out to be unwilling or unable to pay, the seller has to recover the goods or find an alternative buyer.

Chart 3-3 Documentary Credit vs. Documentary Collection

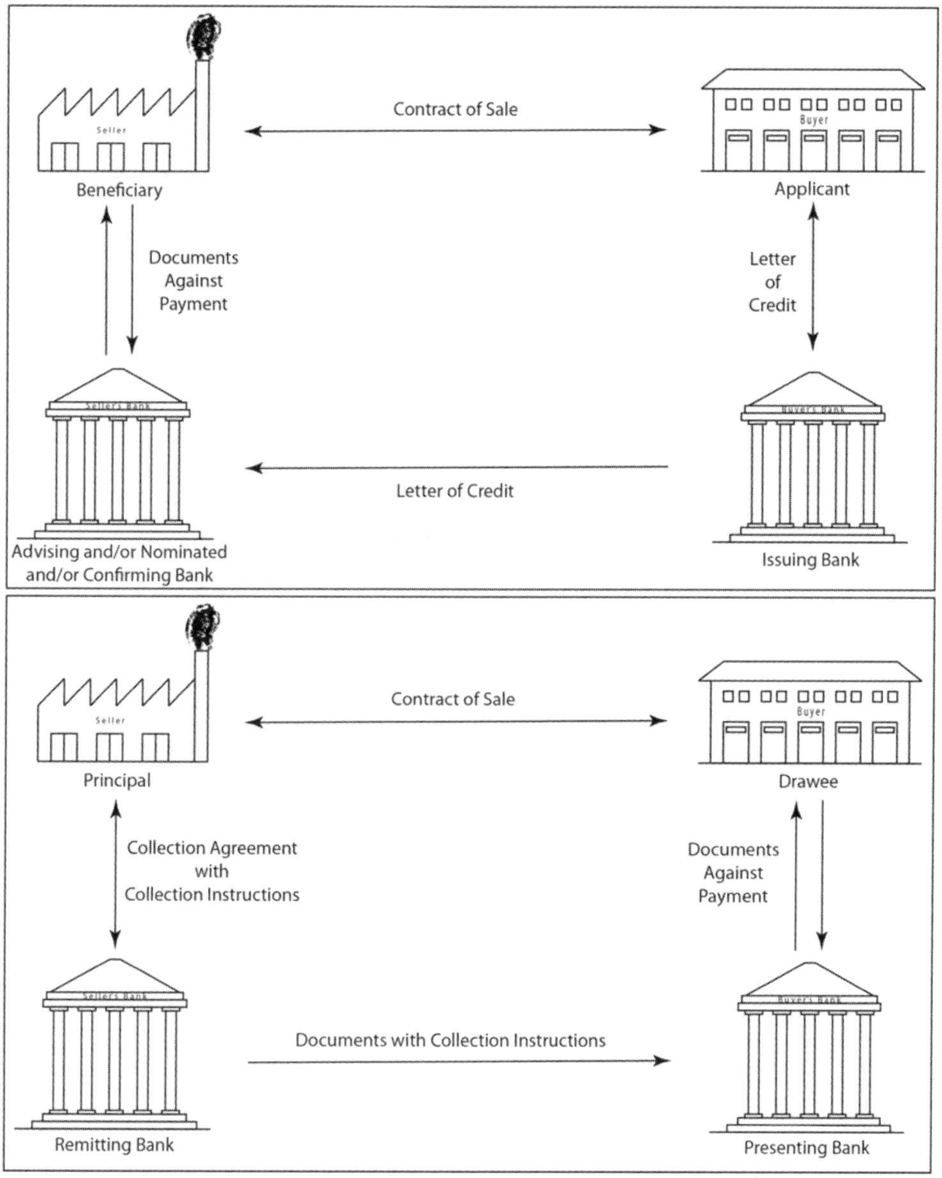

The practical steps for the implementation of a documentary collection are the following:

1. The seller and buyer enter into a contract of sale and specify documentary collection as the payment method.

2. The seller prepares the goods for shipment and obtains any other documents required under the contract of sale, for example, an insurance contract, an inspection certificate, and whatever export clearances or formalities may be required under his country's laws.

3. The seller takes the goods to the carrier and receives a bill of lading (BoL) in return.

4. The seller initiates the payment procedure by going to Seller's Bank with the documents and asking his bank to perform a documentary collection in the buyer's country. Seller's Bank becomes the "remitting bank."

5. Seller's Bank identifies a bank in the buyer's country with which it has a business relationship and asks it to act as the "collecting bank," i.e., to become an agent of the remitting bank for the purpose of the documentary collection. If the "collecting bank" is conveniently located for the buyer, it may also become the "presenting bank." If not, another bank near the buyer or Buyer's Bank will be asked to present the documents to the buyer in exchange for payment.

6. The presenting bank sells the documents to the buyer and then transfers the money, minus its fees, to the collecting bank and onward to Seller's Bank.

7. The buyer takes the documents to the carrier to receive her goods, while the seller receives his payment from his bank.

If the collection is D/P, the seller/principal will send, along with the other documents, a Sight Draft or Sight Bill, i.e., a demand for payment at sight. If the collection is D/A, the seller/principal will send, along with the other documents, a Time Draft or Term Bill, i.e., a demand for payment at a future maturity date. In the latter case, the documents will be released to the buyer/drawee if she "accepts" the future payment obligation. When the buyer/drawee accepts and signs the time draft, it becomes a Term Bill of Exchange, which in this case is comparable to a postdated check. Bills of Exchange are more flexible than checks, however. For example, they can stipulate that a discount will be given for early payment and/or that interest is due for late payment by the drawee. With an accepted term bill, the seller can access the money prior to maturity by discounting the bill—i.e., selling it to a discounting bank. If the discounting is done with recourse, the discounting bank can come back to the drawer in case the drawee/acceptor does not honor the bill. If the discounting is done without recourse, e.g., in forfaiting, the discounting bank bears this risk.

In most cases, documentary collections are governed by the ICC Uniform Rules for Collection URC 522 (Documents, p. I-569). More recently, the ICC has adopted supplementary rules for paperless documentary collection, the ICC Uniform Rules for Collections Supplement for Electronic Presentations (eURC) Version 1.0 (Documents, p. I-577).

Notes and Questions

1. When does it make sense for sellers and buyers to rely on documentary collection rather than opting for a letter of credit? Are these considerations any different for perishable or custom-made goods or time-sensitive shipments?

2. From the perspective of the seller, what are the advantages and disadvantages of accepting payment by means of a Term Bill of Exchange, i.e., D/A? What about the perspective of the buyer?

3. One of the advantages of a Bill of Exchange is its flexibility. For example, a drawer can instruct the drawee to make payment to a third-party payee at maturity. How and why can this be of interest?

4. While a Bill of Exchange is an order from a creditor to a debtor to pay a certain amount to a certain person at a certain time, which is then accepted by the debtor, a Promissory Note is a promise by a debtor to pay a certain amount at a certain time. What is the difference?

5. What are the options of the seller/drawer/creditor/payee if the buyer/drawee/debtor does not pay at maturity, dishonoring the Bill of Exchange? Is there a difference in this regard between nonpayment on a Bill of Exchange and nonpayment on a Promissory Note?

6. If the seller/drawer is worried about the ability of the buyer/drawee to pay at maturity, he can ask a third party, for example buyer's bank, to "avalize" the Term Bill of Exchange. By endorsing the back of the Bill of Exchange, the bank guarantees payment at maturity. In such a case, why don't the parties simply opt for an L/C instead?

———————

The following case illustrates the position of a seller who does not get paid in a documentary collection:

Case 3-7

Amardeep Garments Indus. PVT. v. Cathay Bank

2012 WL 12886849 (C.D. Cal. 2012)
(Paragraph numbers added.)
Judge A. Howard Matz

I. Background

[2] This case arises out of a series of garment sales transactions. . . . Plaintiffs manufacture and export garments from Nepal and Bangladesh. . . . From 2003 until 2008, Plaintiffs contracted with 4004 Inc. to manufacture ready-made clothing and export it to the United States. . . . In 2008, 4004 Inc. declared bankruptcy and failed to pay Plaintiffs for their final shipments of garments. . . . Plaintiffs now seek recovery from 4004 Inc.'s bank, Defendant Cathay Bank, which acted as an intermediary for these sales transactions.

[3] In connection with these failed garment sales transactions, Plaintiffs allege the following fourteen causes of action against Defendant Cathay Bank:

(1) conversion,

(2) statutory conversion,

(3) breach of contract,

(4) breach of the covenant of good faith and fair dealing,

(5) breach of fiduciary duties,

(6) negligence and negligent misrepresentation,

(7) statutory negligence,

(8) intentional misrepresentation,

(9) statutory deceit,

(10) statutory concealment,

(11) statutory fraud,

(12) aiding and abetting 4004 Inc.'s breaches,

(13) civil conspiracy, and

(14) punitive damages. . . .

II. Facts

[6] Between August 2005 and February 2008, the transactions between Plaintiffs, 4004, Inc., and Cathay Bank took the same form. Plaintiffs would ship garments to the United States and simultaneously deliver by courier title documents, payment instructions, and "bills of exchange" to Defendant Cathay Bank. Cathay Bank would act as Plaintiffs' consignee for the goods and would release the title and shipping documents to 4004 Inc. only after paying Plaintiffs on 4004 Inc.'s behalf. . . . This kind of a transaction is called a "documents against payment" ("D/P") transaction—documents of title are released only upon payment. . . .

[7] During this time, Cathay Bank was listed on Plaintiffs' bills of exchange as the "drawee." According to Plaintiff, this fact is significant because it means that Defendant Cathay was providing "banker's acceptance"—"a bank guarantee that funds were available and would remain available at maturity of the credit on account of 4004 Inc."

[8] In February 2008, 4004 Inc. asked Plaintiffs to ship garments based on a promise of payment 60 to 90 days later. . . . Plaintiffs acceded to this request and switched to "documents against acceptance" ("D/A") transactions. . . . D/A transactions and D/P transactions differ in one important respect: with D/P transactions the buyer (here, 4004 Inc.) must remit payment before the consignee (here, Cathay Bank) is authorized to release the title documents, but with D/A transactions the buyer need merely "accept" the terms of the transaction. Once the buyer indicates acceptance, the consignee releases the documents. . . .

[9] Plaintiffs claim that they agreed to these transactions because they assumed that Cathay Bank would continue to be listed as "drawee" on Plaintiff's bills of exchange and would therefore guarantee payment. This assumption proved false. Soon after Plaintiffs shipped the goods and sent the necessary title and shipment documents to Cathay Bank, Cathay Bank contacted each Plaintiff and asked it to change the drawee on the bills of exchange to 4004 Inc. According to Plaintiffs, Cathay Bank knew or should have known at this time that 4004, Inc. was experiencing financial difficulties. . . .

[10] Each Plaintiff agreed to Cathay Bank's request and drew up fresh bills of exchange that listed 4004 Inc. as the drawee. Cathay Bank then presented these documents to 4004 Inc., and 4004 Inc. "accepted" the transaction. Subsequently, 4004 Inc. declared bankruptcy and Plaintiffs have not been paid for these final garment shipments. Plaintiffs seek recovery of $2,695,653.53 for the alleged value of their garment shipments as well as additional compensatory and punitive damages. . . .

IV. Analysis

A. Governing Law

[14] For the following reasons, California law and Article 9 of the Uniform Rules for Collections Publication No. 522 (URC 522) govern the transactions at issue in this case.

[15] Following a transfer of venue for "convenience," a federal court in a diversity case must apply the law of the state in which the action was originally filed. . . . This diversity case was originally filed in the Southern District of New York, and that Court subsequently granted Defendants a "convenience" transfer of venue. Therefore, this Court must apply New York law. New York law, in turn, states that,

> "the liability of a bank for action or non-action with respect to any item handled by it for purposes of presentment, payment or collection is governed by the law of the place where the bank is located. In the case of action or non-action by or at a branch or separate office of a bank, its liability is governed by the law of the place where the branch or separate office is located." (New York Uniform Commercial Code Section 4-102(2))

[16] . . . Cathay Bank is located in California, is a California corporation, and has its principal place of business in California. . . . In addition, Cathay Bank's California offices conducted the transactions at issue in this case. . . . Therefore, under New York law, California law governs the transactions at issue in this case.

[17] Plaintiffs argue that Ohio law should govern their conversion claim because the final shipping destination for all of Plaintiffs' goods was Ohio. . . . The Court does not agree. Plaintiffs' allegations—even the allegations of conversion—are all based on Cathay Bank's presentment and collection activities on behalf of Plaintiffs. Therefore, as described above, New York law specifies that California, and not Ohio, law should govern these transactions.

[18] In addition, Plaintiffs allege, and Defendants do not contest, that Article 9 of URC 522 applies to the parties' transactions.

B. Breach of Contract (Counts III and IV)

[19] Plaintiffs claim that Cathay Bank breached its agreement to handle these garment-sales transactions. . . . The complaint does not clearly explain how Cathay allegedly breached this agreement, but, based on the other allegations in the complaint, the Court assumes that this breach of contract claim is based on Cathay's failure to guarantee the transactions at issue in this case. Plaintiffs' own facts, however, do not establish that Cathay Bank agreed to guarantee the transactions between Plaintiffs and 4004 Inc.

[20] Under California law, "[t]he interpretation of a written instrument is a judicial function to be exercised according to the generally accepted canons of interpretation, unless the interpretation turns upon the credibility of extrinsic evidence." *Sunniland Fruit, Inc. v. Verni*, 233 Cal. App. 3d 892, 284 Cal. Rptr. 824 (Ct. App. 1991). In interpreting an instrument, "express terms prevail." Cal. Comm. Code. §1303.

[21] A fair reading of the complaint shows that Plaintiffs' breach of contract claim is premised on the previous course of conduct between the parties and the duty of good faith and fair dealing. . . . The Court considers these factors as well as the express terms of the parties' agreements.

1. Express terms

[22] Here, considering the Complaint's allegations in the light most favorable to Plaintiffs, Cathay Bank did not agree to guarantee Plaintiffs' sales to 4004 Inc. Plaintiffs' bills of exchange initially listed Cathay Bank as the drawee—the person obliged to pay. Cathay Bank apparently complied with its duties during that period, but later it asked Plaintiffs to substitute the buyer, 4004 Inc., as drawee. Plaintiffs acceded to this request and provided Cathay Bank new bills of exchange that listed 4004 Inc. as drawee. Cathay Bank then acted on these new documents. Therefore, the express terms of the agreements between Plaintiffs and Cathay Bank indicate that, as to the alleged breaches, Cathay was not the drawee and was not obliged to pay Plaintiffs.

2. Prior course of conduct

[23] According to Plaintiffs, Cathay Bank had a duty to act as drawee because, through a prior course of conduct, it had established a "custom and practice" of acting as the payor. . . .

[24] This argument fails for two reasons. First, under California law, the express terms of an agreement take priority over a prior course of conduct. Cal. Comm. Code. §1303. In this case, the express terms required 4004 Inc., not Cathay Bank, to act as drawee.

[25] Second, Plaintiffs' facts indicate that this transaction was *not* part of the prior course of conduct. Previous transactions were D/P transactions in which 4004 Inc. paid the Plaintiffs before receiving the garment shipments. The transactions at issue

here, however, were D/A transactions in which payment was not due for 60 to 90 days. In addition, in the case of these transactions, Cathay specifically indicated that it would not proceed if it was listed as the drawee on the bills of exchange.

[26] Plaintiff, therefore, has not stated sufficient facts to allow this Court to plausibly infer that this transaction was governed by the parties' prior course of dealings. To the contrary, Plaintiffs' facts indicate that this transaction was not governed by the parties' prior course of conduct.

3. Good faith and fair dealing

[27] Plaintiffs claim that Cathay Bank violated implied duties of good faith and fair dealing imposed by California law and URC 522.... These claims are without merit.

[28] The implied covenant of good faith and fair dealing concerns the performance of an agreement, not the negotiation of the agreement.... Furthermore, it cannot be used to create obligations not contemplated by the specific terms of the contract. *Carma Developers (Cal.) Inc. v. Marathon Development California, Inc.*, 2 Cal. 4th 342, 373-74, 6 Cal. Rptr. 2d 467, 826 P.2d 710 (1992);....

[29] Here, Plaintiffs do not allege any facts to indicate that Cathay Bank impeded or acted in bad faith in performing any of the terms of its agreement with Plaintiffs. Instead, Plaintiffs basically allege that Cathay Bank acted in bad faith in asking Plaintiffs to rewrite the bills of exchange.... This allegation is insufficient to support Plaintiffs' claim that Cathay Bank breached its contract with Plaintiffs.

[30] Plaintiffs breach of contract claims (counts III and IV) are dismissed.

C. Fraud (Counts VIII-XI)

[31] Plaintiffs assert four causes of action for intentional misrepresentation, deceit, concealment, and statutory fraud.... California Civil Code § 1709 provides a cause of action for fraudulent deceit. Intentional misrepresentation and concealment are merely two species of actionable deceit and are not separate causes of action. Cal. Civ. Code §§ 1709, 1710. Plaintiff has also pled a "statutory fraud" cause of action, as provided for by California Civil Code 1572, which is essentially identical to an action for fraudulent deceit.... Therefore, the Court will address these four claims together and refer to them as Plaintiffs' fraud claims.

[32] Plaintiffs' fraud claims are based on two theories—(1) that Cathay Bank failed to disclose that it was not guaranteeing these transactions and (2) that Cathay failed to disclose its knowledge of 4004 Inc.'s growing credit risk. Cathay Bank moves to dismiss these fraud claims on the grounds that (i) Plaintiff has not met the pleading requirements of Rule 9(b), (ii) the statements in question did not contain any misrepresentations, and (iii) Cathay Bank had no duty of disclosure to Plaintiffs.

1. Rule ((b)

[33] The allegations of fraud satisfy Rule 9(b)'s heightened pleading standard. Rule 9(b) requires a plaintiff to "state with particularity the circumstances constituting

fraud or mistake." Fed. R. Civ. P 9(b). To satisfy the rule, a pleading must satisfy the "who, what, when, where, and how of the misconduct charged." *Vess v. Ciba-Geigy Corp.*, 317 F.3d 1097, 1106 (9th Cir. 2003).

[34] Plaintiffs have alleged the circumstances constituting fraud in detail. Plaintiffs have identified each communication with Cathay Bank that they considered fraudulent. In addition, Plaintiffs have provided the date, the time, the source, and the recipient of each communication. Plaintiffs have provided enough detail to satisfy the purpose of Rule 9(b), which is to "ensure[] that allegations of fraud are specific enough to give defendants notice of the particular misconduct which is alleged to constitute the fraud charged so that they can defend against the charge and not just deny that they have done anything wrong." *See Semegen v. Weidner*, 780 F.2d 727, 731 (9th Cir. 1986)

2. Intentional misrepresentation

[35] Plaintiffs' first theory of fraud—that Cathay Bank intentionally failed to disclose that it was not guaranteeing available funds—is fatally flawed. There are no facts to indicate that Cathay Bank intentionally misstated its role in this transaction. In fact, the complaint indicates that Cathay Bank specifically informed each Plaintiff that it would not act as "drawee." Even if Plaintiffs did not understand the true significance of this change, nothing supports the allegation that Cathay Bank intentionally attempted to withhold this information from Plaintiffs.

[36] The second theory of fraud—that Cathay Bank failed to disclose its knowledge about 4004 Inc.—is stronger with respect to a material omission. Here, Plaintiffs allege that Cathay Bank had special information about 4004 Inc.'s deteriorating credit by virtue of being 4004's bank. Cathay Bank's communications to Plaintiffs, which asked Plaintiffs to remove Cathay as the drawee, did not disclose this material information.

3. Duty to disclose

[37] Cathay Bank argues that it did not have a duty to disclose information regarding 4004 Inc. to Plaintiffs.

[38] Non-disclosure "may constitute actionable fraud . . . when the defendant had exclusive knowledge of material facts not known to plaintiff." *LiMandri v. Judkins*, 52 Cal. App. 4th 326, 336, 60 Cal. Rptr. 2d 539 (Ct. App. 1997); *Wells v. John Hancock Mut. Life Ins. Co.*, 85 Cal. App. 3d 66, 71, 149 Cal. Rptr. 171 (Ct. App. 1978). Whether a duty exists in a specific case and the scope of that duty are questions of law to be determined on a case-by-case basis. *Parsons v. Crown Disposal Co.*, 15 Cal 4th 456, 472, 63 Cal. Rptr. 2d 291, 936 P.2d 70 (1997); see, e.g., *Wells* (determining, as a matter of law, the disclosure duty of an insurance company).

[39] Even if Plaintiffs are correct that Cathay Bank had exclusive knowledge of 4004 Inc.'s financial position, Cathay was under no duty to disclose this information. In fact, California law expressly forbids a bank from disclosing the private information

of its customers to third parties—even when the disclosure would protect the third party from harm. *Chicago Title Insurance Co. v. Superior Court*, 174 Cal. App. 3d 1142, 1158-59, 220 Cal. Rptr. 507 (1985) (holding that a bank owed no duty of disclosure where it suspected that a customer account was being used in a check-kiting scheme); see also *Burrows v. Superior Court*, 13 Cal. 3d 238, 243, 118 Cal. Rptr. 166, 529 P.2d 590 (1974) ("A bank customer's reasonable expectation is that, absent compulsion by legal process, the matters he reveals to the bank will be utilized by the bank only for internal banking purposes.").

[40] The complaint, as pled, does not state any cause of action for fraud against Cathay Bank. Plaintiffs' first theory of fraud—that Cathay failed to disclose it would not guarantee the transactions—is flawed because Plaintiffs cannot point to a misrepresentation of fact. Plaintiffs' second theory, premised on Cathay's failure to disclose information about 4004 Inc., cannot succeed because Cathay had no duty to disclose this information. Accordingly, the Court dismisses Plaintiffs' claims for fraud (counts VIII—XI).

D. Breach of Fiduciary Duty (Count V)

[41] Plaintiffs allege that Cathay Bank owed them certain fiduciary duties as their "agent, consignee and bailee" and that Cathay breached these duties, presumably by asking Plaintiffs to remove Cathay as drawee or by failing to disclose information about 4004 Inc. . . .

[42] Plaintiffs may be correct that Cathay Bank owed them fiduciary duties in relation to these sales transactions. But any such duties could come into effect only *after* Cathay Bank agreed to act as Plaintiffs' "agent, consignee and bailee." Nothing in the complaint supports an inference that Cathay owed Plaintiffs fiduciary duties before this point. Furthermore, as the Court explained previously, Cathay did not have a duty to disclose information about 4004 Inc. to Plaintiffs.

[43] The Court therefore dismisses Plaintiffs' claims for breach of fiduciary duty.

E. Conversion (Counts I & II) . . .

[45] Conversion is the "exertion of wrongful dominion over the personal property of another. . . ." *George v. Bekins Van Storage Co.*, 33 Cal. 2d 834, 837, 205 P.2d 1037 (1949). There is no conversion "where an owner either expressly or impliedly assents to or ratifies the taking, use or disposition of his property." *Farrington v. A. Teichert & Son*, 59 Cal. App. 2d 468, 474, 139 P.2d 80 (Dist. Ct. App. 1943). However, if the owner's consent is obtained by fraud or misrepresentation, the consent is invalid and the taking amounts to a conversion. Restatement 2d Torts § 252A

[46] In this case, Cathay Bank argues that Plaintiffs consented to Cathay's release of the garment shipments to 4004 Inc. Plaintiffs respond that their consent was invalid due to Cathay's misrepresentations. But as discussed above, Plaintiffs have not stated a viable claim for fraud or misrepresentation. As a result, Plaintiffs cannot state a claim for conversion either, because they cannot show that their consent was invalid. As a result, Plaintiffs claims for conversion are dismissed.

F. Negligence & Negligent Misrepresentation (Counts VI & VII)

[47] Plaintiffs' assert claims for statutory negligence, negligence, and negligent misrepresentation. These claims are pled with nearly identical language and will be addressed together. . . . The crux of Plaintiffs' negligence claims is that Cathay Bank owed Plaintiffs a duty of ordinary care and breached that duty through its "wrongful acts and omissions, including each of its representations and misrepresentations." . . . The two allegedly wrongful acts described in the complaint are:

(1) Cathay's failure to disclose that it would not guarantee payment and

(2) Cathay's failure to disclose 4004 Inc.'s precarious financial position.

[48] As the Court has already explained, Cathay was under no duty to disclose 4004 Inc.'s financial situation. Therefore, Plaintiffs' negligence claim must rest on the argument that Cathay failed to disclose that it was not guaranteeing payment and that this failure to disclose was below the standard of ordinary care applied to banks. See Cal. Comm. Code § 4103 (establishing ordinary care as the applicable standard of care for banks). Although Cathay Bank did inform Plaintiffs that it would not act as "drawee," the implications of that statement may not have been clear. The question whether Cathay's statements to Plaintiffs were clear enough to satisfy the standard of ordinary care cannot be determined on a motion to dismiss. At this time, the Court finds that Plaintiffs have stated a plausible claim that Cathay Bank's communications negligently failed to disclose that Cathay would not act as guarantor.

[49] Plaintiffs' negligence claims are dismissed to the extent they are based on Cathay Bank's failure to disclose 4004 Inc.'s financial condition.

G. Aiding & Abetting (Count XII)

[50] Plaintiffs' claim that Cathay Bank aided and abetted 4004 Inc.'s conversion of Plaintiffs' merchandise. . . . This claim is inadequately pled.

[51] Under California law, "[l]iability may . . . be imposed on one who aids and abets the commission of an intentional tort if the person (a) knows the other's conduct constitutes a breach of duty and gives substantial assistance or encouragement to the other to so act or (b) gives substantial assistance to the other in accomplishing a tortious result and the person's own conduct, separately considered, constitutes a breach of duty to the third person." *Austin B. v. Escondido Union School Dist.*, 149 Cal. App. 4th 860, 879, 57 Cal. Rptr. 3d 454 (Cal. Ct. App. 2007). "Mere knowledge that a tort is being committed and the failure to prevent it does not constitute aiding and abetting." . . .

[52] Under both of Austin's tests, a plaintiff must demonstrate that the defendant substantially assisted another person's intentional tort. Here, the complaint does not allege facts that show that 4004 Inc.'s conduct was tortious. Plaintiffs simply allege that 4004 Inc. "converted" Plaintiffs' property, but that is a legal conclusion and not a factual statement. There are no facts to indicate that 4004 Inc. obtained title to Plaintiffs' property without consent or through fraud.

[53] Plaintiffs' aiding and abetting claim is dismissed.

H. Conspiracy (Count XIII)

[54] Plaintiffs' allegations regarding conspiracy are entirely conclusory. According to Plaintiffs, "Cathay Bank is responsible for the harm to Plaintiffs because it was part of a conspiracy to misrepresent, deceive, conceal and defraud Plaintiffs in order to ultimately convert title to the Goods without payment." . . . Plaintiffs further state that "Cathay Bank was aware that 4004 . . . planned not to pay" and that "Cathay Bank agreed with 4004 Inc." The Supreme Court has explained that "bare assertion[s]" of this type are not sufficient to state a claim for conspiracy. See *Bell Atlantic Corp. v. Twombly*, 550 U.S. 544, 556, 127 S. Ct. 1955, 167 L. Ed. 2d 929 (2007).

[55] Plaintiffs' conspiracy claim is dismissed.

I. Punitive Damages (Count XIV)

[56] As Plaintiffs recognize, a claim for punitive damages is not a cause of action but a form of relief that is derivative of other claims. . . . This claim is therefore dismissed.

V. Conclusion

[57] For the reasons stated above, Plaintiffs' claims, with the exception of Plaintiffs' negligence claims, are dismissed. Plaintiffs' negligence claim is dismissed only to the extent that it is based on Defendant's alleged failure to disclose information regarding 4004 Inc; to the extent that it is based on the notion that Cathay had a duty to explain more clearly the disclosure that it would not guarantee payment, the claim may be pursued. . . .

Notes and Questions

1. This case is a fairly straightforward dispute over the bank's liability in D/P versus D/A transactions. It is made only marginally more interesting by the broad range of claims presented by plaintiffs' attorneys.

The first thing we learn is a rule found in many jurisdictions: banks have to be sued in their home court and the applicable law—to the extent it is not the UCP 600 or the URC 522 or a similar set of rules incorporated by agreement/clauses in the contract—is the home country law of the bank. This is one of the reasons why a seller may want to get a confirmed letter of credit or a guarantee from a bank in his or her own jurisdiction, to avoid having to pursue claims in a foreign jurisdiction under a foreign legal system.

2. An argument that a bank somehow implicitly accepted a guarantee or other form of payment obligation is virtually never going to succeed. Why not?

3. Why did the bank no longer want to be the drawee when the payment terms changed to 30, 45, or 60 days? Was it because they no longer had confidence in the ability of the buyer to pay? Or was there some other impediment for the bank to be drawee on a term bill rather than a sight bill?

4. What do you think of plaintiffs' theory that the bank should have informed them if and when the financial position of 4004 Inc. had become precarious? What kind of a precedent would be set by a court decision to this effect?

5. After plaintiffs submitted additional arguments with regard to negligence, Percy Anderson, District Judge, decided on March 28, 2013, as follows:

> ... As a collecting bank under the California Commercial Code, Defendant was required to "exercise ordinary care in ... presenting an item or sending it for payment." Cal. Comm. Code § 4202(a)(1). Cal. Com. Code § 3103(a)(7) provides that "[o]rdinary care in the case of a person engaged in business means observance of reasonable commercial standards, prevailing in the area in which the person is located, with respect to the business in which the person is engaged." Article 9 of the URC 522 states that "Banks will act in good faith and exercise reasonable care." While Plaintiffs identify general duties of care, they have cited no legal authority providing that a bank has a duty to explain that it is not guaranteeing payment.
>
> In the sworn declaration of Donald R. Smith dated March 10, 2013 ... , Plaintiffs' expert admits that, based on international standard banking practice, Defendant did not have a specific duty to explain more clearly the disclosure that it would not be guaranteeing payment. Despite this admission, Plaintiffs argue that Defendant may have had a duty to explain more clearly the fact that it was not guaranteeing that funds would be available in the importer's account at maturity. However, the April 12 Order already dismissed Plaintiff's negligence claim to the extent that it is based on Defendant's alleged failure to disclose information regarding 4004 Inc. (the importer). Plaintiffs' Motion for Reconsideration to expand the scope of their negligence claims was denied.
>
> Further, it is undisputed that Defendant notified the various Plaintiffs' remitting banks by SWIFT that new drafts were needed to state drawn on drawee (i.e., 'to: 4004 Inc.' and deleting 'drawn under Cathay Bank'). The remitting banks prepared, signed and forwarded new Instructions with amended BOEs listing 4004 Inc. as drawee. The standard method through which a collecting/presenting bank guarantees payment of a time bill of exchange or draft is through affixation of an aval by the bank. It is industry custom and practice that if a collecting/presenting bank is to act as a guarantor, then that information is expressly stated in the instructions accompanying the documentary draft. The lack of an aval on any of the BOEs was a disclosure that Defendant was not guaranteeing payment. The Court finds that Defendant did not have a duty to explain more clearly the disclosure that it would not guarantee payment. (*Amardeep Garments Industries Pvt. Ltd. et al. v. Cathay Bank*, United States District Court, C.D. California, No. CV 11-2849 PA (RZx). March 28, 2013, 2013 WL 1499602).

Reconsider your answer to question 2 in light of this decision.

Consequently, at least in B2B transactions, who has to bear the consequences of not fully understanding what they are doing?

6. Finally, what should the plaintiffs have done when the buyer asked for 30, 45, or 60 days and the documentary collection was modified from D/P to D/A and the bank no longer wanted to be drawee?

Section 7. Payment on Open Account and Cash After Delivery

"Payment on open account" refers to a wire transfer from the buyer to the seller after the goods have been received (push option). If payment terms require "cash after delivery," the buyer makes payment by sending a check or Bill of Exchange in the mail (pull option).

The advantage of the wire transfer is the modest cost. The disadvantage for the seller is the late arrival of the funds, since the seller has to advance all of his performance and has no guarantee that the buyer is still going to be willing and able to pay after she has received the goods.

The situation is even more extreme with a Bill of Exchange, which the seller has to take to his bank. Funds will only be credited to his account if and when the Bill has been honored by the buyer and her bank.

Both options are commonly used if four conditions are met:

- the parties have a high level of trust in each other;

- there is limited or no country risk, namely that trade sanctions or other forms of political upheaval could jeopardize the payment;

- the seller operates in a competitive industry and needs to offer generous terms to win his buyers; and

- there are significant delays between the placement of the order with the seller, when terms are agreed, and the time when the buyer gets paid by her own customers.[31] Therefore, it is customary for sellers to offer 30, 45, 60, 90, and even up to 180 days "same as cash" (also referred to as "Net 30," "Net 45," etc. in invoices), and more, if some modest interest is agreed upon.

The longer the period between the placement of the order, when the seller will start spending money on supplies and production, and the time when payment from the buyer finally arrives, the more likely it is that the seller has to find financing or credit options.

---

31. An example would be the fashion industry. Colors and fabrics are usually selected and materials are ordered about a year in advance. Orders for fall and winter fashions are placed in the spring. Deliveries are made during the summer, and final sales do not happen until the fall or end of the year.

A. Credit Options for the Seller[32]

Even if goods are sold off the shelf from one country to another, it will usually take several weeks before they arrive and may have to be paid for by the buyer. If they have to be manufactured first by the seller, and in particular if the seller has to agree to payment terms such as 30/45/60/90/180 days after arrival, the seller has to advance the cost of production and potentially the cost of shipping and insurance for weeks and possibly months. Although the seller's options to obtain financing are not usually international, we shall briefly list the most important options here:

- Traditional bank loans or revolving lines of credit using other collateral: The seller's bank is funding the production and other expenses incurred by the seller using the seller's other assets, such as real estate, and creditworthiness as collateral; the seller pays interest to his bank at a rate depending on the prevailing interest rates in the country and the seller's credit rating.

- Bank loan using accounts receivable from the buyer as collateral: This is an option if the seller does not otherwise have sufficient collateral or creditworthiness. However, banks will be hesitant to accept receivables from abroad unless they are accompanied by some kind of assurance—for example, a bank draft endorsed by a bank guaranteeing that the buyer will pay at the appointed time.

- The seller can try to sell the receivables instead of borrowing against them: In this option, the seller has to find a bank or other financier who will purchase his future claims against the buyer at a discount. This kind of transaction is often referred to as *factoring*, in particular if it also involves collection services; the financier buying the discounted accounts receivable is called a *factor*. Specialized export financing companies assess the maturity of the claim, the buyer's creditworthiness, and other risk factors, such as general country risk and enforceability. The discount is rarely less than 10% and can be as high as 50%. Sellers can reduce the discount by accepting the financier's recourse in case the buyer does not pay, meaning that the financier can recover what he paid to the seller and possibly as much as 100% of the claim in case of the buyer's default. Factoring is usually available for payment terms up to 180 days but rarely longer. Sellers should be aware that collection of accounts receivable by a factor can negatively impact their relations with the buyer.[33]

- An option similar to factoring is called *forfaiting*: This option is mostly used for larger and/or infrastructure projects with longer time horizons, in particular if they are implemented in developing countries. If the seller has to advance the cost of the IBT for more than 180 days and perhaps for several years, he can

---

32. This part was inspired by Edward G. Hinkelman: *A Short Course in International Payments*, World Trade Press, 2nd ed. 2003, pp. 29–35.

33. For further discussion of receivables financing and factoring, see Jan Dalhuisen, *Dalhuisen on Transnational Comparative, Commercial, Financial and Trade Law*, Hart Publishing 2013, Vol. III, pp. 182–206; see also credit options for the buyer, above, pp. 421–423.

require the buyer to get a guarantee from a reputable bank or from her government for the accounts receivable. The receivables, backed up by the guarantee, can then be sold to a financier, here called the *forfaiter*, at a discount and without recourse. The forfaiter takes over the risk of nonpayment and the onus of collection.

- The seller may also be able to obtain a loan or at least a loan guarantee from his government: Many countries have created export promotion organizations that provide loan guarantee programs or export credit insurance. If a seller obtains a loan guarantee or insurance on the receivables from the buyer, he can usually obtain much better terms from his bank for one of the above-mentioned options. In this way, the Export-Import Bank of the United States (http://www.exim.gov/) makes many export transactions possible that would otherwise not happen or would place much greater risk and cost on American manufacturers.[34]

- Finally, the seller can purchase export credit insurance and/or political risk insurance from private companies like Euler Hermes or via brokers like Global Commercial Credit LLC (GCC).

Whichever financing option the seller chooses, the overall cost of financing the transaction will have to be reflected in the price of the goods or it will cut into the seller's profit margin.

B. Transfer of Funds from Buyer in Country B to Seller in Country S

The mechanics of the transfer of funds from buyer in B to seller in S have been discussed above, on pp. 424–428, and should be reviewed at this time.

Notes and Questions

1. What are the options for sellers who want to give generous payment terms to their clients but still need to contain the risk of nonpayment?

2. Who is in a better position to secure financing for the transaction, the seller or the buyer? Why should a seller go out of his way and accept delayed payment in

---

34. Most European countries have similar export promotion agencies and banks (see, for example, the German KfW IPEX Bank, https://www.kfw-ipex-bank.de/International-financing /KfW-IPEX-Bank/). To prevent market distortions that could occur if different European countries would compete in how much support they can give to their exporters, the European Union adopted *Directive 98/29 on the Harmonisation of the Main Provisions Concerning Export Credit Insurance for Transactions with Medium and Long-Term Cover* (OJ 1998 L 148, pp. 22-32). Export Development Canada EDC offers comparable solutions for Canadian exporters (http://www.edc .ca/EN/Pages/default.aspx). Since 2001, even the Chinese government offers these kind of services via the China Export & Credit Insurance Corporation SINOSURE (http://www.sinosure.com.cn /sinosure/english/English.html). The same is true for many other countries.

spite of the financing cost, the counter-party risk, the country risk, and the risk of exchange rate fluctuations?

Section 8. Consignment Sale

In a consignment sale, the buyer/reseller/distributor gets even more time than under payment terms "open account" and "cash after delivery." Rather than after a fixed time limit, e.g., 90 days same as cash, the buyer/distributor only has to pay the seller once she has herself sold the goods to her customers or end users. To secure the rights and interests of the seller, he retains title to the goods and the buyer / distributor essentially acts as an agent on behalf of the seller. Nevertheless, the risk is high for the original seller because the goods are under the physical control of the buyer and not easily recovered from a foreign country if unpaid.

Consignment sales are common in agency-type arrangements and/or when the foreign buyer/distributor needs to have demo versions of the goods or a certain level of inventory to be competitive. They can also be a way for the original seller to reduce his own inventory and storage costs and have the goods close to the end customers if quick delivery can provide a competitive advantage. Advantages from the buyer/distributor point of view include the fact that she does not have to carry the financing costs of her inventory and receives a predetermined commission for each sale, which makes planning easier. Distribution agreements on consignment basis should be clear on exclusive and nonexclusive territorial rights and the distribution of marketing and other promotional costs and obligations.

Since the goods remain the property of the seller, he should maintain insurance coverage unless different arrangements have been agreed upon with the buyer/ distributor.

Financing options of the seller for the time until the goods are sold by the foreign distributor were discussed on p. 534 and should be reviewed in this context.

Section 9. Satisfaction of Payment Obligations by Other Means[35]

In addition to the handing over of cash (coins and bills) and a bank or wire transfer, payment obligations can also be satisfied via set-off with a counterclaim, replacement with a new obligation (novation), or if the creditor agrees to waive her claims or otherwise release the debtor from his obligation. Since the first two

35. For details, see, in particular, Jan H. Dalhuisen: *Dalhuisen on Transnational Comparative, Commercial, Financial and Trade Law, Vol. III Financial Products, Financial Services and Financial Regulations*, Hart Publishing 5th ed. 2013, pp. 295 et seq.

options in particular are quite frequently used also in international business transactions, they shall be briefly discussed as well.

By contrast to these voluntary forms of payment, a financial obligation can also be satisfied via the enforcement of a court decision or an arbitration award. Some practical aspects of these involuntary forms of payment are discussed in the Part Six on Dispute Settlement, pp. 694 et seq.

Finally, a payment obligation may be deferred by a promise to pay at a later time. Such a promise can be in the form of a check, a bill of exchange, or a promissory note, or even by signing a credit card imprint. A commercial letter of credit, strictly speaking, also falls into this category. These transactions are not payments themselves but facilitate or initiate a bank transfer that follows at a later point in time. The most important legal aspects were discussed in earlier sections of this Part.

A. Set-Off and Netting

If parties have mutual payment obligations, it can make a lot of sense for them to set off their obligations and make only one transfer for the difference. For example, if A owes 100 to B with a maturity on April 1, but B will owe 150 to A a month later, the parties can agree that instead of making two transfers, A will not pay B in April and B will just transfer 50 in May.

Lexis PSL Banking & Finance lists five types of set-off:[36]

- Legal set-off: In court proceedings, the court approves some or all of the claims of A against B, but also some or all of the (related or unrelated) counterclaims of B against A. As a result, the claims are set off against each other and only one payment has to be made by the party owing the larger amount, reduced by the set-off.

- Equitable or transaction set-off: Claims of A against B are reduced because performance by A was defective and B, therefore, has directly related counterclaims for price reduction and/or damages.

- Contractual set-off: Like the example above, the parties agree to set off related or unrelated claims with the same or even different maturity.

- Insolvency set-off: If a debtor becomes insolvent, mandatory rules of bankruptcy law provide for set-off to ensure that multiple creditors will be treated fairly; for example, every debtor in a certain unsecured category receives 20 cents on the dollar.

- Banker's set-off: Banks generally reserve the right to set off multiple accounts belonging to the same natural or legal person. For example, if A's account #1 is overdrawn by 100, while the account #2 is in balance, the bank may apply

---

36. See https://www.lexisnexis.com/uk/lexispsl/bankingandfinance/document/391289/55KB -65S1-F185-X13T-00000-00/Set_off_and_netting_overview.

a payment of 95 coming into account #2 to the debit balance in account #1 before A can withdraw the funds from account #2.

While set-off is essentially a one-time transaction, netting involves the maintenance of mutual accounts between two or more parties with ongoing business relationships. It was described in some detail on pp. 417–418 above.

Since set-off and netting reduce payment obligations, they are a form of payment or at least a form of meeting a payment obligation. The practical importance is twofold:

First, set-off and netting reduce the number of transactions to be made and, therefore, the total cost of the transactions.

Second, set-off and netting become very important if one of the parties defaults and files for bankruptcy: If A owes 100 to B today but B will owe 150 to A next month, should A have to pay today if it becomes clear that B is going to default on its obligations? While different jurisdictions have different rules about bankruptcy, many countries provide "that in bankruptcy all claims against the bankrupt mature immediately," with the effect that creditors can set off their own payment obligations.[37]

B. Novation

Novation is the replacement of an older contractual payment obligation with a new one. It requires the consent of all participants and results in the satisfaction and extinction of the old contract. The new contract with new terms can be between the same parties, e.g., if a debt is restructured, or between different parties, e.g., in case of debtor substitution.

Novation should be distinguished from an assignment of the older contractual payment obligation. The assignment by a creditor of her rights under an existing contract to a third party does not require the consent of the debtor and does not replace the existing contract and its terms. Assignment has the effect of creditor substitution and does not result in a satisfaction and extinction of the old contract.

C. Release

Release by a creditor is a declaration that a debt has been satisfied or is otherwise no longer being pursued. The most common reason for a release is the satisfaction/payment of the debt. If a payment obligation was established by a court decision, the debtor should obtain a statement of satisfaction and release in exchange for

---

37. For detailed discussion, see Dalhuisen, pp. 313–334. The quoted passage is on p. 316. See also Pascal Pichonnaz & Louise Gullifer, *Set-Off in Arbitration and Commercial Transactions*, Oxford Univ. Press 2014; as well as William Johnston, Thomas Werlen & Frederick Link (eds.), *Set-Off Law and Practice*, Oxford Univ. Press, 3rd ed. 2018, with comparative analysis of 34 jurisdictions.

payment, which then becomes public record just like the judgment itself, protects the debtor from being pursued by creditors of the other party to the lawsuit, and prevents further damage to the credit of the debtor. Outside of a litigation context, a statement of satisfaction and release, which refers to a particular debt and a particular creditor and is thus more specific than an invoice for payment, protects the debtor against debt collectors who may have acquired the debt as part of a larger batch of obligations from the original creditor.

Release can also be granted if the debt has been at least partly satisfied in forms other than direct payment. Examples would be the transfer of shares or other forms of equity from the debtor to the creditor, or the performance of certain services in lieu of payment.

Finally, release can be a gift by a creditor who wants to facilitate a new start or has given up hope of getting paid and takes a tax write-off instead.

Part Four

The Documentary Sale 3 of 4: Shipping Contracts

This Part, on shipping or carriage of goods, is organized as follows: In the first Section, we learn about the shipping industry in general; its distinguishing features as a global industry; the market shares of maritime shipping versus air, road, and rail; and some of the major players in the markets. Section 2 is dedicated to the law governing the international carriage of goods, which is a complex web of international conventions, national statutes, and case law; and how to find the specific rules that govern a particular transaction contracted between a shipper from country A, with a carrier based in country B, for the transport of goods from country C to country D, on a ship registered in country E, and delivery to a customer in country F. Since party autonomy in this area is also far reaching, in Section 3 we take a closer look at contracts of carriage, in particular the Bill of Lading. Section 3 also includes a number of practical examples from case law. While the first Sections focus on maritime shipping, Section 4 will provide a few remarks about transport by air, road, and rail.

Section 1. The Past, Present, and Future of Shipping — From Adventurers to Hyper-Efficient Integrated Logistics Providers

A. The Efficiency Revolution in International Business Transactions

In Part Two, we discussed how dramatically international business and trade has changed from the time when Marco Polo sailed to China, taking a year to get there and another year to get back. In our modern age, thousands of satellite-tracked containers on huge container ships, and highly specialized bulk carriers for grain, coffee, oil, or liquified natural gas, are running on schedules almost as reliable as trains in Switzerland, and cross the entire Pacific in less than a week.

One of the consistent themes of this book is the efficiency revolution in international trade, which has brought down the cost of buying or selling goods and services around the globe. As lawyers, we have to play our part in this efficiency revolution and supply our services at competitive rates. Otherwise, we are doomed

541

to the same fate as the sailing ships of old and other outdated tools that we now admire only in museums.

A small case description can illustrate the logistical challenges of our integrated global economy and the kind of legal challenges that follow. BMW, the German car manufacturer, has one of its largest plants in Dingolfing, about an hour's drive northeast of Munich, Germany. About 350,000 cars of the 3, 4, 5, 6, and 7 series are made there every year. The steering wheels for at least some of these cars are supplied by the Swedish/American company Autoliv. The steel column and wheels are manufactured in France and then shipped to Tunisia for the leather to be applied. Final assembly, including the electronics for cruise control, and the airbag system, etc., is done at an Autoliv facility near Dingolfing. Once assembled, the steering wheels have to be supplied to the BMW factory not only "just in time" but also "just in sequence." This means that BMW gives specific instructions to Autoliv for each steering wheel about two months in advance and Autoliv then has to supply each unit on the day and at the appointed time exactly as specified, including the color and type of leather, and the specific electronic setup. BMW basically does no warehousing at all and Autoliv has to supply directly to the assembly line. Obviously, this setup is highly efficient for BMW. One of the challenges for Autoliv, however, is the quality control by BMW at the time of delivery. Among other things, BMW carefully inspects the leather and the stitching and rejects a steering wheel if certain tolerances and standards are not met. In such a case, Autoliv cannot just take the next steering wheel in a given shipment since it won't be "in sequence" with the correct specifications. Instead, Autoliv immediately has to produce a replacement wheel that matches the required specifications and do so before BMW has to stop the assembly line.

As lawyers, we not only have to adjust the price of our own work for our clients, but we also have to help them find the best solutions at the lowest price for the main contracts of sale and for the payment arrangements discussed in Parts Two and Three, the shipping arrangements we are now going to analyze, and the insurance options we will be looking at in Part Five. Finally, we have to build safeguards into our contracts in case a dispute does arise, as described in Part Six. There is no point in squeezing out the last penny of inefficiency in container transportation or just-in-time delivery if the lawyers are causing significant unnecessary expenses with overly complex contracts, poorly chosen laws, or predictable losses due to unenforceable claims.

After discussing the contracts of sale and the arrangements for financing international business transactions, we now turn to shipping and contracts of carriage to show how they can be arranged for maximum efficiency to enable our large and small producers to make use of cost differentials and comparative advantages in different countries and ultimately bring to the consumer the best possible products at the lowest possible price.

Commercial efficiency is not the only goal, however, that should and does matter to us as lawyers, consumers, citizens, parents, and responsible human beings.

Therefore, in this Part, as in all of our work, we need to consider how modern democracies protect their markets against products that are or may be unsafe for our health or environment. After all, we want the *best possible* product at the lowest possible price, not the cheapest product as such. This approach will also be reflected in the Notes and Questions for your consideration. We would invite you to keep it in mind, as we are going to analyze the logistics of the global economy and its increasingly complex international supply chains.

B. The Sheer Volume of Trade and the Corresponding Number of Transactions

From 1948 to 2020, the volume of global export trade in goods grew from about $60 billion US/year to almost $20,000 billion US/year. In addition, some $6 billion US/year in commercial services are exported around the world every year. NAFTA countries contribute about 14% to global export trade. All Asian countries together make up for about 30%. Although China is the country most often talked about, its share of all global exports is "only" 11%, a percentage point or two ahead of the USA and Germany. What may surprise the reader is that the EU Member States are still in the lead, collectively counting for some 40% of all global export trade in goods. By contrast, South and Central America (4%) and Africa (3.5%) are almost insignificant exporters. The import statistics are not much different. NAFTA countries import about 17.5% of all traded goods, Asia imports 27.5%, with China counting for a little over 8%, and the share of the EU Member States is about 42%. Both the USA and EU have a slight deficit in trade with the rest of the world, while Asia, in particular China, as well as the Middle East and other oil producers tend to have a surplus.[1] To some extent, countries with deficits in trade in goods can make up for these with trade in services and/or net investment inflows.

In intercontinental and long distance trade, more than 90% of goods are carried by sea. For this reason, we will focus on maritime shipping in this Part, even if rail and road play a bigger role within NAFTA and within the EU.

In maritime shipping, cargo is usually divided into several categories that require separate vessels and contractual arrangements:

Bulk cargo is either dry (grain, coffee) or liquid (crude oil, liquefied natural gas) and typically requires specialized loading/off-loading facilities and vessels. A single consignment usually fills an entire ship and may be covered by a single transport contract or Bill of Lading. The ships themselves are often owned by the cargo owners, for example, oil tankers are usually owned by large oil companies.

Containerized cargo is all kinds of cargo fitted into standard containers of 20, 40, or 45 feet in length, not exceeding about 20 tons in gross weight. Transport in

---

1. Data from World Trade Organization, available at https://www.wto.org/english/res_e/statis _e/statis_e.htm.

containers has the advantage of protecting the cargo while making handling easy and efficient, allowing for predictable shipping times and pricing. The largest container ships can carry more than 10,000 TEUs (twenty-foot-equivalent units), each of which may be covered by a separate transport contract or Bill of Lading. The ships are used exclusively for container trade and are usually owned by liner shipping companies running them on fixed schedules and routes.

Non-containerized break bulk cargo is generally too small to fill an entire container or too big to fit in one and is presented instead on pallets or in bales or slings. The lack of uniformity of the parcels makes efficient loading and stacking difficult and increases loading times and general transport costs considerably. Separate transport contracts or Bills of Lading are either prepared for each parcel or for each consignment of parcels belonging together. The multipurpose ships are also usually owned by liner shipping companies but may not run on fixed schedules.

Specialized cargo falls somewhere between bulk and break bulk, but usually requires specialized vessels. Examples include Roll-on/Roll-off (RoRo) ships for cars and trucks, ships for specialized chemicals or liquids like drinking water, orange juice concentrate, or edible oils, as well as refrigerated cargo vessels for frozen food with holds cooled to as low as -260F/-160C. More likely than not, an entire ship will sail under a single transport contract or Bill of Lading and may be owned by the cargo owner or chartered by them.

For transactional lawyers, container shipping is the most lucrative because it generates the largest number of transactions or contracts, while break bulk shipping may be the most challenging because no two contracts are alike and more things can go wrong. By contrast, the bulk and specialized contracts of carriage are more often done in-house by the cargo owners and are relatively standardized.[2]

Chart 4-1
The Top 20 Container Ports in the World (UNCTAD, World Shipping Council)

	Port	Country	2010 TEUs	2014 TEUs	2018 TEUs
#1	Shanghai	China	29,069,000	35,290,000	42,010,000
#2	Singapore	Singapore	28,431,000	33,869,000	36,600,000
#3	Shenzhen	China	22,510,000	24,040,000	27,740,000

---

2. For more information see, *inter alia*, Yvonne Baatz et al., *Maritime Law*, Routledge 4th ed. 2017; Rose George, *Ninety Percent of Everything—Inside Shipping, the Invisible Industry that Puts Clothes on Your Back, Gas in Your Car, and Food on Your Plate*, Metropolitan Books 2013; Stephen D. Gervin, *Carriage of Goods by Sea*, Oxford Univ. Press 2nd ed. 2011; Pietra Rivoli, *The Travels of a T-Shirt in the Global Economy—An Economist Examines the Markets, Power, and Politics of World Trade*, Wiley 2005; David Robertson, Steven Friedell & Michael Sturley, Admiralty and Maritime Law in the United States—Cases and Materials, Carolina Academic Press 3rd ed. 2015; Anthony Rogers, Jason Chuah & Martin Dockray, *Cases and Materials on the Carriage of Goods by Sea*, Routledge 4th ed. 2016; Michiel Spanjaart, *Multimodal Transport Law*, Routledge 2018.

	Port	Country	2010 TEUs	2014 TEUs	2018 TEUs
#4	Ningbo	China	13,147,000	19,450,000	26,350,000
#5	Guangzhou	China	12,546,000	16,610,000	21,870,000
#6	Busan	Korea	14,194,000	18,678,000	21,660,000
#7	Hong Kong	China	23,699,000	22,200,000	19,600,000
#8	Qingdao	China	12,012,000	16,580,000	18,260,000
#9	Tianjin	China	10,080,000	14,060,000	16,000,000
#10	Dubai	UAE	11,600,000	15,200,000	14,950,000
#11	Rotterdam	Netherlands	11,148,000	12,298,000	14,510,000
#12	Port Klang	Malaysia	8,870,000	10,946,000	12,320,000
#13	Antwerp	Belgium	8,468,000	8,878,000	11,400,000
#14	Kaohsiung	Taiwan	8,872,000	10,593,000	10,450,000
#15	Dalian	China	5,242,000	10,130,000	10,130,000
#16	Xiamen	China	5,820,000	8,572,000	10,000,000
#17	Los Angeles	USA	7,832,000	8,340,000	9,460,000
#18	Tanjung Pelepas	Malaysia	6,530,000	8,500,000	8,960,000
#19	Hamburg	Germany	7,900,000	9,729,000	8,730,000
#20	Long Beach	USA	6,264,000	6,820,000	8,090,000
Total	Top 20 together		254,434,000	310,418,000	384,430,000[3]

Chart 4-2
Average Container Freight Rates (for TEUs/20 ft equivalent)[4]
(UNCTAD, Clarkson Research Container Intelligence Monthly, Worldfreightrates.com)

Trans-Pacific		2010	2015	2020[5]
From Shanghai	to US West Coast	US$1,300	US$1,000	US$1,200
From Shanghai	to US East Coast	US$2,000	US$1,900	US$2,300

---

3. This is about half of the total global TEU throughput.

4. In addition to these freight rates, exporters and importers will encounter some or all of the following surcharges and other items before a container is delivered door to door: pickup charges, insurance, surcharges for fuel and/or handling of hazardous material, surcharges for certain routes (e.g., Panama Canal), terminal handling charges, storage, customs security and processing, customs brokerage, customs duties, and delivery.

5. These numbers were done before the SARS-CoV-2 or Corona Virus struck widely around the world. At the time the book was finalized, it was too early to estimate the impact of the pandemic on freight rates.

Trans-Pacific		2010	2015	2020
Far East—Europe				
From Shanghai	to Northern Europe	US$1,790	US$1,160	US$2,300
From Shanghai	to Mediterranean	US$1,740	US$1,250	US$1,200
North-South				
From Shanghai	to South America (Santos)	US$2,240	US$1,100	US$1,200
From Shanghai	to Australia (Melbourne)	US$1,190	US$680	US$600
From Shanghai	to West Africa (Lagos)	US$2,300	US$1,840	US$2,100
From Shanghai	to South Africa (Durban)	US$1,480	US$760	US$1,600
Intra-Asian				
From Shanghai	to Singapore	US$320	US$230	US$250
From Shanghai	to Japan East Coast	US$320	US$275	US$250
From Shanghai	to Korea (Busan)	US$195	US$190	US$250
From Shanghai	to Hong Kong	US$120	US$65	US$250
From Shanghai	to Persian Gulf (Dubai)	US$925	US$820	US$450

C. The Future of International Shipping

In our age of rapid change, it has become almost impossible to predict the future more than a few years out and have at least some level of usefulness. Books like *The Next 100 Years—a Forecast for the 21st Century* by George Friedman should be taken as entertainment from the realm of science fiction rather than meaningful, let alone scientific, predictions.[6] That being said, several cautious predictions can be made about the future of international shipping or trade, although this does not take into account the impact of the Covid-19 virus, which is hard to predict at the time the manuscript for this book was finalized:

1. Between 1947 and 2007, the growth rate of international shipping was roughly twice the economic growth rate, as countries diversified their economies and the private sector developed its global supply chains. It is unlikely that the expansion of trade will stay at a level of twice the expansion of the economy overall. At some point, a large majority of items that can be produced cheaper elsewhere are already being produced elsewhere and it will become more difficult to find additional, new opportunities abroad. While trading patterns will continue to evolve—for

---

6. Friedman's goal is clearly to sell books rather than predict the future. Claims such as "2020: China Fragments" or "2050: Global War Between U.S., Turkey, Poland, and Japan—the New Great Powers" demonstrate that Friedman is either an idiot or a charlatan. See—but don't buy—George Friedman, *The Next 100 Years*, Doubleday 2009.

example, some goods that were made in China in recent years will move to even cheaper countries like Vietnam or Cambodia as wages and other cost factors in China increase and some economies, like the U.S., impose tariffs and other trade restrictions—the overall growth of international trade is going to slow down and be more aligned with the overall growth of the global economy in general.

2. After an uneven recovery from the 2008 global economic crisis, there is limited appetite for new free trade agreements and other top-down changes providing further impetus for globalization and trade. Although the current swing of the pendulum in the direction of global protectionism is unlikely to last, it is also unlikely that countries will resume aggressive trade liberalization anytime soon.

3. China in particular is increasingly challenging the economic dominance of the U.S. and EU. This may cause policy changes toward more protectionism, as we experienced it against Japan in the 1980s. At the same time, rising standards of living in China are increasing the cost of production there. As a consequence, some production may relocate. While lateral movements of production from, for example, China to Vietnam will only change, but not increase or decrease, global trade flows, they will still produce new challenges for lawyers.

4. Developing nations have largely been cheap suppliers of raw materials and natural resources in the past. More recently, many of them have also become important manufacturing centers. At the same time, their (urban) populations have seen steady increases in income and purchasing power, which directly translates to increased demand for imported goods. However, these countries are often not well connected and have not invested enough into ports and other infrastructure. As a result, the goods produced in these countries are less competitive in international markets, for example when compared with China, and goods imported by these countries are also more expensive than elsewhere, because shipping is not as efficient. It has been estimated that Latin America and the Caribbean alone have an investment gap of several hundreds of millions of dollars or some five to six percent of GDP *per year* to upgrade their infrastructure to the needs of the global economy. Oxford Economics estimates the global infrastructure investment needs to be US$94 trillion from 2016 to 2040, equivalent to some 3.5% of global GDP.[7] This includes not only shipping and transport infrastructure but also power plants, water supply systems, and communication networks. If sufficient investments are not undertaken—or rather undertaken only in some parts of the world and not in others—shortfalls in economic development and quality of life will not only continue but increase. As investment, business, and trade lawyers, we can make a contribution to reducing inequality and promoting sustainable growth to better serve the people, in particular in less developed countries and regions.

---

7. Oxford Economics (ed.), *Global Infrastructure Outlook—Infrastructure Investment Needs [in] 50 Countries, 7 Sectors to 2040*, available at https://www.oxfordeconomics.com/recent-releases /Global-Infrastructure-Outlook.

5. Although more than half of all merchant ships (by tonnage) are owned by companies from Greece, Japan, China, Germany, and Singapore, very few of the ships are actually registered in these countries. Instead, almost half of the global fleet is registered in Panama, Liberia, and the Marshall Islands, where next to no shipowners are actually domiciled. More and more ships are registered under these "flags of convenience" because health and safety regulations, environmental regulations, and labor laws for the crews may be less strict, and taxes may be lower. The flag states make money from registration fees, largely without investing into regulatory and administrative oversight. Some countries are fighting back by inspecting ships calling into their ports and may impose financial penalties and detain ships until egregious issues are fixed and fines are paid.[8]

6. The containerization and other efficiency revolutions have been major drivers of global trade in the past and have enabled our current level of global supply chains. Major new developments in technology may provide completely new opportunities and disrupt current trading patterns and players in ways that we cannot even imagine today. Blockchain-based software—directly connecting all points of contact in a global supply chain, allowing real-time monitoring of cargo flows, supplying standardized electronic documents, and ensuring automatic payments when predetermined benchmarks are met—is being rolled out as of 2019.[9] These kind of efficiency boosters may push international trade back into growth levels above the general growth of the global economy. Regardless of their impact on overall growth in trade, they are certain to disrupt the legal profession, providing both new challenges and new opportunities.

---

8. Twenty-five coastal countries of the EU plus Canada and Russia participate in the Paris MoU on Port State Control (parismou.org). Twenty countries in the Asia-Pacific region collaborate under the Tokyo MoU on Port State Control (tokyo-mou.org). There is also an Indian Ocean MoU, a Mediterranean MoU, the Acuerdo de Vina del Mar for Central and Latin America, the Caribbean MoU, the Abuja MoU, the Black Sea MoU, and the Riyadh MoU.

Specifically with regard to environmental protection, the International Convention for the Prevention of Pollution from Ships (MARPOL), plays an important role. It is administered by the International Maritime Organization (IMO) (imo.org). Larger oceangoing vessels have traditionally relied on low-quality bunker fuel, a thick and heavy leftover from crude oil refining procedures. This has caused the global shipping industry to be one of the worst polluters on the planet. Things are getting better, however. The IMO has lowered the permitted sulphur levels in bunker fuel from 3.5% to 0.5% as of January 2020. Whether port state control will be able to ensure universal adherence remains to be seen.

9. See, for example, www.laneaxis.com. Geolocation data and location analytics software is provided by companies like esri, see www.esri.com.

Section 2. The Law Governing the International Carriage of Goods

A. Sources of Maritime Law

Maritime law consists of international conventions, regulations and directives of the European Union, national statutory law, and industry codes, as well as case law. Since international business transactions are, by definition, between parties in different countries, multiple sets of rules may apply and provide mutually incompatible rights and obligations for the parties. In addition to the laws to be applied, another question is the jurisdiction of courts or arbitral tribunals to settle any disputes between the parties. These issues have to be addressed with the appropriate rules on conflict of laws or private international law.

Readers may remember the fundamental principle that parties to a B2B agreement enjoy wide discretion as to the content of their agreement, including the possibility of writing up an entire set of rules directly in a contract that largely overrides any applicable national laws, the right to choose the applicable national law or industry codes, and the forum for dispute settlement. When it comes to shipping contracts, international conventions like the Hague and Hague-Visby Rules, and the national laws that implement them,[10] already include far-reaching limitations on carrier liability. Therefore, the shipping contracts themselves, in particular the most common Bills of Lading, are usually not very detailed. They typically do include choice of law and forum clauses, however. Beyond that, conflict rules/private international law rules remain important in two cases: (i) if the parties to an agreement did not include a choice of law and/or forum clause or if any clauses turn out to be invalid or ineffective; and (ii) if there is no agreement between the parties to a dispute, e.g., in case of a maritime accident or collision.

The most important legal regime for maritime law is English law, which is largely based on common law but also includes the Carriage of Goods by Sea Act (UK) and the Marine Insurance Act (UK). The acts, in turn, implement a number of international conventions developed by the International Maritime Organization (IMO), a specialized agency of the UN, and the Comité Maritime International (CMI). English law is important because it is often chosen as the applicable law for contracts of carriage (bills of lading), as well as insurance contracts, even if the parties

---

10. The 1924 International Convention for the Unification of Certain Rules of Law Relating to Bills of Lading (the "Hague Rules," UNTC #2764, Documents, p. I-648) has been implemented by the U.S. in the form of the 1936 Carriage of Goods by Sea Act ("COGSA", 46 USC, §§ 1300–1315, Documents, p. I-708). Only in certain cases where the COGSA does not apply, the Harter Act of 1893 may still play a role. It does not allow as many exclusions of liability as the COGSA. The Hague Rules with the 1968 Protocol Amending the International Convention for the Unification of Certain Rules of Law Relating to Bills of Lading (the "Hague-Visby Rules", UNTS #23643, Documents, p. I-655) have been implemented by the UK in the form of the English Carriage of Goods by Sea Act 1971, as last amended by the Carriage of Goods by Sea Act 1992 (http://www.legislation.gov.uk/ukpga/1992/50/pdfs/ukpga_19920050_en.pdf).

are not located in the UK. Even if English law is not formally applicable, it is often the point of reference for courts and lawyers in other countries. For example, the U.S. has not codified maritime law much beyond the Carriage of Goods by Sea Act (COGSA)[11] and the Jones Act.[12] Many claims are subject to common law and American courts have developed their case law in rather close reliance on English law and court practice. The same is true for India, Pakistan, Singapore, and a number of other Commonwealth countries.

B. The Evolution of the Law Governing Bills of Lading from The Hague to Rotterdam

In the absence of international agreements or conventions, each country regulates independently the rights and obligations of shippers and carriers. For example, in English law, in the absence of contractual limitations of liability, the carrier would be liable to the cargo owner in two important cases: If the carrier does not deliver the goods at all, she could be liable for the tort of conversion. And if the carrier delivers only part of the goods or delivers some or all of them in a damaged state, she may be liable for the tort of negligence.[13] Unsurprisingly, carriers have traditionally excluded any liability as far as possible in the contract of carriage, i.e., the Bill of Lading (BoL).

In an effort at harmonizing the rules and providing minimum standards of liability for carriers, a number of countries negotiated in 1924 and subsequently ratified the International Convention for the Unification of Certain Rules of Law Relating to Bills of Lading, the so-called Hague Rules (Documents, p. I-648). Pursuant to Article 3 of the Hague Rules, the carrier has to "exercise due diligence" *before* the beginning of the voyage to:

(a) Make the ship seaworthy.

(b) Properly man, equip, and supply the ship.

(c) Make the holds, refrigerating and cool chambers, and all other parts of the ship in which goods are carried, fit and safe for their reception, carriage, and preservation.

In addition, the carrier is obliged to issue a BoL to the shipper that meets certain minimum standards (Article 3(3)). These obligations cannot be contractually excluded (Article 3(8)).

---

11. Documents, p. I-708.

12. Under the Merchant Marine Act of 1920, commonly referred to as the "Jones Act" (46 USC § 50101 et seq.), goods can only be carried between U.S. ports by U.S.-flagged ships with at least 75% U.S. crews and 75% U.S. ownership. Only international routes can be served by foreign-flagged, manned, and owned vessels.

13. For more information see Charles Debattista, *Cargo Claims and Bills of Lading*, in Yvonne Baatz (ed.), *Maritime Law*, Routledge 3rd ed. 2014, pp. 178–208, in particular p. 181.

Article 4 provides for a number of limitations of carrier liability, including for any "[a]ct, neglect, or default of the master, mariner, pilot, or the servants of the carrier in the navigation or in the management of the ship" *after departure* from the port of lading (Article 4(2)(a)). Even if a liability can be established in spite of the far-reaching exclusions, "[n]either the carrier nor the ship shall in any event be or become liable for any loss or damage to or in connexion with the goods in an amount exceeding 100 pounds sterling per package or unit, . . . unless the nature and value of such goods have been declared by the shipper before shipment and inserted in the bill of lading." (Article 4(5)).

The Hague Rules "apply to all bills of lading issued in any of the contracting States" (Article 10). Among these Contracting States are the U.S., and the United States Carriage of Goods by Sea Act of 1936 (COGSA, Documents, p. I-708) is a faithful implementation of the Hague Rules.

The Hague Rules were subsequently updated and evolved into the Hague-Visby Rules. The basic system of carrier liability limitation remained unchanged. The maximum liability of the carrier—unless a higher value of the goods was included in the BoL—was raised to 666.67 units of account[14] per package or unit or "2 units of account per kilo of gross weight" (Article IV(5)(a)). The scope of application was "extended beyond bills of lading issued in a contracting State to also cover carriage . . . from a port in a contracting State," as well as cases where "the contract contained in or evidenced by the bill of lading provides that [the Hague-Visby] Rules or legislation of any State giving effect to them are to govern the contract" (Article X). While the U.S. did not ratify these amendments and continues to apply the 1924 Hague Rules only, the Hague-Visby Rules were ratified *inter alia* by the UK and implemented via the Carriage of Goods by Sea Act (UK), as last amended in 1992. Other signatories include Australia, Canada, Japan, New Zealand, Singapore, and many of the EU Member States.

Neither the Hague Rules nor the Hague-Visby Rules are particularly suitable for modern shipping practices. First, they are limited to carriage by sea and not applicable to multimodal transport. Second, they ignore the fundamental changes brought about by the containerization of break bulk transport. Finally, the limitations of carrier liability have not kept up with modern technology and the improved options for securing and monitoring cargo. For these reasons, the UN Conference on Trade and Development (UNCTAD) developed the 1978 UN Convention on the Carriage of Goods by Sea, the so-called **Hamburg Rules** (Documents, p. I-661).

---

14. Units of Account—often also referred to as Special Drawing Rights (SDRs)—are a reference currency maintained by the IMF to have a standard that is disconnected from any one national currency and instead relies on a basket of currencies, including the U.S. Dollar, the Euro, the Chinese Yuan, the Japanese Yen, and the British Pound. In effect, the basket moderates fluctuations in the currency markets, for example if the Dollar gains or loses relative to the Euro. Websites and Apps like XE provide information on the exchange rate of the units of account versus real currencies under the code XDR.

The main innovation of the Hamburg Rules was a rather dramatic expansion of the liability of carriers. In essence, under the Hague and Hague-Visby Rules, the shipper or cargo owner has to prove that the ship had not been seaworthy or properly manned and equipped at the beginning of the voyage to get any compensation. Among the protections for the carriers is the clause that neither the ship nor the carrier can be held accountable for any "[a]ct, neglect, or default of the master, mariner, pilot, or the servants of the carrier" (Article 4(2)(a) Hague Rules and Article IV(2)(a) Hague-Visby Rules). By contrast, the Hamburg Rules provide that "[t]he carrier is liable for loss resulting from loss of or damage to the goods, as well as from delay in delivery, if the occurrence which caused the loss, damage or delay took place while the goods were in his charge . . . , *unless the carrier proves that he, his servants or agents took all measures that could reasonably be required to avoid the occurrence and its consequences*" (Article 5(1), emphasis added). This clause expands the carrier's obligations of care beyond the time before the departure of the ship to cover the entire voyage by providing an important reversal of the burden of proof.

In this way, the Hamburg Rules are a reflection of the membership of the UN, where second- and third-world countries have a clear majority, while most carriers are based in first-world countries. As was to be expected, the Hamburg Rules were ratified mainly by developing countries and largely ignored by the largest trading nations, although the rules make a lot of sense and hardly impose an unreasonable burden on international carriers.

To take account of multimodal transport and electronic contracting, the United Nations Commission on International Trade Law (UNCITRAL) developed the 2008 UN Convention on Contracts for the International Carriage of Goods Wholly or Partly by Sea, the so-called Rotterdam Rules (Documents, p. I-676). The Rotterdam Rules are a truly modern and comprehensive codification with many qualities. However, they also track closer to the Hamburg Rules than the Hague Rules with regard to carrier liability. Although they were signed by some 25 countries in 2009, including the U.S., as of January 2020, only Benin, Cameroon, Congo, Spain, and Togo have ratified. Since entry into force requires 20 ratifications, we may safely assume that the Rotterdam Rules will not assume the intended role of consolidating and modernizing a uniform regime for international bills of lading anytime soon.[15]

---

15. For more information, see Alexander von Ziegler, Johan Schelin & Stefano Zunarelli (eds.), *The Rotterdam Rules 2008—Commentary to the United Nations Convention on Contracts for the International Carriage of Goods Wholly or Partly by Sea*, Wolters Kluwer 2010.

Section 3. Understanding a Bill of Lading for Maritime Shipping

A. The Triple Nature of a Bill of Lading: Contract of Carriage, Receipt for the Goods, and Document of Title

Before we discuss the functions of a Bill of Lading (BoL) in some detail, we need to review once again the normal implementation of a documentary sale (see pp. 72–76). In order to get paid for delivery of the goods, the seller has to present all required documents with the Letter of Credit (L/C) to his bank. In particular, if the INCOTERM® in the contract of sale and in the L/C is FOB or CIF (FCA or CIP for multimodal transport), one of the required documents is usually the BoL. The seller obtains the BoL from the carrier in exchange for the goods. Thus, if the seller has the BoL and takes it to the bank, together with the other required documents, the BoL confirms that the goods have been handed over to the carrier for shipment and are no longer under the control of the seller. If the bank accepts the presentation as compliant, the seller gets paid and the documents are forwarded to the buyer. The buyer then meets the carrier upon arrival and collects the goods in exchange for the BoL.

In the relationship between shipper/seller and carrier on the one side, and carrier and consignee/buyer on the other side, the BoL fulfills several functions:

First, the BoL is the **contract of carriage** between the shipper, i.e., the party who buys the transport services, and the carrier, i.e., the party who owns or rents vessels and sells transport services. As a regular contract for works or services, it stipulates the terms of the carriage or shipment, in particular the port of departure, the port of destination, the date of departure and arrival, some information about the goods, as well as the obligations of the carrier and any limitations of her liability.

Second, the BoL serves as a **receipt for the goods**, issued by the carrier. If the carrier confirms having received the goods in apparent good order, she issues a "clean" BoL (see, for example, 3(3)(c) of the 1924 Hague Rules). If the goods are not in apparent good order, for example because packages are missing, the packaging is damaged or damp, or oil or water are leaking from a container, the carrier will make a notation to this effect on the BoL because she does not want to be responsible for damage to the quality or quantity of the goods that may already been present when she received the goods from the shipper/seller. A BoL with notations is a "soiled," "unclean," "dirty," "claused," or "foul" BoL. Such a BoL will never be accepted by a bank where a presentation of documents for payment under an L/C is made (see Article 27 UCP 600).

For this reason, shippers sometimes offer carriers a letter of indemnity if they issue a clean BoL. In effect, the shipper is promising to compensate the carrier in case claims are brought for damage to the goods supposedly sustained between the time when a clean BoL was issued and the time when the goods are handed over to the consignee at the end of the voyage. However, by agreeing to such a transaction, the carrier or master of the ship may become an accessory to a fraudulent act committed against the bank, the buyer, and the insurance company by the seller, and potentially incur criminal liability. Furthermore, to discourage this kind of fraud, many countries refuse to enforce such letters of indemnity, if the seller does not pay voluntarily. For the same reason, the carrier or the master should also refuse to pre-date or post-date the BoL.

Another requirement for getting paid under the L/C is that the BoL must not be "stale," i.e., it has to be presented, together with all other required documents, within 21 days of the date of shipment, to ensure that the goods can be promptly picked up at the other end of the voyage (see Article 14c. UCP 600). If the documents are not in the hands of the consignee/buyer by the time the vessel arrives at the port of discharge, the carrier may have no choice but to put the goods in storage. Since space is always at a premium in the bonded area of the port, i.e., before customs processing, this storage is rather expensive. In addition, the carrier, who has a statutory lien on the goods until she is paid for her services, may not be happy to give up the goods in case the payment was to be collected from the consignee/buyer. Finally, the goods may be time-sensitive or perishable. One way of ensuring that the BoL gets to the buyer in time for the arrival of the goods is to mark it as "express BoL" or "no original required." Such a BoL can be transmitted by pdf attachment and is not a document of title.

Finally, most L/Cs stipulate that a clean "on-board" BoL has to be presented (compare Article 20a.ii. UCP 600). "On board" means that the cargo has been loaded onto the vessel and has departed from the port of dispatch or departure is imminent. This provides a reasonably good guarantee for the buyer that the goods will arrive on time. By contrast, if the carrier issues only a "received for shipment" BoL, there is no guarantee that the goods will be shipped in a timely fashion and not left behind at the port or storage facility. "On board" should not be confused with "on deck." If a BoL stipulates that the cargo is stored "on deck," this means that the cargo is not below deck and potentially more exposed to the elements. In several of the cases we will be looking at, this caused a problem with the insurance companies, who generally don't want to be held responsible in these cases (see below, pp. 647 et seq.).

If the shipper/seller cannot obtain a clean on-board BoL from the carrier, or he cannot present it to the bank before it becomes stale or before the L/C expires, he is in a difficult position. There is usually no need to seek a waiver from the buyer because the buyer will want to wait and see whether the goods arrive on time and in good condition before authorizing disbursement of the funds. Thus, the intended payment method via the L/C will fail. The shipper/seller has the choice of allowing the release of the goods to the buyer to go ahead, giving up control over the documents, and hoping that the buyer, after inspecting the goods, will indeed pay. A good contract of sale with a good dispute settlement clause will be reassuring in such a case. Alternatively, the shipper/seller can hold back the documents, preventing the buyer from gaining access to the goods for an inspection, and triggering a breach of contract by the seller. With a bit of luck, the shipper/seller may be able to involve an agent at the port of discharge who receives the goods, facilitates an inspection by the buyer and, if approved by the buyer, hands them over in exchange for payment. Since the L/C has already failed as a method of payment, the seller may be able to secure payment by asking a bank in the buyer's country to handle a documentary collection (see above, p. 520 et seq.).

Third, the BoL serves as a **document of title**. If the BoL is "negotiable," which means transferrable with an endorsement, whoever holds the BoL can claim the goods from the carrier upon arrival. This is important in several scenarios. When the carrier receives the goods, she confirms receipt with the BoL, which secures the rights of the shipper/seller who has just given up the goods themselves and has not yet been paid. In a worst-case scenario, the shipper/seller can use the BoL to regain control of the goods or to sell them onward to a third party. The normal procedure, however, is for the shipper/seller to take the BoL and any other required documents to the bank with the L/C and get paid in exchange for handing over the documents. Now the shipper/seller is paid and has no further interest in the goods. By contrast, the nominated bank will hold on to the BoL until it is reimbursed by the issuing bank or by the buyer. In a worst-case scenario, if the buyer is no longer willing or able to pay her bank, the bank can use the BoL to gain control of the goods and sell them onward to a third party to recover at least part of the money it handed over to the seller. By contrast, if all goes well, the bank will surrender the documents to the buyer in exchange for getting reimbursed for its payment to the seller. The buyer will then go to the port to meet the carrier and receive the goods in exchange for a return of the BoL to the carrier. Thus, at least three parties will be rightful holders of the title to the goods in the course of a normal transaction.

The fact that the BoL is negotiable also enables transactions where the ultimate consignee is not even known at the time when the goods are handed over to the carrier. This is by no means uncommon. For example, if the original buyer is a commodity trader, she may have no interest whatsoever in taking physical control of the goods upon arrival. Instead, the original buyer will seek to sell the goods—with a profit—to the final recipient while they are en route to the port of discharge. In exchange for payment, the original buyer hands over the BoL and the final recipient collects the goods at the port. BoLs are by default negotiable. If they are made out to a named consignee, they need to be endorsed by that named consignee to confirm that a third person is in lawful possession of the BoL. The same is true if they are additionally marked "to order." By contrast, if a BoL is made out to "bearer," no endorsement is needed and any person in possession of the BoL can obtain the goods from the carrier at the port of discharge. If it later turns out that the goods were handed over to the wrong person, the carrier has no liability.

In some cases a BoL is marked as "straight" or "not negotiable." Such a BoL is not transferable and only entitles the named consignee to pick up the goods at the port of discharge. Thus, the straight BoL is not a document of title. Although reliance on a straight or nonnegotiable BoL is still common in practice, the UCP 600 refers to nonnegotiable transport documents as Sea Waybill (SWB) instead of a BoL. Since all major sets of rules require the carrier to issue a negotiable BoL upon receipt of the goods (see, in particular, Article 3 of the Hague Rules and Article III of the Hague-Visby Rules), the replacement of the BoL with a Sea Waybill requires the consent of the shipper. Like a straight BoL, a Sea Waybill is not negotiable and not a document of title. Thus, the buyer is protected, in particular if she has prepaid the goods, since a third party who may have come in possession of the straight BoL or SWB cannot claim the goods. Like with the straight BoL, an SWB serves as a receipt for the shipper and determines the consignee who simply needs to present identification to pick up the goods. Neither the straight BoL nor the SWB need to be sent in the original version to the consignee, which saves time and money. Indeed, both are often transmitted as pdf attachments to e-mails these days. Both the straight BoL and the SWB are used only if there is a high level of trust between the seller and the buyer and/or the goods have been prepaid, and if the goods will neither be used as collateral of a bank nor sold to a third party while in transit. Since transmission of original documents is no longer required, an SWB, in particular, also opens up possibilities of the use of electronic documents without paper versions ever being issued.[16] Practical and legal questions related to Electronic Data Interchange (EDI), Electronic Signatures, Electronic Contracts, and Electronic Bills of Lading are discussed in Section C.

B. Non-Maritime Transport

The word "shipping" is used even when no ships are involved. Similarly, while the term "Bill of Lading" was historically used only for maritime shipping, today Bills of Lading may be issued for any mode of transport. As a rule of thumb, if a document is titled "Bill of Lading," we assume that it is intended to fulfill all three functions: contract, receipt, and document of title.

A special form of BoL covers a voyage end-to-end, i.e., from seller's premises in country S to buyer's premises in country B, including the domestic or inland legs of the journey. Such a BoL is commonly referred to as a Through Bill of Lading and is by definition a Multimodal Bill of Lading. The carrier issuing the Through BoL is often subcontracting with local/other carriers for specific parts of the journey. A Through BoL often includes a Clause Paramount, making a particular legal regime applicable to all legs of the journey. This avoids a situation where different legs might have to be litigated in different courts and under different legal provisions. This is of particular interest if it is not clear at what time during the journey the goods may have been damaged. For example, a Clause Paramount might provide for dispute settlement in New York and incorporate the Carriage of Goods by Sea Act (COGSA)

---

16. In this context, see also the Comité Maritime International (CMI) Uniform Rules for Sea Waybills, available at http://www.comitemaritime.org/Uniform-Rules-for-Sea-Waybills/0,2729, 12932,00.html.

to cover all legs of the voyage. If the Clause Paramount is in a BoL issued outside of the U.S., it is more likely to refer to the Hague or Hague-Visby Rules. The result is largely the same, however. Any Bill of Lading might additionally include a Himalaya Clause to extend the COGSA or Hague or Hague-Visby limitations on liability beyond the main carrier to any agents handling the cargo at one point or another, including local trucking companies, but also stevedores and longshoremen, etc.

If a transport document is not supposed to be a document of title and, in particular, if it covers only one leg of a voyage, it can also be issued as a Sea Waybill (see above), an Air Waybill, a Consignment Note (CMR) for road transport, or a Consignment Note (CIM) for rail transport. These are generally used as contracts of carriage, but they may not be receipts for the goods, in particular if they are prepared by the shipper rather than the carrier. We will briefly look at non-maritime transport in Section 4, at the end of this Part (pp. 588 et seq.).

C. A Closer Look at a Bill of Lading

The BoL is issued by the master of the ship or another agent of the carrier upon receipt of the goods. Many of the terms of the BoL are typically already negotiated when the shipper makes the reservation with the carrier, for example, the place and time the goods are handed over to the carrier, the port of departure (port of landing) and the port of destination (port of discharge), and the price to be paid for the carriage, including whether the price will be prepaid by the shipper/seller (CIF) or collected upon delivery from the consignee/buyer (FOB). Nevertheless, only the final terms entered into the actual BoL by the master, *and accepted by the shipper*, make it into the contract.

Traditionally, BoLs are issued in three paper originals. Since each original can theoretically be used independently to claim the goods on arrival, the nominated bank will require a "full set" before making payment under a letter of credit. If the nominated bank is confirming, it will keep one original and send the other two to the issuing bank. The issuing bank keeps another original and gives the last one to the consignee/buyer. The buyer then proceeds to the port to meet the carrier and receive the goods. The moment the carrier hands over the goods in exchange for one (endorsed) original BoL, the other two originals become void. If anything should happen to the buyer or the third original, the bank or banks, who have paid for the goods, can claim the goods with their respective originals or negotiate/sell the right to claim the goods to another buyer.

Since original documents cannot be faxed or e-mailed to the consignee/buyer but have to be sent by courier at considerable expense, efforts at developing secure forms for the transmission of Electronic Bills of Lading started in the 1990s. The problem is that documentary sales involve a wide range of documents, and a large number of actors in a large number of countries. Documents are issued or handled by the seller/shipper/consignor, insurance companies, inspection companies, freight forwarders, warehouse operators, carriers, banks, terminal operators, customs agents, customs authorities, buyers/importers/consignees, and potentially other service providers. Flexibility is also required if goods are sold while in transit, documents are negotiated, instructions change, or if something goes wrong. Thus, a fully functional equivalent electronic system would require that all document types that may be needed in a documentary sale and all participating actors have agreed to and are able to use the same electronic communication standard and platform. Since transferable L/Cs and BoLs can be extremely valuable, any electronic communication standard and platform has to provide a significant level of security, hence encryption, while remaining accessible to users with different levels of experience. Moreover, the same terms and instructions would have to be comprehensible to many individuals speaking different languages in different countries. This challenge has proved formidable and even 30 years after their introduction, electronic bills of lading are struggling to displace paper BoLs.

In 2018, UNCITRAL adopted the Model Law on Electronic Transferable Records (MLETR). The Model Law can be used as guidance by legislative drafters and parliaments around the world. It provides that "[a]n electronic transferable record may replace a [paper based] transferable document or instrument if a reliable method for the change of medium is used." (Article 17(1)). But MLETR itself does not provide or even endorse any particular method. Thus, it may provide the legal basis for change, but will not provide the actual solutions for wider acceptance of electronic bills of lading and other documents in trade. As a consequence, electronic documents are primarily used between large actors with long-standing business relationships that can all use the same system for electronic signatures, for example DocuSign or Adobe Sign. The largest network uses CargoDocs, a software platform adopted by some 5,000 companies around the world.[17] A number of startups are currently working on Blockchain-based solutions, which would take security to another level.[18] It remains to be seen, however, which system or systems will achieve the widest possible acceptance and use.

Sample Document 4-1 is a long-form Bill of Lading used in international maritime transport.

---

17. https://www.essdocs.com/solutions/cargodocs.

18. See, for example, https://cargox.io/welcome/. For further analysis, see Elson Ong, *Blockchain Bills of Lading*, NUS Law Working Paper No. 2018/020, available at SSRN: http://dx.doi.org/10.2139/ssrn.3225520; David Saive, *Blockchain Documents of Title—Negotiable Electronic Bills of Lading Under German Law*, January 23, 2019, available at SSRN: https://ssrn.com/abstract=3321368; Koji Takahashi, *Blockchain Technology and Electronic Bills of Lading*, J. Int'l Mar. L. 2016, pp. 202–211; Stefan Wunderlich & David Saive, *The Electronic Bill of Lading—Challenges of Paperless Trade*, in J. Prieto, A. Das, S. Ferretti, A. Pinto & J. Corchado (eds.), *Blockchain and Applications. BLOCKCHAIN 2019. Advances in Intelligent Systems and Computing*, Vol. 1010, Springer 2020.

Sample Doc 4-1: Marine Bill of Lading

Ship From:[1]
    Name of Shipper:...
    Address...
    Point of Origin...
Date and Time of Receipt of Goods:[2]...............
Ship To:[3]
    Consignee...
    Address...
    Date of Departure and Route...........................
Special Instructions[4]...

Package	Description of Contents[5]	Weight	Size
Total number of packages............			

Declared value (CIF)[6] $...

Bill of Lading Number:[7] ....
Initial Carrier[8]...
□ Truck □ Rail □ Air □ Marine
Vehicle Name and Number..............................
Main Carrier...
□ Truck □ Rail □ Air □ Marine
Vessel Name and Number...........................
Delivering Carrier...
□ Truck □ Rail □ Air □ Marine
Vehicle Name and Number...........................

Payment[9]
COD Amount $...
□ Prepaid □ Collect □ 3rd Party
Partial Pre-Payment Received $.....................

The carrier shall not make delivery of this shipment without payment of freight and all other lawful charges.

Shipper signature...

Without Recourse:[10] Per standard Bill of Lading terms, the shipper is ultimately liable for freight charges, even when the shipment is sent on a collect basis to the consignee. By signing this statement, the shipper is released from the liability of freight charges for collect shipments delivered by the carrier to the consignee.
(For pre-paid shipments leave blank)

....

This Bill of Lading shall be subject to the Hague-Visby Rules.[11] Goods have been received subject to individually agreed rates and conditions as per the present document. In the absence of individually agreed provisions evidenced above, the rates, classifications and rules established by the carrier shall apply, as made available, on request, to the shipper, as well as all applicable statutory laws and regulations.[12]

For the Shipper
Agent name...
Signature...

For the Carrier
Agent name...
Signature...

1) DEFINITIONS: On this Bill of Lading, "we," "our" and "us" refer to THE CARRIER INC. and its employees, agents and independent contractors. "You" and "your" refer to the consignor, shipper, merchant, consignee and its/their employees, principals and agents.
2) AGREEMENT TO TERMS: By giving us your shipment, you agree, regardless of whether you sign the front of this Bill of Lading for yourself or as agent for any other person having an interest in this shipment, to all terms on this NON-NEGOTIABLE Bill of Lading, any applicable tariff and these Terms & Conditions of Service
3) THE BILL OF LADING: Our Bill is NON-NEGOTIABLE, and you acknowledge that the Bill has been prepared by you or by us on your behalf and as you directed. By giving us your shipment, you warrant that you are the owner or authorized agent of the owner of the goods to be transported and that you accept our terms and conditions for yourself and as agent for any other person having any interest in the shipment.
4) YOUR OBLIGATIONS AND ACKNOWLEDGMENTS: You warrant that each item in the shipment is properly described on this Bill of Lading, including any insured value, and is acceptable for transport by us, and that the shipment is properly marked, addressed and packed by you to ensure safe transportation with ordinary care in handling. You hereby acknowledge that we may abandon and/or release, without incurring any liability whatsoever to you, any item consigned by you to us which we have declared to be unacceptable or which you have undervalued for customs' purposes or mis-described on this Bill of Lading, whether intentionally or otherwise. You agree to protect, defend, indemnify and hold us harmless from all claims, damages, fines and expenses arising from our abandonment or release of such item(s). You agree that you will be liable for all costs and expenses related to the shipment and for costs incurred in either returning such item(s) to you or the warehousing of such item(s), pending final disposition. You are responsible for all charges, including transportation charges, duties, customs assessments, governmental penalties and fines, taxes and our attorney fees and legal costs related to this shipment.
5) RIGHT OF INSPECTION OF SHIPMENT: We have the right, but not the obligation, to inspect any shipment, including, without limitation, opening the shipment.
6) LIEN ON SHIPMENT: We have a lien on any shipment in our possession for all money due and payable to us, including all lien and collection related costs, including, but not limited to, all transport charges, customs duties, advances or other charges of any kind arising out of the transportation. In the event of non-payment, interest will be accrued at the legal rate of interest per month from the payment due date. Our charges are not subject to set-off, counterclaim or reduction based on any claim you may feel that you have against us.
7) LIMITATIONS ON LIABILITY: You agree that the declared value listed by you or by us at your direction on this Bill of Lading is the true value of your shipment. We recommend a listing be provided with each shipment by numbering each piece, then describing the contents with each piece and assigning a value to each of the contents. Notwithstanding the amount listed as the value, we limit the amount of damages payable by us under this bill of lading. In consideration of the rates offered you, you agree that we will only be liable for loss or damage resulting from our negligence or fault; our liability is limited to the lesser of: (I) the amount of damages sustained: (ii) U.S. $0.50 per pound per piece (where no value is declared) multiplied by the number of pounds that are actually lost or damaged (but not less than U.S. $75.00 per shipment); or (iii) the declared value in case of loss or damage of the entire shipment (but not less than U.S. $75.00 per shipment). Declared value coverage is for damages or loss of the "actual loss" and is not "replacement cost" type insurance. In the event loss or damage occurs to part of the shipment and no itemized listing has been provided prior to shipment, the average declared value shall be determined by dividing the total value of the shipment by the number of pieces in the shipment to derive a par value. For each piece maximum declared value for carriage will be no more than U.S. $5,000 for any one item, and U.S. $30,000 for any one shipment.
8) HIGH VALUE SHIPMENTS GREATER THAN U.S. $30,000: Special higher declared value, may be obtained at the cost of $2.50 per $100.00 of value. Arrangements must be made one week prior to shipment. We will make reasonable efforts to obtain marine, theft and/or other insurance upon the goods only after specific written instructions have been received from you by us in sufficient time prior to the shipment from the point of origin, which instructions must state specifically the kind and amount of insurance to the placed. We cannot guarantee that insurance can or will be placed. Unless you have your own open marine policy and instruct us to arrange for insurance under such policy, insurance may be obtained with one or more insurance companies, or other underwriters of our choice. Any such insurance shall be governed by the certificate or policy issued and will only be effective when accepted by such insurance companies or other underwriters. Should an insurer dispute its liability for any reason, the insured shall have recourse against the insurer only and we shall not be liable in relation thereto, even if the shipment was insured under a policy in our name. Insurance premiums and our charges for arranging the same shall be at your expense. If for any reason the goods are held in warehouse, or elsewhere, the same will not be covered under any insurance, unless we receive written instructions from you. Unless specifically agreed in writing, we assume no responsibility to obtain insurance on any export or import shipment which we do not handle.
9) LIABILITIES NOT ASSUMED:
WE WILL NOT BE LIABLE for your acts or omissions, including, but not limited to, improper or insufficient packing, securing, marking or addressing; violation of any terms of this agreement; loss or damage to materials not acceptable for transport or prohibited items; loss, damage or delay caused by events we cannot control, including, but not limited to, electrical or magnetic injury, erasure, acts of God, perils of the air, weather conditions, mechanical delay, acts of public enemies, war, strikes, civil commotion or acts of public authorities with actual or apparent authority.
WE WILL NOT BE LIABLE for delays in pick-up, transportation or delivery of any shipment, regardless of the cause of such delay.
WE WILL NOT BE LIABLE in any event for any indirect, special, incidental, punitive, consequential or statutory damages including, but not limited to loss of profits, income, utility, interest or loss of market, whether or not we had knowledge that such damage might be incurred.
WE WILL NOT BE LIABLE in any event for loss or damage to electronic or photographic images or recordings in any form, or loss of or damage to digital or electronic equipment.
10) LIMITATIONS ON LIABILITY, INTERNATIONAL SHIPMENTS: You agree that this Bill of Lading is governed by the Hague-Visby Rules as amended by the Brussels Protocol of 1968 to the extent that our liability is not limited specifically by this bill of lading and these terms & conditions of service as per our agreement. International ocean carriage may alternatively be subject to the rules relating to the liability established by the Carriage of Goods by Sea Act of the United States of America.
11) FILING A CLAIM: You must make all claims in writing and notify us of your claim within thirty (30) days of the date of shipment. Our charges are not subject to setoff, counterclaim or reduction based on any claim you may feel that you have against us. Within fifteen (15) days after you notify us of your claim, you must send us all information you have about the claim. We are not obligated to act on any claim until you have paid all the transportation charges, and you may not off-set, deduct or reduce the amount of your claim from those charges. You agree to retain all packing material for any damaged shipment and make shipment available for survey and inspection at our convenience.
12) MATERIAL NOT ACCEPTABLE FOR TRANSPORT: Unless specifically agreed in writing, we will not provide transportation for: currency, stamps, works of art, jewelry, precious metals, precious stones, bullion, firearms, explosives, cashier's checks, money orders, traveler's checks, antiques, plants, animals, pharmaceuticals, drugs, food stuffs, liquor, tobacco, perishables, negotiable instruments in bearer form, lewd, obscene or pornographic materials, industrial carbons and diamonds. If the combined Bill of Lading includes air transport, we will also not provide transportation for any IATA restricted items, including dangerous goods and hazardous or combustible materials. In any case, we will not transport any material prohibited from transport by any law, regulation, or statue of any country in which the shipment may be carried.
13) C.O.D. AMOUNTS: We will under no circumstances be responsible for the form of payment by consignee unless specifically requested otherwise, in writing, by the shipper. We will not be liable for any fraudulent certified or cashier's check. Applicable charges for handling a C.O.D. shipment will be billed.
14) SUBSTITUTION OF MODE OR EQUIPMENT: You hereby authorize us to choose a carrier or other company to transport this shipment, and our obligation is limited to delivery of your shipment to any such company. Transportation of the shipment is subject to availability of equipment and the space therein. We shall have the right to (I) substitute alternative carriers or other means of transportation (ii) select the routing or deviate from that shown on the face hereof.
15) RIGHT OF REJECTION: We reserve the right to reject a shipment (I) when such shipment would be likely to cause delay or damage to other shipments, equipment or personnel; (ii) or the shipment is prohibited by law; (iii) or the shipment would violate any terms of this Bill of Lading and these Terms & Conditions of Service.
16) LIABILITY FOR CHARGES: You, the consignee and the third party, if applicable shall be liable, jointly and severally, (I) for all unpaid charges on account of a shipment pursuant to this contract, including, but not limited to, the cost of collection, court costs and attorney fees; and (ii) to pay or indemnify us for all claims, fines, penalties, damages, costs or other sums which may be incurred by us by reason of any violation of this contract or any other default.
17) FINAL DISPOSITION: In the event of failure or inability of the consignee to take delivery of the shipment, we will notify you in writing at the address shown on the Bill of Lading and request disposition instructions. If you fail to provide final disposition instructions within thirty (30) days after the date of notification, we will dispose of the shipment at private or public auction and pay out of the net proceeds of the sale for charges due us and remit the balance to the shipper. You, the consignee and any third party, if applicable, remain jointly and severally liable for any deficiency.
18) INVALID PROVISIONS: If any provision of this contract and any other terms and conditions incorporated by reference, are determined to be invalid or unenforceable, the remainder of this contract shall not be affected thereby.
19) CONSTRUCTION OF TERMS AND VENUE: The foregoing terms and conditions shall be construed according to the laws of the Commonwealth of Virginia. Unless otherwise consented to, in writing, by us, no legal proceeding against us may be instituted by you, your assigns or subrogee except in the County of Fairfax, Commonwealth of Virginia.
20) TIME FOR SUIT: We shall be discharged of all liability unless suit is brought in the proper forum within one year after the delivery of the goods or the day that the goods should have been delivered, two years if the shipment is international. In the event that a one year time period shall be found contrary to any convention or law that is compulsory applicable, the period prescribed by such convention or law shall apply.

(Based on the general terms and conditions in the air waybill of EXPRESS VA Inc.)

Long Form Bill of Lading Explained:

This is a regular or "Long Form" BoL, which is by default transferable/negotiable. By contrast, a so-called "Short Form" BoL does not have general terms on the back side, and a so-called "Straight" BoL is not transferable.

#1 The "shipper" is the party contracting with the carrier. If the BoL is only for the maritime leg of the transaction, this will be the seller under CIF and the buyer under FOB. As with all contracts, a contact person should be specified, including phone and e-mail address, in case urgent notifications have to be sent.

#2 The BoL is issued by the master of the ship at the time the goods are handed over. The BoL confirms that the carrier now has control of the goods. The shipper or seller can only regain control if he surrenders the BoL. In the same way, the bank or the buyer must obtain and hold on to the BoL if they want to secure control of the goods upon arrival.

#3 The consignee is the person entitled to receive the goods at the port of destination. However, since the BoL is transferable, the carrier will hand over the goods to anyone showing up with an original BoL. A specific consignee is mainly important in a Straight BoL, which is not transferable. Otherwise, a BoL can also be made out to "Bearer."

#4 Special instructions refer to any other contract clauses. The master of the ship might confirm "on board" on a certain date. The carrier might concede a certain number of days "free demurrage" at the port of destination, etc.

#5 The master of the ship will focus on information she can verify from the outside (number of packages or containers, size, weight, serial numbers, and other markings). Alternatively, the master can copy/paste information given by the shipper. This is usually marked as "SLAC" for "shipper's load, stow and count." The description of the contents (what is inside the container or boxes) is provided by the shipper and mainly needed for customs processing. This information may be identified as "STC" or "said to contain" by the master, to show that she is relying on the carrier's information and did not verify the content. As we saw in Part Three, the description has to match the requirements of the L/C. Otherwise, the bank will not honor the L/C.

#6 The value to be declared to customs upon arrival/importation is the CIF value because the customs value is defined as the value of the goods, including any charges incurred for transport and insurance up to the customs office. Thus, the CIF value has to be disclosed, even if the sales contract provides for FOB.

#7 Each BoL has a unique identifier.

#8 The initial carrier is charged with transport from the seller's premises to the port of origin. The main carrier is the maritime or international carrier. The delivering carrier is charged with transport from the port of origin to the buyer's premises. It is not necessary to identify all carriers and potentially other parties, like warehouses, who will be handling the goods at some point. However, it is highly recommended to clearly identify the two parties who are charged with "delivery," i.e., the passing of the risk from seller to buyer. For example, if the contract is FOB, it matters who has to bring the goods to the port and take care of them until they pass the ship's rail. By contrast, the arrangements made by the buyer for handling in her country is of limited or no interest to the seller and if something happens to the goods at that point, the buyer has only herself to blame.

#9   Payment refers to payment for the carriage. Several options have to be distinguished. Most commonly, carriage is either fully prepaid by the seller (under C- and D-terms), or the carrier "collects" from the buyer on arrival (F-terms).

#10   Under all applicable laws, the carrier has a lien on the goods until she is fully paid. Nevertheless, a right to the goods may not be satisfactory for the carrier if the goods are low or negative in value (scrap metal, trash) or hard to sell (highly customized equipment). Thus, the shipper is normally liable even if the consignee is supposed to receive the goods and pay on delivery. If the carrier is signing this statement, she is waiving her right to come back to the shipper in case the consignee does not pay.

#11   Every BoL should state the applicable legal rules. For discussion of the Hague-Visby Rules, see above, p. 551.

#12   A reference along these lines determines the hierarchy of norms. Mandatory public laws applicable in the respective countries cannot be avoided and stand at the top. The individually negotiated terms—this front page of the BoL—are next in line. Next, per the present clause, are "rates, classifications and rules established by the carrier," i.e., the general terms in the back of the BoL and any general terms on the website, etc., of the carrier. Then come the non-mandatory public law provisions, beginning with the Hague-Visby Rules, followed by any statutory laws and regulations applicable to the carrier in her home country and to the BoL per conflict rules. Finally, as for all contracts, any remaining gaps are filled by reference to industry customs and general principles of law.

The present example includes a choice of law and a choice of forum clause in paragraph 19 of the general terms. By signing the BoL, the shipper accepts these choices and is bound accordingly in case a dispute should arise.

Notes and Questions

1. How detailed should the description of the goods be in the BoL? Who is interested in a more detailed description? Who is interested in a less detailed description? Why?

2. What are the advantages and disadvantages of a "straight" BoL?

D. Charterparties

A charterparty (or charter-party) is a contract between a shipowner and a cargo owner/shipper/seller for the charter of an entire vessel. The charter contract can be a time charter, e.g., for several months and multiple voyages, or a voyage charter, for one specific voyage. Normally, the shipowner provides the vessel and the crew, as well as fuel and other supplies. Under a bareboat charter, the charterer has to bring all of these. If the cargo owner does not want the entire vessel but only a part of it, the contract is usually referred to as affreightment, and involves one or more BoLs being issued.

Since the carriage of goods belonging to one person, the shipper, under a charterparty agreement among another person, the charterer, and a third person (the ship owner) can create questions with regard to the distribution of rights and responsibilities (for example, who the carrier is), a BoL has to state whether it is issued under a charterparty agreement (see also Article 22 UCP 600). If a BoL is issued to the charterer, it is a receipt for the goods and a document of title but not a contract of carriage, because it is superseded by the charterparty agreement. If the charterparty so allows, any BoLs issued under it can supply additional terms and conditions.

E. Practical Examples of the Rights and Obligations of Shipper and Carrier

Disputes over the rights and obligations under a Bill of Lading are relatively common. As we have seen, the Hague Rules and the Hague-Visby Rules allow very far-reaching limitations of carrier liability. We take a look at four decisions. The first discusses the obligations of the carrier to ensure timely arrival of the goods. The second and third rulings are about goods getting damaged during transit and the limitation of liability we find in the Hague and Hague-Visby Rules, or in this case the implementation of the Hague Rules by way of the United States Carriage of Goods by Sea Act (COGSA) (Documents, p. I-708). Finally, in the fourth decision, the court looks at problems on arrival, if the consignee is not present or the delivery can otherwise not be done in a timely manner and the goods have to be entrusted to a third party for storage.

Case 4-1

Sea-Land Service Inc. v. Lozen International LLC

285 F.3d 808 (9th Cir. 2002)
(Paragraph numbers added, footnotes omitted.)
Before Beezer, Tashima and Graber, Circuit Judges

Factual and Procedural Background

[4] Dean Myring, Lozen's president, arranged with Sea-Land to transport three 40-foot containers of grapes from Hermosillo, Mexico, to Felixstowe, England. The containers were to travel by truck from Hermosillo to Long Beach, California. From there, they were to be transported by rail to Elizabeth, New Jersey, where they were to be loaded on the Mathilde Maersk (Maersk), an ocean vessel that would be stopping in Felixstowe. The estimated departure date of the Maersk was June 20, 1999, with an estimated arrival in Felixstowe on June 28, 1999.

[5] Unfortunately, Sea-Land's railroad agent [—the rail company CSX—] placed the containers on the wrong train. As a result, Lozen's grapes did not arrive in New Jersey in time for the sailing of the Maersk. Sea-Land notified Lozen of the problem

and asked whether the company preferred to send the containers on the next week's vessel or, instead, to sell them domestically. After its customer in England agreed to buy the delayed grapes only at a reduced price, Lozen elected to sell them domestically at lower prices than it would have received under its original contract with the customer in England. A week's delay in arrival of the grapes in England was critical because, by then, cheaper European grapes were expected to "flood the market."

[6] Sea-Land filed this action to recover the full amount of its contract with Lozen to transport the containers of grapes. Lozen answered and counterclaimed, arguing that, as a result of Sea-Land's delay in transporting the containers, it suffered damages when it sold its grapes domestically at distressed prices. . . .

B. Terms of the Parties' Agreement

[13] Lozen and Sea-Land dispute the nature of the agreement between them and the terms governing that agreement. Lozen argues that the parties entered into a special oral contract whereby Sea-Land expressly promised to deliver the three containers of grapes by a certain date. Sea-Land, on the other hand, argues that the terms of its international bills of lading constitute the parties' agreement. Those terms provided Sea-Land with some latitude as to the date by which it was required to deliver the three containers. The district court adopted the latter construction of the parties' agreement, and we agree.

[14] This dispute arises because Lozen requested that express Sea waybills of lading be used in the transportation of its grapes. Had this been a traditional shipment, documents incorporating the terms on Sea-Land's international bills of lading would have been printed by Sea-Land and given to Lozen. However, express sea waybills are issued electronically, and Sea-Land did not give a printed copy to Lozen.

[15] Lozen claims that, when it entered into the shipping agreement, it was unaware that the terms printed on Sea-Land's international bills of lading also typically apply to shipments sent via its electronic sea waybills. Lozen further asserts that, regardless of the terms applicable to other shipments of this type, the parties entered into a special oral agreement with respect to this particular shipment and that Sea-Land expressly guaranteed the date by which the grapes would arrive.

[16] Those arguments are unpersuasive on this record. Dean Myring, Lozen's president, twice conceded in his deposition that he could recall no specific details about the formation of the alleged special oral contract. He also admitted that Sea-Land, like other carriers, never guaranteed specific delivery times:

> They are not guaranteed. In fact—well, if they were guaranteed Sea-Land would be opening themselves up to—any carrier would be opening themselves up to all sorts of fun and games if they put a cast iron guarantee on something.

[17] As demonstrated by a fax that he sent to a domestic agent, Myring knew that "the carriers (SeaLand, Maersk, Mitsui, all of them!) have an 'out' based on International Shipping regulations and so a week[']s delay is not considered 'late'. Moreover, ANY

shipping line doesn't totally guarantee a timely delivery, an 'ETA' is exactly what it says, an ESTIMATED time of arrival."

[18] Myring's deposition also reveals that he had shipped cargo several times before under Sea-Land's traditional bills of lading. In addition, Myring admitted that he had read the reverse side of Sea-Land's bills of lading before initiating the shipment at issue here. Perhaps most importantly, Myring demonstrated his awareness that the terms printed on traditional bills of lading generally apply to express sea waybills:

> Q: Was it your understanding that when cargo was moving under an express sea way bill that it was still moving under the terms and conditions of Sea-Land's bills of lading? . . .
>
> A. I think that is a fair statement.

[19] This evidence alone justifies a conclusion that the terms printed on Sea-Land's non-electronic bills of lading control the parties' agreement. We have held that "actual possession of the bill of lading" is unnecessary in situations like this one, in which a shipper is "familiar as a matter of commercial practice with the terms and limitations of Sea-Land's bill of lading." *Royal Ins. Co. v. Sea-Land Serv. Inc.*, 50 F.3d 723, 727 (9th Cir.1995); see also *Travelers Indem. Co. v. Vessel Sam Houston*, 26 F.3d 895, 899 (9th Cir.1994) (holding that a sophisticated shipper who had used the carrier on previous occasions and was familiar with its bill of lading failed to raise a question of material fact as to whether it was denied a fair opportunity to opt out of the liability clause in the bill of lading).

[20] Sea-Land submitted other evidence, in addition to the deposition testimony, that Myring had read the terms on Sea-Land's bills of lading and understood that they controlled the parties' agreement. For example, in an e-mail to Sea-Land, Myring wrote: "I understand what's written on the back of your b/l's [bills of lading] and you can't guarantee deliveries due to certain circumstances." Similarly, in an e-mail to Lozen's customer in England, Myring wrote: "Sorry about this but, as Sea-Land have [sic] politely pointed out, read the back of any ocean bill and there is no 'guarantee' of delivery date and so for a week's delay there's bugger all that they're going to do about it."

[21] In the face of this evidence, Lozen concedes that Sea-Land did not agree to deliver the containers of grapes to *England* by a certain date but, instead, asserts that Sea-Land promised that the containers would be shipped to *New Jersey* in time to be loaded on the Maersk. The record does not allow that inference.

[22] Sea-Land presented considerable evidence that it did not guarantee that the containers would be delivered to any location by a specific date, that it is not the practice of Sea Land or other carriers to make such guarantees, and that Lozen knew that the terms on Sea-Land's international bills of lading governed both the inland and oversea legs of the shipment. In response, Lozen presented no evidence that Sea-Land orally guaranteed timely delivery of the grapes to New Jersey but, instead, offered only bare allegations as to the existence of a special agreement. Accordingly,

there is no genuine issue of fact as to whether Myring had read Sea-Land's bills of lading and knew that they, rather than an alleged oral "guarantee," governed the parties' agreement.

C. Application of COGSA to the Parties' Agreement

[23] The district court applied COGSA in its analysis of the extent of Sea-Land's liability. Lozen argues that, instead, the court should have applied either the Carmack Amendment or the Harter Act, 46 U.S.C.App. § 190.

[24] COGSA applies to "[e]very bill of lading or similar document of title which is evidence of a contract for the carriage of goods by sea *to or from ports of the United States,* in foreign trade." 46 U.S.C.App. § 130046 U.S.C.App. § 1300 (emphasis added). Lozen argues that, because Sea-Land was hired to transport the containers of grapes from Hermosillo, Mexico, to Felixstowe, England, the district court erred in holding that COGSA applies to the shipment. See, e.g., *People's Ins. Co. of China v. M/V Damodar Tanabe (In re Damodar Bulk Carriers, Ltd.),* 903 F.2d 675, 677 (9th Cir.1990) (finding COGSA inapplicable to a shipment from Chile to China, despite the fact that the ocean carrier made a scheduled stop in Hawaii).

[25] Lozen's point is correct but, in the circumstances here, incomplete. Even though COGSA does not apply by its own force to the shipment, Sea-Land's international bills of lading contain a "Clause Paramount" that explicitly incorporates the statute into the contract between the parties. We have repeatedly enforced such clauses. See, e.g., *Royal Ins.,* 50 F.3d at 726–27; *Inst. of London Underwriters v. Sea-Land Serv., Inc.,* 881 F.2d 761, 764–66 (9th Cir.1989). Accordingly, the district court did not err in holding that COGSA applied to the parties' agreement as a matter of contract.

[26] The district court also properly concluded that no other statute applied. First, the Carmack Amendment is inapplicable because (as potentially relevant here) that statute determines carrier liability only for "transportation in the United States between a place in . . . the United States and another place in the United States through a foreign country; or the United States and a place in a foreign country." 49 U.S.C. § 10501(a)(2)(E), (F); . . . Lozen's containers were to be shipped from Mexico to England.

[27] For a similar reason, the Harter Act does not apply to the shipment at issue: "To the extent that the Harter Act governed international trade leaving from or entering American ports, it was superseded in 1936 by the Carriage of Goods by Sea Act. . . . The Harter Act therefore only governs domestic trade." *N. River Ins. Co. v. Fed Sea/Fed Pac Line,* 647 F.2d 985, 987 (9th Cir.1981); see also *Sunkist Growers, Inc. v. Adelaide Shipping Lines, Ltd.,* 603 F.2d 1327, 1333–34(9th Cir.1979) ("It is well recognized that The Hague Rules or COGSA have superseded the Harter Act with respect to foreign trade. . . ."). Moreover, because COGSA is incorporated by contract into Sea-Land's bills of lading, "it, rather than the Harter Act, controls." *N. River Ins.,* 647 F.2d at 987.

D. "Unreasonable Deviation" and Sea-Land's "Liberty Clauses"

[28] Lozen argues that delay caused by CSX, Sea-Land's railroad agent, constituted an unreasonable deviation, which releases Lozen from the terms of Sea-Land's bills of lading. Sea-Land responds that the agent's behavior did not rise to the level of an unreasonable deviation and that, therefore, two "liberty clauses" in its bills of lading protect it from liability.[7]

[29] A "deviation" is defined under admiralty law as a "'voluntary departure without necessity, or any reasonable cause, from the regular and usual course' of the voyage." *Vision Air Flight Serv., Inc. v. M/V Nat'l Pride,* 155 F.3d 1165, 1175–76 n. 12 (9th Cir.1998) (quoting *Constable v. Nat'l S.S. Co.,* 154 U.S. 51, 66, 14 S.Ct. 1062, 38 L.Ed. 903 (1894)). In order for a deviation to be "unreasonable," the carrier must intentionally have caused damage to the shipper's goods. *Id.* at 1175. Even when a carrier has engaged in "gross negligence or recklessness," such behavior does not constitute an unreasonable deviation. *Id.*

[30] Lozen concedes that the initial misrouting of its containers was an accident and that this error alone did not constitute an unreasonable deviation. See *Vistar, S.A. v. M/V Sea-Land Express,* 792 F.2d 469, 472 (5th Cir.1986) (holding that there was no unreasonable deviation in the absence of evidence that a truck driver "intentionally and deliberately deviated from the instructed route"). Instead, Lozen argues that CSX's behavior *after discovering the error* was an unreasonable deviation. It asserts that Sea-Land attempted to minimize the delay caused by the misrouting error, but that CSX deliberately refused to cooperate despite its knowledge of the damaging consequences. According to Lozen, CSX's inaction amounted to intentional causation of damage and, accordingly, constituted an unreasonable deviation.

[31] In Exhibit 4, an internal company e-mail, one of Sea-Land's employees admitted:

> I got with CSX to see if we could get containers taken from the train. . . . I'm not sure why CSX decided to rail them. Had we been able to truck these units, we could've made the vessel. . . . [W]e had plenty of time to get these units, had CSX allowed us to get our hands on them as we asked (repeatedly). I kept telling Lisa Tapley that these units were vessel protected loads, and they had to make the vessel. There was no ambiguity in my needs, with regards these units. It comes down to me wanting to truck these units, from Syracuse, as our recovery plan, but CSX, in their infinite wisdom, decided not to allow us to do this. This is totally, and completely a CSX failure.

---

7. Clauses Three and Four are the "liberty clauses." Clause Three in Sea-Land's bills of lading states: "Carrier shall have the right, without notice, to substitute or employ a vessel, watercraft, or other means rather than the vessel named herein to perform all or part of the carriage." Clause Four states: "Goods shut out or not loaded on a vessel for any reason can be forwarded on a subsequent vessel or by feederships, lighters, aircraft, trucks, trains or other means in addition to the ocean vessel, or its substitute, to accomplish the carriage herein."

[32] Sea-Land also wrote a letter to Lozen, stating in part:

> We are very disappointed in the unfortunate delay caused by the rail and our inability to get cooperation from the rail operators. While we did track and trace these reefer loads most diligently, the railroad failed to follow our instructions and deramp the loads so we could truck them the rest of the way to Elizabeth port.

Together, these two communications permit a reasonable finder of fact to infer that CSX intentionally caused the damage that Lozen suffered. There is, therefore, a genuine issue of fact as to whether CSX committed an unreasonable deviation.

[33] For this reason, the "liberty clauses" in Sea-Land's bills of lading cannot unequivocally insulate the company from liability. Although these provisions are generally enforceable "transship clauses," a liability limitation in a bill of lading is unenforceable to the extent that it authorizes the carrier to engage in an unreasonable deviation. *Yang Mach. Tool Co. v. Sea-Land Serv., Inc.*, 58 F.3d 1350, 1353 (9th Cir.1995). Because there is a genuine issue of fact as to whether Sea-Land's behavior constituted an unreasonable deviation, summary judgment was not appropriate.

Notes and Questions

1. The average lawyer may find the outcome of this dispute surprising. First, the carrier did not provide the shipper/customer with their general terms and instead relied on the customer's familiarity with industry customs and practices. Second, the carrier's agent made the crucial mistake that caused the shipment to miss the intended boat and be delayed by a week. Up to now, the court would absolutely have affirmed the decision that the carrier has no liability, based on the liberty clauses in its general terms. What do you think of these "liberty clauses" in this regard? Should a party to a contract be able to include this level of "liberty"? Why or why not? Are shipping contracts, historically speaking, special in this regard? If so, is this special treatment still warranted in the twenty-first century? Why or why not?

2. The balance was only tipped in favor of the shipper by another crucial factor: Once the mistake was discovered, the carrier's agent knowingly and deliberately obstructed any attempts to minimize the damage. This will rarely happen in practice and, if it does happen, the shipper may never be able to prove it. What are the options for the shipper to protect herself against mistakes by the carrier or his agents that lead to substantial delay without giving any recourse against the carrier? Could the shipper ask for different terms in the BoL or Sea Waybill? What would happen if she did? Could the shipper buy insurance against delay? What does a normal cargo insurance contract cover and what does it not cover? What other options might the shipper have?

3. Can Sea-Land recover from CSX? What would the legal basis for such an action have to be?

Case 4-2

Insurance Co. of North America v. M/V Ocean Lynx

901 F.2d 934 (11th Cir. 1990)
(Paragraph numbers added.)
Before Johnson, Hill and Henley, Senior Circuit Judges

I. Facts

A. Background

[2] Educational Innovation Systems International, Inc. ("Edusystems") shipped 59 boxes of vocational and agricultural equipment to Asuncion, Paraguay on May 9, 1985. Through a freight forwarder in Miami, Meadows Wye and Company ("Meadows"), Edusystems entered into a contract with Mar, which is a non-vessel-operating common carrier, for transportation of the cargo from Miami to Paraguay. Mar, acting as Edusystems' agent, entered into a carriage contract with Bottacchi for shipment of the cargo from Miami to Buenos Aires, Argentina. Bottacchi loaded the cargo onto the M/V Ocean Lynx, a vessel chartered by Bottacchi and owned by Nabadi Maritime, S.A. On June 7, 1985, the Ocean Lynx encountered rough weather, and the container holding the cargo was lost at sea.

[3] Both Mar and Bottacchi supplied bills of lading. The Mar bill of lading consists of one piece of paper. The front identifies the parties and contains a block where the shipping cost is calculated. The back contains twenty-seven clauses in extremely fine print. Clause one states that the carriage contract is subject to COGSA, and clause sixteen recites provisions of COGSA section 4(5), 46 U.S.C.A. App. § 1304(5), limiting Mar's liability for loss to $500 per package. Clause sixteen states,

> In case of any loss or damage to or in connection with the goods exceeding $500.00 . . . the value of the goods shall be deemed to be $500.00 per package . . . unless the nature of the goods and a valuation higher than $500.00 shall have been declared in writing by the shipper upon delivery to the carrier and inserted in this bill of lading and extra freight paid if required . . . [in which case] the carrier's liability, if any, shall not exceed the declared value. . . .

The Bottacchi bill of lading states that it binds the owner of the cargo and that it supersedes all other agreements covering the shipment. The back of the bill of lading is also in fine print and contains provisions identical to the Mar bill of lading.

[4] Mar had filed a tariff with the Federal Maritime Commission. The tariff included a copy of Mar's bill of lading. Rule Twelve of the tariff provided for a declaration of increased valuation that would increase Mar's liability beyond $500 per package. In case of a declaration of excess value, Mar's tariff provided for additional freight charges. Bottacchi also had filed a tariff with the Federal Maritime Commission. Rule Twelve, "Ad Valorem Rates," states that "[a]n ad valorem or 2% value to be

declared on bill of lading, shall be assessed on the following: Currency, Specie, Gold or Silver Bullion, Precious Metals N.O.S., and Negotiable Securities. Minimum bill of lading charge — $101.50."

[5] Edusystems' freight forwarder, Meadows, and Mar's freight forwarder, Continental, had dealt with one another on numerous occasions. Meadows has acted as freight forwarder for Edusystems hundreds of times. On none of these occasions did Edusystems' representative declare the value of a shipment and pay added freight charges.

B. Proceedings in the District Court

[6] On March 28, 1986, Edusystems' insurer, Insurance Company of North America (the "plaintiff"), filed a complaint against the M/V Ocean Lynx, in rem, Mar, Bottacchi, and Nabadi Maritime, S.A., claiming $244,820 in damages for the lost cargo. Mar and Bottacchi answered asserting that their liability was limited to $500 per package under COGSA. Mar also filed a cross-claim against Bottacchi for Mar's damages, interest and costs in the action. . . .

[8] The district court held a bench trial on September 8–9, 1987. The court found that under COGSA section 4(5) Mar's and Bottacchi's liability was limited to $500 per package lost. The court rejected the plaintiff's argument that Mar's bill of lading was illegible and therefore did not invoke COGSA section 4(5)'s limitation on liability. The court found that the print on the back of the Mar bill of lading appeared blurry, but stated that "[w]ith the aid of a magnifying glass . . . most of the words and numerals can be read by a party examining the words and conditions stated therein." Nevertheless, the court found that the Mar bill of lading was sufficient to incorporate COGSA section 4(5)'s limitation of liability.

[9] The court also rejected the plaintiff's argument that COGSA section 4(5) did not apply because Mar and Bottacchi did not present Edusystems with an opportunity to declare the cargo's value. The court stated that incorporation of COGSA in the bills of lading provided a fair opportunity to declare excess value as a matter of law. The court also found that Mar's tariff was valid and presented the plaintiff with an opportunity to declare the cargo's value. Accordingly, the district court entered judgment for the plaintiff against Mar for $29,500 on the plaintiff's complaint and judgment for Mar against Bottacchi for $29,500 on Mar's cross-claim.

[10] On January 8, 1988, Mar moved to recover attorneys' fees and costs from Bottacchi for defending against the plaintiff's claim and to recover costs from the plaintiff. Mar claimed that it was entitled to attorneys' fees from Bottacchi for defending the main claim because it was an indemnitee of Bottacchi. . . .

[12] In this appeal, we first consider whether the district court erred in holding that Mar and Bottacchi have limited liability under COGSA section 4(5). Second, we consider whether the district court erred in holding that Mar could recover attorneys' fees from Bottacchi for the cost of defending against the plaintiff's claim. . . .

III. Analysis

A. Limited Liability

[14] COGSA section 4(5) provides as follows:

> Neither the carrier nor the ship shall in any event become liable for any
> loss or damage to or in connection with the transportation of goods in an
> amount exceeding $500 per package . . . unless the nature and value of such
> goods have been declared by the shipper before shipment and inserted in
> the bill of lading. 46 U.S.C.A. App. § 1304(5).

Congress enacted the COGSA limitation on liability in 1936 in order to restrain the
superior bargaining power wielded by carriers over shippers by setting a reasonable
limitation on liability that the carriers could not reduce by contract. *Sony Magnetic
Prods., Inc. v. Merivienti O/Y*, 863 F.2d 1537, 1542 (11th Cir.1989).

[15] Courts have developed two preconditions to invoking COGSA section 4(5)'s
limitation on liability. First, the carrier must give the shipper adequate notice of
the $500 limitation by including a "clause paramount" in the bill of lading that
expressly adopts the provisions of COGSA. *Brown & Root, Inc. v. M/V Peisander*,
648 F.2d 415, 420 (5th Cir.1981); *General Elec. Co. v. MV Nedlloyd*, 817 F.2d 1022,
1029 (2d Cir.1987); 46 U.S.C.A. App. § 131246 U.S.C.A. App. § 1312. Second, the carrier must give the shipper a fair opportunity to avoid COGSA section 4(5)'s limitation by declaring excess value. *Brown & Root*, 648 F.2d at 420 & n. 11; *General Elec.*,
817 F.2d at 1028.

[16] The clause paramount establishes three things. First, it makes COGSA applicable
at times when it would not apply of its own force. *Brown & Root*, 648 F.2d at 420.
Second, COGSA's provisions are deemed incorporated into the bill of lading. *Id.*
Third, nothing in the bill of lading can increase the carrier's liability under COGSA,
which overrules any clause in the bill of lading that conflicts with COGSA. *Id.*

[17] The *Brown & Root* court discussed what is necessary for a carrier to meet the
second precondition to invoking COGSA section 4(5)'s limitation on liability: that
the carrier afford an opportunity for the shipper to declare excess value. In *Brown
& Root*, the carrier had included a clause paramount in its bill of lading. The bill of
lading, however, also included a clause stating that "in no case" would the liability
of the carrier exceed $500. Moreover, the bill of lading contained no blank space
where the shipper could write in excess valuation. Nevertheless, the court found
that the shipper had an opportunity to declare excess valuation for two reasons:

> First, COGSA was expressly incorporated in the bill of lading to thereby
> bring into play § 4(5). Next, and far more significantly, the published tar-
> iff which has the effect of law very carefully gave [the s]hipper a choice of
> valuations by a choice of precisely definable freight rates. *Id.* at 424 (cita-
> tions omitted).

Brown & Root thus adopted a system of constructive notice of an opportunity to
declare excess valuation. *Id.* Either a clause paramount in the bill of lading or a valid

tariff filed with the Federal Maritime Commission that includes an opportunity to declare excess value according to COGSA section 4(5)'s provisions is sufficient to afford the shipper an opportunity to declare excess value. *Brown & Root*, 648 F.2d at 424.

[18] In the present case, the plaintiff first argues that the Mar bill of lading was illegible and therefore did not provide shippers with notice of COGSA section 4(5)'s limitation on liability. The plaintiff also argues that Bottacchi's tariff failed to provide shippers with an opportunity to declare excess value.

1. Mar's Bill of Lading

[19] The district court found that the back of Mar's bill of lading, which contained a clause paramount and a clause reciting COGSA section 4(5), could not be read without the aid of a magnifying glass. In *Nemeth v. General S.S. Corp.*, 694 F.2d 609, 611–12 (9th Cir.1982), the Ninth Circuit held that "microscopic" print on a bill of lading was insufficient to give the shipper a fair opportunity to avoid COGSA section 4(5). This holding is persuasive; print that cannot be read with the naked eye can hardly impart notice. In the present case, however, Meadows, Edusystems' agent, maintained multiple copies of the Mar master bill of lading in its files, and yet Meadows' representative, Albert Fabrikant, testified that in preparing hundreds of bills of lading for Edusystems he had never read the provisions on the reverse side. Meadows certainly had an opportunity to read these copies of Mar's bill of lading. Accordingly, the plaintiff's argument that Edusystems was not afforded an opportunity to avoid COGSA section 4(5)'s limitation of liability lacks merit. . . .

[20] The plaintiff also fails to address the district court's holding that Edusystems did not desire to avoid COGSA section 4(5)'s limitation on liability by opting for a higher freight charge. The court found that Edusystems had chosen to rely on its policy with the plaintiff to cover any losses. In *General Elec.*, the Second Circuit ruled that where the shipper was experienced and the record showed that the shipper had never taken any steps toward actually declaring excess value, the court would not allow the shipper to challenge the adequacy of its opportunity to declare excess value. *General Elec.*, 817 F.2d at 1029. Similarly, in the present case, Edusystems had made hundreds of shipments with Mar without ever inquiring into declaring excess value. Under these circumstances it is reasonable to conclude that Edusystems did not wish to insure against losses twice and chose to rely on its policy with the plaintiff.

2. Bottacchi's Tariff

[21] Rule 12 of Bottacchi's tariff provides that an ad valorem rate shall be applied to shipments of certain commodities. It does not provide for the method through which a shipper of goods other than the listed commodities can avoid COGSA section 4(5)'s limitation on liability. Bottacchi's bill of lading, however, does contain a clause paramount invoking the provisions of COGSA, and clause sixteen of Bottacchi's bill of lading recites the provisions of COGSA section 4(5). In *Brown & Root*, the court found that such a clause was sufficient to give the shipper constructive

notice of a fair opportunity to declare excess value. "COGSA was expressly incorporated into the bill of lading to thereby bring into play §4(5)." *Brown & Root*, 648 F.2d at 424. Once COGSA was incorporated, the court held, the provisions of COGSA section 4(5) spelled out how a shipper could declare excess value, and the burden was on the shipper to declare excess value. *Id.* at 425.

> COGSA §4(5) does not prescribe that the face of the bill of lading contain a specific space or blank in which the increased valuation is to be inserted nor does it provide that the carrier rather than the shipper must actually make the notation. The phrase "unless the nature and value of such goods have been declared by the shipper before shipment and inserted into the bill of lading" [, COGSA §4(5),] clearly puts the burden on the shipper to make the determination as between value limitations and the making of the declarations. *Id.* at 424.

Accordingly, the plaintiff's argument based on Bottacchi's tariff lacks merit.

B. Attorneys' Fees

1. Indemnity Action

[22] Bottacchi argues that the district court erred in awarding attorneys' fees to Mar for defending against the plaintiff's claim. Bottacchi argues that Mar's claim is governed by COGSA, which does not provide for attorneys' fees, and therefore under the American Rule Mar cannot recover attorneys' fees. Mar argues that it was Bottacchi's indemnitee and therefore can recover attorneys' fees expended in defending against the plaintiff's claim.

[23] Congress has not explicitly provided for the award of attorneys' fees in COGSA actions. *Noritake Co. v. M/V Hellenic Champion*, 627 F.2d 724, 730 (5th Cir. Unit A 1980). In admiralty cases, moreover, the general rule is that attorneys' fees are not awarded. *Plataro Ltd. v. Unidentified Remains of a Vessel*, 695 F.2d 893, 905 (5th Cir.1983). In the case of an indemnitee, however, the indemnitee can recover attorneys' fees from his indemnitor as part of the reasonable expenses of defending a claim. See *Cotten v. Two "R" Drilling Co.*, 508 F.2d 669, 671 (5th Cir.1975); *Noritake*, 627 F.2d at 724 n. 5; see also *Maseda v. Honda Motor Co.*, 861 F.2d 1248, 1256 (11th Cir.1988) (Florida law); *Nitram, Inc. v. Cretan Life*, 599 F.2d 1359, 1372 (5th Cir. 1979).

[24] Bottacchi claims that the present case was not an indemnity action, pointing to the form of the district court's judgment, which did not use the term "indemnity." Bottacchi also argues that COGSA provided Mar's exclusive remedy in this case, and that therefore Mar's case could not have been one for indemnification. Mar argues that the pre-trial order in this case stipulated that indemnification was an issue, and that the district court's February 22, 1989 order found that Mar was an indemnitee.

[25] Mar's cross-claim against Bottacchi stated a prima facie case under COGSA. The joint pre-trial stipulation of Mar and Bottacchi, however, stated that Mar "would

claim reasonable attorney's fees against A. Bottacchi, S.A. pursuant to [Mar's] cross claim for indemnity." The pre-trial order controls the future course of the action, and Mar was not required to amend the pleadings to reflect the indemnity issue. *Feazell v. Tropicana Prods.*, Inc., 819 F.2d 1036, 1040 (11th Cir.1987) (pre-trial stipulation); Fed.R.Civ.P. 16(e); 3 J. Moore, *Moore's Federal Practice* ¶ 16.12 (2d ed. 1989).

[26] The real parties in interest in this case were the plaintiff and Bottacchi, and any claims recoverable by the plaintiff against Mar also would have been recoverable by Mar against Bottacchi. Mar's expenditures defending the main claim, moreover, benefitted Bottacchi by limiting Bottacchi's liability. Under these circumstances, we hold that Mar was an indemnitee of Bottacchi and can recover attorneys' fees. . . .

2. Attorneys' Fees and COGSA Section 4(5)

[27] Bottacchi also argues that Mar's attorneys' fees are part of Mar's overall damages in this case and therefore limited by COGSA section 4(5). Mar argues that attorneys' fees are excluded from the calculation of general damages under COGSA, and that therefore attorneys' fees do not fall under the $500 per package limitation that is applied to damages under COGSA. The district court found that the language in clause sixteen of Bottacchi's bill of lading, which recited provisions of COGSA section 4(5), was distinguishable from "red letter" clauses limiting liability for "any claim." The court found that

> [c]lause sixteen attempts to do no more than protect a carrier against exposure to substantial liability for the loss of highly valuable cargo when the shipper has not declared the higher value and paid an additional freight charge on it. For this reason, clause sixteen does not operate as a red-letter clause.

[28] The district court's interpretation of COGSA section 4(5) is correct. The statute does not purport to include all types of claims in the $500-per-package limitation. Cf. *Noritake*, 627 F.2d at 729 (awarding pre-judgment interest in a COGSA action). Accordingly, Mar's attorneys' fee claims are not limited by COGSA section 4(5).

Notes and Questions

1. When analyzing a case like this one, with multiple parties making claims against each other, be sure to make a relationship chart to identify who is who and who is whose agent or representative.

2. Why did the district court award US$29,500, when the liability is limited to US$500 per package and only one container went overboard? Check the following decision in *Monica Textile* for the answer.

3. What do you think of the analysis of the legislative intent underpinning the adoption of COGSA in 1936 (see para. 14)? What is the "bargaining power" relationship between carriers and shippers today? What about the idea that carriers should not be able to limit their liability *below* US$500 per package? What is the real problem with carrier liability today? Does any of this suggest that it might be time

for an update to COGSA? If so, why and how would you update the law? Could this be done by Congress without any action on U.S. status as a signatory of the Hague Rules?

4. What does the court mean in paragraph 20 when it declares that the shipper could have declared a higher value to escape the US$500 limit of COGSA but "did not wish to insure against losses twice"?

5. On attorney fees, the defendant/carrier tries to argue, *inter alia*, that any reimbursement of attorney fees is part of the overall damages limited by COGSA to US$500. Based on the decision of the court, can you see scenarios in which this argument would succeed?

6. What is meant by "the American Rule" in paragraph 22? Check Part Six pp. 786 and 1038 for the answer.

Case 4-3

Monica Textile Co. v. S.S. Tana et al.

952 F.2d 636 (2d Cir. 1991)
(Paragraph numbers added.)
Before Kearse, Pratt and Mclaughlin, Circuit Judges

Opinion

[1] We are (once again) presented with "the latest skirmish in the age old war between shippers and carriers over their respective rights and liabilities." *Matsushita Elec. Corp. v. S.S. Aegis Spirit*, 414 F.Supp. 894, 897 (W.D.Wash.1976). This case requires us to revisit the issue whether a massive shipping container is a "package" for purposes of the $500 per-package limitation on liability of the Carriage of Goods by Sea Act ("COGSA"), 46 U.S.C.App. § 1304(5).

[2] Holding that the single shipping container was the relevant COGSA package, the district court entered a $500 judgment for the shipper. We now reverse and hold that each of the 76 bales of cloth stowed inside the container is a separate package for COGSA purposes.

Background

[3] Monica Textile Corporation ("Monica" or the "shipper") engaged the defendants-carriers to transport a single 20-foot shipping container from Africa to Savannah, Georgia. The parties' bill of lading disclosed that the container, which Monica had stuffed and sealed, held 76 bales of cotton cloth. The goods were damaged in transit and Monica brought suit in the District Court for the Southern District of New York (Sand, J.) to recover for the loss.

[4] The carriers moved for partial summary judgment limiting their liability to $500 pursuant to COGSA's liability limitation provision, 46 U.S.C.App. § 1304(5). The district court initially denied the motion, holding "that where the bill of lading prepared by the carrier's agent discloses a specific number of identifiable units as the

contents of the container, those units [the bales of cloth] constitute the package" for purposes of COGSA's limitation on liability. *Monica Textile Corp. v. S.S. Tana*, 731 F.Supp. 124, 127 (S.D.N.Y.1990) [*"Monica I"*].

[5] Shortly thereafter, this court decided *Seguros "Illimani" S.A. v. M/V Popi P*, 929 F.2d 89 (2d Cir.1991), which held that for COGSA purposes the number of packages specified in the "No. of Pkgs." column of the bill of lading is generally controlling. *Id.* at 94. In the present case, though the "DESCRIPTION OF GOODS" column of the bill of lading stated that the contents of the container consisted of 76 bales of cotton cloth, the "No. of Pkgs." column of the bill of lading had the number "1" typed in, and a line labeled "Total Number of Packages or Units in Words (Total Column 19 [No. of Pkgs. column])," had the word "ONE" typed in. In light of these facts, Judge Sand permitted the carriers to renew their summary judgment motion to limit their liability to $500, and the district court reversed itself, holding that our intervening decision in *Seguros* compelled a finding that the single container, rather than the 76 bales stowed therein, was the relevant COGSA package. See *Monica Textile Corp. v. S.S. Tana*, 765 F.Supp. 1194, 1195-96 (S.D.N.Y.1991) [*"Monica II"*]. Because the carriers conceded liability, the district court entered judgment for Monica in the amount of $500.

[6] Monica appeals the judgment of the district court, maintaining that the 76 individual bales of cloth, not the solitary shipping container, were the appropriate COGSA packages. We agree and therefore reverse the judgment of the district court.

Discussion

[7] The district court reversed itself in *Monica II* on the basis of *Seguros*, which it read

> as establishing a bright-line rule for determining the number of COGSA packages from the bill of lading. The number of packages is the number appearing in the "No. of Pkgs." column of the bill, unless other evidence of the parties' intent plainly contradicts the applicability of that number, or unless the item referred to by that number is incapable of qualifying as a COGSA package. *Monica II*, 765 F.Supp. at 1195-96.

The district court's characterization of the *Seguros* rule is accurate, as far as it goes. *Seguros*, however, involved 600 separate steel-strapped bundles, each containing 15 tin ingots. The issue therefore was whether there were 600 "packages" or 9,000 (600 × 15) "packages". Most significantly, our *Seguros* decision did not purport to apply to containers, and the district court's application of the *Seguros* rule to the container context was erroneous. An understanding of the "container" cases is necessary to appreciate our present holding that *Seguros* should not be extended to containers.

The Container Cases

[8] Long before COGSA was enacted, industrialized nations recognized the need to reconcile the desire of carriers to limit their potential liability with their vastly

superior bargaining power over shippers. See H.R.Rep. No. 2218, 74th Cong., 2d Sess. 6–9 (1936); *Mitsui & Co. v. America Export Lines, Inc.*, 636 F.2d 807, 814-15 (2d Cir.1981); Comment, Containerization, the Per Package Limitation, and the Concept of "Fair Opportunity," 11 Mar.Law. 123, 124 (1986). The nations at the Brussels Convention of 1924 balanced these competing concerns with a per-package limitation on liability. See International Convention for the Unification of Certain Rules Relating to Bills of Lading, Aug. 25, 1924, 51 Stat. 233, 120 L.N.T.S. 155 (1931-32), reprinted in A. Knauth, *The American Law of Ocean Bills of Lading* 37-72 (4th ed. 1953); Note, *Defining "Package" in the Carriage of Goods by Sea Act*, 60 Tex.L.Rev. 961, 964–66 (1982). The principles established by the Brussels Convention [the Hague Rules,] became the template for COGSA. See *Robert C. Herd & Co. v. Krawill Mach. Corp.*, 359 U.S. 297, 301, 79 S.Ct. 766, 769, 3 L.Ed.2d 820 (1959) ("[t]he legislative history of the Act shows that it was lifted almost bodily from the Hague Rules of 1921, as amended by the Brussels Convention of 1924").

[9] Unhappily, neither the statute nor its legislative history provides any clue as to the meaning of "package" in the Act. See *Aluminios Pozuelo Ltd. v. S.S. Navigator*, 407 F.2d 152, 154 (2d Cir. 1968). Despite the difficulties this lack of guidance engendered, courts managed to muddle through this oft-litigated issue by generally deferring to the intent of the contracting parties when that intent was both clear and reasonable. This intent-approach later became strained by technological advances in the shipping industry. Indeed, "[f]ew, if any, in 1936 could have foreseen the change in the optimum size of shipping units. . . ." *Standard Electrica, S.A. v. Hamburg Sudamerikanische Dampfschifffahrts-Gesellschaft*, 375 F.2d 943, 945 (2d Cir.), cert. denied, 389 U.S. 831, 88 S.Ct. 97, 19 L.Ed.2d 89 (1967). Compare, e.g., *Hartford Fire Ins. Co. v. Pacific Far East Line, Inc.*, 491 F.2d 960, 965 (9th Cir.) (holding that 18-ton electrical transformer bolted to a skid was not a COGSA package), cert. denied, 419 U.S. 873, 95 S.Ct. 134, 42 L.Ed.2d 112 (1974) with *Aluminios Pozuelo Ltd. v. S.S. Navigator*, 407 F.2d 152, 155 (2d Cir.1968) (holding that a 3-ton toggle press bolted to a skid was a COGSA package). See generally *id.* at 154-56 (discussing pre-container cases).

[10] We first addressed COGSA's application to shipping innovations in *Standard Electrica*, which required us to determine which was the relevant COGSA package: each 60-pound carton or the pallets on which the cartons were bound together. Divining the parties' intent, we held the pallet to be the relevant COGSA package. See *id.* at 946.

[11] The so-called "container revolution", however, "added a new dimension to the problem." *Mitsui*, 636 F.2d at 816. See generally Schmeltzer & Peavy, *Prospects and Problems of the Container Revolution*, 1 J.Mar.L. & Com. 203 (1970). Shippers, carriers and industry commentators "speculated at the time whether the courts would adopt the analysis of Standard Electrica or fashion a new rule to apply to containers." Note, *The Shipping Container as a COGSA Package: The Functional Economics Test is Abandoned*, 6 Mar.Law. 336, 340 n. 16 (1981) (collecting citations). Our decision in *Leather's Best, Inc. v. S.S. Mormaclynx*, 451 F.2d 800 (2d Cir.1971) (Friendly,

C.J.), settled the issue, distinguishing *Standard Electrica* and veering away from our pre-container cases because of our

> belief that the purpose of §4(5) of COGSA was to set a reasonable figure below which the carrier should not be permitted to limit his liability and that "package" is thus more sensibly related to the unit in which the shipper packed the goods and described them than to a large metal object, functionally a part of the ship, in which the carrier caused them to be "contained." . . .

Leather's Best thus stood foursquare for the proposition "that a container rarely should be treated as a package." *Smythgreyhound v. M/V "Eurygenes"*, 666 F.2d 746, 748 n. 5 (2d Cir.1981) (quoting *Croft & Scully Co. v. M/V Skulptor Vuchetich*, 508 F. Supp. 670, 678 (S.D.Tex.1981), aff'd in relevant part, 664 F.2d 1277 (5th Cir.1982)).

[12] Although other courts subsequently embraced Leather's Best, see, e.g., *Matsushita Elec. Corp. v. S.S. Aegis Spirit*, 414 F.Supp. 894, 907 (W.D.Wash.1976), cited with approval in *Mitsui*, 636 F.2d at 819-20, we began to stray from it, in favor of a so-called "functional economics test." Whereas *Leather's Best* held that treating a container as a COGSA package is inconsistent with congressional intent and therefore strongly disfavored, see *Leather's Best*, 451 F.2d at 815; accord *Mitsui*, 636 F.2d at 820-21, the functional economics approach ignored congressional intent in favor of a "law and economics" analysis. See, e.g., *Royal Typewriter Co. v. M/V Kulmerland*, 483 F.2d 645, 648-49 (2d Cir.1973) (container is presumptively the package where the units inside are not suitable for breakbulk shipment); *Cameco, Inc. v. S.S. American Legion*, 514 F.2d 1291, 1298-99 (2d Cir.1974).

[13] The reaction to our functional economics approach was swift and overwhelmingly negative, as courts and commentators roundly criticized us for it. See *Croft & Scully Co. v. M/V Skulptor Vuchetich*, 664 F.2d 1277, 1281 n. 10 (5th Cir.1982) (functional economics test "necessitated much judicial guessing work, and we are well rid of it"); *Allstate Ins. Co. v. Inversiones Navieras Imparca, C.A.*, 646 F.2d 169, 172 (5th Cir. Unit B May 1981) (test "was subject to severe criticism from all corners"); *Matsushita*, 414 F.Supp. at 906 (rejecting the test "as contrary to the statute, commercially impracticable and unwise"); DeOrchis, *The Container and the Package Limitation—The Search for Predictability*, 5 J.Mar.L. & Com. 251, 257 (1974); Simon, *The Law of Shipping Containers* (pt. 1), 5 J.Mar.L. & Com. 507, 522 (1974).

[14] Recognizing that the functional economics test was "basically inconsistent with the holding of *Leather's Best*," and acknowledging the criticism the new approach had drawn, we eventually abandoned it. See *Mitsui*, 636 F.2d at 818-21. Judge Friendly, who had earlier written *Leather's Best*, also authored the *Mitsui* decision, and circulated it to the entire court. *Mitsui* held that when a bill of lading discloses on its face what is inside the container, and those contents may reasonably be considered COGSA packages, then the container is not the COGSA package. See *id.*; *Smythgreyhound*, 666 F.2d at 753. *Mitsui* settled the law in container cases for this Circuit and has been steadfastly followed. . . .

[15] Although Mitsui was concerned with containers, a district court later extended it to pallets. See *Allied Int'l Am. Eagle Trading Corp. v. S.S. "Yang Ming"*, 519 F.Supp. 187, 190 (S.D.N.Y.1981), rev'd, 672 F.2d 1055 (2d Cir.1982). We reversed, holding that containers and pallets are quite different and that "Standard Electrica . . . is still the law with regard to pallets." *Yang Ming*, 672 F.2d at 1061. In so doing, we methodically documented why our decisions in *Standard Electrica* and *Leather's Best* required distinct analyses for container and non-container cases. See id. at 1058-61. We explained:

> [T]he container cases involve factors not found in pallet cases. Because of their size and their function in the shipping industry, containers are ordinarily not considered "packages." . . . .
>
> . . . In Mitsui . . . as in other container cases, the courts must look askance at an agreement which purports to define a container as a "package" because the results of such a limitation can be ludicrous. *Id.* at 1061, 1062.

[16] We thus rejected any notion that container and non-container cases were interchangeable; they were then and remain now separate lines of authority. They had been uniformly so construed until the present case. See, e.g., *St. Paul Fire & Marine Ins. Co. v. Sea-Land Serv., Inc.*, 735 F.Supp. 129, 133 (S.D.N.Y.1990) ("containers present different considerations than pallets"); E. Flynn & G. Raduazzo, *Benedict on Admiralty* § 167, at 16-28 (7th ed. 1991) ("These standards [for determining the relevant COGSA package] vary according to whether or not the cargo is shipped in a container, and the discussion here will therefore treat non-containerized and containerized shipments separately.").

Seguros "Illimani"

[17] We now turn to *Monica II's* application of our *Seguros* decision. The dispute in *Seguros* was whether each bundle of 15 tin ingots, or each individual ingot, constituted the relevant COGSA package. See *Seguros "Illimani" S.A. v. M/V Popi P*, 929 F.2d 89, 92 (2d Cir.1991). We therefore adopted the following test to settle such controversies:

> The number appearing under the heading "NO. OF PKGS." is our starting point for determining the number of packages for purposes of the COGSA per-package limitation, and unless the significance of that number is plainly contradicted by contrary evidence of the parties' intent, or unless the number refers to items that cannot qualify as "packages," it is also the ending point of our inquiry. "Package" is a term of art in the ocean shipping business, and parties to bills of lading should expect to be held to the number that appears under a column whose heading so unmistakably refers to the number of packages. Seguros, 929 F.2d at 94.

As between bales, boxes, bundles, cartons, cases, crates and other COGSA packages, the Seguros rule is as sensible as it is straightforward. But all "packages" were not created equal, as our container cases make plain. Containers raise unique issues which we have addressed in a distinct line of case law.

[18] In light of our significant container jurisprudence, the *Seguros* rule is inapposite in the container context. In *Seguros*, the parties disputed whether the ingots or the bundles containing the ingots should be considered the relevant COGSA packages. No one even questioned the district court's holding that "[i]t is clear that the container is not the appropriate 'package' in this case." *Seguros "Illimani" S.A. v. M/V Popi P*, 735 F.Supp. 108, 111 (S.D.N.Y.1990), aff'd, 929 F.2d 89 (2d Cir.1991). Viewed in context, then, *Seguros* simply does not purport to apply when a container is alleged to be the relevant COGSA package. Indeed, that *Seguros* would, in dictum, overrule sub silentio a long line of Second Circuit precedent is inconceivable. Notwithstanding the insertion in the number-of-packages column(s) of the bill of lading of a number reflecting the number of containers, where the bill of lading discloses on its face what is inside the container(s) and those contents may reasonably be considered COGSA packages, the latter, not the container(s), are the COGSA packages. The district court's holding to the contrary in *Monica II* is erroneous.

Parties' Intent and Bill of Lading

[19] We next consider the carriers' argument that the bill of lading manifests the parties' agreement that the container is the relevant COGSA package.

[20] In non-container cases we have generally deferred to the parties' intent, as manifested by their bill of lading, in determining what unit is the relevant COGSA package. See, e.g., *Seguros*, 929 F.2d at 95; *Standard Electrica*, 375 F.2d at 946. Such deference to the parties' wishes permits commercial flexibility without offending the statute.

[21] COGSA, however, requires that we view container cases through a different prism. Thus, in container cases we must "'take a critical look'" at clauses purporting to define the container as the COGSA package, *Smythgreyhound*, 666 F.2d at 750 (quoting *Mitsui*, 636 F.2d at 815). Accordingly, we have consistently cast a jaundiced eye upon language purporting to embody such an agreement.

[22] The reason for this skepticism is that such agreements run against the grain of COGSA. See *id.; Binladen*, 759 F.2d at 1012-13 ("classification of [the container] as a 'package' would violate the purpose of §4(5) by permitting the carrier to limit its liability unduly"); *Yang Ming*, 672 F.2d at 1062 ("the courts must look askance at an agreement which purports to define a container as a 'package'"); *Mitsui*, 636 F.2d at 817 (*Leather's Best* "acknowledg[ed] that treating the containers as packages . . . was precluded by the underlying purpose of [COGSA] §4(5)"). Thus, "our repeatedly-expressed reluctance for sound reasons to treat a container as a package", *Binladen*, 759 F.2d at 1015, compels us to scrutinize the carriers' claim that they agreed with Monica to treat the container as the COGSA package.

[23] The bill of lading in this case discloses on its face that 76 bales of cloth were stowed in the container. Even though that disclosure triggers *Mitsui's* presumption that the container is not the COGSA package, see *Mitsui*, 636 F.2d at 821; see also *Smythgreyhound*, 666 F.2d at 752 ("[*Mitsui*] adopted a general rule that where the bill of lading discloses the contents of the container, then the container is not the

COGSA package.") (brackets in original), the carriers maintain that the bill of lading nevertheless discloses an agreement with Monica that the single container was the relevant package.

[24] They emphasize two clauses appearing on the reverse of the carriers' standard bill of lading forms.[3] Clause 2 of the bill of lading provides, in relevant part:

> The word "package" shall include each container where the container is stuffed and sealed by the Merchant or on his behalf, although the Shipper may have furnished in the Particulars herein the contents of such sealed container. (See Clause 11).

Clause 11 states:

> Neither the Carrier nor the vessel shall in any event be or become liable for any loss or damage to or in connection with the transportation of goods in an amount exceeding U.S. $500 per package. . . . Where container(s) is stuffed by Shipper or on his behalf, and the container is sealed, the Carrier's liability will be limited to U.S. $500 with respect to the contents of each container, except when the Shipper declares value on the face hereof (Box 26) and pays additional charges on such declared value (Box 23). The freight charged on sealed containers when no higher valuation is declared by the Shipper is based on a value of U.S. $500 per container.

The carriers maintain that these clauses articulate an agreement between them and Monica to treat the container as the package.

[25] The carriers' argument is premised on dicta in our container cases suggesting that parties to a bill of lading have the right to agree to treat a container as the relevant COGSA package. For example, in *Smythgreyhound*, we remarked in a footnote that parties may

> agree between themselves that the container will be the COGSA "package," especially in cases where COGSA does not apply *ex proprio vigore*. . . . [W]e hold today that in the absence of clear and unambiguous language indicating agreement on the definition of "package," then we will conclusively presume that the container is not the package where the bill of lading discloses the container's contents. Smythgreyhound, 666 F.2d at 753 n. 20 (emphasis in original).

Thus, the otherwise "clear rule that where the contents of the container are disclosed in the bill of lading then the container is not the COGSA package", *id.* at 753, seemingly has an exception: we will treat the container as the "package" if the bill of lading discloses that the parties have so agreed in terms that are explicit and unequivocal.

---

3. The district court was generous in its characterization of the typeface on the reverse of the bill of lading as "minuscule [sic]." *Monica I*, 731 F.Supp. at 126. Whereas standard typeface (like the body of this opinion) has six lines per inch, the carriers' boilerplate has sixteen lines per inch.

[26] This supposed exception to the Mitsui rule, however, is more apparent than real. No appellate precedent has been found applying this exception to a bill of lading like the one before us now. And for good reason: our container cases recognize that when a bill of lading refers to both containers and other units susceptible of being COGSA packages, it is inherently ambiguous. In *Smythgreyhound*, we candidly admitted "that no shipper ever actually intends that its recovery will be limited to $500 per container, or that any carrier, in the absence of an express agreement, intends that the recovery should exceed $500 per container." *Smythgreyhound*, 666 F.2d at 748 n. 4; see also *id*. at 751 ("on their face the bills of lading reflect the lack of agreement, insofar as they refer to both 'containers' and 'cartons'"); *Matsushita*, 414 F.Supp. at 906 ("it is clear that there was not and, realistically, could not have been any mutual understanding between [the shipper and carrier] with respect to the COGSA package"). *Mitsui* and its progeny resolve this ambiguity against the carriers. See Mitsui, 636 F.2d at 822-23.

[27] It is not without significance that the two boilerplate clauses upon which the carriers rely have consistently failed to persuade us in the past that the container is intended to be the package. Clause 11, for example, is essentially the same one we ignored in Leather's Best, even though in Leathers Best the clause appeared on the front of the bill of lading in capital letters:

> SHIPPER HEREBY AGREES THAT CARRIER'S LIABILITY IS LIMITED TO $500 WITH RESPECT TO THE ENTIRE CONTENTS OF EACH CONTAINER EXCEPT WHEN SHIPPER DECLARES A HIGHER VALUATION AND SHALL HAVE PAID ADDITIONAL FREIGHT ON SUCH DECLARED VALUATION PURSUANT TO APPROPRIATE RULE IN THE CONTINENTAL NORTH ATLANTIC WESTBOUND FREIGHT CONFERENCE TARIFF. *Leather's Best*, 451 F.2d at 804.

Compare *Monica I*, 731 F.Supp. at 126 (similar clause "in minuscule [sic] type face" on reverse of bill of lading).

[28] Similarly, Clause 2 is virtually indistinguishable from one rejected in Matsushita which provided:

> where the cargo has been either packed into container(s) or unitized into similar article(s) of transport by or on behalf of the Merchant, it is expressly agreed that the number of such container(s) or similar article(s) of transport shown on the face hereof shall be considered as the number of the package(s) or unit(s) for the purpose of the application of the limitation of liability provided for herein. *Matsushita*, 414 F.Supp. at 899;

see also *St. Paul Fire & Marine Ins.*, 735 F.Supp. at 132 ("Allowing the carrier . . . to insert an essentially unbargained-for definition of 'package' in the bill of lading would effectively eliminate the protection COGSA was meant to afford shippers."); *Monica I*, 731 F.Supp. at 127 (*Mitsui* and its progeny "control[ ] despite the language of clause 11").

[29] Because the bill of lading in this case is ambiguous on its face and Clauses 2 and 11 are unbargained-for boilerplate, we cannot say that Monica and the carriers unequivocally agreed to treat the container as the COGSA package. Thus, the exception to *Mitsui's* rule is not applicable; and the 76 bales, not the container, are the relevant units for determining the extent of the carriers' liability under the statute.

[30] This conclusion is consistent with our longstanding recognition of what every shipper knows: that "bills of lading are contracts of adhesion ambiguities in which must be resolved against the carrier. . . ." *Mitsui*, 636 F.2d at 822-23. Clauses 2 and 11, like others printed on the back of a form bill of lading, "carr[y] little weight toward establishing intent, being [ ] unilateral, self-serving declaration[s] by the carrier which w[ere] not negotiated by the parties and could scarcely be discerned by the unaided eye in the maze of microscopic and virtually illegible provisions on the back[ ] of the bill[ ] of lading." *Matsushita*, 414 F.Supp. at 906 n. 52; see also *St. Paul Fire & Marine Ins. Co. v. Sea-Land Serv., Inc.*, 735 F.Supp. 129, 132 & n. 4 (S.D.N.Y.1990).

Conclusion

[31] *Seguros* provides a bright-line rule in non-container cases that, "the more consistently it is followed, the more it should minimize disputes." *Seguros*, 929 F.2d at 94. Similarly, *Mitsui* and its progeny continue to provide a simple rule in container cases, a rule that is easily administered by the courts and readily amenable to *ex ante* application by contracting parties. Together, these rules foster predictability in this nettlesome area of the law. Applied faithfully and consistently, they should assist carriers, shippers and the courts to "avoid the pains of litigation." *Standard Electrica*, 375 F.2d at 945.

Notes and Questions

1. On the one hand, the idea that carrier liability should, or even could be, limited to US$500 per container seems unreasonable. The box alone costs more than that. However, the distinction between packages and containers is neither found in COGSA, nor is particularly persuasive. Throughout this book, we have seen that in B2B transactions, the freedom of contract is far reaching and parties will be held to their agreements, even if they are unfavorable to one side or the other.[19] Here, we suddenly overrule not just the language of COGSA, but also the general terms (back side) of the BoL *and even specific clauses included in boldface on the front of a BoL* (see para. 27). What is the justification for such an approach by the courts? Do you find the argument persuasive that the clauses are ambiguous, and ambiguity should be interpreted against the drafter *(contra proferentem)*?

---

19. To give an extreme example, in *Bristow US LLC v. Wallenius Wilhelmsen Logistics, AS*, the United States District Court, S.D. New York, held that an entire helicopter was "a package" under the COGSA. Since the COGSA was applicable per Bill of Lading and the shipper had not contracted and paid for higher liability, the carrier was liable for no more than $500 for dropping it. See 369 F. Supp. 3d 519.

2. Do you agree with the court's self-congratulatory conclusion in paragraph 31 that they have created a bright-line rule that is easily administered and should minimize disputes? If this rule is so obvious and easy, can you formulate it in one or two sentences? Is the court maybe just whistling in the dark?

3. How would you advise carriers seeking to limit their liability in container trade?

4. On behalf of the shipper, how would you draft the description of the goods to be entered in a BoL? What are potential repercussions for letters of credit, customs declarations, and insurance contracts?

5. Even if a shipper is awarded US$500 for each of 76 bales in a container, the total amount may fall far short of the actual value of the cargo. How can a shipper protect her interests?

Case 4-4

The 'ARAWA'

Before Lord Denning M.R., Lord Justice Bridge and Sir David Cairns
Court of Appeal, December 12 and 13, 1979
Lloyd's Law Reports [1980] Vol. 2, p. 135
(Paragraph numbers added.)

The case concerned shipment of a consignment of frozen lamb meat from New Zealand to the United Kingdom. The ship was going to arrive in London on a weekend followed by a public holiday. The carrier wanted to avoid delays with unloading since the ship was scheduled to return immediately to New Zealand. Therefore, the carrier notified the cargo owners proposing that he would contract a cold storage company at his own expense so that the cargo could be unloaded immediately and would be taken care of until the consignee would take delivery after the holiday. The cargo owners did not reply to the notification and the carrier proceeded as proposed. Unfortunately, due to a labor dispute, the cargo was not taken into cold storage quickly enough and part of it was spoiled. The trial court ruled in favor of the cargo owners. The carrier appealed.

Judgment

[1] Lord DENNING, M.R.: As long ago as 1970 a vessel, *Arawa,* belonging to Shaw Savill and Albion carried a cargo of lamb carcasses from Auckland, New Zealand, to London. She was also a vessel which carried passengers. We are particularly concerned here with a cargo of lamb carcasses which was shipped under 24 bills of lading issued by the Shaw Savill Line.

[2] This vessel was due to come into London ready to discharge at the King George V Dock below Tower Bridge on May 23, 1970. That was just before the bank holiday. It was a Saturday. There would not be any unloading of the vessel over the holiday until the Tuesday. The turnround of this vessel would be delayed. She had been booked to go back to New Zealand on an early voyage. All the notices had been advertised for the passengers, and so forth.

[3] The delay over the holiday so concerned the shipowners that they told the cargo-owners—the receivers who were going to receive this cargo of lamb—that they would like to make other arrangements. Instead of waiting at the King George V Dock and holding up the ship for some days, their proposal was that all these carcasses of lamb should be unloaded into lighters alongside the ship and taken to a wharf near Deptford called Chambers Wharf. The carcasses could be unloaded there, sorted out, and, if need be, put into cold store. The receivers could collect them from Chambers Wharf. By so doing the ship would be unloaded quickly, and could get away on time.

[4] The shipowners realized that it would be necessary to have the agreement of the receivers of the cargo to this proposal. So, some four or five days before the vessel was due to arrive, they wrote a letter to them to see if they would agree to it. The letter is so important that I would read it in full. It is dated May 19, 1970. It is from Shaw Savill Line to all the cargo receivers. It says:

> This vessel, carrying passengers and refrigerated cargo from New Zealand, is due to arrive in London on 23rd May but, because of the week-end and Spring Public Holiday, will not commence discharging her cargo until 26th.
>
> Being a passenger liner "ARAWA" operates on a fixed and predetermined schedule which is widely publicised and in order to meet her next outward commitment it will be necessary for us to improve considerably on the time that it is estimated will be required to discharge all of her cargo. Consequently it has been decided that one complete hatch will be discharged "direct overside" into barge for conveyance, at our expense, to Chambers Wharf & Cold Stores Limited, at Chambers Street, London, S.E.16.
>
> Any freight due to us should be paid and Bills of Lading presented for release at this Office in the customary manner. You are asked then to take delivery of your consignment(s) at Chambers Wharf where you will be debited with the Port of London Authority's P.O.Q. [-pass over quay -] charges at the rate current at the time of discharge from the vessel. We understand that, at the time of writing, this is 65/3d. per ton. Customs Clearance will be affected at ship's side in the usual manner.
>
> Free storage for twenty-eight days from the time of breaking bulk of the vessel, will be granted you and whilst we regret any inconvenience which may be incurred by you we sincerely trust that it will be minimal . . .

[5] There was no dissent from that letter. Indeed, there was no reply. It is quite plain from the conduct of the parties that all the cargo receivers were content to let the cargo be dealt with on those lines.

[6] Unfortunately the plan went awry. The lamb carcasses were unloaded into lighters. They were taken to Chambers Wharf at Deptford. But at that wharf there was a "go-slow" by the men who were handling the lighters and the men on the quay alongside. The result of the "go slow" was that the lighters were not unloaded promptly when they arrived at Chambers Wharf. It took some days . . . before the lighters could get

alongside and unload at Chambers Wharf. In some cases several days elapsed before the lighters were unloaded. Even then they had to be taken on to the roof there and sorted out before they could be put into cold store. It was all a consequence of this "go-slow".

[7] Eventually the receivers took up the documents. They presented the bills of lading at the offices of Shaw Savill and Albion in Leadenhall Street. Then they went to Chambers Wharf to take up the carcasses. They found that the carcasses had gone soft and were inedible. It was due—as the Judge found—to the long delay because of the "go-slow".

[8] The receivers of the cargo then sued the shipowners. They said it was their responsibility, because their contractors had not handled the goods properly. Therefore the shipowners ought to be made liable. That is the only point remaining in this case. . . .

[9] The shipowners relied on cl. 2 (a) of the bill of lading—which says:

> Prior to the loading of the goods on or subsequent to their discharge from the vessel, whether or not the goods are in the custody of the Carrier, his agents or servants as warehousemen or otherwise and whether in craft or landed, the Carrier, his agents and servants and the vessel shall not be liable for any loss, detention or damage of or to the goods whatsoever even if caused by the negligence of the Carrier, his agents or servants or other persons for whom the Carrier is responsible . . .

[10] How is that clause to be got over? The Judge overcame it in this way. He said that, as a result of the letter of May 19, 1970, and its implied acceptance by the cargo receivers, there was a new contract—a new contract which applied to the transit to Chambers Wharf—in which there were no exception clauses. He held that the bill of lading conditions did not apply to that transaction: and, accordingly, the shipowners were liable because the bill of lading exception was not available. He said that if the shipowners had wanted it to be available, they ought to have inserted it in the letter which they wrote. Not having inserted it, he held that the shipowners were liable upon a separate contract in which there were no exceptions.

[11] It is a very short point. It seems to me, as a result of the discussion we have heard, that the Judge did fall into error. The question is simply this: Did the bill of lading terms apply to the transit up to Chambers Wharf and delivery there? The proper way of testing it is to ask whether the agreement relating to it was just a mere variation of the bill of lading contract? Or was it a new agreement dealing with a different subject matter? The difference between variation and rescission goes back a long time. It was much discussed in the Statute of Frauds cases. I cannot look upon this agreement about Chambers Wharf as anything more than a variation of the bill of lading contract—a variation just as to the place at which delivery could be taken. It is as simple as that. The terms of the bill of lading contract all apply so far as they are applicable—especially when one reads the third paragraph of the letter of May 19:

. . . Any freight due to us should be paid and Bills of Lading presented for release at this office in the customary manner.

[12] It seems to me that the bills of lading exceptions apply to the whole of this additional transaction.

[13] I need not go into the other points which have been discussed today. To my mind cl. 2 (a) of the bill of lading applies and exempts shipowners from liability in this case. I would allow the appeal accordingly.

[14] Lord Justice BRIDGE: I agree. The question at issue is whether the effect of the arrangements made to lighten these cargoes at Chambers Wharf was to rescind the bills of lading contract from the moment the cargoes were discharged from the vessel to the lighters, on the one hand, or whether, on the other hand, this arrangement left the bills of lading contracts subsisting and merely varied them as to the mode whereby the delivery of the cargoes was to be effected.

[15] The principles whereby the rescission of an existing contract is to be distinguished from a mere variation of it are very clearly stated in par. 1372 of the current edition of Chitty on Contracts. I will not take up time by reading but it seems to me, with all respect, that the learned Judge never applied those principles in asking himself whether there had been a mere variation or a rescission pro tanto of the bills of lading contracts. He assumed that the Chambers Wharf agreement was a completely fresh agreement, and then asked himself the question whether the relevant exempting clause in the bills of lading was to be found either expressly or by implication as a term of that contract. With all respect, in my judgment, that was an erroneous approach to the issue; and, if the learned Judge had approached it with the principles distinguishing rescission from variation in mind, he would inevitably have reached the answer stated by Lord Denning, M.R., that this was a mere variation.

I too would allow this appeal.

Sir DAVID CAIRNS: I agree that the appeal should be allowed. . . .

Notes and Questions

1. It is already quite striking how far the liability of carriers is limited by law under the Hague Rules, the Hague-Visby Rules, and the more modern Hamburg and Rotterdam Rules. Note in this case how the carrier, via preprinted clauses in the Bill of Lading, is able to further limit her liability, including for negligence. The Court of Appeal does not question for a moment the validity of that clause.

What may be even more striking, however, is the extension of the liability limits beyond the actual carriage of the goods to any acts or omissions that may occur on land, prior to and after the physical voyage. Essentially, this means that from the moment the goods are handed over to the custody of the carrier until the moment when they are claimed and obtained by the consignee, the only cause of action for deterioration or loss against the carrier would be for gross negligence or intent.

2. Given the fact that the change of the unloading arrangements was unilaterally requested and initiated by the carrier for her own benefit and became a direct cause of the loss, the trial judge must have felt uneasy with burdening the cargo owners. Do you agree with the Court of Appeal that the trial judge should have consulted Chitty's hornbook on Contracts, i.e., made a fundamental mistake in interpreting the applicable contract law? What exactly was the mistake of the trial judge?

3. How can cargo owners protect themselves against losses such as this? In answering this question, you have to assume that other carriers will use similar exclusion clauses in their contracts.

Section 4. Specifics of Air, Road and Rail Transport

A. Air Transport

In terms of volume or weight of overall transported goods, air transport is relatively insignificant (about 2%), compared to maritime transport, as well as road and rail transport (the other 98%). The significance is even higher when it comes to the value of the transported goods (between 35 and 40%). The real importance of air transport, however, is in the transportation of people and their luggage, as well as airmail. In early 2020, before the coronavirus struck, at any given moment about 10,000 commercial aircraft with a total number of 1.5 million passengers were in the air around the globe. In total, about 5 billion passengers were supposed to take to the air in 2020.

Since transport of goods by air is important in some industries—for example, for certain perishable goods or high-value electronics, and in just-in-time supply chain arrangements—it makes sense to take a brief look at the parties to transport contracts, the legal framework, and some of the typical problems.

The air cargo market is served by several types of companies:

- dedicated air cargo operators like Cargolux, AirBridgeCargo, Polar Air Cargo, or Nippon Cargo Airlines; these carriers do not offer regular passenger service but they often operate scheduled service for cargo;

- regular airlines operating at least some of their aircraft to transport only or mainly cargo, for example, Emirates, China Southern, or Lufthansa;

- other airlines selling cargo space in passenger aircraft;

- integrated logistics providers offering door-to-door services that may or may not include air transport, depending on the distance and the delivery time contracted with the customer; the world's largest are Federal Express and UPS, followed at some distance by DHL and TNT;

- specialized carriers offering services for unconventional cargo that does not fit into regular aircraft cargo holds, e.g., larger live animals, heavy vehicles or machinery, etc.

The regulatory authority in the U.S. is with the Department of Transport (DoT) and, in particular, with the Federal Aviation Authority (FAA), within the DoT. Civil aviation accidents are investigated by an independent agency, the National Transportation Safety Board (NTSB). The Department of Homeland Security (DHS), with the Transportation Security Administration (TSA) and the Customs and Border Protection Service (CBP) are in charge of airport security, passenger security screening, immigration, and customs processing of incoming cargo.

On the domestic level, the U.S. has adopted 49 U.S. Code Title 49 — Transportation, with Subtitle VII dedicated to Aviation Programs (§§ 40101–50105). Section 14 CFR Part 121 deals with air carriers and issues such as certification of an airline, route requirements, navigation, airplane performance requirements, training, service and maintenance requirements, etc. Operating rules and standards for domestic and foreign air carriers can also be found in 14 CFR Parts 91 and 129. Beyond the technical rules, the regulatory framework for international carriage of passengers and cargo by air is based on the 1929 Convention for Unification of Certain Rules Relating to International Carriage by Air, the so-called Warsaw Convention (Documents, p. I-721). The Convention itself was ratified by some 152 countries and was the standard for air transport contracts (passenger tickets, luggage tickets, and air cargo consignment notes), as well as liability limitations in favor of the carriers, for decades. While Articles 17, 18, and 19 generally provide for liability of the carrier in case of physical injury to passengers, damage to or loss of luggage and cargo, as well as delay, Article 20 provides that:

> 1. The carrier is not liable if he proves that he and his agents have taken all necessary measures to avoid the damage or that it was impossible for him or them to take such measures.

> 2. In the carriage of goods and luggage the carrier is not liable if he proves that the damage was occasioned by negligent pilotage or negligence in the handling of the aircraft or in navigation and that, in all other respects, he and his agents have taken all necessary measures to avoid the damage.

Furthermore, Article 22(2) limits the liability of the carrier for lost or damaged luggage or cargo to 250 francs per kilogram, unless otherwise agreed in the air cargo consignment note.

The Warsaw Convention was updated by the 1955 Hague Protocol, which was ratified by about 137 countries. In 1999, the members of the International Civil Aviation Organization (ICAO) adopted a complete revision in the form of the 1999 Convention for the Unification of Certain Rules for International Carriage by Air, the so-called Montreal Convention (Documents, p. I-729). This update was ratified by about 136 countries to date, including the United States, the Member States of the European Union (EU), and other important countries like Australia, Brazil, Canada, China, India, Japan, Russia, and the UK. The Montreal Convention rules on passenger tickets (Article 3), and air waybills for air cargo transport (Articles 4–16), as well as the limitation of the carrier's liability for damage to or loss of cargo

(Articles 18–22), are the de facto standard today. Per Article 22(3), the carrier liability for cargo "destruction, loss, damage or delay" is limited to 17 SDRs per kilogram, about US$25 per kilo, unless otherwise stipulated in the air waybill.

B. Road and Rail Transport

Since road or rail transport rarely occurs from one continent to another, there are no global conventions comparable to the Hague or Hague-Visby Rules (maritime transport) or the Warsaw and Montreal Conventions (air transport) to govern the contract of carriage, the rights and obligations of the shipper and carrier, and the liability of the carrier in case of damage to or loss of the cargo.

In most countries, rail transport services are provided by one national carrier who also owns and controls the rail infrastructure. The 1980 Convention Concerning International Carriage by Rail (COTIF Convention) is administered by the Intergovernmental Organisation for International Carriage by Rail (OTIF) in Berne, Switzerland. It applies mostly to countries in Europe, the Middle East, North Africa, the Caucasus, and Central Asia. Based on the Convention, OTIF has developed Uniform Rules for the Contract of International Carriage of Goods by Rail (CIM).[20]

The 1956 UNECE Convention on the Contract for the International Carriage of Goods by Road (CMR Convention)[21] was ratified by some 56 countries across Europe, the Middle East, North Africa, the Caucasus, and Central Asia.[22] It is the de facto law governing road transport in these countries.

In Articles 4 to 16, the CMR Convention regulates the required elements of the contract of carriage (CMR Consignment Note or CMR Waybill) and the rights and obligations of the parties under it. This triggered the de facto standardization of the CMR Waybill and makes this form of contracting rather straightforward in the participating countries. Three copies have to be produced — one for the shipper/cargo owner, one for the carrier, and one to travel with the goods. Since the CMR Note is not a document of title, it was relatively easy for the Contracting Parties to agree in 2008 on an additional protocol introducing an electronic consignment note.

---

20. https://otif.org/fileadmin/user_upload/otif_verlinkte_files/07_veroeff/03_erlaeut/05_Appendix_B.pdf.

21. https://www.unece.org/fileadmin/DAM/trans/conventn/cmr_e.pdf, last amended in 1978.

22. Albania, Armenia, Austria, Azerbaijan, Belarus, Belgium, Bosnia and Herzegovina, Bulgaria, Croatia, Cyprus, Czech Republic, Denmark, Estonia, Finland, France, Georgia, Germany, Greece, Hungary, Iran (Islamic Republic of), Ireland, Italy, Jordan, Kazakhstan, Kyrgyzstan, Latvia, Lebanon, Lithuania, Luxembourg, Malta, Mongolia, Montenegro, Morocco, Netherlands, Norway, Poland, Portugal, Republic of Moldova, Romania, Russian Federation, Serbia, Slovakia, Slovenia, Spain, Sweden, Switzerland, Syrian Arab Republic, Tajikistan, The former Yugoslav Republic of Macedonia, Tunisia, Turkey, Turkmenistan, Ukraine, United Kingdom of Great Britain and Northern Ireland, and Uzbekistan.

Article 17 of the CMR Convention defines the liability of the carrier as follows:

1. The carrier shall be liable for the total or partial loss of the goods and for damage thereto occurring between the time when he takes over the goods and the time of delivery, as well as for any delay in delivery.

2. The carrier shall, however, be relieved of liability if the loss, damage or delay was caused by the wrongful act or neglect of the claimant, by the instructions of the claimant given otherwise than as the result of a wrongful act or neglect on the part of the carrier, by inherent vice of the goods or through circumstances which the carrier could not avoid and the consequences of which he was unable to prevent.

3. The carrier shall not be relieved of liability by reason of the defective condition of the vehicle used by him in order to perform the carriage, or by reason of the wrongful act or neglect of the person from whom he may have hired the vehicle or of the agents or servants of the latter.

4. Subject to article 18, paragraphs 2 to 5, the carrier shall be relieved of liability when the loss or damage arises from the special risks inherent in one more of the following circumstances:

   (a) Use of open unsheeted vehicles, when their use has been expressly agreed and specified in the consignment note;

   (b) The lack of, or defective condition of packing in the case of goods which, by their nature, are liable to wastage or to be damaged when not packed or when not properly packed;

   (c) Handling, loading, stowage or unloading of the goods by the sender, the consignee or person acting on behalf of the sender or the consignee;

   (d) The nature of certain kinds of goods which particularly exposes them to total or partial loss or to damage, especially through breakage, rust, decay, desiccation, leakage, normal wastage, or the action of moth or vermin;

   (f) Insufficiency or inadequacy of marks or numbers on the packages;

   (g) The carriage of livestock.

5. Where under this article the carrier is not under any liability in respect some of the factors causing the loss, damage or delay, he shall only be liable the extent that those factors for which he is liable under this article have contributed to the loss, damage or delay.[23]

The situation in the U.S. is quite different. Almost all rail cargo carriers are privately owned and they usually also own their respective rail lines with adjacent infrastructure. There is no national network and one railway can only use the lines of another

---

23. Pursuant to Article 18, the carrier has the burden of proof when relying on paragraphs (2) or (4) to limit her liability.

if they have entered into a contract. The railways are divided by class. Seven railways with annual turnover of more than US$463 million form Class I and have somewhat more stringent supervision and reporting requirements. In addition, there are more than 500 Class II and Class III railways with smaller regional and local operations. This does not include passenger transport systems like Amtrak, several local systems in Florida and California, as well as the commuter railways in the bigger cities.

The Interstate Commerce Commission (ICC) exercised oversight over the larger cargo carriers until 1996. Today, the Surface Transportation Board (STB) regulates issues like rates, conditions for entry and exit of service, as well as remedies regarding rates, classifications, and rules per the Interstate Commerce Commission Termination Act of 1995 ("ICCTA") (49 U.S.C.A. § 10101 et seq.). The ICCTA preempts the application of state law.

By contrast, the Federal Railroad Administration under the Department of Transportation is the safety regulator and applies, *inter alia*, the Federal Railroad Safety Act of 1970 ("FRSA").

In the United States, liability for damages to cargo transported by road across state lines is regulated by federal law, the so-called Carmack Amendment of 1935.[24] If the shipper or cargo owner can prove that the cargo was in good condition when handed over to the carrier and it was no longer in good condition upon delivery, the shipper can claim damages from the carrier for the diminution in the value of the goods.[25] However, the carrier can limit her liability by inserting a provision to this end in the contract of carriage.

To provide a level of harmonization, CFR Title 49, Subtitle B, Chapter X, Subchapter A, Part 1035 provides a Uniform Straight Bill of Lading for Domestic Interstate Transport by Road, Rail, or Water. Appendix A contains a Model BoL (front of the contract) and Appendix B provides the Contract Terms and Conditions (back of the contract).[26] Not least because these model rules allow wider exclusions of liability of the carrier, they are the de facto standard used by most carriers based in the U.S.

C. Multimodal Transport

At the national level, multimodal transport is mostly regulated in bits and pieces by the agencies and rules already mentioned in the context of maritime, air, road, and rail transport above. Five international conventions play a role in multimodal transport, although three of them have not been ratified by the U.S. The Hague Rules (Documents, p. I-648) are binding in the U.S. via the COGSA (Documents,

---

24. 49 U.S. Code § 14706—Liability of Carriers Under Receipts and Bills of Lading.

25. There are statutory exceptions for act of God, acts by public enemies, losses due to the fault of the shipper, acts of public authorities, and the inherent vice or nature of the goods.

26. Available, for example, at https://www.law.cornell.edu/cfr/text/49/part-1035.

p. I-708). Air transport is covered by the Montreal Convention (Documents, p. I-729), which has also been ratified by the U.S. By contrast, the Uniform Rules Concerning the Contract of International Carriage of Goods by Rail (CIM), the UNECE Convention on the Contract for the International Carriage of Goods by Road (CMR), and the Budapest Convention on the Contract for the Carriage of Goods by Inland Waterway (CMNI), are relevant mostly for transport in Europe.

The 1980 UN Convention on International Multimodal Transport of Goods[27] was intended to provide a level of harmonization for all countries and all modes of transport. However, this Convention was sponsored by UNCTAD and, like the Hamburg and Rotterdam Rules (above, pp. 550–552) and the UNCTAD Model Clauses for Marine Cargo Insurance (Documents, p. I-771), it is rather developing-country-friendly and imposes more stringent requirements than those currently applicable to carriers and insurers who are mostly based in developed countries. As a consequence, it has only been ratified by 11 countries as of January 2020, not including the U.S., Canada, or any of the EU Member States. It seems safe to say that it will not play a significant role for multimodal transport in the foreseeable future.

We will look at a typical case for multimodal transport, somewhere between federal and state law, and with transport documents prepared and contracts entered into abroad. The reader should look, in particular, at the way the contracts of carriage can achieve far-reaching limitations of liability.

Case 4-5

Norfolk Southern Railway Co. v. James N. Kirby, Pty Ltd.

543 U.S. 14 (2004)
(Paragraph numbers added.)

Justice O'Connor

[1] This is a maritime case about a train wreck. A shipment of machinery from Australia was destined for Huntsville, Alabama. The intercontinental journey was uneventful, and the machinery reached the United States unharmed. But the train carrying the machinery on its final, inland leg derailed, causing extensive damage. The machinery's owner sued the railroad. The railroad seeks shelter in two liability limitations contained in contracts that upstream carriers negotiated for the machinery's delivery

I.

[2] This controversy arises from two bills of lading (essentially, contracts) for the transportation of goods from Australia to Alabama. A bill of lading records that a

---

27. See https://unctad.org/en/PublicationsLibrary/tdmtconf17_en.pdf. For discussion, see, *inter alia*, Kurosh Nasseri, *The Multimodal Convention*, J. Mar. L. & Com. 1988, Vol. 19, No. 2, pp. 231–260. Nasseri discusses the strengths and weaknesses of the convention, as well as the arguments for and against ratification by the U.S.

carrier has received goods from the party that wishes to ship them, states the terms of carriage, and serves as evidence of the contract for carriage. See 2 T. Schoenbaum, *Admiralty and Maritime Law* 58–60 (3d ed.2001) (hereinafter Schoenbaum); Carriage of Goods by Sea Act (COGSA) . . . 46 U.S.C.App. § 1303. Respondent James N. Kirby, Pty Ltd. (Kirby), an Australian manufacturing company, sold 10 containers of machinery to the General Motors plant located outside Huntsville, Alabama. Kirby hired International Cargo Control (ICC), an Australian freight forwarding company, to arrange for delivery by "through" (i.e., end-to-end) transportation. (A freight forwarding company arranges for, coordinates, and facilitates cargo transport, but does not itself transport cargo.) To formalize their contract for carriage, ICC issued a bill of lading to Kirby (ICC bill). The bill designates Sydney, Australia, as the port of loading, Savannah, Georgia, as the port of discharge, and Huntsville as the ultimate destination for delivery.

[3] In negotiating the ICC bill, Kirby had the opportunity to declare the full value of the machinery and to have ICC assume liability for that value. Cf. *New York, N.H. & H.R. Co. v. Nothnagle*, 346 U.S. 128, 135 . . . (1953) (a carrier must provide a shipper with a fair opportunity to declare value). Instead, and as is common in the industry, see Sturley, *Carriage of Goods by Sea*, 31 J. Mar. L. & Com. 241, 244 (2000), Kirby accepted a contractual liability limitation for ICC below the machinery's true value, resulting, presumably, in lower shipping rates. The ICC bill sets various liability limitations for the journey from Sydney to Huntsville. For the sea leg, the ICC bill invokes the default liability rule set forth in the COGSA. The COGSA "package limitation" provides:

> "Neither the carrier nor the ship shall in any event be or become liable for any loss or damage to or in connection with the transportation of goods in an amount exceeding $500 per package lawful money of the United States . . . unless the nature and value of such goods have been declared by the shipper before shipment and inserted in the bill of lading." 46 U.S.C.App. § 1304(5).

[4] For the land leg, in turn, the bill limits the carrier's liability to a higher amount.[1] So that other downstream parties expected to take part in the contract's execution

---

1. The bill provides that "the Freight Forwarder shall in no event be or become liable for any loss of or damage to the goods in an amount exceeding the equivalent of 666.67 SDR per package or unit or 2 SDR per kilogramme of gross weight of the goods lost or damaged, whichever is the higher, unless the nature and value of the goods shall have been declared by the Consignor." App. to Pet. for Cert. 57a, cl. 8.3. An SDR, or Special Drawing Right, is a unit of account created by the International Monetary Fund and calculated daily on the basis of a basket of currencies. Liability computed per package for the 10 containers, for example, was approximately $17,373 when the bill of lading issued in June 1997, $17,231 when the goods were damaged on October 9, 1997, and $9,763 when the case was argued. . . . Respondents claim that liability computed by weight is higher. The machinery's weight is not in the record. In any case, because we conclude that Norfolk is also protected by the $500 per package limit in the second bill of lading at issue here, see Part III-B, infra, and thus cannot be liable for more than $5,000 for the 10 containers, each holding one machine, the precise liability under the ICC bill of lading does not matter.

could benefit from the liability limitations, the bill also contains a so-called "Himalaya Clause."[2] It provides:

> "These conditions [for limitations on liability] apply whenever claims relating to the performance of the contract evidenced by this [bill of lading] are made against any servant, agent or other person (including any independent contractor) whose services have been used in order to perform the contract." . . .

[5] Meanwhile, Kirby separately insured the cargo for its true value with its co-respondent in this case, Allianz Australia Insurance Ltd. (formerly MMI General Insurance, Ltd.).

[6] Having been hired by Kirby, and because it does not itself actually transport cargo, ICC then hired Hamburg Südamerikanische Dampfschiffahrts-Gesellschaft Eggert & Amsinck (Hamburg Süd), a German ocean shipping company, to transport the containers. To formalize their contract for carriage, Hamburg Süd issued its own bill of lading to ICC (Hamburg Süd bill). That bill designates Sydney as the port of loading, Savannah as the port of discharge, and Huntsville as the ultimate destination for delivery. It adopts COGSA's default rule in limiting the liability of Hamburg Süd, the bill's designated carrier, to $500 per package. See [§ 1304(5)]. It also contains a clause extending that liability limitation beyond the "tackles"—that is, to potential damage on land as well as on sea. Finally, it too contains a Himalaya Clause extending the benefit of its liability limitation to "all agents . . . (including inland) carriers . . . and all independent contractors whatsoever." . . .

[7] Acting through a subsidiary, Hamburg Süd hired petitioner Norfolk Southern Railway Company (Norfolk) to transport the machinery from the Savannah port to Huntsville. The Norfolk train carrying the machinery derailed en route, causing an alleged $1.5 million in damages. Kirby's insurance company reimbursed Kirby for the loss. Kirby and its insurer then sued Norfolk in the United States District Court for the Northern District of Georgia, asserting diversity jurisdiction and alleging tort and contract claims. In its answer, Norfolk argued, among other things, that Kirby's potential recovery could not exceed the amounts set forth in the liability limitations contained in the bills of lading for the machinery's carriage.

[8] The District Court granted Norfolk's motion for partial summary judgment, holding that Norfolk's liability was limited to $500 per container. Upon a joint motion from Norfolk and Kirby, the District Court certified its decision for interlocutory review pursuant to 28 U.S.C. § 1292(b).

[9] A divided panel of the Eleventh Circuit reversed. It held that Norfolk could not claim protection under the Himalaya Clause in the first contract, the ICC bill. It construed the language of the clause to exclude parties, like Norfolk, that had not been in privity with ICC when ICC issued the bill. . . . The majority also suggested

---

2. Clauses extending liability limitations take their name from an English case involving a steamship called *Himalaya*. See *Adler v. Dickson*, [1955] 1 Q.B. 158 (C.A.).

that "a special degree of linguistic specificity is required to extend the benefits of a Himalaya clause to an inland carrier." ... As for the Hamburg Süd bill, the court held that Kirby could be bound by the bill's liability limitation "only if ICC was acting as Kirby's agent when it received Hamburg Süd's bill." ... And, applying basic agency law principles, the Court of Appeals concluded that ICC had not been acting as Kirby's agent when it received the bill. ... Based on its opinion that Norfolk was not entitled to benefit from the liability limitation in either bill of lading, the Eleventh Circuit reversed the District Court's grant of summary judgment for the railroad. We granted certiorari to decide whether Norfolk could take shelter in the liability limitations of either bill ... and now reverse.

II.

[10] The courts below appear to have decided this case on an assumption, shared by the parties, that federal rather than state law governs the interpretation of the two bills of lading. Respondents now object. They emphasize that, at bottom, this is a diversity case involving tort and contract claims arising out of a rail accident somewhere between Savannah and Huntsville. We think, however, borrowing from Justice Harlan, that "the situation presented here has a more genuinely salty flavor than that." *Kossick v. United Fruit Co.*, 365 U.S. 731, 742 ... (1961). When a contract is a maritime one, and the dispute is not inherently local, federal law controls the contract interpretation. *Id.*, at 735. ...

[13] The ICC and Hamburg Süd bills are maritime contracts because their primary objective is to accomplish the transportation of goods by sea from Australia to the eastern coast of the United States. See G. Gilmore & C. Black, Law of Admiralty 31 (2d ed.1975) ("Ideally, the [admiralty] jurisdiction [over contracts ought] to include those and only those things principally connected with maritime transportation" (emphasis deleted)). To be sure, the two bills call for some performance on land; the final leg of the machinery's journey to Huntsville was by rail. But under a conceptual rather than spatial approach, this fact does not alter the essentially maritime nature of the contracts. ...

[15] We have reiterated that the "'fundamental interest giving rise to maritime jurisdiction is *the protection of maritime commerce.*'" *Exxon Corp. v. Central Gulf Lines, Inc.*, 500 U.S. 603, 608 (emphasis added) (quoting *Sisson v. Ruby*, 497 U.S. 358, 367 ... (1990), in turn quoting *Foremost Ins. Co. v. Richardson*, 457 U.S. 668, 674, ... (1982). The conceptual approach vindicates that interest by focusing our inquiry on whether the principal objective of a contract is maritime commerce. While it may once have seemed natural to think that only contracts embodying commercial obligations between the "tackles" (i.e., from port to port) have maritime objectives, the shore is now an artificial place to draw a line. Maritime commerce has evolved along with the nature of transportation and is often inseparable from some land-based obligations. The international transportation industry "clearly has moved into a new era—the age of multimodalism, door-to-door transport based on efficient use of all available modes of transportation by air, water, and land." 1 Schoenbaum 589 (4th ed. 2004). The cause is technological change: Because goods

can now be packaged in standardized containers, cargo can move easily from one mode of transport to another. Ibid. See also *NLRB v. Longshoremen*, 447 U.S. 490, 494 . . . (1980) ("'[C]ontainerization may be said to constitute the single most important innovation in ocean transport since the steamship displaced the schooner'"; G. Muller, *Intermodal Freight Transportation* 15–24 (3d ed.1995).

[16] Contracts reflect the new technology, hence the popularity of "through" bills of lading, in which cargo owners can contract for transportation across oceans and to inland destinations in a single transaction. . . . Put simply, it is to Kirby's advantage to arrange for transport from Sydney to Huntsville in one bill of lading, rather than to negotiate a separate contract—and to find an American railroad itself—for the land leg. The popularity of that efficient choice, to assimilate land legs into international ocean bills of lading, should not render bills for ocean carriage nonmaritime contracts.

[17] Some lower federal courts appear to have taken a spatial approach when deciding whether intermodal transportation contracts for intercontinental shipping are maritime in nature. They have held that admiralty jurisdiction does not extend to contracts which require maritime and nonmaritime transportation, unless the nonmaritime transportation is merely incidental—and that longdistance land travel is not incidental. See, e.g., *Hartford Fire Ins. Co. v. Orient Overseas Containers Lines (UK) Ltd.*, 230 F.3d 549, 555–556 . . . ("Transport by land under a bill of lading is not 'incidental' to transport by sea if the land segment involves great and substantial distances," and land transport of over 850 miles across four countries is more than incidental); *Sea-Land Serv., Inc. v. Danzig*, 211 F.3d 1373, 1378 . . . (holding that intermodal transport contracts were not maritime contracts because they called for "substantial transportation between inland locations and ports both in this country and in the Middle East" that was not incidental to the transportation by sea); *Kuehne & Nagel (AG & Co.) v. Geosource, Inc.*, 874 F.2d 283, 290 . . . (holding that a through bill of lading calling for land transportation up to 1,000 miles was not a traditional maritime contract because such "extensive land-based operations cannot be viewed as merely incidental to the maritime operations"). As a preliminary matter, it seems to us imprecise to describe the land carriage required by an intermodal transportation contract as "incidental"; realistically, each leg of the journey is essential to accomplishing the contract's purpose. In this case, for example, the bills of lading required delivery to Huntsville; the Savannah port would not do.

[18] Furthermore, to the extent that these lower court decisions fashion a rule for identifying maritime contracts that depends solely on geography, they are inconsistent with the conceptual approach our precedent requires. See *Kossick*, supra, at 735 . . . . Conceptually, so long as a bill of lading requires substantial carriage of goods by sea, its purpose is to effectuate maritime commerce—and thus it is a maritime contract. Its character as a maritime contract is not defeated simply because it also provides for some land carriage. Geography, then, is useful in a conceptual inquiry only in a limited sense: If a bill's sea components are insubstantial, then the bill is not a maritime contract.

[19] Having established that the ICC and Hamburg Süd bills are maritime contracts, then, we must clear a second hurdle before applying federal law in their interpretation. Is this case inherently local? For not "every term in every maritime contract can only be controlled by some federally defined admiralty rule." *Wilburn Boat Co. v. Fireman's Fund Ins. Co.*, [below, p. 618] (applying state law to maritime contract for marine insurance because of state regulatory power over insurance industry). A maritime contract's interpretation may so implicate local interests as to beckon interpretation by state law. See *Kossick*, 365 U.S., at 735 .... Respondents have not articulated any specific Australian or state interest at stake, though some are surely implicated. But when state interests cannot be accommodated without defeating a federal interest, as is the case here, then federal substantive law should govern. See *id.*, at 739 ... (the process of deciding whether federal law applies "is surely . . . one of accommodation, entirely familiar in many areas of overlapping state and federal concern, or a process somewhat analogous to the normal conflict of laws situation where two sovereignties assert divergent interests in a transaction"); 2 Schoenbaum 61 ("'Bills of lading issued outside the United States are governed by the general maritime law, considering relevant choice of law rules'").

[20] Here, our touchstone is a concern for the uniform meaning of maritime contracts like the ICC and Hamburg Süd bills. We have explained that Article III's grant of admiralty jurisdiction "'must have referred to a system of law coextensive with, and operating uniformly in, the whole country. It certainly could not have been the intention to place the rules and limits of maritime law under the disposal and regulation of the several States, as that would have defeated the uniformity and consistency at which the Constitution aimed on all subjects of a commercial character affecting the intercourse of the States with each other or with foreign states.'" *American Dredging Co. v. Miller*, 510 U.S. 443, 451 ... (1994) (quoting *The Lottawanna*, 21 Wall. 558, 575, 22 L.Ed. 654 (1875)). ...

[21] Applying state law to cases like this one would undermine the uniformity of general maritime law. The same liability limitation in a single bill of lading for international intermodal transportation often applies both to sea and to land, as is true of the Hamburg Süd bill. Such liability clauses are regularly executed around the world. . . . See also 46 U.S.C.App. § 1307 (permitting parties to extend the COGSA default liability limit to damage done "prior to the loading on and subsequent to the discharge from the ship"). Likewise, a single Himalaya Clause can cover both sea and land carriers downstream, as is true of the ICC bill. See Part III-A, infra. Confusion and inefficiency will inevitably result if more than one body of law governs a given contract's meaning. As we said in *Kossick*, when "a [maritime] contract . . . may well have been made anywhere in the world," it "should be judged by one law wherever it was made." 365 U.S., at 741 . . . . Here, that one law is federal.

[22] In protecting the uniformity of federal maritime law, we also reinforce the liability regime Congress established in COGSA. By its terms, COGSA governs bills of lading for the carriage of goods "from the time when the goods are loaded on to the time when they are discharged from the ship." 46 U.S.C.App. § 1301(e). For

that period, COGSA's "package limitation" operates as a default rule. § 1304(5). But COGSA also gives the option of extending its rule by contract. See § 1307 ("Nothing contained in this chapter shall prevent a carrier or a shipper from entering into any agreement, stipulation, condition, reservation, or exemption as to the responsibility and liability of the carrier or the ship for the loss or damage to or in connection with the custody and care and handling of goods prior to the loading on and subsequent to the discharge from the ship on which the goods are carried by sea"). As COGSA permits, Hamburg Süd in its bill of lading chose to extend the default rule to the entire period in which the machinery would be under its responsibility, including the period of the inland transport. Hamburg Süd would not enjoy the efficiencies of the default rule if the liability limitation it chose did not apply equally to all legs of the journey for which it undertook responsibility. And the apparent purpose of COGSA, to facilitate efficient contracting in contracts for carriage by sea, would be defeated.

III. A.

[23] Turning to the merits, we begin with the ICC bill of lading, the first of the contracts at issue. Kirby and ICC made a contract for the carriage of machinery from Sydney to Huntsville, and agreed to limit the liability of ICC and other parties who would participate in transporting the machinery. The bill's Himalaya Clause states:

> "These conditions [for limitations on liability] apply whenever claims relating to the performance of the contract evidenced by this [bill of lading] are made against any servant, agent or other person (including any independent contractor) whose services have been used in order to perform the contract." . . . (emphasis added).

[24] The question presented is whether the liability limitation in Kirby's and ICC's contract extends to Norfolk, which is ICC's sub-subcontractor. The Circuits have split in answering this question. Compare, e.g., *Akiyama Corp. of America v. M.V. Hanjin Marseilles*, 162 F.3d 571, 574 . . . (privity of contract is not required in order to benefit from a Himalaya Clause), with *Mikinberg v. Baltic S.S. Co.*, 988 F.2d 327, 332 . . . (a contractual relationship is required).

[25] This is a simple question of contract interpretation. It turns only on whether the Eleventh Circuit correctly applied this Court's decision in *Robert C. Herd & Co. v. Krawill Machinery Corp.*, 359 U.S. 297 . . . (1959). We conclude that it did not. In *Herd*, the bill of lading between a cargo owner and carrier said that, consistent with COGSA, "'the Carrier's liability, if any, shall be determined on the basis of $500 per package.'" *Id.*, at 302 . . . . The carrier then hired a stevedoring company to load the cargo onto the ship, and the stevedoring company damaged the goods. The Court held that the stevedoring company was not a beneficiary of the bill's liability limitation. Because it found no evidence in COGSA or its legislative history that Congress meant COGSA's liability limitation to extend automatically to a carrier's agents, like stevedores, the Court looked to the language of the bill of lading itself. It reasoned that a clause limiting "'the Carrier's liability'" did not "indicate that the contracting

parties intended to limit the liability of stevedores or other agents. . . . If such had been a purpose of the contracting parties it must be presumed that they would in some way have expressed it in the contract." *Ibid.* The Court added that liability limitations must be "strictly construed and limited to intended beneficiaries." *Id.,* at 305 . . . .

[26] The Eleventh Circuit, like respondents, made much of the *Herd* decision. Deriving a principle of narrow construction from *Herd*, the Court of Appeals concluded that the language of the ICC bill's Himalaya Clause is too vague to clearly include Norfolk. 300 F.3d, at 1308. Moreover, the lower court interpreted *Herd* to require privity between the carrier and the party seeking shelter under a Himalaya Clause. 300 F.3d, at 1308. But nothing in *Herd* requires the linguistic specificity or privity rules that the Eleventh Circuit attributes to it. The decision simply says that contracts for carriage of goods by sea must be construed like any other contracts: by their terms and consistent with the intent of the parties. If anything, *Herd* stands for the proposition that there is no special rule for Himalaya Clauses.

[27] The Court of Appeals' ruling is not true to the contract language or to the intent of the parties. The plain language of the Himalaya Clause indicates an intent to extend the liability limitation broadly—to "*any* servant, agent or other person (including any independent contractor)" whose services contribute to performing the contract. . . . (emphasis added). "Read naturally, the word 'any' has an expansive meaning, that is, 'one or some indiscriminately of whatever kind.'" *United States v. Gonzales,* 520 U.S. 1, 5 . . . (1997) (quoting Webster's Third New International Dictionary 97 (1976)). There is no reason to contravene the clause's obvious meaning. See *Green v. Biddle,* 8 Wheat. 1, 89–90, 5 L.Ed. 547 (1823) ("[W]here the words of a law, treaty, or contract, have a plain and obvious meaning, all construction, in hostility with such meaning, is excluded"). The expansive contract language corresponds to the fact that various modes of transportation would be involved in performing the contract. Kirby and ICC contracted for the transportation of machinery from Australia to Huntsville, Alabama, and, as the crow flies, Huntsville is some 366 miles inland from the port of discharge. . . . Thus, the parties must have anticipated that a land carrier's services would be necessary for the contract's performance. It is clear to us that a railroad like Norfolk was an intended beneficiary of the ICC bill's broadly written Himalaya Clause. Accordingly, Norfolk's liability is limited by the terms of that clause.

B.

[28] The question arising from the Hamburg Süd bill of lading is more difficult. It requires us to set an efficient default rule for certain shipping contracts, a task that has been a challenge for courts for centuries. See, e.g., *Hadley v. Baxendale,* 9 Exch. 341, 156 Eng. Rep. 145 (1854). ICC and Hamburg Süd agreed that Hamburg Süd would transport the machinery from Sydney to Huntsville, and agreed to the COGSA "package limitation" on the liability of Hamburg Süd, its agents, and its independent contractors. The second question presented is whether that liability limitation, which ICC negotiated, prevents Kirby from suing Norfolk (Hamburg

Süd's independent contractor) for more. As we have explained, the liability limitation in the ICC bill, the first contract, sets liability for a land accident higher than this bill does. See n. 1, supra. Because Norfolk's liability will be lower if it is protected by the Hamburg Süd bill too, we must reach this second question in order to give Norfolk the full relief for which it petitioned.

[29] To interpret the Hamburg Süd bill, we turn to a rule drawn from our precedent about common carriage: When an intermediary contracts with a carrier to transport goods, the cargo owner's recovery against the carrier is limited by the liability limitation to which the intermediary and carrier agreed. The intermediary is certainly not automatically empowered to be the cargo owner's agent in every sense. That would be unsustainable. But when it comes to liability limitations for negligence resulting in damage, an intermediary can negotiate reliable and enforceable agreements with the carriers it engages.

[30] We derive this rule from our decision about common carriage in *Great Northern R. Co. v. O'Connor*, 232 U.S. 508 . . . (1914). In *Great Northern*, an owner hired a transfer company to arrange for the shipment of her goods. Without the owner's express authority, the transfer company arranged for rail transport at a tariff rate that limited the railroad's liability to less than the true value of the goods. The goods were lost en route, and the owner sued the railroad. The Court held that the railroad must be able to rely on the liability limitation in its tariff agreement with the transfer company. The railroad "had the right to assume that the Transfer Company could agree upon the terms of the shipment"; it could not be expected to know if the transfer company had any outstanding, conflicting obligation to another party. *Id.*, at 514 . . . . The owner's remedy, if necessary, was against the transfer company. *Id.*, at 515 . . . .

[31] Respondents object to our reading of *Great Northern*, and argue that this Court should fashion the federal rule of decision from general agency law principles. Like the Eleventh Circuit, respondents reason that Kirby cannot be bound by the bill of lading that ICC negotiated with Hamburg Süd unless ICC was then acting as Kirby's agent. Other Courts of Appeals have also applied agency law to cases similar to this one. See, e.g., *Kukje Hwajae Ins. Co. v. The M/V Hyundai Liberty*, 294 F.3d 1171, 1175–1177 . . . (an intermediary acted as a cargo owner's agent when negotiating a bill of lading with a downstream carrier).

[32] We think reliance on agency law is misplaced here. It is undeniable that the traditional indicia of agency, a fiduciary relationship and effective control by the principal, did not exist between Kirby and ICC. See Restatement (Second) of Agency § 1 (1957). But that is of no moment. The principle derived from *Great Northern* does not require treating ICC as Kirby's agent in the classic sense. It only requires treating ICC as Kirby's agent for a single, limited purpose: when ICC contracts with subsequent carriers for limitation on liability. In holding that an intermediary binds a cargo owner to the liability limitations it negotiates with downstream carriers, we do not infringe on traditional agency principles. We merely ensure the reliability of downstream contracts for liability limitations. In *Great Northern*, because the

intermediary had been "entrusted with goods to be shipped by railway, and, nothing to the contrary appearing, the carrier had the right to assume that [the intermediary] could agree upon the terms of the shipment." 232 U.S., at 514 . . . . Likewise, here we hold that intermediaries, entrusted with goods, are "agents" only in their ability to contract for liability limitations with carriers downstream.

[33] Respondents also contend that any decision binding Kirby to the Hamburg Süd bill's liability limitation will be disastrous for the international shipping industry. Various participants in the industry have weighed in as *amici* on both sides in this case, and we must make a close call. It would be idle to pretend that the industry can easily be characterized, or that efficient default rules can easily be discerned. In the final balance, however, we disagree with respondents for three reasons.

[34] First, we believe that a limited agency rule tracks industry practices. In intercontinental ocean shipping, carriers may not know if they are dealing with an intermediary, rather than with a cargo owner. Even if knowingly dealing with an intermediary, they may not know how many other intermediaries came before, or what obligations may be outstanding among them. If the Eleventh Circuit's rule were the law, carriers would have to seek out more information before contracting, so as to assure themselves that their contractual liability limitations provide true protection. That task of information gathering might be very costly or even impossible, given that goods often change hands many times in the course of intermodal transportation. . . .

[35] Second, if liability limitations negotiated with cargo owners were reliable while limitations negotiated with intermediaries were not, carriers would likely want to charge the latter higher rates. A rule prompting downstream carriers to distinguish between cargo owners and intermediary shippers might interfere with statutory and decisional law promoting nondiscrimination in common carriage. Cf. *ICC v. Delaware, L. & W.R. Co.*, 220 U.S. 235, 251–256 . . . (1911) (common carrier cannot "sit in judgment on the title of the prospective shipper"); Shipping Act, 46 U.S.C.App. § 1709 (nondiscrimination rules). It would also, as we have intimated, undermine COGSA's liability regime.

[36] Finally, as in *Great Northern*, our decision produces an equitable result. . . . Kirby retains the option to sue ICC, the carrier, for any loss that exceeds the liability limitation to which they agreed. And indeed, Kirby has sued ICC in an Australian court for damages arising from the Norfolk derailment. It seems logical that ICC — the only party that definitely knew about and was party to both of the bills of lading at issue here — should bear responsibility for any gap between the liability limitations in the bills. Meanwhile, Norfolk enjoys the benefit of the Hamburg Süd bill's liability limitation.

IV.

[37] We hold that Norfolk is entitled to the protection of the liability limitations in the two bills of lading. Having undertaken this analysis, we recognize that our decision does no more than provide a legal backdrop against which future bills of lading

will be negotiated. It is not, of course, this Court's task to structure the international shipping industry. Future parties remain free to adapt their contracts to the rules set forth here, only now with the benefit of greater predictability concerning the rules for which their contracts might compensate. . . .

Notes and Questions

1. Why would a cargo owner accept a limitation of the carrier's liability to a mere US$500 per package under COGSA when they could simply put a higher value into the Bill of Lading?

2. What is a Himalaya Clause and what is it supposed to do?

3. In paragraph 7, the Court states that Kirby, the shipper, was compensated by the insurance company for his loss. Why would Kirby then join the insurer in suing Norfolk Southern Railway, the carrier?

4. What do you make of the umpteenth discussion of the applicability of federal versus state law to the contract at hand? Can you explain "the conceptual approach" taken by the Supreme Court versus "the spatial approach" taken by the Eleventh Circuit? Do you find Justice O'Connor's reasoning in this regard persuasive? Why or why not?

5. What is meant by the sentence used by Schoenbaum and quoted at the end of paragraph 19: "Bills of lading issued outside the United States are governed by the general maritime law, considering relevant choice of law rules."

6. What was different in *Herd* compared to *Kirby*? Why did the Supreme Court not extend the limitation of liability to the agents and subcontractors in *Herd*, whereas it did so in *Kirby*? Check paragraph 25 for the answer.

7. With regard to the Bill of Lading issued by Hamburg Süd, the Supreme Court enters into a discussion of agency law. The Eleventh Circuit had concluded that there was no agency to justify the extension of the liability limitation. The Supreme Court agreed that there was no agency because "the traditional indicia of agency . . . did not exist between Kirby and ICC." However, the Supreme Court continued by inventing some kind of limited agency to justify the extension of the limitation of liability. How does this argument work and do you find it persuasive? Why or why not?

8. As the lawyers working for a shipper/cargo owner, what do you need to do in order to secure your client's interests and protect them against surprises if their cargo should get lost or damaged somewhere between the seller's and the buyer's premises?

Part Five

The Documentary Sale 4 of 4: Insurance Contracts

In the context of International Business Transactions, under the heading "insurance," several different types of insurance have to be considered. First, the cargo itself should normally be insured against loss or damage that may occur due to damaging weather conditions, fire, theft, careless handling by carriers, their employees, dock workers, etc., or more unusual hazards like piracy, terrorist attacks, or war. Second, the various carriers will usually want insurance for their vehicles and vessels, in particular if they cannot hold cargo owners responsible for damage to their vessel, let alone a complete loss. Third, in particular when aircraft or drones are involved, the owners and operators may be required or may want to carry third-party liability insurance. Finally, if a seller does not get paid in advance and does not have a confirmed letter of credit that ensures that he will get paid, the seller may want to purchase insurance against nonpayment by the buyer.

In this Part, we will focus on cargo insurance as it is a standard component of export/import transactions. We will not go into hull insurance, other insurance for vehicles or vessels, or third party liability insurance, since these are quite specialized topics and generally not of great interest to the seller and buyer in the kind of IBTs we are focusing on in this book.

Section 1. The Origins and History of Cargo Insurance[1]

Interest on loans was prohibited during much of Christian history. As a way of making money from money lending, pawn shops were invented in Italy in the fifth century AD, where money was provided in a kind of sale-repurchase agreement and the profit for the lender was derived from the higher repurchase price. Over time, this created a wealthy class of bankers, including families such as the Medici in Florence. Escaping endless wars in Northern Italy, a number of wealthy merchant and banking families migrated from Lombardy to England in the thirteenth century. These "Lombards" soon became involved in two types of financing transactions

---

1. This section is based on Özlem Gürses, *Marine Insurance Law*, London/New York 2015, in particular pp. 1–6; and "Our History" on www.lloyds.com.

with English seafarers. In return for a share of the profits, the Lombards would finance a marine voyage. If they took the ship itself as security, the transaction was referred to as a "bottomry bond" and if the cargo was used as security, it was referred to as "respondentia." Since the loan did not have to be repaid by the ship owner if the ship and/or the cargo was lost, there was not only a profit-sharing, but also a risk-sharing component. Although the basic idea of bottomry goes back to the Babylonians around 3000 BC, the work of the Lombards became the foundation of modern marine cargo insurance.

The discovery of the Americas, the development of colonies across the globe, and the defeat of the Spanish Armada in 1588 created many opportunities for trade and investment in England from the fifteenth century onward. To contain speculative "bubbles" where trading companies sought large sums from many investors for their exploration of foreign lands, the British Government passed the "Bubble Act" in 1720 and restricted the business of insurance to only two chartered companies: the Royal Exchange Assurance Corporation and the London Assurance Corporation. However, the Bubble Act prohibited only insurance by corporations, societies, and partnerships but not by individuals. In response, Lloyd's and other "protection and indemnity clubs" (P&I Clubs) were formed, which brought together individual investors called "underwriters." Lloyd's started out in 1688 as a coffee shop on Tower Street in the City of London where merchants, ship owners, bankers, and investors liked to meet. Soon enough, it was known as the best place for finding business partners and information about business opportunities related to maritime trade. In 1691, Lloyd's relocated to Lombard Street and soon after, it was officially recognized as the location where marine insurance was underwritten by groups of individuals. Lloyd's List, first published in 1734, is one of the oldest journals in the world, providing shipping and insurance news, weekly at first, daily from the 1830s to 2013, and continuously updated online since then. Initially, Lloyd's grew partly because the Bubble Act severely limited its competition. However, superior information and know-how played a role from the start. In 1811, Lloyd's started building a network of Agents around the world that would send home valuable information about international markets on a regular basis and offer insurance contracts wherever Lloyd's had offices and interests. In 1824, the Bubble Act was repealed and Lloyd's had to deal with new competitors—for example, the Alliance Assurance Company of the Rothschild family. To be able to compete with large corporations, Lloyd's created larger syndicates where more underwriters could share in the risk. Via the First Lloyd's Act, the British Parliament incorporated the Society of Lloyd's in 1871. Soon after, Lloyd's expanded into the reinsurance business.

The San Francisco earthquake in 1906 caused such catastrophic damage that many insurance companies in the U.S. were unable to honor their commitments. However, Lloyd's instructed their San Francisco agent to "pay all of our policyholders in full, irrespective of the terms of their policies" and established itself as the most trustworthy insurance company in the Americas. Today, Lloyd's is number three in the global reinsurance market, after Swiss Re and Munich Re. In the direct insurance business Lloyd's is still a marketplace, bringing together clients from around the world and underwriters who form syndicates to share the risk of a particular insurance transaction. Its reputation and continuous expansion over more than 300 years has contributed significantly to the establishment of London as the preeminent marketplace for (marine) cargo insurance.

Our first case illuminates the specific legal nature of Lloyd's of London and some of its legal consequences. It was brought by American investors who had applied to and been accepted as Lloyd's underwriters, also called "Names." They were unhappy when they had to cover higher insurance payments than expected.

Case 5-1

Roby v. Corporation of Lloyd's of London

796 F. Supp. 103 (S.D.N.Y. 1992)
(Paragraph numbers added.)

LASKER, District Judge.

[1] This action alleges violations of the federal securities laws and RICO[1] against various entities which are part of the enterprise known as Lloyd's of London. The 91 investor-plaintiffs allege that solicitation of investor/underwriters in the United States by Lloyd's agents constitutes "sale of securities" and that Lloyd's syndicates are "issuers" within the meaning of the securities laws. They assert that they were deceived as to, inter alia, the types of risks assumed by, and the experience of the underwriters of, the syndicates in which they invested. The syndicates are groups of insurer-investors which are organized for the purpose of assuming insurance risks.

[2] The Syndicate Defendants move to dismiss the action as to them pursuant to Rule 12(b) (1) and Rule 12(b) (6) of the Fed.R.Civ. P., on the ground that they are not legal entities capable of being sued. The dispositive question is whether a syndicate exists as a separate legal entity apart from the investors in the syndicates (who are generally known as Names); or whether, as the syndicates claim, they are merely "groupings" of individual Lloyd's underwriters who severally undertake insurance obligations.

[3] The syndicates contend that the law of England controls the question of their legal existence England being the syndicates' home jurisdiction and the forum designated under plaintiffs' various agreements with the Lloyd's community, or failing that, that the law of New York, the situs of this action, controls. The plaintiffs submit that federal law, in particular the Securities Act of 1933 and the Securities and Exchange Act of 1934 in combination with Fed. R.Civ.P. 17(b), controls.

[4] The syndicates' motion is granted.

---

1. The RICO counts are predicated exclusively on the alleged securities violations.

I.

[5] Lloyd's of London is a venerable institution, dating back to the latter part of the seventeenth century, long known for its insurance business. Although Lloyd's is generally considered to be a unitary organization, it actually is not, and in fact bears little resemblance to the typical corporate insurer. It issues no insurance policies. Rather, it acts as a market for the buying and selling of insurance risks.

[6] According to the syndicates, the closest American analogue to Lloyd's is the New York Stock Exchange. Lloyd's provides the premises, administrative staff and support services for the market; it also issues rules and regulations and monitors transactions that occur in the market. Like the New York Stock Exchange, Lloyd's does not participate in individual decisions made by its brokers, members or underwriters.

[7] The persons who carry on the business at Lloyd's are, respectively, the brokers, active underwriters, member's agents, managing agents, and Names (who make up the syndicates). The Names are the individual investors. They pay fees and delegate complete authority to conduct Lloyd's affairs to "member's agents." Although Names are the ultimate underwriters of the insurance, they do not participate actively in the underwriting process or in the recruiting of other Names to the syndicates. They have no management authority and cannot bind their fellow members or the syndicate. Membership in a Lloyd's syndicate is personal and not transferable and terminates upon the death of the member.

[8] Member's agents recruit new Names and handle the admission of Names to Lloyd's membership. Member's agents are ordinarily also chosen to act as Names' underwriting agents[2] and, in that role, are responsible for placing Names in syndicates. In connection with the latter, the member's agent contracts with a "managing agent" to place the member in a group comprised of two to several hundred other Names. These groups constitute the syndicates. Managing agents run the syndicates. They hire the syndicate's active underwriter and maintain the syndicates' accounts and other records, among other things.

[9] An employee of the managing agent, known as the "active underwriter," acts on behalf of the Names in a syndicate in the "buying" and "selling" of insurance risks. Active underwriters are seated on the underwriting floor at Lloyd's in London. Brokers approach the active underwriter at his desk in Lloyd's parlance "the box" to solicit the underwriter's agreement to accept a risk. The active underwriter decides which of the risks, offered to him by brokers, to accept and at what premium, and negotiates the conditions of coverage and the proportion of risk his syndicate will assume. See *Syndicate 420 at Lloyd's London v. Early American Insurance Co. Ltd*, 796 F.2d 821, 824 (5th Cir. 1986).

---

2. Managing agents, discussed below, can also be chosen to act as the Names' underwriting agents to perform the function of placing Names in syndicates, but ordinarily a member's agent is chosen.

[10] Through their syndicates, Names subscribe to a certain percentage of the risk on policies, in return for a certain percentage of the premium paid to the syndicate by the insured. Normally, syndicates do not insure 100% of a risk. Rather, a number of syndicates agree to subscribe, each assuming a specified portion of the total risk. A syndicate member is entitled to a specified (contracted-for) share of the profits from the syndicate's business and is responsible for that share of loss only.

[11] Although Names have unlimited personal liability for their respective share of the risk, a Name has no responsibility whatsoever for the liability of his fellow syndicate members. Section 8(I) of the Lloyd's Act of 1982 states: "An underwriting member shall be a party to a contract of insurance underwritten at Lloyd's only if it is underwritten with several liability, each underwriting member for his own part and not one for another and if the liability of each underwriting member is accepted solely for his own account."

[12] In addition, when a Name becomes a member of a syndicate, the contract he or she signs specifies that "[nothing in his or her agreement with the relevant member's agent or managing agent] shall constitute a partnership between the Name and the Agent or between the Name and any or all of the other members of the Contracted Syndicates." Schedule 1, Clause 16.1, Lloyd's Byelaw No. 8 of 1988 Agency Agreements. "Nothing in this Agreement shall constitute any partnership between . . . the Name and any other person or persons whomsoever. . . ." Schedule 1, Clause 20, to Lloyd's Byelaw No. 1 of 1985 Agency Agreements.

[13] Syndicates exist for one year, at the end of which they are dissolved and reconstituted. However, although syndicates are identified by numbers (e.g., Syndicate No. 670), the numbers are often reused from year to year and often, at their option, many of the same Names remain members. The Names elect each year which syndicates they wish to join. A syndicate closes its accounts for a given year by transferring its potential liabilities to the members of the syndicate in the following year of account, a practice called "reinsurance to close," and the same managing agents usually run the syndicates from year to year.

[14] There are approximately 365 syndicates in the Lloyd's system. 300 of them, identified by numerical reference in the caption to the complaint, are named as defendants in this action. They are the syndicates to which the 91 plaintiff-investors belonged.

II.

[15] The Syndicate Defendants argue, and ordinarily it would be the case, that either English or New York law controls as to the legal status of the syndicates. It is syndicates' position that their legal status in England is controlling on the issue of whether they are amenable to suit here and that New York law, if it applies, supports their position. However, according to plaintiffs, federal law controls and that federal law is said to be found in the Securities Acts together with the provisions of Fed. R.Civ.P. 17(b). In brief, plaintiffs assert that Congress legislated that "persons" that are "issuers" are subject to the Securities Act of 1933 and the Securities

and Exchange Act of 1934 and automatically have legal existence. Plaintiffs contend that Fed.R.Civ.P. 17(b) makes clear "the rule-maker's goal of removing any procedural obstacles to fulfillment of Congress's intent." (Letter to Court from Plaintiffs' Counsel (March 26, 1992)).

[16] We conclude that English law applies, but whether the test be under English or New York or federal law, the syndicates do not have legal existence.

III.

[17] It is undisputed that under the law of England, the syndicates do not constitute legal entities. Plaintiffs themselves have submitted a barrister's affidavit that squarely concedes the proposition: "As a matter of law, English courts would be bound to treat the syndicates as unincorporated groups of separate traders, without legal personalities, that could not be sued other than by proceeding against all their individual members or against a representative member or members." Affidavit of Anthony Colman, ¶ 28.

[18] Plaintiffs concede that under English common law, the syndicates would not be amenable to suit under any claims plaintiffs might bring in the United Kingdom. All of the literature concerning Lloyd's defines syndicates as a group of Names on behalf of whom an underwriter accepts insurance business. Standard reference works are replete with comments such as the following: "a syndicate is not a legal entity;"[3] "all Names are . . . sole traders;"[4] "the syndicate itself is not an insuring entity, simply an 'annual venture' between individual Names;"[5] and "Lloyd's structure [is] of a Society of Names trading as sole traders."[6] Furthermore, the informational packets provided to the prospective Names and thus every plaintiff-investor here , as well as the membership documents signed by each Name, specify that syndicates are not legal entities.[7]

[19] If English law applies, therefore, the syndicates' motion must be granted.

* * *

[20] To become a Name, an individual must be nominated and seconded and have established certain minimum financial net worth tests. Under Lloyd's bylaws, the Name is required to travel to London to submit to an interview at Lloyd's. Upon acceptance into the Society of Lloyd's, the individual executes a number of documents, among which are the premium trust deed, a member's agent agreement, and a managing agent agreement. Each of the documents provides that it is to be

---

3. J. Cowen, Lloyd's Regulatory Requirements (Chartered Insurance Institute 1991) (glossary).

4. Stephen Lewis & Jan Woloniecki, "Lloyd's: The Market Structure," in Lloyd's, the ILU and the London Insurance Market, at 39 (PLI Comm.L. & Prac. No. 472 1988).

5. Lloyd's: A Route Forward (1992) (a task force report).

6. Id.

7. The membership brochures state: "A syndicate is not a legal entity. Each member of the syndicate is responsible only for the proportion of business written on his behalf. It is a matter of each for his own part and not one for another."

governed by the law of England. Each by its terms provides for dispute resolution either in the courts or in arbitration, as the document may be, in England. There are presently approximately 26,000 names worldwide; 21,000 plus, or 80 percent, are English citizens. The syndicates argue that because the English Names vastly predominate in the group, because the documents which they execute specify the application of English law and the disposition of disputes in England, and because the documents were all executed in England, English law applies.

[21] In addition, this outcome makes particular sense in this case, according to the syndicates, because it involves agreements with Names throughout the world. As the syndicates reasonably note, it would destroy uniformity of treatment and undermine commercial stability if the determination of the legal existence of the Lloyd's syndicates depended on the fortuitous fact of where a Name's lawyer's office was located, which Name sues, where he or she sues, or what cause of action he or she sues on.

[22] In *Carl Zeiss Stiftung v. VEB Carl Zeiss Jena*, 433 F.2d 686, 698 (2d Cir.1970), cert. denied, 403 U.S. 905, 91 S. Ct. 2205, 29 L. Ed. 2d 680 (1971), the court, quoting then District Judge Mansfield, held that the legal existence of a foreign corporate entity "must be determined by the laws of the country where it has been created and continues to exist." *Id.*[8] It is true that the quoted statement in *Carl Zeiss* was dicta with regard to legal existence because the sole issue there was that of identity between successor entities. Nevertheless, the rule enunciated is still persuasive authority.

[23] New York choice of law rules would reach the same result. In choice of law cases, New York courts apply the criterion of "interests analysis," under which "the law of the jurisdiction which, because of its relationship or contact with the occurrence or the parties, has the greatest concern with the specific issue raised in the litigation," controls. *Istim, Inc. v. Chemical Bank*, 78 N.Y.2d 342, 581 N.E.2d 1042, 575 N.Y.S.2d 796 (Ct.App.1991). Under this standard, because Lloyd's is based in London and approximately 80% of the Names are English citizens, English law governs.

IV.

[24] Although I conclude that English law governs, the application of substantive New York law would result in the same outcome.

[25] This court has previously considered the question whether syndicates qualify under the New York statutory definition of "unincorporated associations," which is the only possible legal classification the syndicates could belong to, since they are neither corporations, partnerships nor individuals.[9] In *Bobe v. Lloyd's*, 27 F.2d

---

8. Carl Zeiss states: ". . . the legal existence, status, identity, and domicile of a foreign corporate entity or juristic personality, such as the Foundation here, must be determined by the laws of the country where it has been created and continues to exist." Id. (quoting the district court decision by Judge Mansfield, 293 F. Supp. 892, 898 (S.D.N.Y.1968)).

9. Plaintiffs more or less concede that the syndicates are not partnerships which would appear to be an obvious conclusion since syndicates lack the essential characteristic of a partnership—joint

340, 345 (S.D.N.Y. 1927), *aff'd per curiam*, 27 F.2d 347 (2d Cir.1928), the court held that the syndicates do not constitute unincorporated associations within the meaning of Section 13 of the New York General Associations Law, the controlling provision. In *Bobe*, a Special Master considered the issue of the syndicates' legal existence under New York statutory law and held, in a report which the court confirmed, that Lloyd's syndicates were not unincorporated associations under New York law, after noting that the Names' "liability was several, not joint, and that each underwriter was obligated only for the amount of his individual underwriting, irrespective of the obligation of any of the other underwriters." *Id.* . . .

V.

[27] As indicated above, plaintiffs take the position that United States law controls. They argue that the Securities Acts together with Fed.R.Civ.P. 17(b) establish the legal existence of the syndicates.

A. Plaintiffs' Contentions under Securities Laws

[28] As we understand plaintiffs' argument, . . . the only question before the Court is whether the syndicates constitute "persons" under the federal securities laws. They argue that, as issuers of securities, the syndicates are by definition, that is, without more, suable under the United States securities laws. But this argument begs the very question which must be decided. In *Dean v. Barber*, 951 F.2d 1210 (11th Cir.1992), the Eleventh Circuit explicitly rejected a similar contention. . . .

[29] The American legal system distinguishes between the concepts of causes of action, on the one hand, and persons who can be sued, on the other. The Securities Acts, supplemented by judicial decisions, do, of course, create various causes of action. But nowhere do they purport to confer legal existence. The Securities Acts provide only that "issuers" are persons who issue securities, and "persons" include "unincorporated associations"[11] or "organized group of persons,"[12] but these provisions do not solve the problem posed by this case because they give no definition of what constitutes an "unincorporated association" or "organized group of persons," and the cases which plaintiffs rely upon for such further definition do not deal with the Securities Acts or their terminology.

[30] *United Mine Workers v. Coronado Coal Co.*, 259 U.S. 344, 351, 42 S. Ct. 570, 66 L. Ed. 975 (1922), is a case upon which plaintiffs place substantial reliance. There, the Supreme Court held that unincorporated labor unions, such as the United Mine

---

liability. However, in a footnote to their brief, they remark: "Although ostensibly Names are not jointly and severally liable for syndicates' debts, discovery may show that the syndicates are also partnerships by estoppel under Section 27 of the New York Partnership Law, at least for purposes of their transactions in the United States."

No indication whatsoever has been provided as to what type of evidence plaintiffs expect to uncover through discovery that might establish a relationship of "partnerships by estoppel."

11. Section 2(2) of the Securities Act, 15 U.S.C. §77b(2).

12. Section 3(a)(9) of the Securities and Exchange Act, 15 U.S.C. §78c(a)(9) and section 3(a)(19), 15 U.S.C. §78c(a)(19).

Workers of America, and its district and local branches—recognized as distinct entities by numerous acts of Congress, as well as by the laws and decisions of many states—were suable under the Sherman Act. However, the Sherman Act, in contrast to the Securities Acts, includes a precise definition of the extent to which an association or group might be held liable as a "person" under the act:

> § 7. 'Person' defined: "The word 'person', or 'persons', wherever used in sections 1 to 7 of this title shall be deemed to include corporations and associations existing under or authorized by the laws of either the United States, the laws of any of the Territories, the laws of any State, or the laws of any foreign country. Sherman Act, 15 U.S.C. § 7.

[31] The securities laws provide no such guidance as to who can be sued under them. Plaintiffs themselves concede that neither the Securities Act of 1933 nor the Securities and Exchange Act of 1934 defines an "unincorporated association" and rely on federal judicial decisions to provide the definition of that term, but, as stated above, the cited decisions do not construe the Securities Acts.

[32] Moreover, no provision of the Securities Acts indicates a legislative intent to confer legal existence on any entity that was not suable prior to enactment of the Securities Acts, and plaintiffs point us to no authority, either in the legislative history of the Acts or judicial decisions, which supports their argument.

[33] Finally, whatever authority there is as to whether the syndicates are "issuers" altogether undermines the plaintiffs' position and specifically the position of the named plaintiff in this case. In a letter to Congressman Don J. Pease of the United States House of Representatives from Mary E.T. Beach, Senior Associate Director of the SEC, dated August 5, 1991, in response to a letter from him forwarding questions raised by his constituent, John S. Roby (the lead plaintiff here), Ms. Beach states: "The staff of the Commission's Division of Corporation Finance has had discussions on two occasions with Lloyd's concerning the applicability of the Securities Act of 1933 . . . and the Securities and Exchange Act of 1934 . . . to the solicitation of U.S. Citizens to participate in Lloyd's. It is the Division's position that the solicitation of participations involves the sale of a security, with the issuer of that security being the particular Members' Agent [not the syndicate] involved."

[34] Thus such authority as there is refutes the argument that, in plaintiffs' words, Congress "deemed" syndicates to be among the class of possible defendants under the federal securities laws.

B. Plaintiffs' Contentions under Rule 17(b)

[35] Rule 17(b) provides in pertinent part:

> *Capacity to Sue or be Sued.* The capacity of an individual, other than one acting in a representative capacity, to sue or be sued shall be determined by the law of the individual's domicile. The capacity of a corporation to sue or be sued shall be determined by the law under which it was organized. In all other cases capacity to sue or be sued shall be determined by the law

of the state in which the district court is held, *except (1) that a partnership or other unincorporated association, which has no such capacity by the law of such state, may sue or be sued in its common name for the purpose of enforcing for or against it a substantive right existing under the Constitution or laws of the United States, ...* (emphasis added).

[36] Plaintiffs argue that because they "have sued the syndicates only under the federal securities and RICO laws, and hence seek to enforce only federal substantive rights, the syndicates' capacity to be sued is [ ] governed by Fed.R.Civ.P. 17(b)." As the plaintiffs' counsel states in his letter to the court of April 2, 1992: ". . . in promulgating Fed.R.Civ.P 17(b) in 1937, the Supreme Court consciously acted to federalize the definition of an 'unincorporated association' where, as here, Congress through specific legislation intended to render an unincorporated association subject to suit, notwithstanding any contrary bar or absence of authority under otherwise applicable law, whether state or foreign."

[37] The Syndicate Defendants respond that plaintiffs' theory is analytically flawed. They contend that, as a rule of civil procedure, Rule 17(b) confers no substantive rights and is not triggered until a Court has first made the threshold determination that the party in question is a legal entity. They maintain that Rule 17(b) does not purport to, and cannot constitutionally, establish the legal existence of a particular entity. Creation of a legal entity, other than an individual, according to the syndicates, can be accomplished only by legislation, not by a rule of procedure.

1. Legal existence and capacity to sue and be sued are distinct concepts on their face

[38] Capacity to be sued and legal existence are separate and distinct concepts. Both capacity to be sued and legal existence are prerequisites to the suability of an entity, but Rule 17(b) speaks only to capacity to sue or be sued.

[39] That legal existence and capacity to be sued are distinct concepts is made clear by the language of Rule 9(a) of the Fed. R.Civ.P. which specifically distinguishes between the "legal existence of any party," on the one hand, and "the capacity of any party to sue or be sued," on the other.[13] Judicial decisions even those cited by plaintiffs demonstrate that Rule 17(b) addresses only the question of capacity to sue or be sued. See, e.g., *Klinghoffer v. S.N.C. Achille Lauro*, 739 F. Supp. 854, 858, 865-66 (S.D.N.Y.1990) (treating issue of legal existence and capacity to sue separately), *vacated on other grounds*, 937 F.2d 44 (2d Cir.1991) (on other grounds); *Associated Students v. Kleindienst*, 60 F.R.D. 65, 67 (C.D.Cal.1973) (same).[14]

---

13. Rule 9. Pleading Special Matters: "(1) Capacity. It is not necessary to aver the capacity of a party to sue or be sued or the authority of a party to sue or be sued in a representative capacity or the legal existence of an organized association of persons that is made a party. . . ."

14. Plaintiffs refer to *United Mine Workers v. Coronado Coal Co.*, 259 U.S. 344, 351, 42 S. Ct. 570, 66 L. Ed. 975 (1922), supra, and an article written by Dean (later Judge) Clark and Professor Moore, "A New Federal Procedure II. Pleading and Practice," 44 Yale L.J. 1291, 1312–17 (1935), interpreting the Federal Rules of Civil Procedure prior to their adoption. In these works, there is at times a lack

[40] Put another way, the reach of Rule 17(b) is limited to providing that partnerships or other unincorporated associations which have no capacity under state law to sue or be sued may nevertheless sue or be sued in their common name in federal court for the purpose of enforcing for or against them a substantive right existing under the Constitution or laws of the United States, but Rule 17(b) does not confer legal existence or create new types of legal entities.

[41] Plaintiffs contend that formal organization or compliance with an organizational statute is not required to permit an unincorporated association to be sued on a federal question. But "unincorporated association" is a term of art every group that is not a corporation or partnership is not automatically an unincorporated association. "It is well settled that it must appear that an association, if it is not a corporation, has received by appropriate legislation a legal status before it, or its members, may be sued in the name of the group." *United Mine Workers v. Coronado Coal Co.*, 259 U.S. 344, 351, 42 S. Ct. 570, 66 L. Ed. 975 (1922). Plaintiffs have failed to establish that the syndicates are unincorporated associations under any possibly applicable law English, federal or New York State and indeed English and New York law are directly to the contrary.

2. Legal existence is a substantive proposition that cannot be controlled by a rule of procedure

[42] A further proposition which undermines the plaintiffs' contention that Rule 17(b) confers legal existence on the syndicates is that to do so would violate the Rules Enabling Act, 28 U.S.C. § 2072(b), which provides that the Federal Rules of Civil Procedure may not "abridge, enlarge or modify any substantive right." As the United States Supreme Court has construed the Rules Enabling Act: "An authority conferred upon a court to make rules of procedure for the exercise of its jurisdiction is not an authority to enlarge that jurisdiction; and the Act . . . authorizing this Court to prescribe rules of procedure in civil actions gave it no authority to modify, abridge or enlarge the substantive rights of litigants or to enlarge or diminish the jurisdiction of federal courts." *United States v. Sherwood*, 312 U.S. 584, 589-590, 61 S. Ct. 767, 771, 85 L. Ed. 1058 (1941).

[43] The syndicates submit that if Rule 17(b) were construed to create a legal entity, the court would be performing a legislative rather than a judicial function. That argument has merit.

[44] The plaintiffs acknowledge that if the issue of legal existence is a substantive proposition, Rule 17(b) could not control it. The plaintiffs, however, take the

---

of clarity concerning a distinction between the concepts of "legal existence" and "capacity to sue or be sued" which plaintiffs contend proves their point that Rule 17(b) performs the function of providing for both concepts (or that the two concepts are identical). But regardless of what Clark and Moore in their article may or may not say, there is no question that courts have consistently recognized a distinction between the concepts of legal existence and capacity to sue or be sued in the interpretation of Rule 17(b). . . .

position, without citing any authority, that the question of legal existence is procedural, not substantive. While the authority on the point is slim perhaps because the answer to the question is obvious , it favors the syndicates' position. For example, in his discussion of the subject in *Busby v. Electric Utilities Employees Union*, 323 U.S. 72, 76-77, 65 S. Ct. 142, 145, 89 L. Ed. 78 (1944) (concurring), Justice Frankfurter distinguishes between "suability" and "status" and characterizes "suability" as a "procedural matter" and "determination of status" as a "substantive issue." *Id.*

C. Plaintiffs' miscellaneous contentions

[45] In a number of cases in the United States, syndicates have been sued and been treated as legal entities, and some syndicates have themselves sued or asserted counterclaims. Plaintiffs argue that such actions and determinations contradict the syndicates' claim of non-existence. However, in none of the cases referred to was the question of the syndicates' legal existence ever raised, nor is there any assertion that any syndicate which is a defendant here was a party to the earlier litigation. The issue of legal existence arose, if at all, only indirectly, in the context of determining what kind of entity a syndicate was for purposes of determining diversity jurisdiction. See *International Insurance Co. v. Certain Underwriters at Lloyd's London*, 1991 WL 349914, 1991 U.S.Dist. LEXIS 12,937 (N.D.Ill.1991) and *Graham v. Lloyd's of London*, 371 S.E.2d 801, 296 S.C. 249 (S.C.App.1988).

[46] The plaintiffs also suggest that the syndicates must have legal existence because they own property interests in the $9 billion Lloyd's American Trust Fund ("LATF") held by Citibank, N.A., in New York. Even assuming for the moment that the syndicates have an ownership in the funds, plaintiffs have not shown that such ownership would alone confer legal existence upon the syndicates under English, New York or federal law.

[47] Moreover, there is sufficient undisputed material before the Court in the form of affidavits submitted by both sides to support a conclusion that at best the nature of the syndicates' interest is not that of an owner or beneficiary but that of a nominee or fund manager. The record is incomplete on this point, but at best what has been presented even by the plaintiffs leaves considerable doubt whether the syndicates own property interests in the LATF. For example, in a post-argument motion filed by the plaintiffs under Fed.R.Civ.P. 56(f) for further discovery on the subject, a supporting barrister's affidavit states: "I would emphasize that there is no money in the LATF that is not Names' money." The direct beneficiaries of the fund appear to be the policy holders, to the extent of their justified insurance claims; the Names having a reversionary interest in any funds left in the LATF after payout of claims.

[48] In sum: English law controls, and under English law the syndicates have no legal existence. The result is the same under New York or federal law. Accordingly, the motion to dismiss pursuant to Fed.R.Civ.P. 12(b) (6) is granted. It is unnecessary to determine whether the complaint is defective also under Fed.R.Civ.P. 12(b) (1).

The complaint is dismissed as to the Syndicate Defendants. It is so ordered.

Notes and Questions

1. After Judge Lasker granted the motion to dismiss for lack of suability with regard to the syndicates, Judge Lasker, on August 18, 1992, also dealt with the other defendants' motion to dismiss for improper venue. The judge held that the investors' claims were governed by English forum selection and arbitration clauses (824 F. Supp. 336). Of course, referral to the courts of England would also secure that Lloyd's as such would not be regarded as a suable entity.

On appeal against these decisions, the U.S. Court of Appeals for the Second Circuit, affirmed, leaving it open whether the syndicates did or did not have entity existence. The Court of Appeals held that "even if we assume the syndicates to have entity existence, we would affirm the dismissal of the Roby Names' complaint on the basis of improper venue" (996 F.2d 1353). It referred to Paragraph 2.2 of the General Undertaking between any Name and the Lloyd's governing bodies, which includes the following forum choice: "Each party hereto irrevocably agrees that the courts of England shall have exclusive jurisdiction to settle any dispute and/or controversy of whatsoever nature arising out of or relating to the [Name's] membership of, and/or underwriting of insurance business at, Lloyd's." The Supreme Court denied certiorari on November 1, 1993 (114 S. Ct. 385).

The consequence of these decisions is that Lloyd's as such cannot be sued in the U.S. because its contracts refer to the courts of England. Even if the matter is outside of contract law—for example arising in tort or property—Lloyd's as such can probably not be sued in the U.S. (or in the UK) because it is not a legal person. This is an enviable position for an entity that holds more than US$70 billion in assets, underwrites some US$45 billion in insurance premiums annually, and is number three in the global reinsurance market.

However, does the fact that Lloyd's is not a legal person mean that they can never be sued by insured parties anywhere? Or by Names/investors? Who are "they" in this context? How could Lloyd's possibly be so successful over such a long period of time, if it cannot be held legally accountable? Remember the analogy with the New York Stock Exchange and similar marketplaces when pondering the answer to this question.

2. In the present case, about 91 American Names sued Lloyd's, claiming that they were deceived about the risk and types of risks they were agreeing to secure. Judge Lasker, in paragraph 23, refers to the "interest analysis" in New York choice of law rules. In plain English, the applicable law should be the one of the jurisdiction that has the greatest interest in the specific dispute. In paragraphs 20 and 21, the judge prioritizes the interest of Lloyd's in uniformity of treatment over the interests of the American Names. Similarly, the Court of Appeals held that "the syndicates have a pecuniary interest in the certainty and consistency of litigating in one nation's courts under one nation's laws" (at p. 1359). However, by contrast to Judge Lasker, the Court of Appeals emphasized the fact that the General Undertakings signed between the Names and Lloyd's governing bodies not only contained a clear and

unambiguous forum choice in Paragraph 2.2, but "Paragraph 2.1 is equally broad and provides for the application of English law" (Id.). In concluding, the Court of Appeals held "that the Roby Names' contract clauses [with choices for English law and English courts] cover the scope of, and the parties named in, the complaint and that the Roby Names have remedies under English law adequate not only to vindicate their substantive rights but also to protect the public policies established by the United States securities laws" (at p. 1366).

The UK Marine Insurance Act of 1906, as the first modern codification of marine insurance law, not only bolstered the position of the City of London in this regard but has also informed marine cargo insurance law in the U.S., where this subject is not codified, but developed via federal common law based on the Admiralty Clause in the U.S. Constitution. Professor Schoenbaum describes the symbiotic relationship between English and American law as follows: "The American law of marine insurance took its cue from English law; there was no American statute, and English legal precedents were cited routinely in American courts. For 50 years after the English law was codified in the Marine Insurance Act 1906 (MIA), it could truly be said that there was a unified Anglo-American law of marine insurance, and that English law was part of the 'general maritime law' of the United States."[2]

As late as 1953, the U.S. Court of Appeals for the Fifth Circuit held in a purely domestic case that "[i]t is the settled doctrine that a marine contract of insurance is 'derived from' is 'governed by', and is a 'part of' the general maritime law of the world." (*Wilburn Boat Co. v. Fireman's Fund Ins. Co.*, 201 F.2d 833, 1953 A.M.C. 284). However, things got a lot more complicated right afterward because the U.S. Supreme Court reversed and the cause was remanded with directions:

Case 5-2

Wilburn Boat Co. v. Fireman's Fund Ins. Co.

(Paragraph numbers added, some footnotes omitted.)
348 U.S. 310 (1955)

[2] Since the insurance policy here sued on is a maritime contract the Admiralty Clause of the Constitution brings it within federal jurisdiction. *New England Mutual Marine Insurance Co. v. Dunham*, 11 Wall. 1, 20 L.Ed. 90. But it does not follow, as the courts below seemed to think, that every term in every maritime contract can only be controlled by some federally defined admiralty rule. In the field of maritime contracts as in that of maritime torts, the National Government has left much regulatory power in the States. . . . [T]his state regulatory power, exercised with federal consent or acquiescence, has always been particularly broad in relation to insurance companies and the contracts they make. . . .

---

2. Thomas J. Schoenbaum, *Key Divergences Between English and American Law of Marine Insurance: A Comparative Study*, Cornell Maritime Pr/Tidewater Pub 1999, at p. 12.

[9] Under our present system of diverse state regulations, which is as old as the Union, the insurance business has become one of the great enterprises of the Nation. Congress has been exceedingly cautious about disturbing this system, even as to marine insurance where congressional power is undoubted. We, like Congress, leave the regulation of marine insurance where it has been—with the States. . . .

[The treatment of maritime insurance as just another form of insurance and, consequently, the blanket rejection of federal rules—developed by federal courts in harmony with English maritime insurance law—by Justice Black, writing for the majority, was immediately criticized by Justice Frankfurter in a "limiting concurrence":]

[10] This case concerns a marine insurance policy covering a small houseboat yacht, . . . plying the waters of Lake Texoma, an artificial inland lake between Texas and Oklahoma. . . . After [the boat] was destroyed by fire while lying idle on Lake Texoma, it was discovered that certain warranties of the insurance policy had been ignored by petitioner. Under a uniform rule of admiralty law governing breach of such warranties, petitioner probably would be unable to recover on the policy. Texas statute law, however, might excuse the breaches of warranty, although this is by no means clear. Our problem is whether this situation—involving a marine policy such as is the basis of litigation—calls for a uniform rule throughout the country applicable to breaches of warranty of all similar marine insurance contracts.

[11] There is no doubt that as to some matters affecting maritime affairs the States are excluded from indulging in variant state policies. E.g., *Chelentis v. Luckenbach S.S. Co.*, 247 U.S. 372, 38 S.Ct. 501, 62 L.Ed. 1171, *The Lottawanna*, 21 Wall. 558, 22 L.Ed. 654. Equally, there is no doubt that some matters are so predominantly restricted in the range of their significance that a uniform admiralty rule need not be recognized or fashioned. E.g., *Madruga v. Superior Court*, 346 U.S. 556, 74 S.Ct. 298, 98 L.Ed. 290; *C. J. Hendry Co. v. Moore*, 318 U.S. 133, 63 S.Ct. 499, 87 L.Ed. 663; *The Hamilton*, 207 U.S. 398, 28 S.Ct. 133, 52 L.Ed. 264. Therefore the question, and the only question now to be decided, is whether the demands of uniformity relevant to maritime law require that marine insurance on a houseboat yacht brought to Lake Texoma for private recreation should be subject to the same rules of law as marine insurance on a houseboat yacht 'confined,' after arrival, to the waters of Lake Tahoe or Lake Champlain. The provision of the policy whereby the insured warranted 'that the vessel will be confined to Lake Texoma' conveys the emphasis of the situation—the essentially localized incidence of the transaction despite the interstate route followed in reaching the circumscribed radius within which the yacht was to move. It is reasonable to conclude that the interests concerned with shipping in its national and international aspects are substantially unconcerned with the rules of law to be applied to such limited situations. I join in a result restricted within this compass.

[12] Unfortunately, for reasons that I do not appreciate, the Court's opinion goes beyond the needs of the problem before it. Unless I wholly misconceive that opinion, its language would be invoked when cases so decisively different in degree as to be different in kind come before this Court. It seems directed with equal force to

ocean-going vessels in international maritime trade, as well as coastal, intercoastal and river commerce. Is it to be assumed that were the Queen Mary, on a world pleasure cruise, to touch at New York City, New Orleans and Galveston, a Lloyds policy covering the voyage would be subjected to the varying insurance laws of New York, Louisiana and Texas? Such an assumption, I am confident, would not prevail were decision necessary. The business of marine insurance often may be so related to the success of many manifestations of commercial maritime endeavor as to demand application of a uniform rule of law designed to eliminate the vagaries of state law and to keep harmony with the marine insurance laws of other great maritime powers. . . . It cannot be that by this decision the Court means suddenly to jettison the whole past of the admiralty provision of Article III and to renounce requirements for nationwide maritime uniformity, except insofar as Congress has specifically enacted them, in the field of marine insurance. . . .

[Justices Reed and Burton, dissenting, were even more outspoken:]

[18] . . . Our admiralty laws, like our common law, came from England. As a matter of American judicial policy, we tend to keep our marine insurance laws in harmony with those of England. *Queen Ins. Co. of America v. Globe & Rutgers Fire Ins. Co.*, 263 U.S. 487, 493, 44 S.Ct. 175, 176, 68 L.Ed. 402; *Calmar Steamship Corp. v. Scott*, 345 U.S. 427, 442—443, 73 S.Ct. 739, 747, 97 L.Ed. 1125. Before our Revolution, the rule of strict compliance with maritime insurance warranties [i.e., the doctrine of uberrimae fidei] had been established as the law of England. That rule persists. While no case of this Court has been cited or found that says specifically that the rule of strict compliance is to be applied in admiralty and maritime cases, that presupposition has been consistently adopted as the basis of reasoning from our earliest days. Other courts have been more specific. No case holds to the contrary. . . .

[20] This brings me to the crucial phase of the Court's decision which, so the Court says, 'leaves the regulation of maritime insurance where it has been—with the States.' This is the dominant issue here, and the Court's decision strikes deep into the principle of a uniform admiralty law and will have the result of unduly burdening maritime commerce. . . .

[21] One rule of laws stands unquestioned. That is that all courts, state and federal, which have jurisdiction to enforce maritime or admiralty substantive rights must do so according to federal admiralty law. See particularly the excellent discussion of Judge Magruder in *Doucette v. Vincent*, 1 Cir., 194 F.2d 834, 841 et seq. The issue of an insurer's liability upon an insured's broken warranty is clearly a matter of substantive law. . . .

[22] . . . The answer as to whether state or federal law governs marine insurance contracts lies in the nature of the federal admiralty jurisdiction.

[23] The Constitution, Art. III, s 2 provides that 'The judicial Power shall extend * * * to all Cases of admiralty and maritime Jurisdiction * * *.' The First Congress enacted that the district courts 'shall also have exclusive original cognizance of all civil causes of admiralty and maritime jurisdiction * * * saving to suitors, in all

cases, the right of a common law remedy, where the common law is competent to give it * * *.' In this manner national control was asserted over maritime litigation. It was needed because the Republic bordered a great length of the Atlantic littoral and the navigable waters furnished the best avenue of transportation.

[24] Although congressional authority over maritime trade was not expressly granted by the Constitution, the grant of admiralty jurisdiction together with the Necessary and Proper Clause has been found adequate to enable Congress to declare the prevailing maritime law for navigable waters throughout the Nation. The Commerce Clause aids where interstate commerce is affected, but has not the scope of 'navigable waters.' . . .

[26] State authority, however, although it may provide remedies, does not extend to changing the general substantive admiralty law. That is the maritime law existing as a body of law enforceable in admiralty. The extent of the states' power to grant rights arising from maritime incidents is not subject to definition. It may vary as the course or manner of navigation or commerce changes. It exists in some circumstances, . . . and . . . must be determined in each situation. The principles which control the validity of an assertion of state power in the admiralty sphere are, however, clear. State power may be exercised where it is complementary to the general admiralty law. It may not be exercised where it would have the effect of harming any necessary or desirable uniformity. The cases decided by this Court make it plain that state legislation will not be permitted to burden maritime commerce with variable rules of law that destroy that uniformity.

[27] Since Congress has power to make federal jurisdiction and legislation exclusive, the situation in admiralty is somewhat analogous to that governing state action interfering with interstate commerce. In the absence of congressional direction, it is this Court that must bear the heavy responsibility of saying when a state statute has burdened the required federal uniformity. It is one thing to allow the States to add a remedy or create a new cause of action for certain incidents arising out of maritime activity. It is quite another thing to relinquish an entire body of substantive law making for a whole phase of maritime activity to the States. Such action does violence to the premise upon which the admiralty jurisdiction was constructed.

[28] . . . A vessel moves from State to State along our coasts or rivers. State lines may run with the channel or across it. Under maritime custom an insurance policy usually covers the vessel wherever it may go. If uniformity is needed anywhere, it is needed in marine insurance. . . .

Notes and Questions

1. What are the pros and cons of giving the regulatory power over marine insurance issues to the states instead of the federal government? How would you argue the case on behalf of the states?

2. What do you think of the Commerce Clause analogy presented in the dissenting opinion? What is the scope of the Interstate Commerce Clause? Could the

federal government adopt a sales law along the lines of the UCC and make it binding for all transactions that cross state (or national) borders? What would be the pros and cons of such a federal law?

3. After the *Wilburn Boat* decision, many commentators and courts tried to limit its impact to cases that are either confined to a single state or at least not international cases.[3] Some courts basically ignored it altogether. References to English law, and in particular the UK Marine Insurance Act (last amended in 2012, Documents p. I-744), became fewer in American courts but did not stop completely. When reading the following cases, make sure to note whether a reference is based on a choice of law by the parties or the conviction of the judges that American marine insurance law continues—and should continue—to be aligned with English marine insurance law.[4]

Case 5-3

St. Paul Ins. Co. v. Great Lakes Turnings, Ltd.

829 F. Supp. 982 (N.D. Ill. 1993)
(Paragraph numbers added, some footnotes omitted.)
Opinion, Brian Barnet Duff, D.J.

[1] This is a marine insurance case. Counts II and III of the Second Amended Complaint ask for rescission of an insurance policy under the doctrine of *uberrimae fidei* (utmost good faith and honesty) based on misrepresentations and nondisclosures which the Defendant assureds allegedly made to the Plaintiff insurer. The Defendants have filed a motion to dismiss Counts II and III of the Second Amended Complaint. They assert that *uberrimae fidei* is not applicable and that, accordingly, the Illinois doctrine of ordinary good faith in insurance contracts governs this dispute. Under this doctrine, the Defendants assert that the Plaintiff has not stated a claim for relief. For the following reasons, the motion to dismiss is denied.

Background

[2] The Plaintiff, St. Paul Insurance Company of Illinois, insures ship charterers against liabilities incurred on chartered voyages. The Defendant, Great Lakes Turnings, Ltd. ("Great Lakes"), fashions and transports steel turnings. In June 1987, Defendant Great Lakes took out a one-year charterer's protection and indemnity "open policy" with the Plaintiff to insure voyages it would charter to ship its steel turnings between the Great Lakes area and Spain ("the Policy"). An open marine insurance policy is one for which a premium is typically paid for each individual

---

3. The next case, *St. Paul Insurance v. Great Lakes Turnings*, illustrates how this particular American court disagrees with the majority opinion in *Wilburn Boat* and basically follows Justice Frankfurter's approach of differentiating purely localized versus international transactions (see paras. 15 et seq., in particular paras. 19 and 23–25).

4. For further analysis, see, for example, Robert Bocko et al., *Marine Insurance Survey; A Comparison of United States Law to the Marine Insurance Act of 1906*, 20 Tul. Mar. L.J. 5, 8 (1995).

voyage. . . . Unlike a "valued" policy, the assured is usually required to declare each voyage made within the duration of the policy. . . . The Policy was renewed in 1988, 1989 and 1990. Between 1987 and 1990, the Defendants chartered thirty-seven voyages and informed the Plaintiff of and paid the premium for five of these.

[3] Clauses 10 and 14 of the Policy provide that the assured must give prompt notice of changes in policy conditions and pay additional premiums if necessary, and that "(t)he Assured agrees to advise the Assurer as soon as practicable the Name, Tonnage, and On Hire and Off Hire date of all vessels chartered during the currency of the policy." The Plaintiff asserts that Form SP 23 (a standard marine P & I form) was also part of the Policy. In relevant part, the Form SP 23 provides that the Defendant will promptly notify and forward to the Plaintiff information about any occurrence which may result in liability.

[4] On or about February 10, 1990, the Defendants chartered the *M/V Star I* to transport steel turnings from a port in Louisiana to Pasajes, Spain. This charter was not one of the five which was declared or for which a premium was paid to the Plaintiff. The ship arrived in port at Pasajes on or about March 6, 1990. Sometime on March 7, 1990, the ship was allegedly damaged by a fire in the cargo holds. The owner of the *Star I* is presently suing Defendant Great Lakes in the United States District Court for the Southern District of New York, alleging that the negligence of its agents and/or employees caused the fire which damaged the ship. The Plaintiff has brought the instant suit seeking a declaratory judgment that the Policy did not cover this damage. In Counts II and III, which are the object of this motion to dismiss, the Plaintiff alleges that the misrepresentations and nondisclosures of the Defendants were violations of the admiralty standard of utmost good faith in marine contracts (*uberrimae fidei*) and allow the Plaintiff to rescind the Policy.

Discussion . . .

[6] It is undisputed that marine contracts, including marine insurance contracts, fall under federal admiralty jurisdiction in Article 3, 2 of the United States Constitution. *The New England Marine Insurance Co. v. Dunham,* 78 U.S. (11 Wall.) 1, 31 (1871); *Kossick v. United Fruit Co.,* 365 U.S. 731, 735 . . . (1961); *Albany Ins. Co. v. Anh Thi Kieu,* 1991 AMC 2211, 2214, 927 F.2d 882, n.2 (5 Cir.), *cert. den.* 502 U.S. __, 1992 AMC 2701 (1991); *Albany Ins. Co. v. Wisniewski,* 1985 AMC 689, 702, 579 F.Supp. 1004, 1013 (D.R.I. 1984). However, Congressional acquiescence to state insurance regulation has established a broad presumption that state codes regulating marine insurance contracts are valid notwithstanding the federal nature of admiralty law. *Wilburn Boat Co. v. Fireman's Fund Ins. Co.* [above, p. 618] (1955), *citing* the McCarran-Ferguson Act, 15 U.S.C. 1011 *et seq.*

[7] When no particular state code exists to govern a marine insurance dispute, but the state does possess a general regulatory scheme over insurance contracts, state law will govern if the state has a substantial and legitimate interest in the furtherance of its own laws in the dispute and there is no relevant established federal precedent. *Kossick,* 365 U.S. 731 . . . ; *Wilburn Boat,* 348 U.S. 310 . . . .

I. Substantial and Legitimate State Interest in Marine Insurance.

[8] Illinois has no substantial and legitimate interest in the application of its regulatory scheme concerning insurance nondisclosures and misrepresentations to the dispute at bar. As noted above, state insurance regulatory schemes do not govern marine insurance disputes if the state does not have a substantial and legitimate interest in the application of its law. *Kossick*, 365 U.S. at 738 . . . ; *Albany*, . . . 927 F.2d at 887. In other words, unless the local interest in the controversy materially exceeds the federal marine concerns, federal admiralty law will apply. *Id.*

[9] In *Kossick*, a seaman on shore in New York made an oral agreement by telephone with his employer regarding medical treatment. Under the New York Statute of Frauds, the oral agreement was not a contract; however, under federal admiralty law, the oral agreement was a contract. The *Kossick* court ruled that the controlling question for deciding whether state or federal law applies to a marine contract dispute is "whether the alleged contract, though marine, is 'maritime and local.'" *Id.* 365 U.S. at 738 . . . (citation omitted). This balancing of state and federal interests addresses the "process of accommodation, entirely familiar in many areas of overlapping state and federal concern," that allows states to maintain an interest in the "status and wellbeing" of its citizens. *Kossick*, 365 U.S. at 739 . . . . The Supreme Court found that the application of state law would disturb the uniformity of marine law because such an oral contract "may well have been made anywhere in the world, and that the validity of it should be judged by one law wherever it was made." *Id.* 365 U.S. at 741 . . . . Moreover, the Supreme Court held that the contract at issue was not "peculiarly a matter of state and local concern." *Id.* (citation omitted).

[10] Likewise, in the case at bar, the contract at issue is not peculiarly a matter of state and local concern.[2] First, the Illinois statute on point, 215 ILCS 5/154, specifically excludes marine insurance from its scope: "(t)his section shall not apply to policies of marine. insurance." 215 ILCS 5/154. The statute requires an insurer to request specific information and for the insured to intentionally provide a false reply before a policy can be avoided. 215 ILCS 5/154 (Michie 1993); *Preferred Risk Mutual Insurance Company v. Hites*, 125 Ill. App. 2d 144 (1970). This standard demands substantially less strict behavior of assureds than the federal standard in which any nondisclosure or misrepresentation, even if made unknowingly, will void the policy if it pertains to information material to the risk assumed by the insurer. *Ingersoll Mill. Mach. Co. v. M/V Bodena*, [below, p. 647]. Thus, 215 ILCS 5/154 indicates that Illinois has not asserted any particular interest in the dispute at bar.

[11] Second, the international and commercial nature of the case at bar puts this dispute outside the sort of concerns contemplated by Illinois insurance regulations.

---

2. The states generally exempt marine insurance from the kind of licensing and rate regulations that apply to other types of insurance. See generally Thomas J. Schoenbaum and A. N. Yannapoulos, Admiralty and Maritime Law: Cases and Materials 525–26. *See also* 215 ILCS 5/154 (*"This section shall not apply to policies of marine. insurance."*) and 215 ILCS 5/4 (exempting from class of marine insurance the loss from various perils of the sea and waterways).

Cases in which the federal courts applied state insurance laws involve particularly local or regional maritime matters. For example, in *Irwin v. Eagle Star Insurance Co.*, . . . 455 F.2d 827 (5 Cir. 1972), the state law was applied because the insurer and the broker were Florida registered business agents, the plaintiff was a Florida resident, and the damaged yacht at issue was anchored in Florida waters when she sank. *Id.*, . . . 455 F.2d at 830. In contrast, in the case at bar, the controversy involves an insurance policy covering ocean crossing charters from the Great Lakes to Europe for the carriage of international commerce. . . .

[13] Accordingly, since Illinois has only a minimal interest if any in this dispute, *uberrimae fidei* governs this case. Even if Illinois did have a substantial and legitimate interest though, as discussed below, *uberrimae fidei* would still apply.

II. *Uberrimae Fidei* is Established Federal Precedent.

[14] Prior to 1955, it was generally accepted that *uberrimae fidei* applied to all of the conduct which assureds and insurers accorded each other regarding marine insurance. *See generally* Graydon S. Staring, *Admiralty and Maritime Law: Selected Topics*, 26 Tort & Ins. L.J. 538 (Spring 1991). Some confusion sprang up that year when *Wilburn Boat Co. v. Fireman's Fund Ins. Co.* constricted the range of scenarios to which *uberrimae fidei* applied. *Id.*

[15] In *Wilburn Boat*, the Supreme Court ruled that because Congress established a strong presumption that states should regulate insurance contracts, if there was not an established federal precedent of applying federal admiralty law to a particular type of marine insurance dispute, then the state insurance regulatory scheme would govern. Because at that time there was not a federal admiralty doctrine concerning the discharge of express and discrete contractual duties, i.e., *express warranties*, the Supreme Court declined to expand the federal admiralty standard into a new area and instead allowed the strong presumption of state regulation to prevail.

[16] In that case, the owner of a small houseboat which operated on Lake Texoma, a small artificial lake between Texas and Oklahoma, had taken out a marine insurance policy to cover loss by fire. Within the duration of the policy, the owners used the boat for commercial purposes to transport passengers and also transferred legal title of the boat. Both commercial use and title transfer were breaches of express warranties of the insurance policy. The boat was destroyed by fire, and the owners sought to collect on the policy. Under Texas law, the insurance company could not rescind the policy based on the assured's breaches of warranties. The insurer relied instead on the federal doctrine of utmost good faith in admiralty law in refusing payment for the loss. After finding no federal precedent for applying the standard of utmost good faith to express warranties, the Supreme Court ruled that Texas insurance law and not federal admiralty law applied to this dispute.

[17] Subsequent to *Wilburn Boat*, the courts have differed in the types of factual scenarios in which they concluded that there is established federal precedent. The rulings in the other courts of appeals on the extent to which *uberrimae fidei* applies in a marine insurance setting have ranged from automatic application of the federal

rule, e.g., *Knight v. U.S. Fire Ins. Co.*, . . . 804 F.2d 9, 13 (2 Cir. 1986) ("It is well-established under the doctrine of *uberrimae fidei* that the parties to a marine insurance policy must accord each other the highest degree of good faith."); *Puritan Ins. Co. v. Eagle S.S. Co. S.A.*, . . . 779 F.2d 866, 870 (2 Cir. 1985); *Ingersoll Mill. Mach. Co. v. M/V Bodena*, . . . 829 F.2d 293, 308 (2 Cir. 1987); to reluctant application of the state rule, e.g., *Albany*, . . . 927 F.2d at 889 ("(N)o opinion of this Court has ever explicitly authorized the application of the *uberrimae fidei* doctrine to invalidate a marine insurance policy. We conclude, albeit with some hesitation, that the *uberrimae fidei* doctrine is not 'entrenched federal precedent.'")

[18] The Seventh Circuit is among those which have not yet addressed *Wilburn Boat*, nor ruled at all on this aspect of marine insurance contracts. This court is therefore obliged to determine the extent to which *uberrimae fidei* should apply to marine insurance disputes in this circuit. As an initial matter, this court notes that the case at bar is factually distinguishable from *Wilburn Boat* for two reasons. First, *Wilburn Boat* involved discrete contractual duties (i.e., express warranties) which the assured allegedly breached, whereas at bar the dispute covers an ongoing obligation to report changes material to the risk assumed by the insurer. Second, *Wilburn Boat* involved an inland marine matter while the case at bar involves a trans-ocean commercial setting.

[19] Given that the case at bar is distinguishable, the court must determine if there is established federal precedent governing this particular dispute. The court notes two dispositive points. First, if it applies anywhere, *uberrimae fidei* applies to those elements of a marine insurance policy which establish ongoing and continuous contractual duties between the parties. Second, the need for a single national voice in the field of international trade, and the need for harmonization of marine insurance laws with the laws of Great Britain, have both long been recognized as justifications for applying a uniform federal doctrine to marine disputes.[4]

[20] The standard of utmost good faith in an assured's ongoing contractual obligations has numerous purposes, including: protecting insurance company assets and the assets of policy holders; deterring the submission of misleading information; promoting personal integrity by imposing harsh penalties on dishonesty; preventing the imposition of frauds and perjuries on the court; and injecting certainty, predictability and uniformity into the law. See generally Duncan B. Cooper III, *Misrepresentations and False Warranties in Insurance Applications*, 58 Ill. Bar J. 962 (Aug. 1970); cf. *Stone v. Those Certain Underwriters at Lloyds*, 81 Ill. App. 3d 333, 336–37 (5th Dist. 1980) ("(T)he law relating to an insured's duty to make truthful disclosures and representations in applications for insurance arose from maritime law applications.").

---

4. See, e.g., Schoenbaum and Yannopoulos, supra, at 511, for an interesting description of how marine insurance played a determinative role in the decline of the Spanish Empire in the sixteenth century, summarized from *Spanish Wool and Dutch Rebels: The Middleburg Incident of 1574*, 82 Am. Hist. Rev. 312 (Apr. 1977).

[21] One treatise on insurance law contains an eloquent statement of why utmost good faith applies particularly to parties to a marine insurance contract. "(I)t must be recognized that marine insurance is big business. The amounts involved in such policies, usually, are comparatively large. The parties requesting insurance are not unskilled laymen venturing into an unknown field. Shipowners are experts in their field and it would create an intolerable situation to permit such people to shift their losses through subterfuge or nondisclosure of facts available to them. The subject of insurance is not always available for inspection by the underwriter. Ships and cargo may be at sea when coverage is requested." 7 Appleman 4541 (citations omitted). *See also, Knight*, . . . 804 F.2d at 10–12. Ongoing contractual obligations, such as the duty in the Policy at bar to declare newly chartered voyages, thus have long operated under a standard of utmost honesty between the parties of a marine insurance contract. *Higgie v. American Lloyds*, 14 Fed. 143 (N.D. Ill. 1882) (holding that a misrepresentation of a material fact essential to the determination of the risk under a marine insurance contract renders it voidable by the insurer) . . . .

[22] Maritime disputes which call for a single national standard, such as those based on facts of an international and commercial nature, are particularly susceptible to federal admiralty jurisdiction. In *Moragne v. States Marine Lines*, 398 U.S. 375 . . . (1970), for example, the Supreme Court confirmed common law wrongful death recovery in all federal waters with the goal of removing the tensions and discrepancies that have resulted from the necessity to accommodate state remedial statutes to exclusively maritime substantive concepts (citations omitted). Such uniformity will give effect to the constitutionally based principle that federal admiralty law should be "a system of law coextensive with, and operating uniformly in, the whole country." *The Lottawanna*, 88 U.S. (21 Wall.) 558, 575 (1875). *Id.*, 398 U.S. at 401–2, 1970 AMC at 987–88. Moreover, the Jones Act, 46 U.S.C. app. 688, the Death on the High Seas Act, 46 U.S.C. app. 761–68, and the Carriage of Goods by Sea Act, 46 U.S.C. app. 1300–15, are just three examples of Congressional will exerted to assure uniform treatment of legal liability on behalf of citizens and corporations engaged in international trade and commerce on the oceans. See Appleman 7468 ("The interpretation of a marine policy has been considered not to be a question of morals or of public policy, the important thing being to secure uniformity of an interpretation in a commercial world embracing more than one continent and more than one ocean.").

[23] The custom of marine shippers and American courts to harmonize their interpretation of marine insurance policies with the laws of Great Britain illustrates that maritime disputes with an international flavor require a single national voice for resolution. *See Queen Insurance Co. v. Globe & Rutgers Fire Ins. Co.*, 263 U.S. 487, 493 . . . (1924) ("There are special reasons for keeping in harmony with the marine insurance laws of England, the great field of this business."); *Calmar S. S. Corp. v. Scott*, 345 U.S. 427, 443 . . . (1953) (expressing need for harmony of laws with England); *Antilles Steamship Co. Ltd. v. Members of the American Hull Insurance*

Syndicate, . . . 733 F.2d 195, 198 (2 Cir. 1984) (following English version of meaning of disputed clause).

[24] The British Marine Insurance Act of 1906 . . . ("the Act"), was "basically a codification of settled judicial doctrine relating to disclosures and representations." Schoenbaum and Yannopoulos, *supra*, at 528. As such, it is cited by American courts seeking information on which doctrines are actually established maritime precedent. *E.g., Lenfest v. Coldwell, . . .* 525 F.2d 717, n.15 and accompanying text (2 Cir. 1975) ("It is the general rule in this country that American courts will look to British law for meaning and definition in this field."); *Delta Supply Co. v. Liberty Mut. Ins. Co.*, 1963 AMC 1540, 211 F.Supp. 429 (S.D. Tex. 1962) (asserting that federal courts look to the laws of England to interpret marine insurance unless public policy requires following a different rule). Among the provisions in the Act is the following: "*Insurance is uberrimae fidei* 17. A contract of marine insurance is a contract based upon the utmost good faith, and, if the utmost good faith be not observed by either party, the contract may be avoided by the other party." Schoenbaum and Yannopoulos, *supra*, at 528, quoting the Act. The acceptance of the Act for purposes of interpretation in the federal courts demonstrates that it is "entrenched federal precedent" to apply the *uberrimae fidei* doctrine to marine insurance contracts, especially to those involving issues of international trade or commerce.

[25] Judicial precedent should not be casually dismissed by allowing a local regulatory scheme to interfere with international transactions. Even though some circuits have acquiesced to ordinary state insurance regulation, they have done so on facts pertaining to local economic interests. *See, e.g., Irwin, . . .* 455 F.2d 827. Indeed, to decide that *uberrimae fidei* is not established federal precedent in this dispute would require this court to ignore four hundred years of judicial decisions, the entire history of insurance, and the need for uniformity and coherence of a vital international industry.[6]

[26] Accordingly, the federal admiralty doctrine of *uberrimae fidei* applies to marine insurance disputes over ongoing contractual obligations between parties engaged in international and commercial matters. Given this court's decision that *uberrimae fidei* applies (both because Illinois has a minimal interest if at all in the dispute and because *uberrimae fidei* is established federal precedent for the type of dispute at bar), and accepting the well-pleaded facts in the Second Amended Complaint as true, the Plaintiff has stated a claim for relief under the federal doctrine of *uberrimae fidei*. The alleged misrepresentations and nondisclosures concerning the declaration of new charters, the payment of premiums, and the occurrence of events material to assumed risk, if proven true, would support a finding that the Defendants breached the duty of utmost good faith. Accordingly, the Defendants' Motion to Dismiss is denied.

---

6. The court expresses no opinion on whether the doctrine of *uberrimae fidei* would apply to maritime insurance on facts of a less commercial or international scope. Nor is it necessary to ponder whether the Plaintiff has asserted a claim for relief under Illinois insurance law.

Notes and Questions

1. What does *uberrimae fidei* mean, when is the standard violated, and what are the consequences for insurance contracts subject to this doctrine?

2. The doctrine of *uberrimae fidei* comes to the U.S. from the UK. The present court considers it part of federal admiralty law. By contrast, at least some of the states do not require *uberrimae fidei* from assured parties. How could an Illinois standard be formulated? Check paragraph 10 to help with the answer to this question. Check also the *Wilburn Boat* decision, above p. 618, for the Texas standard.

3. From a policy point of view, does the standard of *uberrimae fidei* or the state standard make more sense? Why? Consider the arguments in favor of *uberrimae fidei* in paragraph 21 as you consider the pros and cons of the two options. Does the answer to this question depend on the context, i.e., whether an insurance contract is for a purely local risk or for an interstate risk or for an international risk?

4. How does the *Great Lakes* court apply the *Wilburn* doctrine for the distinction between insurance contracts subject to federal law versus state law? Do you think this approach is what the majority in *Wilburn* had in mind?

5. Hypothetically, if a clear majority of American jurists came to the conclusion that the state standard referred to in questions 2 and 3 made more sense than the standard of *uberrimae fidei*, how could this be implemented in Federal admiralty law?

Section 2. The Law Governing Marine Cargo Insurance

A. Statutory and Industry Rules

As we have seen, the law governing marine insurance is a complex web of federal and state laws that altogether provide little guidance on insurance contracts between commercial actors. State law is much more relevant for insurance contracts entered into by consumers, but this is not the focus of our analysis. In the absence of statutory and/or case law requirements for B2B insurance contracts, the rights and obligations of the parties are heavily determined by the contracts themselves, including the standard clauses in the back of an insurance policy or contract. Whenever a policy is purchased at the London market—Lloyd's being an important but not the only provider—it is usually subject to the UK Marine Insurance Act of 1906 (as amended) and the Institute Cargo Clauses developed by the International Underwriting Association. For the American market, the American Institute of Marine Underwriters has developed its own sets of standardized clauses, usually referred to as the American Institute Cargo Clauses (see https://www.aimu.org/formsmenu.html).

The UK Marine Insurance Act of 1906 included a standardized insurance contract form in an annex, the so-called SG policy (ship and goods). Lord Chalmers, the author of the Act, intended to codify existing practice and case law, rather than to create new rules. In the same fashion, the SG policy can be traced back to the late eighteenth century. Unsurprisingly, its language is archaic and hardly comprehensible. Nevertheless, it was widely used until the 1980s, when the general clauses of the SG policy were updated and presented as the 1982 Institute Cargo Clauses by the Institute of London Underwriters, today known as the International Underwriting Association of London (IUA). An insurance contract procured in the London Market will typically consist of individually negotiated clauses based on the policy application by the assured (front of the contract), and the Institute Cargo Clauses (back of the contract). In an effort to standardize the format and the questions asked in the policy application, Lloyd's developed a number of form contracts, including the Lloyd's Marine Policy (MAR).

The Institute Clauses offer three levels of assurance: level A for "all risks," level B for intermediate cover, and level C for restricted or minimum cover cargo insurance. Under level A, all risks are covered except for those spelled out in the clauses (negative list). Under levels B and C, only those risks are covered that are spelled out in the clauses (positive list). These basic insurance clauses continue to be widely applied. However, the IUA has added many more specific cargo clauses, for example for frozen food, commodity trades, bulk oil, other specialized goods like jute, natural rubber, timber, etc., as well as specialized clauses covering war risks, strikes, and other issues otherwise excluded from insurance coverage. The general clauses were updated in 2009.

The INCOTERMS 2020® require only the restricted or minimum cover at level C if the INCOTERM® CIF is used, unless otherwise agreed by the parties. However, if the INCOTERM® CIP is used — recommended *inter alia* for multimodal transport — the required coverage is A for All Risks. The same is usually true if the transaction is financed via a Letter of Credit: Issuing banks typically require All Risks insurance (see UCP600 Article 28(h)). This is very important for the seller who will not get paid by the advising, confirming, and/or issuing bank, if he has to procure insurance unless it is procured at level A, even if the INCOTERM® is otherwise CIF.

The 2009 Institute Cargo Clauses (A) and (C), are reproduced in the Documents Collection on facing pages to make comparison easier (see pp. I-789).[5] The 2004 American Institute Cargo Clauses "All Risks" are also included on p. I-800. Finally, the UK Marine Insurance Act can be found on p. I-744.

While the Institute clauses were drafted by or on behalf of the insurance industry, and American state and federal common law is somewhat intransparent and unpredictable, the UK Marine Insurance Act provides a reasonably balanced and straightforward set of rights and obligations. Therefore, it would make a lot of sense for the shipper/cargo owner to select the UK Marine Insurance Act explicitly as

---

5. For detailed analysis, see N. Geoffrey Hudson, Tim Madge & Keith Sturges, *Marine Insurance Clauses*, Routledge 5th ed. 2012.

the applicable law and the Institute Cargo Clauses only to the extent that the UK Act does not provide a clear and comprehensive answer to a question. However, in commercial reality, the insurance contracts are prepared by the insurance companies and usually select the Institute Cargo Clauses first and the UK Marine Insurance Act second. In tandem, the parties should either select English courts as the courts with the most experience in applying the UK Act—and maritime law in general—or they should select arbitration as the applicable method of dispute settlement. Unfortunately, most insurers won't negotiate the applicable law and jurisdiction and largely expect their customers to simply sign at the bottom of whatever is offered to them.

B. The Cargo Insurance Contract

Insurance cover can be purchased on a voyage basis (also referred to as "single cargo shipments" or "single goods-in-transit consignments"), or on a time basis (usually referred to as "open cover"). Applications may also be for a valued policy, disclosing or fixing the value of the insured cargo in advance. If a total loss occurs, the insurer will pay the declared value. In a partial loss, the insurer will cover a percentage of that value. Alternatively, the application can be for an unvalued policy, where the value of the goods lost or damaged is determined after an event, usually based on market prices at the time of the loss, and cover is provided up to the limit of the insurance contract.

Cargo owners who need to ship goods—depending on the INCOTERM®, this could be the seller (C or D terms) or the buyer (E and F terms)—can either fill in an application directly on the website of an insurance provider or involve an insurance broker to find them a good match for the required cover. Whether the cargo owner/shipper fills in the application or gets a broker to do it, all questions in the form have to be answered truthfully and any information that might affect the risk or the willingness of the underwriters to contract cover at the given rate has to be provided in the application or at the time when such information becomes known. Failure to provide complete and truthful information voids the policy if the principle of *uberrimae fidei* is applicable.

We will look at an application for open cover, i.e., a policy that will be valid for a period of time. The application for a particular voyage cover is very similar, except that it will not ask for the time period and the expected average shipments during that time, but for details of the particular voyage to be covered. After an application or slip is submitted—today mostly online—it is treated as an offer and reviewed by an underwriter on behalf of an insurance company or one or more Lloyd's syndicates or Names. If accepted,[6] a voyage cover provides insurance for the specific voyage and up to the amount agreed in the contract. By contrast, an open cover

---

6. If an application is submitted to the manager of a Lloyd's syndicate, the manager will solicit acceptance from different Names who can individually subscribe to a chosen percentage of the risk

policy will be good for a definite period of time—usually a year—and cover all voyages notified to the insurance company during this time and each one up to the amount agreed in the contract.

The position of the insurance broker is not always entirely clear. On the one hand, the brokers are usually retained by the parties seeking insurance. On the other hand, it is customary in many markets that they are actually paid by the insurance companies, namely by getting a discount on the premiums they are forwarding on behalf of the assured. As long as the commissions for the brokers are in line with market rates, they are deemed not to affect the position of the brokers as agents of the assured. As a consequence, even if the commission of the broker is paid by the insurance company, the broker has primary duties of loyalty to the assured party. However, as an agent of the assured, the broker also has disclosure obligations toward the insurance company.

The insurance contract can be void or avoided under general contract law, for example, if a mistake was made or a party lacked capacity to contract. In addition, two important vitiating factors are specific to insurance law. We have already heard about the principle of *uberrimae fidei,* an enhanced standard of misrepresentation and nondisclosure. The other factor is the lack of an insurable interest. This requires loss of or damage to an actual or existing right of the assured and excludes mere hopes and expectations. It also excludes claims made on behalf of others, for example, where a shareholder seeks to collect insurance for losses sustained by the company, even if he is the majority or sole shareholder. Finally, it prevents insurance claims where the assured has already received compensation from other parties. A practical application of the requirement of insurable interest is a claim by a seller in an export/import transaction where the risk has already passed to the buyer under FOB. Finally, a marine insurance provider is only liable if the loss or damage was caused by the risk insured against. The standard is that of proximate cause.

---

to be covered. Once enough Names have signed up to cover 100% of the policy, the manager will communicate acceptance to the applicant.

The underwriter may also return a counteroffer, for example excluding certain risks, lowering the limit of the sum insured, or requiring full payment of the premium for coverage to begin.

Sample Document 5-1
Application for Open Cover Policy

Insurance Company Name & Logo
Contact Person [1] ....
Street Address ....
City, Zip Code & Country ....
Phone, Fax and e-mail ....

Ocean Cargo Application [2]
Date of Application.......................................
Proposed Beginning ....
and End of Insurance Cover .... [3]
Customer Reference ....[4]

Insurance Broker (if any) [5]
Name and Address ....
Contact Person, with Phone, Fax and e-mail ....

Information About the Applicant [6]
Company Name ....
Website ....
Contact Person ....
City, Zip Code & Country ....
Phone, Fax and e-mail ....

1. Describe applicant's business ....[7]
2. Number of years in business ....[8]
3. List all operating names used in the last five years by applicant, any subsidiaries, and parents companies
   ....[9]
4. Names of current and past insurance carriers in the past five years
   Companies .... from when to when ....[10]
5. Has any policy or cover been canceled or not renewed in the past five years? ☐ Yes ☐ No
   If yes, explain ....[11]
6. Has the applicant or any of its subsidiaries or parent companies or principal owners declared bankruptcy in the past five years? ☐ Yes ☐ No
   If yes, explain ....[12]
7. Revenue details and values shipped [13]

Time frame	Gross sales	Values shipped domestic / int'l	Values insured domestic / int'l
current year	....	....	....
past year	....	....	....
next year (anticipated)	....	....	....

Insurance Cover Required
8. Principal goods to be insured ....[14]
9. Detailed description of packing ....[15]
10. Main destination countries ....[16]
11. Details of mode(s) of transport ....[17]
12. Details of carriers and warehouses involved ....[18]
13. Average and maximum insurance cover required: Number of voyages anticipated ....
    Average value to be covered .... Maximum value to be covered ....[19]
13. Valuation basis: ☐ 110% of CIF Value   ☐ Other: ....[20]
14. Insurance conditions: ☐ All Risks ICC (A) ☐ Free of Particular Average ICC (C) ☐ Other: ....[21]
15. Special conditions required: ☐ War Risk   ☐ SR&CC
    ☐ Domestic inland transit ☐ Foreign inland transit ☐ Warehouse coverage ☐ Increased value (IV)[22]
16. Requested deductible ....[23]

Loss History

17. Five year premium and loss experience [24]

Time frame	Total premiums paid	Total losses claimed	Pending claims
current year	....	....	....
previous year	....	....	....
2 years ago	....	....	....
3 years ago	....	....	....
4 years ago	....	....	....
5 years ago	....	....	....

18. Describe all losses and insurance claims greater than US$10,000 in the past five years ....
.... [25]

19. List all countries involved in losses in the past five years ....

20. Describe any lawsuits or ADR procedures over cargo losses or insurance claims in the past five years.[26]

21. Are any other insurance companies expected to provide cover during the time frame covered by the current application? ☐ No   ☐ Yes .... % of total; Providers .... [27]

Declaration

I hereby confirm that I have read and understood this proposal form and that I have answered all questions and provided all information to the best of my knowledge and have not withheld any information that might influence the decision of the underwriters with regard to this proposal. I am aware that any incorrect or incomplete statements can void my protection. I agree that the information in this proposal can be shared for underwriting and reinsurance purposes. Furthermore, I agree that this proposal will become the basis of insurance issued by the underwriters if accepted and a policy is issued. [28]

....
Name and Signature   Place and Date

Cargo Insurance Contracts Explained:

#1   Applications for insurance cover like this one are typically accessed on the website of a broker or insurance company. If a specific person is suggested by the insurer or has already dealt with the applicant, the information should be entered here.

#2   The form is mainly designed for maritime transport but it can be used, with few modifications, for other modes of international shipping.

#3   The applicant can enter any time frame for the beginning and end of the open cover. Six months or a year are most common.

#4   The applicant can enter their internal filing reference here.

#5   If the applicant is using an insurance broker or if the application is made via a broker, this needs to be disclosed here.

Information About the Applicant

#6   The applicant is the natural person or corporate entity that carries an insurable risk and seeks to become the beneficiary of the insurance cover.

#7   The applicant needs to describe in some detail the kind of business activities they are involved in, including those not directly relevant to the cargo insurance at issue.

#8   The applicant should disclose the year of incorporation and the number of years they have been conducting the business activities described under #7 and the activities relevant to the cargo insurance at issue.

#9   The applicant has to disclose any corporate and commercial names and trademarks they have been using and that are potentially relevant to the cargo insurance at issue.

#10   The applicant has to disclose all insurers they have been using over the past five years.

#11   The applicant has to disclose whether they have been rejected by any insurers over the past five years.

#12   The applicant has to disclose any bankruptcies in the group of companies relevant to the cargo insurance at issue.

#13   The applicant has to disclose the overall turnover and the volume and share of domestic and international sales and shipments.

Insurance Cover Required

#14   The applicant has to explain in some detail the kind of goods that will be shipped under the cargo policy. This includes information about the origin of the goods, the owners of the goods, whether they are new or used, the consignees or buyers, the use to be made of the goods, the extent to which shipments are time-sensitive, and any information an insurer would want to have about hazards, particularly high values etc. Some insurers use forms that specifically ask about perishable goods, live animals, jewelry, precious metals or stones, works of art, and any goods potentially subject to export or import restrictions.

#15   The insurer wants to know who is packing and unpacking the goods, where they will be packed or unpacked, whether they will be accessed anywhere else, and how they will be packed, in particular whether they will be containerized. It is not uncommon that pictures of the cargo before and after packing are required, in particular if the cargo is nonstandard in size or type.

#16   Under an open cargo policy, the applicant purchases insurance for a range of yet-to-be-determined shipments over the contracted period of time. One of the benefits is the flexibility provided to the applicant, namely to be sure of cover for all voyages within the confines of the policy. In light of the flexibility given to the assured, the insurer needs to know the main destination countries to understand the risk associated with the shipments.

#17   The applicant has to provide details of the shipments from door to door, i.e., where the shipment originates, how they are taken to the port, whether they will be stored at the terminal, whether the main ocean voyage will be direct or whether transshipment is expected, and how the goods will be taken from the port of destination to the final inland destination.

#18   To the extent this information is already available, the applicant has to provide information about all carriers, terminals, warehouses, and other intermediaries expected to handle the cargo at one point or another.

#19   In this section, the applicant has to provide estimates of the overall volume of cargo to be insured under the policy. This is done via a multiplication of the average value to be insured multiplied by the anticipated number of voyages. The insurer will also want to know the highest anticipated value of any one cargo shipment. This information, together with the information about the applicant, the types of goods, and the loss history, will be used for the determination of the price range, i.e., the premium as a percentage of the insured value to be offered by the insurer. The applicant will still have to provide notice of each voyage and the specific value of the cargo to be insured. However, at that point, the applicant will pay a fixed percentage of the insured value instead of having to negotiate the premium every time. Furthermore, the applicant will usually have cover even if he does not provide notice of a particular shipment and pay the premium before the actual departure of the goods.

#20   The standard valuation is CIF + 10%. This is also the insurance cover required under CIF. A lower cover is usually achieved via deductibles. Any higher valuation will need to be explained and will result in higher premiums.

#21   The most common general terms or conditions are the ICC (A) Clauses for "All Risks" and the ICC (C) Clauses for restricted or minimum cover. In most cases, the shipper will need to purchase "All Risks" insurance, either because of obligations to the cargo owner to whom the risk has already passed (CIP), or because the bank that guarantees payment via a Letter of Credit requires it. Only if the shipper owns the cargo outright and does not anticipate problems, should she consider restricted cover.

#22   Even "All Risks" insurance does not really cover all risks. In some cases, per agreement with the consignee and/or the banks, insurance has to be purchased to also cover Strikes, Riots, and Civil Commotions (SR&CC) or even War Risks, which are otherwise not included.

While CIF + 10% is normally taking care of the additional cost of replacing the cargo if there is a total loss, in some cases the additional costs will be more than the 10% provided under standard cover. IV insurance can provide the full replacement costs.

The applicant can also decide at this point to purchase door-to-door insurance or only insurance for the main or marine voyage.

#23   As in any insurance contract, a deductible can reduce the cost. It means that the assured will have to cover the first US$5,000 or $10,000 herself.

#24 to #26   The insurer has limited options to determine the risk involved with a particular application for cover. One important way of getting to know the applicant and the riskiness of her business is to look at the last five years of loss history.

#27 If the applicant is running a larger operation with many shipments, it is not uncommon that she will be dealing with multiple insurers at the same time. The insurers will want to have transparency about the arrangements since none of them wants to be the one saddled with the high-risk parts of the business unless this was agreed upon and paid for.

#28 The declaration is a reminder of the principle of *uberrimae fidei*.

Section 3. The Practice of (Marine) Insurance Law[7]

Our first case illustrates the typical contracting procedure. The client, Sealink, approaches an insurance broker, Frenkel, and requests procurement of suitable insurance cover. The client has to fill out an application form. In this case, a "London Market Protection and Indemnity Insurance Application Form" was used. These forms can be viewed online and are similar to the application form included above.[8] If and when problems with the insurance arise, one of the typical disputes is between the client and the broker about whether information was conveyed correctly in both directions, and whether the broker procured the most suitable cover at the best price.

Case 5-4
Sealink v. Frenkel
U.S. District Court, D. Puerto Rico, 31 July 2006,
441 F. Supp. 2d 374 (D.P.R. 2006)
(Paragraph number added.)
Domínguez, J.

III. Factual and Procedural Background [emphasis in original]

[12] . . . The following facts are undisputed. Sealink is a corporation organized and existing under the laws of Puerto Rico, and engaged in the business of maritime cargo carriage in and about the Caribbean Basin. . . . Sealink is the owner of a cargo vessel known as the M/V Sealink Express. . . . Frenkel is an international insurance

---

7. For further reading, see, *inter alia*, John Dunt, *Marine Cargo Insurance*, Informa Law/Routledge, 2nd ed. 2016; Jonathan Gilman et al., *Arnould Law of Marine Insurance and Average*, Sweet & Maxwell 19th ed. 2019; Özlem Gürses, *Marine Insurance Law*, Routledge 2nd ed. 2016; Susan Hodges, *Cases and Materials on Marine Insurance Law*, Routledge-Cavendish 1999; F.D. Rose, *Marine Insurance: Law and Practice*, Routledge 2nd ed. 2012; and Thomas J. Schoenbaum, *Key Divergences Between English and American Law of Marine Insurance: A Comparative Study*, Cornell Maritime Pr/Tidewater Pub. 1999.

8. See, for example, https://www.mnkre.com/protection-and-indemnity-application-form .html or https://www.thomasmillerspecialty.com/fileadmin/uploads/tms/Documents/Product_Do cuments/P_I/P_I__U.S__APP.pdf.

brokerage firm, which provides businesses and individuals with insurance and risk management services. . . . Frenkel procures insurance policies for marine exposures, property, and casualty. . . .

[13] In providing its services, Frenkel obtains information directly from the client pertinent to their businesses and related risks, and then procures what it believes should be proper insurance to protect the assets. . . . On November 12, 1997, Sealink sought out Frenkel's services and filled out a "London Market Protection and Indemnity Insurance Application Form." . . . The application was completed almost entirely by Kristian Meszaros, Sealink's President and Chief Executive Officer, on Sealink's behalf. . . . By signing the application, Meszaros warranted that the information provided was "complete and accurate", and acknowledged that underwriters would rely on the information and representations listed therein in determining acceptability, rates, and conditions of coverage. . . . By signing the application, Sealink also understood that any misrepresentation or omission would constitute "ground for immediate cancellation of coverage and denial of claims." . . . Further, by signing the application, Sealink noted and acknowledged that it was "under a continuing obligation" to notify underwriters of any material alteration to the "nature, extent or size" of the operation. . . . Meszaros reviewed the application after completing it, to make sure it was accurate, and sent it to Joseph Valenza, Frenkel's representative. . . . Frenkel did not review the application to determine if the responses were correct, but only to ascertain it was signed. . . .

[14] During 1997 and 1998, Frenkel, through Valenza, procured two insurance policies for Sealink. . . . One policy was for Protection and Indemnity (hereinafter "P & I") coverage through a British company, Terra Nova; the other for Hull & Machinery (hereinafter "H & M") coverage through an American company, St. Paul Fire and Marine. . . . The H & M policy that expired in 1998 was not renewed in 1999 due to Sealink's "severe cash problems." . . . In late 1999, Frenkel procured a new H & M policy for Sealink. . . . While procuring H & M coverage, Frenkel also procured new P & I coverage for Sealink. . . . Sealink's P & I policy was approved and renewed on February 5, 2000 for one year. . . . The P & I policy was issued by Terra Nova. . . . The P & I policy accepted and approved by Sealink contained and [sic] arbitration and selection clause. . . . Specifically, the clause read "[a]ny dispute arising under or in connection with this Insurance is to be referred to arbitration on London . . .". . . . Meszaros was aware that the P & I policy contained the provision requiring arbitration in London. On February 22, 2000, Sealink advised Frenkel that it had forwarded the proposed H & M coverage to the Economic Development Bank of Puerto Rico (hereinafter "EDB"), as secured creditor of Sealink and co-assured, for their comments. . . . Sealink notes that the policy [Frenkel] forwarded failed to include a "MAR 91 — Slip Copy" nor made any mention of a forum selection clause. [MAR 91 is a standardized hull insurance contract form.]

[15] The EDB requested that the valuation of the vessel be increased to $4 million. . . . As a result, Sealink requested Frenkel to cause the issuance of H & M policies as follows: 1) H & M coverage at $3.2 million, and 2) Increased Valuation (hereinafter

"IV") at $800,000. . . . On February 29, 2000, Frenkel received confirmation that coverage had been bound by both H & M and IV underwriters, Lloyd's of London. . . .

[16] On April 23, 2000, a fire was reported aboard the Sealink Express in the engine room. . . . The fire occurred at dockside in the Dominican Republic while the Sealink Express was being repaired for previous flood damages not claimed in the instant case. . . . The fire was contained by the local Dominican fire crew. . . . On that same day, Meszaros informed Frenkel of the casualty by phone and fax. . . . Shortly after the fire, Sealink filed a claim with the H & M underwriter, Lloyd's of London, seeking payment of the policy amounts. . . . On April 26, 2000, as a result of Frenkel's notice to the insurer, Capt. D. Weston, a marine and cargo surveyor of Schad Insurance in the Dominican Republic, was appointed to act on behalf of the H & M underwriter. . . . Capt. Weston was appointed by Frenkel and entrusted with performing a survey/investigation surrounding the case, nature, and extent of damages incurred by the vessel. . . . Capt. Weston's initial investigation suggested possible foul play by ex-crew of the Sealink Express. . . . On June 30, 2000, Weston rendered another report suggesting that, considering the cost of repairs, the underwriters may wish to consider the vessel a constructive total loss.[2] . . . On July 6, 2000, as a result of this casualty, and based on Sealink's opinion that the cost of repairs of the vessel would exceed the insurance value, the Sealink Express was declared a constructive total loss and a Notice of Abandonment of the vessel to the underwriters was issued. . . .

[17] On December 29, 2000, Sealink requested from Frenkel copies of the Cover Notes of the policies, the complete policies, and a breakdown of the Lloyd's of London syndicates for the H & M and P & I policies. . . . Sealink asserts that Meszaros requested this information because it had not been previously provided to him. . . .

[18] On or about January of 2001, Sealink first learned what "MAR 91 — Slip Copy"[3] meant when counsel for the H & M underwriter advised that they would possibly avoid insurance, and that arbitration was mandated. . . . The document containing the MAR 91 clause confirms that the insurance "shall be subject to the exclusive jurisdiction of the English Courts, except as may be expressly provided herein to the contrary." . . . [It is this specific clause that gives rise to Sealink's claim that the

---

2. A constructive total loss is when the cost of repairing the damage sustained in a vessel exceeds the insurance value. 12 Lee R. Russ & Thomas F. Segalla, Couch on Insurance 3d § 183–10 (1997).

3. The term MAR 91 has its origins in London, England. The Marine Insurance Act was passed in England in the year 1906, which codified the previous common law related to insurance matters. In the 19th century, Lloyd's and the Institute of London Underwriters developed between them standardized clauses for the use of marine insurance, which are known as the Institute Clauses. The Marine Insurance Act includes a standard policy, which parties were at liberty to use if they wished, but they were expressed in archaic terms. In 1991, the London market produced a new standard policy wording known as the MAR 91 form. The MAR form is a general statement of insurance; the Institute Clauses are used to set out the detail of the insurance coverage. In practice, the policy document usually consists of the MAR form used as a cover, with the Clauses stapled to the inside.

broker was not diligent, and thus, liable.] On February 27, 2001, Frenkel sent Sealink a letter, from the H & M underwriter's counsel advising that Lloyd's of London
had formally denied the claim under the H & M policy due to "serious misrepresentations, material nondisclosures and the breach of the utmost duty of good faith by
Sealink". . . .

[19] On June 8, 2000, the EDB, as secured creditor and co-assured, brought suit against
Sealink. . . . The EDB sued Sealink, Meszaros and the Lloyd's of London underwriters seeking to collect amounts due under the loan agreement. . . . On February 12,
2003, the Superior Court of Puerto Rico, in Carolina, rendered judgment and stated:
"[f]rom the materials submitted in support for the arguments of the parties it does
not appear that the insured [. . .] had ever raised a question or concern [. . .]". . . .
The [State Superior C]ourt dismissed the claims against the underwriters. . . . The
Superior Court also noted that it could not ignore that Sealink had delegated certain
responsibilities onto Frenkel as its broker [and that Sealink had ample opportunity
to inquire as to the terms and conditions of this new policy]. . . .

[20] Nonetheless, the Court imputed onto Sealink the knowledge of the terms and
conditions negotiated on its behalf by persons with knowledge of what is being
negotiated. . . .

[21] On October 22, 2001, legal proceedings were initiated by Sealink before the
United States District Court in Puerto Rico against the Lloyd's H & M and IV
underwriters seeking to collect the value of the policies. . . . Sealink did not join
Frenkel as a defendant in this lawsuit. . . . On October 24, 2003, the Court dismissed
the complaint by upholding the forum selection clause incorporated in "MAR 91 —
Slip Policy." . . .

[22] In early 2002, H & M underwriters, Lloyd's of London, also commenced arbitration proceedings against Sealink and EDB seeking avoidance of the H & M policy
and breach of contract damages. . . . The parties settled for $25,000.00, agreeing
that such payment completely discharged and released the H & M and IV underwriters from any liability with respect to the premium and all liability arising out
for the H & M and IV policies. . . .

[23] On July 15, 2003, two years and five months after the H & M underwriter had
voided the policy, [and one year and five months after the Puerto Rico State Court
dismissed the EDB's complaint], Sealink sent a formal demand letter to Frenkel
complaining of Frenkel's failure to advise Sealink as to the "meaning and purport"
of MAR 91. . . .

[24] On February 12, 2004 Sealink filed the instant claim requesting damages pursuant to the denied coverage and voidance of the insurance policy placed by Frenkel, and loss of business opportunities. . . . An amended claim was filed on July 13,
2004 adding to the allegations that Frenkel had failed in its duties as an insurance
broker. Sealink contends that Frenkel breached their contract for failure to place
a proper insurance policy and properly negotiate claims on Sealink's behalf. . . .
The amended claim failed to include, however, a breach of contract claim. Rather,

Sealink's claim for breach of contract was first alleged in the opposition to Frenkel's motion for summary judgment. . . .

[25] On February 15, 2006 Frenkel filed a motion for summary judgment alleging that Sealink's action was time barred by the statute of limitations applicable to tort actions; that Sealink's allegation of Frenkel's breach of fiduciary duty is without merit; and that Frenkel's alleged negligence was not the proximate cause of Sealink's injuries stemming from the voidance of its insurance policy. . . .

[26] On March 27, 2006, Sealink filed an opposition to Frenkel's motion for summary judgment. . . . Sealink contends that Frenkel failed to act with the sufficient skill, care, and diligence required as an insurance broker. . . .

IV. Insurance Broker Duties Under Marine Insurance

[28] The contract of marine insurance is a contract whereby the insurer undertakes to indemnify the assured, in the manner and to the extent thereby agreed, against the losses incident to the marine adventure. See 2 Thomas J. Shoenbaum, *Admiralty and Maritime Law,* § 19-1 (4th ed.2004). There are three principal categories of marine insurance policies: H & M insurance; cargo insurance; and protection and indemnity insurance. The hull insurance is taken by the shipowner to insure the vessel and its equipment on a time basis and certain liabilities for collision as well as general average and salvage charges. A hull policy on a commercial vessel typically insures against physical damage and losses from certain perils. . . .

[29] The basic substantive law of marine insurance contract is federal maritime law. District courts have original jurisdiction in admiralty matters, as conferred in 28 U.S.C.A. § 1333(1), stating that "[t]he district courts shall have original jurisdiction, exclusive of the courts of the States, of (1)[a]ny civil case of admiralty or maritime jurisdiction, saving to suitors in all cases all other remedies to which they are otherwise entitled [. . .]". However, a federal district court sitting in admiralty applies state law to disputes over contracts of marine insurance. See *Wilburn Boat Co. v. Fireman's Fund Ins. Co.,* [above, p. 618] (1955). Specifically, when neither party claims that a federal statute or rule of maritime law governs the current situation, courts must look to state law to resolve the issues. *Id.* Although, the *Wilburn Boat* doctrine was applied by certain courts to contracts to procure maritime insurance and disputes arising from the relationship between the insurance broker and the assured, *Graham v. Milky Way Barge, Inc.,* 923 F.2d 1100, 1105 (5th Cir.1991); *Illinois Constructors Corp. v. Morency & Assoc., Inc.,* 802 F.Supp. 185, 187 (N.D.Ill.1992), the Supreme Court of the United States concluded that Courts must determine the boundaries of admiralty jurisdiction looking at the purpose of the relationship or transaction at hand. *Exxon Corp. v. Central Gulf Lines, Inc.,* 500 U.S. 603, 608 . . . (1991). Justice Marshall further stressed that the admiralty jurisdiction is designed to protect maritime commerce and mandates lower courts to look at the nature and subject matter of the relationship in controversy to assess if the admiralty jurisdiction stands. *Id.,* at 612.

[30] Since issuance of said mandate, only two district courts have had to discern whether the procurement contract before them were related to maritime commerce to such an extent as to warrant their falling within those court's admiralty jurisdiction. See *Lewco Corp. v. One 1984 23' Chris Craft Motor Vessel*, 889 F.Supp. 1114, 1995 A.M.C. 2994 (D.Minn.1995); *Illinois Constructors Corp. v. Morency & Associates, Inc.*, 794 F.Supp. 841, 1993 A.M.C. 203 (N.D.Ill.1992). In *Illinois Constructors* the Northern District Court of Illinois held tat the agreement to procure maritime insurance did in fact fall within the Court's admiralty jurisdiction for it was the broker who failed to secure insurance which contains pollution coverage—coverage integral to the maritime activities of the vessel in lieu of the devastation to maritime commerce resulting engendered by accidents at sea and the overwhelming costs of clean-up. *Id.* at 843. The *Illinois Constructors* Court, however, did not reach this conclusion without first emphasizing that, when analyzing the subject matter of the agreement to procure maritime insurance and the relationship between the parties with a view **toward protection of maritime commerce**, courts must be "cautious to open the courthouse doors to a surge of litigation concerning transactions that may only tangentially involve a maritime business or ship owner merely because one is a party in the dispute." *Id.* The *Lewco Corp.* Court sheds further light onto this subject. Particularly, *Lewco Corp.*, citing to Charles L. Black, Jr., *Admiralty Jurisdiction: Critique and Suggestions*, 50 Col.L.Rev. 259, 264, specified that "[m]aritime insurance, yes [falls within the admiralty jurisdiction]; a contract to procure it, no [falls outside admiralty jurisdiction]." *Lewco Corp.*, 889 F.Supp. at 1116.

[31] Understanding that the contract object of the instant complaint is one to procure maritime insurance and the duties of the broker thereto, and concluding that the subject matter of the maritime insurance brokered to be procured does not involve a maritime business or affects maritime commerce, the Court chooses to be cautious and closes the courthouse doors to this suit in admiralty for the parties' controversy regarding the interpretation and/or duties of the procurement contract falls **only** within state insurance law and interpretative case law. Notwithstanding, because there is clear diversity between the parties, the Court proceeds to address the issues on the merits while applying exclusively state law.

[32] The parties to a contract of insurance are generally the assured and the insurer or underwriter. Often times, due to the specialized nature of the insurance industry, an insurance broker is consulted as an intermediary between assured and insurer. An insurance broker, according to Article 9.020 of the Puerto Rico Insurance Code, "is an individual, firm or corporation who for compensation as an independent contractor, in any manner solicits, negotiates, or procures insurance or the renewal or continuance thereof, on behalf of insureds or prospective insured other than himself, and not on behalf of an insurer or agent". P.R. Laws Ann. tit. 26 §902. The role of the insurance broker can vary depending on the circumstances of their actions and on whose behalf the broker acts—they can be considered agents of the assured when they procure an insurance contract from various insurers; or they can be considered agents of the insurer when they receive and transmit payments

for the policies issued. 3 Lee R. Russ & Thomas F. Segalla, *Couch on Insurance 3d* §§ 45:1–45:10 (1997); see also *Wilburn Boat Co. v. Fireman's Fund Ins. Co.*, [above, p. 618] (1955); *Graham v. Milky Way Barge, Inc.*, 923 F.2d 1100, 1105 (5th Cir.1991).

[33] As an agent to the assured, the insurance broker has the following duties: (1) to carry out the assured's instructions; (2) to exercise reasonable care in carrying out his duties; (3) to avoid conflicts of interest with respect to his client as part of his fiduciary duties; and (4) payment and return of the premium. See Shoenbaum, *supra*, at § 19-5.

broker

[34] The duty to carry out the assured's instructions relate to the broker's approach of suitable underwriters, and to use his best efforts to obtain suitable coverage within a reasonable time. He is also responsible for disclosing to an insurer material facts concerning the risk. However, the broker will not be liable if the assured's instructions are incomplete or ambiguous. In order to exercise reasonable care, the broker must select responsible insurers and apply their specialist knowledge while still carrying out the assured's instructions. As mentioned above, an insurance broker may also be called to protect the fiduciary relationship with the assured and, thus, must avoid conflicts of interest with other parties to the insurance contract. An exception to avoiding conflicts of interest is, for example, when brokers disclose and have consent from the parties involved. In general, brokers acquire express and fully informed consent to the assureds and insurers so they can act on behalf of both parties. Brokers are directly responsible to the insurer for premium payments received by the assured upon issuance of the insurance contract. They are also directly responsible to the assured to pay the losses covered in the insurance policy and for the return of the unused portion of the premium upon policy cancellation. See Russ & Segalla, *supra*, at §§ 45:1–45:10.

[35] Specifically, the Supreme Court of Puerto Rico has addressed the issue of whether the insurance broker is responsible to the assured when the insurer denies coverage. In *González v. The Commonwealth Ins. Co.*, 140 P.R. Dec. 673, 691 (1996), the Supreme Court of Puerto Rico held that between the insurance broker and the assured exists an agency relationship to procure insurance. As such, applying Article 1610 of the Civil Code of Puerto Rico, P.R. Laws Ann. tit. 31, § 4442, if the broker carries out the instructions given by the assured, the insurance broker cannot be held responsible for the result of those actions. The same is true in the absence of such instructions when the broker acts according to the character of the business.

[36] Under a marine insurance contract, as for any other insurance contract, the duties of the assureds are to pay the insurance policy premium; notify the insurer or broker of any claims covered by the insurance policy in a timely manner; and make truthful and complete representations on the insurance application of material matters. The insurance industry considers material matters to be the information that would aid the underwriters in making their determination of assuming the risk and, if choosing to assume the risk, decide the premium to be charged. The query the Court must now address is, under a broker-assured relationship, whose responsibility is it to properly fill out the insurance application and ensure the accuracy

and completeness of the information contained therein. From the text of the Insurance Code of Puerto Rico, the Civil Code of Puerto Rico, and interpretations of the Supreme Court of Puerto Rico, the Court can only conclude that **it is the sole responsibility of the assured to complete the insurance application and ensure its accuracy.**

[37] The insurance industry, in general, requires of the parties involved in an insurance contract the utmost good faith on all aspects of their relationship. Often, the insurer, agent, or broker lacks the means for verifying the accuracy or completeness of the information provided by the insurance applicants for purposes of their risk analyses. Consequently, the doctrine of *uberrimae fidei*:

> "puts the burden on the assured to 'disclose to the insurer all known circumstances that materially affect the risk being insured'—whether or not the insurer asks about them—on the theory that '[s]ince the assured is in the best position to know of any circumstances material to the risk, he must reveal those facts to the underwriter, rather than wait for the underwriter to inquire' (Citations omitted). The assured's failure to make such disclosure entitles the underwriter to void the policy *ab initio.*" *Commercial Union Ins. Co. v. Flagship Marine Services, Inc.,* 982 F.Supp. 310, 313 (S.D.N.Y.,1997).

[38] In marine insurance, contrary to other kinds of insurance, "a mistake or omission material to a marine risk, whether it be willful or accidental, fraudulent or resulting from a mistake, negligence, or voluntary ignorance, **avoids the policy**". *See* Russ & Segalla, *supra,* at § 99:6 (emphasis added). The reason the policy is void under these circumstances is that the risk assumed is not the one intended to be assumed by the insurer.

[39] The Supreme Court of Puerto Rico has implemented the principle of utmost good faith when resolving cases related to breach of insurance contracts or of the duties of any of the parties. In *Serrano Ramírez v. Clínica Perea, Inc.,* 108 P.R. Dec. 477 (1979), the Court upheld the avoidance for coverage of an insurance policy when, in the course of a medical malpractice suit against the assured, the insurer learned the assured had omitted certain material information from the insurance application that if the insurer had known, would have not issued the policy. The Court stressed the importance of acting in utmost good faith in insurance contracts based on the nature of the insurance industry, the risks involved in it, and also because the end result is the rescission of the contract for vitiated consent. . . .

[41] The Supreme Court of Puerto Rico has also allowed an exception to the assureds' duty to make truthful and complete representations in the insurance application. When the assured truthfully has no knowledge of the information requested in the application, the assured or beneficiary, upon avoidance of coverage, may show evidence that the assured had neither knowledge of nor reason to know the information inquired in the insurance application. That was the situation in *Sandoval Figueroa v. Puerto Rican Life Ins. Co.,* 99 P.R. Dec. 287 (1970), wherein the insurer denied payment to the beneficiaries of a life insurance policy because the assured

had completed the application shortly before dying of cancer, and made no such disclosures in the application. The beneficiaries of the policy presented evidence that neither them nor the assured had prior knowledge of her condition. The Court determined the insurer had to submit payment to the beneficiaries because the principle of utmost good faith had not been breached.

[42] Consequently, the Court must conclude from the discussion set forth that, in accordance with the principle of utmost good faith, it is the assureds' obligation to provide accurate and complete information in their insurance application. This obligation persists despite the intervention of insurance brokers or other intermediaries between the relationship of assureds and insurers. In so doing, the insurance contract could not be avoided and coverage should not be denied on grounds of misstatements or non-disclosures.

V. Analysis

[43] Sealink alleges they suffered a loss due to the cancellation of the policy. Sealink argues that this loss was a result of Frenkel's lack of reviewing thoroughly the insurance application for completeness and correctness, other than just ensuring it was signed. In doing so, Sealink alleges Frenkel failed to act with the sufficient skill, care, and diligence required of it as a broker, as instructed in the Insurance Code of Puerto Rico. . . .

[44] In this case there is no evidence on record that Frenkel, in acting as an insurance broker to Sealink, acted differently than any other broker would have acted under the same circumstances. Sealink alleges that Frenkel breached their fiduciary duty because they only reviewed the insurance application to ensure it was signed, not to ensure its accuracy or completeness. However, there is no recognized duty of an insurance broker to review the insurance application for the truthfulness or accuracy of the information contained therein and supplied by the assured before sending it to the underwriters. On the contrary, it is the assured who carries the burden for the accuracy of the representations and disclosures included in the insurance application, subject to cancellation of the insurance policy for any material misrepresentations or omissions.

[45] Furthermore, Sealink alleges that because they were a new client of Frenkel's by 1998, the time when the insurance application was completed, Frenkel "should have been aware that his new client would require guidance in filling out an application of insurance, where a wrong or misleading answer would result in denial of insurance". . . . In essence, Sealink is asking the Court to conclude that because they were a new customer to Frenkel, they were also new to marine insurance. However, Exhibit 1 of plaintiff's Motion for Summary Judgment, . . . shows an executive summary in which it represents that Mr. Meszaros' experience in the maritime transportation industry was of almost twenty (20) years at the time he completed the insurance application with Frenkel. . . . Hence, it would be unreasonable to deem that 1998 was the first time Mr. Meszaros encountered an application for maritime insurance, thereby requiring guidance in filling out an insurance application.

[46] This Court stresses that the instant case is not one in which the nature of the insurance is the cause of the voidance, but, instead, one in which the correct insurance policy is based on misrepresentations provided by the insured to the insurance company, thus, causing voidance. The Court simply cannot envision placing responsibility on Frenkel for Sealink's misleads as to prior material misrepresentations as to bankruptcy applications and/or detentions by the Coast Guard due to poor maintenance and/or prior structural vessel damage and/or providing true market value of the vessel and/or prior grounding of the vessel.

[47] Based on the above, the Court cannot accept Sealink's allegation that it had no knowledge of the omissions and nondisclosures that resulted in the cancellation of its insurance policy, or that Mr. Meszaros did not know how to complete the insurance application. Along the same line, the Court cannot hold that Frenkel breached its duty as an insurance broker due to Frenkel's own lack of knowledge of the term MAR 91. The issue of fiduciary duty or providing the wrong policy had no relationship with the cancellation of Sealink's insurance policy.[6] In acting within the limits and duties of an insurance broker, Frenkel is not liable to Sealink for failing to review the insurance application for its completeness or accuracy, or for the lack of knowledge of the term MAR 91 simply because the policy was cancelled due to material misrepresentations as set forth at Note 6, infra.

[48] Therefore the Court holds that Frenkel was not negligent and did not have the duty to provide facts that were the exclusive knowledge of the assured regarding the broker's obligations as Sealink's insurance broker. Accordingly, Sealink's negligence and loss of business opportunities claims are hereby DISMISSED WITH PREJUDICE.

Notes and Questions

1. The *Sealink* case provides a good example of the convoluted mess that calls itself American maritime or admiralty law (see also paras. 24 to 29 in *Ingersoll*, below). Some aspects are part of federal law, others are not, and the jurisdiction of the federal courts is not unambiguous either. Even in diversity cases, the federal courts may end up applying state law. This is a bonanza for attorneys who know their way around the mess, and a nightmare for the clients who end up with unpredictable outcomes and exorbitant attorney fees. What would be a sensible strategy for American shipping and insurance companies to minimize the problems and reduce the cost of disputes?

---

6. The insurance policy was cancelled for the following reasons: (1) material misrepresentations on the application related to the affiliation with an entity involved in bankruptcy proceedings; (2) failure to disclose uncommonly high number of detentions by the U.S. Coastguard due to the poor maintenance and structural damage to the vessel; (3) failure to disclose threats of physical violence made by the crew while on the Dominican Republic during a wage dispute; (4) material misrepresentation or failure to disclose the true market value of the vessel; and (5) material failure to disclose grounding and repeated instances of contact damage and casualty loss history. All of these reasons were deemed material to assuming the risk and to determine the insurance coverage. . . . These misrepresentations have not been sufficiently challenged by plaintiff.

2. In the triangle among insured party, insurance, and insurance broker, can you outline the rights and obligations of each party? Who are the parties to the insurance contract? What is the position of the broker?

3. What is P & I coverage and what is H & M coverage (compare para. 14)? What is meant by Increased Valuation (IV) in paragraph 15? What is the role of the EDB in the present case? What is a "total constructive loss"? What is a Notice of Abandonment (para. 16)? What is an MAR 91 Slip Copy?

4. What is the requirement of utmost good faith in insurance contracts? Who is bound by it and who is not? What are the limitations of the requirement? Why could Sealink not benefit from the limitations in the present case?

5. Do you agree with the outcome of the case? Why or why not?

———————

The next case, *Ingersoll*, may well be the most complicated presented in this book. It illustrates a number of challenges: First, it is a multiparty litigation between a shipper/cargo owner (Ingersoll) and its insurance company (Fireman's), involving also the supplier of the goods (Waldrich), the carrier (Taiwan), the ship (the M/V Bodena), the owner of the ship (Excellent Marine), a shipping agent approached by the cargo owner (Gryphon), a shipping agent working for the carrier (Mid-Gulf), and an insurance broker (Bernard) (for details, see the District Court judgment of September 4, 1985, 619 F. Supp. 493). Second, the liability of the insurance, for example, whether certain exclusions could be applied, turns on the substance of the contract between the shipper and the carrier. The court has to address the question whether or not the exclusions in the insurance contract were ambiguous, whether the contract of carriage was exclusively the Bill of Lading, whether the carrier breached its contractual obligations, and whether the shipper was or should have been aware of the breach and should have informed the insurance company.

You are strongly advised to take the time to carefully dissect this case, beginning with a relationship chart of the parties involved and a time line of the events. Then you should identify possible claims and break them down into binary relationships. Once this is accomplished, you are ready for a thorough reading of the court's analysis and the questions proposed at the end of the case, including whether you agree with the various findings of the court and why or why not.

Case 5-5

Ingersoll Mill. Mach. Co. v. M/V Bodena

829 F.2d 293 (2d Cir. 1987)
(Paragraph numbers added.)
PIERCE, Circuit Judge:

[1] These appeals are from a final judgment filed in the United States District Court for the Southern District of New York on April 28, 1986, following a bench trial before Judge Robert L. Carter. The judgment (1) awarded plaintiff-appellee The

Ingersoll Milling Machine Co. ("Ingersoll") damages and prejudgment interest against defendants-appellants Taiwan International Line Ltd. ("Taiwan"), J.E. Bernard Co. ("Bernard"), and Fireman's Fund Insurance Co. ("Fireman's Fund" or the "Fund") jointly and severally, (2) awarded Ingersoll attorney's fees and litigation expenses against Fireman's Fund, (3) awarded Fireman's Fund a right of subrogation against Taiwan and Bernard, and (4) dismissed claims of Taiwan and Bernard against each other.

[2] Ingersoll cross-appeals seeking to increase its award of damages and prejudgment interest.

[3] Appellants each raise a number of issues on appeal. We consider them seriatim, and we affirm the determinations of the district court except with regard to the award of attorney's fees and litigation expenses.

Background

[4] This case arises from the shipment of certain cargo from the United States to South Korea. The cargo, which was insured, and consisted of 20 packages, 18 of which were stowed on the deck of the ship, was damaged in transit. Simply stated, we must determine whether the district court properly decided who is responsible for the damage and that the insurer improperly refused to cover the loss. We set forth the essential evidence in this section, as found by the district court, 619 F. Supp. 493 (S.D.N.Y. 1985), with details to be provided later as necessary.

[5] In January 1978, Waldrich Siegen, GmbH ("Waldrich") of West Germany contracted to sell heavy, specially designed machines to Hyundai International, Inc., in Korea. Waldrich engaged its affiliate, Ingersoll, a manufacturer of special design machinery, as a subcontractor to manufacture Shop Order 24441 ("Order # 24441") and to arrange for its shipment to Korea. Order # 24441 consisted of a ram type, horizontal spindle, traveling column machinery center, and was valued in excess of $2 million.

[6] In the summer of 1979, Ingersoll, located in Rockford, Illinois, contacted Gryphon Shipping Service, Inc. ("Gryphon"), a broker and steamship agent in Chicago, to arrange for shipment of Order # 24441 to Korea.[1] Gryphon, in turn, contacted Taiwan, which had time chartered the M/V Bodena from its owner Excellent Marine, Inc. ("Excellent Marine"). Gryphon arranged with Taiwan in August 1979 for the cargo to be shipped in September 1979 from New Orleans aboard the M/V Bodena. A contract of carriage arose between Ingersoll and Taiwan in August 1979 when Ingersoll accepted the terms arranged by Gryphon and informed Gryphon that the shipment of Order # 24441 would be in twenty boxes. The district court found that, at the time of booking, there was no evidence that Ingersoll had agreed to on deck stowage. Gryphon's commission was to be paid by Taiwan, and Gryphon was found by the district court to be Taiwan's agent.

---

1. Gryphon is not a party to this action.

[7] In connection with the shipment, Ingersoll also retained Bernard, a freight for-warder doing business in Elk Grove Village, Illinois, to perform various freight for-warding tasks. In addition to other duties to be performed by Bernard, Ingersoll, by letter dated September 10, 1979, requested that Bernard secure "three originals and four copies of *clean* on-board bills of lading" (emphasis added). In response to this letter, Bernard prepared two master ditto forms of the bill of lading and also the shipper's export declaration. One of the master ditto forms was sent to Mid-Gulf Shipping, Inc. ("Mid-Gulf"), Taiwan's agent in New Orleans, to be used in the preparation of the original bills of lading; the other was sent to Gryphon. In addi-tion, the master ditto was used to prepare an advance notice of shipment which was sent by Bernard to Ingersoll on September 25, 1979. Neither the master ditto nor the advance notice contained any notation as to stowage. Ingersoll informed Bernard that all the information on the advance notice was correct except that the port of discharge should be changed.

[8] The Ingersoll cargo, which had arrived in New Orleans from Illinois by truck and rail, was loaded on board the M/V Bodena on September 26 and 27, 1979. Of the twenty boxes which comprised Order # 24441, eighteen were initially stowed on deck and two were stowed below deck. Mid-Gulf, Taiwan's agent, was responsible for the issuance of bills of lading. Prior to sailing, Mid-Gulf took the ditto form sup-plied by Bernard and added the phrase "on deck shipper's risk" to its face. Mid-Gulf then used the altered ditto to run off three original bills of lading and mailed the originals with thirteen copies to Gryphon in Chicago.

[9] Ingersoll received the originals and four copies on October 1, 1979. Fred Woy-wod, Ingersoll's contract administrator, saw the documents that day but either did not notice the addition of the words "on deck shipper's risk" or if he did notice them, did not understand their legal significance. Bernard, too, received copies of the bills of lading on October 1 but failed to examine the issued bills to determine whether they were in fact clean, and, consequently, failed to inform Ingersoll that Taiwan had not followed the instructions to issue clean bills of lading.

[10] The M/V Bodena, which had made several intermediate stops at various East Coast ports, set sail from Savannah, Georgia, for Korea on October 14, 1979. At the time of sailing, seventeen of Ingersoll's boxes were stowed on deck, one of the boxes initially stowed on deck having been moved below deck. The voyage to Korea lasted more than one month and was beset with storms, heavy seas, and high winds. As a result of heavy rolling and pitching during the voyage, the seventeen boxes on the deck were severely damaged. Some boxes were broken; others were thoroughly soaked by sea water. Because of the damage, Order # 24441 had to be sent from Korea to Waldrich in Germany for repair. None of the three boxes stowed under deck was damaged.

[11] Ingersoll maintained an all risk insurance policy with Fireman's Fund. That policy had been issued as an open cargo policy, designed to cover all of Ingersoll's shipments. In other words, a particular shipment would become covered under the policy either when Ingersoll filled out and sent to Fireman's Fund a certificate of

insurance for each shipment, indicating the contents, value, destination, and carrier of the cargo, or when Ingersoll sent to the Fund a monthly declaration of shipments. As testified to by Fireman's Fund officials, such a policy was designed to provide automatic coverage such that even if the certificate or monthly declaration was sent after a loss had occurred, the shipment would nevertheless be covered.

[12] The particular policy in question contained separate clauses for insuring under deck shipments and on deck shipments.[2] Clause 17(a) insured under deck shipments and specifically contained broader terms of coverage. Those terms provided coverage against all risks of physical loss or damage. Clause 17(b), which did not contain broader terms, provided coverage for on deck shipments known as free of particular average ("FPA"). FPA coverage does not cover a partial loss of the subject matter insured unless certain contingencies not relevant herein occur. Another provision of the policy, clause 8(B)(2), limited coverage to $175,000 for shipments subject to an on deck bill of lading or shipments stowed on deck with the consent of the insured.[3]

[13] In August 1979, Ingersoll sent to Fireman's Fund a certificate of insurance to cover Order # 24441. The certificate, which took effect before the boxes were

---

2. The pertinent provisions of the policy are set forth below in full:

17. (a) UNDER DECK shipments—Including containerized shipments under optional On Deck /Or Under Deck bill(s) of lading are insured. Warranted free from Particular Average unless the vessel or craft be stranded, sunk, or burnt, but notwithstanding this warranty this Company is to pay any loss of or damage to the interest insured which may reasonably be attributed to fire, collision or contact of the vessel and/or craft and/or conveyance with any external substance (ice included) other than water, or to discharge of cargo at port of distress. *The foregoing warranty, however, shall not apply where broader terms of Average are provided for hereinafter.*
BROADER TERMS:—
Insured against all risks of physical loss or damage from any external cause irrespective of percentage, including theft, pilferage and/or non-delivery, but excluding, nevertheless, the risks of war, strikes, riots, seizure, detainment, confiscation, requisition, nationalization and other risks excluded by the "F.C. S. and/or S.R. C.C." warranties in the printed portion of the policy except to the extent that such risks may be specifically covered by endorsement, also warranted free from any claims arising out of the inherent vice of the goods insured or consequent upon loss of time and/or market.
(b) ON DECK shipments are insured:—Warranted free of particular average unless caused by the vessel and/or interest insured being stranded, sunk, burnt, on fire or in collision with another ship or vessel or with ice or with any substance other than water, but liable for jettison and/or washing overboard, irrespective of percentage. *The foregoing warranty, however, shall not apply when broader terms of Average are provided for hereinafter.*
BROADER TERMS:—[None provided]
Fireman's Fund Insurance Company, Marine Open Cargo Policy No. WB 20737, (italics in original), *also quoted in* 619 F.Supp. 493, 498–99 (S.D.N.Y. 1985).

3. Clause 8(B)(2) reads in full as follows:

B. Of the limit of liability expressed above, this Company shall not be liable for more than . . .
(2) *$175,000.00* in respect of cargo shipped subject to On Deck ocean bill(s) of lading or stowed On Deck with consent of the Assured.

actually loaded aboard the M/V Bodena, stated that the machinery was laden under deck. When Ingersoll learned of the damage to the cargo in December 1979, it notified Fireman's Fund of its loss. After an investigation, Fireman's Fund, on May 23, 1980, denied Ingersoll's claim under its policy for full indemnity for the repairs undertaken by Ingersoll.

[14] The district court found that Taiwan and Bernard were jointly and severally liable for Ingersoll's damages, and accordingly, awarded Ingersoll $977,899 plus prejudgment interest. Fireman's Fund too was found jointly and severally liable to Ingersoll in the same amount under the insurance policy; and it was ordered that to the extent that Fireman's Fund makes payment to Ingersoll for damages assessed, it will be entitled to recover such payment from Taiwan and Bernard, including taxable costs but not including attorney's fees and litigation expenses. Additionally, the district judge ruled that Ingersoll was entitled to recover attorney's fees and litigation expenses from Fireman's Fund. Finally, the district court dismissed the claims of Taiwan and Bernard against each other, as well as Ingersoll's claim against Excellent Marine. This appeal followed.

Discussion

I. Taiwan

[15] Ingersoll's claim against Taiwan can be characterized simply as a claim for breach of contract. There is no dispute that a contract of carriage existed between Ingersoll and Taiwan. Telephone conversations in August 1979 between representatives of Ingersoll, Gryphon, and Taiwan, in which the cargo was booked, led to a binding contract when Ingersoll informed Gryphon that it accepted Taiwan's terms. As the district court found, this contract constituted the contract of carriage. The open question then was what were the terms of the contract. More specifically, did the contract call for on deck or below deck stowage.

[16] Absent an express agreement by the shipper permitting cargo to be stowed on deck or a general port custom permitting on deck stowage, a shipper is entitled to expect below deck stowage under a clean bill of lading. . . . *see* 2A E. Benedict, *Benedict on Admiralty* § 123, at 12–11 (7th ed. 1987) ("[g]oods stowed on deck without the shipper's consent are at the ship's risk, the shipowner being liable for any loss or damage thereto.") To reiterate, a shipper's reasonable expectation on booking cargo for shipment is that it will be stowed below deck, unless the shipper agrees to the contrary or a general port custom permits above deck stowage. The burden is on the carrier to prove that the shipper consented to something other than the usual and customary arrangement. *See Gemini Navigation, Inc. v. Philipp Bros. Div. of Minerals Chemicals Philipp Corp.,* 499 F.2d 745, 751 (2d Cir. 1974).

[17] Although the district court found that "[t]here is no evidence that Ingersoll specified below deck stowage," 619 F.Supp. at 500, it also found that "there is no credible evidence that Ingersoll agreed to an on deck shipment," *id*. Thus, the terms of the contract of carriage were established by the industry custom that stowage would be below deck. The district court correctly found that Taiwan had failed to

meet its burden of proof that Ingersoll agreed to on deck stowage and that Taiwan was liable for not performing its contract obligations.

[18] Taiwan presents a number of arguments in support of its contention that it is not liable for breach of contract.[4] First, Taiwan argues that Ingersoll waived its right to below deck stowage of its cargo. Specifically, Taiwan claims that by receiving the bill of lading on October 1, 1979, with the notation "on deck shipper's risk," Ingersoll had constructive notice that its goods had been stowed on deck. Therefore, Taiwan argues, Ingersoll had a duty to notify Taiwan that on deck stowage was unacceptable so that Taiwan could have either shifted the cargo to a below deck location or unloaded the cargo at another port of call at which the M/V Bodena docked prior to embarking for Korea on October 14, 1979.

[19] The district court did indeed find that Ingersoll had constructive notice that its goods were being carried on the deck of the M/V Bodena at Ingersoll's risk. 619 F. Supp. at 501. However, a party asserting a waiver defense bears the burden of proof in establishing that defense. Taiwan, in our view, cannot make out a defense of waiver. Waiver is generally defined as an intentional relinquishment of a known right. . . . An intent to waive a contractual right must be manifest in a party's failure to object. *See Saverslak v. Davis-Cleaver Produce Co.*, 606 F.2d 208, 213 (7th Cir. 1979), *cert. denied*, 444 U.S. 1078 . . . (1980).

[20] Ingersoll's contract with Taiwan, as the district court interpreted it, called for under deck stowage. We find no basis in the record upon which to conclude that Ingersoll intentionally relinquished its right to under deck stowage. Ingersoll's silence after receiving constructive notice of the on deck shipment lacks the requisite manifest intent to constitute a waiver. Ingersoll's silence and failure to act can better be characterized as an oversight or carelessness rather than as a waiver of a contractual right. The mere fact that Ingersoll can be deemed to have been informed that its machinery was being shipped to Korea on deck does not mean that the conclusion must be drawn that it knowingly consented to a modification of the original contract.

[21] Next, Taiwan contends that Gryphon was Ingersoll's agent and therefore that Ingersoll was bound by the contracts entered into by Gryphon. Taiwan claims that if Gryphon was aware during booking that Order # 24441 was going to be shipped on deck, Ingersoll would be bound by that knowledge. However, the district court specifically found that Gryphon was Taiwan's agent.[5] This finding may not be reversed

---

4. Taiwan's argument that the district court improperly interpreted the meaning of "clean" on board bills of lading is not relevant. The contract of carriage between Ingersoll and Taiwan was formed in August 1979 when the cargo was booked. It did not contain any reference to bills of lading. Interpretation of the meaning of "clean" bills of lading is relevant only in assessing Ingersoll's claims against Bernard. See *infra* section IIB.

5. Taiwan asserts that the agency issue had already been decided in a related action in the Northern District of Illinois. *Ingersoll Mill. Mach. Co. v. J.E. Bernard Co.*, 508 F.Supp. 907 (N.D.Ill. 1981). However, that court concluded only that Gryphon was more likely Ingersoll's agent than

unless clearly erroneous. *O'Connell Mach. Co. v. M.V. "Americana"*, 797 F.2d 1130, 1133 (2d Cir. 1986). It appears that there is sufficient evidence in the record to support this finding. For instance, Gryphon paid Bernard its brokerage commission on Taiwan's behalf. Bernard also sent a copy of the master ditto bill of lading to Gryphon to prepare the bill of lading, which Gryphon would be likely to do if it was Taiwan's agent. Moreover, Taiwan paid Gryphon a finder's fee for obtaining the Ingersoll cargo for Taiwan.

[22] Taiwan also contends that even if the initial oral contract called for below deck stowage, Ingersoll's receipt of the bill of lading with the new terms changed the parties' obligations. As Taiwan would have it, only the bill of lading, even if it contains unauthorized terms, represents the contract of carriage. In other words, Taiwan contends it is solely the bill of lading which governs and determines the proper stowage of the cargo. While it is true that a bill of lading may under certain circumstances constitute the contract of carriage between the parties, *see CIA. Platamon de Navegacion, S.A. v. Empresa Colombiana de Petroleos,* 478 F.Supp. 66, 67 (S.D.N.Y. 1979); *see generally* 2A *Benedict on Admiralty* §34, at 4–13, Taiwan's argument is not at all persuasive on the evidence in this case. A carrier such as Taiwan may not unilaterally alter a bill of lading so as to bind the shipper without the authorization of the shipper. *See West India Indus. v. Tradex, Tradex Petroleum Services,* 664 F.2d 946, 949–50 n. 5 (5th Cir. 1981). A carrier cannot impose on deck stowage on a shipper merely by including a notation in the bill of lading which it delivers after the voyage commences. To allow a carrier after the fact to impose on the shipper an unauthorized change of terms would run counter to the general proposition that without its contrary agreement, a shipper is entitled to expect below deck stowage. *See St. Johns N.F. Shipping Corp.,* 263 U.S. at 124, 44 S.Ct. at 30; *Encyclopaedia Britannica, Inc.,* 422 F.2d at 14 n. 5. Under the circumstances presented herein, the contract of carriage which governed the obligations of Ingersoll and Taiwan was the one orally entered into in August 1979 and not the altered bill of lading.

[23] Finally, Taiwan argues that Ingersoll had the burden of showing that the damage was caused by Taiwan's negligence and, in any case, that its liability should be limited to $500 per package pursuant to the Carriage of Goods by Sea Act ("COGSA"), 46 U.S.C. § 1300 *et seq.* (1982 Supp. 1983), which the bill of lading incorporated by reference. We reject both of these contentions. First, as shown above, Taiwan's stowage of Ingersoll's cargo on deck without Ingersoll's permission was a breach of the contract of carriage. A showing that Taiwan was negligent by such stowage is not relevant to or necessary for establishing a breach of contract. Second, where, as here,

---

Taiwan's. *Id.* at 912. Moreover, the district judge was not bound by that decision because it was rendered on a motion to dismiss for lack of jurisdiction before discovery, and without the benefit of testimony and the emergence of all the evidence. We do not believe the issue had been fully and fairly litigated so as to preclude the district judge from making his own independent finding. *Saylor v. Lindsley,* 391 F.2d 965, 968 (2d Cir. 1968); *see also Saez Rivera v. Nissan Mfg. Co.,* 788 F.2d 819, 821 (1st Cir. 1986).

a carrier has materially deviated from the terms of the contract of carriage, monetary limits contained in COGSA and in bills of lading are inapplicable; rather, the carrier is liable in full as an insurer of the cargo. *General Elec. Co. Int'l Sales Div. v. S.S. Nancy Lykes,* 706 F.2d 80, 87 (2d Cir.), *cert. denied,* 464 U.S. 849, 104 S.Ct. 157, 78 L.Ed.2d 145 (1983); *Calmaquip Eng'g West Hemisphere Corp.,* 650 F.2d at 638–39; *Encyclopaedia Britannica, Inc.,* 422 F.2d at 18. Therefore, because Ingersoll's cargo was stowed on deck in breach of the contract of carriage, Ingersoll's recovery is not contingent upon a showing of negligence, and Taiwan cannot benefit from the limits of liability in the bill of lading or in COGSA.

II. Bernard

A. Admiralty Jurisdiction

[24] As a preliminary matter, Bernard challenges the district court's assertion of subject matter jurisdiction. Since there does not appear to be diversity or federal question jurisdiction, subject matter jurisdiction must reside, if at all, under 28 U.S.C. § 1333, which provides for admiralty or maritime jurisdiction in the federal courts. Bernard, seeking to avoid the application of admiralty jurisdiction, characterizes its contract with Ingersoll as one for preliminary brokerage services only incidentally related to the maritime contract between Ingersoll and Taiwan. The district court, after observing that "[f]ederal courts have traditionally exercised admiralty jurisdiction over shipper's claims against freight forwarders," 619 F.Supp. at 503, held that the services Bernard performed were not preliminary in nature. While we decline to lay down a general rule that freight forwarders are always subject to admiralty jurisdiction, we do hold, for reasons discussed below, that in this instance, Bernard's freight forwarding contract with Ingersoll involved enough tasks of a non-preliminary nature to support admiralty jurisdiction.

[25] We have recognized that "[t]he precise categorization of the contracts that warrant invocation of the federal courts' admiralty jurisdiction has proven particularly elusive." *CTI-Container Leasing Corp. v. Oceanic Operations Corp.,* 682 F.2d 377, 379 (2d Cir. 1982). The Supreme Court has cautioned that "[t]he boundaries of admiralty jurisdiction over contracts—as opposed to torts or crimes—being conceptual rather than spatial, have always been difficult to draw." *Kossick v. United Fruit Co.,* 365 U.S. 731, 735 . . . (1961). A long-recognized principle for determining whether a contract is maritime is that agreements preliminary to maritime contracts are not cognizable in admiralty. *Peralta Shipping Corp. v. Smith Johnson (Shipping) Corp.,* 739 F.2d 798, 801 (2d Cir. 1984), *cert. denied,* 470 U.S. 1031 . . . (1985); 1 *Benedict on Admiralty* § 184, at 11-8 (7th ed. 1985). Applying this principle, our Court, despite questioning its continuing validity, has recently affirmed the longstanding, well settled rule laid down by the Supreme Court in *Minturn v. Maynard,* 58 U.S. (17 How.) 477, 15 L.Ed. 235 (1854), that general agency contracts are not cognizable in admiralty. *Peralta Shipping,* 739 F.2d at 804. General agency contracts are those that call for the "husbanding" of a vessel, that is, arranging for performance of a variety of services preliminary to maritime contracts, such as soliciting cargo or passengers,

and procuring supplies, crews, stevedores, and tugboats. Thus, in *Peralta Shipping*, this Court held that a contract which included a duty to supervise the performance of maritime contracts did not warrant admiralty jurisdiction. *Id.* at 803.

[26] Bernard argues that freight forwarding contracts fall within the ambit of general agency contracts and are therefore excluded from admiralty consideration. Courts that have specifically dealt with admiralty jurisdiction over freight forwarders appear to have arrived at different conclusions. *Compare Outbound Maritime Corp. v. P.T. Indonesian Consortium of Constr. Indus.*, 575 F.Supp. 1222, 1223–24 (S.D.N.Y. 1983) (freight forwarder subject to admiralty jurisdiction) *with Johnson Products Co. v. M/V La Molinera*, 619 F.Supp. 764, 767 (S.D.N.Y. 1985) (freight forwarder not subject to admiralty jurisdiction). However, the focus of our inquiry must be not on the name assigned to the contract, but rather on the nature of the services to be performed. It is the character of the work to be performed under the contract that is determinative of whether the agreement was maritime. . . . If the subject matter of the contract "'relat[es] to a ship in its use as such, or to commerce or to navigation on navigable waters, or to transportation by sea or to maritime employment'" it is fairly said to constitute a maritime contract. *CTI-Container Leasing Corp.*, 682 F.2d at 379 (quoting 1 *Benedict on Admiralty* § 183, at 11-6 (7th ed. 1981)). Accordingly, we turn to an examination of the services to be performed by Bernard under its contract with Ingersoll.

[27] Of the thirteen services listed by the Federal Maritime Commission which a freight forwarder may perform at the request of a shipper, 46 C.F.R. § 510.2(h), Ingersoll asked Bernard to undertake six. Bernard was obligated to prepare and process export declarations; to prepare and process delivery orders or dock receipts; to prepare and process ocean bills of lading, including the preparation and forwarding of a master ditto; to prepare and send advance notification of shipments or other documents to banks, shippers, or consignees; to handle freight or other monies advanced by the shipper or to remit or advance freight or other monies or credit in connection with the dispatching of shipments; and together with Ingersoll, to coordinate the movement of shipments from origin to vessel.

[28] Although Bernard's services may not have included *all* the services a freight forwarder traditionally performs for a shipper, it is not upon the number of services that we focus but rather on their nature. The preparation and processing of export declarations, delivery orders, dock receipts, bills of lading, and advance notification of shipment are not services rendered preliminary to a voyage rather they are essential to it. Without these, there can be no voyage. Specifically, we note that the district court found that Bernard's obligation with regard to the bills of lading was twofold. First, Bernard was engaged to *secure* clean on board bills of lading. Additionally, on receipt of the bills of lading, Bernard was to *review* the copies it received and to *advise* Ingersoll if in fact they were not clean. 619 F.Supp. at 502. Bernard's duty to secure clean bills of lading is akin to the issuance of bills of lading themselves. An obligation to procure a bill of lading for an ocean shipment, in our view, is a contract relating to transportation by sea. The procurement of the proper papers

and documents relating to a shipment by sea is an essential and integral part of the shipping process; a contract to obtain those papers, therefore, falls squarely within the admiralty jurisdiction of the federal courts. . . .

B. Breach of Contract

[30] Bernard's contract with Ingersoll called for Bernard to perform a number of services typically associated with a general freight forwarder. Bernard's contention that its duties were more limited in scope than those generally performed by freight forwarders is not pivotal in determining whether Bernard breached its contract with Ingersoll. Our focus must be on the specific obligations involved and whether Bernard satisfactorily performed them. As noted, the district court found that two of the tasks to be performed by Bernard related to the bills of lading. Bernard was bound initially to secure clean on board bills of lading for Ingersoll. Moreover, Bernard was bound to examine the bills of lading once they had been issued by Taiwan and to inform Ingersoll of any imperfections. The district court held that Bernard failed in both respects: it failed in its obligation to procure clean bills, and it failed to examine the copies it received and to advise Ingersoll that in fact they were not clean. 619 F.Supp. at 502. We find no clear error in the district court's finding that Bernard failed in its primary duty, namely, to supply the clean bills. We therefore find it unnecessary to reach the secondary question, whether Bernard also failed to review the bills for imperfections.

1. "Clean" on Board Bills of Lading

[31] Bernard contends that the bills of lading that it supplied were in fact clean. According to Bernard, the notation of the words "on deck shipper's risk" did not render the bills unclean. In Bernard's view, a "clean" bill of lading requires only that the shipping document bear no notation on its face that expressly declares a defective condition of the goods. In other words, it contends, a "clean" bill of lading indicates that the goods were not received by the carrier in damaged condition at the time of shipment. The phrase "on deck shipper's risk," Bernard argues, is a clause which does not describe the physical condition of the goods at the time of receipt by the carrier, but rather relates instead to who bears the risk during voyage. So interpreted, a notation declaring that the shipper bears the risk of damage during the voyage would not affect the cleanliness of the bills. We disagree with Bernard's interpretation.

[32] It is no doubt true, as Bernard claims, that a "clean" bill of lading refers to the undamaged condition of the cargo at the time it is received by the carrier. *Vana Trading Co. v. S.S. "Mette Skou"*, 556 F.2d 100, 103 n. 4 (2d Cir.), *cert. denied*, 434 U.S. 892 . . . (1977); C. Gilmore C. Black, *The Law of Admiralty* § 3-13, at 122 (2d ed. 1975). However, a "clean" bill of lading refers to more than just the condition of the goods. It has long been recognized in admiralty custom and practice that a "clean" bill of lading refers also to the place on a ship where cargo is to be stowed.[6] "[A] clean

---

6. The meaning of a "clean" bill of lading is one firmly established by the custom and practice of the maritime industry. Its meaning is not ambiguous, and, therefore, the parties' intention in using

bill of lading imports that the goods are to be safely and properly stowed *under deck.*" *The Delaware*, 81 U.S. (14 Wall.) 579, 602, 20 L.Ed. 779 (1871) (emphasis added); *see Seguros Banvenez, S.A. v. S/S Oliver Drescher*, 761 F.2d 855, 859 (2d Cir. 1985). Noted admiralty commentators agree that a "clean" bill of lading denotes a bill that is either silent as to stowage, thereby imputing that the cargo is to be stowed below deck, or provides for under deck stowage. 2A *Benedict on Admiralty* § 97, at 9–12 (7th ed. 1987) ("[t]he issuance of a clean bill of lading—one which does not specifically provide for on-deck stowage—obligates the carrier to stow the cargo under deck"); *id.* § 123, at 12–10 ("[a] clean bill of lading imputes under-deck stowage"); A. Knauth, *Ocean Bills of Lading* 237 (2d ed. 1941) ("[a] 'clean' bill of lading is an unwritten representation that the cargo would be carried under deck"). Thus, when a shipper requests a "clean" bill of lading it expects to receive from the carrier a document which either specifically notes that stowage is under deck, *see Thyssen, Inc. v. S.S. Fortune Star*, 777 F.2d 57, 59 (2d Cir. 1985), or is silent as to stowage, *see The Idefjord*, 114 F.2d 262, 266 (2d Cir.), *cert. denied*, 311 U.S. 707 . . . (1940). If the document is silent as to stowage, the assumption is that the goods have been stowed below deck. In other words, a request for a "clean" bill of lading is an implied request for stowage below deck.

[33] Ingersoll's instruction to Bernard in its letter of September 10, 1979, was to provide "clean" on board bills of lading. Bernard, therefore, was duty bound to supply bills that noted or implied that stowage was below deck. Contrary to Ingersoll's instruction, the bills actually provided by Bernard contained a notation indicating that the goods had been stowed on deck. Thus, Bernard plainly breached its contract with Ingersoll. → seller ＼ carrier

2. Causation

[34] Bernard also contends that even if it failed to supply "clean" bills of lading to Ingersoll, its breach of contract was not causally connected to the damage to Order # 24441. Essentially, Bernard argues that even if it had reviewed the bills and found the notation, the damage to the cargo would still have occurred. By the time the notation was detected, the cargo was already on deck and at sea. Therefore, according to Bernard, its failure to advise Ingersoll that the bills bore the clause "on deck" did not cause or contribute to the damage.

[35] Bernard's contention might have some merit were its only contractual duty to review the bills after they had been issued. In such case, given that Bernard received the documents on October 1 and that the M/V Bodena did not actually leave the United States bound for Korea until October 14, the feasibility of unloading the cargo at another U.S. port prior to sailing would be a crucial issue. The district court did not decide whether unloading was a viable option because of a dearth of

---

that term does not govern, as Bernard argues it should. The district court properly did not employ contractual rules of construction, such as the intent of the parties at the time of contracting, in interpreting its meaning.

evidence. 619 F.Supp. at 502. However, the question of whether the cargo could have somehow been saved between October 1 and October 14 is not determinative of Bernard's liability. Bernard's contractual obligation was not only to review the bills of lading for defects but also to secure clean bills in the first instance. Having failed to ensure that the cargo was placed below deck, thereby breaching its contract by causing a bill that was not "clean" to be issued, Bernard can be said to have proximately caused Ingersoll's damages. . . .

III. Cross-Claims of Taiwan and Bernard

[37] The district court properly dismissed the claims asserted by Taiwan and Bernard for indemnity against each other. Indemnity rests upon the principle that the true wrongdoer should bear the ultimate burden of payment. *Ross v. Penn Cent. Transp. Co.*, 433 F.Supp. 306, 309 (W.D. N.Y. 1977). There can be no indemnity as between parties that each bear primary responsibility for a wrong regardless of their relative degrees of fault. *Philadelphia Elec. Co. v. Hercules, Inc.*, 762 F.2d 303, 318 (3d Cir.), *cert. denied*, 474 U.S. 980 . . . (1985). Having concluded that Taiwan and Bernard each breached their separate contracts with Ingersoll, the district court properly held them jointly and severally liable and dismissed their respective claims for indemnity.

IV. Fireman's Fund

A. Liability on the Policy

[38] Fireman's Fund contends that the district court erred in finding that Ingersoll's policy covered the damage sustained by Order # 24441. Essentially, the Fund contends on appeal that clause 17(b) of the policy, which denies coverage for partial loss of on deck shipments, should apply to deny coverage because part of Ingersoll's cargo was actually stowed on deck. We disagree. As we discuss below, the district court was justified in finding the policy ambiguous, construing it against Fireman's Fund, and applying clause 17(a) of the policy, which covers all risks of loss in cases of under deck shipments.

[39] Ingersoll's policy with Fireman's Fund was an open cargo policy. Such a policy is a master policy which covers all of an insured's shipments. An insured declares a particular shipment either by sending the Fund a copy of an insurance certificate or a monthly declaration of shipments. One of the advantages of this type of policy is that an insured has automatic coverage for a shipment even if it neglects to declare the shipment, or if the certificate is not issued until the cargo has arrived and a loss has already occurred. Under the subject policy, different types of shipments were accorded different types of coverage. Certain shipments were insured on an all risk basis (clause 17(a)), that is, against all risks of physical loss or damage from any external cause; other types of shipments were insured free of particular average (clause 17(b)), that is, partial losses were not covered; still others were subject to monetary limits (clause 8(B)(2)).

[40] In August 1979, before shipping Order # 24441, Ingersoll sent Fireman's Fund an insurance certificate to declare and insure the machine. The certificate stated that

the goods were stowed under deck and were insured against all risks. The certificate became effective on August 31, 1979. In fact, the bulk of the shipment was stowed on deck and the bill of lading was marked "on deck shipper's risk" without Ingersoll's consent. Ingersoll notified Fireman's Fund of the damage to the cargo in December 1979. The Fund denied Ingersoll's claim by letter dated May 23, 1980.

[41] Marine insurance contracts are governed by federal admiralty law when there is an established federal rule, and by state law when there is not. *Wilburn Boat Co. v. Fireman's Fund Ins. Co.,* [above, p. 618] (1955); *Ionian Shipping Co. v. British Law Ins. Co.,* 426 F.2d 186, 190 (2d Cir. 1970). The parties do not dispute that to the extent that federal admiralty rules do not exist, the interpretation of the policy is governed by Illinois law.

[42] The starting point in interpreting an insurance policy is to determine whether the policy terms are ambiguous. As a general rule, plain or unambiguous language will be given its ordinary meaning and effect, and the need to resort to rules of construction arises only when an ambiguity exists. . . . Courts may not create an ambiguity where none exists. . . . If an insurance contract is ambiguous it will generally be construed against the insurer who drafted it in order to promote coverage for losses to which the policy relates. *Karaganis,* 811 F.2d at 361; *FSC Paper Corp. v. Sun Ins. Co. of N.Y.,* 744 F.2d 1279, 1282 (7th Cir. 1984). This principle applies to all types of insurance policies including maritime policies. *Kalmbach, Inc. v. Insurance Co. of Pa.,* 529 F.2d 552, 555 (9th Cir. 1976) (citing Illinois cases). The rule that insurance policies are to be construed in favor of the insured is most rigorously applied in construing the meaning of exclusions incorporated into a policy of insurance or provisions seeking to narrow the insurer's liability. *Sears, Roebuck Co. v. Reliance Ins. Co.,* 654 F.2d 494, 499 (7th Cir. 1981). Accordingly, we turn first to the question of whether Ingersoll's policy is ambiguous.

[43] Fireman's Fund's argument that the policy provisions are unambiguous has surface appeal. Clause 17(a) is encaptioned "UNDER DECK shipments" and clause 17(b) is encaptioned "ON DECK shipments." At first glance, these captions would seem to indicate that it is the actual, physical place of stowage which governs the applicability of the clauses. Cargo actually stowed under deck would be governed by clause 17(a), and cargo actually stowed on deck would fall within clause 17(b). However, a closer, more careful reading of the policy reveals that the provisions at issue are in fact ambiguous.[7]

---

7. Fireman's Fund contends that the district court improperly considered parol evidence (testimony of Fund officials to the effect that cargo on deck without the insured's consent but with an under deck bill of lading would be covered by clause 17(a)) in finding an ambiguity in the policy. We disagree. As explained, the district court could properly have found the policy ambiguous on its face. Moreover, under Illinois law, "[i]n determining whether an ambiguity exists, as a matter of law, the trial court may consider parol and extrinsic evidence." *Sunstream Jet Express, Inc. v. International Air Serv. Co.,* 734 F.2d 1258, 1268 (7th Cir. 1984) (citing cases).

[44] Looking at the insurance contract as a whole, as we must, *Michigan Chem. Corp. v. American Home Assurance Co.*, 728 F.2d 374, 377 (6th Cir. 1984) (applying Illinois law), we find clauses 17(a) and 17(b) subject to varying interpretations. A contract that is reasonably and fairly susceptible of more than one meaning is said to be ambiguous. *Karaganis*, 811 F.2d at 361; *Sunstream Jet Express, Inc. v. International Air Serv. Co.*, 734 F.2d 1258, 1269 (7th Cir. 1984). Neither clause 17(a) or 17(b) makes reference on its face to the bills of lading or to the contract of carriage under which the shipments were to travel.[8] Nor do clauses 17(a) or 17(b) refer to the consent of the insured in deciding where its cargo is to be placed. However, another provision of the policy, clause 8(B)(2), specifically places a monetary ceiling on shipments that travel either "subject to On Deck ocean bill(s) of lading" or are "stowed On Deck with consent of the Assured." Where one part of the policy is specific and another general, it is incumbent upon the court to resolve the question of what relationship each part bears to the other. Clauses 17(a) and 17(b) could conceivably refer to any one or to a combination of many possible situations. Coverage under these clauses might be determined by the actual physical place of stowage, the bill of lading under which the cargo traveled, the contract of carriage for the shipment, or the consent of the insured as to where its cargo should be stowed. It simply is not clear from the face of the policy when coverage under clauses 17(a) or 17(b) would be in effect.

[45] Having concluded that the policy terms are ambiguous, we turn next to the construction of those terms. In our view, the district court properly construed the policy in favor of the insured. We think a fair and reasonable interpretation of the policy suggests that "UNDER DECK shipments" of clause 17(a) refers to shipments that were supposed to travel under deck. In other words, when an insured has contracted with its carrier for shipment of cargo below deck, clause 17(a) applies. It is irrelevant whether the cargo actually traveled below deck or whether the cargo was shipped pursuant to an under deck bill of lading, or, as in this case, pursuant to an unauthorized on deck bill of lading. The place of physical stowage or the bill of lading is not determinative of coverage; it is the contract of carriage that governs. As long as the shipper intended the cargo to be stowed below deck and so manifested its intent in its contract of carriage, clause 17(a) applies. Similarly, "ON DECK shipments" of clause 17(b) refers to all shipments that were supposed to travel on deck. In such an instance, a lesser degree of coverage is provided. In those cases, coverage is provided only for a total loss and only when that loss occurs as a result of certain perils. No coverage whatsoever is provided for fortuitous partial losses caused even by an insured-against peril. Furthermore, clause 8(B)(2) would appear to provide an additional limitation on clause 17(b), limiting the maximum possible recovery to $175,000 if the cargo was shipped subject to an on deck bill of lading or stowed on deck with the insured's consent. Construction of the policy in this manner

---

8. Clause 17(a) does refer to the bills of lading under which *containerized* shipments travel. It does not, however, mention bills of lading with regard to other types of shipments. Mentioning one type of shipment and not other types, in our view, only adds to the ambiguity of the clause.

comports with the logical assumption that an insurance company would provide, and an insured would buy, greater protection for shipments that were supposed to travel under deck than for shipments intended to be placed on deck. Accordingly, applying this construction to the facts herein, we believe it is clear that clause 17(a) is the operative provision. As discussed, Ingersoll's contract of carriage with Taiwan required under deck stowage. This being so, the provision which relates to shipments that were intended to travel below deck, namely clause 17(a), must govern.

[46] Under clause 17(a), Ingersoll's loss would have been covered. Clause 17(a) insures against "all risks of physical loss or damage from any external cause." All risk coverage covers all losses which are fortuitous no matter what caused the loss, including the insured's negligence, unless the insured expressly advises otherwise. *Goodman v. Fireman's Fund Ins. Co.*, 600 F.2d 1040, 1042 (4th Cir. 1979). A loss is fortuitous unless it results from an inherent defect, ordinary wear and tear, or intentional misconduct of the insured. *Id.* An insured satisfies its burden of proving that its loss resulted from an insured peril if the cargo was damaged while the policy was in force and the loss was fortuitous. *Atlantic Lines Ltd. v. American Motorists Ins. Co.*, 547 F.2d 11, 12 (2d Cir. 1976); *accord Morrison Grain Co. v. Utica Mut. Ins. Co.*, 632 F.2d 424, 430–31 (5th Cir. 1980). The circumstances surrounding the placement of the Ingersoll cargo on deck and the resultant loss can fairly be characterized as fortuitous. It was the carrier that breached the contract of carriage by placing the cargo on deck. Ingersoll certainly did not engage in any intentional misconduct to cause the misplacement of its cargo. Moreover, even if the carrier was negligent in placing the cargo outside the area of the ship's hold, all risk coverage would still apply.

[47] Construing Ingersoll's policy as providing full coverage for shipments stowed on deck without the shipper's consent is consistent with the purpose for which the policy was issued. All risk open cargo policies, such as the one issued to Ingersoll, provide broad coverage for shippers. *See, e.g., Greene v. Cheetham*, 293 F.2d 933 (2d Cir. 1961); *Groban v. S.S. Pegu*, 331 F.Supp. 883 (S.D.N.Y. 1971), *aff'd sub nom. Groban v. American Casualty Ins. Co.*, 456 F.2d 685 (2d Cir. 1972). A shipper not located near a port has no practical control over how a steamship line may ultimately carry and protect its cargo. Even if it issues clear instructions as to stowage directly to the carrier, it has no guarantee that the carrier will comply. A carrier may negligently or inadvertently place cargo intended to be stowed below deck, above deck. A shipper may reasonably seek to avoid exposing itself to the potential risk of damage and to consequential losses by procuring insurance. To hold that Ingersoll's loss was not covered would be to render the insurance that it purchased from Fireman's Fund meaningless. It is not at all unreasonable to assume that Ingersoll procured insurance precisely to cover itself in situations such as this one—where the carrier placed its cargo on deck without Ingersoll's consent.

[48] Fireman's Fund also argues that it should not be held liable under the policy because Ingersoll had a duty to inform the Fund after it learned of the on deck placement of its cargo on October 1, 1979. The Fund contends that had it been so

advised, it would have instructed Ingersoll to get the cargo under deck or off the ship before the M/V Bodena sailed for Korea on October 14.[9] Violation of this duty to disclose, the Fund claims, voids the policy under the doctrine of *uberrimae fidei.*

[49] The doctrine of *uberrimae fidei* requires a party seeking marine insurance to disclose all circumstances known to it which materially affect the risk. . . . If a party omits to disclose material information applicable to the risk involved, the policy is void. . . . However, in our view, the doctrine is not applicable in the instant case. As discussed, clause 17(a) of Fireman's Fund's policy provided coverage for shipments traveling pursuant to under deck contracts of carriage. As interpreted hereinabove, Ingersoll's contract of carriage with Taiwan was one for under deck stowage. The fact that Ingersoll's cargo was actually stowed on deck, in breach of the contract of carriage, did not change the terms of the contract. Similarly, the fact that Ingersoll had constructive notice as of October 1 of that breach also did not change the terms of the contract of carriage or Ingersoll's rights thereunder. See section I, *supra.* Ingersoll's contract remained one for under deck shipment throughout the voyage. Since there was never any change in Ingersoll's contract of carriage, there was no change in circumstances affecting the risk insured which Ingersoll might have been required to disclose. The subject open cargo policy does not distinguish between under deck contract of carriage that are performed and those that are breached. Coverage is provided for all shipments traveling pursuant to under deck contracts of carriage. Consequently, Ingersoll had no duty to inform Fireman's Fund that its cargo had been stowed on deck in breach of the contract of carriage. Indeed, it was to protect against just such an occurrence that Ingersoll most likely contracted for insurance in the first place.

B. Fireman's Fund's Right of Subrogation Against Bernard and Taiwan

[50] The district court properly ordered that to the extent Fireman's Fund makes payments to Ingersoll under its policy, it is entitled to recover such payments from Taiwan and Bernard, including taxable costs but excluding attorney's fees and litigation expenses. It is well settled that an insurer has an equitable right of subrogation as a matter of law upon making payment to its insured for a cargo loss. *Meredith v. The Ionian Trader,* 279 F.2d 471, 474 (2d Cir. 1960). Bernard errs in contending that the Fund's failure to fulfill its contractual obligation to Ingersoll precludes it from being granted equitable subrogation. An insurance company retains its right of subrogation even after it litigates coverage and suffers a judgment requiring payment to

---

9. Fireman's Fund makes a similar argument with regard to mitigation of damages. The Fund argues that Ingersoll failed to take any steps to remove the cargo from danger despite its knowledge as of October 1 that the cargo was stowed on deck and likely to incur damage. However, the burden of proving a failure to mitigate damages falls on the insurer. *Emmco Ins. Co. v. Wallenius Caribbean Line, S.A.,* 492 F.2d 508, 514 (5th Cir. 1974). The district court concluded that there was a "dearth of evidence" to show that unloading was a real and viable option and that appellants failed to meet their burden. 619 F.Supp. at 502.

the insured. *Id.; see also Bunge Corp. v. London Overseas Ins. Co.,* 394 F.2d 496, 497 (2d Cir.), *cert. denied,* 393 U.S. 952 . . . (1968).

C. Attorney's Fees and Litigation Expenses

[51] The district court awarded Ingersoll attorney's fees ($590,381.96) and litigation expenses ($226,250.96) against Fireman's Fund for costs it incurred in prosecuting its suit against Fireman's Fund and the other defendants. Although the district court did not specifically apportion the fees and expenses allocable to the various defendants, it did advance two different theories to support the award. First, Ingersoll's fees and expenses incurred in suing Bernard, Taiwan, and Excellent Marine were awarded as compensatory damages, to make Ingersoll whole. Second, the fees and expenses incurred in suing the Fund were awarded because of the Fund's apparent bad faith in denying Ingersoll's claim.

[52] Apropos the fees and expenses attributable to Ingersoll's suit against Bernard, Taiwan, and Excellent Marine, those fees were a direct and foreseeable consequence of Fireman's Fund's breach. As a result of the refusal of Fireman's Fund to cover the loss, Ingersoll was forced to sue third parties and to bear the burdens of complex litigation. Where a breach of contract has caused a party to maintain a suit against a third person, courts have permitted recovery from the breaching party of counsel fees and other litigation expenses incurred in the suit. *Artvale, Inc. v. Rugby Fabrics Corp.,* 232 F.Supp. 814, 826 (S.D.N.Y. 1964), *aff'd,* 363 F.2d 1002 (2d Cir. 1966); *accord Ranger Constr. Co. v. Prince William County School Bd.,* 605 F.2d 1298, 1301 (4th Cir. 1979); *see Freed v. Travelers,* 300 F.2d 395, 399 (7th Cir. 1962) (attorney's fees and expenses of litigation incurred in action against third parties proper elements of damage in action against insurer). Therefore, since Fireman's Fund's breach necessitated Ingersoll's suit against other defendants, the Fund was properly held responsible for Ingersoll's attorney's fees and litigation expenses. Fireman's Fund may not recover those costs from the other defendants, as it argues it should, because in the ordinary course, it could have paid Ingersoll's claim and then commenced its own litigation against the other defendants as Ingersoll's subrogee. In such an action, the Fund would have had to bear its own fees and expenses.

[53] Second, apropos the fees and expenses attributable to Ingersoll's suit against Fireman's Fund, the general rule is that the award of fees and expenses in admiralty actions is discretionary with the district judge upon a finding of bad faith. *Seguros Banvenez, S.A.,* 761 F.2d at 861–62. As a party subject to admiralty jurisdiction, *Big Lift Shipping Co. (N.A.) v. Bellefonte Ins. Co.,* 594 F.Supp. 701, 704 (S.D.N.Y. 1984), marine insurers also are subject to this rule. *See Puritan Ins. Co.,* 779 F.2d at 873. We acknowledge an awareness of the district judge's dissatisfaction with Fireman's Fund for refusing to pay Ingersoll's claim. Judge Carter characterized explanations given by Fireman's Fund as *"contrived, concocted* solely to keep from paying" its obligations under the policy. 619 F.Supp. at 506 (emphasis added). Moreover, noting conflicting and inconsistent testimony among Fund officials, he observed that "Fireman's Fund had *conjured* up its *strained* reading of the insurance policy

solely in an effort to avoid accepting the liability the policy imposed." *Id.* at 507 (emphasis added). However, we note that the district court never explicitly found that Fireman's Fund acted in bad faith in denying Ingersoll's claim. In light of the ambiguity inherent in the Fund's policy and our lengthy discussion herein necessary to analyze the ambiguity, we cannot conclude that the Fund was unjustified in rejecting Ingersoll's claim. Whether the damage to Order # 24441 was covered under the Fireman's Fund open cargo policy seems to us to be a difficult issue, one which constitutes a perfectly valid basis for contest and litigation. Accordingly, we reverse the award of attorney's fees and litigation expenses insofar as they are allocable to Ingersoll's suit against Fireman's Fund. We remand to the district court to determine, using the method it deems appropriate, how much of the sum total of Ingersoll's attorney's fees and litigation expenses is attributable to its suit against Fireman's Fund and how much to its suit against each of the other defendants and to apportion accordingly.

[54] In its final judgment, dated April 25, 1986, the district court apparently included only those attorney's fees and litigation expenses incurred through August 31, 1985, leaving subsequent expenditures for calculation after any appeal. While we decline to impose attorney's fees and litigation expenses against Fireman's Fund in this Court for prosecuting either a frivolous appeal, Fed.R.App.P. 38, or one calculated to achieve delay, 28 U.S.C. § 1912, we do note that in calculating expenditures after August 31, 1985, the district court, in its discretion, in order to make Ingersoll whole, might include those amounts that properly can be attributed to Ingersoll's defending the appeal taken by Bernard and Taiwan. Of course, those fees and expenses that relate to Ingersoll's defense of Fireman's Fund's appeal, as well as those attributable to Ingersoll's cross-appeal, are beyond the scope of the compensatory damage rationale.

V. Damages and Prejudgment Interest

A. Damages

[55] Both Fireman's Fund and Ingersoll dispute the district court's computation of total damages of $977,899. Fireman's Fund seeks to *reduce* the total award by $90,970 which was awarded as damages representing the interest for delay in Ingersoll's receiving contract payments from Hyundai. The Fund claims that interest for delay is not properly recoverable under its policy. On the other hand, Ingersoll seeks to *increase* its award by $48,287 which represents Waldrich's expense of financing the costs of repairing Order # 24441 and by $157,585 which is said to represent Waldrich's corporate overhead and profit.

[56] Ordinarily, a district court's computation of damages in a cargo case is a factual determination that will not be disturbed on appeal unless it is clearly erroneous. *Seguros Banvenez, S.A.*, 761 F.2d at 861. In our view, the district judge carefully considered all items submitted to him by the parties as elements of damages; he awarded some, and rejected others. As to Fireman's Fund's claim that damages should be reduced, under its policy it was obligated to indemnify Ingersoll in full

for its loss which includes Ingersoll's damage for the loss of use of contract payments. As to Ingersoll's claim that damages should be increased, financing costs can reasonably be viewed as a part of overhead; what amount of overhead and profits to award was specifically considered by the district court and included in the final calculation. We find no error in the computation of damages.

B. Interest Rate on Prejudgment Interest

[57] In accordance with our direction that in admiralty cases prejudgment interest "should be granted in the absence of exceptional circumstances," *Mitsui Co. v. American Export Lines,* 636 F.2d 807, 823 (2d Cir. 1981), the district court calculated prejudgment interest from the date of payment for the repairs through the date of judgment. Ingersoll objects to the rate of interest used, contending that the proper rate should have been the rate at which Ingersoll actually invested its excess cash during the periods in question, or alternatively, a single, uniform, constant rate based on the rate for federal paper, as specified in 28 U.S.C. § 1961, which sets forth the method for computation of *postjudgment* interest. The rule in this Circuit, however, is that the rate of interest used in awarding *prejudgment* interest rests firmly within the sound discretion of the trial court. *Independent Bulk Transp., Inc. v. The Vessel "MORANIA ABACO",* 676 F.2d 23, 26 (2d Cir. 1982). A "[p]laintiff is entitled to the income which the monetary damages would have earned, and that should be measured by interest on short-term, risk-free obligations." *Id.* at 27. In exercising its discretion, the district court determined that rather than using a single Treasury Bill rate applied retroactively over the relevant periods as initially proposed, using an average rate for each period would be fairer because the rate on Treasury Bills was subject to wide fluctuation during those periods. Accordingly, the district court applied rates ranging between 9.676% and 10.112%. We cannot say that in determining prejudgment interest based upon an average of prevailing Treasury Bill rates, which are short-term, risk-free obligations, the district court abused its discretion.

Conclusion

[58] To summarize: we hold that (1) Taiwan, Bernard, and Fireman's Fund all breached their respective contracts with Ingersoll and are therefore jointly and severally liable to Ingersoll for damages and prejudgment interest as determined by the district court; (2) Fireman's Fund was properly held responsible only for Ingersoll's attorney's fees and litigation expenses allocable to its suit against Bernard, Taiwan, and Excellent Marine but not for those allocable to its suit against Fireman's Fund; (3) Fireman's Fund may recover from Bernard and Taiwan to the extent it actually pays Ingersoll's damages (excluding attorney's fees and litigation expenses); and (4) the claims of Bernard and Taiwan against each other for indemnification were properly dismissed. . . .

Notes and Questions

1. The case is useful because it illustrates the entire process of contracting for insurance cover, including what can go wrong in the related shipping arrangements.

Do you remember the triple nature of the Bill of Lading (BoL)? Given the fact that the BoL is the contract of carriage, we need to review who drafts the BoL and how the contract is formed. What does it mean if the master of the ship adds a notation, for example that the cargo is lighter or heavier than anticipated or that the packaging is damaged? From a contracting perspective, how would such a notation be different from a notation like the one added here "on deck shipper's risk"? What is a "clean" and an "unclean" BoL in this context? Why?

2. In light of what we discussed earlier with regard to the open cargo policy on p. 633 and the discussion in paragraph 11 of *Ingersoll*, do you now understand how an open cargo policy works in practice and how a particular shipment gets covered and how the insurance gets paid?

3. What do you think of the argument presented by the carrier that the shipper had "constructive notice" that the bulk of its goods had been stored on deck and, given the fact that they did not object, should be deemed to have accepted this change of plan? The court discusses the question whether Ingersoll waived the right to have the cargo moved under deck. Why did Ingersoll not react to the notice and how or why does it matter?

4. How can we best describe the roles of Gryphon and Bernard? What are their respective rights and obligations?

5. Under the COGSA, carrier liability is limited to US$500 per package. Does this not apply in the present case? Why or why not? What are the specific provisions in the COGSA that determine the extent of carrier liability?

6. According to the Federal Maritime Commission, a freight forwarder shall (may?) provide 13 services for the shipper. Which did Bernard provide and which did he not? What are the consequences?

7. What do you think of the court's analysis of the exclusion clause in the insurance policy denying coverage for partial loss of "on deck" shipments (paras. 38 et seq.)? The insurance excluded cover for "on deck" cargo. The cargo was on deck. How and why does the court not accept the exclusion? What could Fireman's have conceivably done differently to avoid liability for "on deck" cargo?

8. Fireman's also argued that Ingersoll could have and should have notified them that the cargo ended up on deck so the insurance could have insisted on a relocation of the cargo. Was there time for this? Why did Ingersoll not notify Fireman's of the problem? Why did the court not hold it against Ingersoll in the end?

9. Can you explain in plain English what the court decided about attorney fees and litigation expenses?

10. The damages were in the magnitude of US$1 million. By the time the Court of Appeals was done with the case, the attorney fees alone were already more than US$590,000, plus litigation expenses of more than US$220,000. If we add interest at around 10%, wouldn't it have made more sense for Fireman's to pay Ingersoll on demand and pursue Taiwan and the other defendants instead? How could

Fireman's have achieved such a result? What would have been the risk in pursuing this strategy?

11. The District Court awarded interest at a rate between 9.676% and 10.112%, taking into account fluctuations in capital markets. This seems a rather generous rate. Why did Ingersoll object? How should interest be calculated? What is supposed to be compensated? Why did the Court of Appeals refuse to review the method applied by the District Court?

Our next case is about the risks covered. The policy was for "perils of the sea." The damage, however, was done by rough handling at dockside. Let's see what is and what is not included in the insurance coverage and why.

Case 5-6

Plymouth Rubber Co. v. Insurance Company of North America, Inc.

18 Mass. App. Ct. 364, 465 N.E.2d 1234 (1984)
(Paragraph numbers added.)
KASS, J.

[1] Plymouth Rubber Co., Inc. (Plymouth Rubber), seeks to recover under a marine insurance policy issued by Insurance Company of North America, Inc. (INA), for cargo damage resulting from rough handling and improper storage on the dock at Khorramshahr, Iran. We have the following facts from the pleadings, affidavits, and a deposition filed in connection with a motion for summary judgment.

[2] In May of 1973, Clarence H. Tenney, then Plymouth Rubber's quality control agent, travelled to the port of Khorramshahr to collect samples of pipewrapping material and adhesive primer which Plymouth had shipped there. Tenney's mission was stimulated by rejection of the goods as nonconforming by Plymouth Rubber's customer, United Iranian Oil Company. On the basis of Tenney's observation that Plymouth Rubber's goods were stored outdoors at the dock and that some of the packaging was damaged from exposure to the weather, Plymouth Rubber took out a "Special Marine Policy" of insurance. The INA policy, obtained through Fred S. James & Co. of New England, Inc. (James), covered Plymouth Rubber's "Pipe wrap, PVC tape, [and] chemicals . . . [w]hile at: Dockside Khoranshak [sic], Iran." The policy, which was effective May 11, 1973, did not cover a vessel.

[3] On two subsequent trips to Iran in the spring and summer of 1974, Tenney observed that many of Plymouth Rubber's goods, which remained stored outdoors, were damaged. Some PVC tapes had melted from exposure to the sun, drum tops had rusted, and there was evidence of water contamination. In addition, several rolls of pipe wrapping were cut, unwound, dirty or broken. During his visits, Tenney saw that other cargo at the port was handled roughly. He reported that the storage area was extremely congested, that cranes and forklift trucks were operated at speeds too fast for the crowded conditions, and that cargo was frequently dropped

from cranes onto tall piles of goods which collapsed from the extra weight. Tenney felt that much of the damage to Plymouth Rubber's goods, such as loose and flattened rolls and broken spools, resulted from such rough handling at dockside.

[4] Plymouth Rubber brought an action against INA and James, seeking to recover from INA under the terms of the policy. In the alternative, i.e., if the policy did not cover the damage to the goods, Plymouth Rubber's complaint charged James with failure to perform its contract to secure insurance for damage to the goods stored at Khorramshahr and, in consequence, with a violation of G.L.c. 93A, §2(a). In addition, Plymouth Rubber charged INA with James' breach of contract under an agency theory and—it seems inevitably—with a violation of G.L.c. 93A, §2(a).

[5] A judge of the Superior Court granted INA's motion for summary judgment on those counts of the complaint which alleged that INA was liable to Plymouth Rubber under the terms of the policy, and that INA had violated G.L.c. 93A. Plymouth Rubber waived the count which sought to bind INA, under an agency theory, for James' breach of contract. Upon allowance of a motion under Mass.R.Civ.P. 54(b), 365 Mass. 821 (1974), the judgment in favor of INA became final and Plymouth Rubber appealed. Plymouth Rubber's claims against James remain to be tried.

[6] INA seeks to limit its liability under the policy to a standard clause in the insurance form, the "Shore Clause," on the basis of typewritten language on the face of the contract which reads, "Coverage as per Shore Clause above" followed by a schedule of the amount of insurance for various time periods. Plymouth Rubber argues that the policy of insurance is not so limited and that INA must also be liable for damage falling within the "Perils Clause," another standard clause in the insurance form. Although typewritten language in a contract normally controls if it is inconsistent with other printed language, *Bluewaters, Inc.* v. *Boag,* 320 F.2d 833, 835 n. 4 (1st Cir.1963), we need not decide if any inconsistency arises from the typewritten language in the instant case. The only clause in addition to the Shore Clause upon which Plymouth Rubber seizes is the Perils Clause, and we have no difficulty in deciding that the damage to Plymouth Rubber's goods while dockside at Khorramshahr does not fall within the coverage of that clause.

[7] The Perils Clause provides, "PERILS CLAUSE: Touching the adventures and *perils* which this Company is contented to bear, and takes upon itself, they are *of the seas,* fires, assailing thieves, jettisons, barratry of the master and mariners, *and all other like perils,* losses and misfortunes (illicit or contraband trade excepted in all cases), that have or shall come to the hurt, detriment or damage of the said goods and merchandise, or any part thereof" (emphasis supplied). To prevail on its theory that the damage to its cargo falls within the coverage of the Perils Clause, Plymouth Rubber must show that such damage resulted from "perils of the seas" or "other like perils."

[8] The Supreme Court has construed "perils of the seas" to include "losses from *extraordinary occurrences* only; such as stress of weather, winds and waves, lightning, tempests, rocks, [etc.] . . . and not those ordinary perils which every vessel

must encounter." *Hazard* v. *New England Marine Ins. Co.,* 33 U.S. (8 Pet.) 557, 585 (1834) (emphasis supplied). Thus, in *Hazard,* the Supreme Court upheld an instruction to a jury that if damage to a vessel by worms was an ordinary occurrence in the Pacific Ocean, then damage of that kind was not covered under the Perils Clause. In *Commercial Trading Co.* v. *Hartford Fire Ins. Co.,* 466 F.2d 1239, 1245 (5th Cir.1972), misdelivery of the cargo was held not to come within the "other like perils" portion of the clause, since that phrase referred to perils "very similar to or very much like th[ose] enumerated [in the Perils Clause]," quoting from *Feinberg* v. *Insurance Co. of No. America,* 260 F.2d 523, 527 (1st Cir.1958).

[9] In the instant case, the damage to Plymouth Rubber's goods while stored on land at Khorramshahr resulted neither from an extraordinary risk nor one "peculiarly associated with maritime voyages." See *Southport Fisheries, Inc.* v. *Saskatchewan Govt. Ins. Office,* 161 F.Supp. 81 (E.D.N.C. 1958). 11 Rhodes, Couch's Cyclopedia of Insurance Law § 43:87, at 67 (2d ed. rev. 1982). See also *id.* §§ 43:92–43:125. *Underwriters' Agency* v. *Sutherlin,* §§ Ga. 266, 272 (1875), on which Plymouth Rubber relies to support its position that damage to the stored goods by rain should fall within the Perils Clause, is inapposite. The court in *Sutherlin* was faced with construction of the "perils of navigation" clause, which is broader than the "perils of the seas" clause. See *Lipshitz* v. *New Zealand Ins. Co.,* 34 Ga.App. 825, 834 (1926).

[10] Even in its extremity, the plaintiff in *Commercial Trading Co.* v. *Hartford Fire Ins. Co.,* 466 F.2d at 1245, felt compelled, in order to make its case, to argue that the mishap it had suffered "reeked with the smell of the sea." While chary of adopting sniff tests as a basis for construing clauses in an insurance policy, we find the metaphor helpful. As its Eighteenth Century style suggests, the Perils Clause of an open marine cargo policy has a long tradition. *Id.* at 1240 and 1242. It has been construed to refer to damage from the sea and occurring at sea, or, at least, on the water. *Cary* v. *Home Ins. Co.,* 235 N.Y. 296, 300 (1923). 11 Rhodes, Couch's Cyclopedia of Insurance Law § 43:101 (2d ed. rev. 1982). Although a vessel need not be on the high seas to invoke the Perils Clause, it must be water borne. See *Hill* v. *Union Ins. Soc. of Canton, Ltd.,* 61 Ont. L.R. 201, 206 (1927). Compare *Swift* v. *Union Mut. Marine Ins. Co.,* 122 Mass. 573, 575 (1877), where the Perils Clause covered loss of a ship which came apart while beached for repairs in Panama, but where the injury to the ship occurred when she struck floating ice while cruising for whales in the Arctic Ocean. Compare also *Ellery* v. *New England Ins. Co.,* 8 Pick. 14 (1829), in which the insurer was held liable where the ship was only partially water borne and was lost when a gust blew her over while she was being hauled out on a railway. There is, however, nothing redolent of the sea and its hazards that we associate with driving fork lifts as if they were "dodge 'ems" in an amusement park.

[11] So, for example, loss of cargo by reason of negligence in loading or unloading does not come within the perils of the seas coverage. *J.A. Jones Constr. Co.* v. *Niagara Fire Ins. Co.,* 170 F.2d 667, 668 (4th Cir.1948). Mishandling of cargo which causes a leaky barge to capsize, i.e., the intervention of negligent management of the vessel, has been held to fall outside the coverage of the clause. *Cary* v. *Home Ins. Co.,*

235 N.Y. at 300–301. See to the same effect, although based on slightly different language in the insurance contract, *Paddock* v. *Franklin Ins. Co.,* 28 Mass. 227, 235–236 (1831).

[12] Perhaps recognizing that conventional construction of the Perils Clause would not cover this damage, which was neither extraordinary nor "of the seas," Plymouth Rubber urges that the insurance contract must be read in light of the circumstances existing at the time the contract was made. See *Oakes* v. *Manufacturers' Fire & Marine Ins. Co.,* 131 Mass. 164, 165 (1881); *Trustees of Thayer Academy* v. *The Corp. of the Royal Exch. Assur. of London.,* 281 Mass. 150, 155 (1932). Because the policy was issued for goods "at dockside" and did not cover a vessel, Plymouth Rubber argues that these circumstances require that the Perils Clause be extended to cover risks reasonably expected when the goods are on land.

[13] Commercial context is of assistance in construing ambiguous provisions in a contract, or when it is necessary to fill in missing pieces. *Robert Indus., Inc.* v. *Spence,* 362 Mass. 751, 755 (1973). *Fay, Spofford & Thorndike, Inc.* v. *Massachusetts Port Authy.,* 7 Mass.App.Ct. 336, 342 (1979). Restatement (Second) of Contracts §202 (1979). Courts cannot, however, use commercial context to override express provisions in a contract. A decisional patina of several centuries makes the Perils Clause inapplicable. Had the insured examined its policy, it could not reasonably have understood that it afforded protection against loss from negligent handling of its property on the dock in Khorramshahr, even though that may have been precisely what Plymouth Rubber was trying to insure against. Compare *Slater* v. *United States Fid. & Guar. Co.,* 379 Mass. 801, 803 (1980). Unlike the policy in the *Slater* case, Plymouth Rubber did not receive an "all risks" policy. Compare also *By's Chartering Serv., Inc.* v. *Interstate Ins. Co.,* 524 F.2d 1045, 1047 nn. 1 & 2 (1st Cir.1975), which draws a distinction between the coverage of a Perils Clause and an all risks policy. The damage to Plymouth Rubber's goods while stored at Khorramshahr simply was not the type of damage contemplated by the "perils of the seas" or "other like perils" portions of the Perils Clause.

[14] The other clause under which Plymouth Rubber seeks to recover is the Shore Clause. That clause provides, "SHORE CLAUSE: Where this insurance by its terms covers while on docks, wharves or elsewhere on shore, and/or during land transportation, it shall include the risks of collision, derailment, overturning or other accident to the conveyance, fire, lightning, sprinkler leakage, cyclones, hurricanes, earthquakes, floods (meaning the rising of navigable waters), and/or collapse or subsidence of docks or wharves, even though the insurance be otherwise F.P.A." Plymouth Rubber argues that the term "collision" is ambiguous, since it could refer to generic collisions (such as a forklift bumping into cargo on dock), or only to collisions of the conveyance. Given this alleged ambiguity, Plymouth contends that the Shore Clause must be construed against the drafter, INA, and in favor of coverage.

[15] We see no reason to torture the language of the Shore Clause. The term "collision" appears in the context of a phrase which refers to "risks of collision, derailment, overturning *or other accident to the conveyance* . . ." (emphasis added). The

word "collision" does not stand in isolation, but must be read in conjunction with the remainder of the phrase. In context, we construe the risk of collision as referring to the conveyance, e.g., a truck or rail car. "When . . . words are plain and free from ambiguity they must be construed in their usual and ordinary sense." *Sherman* v. *Employers' Liab. Assur. Corp.*, 343 Mass. 354, 356 (1961). See generally as to the Shore Clause, Buglass, Marine Insurance & General Average in the United States 66–67 (2d ed. 1981). . . .

Judgment affirmed.

Notes and Questions

1. In this case, the plaintiff, after having seen the rough handling at the port, took out a "Special Marine Policy" of insurance (para. 2) to protect its interests in the cargo. The insurance agent Fred James procured the policy from INA covering Plymouth Rubber's goods "while at Dockside Khoramshar." It may be understandable that the policy clause about perils of the sea would not cover damage done by rough handling dockside. The question in that regard is why such a clause would even be included in the policy, when there was no vessel and the cargo was not supposed to go anywhere. What is harder to understand is why the shore clause was considered not to cover the damage done on shore. What should a cargo owner do differently to be sure that they will be covered in case the goods get damaged, lost, or stolen? Remember in this context that insurance contracts are pre-formulated by the insurance company and clauses are not commonly subject to negotiation. Some commentators have referred to these contracts as "contracts of adhesion," essentially based on the idea of "take it or leave it," rather than B2B negotiations of equally powerful and knowledgeable partners.

2. What do you think of the narrow interpretation of the shore clause by the court?

3. As a consequence of this decision, the cargo owner (Plymouth Rubber) is left only with a claim against the insurance broker (Fred James). Would a future court deciding the merits of such a claim be bound by the present judgment or could they say that James did no wrong in procuring the policy with the shore clause since it should have protected the owner?

4. Having to pursue the broker is a triple burden and risk for the cargo owner. First, they will need to expend time and resources to bring another lawsuit, hoping that the statute of limitations has not expired. Second, they bear the risk that another court might not find fault with the services provided by the broker. Third, even if they can secure a judgment in their favor, the broker might not have sufficient resources to cover the claims. From a policy perspective, wouldn't it make more sense for the insurance company to cover the damage and pay the owner and then bear the risk of getting their money back from the broker? What could the legal basis be for a claim by the insurance company against the broker?

Our final cases are about untypical losses to cargo and vessels, where bad faith may have played a role. Let's see to what extent insurance coverage can be claimed for atypical or suspicious losses.

Case 5-7

Coast to Coast Seafood v. Assurances Generales de France

50 P.3d 662(Wash. Ct. App. 2002)
(Paragraph numbers added, footnotes omitted.)
Coleman, J.

[1] Coast to Coast Seafoods, Inc., ordered large amounts of shrimp from suppliers in Thailand that were to arrive in sealed containers in separate shipments involving various vessels. Although some containers arrived with the shrimp as ordered, others did not. Rather, certain containers had just blocks of ice with a thin layer of shrimp while others contained a mixed array of seafood. When Coast to Coast filed a claim under its marine insurance policy, the various appellants (Underwriters) refused to provide coverage. Coast to Coast sued Underwriters. The trial court granted summary judgment to Coast to Coast. Underwriters appeal arguing that the policy does not cover the loss. Because we conclude that Coast to Coast has not met its burden in proving coverage, we reverse.

Facts

[2] In February or March 1997, David Seto of Springland (a trading company) called Stuart Kozloff, president of Coast to Coast, and offered five containers of black tiger prawns from Magnet & Syndicate, a company in Thailand. Coast to Coast was familiar with the Thai company since it had purchased black tiger prawns and other shrimp from it since 1994. After negotiations over the telephone and a face-to-face meeting with Seto and Ben Chui, a principal of Springland, the parties reached an agreement. Coast to Coast paid 70 percent upon receipt of the copies of the bills of lading and the balance after inspection. The shipment arrived without incident.

[3] Thereafter, Coast to Coast agreed to purchase a larger shipment of black tiger prawns. For 24 containers, Coast to Coast advanced 80 percent of the negotiated price upon receipt of the bills of lading and planned to pay 20 percent after arrival and clearance by the FDA. The terms of the deal were "C & F" (cost and freight). Each of the 24 containers commenced transit in either Bangkok or Laem Chabang, Thailand. Various feeder vessels carried most of the containers to Kaohsiung, Taiwan; Busan, South Korea; or Singapore for loading onto vessels headed for Los Angeles or Long Beach, California. Only three of the shipments cruised directly to Los Angeles from Laem Chabang. Despite the numerous vessels involved, the bills of lading uniformly described the contents as "FROZEN SEAFOOD PRODUCTS SHRIMP." Many bills listed the various shipment weights along with disclaimers such as "SAID TO WEIGHT [sic]" or "SHIPPER LOADED & COUNT."

[4] Upon delivery, Coast to Coast discovered a problem with the packing after inspecting the sixth and subsequent containers. Frank Sipin, a branch manager, found

shrimp only on the upper quarter of a block of ice. Normally, there would be several layers of shrimp throughout the block of ice. Sipin also discovered that some of the shrimp were headless, shell-on shrimp that were poor in quality. Upon an inspection of other containers, he found cuttlefish, scad, trevally, and other seafood items. Sipin described the mixed packing: "The fish products were apparently stowed in the mid and innermost areas of the containers while the shrimp was at the tailgate of the container, obviously to avoid any suspicion/detection of fraud by customs inspectors."

[5] Bennett Kozloff, Coast to Coast's CEO, notified its insurance carrier and his brother, Stuart, who was out of town. Stuart returned immediately and called David Seto who seemed surprised and promised to investigate. Stuart also contacted Ben Chui, after several unsuccessful attempts. Chui had planned to come to Seattle but then went directly to Thailand to investigate. Seto and Chui told Kozloff that it was possible that they had mixed up containers and that they would find out what had happened. After a period, however, Kozloff was unable to reach Seto, Chui, or anyone else at Springfield by telephone. Coast to Coast notified United States Customs, the Federal Bureau of Investigation, and the Thai Embassy about the problem and hired law firms in Hong Kong and Thailand to investigate. It also attempted to obtain shipping details through a customs broker and requested Wells Fargo to locate Seto and Frank Zho, a Springland director. Needless to say, Coast to Coast was unable to recover its losses from Springland or Magnet & Syndicate. As for the shipment, Coast to Coast sold the shrimp through its normal markets and sold the majority of the other seafood as cat food.

[6] After Underwriters denied coverage, Coast to Coast sued them seeking coverage under its marine insurance policy. According to the policy language, the insurance attaches when the goods leave the warehouse: "This insurance attaches from the time the goods leave the warehouse . . . for the commencement of transit and continues during the ordinary course of transit until the goods are delivered to the final warehouse[.]" (Warehouse to warehouse clause.) A "shore perils" clause insured the shipments against all risks in transit and on land: "(S)hipments insured 'All Risks' while waterborne are insured 'All Risks' while in transit or otherwise on land." The term "All Risks" included physical loss or damage to perishable cargo from any external cause, but excluding a preshipment condition, among other things.

[7] Both parties moved for summary judgment based on the policy language. In its crossmotion for summary judgment, Coast to Coast relied primarily on the "unexplained shortage" clause in seeking coverage:

> This insurance is also specially to cover unexplained shortages of goods insured shipped in sealed container(s) whether or not the original seals are intact upon arrival at the final destination, provided that:
>
> A. the coverage for the shipment includes loss caused by theft; [and]
>
> B. the Assured makes every attempt to recover the loss from anyone who may have been responsible for the shortage through involvement in stuffing the container.

It is a condition precedent to this coverage that the Assured shall not divulge the existence of this coverage to any party. Such disclosure shall void coverage provided by this clause. (Emphasis in original.)

[8] After reviewing many documents, the trial court granted summary judgment in favor of Coast to Coast. Underwriters appeal.

Discussion

[9] We review a summary judgment order de novo. *Kirnta. AS v. Royal Ins. Co.,* 102 Wash.App. 716, 720, 9 P.3d 239 (2000), *review denied* 142 Wash.2d 1029, 21 P.3d 1150 (2001). The parties first disagree as to whether federal or state law governs this case. State law governs the interpretation of a marine insurance policy only in the absence of applicable federal statute, judicially created maritime law, or a need for uniform admiralty rules. *Kimta,* 102 Wash.App. at 722, 9 P.3d 239. Underwriters contend that judicially established federal maritime law places the burden on Coast to Coast to prove coverage under the policy. Similarly, state law also places the burden on the insured to prove coverage and, once met, shifts the burden to the insurer to establish a policy exclusion. *Compare American Star Ins. Co. v. Grice,* 121 Wash.2d 869, 875, 854 P.2d 622; 865 P.2d 507 (1993) *and Diamaco, Inc. v. Aetna Cas. & Sur. Co.,* 97 Wash.App. 335, 337, 983 P.2d 707 (1999) *with New Hampshire Ins. Co. v. Martech USA, Inc.,* 993 F.2d 1195, 1200 (1993). *As* in *Martech,* we need not decide whether federal maritime law or state law sets the burden of proof because each standard produces the same result. *Martech,* 993 F.2d at 1198–99.

[10] As for interpreting the language in the policy itself, both parties cite to Washington case law for familiar rules of construction. In their reply brief, Underwriters admit that there is no specific federal rule governing the construction of marine insurance contracts. *Commercial Union Ins. Co. v. Flagship Marine Servs., Inc.,* 190 F.3d 26, 30 (2d Cir.1999). We therefore look to state law to interpret the contract. Washington courts interpret insurance policies as an average purchaser would. *Hayden v. Mut. of Enumclaw Ins. Co.,* 141 Wash.2d 55, 64, 1 P.3d 1167 (2000). Absent mutual agreement on the technical meaning of certain language, we give words their plain, ordinary meaning. *Wolstein v. Yorkshire Ins. Co., Ltd.,* 97 Wash. App. 201, 210, 985 P.2d 400 (1999). Courts construe insurance policies as a whole, with force and effect given to each clause. *Wolstein,* 97 Wash.App. at 210, 985 P.2d 400. All risks marine insurance is not a performance bond and may not provide coverage even when no express exclusion applies. *Wolstein,* 97 Wash.App. at 213–14, 985 P.2d 400. *But c.f.* 2 Thomas J. Schoenbaum, *Admiralty & Maritime Law* § 19-9, at 469 (3d ed. 2001) ("All risks marine insurance covers all risks of loss or damage that are not expressly excluded.")

[11] Coast to Coast relies mainly upon the unexplained shortage clause in seeking coverage: "This insurance is also specially to cover unexplained shortages of goods insured shipped in sealed container(s) whether or not the original seals are intact upon arrival at the final destination[.]" According to Coast to Coast, this clause expands the already broad "all risk" coverage and insures against losses sustained

when shipping containers arrive with the product missing, even if the original seals are intact. Underwriters contend that Coast to Coast failed to establish that the insurance attached with proof that the promised goods left the warehouse and commenced transit before a physical loss occurred, citing the warehouse to warehouse clause and *Pacific Tall Ships Co. v. Kuehne & Nagel, Inc.,* 76 F.Supp.2d B8G, 892–93 (N.D.Ill. l999) (defining transit and construing a warehouse-to-warehouse clause). Coast to Coast responds that by including coverage for goods shipped in containers that arrive with their seals intact, the unexplained shortage clause covers cases in which the shipper fails to load the goods into the containers prior to sealing. We disagree. By providing coverage for unexplained shortages in sealed containers, the policy merely accounts for the possibility that the loss could have occurred while in the carrier's possession, even though the seals remained intact. *See Bally, Inc. v. M. V Zim America,* 22 F.3d 65, 70 (2d Cir.1994) ("Delivery by a carrier of a container with an intact seal does not conclusively prove that loss did not occur while the container was in the carrier's possession.") In reading the policy as a whole, we find that if the goods had left the warehouse and commenced transit but arrived at the final destination inexplicably short, then the unexplained shortages clause may have applied. We conclude, however, that the unexplained shortages clause does not relate back in time and provide coverage for a loss that occurred before the goods left the warehouse. Accordingly, the policy does not cover situations where the shipper fails to pack the goods into the containers prior to sealing.

[12] Nonetheless, Coast to Coast maintains that the broad all risk coverage provisions of the insurance policy cover the loss, even if the cargo was nonexistent, citing *Chemical Bank v. Affiliated FM Ins. Co.,* 815 F.Supp. 115 (S.D.N.Y. 1993). *Chemical Bank* involved false bills of lading issued by a Columbian exporting company to obtain advance payments under letters of credit for nonexistent shipments of coffee. *Chemical Bank,* 815 F.Supp. at 116–17. When the coffee purchaser and its banks discovered the fraudulent scheme, they tried to obtain coverage from its insurers. *Chemical Bank.* 815 F.Supp. at 117. Because the insurance contract clearly covered a loss caused by the acceptance of fraudulent bills of lading without limiting coverage to physical goods actually in existence, the court entered partial summary judgment in favor of the plaintiffs. *Chemical Bank,* 815 F.Supp. at 118–19, 122. *Chernical Bank* is distinguishable, however, because there is no similar provision in the insurance policy here that covers a loss arising from fraudulent bills of lading. As a result, the policy does not provide coverage for nonexistent goods.

[13] Under our reading of the policy as a whole, Coast to Coast has the burden to prove that the containers left the warehouse and commenced transit with the ordered goods. In its cross-motion for summary judgment, Coast to Coast submitted bills of lading to the trial court as proof of goods shipped. Bills of lading may constitute prima facie evidence that the carrier received the goods as described by identifying marks, number, quantity, or weight. 46 U.S.C.App. §§ 1303(3), (4) (Carriage of Goods by Sea Act or COGSA). Disclaimers such as, "said to weigh" and "shipper's load and count" do not affect the evidentiary value of the bills of

lading in this regard. *Daewoo Int'l (America) Corp. v. Sea-Land Orient Ltd.*, 196 F.3d 481, 485 (3d Cir.l999); *Bally*, 22 F.3d at 69 (quoting *Westway Coffee Corp. v. M. V. Netuno*, 675 F.2d 30, 32 (2d Cir.1982)); *Fox & Assocs., Inc. v. M/V Hanjin Yokohama*, 977 F.Supp. 1022, 1028 (C.D.Cal.1997). *But c.f Plastique Tags, Inc. v. Asia Trans Line, Inc.*, 83 F.3d 1367, 1370 (11th Cir.l996) (bills of lading were not prima facie proof of amount because the bills contained limiting language and the amount was not verifiable in a sealed container). . . .

[15] Anticipating that the disclaimers would not apply, Underwriters argue that the loss of shrimp did not occur during the shipment because the weights of the containers on arrival matched the listed weights of the containers on departure. They cite the warehouse to warehouse clause and maintain that the insurance policy applies only to physical loss or damage suffered *in transit* due to an external cause. Many of the cases construing COGSA in determining whether bills of lading constitute prima facie evidence of shipped goods have focused on the weight of the cargo at the outturn or upon arrival. *E.g., Bally*, 22 F.3d at 69–70; *Cont'l Distrib. Co. v. M/V Sea-Land Commitment*, 1992 WL 75067, 3–4 (S.D.N.Y.1992). For instance, carriers are liable for shortage of cargo where the weight measured upon arrival is less than the weight listed in the bill of lading. *Westway*, 675 F.2d at 32. If the goods weight is the same, such evidence may rebut the prima facie case. *Bally*, 22 F.3d at 70 (construing *Westway*, 675 F.2d at 33 n. 4). Underwriter's citations to the record, however, do not demonstrate that the weights on the bills of lading are the same as the weights at the outturn. According to our reading of Frank Sipin's declaration, he merely recites the information contained in the bills of lading and does not mention the weights at the outturn. Furthermore, this statement is not determinative because there was a substitution of goods rather than just a shortage.

[16] Although a bill of lading may constitute prima facie evidence of the weight of goods shipped, it is not prima facie evidence of the contents or the condition of goods shipped in a sealed container, even if the bill attests to the "apparent good order and condition" as here. *Daewoo*, 196 F.3d at 485. This is so because the contents of a sealed container are not readily verifiable by external examination of the sealed container. *Daewoo*, 196 F.3d at 485. In *Daewoo*, a Hong Kong company agreed to ship over one million plastic videocassette holders to Daewoo in the United States. *Daewoo*, 196 F.3d at 482–83. Similar to the situation here, the Hong Kong company received payment upon presentation of the shipping documents to the bank issuing the letters of credit. *Daewoo*, 196 F.3d at 483. When Daewoo's agents opened the containers, they discovered cement blocks instead of videocassette holders and incorrect weights listed on the bills of lading. *Daewoo*, 196 F.3d at 483. Like here, the seals of the containers were intact upon arrival and the Hong Kong company had disappeared. *Daewoo*, 196 F.3d at 483–84. In Daewoo's lawsuit against the carriers, the Third Circuit held that Daewoo could not recover based on the bills of lading because it failed to prove that the carriers received the cargo in good condition before shipment. *Daewoo*, 196 F.3d at 485. The court suggested that

Daewoo could have designated an agent to inspect the packing of the cargo into the containers prior to sealing. *Daewoo,* 196 F .3d at 485. We find *Daewoo* instructive.

[17] Here, the bills of lading do not prove the contents of the sealed containers upon leaving the warehouse and commencing transit. According to the warehouse to warehouse clause, the insurance does not attach until the goods leave the warehouse for the commencement of transit. Coast to Coast has not presented any evidence that the sealed containers left the warehouse with the ordered goods. In fact, in his declaration, Frank Sipin notes that whoever packed the substituted goods did so in a fraudulent manner, placing the substituted fish products in the mid and innermost areas of the containers in an effort to deceive customs inspectors. Besides the substitution of fish, other shipments arrived with blocks of ice containing only a thin layer of shrimp, and much of it was poor in quality. There were a number of shipments, 24 containers in all, loaded aboard various vessels on different dates, passing through numerous ports, and yet almost the entire shipment arrived with either substituted goods or thinly packed shrimp that was substantially poor in quality. A different situation might arise if only one shipment arrived in this manner. Since virtually all the shipments arrived in the same condition, there is an insurmountable inference that the loss or substitution did not occur during transit. The facts indicate that the substituted goods and thin layers of shrimp were packed before the containers left the warehouse pursuant to a scheme to defraud Coast to Coast. In other words, the only reasonable inference is that the goods ordered were never shipped. Based on the totality of the circumstances, Coast to Coast has failed to demonstrate that the loss occurred subsequent to the time that the insurable interest attached. Accordingly, we conclude that Coast to Coast has not met its burden in proving coverage under the insurance policy. To conclude otherwise, would transform the insurance policy into a performance bond.

Conclusion

[18] Because Coast to Coast failed to establish that the loss occurred after the shipment left the warehouse and commenced transit, it did not meet its burden in proving insurance coverage. For this reason, we do not address the shifting burden on Underwriters to prove an applicable exclusion or Coast to Coast's request for attorney fees and costs on appeal pursuant to *Olympic S.S. Co. v. Centennial Ins. Co.,* 117 Wash.2d 37, 811 P.2d 673 (1991). We reverse summary judgment in favor of Coast to Coast and direct that judgment be entered in favor of Underwriters.

Notes and Questions

1. Once again, we have a cargo owner seeking comprehensive insurance cover, including for cases of theft. Like in *Plymouth Rubber,* the efforts fail. How did the court come to the conclusion that the policy, with the warehouse-to-warehouse clause, the additional shore clause, and the clause covering unexplained shortages of goods still did not require indemnification of the cargo owner?

2. What is the effect of a notation on the Bill of Lading along the lines of "shippers load & count" or "said to weigh" (or, in other cases, "shipper's load, stow and count" or SLAC)?

3. Note the analysis of the crime, the packing of the fraudulent cargo in the middle and rear of the containers, where they would not easily be discovered by customs and other inspectors. How could Coast to Coast protect itself against this kind of fraud?

4. From a policy perspective, should the insurance have to cover the losses of Coast to Coast? What are the arguments in favor and against?

———

Our final case concerns insurance claims presented by the assured party that are at least partly untrue.

Professor Sooksripaisarnkit has identified five forms of potentially fraudulent claims:[9]

1. Where the assured procures or causes the loss deliberately and knowingly (or with reckless indifference to the truth) presents a claim for an indemnity in respect of that loss;

2. Where the assured suffers no loss, but manufactures or invents a loss for presentation to the insurer;

3. Where the assured suffers a genuine loss but presents the claim in such a way as knowingly (or with reckless indifference to the truth) to disguise the fact that the insurer has or might have a defence to the claim;

4. Where the assured suffers a genuine loss, which is indemnifiable under the insurance contract, but the assured knowingly (or with reckless indifference to the truth) exaggerates the claim to a not insignificant extent; and

5. Where the assured suffers a genuine loss, which is indemnifiable under the insurance contract, but the assured deploys a fraudulent device with the intention of (not insignificantly) improving his prospects vis-à-vis the insurer.

As you read the decision from the UK Court of Appeals, see whether you can place the problem into the correct category and whether you agree with the distinction of untrue claims made in contract negotiations versus untrue claims made during litigation.

———

9. Poomintr Sooksripaisarnkit, *Chapter 8 — Marine Insurance*, in Mary Thomson (ed.), *Maritime Law and Practice in Hong Kong*, Sweet & Maxwell 2015, pp. 269–353, at p. 339.

Case 5-8

Agapitos v. Agnew

UK Court of Appeal (Civil Division)
Judgment of 6 March 2002, [2002] EWCA Civ 247, 2002 WL 226160
Lord Justice Mance

Introduction

[1] It has been said that the more cases there are endorsing a particular proposition, the shakier it may be (cf Posner, *The Problems of Jurisprudence*, Harvard University Press, p. 83). The waves of insurance litigation over the last 20 years have involved repeated examination of the scope and application of any post-contractual duty of good faith. The opacity of the relevant principles—whether originating in venerable but cryptically reasoned common law cases or enshrined, apparently immutably, in s.17 of the Marine Insurance Act 1906—is matched only by the stringency of the sanctions assigned. Not surprisingly, recent clarification of aspects of these principles has been influenced by this stringency, particularly in the context of s.17: see e.g., *Manifest Shipping Co. Ltd. v. Uni-Polaris Shipping Co. Ltd. (The "Star Sea")* [2001] 2 WLR 170 . . . .

[2] The older common law cases (particularly, *Levy v. Baillie* (1831) 7 Bing. 349, *Goulstone v. Royal Insurance Co.* (1858) 1 F & F 276, and *Britton v. Royal Insurance Co.* (1866) 4 F & F 905) stand for a rule of law, applicable even where there is no express clause in the policy, to the effect that an insured who has made a fraudulent claim forfeits any lesser claim which he could properly have made: see *The "Star Sea"* at para. 62, per Lord Hobhouse. It was unnecessary in *The "Star Sea"* to consider whether the whole policy is (at least if it is a marine policy) then also voidable, by application of or analogy with s.17 . . . . Nor did that issue arise in either of the modern decisions to which Lord Hobhouse there referred—*Orakpo v. Barclays Insurance Services* [1995] LRLR 443 . . . , and *Galloway v. Guardian Royal Exchange* (UK) Ltd. [1999] LRLR 209 . . . .

[3] [UK Marine Insurance Act 1906] S.17 provides: "Insurance is uberrimae fidei

> 17 A contract of marine insurance is a contract based upon the utmost good faith, and, if the utmost good faith be not observed by either party, the contract may be avoided by the other party."

[4] The present appeal raises for consideration (a) whether and in what circumstances the common law rule of law and/or s.17 can apply in the event of use of fraudulent means or devices ("fraudulent devices" for short) to promote a claim, which claim may prove at trial to be in all other respects valid, (b) whether (if so) the application of that rule and section ceases with the commencement of litigation and (c) whether, in the light of the answers to these questions, the judge should have allowed the appellant insurers to amend their defence to assert (in short) that the respondents, during the course of the present litigation, maintained a case involving lying representations, as to the date when hot works commenced on the insured vessel.

The Facts

[5] The litigation arises from the loss of the passenger ferry "Aegeon" following a fire on 19th February 1996. She belonged to Ioannis Agapitos. He issued proceedings on 27th January 1997. Since his death on 15th November 1999, the proceedings have been pursued by his son, Konstantinos Agapitos, as his successor in title.

[6] The Aegeon was insured against hull and machinery port risks under a slip policy for six months at 9th August 1995 "whilst laid up and undergoing general and cosmetic maintenance at Neo Molo Drapetsona, Greece". The conditions included "Wtd no hot work". After a spell spent at Eleusis, with insurers' permission, a further endorsement initialled on 12th January 1996 noted that she was again moored at Neo Molo, and that "Refurbishment/maintenance works have recommenced and Hot Works on decks is due to commence soon". It further provided "Wtd LSA certificate and all recs. complied with prior commencement of hot work". A fax transmission dated 25th January 1996 (shown, it appears, by the brokers to the leading underwriters on 26th and 30th January 1996) communicated the vessel's managers' advice "that as from yesterday 24.01.96 hot works are carried out on the above vessel".

[7] The brokers responded on 26th January 1996 that the (first) leading underwriter had noted the contents of the fax, but that "We would stress, however, that coverage of this vessel is warranted LSA certificate updated and all recommendations complied with prior to commencement of hot work. For the sake of good order please confirm that this has been carried out." On 29th January 1996 the owner asked the Salvage Association "Pls appoint Mr Costouros in order to give us a new mooring approval plus L.S.A. certificate in Neo Molo Drapetsona". The Salvage Association instructed Mr Costouros. There followed some conversations between him and representatives of Mr Ioannis Agapitos, the contents of which are in issue. But it is common ground that Mr Costouros did not actually survey the vessel or issue any new certificate prior to the casualty on 19th February 1996. On 30th January 1996 the brokers informed owners that all leading underwriters had now seen the fax of 25th January, and repeated their warning and request regarding the warranty. By a further endorsement on 6th February 1996 underwriters agreed to extend cover for a further two months from 9th February 1996 at pro rata additional premium, on terms "Wtd LSA cert updated". On 19th February 1996 the fire occurred during hot works.

[8] In their defence served on 21st April 1997, underwriters alleged a number of breaches of warranty. That presently material related to alleged failure to obtain a Salvage Association certificate (a) prior to commencement of hot works as required by the endorsement of 12th January 1996 and/or (b) on or shortly after 9th February 1996 as allegedly required by the endorsement of 6th February 1996. (Recently, underwriters have amended to assert that the endorsement of 6th February 1996 warranted that such a certificate had already been obtained.) Underwriters asserted in support of (a) that hot works commenced by or from 16th January 1996 [or by 24th January or by 19th February 1996]. In his original reply of 13th June 1997,

the insured denied any breach of warranty, and alleged that hot works began on 12th February 1996 and that, in so far as there was any warranty, the failure of the designated surveyor, Mr Costouros, to make himself available prior to the commencement of the hot works constituted a change of circumstance which excused non-compliance under s.34(1).

[9] Underwriters sought in this light to resolve the proceedings by proposing preliminary issues, relying on the fax dated 25th January 1996 to establish the date when hot works began. In evidence in reply on 24th June 1998 the claimant alleged that an oxyacetylene tool had been used for a collateral purpose for a few hours on 24th January 1996, but that this did not constitute "hot works" within the meaning of any of the endorsements. Shortly thereafter on 28th August 1998 the reply was amended to plead this, to delete the s.34(1) defence and to assert that underwriters had waived or were estopped from relying on any warranty that a LSA certificate would be obtained, having regard to the fax of 25th January 1996 and the endorsement of 6th February 1996. On 22nd November 2000 the reply was further amended to rely on the conversations between Mr Costouros and representatives of the claimant on or about 30th January and/or 8th February 1996, and to allege that during them Mr Costouros agreed to hot works starting without any survey of the vessel.

[10] In disclosure in early 2001 the claimant disclosed sworn statements taken from two workmen immediately after the casualty, which attested that hot works of a substantial nature had been carried out from as early as 1st February 1996. On 30th July 2001 underwriters' solicitors wrote drawing attention to this, claiming inter alia to avoid the policy for fraud and inviting consent to amendments to their defence to plead such fraud. More specifically the proposed amendments assert that both Mr Ioannis Agapitos . . . and Mr Konstantinos Agapitos . . . have knowingly, falsely and fraudulently mis-represented that no hot works were carried out prior to 12th February 1996 and/or were in breach of their duty to act with utmost good faith, in the latter case entitling the asserted avoidance. In support of these pleas, underwriters propose to plead that "Both the claimant and his late father were closely involved in the refurbishment works on the vessel and would have known when hot works commenced" and that "It can be assumed that pleadings in this action and the affidavits relied on by Ioannis Agapitos and latterly [Konstantinos Agapitos] were settled on their instructions". . . .

The Scope and Inter-relationship of the Common Law Rule and s.17 . . .

[14] The fullest description of the common law rule appears in *Britton* in Willes J's summing up to the jury:

"Of course, if the assured set fire to his house, he could not recover. That is clear. But it is not less clear that, even suppose that it were not wilful, yet as it is a contract of indemnity only, that is, if the claim is fraudulent, it is defeated altogether. That is, suppose the insured made a claim for twice the amount insured and lost, thus seeking to put the office off its guard, and in the result recover more than he is entitled to, that would be a wilful fraud, and the consequence is that he could not recover anything. This is a defence quite different from that of wilful arson. It gives the go-by to the origin of the fire, and it amounts to this — that the assured took advantage of the fire to make a fraudulent claim. The law upon such a case is in accordance with justice, and also with sound policy. The law is, that a person who has made such a fraudulent claim could not be permitted to recover at all. The contract of insurance is one of perfect good faith on both sides, and it is most important that such good faith should be maintained. It is the common practice to insert in fire-policies conditions such that they shall be void in the event of a fraudulent claim; and there was such a condition in the present case. Such a condition is only in accordance with legal principle and sound policy. It would be most dangerous to permit parties to practise such frauds, and then, notwithstanding their falsehood and fraud in the claim, to recover the real value of the goods consumed. And if there is wilful falsehood and fraud in the claim, the insured forfeits all claim upon the policy."

The simple rationale is in Lord Hobhouse's words (para. 62 in *The "Star Sea"* that:

"The fraudulent insured must not be allowed to think: if the fraud is successful, then I will gain; if it is unsuccessful, I will lose nothing".

The policy of the law to discourage the making of fraudulent claims had previously been emphasised by both Lord Woolf MR and Millett LJ in *Galloway*. Millett LJ, at p. 214 described the fraudulent claim rule "as a necessary and salutary rule which deserves to be better known by the public" and one which he "would be most unwilling to dilute . . . in any way".

[15] It is convenient at the outset to consider two points on which the scope of the common law rule is not entirely clear. The first is whether a claim, which is honestly believed in when initially presented, may become fraudulent for the purposes of the rule, if the insured subsequently realises that it is exaggerated, but continues to maintain it. The second is whether the fraud must relate, in some narrow sense, to the subject matter of the claim, or may go to any aspect of its validity, including therefore a defence. The first point was left open by Lord Scott in *The "Star Sea"* . . . . But I believe that the correct answer must be in the affirmative. As a matter of principle, it would be strange if an insured who thought at the time of his initial claim that he had lost property in a theft, but then discovered it in a drawer, could happily maintain both the genuine and the now knowingly false part of his claim, without risk of application of the rule. . . .

[18] As to the second point, a claim cannot be regarded as valid, if there is a known defence to it which the insured deliberately suppresses. To that extent, at least, fraud in relation to a defence would seem to me to fall within the fraudulent claim rule. Further, I do not consider that it should make any difference in this connection if the known defence consists of breach of warranty or a known right to avoid for misrepresentation or non-disclosure. . . .

[19] I turn to examine the scope of the rule and the section more closely. Where there is a fraudulent claim, the law forfeits not only that which is known to be untrue,

but also any genuine part of the claim. In contrast, where the use of fraudulent devices occurs, the whole claim is by definition otherwise good. The present appeal raises for consideration whether, as a matter of policy, the underlying rationale of the fraudulent claim principle should extend to invalidate not merely the whole of a claim where part proves good, but the whole of a claim where the whole proves otherwise good. . . .

[20] Mr Popplewell QC for the appellant insurers in the present case argues persuasively that the rationale of the common law rule regarding fraudulently exaggerated claims has force in the wider context of use of fraudulent devices to promote an insurance claim. If an insured uses fraudulent devices to support a claim, he does so, normally, because he believes that it is necessary or expedient to do so. He uses such devices, precisely because he cannot be sure that his claim is otherwise good. Mr Popplewell therefore submits that it should be irrelevant for an assured to show subsequently that the claim was all along good or that his fraudulent devices were superfluous. If the deception succeeds, and the insured wins, either at trial or because insurers settle on the basis that the facts were or may be as presented to them, the insured gains, because he avoids consideration of what he perceives as his true but weaker case. Assuming that the claim was in truth good all along, he will still successfully have gilded the lily (and may achieve a better settlement thereby). If the deception is revealed, either before or at trial, the insured cannot, Mr Popplewell submits, be allowed to think that he will lose nothing. The whole claim, if not the whole policy, must be forfeit, so as to introduce an incentive not to lie, paralleling that already recognised by the common law rule. . . .

[30] That some distinctions exist between fraudulent claims, in the narrow sense of cases of no or exaggerated loss, and the use of fraudulent devices is clear. A fraudulent claim exists where the insured claims, knowing that he has suffered no loss, or only a lesser loss than that which he claims (or is reckless as to whether this is the case). A fraudulent device is used if the insured believes that he has suffered the loss claimed, but seeks to improve or embellish the facts surrounding the claim, by some lie. There may however be intermediate factual situations, where the lies become so significant, that they may be viewed as changing the nature of the claim being advanced. . . .

[31] The authorities also indicate that there are differences between, on the one hand, a fraudulent claim to recover a non-existent or exaggerated loss and, on the other, a breach of the duty of good faith under s.17. . . .

[32] . . . Lord Woolf MR explained . . . the need for "substantial" fraud as intended to exclude fraud which could be regarded as "immaterial" (or, in Visc. Sumner's words in *Lek v. Mathews*, so "unsubstantial as to be de minimis").

[33] . . . [To] the extent that loss claimed is non-existent, the claim will fail anyway and the fraud is clearly material in so far as it amounted to an attempt to recover for non-existent loss. But the real bite of the fraudulent claim rule is to forfeit even the genuine part of any claim; and the fraud by definition is not material in any

ordinary sense to the genuine part. Thus, it is sufficient for the rule to apply that the fraud occurs in making a claim and relates to a part of the claim which, when viewed discretely, is not itself immaterial or "unsubstantial".

[34] In contrast, it is a general requirement of s.17 that the matter fraudulently misrepresented or undisclosed should have been material. In *Royal Boskalis*, Rix J considered that, if the duty under s.17 extended at the claims stage to non-fraudulent, albeit culpable non-disclosure, then: ". . . it seems to me to make sense that the test of materiality should depend on the ultimate legal relevance to a defence under the policy of the non-disclosure or misrepresentation relied on as a breach" (p.588) and "The result would be that non-fraudulent breach of duty in relation to claim A would only be proved if the matter misrepresented or concealed justified a defence to that claim, but upon such proof the insurer would be shown to be justified, if he so chooses, to avoid the policy as a whole." . . .

[35] If one were to apply the test of materiality developed in *Royal Boskalis* . . . to the use of a fraudulent device, two consequences would follow. First, the use of a fraudulent device would itself commonly become immaterial. With regard to the claim itself, if that was bad in any case, it would fail because it was bad, and any finding that a fraudulent device was used would add nothing. With regard to the policy generally, a finding of use of a fraudulent device could only add something, if one were to assume that (a) either s.17 creates a right of avoidance or the common law rule of forfeiture affects future claims as well as the claim to which the device related and (b) some other past claim(s) had been paid (which insurers decided that they wished to recover by avoiding the whole policy) or some future claim had arisen (which insurers wished to avoid paying). Secondly, there could be no preliminary issue to determine whether a claim failed for use of a fraudulent device. The proceedings would have to be litigated to trial to determine whether "the matter misrepresented or concealed justified a defence to [the] claim".

[36] What relationship need there then be between any fraud and the claim, if the fraudulent claim rule is to apply? And need the fraud have any effect on insurers' conduct? Speaking here of a claim for a loss known to be non-existent or exaggerated, the answers seem clear. Nothing further is necessary. The application of the rule flows from the fact that a fraudulent claim of this nature has been made. Whether insurers are misled or not is in this context beside the point. The principle only arises for consideration where they have not been misled into paying or settling the claim, and its application could not sensibly depend upon proof that they were temporarily misled. The only further requirement is that the part of the claim which is non-existent or exaggerated should not itself be immaterial or unsubstantial: see paragraphs 32–33 above. That also appears consistent with general principle, even though, in a pre-contract context, no significance or sanction attaches to a fraudulent misrepresentation or non-disclosure unless it has, by misleading insurers, induced them to enter a contract. Thus, Lord Mustill considered in *Pan Atlantic Insurance Ltd. v. Pine Top Insurance Ltd.* [1995] 1 AC 501 , 533B that the texts and the relevant cases leave no room for doubt that — whereas, if the representation

inducing a contract was either fraudulent or a "warranty" of the contract, "its false-hood would invariably give a right to avoid"—an innocent misrepresentation inducing the contract would in contrast "give the underwriter a right to avoid only if it was material".

[37] What is the position where there is use of a fraudulent device designed to promote a claim? I would see no reason for requiring proof of actual inducement here, any more than there is in the context of a fraudulent claim for non-existent or exaggerated loss. As to any further requirement of "materiality", if one were to adopt in this context the test identified in *Royal Boskalis* . . . , then, as I have said, the effect is, in most cases, tantamount to saying that the use of a fraudulent device carries no sanction. It is irrelevant (unless it succeeds, which only the insured will then know). On the basis (which the cases show and I would endorse) that the policy behind the fraudulent claim rule remains as powerful today as ever, there is, in my view, force in Mr Popplewell's submission that it either applies, or should be matched by an equivalent rule, in the case of use of a fraudulent device to promote a claim—even though at the end of a trial it may be shown that the claim was all along in all other respects valid. The fraud must of course be directly related to and intended to promote the claim. . . . Whenever that is so, the usual reason for the use of a fraudulent device will have been concern by the insured about prospects of success and a desire to improve them by presenting the claim on a false factual basis. If one does use in this context the language of materiality, what is material at the claims stage depends on the facts then known and the strengths and weaknesses of the case as they may then appear. It seems irrelevant to measure materiality against what may be known at some future date, after a trial. The object of a lie is to deceive. The deceit may never be discovered. The case may then be fought on a false premise, or the lie may lead to a favourable settlement before trial. Does the fact that the lie happens to be detected or unravelled before a settlement or during a trial make it immaterial at the time when it was told? In my opinion, not. Materiality should take into account the different appreciation of the prospects, which a lie is usually intended to induce on insurers' side, and the different understanding of the facts which it is intended to induce on the part of a judge at trial.

[38] . . . In the context of use of a fraudulent device or means, one can contemplate the possibility of an obviously irrelevant lie—one which, whatever the insured may have thought, could not sensibly have had any significant impact on any insurer or judge. Tentatively, I would suggest that the courts should only apply the fraudulent claim rule to the use of fraudulent devices or means which would, if believed, have tended, objectively but prior to any final determination at trial of the parties' rights, to yield a not insignificant improvement in the insured's prospects—whether they be prospects of obtaining a settlement, or a better settlement, or of winning at trial. . . .

[45] What then is the appropriate approach for the law to adopt in relation to the use of a fraudulent device to promote a claim, which may (or may not) prove at trial to be otherwise good, but in relation to which the insured feels it expedient to tell lies

to improve his prospects of a settlement or at trial? The common law rule relating to cases of no or exaggerated loss arises from a perception of appropriate policy and jurisprudence on the part of our 19th century predecessors, which time has done nothing to alter. The proper approach to the use of fraudulent devices or means is much freer from authority. It is, as a result, our duty to form our own perception of the proper ambit or any extension of the common law rule. In the present imperfect state of the law, fettered as it is by s.17, my tentative view of an acceptable solution would be:

> a) to recognise that the fraudulent claim rule applies as much to the fraudulent maintenance of an initially honest claim as to a claim which the insured knows from the outset to be exaggerated,

> b) to treat the use of a fraudulent device as a sub-species of making a fraudulent claim—at least as regards forfeiture of the claim itself in relation to which the fraudulent device or means is used. (The fraudulent claim rule may have a prospective aspect in respect of future, and perhaps current, claims, but it is unnecessary to consider that aspect or its application to cases of use of fraudulent devices.)

> c) to treat as relevant for this purpose any lie, directly related to the claim to which the fraudulent device relates, which is intended to improve the insured's prospects of obtaining a settlement or winning the case, and which would, if believed, tend, objectively, prior to any final determination at trial of the parties' rights, to yield a not insignificant improvement in the insured's prospects—whether they be prospects of obtaining a settlement, or a better settlement, or of winning at trial, and

> d) to treat the common law rules governing the making of a fraudulent claim (including the use of fraudulent device) as falling outside the scope of s.17 . . . . On this basis no question of avoidance ab initio would arise. . . .

The Application of the Fraudulent Claim Rule after Litigation [Is Initiated]

[47] In *The "Star Sea"* Lord Clyde said at para. 4:

"As regards the obligations in law of an insured at the stage of a disputed claim I take the view that there is no duty upon the insured to make a full disclosure of his own case to the other side in a litigation. I see no practical justification for such an obligation at that stage. Unlike the initial stage when the insurer may rely very substantially upon the openness of the insured in order to decide whether or not to agree to provide insurance cover, and if so at what level of premium, the insurer has open to him means of discovery of any facts which he requires to know for his defence to the claim. . . . . The idea of a requirement for full disclosure superseding the procedural controls for discovery in litigation is curious and unattractive, and one which would require to be soundly based in authority or principle."

[48] Lord Hobhouse dealt with the matter more fully at paras. 73–78, where he said this: "In Litigation:

73. The point here is whether the obligation of good faith and disclosure continues to apply unqualified once the parties are engaged in hostile litigation before the courts. There is no authority directly on this point. . . . It is therefore right to consider what effect the commencement of legal proceedings has upon the relationship of the parties. . . .

74. Before the litigation starts the parties' relationship is purely contractual subject to the application of the general law. . . .

75. When a writ is issued the rights of the parties are crystallised. The function of the litigation is to ascertain what those rights are and grant the appropriate remedy. The submission of the defendants in this case is that, notwithstanding this, one party's conduct of the litigation can not only change that party's substantive rights but do so retrospectively avoiding the contract ab initio. It cannot be disputed that there are important changes in the parties' relationship that come about when the litigation starts. There is no longer a community of interest. The parties are in dispute and their interests are opposed. Their relationship and rights are now governed by the rules of procedure and the orders which the court makes on the application of one or other party. The battle lines have been drawn and new remedies are available to the parties. The disclosure of documents and facts are provided for with appropriate sanctions; the orders are discretionary within the parameters laid down by the procedural rules. Certain immunities from disclosure are conferred under the rules of privilege. If a party is not happy with his opponent's response to his requests he can seek an order from the court. If a judgment has been obtained by perjured evidence remedies are available to the aggrieved party. The situation therefore changes significantly. There is no longer the need for the remedy of avoidance under s.17; other more appropriate remedies are available. . . .

[51] . . . [The] duty of good faith under s.17 is superseded or exhausted by the rules of litigation, once litigation is begun. . . .

[52] For my part, I consider that it would be inappropriate to introduce a distinction between the duration of impact of the fraudulent claim rule (including in that any extension to cover the use of fraudulent devices to promote a claim) and of the s.17 duty. . . . The same policy considerations that led Lord Hobhouse to restrict the latter duty to the pre-litigation period militate strongly in favour of a similar restriction of the duration of the common law duty.

[53] I therefore conclude that the proposed amendments raise a case which would be obviously bad, in so far as it depends on the assertion of lying in breach of either a common law duty or a duty under s.17 continuing after the commencement of litigation. . . . For this reason . . . underwriters' appeal should in my view be dismissed. . . .

Mr. Justice Park [concurring]:

[58] A regrettable but not uncommon phenomenon in the civil courts is the litigant, whether a claimant or a defendant, who thinks that he has a fairly good case but is worried that he just might lose, so he tries to improve his chances by embellishing the evidence and telling a few lies. Suppose that at the trial his lies are exposed, but the judge takes the view that he would have won the case anyway without them. Does he lose the case because he lied? The answer is: no. If his case is a good one anyway, he wins. It is deplorable that he lied, but he is not deprived of his victory in consequence.

[59] The present case raises the question whether it is any different if the litigant who tells lies is an insured claimant, the defendant is the insurer, and the insured is attempting to improve his chances of securing judgment for his claim under the policy. In my judgment, for the reasons which Mance LJ explains, it is not any different. The point arises because, if the litigant had told his lies, not in the course of the court proceedings, but at the earlier stage when he was pressing his claim upon the insurer, it is likely that the lies, if discovered, would have provided the insurer with a defence at common law under the fraudulent claims principle. The case for the insurers is that the position is exactly the same if the litigant tells his lies in the course of the litigation, but in my view it is not. . . .

[61] In this case the insured has said that hot works did not commence on the vessel until 12 February 1996. The insurers say that that was a lie: they say that recent disclosures reveal that hot works had begun not later than on or about 1 February 1996, and that both of the Messrs Agapitos (the father, now deceased, and the son) must have known that they had begun by then. The relevance of the point is that 8 February was the earliest date on which, according to the insured's case, a London Salvage Association certificate was in force (or, if a certificate was not in force, the designated surveyor of the LSA had confirmed that, if hot works commenced thereafter, there would be no breach of the insured's warranty). The insured had warranted that hot works would not begin until a LSA certificate was in force. So, if hot works had begun by 1 February, the insurers have an arguable case that the insured was in breach of warranty. The result would be that the insurers would not be liable under the policy for the consequences of the fire which destroyed the vessel on 19 February. On the other hand, if hot works did not begin until 12 February the insured has a maintainable case that there was no breach of warranty. . . .

[62] It is of course open to the insurers on the pleadings as they presently stand to advance at trial the case that hot works had begun on 1 February (before the LSA certificate or anything equivalent from the LSA's surveyor was in place), that in consequence the insured was in breach of warranty, and that therefore the case should be decided in favour of the insurers. However, the insurers want to amend their pleadings so as to put forward in addition the more root and branch case that the claimant, an insured who owes a duty of good faith to his insurers, has told a significant lie in advancement of his insurance claim, and that for that reason alone his claim should be dismissed.

[63] If the insured's statement (the alleged lie) that hot works did not commence until 12 February had been made to the insurers in the course of pre-litigation discussions and negotiations about the policy claim, it would, I believe, follow from the

principles which Mance LJ has described that permission should be given to amend the defence so as to raise the plea which the insurers wish to advance. However, the statement was not made to the insurers in pre-litigation discussions and negotiations: it was made in a pleading in the course of the litigation. Mance LJ's conclusion is that that circumstance removes it from the ambit of the fraudulent claims principle. I respectfully agree with him, both in the result and in the reasons for it. In my opinion the case simply becomes one, such as I described in the first paragraph of this short concurring judgment, where a litigant is alleged to have lied in support of his case. If a litigant did lie that is reprehensible, and the fact that he thought it necessary or desirable to lie obviously causes one to suspect that his case, stripped of the lies in support of it, may not be a good one. But it is not the law that, if his case is a good one after all, the fact that he lied in support of it is in itself a ground for judgment being given against him.

Notes and Questions

1. Pursuant to paragraph 30, "[a] fraudulent claim exists where the insured claims, knowing that he has suffered no loss, or only a lesser loss than that which he claims (or is reckless as to whether this is the case). A fraudulent device is used if the insured believes that he has suffered the loss claimed, but seeks to improve or embellish the facts surrounding the claim, by some lie." The first scenario is self-explanatory. The second not so much. An example would be the homeowner who has been robbed. If she seeks to recover an amount for her jewelry that is clearly much greater than the real value of the stolen goods, there is a fraudulent claim. If she claims the true value of the stolen goods but falsely claims that the alarm system had been engaged, a fraudulent device is being used.

Under English common law, if an insured party makes a fraudulently exaggerated claim, she forfeits her entire claim, including that for the genuine loss. The common law does not clearly stipulate the consequences of the use of fraudulent devices, however.

Section 17 of the English Marine Insurance Act 1906 (MIA) stipulates that insurance is *uberrimae fidei*. In other words: "A contract of marine insurance is a contract based upon the utmost good faith, and, if the utmost good faith be not observed by either party, the contract may be avoided by the other party."

The court has to decide whether the use of a fraudulent device should always result in the complete denial of an otherwise honest claim. Furthermore, the court has to locate the remedy for use of fraudulent devices either in the common law claim of fraud, or in Sec. 17 of the MIA.

2. Whether there is fraud or the use of fraudulent devices, distinctions could be made between serious or substantial fraud on the one side and immaterial, unsubstantial, or *de minimis* fraud on the other (see paras. 32–33).

Another distinction could be between active misrepresentation on the one side and passive nondisclosure on the other (para. 34).

Regardless of which is which, should the outcome be the same, whether there was fraud in the claim or merely use of fraudulent devices? (para. 37)

3. Ultimately, the court takes a strict approach to fraud and the use of fraudulent devices during the time when a claim is first presented and then investigated, granting at best a very narrow exception if the fraud or the use of fraudulent devices was entirely insignificant. However, Lord Justice Mance wants to locate both fraud and fraudulent devices in the common law and outside of Sec. 17 (see para. 45 d)). Why? How do the consequences of the application of the common law of fraud (potentially) differ from the application of Sec. 17 MIA? Check paragraph 35 to find the answer.

4. If both fraud and the use of fraudulent devices are subject to the common law of fraud, what is the scope of application remaining for Sec. 17 MIA, if any?

5. Up to paragraph 45 it seemed a foregone conclusion that the insurer would win and would not have to indemnify the shipowners. What happens then?

Part Six

Dispute Settlement

In the business world, the parties to an IBT share the desire for conducting a profitable transaction. However, in the details, their interests are opposed. The seller would like to get the highest possible price with the lowest possible level of obligations and liabilities for her goods or services, while the buyer wants to pay the lowest possible price and get the highest possible level of assurances and performance. If the parties can come to an agreement on the goods or services to be sold, the price to be paid, and various terms and practical arrangements, a contract for an IBT is formed. The provisions of the contract can be very basic—a handshake or a verbal agreement identifying only the goods and the parties, if there is a market price or another way of figuring out the price; or it can be very elaborate—a written agreement of dozens or even hundreds of pages. Disputes can arise at any stage of the negotiations, the contract formation, and the performance of the contract. They can arise as early as the first interactions of the parties—for example, if one party is physically injured or experiences a data breach in the early stages of negotiations with the other party—or as late as years after the contract was performed and the goods or services were delivered—for example, if goods break while they are still covered by a warranty. If one party claims a right to receive something from the other party—a refund of monies paid, delivery of additional or alternative goods or services, damages, etc.—and the other party denies this right or claim, a dispute arises.

Professor Galanter wrote in this context that:

> [d]isputes are not discrete events like births or deaths; they are more like such constructs as illnesses and friendships. . . . Disputes are drawn from a vast sea of events, encounters, collisions, rivalries, disappointments, discomforts and injuries. . . . Some things in this sea of 'proto-disputes' become disputes through a process in which injuries are perceived, persons or institutions responsible for remedying them are identified, forums for presenting these claims are located and approached, claims are formulated acceptably to the forum, appropriate resources are invested, and attempts at diversion resisted. The disputes that arrive at courts can be seen as the survivors of a long and exhausting process.[1]

---

1. Marc S. Galanter, *Reading the Landscape of Disputes: What We Know and Don't Know (and Think We Know) About Our Allegedly Contentious and Litigious Society*, 31 UCLA L. Rev. 1983, pp. 4–71, at p. 12.

Galanter continues that:

> [w]e begin, in effect, with all human experience which might be identified as injurious. . . . First, a very large number of injuries go unperceived. . . . Even where injuries are perceived, a common response is resignation, that is, 'lumping it.' . . . 'Lumping it' is done not only by naive victims who lack information about or access to remedies, but also by those who knowingly decide that the gain is too low, or the cost too high, including the psychic costs of pursuing the claim. . . . Among . . . perceived injurious experiences, some may be seen as deserved punishment, some as the result of assumed risk or fickle fate; but a subset is viewed as violations of some right or entitlement caused by a human agent (individual or collective) and susceptible of remedy. These, . . . are grievances. . . . When such grievances are voiced to the offending party they become claims. Many will be granted. Those claims not granted become disputes.[2]

Most parties to an IBT find disputes undesirable—a distraction from their actual business, something they would like to avoid, contain, and end as swiftly and cost-effectively as possible. This is another interest both sides usually share. The best lawyers and in-house legal counsel will focus more on conflict prevention than on conflict or dispute resolution.[3] Even if a problem does arise, many disputes can be resolved via negotiations and some kind of settlement and do not require the involvement of third parties, which invariably costs time and money.[4] However, some disputes cannot be resolved so easily and if sufficiently valuable assets or interests are at stake, either or both of the parties may find it useful or even necessary to take recourse to one or more formal dispute settlement procedures.

If purely bilateral negotiations did not lead to a resolution of the dispute, the parties may call upon good offices of third parties in the hope that a negotiated solution can be found. These third parties can use their prestige or experience to ensure that the disputing parties negotiate in good faith, understand all undisputed facts, fairly assess the evidence for or against disputed facts, and are aware of the legal rules potentially applicable to their dispute and how they could or should be understood. If the third party is called a facilitator, the procedure may be referred to as conciliation. Some experts and some dispute settlement institutions also refer to this kind of service as mediation. If, in addition, a third party makes proposals for a resolution of the dispute, we usually speak of mediation or evaluative mediation.[5]

---

2. Ibid., pp. 12–15, with referenes, *inter alia*, to William L.F. Felstiner, Richard Abel & Austin Sarat, *The Emergence and Transformation of Disputes: Naming, Blaming, Claiming . . .* , 15 Law & Soc'y Rev. 631 (1980–1981), as well as Richard Miller & Austin Sarat, *Grievances, Claims, and Disputes: Assessing the Adversary Culture*, 15 Law & Soc'y Rev. 525, 527 (1980–1981).

3. See, for example, Deborah Masucci & Shravanthi Suresh: *Transforming Business Through Proactive Dispute Management*, Cardozo J. Confl. Res. 2017, Vol. 18, No. 3, pp. 659–676.

4. For more on this, see below, pp. 866 et seq.

5. As can be seen, the terminology is not always consistent. While the International Institute for Conflict Prevention & Resolution (CPR), for example, acknowledges that a mediator may "alert

All cases are so far characterized by the freedom of the parties to accept or reject a negotiated outcome. An involvement of attorneys or other legal professionals is so far entirely optional and by no means always advisable since it invariably costs more money and may lead to an escalation of the dispute. However, while a mediator does not have to be a trained lawyer, she should be trained and qualified in the do's and don'ts of mediation.

If neither of these procedures brings about a resolution of the dispute, the party or parties have to decide whether or not to initiate adversarial procedures before a court or tribunal. Unless it was contractually excluded, a party always has the right to call upon a public court for help. Although different countries have different rules in this regard, it is virtually universally accepted that a plaintiff may bring a case against a defendant in the court district where the defendant has his or her domicile, the so-called defendant court.[6] We will discuss in some detail the pros and cons of calling upon the courts of various states around the world and certain other choices parties may be able to make. Calling upon one or more public courts for the resolution of a dispute resulting from an IBT is called international or transnational litigation. The result is typically a judgment and the victorious party or parties can call upon the police powers of the respective state to have it enforced. However, if

---

[the parties] to a resolution that may further [their] interests" and, "if requested by both parties, the mediator may eventually (1) offer an opinion on the parties likelihood of success in an adjudicated proceeding, and/or (2) offer a proposed 'best resolution' that the mediator considers is the fairest, most commercially rational outcome to the dispute," as long as it is clear that "the mediator has no authority to impose an outcome on the parties and controls only the process of the mediation itself, not its result" (CPR's ADR Primer), Professor Love, the well-known director of Cardozo's Kukin Program for Conflict Resolution, is strongly opposed to any "evaluative" input where a mediator "gives advice, makes assessments, states opinions—including opinions on the likely court outcome, proposes a fair or workable resolution to an issue or the dispute, or presses the parties to accept a particular resolution." (Lela Love, *The Top Ten Reasons Why Mediators Should Not Evaluate*, Fla. St. Univ. L. Rev. 1997, Vol. 24, pp. 937–948, at p. 938). A similar approach is taken by the Centre for Effective Dispute Resolution (CEDR) in London, the leading international mediation training provider, although the CEDR Model Mediation Procedure allows proposals by mediators if both parties so agree.

We will use the terms "facilitation" and "conciliation" for the services envisaged by Prof. Love and we will use the terms "mediation" and "mediator" to allow an evaluation of facts, evidence and law, as well as proposals for the resolution of the conflict, unless clearly stated otherwise in the agreement between the parties.

Both approaches are consistent with the 2005 Model Standards of Conduct for Mediators jointly approved by the American Arbitration Association, American Bar Association, and Association for Conflict Resolution. This may not be self-evident in other countries, however. In Switzerland, for example, mediation is supposed to be nonevaluative, while conciliation allows the neutral to express a nonbinding opinion how the dispute should be resolved (see Michael McIlwrath & John Savage: *International Arbitration and Mediation—A Practical Guide*, Wolters Kluwer 2010, at p. 174). This is rather the opposite of the speech convention we will be using and demonstrates that all parties to an IBT *and their chosen neutrals* need to make sure that they have the same understanding of their intended ADR procedure.

6. There are some exceptions where countries declare certain mandatory and exclusive jurisdictions, for example, in real estate cases, the court where the property is located.

the losing party or parties do not have sufficient assets in the respective state or enforcement has to be sought in other states for other reasons, recognition and enforcement of a foreign judgment in these other states is by no means automatic.

If both parties to an IBT agree, either at the time their contract is concluded or later, when the dispute has arisen, they can go to arbitration instead of litigation. To this end, they can either call upon institutional arbitration offered by a national or international organization such as the American Arbitration Association (AAA) or the International Chamber of Commerce (ICC), or they can pursue a more informal approach called ad hoc arbitration. In either case, an arbitral tribunal of one or three arbitrators will be composed specifically for the dispute. Eventually, the arbitrators, after hearing the arguments of the parties and reviewing the evidence and any applicable laws, will issue an award granting or denying some or all of the claims of the parties. Arbitral awards are enforceable domestically pursuant to the national law of the seat of the tribunal. The recognition and enforcement by other states is usually mandated by the New York Convention.

In addition to questions of choice of (substantive) law already discussed in Part Two (above, pp. 113 et seq.), we now have to analyze the pros and cons of different choices of international or transnational dispute settlement.

Section 1. The International Dimension and the Consequences for Dispute Settlement

Whenever parties to a commercial transaction come from different countries, any issues connected to the settlement of potential disputes take on several additional and complicated dimensions:

- **Choice of law:** The business transaction and the resulting rights and obligations of the parties—and the consequences of any breaches of those obligations—have to be determined by reference to only one legal system. This is the substantive law applicable to the transaction, primarily the contract law. It could be seller's law or buyer's law or another legal system, but it cannot be a mix of the legal systems of both parties.[7]

---

7. There is one exception to the latter rule, namely if the parties, by incorporation into their agreement, essentially write an entire contract law themselves and draw upon provisions borrowed from both or even multiple legal systems. The only justification for doing this would be if there is no single legal system available that the parties could simply refer to and thus obtain a just, balanced, and efficient set of rules for their contractual rights and obligations. Given the fact that parties in B2B transactions literally have the choice among almost 200 national legal systems and at least three international contract laws, this argument cannot seriously be made. At a maximum, parties could decide to choose the contract law regime that most closely resembles their agreement and then modify just a handful of select clauses of that regime to obtain a perfect fit. Doing otherwise creates a real danger of mutually contradictory or at least incompatible provisions because it

- **Choice of forum:** The form of dispute settlement (litigation versus arbitration) and the specific venue or forum (which specific court, arbitration institution, or tribunal) have to be determined unambiguously to avoid parallel proceedings in different fora with potentially conflicting outcomes and/or proceedings in a forum that does not or should not have jurisdiction and may produce an unenforceable result. Obviously, the parties will have preferences in favor of or against certain fora. The location or proximity of the court is only the beginning of these considerations. While the parties can usually choose the substantive law, a court will always apply its own procedural law, which could be a factor making it attractive for one party and unattractive for the other party. Various other factors will be discussed below.

- **Recognition and enforcement of foreign judgments or awards:** International litigation results in a judgment or similar judicial decision and international arbitration results in an award that may need to be recognized and enforced in a country other than the country where it was adopted.

In the context of commercial transactions, there are two options for the determination of the applicable law and the applicable forum:

- On the basis of the universally recognized principles of freedom of contract and party autonomy, the parties to a Business-to-Business (B2B) contract — by contrast to Business-to-Consumer (B2C) contracts — can freely choose the applicable law and the applicable forum. This is generally done either when a contract is first concluded or when a dispute first arises. While a choice of law is almost always respected during dispute settlement, not every forum will accept every case thrown at it and some fora may be considered or consider themselves *forum non conveniens*. In such a case, the party choice may turn out to be invalid or ineffective.

- If the parties did not make a choice or if a choice is invalid or ineffective, the applicable law and/or the applicable forum will be determined by reference to the rules of private international law, also called international conflict of laws. A party choice is invalid if it does not meet certain form requirements, e.g., is not in writing, or refers to a subject matter where the law does not allow party

---

is not easy to ensure that all provisions in a large document, which often draws on multiple drafts used in earlier transactions, are always in line with all other provisions.

Nevertheless, the large number of international contracts that clock in at 80 or 100 pages and have their own self-contained contract law regime, demonstrates that attorneys often do not follow this rule. If confronted about the sensibility of their elaborations, they will surely claim that every single clause is trying to get the best possible deal for their clients. As we have already discussed earlier (see pp. 111–113),), this argument can also not seriously be made. The truth of the matter is, unfortunately, that the attorneys are primarily billing for a lot of work that is of no use or value to the client and not infrequently actually harms the position of the party that has to pay for it. (see also Ken Adams, A Manual on Style for Contract Drafting, ABA Publishing, 4th ed. 2017, p. xxxvi ("Traditional Contract Language is Dysfunctional"), and on his website https://www.adamsdrafting .com/).

choice, e.g., certain transactions affecting real estate or public registers. A party choice is ineffective if the chosen law does not cover the respective issues, e.g., the CISG does not cover fraud or mistake in the formation of the contract, or if the chosen forum does not exist or does not accept jurisdiction over the dispute. Most commonly, however, the rules of private international law come into play because the parties were unable to agree on a specific law and forum and simply left the question open.

The application of one legal system rather than another and one forum rather than another typically affects the parties in several ways:

- Neither the party herself nor her usual legal counsel will normally be familiar with a foreign legal system, which may create a bias for "their own" legal system to be applied, even if this may be unfavorable in substantive or procedural terms.

- Since the usual legal counsel will normally not be admitted to the bar in the foreign jurisdiction, the party can either insist on settling the dispute in her own court—even if that may be unfavorable in other respects—or she will have to retain additional foreign counsel to represent her in the foreign forum.

- The applicability of one legal system rather than another can cause unpredictable outcomes if the judges are unfamiliar with the applicable law.

- Certain fora are undesirable for reasons such as excessive delays (the courts of India and Italy are notorious examples), potential bias against foreign parties, and other issues related to incompetence, corruption, and general shortcomings with the rule of law (Russia is a prominent example here).

- Even if there are no problems with a foreign court as such, the retention of additional foreign counsel, translation of potentially large numbers of documents,[8] as well as travel expenses of parties, attorneys, witnesses, and experts, can add substantially to the cost of the dispute settlement.

As a consequence, the "default" for most American lawyers—and, for that matter, most lawyers anywhere in the world who are educated and experienced only in their own legal system—is to insist on contract clauses that provide for the application of their own legal system and for litigation in their own courts of law. This, however,

---

8. Acknowledging the preponderance of English as the language of international commerce, the French government recently opened an "International Chamber" at the Paris Court of Appeal, to allow appeals in English against decisions of the International Chamber of the First Instance Commercial Court in Paris. The latter has already been in operation for several years. Besides allowing proceedings in languages other than French, the courts also have some flexibility with procedures, for example allowing foreign attorneys to plead, as long as they are accompanied by a French attorney. Furthermore, strict deadlines apply for the duration of proceedings. For more information, see https://blogs.lexisnexis.co.uk/dr/frances-international-court-for-dispute-resolution/.

It remains to be seen, however, whether this innovative approach will succeed in competing with London courts and international arbitration. Several limitations remain, in particular the fact that written pleadings still have to be submitted in French and the judgments are also rendered in French and then translated.

will not allow for an agreement if the other side also insists on the application of their own laws and courts. Moreover, application of one's own law and litigation in one's own courts is not always in the client's best interests:

- The extent of the substantive rights and obligations of the parties may vary, depending on the applicable law; for example, the standard for the required performance by the seller tends to be stricter under the UCC compared to a variety of continental European legal systems, as well as the CISG, let alone English law (see above, p. 301).

- Procedural rights and obligations of the parties may vary, depending on the applicable law; for example, the time limits for the buyer to notify defects with the seller's performance.

- A decision by an American court against an American party will be very easily enforceable in America in favor of the foreign party. By contrast, a decision by an American court in favor of an American party will not be so easily enforceable abroad against the foreign party (China, for example, generally does not enforce foreign judgments).

The purpose of Part Six is to explain in some detail the differences between international commercial litigation and international commercial arbitration and to highlight the pros and cons of different forms of dispute settlement in different jurisdictions for different kinds of commercial transactions. In the end, readers will be able to make sensible choices of law and forum for different contracts (*ex ante*) and to plan and implement a strategy for commercial litigation abroad, or for international commercial arbitration after a dispute has arisen (*ex post*).[9]

Section 2. International Commercial Litigation[10]

Private international law, the continental European equivalent of *international conflict of laws*, is concerned with three primary problems:

---

9. For additional analysis, see also Adrian Biggs, *Agreements on Jurisdiction and Choice of Law*, Oxford Univ. Press 2008.

10. For deeper analysis, see, in particular, Gary Born & Peter Rutledge, *International Civil Litigation in United States Courts*, Wolters Kluwer 5th ed. 2011; David Epstein & Charles Baldwin, *International Litigation*, 4th ed. Martinus Nijhoff 2010; Richard Fentiman: *International Commercial Litigation*, Oxford Univ. Press 2nd ed. 2015; Ralph Folsom, *Principles of International Litigation and Arbitration*, West Academic 2015; John Haley: *Fundamentals of Transnational Litigation: The United States, Canada, Japan, and the European Union*, LexisNexis 2nd ed. 2015; Trevor Hartley, *International Commercial Litigation — Text, Cases and Materials on Private International Law*, Cambridge Univ. Press 2nd ed. 2015; Barton Legum, Theodore Edelman & Ethan Berghoff (eds.), *International Litigation Strategies and Practice: International Practitioner's Deskbook Series*, American Bar Association 2nd ed. Chicago 2015; Stephen McCaffrey & Thomas Main, *Transnational Litigation in Comparative Perspective*, Oxford Univ. Press 2010; J.G. Merrills, *International Dispute Settlement*, Cambridge Univ. Press 5th ed. 2011; Russell J. Weintraub, *International Litigation and Arbitration — Practice and Planning*, Carolina Academic Press 6th ed. 2011.

- determining which courts of which country have *jurisdiction* to hear disputes in a given civil or commercial case;[11]
- determining the *applicable law* for the given civil or commercial case; and
- providing whether and under what conditions a foreign judgment shall be *recognized* and *enforced* domestically.

In spite of its name, private international law is traditionally not international law at all. Rather, each country—and in some cases each subnational jurisdiction— determines in its national law whether its courts shall have jurisdiction over a dispute with an international element, when its national law shall be applied to a case with an international element, and when and under what conditions it will recognize and enforce a foreign judgment. For example, in Switzerland the rules of private international law were largely based on case law until they were codified in the Federal Law of Private International Law (PIL) in 1987.[12] By contrast, in the United States, federal rules on conflict of laws, jurisdiction, and venue are codified, while state rules remain largely uncodified and thus determined by common law. Theoretically, understanding the state-level common law would require extensive and time-consuming research of case law in 50 jurisdictions and the District of Columbia. However, the Restatement (Second) of Conflict of Laws provides an excellent summary of the common law. Some additional information on the U.S. and its most important trading partners is provided below, at pp. 827 et seq.

Naturally, uncoordinated national rules for cases with international dimensions can and will differ and lead to contradictory results. For example, country A may stipulate that disputes related to international commercial transactions have to be brought in the courts that have jurisdiction over the defendant (defendant's court), while the applicable law should be the one of the party that has to make the characteristic performance under the contract (usually seller's law). By contrast, country B may stipulate that its courts shall always have jurisdiction if a dispute involves one of its nationals and that its courts shall normally apply their own law. As is easy to see, commercial disputes between a seller from A and a buyer from B could end up being litigated in A under the laws of A or in B under the laws of B, depending on who brings the first claim and where. This can trigger what is sometimes referred to as a "race to the courthouse" because the first mover may be able to determine the applicable law, the forum, or both. This is widely considered undesirable, however, since it can pressure the parties to a commercial transaction into moving from negotiation to litigation at a time when there were still realistic chances for an amicable settlement of the dispute. Furthermore, the choices made by the first mover may subsequently be challenged by the other party, which means that a first lawsuit

---

11. See also above, Part Two, pp. 40–44, 113 et seq., and 145 et seq.

12. See François Dessemontet & Walter Stoffel, *Private International Law*, http://www.unil.ch /files/live//sites/cedidac/files/shared/Articles/Intro%20Sw%20Law.pdf.

or at least a preliminary stage in the main lawsuit will be conducted over questions of jurisdiction and choice of law, which is inefficient from a business point of view.

The issues related to *choice of law* by the parties—respectively the applicable law determined by the rules of private international law if the parties have not made a choice of law or have made an ineffective choice—have been discussed above, in Part Two. At the present time, we will focus on issues related to *choice of forum* by the parties—respectively the rules of private international law that determine the forum in cases where the parties have not made a choice of forum or have made an ineffective choice, as well as certain aspects of *recognition and enforcement* of foreign judgments.

A. International Jurisdiction of National Courts

With regard to jurisdiction of courts in international settings, the following questions must be answered by the parties to a dispute:

- Which court or courts in which countries have jurisdiction to hear a case concerning the dispute?

- Does it matter in this regard whether a party—for example, the seller—takes the initiative and brings a case as applicant or waits for the other party—in this, case the buyer—to bring the case, making the seller the defendant in the dispute?

- If there is more than one court where a case might be brought and/or if it makes a difference for the question of jurisdiction whether a party is applicant or defendant, which court is preferable from the perspective of the party, and why?

- In practical terms, how can a party ensure that the most favorable court will hear her case or at least prevent it from going to the least favorable court?

1. Basic Rules on Jurisdiction or Venue

"Jurisdiction"—literally "to speak law"—is the power of a court to make binding decisions regarding a specific dispute in front of it. We must distinguish between jurisdiction over the parties (*in personam*) and over the subject matter (*in rem*), as well as the power of a court to grant the specific remedy requested of it. The Restatement (Second) of Conflict of Laws uses the term "judicial jurisdiction" to distinguish the concepts we are discussing here from the "prescriptive jurisdiction" of states to regulate the status of people or property and to provide rules for various types of transactions and activities.[13] Finally, there is also the "enforcement jurisdiction" of states, which refers to the possibilities of a state, in law and in fact,

---

13. See above, Part One, Section 3, pp. 28–32. For further discussion, see also Curtis A. Bradley, *International Law in the U.S. Legal System*, Oxford Univ. Press 2nd ed. 2015, pp. 186–194.

to enforce its regulatory and judicial decisions for and against specific natural and legal persons. Our focus here will be on *judicial jurisdiction*.

In most cases, jurisdiction is determined by the law applicable at the seat of the court. In international cases this means that jurisdiction is determined by the private international law or the law on international conflict of laws in force in the country where the court is located. Naturally, these rules may differ from one country to another. Thus, it may make a difference to the parties to a dispute whether one party or the other initiates litigation, and where.

When an applicant approaches a court, this voluntary submission usually establishes jurisdiction *in personam* over the applicant if the applicant and/or the defendant and/or the subject matter have a sufficiently close connection to that court. The question to be answered is whether the court also has jurisdiction over the other party, the defendant. The basic and universally acknowledged principle is that the court or courts in whose district the defendant has her *domicile* have jurisdiction over the defendant. In the civil law countries, this jurisdiction over the defendant is established by law and service of process is an independent requirement that will be taken care of by the court itself.

By contrast, in the U.S. and other common law countries, service of process is a requirement of jurisdiction over the defendant and the responsibility of the plaintiff. Thus, in the U.S. the plaintiff has to initiate proceedings in a suitable forum *and* effect service of process to establish jurisdiction of that court. A forum is suitable if it has a sufficient connection to either or both parties and/or the matter in dispute (see below) and does not conflict with rules on special or exclusive jurisdiction and is not otherwise a *forum non conveniens*.

In general, a natural or legal person can always be sued in her own court, the defendant court. However, there may be another court or even several courts that also have jurisdiction over the defendant. If two or more courts have jurisdiction over the defendant and neither of them is an exclusive jurisdiction, the plaintiff can choose among these different courts, something generally referred to as *forum shopping*. While national systems are not all alike, there are usually four possible answers to the question of which court or courts have jurisdiction over the defendant. Since there is a hierarchical relationship between different grounds for jurisdiction, the sequencing of the answers is important:

1. A court may have jurisdiction because the subject matter establishes a special jurisdiction that is independent of domicile. If the special jurisdiction is also an exclusive jurisdiction, it preempts any other courts from taking on the dispute. For example, many countries provide a special and exclusive jurisdiction for disputes over real estate on behalf of the court where the real estate is located.

2. Jurisdiction of a particular court may also be established by a prior and valid choice of court agreement between the parties, provided the court and its respective legal system accept the choice of the parties; such *ex ante*

agreements are typically included in the sales contract or any other contract underlying an IBT; a valid choice of court agreement usually creates an exclusive jurisdiction on behalf of the chosen court; however, if another court has exclusive jurisdiction by law, for example, the court where the real estate is located, any party agreement designating another court would be invalid.

3. Alternatively, jurisdiction of a particular court may be established by the parties *ex post*, after a dispute has arisen; such an ad hoc agreement of the parties to litigate in front of a particular court can be effected via a separate contract or an addendum to the original IBT; more commonly, an *ex post* agreement is implied if both parties to a dispute make an appearance in front of a particular court and present arguments on the merits of the case (so-called *prorogation*), provided the court and its respective legal system accept the choice of the parties and no other court has exclusive jurisdiction over the dispute.

4. In the absence of alternative grounds, jurisdiction over the defendant is usually established by law in the court district where the defendant is domiciled — the default jurisdiction. However, national law in the plaintiff's country may also allow a case to be brought in plaintiff court, where a contract was negotiated or to be performed, where a tort was committed or the damages were incurred, or another court with some connection to the parties or the matter in dispute. The defendant's country may consider some of these alternative jurisdictions to be exorbitant jurisdictions and refuse to recognize them and the resulting decisions.

The various concepts introduced in the preceding paragraphs need further elaboration at this point and have to be well understood. Starting proceedings in a court that has jurisdiction is of crucial importance. If a defendant is not subject to the jurisdiction of a particular court, she should not be dragged before it against her will, and should not see judgments in default enforced against her.

Jurisdiction is not only a geographic question of finding the right court district. Most national legal systems have different courts for different subject matters and usually provide trial or first instance courts, as well as appellate courts. For example, in Germany, separate courts exist for civil and criminal cases, administrative cases, tax cases, labor disputes, and social security matters. If a case is brought in a court that lacks jurisdiction *in rem*, the court may or may not pass the matter on to the right court. In such cases, the statute of limitations will not be tolled until the case is in front of the right court.

If a case is brought in a court that may not have *in personam* jurisdiction over the defendant, the court may of its own motion examine whether it has jurisdiction. Alternatively, the defendant may file a motion or make an appearance merely to contest jurisdiction. If the defendant leaves it at that and does not file any claims on the merits of the case, the court will not consider that the defendant has "entered an appearance" and will not consider that she has voluntarily submitted to the jurisdiction of the court (more on this below, at pp. 759 et seq.).

If doubts about a court's jurisdiction arise after it has been approached by one or both parties, it is generally for that court to decide whether or not it has jurisdiction and will hear the case. This principle is called *Kompetenz-Kompetenz*, i.e., the competence to decide its own competence. Another way of saying the same thing is that the court has jurisdiction to determine its jurisdiction. Whether the decision will be recognized by the country where enforcement of the final judgment is sought, however, is another question, in particular if the other country may consider the jurisdictional base of the first seized court to be exorbitant or in violation of its own rules on special and exclusive jurisdictions (for more on this, see below pp. 703 and 706).

If one party approaches the court in A while the other party approaches the court in B, the two courts may both come to the conclusion that they have jurisdiction over the dispute. This may lead to parallel proceedings and potentially conflicting outcomes. Since this is undesirable from several perspectives — waste of court resources, duplication of attorney fees and other expenses for the parties, as well as damage to the authority of the courts if they end up contradicting each other — private international law seeks to reduce the probability of parallel cases via the principle of *lis pendens*. According to this principle, the first seized court has priority to decide the dispute and any subsequently seized courts should refuse, suspend, or terminate proceedings brought to them. This bar, however, is in effect only as long as the first seized court occupies itself with the dispute. Should the first seized court decide that it does not have jurisdiction — or should it discontinue the matter for other procedural reasons — a second seized court may accept or resume proceedings regarding the dispute.[14] Even if the defendant in a proceeding raises the fact that the same matter is already pending elsewhere, not all courts in all countries always respect the principle of *lis pendens*.

Should the first seized court not only uphold its jurisdiction over the dispute, but also come to a final decision on the merits, the bar for any other courts to take on the dispute becomes permanent. The principle of *res judicata* should be respected not only within the same country but across the globe and prevent the same parties from relitigating the same questions — at least to the extent that they have been decided by the first court — for a potentially different outcome.[15] An exception applies, of course, for the court holding appellate jurisdiction over the decision of the first court. Again, not all courts in all countries always respect the principle of *res judicata*.

In both cases, if a court accepts proceedings although the same matter is already pending elsewhere, or if a court accepts proceedings although the matter has been decided and the decision has become *res judicata* elsewhere, the resulting decision will usually be enforceable only in the country where the second seized court is

---

14. For details, see, for example, Campbell McLachlan, *Lis Pendens in International Litigation*, Martinus Nijhoff Publishers/Brill Academic Publishers 2009.

15. For further discussion, see Peter R. Barnett, *Res Judicata, Estoppel and Foreign Judgments — The Preclusive Effects of Foreign Judgments in Private International Law*, Oxford Univ. Press 2001.

located. If recognition and enforcement are sought elsewhere, the defendant in the second proceeding can usually rely on *lis pendens* and/or res judicata to prevent recognition and enforcement. However, this is not enough if the defendant in the second proceeding has assets in the country where the second seized court is located and cannot remove them in time.

2. Special Jurisdictions

In addition to the general jurisdiction of the defendant court, many legal systems provide special jurisdictions for special subject matters or cases. Such special jurisdictions are generally alternatives to the general jurisdiction at the domicile of the defendant. Thus, several courts within the same country may have jurisdiction over a given dispute, giving the plaintiff some limited choices. For example, in tort cases, many legal systems provide jurisdiction at the place where the tort was committed and/or where the damages occurred. The injured party, therefore, does not have to go to the domicile of the defendant, which may be far away, but can also bring the case where the tortious act occurred. Similarly, many legal systems provide consumer protection rules pursuant to which the consumer in a B2C transaction can sue at her own domicile and does not have to go to the merchant's domicile. Even for B2B transactions, some legal systems provide jurisdiction at the place where the contract was concluded or where it was to be performed. Some alternative forum choices based on special jurisdictions may also be available in international or transnational litigation.

Whenever several alternative jurisdictions are available, none of which is exclusive, the party making the first move gets to make the choice regarding the court to hear the dispute. As mentioned above, this is sometimes referred to as forum shopping.[16] The following case illustrates jurisdictional choices for certain parties.

Case 6-1

Handelskwekerij G.J. Bier BV v. Mines de Potasse d'Alsace SA

European Court of Justice, Case 21/76
Judgment of 30 November 1976, 1976 ECR 1735

The applicant operates a horticultural business in the Netherlands and uses water from the river Rhine for irrigation. The defendant is a potassium mine in France, some 700 km or 400+ miles upstream on the Rhine. The applicant is seeking compensation for damage done to its business by defendant's massive discharge of saline waste into the river. The applicant brought the case in front of the courts in the Netherlands. After the trial court declined jurisdiction, the applicants appealed and the Gerechtshof in the Hague referred a question about the interpretation of Article 5(3) of the Convention on Jurisdiction and the Enforcement of Judgments in Civil

---

16. For in-depth analysis, see Andrew Bell, *Forum Shopping and Venue in Transnational Litigation*, Oxford Univ. Press 2003.

and Commercial Matters (the "Brussels Convention") to the European Court of Justice. This Convention has meanwhile been replaced by EU Regulation 1215/2012 of 12 December 2012 on Jurisdiction and the Recognition and Enforcement of Judgments in Civil and Commercial Matters (the "Brussels I or I *bis* Regulation"), which is largely congruent to the earlier Brussels Convention but is directly applicable law in all EU Member States (see below, p. 713). The following are excerpts from the judgment:

[7] Article 5 of the Convention provides: 'A person domiciled in a Contracting State may, in another Contracting State, be sued: . . . (3) in matters relating to tort, delict or quasi-delict, in the courts for the place where the harmful event occurred'.

[8] That provision must be interpreted in the context of the scheme of conferment of jurisdiction which forms the subject-matter of Title II of the Convention.

[9] That scheme is based on a general rule, laid down by Article 2, that the courts of the State in which the defendant is domiciled shall have jurisdiction.

[10] However, Article 5 makes provision in a number of cases for a special jurisdiction, which the plaintiff may opt to choose.

[11] This freedom of choice was introduced having regard to the existence, in certain clearly defined situations, of a particularly close connecting factor between a dispute and the court which may be called upon to hear it, with a view to the efficacious conduct of the proceedings.

[12] Thus in matters of tort, delict or quasi-delict Article 5 (3) allows the plaintiff to bring his case before the courts for 'the place where the harmful event occurred'.

[13] In the context of the Convention, the meaning of that expression is unclear when the place of the event which is at the origin of the damage is situated in a State other than the one in which the place where the damage occurred is situated, as is the case inter *inter alia* with atmospheric or water pollution beyond the frontiers of a State.

[14] The form of words 'place where the harmful event occurred', used in all the language versions of the Convention, leaves open the question whether, in the situation described, it is necessary, in determining jurisdiction, to choose as the connecting factor the place of the event giving rise to the damage, or the place where the damage occurred, or to accept that the plaintiff has an option between the one and the other of those two connecting factors.

[15] As regards this, it is well to point out that the place of the event giving rise to the damage no less than the place where the damage occurred can, depending on the case, constitute a significant connecting factor from the point of view of jurisdiction.

[16] Liability in tort, delict or quasi-delict can only arise provided that a causal connexion can be established between the damage and the event in which that damage originates.

[17] Taking into account the close connexion between the component parts of every sort of liability, it does not appear appropriate to opt for one of the two connecting

factors mentioned to the exclusion of the other, since each of them can, depending on the circumstances, be particularly helpful from the point of view of the evidence and of the conduct of the proceedings.

[18] To exclude one option appears all the more undesirable in that, by its comprehensive form of words, Article 5 (3) of the Convention covers a wide diversity of kinds of liability.

[19] Thus the meaning of the expression 'place where the harmful event occurred' in Article 5 (3) must be established in such a way as to acknowledge that the plaintiff has an option to commence proceedings either at the place where the damage occurred or the place of the event giving rise to it.

[20] This conclusion is supported by the consideration, first, that to decide in favour only of the place of the event giving rise to the damage would, in an appreciable number of cases, cause confusion between the heads of jurisdiction laid down by Articles 2 and 5 (3) of the Convention, so that the latter provision would, to that extent, lose its effectiveness.

[21] Secondly, a decision in favour only of the place where the damage occurred would, in cases where the place of the event giving rise to the damage does not coincide with the domicile of the person liable, have the effect of excluding a helpful connecting factor with the jurisdiction of a court particularly near to the cause of the damage. . . .

[24] Thus it should be answered that where the place of the happening of the event which may give rise to liability in tort, delict or quasidelict and the place where that event results in damage are not identical, the expression 'place where the harmful event occurred', in Article 5 (3) of the Convention, must be understood as being intended to cover both the place where the damage occurred and the place of the event giving rise to it.

[25] The result is that the defendant may be sued, at the option of the plaintiff, either in the courts for the place where the damage occurred or in the courts for the place of the event which gives rise to and is at the origin of that damage.

Notes and Questions

1. In plain English, what is the European Court of Justice saying? Where can a case be brought by a plaintiff who claims to be the victim of a tortious act?

2. Why would the applicant fight a battle all the way to the European Court of Justice over the question of jurisdiction, instead of simply bringing the case in defendant court? What kind of benefits might a party gain from forum shopping?

3. The present case concerns a tort or delict situation and is in that regard different from most international business transactions. Why, then, is it in this book?

4. Look at the discussion of available forum choices in different countries (below, pp. 707 et seq.) and try to construct situations where a party to an international

business transaction may have similar opportunities for forum shopping as granted to the applicant in *Mines de Potasse d'Alsace*.

3. Exclusive Jurisdictions

For certain categories of cases or subject matter, many legal systems prescribe specific and exclusive jurisdiction. Such cases are exceptions to the principle that a case can always be brought in defendant court. Instead, only one court will be competent to hear the case, regardless of the domicile of the parties or the specifics of the case. The most common example is jurisdiction over immovable property, which most countries give exclusively to the court where the property is located. Other exclusive jurisdictions specified by many countries concern disputes over entries in public registers (the court where the register is kept), as well as disputes over status questions of corporations and other legal persons (the court where the entity is incorporated). If a country gives exclusive jurisdiction to a particular court, this not only excludes jurisdiction of other courts, but also of arbitral tribunals. These exclusive jurisdictions are largely undisputed. Thus, a judgment from a court that has exclusive jurisdiction will usually be recognized and enforced elsewhere and the recognition and enforcement of a competing judgment from another court, for example the defendant court, can be opposed because the other court did not have jurisdiction.

4. Exorbitant Jurisdictions

Because of the general principle that claims should be brought in defendant court, countries should not entertain lawsuits brought in places other than defendant's domicile, unless they have good reasons for doing so. While a number of special jurisdictions for the protection of injured or weaker parties, and certain exclusive jurisdictions where local ties matter, are all widely accepted, some countries allow applicants additional choices that are not so easily accepted elsewhere. These are commonly referred to as exorbitant jurisdictions because they go beyond what is mutually acceptable and infringe on the rights of other countries and their citizens. Clermont and Palmer define exorbitant jurisdictions as "classes of jurisdiction, although exercised validly under a country's rules, that nonetheless are unfair to the defendant because of a lack of significant connection between the sovereign and either the parties or the dispute."[17]

An example of an exorbitant jurisdiction is the French rule that a French citizen or corporation can always bring a lawsuit against a foreign party in France (Article 14 of the French Code Civil[18]). A summary of the jurisdictional options provided by the U.S. and some of its most important trading partners is provided below, at pp. 707–725.

---

17. See Kevin M. Clermont & John R.B. Palmer, *Exorbitant Jurisdiction*, Maine L. Rev., Vol. 58, No. 2, pp. 473–505, at p. 474.

18. A semi-official English version of the French Code Civil is available on the website of the French government, https://www.legifrance.gouv.fr.

While the party that is favored by an exorbitant jurisdiction may consider herself lucky, problems may soon occur when it comes to the recognition and enforcement of the resulting judgment. In general, the courts of a country will not recognize and enforce a foreign judgment, if they consider that the foreign court should not have exercised its jurisdiction. As a result, if a court entertains a lawsuit on the basis of an exorbitant jurisdiction, the resulting judgment will mainly be enforceable in that same country—provided, of course, that the defendant has assets there. If the defendant does not have assets in that country, it may well be a waste of time and money to go to court on the basis of an exorbitant jurisdiction.

5. *Different National Rules on Jurisdiction or Venue and the Attractiveness of a Particular Forum*

As we saw in Part Two, the parties to a B2B transaction can literally choose any legal system out of about 200 national legal systems and at least three international legal systems, and they can even craft their own. Of course, some choices of *law* are smarter than others but the freedom is virtually unlimited.

The same is not true for the choice of *forum*. While parties to a B2B transaction are almost always free to chose arbitration, including virtually any arbitration tribunal (see below, pp. 866 and 944), they cannot choose any court they want for the settlement of their dispute. If they could, one might expect a lot of cases from around the world going to just two dozen countries or so.[19] It is easy to see why this cannot work and why courts are usually reluctant to accept international cases. First, courts are public institutions and are usually supported by taxpayers of that country because court fees don't cover all expenses. This would make it problematic to allow almost anyone from around the world to bring their cases, especially if they are completely unrelated to the respective country or jurisdiction. Furthermore, courts are very busy and in many cases overburdened, resulting in long delays for litigants—another reason not to open the door for additional litigants that could and should go elsewhere. Third, international cases often pose additional problems—for example, if foreign law has to be applied, if documents are not available in the official language of the court, if witnesses are unwilling or unable to travel to the seat of the court, etc. This increases the risk for the judges and the courts to "get it wrong" and end up with criticism in spite of extraordinary expenditure of time and effort. Even if a foreign court were to accept jurisdiction over a dispute, there may be problems with recognition and enforcement of the judgment at the place of business of

---

19. For the most part, all the other countries and their courts and legal systems are not attractive fora for litigants—at least not for those that actually want to see their dispute settled in a fair and equitable way within a reasonable time. Either the legal systems and court procedures are excessively cumbersome and slow, or the outcomes are often unpredictable and seemingly arbitrary, leaving the losing party to speculate whether incompetence, corruption, or the actual law cost them their victory. For additional discussion, see below, p. 880, as well as Frank Emmert, *Global Failure of Justice Systems—Causes and Consequences*, available at https://www.researchgate .net/profile/Frank_Emmert2.

the parties. Finally, issues of procedural economy may need to be considered—for example, if the majority of documents and other evidence does not exist in the official language of a chosen court and/or if the parties, lawyers, and witnesses will all incur significant travel expenses to get to that court—as well as issues that make a court more or less attractive, as discussed above.

For these reasons, it is important for parties and their legal counsel to know which jurisdictions can be selected in which cases before a choice of forum is made in a contract clause.

The rules on whether or not an international case can be brought in a specific forum vary from one country to another and they evolve over time. Therefore, only some general guidelines can be provided here.[20]

Canada: The federal system of Canada is quite similar, in many respects, to the federal system in the U.S. Certain legislative powers belong to the provinces and will be exercised differently in some provinces than in others. Other legislative powers belong to the federal government and will be exercised for the entire territory of Canada. Also, Quebec—like the U.S. state of Louisiana—follows a civil law tradition and does not apply the common law that is applied by the other provinces, respectively the other U.S. states. One important difference is the power of the Supreme Court of Canada to hear appeals against the final decisions of the provincial courts of appeal. In so doing, the Supreme Court of Canada becomes the final arbiter of provincial law, as well as federal law.

To determine which of the many courts in Canada has jurisdiction over a particular dispute, a distinction is made whether the parties have included a "forum selection clause" in their business contract or not. Canadian courts have recognized "permissive" forum selection clauses that add an alternative forum to those available by law, as well as "mandatory" forum selection clauses that exclude any other fora. Like in the U.S., the Canadian courts treat inter-provincial cases essentially like international cases. The leading case in this regard is *Z.I. Pompey v. ECU Line.*[21] Polyfibron Technologies Inc. had purchased machines from Z.I. Pompey in France for shipment from Antwerp (Belgium) to Seattle (USA). Polyfibron engaged John James Co., a freight forwarder, to arrange for shipment and importation. John James hired SLMN Shipping in France, which in turn made arrangements with ECU Line Belgium for carriage by sea. The Bill of Lading stipulated "The contract evidenced by or contained in this bill of Lading [sic] is governed by the law of Belgium, and any claim or dispute arising hereunder or in connection herewith shall

---

20. For additional analysis, see Mukarrum Ahmed, *The Nature and Enforcement of Choice of Court Agreements: A Comparative Study,* Hart Publishing 2017; Adrian Briggs, *Agreements on Jurisdiction and Choice of Law,* Oxford Univ. Press 2008.

21. 2003 SCC 27, 2003 CSC 27, Supreme Court of Canada, judgment of May 1, 2003. For further discussion, see, *inter alia,* Geneviève Saumier & Jeffrey Bagg, *Forum Selection Clauses Before Canadian Courts: A Tale of Two (or Three?) Solitudes,* 46 UBC L. Rev. 439 (2013).

be determined by the courts in Antwerp and no other Courts."²² The general terms on the back of the BoL provided, *inter alia*, "(1) The Carrier may ant [sic] any time and without notice to the Merchant: use any means of transport or storage whatsoever; load or carry the Goods on any vessel whether named on the front hereof or not; transfer the Goods from one conveyance to another including transshipping or carrying the same on another vessel than that named on the front hereof or by any other means of transport whatsoever; at any place unpack and remove Goods which have been stuffed in or on a Container and forward the same in any manner whatsoever; proceed at any speed and by any route in his discretion (whether or not the nearest or most or customary or advertised route) and proceed to or stay at any place whatsoever once or more often and in any order; load or unload the Goods from any conveyance at any place (whether or not the place is a port named on the front hereof as the intended Port of Loading or intended Port of Discharge);.... (2) The liberties set out in (1) above be [sic] invoked by the Carrier for any purposes whatsoever whether or not connected with the Carriage of the Goods. Anything done accordance [sic] with (1) above or any delay arising therfrom [sic] shall be deemed to be within the contractual Carriage and shall not be a deviation or whatsoever nature or degree."²³

Instead of going all the way to Seattle by ship, the machines were unloaded in Montreal and carried by rail to Seattle. Upon arrival, they were damaged. Since a clean BoL had been issued in Antwerp, Pompey sued ECU Line in the Federal Court of Canada for some CA$60,000 in damages. ECU Line claimed, *inter alia*, that the dispute could only be decided by the courts of Antwerp. The trial court disagreed and eventually ECU Line brought the case before the Supreme Court of Canada.

In its decision, the Supreme Court of Canada referenced a well-known precedent from England:

¹⁹ Pursuant to s. 50(1) of the Federal Court Act, the court has the discretion to stay proceedings in any cause or matter on the ground that the claim is proceeding in another court or jurisdiction, or where, for any other reason, it is in the interest of justice that the proceedings be stayed. For some time, the exercise of this judicial discretion has been governed by the "strong cause" test when a party brings a motion for a stay of proceedings to enforce a forum selection clause in a bill of lading. Brandon J. set out the test as follows in "Eleftheria" (The),[24] at p. 242:

"(1) Where plaintiffs sue in England in breach of an agreement to refer disputes to a foreign Court, and the defendants apply for a stay, the English Court, assuming the claim to be otherwise within the jurisdiction, is not bound to grant a stay but has a discretion whether to do so or not. (2) The

22. Ibid., para. 4 of the judgment.
23. Ibid.
24. *Owners of Cargo Lately Laden on Board the Eleftheria v Owners of the Eleftheria*, Probate, Divorce & Admiralty Division, 31 January 1969, [1969] 2 W.L.R. 1073; [1969] 2 All E.R. 641; [1969] 1 Lloyd's Rep. 237, at 242; (1969) 113 S.J. 407.

discretion should be exercised by granting a stay unless strong cause for not doing so is shown. (3) The burden of proving such strong cause is on the plaintiffs. (4) In exercising its discretion the Court should take into account all the circumstances of the particular case. (5) In particular, but without prejudice to (4), the following matters, where they arise, may be properly regarded: (a) In what country the evidence on the issues of fact is situated, or more readily available, and the effect of that on the relative convenience and expense of trial as between the English and foreign Courts. (b) Whether the law of the foreign Court applies and, if so, whether it differs from English law in any material respects. (c) With what country either party is connected, and how closely. (d) Whether the defendants genuinely desire trial in the foreign country, or are only seeking procedural advantages. (e) Whether the plaintiffs would be prejudiced by having to sue in the foreign Court because they would (I) be deprived of security for that claim; (ii) be unable to enforce any judgment obtained; (iii) be faced with a time-bar not applicable in England; or (iv) for political, racial, religious or other reasons be unlikely to get a fair trial."

[20] Forum selection clauses are common components of international commercial transactions, and are particularly common in bills of lading. They have, in short, "been applied for ages in the industry and by the courts" .... These clauses are generally to be encouraged by the courts as they create certainty and security in transaction, derivatives of order and fairness, which are critical components of private international law.... The "strong cause" test remains relevant and effective and no social, moral or economic changes justify the departure advanced by the Court of Appeal. In the context of international commerce, order and fairness have been achieved at least in part by application of the "strong cause" test. This test rightly imposes the burden on the plaintiff to satisfy the court that there is good reason it should not be bound by the forum selection clause. It is essential that courts give full weight to the desirability of holding contracting parties to their agreements. There is no reason to consider forum selection clauses to be non-responsibility clauses in disguise. In any event, the "strong cause" test provides sufficient leeway for judges to take improper motives into consideration in relevant cases and prevent defendants from relying on forum selection clauses to gain an unfair procedural advantage. . . .

[29] Bills of lading are typically entered into by sophisticated parties familiar with the negotiation of maritime shipping transactions who should, in normal circumstances, be held to their bargain. . . . The parties in this appeal are corporations with significant experience in international maritime commerce. The respondents were aware of industry practices and could have reasonably expected that the bill of lading would contain a forum selection clause. A forum selection clause could very well have been negotiated with the appellant, in light of the respondent John S. James Co.'s insistence that S.L.M.N. Shipping transport the cargo solely by sea. There is no evidence that this bill of lading is the result of grossly uneven bargaining power that would invalidate the forum selection clause contained therein.

[The Supreme Court of Canada then had to address the question whether the BoL had terminated in Montreal and/or whether the deviation from the agreed-upon shipping route was a sufficiently serious breach of the shipping contract to invalidate the forum selection clause:]

[31] Issues respecting an alleged fundamental breach of contract or deviation therefrom should generally be determined under the law and by the court chosen by the parties in the bill of lading. The "strong cause test", once it is determined that the bill of lading otherwise binds the parties (for instance, that the bill of lading as it relates to jurisdiction does not offend public policy, was not the product of fraud or of grossly uneven bargaining positions), constitutes an inquiry into questions such as the convenience of the parties, fairness between the parties and the interests of justice, not of the substantive legal issues underlying the dispute. . . . Put differently, a court, in the context of an application for a stay to uphold a forum selection clause in a bill of lading, must not delve into whether one party has deviated from, or fundamentally breached an otherwise validly formed contract. Such inquiries would render forum selection clauses illusory since most disputes will involve allegations which, if proved, will make the agreement terminable or voidable by the aggrieved party. Moreover, while the choice of forum for the determination of the existence of the agreement would be made without reference to the forum selection clause in the contract, if the agreement were found to remain intact, resort to the said clause would presumably be necessary to decide the appropriate forum in which to settle the rights of the parties under the agreement.

[32] [To conclude otherwise] would remove many disputes from the reach of a widely framed forum selection clause by the mere allegation of various types of wrongful conduct. [Where] . . . the parties agree that claims or disputes arising under or in connection with a bill of lading are to "be determined by the courts in Antwerp and no other Courts", a proceeding in which one party contends that the other party deviated from the agreement such as to give the former the right to terminate or void the contract remains a proceeding in respect of a claim or dispute arising under or in connection with the bill of lading. . . .

[36] [In conclusion, there is no need to] address . . . the relationship between deviation and fundamental breach. Suffice it to say that, in this case, either allegation concerns a dispute arising under or in connection with the bill of lading. There is no need to consider the applicability of the doctrine of separability.

The situation is a bit different if the parties have not made a valid forum choice. The approach is, however, similar to the one taken in the U.S. The basic requirement has been formulated as follows:

> 1. An action must be brought before the court of the province, territory, state, or country with which the parties, the action, or the matter have a real and substantial connection.

> 2. Once it has jurisdiction, the court must apply the law that has the most real and substantial connection with the issue to be decided.

3. A foreign judgment will be recognized and enforced only if the original court had jurisdiction based on a real and substantial connection with the parties and/or the action.[25]

China: The courts in China are generally conservative when it comes to accepting cases with foreign elements, in particular if the choice of law is not for Chinese law and the language of the contract is anything other than Mandarin.[26] In addition, it is difficult and often impossible to get Chinese courts to enforce foreign judgments. Therefore, foreign parties entering into contracts with Chinese parties usually have only two options if they want to make sure that a decision in a dispute can be enforced in China: Either select a Chinese court as the exclusive jurisdiction by party choice, as well as Chinese law and Chinese language for the contract, or select international commercial arbitration. The choice of Chinese courts also has to be considered carefully. Many trial court judges in China, even today, are not lawyers but retired military officers. Since many companies in China are wholly or partly owned by the military, a foreign party cannot expect as self-evident that a trial court in China will give it a fair hearing and decision. Furthermore, in sufficiently important cases, Chinese judges may receive instructions directly from the Communist Party headquarters in Beijing. Against this background, even Chinese parties sometimes try to escape their own courts and include foreign forum choices in their contracts. A case in point was recently decided in China. A Chinese seller and a Chinese carrier had used a Bill of Lading for a shipment to Turkey with a choice of forum clause for Genova, Italy. When the seller sued the carrier in a Chinese court, the carrier disputed jurisdiction but the Chinese court declared the forum choice invalid. Under Chinese law, the parties to a contract can select the defendant's domicile, the applicant's domicile, the place where the contract was signed or has to be performed, the location of the subject matter, or any other location

---

25. See Jean-Gabriel Castel, *The Uncertainty Factor in Canadian Private International Law*, 52 McGill L.J. 555, at 557 (footnotes omitted). While Quebec has clear guidelines in its Civil Code of Quebec, the provinces relying on common law have seen many inconsistent decisions based on the real and substantial connection test. As Castel puts it, "[T]he application of the real and substantial connection test does not predict a single definite result when taking into account the many connecting factors present in a particular case. It can produce a variety of outcomes depending on their evaluation by different courts and makes it difficult, if not impossible, to achieve predictability and uniformity of result. Thus, a systematic application of the real and substantial connection test introduces an unavoidable element of uncertainty into private international law that is contrary to the objective of predictability of results so needed in international business.

Furthermore, the principle of proximity encourages forum shopping and prolongs litigation. Where there is an element of uncertainty, the door is open for a resourceful lawyer to attempt to change the application of the law; a clear rule of law, by contrast, promotes settlement. . . .

When jurisdiction, contracts, and foreign judgments are at issue, the result of the case will often depend on chance since, in the absence of prescribed connecting factors, the courts are usually analyzing and weighing facts. . . .

Consequently, private international law jurisprudence, in which courts apply the real and substantial connection test, is in disarray because the courts are often at odds with one another. . . ." (Ibid., pp. 557–558).

26. Additional analysis is provided by Guangjian Tu, *Private International Law in China*, Springer 2016.

that has an actual connection with the parties or the transaction as the place where a dispute has to be brought to court. Since neither Genova nor Italy had any connection to the case, the clause was held invalid and jurisdiction at the port of loading was established instead. See *Tianjin Maritime Court, People's Republic of China*, Case no. [2014] JHFSCZ No. 81-1, 17 April 2014.

European Union: The EU is progressively establishing an *Area of Freedom, Justice and Security* with a high level of cooperation between the courts and authorities of the Member States. Among the goals are the facilitation of access to justice for EU citizens across all 27 Member States, equal treatment for litigants regardless of nationality, and the automatic recognition and easy enforcement of judicial and extrajudicial decisions of the other Member States. With regard to the courts having jurisdiction over a dispute, the rules are different for cases where the defendant is domiciled in the EU versus cases where the defendant is not domiciled in the EU. The former fall under EU law, namely Regulation 1215/2012 of 12 December 2012 on Jurisdiction and the Recognition and Enforcement of Judgments in Civil and Commercial Matters, the so-called "Brussels Ia or I *bis* Regulation" (Documents, p. II-92).[27] By contrast, whether or not a case can be brought in an EU Member State against a defendant who is not domiciled in the EU is subject to the national law of the respective Member State.

Regulation 1215/2012 applies "in civil and commercial matters whatever the nature of the court or tribunal" (Art. 1(1)). It does not apply to "revenue, customs or administrative matters or to the liability of the State for acts and omissions in the exercise of State authority (*acta iure imperii*)" (Art. 1(1)). It also does not apply to:

(a) the status or legal capacity of natural persons, rights in property arising out of a matrimonial relationship or out of a relationship deemed by the law applicable to such relationship to have comparable effects to marriage;

(b) bankruptcy, proceedings relating to the winding-up of insolvent companies or other legal persons, judicial arrangements, compositions and analogous proceedings;

(c) social security;

(d) arbitration;

(e) maintenance obligations arising from a family relationship, parentage, marriage or affinity;[28]

---

27. As such, the Regulation only applies to the 27 Member States of the European Union. However, by virtue of the parallel provisions of the Lugano Convention, its effects are extended to Iceland, Norway, and Switzerland; see OJ 2007 L 339, p. 3, as well as the update in OJ 2009 L 147, p. 5.

For in-depth analysis, see Andrew Dickinson & Eva Lein, *The Brussels I Regulation Recast*, Oxford Univ. Press 2015; Peter Mankowski & Ulrich Magnus (eds.), *Brussels Ibis Regulation — European Commentaries on Private International Law*, Sellier European Law Publishers 2015.

28. Many of these issues are covered by the so-called "Brussels IIbis" *Regulation 2201/2003 Concerning Jurisdiction and the Recognition and Enforcement of Judgments in Matrimonial Matters and the Matters of Parental Responsibility*, OJ 2003 L 338, p. 1, as amended. For detailed analysis of

(f) wills and succession, including maintenance obligations arising by reason of death.[29]

Pursuant to Article 4(1) of the Regulation, "persons domiciled in a Member State shall, whatever their nationality, be sued in the courts of that Member State."[30] This is the general principle that disputes should be brought in defendant's court. However, in the following cases—and this list is finite—a person domiciled in one Member State may *alternatively* be sued in the courts of another Member State:

Article 7 [Alternative Non-Exclusive Jurisdictions]

(1)(a) in matters relating to a contract, in the courts for the place of performance of the obligation in question;

(b) for the purpose of this provision and unless otherwise agreed, the place of performance of the obligation in question shall be:

— in the case of the sale of goods, the place in a Member State where, under the contract, the goods were delivered or should have been delivered,

— in the case of the provision of services, the place in a Member State where, under the contract, the services were provided or should have been provided;

(c) if point (b) does not apply then point (a) applies;

(2) in matters relating to tort, delict or quasi-delict, in the courts for the place where the harmful event occurred or may occur;[31]

(3) as regards a civil claim for damages or restitution which is based on an act giving rise to criminal proceedings, in the court seised of those proceedings, to the extent that that court has jurisdiction under its own law to entertain civil proceedings;

(4) as regards a civil claim for the recovery, based on ownership, of a cultural object as defined in point 1 of Article 1 of Directive 93/7/EEC initiated by the person claiming the right to recover such an object, in the courts for the place where the cultural object is situated at the time when the court is seised;

---

that Regulation, see Ulrich Magnus & Peter Mankowski (eds.), *Brussels IIbis Regulation, European Commentaries on Private International Law*, Sellier, Munich 2012.

29. See Article 1(2) of the Regulation. For some of the matters not covered by Reg. 1215/2012 see Regulation 2201/2003, note 28 supra.

30. Pursuant to Article 62 of the Regulation, the notion of "domicile" is to be determined by the national law of the forum state. For legal persons, Article 63 of the Regulation provides a choice between "statutory seat," "central administration," and "principal place of business."

31. In the important judgment of 30 November 1976 in *Case 21/76 Handelskwekerij Bier v Mines de Potasse d'Alsace* [1976] ECR 1735, the European Court established the principle of ubiquity for tort cases. Pursuant to this principle, the injured party can choose between the courts of the place where the tortious act was committed and the courts of the place where the damages occurred. See above, p. 703.

(5) as regards a dispute arising out of the operations of a branch, agency or other establishment, in the courts for the place where the branch, agency or other establishment is situated;

(6) as regards a dispute brought against a settlor, trustee or beneficiary of a trust created by the operation of a statute, or by a written instrument, or created orally and evidenced in writing, in the courts of the Member State in which the trust is domiciled;

(7) as regards a dispute concerning the payment of remuneration claimed in respect of the salvage of a cargo or freight, in the court under the authority of which the cargo or freight in question:

(a) has been arrested to secure such payment; or

(b) could have been so arrested, but bail or other security has been given; provided that this provision shall apply only if it is claimed that the defendant has an interest in the cargo or freight or had such an interest at the time of salvage.

Article 8 [Jurisdiction for Related Claims]

A person domiciled in a Member State may also be sued:

(1) where he is one of a number of defendants, in the courts for the place where any one of them is domiciled, provided the claims are so closely connected that it is expedient to hear and determine them together to avoid the risk of irreconcilable judgments resulting from separate proceedings;

(2) as a third party in an action on a warranty or guarantee or in any other third-party proceedings, in the court seised of the original proceedings, unless these were instituted solely with the object of removing him from the jurisdiction of the court which would be competent in his case;

(3) on a counter-claim arising from the same contract or facts on which the original claim was based, in the court in which the original claim is pending;

(4) in matters relating to a contract, if the action may be combined with an action against the same defendant in matters relating to rights in rem in immovable property, in the court of the Member State in which the property is situated.

Articles 10–16 of the Regulation deal with special, non-exclusive, i.e., alternative jurisdictions "in matters relating to insurance" for the benefit of the insured parties; Articles 17–19 provides similar alternative jurisdictions for consumers, and Articles 20–23 for employees regarding disputes with their employers. A number of exclusive jurisdictions are regulated as follows:

Article 24 [Exclusive Jurisdictions Regardless of Domicile]

The following courts of a Member State shall have exclusive jurisdiction, regardless of the domicile of the parties:

(1) in proceedings which have as their object rights in rem in immovable property or tenancies of immovable property, the courts of the Member State in which the property is situated.

However, in proceedings which have as their object tenancies of immovable property concluded for temporary private use for a maximum period of six consecutive months, the courts of the Member State in which the defendant is domiciled shall also have jurisdiction, provided that the tenant is a natural person and that the landlord and the tenant are domiciled in the same Member State;

(2) in proceedings which have as their object the validity of the constitution, the nullity or the dissolution of companies or other legal persons or associations of natural or legal persons, or the validity of the decisions of their organs, the courts of the Member State in which the company, legal person or association has its seat. In order to determine that seat, the court shall apply its rules of private international law;

(3) in proceedings which have as their object the validity of entries in public registers, the courts of the Member State in which the register is kept;

(4) in proceedings concerned with the registration or validity of patents, trade marks, designs, or other similar rights required to be deposited or registered, irrespective of whether the issue is raised by way of an action or as a defence, the courts of the Member State in which the deposit or registration has been applied for, has taken place or is under the terms of an instrument of the Union or an international convention deemed to have taken place.

Without prejudice to the jurisdiction of the European Patent Office under the Convention on the Grant of European Patents, signed at Munich on 5 October 1973, the courts of each Member State shall have exclusive jurisdiction in proceedings concerned with the registration or validity of any European patent granted for that Member State;

(5) in proceedings concerned with the enforcement of judgments, the courts of the Member State in which the judgment has been or is to be enforced.

Finally, Articles 25 and 26 deal with prorogation, first by written agreement,[32] and second by entering an appearance without contesting the jurisdiction of the seized court (see below, pp. 759 et seq.). The full text of the Regulation is reproduced in the Documents Supplement (p. II-92). Its provisions can generally be taken as a reasonably good reflection of the most common rules of private international law found at the national level.

---

32. For further analysis, see Ilaria Queirolo, *Choice of Court Agreements in the New Brussels I-bis Regulation: A Critical Appraisal*, in Petar Šarčević et al. (eds.), *Yearbook of Private International Law*, Vol. XV, 2013/2014, pp. 113–142.

France: In cases where defendants are not in the EU, France allows French nationals and corporations to sue in France regardless of the rule that a suit should be brought in defendant court (Article 14 Code Civil). This is a very far-reaching exorbitant jurisdiction because it does not require any connection between the defendant and France.[33]

Germany: In cases where defendants are not in the EU, Germany allows a suit to be brought in German courts if the defendants have property in Germany regardless of the rule that a suit should be brought in defendant court. This is also an exorbitant jurisdiction, although it is not as far reaching as the French provision, since Germany does require some connection with the defendant before a case can be brought in Germany.

Hague Convention on Choice of Court Agreements (2005): Similar to EU Regulation 1215/2012 (the so-called Brussels I Regulation), the 2005 Hague Convention provides a summary of the internationally accepted principles on jurisdiction based on choice of court agreements, otherwise known as forum selection clauses. Although it has been ratified by and is binding on only 30 states, its provisions enjoy broader respect.[34] Article 3 defines an "exclusive choice of court agreement" as "an agreement concluded by two or more parties that . . . designates, for the purpose of deciding disputes which have arisen or may arise in connection with a particular legal relationship, the courts of one Contracting State or one or more specific courts of one Contracting State to the exclusion of the jurisdiction of any other courts." Such an agreement "shall be deemed to be exclusive unless the parties have expressly provided otherwise." It has to be in writing or "by any other means of communication which renders information accessible so as to be useable for subsequent reference." The 2005 Hague Convention also affirms the well-established principle of separability of the dispute settlement clause in its Article 3(d): "an exclusive choice of court agreement that forms part of a contract shall be treated as an agreement independent of the other terms of the contract. The validity of the exclusive choice of court agreement cannot be contested solely on the ground that the contract is not valid." Article 5 of the Convention stipulates:

> (1) The court or courts of a Contracting State designated in an exclusive choice of court agreement shall have jurisdiction to decide a dispute to which the agreement applies, unless the agreement is null and void under the law of that State.

---

33. For more information, see Sandie Calme, *French Private International Law*, Vandeplas Publ. 2nd ed. 2020.

34. The text of the Convention and a table of Contracting Parties is in the Documents collection at p. II-11. See also Stefan Reuter & Gerhard Wegen, *Das Haager Übereinkommen über Gerichtsstandsvereinbarungen vom 30. 6. 2005 — Entstehung, Charakteristika, Erfolgschancen*, Zeitschrift für Vergleichende Rechtswissenschaft 2017, pp. 382–417.

(2) A court that has jurisdiction under paragraph 1 shall not decline to exercise jurisdiction on the ground that the dispute should be decided in a court of another State.

Article 6 also contains rules for other courts, namely

A court of a Contracting State other than that of the chosen court shall suspend or dismiss proceedings to which an exclusive choice of court agreement applies unless

a) the agreement is null and void under the law of the State of the chosen court;

b) a party lacked the capacity to conclude the agreement under the law of the State of the court seised;

c) giving effect to the agreement would lead to a manifest injustice or would be manifestly contrary to the public policy of the State of the court seised;

d) for exceptional reasons beyond the control of the parties, the agreement cannot reasonably be performed; or

e) the chosen court has decided not to hear the case.

Finally, Articles 8 to 26 of the 2005 Hague Convention deal with recognition and enforcement of foreign judgments. Pursuant to Article 8(1) "A judgment given by a court of a Contracting State designated in an exclusive choice of court agreement shall be recognised and enforced in other Contracting States in accordance with this Chapter. Recognition or enforcement may be refused only on the grounds specified in this Convention."[35]

Italy: In cases where defendants are not in the EU, Italy goes even further than France and allows anyone with a domicile in Italy to sue in Italy, regardless of the rule that a suit should be brought in defendant court.[36] This is a very far-reaching exorbitant jurisdiction.

Mexico: Based on nationalist policy preferences, Mexico adopted rules in the 1930s excluding the application of foreign law by its courts and providing for jurisdiction over everyone domiciled in the country or otherwise personally present (*ad personam*). In the 1970s, Mexico started modernizing its private international law and ratified a number of Inter-American conventions. Based on Article 133 of the Mexican Constitution, these conventions enjoy supremacy throughout the country and can be invoked and must be respected and applied by every judge in the country. In the context of the ratification and implementation of NAFTA in 1988, Mexico

---

35. See also Trevor Harley: *Choice-of-Court Agreements Under the European Instruments and the Hague Convention—The Revised Brussels I Regulation, the Lugano Convention, and the Hague Convention*, Oxford Univ. Press 2013.

36. Legge n. 218, 31 May 1995, Art. 3. For discussion, see Andrea Giardina: *Italy: Reforming the Italian System of Private International Law*, 35 I.L.M. 760 (1996); as well as Irene Grassi: *The Reform of Italian Private International Law*, European J. L. Reform 1999, Vol. 1, No. ½, pp. 153–162.

reformed its private international law provisions, i.e., the rules on conflict of laws in the Federal Code of Civil Procedure, the Civil Code for the Federal District, and the Code of Civil Procedure for the Federal District. Since the states in Mexico tend to follow the codes applied in the Federal District, the reforms, for all practical purposes, cover the entire country. In essence, the reforms implement nine important Inter-American conventions in the area of private international law and simplify considerably the application of the rules. Among other changes, Mexican courts now have to apply foreign law if so required by an international convention (Article 12 Civil Code for the Federal District). Jurisdiction of Mexican courts is established primarily if the defendant is domiciled in the court district. However, it can also be established by "business ties, tortious action, or even a contract to be performed in the forum state."[37] By contrast, Mexico does not recognize so-called *transient jurisdiction* established by serving a defendant on a merely transient visit to the country.[38]

Switzerland: As mentioned earlier, Swiss conflict rules were largely based on case law until the codification of the Federal Act on Private International Law in 1987.[39] Not least because Switzerland is a party to the Lugano Convention, which largely parallels the provisions of EU Regulation 1215/2012 (see above, p. 713), the Swiss Federal Act on Private International Law is mainly applicable if at least one party to the dispute is domiciled outside of the area covered by the Lugano Convention, which comprises the 27 EU Member States, as well as Switzerland, Norway, Iceland, and Liechtenstein.[40] The Federal Act would apply, for example, to disputes between a U.S. and a Swiss party. Chapter 1 deals with general questions of jurisdiction and applicable law, as well as recognition and enforcement of foreign decisions. Chapter 2 deals with jurisdiction in matters of personal status. Chapter 3 covers issues related to marriage and divorce, including measures relating to marital property. A new Chapter 3a provides rules for registered partnerships. Chapter 4 deals with parent-child relationships, including adoption. Chapter 5 deals with guardianship and related matters. Chapter 6 covers inheritance. Chapter 7 provides rules for real property, moveable or personal property, as well as cultural property. Chapter 7a deals specifically with securities held by intermediaries. Chapter 8 covers intellectual property. Chapter 9 is of specific importance for IBTs because it deals with obligations arising from contracts, unjust enrichment, torts, and related matters. Chapter 9a contains specific rules for trusts. Chapter 10 deals with companies,

---

37. Jason Farber, *NAFTA and Personal Jurisdiction: A Look at the Requirements for Obtaining Personal Jurisdiction in the Three Signatory Nations*, Loy. L.A. Int'l & Comp. L. Rev. 1997, Vol. 19, No. 2, pp. 449–477, at p. 458.

38. Ibid. For transient jurisdiction in the U.S. see below, p. 722.

39. Swiss legislation is generally published in three official languages: German, French, and Italian. Thus, this title is not official but taken from the unofficial but widely used English translation provided by Andreas Bucher and available online at http://www.andreasbucher-law.ch/images /stories/pil_act_1987_as_amended_until_1_7_2014.pdf.

40. The 1988 Lugano Convention was revised in 2007 and can be found at https://www.rhf .admin.ch/rhf/de/home/zivilrecht/rechtsgrundlagen/sr-0-275-12.html in English, French, German, and Italian. Further official language versions can be accessed via the website of the EU.

including M&A transactions. Chapter 11 provides for bankruptcy cases. Finally, and this is of great interest given the importance of Switzerland as a seat of international arbitrations, Chapter 12 provides rules for international arbitration, including arbitrability of subject matter, validity of arbitration agreements, composition of arbitral tribunals, interim relief, evidence before arbitral tribunals, awards, and enforcement. To the best knowledge of this author, the Swiss Federal Act is the most comprehensive piece of legislation of its kind anywhere in the world.

United Arab Emirates (UAE), Saudi Arabia, and Gulf Cooperation Council (GCC): In general, the contract and commercial law systems of the Middle Eastern countries, with the exception of Israel, are based on the Egyptian Civil Code, which is a translation and adaptation of the French Code Civil, accomplished by the Egyptian scholar El Sanhuri in 1949 (see above, p. 119). Thus, as far as substantive law goes, international lawyers familiar with the continental European legal tradition, including the CISG, will find few surprises in the civil codes of Egypt, Syria, Lebanon, the UAE, and even Saudi Arabia. However, while Egypt, Syria, and Lebanon have traditionally trained judges, most judges in the UAE, Saudi Arabia, and the other GCC countries are mainly trained in Sharia or Islamic law. Since Sharia does not contain a sophisticated contract law regime, bringing a case before a court in the UAE, Kuwait, Bahrein, Qatar, Oman, or Saudi Arabia can lead to unexpected outcomes.

In an effort at attracting investment beyond oil and gas, the UAE has created a number of free zones where goods can be imported, stored, worked on, and re-exported largely without incurring duties or taxes. By contrast to free zones in most other countries, the free zones in the UAE are also largely exempt from the application of the UAE legal system, including the usual 51% local ownership requirements and the problematic *kafala* employment system. Interestingly, at least one of these free zones, the Dubai International Finance Center (DIFC), also has its own courts, which are largely staffed by retired English judges who hear and decide cases in English, and essentially apply a mix of English and international trade law. Originally, the DIFC courts only had jurisdiction over parties domiciled in the DIFC free zone. However, on the basis of a law adopted in 2011, the DIFC courts are allowed to accept cases from outside the zone if the parties have made a valid choice of court agreement to that effect. Thus, at least in theory, parties doing business in the UAE now have a choice between the regular state courts applying UAE law and the DIFC courts applying English common law. Enforcement of the DIFC judgments in the UAE should be unproblematic. Enforcement across the GCC should be reasonably easy, provided the decisions do not conflict with Sharia.[41]

After the Sharia courts in Saudi Arabia were criticized for some decisions that did not align with international law and practice—for example, the denial of IP

---

41. For more information, see Amgad Husein & Jonathan Burns, *Choice of Forum in Contracts with Saudi Arabian Counterparties: An Analysis of the DIFC Common Law Courts from a Saudi Arabian Perspective*, The Int'l Lawyer 2015, Vol. 48, No. 3, pp. 179–190.

licensing fees because of the judge's conviction that any secular music is incompatible with Sharia — the Saudi government has recently begun creating "Committees" charged with the settlement of certain types of cases. For example, the Banking Disputes Committee is now in charge of disputes between banks and their customers and can even enforce contracts that provide for payment of interest. Another Committee has been established to take charge of the recognition and enforcement of foreign judgments and arbitral awards, which previously were subject to review on the merits for Sharia compliance before the Board of Grievances.

United Kingdom: The UK grants jurisdiction to its courts if the document instituting the proceedings has been served on the defendant during a temporary presence in the UK, if the defendant has property in the UK, and/or if the plaintiff was able to seize property of the defendant in the UK. These are also far-reaching exorbitant jurisdictions; however, they maintain at least a minimum level of connection of the defendant to the UK.

United States: In the United States, the subject of "private international law" is generally referred to as "conflict of laws" and deals with the questions of jurisdiction, choice of law, and recognition and enforcement of judgments. By and large, the rules applicable to parties from different U.S. states (interstate cases) are applied also to parties from different countries (international cases). Within the U.S. and between federal and state courts, the party choices are not unlimited however, even in B2B cases. Although parties may opt for a certain court and set of laws, the rules on venue and jurisdiction have the final say on which courts — in a geographic sense — can be called upon to hear a case and which courts — state or federal — are competent to hear certain subject matter, respectively. These rules may override the desire and choices of the parties.

U.S. federal courts[42] have jurisdiction to hear cases about federal questions[43] and in diversity cases.[44] In all other cases, the courts of the states have jurisdiction. Until

---

42. The U.S. has 94 district courts (trial level), 13 circuit courts (appellate), and one Supreme Court. In addition, the United States Court of International Trade in New York has exclusive jurisdiction (at the first instance or trial level) to hear cases regarding U.S. customs and trade laws and the United States Court of Federal Claims in Washington, D.C., has exclusive jurisdiction (at the first instance or trial level) over claims against the federal government. The Court of Appeals for the Federal Circuit has exclusive jurisdiction to hear appeals against the decisions of these two courts, and over certain specialized cases, for example involving patents.

43. Article III of the U.S. Constitution is the original source for federal question jurisdiction. It provides that the "judicial power shall extend to all cases, in Law and Equity, arising under this Constitution, the Laws of the United States, and Treaties made, or which shall be made, under their Authority." These jurisdictional bases have been subsequently codified in U.S. Code Title 28 — Judiciary and Judicial Procedure, specifically in Chapter 81 on the Supreme Court (§§ 1251 to 1260), Chapter 83 on the Federal Courts of Appeals (§§ 1291 to 1296), and Chapter 85 on Federal District Courts (§§ 1330 to 1369).

44. So-called diversity cases involving "citizens of different States" of the U.S., "citizens of a State and citizens or subjects of a foreign state" unless the foreigner is "lawfully admitted for permanent residence in the United States and are domiciled in the same State [as the other party],"

the middle of the twentieth century, jurisdiction depended on the closest territorial link.[45] In 1945, the Supreme Court decided *International Shoe Co. v. Washington*,[46] wherein it fashioned the idea that a state has jurisdiction over a nonresident if that nonresident had "minimum contacts" with the state. Subsequent cases involving foreign litigants applied the *International Shoe* requirements to the foreign litigants the same way it was applied in interstate cases.[47]

In the federal code as well as in the various state common laws, jurisdiction of a particular court over a defendant is, therefore, established by "the requirement that the defendant 'have certain minimum contacts with [the forum] such that maintenance of the suit does not offend *traditional notions of fair play and substantial justice.*'"[48] The latter condition is usually referred to as the due process clause.

The problem is that "minimum contacts" offers a myriad of interpretations and this generates about 500 cases per year focusing on the question of personal jurisdiction if a suit involves at least one party from another U.S. state—the Restatement speaks of a "sister State"—or a foreign country.[49]

One specific example of minimum contact is the rule in 28 U.S. Code § 1391(b) (3), also referred to as *transient jurisdiction,* because it gives a court powers over a foreign defendant merely because she was served with process in the court district, even if she only came for a brief visit.[50] This is generally considered an exorbitant jurisdiction.

The laws of many states of the U.S. not only mirror the jurisdictional rules of the federal courts but go further to include so-called *attachment jurisdiction*, which can be established by arresting someone's property located in the state,[51] as well as

---

as well as "citizens of different States and in which citizens or subjects of a foreign state are additional parties" (28 U.S. Code § 1332 (a)) can be brought directly in federal district court or can be removed from a State court to a Federal district court, as long as "the matter in controversy exceeds the sum or value of $75,000, exclusive of interests and costs" (ibid.).

45. *Pennoyer v. Neff*, 95 U.S. 714 (1877).

46. *Int'l Shoe Co. v. Washington*, 326 U.S. 310 (1945).

47. For further analysis, see Gary B. Born, *Reflections on Judicial Jurisdiction in International Cases*, 17 Ga. J. Int'l & Comp. L. 1 (1987).

48. Peter Hay, Russel J. Weintraub & Patrick J. Bochers, *Conflict of Laws—Cases and Materials*, 12th ed. 2004, at p. 4, citing the U.S. Supreme Court decision in *Int'l Shoe v. Washington*, 326 U.S. 310 (1945).

49. Hay, Weintraub & Borchers, p. 4. Restatement (Second) of Conflict of Laws (1971), §§ 93-121.

50. Transient jurisdiction was upheld when a New Jersey resident was served while visiting his children in another state; see *Burnham v. Superior Court of California, Cty. of Marin*, 495 U.S. 604 (1990). This was later applied to defendants from other countries. For comments see Peter Hay, *Transient Jurisdiction, Especially Over International Defendants: Critical Comments on* Burnham v. Superior Court of California, 1990 U. Ill. L. Rev. 593 (1990).

51. The Supreme Court requires some kind of "reasonableness test," however, if the presence of the property is the only connection of the defendant to the State, see *Shaffer v. Heitner*, 433 U.S. 186 (1977).

jurisdiction based on the fact that the defendant was "doing business" in the state.[52] An extreme example is provided by the *Asahi Metal* case. Asahi manufactured valve assemblies for tires in Japan and sold them to Cheng Shin, a tire manufacturer in Taiwan. Some of the Taiwanese tires eventually found their way into the U.S. Asahi was aware of the tire sales to the U.S. but "never contemplated that its sales to Cheng Shin in Taiwan would subject it to lawsuits in California." When a tire from Taiwan failed and caused an accident in California, a product liability case was brought *inter alia* against Asahi. The California Supreme Court decided that "[Asahi's] intentional act of placing its assemblies into the stream of commerce by delivering them to Cheng Shin in Taiwan, coupled with its awareness that some of them would eventually reach California, were sufficient to support state court jurisdiction."[53]

A good summary of the state rules is provided in the Restatement (Second) of Conflict of Laws.

Whether a particular federal district court or a particular state court is also the appropriate *venue*—or whether this particular court is a *forum non conveniens*[54] and another court with jurisdiction would be more appropriate—is a separate question, however. Pursuant to 28 U.S. Code § 1391

> (b) Venue in General.—A civil action may be brought in—(1) a judicial district in which any defendant resides, if all defendants are residents of the State in which the district is located; (2) a judicial district in which a substantial part of the events or omissions giving rise to the claim occurred,

---

52. The question whether it is enough if a foreign company has a website that can be accessed and through which orders can be placed from the U.S. to establish jurisdiction based on their "doing business" in the U.S. is discussed below at pp. 741–744.

53. Judgment (en banc) of 25 July 1985; 39 Cal.3d 35, 216 Cal.Rptr. 385, 702 P.2d 543. The decision was reversed by the U.S. Supreme Court, see *Asahi Metal Industry v. Superior Court of California*, 107 S.Ct. 1026. It found that ". . . Asahi does not do business in California. It has no office, agents, employees, or property in California. It does not advertise or otherwise solicit business in California. It did not create, control, or employ the distribution system that brought its valves to California. . . . There is no evidence that Asahi designed its product in anticipation of sales in California. . . . On the basis of these facts, the exertion of personal jurisdiction over Asahi by the Superior Court of California exceeds the limits of due process. . . . [T]he determination of the reasonableness of the exercise of jurisdiction in each case will depend on an evaluation of several factors. A court must consider the burden on the defendant, the interests of the forum State, and the plaintiff's interest in obtaining relief. It must also weigh in its determination 'the interstate judicial system's interest in obtaining the most efficient resolution of controversies; and the shared interest of the several States in furthering fundamental substantive social policies.' *World-Wide Volkswagen*, 444 U.S., at 292, 100 S.Ct., at 564." It is easy to see that these criteria are not exactly straightforward and international enterprises should not assume that they are safe from the approach taken by the California court.

54. "The doctrine that an appropriate forum—even though competent under the law—may divest itself of jurisdiction if, for the convenience of the litigants and the witnesses, it appears that the action should proceed in another forum in which the action might also have been properly brought in the first place." *Forum non conveniens, Black's Law Dictionary* (10th ed. 2014). For comprehensive analysis see Ronald Brand & Scott Jablonski: *Forum Non Conveniens: History, Global Practice, and Future under the Hague Convention on Choice of Court Agreements*, Oxford 2007.

or a substantial part of property that is the subject of the action is situated; or (3) if there is no district in which an action may otherwise be brought as provided in this section, any judicial district in which any defendant is subject to the court's personal jurisdiction with respect to such action.

(c) Residency.—For all venue purposes—(1) a natural person, including an alien lawfully admitted for permanent residence in the United States, shall be deemed to reside in the judicial district in which that person is domiciled; (2) an entity with the capacity to sue and be sued in its common name under applicable law, whether or not incorporated, shall be deemed to reside, if a defendant, in any judicial district in which such defendant is subject to the court's personal jurisdiction with respect to the civil action in question and, if a plaintiff, only in the judicial district in which it maintains its principal place of business; and (3) a defendant not resident in the United States may be sued in any judicial district, and the joinder of such a defendant shall be disregarded in determining where the action may be brought with respect to other defendants.

The Supreme Court decision in *Piper Aircraft Co. v. Reyno*,[55] (below, p. 727), and the additional cases mentioned in the Notes and Questions, provide a general discussion of venue and *forum non conveniens* as applied today in the U.S. federal courts.

Given the federal structure of the U.S. and the fact that contract law exists both at the federal and state levels, the complicated rules on jurisdiction and venue have a direct impact on the applicable substantive law if the parties have not made a valid choice of law in an IBT. In the absence of a valid party choice, the applicable law inside the U.S. is determined by conflict rules and the courts in one jurisdiction, whether a federal court or the courts of a particular state of the U.S., do not automatically apply their own law to every case that comes before them. In 1938, the Supreme Court decided in *Erie R. Co. v. Tompkins* that in a case involving diversity, federal courts are to apply state law rather than federal law on substance but may apply federal procedural rules.[56] Thus, although a case may be decided by a federal district court, the law applied may be specific to a particular state. The question *which* state law, if several states have a connection to the case, is only one of the many problems resulting from the *Erie* doctrine.[57] This makes it all the more

---

55. *Piper Aircraft Co. v. Reyno*, 454 U.S. 235 (1981).

56. *Erie R. Co. v. Tompkins*, 304 U.S. 64 (1938) (a federal court applies federal procedural law but state substantive law, except in certain circumstances).

57. The literature on the *Erie* doctrine is vast and it would exceed the scope of the present book even to try to list the most important or influential articles that analyze it. The following quote shall suffice to give the uninitiated readers an idea of the problem: "The *Erie* doctrine is still a minefield. It has long been a source of frustration for scholars and students. . . . In its present form, the *Erie* doctrine fails to protect any coherent vision of the structural interests that supposedly are at its core—federalism, separation of powers, and equality." Alan M. Trammell, *Toil and Trouble: How the* Erie *Doctrine Became Structurally Incoherent (and How Congress Can Fix It)*, 82 Fordham L. Rev. 3249 (2013–2014), at p. 3249.

important that parties include a valid choice of law in their contracts whenever one or both of them, or the transaction itself, has a connection to the U.S.[58]

After this overview of the options available in different countries, we now turn specifically to the attractiveness of some courts versus others from the point of view of the parties. There are a number of considerations that make a particular court attractive or unattractive.

For the plaintiff or applicant, it is usually important to get a favorable outcome within the shortest possible time and at the lowest possible cost, provided it is also effectively enforceable against the defendant or respondent. On the other hand, the defendant or respondent would usually not want the proceedings to begin in the first place, to be slow if they cannot be avoided, and to result in a decision that is either unfavorable for the plaintiff or at least hard to enforce against the defendant or respondent.

Thus, a plaintiff and a defendant will be looking at the following qualities, for some of which the interests will be aligned (=) and for others, they will be diametrically opposed (↔):

Chart 6-1
Party Interests in International Commercial Litigation

Plaintiff wants		Defendant wants
proximity to plaintiff to keep his travel expenses low	↔	proximity to defendant to keep her travel expenses low and (potentially) discourage the plaintiff from bringing the case in the first place
court fees known to be reasonable or low	=	although higher court fees may discourage the plaintiff, they will either be shared by both parties or shifted to the losing party in the end
working language of the court corresponds to the language used by the parties in their agreement and the language of any other relevant documents, witnesses, etc. to avoid or reduce translation and interpretation expenses	=	although anticipated higher expenses for translation and interpretation may discourage the plaintiff, they will either be shared by both parties or shifted to the losing party in the end

---

58. The U.S. has signed but not ratified yet the 2005 Hague Convention on Choice of Court Agreements (see above, p. 717). The validity and effects of party agreements on choice of court are, therefore, subject to U.S. law alone. By contrast, party agreements choosing arbitration are binding on the U.S. pursuant to the 1958 New York Convention (see below, pp. 1014 et seq., as well as Documents, p. II-500).

Plaintiff wants		Defendant wants
jurisdiction over both parties and the subject matter not in question	?	although doubts about jurisdiction may discourage the plaintiff, a useless lawsuit in the wrong forum as a prelude to another lawsuit in the right forum will invariably add expenses for both parties
favorable rules on access to court, including quick and easy service on the defendant	↔	stricter or narrower rules on access to court and more cumbersome rules on service may discourage the plaintiff
familiarity of the plaintiff and his counsel with procedural rules applied by the court; ideally, plaintiff's usual legal counsel is admitted to practice before the court	↔	familiarity of the defendant and her counsel with procedural rules applied by the court; ideally, defendant's usual legal counsel is admitted to practice before the court
familiarity of the court with the substantive law to be applied to the case on account of party agreement or rules of private int'l law	=	familiarity of the court with the substantive law avoids surprises, which can always go both ways
duration of proceedings known to be reasonable or short	?	although lengthy trials can be in defendant's interest, delaying any negative outcomes of a trial, it is often not in the best interest of a business to have claims pending against it; inefficient proceedings also add expenses and may be detrimental to any counterclaims
any bias of the judges and/or the procedural law and/or the substantive law to be applied would be in favor of the plaintiff or at least not to his disadvantage	↔	any bias of the judges and/or the procedural law and/or the substantive law to be applied would be in favor of the defendant or at least not to her disadvantage
enforceability of the decision is virtually guaranteed against the defendant on account of location of defendant assets and/or well-functioning agreements for mutual recognition and enforcement of judgments with the country or countries where any assets are located	↔	if easy enforceability is by no means guaranteed, the plaintiff may settle for a much smaller amount than he did or might get from a judgment; if a counterclaim is brought, the defendant becomes the plaintiff and things reverse

As a result of this distribution of interests, business parties located in different countries, at least if they are basically fair-minded and interested in continuing the business relationship, should actually agree on neutral and efficient third-country courts familiar with the language of their transactions. Since international business is, by and large, conducted in English these days, many parties might want to go to court in the UK or the U.S., even if they have few or no connections to these countries, potentially placing a heavy burden on these courts.

6. Forum Non Conveniens

One way national legal systems and national courts can control the influx of foreign cases is via the doctrine of *forum non conveniens*. The following case includes a good discussion of the doctrine.

Case 6-2

Piper Aircraft Co. v. Reyno

454 U.S. 235 (1981)
(Paragraph numbers added, some footnotes omitted.)
JUSTICE MARSHALL delivered the opinion of the Court.

[1] These cases arise out of an air crash that took place in Scotland. Respondent, acting as representative of the estates of several Scottish citizens killed in the accident, brought wrongful-death actions against petitioners that were ultimately transferred to the United States District Court for the Middle District of Pennsylvania. Petitioners moved to dismiss on the ground of *forum non conveniens*. After noting that an alternative forum existed in Scotland, the District Court granted their motions. 479 F. Supp. 727 (1979). The United States Court of Appeals for the Third Circuit reversed. 630 F.2d 149 (1980). The Court of Appeals based its decision, at least in part, on the ground that dismissal is automatically barred where the law of the alternative forum is less favorable to the plaintiff than the law of the forum chosen by the plaintiff. Because we conclude that the possibility of an unfavorable change in law should not, by itself, bar dismissal, and because we conclude that the District Court did not otherwise abuse its discretion, we reverse.

I. A

[2] In July 1976, a small commercial aircraft crashed in the Scottish highlands during the course of a charter flight from Blackpool to Perth. The pilot and five passengers were killed instantly. The decedents were all Scottish subjects and residents, as are their heirs and next of kin. There were no eyewitnesses to the accident. At the time of the crash the plane was subject to Scottish air traffic control.

[3] The aircraft, a twin-engine Piper Aztec, was manufactured in Pennsylvania by petitioner Piper Aircraft Co. (Piper). The propellers were manufactured in Ohio by petitioner Hartzell Propeller, Inc. (Hartzell). At the time of the crash the aircraft was registered in Great Britain and was owned and maintained by Air Navigation

and Trading Co., Ltd. (Air Navigation). It was operated by McDonald Aviation, Ltd. (McDonald), a Scottish air taxi service. Both Air Navigation and McDonald were organized in the United Kingdom. The wreckage of the plane is now in a hangar in Farnsborough, England.

[4] The British Department of Trade investigated the accident shortly after it occurred. A preliminary report found that the plane crashed after developing a spin, and suggested that mechanical failure in the plane or the propeller was responsible. At Hartzell's request, this report was reviewed by a three-member Review Board, which held a 9-day adversary hearing attended by all interested parties. The Review Board found no evidence of defective equipment and indicated that pilot error may have contributed to the accident. The pilot, who had obtained his commercial pilot's license only three months earlier, was flying over high ground at an altitude considerably lower than the minimum height required by his company's operations manual.

[5] In July 1977, a California probate court appointed respondent Gaynell Reyno administratrix of the estates of the five passengers. Reyno is not related to and does not know any of the decedents or their survivors; she was a legal secretary to the attorney who filed this lawsuit. Several days after her appointment, Reyno commenced separate wrongful-death actions against Piper and Hartzell in the Superior Court of California, claiming negligence and strict liability. Air Navigation, McDonald, and the estate of the pilot are not parties to this litigation. The survivors of the five passengers whose estates are represented by Reyno filed a separate action in the United Kingdom against Air Navigation, McDonald, and the pilot's estate. Reyno candidly admits that the action against Piper and Hartzell was filed in the United States because its laws regarding liability, capacity to sue, and damages are more favorable to her position than are those of Scotland. Scottish law does not recognize strict liability in tort. Moreover, it permits wrongful-death actions only when brought by a decedent's relatives. The relatives may sue only for "loss of support and society."

[6] On petitioners' motion, the suit was removed to the United States District Court for the Central District of California. Piper then moved for transfer to the United States District Court for the Middle District of Pennsylvania, pursuant to 28 U.S.C. 1404(a).[4] Hartzell moved to dismiss for lack of personal jurisdiction, or in the alternative, to transfer. . . .

B

[7] In May 1978, after the suit had been transferred, both Hartzell and Piper moved to dismiss the action on the ground of *forum non conveniens*. The District Court granted these motions in October 1979. It relied on the balancing test set forth by

---

4. Section 1404(a) provides: "For the convenience of parties and witnesses, in the interest of justice, a district court may transfer any civil action to any other district or division where it might have been brought."

this Court in *Gulf Oil Corp. v. Gilbert*, 330 U.S. 501 (1947), and its companion case, *Koster v. Lumbermens Mut. Cas. Co.*, 330 U.S. 518 (1947). In those decisions, the Court stated that a plaintiff's choice of forum should rarely be disturbed. However, when an alternative forum has jurisdiction to hear the case, and when trial in the chosen forum would "establish . . . oppressiveness and vexation to a defendant . . . out of all proportion to plaintiff's convenience," or when the "chosen forum [is] inappropriate because of considerations affecting the court's own administrative and legal problems," the court may, in the exercise of its sound discretion, dismiss the case. *Koster, supra*, at 524. To guide trial court discretion, the Court provided a list of "private interest factors" affecting the convenience of the litigants, and a list of "public interest factors" affecting the convenience of the forum. *Gilbert*, supra, at 508–509.[6]

[8] After describing our decisions in *Gilbert* and *Koster*, the District Court analyzed the facts of these cases. It began by observing that an alternative forum existed in Scotland; Piper and Hartzell had agreed to submit to the jurisdiction of the Scottish courts and to waive any statute of limitations defense that might be available. It then stated that plaintiff's choice of forum was entitled to little weight. The court recognized that a plaintiff's choice ordinarily deserves substantial deference. It noted, however, that Reyno "is a representative of foreign citizens and residents seeking a forum in the United States because of the more liberal rules concerning products liability law," and that "the courts have been less solicitous when the plaintiff is not an American citizen or resident, and particularly when the foreign citizens seek to benefit from the more liberal tort rules provided for the protection of citizens and residents of the United States." 479 F. Supp., at 731.

[9] The District Court next examined several factors relating to the private interests of the litigants, and determined that these factors strongly pointed towards Scotland as the appropriate forum. Although evidence concerning the design, manufacture, and testing of the plane and propeller is located in the United States, the connections with Scotland are otherwise "overwhelming." *Id.*, at 732. The real parties in interest are citizens of Scotland, as were all the decedents. Witnesses who could testify regarding the maintenance of the aircraft, the training of the pilot, and the investigation of the accident—all essential to the defense—are in Great Britain.

---

6. The factors pertaining to the private interests of the litigants included the "relative ease of access to sources of proof; availability of compulsory process for attendance of unwilling, and the cost of obtaining attendance of willing, witnesses; possibility of view of premises, if view would be appropriate to the action; and all other practical problems that make trial of a case easy, expeditious and inexpensive." *Gilbert*, 330 U.S., at 508 . The public factors bearing on the question included the administrative difficulties flowing from court congestion; the "local interest in having localized controversies decided at home"; the interest in having the trial of a diversity case in a forum that is at home with the law that must govern the action; the avoidance of unnecessary problems in conflict of laws, or in the application of foreign law; and the unfairness of burdening citizens in an unrelated forum with jury duty. Id., at 509.

Moreover, all witnesses to damages are located in Scotland. Trial would be aided by familiarity with Scottish topography, and by easy access to the wreckage.

[10] The District Court reasoned that because crucial witnesses and evidence were beyond the reach of compulsory process, and because the defendants would not be able to implead potential Scottish third-party defendants, it would be "unfair to make Piper and Hartzell proceed to trial in this forum." *Id.*, at 733. The survivors had brought separate actions in Scotland against the pilot, McDonald, and Air Navigation. "[I]t would be fairer to all parties and less costly if the entire case was presented to one jury with available testimony from all relevant witnesses." Ibid. Although the court recognized that if trial were held in the United States, Piper and Hartzell could file indemnity or contribution actions against the Scottish defendants, it believed that there was a significant risk of inconsistent verdicts.[7]

[11] The District Court concluded that the relevant public interests also pointed strongly towards dismissal. The court determined that Pennsylvania law would apply to Piper and Scottish law to Hartzell if the case were tried in the Middle District of Pennsylvania.[8] As a result, "trial in this forum would be hopelessly complex and confusing for a jury." *Id.*, at 734. In addition, the court noted that it was unfamiliar with Scottish law and thus would have to rely upon experts from that country. The court also found that the trial would be enormously costly and time-consuming; that it would be unfair to burden citizens with jury duty when the Middle District of Pennsylvania has little connection with the controversy; and that Scotland has a substantial interest in the outcome of the litigation.

[12] In opposing the motions to dismiss, respondent contended that dismissal would be unfair because Scottish law was less favorable. The District Court explicitly rejected this claim. It reasoned that the possibility that dismissal might lead to an unfavorable change in the law did not deserve significant weight; any deficiency in the foreign law was a "matter to be dealt with in the foreign forum." *Id.*, at 738.

---

7. The District Court explained that inconsistent verdicts might result if petitioners were held liable on the basis of strict liability here, and then required to prove negligence in an indemnity action in Scotland. Moreover, even if the same standard of liability applied, there was a danger that different juries would find different facts and produce inconsistent results.

8. Under *Klaxon v. Stentor Electric Mfg. Co.*, 313 U.S. 487 (1941), a court ordinarily must apply the choice-of-law rules of the State in which it sits. However, where a case is transferred pursuant to 28 U.S.C. 1404(a), it must apply the choice-of-law rules of the State from which the case was transferred. *Van Dusen v. Barrack*, 376 U.S. 612 (1946). Relying on these two cases, the District Court concluded that California choice-of-law rules would apply to Piper, and Pennsylvania choice-of-law rules would apply to Hartzell. It further concluded that California applied a "governmental interests" analysis in resolving choice-of-law problems, and that Pennsylvania employed a "significant contacts" analysis. The court used the "governmental interests" analysis to determine that Pennsylvania liability rules would apply to Piper, and the "significant contacts" analysis to determine that Scottish liability rules would apply to Hartzell.

C

[13] On appeal, the United States Court of Appeals for the Third Circuit reversed and remanded for trial. The decision to reverse appears to be based on two alternative grounds. First, the Court held that the District Court abused its discretion in conducting the *Gilbert* analysis. Second, the Court held that dismissal is never appropriate where the law of the alternative forum is less favorable to the plaintiff.

[14] The Court of Appeals began its review of the District Court's *Gilbert* analysis by noting that the plaintiff's choice of forum deserved substantial weight, even though the real parties in interest are nonresidents. It then rejected the District Court's balancing of the private interests. It found that Piper and Hartzell had failed adequately to support their claim that key witnesses would be unavailable if trial were held in the United States: they had never specified the witnesses they would call and the testimony these witnesses would provide. The Court of Appeals gave little weight to the fact that Piper and Hartzell would not be able to implead potential Scottish third-party defendants, reasoning that this difficulty would be "burdensome" but not "unfair," *639 F.2d, at 162.*[9] Finally, the court stated that resolution of the suit would not be significantly aided by familiarity with Scottish topography, or by viewing the wreckage.

[15] The Court of Appeals also rejected the District Court's analysis of the public interest factors. It found that the District Court gave undue emphasis to the application of Scottish law: "'the mere fact that the court is called upon to determine and apply foreign law does not present a legal problem of the sort which would justify the dismissal of a case otherwise properly before the court.'" *Id.*, at 163 (quoting *Hoffman v. Goberman*, 420 F.2d 423, 427 (CA3 1970)). In any event, it believed that Scottish law need not be applied. After conducting its own choice-of-law analysis, the Court of Appeals determined that American law would govern the actions against both Piper and Hartzell.[10] The same choice-of-law analysis apparently led it to conclude that Pennsylvania and Ohio, rather than Scotland, are the jurisdictions with the greatest policy interests in the dispute, and that all other public interest factors favored trial in the United States.[11]

---

9. The court claimed that the risk of inconsistent verdicts was slight because Pennsylvania and Scotland both adhere to principles of res judicata.

10. The Court of Appeals agreed with the District Court that California choice-of-law rules applied to Piper, and that Pennsylvania choice-of-law rules applied to Hartzell, see n. 8, supra. It did not agree, however, that California used a "governmental interests" analysis and that Pennsylvania used a "significant contacts" analysis. Rather, it believed that both jurisdictions employed the "false conflicts" test. Applying this test, it concluded that Ohio and Pennsylvania had a greater policy interest in the dispute than Scotland, and that American law would apply to both Piper and Hartzell.

11. The court's reasoning on this point is somewhat unclear. It states: "We have held that under the applicable choice of law rules Pennsylvania and Ohio are the jurisdictions with the greatest policy interest in this dispute. It follows that the other public interest factors that should be considered under the Supreme Court cases of *Gilbert* and *Koster* favor trial in this country rather than Scotland." 630 F.2d, at 171.

[16] In any event, it appears that the Court of Appeals would have reversed even if the District Court had properly balanced the public and private interests. The court stated:

> "[I]t is apparent that the dismissal would work a change in the applicable law so that the plaintiff's strict liability claim would be eliminated from the case. But . . . a dismissal for forum non conveniens, like a statutory transfer, 'should not, despite its convenience, result in a change in the applicable law.' Only when American law is not applicable, or when the foreign jurisdiction would, as a matter of its won choice of law, give the plaintiff the benefit of the claim to which she is entitled here, would dismissal be justified." 630 F.2d, at 163-164 (footnote omitted) (quoting *DeMateos v. Texaco, Inc.*, 562 F.2d 895, 899 (CA3 1977), cert. denied, 435 U.S. 904 (1978)).

[17] In other words, the court decided that dismissal is automatically barred if it would lead to a change in the applicable law unfavorable to the plaintiff.

[18] We granted certiorari in these case to consider the questions they raise concerning the proper application of the doctrine of *forum non conveniens*. 450 U.S. 909 (1981).[12]

II

[19] The Court of Appeals erred in holding that plaintiffs may defeat a motion to dismiss on the ground of *forum non conveniens* merely by showing that the substantive

---

The Court of Appeals concluded as part of its choice-of-law analysis that the United States had the greatest policy interest in the dispute. See n. 10, *supra*. It apparently believed that this conclusion necessarily implied that the *forum non conveniens* public interest factors pointed toward trial in the United States.

12. We granted certiorari in No. 80-848 to consider the question "[w]hether, in an action in federal district court brought by foreign plaintiffs against American defendants, the plaintiffs may defeat a motion to dismiss on the ground of *forum non conveniens* merely by showing that the substantive law that would be applied if the case were litigated in the district court is more favorable to them than the law that would be applied by the courts of their own nation." We granted certiorari in No. 80-883 to consider the question whether "a motion to dismiss on grounds of *forum non conveniens* [should] be denied whenever the law of the alternate forum is less favorable to recovery than that which would be applied by the district court."

In this opinion, we begin by considering whether the Court of Appeals properly held that the possibility of an unfavorable change in law automatically bars dismissal. Part II, infra. Since we conclude that the Court of Appeals erred, we then consider its review of the District Court's *Gilbert* analysis to determine whether dismissal was otherwise appropriate. Part III, *infra*. We believe that it is necessary to discuss the *Gilbert* analysis in order to properly dispose of the cases.

The questions on which certiorari was granted are sufficiently broad to justify our discussion of the District Court's *Gilbert* analysis. However, even if the issues we discuss in Part III are not within the bounds of the questions with respect to which certiorari was granted, our consideration of these issues is not inappropriate. An order limiting the grant of certiorari does not operate as a jurisdictional bar. We may consider questions outside the scope of the limited order when resolution of those questions is necessary for the proper disposition of the case. See *Olmstead v. United States*, 277 U.S. 438 (1928); *McCandless v. Furlaud*, 293 U.S. 67 (1934); *Redrup v. New York*, 386 U.S. 767 (1967).

law that would be applied in the alternative forum is less favorable to the plaintiffs than that of the present forum. The possibility of a change in substantive law should ordinarily not be given conclusive or even substantial weight in the *forum non conveniens* inquiry.

[20] We expressly rejected the position adopted by the Court of Appeals in our decision in *Canada Malting Co. v. Paterson Steamships, Ltd.*, 285 U.S. 413 (1932). That case arose out of a collision between two vessels in American waters. The Canadian owners of cargo lost in the accident sued the Canadian owners of one of the vessels in Federal District Court. The cargo owners chose an American court in large part because the relevant American liability rules were more favorable than the Canadian rules. The District Court dismissed on grounds of *forum non conveniens*. The plaintiffs argued that dismissal was inappropriate because Canadian laws were less favorable to them. This Court nonetheless affirmed:

> "We have no occasion to enquire by what law rights of the parties are governed, as we are of the opinion that, under any view of that question, it lay within the discretion of the District Court to decline to assume jurisdiction over the controversy. . . . '[T]he court will not take cognizance of the case if justice would be as well done by remitting the parties to their home forum.'" *Id.*, at 419–420 (quoting *Charter Shipping Co. v. Bowring, Jones & Tidy, Ltd.*, 281 U.S. 515, 517 (1930).

[21] The Court further stated that "[t]here was no basis for the contention that the District Court abused its discretion." 285 U.S., at 423.

[22] It is true that *Canada Malting* was decided before *Gilbert*, and that the doctrine of *forum non conveniens* was not fully crystallized until our decision in that case.[13] However, *Gilbert* in no way affects the validity of *Canada Malting*. Indeed, by holding that the central focus of the *forum non conveniens* inquiry is convenience, *Gilbert*

---

13. The doctrine of *forum non conveniens* has a long history. It originated in Scotland, see Braucher, *The Inconvenient Federal Forum*, 60 Harv. L. Rev. 908, 909–911 (1947), and became part of the common law of many States, see id., at 911–912; Blair, *The Doctrine of Forum Non Conveniens in Anglo-American Law*, 29 Colum. L. Rev. 1 (1929). The doctrine was also frequently applied in federal admiralty actions. See, e.g., *Canada Malting Co. v. Paterson Steamships, Ltd.*; see also Bickel, *The Doctrine of Forum Non Conveniens As Applied in the Federal Courts in Matters of Admiralty*, 35 Cornell L. Q. 12 (1949). In *Williams v. Green Bay & Western R. Co.*, 326 U.S. 549 (1946), the Court first indicated that motions to dismiss on grounds of *forum non conveniens* could be made in federal diversity actions. The doctrine became firmly established when *Gilbert* and *Koster* were decided one year later.

In previous *forum non conveniens* decisions, the Court has left unresolved the question whether under *Erie R. Co. v. Tompkins*, 304 U.S. 64 (1938), state or federal law of *forum non conveniens* applies in a diversity case. *Gilbert*, 330 U.S., at 509; *Koster*, 330 U.S., at 529; *Williams v. Green Bay & Western R. Co.*, supra, at 551, 558–559. The Court did not decide this issue because the same result would have been reached in each case under federal or state law. The lower courts in these cases reached the same conclusion: Pennsylvania and California law on *forum non conveniens* dismissals are virtually identical to federal law. See 630 F.2d, at 158. Thus, here also, we need not resolve the Erie question.

implicitly recognized that dismissal may not be barred solely because of the possibility of an unfavorable change in law.[14] Under *Gilbert*, dismissal will ordinarily be appropriate where trial in the plaintiff's chosen forum imposes a heavy burden on the defendant or the court, and where the plaintiff is unable to offer any specific reasons of convenience supporting his choice.[15] If substantial weight were given to the possibility of an unfavorable change in law, however, dismissal might be barred even where trial in the chosen forum was plainly inconvenient.

[23] The Court of Appeals' decision is inconsistent with this Court's earlier *forum non conveniens* decisions in another respect. Those decisions have repeatedly emphasized the need to retain flexibility. In *Gilbert*, the Court refused to identify specific circumstances "which will justify or require either grant or denial of remedy." 330 U.S., at 508 . Similarly, in *Koster*, the Court rejected the contention that where a trial would involve inquiry into the internal affairs of a foreign corporation, dismissal was always appropriate. "That is one, but only one, factor which may show convenience." 330 U.S., at 527. And in *Williams v. Green Bay & Western R. Co.*, 326 U.S. 549, 557 (1946), we stated that we would not lay down a rigid rule to govern discretion, and that "[e]ach case turns on its facts." If central emphasis were placed on any one factor, the *forum non conveniens* doctrine would lose much of the very flexibility that makes it so valuable.

[24] In fact, if conclusive or substantial weight were given to the possibility of a change in law, the *forum non conveniens* doctrine would become virtually useless. Jurisdiction and venue requirements are often easily satisfied. As a result, many plaintiffs are able to choose from among several forums. Ordinarily, these plaintiffs will select that forum whose choice-of-law rules are most advantageous. Thus, if the possibility of an unfavorable change in substantive law is given substantial weight in the *forum non conveniens* inquiry, dismissal would rarely be proper.

[25] Except for the court below, every Federal Court of Appeals that has considered this question after *Gilbert* has held that dismissal on grounds of *forum non conveniens* may be granted even though the law applicable in the alternative forum is less favorable to the plaintiff's chance of recovery. See, e. g., *Pain v. United Technologies Corp.*, 205 U.S. App. D.C. 229, 248–249, 637 F.2d 775, 794–795 (1980); *Fitzgerald v. Texaco, Inc.*, 521 F.2d 448, 453 (CA2 1975), cert. denied, 423 U.S. 1052 (1976); *Anastasiadis v. S.S. Little John*, 346 F.2d 281, 283 (CA5 1965), cert. denied, 384 U.S. 920 (1966). Several Courts have relied expressly on *Canada Malting* to hold that the possibility of an unfavorable change of law should not, by itself, bar dismissal. See

---

14. See also *Williams v. Green Bay & Western R. Co.*, supra, at 555, n. 4 (citing with approval a Scottish case that dismissed an action on the ground of *forum non conveniens* despite the possibility of an unfavorable change in law).

15. In other words, *Gilbert* held that dismissal may be warranted where a plaintiff chooses a particular forum, not because it is convenient, but solely in order to harass the defendant or take advantage of favorable law. This is precisely the situation in which the Court of Appeals' rule would bar dismissal.

Fitzgerald v. Texaco, Inc., supra; *Anglo-American Grain Co. v. The S/T Mina D'Amico*, 169 F. Supp. 908 (ED Va. 1959).

[26] The Court of Appeals' approach is not only inconsistent with the purpose of the *forum non conveniens* doctrine, but also poses substantial practical problems. If the possibility of a change in law were given substantial weight, deciding motions to dismiss on the ground of *forum non conveniens* would become quite difficult. Choice-of-law analysis would become extremely important, and the courts would frequently be required to interpret the law of foreign jurisdictions. First, the trial court would have to determine what law would apply if the case were tried in the chosen forum, and what law would apply if the case were tried in the alternative forum. It would then have to compare the rights, remedies, and procedures available under the law that would be applied in each forum. Dismissal would be appropriate only if the court concluded that the law applied by the alternative forum is as favorable to the plaintiff as that of the chosen forum. The doctrine of *forum non conveniens*, however, is designed in part to help courts avoid conducting complex exercises in comparative law. As we stated in *Gilbert*, the public interest factors point towards dismissal where the court would be required to "untangle problems in conflict of laws, and in law foreign to itself." 330 U.S., at 509.

[27] Upholding the decision of the Court of Appeals would result in other practical problems. At least where the foreign plaintiff named an American manufacturer as defendant,[17] a court could not dismiss the case on grounds of *forum non conveniens* where dismissal might lead to an unfavorable change in law. The American courts, which are already extremely attractive to foreign plaintiffs,[18] would become even

---

17. In fact, the defendant might not even have to be American. A foreign plaintiff seeking damages for an accident that occurred abroad might be able to obtain service of process on a foreign defendant who does business in the United States. Under the Court of Appeals' holding, dismissal would be barred if the law in the alternative forum were less favorable to the plaintiff—even though none of the parties are American, and even though there is absolutely no nexus between the subject matter of the litigation and the United States.

18. First, all but 6 of the 50 American States—Delaware, Massachusetts, Michigan, North Carolina, Virginia, and Wyoming—offer strict liability. CCH Prod. Liability Rep. 4016 (1981). Rules roughly equivalent to American strict liability are effective in France, Belgium, and Luxembourg. West Germany and Japan have a strict liability statute for pharmaceuticals. However, strict liability remains primarily an American innovation. Second, the tort plaintiff may choose, at least potentially, from among 50 jurisdictions if he decides to file suit in the United States. Each of these jurisdictions applies its own set of malleable choice-of-law rules. Third, jury trials are almost always available in the United States, while they are never provided in civil law jurisdictions. G. Gloss, Comparative law 12 (1979); J. Merryman, the Civil Law Tradition 121 (1969). Even in the United Kingdom, most civil actions are not tried before a jury. G. Keeton, The United Kingdom, The Development of its Laws and Constitutions 309 (1955). Fourth, unlike most foreign jurisdictions, American courts allow contingent attorney's fees, and do not tax losing parties with their opponents' attorney's fees. R. Schlesinger, Comparative Laws: Cases, Text, Materials 275–277 (3d ed. 1970); Orban, Product Liability: A Comparative Legal Restatement—Foreign National Law and the EEC Directive, 8 Ga. J. Int'l & Comp. L. 342, 393 (1978). Fifth, discovery is more extensive in American than in foreign courts. R. Schlesinger, supra, at 307, 310, and n. 33.

more attractive. The flow of litigation into the United States would increase and further congest already crowded courts.[19] . . .

[31] We do not hold that the possibility of an unfavorable change in law should never be a relevant consideration in a *forum non conveniens* inquiry. Of course, if the remedy provided by the alternative forum is so clearly inadequate or unsatisfactory that it is no remedy at all, the unfavorable change in law may be given substantial weight; the district court may conclude that dismissal would not be in the interests of justice.[22] In these cases, however, the remedies that would be provided by the Scottish courts do not fall within this category. Although the relatives of the decedents may not be able to rely on a strict liability theory, and although their potential damages award may be smaller, there is no danger that they will be deprived of any remedy or treated unfairly.

III

[32] The Court of Appeals also erred in rejecting the District Court's *Gilbert* analysis. The Court of Appeals stated that more weight should have been given to the plaintiff's choice of forum, and criticized the District Court's analysis of the private and public interests. However, the District Court's decision regarding the deference due plaintiff's choice of forum was appropriate. Furthermore, we do not believe that the District Court abused its discretion in weighing the private and public interests.

---

19. In holding that the possibility of a change in law unfavorable to the plaintiff should not be given substantial weight, we also necessarily hold that the possibility of a change in law favorable to defendant should not be considered. Respondent suggests that Piper and Hartzell filed the motion to dismiss, not simply because trial in the United States would be inconvenient, but also because they believe the laws of Scotland are more favorable. She argues that this should be taken into account in the analysis of the private interests. We recognize, of course, that Piper and Hartzell may be engaged in reverse forum-shopping. However, this possibility ordinarily should not enter into a trial court's analysis of the private interests. If the defendant is able to overcome the presumption in favor of plaintiff by showing that trial in the chosen forum would be unnecessarily burdensome, dismissal is appropriate—regardless of the fact that defendant may also be motivated by a desire to obtain a more favorable forum. Cf. *Klöckner Reederei und Kohlenhandel v. A/S Hakedal*, 210 F.2d 754, 757 (CA2) (defendant not entitled to dismissal on grounds of *forum non conveniens* solely because the law of the original forum is less favorable to him than the law of the alternative forum), cert. dism'd by stipulation, 348 U.S. 801 (1954).

22. At the outset of any *forum non conveniens* inquiry, the court must determine whether there exists an alternative forum. Ordinarily, this requirement will be satisfied when the defendant is "amenable to process" in the other jurisdiction. *Gilbert*, 330 U.S., at 506-507. In rare circumstances, however, where the remedy offered by the other forum is clearly unsatisfactory, the other forum may not be an adequate alternative, and the initial requirement may not be satisfied. Thus, for example, dismissal would not be appropriate where the alternative forum does not permit litigation of the subject matter of the dispute. Cf. *Phoenix Canada Oil Co. Ltd. v. Texaco, Inc.*, 78 F. R. D. 445 (Del. 1978) (court refuses to dismiss, where alternative forum is Ecuador, it is unclear whether Ecuadorean tribunal will hear the case, and there is no generally codified Ecuadorean legal remedy for the unjust enrichment and tort claims asserted).

A

[33] The District Court acknowledged that there is ordinarily a strong presumption in favor of the plaintiff's choice of forum, which may be overcome only when the private and public interest factors clearly point towards trial in the alternative forum. It held, however, that the presumption applies with less force when the plaintiff or real parties in interest are foreign.

[34] The District Court's distinction between resident or citizen plaintiffs and foreign plaintiffs is fully justified. In *Koster*, the Court indicated that a plaintiff's choice of forum is entitled to greater deference when the plaintiff has chosen the home forum. 330 U.S., at 524.[23] When the home forum has been chosen, it is reasonable to assume that this choice is convenient. When the plaintiff is foreign, however, this assumption is much less reasonable. Because the central purpose of any *forum non conveniens* inquiry is to ensure that the trial is convenient, a foreign plaintiff's choice deserves less deference.[24]

---

23. In *Koster*, we stated that "[i]n any balancing of conveniences, a real showing of convenience by a plaintiff who has sued in his home forum will normally outweigh the inconvenience the defendant may have shown." 330 U.S., at 524. See also *Swift & Co. Packers v. Compania Colombiana del Caribe*, 339 U.S. 684, 697 (1950) ("suit by a United States citizen against a foreign respondent brings into force considerations very different from those in suits between foreigners"); *Canada Malting Co. v. Paterson Steamships, Ltd.*, 285 U.S., at 421 ("[t]he rule recognizing an unqualified discretion to decline jurisdiction in suits in admiralty between foreigners appears to be supported by an unbroken line of decisions in the lower federal courts").

As the District Court correctly noted in its opinion, 479 F. Supp., at 731; see also n. 10, supra, the lower federal courts have routinely given less weight to a foreign plaintiff's choice of forum. See, e. g., *Founding Church of Scientology v. Verlag*, 175 U.S. App. D.C. 402, 408, 536 F.2d 429, 435 (1976); *Paper Operations Consultants Int'l, Ltd. v. SS Hong Kong Amber*, 513 F.2d 667, 672 (CA9 1975); *Fitzgerald v. Texaco, Inc.*, 521 F.2d 448, 451 (CA2 1975), cert. denied, 423 U.S. 1052 (1976); *Mobil Tankers Co. v. Mene Grande Oil Co.*, 363 F.2d 611, 614 (CA3), cert. denied, 385 U.S. 945 (1966); *Ionescu v. E. F. Hutton & Co. (France)*, 465 F. Supp. 139 (SDNY 1979); *Michell v. General Motors Corp.*, 439 F. Supp. 24, 27 (ND Ohio 1977).

A citizen's forum choice should not be given dispositive weight, however. See *Pain v. United Technologies Corp.*, 205 U.S. App. D.C. 229, 252–253, 637 F.2d 775, 796–797 (1980); *Mizokami Bros. of Arizona, Inc. v. Baychem Corp.*, 556 F.2d 975 (CA9 1977), cert. denied, 434 U.S. 1035 (1978). Citizens or residents deserve somewhat more deference than foreign plaintiffs, but dismissal should not be automatically barred when a plaintiff has filed suit in his home forum. As always, if the balance of conveniences suggests that trial in the chosen forum would be unnecessarily burdensome for the defendant or the court, dismissal in proper.

24. See *Pain v. United Technologies Corp.*, supra, at 253, 637 F.2d, at 797 (citizenship and residence are proxies for convenience); see also Note, *Forum Non Conveniens and American Plaintiffs in the Federal Courts*, 47 U. Chi. L. Rev. 373, 382–383 (1980).

Respondent argues that since plaintiffs will ordinarily file suit in the jurisdiction that offers the most favorable law, establishing a strong presumption in favor of both home and foreign plaintiffs will ensure that defendants will always be held to the highest possible standard of accountability for their purported wrongdoing. However, the deference accorded a plaintiff's choice of forum has never been intended to guarantee that the plaintiff will be able to select the law that will govern the case. See *supra*, at 247–250.

B

[35] The *forum non conveniens* determination is committed to the sound discretion of the trial court. It may be reversed only when there has been a clear abuse of discretion; where the court has considered all relevant public and private interest factors, and where its balancing of these factors is reasonable, its decision deserves substantial deference. *Gilbert*, 330 U.S., at 511-512; *Koster*, 330 U.S., at 531. Here, the Court of Appeals expressly acknowledged that the standard of review was one of abuse of discretion. In examining the District Court's analysis of the public and private interests, however, the Court of Appeals seems to have lost sight of this rule, and substituted its own judgment for that of the District Court.

(1)

[36] In analyzing the private interest factors, the District Court stated that the connections with Scotland are "overwhelming." 479 F. Supp., at 732. This characterization may be somewhat exaggerated. Particularly with respect to the question of relative ease of access to sources of proof, the private interests point in both directions. As respondent emphasizes, records concerning the design, manufacture, and testing of the propeller and plane are located in the United States. She would have greater access to sources of proof relevant to her strict liability and negligence theories if trial were held here.[25] However, the District Court did not act unreasonably in concluding that fewer evidentiary problems would be posed if the trial were held in Scotland. A large proportion of the relevant evidence is located in Great Britain.

[37] The Court of Appeals found that the problems of proof could not be given any weight because Piper and Hartzell failed to describe with specificity the evidence they would not be able to obtain if trial were held in the United States. It suggested that defendants seeking *forum non conveniens* dismissal must submit affidavits identifying the witnesses they would call and the testimony these witnesses would provide if the trial were held in the alternative forum. Such detail is not necessary.[26] Piper and Hartzell have moved for dismissal precisely because many crucial witnesses are located beyond the reach of compulsory process, and thus are difficult to identify or interview. Requiring extensive investigation would defeat the purpose of their motion. Of course, defendants must provide enough information to enable the District Court to balance the parties' interests. Our examination of the record convinces us that sufficient information was provided here. Both Piper and Hartzell

---

25. In the future, where similar problems are presented, district courts might dismiss subject to the condition that defendant corporations agree to provide the records relevant to the plaintiff's claims.

26. The United States Court of Appeals for the Second Circuit has expressly rejected such a requirement. *Fitzgerald v. Texaco, Inc.*, supra, at 451, n. 3. In other cases, dismissals have been affirmed despite the failure to provide detailed affidavits. See *Farmanfarmaian v. Gulf Oil Corp.*, 437 F. Supp. 910, 924 (SDNY 1977), aff'd., 588 F.2d 880 (CA2 1978). And in a decision handed down two weeks after the decision in this case, another Third Circuit panel affirmed a dismissal without mentioning such a requirement. See *Dahl v. United Technologies Corp.*, 632 F.2d 1027 (1980). . . .

submitted affidavits describing the evidentiary problems they would face if the trial were held in the United States.[27]

[38] The District Court correctly concluded that the problems posed by the inability to implead potential third-party defendants clearly supported holding the trial in Scotland. Joinder of the pilot's estate, Air Navigation, and McDonald is crucial to the presentation of petitioners' defense. If Piper and Hartzell can show that the accident was caused not by a design defect, but rather by the negligence of the pilot, the plane's owners, or the charter company, they will be relieved of all liability. It is true, of course, that if Hartzell and Piper were found liable after a trial in the United States, they could institute an action for indemnity or contribution against these parties in Scotland. It would be far more convenient, however, to resolve all claims in one trial. The Court of Appeals rejected this argument. Forcing petitioners to rely on actions for indemnity or contributions would be "burdensome" but not "unfair." 630 F.2d, at 162. Finding that trial in the plaintiff's chosen forum would be burdensome, however, is sufficient to support dismissal on grounds of *forum non conveniens*.[28]

(2)

[39] The District Court's review of the factors relating to the public interest was also reasonable. On the basis of its choice-of-law analysis, it concluded that if the case were tried in the Middle District of Pennsylvania, Pennsylvania law would apply to Piper and Scottish law to Hartzell. It stated that a trial involving two sets of laws would be confusing to the jury. It also noted its own lack of familiarity with Scottish law. Consideration of these problems was clearly appropriate under *Gilbert*; in that case we explicitly held that the need to apply foreign law pointed towards dismissal.[29] The Court of Appeals found that the District Court's choice-of-law analysis was incorrect, and that American law would apply to both Hartzell and Piper. Thus, lack of familiarity with foreign law would not be a problem. Even if the Court of Appeals' conclusion is correct, however, all other public interest factors favored trial in Scotland.

---

27. ... The affidavit provided to the District Court by Piper states that it would call the following witnesses: the relatives of the decedents; the owners and employees of McDonald; the persons responsible for the training and licensing of the pilot; the persons responsible for servicing and maintaining the aircraft; and two or three of its own employees involved in the design and manufacture of the aircraft.

28. See *Pain v. United Technologies Corp.*, 205 U.S. App. D.C., at 244, 637 F.2d, at 790 (relying on similar argument in approving dismissal of action arising out of helicopter crash that took place in Norway).

29. Many *forum non conveniens* decisions have held that the need to apply foreign law favors dismissal. See, e.g., *Calavo Growers of California v. Belgium*, 632 F.2d 963, 967 (CA2 1980), cert. denied, 449 U.S. 1084 (1981); *Schertenleib v. Traum*, 589 F.2d, at 1165. Of course, this factor alone is not sufficient to warrant dismissal when a balancing of all relevant factors shows that the plaintiff's chosen forum is appropriate. See, e. g., *Founding Church of Scientology v. Verlag*, 175 U.S. App. D.C., at 409, 536 F.2d, at 436; *Burt v. Isthmus Development Co.*, 218 F.2d 353, 357 (CA5), cert. denied, 349 U.S. 922 (1955).

[40] Scotland has a very strong interest in this litigation. The accident occurred in its airspace. All of the decedents were Scottish. Apart from Piper and Hartzell, all potential plaintiffs and defendants are either Scottish or English. As we stated in *Gilbert*, there is "a local interest in having localized controversies decided at home." 330 U.S., at 509 . Respondent argues that American citizens have an interest in ensuring that American manufacturers are deterred from producing defective products, and that additional deterrence might be obtained if Piper and Hartzell were tried in the United States, where they could be sued on the basis of both negligence and strict liability. However, the incremental deterrence that would be gained if this trial were held in an American court is likely to be insignificant. The American interest in this accident is simply not sufficient to justify the enormous commitment of judicial time and resources that would inevitably be required if the case were to be tried here.

IV

[41] The Court of Appeals erred in holding that the possibility of an unfavorable change in law bars dismissal on the ground of *forum non conveniens*. It also erred in rejecting the District Court's *Gilbert* analysis. The District Court properly decided that the presumption in favor of the respondent's forum choice applied with less than maximum force because the real parties in interest are foreign. It did not act unreasonably in deciding that the private interests pointed towards trial in Scotland. Nor did it act unreasonably in deciding that the public interests favored trial in Scotland. Thus, the judgment of the Court of Appeals is *Reversed. . . .*

JUSTICE STEVENS, with whom JUSTICE BRENNAN joins, dissenting.

[45] In No. 80-848, only one question is presented for review to this Court:

> "Whether, in an action in federal district court brought by foreign plaintiffs against American defendants, the plaintiffs may defeat a motion to dismiss on the ground of *forum non conveniens* merely by showing that the substantive law that would be applied if the case were litigated in the district court is more favorable to them than the law that would be applied by the courts of their own nation." Pet. for Cert. in No. 80-848, p. I.

[46] In No. 80-883, the Court limited its grant of certiorari, see 450 U.S. 909, to the same question:

> "Must a motion to dismiss on grounds of *forum non conveniens* be denied whenever the law of the alternate forum is less favorable to recovery than that which would be applied by the district court?" Pet. for Cert. in No. 80-883, p. I.

[47] I agree that this question should be answered in the negative. Having decided that question, I would simply remand the case to the Court of Appeals for further consideration of the question whether the District Court correctly decided that Pennsylvania was not a convenient forum in which to litigate a claim against a Pennsylvania company that a plane was defectively designed and manufactured in Pennsylvania.

Notes and Questions

1. This is a leading case on the doctrine of *forum non conveniens* and neatly summarizes earlier case law. Can you formulate the doctrine in two or three clear and straightforward sentences?[59]

2. In paragraph 23, the Justice Marshall refers to the "flexibility" of the doctrine of *forum non conveniens*. What does he mean by that? Isn't there a conflict between predictability or legal certainty on the one hand and flexibility on the other?

3. Paragraph 26 outlines how the Court of Appeals would force American courts to analyze cases both under American and foreign law in order to make a determination whether the foreign law applied by the foreign court would be less favorable for the plaintiff. How would this even be possible in practice? And why would the Court of Appeals think that a plaintiff—basically any plaintiff, including any foreigner—is entitled to have her case heard in the U.S. court system merely because that would lead to a more favorable outcome for her? Would the Court of Appeals *always* grant access to American courts if a trial in the foreign court would lead to a less favorable outcome? Check paragraph 13 for the answer. By overruling the Court of Appeals, is the Supreme Court saying that a more favorable outcome alone can *never* justify access to American courts? Check paragraph 31 for the latter point.

4. Can you explain what the Supreme Court is talking about in note 25?

5. In note 17, the Supreme Court suggests that it could be enough for a foreign case to be brought to U.S. courts that a foreign company also does business in the U.S. An extreme example confirming this concern occurred after a high-speed train of the German state-owned railway Deutsche Bahn derailed in 1998 near the town of Eschede, Germany, killing 101 people and injuring 88 more. Deutsche Bahn offered about $15,000 to the families of each deceased person. Outraged by this offer, a self-help group of victims' families sought to bring a lawsuit in the United States. As in *Piper*, the accident did not occur in the U.S. and the victims were not American citizens. However, in contrast to *Piper*, the defendant was not a U.S. corporation, nor were the defective wheels designed or manufactured in the U.S. The claim that American courts should nevertheless have jurisdiction was based on the fact that tickets for train trips with Deutsche Bahn were sold, *inter alia*, over the internet, hence available in the United States. Thus, Deutsche Bahn was supposedly doing business in the U.S. and claims by German citizens against the German railway over an accident in Germany were indeed attempted in the District Court of New York, claiming gross negligence, and seeking punitive damages. The U.S. court ultimately declined jurisdiction. That was probably a wise decision but how about

---

59. For further analysis, see Ronald A. Brand & Scott R. Jablonski, *Forum Non Conveniens—History, Global Practice, and Future under the Hague Convention on Choice of Court Agreements*, Oxford Univ. Press 2007.

if the case had been brought by an American family over the death of an American citizen who had indeed purchased the ticket from America over the internet?[60]

U.S. case law is not consistent regarding the question whether doing business over the internet establishes jurisdiction wherever the websites can be accessed. Many U.S. states have so-called *long-arm jurisdiction* statutes pursuant to which jurisdiction can be exercised over out-of-state (or foreign) defendants. A common ground for the exercise of long-arm jurisdiction is conduct of business in the state. But what does "conduct of business" mean in the day and age of e-commerce? An important precedent is *Zippo Mfg. Co. v. Zippo Dot Com, Inc.*, 952 F. Supp. 1199 (W.D. Pa. 1997):

[9] The Constitutional limitations on the exercise of personal jurisdiction differ depending upon whether a court seeks to exercise general or specific jurisdiction over a non-resident defendant. *Mellon Bank (East) PSFS, Nat. Ass'n v. Farino*, 960 F.2d at 1221. General jurisdiction permits a court to exercise personal jurisdiction over a non-resident defendant for non-forum related activities when the defendant has engaged in "systematic and continuous" activities in the forum state. *Helicopteros Nacionales de Colombia, S.A. v. Hall*, 466 U.S. 408, 414-16 . . . (1984). In the absence of general jurisdiction, specific jurisdiction permits a court to exercise personal jurisdiction over a non-resident defendant for forum-related activities where the "relationship between the defendant and the forum falls within the 'minimum contacts' framework" of *International Shoe Co. v. Washington*, 326 U.S. 310 . . . (1945) and its progeny. *Mellon*, 960 F.2d at 1221. . . .

[10] A three-pronged test has emerged for determining whether the exercise of specific personal jurisdiction over a non-resident defendant is appropriate: (1) the defendant must have sufficient "minimum contacts" with the forum state, (2) the claim asserted against the defendant must arise out of those contacts, and (3) the exercise of jurisdiction must be reasonable. *Id*. The "Constitutional touchstone" of the minimum contacts analysis is embodied in the first prong, "whether the defendant purposefully established" contacts with the forum state. *Burger King Corp. v. Rudzewicz*, 471 U.S. 462, 475 . . . (1985) (citing *International Shoe Co. v. Washington*, 326 U.S. 310, 319 . . . (1945)). Defendants who "'reach out beyond one state' and create continuing relationships and obligations with the citizens of another state are subject to regulation and sanctions in the other State for consequences of their actions." *Id*. (citing *Travelers Health Assn. v. Virginia*, 339 U.S. 643, 647 . . . (1950)). "[T]he foreseeability that is critical to the due process analysis is . . . that the defendant's conduct and connection with the forum State are such that he should reasonably expect to be haled into court there." *World-Wide Volkswagen Corp. v. Woodson*, 444 U.S. 286, 297 . . . (1980). This protects defendants from being forced to answer for their actions in a foreign jurisdiction based on "random, fortuitous or attenuated" contacts. *Keeton v. Hustler Magazine, Inc.*, 465 U.S. 770, 774 . . . (1984). "Jurisdiction

---

60. See *Reers v. Deutsche Bahn AG*, 320 F. Supp. 2d 140 (S.D.N.Y. 2004).

is proper, however, where contacts proximately result from actions by the defendant himself that create a 'substantial connection' with the forum State." *Burger King*, 471 U.S. at 475, 105 S.Ct. at 2183-84 (citing *McGee v. International Life Insurance Co.*, 355 U.S. 220, 223 . . . (1957)).

[11] The "reasonableness" prong exists to protect defendants against unfairly inconvenient litigation. *World-Wide Volkswagen*, 444 U.S. at 292 . . . . Under this prong, the exercise of jurisdiction will be reasonable if it does not offend "traditional notions of fair play and substantial justice." *International Shoe*, 326 U.S. at 316 . . . . When determining the reasonableness of a particular forum, the court must consider the burden on the defendant in light of other factors including: "the forum state's interest in adjudicating the dispute; the plaintiff's interest in obtaining convenient and effective relief, at least when that interest is not adequately protected by the plaintiff's right to choose the forum; the interstate judicial system's interest in obtaining the most efficient resolution of controversies; and the shared interest of the several states in furthering fundamental substantive social policies." *World-Wide Volkswagen*, 444 U.S. at 292 . . . (internal citations omitted). . . .

[13] . . . The Internet makes it possible to conduct business throughout the world entirely from a desktop. . . . [T]he development of the law concerning the permissible scope of personal jurisdiction based on Internet use is in its infant stages. The cases are scant. Nevertheless, our review of the available cases and materials . . . reveals that the likelihood that personal jurisdiction can be constitutionally exercised is directly proportionate to the nature and quality of commercial activity that an entity conducts over the Internet. This sliding scale is consistent with well developed personal jurisdiction principles. At one end of the spectrum are situations where a defendant clearly does business over the Internet. If the defendant enters into contracts with residents of a foreign jurisdiction that involve the knowing and repeated transmission of computer files over the Internet, personal jurisdiction is proper. E.g., *CompuServe, Inc. v. Patterson*, 89 F.3d 1257 (6th Cir.1996). At the opposite end are situations where a defendant has simply posted information on an Internet Web site which is accessible to users in foreign jurisdictions. A passive Web site that does little more than make information available to those who are interested in it is not grounds for the exercise personal jurisdiction. E.g., *Bensusan Restaurant Corp., v. King*, 937 F.Supp. 295 (S.D.N.Y.1996). The middle ground is occupied by interactive Web sites where a user can exchange information with the host computer. In these cases, the exercise of jurisdiction is determined by examining the level of interactivity and commercial nature of the exchange of information that occurs on the Web site. E.g., *Maritz, Inc. v. Cybergold, Inc.*, 947 F.Supp. 1328 (E.D.Mo.1996).

[14] Traditionally, when an entity intentionally reaches beyond its boundaries to conduct business with foreign residents, the exercise of specific jurisdiction is proper. *Burger King*, 471 U.S. at 475 . . . . Different results should not be reached simply because business is conducted over the Internet. . . .

On the basis of *Zippo*, can you now answer the question whether an American citizen injured in the train accident in Germany could have sued Deutsche Bahn in the U.S. based on the purchase of her ticket from the U.S. via the internet?

6. The dissenting justices apparently saw nothing wrong with the idea of suing an American company in an American court over a defect that was manufactured or caused in America. With whom do you agree? What about the default rule that suits have to be brought in defendant court? Where was the defendant court for *Piper Aircraft*? What about the fact that Piper first moved to have the case transferred to the Pennsylvania court and then claimed that it was a *forum non conveniens* (see paras. 6 and 7)? What *should* the rules be about *forum non conveniens*?

7. As pointed out above, pp. 713 et seq., the jurisdiction of courts in the EU in cases with international dimensions is determined by the so-called Brussels I Regulation. If the defendant is domiciled in an EU Member State, whatever her nationality, she can only be sued in that Member State (Article 2), unless one of the exceptions specifically listed in the Regulation applies (Article 3). In 2005, the European Court of Justice had to respond to a request for a preliminary ruling sent from a British court. The case before the national court involved a British national suing a Jamaican resort and its British co-owner over injuries sustained during a vacation in Jamaica. The British judge wanted to know whether he could decline to hear the case based on *forum non conveniens*. Here are the pertinent parts of the Judgment of the ECJ of March 1, 2005, in *Case C-281/02, Owusu v. Jackson et al.* ([2005] ECR I-1445):

[34] [T]he uniform rules of jurisdiction contained in the Brussels [Regulation] are not intended to apply only to situations in which there is a real and sufficient link with the working of the internal market, by definition involving a number of Member States. . . .

[35] . . . Article 2 of the Brussels [Regulation] applies to circumstances such as those in the main proceedings, involving relationships between the courts of a single [EU Member] State and those of a [Non-Member] State rather than relationships between the courts of a number of [EU Member] States.

[36] It must therefore be considered whether, in such circumstances, the Brussels [Regulation] precludes a court of [an EU Member] State from applying the *forum non conveniens* doctrine and declining to exercise the jurisdiction conferred on it by Article 2 of that [Regulation].

The compatibility of the *forum non conveniens* doctrine with the Brussels [Regulation]

[37] It must be observed, first, that Article 2 of the Brussels [Regulation] is mandatory in nature and that, according to its terms, there can be no derogation from the principle it lays down except in the cases expressly provided for by the [Regulation] (see, as regards the compulsory system of jurisdiction set up by the Brussels [Regulation], *Case C-116/02 Gasser* [2003] ECR 1-14693, paragraph 72, and *Case C-159/02 Turner* [2004] ECR I-3565, paragraph 24). It is common ground that no exception

on the basis of the *forum non conveniens* doctrine was provided for by the authors of the [Regulation . . .].

[38] Respect for the principle of legal certainty, which is one of the objectives of the Brussels [Regulation . . .], would not be fully guaranteed if the court having jurisdiction under the [Regulation] had to be allowed to apply the *forum non conveniens* doctrine.

[39] According to its preamble, the Brussels [Regulation] is intended to strengthen in the [EU] the legal protection of persons established therein, by laying down common rules on jurisdiction to guarantee certainty as to the allocation of jurisdiction among the various national courts before which proceedings in a particular case may be brought. . . .

[40] The Court has thus held that the principle of legal certainty requires, in particular, that the jurisdictional rules which derogate from the general rule laid down in Article 2 of the Brussels [Regulation] should be interpreted in such a way as to enable a normally well-informed defendant reasonably to foresee before which courts, other than those of the State in which he is domiciled, he may be sued. . . .

[41] Application of the *forum non conveniens* doctrine, which allows the court seised a wide discretion as regards the question whether a foreign court would be a more appropriate forum for the trial of an action, is liable to undermine the predictability of the rules of jurisdiction laid down by the Brussels [Regulation], in particular that of Article 2, and consequently to undermine the principle of legal certainty, which is the basis of the [Regulation].

[42] The legal protection of persons established in the Community would also be undermined. First, a defendant, who is generally better placed to conduct his defence before the courts of his domicile, would not be able, in circumstances such as those of the main proceedings, reasonably to foresee before which other court he may be sued. Second, where a plea is raised on the basis that a foreign court is a more appropriate forum to try the action, it is for the claimant to establish that he will not be able to obtain justice before that foreign court or, if the court seised decides to allow the plea, that the foreign court has in fact no jurisdiction to try the action or that the claimant does not, in practice, have access to effective justice before that court, irrespective of the cost entailed by the bringing of a fresh action before a court of another State and the prolongation of the procedural time-limits.

[43] Moreover, allowing *forum non conveniens* in the context of the Brussels [Regulation] would be likely to affect the uniform application of the rules of jurisdiction contained therein in so far as that doctrine is recognised only in a limited number of [EU Member States], whereas the objective of the Brussels [Regulation] is precisely to lay down common rules to the exclusion of derogating national rules.

[44] The defendants in the main proceedings emphasise the negative consequences which would result in practice from the obligation the English courts would then be under to try this case, inter alia as regards the expense of the proceedings, the possibility of recovering their costs in England if the claimant's action is dismissed, the

logistical difficulties resulting from the geographical distance, the need to assess the merits of the case according to Jamaican standards, the enforceability in Jamaica of a default judgment and the impossibility of enforcing cross-claims against the other defendants.

[45] In that regard, genuine as those difficulties may be, suffice it to observe that such considerations, which are precisely those which may be taken into account when *forum non conveniens* is considered, are not such as to call into question the mandatory nature of the fundamental rule of jurisdiction contained in Article 2 of the Brussels [Regulation], for the reasons set out above.

[46] In the light of all the foregoing considerations, the answer to the first question must be that the Brussels [Regulation] precludes a court of [an EU Member State] from declining the jurisdiction conferred on it by Article 2 of that [Regulation] on the ground that a court of a [Non-Member] State would be a more appropriate forum for the trial of the action even if the jurisdiction of no other [EU Member] State is in issue or the proceedings have no connecting factors to any other [EU Member] State.

What do you think of the European approach compared to the U.S. approach to *forum non conveniens*? In response to the concerns voiced by the ECJ in paragraph 42, many U.S. courts stipulate conditions before dismissing a case, namely that the defendant who claims *forum non conveniens* promises to accept service of process and jurisdiction of the foreign court, that any statute of limitations will be waived and not prevent the litigation, and sometimes even that the defendant promises to respect a judgment of the foreign court one way or the other and pay whatever he or she may be ordered to pay.[61]

8. *Forum non conveniens* was also invoked in a very different type of case that led to the 1980 decision in *Filártiga v. Peña-Irala*. In the 1970s, Dr. Joel Filártiga was a well-known critic of the Paraguayan dictator Alfredo Stroessner. On March 29, 1976, his 17-year-old son Joelito was kidnapped and tortured to death by Americo Peña-Irala, the Inspector General of Police in Asunción, the capital of Paraguay. Peña-Irala showed the body to Dolly Filártiga, the sister of Joelito, and told her to pass the message "to shut up" to her father. Dr. Filártiga initiated criminal proceedings for murder in Paraguay but the only result was the arrest of his attorney. Years later, both Dolly Filártiga and Peña-Irala met again in the United States where she had applied for political asylum and he had overstayed a tourist visa. Filártiga reported the crime to the U.S. Immigration and Naturalization Service, who arrested Peña-Irala and ordered his deportation back to Paraguay. While he was still in custody pending deportation, Filártiga brought an action against Peña-Irala in the Federal District Court for the Eastern District of New York, alleging that he had wrongfully caused the death of her brother by torture and seeking compensatory and punitive

---

61. See Ralph H. Folsom, *Principles of International Litigation and Arbitration*, West Academic 2016, at p. 39.

damages of US$10 million. Peña-Irala moved to dismiss the complaint for lack of subject matter jurisdiction and *forum non conveniens*. Judge Nickerson, for the district court, dismissed the complaint on jurisdictional grounds, and Peña-Irala was deported. On appeal, Irving Kaufman, Circuit Judge, wrote the judgment for the United States Court of Appeals for the Second Circuit:[62]

[12] II. Appellants rest their principal argument in support of federal jurisdiction upon the Alien Tort Statute, 28 U.S.C. s 1350, which provides: "The district courts shall have original jurisdiction of any civil action by an alien for a tort only, committed in violation of the law of nations or a treaty of the United States." Since appellants do not contend that their action arises directly under a treaty of the United States, a threshold question on the jurisdictional issue is whether the conduct alleged violates the law of nations. In light of the universal condemnation of torture in numerous international agreements, and the renunciation of torture as an instrument of official policy by virtually all of the nations of the world (in principle if not in practice), we find that an act of torture committed by a state official against one held in detention violates established norms of the international law of human rights, and hence the law of nations. . . .

[25] Having examined the sources from which customary international law is derived the usage of nations, judicial opinions and the works of jurists we conclude that official torture is now prohibited by the law of nations. The prohibition is clear and unambiguous, and admits of no distinction between treatment of aliens and citizens. Accordingly, we must conclude that the dictum in *Dreyfus v. von Finck*, . . . 534 F.2d at 31, to the effect that "violations of international law do not occur when the aggrieved parties are nationals of the acting state," is clearly out of tune with the current usage and practice of international law. The treaties and accords cited above, as well as the express foreign policy of our own government, all make it clear that international law confers fundamental rights upon all people vis-a-vis their own governments. While the ultimate scope of those rights will be a subject for continuing refinement and elaboration, we hold that the right to be free from torture is now among them. We therefore turn to the question whether the other requirements for jurisdiction are met.

[26] III. Appellee submits that even if the tort alleged is a violation of modern international law, federal jurisdiction may not be exercised consistent with the dictates of Article III of the Constitution. The claim is without merit. Common law courts of general jurisdiction regularly adjudicate transitory tort claims between individuals over whom they exercise personal jurisdiction, wherever the tort occurred. Moreover, as part of an articulated scheme of federal control over external affairs, Congress provided, in the first Judiciary Act, s 9(b), 1 Stat. 73, 77 (1789), for federal jurisdiction over suits by aliens where principles of international law are in issue.

---

62. 630 F.2d 876 (2d Cir. 1980), most footnotes omitted.

The constitutional basis for the Alien Tort Statute is the law of nations, which has always been part of the federal common law.

[27] It is not extraordinary for a court to adjudicate a tort claim arising outside of its territorial jurisdiction. A state or nation has a legitimate interest in the orderly resolution of disputes among those within its borders, and where the lex loci delicti commissi is applied, it is an expression of comity to give effect to the laws of the state where the wrong occurred. Thus, Lord Mansfield in *Mostyn v. Fabrigas*, 1 Cowp. 161 (1774), quoted in *McKenna v. Fisk*, 42 U.S. (1 How.) 241, 248, 11 L.Ed. 117 (1843) said:

> (I)f A becomes indebted to B, or commits a tort upon his person or upon his personal property in Paris, an action in either case may be maintained against A in England, if he is there found. . . . (A)s to transitory actions, there is not a colour of doubt but that any action which is transitory may be laid in any county in England, though the matter arises beyond the seas.

[28] *Mostyn* came into our law as the original basis for state court jurisdiction over out-of-state torts, *McKenna v. Fisk*, supra, 42 U.S. (1 How.) 241, 11 L.Ed. 117 (personal injury suits held transitory); *Dennick v. Railroad Co.*, 103 U.S. 11 . . . (1880) (wrongful death action held transitory), and it has not lost its force in suits to recover for a wrongful death occurring upon foreign soil, *Slater v. Mexican National Railroad Co.*, 194 U.S. 120 . . . (1904), as long as the conduct complained of was unlawful where performed. Restatement (Second) of Foreign Relations Law of the United States s 19 (1965). Here, where in personam jurisdiction has been obtained over the defendant, the parties agree that the acts alleged would violate Paraguayan law, and the policies of the forum are consistent with the foreign law, state court jurisdiction would be proper. Indeed, appellees conceded as much at oral argument. . . .

[34] Thus, it was hardly a radical initiative for Chief Justice Marshall to state in *The Nereide*, 13 U.S. (9 Cranch) 388, 422, 3 L.Ed. 769 (1815), that in the absence of a congressional enactment,[20] United States courts are "bound by the law of nations, which is a part of the law of the land." These words were echoed in *The Paquete Habana*, supra, 175 U.S. at 700 . . . : "(i)nternational law is part of our law, and must be ascertained and administered by the courts of justice of appropriate jurisdiction, as often as questions of right depending upon it are duly presented for their determination."

[35] The Filartigas urge that 28 U.S.C. s 1350 be treated as an exercise of Congress's power to define offenses against the law of nations. While such a reading is possible, see *Lincoln Mills v. Textile Workers*, 353 U.S. 488 . . . (1957) (jurisdictional statute authorizes judicial explication of federal common law), we believe it is sufficient

---

20. The plainest evidence that international law has an existence in the federal courts independent of acts of Congress is the long-standing rule of construction first enunciated by Chief Justice Marshall: "an act of congress ought never to be construed to violate the law of nations, if any other possible construction remains. . . ." *The Charming Betsy*, 6 U.S. (2 Cranch), 34, 67, 2 L.Ed. 208 (1804), quoted in *Lauritzen v. Larsen*, 345 U.S. 571, 578, 73 S.Ct. 921, 926, 97 L.Ed. 1254 (1953).

here to construe the Alien Tort Statute, not as granting new rights to aliens, but simply as opening the federal courts for adjudication of the rights already recognized by international law. . . .

[36] Although the Alien Tort Statute has rarely been the basis for jurisdiction during its long history, in light of the foregoing discussion, there can be little doubt that this action is properly brought in federal court. This is undeniably an action by an alien, for a tort only, committed in violation of the law of nations. The paucity of suits successfully maintained under the section is readily attributable to the statute's requirement of alleging a "violation of the law of nations" (emphasis supplied) at the jurisdictional threshold. Courts have, accordingly, engaged in a more searching preliminary review of the merits than is required, for example, under the more flexible "arising under" formulation. Compare *O'Reilly de Camara v. Brooke*, 209 U.S. 45, 52 . . . (1907) (question of Alien Tort Statute jurisdiction disposed of "on the merits") (Holmes, J.), with *Bell v. Hood*, 327 U.S. 678 . . . (1946) (general federal question jurisdiction not defeated by the possibility that the averments in the complaint may fail to state a cause of action). Thus, the narrowing construction that the Alien Tort Statute has previously received reflects the fact that earlier cases did not involve such well-established, universally recognized norms of international law that are here at issue. . . .

[41] IV. Pena argues that the customary law of nations, as reflected in treaties and declarations that are not self-executing, should not be applied as rules of decision in this case. In doing so, he confuses the question of federal jurisdiction under the Alien Tort Statute, which requires consideration of the law of nations, with the issue of the choice of law to be applied, which will be addressed at a later stage in the proceedings. The two issues are distinct. Our holding on subject matter jurisdiction decides only whether Congress intended to confer judicial power, and whether it is authorized to do so by Article III. The choice of law inquiry is a much broader one, primarily concerned with fairness, see *Home Insurance Co. v. Dick*, 281 U.S. 397 . . . (1930); consequently, it looks to wholly different considerations. . . .

[42] Pena also argues that "(i)f the conduct complained of is alleged to be the act of the Paraguayan government, the suit is barred by the Act of State doctrine." This argument was not advanced below, and is therefore not before us on this appeal. We note in passing, however, that we doubt whether action by a state official in violation of the Constitution and laws of the Republic of Paraguay, and wholly unratified by that nation's government, could properly be characterized as an act of state. See *Banco Nacionale de Cuba v. Sabbatino*, supra, 376 U.S. 398 . . . ; *Underhill v. Hernandez*, 168 U.S. 250 . . . (1897). . . .

Can *Piper Aircraft* be reconciled with *Filártiga v. Peña-Irala*? Or are the two courts applying different standards, which may be justified by the differences in fact and subject matter?

Given what is going on around the world on a daily basis, *Filártiga v. Peña-Irala* could have opened up the U.S. court system to a great many lawsuits from foreigners who were tortured in one of the many countries where effective judicial remedies are generally not available or at least not to those in opposition to the government. Would that be a good or a bad development? Why?[63] See the decisions in *Tel-Oren v. Libyan Arab Republic*, 517 F. Supp. 542 (D.D.C. 1981), *Argentine Republic v. Amerada Hess Shipping Corporation*, 488 U.S. 428 (1989), and more recently in *Kiobel v. Royal Dutch Petroleum*, 133 S. Ct. 1659 (2013), to find out how and why the American courts have largely eliminated access for plaintiffs like the Filártiga family in more recent years.[64]

Finally, do you agree that international law should have the kind of influence in U.S. domestic law that was originally granted to it by Chief Justice Marshall in 1804 (see note 20 and para. 34 above)? Why or why not? Do we still do this today? Why or why not?[65]

7. Serving a Claim in a Foreign Jurisdiction

The initiation of legal proceedings has important consequences. For example, the statute of limitations is tolled or halted, the dispute is considered to be pending before the seized court, the defendant is forced to participate in the proceedings since nonparticipation may result in an enforceable judgment in default against the defendant, and the defendant may be saddled with court and attorney fees even if she ultimately prevails in the dispute. Thus, by contrast to negotiation, mediation, and arbitration, the defendant is usually not a voluntary participant in litigation.

In order to ensure that the date and time of initiation of proceedings is known, a court or tribunal with jurisdiction over the parties is clearly identified, and the defendant is aware of the proceedings against her and has sufficient time and opportunity to prepare and present her defense, most jurisdictions have elaborate rules on how service of process must be effected. Often, they also have similar rules about how other legal documents, such as motions, requests to produce evidence,

---

63. In support of *Filártiga*, in particular, Blum & Steinhardt, *Federal Jurisdiction Over International Human Rights Claims: The Alien Tort Claims Act After* Filártiga v. Pena-Irala, 22 Harv. Int'l L.J. 53 (1981); as well as Beth Stephens, *Translating Filártiga: A Comparative and International Law Analysis of Domestic Remedies For International Human Rights Violations*, 27 Yale J. Int'l L. 1 (2002); in opposition, *inter alia*, Farooq Hassan, *A Conflict of Philosophies: The* Filártiga *Jurisprudence*, 32 Int. & Comp. L.Q. 250 (1983). For a rather nuanced assessment, see Karen E. Holt, Filártiga v. Pena-Irala *After Ten Years: Major Breakthrough or Legal Oddity?*, Ga. J. Int'l & Comp. L., Vol. 20, pp. 543–569.

64. For further discussion, see Jonathan L.H. Blaine, *Sosa, Kiobel and Pirates Inc.: Defining the "Modern" Parameters of the Archaic Alien Tort Statute*, Hague Yearbook of Int'l Law 2013, Vol. 26, pp. 116–140; Sarah H. Cleveland, *Commentary on* Kiobel v. Royal Dutch Petroleum — The Kiobel *Presumption and Extraterritoriality*, Colum. J. Transnat'l L., Vol. 52, pp. 8–27; and, more generally, David Nersessian, *International Human Rights Litigation: A Guide for Judges*, Federal Judicial Center 2016.

65. For useful discussion of the subject in general, see John Quigley, *A Tragi-Comedy of Errors Erodes Self-Execution of Treaties:* Medellín v. Texas *and Beyond*, 45 Case W. Res. J. Int'l L. 403 (2012).

or requests for arbitration have to be served in order to be valid and produce legal effects.

In principle, these rules can provide for different forms of service:

1. The most basic and simple form is service by mail. However, if a document is simply mailed by the applicant to the defendant, she may deny having received the mail and the applicant may not be able to prove otherwise. Even if the documents are sent by registered mail with return receipt, the sender only holds a confirmation from the addressee that an envelope or package was delivered but not what it contained.

2. In most countries, therefore, the service is effected by the court or by an officer of the court. Thus, the applicant initiates proceedings by filing in court and the court then effects service on the defendant. This may be done by registered mail or by in-person service. If documents are sent by the court via registered mail, the addressee cannot normally (credibly) claim that the envelope was empty or contained only irrelevant papers.

3. A third option is for the applicant to make use of specialized process servers, in particular when personal service is required. These are independent professionals who offer services including filing papers in court, retrieving documents (such as entries in public registers) and, in particular, serving legal documents on defendants or other parties to a lawsuit. After handing over the papers to the defendant, the process servers deliver an affidavit of service or proof of service to the applicant. This is a sworn or notarized testimony that the respective papers were personally served on the addressee.

Timely and correct service is crucial for the successful initiation of legal proceedings. If the defendant was not correctly served, she can ignore the summons or other documents and, if the applicant moves ahead with proceedings, any judgments in default against the defendant will be unenforceable.

This creates major problems for transnational litigation because applicants and their legal counsel in one country rarely know how to effect service of process in another country. Furthermore, since countries are sovereign, the courts or authorities of one country cannot engage in official acts in another country, including service of documents, without the latter's permission. One way of overcoming the problem is to hire local counsel in defendant's country or jurisdiction and have them take care of the required formalities. However, many countries do not allow foreign process to be served this way. Moreover, this is a very expensive way of serving documents, in particular if the underlying claims are relatively small and/or it is not clear whether the claims will be disputed.

The traditional approach taken to resolve the problem is for the person or law firm or court seeking to serve a document in another country to engage the help of the authorities of that country via letters rogatory. On the most basic level, letters rogatory are written requests from the courts of one country to the courts of another country for judicial assistance with an ongoing procedure. The assistance can be for service of process or other documents, but it can also be for obtaining evidence via documents, witnesses, or other means. Since many countries do not allow foreign courts to approach their courts, the requests often have to be channeled via diplomatic or consular authorities. These authorities typically check whether the request is valid and does not violate the *ordre public* of the receiving country, and whether reciprocity would be guaranteed. Once accepted, the diplomatic or consular authorities determine the appropriate court in the receiving country and forward the request to that court. That court would then perform the requested act and send confirmation or documentary evidence back to the requesting court, but again via the diplomatic or consular channels. Unsurprisingly, these procedures are very slow.[66] Beginning in the early twentieth century, therefore, countries entered into bilateral and multilateral agreements to simplify and accelerate these procedures. The U.S. has ratified both the Inter-American Convention on Letters Rogatory[67] and the Additional Protocol to that Convention, as well as the 1965 Hague Convention on the Service Abroad of Judicial and Extrajudicial Documents in Civil and Commercial Matters,[68] and the 1970 Hague Convention on the Taking of Evidence Abroad in Civil and Commercial Matters.[69] For practitioners, the State Department maintains a website with country-specific information, in particular for the countries that are not also members of these conventions.[70]

The 1965 Hague Convention has been ratified by 75 countries (as of December 2019), including many important trading partners of the U.S. such as Australia, Canada, China, France, Germany, India, Japan, Korea, Mexico, Russia, and the UK. Pursuant to Article 2, each Contracting State has to designate a "Central Authority" to receive requests from any judicial officer or authority from any other Contracting State. In the annex of the Convention, there are model forms to be used for the requests. They are available in English, French, Chinese, Czech, German, Polish, Russian, Slovak, Spanish, Turkish, and Ukrainian. Whenever a Central Authority receives a request, it verifies that the request complies with the Convention and then proceeds to serve the document pursuant to the rules applicable in the Contracting

---

66. The actual steps are usually as follows: Court in requesting country → Ministry of Justice of requesting country → Ministry of Foreign Affairs of requesting country → Embassy of requesting country in receiving country → Ministry of Foreign Affairs of receiving country → Ministry of Justice of receiving country → Court with jurisdiction over addressee.

67. The U.S. ratified this Convention in 1986 and it entered into effect for and against the U.S. in 1988. The official source is the Organization of American States (OAS), see http://www.oas.org /juridico/english/treaties/b-36.html.

68. The U.S. ratified this Convention in 1967 and it entered into effect for and against the U.S. in 1969. The official source is the Hague Conference on Private International Law (HCCH), see https://www.hcch.net/en/instruments/conventions/specialised-sections/service. The Convention is also reproduced in our Documents, p. II-23.

69. The U.S. ratified this Convention in 1972. The official source is the Hague Conference on Private International Law (HCCH), see https://www.hcch.net/en/instruments/conventions /specialised-sections/evidence. The Convention is also reproduced in the Documents, p. II-32. For discussion, see below, pp. 816–827.

70. See https://travel.state.gov/content/travel/en/legal-considerations/judicial/country.html.

State (Article 5). As soon as service is effected, the Central Authority has to complete a certificate pursuant to another model form annexed to the Convention and return this certificate to the applicant who requested the service. If service was not possible, the Central Authority has to inform the applicant of the reasons that prevented service. The Inter-American Convention follows roughly the same method. Neither of the Conventions prevents alternative methods, such as service via the consular or diplomatic channels, but the procedures under the Conventions are generally easier, cheaper, and faster.

With regard to alternative methods, in particular direct service via mail or process servers from the requesting State, Article 10 of the Hague Convention provides an option for States to object to the direct service of judicial documents on natural or legal persons within their jurisdiction. The Swiss criminal sanctions for anyone trying to commit acts on behalf of foreign public authorities in Switzerland may be the best-known provisions.[71] Another country that has made use of this option is China.[72] The only option to effect service on a party in China is, therefore, the route via the Central Authority designated per Article 2 of the Hague Convention. This is the Ministry of Justice of the People's Republic of China. The address and other specific instructions can be found—for each signatory state of the Convention—on the website of the Hague Conference on Private International Law.[73] If service is not effected in this way, the Chinese party may not attend judicial proceedings abroad and China will not enforce a default judgment obtained against the Chinese party. Many other countries have similar restrictions.

In the U.S., different rules apply depending whether the procedure is initiated in federal or in state court. Pursuant to the Federal Rules of Civil Procedure (FRCP) for the United States District Courts,[74] "[a] civil action is commenced by filing a complaint with the court" (Rule 3). After the plaintiff has filed the complaint, she "may present a summons to the clerk for signature and seal. If the summons is properly completed, the clerk must sign, seal, and issue it to the plaintiff for service

---

71. The most well-known and far-reaching "blocking statute" may be Article 271 of the Swiss Criminal Code. Pursuant to Article 271(1), "[a]ny person who carries out activities on behalf of a foreign state on Swiss territory without lawful authority, where such activities are the responsibility of a public authority or public official, any person who carries out such activities for a foreign party or organisation, any person who encourages such activities, is liable to a custodial sentence not exceeding three years or to a monetary penalty, or in serious cases to a custodial sentence of not less than one year." (unofficial translations provided by the Swiss government are available at https://www.admin.ch/opc/en/classified-compilation/19370083/index.html). The provision is even more important in the realm of pretrial discovery and other procedures by U.S. and other foreign authorities to obtain evidence from Switzerland; see the discussion below, p. 819.

72. China has objected to the option of service via diplomatic or consular agents (Art. 8(2)), service directly by mail (Art. 10(a)), and service directly through judicial officers (Art. 10(b) and (c)). This information, and similar information about all other Contracting States, can be obtained from the website of the Hague Conference, www.hcch.net/en/home.

73. For China, the URL is https://www.hcch.net/en/states/authorities/details3/?aid=243.

74. Effective September 16, 1938, as last amended on December 1, 2016, available at http://www.uscourts.gov/sites/default/files/rules-of-civil-procedure.pdf.

on the defendant. . . ." (Rule 4(b)). Thus, by contrast to most European and civil law countries, the service of process is the responsibility of the plaintiff. Within the U.S., "[a]ny person who is at least 18 years old and not a party may serve a summons and complaint" (Rule 4(c)(2)). Thus, in most cases, the plaintiff will make use of a professional process server. Actual service will be effected either "following state law for serving a summons in an action brought in courts of general jurisdiction in the state where the district court is located or where service is made" (Rule 4(e)(1)), or by "delivering a copy of the summons and of the complaint to the individual personally" or by "leaving a copy of each at the individual's dwelling or usual place of abode with someone of suitable age and discretion who resides there" (Rule 4(e)(2)). Finally, in particular in case of legal persons, service can be made by "delivering a copy of each to an agent authorized by appointment or by law to receive service of process" (ibid.).

Rule 4(f) specifically addresses service abroad and stipulates the following:

(f) SERVING AN INDIVIDUAL IN A FOREIGN COUNTRY. Unless federal law provides otherwise, an individual . . . may be served at a place not within any judicial district of the United States:

(1) by any internationally agreed means of service that is reasonably calculated to give notice, such as those authorized by the Hague Convention on the Service Abroad of Judicial and Extrajudicial Documents;

(2) if there is no internationally agreed means, or if an international agreement allows but does not specify other means, by a method that is reasonably calculated to give notice:

(A) as prescribed by the foreign country's law for service in that country in an action in its courts of general jurisdiction;

(B) as the foreign authority directs in response to a letter rogatory or letter of request; or

(C) unless prohibited by the foreign country's law, by:

(i) delivering a copy of the summons and of the complaint to the individual personally; or

(ii) using any form of mail that the clerk addresses and sends to the individual and that requires a signed receipt; or

(3) by other means not prohibited by international agreement, as the court orders.

The U.S. Federal Rules of Civil Procedure, in particular with their reference to the 1965 Hague Convention, are thus generally in line with our earlier explanations. A problem can arise, however, if a plaintiff is serving a subsidiary of a foreign corporation in the U.S. claiming that the subsidiary is "an agent authorized by appointment or by law" of the foreign corporation. An example is provided by the litigation of Mr. Schlunk against Volkswagen. The plaintiff's parents were killed in an automobile accident and he claimed that defects of the automobile contributed to the cause of their death. Initially, Schlunk brought the case against Volkswagen of America, Inc. (VWoA), claiming that they had "designed or assembled" the car in question. However, VWoA was able to demonstrate that the car had been designed and built in Germany. Schlunk then brought a case against Volkswagenwerk Aktiengesellschaft (VWAG), the German mother company. He attempted service on VWAG by serving VWoA as involuntary agent of VWAG. The Circuit Court of Cook County, Illinois, agreed with Schlunk and denied VWAG's motion that service was improper since it could only be served in accordance with the 1965 Hague Convention. The Circuit Court held that VWoA, as a wholly owned subsidiary of VWAG, could not avoid being an agent of VWAG for the purpose of service of process, and, since service was accomplished in the U.S., adherence to the 1965 Hague Convention was not required. The decision was upheld on appeal and eventually brought before the Supreme Court of the United States. In *Volkswagenwerk Aktiengesellschaft v. Schlunk* (486 U.S. 694), Justice O'Connor wrote for the majority affirming the lower court decisions based on the following reasons:

[9] [T]he Convention does not specify the circumstances in which there is "occasion to transmit" a complaint "for service abroad." But at least the term "service of process" has a well-established technical meaning. Service of process refers to a formal delivery of documents that is legally sufficient to charge the defendant with notice of a pending action. . . . The legal sufficiency of a formal delivery of documents must be measured against some standard. The Convention does not prescribe a standard, so we almost necessarily must refer to the internal law of the forum state. If the internal law of the forum state defines the applicable method of serving process as requiring the transmittal of documents abroad, then the Hague Service Convention applies. . . .

[19] VWAG correctly maintains that the Convention also aims to ensure that there will be adequate notice in cases in which there is occasion to serve process abroad. Thus compliance with the Convention is mandatory in all cases to which it applies, . . . and Articles 15 and 16 provide an indirect sanction against those who ignore it, ... Our interpretation of the Convention does not necessarily advance this particular objective, inasmuch as it makes recourse to the Convention's means of service dependent on the forum's internal law. But we do not think that this country, or any other country, will draft its internal laws deliberately so as to circumvent the Convention in cases in which it would be appropriate to transmit judicial documents for service abroad. For example, there has been no question in this country of excepting foreign nationals from the protection of our Due Process Clause. Under that Clause, foreign nationals are assured of either personal service, which typically will require service abroad and trigger the Convention, or substituted service that provides "notice reasonably calculated, under all the circumstances, to apprise interested parties of the pendency of the action and afford them an opportunity to present their objections." *Mullane v. Central Hanover Bank & Trust Co.*, 339 U.S. 306, 314 . . . (1950).

[20] Furthermore, nothing that we say today prevents compliance with the Convention even when the internal law of the forum does not so require. The Convention provides simple and certain means by which to serve process on a foreign national. Those who eschew its procedures risk discovering that the forum's internal law required transmittal of documents for service abroad, and that the Convention therefore provided the exclusive means of valid service. In addition, parties that comply with the Convention ultimately may find it easier to enforce their judgments abroad. . . . For these reasons, we anticipate that parties may resort to the Convention voluntarily, even in cases that fall outside the scope of its mandatory application.

III

[21] In this case, the Illinois long-arm statute authorized Schlunk to serve VWAG by substituted service on VWoA, without sending documents to Germany. . . .

[22] VWAG explains that . . . as a legal matter, the Due Process Clause requires every method of service to provide "notice reasonably calculated, under all the circumstances, to apprise interested parties of the pendency of the action and afford them an opportunity to present their objections." . . . VWAG argues that, because of this notice requirement, every case involving service on a foreign national will present an "occasion to transmit a judicial . . . document for service abroad" within the meaning of Article 1 [of the 1965 Hague Convention]. . . .

[23] We reject this argument. Where service on a domestic agent is valid and complete under both state law and the Due Process Clause, our inquiry ends and the Convention has no further implications. Whatever internal, private communications take place between the agent and a foreign principal are beyond the concerns of this case. The only transmittal to which the Convention applies is a transmittal abroad that is required as a necessary part of service. And, contrary to VWAG's assertion, the Due Process Clause does not require an official transmittal of documents abroad every time there is service on a foreign national. Applying this analysis, we conclude that this case does not present an occasion to transmit a judicial document for service abroad within the meaning of Article 1. Therefore the Hague Service Convention does not apply, and service was proper. The judgment of the Appellate Court is Affirmed.

The decision of the Supreme Court was widely criticized in academic circles.[75] The Hague Conference on Private International Law convened a Special Commission to discuss concerns over "the danger of permitting domestic service upon a person who had not been expressly designated as an agent to receive such service of process," thereby circumventing the purpose and requirements of the 1965 Convention.[76]

---

75. See, for example, Henry J. Moravec, *Service of Process Abroad—Is There Anything Left of the Hague Service Convention After* Volkswagenwerk A.G. v. Schlunk?, 12 Loy. L.A. Int'l & Comp. L. Rev. 317 (1989).

76. See the report in Russel J. Weintraub, *International Litigation and Arbitration—Practice and Planning*, 6th ed., Carolina Academic Press 2011, at p. 151.

What do you think of the decision of the U.S. Supreme Court? What would be arguments in favor of allowing domestic service on a wholly owned subsidiary of a foreign corporation? What might be arguments against? What if the domestic company is only partly owned by the foreign corporation? A franchisee under different ownership? How about a high-level executive of the foreign corporation traveling to the U.S. on business? On vacation?

While *Schlunk* was pending, the German government declared unambiguously that German courts would not enforce a foreign judgment against a German natural or legal person unless, *inter alia*, service of process had been effected pursuant to the 1965 Hague Convention. What is the use of a decision against a foreign entity if it cannot be enforced in the country where the entity is domiciled? When and why would you, nevertheless, consider domestic service within the U.S. on an involuntary agent of a foreign corporation or person?

Within the European Union, questions of transnational service are subject to EU Regulation 1393/2007 on the Service in the Member States of Judicial and Extrajudicial Documents in Civil and Commercial Matters (OJ 2007 L 324, p. 79), Documents p. II-71. This Regulation is directly applicable and binding in all EU Member States with the exception of Denmark. Within its scope of application, neither national law nor international conventions like the 1965 Hague Convention can be applied.

Pursuant to Article 1(1), the Regulation "shall apply in civil and commercial matters where a judicial or extrajudicial document has to be transmitted from one Member State to another for service there." Thus, the Regulation applies, for example, if an American corporation has a subsidiary in one EU Member State and is being served from another Member State or has to effect service in another Member State. It does not apply, however, if only one of the parties to a dispute is located in an EU Member State. Thus, if the American corporation needs to serve a document on an EU party from the American headquarters, the 1965 Hague Convention applies. The Regulation also does not apply for purely internal situations, for example if both parties are located in France.

Article 2 of the Regulation requires that each EU Member State designate one agency for the transmission of judicial or extrajudicial documents and one agency for the receipt of such documents. Both functions can be entrusted to one agency. Federal states can designate different agencies for different autonomous territories. A natural or legal person in a Member State seeking service of a judicial or extrajudicial document on a natural or legal person in another Member State has to address the request to the transmitting agency in his or her home state. The form to be used is standardized and included in Annex I of the Regulation. The documents to be transmitted and the accompanying form have to be in the official language of the receiving Member State and the applicant has to ensure and pay for any translation that may be necessary before transmission.

Pursuant to Articles 6 and 7 of the Regulation, the receiving agency has to confirm receipt of the request within seven days and has to effect service "as soon as possible, and in any event within one month of receipt" (Article 7(2)). Once service has been completed, the receiving agency sends a Certificate of Service to the transmitting agency, together with a copy of the document(s) served. The transmitting agency forwards the Certificate to the applicant. Pursuant to Article 11, Member States do not charge each other for service via this method.

Service by diplomatic or consular agents is possible pursuant to Articles 12 and 13. Direct (personal) service is possible pursuant to Article 15 unless the receiving Member State does not allow it. Finally, service by postal service is also allowed pursuant to Article 14. However, in the latter case the abovementioned issues with proof of service may arise. In practice, the route via the transmitting and receiving agencies is safe, cost-effective, and straightforward, not least because the forms are standardized and available in all official languages of the EU. In effect, the procedure under the Regulation is not really different from the procedure under the 1965 Hague Convention, except that all Member States, except Denmark, are bound by it and it is faster. An important difference might arise if questions of interpretation of the Regulation should arise. Those would not come under the jurisdiction of the national courts but would have to be submitted to the European Court of Justice pursuant to the preliminary rulings procedure (for examples, see pp. 97, 777, and 1012) for a uniform and authoritative interpretation binding all EU Member States.

So far, in all cases where service on a defendant is to be effected, the plaintiff has to specify where the service should be made, i.e., the plaintiff has to know the place of residence or business or domicile of the defendant and the defendant has to be found at this place. The last question we will address in this context is what a plaintiff can do if she is unable to discover the foreign address where service can be effected or when a foreign defendant is deliberately trying to evade service.

To answer this question we need to remember that service can be performed pursuant to the rules applicable at the seat of the court/forum or at the domicile of the defendant, or both. If a U.S. plaintiff successfully pursues service of process on a foreign defendant via the means prescribed in the 1965 Hague Convention, she has satisfied both sets of rules and the judgment of the court should be enforceable in both/all countries. If a U.S. plaintiff only serves process in accordance with the foreign rules in defendant's country, the proceedings in the U.S. court should not go ahead because the due process clause requires service of process in compliance with the rules binding on the court. Finally, the third option is service of process only in compliance with the rules applicable in the U.S./at the forum and not compatible with the rules applicable in defendant's country. This would be the *Schlunk* scenario. The litigation can go ahead in the plaintiff's country, but the judgment will most likely not be recognized and enforced in the defendant's country (or any other country). Against this background, we can now outline the options for service on elusive foreign defendants:

1. Both the 1965 Hague Convention and the Inter-American Convention require the name and address of the defendant. Thus, the plaintiff should go to considerable lengths to discover the address and include it in the request, even

if the address is outdated. If the defendant is not present at the designated address, the authorities in the receiving country may be able to serve it on another person at the domicile of the defendant or perform another method of substituted service, including service by registered mail. Depending on the locally applicable rules, the authorities in the receiving country may be able to effect substituted service by publication, also referred to as constructive service.[77] In the UK, for example, service may be possible on a known attorney (solicitor) of the defendant. Once service of process has been accomplished in such a way, whether the defendant has actually received the documents or not, the plaintiff will be sent a certificate of service and can go ahead with the litigation.

2. By contrast, service of process only in accordance with the forum laws, for example via service on an involuntary agent or via publication of a notice in the forum State, makes sense only if the following conditions are met:

   a. service pursuant to the Hague Convention or another bilateral or multilateral agreement on judicial assistance or via the traditional letters rogatory has failed or is virtually certain to fail; *and*

   b. the defendant has assets in the forum State.

8. *Choice of Forum Clauses and Submission to the Jurisdiction of a Particular Forum*

As we have discussed, litigation, once initiated in a specific court, can go ahead under the following conditions:

1. The court has or accepts jurisdiction over the plaintiff and the subject matter (*in personam* and *in rem*).

2. The court also has jurisdiction over the defendant, which may be established by law, in particular because the defendant has her domicile in the court district or the law provides a special jurisdiction for the matter in dispute (civil law countries) or because the court has some valid connection to the parties and/or the matter in dispute and service of process was successfully effected on the defendant (common law countries).

Importantly, jurisdiction over the defendant (or even both parties) may also be established by voluntary submission to the jurisdiction of just about any court,

---

77. The U.S. Supreme Court held in *Mullane v. Central Hanover Bank & Trust Co.* (339 U.S. 306 (1950)) that publication of a notice in a local newspaper, while inadequate for persons of known place of residence, can be a valid substitute for persons whose "whereabouts could not with due diligence be ascertained," as long as "the form [of service] chosen is not substantially less likely to bring home notice than other of the feasible and customary substitutes," even if it is unlikely that the person(s) concerned will actually see the publication. Thus, under these conditions, constructive service done pursuant to the rules of the receiving country would also satisfy the due process clause of the forum.

provided that court does not reject the dispute considering itself a *forum non conveniens* (see above, pp. 727 et seq.). Voluntary submission *ex ante* is typically in the form of choice of court or forum clauses in a contract. Voluntary submission *ex post*, after a dispute has arisen, can also be done by contract, i.e., a submission agreement between the parties. However, it is more commonly done implicitly by "making an appearance" before the court and presenting arguments on the merits.

In general, each country applies its own rules of private international law or international conflict of laws to determine whether a choice of forum agreement or a submission by appearance will be respected and create jurisdiction of a court over a given dispute. This can lead to conflicts if the requirements for valid choice of forum agreements vary from one country to another. Similarly, what does or does not constitute "submission" should also be somewhat harmonized internationally or at least clear. The principle that an appearance merely to contest jurisdiction of the forum does not constitute submission to its jurisdiction is widely recognized. However, several grey areas remain where different courts have come out differently, for example when a defendant makes an appearance and contests the jurisdiction of the forum, but also presents arguments on the merits as alternative arguments, just in case her challenge to the jurisdiction should not be successful. Thus, several problems can and do arise in the absence of international agreements or harmonization:

1. If the parties have included a less-than-perfect choice of forum clause in their contract, the seller may rely on the clause and bring a case in the chosen forum while the buyer claims that the clause is invalid and brings parallel proceedings in a different forum. If both fora decide to go ahead with their proceedings, we may end up with two conflicting judgments in default. Which one, if any, will be enforceable in the buyer's and in the seller's country?

   Equally common are the cases where the parties have included a choice of forum clause and only one party initiates proceedings elsewhere. The other party either completely ignores the proceedings or participates only for the purpose of contesting jurisdiction. The first seized court goes ahead regardless and issues a judgment in default. Where would such a judgment be enforceable? What are the options of the other party?

2. If the seller requests interim relief, for example the arrest of contracted goods, from the court where these goods are located, does the seller implicitly accept jurisdiction of that court over the entire contractual dispute? If the buyer makes an appearance and argues against the grant of interim relief, does the buyer implicitly accept jurisdiction of that court over the entire contractual dispute?

3. If one party brings a case in court and the other party makes an appearance to contest jurisdiction of that court but also presents alternative arguments in case her jurisdictional challenge is unsuccessful, did the party implicitly accept jurisdiction of the court after all?

4. If there is a choice of forum clause in an IBT, where can one party apply for an anti-suit injunction to prevent the other party from initiating proceedings in a non-chosen court? Perhaps more practically relevant, if there is an arbitration clause in an IBT, where can one party apply for an anti-suit injunction to prevent the other party from initiating proceedings in court rather than going to arbitration?

The answer to the question how a valid choice of court or choice of forum clause should be drafted or what constitutes submission by appearance is not straight-forward since there are no international standards followed by courts around the world. Thus, in each country and even in each state of the U.S., the courts, to some extent, follow their own rules about jurisdiction and choice of forum agreements when approached for an anti-suit injunction before litigation, or for recognition and enforcement after litigation elsewhere.

The EU Regulation 1215/2012 on Jurisdiction and Enforcement of Judgments in Civil and Commercial Matters (Brussels Ia or Ibis Regulation)[78] provides rather straightforward language for parties making a choice in favor of a court in the EU by agreement (Article 25) or by appearance (Article 26):

Article 25 [Choice of Jurisdiction by Agreement]

1. If the parties, regardless of their domicile, have agreed that a court or the courts of a Member State are to have jurisdiction to settle any disputes which have arisen or which may arise in connection with a particular legal relationship, that court or those courts shall have jurisdiction, unless the agreement is null and void as to its substantive validity under the law of that Member State. Such jurisdiction shall be exclusive unless the parties have agreed otherwise. The agreement conferring jurisdiction shall be either:

    (a) in writing or evidenced in writing;

    (b) in a form which accords with practices which the parties have established between themselves; or

    (c) in international trade or commerce, in a form which accords with a usage of which the parties are or ought to have been aware and which in such trade or commerce is widely known to, and regularly observed by, parties to contracts of the type involved in the particular trade or commerce concerned.

2. Any communication by electronic means which provides a durable record of the agreement shall be equivalent to 'writing'. . . .

5. An agreement conferring jurisdiction which forms part of a contract shall be treated as an agreement independent of the other terms of the contract.

The validity of the agreement conferring jurisdiction cannot be contested solely on the ground that the contract is not valid.

---

78. Documents, p. II-92.

Article 26 [Choice of Jurisdiction by Submission]

1. Apart from jurisdiction derived from other provisions of this Regulation, a court of a Member State before which a defendant enters an appearance shall have jurisdiction. This rule shall not apply where appearance was entered to contest the jurisdiction, or where another court has exclusive jurisdiction by virtue of Article 24.[79]

2. In matters referred to in Sections 3, 4 or 5 [on matters relating to insurance, consumer contracts, and individual contracts of employment] where the policyholder, the insured, a beneficiary of the insurance contract, the injured party, the consumer or the employee is the defendant, the court shall, before assuming jurisdiction under paragraph 1, ensure that the defendant is informed of his right to contest the jurisdiction of the court and of the consequences of entering or not entering an appearance.

As we can see, only certain "weaker" parties will be informed in the EU that their appearance in front of the court establishes jurisdiction of that court unless they only appear to contest jurisdiction. The European Court of Justice has also consistently held that within the scope of application of the Brussels Regulation, a party is *not* considered to have accepted the jurisdiction of a court simply because it makes *alternative* arguments in case its jurisdictional challenge should not be accepted by the court as long as it is clear that these are *subsidiary* to the main argument, which is that the court has no jurisdiction to hear the matter.[80] Lawyers and parties in B2B transactions are expected to be aware of this principle.

Traditional English law follows the same basic principles. As Hartley has outlined:

In addition to jurisdiction based on the service of the claim form, jurisdiction may also be obtained through consent of the defendant. It is traditionally regarded that there are three ways in which this may be given: the defendant may agree expressly that the court will have jurisdiction (choice-of-court agreement); he may plead to the merits without challenging jurisdiction of the court (submission); or he may himself invoke the jurisdiction of the court, in which case he is regarded as consenting to its jurisdiction to make an order against him (for example, as regards costs) and with regard to a counterclaim.[81]

---

79. For Article 24, see above, pp. 715–716.

80. See the Judgment of October 22, 1981 in *Case 27/81 Rohr v. Ossberger*, dealing with the original Brussels Convention (1981 ECR 2431): "Article 18 of the [Brussels Convention] must be interpreted as meaning that it allows the defendant not only to contest the jurisdiction but to submit at the same time in the alternative a defence on the substance of the action without, however, losing his right to raise an objection of lack of jurisdiction." (at pp. 2439–2440). This was recently affirmed for the Brussels Ia or Ibis Regulation 1215/2012 in *Case C-433/16, Bayerische Motorenwerke v. Acacia* (ECLI:EU:C:2017:550, in particular para. 36 of the judgment).

81. Trevor C. Hartley, *International Commercial Litigation — Text, Cases and Materials on Private International Law*, Cambridge 2009, at p. 102.

In the U.S., the question whether a judgment from another court will be recognized and enforced—whether it is a court in another state of the U.S. or a foreign court—is a matter of state law and not of federal law. This includes the recognition and enforcement of judgments based on choice of forum agreements or jurisdiction by submission or appearance if the validity of the proceedings is contested by the other party. Until the early 1970s, courts in the U.S. often looked at choice of forum clauses with suspicion, in particular if a foreign court was chosen by the parties. The U.S. Supreme Court, however, came out rather strongly in favor of choice of forum clauses in B2B contracts in *The Bremen et al. v. Zapata Off-Shore Company* (407 U.S. 1, 1972).[82] The Supreme Court held that choice of forum clauses "freely entered into between two competent parties" (p. 14) should be enforced unless one side "could clearly show that enforcement would be unreasonable or unjust, or that the clause was invalid for such reasons as fraud or overreaching" (p. 15). With regard to the convenience of inconvenience of the foreign forum, the Court continued on p. 17:

We are not here dealing with an agreement between two Americans to resolve their essentially local disputes in a remote alien forum. In such a case, the serious inconvenience of the contractual forum to one or both of the parties might carry greater weight in determining the reasonableness of the forum clause. The remoteness of the forum might suggest that the agreement was an adhesive one, or that the parties did not have the particular controversy in mind when they made their agreement; yet even there the party claiming should bear a heavy burden of proof. . . .

This case, however, involves a freely negotiated international commercial transaction between a German and an American corporation. . . . [S]election of a London forum was clearly a reasonable effort to bring vital certainty to this international transaction and to provide a neutral forum experienced and capable in the resolution of [this type of] litigation. Whatever 'inconvenience' Zapata would suffer by being forced to litigate in the contractual forum as it agreed to do was clearly foreseeable at the time of contracting. In such circumstances it should be incumbent on the party seeking to escape his contract to show that trial in the contractual forum will be so gravely difficult and inconvenient that he will for all practical purposes be deprived of his day in court. Absent that, there is no basis for concluding that it would be unfair, unjust, or unreasonable to hold that party to his bargain.

In an effort at reducing problems resulting from different and inconsistent State court decisions on recognition and enforcement, the Uniform Law Commission drafted first the Uniform Foreign-Money Judgments Recognition Act (1962) and then the revised Uniform Foreign Country Money-Judgment Recognition Act

---

82. For additional analysis, see Kurt H. Nadelmann, *Choice-of-Court Clauses in the United States: The Road to Zapata*, Am. J. Comp. L. 1973, Vol. 21, No. 1, pp. 124–135; and Willis L.M. Reese, *The Supreme Court Supports Enforcement of Choice-of-Forum Clauses*, Int'l Law. 1973, Vol. 7, No. 3, pp. 530–540.

(2005).[83] These have been widely applied in the states and greatly reduced prior inconsistencies.

However, with regard to choice of forum clauses, there is an additional problem in the U.S. While most foreign courts have long treated choice of forum clauses to confer *exclusive* jurisdiction on the chosen court, as long as the choice does not violate any mandatory rules, American courts have done so only if the exclusion of any other is clearly stipulated in the clause. This is based on the notion that a forum selection clause may merely create an *option* of litigating in the chosen forum (pro-rogation or permissive clause) even if that court would not otherwise have jurisdiction, or it may also want to exclude any other fora (derogation or mandatory clause). Different courts have applied different standards as to the language required for the designation of an exclusive jurisdiction, let alone a specific and exclusive venue. Ambiguity is usually decided against the drafter. Furthermore, if a forum selection clause is too narrow with regard to the subject matter ("disputes arising out of the present agreement"), American courts have often limited its application to only some of the claims made in a dispute, with the unfortunate result that parties may have to litigate contractual claims in one court and related tort or statutory claims in another.

The U.S. situation is complicated for U.S. businesses, which are usually forced to involve attorneys even in fairly straightforward contract negotiations. It is exacerbated in IBTs because foreign parties will be even less able to anticipate and understand what is going on in American courts. This can have important consequences on the recognition and enforcement of U.S. court decisions abroad — or rather the refusal to recognize and enforce them. Having diagnosed an imbalance where "U.S. parties often are unable to enforce U.S. judgments abroad with the same degree of success as incoming judgments," the U.S. government encouraged the Hague Conference on Private International Law as early as 1992 to prepare a multilateral convention on the matter.[84] The result is the 2005 Hague Convention on Choice of Court Agreements (COCA) (Documents, p. II-11). "The Convention was designed as the litigation counterpart to the United Nations Convention on the Recognition and Enforcement of Foreign Arbitral Awards (the 'New York Convention')."[85] After securing 30 ratifications, including 27 of the EU Member States, the Convention entered into force in 2015.[86] Although the U.S. was a driving force behind

---

83. Documents, p. II-68.

84. See History of the Hague Convention on Choice of Court Agreements, in Preparatory Note to the Uniform International Choice of Court Agreements Act (Draft for Approval), National Conference of Commissioners on Uniform State Laws 2010, at p. 1.

85. Trevor Hartley & Masato Dogauchi, *Explanatory Report: Convention of 30 June 2005 on Choice of Court Agreements*, available at https://assets.hcch.net/upload/expl37e.pdf, at p. 16.

86. For discussion, see Ronald A. Brand, *The 2005 Hague Choice of Court Convention in the United States*, 18 Annals Fac. L.U. Zenica 31 (2016); Glenn P. Hendrix & Louise Ellen Teitz, *The Hague Convention on Choice of Court Agreements: A Realistic Competitor to the New York Convention?*, NYSBA N.Y. Disp. Res. Law. 2017, Vol. 10, No. 1, pp. 47–51; as well as Nino Sievi, *Enforceability*

the initiative and signed the Convention in 2009, it has so far not completed the ratification. At the present time, it is not clear whether the Trump administration intends to pursue ratification of the Convention in the foreseeable future. Nevertheless, the National Conference of Commissioners on Uniform State Laws has already prepared a Uniform International Choice of Court Agreements Act as guidance for the states on how to implement the 2005 Hague Convention after ratification. The Prefatory Note elaborates that:

> The Hague Choice of Court Agreement Act, in conjunction with federal legislation, will implement the Hague Convention on Choice of Court Agreements in the United States.[87] The Convention, the product of over a decade of multilateral negotiations, validates party autonomy by enforcing exclusive choice of court agreements and the judgments that result from them, as will the Act. The Convention is an immeasurably valuable treaty that will help create certainty and predictability for transactional planning, validate party autonomy, facilitate the free movement of judgments, and provide a foundation for further cooperation and harmonization of law. Implementation through a federal statute including provisions for states to choose to opt into the Uniform Law will allow this area to continue to incorporate state law, facilitating greater consistency with existing state law in the broader area of judgment recognition and enforcement. . . .

> There are several aspects of existing U.S. law that will be affected by the Convention. . . .

> In some respects, there will be less opportunity for variation among existing state law. For example, many states now vary on aspects of formal validity required in a choice of court/forum clause, such as bold type face or size of font required for the clause to be effective. The Convention defines formal validity as requiring a writing or its equivalent (Article 3(c)) and this is included in the Act in the definitions of a "choice of court agreement" and "record" (Section 3(1) and (12).) Nothing more is or may be required by state law for formal validity, thus limiting existing state variations. . . .

> The most significant change is the presumption of exclusivity. Under Article 3 (b), the Convention provides that if a choice of court agreement designates the courts of only one country, the agreement is deemed to be exclusive unless otherwise "expressly provided." This presumption is contrary to that applied by the majority of state courts or federal courts in diversity which generally requires specific language of exclusion. . . .

---

of International Choice of Court Agreements: Impact of the Hague Convention on the US and EU Legal System, Hague Yearbook of Int'l Law 2011, Vol. 24, pp. 95–117.

87. The final implementation structure has not yet been determined by the U.S. Department of State.

A second significant change is in the area of *forum non conveniens*. Article 5(2) of the Convention provides that where a court has jurisdiction, the court "shall not decline to exercise jurisdiction on the ground that the dispute should be decided in a court of another State." The doctrine of *forum non conveniens* exists in federal courts and in most state court systems, providing a mechanism for dismissal of cases that are more appropriately heard by other courts, for reasons which may include the lack of connection to the forum. Approximately 47 states have some version of *forum non conveniens* and not all are identical to federal doctrine. At least twenty-two states have enacted *forum non conveniens* statutes or promulgated rules of civil procedure. Some of these statutes are designed to address certain types of cases, many of which are outside the scope of the Convention. The majority of states have been able to avoid hearing cases which are not sufficiently connected or related to the forum through the doctrine of *forum non conveniens*. This possibility will be circumscribed in connection with those cases that fall under the Convention where the parties have selected an exclusive forum. The application of Article 5(2) then mandates that the chosen court has no discretion to dismiss for *forum non conveniens* in this circumstance.

The Convention does, however, specifically limit the application of Article 5(2) so that a court without subject matter jurisdiction is not forced to hear a case. . . .

The Convention requires that questions of whether an agreement is invalid (null and void) are to be made under "the law of the chosen court," Article 5 (1), with "law" including the choice of law rules of the chosen court. Thus, in a choice of court agreement with Oslo as the chosen forum, the question of validity by a nonchosen Minnesota court would be determined under the whole law of Norway. . . . With regard to the EU] there is the complication of a US state or federal court looking at a choice of court agreement in an international case that selects London for example, being faced with determining the validity of the agreement under English law, including its choice of law rules, and the impact of European Regulation.[88]

Finally, the question of when an appearance will be considered a submission to the jurisdiction of the forum is generally treated the same way in the U.S. as in the EU, although the rules vary somewhat between federal courts and the courts of the states. A "special appearance" for the sole purpose of contesting jurisdiction used to be distinguished from a "general appearance," which constitutes a submission and establishes jurisdiction over the defendant where it may not have existed before.

---

88. See Uniform International Choice of Court Agreements Act, Prefatory Note, available at https://www.uniformlaws.org/HigherLogic/System/DownloadDocumentFile.ashx?DocumentFileKey=da44025b-ccff-c859-2eff-29ff22e67027&forceDialog=0, at pp. 1–4.

Rule 12(b) of the Federal Rules of Civil Procedure does not make this distinction anymore:

> (b) How to Present Defenses. Every defense to a claim for relief in any pleading must be asserted in the responsive pleading if one is required. But a party may assert the following defenses by motion:
>
>> (1) lack of subject-matter jurisdiction;
>>
>> (2) lack of personal jurisdiction;
>>
>> (3) improper venue;
>>
>> (4) insufficient process;
>>
>> (5) insufficient service of process;
>>
>> (6) failure to state a claim upon which relief can be granted; and
>>
>> (7) failure to join a party under Rule 19.
>
> A motion asserting any of these defenses must be made before pleading if a responsive pleading is allowed. If a pleading sets out a claim for relief that does not require a responsive pleading, an opposing party may assert at trial any defense to that claim. *No defense or objection is waived by joining it with one or more other defenses or objections in a responsive pleading or in a motion.* (emphasis added)

In the states, the distinction is often still retained. For example, § 418.10 of the California Code of Civil Procedure has been summarized as follows: "Motions to quash and motions to stay or dismiss the action brought under CCP § 418.10 provide a defendant with an opportunity to end an action immediately *without making a general appearance*, which has the effect of submitting defendant to the court's jurisdiction. Defendants may raise several objections via CCP § 418.10: lack of personal jurisdiction (via motion to quash service of summons), inconvenient forum (via motion to stay or dismiss the action), and dismissal for delay in serving summons (via motion to stay or dismiss the action)" (emphasis added).[89]

9. What to Do About Proceedings in the Wrong Forum?

There are several scenarios in which a party may be confronted with proceedings in the wrong forum:

#1 If the parties to an IBT included a choice of court agreement in their contract but the other party claims that the clause is invalid or does not cover the dispute in question and launches proceedings in a different court;

#2 If the parties to an IBT included a choice of court agreement in their contract and the first party launches proceedings in the chosen court but the

---

89. See Paul R. Kiesel, Peter D. Lichtman, Edith R. Matthai & Richard L. Seabolt, *Matthew Bender Practice Guide: California Pretrial Civil Procedure*, LexisNexis 2017, at 9.07. See also Robert F. Kane and Donald G. Rez, *California Pretrial Practice & Forms*, James Publishing 2018, § 7:223.

other party claims that the choice was invalid or does not cover the dispute in question and launches proceedings in a different court, resulting in parallel proceedings in two different fora;

#3   In a variation of Scenario #2, the first party not only launched proceedings in the chosen court, but also obtained a judgment from it; instead of appealing the judgment, the other party ignores it and launches proceedings in a different court;

#4   If the parties to an IBT included an arbitration clause in their contract but the other party claims that the clause is invalid or does not cover the dispute in question and launches proceedings in court instead;

#5   If there are multiple parties to an IBT and several of them are sued by one or more of the other parties in a forum that may be right for some but not all of them;

#6   The other party, in any of the first four scenarios, has not launched proceedings in the inappropriate forum yet but the first party has reason to believe that such proceedings are imminent.

In general, parties have several defenses or options when confronted with a lawsuit or the threat of a lawsuit in a forum they consider inappropriate.

Scenario #1: The party can make an appearance and dispute jurisdiction of the forum based on the choice of forum agreement in favor of a different court. If the party does not have assets in the country where the proceedings have been initiated, it could also ignore the proceedings and wait for any attempts at enforcing the default judgment in countries where it does have assets. Then it would counter those enforcement efforts with the argument that the court lacked jurisdiction in the first place. We would recommend the latter strategy only if the party can also claim that service of process was not properly done or that it had other reasons for ignoring the proceedings, such as serious reservations about the convenience of the forum or its ability to conduct proceedings pursuant to Western standards of rule of law and due process.

Scenario #2: If the party makes an appearance to dispute jurisdiction of the second seized court, it should present the additional argument that the matter is already pending elsewhere (*lis pendens*). Otherwise, the same advice as for Scenario #1 would apply.

Scenario #3: If the party makes an appearance to dispute jurisdiction of the second seized court, it should present the additional argument that the matter has already been decided elsewhere (res judicata). Otherwise, the same advice as for Scenario #1 would apply.

Scenario #4: This is a variation of Scenario #1. The party should make an appearance and dispute jurisdiction of the forum based on the arbitration agreement. Otherwise, the same advice as for Scenario #1 would apply.

Scenario #5: When IBTs involve more than two parties, it is even more important to have clear and effective choice of law and choice of forum clauses. The alternatives—the rules of private international law or international conflict of laws applied in different countries—are complicated for bilateral agreements. They become byzantine for multilateral contracts and quite unpredictable. However, if no such clauses were included or they have been held to be invalid by some parties and maybe even some courts, the party or parties being haled into the wrong courts basically have the same options as outlined for Scenarios #1, 2, and 3. Their position is weakened, however, if they are considered jointly and severally liable for the performance or any other claims resulting from the IBT. Of course, joint and several liability can also result from tort action rather than a contract and in such cases, there won't be a valid choice of forum clause. An example for the latter is provided by the famous litigation of *Laker Airways* (the original budget airline) against a number of European and American carriers in the U.S. District Court for the District of Columbia, based on alleged violations of U.S. antitrust law. Several of the European airlines responded by filing suit in the High Court of Justice in London, where Laker was based, and obtained an injunction "forbidding Laker from prosecuting its American antitrust action against the foreign defendants."[90] In spite of this anti-suit injunction,[91] Laker pursued its claims in the U.S. and obtained what has been called a "counter anti-suit injunction."[92]

Scenario #6: In most jurisdictions, injunctions can only be obtained if the main claims have also been initiated successfully in the same court. Thus, to obtain an anti-suit injunction, the first party would have to bring proceedings before the chosen court or arbitration tribunal and simultaneously request an anti-suit injunction enjoining the other party from going to court elsewhere or from continuing proceedings elsewhere. This has the disadvantage, however, of forcing the party to escalate the dispute on suspicion that proceedings may be initiated by the other party, although further negotiations might still be promising.

Finally, at least in principle, an anti-suit injunction can also be sought from the chosen court to prevent a second round of litigation if the matter is already res judicata (scenario #3).

----

90. See *Laker Airways Ltd. v. Sabena, Belgian World Airlines*, 731 F.2d 909, at 915.

91. For further discussion see, *inter alia*, George A. Bermann, *The Use of Anti-Suit Injunctions in International Litigation*, 28 Colum. J. Transnat'l L. 589 (1990); Andreas F. Lowenfeld, *Forum Shopping, Antisuit Injunctions, Negative Declarations, and Related Tools of International Litigation*, Am. J. Int'l L. 1997, Vol. 91, No. 2, pp. 314–324; as well as Olivier Luc Mosimann, *Anti-Suit Injunctions in International Commercial Arbitration*, Eleven International Publishing 2010.

92. Ralph Folsom, *Principles of International Litigation and Arbitration*, West Academic 2016, at p. 323.

Although parallel proceedings in different countries are highly undesirable from the points of view of procedural economy, justice, rule of law, due process, and legitimacy of the courts, they are not at all infrequent. In spite of the strategies presented above, the non-chosen court may decide that the choice of forum clause is invalid, or does not cover the matter at hand, or that their party would not get a fair trial in the chosen court. If this should happen, the question turns to the enforceability of the decisions and the location of assets. With few exceptions, the decisions of a court, chosen or not, will be enforceable in the respective country, unless successfully appealed. Other countries will recognize and enforce only decisions they agree with or accept as fundamentally in line with their laws, including their rules on jurisdiction, conflicts, any bilateral and international agreements, and their notions of justice (*ordre public*). In the U.S., the situation is even more complicated because the case law is inconsistent and not all federal and state courts always follow the Zapata standard (above, p. 763) when dealing with the question whether or not a choice of forum agreement will be enforced.

Since recognition and enforcement of foreign judicial decisions is regulated at the supranational level in the EU, some of these issues present themselves a bit differently there. The following judgments of the European Court of Justice and the attached comments and questions show how the EU rules have evolved and how they are applied today:

Case 6-3

Erich Gasser GmbH v. Misat Srl

European Court of Justice, Case C-116/02
Judgment of 9 December 2003, 2003 ECR I-14721

Gasser is based in Austria and had been supplying children's clothing to Misat in Italy for years. In early 2000, Misat fell behind with payment for several shipments. Before Gasser could bring a case in Austria in the court designated by a choice of court agreement, Misat brought a case in Italy seeking a declaration that the contract had ended due to disagreements between the parties and that it owed nothing to Gasser. Misat further sought damages from Gasser "for failure to fulfil the obligations of fairness, diligence and good faith"[93] and for various costs. When Gasser initiated proceedings in Austria several months later for payment pursuant to contractual obligations, Misat disputed jurisdiction of the Austrian court based, inter alia, on *lis pendens*. The trial court in Austria stayed its proceedings to await a decision from Italy. Gasser appealed and the appellate court made a reference to the European Court of Justice. The Court interpreted an earlier version of the Brussels Regulation[94] as follows:

---

93. See para. 12 of the judgment of the ECJ, 2003 ECR I-14721, at I-14728.

94. The European Court of Justice has repeatedly held that its interpretations of the earlier versions of this Regulation apply to the current version "whenever the provisions of the two instruments

²⁸ By its second question, the national court seeks in essence to establish whether [the Brussels Regulation] must be interpreted as meaning that, where a court is the second court seised and has exclusive jurisdiction under an agreement conferring jurisdiction, it may, by way of derogation from [the article on *lis pendens*], give judgment in the case without waiting for a declaration from the court first seised that it has no jurisdiction. . . .

⁴¹ It must be borne in mind at the outset that [the Brussels Regulation] is intended, in the interests of the proper administration of justice within the Community, to prevent parallel proceedings before the courts of different [Member] States and to avoid conflicts between decisions which might result therefrom. Those rules are therefore designed to preclude, so far as possible and from the outset, the possibility of a situation arising such as that referred to in Article [34(3) of the Brussels I Regulation, now Article 45(1)(c) of the Brussels Ibis Regulation], that is to say the non-recognition of a judgment on account of its irreconcilability with a judgment given in proceedings between the same parties in the State in which recognition is sought. . . . It follows that, in order to achieve those aims, [the *lis pendens* provisions in the Brussels Regulation] must be interpreted broadly so as to cover, in principle, all situations of *lis pendens* before courts in [Member] States, irrespective of the parties' domicile. . . .

⁴² From the clear terms of [Article 27 of the original Brussels I Regulation], it is apparent that, in a situation of *lis pendens*, the court second seised must stay proceedings of its own motion until the jurisdiction of the court first seised has been established and, where it is so established, must decline jurisdiction in favour of the latter. . . .

⁴⁷ . . . [T]he application of the procedural rule contained in Article [27 of the Brussels I Regulation] is based clearly and solely on the chronological order in which the courts involved are seised.

⁴⁸ Moreover, the court second seised is never in a better position than the court first seised to determine whether the latter has jurisdiction. . . .

⁴⁹ Thus, where there is an agreement conferring jurisdiction within the meaning of [the Brussels Regulation], not only, as observed by the Commission, do the parties always have the option of declining to invoke it and, in particular, the defendant has the option of entering an appearance before the court first seised without alleging that it lacks jurisdiction on the basis of a choice-of-court clause . . . , but, moreover, in circumstances other than those just described, it is incumbent on the court first seised to verify the existence of the agreement and to decline jurisdiction if it is

---

of EU law may be regarded as equivalent"; see, for example, the Judgment of 16 November 2016 in Case C-417/15 Schmidt, EU:C:2016:881, at para. 26, with further references. For discussion see also Fabrizio Marongiu Buonaiuti: *Lis alibi pendens and Related Actions in the Relationships with the Courts of Third Countries in the Recast of the Brussels I Regulation*, in Petar Šarčević et al. (eds), Yearbook of Private International Law, Vol. XV, 2013/2014, pp. 87–111.

established . . . that the parties actually agreed to designate the court second seised as having exclusive jurisdiction. . . .

[53] Finally, the difficulties of the kind referred to by the United Kingdom Government, stemming from delaying tactics by parties who, with the intention of delaying settlement of the substantive dispute, commence proceedings before a court which they know to lack jurisdiction by reason of the existence of a jurisdiction clause are not such as to call in question the interpretation of any provision of the Brussels [I Regulation], as deduced from its wording and its purpose.

[54] In view of the foregoing, the answer to the second question must be that [the Brussels Regulation] must be interpreted as meaning that a court second seised whose jurisdiction has been claimed under an agreement conferring jurisdiction must nevertheless stay proceedings until the court first seised has declared that it has no jurisdiction.

[55] By its third question, the national court seeks in essence to ascertain whether [these rules of the Brussels Regulation] may be derogated from where, in general, the duration of proceedings before the courts of the [Member] State in which the court first seised is established is excessively long. . . .

[59] According to Gasser, [the Brussels Regulation] must be interpreted in any event as excluding excessively protracted proceedings (that is to say of a duration exceeding three years), which are contrary to Article 6 of the ECHR and would entail restrictions on freedom of movement as guaranteed by Articles 28 EC, 39 EC, 48 EC and 49 EC. It is the responsibility of the European Union authorities or the national courts to identify those States in which it is well known that legal proceedings are excessively protracted.

[60] Therefore, in a case where no decision on jurisdiction has been given within six months following the commencement of proceedings before the court first seised or no final decision on jurisdiction has been given within one year following the commencement of those proceedings, it is appropriate, in Gasser's view, to decline to apply [the *lis pendens* rule of the Brussels I Regulation]. In any event, the courts of the State where the court second seised is established are entitled themselves to rule both on the question of jurisdiction and, after slightly longer periods, on the substance of the case.

[61] The United Kingdom Government also considers that [the Brussels Regulation] must be interpreted in conformity with Article 6 of the ECHR. It observes in that connection that a potential debtor in a commercial case will often bring, before a court of his choice, an action seeking a judgment exonerating him from all liability, in the knowledge that those proceedings will go on for a particularly long time and with the aim of delaying a judgment against him for several years.

[62] The automatic application of [Article 27 of the Brussels I Regulation] in such a case would grant the potential debtor a substantial and unfair advantage which would enable him to control the procedure, or indeed dissuade the creditor from enforcing his rights by legal proceedings.

[63] In those circumstances, the United Kingdom Government suggests that the Court should recognise an exception to Article [27] whereby the court second seised would be entitled to examine the jurisdiction of the court first seised where (1) the claimant has brought proceedings in bad faith before a court without jurisdiction for the purpose of blocking proceedings before the courts of another [Member] State which enjoy jurisdiction under the Brussels [Regulation] and (2) the court first seised has not decided the question of its jurisdiction within a reasonable time. . . .

[65] MISAT, the Italian Government and the Commission, on the contrary, advocate the full applicability of [Article 27 of the Brussels I Regulation], notwithstanding the excessive duration of court proceedings in one of the States concerned. . . .

[67] The Commission states that the Brussels [Regulation] is based on mutual trust and on the equivalence of the courts of the [Member] States and establishes a binding system of jurisdiction which all the courts within the purview of the [Regulation] are required to observe. The [Member] States can therefore be obliged to ensure mutual recognition and enforcement of judgments by means of simple procedures. This compulsory system of jurisdiction is at the same time conducive to legal certainty since, by virtue of the rules of the Brussels [Regulation], the parties and the courts can properly and easily determine international jurisdiction. Within this system, [Sections 7, 8 and 9 of Chapter II of the Brussels I Regulation are] designed to prevent conflicts of jurisdiction and conflicting decisions.

[68] It is not compatible with the philosophy and the objectives of the Brussels [Regulation] for national courts to be under an obligation to respect rules on *lis pendens* only if they consider that the court first seised will give judgment within a reasonable period. Nowhere does the Convention provide that courts may use the pretext of delays in procedure in other contracting States to excuse themselves from applying its provisions.

[69] Moreover, the point from which the duration of proceedings becomes excessively long, to such an extent that the interests of a party may be seriously affected, can be determined only on the basis of an appraisal taking account of all the circumstances of the case. That is an issue which cannot be settled in the context of the Brussels [Regulation]. It is for the European Court of Human Rights to examine the issue and the national courts cannot substitute themselves for it by recourse to Article [27] of the [Regulation]. . . .

[73] In view of the foregoing, the answer to the third question must be that Article [27 of the Brussels I Regulation] must be interpreted as meaning that it cannot be derogated from where, in general, the duration of proceedings before the courts of the Contracting State in which the court first seised is established is excessively long.

Notes and Questions

As the UK government points out, if the first seized court in the EU *always* has jurisdiction to decide whether a choice of forum clause in favor of a different court or arbitration tribunal in the EU is valid or not, and that the other Member States have to respect whatever decision this first seized court comes up with, we would be inviting abuse. For example, parties might have agreed to litigate in the High Court in London. One or even both of the parties may have entered into this agreement in the knowledge that the London court is known for efficiency and competence over the subject matter. Eventually a dispute arises and one party realizes that it does not stand much of a chance of prevailing on substance in the London court. Therefore, they bring a case in Italy, on the basis of the exorbitant rule that allows any party with a domicile in Italy to bring a case in Italian court. Although the initiation of proceedings in Italy is clearly inconsistent with the choice of court agreement, the Italian court would take its own time to examine its jurisdiction. Even if it came to the correct conclusion that the case should be litigated in London, this could be appealed. Altogether, justified claims of the other party could easily be blocked for several years in this way. To counter what has sometimes been called "torpedo actions" like these,[95] a change was made when the earlier Brussels I Regulation 44/2001 was replaced with the current Brussels Ia or Ibis Regulation 1215/2012. Article 31(2) of the new Regulation now gives unconditional priority to the court chosen in a choice of court agreement to establish whether it has jurisdiction:

Article 31

1. Where actions come within the exclusive jurisdiction of several courts, any court other than the court first seised shall decline jurisdiction in favour of that court.

2. Without prejudice to Article 26, where a court of a Member State on which an agreement as referred to in Article 25 confers exclusive jurisdiction is seised, any court of another Member State shall stay the proceedings until such time as the court seised on the basis of the agreement declares that it has no jurisdiction under the agreement.

3. Where the court designated in the agreement has established jurisdiction in accordance with the agreement, any court of another Member State shall decline jurisdiction in favour of that court.

4. Paragraphs 2 and 3 shall not apply to matters referred to in Sections 3, 4 or 5 where the policyholder, the insured, a beneficiary of the insurance contract, the injured party, the consumer or the employee is the claimant and the agreement is not valid under a provision contained within those Sections.

In plain English, if the dispute is between commercial parties and not the B2C kind referred to in paragraph (4), the court chosen in a choice of forum clause gets to decide on the validity of that clause even if it is not the first seized court. The passage "without prejudice . . ." in paragraph (2) provides for only one exception. If one party brings a case in a non-chosen court, and the other party makes an appearance

---

95. See, for example, http://www.lexology.com/library/detail.aspx?g=8c7b00c4-80dd-43e4 -89f3-fdd453a19420.

pursuant to Article 26 *and presents arguments on the merits*, i.e., not appearing only to contest jurisdiction, this appearance will be interpreted as a new party agreement on jurisdiction in favor of the first seized court and will override the original choice of forum clause.

An open question is whether the same principles apply if the choice of forum clause is an arbitration clause.

Case 6-4

Allianz SpA and Assicurazioni Generali SpA v. West Tankers Inc.

European Court of Justice, Case C-185/07
Judgment of 10 February 2009, 2009 ECR I-663

[This case also concerns the interpretation of a provision in Regulation 44/2001 on Jurisdiction and the Recognition and Enforcement of Judgments in Civil and Commercial Matters, the Brussels I Regulation. As outlined earlier, this Regulation has meanwhile been replaced with Regulation 1215/2012 on Jurisdiction and the Recognition and Enforcement of Judgments in Civil and Commercial Matters, the Brussels Ia or I bis Regulation (Documents, p. II-92). According to its Article 1(2)(d), neither the new nor the old Regulation applies to arbitration. As a consequence, the provisions of the Regulation directing applicants to the appropriate courts do not apply when there is an arbitration clause. At the same time, the EU Regulation must not interfere with the older obligations of the EU Member States under the New York Convention on the Recognition and Enforcement of Foreign Arbitral Awards. Thus, pursuant to Article II(1) of the New York Convention, "[e]ach Contracting State shall recognize an agreement in writing under which the parties undertake to submit to arbitration all or any differences which have arisen or which may arise between them in respect of a defined legal relationship, whether contractual or not . . ." (see below, pp. 1014 et seq.). This would suggest that the courts have no role to play when there is an arbitration clause in a contract. However, the EU Regulation does not clearly state *who should decide whether an arbitration clause is actually valid* in a given case. And the New York Convention, in Article II(3), leaves room for some court intervention: "The court of a Contracting State, when seized of an action in a matter in respect of which the parties have made an agreement within the meaning of this article, shall, at the request of one of the parties, refer the parties to arbitration, unless it finds that the said agreement is null and void, inoperative or incapable of being performed." The following case demonstrates how such a conflict can play out. The reader should pay attention to how the House of Lords, called upon by the party that would prefer to arbitrate, wants to be able to grant an anti-suit injunction preventing the other party from going to court, or requiring them to discontinue any proceedings already begun. In considering whether to grant an anti-suit injunction, the House of Lords, as the court with jurisdiction over the place of arbitration, would implicitly have to make a decision on the validity of the arbitration clause. The Tribunale di Siracusa, however, had already been seized by the party that would prefer to litigate and is the court that would have jurisdiction pursuant to the Regulation in the absence of a valid arbitration clause. In considering whether to pursue with the case, the Tribunale would implicitly have to make a decision on the validity of the arbitration clause as well. Thus, the European Court of Justice had to decide which forum should have priority, i.e., whether the exclusion of "arbitration" in the Regulation covers also the question whether an arbitration clause is valid or not.]

The dispute in the main proceedings and the question referred for a preliminary ruling

[9] In August 2000 the *Front Comor*, a vessel owned by West Tankers and chartered by Erg Petroli SpA ('Erg'), collided in Syracuse (Italy) with a jetty owned by Erg and caused damage. The charterparty was governed by English law and contained a clause providing for arbitration in London (United Kingdom).

[10] Erg claimed compensation from its insurers Allianz and Generali up to the limit of its insurance cover and commenced arbitration proceedings in London against West Tankers for the excess. West Tankers denied liability for the damage caused by the collision.

[11] Having paid Erg compensation under the insurance policies for the loss it had suffered, Allianz and Generali brought proceedings on 30 July 2003 against West Tankers before the Tribunale di Siracusa (Italy) in order to recover the sums they had paid to Erg. The action was based on their statutory right of subrogation to Erg's claims, in accordance with Article 1916 of the Italian Civil Code. West Tankers raised an objection of lack of jurisdiction on the basis of the existence of the arbitration agreement.

[12] In parallel, West Tankers brought proceedings, on 10 September 2004, before the High Court of Justice of England and Wales, Queens Bench Division (Commercial Court), seeking a declaration that the dispute between itself, on the one hand, and Allianz and Generali, on the other, was to be settled by arbitration pursuant to the arbitration agreement. West Tankers also sought an injunction restraining Allianz and Generali from pursuing any proceedings other than arbitration and requiring them to discontinue the proceedings commenced before the Tribunale di Siracusa ('the anti-suit injunction').

[13] By judgment of 21 March 2005, the High Court of Justice of England and Wales, Queens Bench Division (Commercial Court), upheld West Tankers' claims and granted the anti-suit injunction sought against Allianz and Generali. The latter appealed against that judgment to the House of Lords. They argued that the grant of such an injunction is contrary to Regulation No 44/2001 [the precursor to Regulation 1215/2012 cited above, p. 713].

[14] The House of Lords first referred to the judgments in Case C-116/02 *Gasser* [above, p. 770] and Case C-159/02 *Turner* [2004] ECR I-3565, which decided in substance that an injunction restraining a party from commencing or continuing proceedings in a court of a Member State cannot be compatible with the system established by

Regulation No 44/2001, even where it is granted by the court having jurisdiction under that regulation. That is because the regulation provides a complete set of uniform rules on the allocation of jurisdiction between the courts of the Member States which must trust each other to apply those rules correctly.

[15] However, that principle cannot, in the view of the House of Lords, be extended to arbitration, which is completely excluded from the scope of Regulation No 44/2001 by virtue of Article 1(2)(d) thereof. In that field, there is no set of uniform Community rules, which is a necessary condition in order that mutual trust between the courts of the Member States may be established and applied. Moreover, it is clear from the judgment in Case C-190/89 *Rich* [1991] ECR I-3855 that the exclusion in Article 1(2)(d) of Regulation No 44/2001 applies not only to arbitration proceedings as such, but also to legal proceedings the subject-matter of which is arbitration. The judgment in Case C-391/95 *Van Uden* [1998] ECR I-7091 stated that arbitration is the subject-matter of proceedings where they serve to protect the right to determine the dispute by arbitration, which is the case in the main proceedings.

[16] The House of Lords adds that since all arbitration matters fall outside the scope of Regulation No 44/2001, an injunction addressed to Allianz and Generali restraining them from having recourse to proceedings other than arbitration and from continuing proceedings before the Tribunale di Siracusa cannot infringe the regulation.

[17] Finally, the House of Lords points out that the courts of the United Kingdom have for many years used anti-suit injunctions. That practice is, in its view, a valuable tool for the court of the seat of arbitration, exercising supervisory jurisdiction over the arbitration, as it promotes legal certainty and reduces the possibility of conflict between the arbitration award and the judgment of a national court. Furthermore, if the practice were also adopted by the courts in other Member States it would make the European Community more competitive vis-à-vis international arbitration centres such as New York, Bermuda and Singapore.

[18] In those circumstances, the House of Lords decided to stay its proceedings and to [make a reference to the European Court of Justice pursuant to Article 267 TFEU].

The question referred for a preliminary ruling

[19] By its question, the House of Lords asks, essentially, whether it is incompatible with Regulation No 44/2001 for a court of a Member State to make an order to restrain a person from commencing or continuing proceedings before the courts of another Member State on the ground that such proceedings would be contrary to an arbitration agreement, even though Article 1(2)(d) of the regulation excludes arbitration from the scope thereof.

[20] An anti-suit injunction, such as that in the main proceedings, may be directed against actual or potential claimants in proceedings abroad. As observed by the Advocate General in point 14 of her Opinion, non-compliance with an anti-suit injunction is contempt of court, for which penalties can be imposed, including imprisonment or seizure of assets.

[21] Both West Tankers and the United Kingdom Government submit that such an injunction is not incompatible with Regulation No 44/2001 because Article 1(2)(d) thereof excludes arbitration from its scope of application.

[22] In that regard it must be borne in mind that, in order to determine whether a dispute falls within the scope of Regulation No 44/2001, reference must be made solely to the subject-matter of the proceedings (*Rich*, paragraph 26). More specifically, its place in the scope of Regulation No 44/2001 is determined by the nature of the rights which the proceedings in question serve to protect (*Van Uden*, paragraph 33).

[23] Proceedings, such as those in the main proceedings, which lead to the making of an anti-suit injunction, cannot, therefore, come within the scope of Regulation No 44/2001.

[24] However, even though proceedings do not come within the scope of Regulation No 44/2001, they may nevertheless have consequences which undermine its effectiveness, namely preventing the attainment of the objectives of unification of the rules of conflict of jurisdiction in civil and commercial matters and the free movement of decisions in those matters. This is so, inter alia, where such proceedings prevent a court of another Member State from exercising the jurisdiction conferred on it by Regulation No 44/2001.

[25] It is therefore appropriate to consider whether the proceedings brought by Allianz and Generali against West Tankers before the Tribunale di Siracusa themselves come within the scope of Regulation No 44/2001 and then to ascertain the effects of the anti-suit injunction on those proceedings.

[26] In that regard, the Court finds, as noted by the Advocate General in points 53 and 54 of her Opinion, that, if, because of the subject-matter of the dispute, that is, the nature of the rights to be protected in proceedings, such as a claim for damages, those proceedings come within the scope of Regulation No 44/2001, a preliminary issue concerning the applicability of an arbitration agreement, including in particular its validity, also comes within its scope of application. This finding is supported by paragraph 35 of the Report on the accession of the Hellenic Republic to the Convention of 27 September 1968 on Jurisdiction and the Enforcement of Judgments in Civil and Commercial Matters (OJ 1978 L 304, p. 36) ('the Brussels Convention'), presented by Messrs Evrigenis and Kerameus (OJ 1986 C 298, p. 1). That paragraph states that the verification, as an incidental question, of the validity of an arbitration agreement which is cited by a litigant in order to contest the jurisdiction of the court before which he is being sued pursuant to the Brussels Convention, must be considered as falling within its scope. [The Brussels Convention is the precursor to Reg 44/2001; the Brussels Convention, Reg 44/2001 and the current Reg 1215/2015 contain parallel provisions regarding the present matter.]

[27] It follows that the objection of lack of jurisdiction raised by West Tankers before the Tribunale di Siracusa on the basis of the existence of an arbitration agreement, including the question of the validity of that agreement, comes within the scope of Regulation No 44/2001 and that it is therefore exclusively for that court to rule on

that objection and on its own jurisdiction, pursuant to Articles 1(2)(d) and 5(3) of that regulation.

[28] Accordingly, the use of an anti-suit injunction to prevent a court of a Member State, which normally has jurisdiction to resolve a dispute under Article 5(3) of Regulation No 44/2001, from ruling, in accordance with Article 1(2)(d) of that regulation, on the very applicability of the regulation to the dispute brought before it necessarily amounts to stripping that court of the power to rule on its own jurisdiction under Regulation No 44/2001.

[29] It follows, first, as noted by the Advocate General in point 57 of her Opinion, that an anti-suit injunction, such as that in the main proceedings, is contrary to the general principle which emerges from the case-law of the Court on the Brussels Convention, that every court seised itself determines, under the rules applicable to it, whether it has jurisdiction to resolve the dispute before it (see, to that effect, *Gasser*, paragraphs 48 and 49). It should be borne in mind in that regard that Regulation No 44/2001, apart from a few limited exceptions which are not relevant to the main proceedings, does not authorise the jurisdiction of a court of a Member State to be reviewed by a court in another Member State (Case C-351/89 *Overseas Union Insurance and Others* [1991] ECR I-3317, paragraph 24, and *Turner*, paragraph 26). That jurisdiction is determined directly by the rules laid down by that regulation, including those relating to its scope of application. Thus in no case is a court of one Member State in a better position to determine whether the court of another Member State has jurisdiction (*OverseasUnion Insurance and Others*, paragraph 23, and *Gasser*, paragraph 48).

[30] Further, in obstructing the court of another Member State in the exercise of the powers conferred on it by Regulation No 44/2001, namely to decide, on the basis of the rules defining the material scope of that regulation, including Article 1(2)(d) thereof, whether that regulation is applicable, such an anti-suit injunction also runs counter to the trust which the Member States accord to one another's legal systems and judicial institutions and on which the system of jurisdiction under Regulation No 44/2001 is based (see, to that effect, *Turner*, paragraph 24).

[31] Lastly, if, by means of an anti-suit injunction, the Tribunale di Siracusa were prevented from examining itself the preliminary issue of the validity or the applicability of the arbitration agreement, a party could avoid the proceedings merely by relying on that agreement and the applicant, which considers that the agreement is void, inoperative or incapable of being performed, would thus be barred from access to the court before which it brought proceedings under Article 5(3) of Regulation No 44/2001 and would therefore be deprived of a form of judicial protection to which it is entitled.

[32] Consequently, an anti-suit injunction, such as that in the main proceedings, is not compatible with Regulation No 44/2001.

[33] This finding is supported by Article II(3) of the New York Convention, according to which it is the court of a Contracting State, when seised of an action in a matter

in respect of which the parties have made an arbitration agreement, that will, at the request of one of the parties, refer the parties to arbitration, unless it finds that the said agreement is null and void, inoperative or incapable of being performed.

[34] In the light of the foregoing considerations, the answer to the question referred is that it is incompatible with Regulation No 44/2001 for a court of a Member State to make an order to restrain a person from commencing or continuing proceedings before the courts of another Member State on the ground that such proceedings would be contrary to an arbitration agreement.

Notes and Questions

1. As can be seen from paragraph 26, the ECJ held that the validity of an arbitration agreement is a preliminary question to a lawsuit falling within the scope of application of the Regulation. Thus, it gave the power to the Tribunale to decide the validity of the arbitration clause, in line with the time-honored principle that if the jurisdiction of a court is disputed, it is for that same court to decide upon its jurisdiction (the so-called "Kompetenz-Kompetenz," see para. 29). In so doing, it rejected the availability of anti-suit injunctions in cases like this one, since the courts or tribunals of one Member State could not prevent the courts of another Member State from exercising their powers to make preliminary decisions regarding jurisdiction. However, the ECJ also held in *Van Uden* and elsewhere that the right to arbitrate falls under the exclusion of Article 1(2)(d) of the Regulation and, therefore, has to be protected by the court with jurisdiction over the place of arbitration. What are the consequences if the Tribunale should decide that the arbitration clause is not valid and that litigation can go ahead in Siracusa, while the House of Lords decides that the arbitration clause is valid and that arbitration can go ahead in London? Where would a judgment from Siracusa be recognized and enforced? Where would an arbitral award from London be recognized and enforced? What about the principle of mutual trust and the obligation of EU Member States to recognize and enforce judicial decisions from other Member States? What about procedural economy?

Please note that the approach taken by the Court in *West Tankers* was specifically endorsed by the Member States when they revised the Brussels I Regulation. Recital 12 of the Preamble of the new Brussels Ia or Ibis Regulation 1215/2012 reads as follows:

> (12) This Regulation should not apply to arbitration. Nothing in this Regulation should prevent the courts of a Member State, when seised of an action in a matter in respect of which the parties have entered into an arbitration agreement, from referring the parties to arbitration, from staying or dismissing the proceedings, or from examining whether the arbitration agreement is null and void, inoperative or incapable of being performed, in accordance with their national law.

> A ruling given by a court of a Member State as to whether or not an arbitration agreement is null and void, inoperative or incapable of being performed

should not be subject to the rules of recognition and enforcement laid down in this Regulation, regardless of whether the court decided on this as a principal issue or as an incidental question.

On the other hand, where a court of a Member State, exercising jurisdiction under this Regulation or under national law, has determined that an arbitration agreement is null and void, inoperative or incapable of being performed, this should not preclude that court's judgment on the substance of the matter from being recognised or, as the case may be, enforced in accordance with this Regulation. This should be without prejudice to the competence of the courts of the Member States to decide on the recognition and enforcement of arbitral awards in accordance with the Convention on the Recognition and Enforcement of Foreign Arbitral Awards, done at New York on 10 June 1958 ('the 1958 New York Convention'), which takes precedence over this Regulation.

This Regulation should not apply to any action or ancillary proceedings relating to, in particular, the establishment of an arbitral tribunal, the powers of arbitrators, the conduct of an arbitration procedure or any other aspects of such a procedure, nor to any action or judgment concerning the annulment, review, appeal, recognition or enforcement of an arbitral award.[96]

2. In spite of the somewhat problematic outcome, the European Court of Justice confirmed its stance regarding the jurisdiction of non-chosen courts to decide on the validity of arbitration clauses in the more recent *Case C-536/13 Gazprom v. Lietuvos Respublika*.[97] The European Court, after reminding the parties that "arbitration does not fall within the scope of Regulation No [1215/2012]," decided as follows:

[43] Since the New York Convention governs a field excluded from the scope of Regulation No [1215/2012], it does not relate to a 'particular matter' within the meaning of Article 71(1) of that regulation. Article 71 governs only the relations between that regulation and conventions falling under the particular matters that come within the scope of Regulation No [1215/2012 . . .].

[44] It follows from all the foregoing considerations that the answer to the questions referred is that Regulation No [1215/2012] must be interpreted as *not* precluding a court of a Member State from recognising and enforcing, or from refusing to recognise and enforce, an arbitral award prohibiting a party from bringing certain claims before a court of that Member State, since that regulation does not govern the recognition and enforcement, in a Member State, of an arbitral award issued by an arbitral tribunal in another Member State. [emphasis added]

---

96. Documents, p. II-92. For the argument that this addition to the Brussels Regulation opens as many questions as it answers, see Neil Dowers & Zheng Sophia Tang, *Arbitration in EU Jurisdiction Regulation: Brussels I Recast and a New Proposal*, Groningen J. Int'l L., Vol. 3, No. 1, pp. 125–146.

97. Judgment of May 13, 2015, *Case C-536/13 Gazprom*, ECLI:EU:C:2015:316.

What does this mean for parallel proceedings in court and in arbitration in the EU? Do you agree with the European Court of Justice? Obviously, the ECJ was just looking at Regulation 1215/2012, including the new provision in the Preamble, but could it have done more to support the New York Convention? Could Gazprom have enforced the arbitration clause in the shareholder agreement? If so, how?

Another important consideration is the cost of defending oneself against a lawsuit brought in the wrong forum. An important example is the case that led to the decision in *Union Discount Co. Ltd. v. Zoller & Ors.* of the United Kingdom Court of Appeal in 2001.[98] Union Cal had entered into a number of contracts with Robert Zoller, each of which provided for exclusive jurisdiction of English courts over any disputes. In accordance with the clauses, Union Cal eventually sued Zoller in England over performance issues. However, Zoller initiated proceedings against Union Cal in New York to deny the claims. Union Cal made an appearance in New York to contest jurisdiction and eventually persuaded the New York court to strike out the proceedings for lack of jurisdiction. Since the laws of New York do not provide for an award of costs in these kind of proceedings, Union Cal went back to England to seek compensation for the costs incurred in New York. The trial court in the UK refused the claims on the grounds that "[c]osts incurred in foreign proceedings cannot be recovered in an English action between the same parties."[99] On appeal, the issue was framed as "whether the defendants are right to assert . . . that: 'As a matter of law the costs of litigation can not be recovered as damages for breach of contract by one party to the said litigation against another' or whether the true principle of law is, as Union Cal asserts . . . that: 'The costs of prior proceedings between the same parties may be recovered as damages for breach of contract if (as in the present case) the party seeking to recover the costs of the prior proceedings as damages could not in the circumstances of the prior proceedings have obtained an order for the payment of those costs as costs'."[100] The Court of Appeal first concluded that there was no hard-and-fast rule about recovery of foreign costs in domestic proceedings and that the decision was to be based on policy considerations. Then it continued as follows, starting at p. 319:

[18] It is important to emphasise that in the present case the following unusual features are all present:

> (i) The costs which the claimant seeks to recover in the English proceedings were incurred by him when he was a defendant in foreign proceedings brought by the defendant in the English proceedings.

---

98. Court of Appeal (Civil Division), Judgment of 21 November 2001, [2001] EWCA Civ 1755, [2002] C.L.C. 314.

99. The court cited *Halsbury's Laws of England* (4th ed. reissue) vol. 12(1) (1988), Damages, para. 828. Halsbury's is not legislation but rather a kind of restatement of English common law.

100. [2002] C.L.C. 314, at p. 316.

(ii) The claimant in the foreign proceedings brought those proceedings in breach of an express term, the EJC, which, it is assumed for present purposes, has the effect of entitling the English claimant to damages for its breach.

(iii) The rules of the foreign forum only permitted recovery of costs in exceptional circumstances.

(iv) The foreign court made no adjudication as to costs.

[19] It is common ground that there is no binding authority which inhibits us from granting Union Cal relief in damages in the present case. That relief is predicated on the assumption, not in issue before us, that the bringing of the New York proceedings itself constituted a breach of contract which has resulted in damages which are prima facie recoverable. Thus it is common ground that the action should not have been struck out unless there are policy reasons which prevent the recovery of these damages.

[20] Mark Hubbard, appearing for Zoller, put forward the following policy reasons which he submitted justified the conclusion of the [UK trial] judge.

The comity argument

[21] He submitted that the rules of comity prevented the recovery of costs of civil proceedings in foreign jurisdictions as damages for breach of contract. The argument went as follows. Costs rules and practices in a state's jurisdiction are a matter for the state in question. One can advance policy arguments in favour of an approach, such as that which prevails in this country, that in general the successful party recovers his costs. Equally one can advance policy arguments in favour of an approach such as that which prevails in New York that in general each side pays its own costs. It would breach international comity if we sought indirectly to apply our approach to litigation which had taken place in the foreign country.

[22] We accept that policy arguments can be made in favour of either approach but we reject the notion that by allowing a party in the position of Union Cal to recover these costs we would be breaching international comity. Comity is, as the editors of *Dicey and Morris on the Conflict of Laws* (13th edn) point out in para. 1-010, a term of very elastic content. Suppose the situation were reversed. A party from a jurisdiction which had an indemnity approach to costs more generous than our own is sued here in breach of an [exclusive jurisdiction clause EJC]. He persuades the English courts that we had no jurisdiction. He asks for costs but only recovers, let us say, a small amount of costs because our courts thought a larger amount was disproportionate to the amount at stake. He then sues for the difference in the jurisdiction named in the EJC and recovers the difference. We can not think that such a happening would be the cause of the slightest concern to this country or its courts if indeed it ever came to their attention.

[23] There is in these cases no reason of comity why our courts should enforce a foreign jurisdiction's policy perception in preference to our own nor why they should enforce ours in preference to theirs.

[24] If, as Berry[101] demonstrates, an English civil court is prepared to give as damages in tort costs which have been refused by an English criminal court, we see no reason based on comity which would prevent an English civil court from giving as damages costs which a foreign court has not awarded. We would not expect to show a foreign court more comity than we show our own.

The res judicata argument

[25] The courts manifestly should avoid two adjudications on the same point. That is common ground. However in cases such as the present where there is assumed to be an independent cause of action then, as Devlin LJ points out in the fourth passage we cite from Berry . . . , what is being adjudicated upon on the second occasion is not the same point.

[26] In the present case . . . there was no adjudication upon costs in the New York court and so res judicata does not arise.

The Henderson v Henderson point

[27] This founds on the well known passage in that case in the Vice-Chancellor's judgement in that case[102] where he said:

"where a given matter becomes the subject of litigation in, and of adjudication by, a court of competent jurisdiction, the court requires the parties to that litigation to bring forward their whole case, and will not (except under special circumstances) permit the same parties to open the same subject of litigation in respect of matter which might have been brought forward as part of the subject in contest, but which was not brought forward, only because they have . . . omitted part of their case."

[28] We accept of course that it is important that there should be an end to litigation but that principle has no sensible application to the present case. Since it was Union Cal's contention that the New York courts had no jurisdiction to consider breaches of the contract between Zoller and Union Cal, the latter could not in New York bring an action for damages caused to Union Cal by the bringing of the action in New York. If it wished to advance that contention it had to do so in England. The principle in Henderson v Henderson is manifestly inapplicable.

The unity of the law point

[29] Mr Hubbard submitted that since the English courts have for years proceeded on the presumption . . . that the litigant who won the earlier proceedings will have got such costs as the law considers he deserves, the same presumption ought to apply

---

101. The Court of Appeal had already referred earlier to *Berry v British Transport Commission*, Court of Appeal, Judgment of 23 June 1961 ([[1962] 1 Q.B. 306; [1961] 3 W.L.R. 450; [1961] 3 All E.R. 65; (1961) 105 S.J. 5870, a purely domestic case about recovery of costs incurred in criminal proceedings pursuant to malicious prosecution.

102. *Henderson v Henderson*, Court of Chancery, Decision of 20 July 1843, [1843–60] All E.R. Rep. 378; 67 E.R. 313; (1843) 3 Hare 100.

whether those earlier proceedings were abroad or here. The law there referred to, it was implicit in his submissions, was the law of the courts in which the earlier proceedings were litigated. He submitted that either the general presumption should be abandoned or it should be kept and universally applied.

[30] While in some ways an attractive proposition, it falls at first base because it was ruled in Berry by this court that it should not apply in malicious prosecution cases. Therefore the unity of the law after which he strives is not available—in any event in this court.

[31] EJCs arise because the parties agree to litigate in one jurisdiction. It may be that one of the considerations which led to the adoption of the EJC in question was the costs regime in the nominated jurisdiction. We see no policy reason connected with either party for allowing one party to the contract to escape from liability for the damages which he has caused to the other by attempting to sue in a country where a different costs regime prevails.

[32] There remains the question whether there is a policy reason or the benefit of society at large which argues in favour of applying the usual rule in cases where the costs sought to be recovered as damages represent the cost of litigation abroad in breach of an EJC. In the present case we can see none unless it be a desire to keep down litigation purely involving costs—often referred to as parasitic litigation. A rationale behind the reluctance to facilitate parasitic litigation is that the state's legal resources should be devoted to central rather than parasitic questions. While this seems attractive, one must note that the amount of costs (or damages in the form of costs) at stake can be very much more than many a sum which otherwise is allowed to be recovered as damages.

The availability of an anti-suit injunction

[33] Mr Hubbard submitted correctly that Union Cal had the option of obtaining an anti-suit injunction in England. The fact that they did not do this but instead chose to apply to strike out the New York proceedings was a tactical decision no doubt motivated, he submitted, by the desire not to expose themselves to a costs order should they fail in the strike out application. This in substance is an argument that Union Cal should have mitigated their damages by trying to obtain an anti-suit injunction. Even if this submission be correct, which we do not have to decide and do not decide, it goes to quantum not to the principle as to whether any damages are recoverable. We confess that it seems to us unattractive for the New York claimant to submit that the English defendant should not have gone to New York to resist the proceedings which the New York claimant had, as a matter of choice, started there.

Conclusion

[34] In circumstances such as the present we do not consider that the public interest requires that the claimant should be deprived of its reasonable expenses in litigating at the instance of the defendant in a jurisdiction which the defendant chose in breach of an EJC. . . .

Notes and Questions

1. The costs of proceedings are generally composed of multiple components. First, there are the court fees themselves, then the attorney fees of each side, and finally other expenses such as travel, expert witnesses, translations, etc. Different jurisdictions apply different models with regard to the distribution of costs and expenses. For our purposes, it is generally sufficient to distinguish between countries or jurisdictions with and without fee shifting. Without fee shifting, the court fees are either paid by the plaintiff or shared, while each side pays its own attorney fees and other expenses. By contrast, if a country applies fee shifting, the losing party will be required to pay not only the court fees and its own attorney fees and expenses, but also reasonable attorney fees and expenses of the winning party. The latter model — also called "the English Rule" — is prevalent in most countries outside of the U.S., as well as in most arbitration procedures. By contrast, under the "American Rule," fee shifting remains an exceptional remedy, mostly reserved for cases where litigation was unjustified or even frivolous, or expenses of the other side were driven up with the intention of forcing an abandonment of a claim or a settlement. Furthermore, contractual arrangements between business parties can overrule statutory provisions on fee shifting, but a court or judge may refuse to enforce them if they are considered unreasonable or unfair. For further analysis see also below pp. 790–793 and 1036 et seq.

2. Prior to *Union Discount v. Zoller*, the courts in the United Kingdom generally did not allow costs and expenses incurred abroad to be claimed as costs or damages in domestic proceedings. This approach was based on the notion that each court or jurisdiction should be entitled to have and enforce its own rules on distribution of costs. However, the Court of Appeal changed the long-standing approach and allowed recovery of foreign costs.

    a. Why did the Court of Appeal feel compelled to deviate from the long-standing practice? How broad or how narrow is the deviation? Can you outline scenarios in which the new rule would allow recovery and others in which recovery of foreign costs would still be refused?

    b. The Court of Appeal discusses comity, res judicata, the *Henderson v. Henderson* precedent, the "unity of law" argument, and the problem of potentially "parasitic litigation." Can you explain each of these policy arguments advanced on behalf of Zoller and why the Court of Appeal was not persuaded?

    c. Union Cal did not ask the court in New York to rule on costs. Did they forget or did they know that they would not get compensation for their attorney expenses? What would have happened in the UK courts if Union Cal had tried but failed to recover costs in New York? (Re-read paragraphs 25 and 26.)

Before we end our analysis of jurisdiction and venue and turn to other practical matters related to litigation abroad, we can formulate some practical rules on how to determine where a dispute resulting from an IBT can be brought to court:

Checklist 6-1
How to Determine the Forum (State) — Which Courts Have Jurisdiction Over a Dispute Resulting from an IBT?

1. Autonomous choice by valid agreement of the parties
   - in writing at the time of the conclusion of the contract
   - in writing after the dispute has arisen

     provided the rules on private international law/international conflict of laws of the chosen country accept the choice and the subject matter does not fall under an exclusive jurisdiction elsewhere;

2. Jurisdiction of the first-seized court if the defendant enters an appearance without contesting jurisdiction;

3. The courts in the country determined by private international law (international conflict of laws); as a rule of thumb, claims have to be brought at the place of residence or incorporation or the seat or the place of business ("domicile") of the defendant;

   N.B. PIL rules are not fully harmonized between countries; most countries provide for certain alternative jurisdictions in addition to domicile of defendant, to protect the weaker parties in tort cases, consumer cases, insurance contracts, employment contracts, etc.; some countries also have alternative jurisdictions falling into the category of exorbitant jurisdictions;

4. If the first-seized court accepts jurisdiction and as long as it occupies itself with the case, the rule of *lis pendens* should block any other courts from hearing a case involving the same parties and the same claims;

5. If the first-seized court adopts a decision on the merits, the rule of *res judicata* should permanently block any other courts from accepting a case involving the same parties and the same claims; an exception applies only for the court having appellate jurisdiction over the decision of the first-seized court;

6. For defendants with a domicile in the EU, the rules of Regulation 1215/2012 are applicable and displace any Member State rules of private international law or conflicts. In other parts of the world, there may also be bilateral or multilateral conventions that need to be considered, in particular Hague Conventions.

B. Procedural Issues in Transnational Litigation

1. Legal Representation in a Foreign Jurisdiction

Whenever a business is forced to bring a claim in a foreign court or — even worse — is forced to defend itself against a claim in a foreign court, one of the early challenges is finding an attorney in that foreign country. In general, legal studies in one country only qualify lawyers to be admitted to the bar or profession in that country. Very few lawyers go to the trouble of getting a second law degree or qualification in order to practice in two, let alone more than two, countries. In the U.S., lawyers generally take the bar exam in the state where they want to practice and for the federal bar. After some years of experience, they can also be admitted relatively easily to the bar in other states of the U.S. However, an American lawyer will rarely be admitted to the bar in more than three or four states. Thus, an attorney may be admitted to practice in New York and in Florida, or in California, but not anywhere else. As a consequence of these localized bar admission rules, the usual counsel of a business will not normally be able to represent it abroad. Naturally, these rules do not serve only or even primarily for the compartmentalization of the market. Difficulties with understanding the law of foreign countries only begin with the language. The procedural rules and requirements—and even the substantive laws—differ greatly from one country to another, and keep on evolving, making it hard for any legal professional to stay fully informed of the rules and requirements in more than one jurisdiction, even if she is fully proficient in the respective languages. Thus, the usual counsel not only cannot represent the client, she can not even provide much advice about the law in the foreign country. Worst of all, she will not even be able to discern whether an attorney retained as local counsel is good at her job or not, before a lot of time and money has been spent.

Lawyers in foreign countries are fully aware of this problem and when approached by a foreign law firm or corporation—in particular if they are from the U.S. or another county that is perceived as wealthy—they may make quite exaggerated demands with regard to their fees. In a recent case, we wanted to know whether a particular corporation in Turkey was registered in the name of a particular individual. The first Turkish attorney we approached looked at the names of the parties to the dispute and then demanded an advance of no less than US$50,000. He probably would have sent a paralegal to search the corporate register, paid less than US$100 for the service, and laughed all the way to the bank.

The question is, therefore, how can we find a lawyer in the foreign jurisdiction who is both good at her job and reasonable in price? Unfortunately, there is no easy answer to this question. The best solution is to use contacts or connections we already have in the foreign country who can recommend the right lawyer for the job. This could be via an association our law firm may have or via another professional network. Use caution, however. The larger the network and the less personal the connection, the less reliable it will be. For example, Law Crossing lists the 30 largest legal networks in the world at https://www.lawcrossing.com/employers/article/900044704/30-Largest-Law-Firm-Networks/. Leading the list are Lex Mundi with 160 law firms in 160 jurisdictions and 21,000 lawyers, and the multi-disciplinary World Services Group (WSG) with 150 firms in 141 jurisdictions and 19,232 legal advisers. Naturally, these networks seek to impose a number of quality standards to secure their reputation as the "go to" place to find help abroad. Thus, "WSG ensures the highest standards across its membership through the implementation of strict admissions criteria, membership bylaws and policies, regular member reviews, peer-to-peer feedback and oversight by the Board of Directors and Regional Councils."[103] However, these are not franchises and they have limited options of imposing uniform standards of quality across their membership. What is demanded, rather, is for members to be "among the leading local, national and/or international firm[s],"[104] i.e., that the members fulfill high *local* standards. These may be quite different from what we are used to in our own jurisdiction.

The next option is to go with what we know, i.e., to work with the largest law firms in the world that have branch offices in many of the places where our clients do business. As of 2020, Dentons was the largest law firm in the world with almost 10,000 lawyers in more than 180 offices in 73 countries. Baker & McKenzie was not far behind, with more than 6,000 lawyers in 46 countries. Some firms have particular strengths in specific regions.[105] For example, Dentons, after merging with the Chinese law firm Dacheng, is particularly well represented in China. CMS, a regional firm based in Vienna, Austria, is recognized for its penetration of Central and Eastern Europe. Cleary Gottlieb Steen & Hamilton are well known for their coverage of Latin America when it comes to corporate and commercial law. Linklaters may be the best firm across Africa. By contrast to the looser associations covered above, the integrated firms, although they may be franchises, generally have more control over the quality of the work and the professionals at their various branches. They may also have to back up their work with a system-wide liability, in case of malpractice. This is not the case with the associations. However, whether we are approaching a global law firm or a global association of local firms, the ease of access, proficiency in English, and assurance of quality comes at a price. While we may not know much else about the individual lawyers who will actually be our local counsel, one thing we know for sure: they will be among the most expensive in those countries.

Whenever the stakes are high, we should not hesitate to hire the most recommended and best reputed lawyers, regardless of cost. But what should we do if the amount in dispute is not so large, even though it may be a question of survival for our client? Or if the client is in financial distress—possibly because of the unfulfilled claims we are trying to help with—and cannot advance the fees of a large international law firm? This is where we need more personalized recommendations from friends, colleagues, fellow alumni, and others we can trust in a foreign country. These informal networks obviously work in both directions: An American lawyer today may seek help with finding local counsel in Poland for a commercial case. Tomorrow, the Polish colleagues may need help with finding a trusts and estates lawyer admitted in Florida.

---

103. https://www.worldservicesgroup.com/joinwsg.asp, last visited March 16, 2020.
104. https://www.worldservicesgroup.com/joinwsg.asp#membershipfees.
105. Chambers in the UK has been ranking the best law firms around the world since 1990 and covers approximately 185 jurisdictions. Their listing of top firms for different regions and specializations is freely accessible at https://www.chambers.com/.

Individual attorneys and smaller boutique firms are sometimes also recommended by the U.S. and other embassies in a particular country[106] and/or by the local chamber of commerce. Finally, the bar associations in different jurisdictions are usually also willing and able to recommend attorneys with different specializations, although these recommendations may sometimes be more based on who-knows-who than on who is objectively a good fit for the client.[107]

The least attractive alternative is usually to search the internet for a phrase like "commercial law firm Ivory Coast." Such a search will yield mainly the firms with fancy websites in English. It won't tell us much or anything about their reputation and quality.

Attorneys and clients looking for local counsel abroad also need to be aware of differences in billing practices. There are multiple models for attorney billing and the only way to avoid or at least reduce frustration when dealing with a foreign attorney is to request comprehensive information up front. In the U.S. and in many other countries, most larger firms still rely on an hourly billing system, which makes it very hard for the client to predict the total cost because it will be hard for either side to predict the number of hours of work that will be needed. It also incentivizes inefficiency, because the attorney gets more money if she takes longer to work on the case. Clients, and in particular foreign clients, seeking help from a U.S. attorney insisting on hourly billing have limited options to predict, let alone contain, the cost. Even if an agreement is made that the attorney will send a note before the work exceeds a certain number of hours, it is not exactly feasible, and certainly not attractive, for the client to pull out and find another lawyer after two-thirds of the work are already completed. The only option is to insist on highly detailed billing so that the client can at least try to review whether the attorney only did useful work related to the case and only spent a realistic amount of time on each line item.

Alternative billing models used in the U.S. and elsewhere include flat-fee arrangements, as well as contingency fee arrangements. Billing a flat fee is highly advantageous for the client since she will have transparency and predictability up front. In addition, it enables the client, if necessary, to shop around for the service. On the other hand, an attorney will only be willing to enter into a flat-fee arrangement if the amount of work is clearly predictable — for example, filing a green card application on behalf of a client — and any liability risk is limited. On its face, a contingency fee billing arrangement seems even more advantageous for the client. In most cases, the attorney will agree to forgo any fees unless her work is successful

---

106. See, for example, https://travel.state.gov/content/travel/en/legal-considerations/judicial/retaining-a-foreign-attorney.html.

107. One of the better services is offered by the Law Society of England and Wales. The "Find a Solicitor" tool on their website offers different areas of specialization and different countries and regions of the world. While the usual large international firms will pop up, in many cases the link includes smaller and medium-sized local firms. See http://solicitors.lawsociety.org.uk/.

The ABA has a Standing Committee on Lawyer Referral and Information Service, but its work is focused on referrals to lawyers in the U.S.

and the client gets paid by the other party. However, if successful, the contingency fee will usually be in the magnitude of 35 or 40% of whatever amount is won. In addition to the contingency fee, the client usually also has to cover other costs of the procedure, such as court fees, travel expenses of the client, witnesses, translation and interpretation services, etc. which often bring the final payment for the client to less than 50% of the amount awarded by the court or tribunal. Furthermore, a contingency fee arrangement may incentivize the attorney to take shortcuts and/or seek a settlement because 40% of US$1 million after a month of work may look a lot more attractive than 40% of US$2 million after a year of work. This is not always in the client's best interests. And while contingency fee arrangements may be the best option for clients who cannot afford to advance a lot of money for lawyers and court fees, many good attorneys will only enter into such arrangements and advance their time and money if they are very confident that they can win the case. Thus, a client with a solid case may well overpay for the legal services in such an arrangement. Today, we more frequently find combinations of these different billing models. For example, an attorney may demand a flat fee to do the basic work but also a contingency fee or percentage of any amounts won beyond a certain threshold.

All of these billing arrangements are essentially legal in the U.S., including contracts between attorneys and clients where the attorneys have limited to no risk and get paid the bulk of any awards won on behalf of the clients. Furthermore, under the American Rule, each side normally pays her own costs and fees, including attorney fees and court fees, regardless of who wins the case.[108]

The billing and payment arrangements can be very different in other countries. First, many countries follow the English Rule for the payment of attorney fees and court fees, pursuant to which the losing party has to pay not only her own fees and expenses, but also the attorney fees of the winning party, at least to the extent they are seen as reasonable by the court, as well as all court fees and other expenses related to the procedure. This so-called fee shifting is also increasingly the norm in arbitration. The way this works in practice is as follows: When the court or tribunal delivers its decision on the claims and counterclaims, it assesses to what extent the plaintiff or claimant has prevailed with her claims and against any counterclaims. The outcomes of the assessment might be along one of the following lines:

1. The plaintiff won all or nearly all of her claims and the defendant did not present any or did not win any of her counterclaims: All reasonable fees and expenses of both sides and the court will be borne by the defendant.

2. The plaintiff lost all or nearly all of her claims (and the defendant won any counterclaims she may have presented): All reasonable fees and expenses of both sides and the court will be borne by the plaintiff.

---

108. There are exceptions to this rule in the U.S., for example under the Civil Rights Attorney's Fees Act of 1976 (42 U.S.C. § 1988(b)).

3. The plaintiff won or lost about half of what she originally claimed: Each side bears its own attorney fees and expenses and they share the court and other expenses equally.

4. The plaintiff won a different share of her claims, other than 100%, 50%, or 0%, or close to these numbers: The fees and expenses will be shared roughly along the lines of the outcome. For example, if a plaintiff claimed US$10 million and won US$2 million, the court will find that she lost 80% of her claims and burden her with 80% of all fees and expenses of both sides and the court. This effect has to be carefully considered by U.S. attorneys going abroad. The common practice in U.S. courts for the plaintiff to demand an outrageous sum of money, say US$100 million, in order to have leverage and be able to settle for much less, for example, US$5 million, would lead a foreign court to decide that the plaintiff lost 95% of her case and should bear all fees and expenses of both sides and the court. Those would then eat up the bulk of the US$5 million the court decided to award. To drive home this point, if the U.S. attorney had asked for US$5 million instead, she would have won 100% of her case and the other side would be paying all fees and expenses.

The importance of presenting realistic claims in countries where the fees are shifted can be illustrated by the following calculation. In Germany, the minimum attorney fees, which are equal to the fees that will be reimbursed under the English Rule, as well as the court fees, are determined by law. Under the Rechtsanwaltsvergütungsgesetz,[109] the attorney fees usually increase progressively with the amount in dispute and have nothing to do with the number of hours expended by the attorney on the case. Thus, a case between one plaintiff and one defendant over US$10 million will cost about €277,000 or US$300,000 at first instance, a further €360,000 or US$400,000 on appeal, and another €475,000 or US$550,000 if appealed to the federal high court for a total of about US$1.25 million. These numbers include attorney fees for both sides and court fees, as well as taxes.[110] However, if the dispute is over US$30 million, the fees climb up to €805,000 plus €1.05 million plus €1.4 million for a total of about US$3.5 million. If there is more than one party to be represented and/or more than one attorney representing a party, the fees can still climb considerably. Thus, if an American attorney goes to court and presents a claim for US$30 million but ends up settling for US$3.5 million, she would be quite proud of herself in the U.S. By contrast, in Germany, the US$3.5 million might not even cover the expenses, if the court, concluding that the party lost almost all of her initial claims, should order her to bear all fees and expenses of both sides.

The situation is further exacerbated by the fact that some countries, like Germany, do not allow contingency fee arrangements between a plaintiff and her attorney. While lawyers in the U.S. will sometimes advertise their services with slogans

---

109. Law on the Remuneration of Attorneys, an unofficial English version is available from the German Federal Ministry of Justice at http://www.gesetze-im-internet.de/englisch_rvg/index.html.

110. The German Lawyer Association (DeutscherAnwaltVerein) provides a convenient online calculator for the fees at https://anwaltverein.de/de/service/prozesskostenrechner.

such as "no fee unless you win," essentially offering to work for free if they do not succeed, such an arrangement would not protect a party from court and attorney fees in jurisdictions where the English Rule is applied.

Furthermore, contingency lawyers often share with third-party litigation (and arbitration) funding firms[111] that they will take a hefty percentage—35–40% and up—if the case is successful. However, while contingency fee arrangements are illegal in many countries (for example, in Western Europe), third-party funding is generally legal in most jurisdictions. Parties just have to ensure that they understand the contract they are entering into and whether it is structured more like a loan—where they have to repay the (bulk of the) funding regardless of the outcome of the litigation or arbitration, or whether it is structured more like a business venture, where the funding party bears most or all of the financial risk of the procedures in exchange for a significant share of the final award, if any.[112]

Finally, different countries also have different rules with regard to the permissibility of class action[113] law suits, as well as demands for punitive or treble damages.[114]

2. Injunctions and Other Forms of Interim or Interlocutory Relief

The initiation of legal proceedings to enforce bona fide claims can be pointless even if the parties have access to a fair-minded and efficient court with undisputed jurisdiction over their dispute. First, even a court in a functioning system subject to rule of law will take nine months to a year to come to a decision at first instance. Complex cases can take much longer. Then there is the option of appeals. Thus, legitimate claims can be frustrated by the mere passing of time until a final judgment can be obtained. The old adage that justice delayed is justice denied is not just a platitude. For example, it is becoming more common for corporations in the U.S. to include noncompete clauses in their employment contracts, prohibiting employees from leaving and working for a competitor, or even just in their profession, for several years after the employment has ended. If a former employee is suing to have such a clause or restrictive covenant annulled, the mere fact that the

---

111. Burford claims to be the leading firm worldwide when it comes to litigation and arbitration funding. See http://www.burfordcapital.com/about/.

112. For further analysis, see David S. Abrams & Daniel L. Chen, *A Market for Justice: A First Empirical Look at Third Party Litigation Funding*, U. Pa. J. Bus. L. 2013, Vol. 15, No. 4, pp. 1075–1109; and Marco de Morpurgo, *A Comparative Legal and Economic Approach to Third-Party Litigation Funding*, Cardozo J. Int'l & Comp. L. 2011, Vol. 19, No. 2, pp. 343–412. Specifically with regard to the lack of uniformity in U.S. state laws, see Victoria A. Shannon, *Harmonizing Third-Party Litigation Funding Regulation*, Cardozo L. Rev. 2015, Vol. 36, No. 3, pp. 861–912.

113. For a comparative analysis, see Deborah R. Hensler, *The Future of Mass Litigation: Global Class Actions and Third-Party Litigation Funding*, Geo. Wash. L. Rev. 2011, Vol. 79, No. 2, pp. 306–323; as well as Samuel Issacharof & Geoffrey P. Miller, *Will Aggregate Litigation Come to Europe?*, Vand. L. Rev. 2009, Vol. 62, No. 1, pp. 179–210.

114. On the latter, see also above pp. 61 and 184, as well as below, pp. 828, 852 et seq., 899, 910 and 1016.

legal proceedings will take as long as the intended restriction makes the proceedings largely pointless for the employee.

Second, in some cases legitimate claims of one party can be frustrated by deliberate acts or omissions of the other party while the proceedings are pending. Such acts or omissions can concern evidence that may be required for the trial, assets and their availability at the end of the trial to satisfy the judgment, and other forms of conduct of the defendant.

Thus, one way of classifying the scenarios where a court may be called upon to make an order granting provisional or interim relief is the following:

- Relevant evidence may need to be secured or protected until it can be taken into account by the court. An example would be a dispute over the conformity of goods with contractual stipulations. If the goods are perishable or intended to be sold or processed further, it may be impossible, by the time the court gets around to it, to determine whether the goods met the contractual requirements at the time they were delivered.

- Relevant evidence located in one country may have to be disclosed and/or produced for a lawsuit in another country. We will deal with this specific problem below at pp. 816 et seq. and pp. 989 et seq.

- Specific conduct by the defendant may be required or prohibited. In the absence of an injunction or another form of temporary order, an ongoing infringement of rights of the plaintiff may be perpetuated or exacerbated before a final decision on the matter can be obtained. An example would be a case where the plaintiff is claiming the infringement of a patent or another intellectual property right by the defendant and wants him to cease and desist from the infringement.

- Finally, and most commonly, assets of the defendant may need to be secured to be available to the plaintiff after she wins her case. This is critically important, in particular, in transnational litigation, since judgments are not easily recognized and enforced in another country and it may be quite easy for a party to remove all assets from one country or jurisdiction where they may be subject to enforcement action, and move them to another country, where they are not. Indeed, a prejudgment attachment of assets (U.S. law), or a freezing order (English law), may have to be put in place simultaneously with or even before service of process.

Continental European law distinguishes three primary types of interim relief: freezing of assets, negative injunctions suspending or preventing certain legal effects or real-world actions, as well as positive or regulatory injunctions ordering certain legal effects or real-world actions.

English legal tradition has developed more subtle distinctions, as elaborated by Park & Cromie:[115]

---

115. See W.D. Park & S.J.H. Cromie, *International Commercial Litigation*, Butterworths 1990, at pp. 288–289.

(i) Negative injunctions: The straightforward type, where the plaintiff alleges that the defendant is acting in violation of his rights. The court will restrain the defendant from so acting until trial.

(ii) Quia timet injunction: The defendant has not yet acted, but the plaintiff fears he will, and wants an order to stop him.

(iii) Mandatory injunction: The defendant is required to do something, to remedy a violation of the plaintiff's rights. Much more difficult to obtain at the interlocutory stage than a negative injunction.

(iv) Mareva injunction: An injunction to prevent the defendant dissipating his assets, so as to defeat any eventual judgment.

(v) Disclosure of assets: Often combined with a Mareva. The defendant must swear an affidavit identifying his assets and their location. If necessary the court may order that the defendant be cross-examined on his affidavit. It may even appoint outside accountants to prepare a schedule of his assets.

(vi) Interim preservation of property: An order that property be detained and held safe pending trial.

(vii) Inspection: An order that the defendant allow the plaintiff to inspect property in the defendant's possession.

(viii) Delivery: An order that the defendant deliver up to the plaintiff property belonging to the plaintiff.

(ix) Anton Piller order: A more extreme order than (vi)-(viii) above and accordingly more popular. The plaintiff is permitted to search the defendant's premises without warning and remove property or evidence.

(x) Discovery: A defendant to an Anton Piller application may be ordered to disclose the identity of the suppliers of the property in question. Much more rarely, the defendant may be cross-examined on the information.

(xi) Writ ne exeat regno: A writ to restrain a defendant from leaving the country, where the defendant's absence would prejudice the plaintiffs case.

Not all of these remedies will be available in all cases and in all jurisdictions. However, in most cases and in most jurisdictions, the following conditions have to be satisfied before any interim relief will be granted:

1. Interim relief is not a stand-alone procedure, but is ancillary to a lawsuit seeking a permanent decision by the court. Thus, interim relief will only be granted if the main claims are already pending or are being brought simultaneously to court. Before granting interim relief, the court must examine its jurisdiction over the matter and the parties and any other questions of admissibility of the main proceedings.

2. Interim relief is intended to protect only legitimate rights and claims. Thus, interim relief will only be granted if the main claims have sufficient merit. Since time is of the essence, a reduced standard of assessment will be applied, namely

whether the claims are prima facie persuasive. In most cases, the court will neither consider counterarguments of the defendant, nor examine any of the evidence offered by the plaintiff. However, once the court has either granted or denied the requested relief, both plaintiff and defendant may appeal the order and seek more detailed review.

3. Interim relief is a simplified procedure that does not allow a full assessment of the facts and the law. Thus, interim relief will only be granted if the plaintiff or applicant can demonstrate **urgency**, namely that his or her rights are likely to be frustrated if interim relief is *not* provided or is delayed until the matter can be examined more carefully.

4. Interim relief is an intervention in a situation of conflict of interest between plaintiff and defendant. If interim relief is granted, the rights of the plaintiff are secured but the freedoms of the defendant are restricted. If interim relief is denied, the freedoms of the defendant are protected but the rights of the plaintiff may be lost. Thus, interim relief will only be granted if a balancing of interests tilts sufficiently in favor of the plaintiff. However, in some cases, the interests of the defendant may be safeguarded by requiring the plaintiff to provide security. If the plaintiff does not prevail in the main proceedings, the defendant can be compensated for his losses from the deposit.

These are the questions the trial court will have to consider before granting or denying interim relief in one form or another. In transnational litigation, a further dimension is added, namely the dimension of the court that is not the trial court being confronted with a request from a court in another country to provide assistance with interim relief. The way courts have handled these questions in practice will be illustrated with the following decisions. Readers should observe, in particular, the conditions the courts have examined before granting the requested relief and the way the courts have sought to strike a balance between the conflicting interests.

Case 6-5

Derby et al. v. Weldon et al. (No. 1)

English Court of Appeal [1989] E.C.C. 283, 29 July 1988

Plaintiffs were the owners of a group of companies managed by defendants. After the group went bankrupt, plaintiffs alleged breach of contract, conspiracy, tort, and fraudulent breach of fiduciary duties and sought about 35 million UK£ in damages from defendants. The assets of the defendants were spread out over several countries. Plaintiffs sought an arrest order—a Mareva injunction—covering as many jurisdictions as possible, commonly referred to as a "worldwide Mareva". The trial court agreed that "there are grounds for supposing that the respondents may have acted dishonestly" and "that they have the ability to lock away assets in inaccessible overseas companies" because "respondents are well used to moving funds world wide."[116] Nevertheless, the trial judge only granted an injunction for the United Kingdom. Respondents appealed against the asset freeze and plaintiffs cross appealed against the geographic limitation of the asset freeze. The Court of Appeal decided as follows (from p. 287):

MAY, L.J.:

[6] In his submissions in the instant appeal, counsel for the respondents submitted that, other things apart, a worldwide Mareva should only be made where there was evidence either that the defendant had in fact secreted or alternatively had attempted to secrete assets of his outside the jurisdiction so as to render nugatory any judgment to which the plaintiff might ultimately be entitled. Counsel based this submission [on a number of precedents in English courts]. As counsel originally submitted, all these authorities show that as wide an order as that sought in the instant case should only be made where there is evidence of previous malpractice or nefarious intent. Counsel originally contended that one could deduce this as a principle of law from the authorities: in his reply, however, he accepted that the highest he could put it was that the cases demonstrated that at least evidence of this nature, or of equivalent persuasive effect, was needed before the court was entitled to make so draconian an order as that sought in this case.

[7] I entirely accept that it will only be in an exceptional case that the court will make such an order. Nevertheless each case must depend on its own facts. . . .

[9] As the learned judge in the instant case pointed out, first, such a wide order can be severely oppressive if the respondents, while preparing for a very complicated trial in England, at the same time find themselves engaged in courts overseas in further applications of a Mareva nature, bearing in mind that plaintiffs with substantial resources may not be slow to engage the respondents in as many courts throughout the world as possible. . . .

[10] I should add that the third particular reason which the learned judge gave for refusing a worldwide order was:

> 'No dishonesty is yet proved and may never be proved. I must assume that the respondents are honest. Furthermore, they are not in breach of any Court order.'

These comments do not lie easily alongside the earlier comments made by the learned judge in his judgment which I have already quoted, to support which there was certainly evidence before him.

[11] In these circumstances my opinion is that it falls to us to decide whether the relief sought should be granted on the learned judge's findings of fact and in the light of the law as I understand this Court has now stated it to be. For my part I have no doubt that with the appropriate safeguards to which I have referred, this is a case in

---

116. [1989] E.C.C. 283, at p. 286.

which a worldwide Mareva injunction ought to be granted, with the concomitant disclosure.

The jurisdictional questions presented by the court of one country granting an injunction that applies to assets of the defendant spread out across the entire world are discussed in the following decision by the English Court of Appeals, and the judge comes up with some useful classifications. He also discusses how the situation is unique when it comes to injunctions within the EU.

Case 6-6

Babanaft International v. Bahaedine Bassatne and Walid Mohamed Bassatne

Court of Appeal (Civil Division), 29 June 1988, [1989] E.C.C. 151.
(Some footnotes omitted.)

[Plaintiffs had won a judgment against defendants for an amount in excess of US$15 million. In order to enforce their claims, they obtained from the trial judge, Vinelott, an order that defendants disclose their assets worldwide. Judge Vinelott also issued a Mareva injunction but only for the United Kingdom. Plaintiffs appealed against the geographic limitation of the injunction and Judge Vinelott issued a modified injunction pursuant to which defendants had to give five days notice to plaintiffs before moving or using any assets worldwide. Plaintiffs notified some 47 individuals and entities, including 24 banks, around the world of the injunction. Defendants appealed and another revised injunction was issued "expressly excluded any effect on any third party, and a further order was made that all persons who had originally been told of the existence of the injunction should be informed that they should disregard it" (at p. 156). The following are the reasons given for the second revised injunction.]

KERR, L.J. . . .

[12] The jurisdiction of the court to grant injunctions is now to be found in section 37 of the Supreme Court Act 1981:

Powers of High Court with respect to injunctions and receivers.

(1) The High Court may by order (whether interlocutory or final) grant an injunction or appoint a receiver in all cases in which it appears to the court to be just and convenient to do so.

(2) Any such order may be made either unconditionally or on such terms and conditions as the court thinks just.

(3) The power of the High Court under subsection (1) to grant an interlocutory injunction restraining a party to any proceedings from removing from the jurisdiction of the High Court, or otherwise dealing with, assets located within that jurisdiction shall be exercisable in cases where that party is, as

well as in cases where he is not, domiciled, resident or present within that jurisdiction.

[13] ... The purpose of subsection (3) was not to restrict the territorial ambit of Mareva injunctions but to ensure that there should be no discrimination against persons not domiciled, resident or present within the jurisdiction. Subsection (3) does not restrict the scope, geographical or otherwise, of subsection (1). And it is perhaps worth noting that the appointment of a receiver pursuant to subsection (1) may extend to assets outside the jurisdiction, whether movable or immovable.

[14] ... [I]n regard to the proper scope of the exercise of the court's discretion, the practice is clearly still in a state of development. ...

[15] The fact that the practice in this field is still in a state of development is also shown by recent decisions concerning orders for the disclosure of assets outside the jurisdiction. In *Ashtiani*,[11] albeit on the particular facts, this Court took a restrictive view of an order for the disclosure of assets situated abroad because, it was said, such a disclosure might enable the plaintiffs to use the disclosed information to obtain an attachment of the defendant's assets in other jurisdictions. That was a pre-judgment case, ... However, two more recent decisions of this Court have held that the position is in any event different in principle once a judgment has been obtained. The first was *Interpool Ltd. v. Galani*[12] which decided that orders for the disclosure of assets after judgment pursuant to Order 48 could properly extend to assets outside the jurisdiction. And in *Maclain Watson & Co. Ltd. v. International Tin Council (No. 2)*[13] this Court held that the defendants should make a full disclosure of their assets, both within and outside the jurisdiction, where the plaintiffs had obtained judgment but were unable to rely on Order 48. The order for extraterritorial disclosure was made pursuant to section 37(1) of the Supreme Court Act 1981.

[16] I therefore proceed on the basis that in appropriate cases, though these may well be rare, there is nothing to preclude our courts from granting Mareva-type injunctions against defendants which extend to their assets outside the jurisdiction.

[17] On that assumption three questions fall to be answered which did not arise or were not raised in *Ashtiani* but which now need to be considered in principle. To take them in the order in which they were raised in the present case, they are as follows.

(1) Should we adopt a different policy in relation to applications made after judgment, in line with the authorities on post-judgment orders for the disclosure of assets, by granting unqualified Mareva injunctions over foreign assets after judgment in appropriate cases? That was the conclusion of Vinelott J. and the main issue argued on this appeal, distinguishing *Ashtiani* on that ground.

---

11. *Ashtiani v. Kashi*, English Court of Appeal (per Dillon L.J.): [1987] Q.B. 888.
12. [1987] 3 W.L.R. 1042 (C.A.).
13. [1987] 3 W.L.R. 1169 (C.A.).

(2) If the answer to (1) is in the negative, because this would involve an exorbitant assertion of extra territorial jurisdiction over third parties, should we restrict such orders expressly so as to bind only the defendant personally by adding a proviso to make it clear that third parties shall not be affected by the order? This was a fallback position suggested on behalf of the defendants as a compromise between upholding the unqualified Mareva injunction, which they submitted was clearly wrong in law, . . . and declining to make any order affecting the defendants' foreign assets, which they recognised to be more or less unacceptable on the facts of this case. . . .

(3) Alternatively to (2), should the terms of the order in such cases take the form of a normal Mareva injunction, but with the qualification that the order shall not affect third parties unless and to the extent that it is enforced by the courts of the State in which the assets are located? This appears to me to be the correct international approach, ...

[18] Three matters should be noted about solutions (2) and (3). First, both are in principle equally relevant before and after judgment. Secondly, neither militates against the reasoning of the judgments of this Court in *Ashtiani*. Thirdly, it may be that in some foreign jurisdictions there would be no real difference between these solutions in their practical effect. Thus, some foreign courts might enforce orders in terms of solution (2) in ways which would affect third parties holding assets of the defendant, and to that extent the proviso to such orders might in practice prove to be nugatory. This is an additional reason, together with those set out hereafter, for the conclusion that in my view solution (3) is the correct approach in principle in those cases where a Mareva-type injunction extending to foreign assets is considered to be appropriate.

[19] However, before coming to these aspects. I must briefly refer to the reasons which led Vinelott J. to adopt solution (1).

[20] The learned judge founded himself squarely on the consideration that in the present case the order was sought after judgment and therefore in aid of execution. In that connection he dealt at length with the judgments in this Court in the *Faith Panton* case which had been an appeal from himself. This Court had there granted a Mareva injunction after judgment to protect an order for costs in favour of the plaintiffs . . . , and the judgments emphasised the difference in approach to orders of this kind when the plaintiff has already obtained a judgment. That is of course understandable. The court is then no longer so concerned to protect the defendant, and there are good reasons for assisting judgment creditors, as shown by *Interpool v. Galani* and *Maclaine Watson v. International Tin Council*. But the *Faith Panton* case had no foreign element of any kind and is no authority for present purposes. In the context of orders which operate extra territorially, wholly different considerations arise, as discussed below. These show that unqualified Mareva- type injunctions applying to foreign assets can never be justified; neither after nor before judgment. None of the counsel could recollect any order of any foreign court—however 'long- arm' the nature of the jurisdiction claimed—which had gone as far as the order made in this case.

²¹ In my view, the key to the proper exercise of any extra territorial jurisdiction must lie in the question whether there is international reciprocity for the recognition and enforcement of the type of order which is under consideration, in this case a Mareva injunction or a variant of it purporting to operate on the defendants' assets abroad. In that context one must have regard to the practice and case law concerning Article 24 of the European Judgments Convention. This was concluded in 1968 between the original six members of the EEC and extended to the United Kingdom (among others) by an Accession Convention of 1978, without any alteration to Article 24. The Convention requires the recognition and enforcement of all judgments or orders which fall within its scope, whether final or interlocutory, subject to limited exceptions which have no application in the present case. . . . [117]

²² But this is not the main reason for the importance of the Convention in the present context. The main reason lies in the fact that it contains the most extensive code evidencing international reciprocity in the recognition and enforcement of judgments and orders issued in foreign jurisdictions, and that it includes Article 24 dealing with provisional and protective measures. The forerunner of the European Judgments Convention had been a network of bilateral Conventions. . . . So the Judgments Convention is now the widest embodiment of international consensus in this field, founded on decades of bilateral Conventions. . . .

²³ With apologies for this lengthy introduction, I then come to the text of Article 24 which is in the following terms:

> 'Application may be made to the courts of a Contracting State for such provisional, including protective, measures as may be available under the law of that State, even if, under this Convention, the courts of another Contracting State have jurisdiction as to the substance of the matter.'

²⁴ Without legislation this provision could not have been used by our courts to grant (for instance) Mareva injunctions over assets situated in this country in aid of substantive proceedings pending in other EEC jurisdictions. To do so would have been contrary to the decision of the House of Lords in *The Siskina v. Distos Compania Naviera S.A.* This had held that, unless our courts were properly seised of the substance of an action, there was no jurisdiction to grant a Mareva injunction over assets in this country in aid of proceedings abroad. The reversal of *The Siskina* and adherence to Article 24 was achieved by section 25 of the 1982 Act. It is unnecessary

---

117. As outlined earlier (p. 97 note 6, and p. 775), the 1968 Convention was later replaced by EU Regulation 44/2001 on Jurisdiction and the Recognition and Enforcement of Judgments in Civil and Commercial Matters (Brussels I Regulation). By contrast to a convention, which has to be implemented via domestic legislation to have direct effect in the country, an EU Regulation is directly applicable legislation in all Member States and has supremacy over potentially conflicting national law. The 44/2001 Regulation has subsequently been updated in the form of EU Regulation 1215/2012 of 12 December 2012 on Jurisdiction and the Recognition and Enforcement of Judgments in Civil and Commercial Matters (the so-called Brussels Ia or I bis Regulation, OJ 2012 L 351; Documents, p. II-92). This law is currently in force in the EU. The original text of Article 24 of the Convention is now contained, unchanged, in Article 35 of the Brussels Ia or Ibis Regulation.

to set this out for present purposes. However, its effect was to focus attention on only one aspect of Article 24: the power of a court in EEC State A, which is not seised of the substantive action, to make some provisional or protective order in aid of a substantive action pending in State B. I will refer to this as the primary effect of Article 24. However, that leaves out of account a secondary and entirely distinct effect of Article 24 to take a corresponding example: the recognition and enforcement by the courts of State A, pursuant to the requirements of the Convention, of provisional or protective orders made by a court in State B pursuant to Article 24 in aid of a substantive action pending before it, which orders purport to have effect in State A. It is this latter aspect which is material in the present context.

[25] Two important decisions of the European Court of Justice on Article 24 indicate that extraterritorial orders akin to Mareva injunctions, made by the courts in one EEC State and purporting to operate on assets located in another EEC State, will be recognised and enforced by the courts of the latter State if they fall within the scope of the Judgments Convention and satisfy certain requirements designed to protect the defendant against whom the orders were made. They are *De Cavel v. de Cavel (No. 1)*[19] and *Denilauler v. SNC Couchet Freres.*[20] Both cases concerned a pre-judgment *saisie conservatorie* [sic] issued by a French court over assets of the defendants located in Germany. . . .

[27] There are three important implications of these decisions.

(A) Viewed purely from the point of view of international comity, and indeed reciprocity, there appears to be no reason why our courts should refrain from granting *inter partes* pre-judgment Mareva injunctions in cases falling within the European Judgments Convention in relation to assets situated in the territories of other EEC States; and the same may soon apply to the territories of all or most of the EFTA States.

(B) However, there can be no question of such orders operating directly upon the foreign assets by way of attachment, or upon third parties, such as banks, holding the assets. The effectiveness of such orders for these purposes can only derive from their recognition and enforcement by the local courts, as should be made clear in the terms of the orders to avoid any misunderstanding suggesting an unwarranted assumption of extraterritorial jurisdiction. However, if the orders fulfil the requirements of (i) and (ii) above, then the local courts will be bound to recognised and enforce them.

(C) Apart from any EEC or EFTA connection, there is in any event no jurisdictional (as opposed to discretionary) ground which would preclude an English court from granting a pre-judgment Mareva injunction over assets situated anywhere outside the jurisdiction, which are owned or controlled by a defendant who is subject to the jurisdiction of our courts, provided

---

19. Case 143/78, [1979] E.C.R. 1055 . . . .
20. Case 125/79, [1980] E.C.R. 1553 . . . .

that the order makes it clear that it is not to have any direct effect upon the assets or upon any third parties outside the jurisdiction save to the extent that the order may be enforced by the local courts. Whether an order which is qualified in this way would be enforced by the courts of States where the defendant's assets are situated would of course depend on the local law, as would the question whether such orders would be recognised and enforced if they refer to the assets of the defendant generally or only if specified assets are mentioned in the order. As the European Court said in *Denilauler*[21]:

> 'The courts of the place ... where the assets subject to the measures sought are located, are those best able to assess the circumstances which may lead to the grant or refusal of the measures sought or to the laying down of procedures and conditions which the plaintiff must observe in order to guarantee the provisional and protective character of the measures ordered.'

That comment applies equally to what I have referred to as the primary as well as to the secondary effect of Article 24.

[28] Before turning to post-judgment orders I would add two further comments on the decision of this court in *Ashtiani*, bearing in mind that none of this case law was brought to the court's attention in that case.

[29] First, Dillon L.J.[22] expressed the view that

> 'if in a future case disclosure of foreign assets is in a proper case ordered on special grounds, it does seem to me that *prima facie* at any rate the plaintiffs should be required to give an undertaking not to use any information disclosed without the consent of the defendant or the leave of the court.'

With all due respect, I do not think that as a general rule this comment can be correct, and it was regarded as 'somewhat surprising' by Rogers J. in the Commercial Court of New South Wales: see *Yandil Holdings Pty. Ltd. v. Insurance Co. of North America*.[23] Its application would deny the intended effect, both primary and secondary, of Article 24. No doubt, as emphasised by Nicholls L.J. at the end of his judgment in the present case, any orders affecting foreign assets should always be considered with great care, since they may have unforeseen and unintended consequences for defendants. But it should also be said, with equal emphasis, that some situations, which are nowadays by no means uncommon, cry out — as a matter of justice to plaintiffs — for disclosure orders and Mareva-type injunctions covering foreign assets of defendants even before judgment. Indeed, that is precisely the philosophy which underlies Article 24 and which has been applied by the development of the common law in Australia.

---

21. At para. [16].
22. At p. 903A.
23. [1987] N.S.W.L.R. 571 at 577.

[30] Secondly, Dillon L.J. in *Ashtiani* cites at length a passage from the transcript of the judgment of Hoffmann J. in *Bayer A.G. v. Winter (No. 3)*[25] . . . . I do not propose to repeat it in full, but the passage concluded as follows:

> 'There are territorial limits to the effectiveness of this Court's own orders. If however there is evidence that a foreign court would be willing to make orders similar in effect to a Mareva injunction upon assets within its jurisdiction, it seems to me that, other things being equal, this Court should not restrict a plaintiff's ability to obtain such relief. It would be a pointless insularity for an English court to put obstacles in the way of a plaintiff who wished, with the aid of foreign courts, to enforce an English judgment against a defendant's assets wherever they might be.' . . .

[32] I appreciate that in this discussion I have strayed a long way from the course which the present appeal in fact took on the basis of the limited issues which were debated. Unfortunately, the important international perspective was only touched on superficially at the end of the hearing and briefly in the subsequent written submissions. But, if one goes back to the suggested alternative solutions numbered (1), (2) and (3) to the problems posed by extraterritorial Mareva-type injunctions which I have set out earlier, I think that I have said enough to indicate my reasons for concluding that solution (1) is clearly unacceptable, and that this appeal therefore had to be allowed to that extent in any event. Unqualified Mareva injunctions covering assets abroad can never be justified, either before or after judgment, because they involve an exorbitant assertion of jurisdiction of an *in rem* nature over third parties outside the jurisdiction of our courts. They cannot be controlled or policed by our courts, and they are not subjected to the control of the local courts, as the European Court advised in *Denilauler*[31] they should be. In consequence, as can be seen from the correspondence between the plaintiffs' solicitors and the 47 or so third parties to whom the injunctions were notified in the present case, any purported assertion of such jurisdiction is unworkable and merely gives rise to problems and disputes.

[33] Solution (3), which I believe to be the correct solution in principle, was never canvassed, for the reasons which I have stated. It obviously binds the defendant personally, in common with solution (2), but would go further and would therefore be more useful. So that leaves our adoption of solution (2) in the present case. For the reasons set out in the judgment of Nicholls L.J. there is clearly no objection to making a personal order binding on the defendant alone. . . . The order which we made in the present case went further, and its terms covered immovable as well as movable property of the defendants. Its crucial difference from the order made by Vinelott J. was that it was qualified by the following proviso:

> 'Provided always that no person other than the defendants themselves shall in any wise be affected by the terms of this order . . . or concerned to

---

25. [1986] E.C.C. 465.
31. At para. [16].

enquire whether any instruction given by or on behalf of either defendant or by anyone else, or any other act or omission of either defendant or anyone else, whether acting on behalf of either defendant or otherwise, is or may be a breach of this order . . . by the defendant.'

³⁴ In addition, to complete the history, we added a paragraph entitling each of the defendants to draw living and other expenses which they claimed to be necessary and for which no allowance had been made below. Since both defendants undertook that these would come exclusively out of income to be generated by their business activities and that they would not dispose of any capital assets, we agreed to the lavish amounts for which they asked, £15,000 per month for B.B. and US $17,000 for W.B. in that connection we bore in mind that the whole position will be reviewed in whatever way may appear to be necessary in the light of the defendants' full evidence which they are required to give pursuant to Order 48. They undertook to supplement their present inadequate affidavits by supplying full details of the nature, value and location of their assets, and they will then be cross-examined upon them.

³⁵ Finally, it is perhaps hardly necessary to add an emphatic note of caution in relation to those parts of this judgment which, as I have indicated, were not canvassed in the arguments of counsel, either before Vinelott J. or on this appeal. In these circumstances, it is obviously particularly likely that there may be errors in what I have said. But, in view of its great general importance, I feel that it is right to air this topic more fully, albeit obiter, than was necessary for the purposes of this particular appeal. Viewed in that way I can summarise my present views as follows:

A. An unqualified Mareva-type injunction purporting to freeze assets situated outside the jurisdiction of our courts is always inadmissible, both after and before judgment.

B. A Mareva-type injunction (perhaps it should be called 'a personal Mareva' for identification) qualified by an express proviso excluding any effect on third parties, which was the order which we made on the present appeal, is clearly unobjectionable in principle. But it is not a satisfactory formulation, because it disregards the realities which a Mareva injunction seeks to achieve. Hobhouse J. recognised this in the Crown Petroleum case when he said that the order 'will be solely binding on the conscience of the defendant . . .'

C. Subject to the note of caution which I have sounded, if the arguments addressed to us had fully deployed the considerations discussed in this judgment, then it would in my view have been equally permissible, and the better course, to have allowed this appeal by making an order in terms of my solution (3), viz. an order in the form of a normal Mareva injunction against both defendants with a qualification that the order should not affect third parties unless and to the extent that it is enforced by the courts of the States in which any of the defendants' assets are located. This would be the logical and internationally appropriate course, and it would have taken the plaintiffs further than the order which we made, without—so far as I can see—any basis for objection by the defendants; nor in principle, for the reasons discussed.

D. Viewed purely jurisdictionally, the comments in B and C above apply equally to orders made after, as well as before, judgment. However, as a matter of discretion, such orders will in practice no doubt be made much more readily after judgment.

E. The orders for the disclosure of the defendants' assets abroad pursuant to R.S.C. Order 48 were not in issue on this appeal, and their jurisdictional justification was not open to question in view of the decisions of this Court in *Interpool* and *Maclaine Watson*. However, in my view there is equally no jurisdictional objection to such orders before judgment. The cautionary comments in the judgments in *Ashtiani* should no doubt be borne in mind in this context. But in extreme situations, which justify a pre-judgment Mareva injunction covering a defendant's assets outside the jurisdiction, orders for the disclosure of the nature and location of such assets must be equally justifiable. Prima facie, both types of orders should be considered in parallel.

Notes and Questions

1. The first distinction to be made in the present context is between an order that the defendant should *disclose* her assets worldwide, and a worldwide Mareva injunction, *freezing* defendant's assets around the globe, and prohibiting any transfer or removal of the assets. Which arguments can be made in favor of and against the disclosure order? The worldwide Mareva injunction? Should the two be treated differently? Why?

2. The second distinction to be made is between orders *before* and *after* a final judgment has been obtained. Is a party in greater or lesser need at the beginning of proceedings or after a judgment has been rendered? Why? Is there a difference in this regard between the plaintiff and the defendant? Is there a third period of time to be distinguished, after a first judgment has been obtained but while an appeal may still be pending? Why or why not?

3. What are the three options referred to in paragraph 32? Can you outline them in your own words?

a. With regard to solution (1), what is the specific problem and why does the Court deem it "clearly unacceptable"?

b. Why is solution (2) not satisfactory from the plaintiff's point of view?

c. What are the strengths and weaknesses of solution (3), as adopted by the Court?

4. To what extent is solution (3) different or the same as the approach mandated within the European Union under the 1968 European Judgments Convention,

today succeeded by Regulation 1215/2012 on Jurisdiction and the Recognition and Enforcement of Judgments in Civil and Commercial Matters?

5. In the U.S., the situation with regard to prejudgment asset freezes abroad is still governed by a controversial precedent. On June 17, 1999, the U.S. Supreme Court decided *Grupo Mexicano De Desarrollo, S.A. v. Alliance Bond Fund, Inc.*[118] American investors wanted to freeze assets of a Mexican toll road operator because of an alleged default on unsecured notes. Justice Scalia wrote the following on behalf of the majority (from p. 318):

III

[15] We turn, then, to the merits question whether the District Court had authority to issue the preliminary injunction in this case pursuant to Federal Rule of Civil Procedure 65.[3] The Judiciary Act of 1789 conferred on the federal courts jurisdiction over "all suits . . . in equity." § 11, 1 Stat. 78. We have long held that "[t]he 'jurisdiction' thus conferred . . . is an authority to administer in equity suits the principles of the system of judicial remedies which had been devised and was being administered by the English Court of Chancery at the time of the separation of the two countries." *Atlas Life Ins. Co. v. W.I. Southern, Inc.*, 306 U.S. 563, 568 . . . (1939). See also, e.g., *Stainback v. Mo Hock Ke Lok Po*, 336 U.S. 368, 382, n. 26 . . . (1949); *Guaranty Trust Co. v. York*, 326 U.S. 99, 105 . . . (1945); *Gordon v. Washington*, 295 U.S. 30, 36 . . . (1935). "Substantially, then, the equity jurisdiction of the federal courts is the jurisdiction in equity exercised by the High Court of Chancery in England at the time of the adoption of the Constitution and the enactment of the original Judiciary Act, 1789 (1 Stat. 73)." A. Dobie, Handbook of Federal Jurisdiction and Procedure 660 (1928). "[T]he substantive prerequisites for obtaining an equitable remedy as well as the general availability of injunctive relief are not altered by [Rule 65] and depend on traditional principles of equity jurisdiction." 11A Charles Alan Wright, Arthur R. Miller, & Mary Kay Kane, Federal Practice and Procedure § 2941, p. 31 (2d ed.1995). We must ask, therefore, whether the relief respondents requested here was traditionally accorded by courts of equity.

A

[16] Respondents do not even argue this point. The United States as amicus curiae, however, contends that the preliminary injunction issued in this case is analogous to the relief obtained in the equitable action known as a "creditor's bill." This remedy was used (among other purposes) to permit a judgment creditor to

---

118. 527 U.S. 308.

3. Although this is a diversity case, respondents' complaint sought the injunction pursuant to Rule 65, and the Second Circuit's decision was based on that rule and on federal equity principles. Petitioners argue for the first time before this Court that under *Erie R. Co. v. Tompkins*, 304 U.S. 64 . . . (1938), the availability of this injunction under Rule 65 should be determined by the law of the forum State (in this case New York). Because this argument was neither raised nor considered below, we decline to consider it.

discover the debtor's assets, to reach equitable interests not subject to execution at law, and to set aside fraudulent conveyances. See 1 D. Dobbs, Law of Remedies §2.8(1), pp. 191–192 (2d ed.1993); 4 S. Symons, Pomeroy's Equity Jurisprudence §1415, pp. 1065–1066 (5th ed.1941); 1 G. Glenn, Fraudulent Conveyances and Preferences §26, p. 51 (rev. ed.1940). It was well established, however, that, as a general rule, a creditor's bill could be brought only by a creditor who had already obtained a judgment establishing the debt. See, e.g., *Pusey & Jones Co. v. Hanssen*, 261 U.S. 491, 497 . . . (1923); *Hollins v. Brierfield Coal & Iron Co.*, 150 U.S. 371, 378–379 . . . (1893); Cates v. Allen, 149 U.S. 451, 457 . . . (1893); *National Tube Works Co. v. Ballou*, 146 U.S. 517, 523–524 . . . (1892); *Scott v. Neely*, 140 U.S. 106, 113 . . . (1891); *Smith v. Railroad Co.*, 99 U.S. 398, 401 . . . (1879); *Adler v. Fenton*, 24 How. 407, 411–413, 16 L.Ed. 696 (1861); see also 4 Symons, *supra*, at 1067; 1 Glenn, *supra*, §9, at 11; F. Wait, Fraudulent Conveyances and Creditors' Bills §73, pp. 110–111 (1884). The rule requiring a judgment was a product, not just of the procedural requirement that remedies at law had to be exhausted before equitable remedies could be pursued, but also of the substantive rule that a general creditor (one without a judgment) had no cognizable interest, either at law or in equity, in the property of his debtor, and therefore could not interfere with the debtor's use of that property. As stated by Chancellor Kent: "The reason of the rule seems to be, that until the creditor has established his title, he has no right to interfere, and it would lead to an unnecessary, and, perhaps, a fruitless and oppressive interruption of the exercise of the debtor's rights." *Wiggins v. Armstrong*, 2 Johns. Ch. 144, 145–146 (N.Y.1816). See also, e.g., *Guaranty Trust Co.*, *supra*, at 106–107, n. 3, 65 S. Ct. 1464; *Pusey & Jones Co.*, *supra*, at 497, 43 S.Ct. 454; *Cates*, *supra*, at 457, 13 S.Ct. 883; *Adler*, *supra*, at 411–413; *Shufeldt v. Boehm*, 96 Ill. 560, 564 (1880); 1 Glenn, *supra*, §9, at 11; Wait, *supra*, §52, at 81, §73, at 113. . . .

[18] Justice GINSBURG concedes that federal equity courts have traditionally rejected the type of provisional relief granted in this case. [See below, opinion concurring in part and dissenting in part]. She invokes, however, "the grand aims of equity," and asserts a general power to grant relief whenever legal remedies are not "practical and efficient," unless there is a statute to the contrary. . . . This expansive view of equity must be rejected. . . .

[19] We do not question the proposition that equity is flexible; but in the federal system, at least, that flexibility is confined within the broad boundaries of traditional equitable relief. To accord a type of relief that has never been available before — and especially (as here) a type of relief that has been specifically disclaimed by long-standing judicial precedent — is to invoke a "default rule," . . . not of flexibility but of omnipotence. When there are indeed new conditions that might call for a wrenching departure from past practice, Congress is in a much better position than we both to perceive them and to design the appropriate remedy. . . .

[Justice GINSBURG concurred in part and dissented in part. She was joined by Justice SOUTER and Justice BREYER (from p. 333):]

I

[38] Uncontested evidence presented to the District Court at the preliminary injunction hearing showed that petitioner Grupo Mexicano de Desarrollo, S.A. (GMD), had defaulted on its contractual obligations to respondents, a group of GMD noteholders (Alliance) . . . , that Alliance had satisfied all conditions precedent to its breach of contract claim . . . , and that GMD had no plausible defense on the merits. . . . Alliance also demonstrated that GMD had undertaken to treat Alliance's claims on the same footing as all other unsecured, unsubordinated debt . . . , but that GMD was in fact satisfying Mexican creditors to the exclusion of Alliance. . . . Furthermore, unchallenged evidence indicated that GMD was so rapidly disbursing its sole remaining asset that, absent provisional action by the District Court, Alliance would have been unable to collect on the money judgment for which it qualified.

[39] Had it been possible for the District Judge to set up "a pie-powder court . . . on the instant and on the spot," *Parks v. Boston*, 32 Mass. 198, 208 (1834) (Shaw, C. J.), the judge could have moved without pause from evidence taking to entry of final judgment for Alliance, including an order prohibiting GMD from transferring assets necessary to satisfy the judgment. Lacking any such device for instant adjudication, the judge employed a preliminary injunction "to preserve the relative positions of the parties until a trial on the merits [could] be held." *University of Texas v. Camenisch*, 451 U.S. 390, 395 . . . (1981). The order enjoined GMD from distributing assets likely to be necessary to satisfy the judgment in the instant case, but gave Alliance no security interest in GMD's assets, nor any preference relative to GMD's other creditors. Moreover, the injunction expressly reserved to GMD the option of commencing proceedings under the bankruptcy laws of Mexico or the United States. . . . In addition, the District Judge recorded his readiness to modify the interim order if necessary to keep GMD in business. . . . The preliminary injunction thus constrained GMD only to the extent essential to the subsequent entry of an effective judgment.

[40] The Court nevertheless disapproves the provisional relief ordered by the District Court, holding that a preliminary injunction freezing assets is beyond the equitable authority of the federal courts. I would not so disarm the district courts. As I comprehend the courts' authority, injunctions of this kind, entered in the circumstances presented here, are within federal equity jurisdiction. Satisfied that the injunction issued in this case meets the exacting standards for preliminary equitable relief, I would affirm the judgment of the Second Circuit.

II

[41] The Judiciary Act of 1789 gave the lower federal courts jurisdiction over "all suits . . . in equity." § 11, 1 Stat. 78. We have consistently interpreted this jurisdictional grant to confer on the district courts "authority to administer . . . the principles of the system of judicial remedies which had been devised and was being

administered" by the English High Court of Chancery at the time of the founding. *Atlas Life Ins. Co. v. W.I. Southern, Inc.*, 306 U.S. 563, 568 . . . (1939).

[42] As I see it, the preliminary injunction ordered by the District Court was consistent with these principles. We long ago recognized that district courts properly exercise their equitable jurisdiction where "the remedy in equity could alone furnish relief, and . . . the ends of justice requir[e] the injunction to be issued." *Watson v. Sutherland*, 5 Wall. 74, 79, 18 L.Ed. 580 (1867). Particularly, district courts enjoy the "historic federal judicial discretion to preserve the situation [through provisional relief] pending the outcome of a case lodged in court." 11A Charles Alan Wright, Arthur R. Miller, & Mary Kay Kane, Federal Practice and Procedure § 2943, p. 79 (2d ed. 1995). The District Court acted in this case in careful accord with these prescriptions, issuing the preliminary injunction only upon well-supported findings that Alliance had "[no] adequate remedy at law," would be "frustrated" in its ability to recover a judgment absent interim injunctive relief, and was "almost certain" to prevail on the merits. . . .

[43] The Court holds the District Court's preliminary freeze order impermissible principally because injunctions of this kind were not "traditionally accorded by courts of equity" at the time the Constitution was adopted. . . . In my view, the Court relies on an unjustifiably static conception of equity jurisdiction. From the beginning, we have defined the scope of federal equity in relation to the principles of equity existing at the separation of this country from England, see, e.g., *Payne v. Hook*, 7 Wall. 425, 430, 19 L.Ed. 260 (1869); *Gordon v. Washington*, 295 U.S. 30, 36 . . . (1935); we have never limited federal equity jurisdiction to the specific practices and remedies of the pre-Revolutionary Chancellor.

[44] Since our earliest cases, we have valued the adaptable character of federal equitable power. See *Seymour v. Freer*, 8 Wall. 202, 218, 19 L.Ed. 306 (1869) ("[A] court of equity ha[s] unquestionable authority to apply its flexible and comprehensive jurisdiction in such manner as might be necessary to the right administration of justice between the parties."); *Hecht Co. v. Bowles*, 321 U.S. 321, 329 . . . (1944) ("Flexibility rather than rigidity has distinguished [federal equity jurisdiction]."). We have also recognized that equity must evolve over time, "in order to meet the requirements of every case, and to satisfy the needs of a progressive social condition in which new primary rights and duties are constantly arising and new kinds of wrongs are constantly committed." *Union Pacific R. Co. v. Chicago, R.I. & P.R. Co.*, 163 U.S. 564, 601 . . . (1896) (internal quotation marks omitted); see also 1 S. Symons, Pomeroy's Equity Jurisprudence § 67, p. 89 (5th ed. 1941) (the "American system of equity is preserved and maintained . . . to render the national jurisprudence as a whole adequate to the social needs. . . . [I]t possesses an inherent capacity of expansion, so as to keep abreast of each succeeding generation and age."). A dynamic equity jurisprudence is of special importance in the commercial law context. As we observed more than a century ago: "It must not be forgotten that in the increasing complexities of modern business relations equitable remedies have necessarily and steadily been expanded, and no inflexible rule has been permitted to circumscribe them."

Union Pacific R. Co., 163 U.S., at 600–601 .... On this understanding of equity's character, we have upheld diverse injunctions that would have been beyond the contemplation of the 18th-century Chancellor.[4] ...

[46] I do not question that equity courts traditionally have not issued preliminary injunctions stopping a party sued for an unsecured debt from disposing of assets pending adjudication. (As the Court recognizes, however . . . , the historical availability of prejudgment freeze injunctions in the context of creditors' bills remains cloudy.) But it is one thing to recognize that equity courts typically did not provide this relief, quite another to conclude that, therefore, the remedy was beyond equity's capacity. I would not draw such a conclusion.

[47] Chancery may have refused to issue injunctions of this sort simply because they were not needed to secure a just result in an age of slow-moving capital and comparatively immobile wealth. By turning away cases that the law courts could deal with adequately, the Chancellor acted to reduce the tension inevitable when justice was divided between two discrete systems. See Wasserman, supra, at 319. But as the facts of this case so plainly show, for creditors situated as Alliance is, the remedy at law is worthless absent the provisional relief in equity's arsenal. Moreover, increasingly sophisticated foreign-haven judgment proofing strategies, coupled with technology that permits the nearly instantaneous transfer of assets abroad, suggests that defendants may succeed in avoiding meritorious claims in ways unimaginable before the merger of law and equity. See LoPucki, The Death of Liability, 106 Yale L.J. 1, 32–38 (1996). I am not ready to say a responsible Chancellor today would deny Alliance relief on the ground that prior case law is unsupportive.

[48] The development of *Mareva* injunctions in England after 1975 supports the view of the lower courts in this case, a view to which I adhere. As the Court observes . . . , preliminary asset-freeze injunctions have been available in English courts since the 1975 Court of Appeal decision in *Mareva Compania Naviera S.A. v. International Bulkcarriers S. A.*, 2 Lloyd's Rep. 509. Although the cases reveal some uncertainty regarding Mareva's jurisdictional basis, the better-reasoned and more recent decisions ground Mareva in equity's traditional power to remedy the "abuse" of legal process by defendants and the "injustice" that would result from defendants

---

4. In a series of cases implementing the desegregation mandate of *Brown v. Board of Education*, 347 U.S. 483 . . . (1954), for example, we recognized the need for district courts to draw on their equitable jurisdiction to supervise various aspects of local school administration. See *Freeman v. Pitts*, 503 U.S. 467, 491–492 . . . (1992) (describing responsibility shouldered by district courts, "in a manner consistent with the purposes and objectives of [their] equitable power," first, to structure and supervise desegregation decrees, then, as school districts achieved compliance, to relinquish control at a measured pace). Similarly, courts enforcing the antitrust laws have superintended intricate programs of corporate dissolution or divestiture. See *United States v. E.I. du Pont de Nemours & Co.*, 366 U.S. 316, 328–331, and nn. 9–13 . . . (1961) (cataloging cases); cf. *United States v. American Tel. & Tel. Co.*, 552 F.Supp. 131 (DDC 1982), aff'd sub nom. *Maryland v. United States*, 460 U.S. 1001 . . . (1983) (approving consent decree that set in train lengthy judicial oversight of divestiture of telephone monopoly).

"making themselves judgment-proof" by disposing of their assets during the pendency of litigation. *Iraqi Ministry of Defence v. Arcepey Shipping Co.*, 1 All E.R. 480, 484–487 (1979) (citations omitted); see Hetherington, Introduction to the Mareva Injunction, in Mareva Injunctions 1, 10–13, and n. 95, 20 (M. Hetherington ed.1983) (explaining the doctrinal basis of this jurisdictional theory and citing cases adopting it). That grounding, in my judgment, is secure.

III A

[49] The Court worries that permitting preliminary injunctions to freeze assets would allow creditors, "'on a mere statement of belief that the defendant can easily make away with or transport his money or goods, [to] impose an injunction on him, indefinite in duration, disabling him to use so much of his funds or property as the court deems necessary for security or compliance with its possible decree.' . . . (quoting *De Beers Consol. Mines, Ltd. v. United States*, 325 U.S. 212, 222 . . . (1945)). Given the strong showings a creditor would be required to make to gain the provisional remedy, and the safeguards on which the debtor could insist, I agree with the Second Circuit "that this 'parade of horribles' [would] not come to pass." 143 F.3d 688, 696 (1998).

[50] Under standards governing preliminary injunctive relief generally, a plaintiff must show a likelihood of success on the merits and irreparable injury in the absence of an injunction. See *Doran v. Salem Inn, Inc.*, 422 U.S. 922, 931 . . . (1975). Plaintiffs with questionable claims would not meet the likelihood of success criterion. See 11A Charles Alan Wright, Arthur R. Miller, & Mary Kay Kane, Federal Practice and Procedure § 2948.3, at 184–188 (as a general rule, plaintiff seeking preliminary injunction must demonstrate a reasonable probability of success). The irreparable injury requirement would not be met by unsubstantiated allegations that a defendant may dissipate assets. See *id.*, § 2948.1, at 153 ("Speculative injury is not sufficient."); see also Wasserman, 67 Wash.L.Rev., at 286–305 (discussing application of traditional preliminary injunction requirements to provisional asset-freeze requests). As the Court of Appeals recognized, provisional freeze orders would be appropriate in damages actions only upon a finding that, without the freeze, "the movant would be unable to collect [a money] judgment." 143 F.3d, at 697. The preliminary asset-freeze order, in short, would rank and operate as an extraordinary remedy.

[51] Federal Rule of Civil Procedure 65(c), moreover, requires a preliminary injunction applicant to post a bond "in such sum as the court deems proper, for the payment of such costs and damages as may be incurred or suffered by any party who is found to have been wrongfully enjoined." As an essential condition for a preliminary freeze order, a district court could demand sufficient security to ensure a remedy for wrongly enjoined defendants. Furthermore, it would be incumbent on a district court to "match the scope of its injunction to the most probable size of the likely judgment," thereby sparing the defendant from undue hardship. See *Hoxworth v. Blinder, Robinson & Co.*, 903 F.2d 186, 199 (C.A.3 1990); cf. App. to Pet. for Cert. 53a (District Court expressed readiness to modify the preliminary injunction if necessary to GMD's continuance in business).

[52] The protections in place guard against any routine or arbitrary imposition of a preliminary freeze order designed to stop the dissipation of assets that would render a court's judgment worthless. Cf. ante, at 1972, 1974–1975. The case we face should be paradigmatic. There was no question that GMD's debt to Alliance was due and owing. And the short span — less than four months — between preliminary injunction and summary judgment shows that the temporary restraint on GMD did not linger beyond the time necessary for a fair and final adjudication in a busy but efficiently operated court. Absent immediate judicial action, Alliance would have been left with a multimillion dollar judgment on which it could collect not a penny.[6] 6 In my view, the District Court properly invoked its equitable power to avoid that manifestly unjust result and to protect its ability to render an enforceable final judgment. . . .

B

[54] Contrary to the Court's suggestion . . . , this case involves no judicial usurpation of Congress' authority. Congress, of course, can instruct the federal courts to issue preliminary injunctions freezing assets pending final judgment, or instruct them not to, and the courts must heed Congress' command. See *Guaranty Trust Co. v. York*, 326 U.S. 99, 105 . . . (1945) ("Congressional curtailment of equity powers must be respected."). Indeed, Congress has restricted the equity jurisdiction of federal courts in a variety of contexts. See *Yakus v. United States*, 321 U.S. 414, 442, n. 8 . . . (1944) (cataloging statutes regulating federal equity power).

[55] The Legislature, however, has said nothing about preliminary freeze orders. The relevant question, therefore, is whether, absent congressional direction, the general equitable powers of the federal courts permit relief of the kind fashioned by the District Court. I would find the default rule in the grand aims of equity. Where, as here, legal remedies are not "practical and efficient," *Payne*, 7 Wall. at 431, 19 L.Ed. 260, the federal courts must rely on their "flexible jurisdiction in equity . . . to protect all rights and do justice to all concerned," *Rubber Co. v. Goodyear*, 9 Wall. 805, 807, 19 L.Ed. 828 (1870). No countervailing precedent or principle holds the federal courts powerless to prevent a defendant from dissipating assets, to the destruction of a plaintiff's claim, during the course of judicial proceedings. Accordingly, I would affirm the judgment of the Court of Appeals and uphold the District Court's preliminary injunction.

---

6. Before the District Court, Alliance frankly acknowledged the existence of other, unrepresented creditors. While acting to protect its own interest, Alliance asked the District Court to fashion relief that "does not just directly benefit us, but benefits . . . the whole class of creditors" by creating "an even playing field" among creditors . . . (Alliance suggests that District Court direct GMD to set up a trust in compliance with Mexican law in order to oversee distributions to creditors). The Court supplies no reason to think that Alliance should have abandoned its rock-solid claim just because other creditors, for whatever reason, failed to bring suit. But cf. ante, . . . ("respondents did not represent all of the holders of the Notes; they were an active few who sought to benefit at the expense of the other [creditors]").

The position of Justice Scalia—ever the originalist—is not only questionable given the high probability that justified claims of the plaintiffs will be frustrated. It also flies in the face of the acclaimed advantage of the common law over the more statute-based civil law systems, namely its flexibility. Consequently, there has been some criticism of *Grupo Mexicano* and some calls for it to be overturned.[119]

6. The European Union has recently taken another important step to ensure that legitimate claims can be successfully pursued across the entire Union. This measure is not only relevant for U.S. corporations with subsidiaries in the EU. It also applies if a U.S. natural or legal person brings a case against any natural or legal person in one Member State, where the courts have jurisdiction on the basis of domicile, incorporation, or location of assets, and wants to secure additional assets for subsequent enforcement across several or all EU Member States. EU Regulation 655/2014 Establishing a European Account Preservation Order Procedure to Facilitate Cross-Border Debt Recovery in Civil and Commercial Matters[120] entered into force on January 18, 2017:

Article 1 Subject Matter

1. This Regulation establishes a Union procedure enabling a creditor to obtain a European Account Preservation Order ('Preservation Order' or 'Order') which prevents the subsequent enforcement of the creditor's claim from being jeopardised through the transfer or withdrawal of funds up to the amount specified in the Order which are held by the debtor or on his behalf in a bank account maintained in a Member State.

2. The Preservation Order shall be available to the creditor as an alternative to preservation measures under national law. . . .

Article 3 Cross-Border Cases

1. For the purposes of this Regulation, a cross-border case is one in which the bank account or accounts to be preserved by the Preservation Order are maintained in a Member State other than:

(a) the Member State of the court seised of the application for the Preservation Order pursuant to Article 6; or

(b) the Member State in which the creditor is domiciled. . . .

Article 5 Availability

The Preservation Order shall be available to the creditor in the following situations:

---

119. See, for example, Anthony DiSarro, *Freeze Frame: The Supreme Court's Reaffirmation of the Substantive Principles of Preliminary Injunctions*, Gonzaga L. Rev. 2011, Vol. 47, No. 1, pp. 51–98; as well as David Capper, *The Need for Mareva Injunctions Reconsidered*, Fordham L. Rev. 2005, Vol. 73, No. 5, pp. 2161–2181.

120. OJ L 189 of June 27, 2014, pp. 59–92.

(a) before the creditor initiates proceedings in a Member State against the debtor on the substance of the matter, or at any stage during such proceedings up until the issuing of the judgment or the approval or conclusion of a court settlement;

(b) after the creditor has obtained in a Member State a judgment, court settlement or authentic instrument which requires the debtor to pay the creditor's claim.

Article 6 Jurisdiction

1. Where the creditor has not yet obtained a judgment, court settlement or authentic instrument, jurisdiction to issue a Preservation Order shall lie with the courts of the Member State which have jurisdiction to rule on the substance of the matter in accordance with the relevant rules of jurisdiction applicable. . . .

3. Where the creditor has already obtained a judgment or court settlement, jurisdiction to issue a Preservation Order for the claim specified in the judgment or court settlement shall lie with the courts of the Member State in which the judgment was issued or the court settlement was approved or concluded. . . .

Article 7 Conditions for Issuing a Preservation Order

1. The court shall issue the Preservation Order when the creditor has submitted sufficient evidence to satisfy the court that there is an urgent need for a protective measure in the form of a Preservation Order because there is a real risk that, without such a measure, the subsequent enforcement of the creditor's claim against the debtor will be impeded or made substantially more difficult.

2. Where the creditor has not yet obtained in a Member State a judgment, court settlement or authentic instrument requiring the debtor to pay the creditor's claim, the creditor shall also submit sufficient evidence to satisfy the court that he is likely to succeed on the substance of his claim against the debtor. . . .

Article 10 Initiation of Proceedings on the Substance of the Matter

1. Where the creditor has applied for a Preservation Order before initiating proceedings on the substance of the matter, he shall initiate such proceedings and provide proof of such initiation to the court with which the application for the Preservation Order was lodged within 30 days of the date on which he lodged the application or within 14 days of the date of the issue of the Order, whichever date is the later. The court may also, at the request of the debtor, extend that time period, for example in order to allow the parties to settle the claim, and shall inform the two parties accordingly.

2. If the court has not received proof of the initiation of proceedings within the time period referred to in paragraph 1, the Preservation Order shall be revoked or shall terminate and the parties shall be informed accordingly. . . .

The procedure is standardized across all EU Member States (see, in particular, Articles 8 and 19). Specific provisions are made for the issuing of the Preservation Order without prior notice to the debtor (Article 11), although once the Order is issued, it has to be served on the debtor (Article 28). Unless a court deems it inappropriate in a particular case, the creditor has to provide security "for an amount sufficient to prevent abuse of the procedure" if she has not yet obtained a judgment confirming her claims (Article 12). If a creditor has already obtained a judgment, she can ask for disclosure of unknown bank account balances in other Member States pursuant to Article 14. The courts of other Member States are obliged to recognize and enforce Preservation Orders "without any special procedure" (Article 22). Banks that do not comply with obligations under the Regulation may be liable for damages (Articles 26, 39).

3. *Evidence*

The general rule in litigation is that the party presenting a claim has the burden of proof. If the party cannot produce enough evidence to persuade the court, the claim will be rejected. As lawyers, we need to consider five types of evidence: Documents, Experts, Witnesses (of fact), Inspection of Locales or Things, as well as the Parties themselves. The canon can easily be remembered via the acronym DEWIP.

The problem in many cases is that evidence may not be in the hands of the party making the claim, but may be controlled by the other party or by third parties. Thus, every jurisdiction has rules on disclosures and discovery that determine whether, when, how, and to what extent a party making a claim, or the court itself, can demand evidence from the other party and from third parties unconnected to the litigation.

In the U.S., Title V of the Federal Rules of Civil Procedure provides the rules applicable in federal courts.[121] Each of the states has its own rules for its own state courts. In general, discovery is part of the pretrial procedures. After the parties have presented their pleadings, motions, defenses, objections, counterclaims, and cross-claims, the court will usually schedule a pretrial conference. One important goal of the conference is to determine any facts that are in dispute, to what extent evidence relevant to these facts is available and admissible, and to what extent disclosures and discovery will be required. The general principle in civil and commercial trials in the U.S. is that a party cannot only ask for relevant and admissible evidence, but also for any other information that may lead to the discovery of relevant and admissible evidence. This principle is based on the notion that a party may not know the

---

121. Rules 26 to 37. The FRCP were last amended on December 1, 2016 and are available online at http://www.uscourts.gov/sites/default/files/rules-of-civil-procedure.pdf.

persons, documents, or things that contain relevant and admissible evidence and needs first "to discover" these.[122] There are some restrictions, of course, for example for privileged attorney-client communications or certain types of trade secrets, but the general rule favors broad access to evidence. Failure to comply with disclosure obligations or discovery requests may constitute contempt of court and entail various sanctions pursuant to Rule 37(b) FRCP.

The problem with getting evidence from parties, third persons, witnesses, or public authorities in another country is in many ways similar to the problem of effecting service of process in another country: The court and the public authorities in the country where the litigation is taking place do not have the power to demand evidence from other countries. Even just attempting such a demand would be an infringement of the sovereign powers of the other country. The traditional answer to the question is to send a request for judicial assistance via the diplomatic and political channels, as described above, pp. 750–759, for service of process. These procedures are slow and they are at the mercy of the political consent of the authorities in the other country. They may comply with the request on the basis of reciprocity (we help you now if you help us next time). They may generally refuse to comply with the request because the political atmosphere between the countries is hostile, the authorities of the other country do not trust informal promises of reciprocity, or the parties concerned in the other country are politically connected and pull some strings in order to ensure that potentially damaging evidence does not get out. Finally, and most commonly, the authorities of the other country may comply with some but not all of the requests. This outcome is common because virtually all other countries in the world think that U.S. rules on pretrial discovery go too far and enable unjustified fishing expeditions and/or frivolous litigation to impede or harass competitors or former business partners after a relationship has

---

122. Rule 26(b) FRCP stipulates as follows: "Unless otherwise limited by court order, the scope of discovery is as follows: Parties may obtain discovery regarding any nonprivileged matter that is relevant to any party's claim or defense and proportional to the needs of the case, considering the importance of the issues at stake in the action, the amount in controversy, the parties' relative access to relevant information, the parties' resources, the importance of the discovery in resolving the issues, and whether the burden or expense of the proposed discovery outweighs its likely benefit. Information within this scope of discovery need not be admissible in evidence to be discoverable."

Rule 34(a) FRCP elaborates: "A party may serve on any other party a request within the scope of Rule 26(b): (1) to produce and permit the requesting party or its representative to inspect, copy, test, or sample the following items in the responding party's possession, custody, or control: (A) any designated documents or electronically stored information — including writings, drawings, graphs, charts, photographs, sound recordings, images, and other data or data compilations — stored in any medium from which information can be obtained either directly or, if necessary, after translation by the responding party into a reasonably usable form; or (B) any designated tangible things; or

(2) to permit entry onto designated land or other property possessed or controlled by the responding party, so that the requesting party may inspect, measure, survey, photograph, test, or sample the property or any designated object or operation on it."

soured. To counter what they consider overly broad discovery demands from U.S. courts and to protect their citizens and businesses against U.S. sanctions, a number of countries have adopted so-called *blocking statutes*. Article 271(1) of the Swiss Criminal Code was quoted above, at p. 753, note 71. If anything, French law may go even further. Pursuant to the French Loi No. 80-538 of 16 July 1980,[123] it is generally prohibited for anyone who is either a French citizen or resident in France or works for a company based in France, to disclose economic, commercial, industrial, financial, or technical information to foreign public authorities, if such disclosure might affect the sovereignty, security, essential economic interests, or the public order of France (Article 1). It is further prohibited for anyone to demand such information, including and in particular any documents or other information that might be used as evidence in foreign judicial or administrative procedures (Article 1bis). Violations are punishable by financial penalties and/or imprisonment of up to six months (Article 3). A number of other countries have similar laws to protect their interests.

To provide procedures for obtaining evidence from abroad that are less cumbersome than the traditional diplomatic and consular channels, and to strike a balance between the interests of the party that is seeking evidence and the party that supposedly has the evidence, the Hague Conference on Private International Law produced the 1970 Hague Convention on the Taking of Evidence Abroad in Civil and Commercial Matters (Documents, p. II-32). The structure and mechanisms of this Convention are somewhat similar to the 1965 Hague Convention on the Service Abroad of Judicial and Extrajudicial Documents in Civil and Commercial Matters, described above, pp. 752 et seq. Each Contracting State has to designate a Central Authority that can be approached with Letters of Request by the courts and judicial authorities of any other Contracting State (Article 2). The format of the Letters of Request is standardized and a model is provided on the website of the HCCH.[124] Once a Letter is accepted as compliant with the requirements under the Convention, it "shall be executed expeditiously" by the judicial authorities of the requested State (Article 9). Compulsion has to be used, if necessary (Article 10). The execution can only be refused on narrow grounds, which do not include different and more restrictive rules on disclosure and discovery in the requested State (Article 12). Finally, the procedure is generally free of charge (Article 13).

---

123. Loi No. 80-538 du 16 juillet 1980 relative à la communication de documents ou renseignements d'ordre économique, commercial ou technique à des personnes physiques ou morales étrangères, Journal Officiel de la République Française [J.O.] [Official Gazette of France], July 16, 1980, p. 1799, available online at https://www.legifrance.gouv.fr/jo_pdf.do?id=JORFTEXT000000 515863&pageCourante=01799.

124. See Article 3 of the Convention and https://assets.hcch.net/docs/5407462f-6e0c-4da9 -a316-73b554a8eef4.pdf. The HCCH even provides a fillable pdf at https://assets.hcch.net/docs /e7b6b267-49e9-4e02-b814-c0780e5b65e3.pdf.

The basic principles of the Convention, in particular Article 12, support the U.S. position, namely that a court, once it has jurisdiction over a party, can apply its own rules on disclosure and discovery and obtain evidence abroad even if the rules in the other country are not as broad. Thus, it was easy for the U.S. to ratify the Convention as early as 1972. However, to alleviate concerns in some countries with regard to the U.S. rules and procedures for pretrial discovery, Article 23 of the Convention allows for any Contracting State to "declare that it will not execute Letters of Requests issued for the purpose of obtaining pre-trial discovery of documents as known in Common Law countries." While this provision made it possible for the Convention to be ratified by a total of 63 countries (as of March 2020), it also reduces its practical value. However, U.S. attorneys should in each case read the text of any reservations and declarations of the foreign country carefully. For example, Switzerland does not exclude all pretrial discovery cooperation. The reservation reads as follows: "Switzerland declares that Letters of Request issued for the purpose of obtaining pre-trial discovery of documents will not be executed if: a) the request has no direct and necessary link with the proceedings in question; or b) a person is required to indicate what documents relating to the case are or were in his/her possession or keeping or at his/her disposal; or c) a person is required to produce documents other than those mentioned in the request for legal assistance, which are probably in his/her possession or keeping or at his/her disposal; or d) interests worthy of protection of the concerned persons are endangered."[125] While this excludes broad fishing expeditions, requests for specific documents with obvious connections to pending proceedings will normally be accepted. Similarly, while France made a general reservation against pretrial discovery, the French government also declared the following: "The declaration made by the French Republic in accordance with Article 23 relating to Letters of Request issued for the purpose of obtaining pretrial discovery of documents does not apply when the requested documents are enumerated limitatively in the Letter of Request and have a direct and precise link with the object of the procedure."[126] Successful pretrial discovery abroad will, therefore, normally require that U.S. attorneys specify rather clearly the documents and other evidence they are requesting.

Unfortunately, the situation has been further complicated by the practice of some American courts of sidestepping the Convention and basically holding foreign parties in contempt if they do not surrender evidence located abroad and requested pursuant to the broad U.S. discovery rules. The leading U.S. Supreme Court case on the matter is *Aérospatiale*.

---

125. See https://www.hcch.net/en/instruments/conventions/status-table/notifications/?csid =561&disp=resdn.

126. See https://www.hcch.net/en/instruments/conventions/status-table/notifications/?csid =501&disp=resdn, translation by the HCCH.

Case 6-7

Société Nationale Industrielle Aérospatiale v. United States District Court

482 U.S. 522 (1987)
(Paragraph numbers added, some footnotes omitted.)

[Plaintiffs were injured in the crash of an airplane made by Aérospatiale in France. They claimed defective design and/or manufacturing and requested that the defendant should "identify the pilots who flew test flights in the [plane] before it was certified for flight by the Federal Aviation Administration" and that the defendants produce all "design specifications, line drawings and engineering plans and all engineering change orders and plans and all drawings concerning the leading edge slats for the Rallye type aircraft manufactured by the Defendants" (p. 545). In front of the trial court, the defendants argued that the request should be submitted via the channels specified in the Hague Convention. However, the trial judge held that "[t]o permit the Hague Evidence Convention to override the Federal Rules of Civil Procedure would frustrate the courts' interests, which particularly arise in products liability cases, in protecting United States citizens from harmful products and in compensating them for injuries arising from use of such products" (pp. 527–528). On appeal, the Court of Appeals for the Eighth Circuit held that "when the district court has jurisdiction over a foreign litigant the Hague Convention does not apply to the production of evidence in that litigant's possession, even though the documents and information sought may physically be located within the territory of a foreign signatory to the Convention."[127] The decision of the Court of Appeals is further reported as follows by the Supreme Court:

> The Court of Appeals disagreed with petitioners' argument that this construction would render the entire Hague Convention "meaningless," noting that it would still serve the purpose of providing an improved procedure for obtaining evidence from nonparties. . . . The court also rejected petitioners' contention that considerations of international comity required plaintiffs to resort to Hague Convention procedures as an initial matter ("first use"), and correspondingly to invoke the federal discovery rules only if the treaty procedures turned out to be futile. The Court of Appeals believed that the potential overruling of foreign tribunals' denial of discovery would do more to defeat than to promote international comity. . . .

After granting certiorari, Justice Stevens wrote on behalf of the majority of the Supreme Court (starting at p. 529, most footnotes omitted)]:

II

[6] In the District Court and the Court of Appeals, petitioners contended that the Hague Evidence Convention "provides the exclusive and mandatory procedures

---

127. 782 F.2d 120 (1986), at p. 124.

for obtaining documents and information located within the territory of a foreign signatory." 782 F.2d, at 124. We are satisfied that the Court of Appeals correctly rejected this extreme position. We believe it is foreclosed by the plain language of the Convention. . . .

III

[9] In arguing their entitlement to a protective order, petitioners correctly assert that both the discovery rules set forth in the Federal Rules of Civil Procedure and the Hague Convention are the law of the United States. . . . This observation, however, does not dispose of the question before us; we must analyze the interaction between these two bodies of federal law. Initially, we note that at least four different interpretations of the relationship between the federal discovery rules and the Hague Convention are possible. Two of these interpretations assume that the Hague Convention by its terms dictates the extent to which it supplants normal discovery rules. First, the Hague Convention might be read as requiring its use to the exclusion of any other discovery procedures whenever evidence located abroad is sought for use in an American court. Second, the Hague Convention might be interpreted to require first, but not exclusive, use of its procedures. Two other interpretations assume that international comity, rather than the obligations created by the treaty, should guide judicial resort to the Hague Convention. Third, then, the Convention might be viewed as establishing a supplemental set of discovery procedures, strictly optional under treaty law, to which concerns of comity nevertheless require first resort by American courts in all cases. Fourth, the treaty may be viewed as an undertaking among sovereigns to facilitate discovery to which an American court should resort when it deems that course of action appropriate, after considering the situations of the parties before it as well as the interests of the concerned foreign state. . . .

[11] We reject the first two of the possible interpretations as inconsistent with the language and negotiating history of the Hague Convention. The preamble of the Convention specifies its purpose "to facilitate the transmission and execution of Letters of Request" and to "improve mutual judicial co-operation in civil or commercial matters." . . . The preamble does not speak in mandatory terms which would purport to describe the procedures for all permissible transnational discovery and exclude all other existing practices.[15] The text of the Evidence Convention itself does not modify the law of any contracting state, require any contracting state

---

15. The Hague Conference on Private International Law's omission of mandatory language in the preamble is particularly significant in light of the same body's use of mandatory language in the preamble to the Hague Service Convention [Documents, p. II-23]. Article 1 of the Service Convention provides: "The present Convention shall apply in all cases, in civil or commercial matters, where there is occasion to transmit a judicial or extrajudicial document for service abroad." . . . [T]he Service Convention was drafted before the Evidence Convention, and its language provided a model exclusivity provision that the drafters of the Evidence Convention could easily have followed had they been so inclined. Given this background, the drafters' election to use permissive language instead is strong evidence of their intent.

to use the Convention procedures, either in requesting evidence or in responding to such requests, or compel any contracting state to change its own evidence-gathering procedures. . . .

[14] An interpretation of the Hague Convention as the exclusive means for obtaining evidence located abroad would effectively subject every American court hearing a case involving a national of a contracting state to the internal laws of that state. Interrogatories and document requests are staples of international commercial litigation, no less than of other suits, yet a rule of exclusivity would subordinate the court's supervision of even the most routine of these pretrial proceedings to the actions or, equally, to the inactions of foreign judicial authorities. As the Court of Appeals for the Fifth Circuit observed in *In re Anschuetz & Co., GmbH*, 754 F.2d 602, 612 (1985), cert. pending, No. 85–98:

> "It seems patently obvious that if the Convention were interpreted as pre-empting interrogatories and document requests, the Convention would really be much more than an agreement on taking evidence abroad. Instead, the Convention would amount to a major regulation of the overall conduct of litigation between nationals of different signatory states, raising a significant possibility of very serious interference with the jurisdiction of United States courts. . . .
>
> While it is conceivable that the United States could enter into a treaty giving other signatories control over litigation instituted and pursued in American courts, a treaty intended to bring about such a curtailment of the rights given to all litigants by the federal rules would surely state its intention clearly and precisely identify crucial terms."

[15] The Hague Convention, however, contains no such plain statement of a pre-emptive intent. We conclude accordingly that the Hague Convention did not deprive the District Court of the jurisdiction it otherwise possessed to order a foreign national party before it to produce evidence physically located within a signatory nation.[25] . . .

---

25. The opposite conclusion of exclusivity would create three unacceptable asymmetries. First, within any lawsuit between a national of the United States and a national of another contracting party, the foreign party could obtain discovery under the Federal Rules of Civil Procedure, while the domestic party would be required to resort first to the procedures of the Hague Convention. This imbalance would run counter to the fundamental maxim of discovery that "[m]utual knowledge of all the relevant facts gathered by both parties is essential to proper litigation." *Hickman v. Taylor*, 329 U.S. 495, 507, 67 S.Ct. 385, 392, 91 L.Ed. 451 (1947).

Second, a rule of exclusivity would enable a company which is a citizen of another contracting state to compete with a domestic company on uneven terms, since the foreign company would be subject to less extensive discovery procedures in the event that both companies were sued in an American court. Petitioners made a voluntary decision to market their products in the United States. They are entitled to compete on equal terms with other companies operating in this market. But since the District Court unquestionably has personal jurisdiction over petitioners, they are subject to the same legal constraints, including the burdens associated with American judicial procedures, as their American competitors. A general rule according foreign nationals a preferred

V

[18] Petitioners contend that even if the Hague Convention's procedures are not mandatory, this Court should adopt a rule requiring that American litigants first resort to those procedures before initiating any discovery pursuant to the normal methods of the Federal Rules of Civil Procedure. . . . The Court of Appeals rejected this argument because it was convinced that an American court's order ultimately requiring discovery that a foreign court had refused under Convention procedures would constitute "the greatest insult" to the sovereignty of that tribunal. . . . We disagree with the Court of Appeals' view. It is well known that the scope of American discovery is often significantly broader than is permitted in other jurisdictions, and we are satisfied that foreign tribunals will recognize that the final decision on the evidence to be used in litigation conducted in American courts must be made by those courts. We therefore do not believe that an American court should refuse to make use of Convention procedures because of a concern that it may ultimately find it necessary to order the production of evidence that a foreign tribunal permitted a party to withhold.

[19] Nevertheless, we cannot accept petitioners' invitation to announce a new rule of law that would require first resort to Convention procedures whenever discovery is sought from a foreign litigant. Assuming, without deciding, that we have the law-making power to do so, we are convinced that such a general rule would be unwise. In many situations the Letter of Request procedure authorized by the Convention would be unduly time consuming and expensive, as well as less certain to produce needed evidence than direct use of the Federal Rules. A rule of first resort in all cases would therefore be inconsistent with the overriding interest in the "just, speedy, and inexpensive determination" of litigation in our courts. See Fed.Rule Civ.Proc. 1.

[20] Petitioners argue that a rule of first resort is necessary to accord respect to the sovereignty of states in which evidence is located. It is true that the process of obtaining evidence in a civil-law jurisdiction is normally conducted by a judicial officer rather than by private attorneys. Petitioners contend that if performed on French soil, for example, by an unauthorized person, such evidence- gathering might violate the "judicial sovereignty" of the host nation. Because it is only through the Convention that civil-law nations have given their consent to evidence-gathering activities within their borders, petitioners argue, we have a duty to employ those procedures whenever they are available. . . . We find that argument unpersuasive. If such a duty were to be inferred from the adoption of the Convention itself, we believe it would have been described in the text of that document. Moreover, the concept of

---

position in pretrial proceedings in our courts would conflict with the principle of equal opportunity that governs the market they elected to enter.

Third, since a rule of first use of the Hague Convention would apply to cases in which a foreign party is a national of a contracting state, but not to cases in which a foreign party is a national of any other foreign state, the rule would confer an unwarranted advantage on some domestic litigants over others similarly situated.

international comity[27] requires in this context a more particularized analysis of the respective interests of the foreign nation and the requesting nation than petitioners' proposed general rule would generate.[28] We therefore decline to hold as a blanket matter that comity requires resort to Hague Evidence Convention procedures without prior scrutiny in each case of the particular facts, sovereign interests, and likelihood that resort to those procedures will prove effective. . . .

[22] American courts, in supervising pretrial proceedings, should exercise special vigilance to protect foreign litigants from the danger that unnecessary, or unduly burdensome, discovery may place them in a disadvantageous position. Judicial supervision of discovery should always seek to minimize its costs and inconvenience and to prevent improper uses of discovery requests. When it is necessary to seek evidence abroad, however, the district court must supervise pretrial proceedings particularly closely to prevent discovery abuses. For example, the additional cost of transportation of documents or witnesses to or from foreign locations may increase the danger that discovery may be sought for the improper purpose of motivating settlement, rather than finding relevant and probative evidence. Objections to "abusive" discovery that foreign litigants advance should therefore receive the most careful consideration. In addition, we have long recognized the demands of comity in suits involving foreign states, either as parties or as sovereigns with a coordinate interest in the litigation. See *Hilton v. Guyot*, [below, p. 834] (1895). American courts should therefore take care to demonstrate due respect for any special problem confronted by the foreign litigant on account of its nationality or the location of its operations, and for any sovereign interest expressed by a foreign state. We do not articulate specific rules to guide this delicate task of adjudication. . . .

---

27. Comity refers to the spirit of cooperation in which a domestic tribunal approaches the resolution of cases touching the laws and interests of other sovereign states. . . . See also *Hilton v. Guyot*, [below, p. 834] (1895): "'Comity,' in the legal sense, is neither a matter of absolute obligation, on the one hand, nor of mere courtesy and good will, upon the other. But it is the recognition which one nation allows within its territory to the legislative, executive or judicial acts of another nation, having due regard both to international duty and convenience, and to the rights of its own citizens or of other persons who are under the protection of its laws."

28. The nature of the concerns that guide a comity analysis is suggested by the Restatement of Foreign Relations Law of the United States (Revised) § 437(1)(c) (Tent.Draft No. 7, 1986) (approved May 14, 1986) (Restatement). While we recognize that § 437 of the Restatement may not represent a consensus of international views on the scope of the district court's power to order foreign discovery in the face of objections by foreign states, these factors are relevant to any comity analysis:

"(1) the importance to the . . . litigation of the documents or other information requested;

"(2) the degree of specificity of the request;

"(3) whether the information originated in the United States;

"(4) the availability of alternative means of securing the information; and

"(5) the extent to which noncompliance with the request would undermine important interests of the United States, or compliance with the request would undermine important interests of the state where the information is located." *Ibid.*

[24] Accordingly, the judgment of the Court of Appeals is vacated, and the case is remanded for further proceedings consistent with this opinion.

It is so ordered.

[25] Justice BLACKMUN, with whom Justice BRENNAN, Justice MARSHALL, and Justice O'CONNOR join, concurring in part and dissenting in part.

[26] Some might well regard the Court's decision in this case as an affront to the nations that have joined the United States in ratifying the Hague Convention on the Taking of Evidence Abroad in Civil or Commercial Matters. . . . The Court ignores the importance of the Convention by relegating it to an "optional" status, without acknowledging the significant achievement in accommodating divergent interests that the Convention represents. Experience to date indicates that there is a large risk that the case-by-case comity analysis now to be permitted by the Court will be performed inadequately and that the somewhat unfamiliar procedures of the Convention will be invoked infrequently. I fear the Court's decision means that courts will resort unnecessarily to issuing discovery orders under the Federal Rules of Civil Procedure in a raw exercise of their jurisdictional power to the detriment of the United States' national and international interests. The Court's view of this country's international obligations is particularly unfortunate in a world in which regular commercial and legal channels loom ever more crucial.

[27] I do agree with the Court's repudiation of the positions at both extremes of the spectrum with regard to the use of the Convention. Its rejection of the view that the Convention is not "applicable" at all to this case is surely correct: the Convention clearly applies to litigants as well as to third parties, and to requests for evidence located abroad, no matter where that evidence is actually "produced." The Court also correctly rejects the far opposite position that the Convention provides the exclusive means for discovery involving signatory countries. I dissent, however, because I cannot endorse the Court's case-by-case inquiry for determining whether to use Convention procedures and its failure to provide lower courts with any meaningful guidance for carrying out that inquiry. In my view, the Convention provides effective discovery procedures that largely eliminate the conflicts between United States and foreign law on evidence gathering. I therefore would apply a general presumption that, in most cases, courts should resort first to the Convention procedures.[1] An individualized analysis of the circumstances of a particular case is

---

1. Many courts that have examined the issue have adopted a rule of first resort to the Convention. See, e.g., Philadelphia *Gear Corp. v. American Pfauter Corp.*, 100 F.R.D. 58, 61 (ED Pa.1983) ("avenue of first resort for plaintiff [is] the Hague Convention"); *Gebr. Eickhoff Maschinenfabrik und Eisengieberei mbH v. Starcher*, W.Va., 328 S.E.2d 492, 504–506 (1985) ("principle of international comity dictates first resort to [Convention] procedures"); *Vincent v. Ateliers de la Motobécane, S.A.*, 193 N.J.Super. 716, 723, 475 A.2d 686, 690 (App.Div.1984) (litigant should first attempt to comply with Convention); *Th. Goldschmidt A.G. v. Smith*, 676 S.W.2d 443, 445 (Tex.App.1984) (Convention procedures not mandatory but are "avenue of first resort"); *Pierburg GmbH & Co. KG v. Superior Court*, 137 Cal.App.3d 238, 247, 186 Cal.Rptr. 876, 882–883 (1982) (plaintiffs must attempt to comply with the Convention); *Volkswagenwerk Aktiengesellschaft v. Superior Court*, 123

appropriate only when it appears that it would be futile to employ the Convention or when its procedures prove to be unhelpful. . . .

Notes and Questions

1. What do you think of the opinion of the trial judge that he could not allow the Hague Evidence Convention to override the FRCP? What is the legal status of an international convention ratified by the U.S. Senate in U.S. law? What is the point of the U.S. ratifying international conventions if any judge who does not like them can set them aside at will? What would such an approach do to the ability of the U.S. to participate in international organizations and to regulate their international relations via conventions and agreements with foreign nations as contemplated in Article II Sec. 2 and Article VI of the U.S. Constitution?

2. What do you think of the decision of the Court of Appeals in this regard? Specifically, what do you think of the argument that the Convention would still serve the purpose of providing an improved procedure for obtaining evidence from nonparties?

3. What do you think of the argument of the Supreme Court in paragraph 6 and the cited decision of the Court of Appeals for the Fifth Circuit that a requirement to apply the Hague Convention would "subject every American court hearing a case involving a national of a Contracting State to the internal laws of that state." Isn't that what mutual respect for national sovereignty is all about and what the U.S. is certainly demanding from foreign authorities in their dealings with U.S. citizens and other persons under U.S. jurisdiction? Do you find the Court's reasoning in note 25 persuasive in this regard? Why? Why not?

4. What do you think of the argument in paragraph 10 that the interests of just, speedy, and inexpensive litigation overrides the interest of foreign parties that the procedures of the Convention should at least be attempted before U.S. discovery rules, including their sanctions, are applied to foreign parties? Consider also the partial dissent of Justices Blackmun, Brennan, Marshall, and O'Connor in this regard.

———

Between the Member States of the European Union, despite their considerable diversity and 24 official languages, disclosure and discovery works more like within the United States. EU Regulation 1206/2001 of 28 May 2001 on Cooperation Between the Courts of the Member States in the Taking of Evidence in Civil and Commercial Matters[128] is directly applicable law in all 27 Member States, with the exception of Denmark. Pursuant to Article 2, requests for taking of evidence can be directly addressed by the courts of one Member State to the courts of another

———

Cal.App.3d 840, 857–859, 176 Cal.Rptr. 874, 885–886 (1981) ("Hague Convention establishes not a fixed rule but rather a minimum measure of international cooperation").

128. OJ 2001 L 174, pp. 1–24. See also Documents, p. II-82.

Member State. The format of the requests is standardized pursuant to Article 4 and the model Form A annexed to the Regulation. Acknowledgment of receipt is likewise standardized per model Form B, and so is the Form H providing information on the outcome of the request. Pursuant to Article 17, a court of a Member State can also ask to directly take evidence itself in another Member State, as long as coercive measures are not required. Finally, pursuant to Article 18, the procedure is free of cost.[129]

C. Recognition and Enforcement of Foreign Judgments

1. Introduction

Once a judgment is obtained in one country, it is generally enforceable only in that country. Because of their sovereignty, countries are under no obligation to recognize and enforce acts of foreign authorities unless they have agreed to do so. Agreement could be general, if both countries have ratified a multilateral or bilateral convention and the conditions laid down in the convention are met. In the absence of a prior general commitment, agreement has to be sought on a case-by-case basis for specific judicial decisions.

While the 1958 New York Convention on Recognition and Enforcement of Foreign Arbitral Awards provides effective mechanisms of enforcement for arbitral awards in most countries (see below, pp. 1014 et seq.), there is no comparable multinational convention on the recognition and enforcement of foreign judgments. Whether a foreign judgment can be recognized and enforced, the criteria it has to meet, and the procedure to be followed, are thus subject to the national law—and sometimes the politics—of the country or countries where enforcement is sought. This is particularly troublesome for international business since it may be unpredictable whether or not a judgment can be enforced abroad and it is not uncommon for assets to be pursued in several countries.

In this Section, we will discuss the enforcement of foreign judgments in the U.S., on the one side, and the enforcement of U.S. judgments abroad, on the other. In the United States, there is no federal law regulating the recognition and enforcement of foreign judgments. Nevertheless, foreign country judgments are usually recognized and enforced by state courts without too many difficulties, much like the state courts recognize and enforce out-of-state judgments from another jurisdiction within the U.S. Therefore, the absence of multinational rules has been commented on by Zeynalova as follows: "while the principle of Comity of Nations, the common law, and individual states' laws do allow American courts to recognize and enforce foreign judgments, foreign courts may not necessarily reciprocate. Enforcing U.S.

---

129. The only expenses to be covered are fees paid to experts and interpreters, videoconferencing expenses, and the like (Article 18(2)). This does not include witness expenses, as it was confirmed by the European Court of Justice in *Case C-283/09, Artur Weryński v. Mediatel 4B spółka* (ECLI:EU:C:2011:85).

court judgments abroad can prove especially difficult in light of divergent rules on jurisdiction, requirements for special service of process, reciprocity, and some foreign countries' public policy concerns over enforcing American jury awards carrying hefty punitive damages. . . . Generally speaking, . . . a foreign claimant will have a faster and easier time enforcing his or her foreign-made judgment in America, while a creditor possessing a U.S.-made judgment can expect a bumpier ride through foreign court bureaucracy."[130] In light of this imbalance, the U.S. has been an active player on the international level (at least until 2016) in the quest for a multilateral solution.

The international community, getting together as the Hague Conference on Private International Law (HCCH), undertook a first effort at harmonizing the rules and procedures in the form of the 1971 Hague Convention on the Recognition and Enforcement of Foreign Judgments in Civil and Commercial Matters (Documents, p. II-43). Pursuant to Article 4 of this Convention, "[a] decision rendered in one of the Contracting States shall be entitled to recognition and enforcement in another Contracting State under the terms of this Convention (1) if the decision was given by a court considered to have jurisdiction within the meaning of this Convention, and (2) if it is no longer subject to ordinary forms of review in the State of origin." Recognition and enforcement could be refused only if it would be "manifestly incompatible with the public policy of the State addressed or if the decision resulted from proceedings incompatible with the requirements of due process of law or if, in the circumstances, either party had no adequate opportunity fairly to present his case" (Article 5 (1) and (2)). A further exception was made for refusal on the basis that the matter was already pending elsewhere (*lis pendens*), or was already decided elsewhere (res judicata) (Article 5(3)). Review on the merits was generally prohibited (Article 8) and the courts addressed for recognition and enforcement were generally bound by the findings of fact of the court of origin (Article 9). A rather straightforward procedure was provided by Articles 13-19 avoiding, in particular, the diplomatic route and the need for legalization. Unfortunately, the Convention was initially only ratified by the Netherlands and Cyprus. Many other countries objected to the notion that they would have to recognize and enforce foreign judgments even if they did not agree that the court of origin had jurisdiction to try the matter, and regardless of whether or not they considered the judgments and any monetary awards compatible with their notions of fairness and justice. The Convention finally entered into force in 2010, after the fifth ratification, but has remained practically insignificant.

In light of the rapid expansion of international trade and the commensurate growth of international business transactions and transnational litigation, a renewed effort was launched in 1992 at the initiative of the U.S. under the umbrella of the HCCH. It avoided the contentious questions related to jurisdiction of the court of origin and culminated in the 1999 Preliminary Draft Convention on Jurisdiction

---

130. Yuliya Zeynalova, *The Law on Recognition and Enforcement of Foreign Judgments: Is It Broken and How Do We Fix It?*, 31 Berkeley J. Int'l L. 150 (2013), at p. 151, footnotes omitted.

and Foreign Judgments in Civil and Commercial Matters.[131] The text was adopted by the drafting commission of the HCCH and "provides for three kinds of jurisdiction (a mixed convention):

> required jurisdiction (the 'white list')—the court of origin may exercise jurisdiction on certain grounds listed in the convention, and if it does, the resulting judgment is entitled to recognition and enforcement in other Contracting States;

> prohibited jurisdiction (the 'black list')—the court of origin may not exercise a judgment based on certain other grounds listed in the convention, but if it does, the resulting judgment is not to be recognised;

> undefined area (the 'grey area')—in all other cases, the court of origin may exercise jurisdiction on grounds under its national law, and if it does, the resulting judgment may be recognised and enforced in accordance with the national law of the court addressed.[132]

Unfortunately, it soon became evident that the HCCH Member States, and in particular the U.S. on the one side and the EU on the other, were unable to agree on a number of key issues, including activity-based jurisdiction—by contrast to jurisdiction based on domicile, protection of consumers and employees—and the impact of internet-based transactions and e-commerce. To salvage parts of the draft convention where agreement was possible, the 2005 Hague Convention on Choice of Court Agreements (above, p. 764) was spun off and opened for ratification.

Meanwhile, at the HCCH, work on a convention on the recognition and enforcement of foreign judgments has continued and recently produced the 2019 Convention on the Recognition and Enforcement of Judgments in Civil and Commercial Matters.[133] The Convention covers "the recognition and enforcement of judgments

131. Available online at https://assets.hcch.net/docs/638883f3-0c0a-46c6-b646-7a099d9bd95e.pdf. For background information and analysis, see, *inter alia*, Samuel Baumgartner, *The Proposed Hague Convention on Jurisdiction and Foreign Judgments*, Mohr Siebeck 2003; Brandon B. Danford, *The Enforcement of Foreign Money Judgments in the United States and Europe: How Can We Achieve a Comprehensive Treaty?*, 2004 Rev. Litig., Vol. 23, pp. 381–434; Peter H. Pfund, *The Project of the Hague Conference on Private International Law to Prepare a Convention on Jurisdiction and the Recognition/Enforcement of Judgments in Civil and Commercial Matters*, 24 Brook. J. Int'l L. 7 (1998); Michael Traynor, *An Introductory Framework for Analyzing the Proposed Hague Convention on Jurisdiction and Foreign Judgments in Civil and Commercial Matters: U.S. and European Perspectives*, 6 Ann. Surv. Int'l & Comp. L. 1 (2000); Arthur T. von Mehren, *Recognition and Enforcement of Foreign Judgments: A New Approach for the Hague Conference?*, 57 L. & Contemp. Probs. 271 (1994); as well as Arthur T. von Mehren, *Drafting a Convention on International Jurisdiction and the Effects of Foreign Judgments Acceptable World-Wide: Can the Hague Conference Project Succeed?*, Am. J. Comp. L. (2001), Vol. 49, No. 2, pp. 191–202.

132. https://www.hcch.net/en/projects/legislative-projects/judgments/preparation-of-a-preliminary-draft-convention-1997-1999-.

133. https://www.hcch.net/en/instruments/conventions/full-text/?cid=137, as well as Documents, p. II-54. This Convention is comprehensive and generally well-crafted. We must hope that it will garner widespread support and will be ratified and binding for many countries, rather than countries opting for supportive but non-binding provisions such as those expressed in the *2020*

relating to civil or commercial matters." (Article 1(1)). Among others, the following subjects are excluded from its scope of application: "revenue, customs or administrative matters"; "insolvency . . . carriage of passengers and goods . . . validity, nullity or dissolution of legal persons . . . and the validity of decisions of their organs; the validity of entries in public registers; . . . intellectual property; [and] anti-trust (competition) matters . . ." (Arts. 1 and 2). For those civil and commercial matters within its scope of application, the Convention provides that "[a] judgment given by a court of a Contracting State (State of origin) *shall be recognised and enforced* in another Contracting State (requested State) . . . . Recognition or enforcement may be *refused only* on the grounds specified in this Convention . . . [and] [t]here shall be *no review of the merits* of the judgment in the requested State." (Article 4(1) and (2), emphasis added). Articles 5 and 6 detail the conditions for a judgment to be recognized and enforced. Articles 7 and 8 specify general rules when recognition and enforcement can or shall be refused. Similar to the 1958 New York Convention, there is a provision for refusals if "recognition or enforcement would be *manifestly incompatible with the public policy* of the requested State, including situations where the specific proceedings leading to the judgment were *incompatible with fundamental principles of procedural fairness* of that State . . ." (Article 7(1)(c), emphasis added). Article 12 extends recognition and enforcement to judicial settlements that have been approved by a court. Article 13 provides a finite list of documents to be produced when recognition and enforcement are sought. The Convention was opened for signature and ratification on July 2, 2019. As of June 2020, it was signed by Ukraine and Uruguay, with no ratifications to date. Whether this Convention will finally result in a system where judgments are regularly recognized and enforced around the world, similar to the New York Convention for arbitral awards, remains to be seen.[134]

2. *Enforcement of Foreign Judgments in the U.S.*

The recognition and enforcement of "foreign" judgments refers both to judgments from another U.S. state (interstate cases), and judgments from another country (international cases). In principle, "[f]ull faith and credit shall be given in each state to the public acts, records, and judicial proceedings of every other state. And the Congress may by general laws prescribe the manner in which such acts, records, and proceedings shall be proved, and the effect thereof." This Full Faith and Credit Clause in Article IV Section 1 of the U.S. Constitution allows courts in one state to recognize and enforce orders and judgments from a court in another state. However, there is not really a federal enabling law dealing with the manner and proceedings, at least not one that would preempt state laws.[135] From the perspective of

---

Asian Principles for the Recognition and Enforcement of Foreign Judgments proposed by ASEAN and some of its regional partners.

134. For analysis of the 2019 Hague Convention, see, *inter alia*, Ronald A. Brand, *Jurisdiction and Judgments Recognition at the Hague Conference: Choices Made, Treaties Completed, and the Path Ahead*, Netherlands Int'l L. Rev. 202, Vol. 67, No. 1, pp. 3–17.

135. The American Law Institute (ALI) has drafted a federal statute for the Recognition and Enforcement of Foreign Judgments in 2006. Congress has yet to take up the proposal, however. For

foreigners, reliance on state law creates a number of challenges that may seem quite forbidding, although in practice the U.S. is more open to the enforcement of foreign judgments than many other countries.

In principle, the law governing recognition and enforcement of foreign judgments in the states is common law, i.e., case law. Researching the details would be a nightmare, in particular for foreign lawyers, but there are two shortcuts. First, to improve on a highly fragmented legal landscape, the Uniform Law Commission has drafted two important model laws for the states to adopt and achieve a level of harmonization. The Revised Uniform Enforcement of Foreign Judgments Act of 1964 (Documents, p. II-66) is applied by 47 of the 50 states to interstate cases and essentially implements the Full Faith and Credit Clause of the Constitution. The Uniform Foreign Money-Judgments Recognition Act of 1962 (Documents, p. II-68) deals with international cases and is applied in 32 of the 50 states in the U.S. It was revised in 2005 and renamed the 2005 Uniform Foreign-Country Money Judgments Recognition Act (UFCMJRA). The revision clarifies the burden of proof, namely that the applicant has the burden of proof that the Act can be applied to the judgment, and any party opposing recognition has the burden of proof that a specific ground for nonrecognition exists (Section 4.(d)). The revision also clarifies the procedure. The applicant has to file an action in the court with jurisdiction over the defendant (*in personam*) or the property (*in rem*) to obtain recognition (Section 6.(a)). Alternatively, recognition can also be sought in a pending case in the form of a counterclaim or defense (Section 6.(b)). Finally, the revision provides a statute of limitations of 10 years for the recognition and enforcement of a foreign country judgment, or when the judgment becomes unenforceable in the country of origin, whichever is earlier (Section 9.). The revision has so far been adopted in some 20 states.[136] In both versions, the Act provides a number of mandatory and optional grounds for refusal of recognition in Section 4 (emphasis added):

(a) Except as otherwise provided in subsections (b) and (c), a court of this state *shall recognize* a foreign-country judgment to which this [act] applies.

(b) A court of this state *may not recognize* a foreign-country judgment if:

(1) the judgment was rendered under a judicial system that does not provide impartial tribunals or procedures compatible with the requirements of due process of law;

(2) the foreign court did not have personal jurisdiction over the defendant; or

(3) the foreign court did not have jurisdiction over the subject matter.

---

comments, see Robert L. McFarland, *Federalism, Finality, and Foreign Judgments: Examining the ALI Judgment Project's Proposed Federal Foreign Judgments Statute*, 45 New Eng. L. Rev. 63 (2010). See also note 138.

136. For the most up-to-date information on state enactment, see http://www.uniformlaws.org /Act.aspx?title=Foreign-Country Money Judgments Recognition Act.

(c) A court of this state *need not recognize* a foreign-country judgment if:

(1) the defendant in the proceeding in the foreign court did not receive notice of the proceeding in sufficient time to enable the defendant to defend;

(2) the judgment was obtained by fraud that deprived the losing party of an adequate opportunity to present its case;

(3) the judgment or the [cause of action] [claim for relief] on which the judgment is based is repugnant to the public policy of this state or of the United States;

(4) the judgment conflicts with another final and conclusive judgment;

(5) the proceeding in the foreign court was contrary to an agreement between the parties under which the dispute in question was to be determined otherwise than by proceedings in that foreign court;

(6) in the case of jurisdiction based only on personal service, the foreign court was a seriously inconvenient forum for the trial of the action;

(7) the judgment was rendered in circumstances that raise substantial doubt about the integrity of the rendering court with respect to the judgment; or

(8) the specific proceeding in the foreign court leading to the judgment was not compatible with the requirements of due process of law.

The Uniform Law Commission provides the following additional explanations:

The primary differences between the 1962 and the 2005 Uniform Acts are as follows:

1. The 2005 Act makes it clear that a judgment entitled to full faith and credit under the U.S. Constitution is not enforceable under this Act. This clarifies the relationship between the Foreign-Country Money Judgments Act and the Enforcement of Foreign Judgments Act. Recognition by a court is a different procedure than enforcement of a sister state judgment from within the United States.

2. The 2005 Act expressly provides that a party seeking recognition of a foreign judgment has the burden to prove that the judgment is subject to the Uniform Act. Burden of proof was not addressed in the 1962 Act.

3. Conversely, the 2005 Act imposes the burden of proof for establishing a specific ground for non-recognition upon the party raising it. Again, burden of proof is not addressed in the 1962 Act.

4. The 2005 Act addresses the specific procedure for seeking enforcement. If recognition is sought as an original matter, the party seeking recognition must file an action in the court to obtain recognition. If recognition is sought in a pending action, it may be filed as a counter-claim, cross-claim

or affirmative defense in the pending action. The 1962 Act does not address the procedure to obtain recognition at all, leaving that to other state law.

5. The 2005 Act provides a statute of limitations on enforcement of a foreign-country judgment. If the judgment cannot be enforced any longer in the country of origin, it may not be enforced in a court of an enacting state. If there is no limitation on enforcement in the country of origin, the judgment becomes unenforceable in an enacting state after 15 years from the time the judgment is effective in the country of origin.[137]

So far, the states have shown limited interest in the implementation of the 2005 Act. This, and the fact that 18 of the 50 states have not even implemented the 1962 Act, are the reasons why calls for a federal statute are becoming more frequent.[138] Nevertheless, even the 1962 Act provides relatively easy access to the rules applicable in a majority of U.S. jurisdictions, including big business states like New York and California.[139]

Importantly, foreign parties cannot avoid the application of state law to their enforcement needs in the U.S. by removing their cases to federal court. Although removal is usually possible on diversity grounds, the federal courts, pursuant to the *Erie* doctrine, would have to apply the same state law that applies wherever the recognition and enforcement is sought.[140]

As early as 1895, the U.S. Supreme Court provided guidelines for the recognition and enforcement of foreign country money judgments in *Hilton v. Guyot*, which are widely followed even today, in particular in states that do not follow a version of the Uniform Foreign Money-Judgments Recognition Act.[141]

---

137. https://www.uniformlaws.org/HigherLogic/System/DownloadDocumentFile.ashx? DocumentFileKey=8313e855-dee3-6d72-7c2c-44b682553285&forceDialog=1

138. The American Law Institute launched an International Jurisdiction and Judgments Project in 1999 and adopted a proposal for a federal statute in 2006, see https://www.ali.org/publications /show/recognition-and-enforcement-foreign-judgments-analysis-and-proposed-federal-statute/. For commentary, see S.I. Strong, *Recognition and Enforcement of Foreign Judgments in U.S. Courts: Problems and Possibilities*, 33 Rev. Litig. (2014), pp. 45–144. See also Violeta I. Balan, *Recognition and Enforcement of Foreign Judgments in the United States: The Need for Federal Legislation*, 37 J. Marshall L. Rev. 229 (2003).

139. For a complete list, see http://www.uniformlaws.org/Act.aspx?title=Foreign%20Money %20Judgments%20Recognition%20Act.

140. For more on this, see above, pp. 45 and 724, and Gary Born & Peter Rutledge, *International Civil Litigation in United States Courts*, 5th ed. 2011, at pp. 10–11.

141. *Hilton v. Guyot*, 159 U.S. 113 (1895). This decision is still widely followed by state courts and mandates that "[w]hen an action is brought in a court of this country by a citizen of a foreign country against one of our own citizens to recover a sum of money adjudged by a court of that country to be due from the defendant to the plaintiff, and the foreign judgment appears to have been rendered by a competent court, having jurisdiction of the cause and of the parties, and upon due allegations and proofs and opportunity to defend against them, and its proceedings are according to the course of a civilized jurisprudence, and are stated in a clear and formal record, the judgment is prima facie evidence, at least, of the truth of the matter adjudged, and it should be held conclusive upon the merits tried in the foreign court unless some special ground is shown for

Case 6-8

Hilton v. Guyot

159 U.S. 113 (1895)

(Paragraph numbers added, footnotes omitted.)

[Hilton and his partner Libbey had been doing business in Paris under the name of Stewart & Co. The French company Fortin acquired a number of claims against Stewart and initiated litigation in Paris in 1879. A judgment in favor of Fortin was rendered in 1883 and confirmed on appeal in 1884, awarding an amount of around 1 million French francs. The liquidator of Fortin, Mr. Gustave Guyot, brought an action for recognition and enforcement in New York courts in 1885 against Mr. Hilton and Mr. Libbey. In the U.S. proceedings, Hilton and Libbey argued that the French judgments had been procured by fraud and should not be recognized. The court, however, rejected these claims and awarded the sum of $277,775.44, equivalent to the French award plus interest, to Guyot. On appeal, Justice Gray wrote the majority opinion (from p. 163)]:

[2] International law, in its widest and most comprehensive sense, — including not only questions of right between nations, governed by what has been appropriately called the 'law of nations,' but also questions arising under what is usually called 'private international law,' or the 'conflict of laws,' and concerning the rights of persons within the territory and dominion of one nation, by reason of acts, private or public, done within the dominions of another nation, — is part of our law, and must be ascertained and administered by the courts of justice as often as such questions are presented in litigation between man and man, duly submitted to their determination.

[3] The most certain guide, no doubt, for the decision of such questions is a treaty or a statute of this country. But when, as is the case here, there is no written law upon the subject, the duty still rests upon the judicial tribunals of ascertaining and declaring what the law is, whenever it becomes necessary to do so, in order to determine the rights of parties to suits regularly brought before them. In doing this, the courts must obtain such aid as they can from judicial decisions, from the works of jurists and commentators, and from the acts and usages of civilized nations. . . .

[4] No law has any effect, of its own force, beyond the limits of the sovereignty from which its authority is derived. The extent to which the law of one nation, as put in force within its territory, whether by executive order, by legislative act, or by judicial decree, shall be allowed to operate within the dominion of another nation, depends upon what our greatest jurists have been content to call 'the comity of nations.' Although the phrase has been often criticised, no satisfactory substitute has been suggested.

---

impeaching the judgment, as by showing that it was affected by fraud or prejudice or that, by the principles of international law and by the comity of our own country, it should not be given full credit and effect" (at pp. 205–206).

[5] 'Comity,' in the legal sense, is neither a matter of absolute obligation, on the one hand, nor of mere courtesy and good will, upon the other. But it is the recognition which one nation allows within its territory to the legislative, executive or judicial acts of another nation, having due regard both to international duty and convenience, and to the rights of its own citizens, or of other persons who are under the protection of its laws.

[6] Mr. Justice Story, in his Commentaries on the Conflict of Laws, treating of the question in what department of the government of any state, in the absence of any clear declaration of the sovereign will, resides the authority to determine how far the laws of a foreign state shall have effect, and observing that this differs in different states, according to the organization of the departments of the government of each, says: 'In England and America the courts of justice have hitherto exercised the same authority in the most ample manner, and the legislatures have in no instance (it is believed) in either country interfered to provide any positive regulations. The common law of both countries has been expanded to meet the exigencies of the times as they have arisen, and, so far as the practice, of nations, or the 'jus gentium privatum,' has been supposed to furnish any general principle, it has been followed out.' Story, Confl. Laws, §§ 23, 24.

[7] Afterwards, speaking of the difficulty of applying the positive rules laid down by the Continental jurists, he says that 'there is, indeed, great truth' in these remarks of Mr. Justice Porter, speaking for the supreme court of Louisiana: 'They have attempted to go too far, to define and fix that which cannot, in the nature of things, be defined and fixed. They seem to have forgotten that they wrote on a question which touched the comity of nations, and that that comity is, and ever must be, uncertain; that it must necessarily depend on a variety of circumstances which cannot be reduced to any certain rule; that no nation will suffer the laws of another to interfere with her own to the injury of her citizens; that whether they do or not must depend on the condition of the country in which the foreign law is sought to be enforced, the particular nature of her legislation, her policy, and the character of her institutions; that in the conflict of laws it must often be a matter of doubt which should prevail; and that, whenever a doubt does exist, the court which decides will prefer the laws of its own country to that of the stranger.' Story, Confl. Laws, § 28 . . . .

[8] Again, Mr. Justice Story says: 'It has been thought by some jurists that the term 'comity' is not sufficiently expressive of the obligation of nations to give effect to foreign laws when they are not prejudicial to their own rights and interests. And it has been suggested that the doctrine rests on a deeper foundation; that it is not so much a matter of comity or courtesy, as a matter of paramount moral duty. Now, assuming that such a moral duty does exist, it is clearly one of imperfect obligation, like that of beneficence, humanity, and charity. Every nation must be the final judge for itself, not only of the nature and extent of the duty, but of the occasions on which its exercise may be justly demanded.' And, after further discussion of the matter, be concludes: 'There is, then, not only no impropriety in the use of the phrase 'comity

of nations,' but it is the most appropriate phrase to express the true foundation and extent of the obligation of the laws of one nation within the territories of another.' Story, Confl. Laws, §§ 33-38.

[9] Chief Justice Taney, likewise, speaking for this court, while Mr. Justice Story was a member of it, and largely adopting his words, said: 'It is needless to enumerate here the instances in which, by the general practice of civilized countries, the laws of the one will, by the comity of nations, be recognized and executed in another, where the rights of individuals are concerned.' 'The comity thus extended to other nations is no impeachment of sovereignty. It is the voluntary act of the nation by which it is offered, and is inadmissible when contrary to its policy, or prejudicial to its interests. But it contributes so largely to promote justice between individuals, and to produce a friendly intercourse between the sovereignties to which they belong, that courts of justice have continually acted upon it as a part of the voluntary law of nations.' 'It is not the comity of the courts, but the comity of the nation, which is administered and ascertained in the same way, and guided by the same reasoning, by which all other principles of municipal law are ascertained and guided.' . . . Story, Confl. Laws, § 38.

[10] Mr. Wheaton says: 'All the effect which foreign laws can have in the territory of a state depends absolutely on the express or tacit consent of that state.' 'The express consent of a state to the application of foreign laws within its territory is given by acts passed by its legislative authority, or by treaties concluded with other states. Its tacit consent is manifested by the decisions of its judicial and administrative authorities, as well as by the writings of its publicists. There is no obligation recognized by legislators, public authorities, and publicists to regard foreign laws; but their application is admitted only from considerations of utility and the mutual convenience of states. . . ." Wheat. Int. Law (8th Ed.) §§ 78, 79. 'No sovereign is bound, unless by special compact, to execute within his dominions a judgment rendered by the tribunals of another state; and, if execution be sought by suit upon the judgment or otherwise, the tribunal in which the suit is brought, or from which execution is sought, is, on principle, at liberty to examine into the merits of such judgment, and to give effect to it or not, as may be found just and equitable. The general comity, utility, and convenience of nations have, however, established a usage among most civilized states, by which the final judgments of foreign courts of competent jurisdiction are reciprocally carried into execution, under certain regulations and restrictions, which differ in different countries.' Id. § 147.

[11] Chancellor Kent says: 'The effect to be given to foreign judgments is altogether a matter of comity in cases where it is not regulated by treaty.' 2 Kent, Comm. (6th Ed.) 120.

[12] In order to appreciate the weight of the various authorities cited at the bar, it is important to distinguish different kinds of judgments. Every foreign judgment, of whatever nature, in order to be entitled to any effect, must have been rendered by a court having jurisdiction of the cause, and upon regular proceedings, and due notice. In alluding to different kinds of judgments, therefore, such jurisdiction,

proceedings, and notice will be assumed. It will also be assumed that they are untainted by fraud, the effect of which will be considered later.

[13] A judgment in rem, adjudicating the title to a ship or other movable property within the custody of the court, is treated as valid everywhere. As said by Chief Justice Marshall: 'The sentence of a competent court, proceeding in rem, is conclusive with respect to the thing itself, and operates as an absolute change of the property. By such sentence the right of the former owner is lost, and a complete title given to the person who claims under the decree. No court of co-ordinate jurisdiction can examine the sentence. The question, therefore, respecting its conformity to general or municipal law can never arise, for no co-ordinate tribunal is capable of making the inquiry.' . . . The most common illustrations of this are decrees of courts of admiralty and prize, which proceed upon principles of international law. . . . But the same rule applies to judgments in rem under municipal law. . . .

[14] A judgment affecting the status of persons, such as a decree confirming or dissolving a marriage, is recognized as valid in every country, unless contrary to the policy of its own law. . . . It was of a foreign sentence of divorce that Lord Chancellor Nottingham, in the House of Lords, in 1678, in Cottington's Case . . . said: 'It is against the law of nations not to give credit to the judgments and sentences of foreign countries till they be reversed by the law, and according to the form, of those countries wherein they were given; for what right hath one kingdom to reverse the judgment of another? And how can we refuse to let a sentence take place till it be reversed? And what confusion would follow in Christendom, if they should serve us so abroad, and give no credit to our sentences!'

[15] Other judgments, not strictly in rem, under which a person has been compelled to pay money, are so far conclusive that the justice of the payment cannot be impeached in another country, so as to compel him to pay it again. For instance, a judgment in foreign attachment is conclusive, as between the parties, of the right to the property or money attached. Story, Confl. Laws (2d Ed.) § 592a. . . .

[16] Other foreign judgments which have been held conclusive of the matter adjudged were judgments discharging obligations contracted in the foreign country between citizens or residents thereof. Story, Confl. Laws, §§ 330-341 . . .

[19] In former times, foreign decrees in admiralty in personam were executed, even by imprisonment of the defendant, by the court of admiralty in England, upon letters rogatory from the foreign sovereign, without a new suit. Its right to do so was recognized by the court of king's bench in 1607 in a case of habeas corpus, cited by the plaintiffs, and reported as follows: 'If a man of Frizeland sues an Englishman in Frizeland before the governor there, and there recovers against him a certain sum, upon which the Englishman, not having sufficient to satisfy it, comes into England, upon which the governor sends his letters missive into England, omnes magistratus infra regnum Angliae rogans, to make execution of the said judgment, the judge of the admiralty may execute this judgment by imprisonment of the party, and he shall not be delivered by the common law; for this is by the law of nations that the

justice of one nation should be aiding to the justice of another nation, and for one to execute the judgment of the other, and the law of England takes notice of this law, and the judge of the admiralty is the proper magistrate for this purpose, for he only hath the execution of the civil law within the realm.' . . . But the only question there raised or decided was of the power of the English court of admiralty, and not of the conclusiveness of the foreign sentence, and in later times the mode of enforcing a foreign decree in admiralty is by a new libel. . . .

[20] The extraterritorial effect of judgments in personam, at law, or in equity may differ, according to the parties to the cause. A judgment of that kind between two citizens or residents of the country, and thereby subject to the jurisdiction in which it is rendered, may be held conclusive as between them everywhere. So, if a foreigner invokes the jurisdiction by bringing an action against a citizen, both may be held bound by a judgment in favor of either; and if a citizen sues a foreigner, and judgment is rendered in favor of the latter, both may be held equally bound.

[21] The effect to which a judgment, purely executory, rendered in favor of a citizen or resident of the country, in a suit there brought by him against a foreigner, may be entitled in an action thereon against the latter in his own country, as is the case now before us, presents a more difficult question, upon which there has been some diversity of opinion. . . .

[47] The law upon this subject as understood in the United States at the time of their separation from the mother country was clearly set forth by Chief Justice Parsons, speaking for the supreme judicial court of Massachusetts, in 1813, and by Mr. Justice Story in his Commentaries on the Constitution of the United States, published in 1833. Both those eminent jurists declared that by the law of England the general rule was that foreign judgments were only prima facie evidence of the matter which they purported to decide; and that by the common law, before the American Revolution, all the courts of the several colonies and states were deemed foreign to each other, and consequently judgments rendered by any one of them were considered as foreign judgments, and their merits re-examinable in another colony, not only as to the jurisdiction of the court which pronounced them, but also as to the merits of the controversy, to the extent to which they were understood to be re-examinable in England. And they noted that, in order to remove that inconvenience, statutes had been passed in Massachusetts, and in some of the other colonies, by which judgments rendered by a court of competent jurisdiction in a neighboring colony could not be impeached. . . . Story, Const. (1st Ed.) §§ 1301, 1302; Id. (4th Ed.) §§ 1306, 1307.

[48] It was because of that condition of the law, as between the American colonies and states, that the United States, at the very beginning of their existence as a nation, ordained that full faith and credit should be given to the judgments of one of the states of the Union in the courts of another of those states. . . .

[51] The decisions of this court have clearly recognized that judgments of a foreign state are prima facie evidence only, and that, but for these constitutional and

legislative provisions, judgments of a state of the Union, when sued upon in another state, would have no greater effect. . . .

[61] But neither in those cases nor in any other has this court hitherto been called upon to determine how far foreign judgments may be re-examined upon their merits, or be impeached for fraud in obtaining them. . . .

[63] In the leading case of *Bissell v. Briggs*, Chief Justice Parsons said: 'A foreign judgment may be produced here by a party to it, either to justify himself by the execution of that judgment in the country in which it was rendered, or to obtain the execution of it from our courts.' 'If the foreign court rendering the judgment had jurisdiction of the cause, yet the courts here will not execute the judgment, without first allowing an inquiry into its merits. The judgment of a foreign court, therefore, is by our laws considered only as presumptive evidence of a debt, or as prima facie evidence of a sufficient consideration of a promise, where such court had jurisdiction of the cause; and, if an action of debt be sued on any such judgment, nil debet is the general issue; or, if it be made the consideration of a promise, the general issue is non assumpsit. On these issues the defendant may impeach the justice of the judgment, by evidence relative to that point. On these issues the defendant may also, by proper evidence, prove that the judgment was rendered by a foreign court, which had no jurisdiction; and, if his evidence be sufficient for this purpose, he has no occasion to impeach the justice of the judgment.' 9 Mass. 463, 464.

[64] In a less known case, decided in 1815, . . . the reasons for this view were forcibly stated by Chief Justice Jeremiah Smith, speaking for the Supreme Court of New Hampshire, as follows:

'The respect which is due to judgments, sentences, and decrees of courts in a foreign state, by the law of nations, seems to be the same which is due to those of our own courts. Hence the decree of an admiralty court abroad is equally conclusive with decrees of our admiralty courts. Indeed, both courts proceed by the same rule, are governed by the same law, — the maritime law of nations (Coll. Jurid. 100), which is the universal law of nations, except where treaties alter it.

'The same comity is not extended to judgments or decrees which may be founded on the municipal laws of the state in which they are pronounced. Independent states do not choose to adopt such decisions without examination. These laws and regulations may be unjust, partial to citizens, and against foreigners. They may operate injustice to our citizens, whom we are bound to protect. They may be, and the decisions of courts founded on them, just cause of complaint against the supreme power of the state where rendered. To adopt them is not merely saying that the courts have decided correctly on the law, but it is approbating the law itself. Wherever, then, the court may have proceeded on municipal law, the rule is that the judgments are not conclusive evidence of debt, but prima facie evidence only. The proceedings have not the conclusive quality which is annexed to the records or proceedings of our own courts, where we approve both of the rule and of the judges who interpret and apply it. A foreign judgment may be impeached. Defendant may show that it is unjust, or that it was irregularly or unduly obtained. Doug. 5, note.' *Bryant v. Ela*, Smith (N. H.) 396, 404.

[65] From this review of the authorities, it clearly appears that, at the time of the separation of this country from England, the general rule was fully established that foreign judgments in personam were prima facie evidence only, and not conclusive of the merits of the controversy between the parties. . . .

[66] In *Taylor v. Bryden* (1811), . . . Chief Justice Kent said: 'The judgment in Maryland is presumptive evidence of a just demand; and it was incumbent upon the defendant, if he would obstruct the execution of the judgment here, to show, by positive proof, that it was irregularly or unduly obtained.' 'To try over again, as of course, every matter of fact which had been duly decided by a competent tribunal, would be disregarding the comity which we justly owe to the courts of other states, and would be carrying the doctrine of re-examination to an oppressive extent. It would be the same as granting a new trial in every case, and upon every question of fact. Suppose a recovery in another state, or in any foreign court, in an action for a tort, as for an assault and battery, false imprisonment, slander, etc., and the defendant was duly summoned and appeared, and made his defense, and the trial was conducted orderly and properly, according to the rules of a civilized jurisprudence, is every such case to be tried again here on the merits? I much doubt whether the rule can ever go to this length. The general language of the books is that the defendant must impeach the judgment by showing affirmatively that it was unjust by being irregularly or unfairly procured.' But the case was decided upon the ground that the defendant had done no more than raise a doubt of the correctness of the judgment sued on. 8 Johns. 173, 177, 178.

[67] Chancellor Kent, afterwards, treating of the same subject in the first edition of his Commentaries (1827), put the right to impeach a foreign judgment somewhat more broadly, saying: 'No sovereign is obliged to execute, within his dominion, a sentence rendered out of it; and, if execution be sought by a suit upon the judgment or otherwise, he is at liberty, in his courts of justice, to examine into the merits of such judgment [for the effect to be given to foreign judgments is altogether a matter of comity, in cases where it is not regulated by treaty]. In the former case [of a suit to enforce a foreign judgment] the rule is that the foreign judgment is to be received, in the first instance, as prima facie evidence of the debt; and it lies on the defendant to impeach the justice of it, or to show that it was irregularly and unduly obtained. This was the principle declared and settled by the house of lords in 1771, in the case of *Sinclair v. Fraser*, upon an appeal from the court of session in Scotland.' In the second edition (1832) he inserted the passages above printed in brackets; and in a note to the fourth edition (1840), after citing recent conflicting opinions in Great Britain, and referring to Mr. Justice Story's reasoning in his Commentaries on the Conflict of Laws (section 607) in favor of the conclusiveness of foreign judgments,

he added: 'And that is certainly the more convenient and the safest rule, and the most consistent with sound principle, except in cases in which the court which pronounced the judgment has not due jurisdiction of the case, or of the defendant, or the proceeding was in fraud, or founded in palpable mistake or irregularity, or bad by the law of the rei judicatae; and in all such cases the justice of the judgment ought to be impeached.' 2 Kent, Comm. (1st Ed.) 102; Id. (later Eds.) 120. . . .

[90] The English courts, however, have since treated that decision as establishing that a judgment of any competent foreign court could not, in an action upon it, be questioned, either because that court had mistaken its own law, or because it had come to an erroneous conclusion upon the facts. . . .

[102] In view of all the authorities upon the subject, and of the trend of judicial opinion in this country and in England, following the lead of Kent and Story, we are satisfied that where there has been opportunity for a full and fair trial abroad before a court of competent jurisdiction, conducting the trial upon regular proceedings, after due citation or voluntary appearance of the defendant, and under a system of jurisprudence likely to secure an impartial administration of justice between the citizens of its own country and those of other countries, and there is nothing to show either prejudice in the court, or in the system of laws under which it was sitting, or fraud in procuring the judgment, or any other special reason why the comity of this nation should not allow it full effect, the merits of the case should not, in an action brought in this country upon the judgment, be tried afresh, as on a new trial or an appeal, upon the mere assertion of the party that the judgment was erroneous in law or in fact. The defendants, therefore, cannot be permitted, upon that general ground, to contest the validity or the effect of the judgment sued on.

[103] But they have sought to impeach that judgment upon several other grounds, which require separate consideration.

[104] It is objected that the appearance and litigation of the defendants in the French tribunals were not voluntary, but by legal compulsion, and, therefore, that the French courts never acquired such jurisdiction over the defendants that they should be held bound by the judgment.

[105] Upon the question what should be considered such a voluntary appearance, as to amount to a submission to the jurisdiction of a foreign court, there has been some difference of opinion in England. . . .

[108] The present case is not one of a person traveling through or casually found in a foreign country. The defendants, although they were not citizens or residents of France, but were citizens and residents of the state of New York, and their principal place of business was in the city of New York, yet had a storehouse and an agent in Paris, and were accustomed to purchase large quantities of goods there, although they did not make sales in France. Under such circumstances, evidence that their sole object in appearing and carrying on the litigation in the French courts was to prevent property in their storehouse at Paris, belonging to them, and within the jurisdiction, but not in the custody, of those courts, from being taken in satisfaction of any

judgment that might be recovered against them, would not, according to our law, show that those courts did not acquire jurisdiction of the persons of the defendants.

[109] It is next objected that in those courts one of the plaintiffs was permitted to testify not under oath, and was not subjected to cross-examination by the opposite party, and that the defendants were therefore deprived of safeguards which are by our law considered essential to secure honesty and to detect fraud in a witness; and also that documents and papers were admitted in evidence, with which the defendants had no connection, and which would not be admissible under our own system of jurisprudence. But it having been shown by the plaintiffs, and hardly denied by the defendants, that the practice followed and the method of examining witnesses were according to the laws of France, we are not prepared to hold that the fact that the procedure in these respects differed from that of our own courts is, of itself, a sufficient ground for impeaching the foreign judgment. . . .

[111] It must, however, always be kept in mind that it is the paramount duty of the court before which any suit is brought to see to it that the parties have had a fair and impartial trial, before a final decision is rendered against either party.

[112] When an action is brought in a court of this country, by a citizen of a foreign country against one of our own citizens, to recover a sum of money adjudged by a court of that country to be due from the defendant to the plaintiff, and the foreign judgment appears to have been rendered by a competent court, having jurisdiction of the cause and of the parties, and upon due allegations and proofs, and opportunity to defend against them, and its proceedings are according to the course of a civilized jurisprudence, and are stated in a clear and formal record, the judgment is prima facie evidence, at least, of the truth of the matter adjudged; and it should be held conclusive upon the merits tried in the foreign court, unless some special ground is shown for impeaching the judgment, as by showing that it was affected by fraud or prejudice, or that by the principles of international law, and by the comity of our own country, it should not be given full credit and effect. . . .

[121] In the case at bar the defendants offered to prove, in much detail, that the plaintiffs presented to the French court of first instance and to the arbitrator appointed by that court, and upon whose report its judgment was largely based, false and fraudulent statements and accounts against the defendants, by which the arbitrator and the French courts were deceived and misled, and their judgments were based upon such false and fraudulent statements and accounts. This offer, if satisfactorily proved, would according to the decisions of the English court of appeal . . . be a sufficient ground for impeaching the foreign judgment, and examining into the merits of the original claim.

[122] But whether those decisions can be followed in regard to foreign judgments, consistently with our own decisions as to impeaching domestic judgments for fraud, it is unnecessary in this case to determine, because there is a distinct and independent ground upon which we are satisfied that the comity of our nation does not require us to give conclusive effect to the judgments of the courts of France; and

that ground is the want of reciprocity, on the part of France, as to the effect to be given to the judgments of this and other foreign countries. . . .

[125] The defendants . . . cited the . . . provisions of the statutes of France, and alleged, and at the trial offered to prove, that by the construction given to these statutes by the judicial tribunals of France, when the judgments of tribunals of foreign countries against the citizens of France are sued upon in the courts of France, the merits of the controversies upon which those judgments are based are examined anew, unless a treaty to the contrary effect exists between the republic of France and the country in which such judgment is obtained (which is not the case between the republic of France and the United States), and that the tribunals of the republic of France give no force and effect, within the jurisdiction of that country, to the judgments duly rendered by courts of competent jurisdiction of the United States against citizens of France after proper personal service of the process of those courts has been made thereon in this country. We are of opinion that this evidence should have been admitted. . . .

[134] Mr. Justice Story said: 'If a civilized nation seeks to have the sentences of its own courts of any validity elsewhere, they ought to have a just regard to the rights and usages of other civilized nations, and the principles of public and national law in the administration of justice.' *Bradstreet v. Insurance Co.*, 3 Sumn. 600, 608, Fed. Cas. No. 1,793. . . .

[136] Mr. Justice Cooley said: 'True comity is equality. We should demand nothing more and concede nothing less.' *McEwan v. Zimmer*, 38 Mich. 765, 769. . . .

[139] By the law of France, settled by a series of uniform decisions of the court of cassation, the highest judicial tribunal, for more than half a century, no foreign judgment can be rendered executory in France without a review of the judgment au fond (to the bottom), including the whole merits of the cause of action on which the judgment rests. . . .

[The Court then proceeds with an examination of the practice, with regard to recognition and enforcement of foreign judgments, in Belgium, Holland, Denmark, Norway, Sweden, Germany, Switzerland, Russia, Poland, Romania, Bulgaria, Austria, Italy, Monaco, Spain, Portugal, Greece, Egypt, Cuba, Puerto Rico, Haiti, Mexico, Peru, Chile, Brazil, and Argentina. Of course, since 1895, the practice in these countries has evolved. The Court continues on p. 227:]

[161] It appears, therefore, that there is hardly a civilized nation on either continent which, by its general law, allows conclusive effect to an executory foreign judgment for the recovery of money. In France and in a few smaller states-Norway, Portugal, Greece, Monaco, and Hayti-the merits of the controversy are reviewed, as of course, allowing to the foreign judgment, at the most, no more effect than of being prima facie evidence of the justice of the claim. In the great majority of the countries on the continent of Europe,—in Belgium, Holland, Denmark, Sweden, Germany, in many cantons of Switzerland, in Russia and Poland, in Roumania, in Austria and Hungary (perhaps in Italy), and in Spain,—as well as in Egypt, in Mexico, and in a

great part of South America, the judgment rendered in a foreign country is allowed the same effect only as the courts of that country allow to the judgments of the country in which the judgment in question is sought to be executed.

[162] The prediction of Mr. Justice Story in section 618 of his Commentaries on the Conflict of Laws, already cited, has thus been fulfilled, and the rule of reciprocity has worked itself firmly into the structure of international jurisprudence.

[163] The reasonable, if not the necessary, conclusion appears to us to be that judgments rendered in France, or in any other foreign country, by the laws of which our own judgments are reviewable upon the merits, are not entitled to full credit and conclusive effect when sued upon in this country, but are prima facie evidence only of the justice of the plaintiffs' claim.

[164] In holding such a judgment, for want of reciprocity, not to be conclusive evidence of the merits of the claim, we do not proceed upon any theory of retaliation upon one person by reason of injustice done to another, but upon the broad ground that international law is founded upon mutuality and reciprocity, and that by the principles of international law recognized in most civilized nations, and by the comity of our own country, which it is our judicial duty to known and to declare, the judgment is not entitled to be considered conclusive. . . .

The UFCMJRA is a shortcut to understand recognition and enforcement of foreign judgments in the 32 states that have implemented it. A second shortcut exists for the 18 U.S. states that still rely entirely on common law for their rules on recognition and enforcement, but it also covers the way all of the states interpret any state laws implementing the 1962 and the 2005 Model Laws:

The Restatement (Third) of Foreign Relations Law (1987) "sets forth the prevailing common and statutory law of states of the United States, not rules of federal or international law"[142] as follows:[143]

§ 481 Recognition and Enforcement of Foreign Judgments

(1) Except as provided in § 482, a final judgment of a court of a foreign state granting or denying recovery of a sum of money, establishing or confirming the status of a person, or determining interests in property, is conclusive between the parties, and is entitled to recognition in courts in the United States.

(2) A judgment entitled to recognition under Subsection (1) may be enforced by any party or its successors or assigns against any other party, its successors or assigns, in accordance with the procedure for enforcement of judgments applicable where enforcement is sought.

---

142. American Law Institute, Comment a. to § 481.

143. *Restatement of the Law Third, Foreign Relations*, copyright 1987 © by the American Law Institute. All rights reserved. Reprinted by permission. See https://www.ali.org/projects/show /foreign-relations-law-united-states/.

§ 482 Grounds for Nonrecognition of Foreign Judgments

(1) A court in the United States may not recognize a judgment of the court of a foreign state if:

   (a) the judgment was rendered under a judicial system that does not provide impartial tribunals or procedures compatible with due process of law; or

   (b) the court that rendered the judgment did not have jurisdiction over the defendant in accordance with the law of the rendering state and with the rules set forth in § 421.

(2) A court in the United States need not recognize a judgment of the court of a foreign state if:

   (a) the court that rendered the judgment did not have jurisdiction of the subject matter of the action;

   (b) the defendant did not receive notice of the proceedings in sufficient time to enable him to defend;

   (c) the judgment was obtained by fraud;

   (d) the cause of action on which the judgment was based, or the judgment itself, is repugnant to the public policy of the United States or of the State where recognition is sought;

   (e) the judgment conflicts with another final judgment that is entitled to recognition; or

   (f) the proceeding in the foreign court was contrary to an agreement between the parties to submit the controversy on which the judgment is based to another forum.

With regard to reciprocity, the Restatement says "A judgment otherwise entitled to recognition will not be denied recognition or enforcement because courts in the rendering state might not enforce a judgment of a court in the United States if the circumstances were reversed. *Hilton v. Guyot* . . . declared a limited reciprocity requirement applicable when the judgment creditor is a national of the state in which the judgment was rendered and the judgment debtor is a national of the United States. Though that holding has not been formally overruled, it is no longer followed in the great majority of State and federal courts in the United States."[144]

Finally, the Restatement also clarifies the procedure:

"No procedures exist in the United States for registration of foreign country judgments, or for their validation by exequatur, (i.e., an endorsement by

144. American Law Institute, Comment d. on § 481. © American Law Institute, last updated June 2020. Reproduced by permission. All Rights Reserved.

order of a court authorizing execution). Therefore, enforcement of a debt arising out of a foreign judgment must be initiated by civil action, and the judgment creditor must establish a basis for the exercise of jurisdiction by the enforcing court over the judgment debtor or his property. . . . In many States, including those that have adopted the Uniform Foreign Money Judgments Recognition Act . . . , an action to enforce a foreign money judgment may be initiated through expedited procedures, such as a motion for summary judgment in lieu of a complaint. Enforcement of a foreign judgment may also be pursued by counterclaim, cross-claim, or affirmative defense."[145]

"The rules of jurisdiction to adjudicate in respect of civil actions generally . . . are applicable to actions or proceedings to enforce foreign judgments. However, whereas under . . . prevailing United States law . . . a state has jurisdiction to adjudicate a claim on the basis of presence of property in the forum *only where the property is reasonably connected with the claim*, an action to enforce a judgment may usually be brought wherever property of the defendant is found, *without any necessary connection* between the underlying action and the property, or between the defendant and the forum. The rationale behind wider jurisdiction in enforcement of judgments is that once a judgment has been rendered in a forum having jurisdiction, *the prevailing party is entitled to have it satisfied out of the judgment debtor's assets wherever they may be located*. The owner of property against which enforcement proceedings are initiated is, of course, entitled to raise all defenses to recognition available under § 482 . . . ."[146]

"Unlike courts in many foreign states, courts in the United States generally give the same direct effect to *default judgments* as to judgments following proceedings in which all parties participated. Neither the Uniform Foreign Money Judgments Recognition Act nor this Restatement distinguishes between contested and default judgments. However, since a judgment rendered by a court not having jurisdiction over the judgment debtor is not entitled to recognition, see § 482(1)(b), a court in the recognizing state will scrutinize the jurisdiction of the rendering court when that issue has not been adjudicated or waived in the rendering forum. If the judgment debtor appeared in the rendering court for the purpose of challenging its jurisdiction and that jurisdiction was upheld, he is generally precluded from renewing the challenge in the state where recognition is sought, unless the proceeding in the foreign court was manifestly unfair or the asserted basis for jurisdiction clearly untenable. . . ."[147]

---

145. American Law Institute, Comment g. on § 481. © 2020. Reproduced by permission. All Rights Reserved.

146. American Law Institute, Comment h. on § 481, emphasis added. © 2020. Reproduced by permission. All Rights Reserved.

147. American Law Institute, Comment i. on § 481, emphasis added. © 2020. Reproduced by permission. All Rights Reserved.

Notes and Questions

1. In *Hilton v. Guyot*, the Supreme Court held that there is no legal obligation to recognize and enforce foreign judgments in the U.S. Instead, the question whether or not a foreign judgment should be recognized and enforced is a matter of "comity." What is "comity"?

2. In paragraph 15, the Supreme Court speaks of judgments being "conclusive" only. More specifically, in paragraphs 47 to 51, the Supreme Court makes the distinction between judgments that are entitled to *full faith and credit* and others that are only *prima facie evidence* for an entitlement. The former will be generally recognized and enforced via a simplified procedure resulting in summary judgment. In the latter cases, the foreign judgments are more akin to a contractual promise that payment will be made. The recognition and enforcement cannot be obtained via a motion for summary judgment. Instead, the court with jurisdiction over the defendant and/or her assets may conduct *de novo* review of the claims.

3. In practice, 32 of the 50 states of the U.S. are today applying the Uniform Foreign Money-Judgments Recognition Act (UFMJRA), while 18 states don't. *Hilton v. Guyot* is still cited quite regularly as a leading precedent in the jurisdictions relying on common law. To what extent are there differences between the standards of *Hilton v. Guyot* and the UFMJRA? In the procedure?

4. With regard to the fraud defense against enforcement of a foreign judgment in the U.S., it has generally been held that the defendant invoking fraud has the burden of proof. In practice, how can a defendant show that a foreign judgment was fraudulently obtained?

5. According to the Restatement (Third), the reciprocity requirement stipulated by the Supreme Court in *Hilton v. Guyot* was "limited" (Comment d.). In what way was it limited?

6. The Restatement also says that the reciprocity requirement is no longer followed in the majority of U.S. jurisdictions. Why do you think many U.S. courts no longer insist on reciprocity? Do you think it is a good idea to give up the reciprocity requirement? From a perspective of general policy? From a perspective of individual justice?

Consider the following examples and whether they impact your answers to these questions:

a. From around 1999, Xia Xuguo, a Chinese national residing in Jiangsu Province, China, and working for KIC Suzhou, a partly American-owned Chinese automotive supply company, began diverting company funds to various personal bank accounts. KIC Suzhou sued Xia Xuguo in China and obtained a well-reasoned summary judgment ordering a return of the stolen funds. It turned out that some of the funds had been transferred to a Chase bank account in Indianapolis in the name of Xia Xuguo's sister, who lived in the U.S. In 2005, Judge McKinney of the United States District Court for the Southern District of Indiana froze the funds in the account and, in 2009, after satisfying himself that the money was indeed part of the stolen funds, the judge recognized and enforced the Chinese judgment, although China generally does not reciprocate.[148]

b. A few months after the Indiana decision, the United States District Court for the Central District of California agreed to recognize and enforce a Chinese judgment against an American defendant, awarding US$6.5 million to two Chinese plaintiffs. Compared to the Indiana case, the California case was both easier and more difficult for the plaintiffs and their U.S. attorneys. On the one hand, this case concerned American defendants. On the other hand, California has implemented the Uniform Foreign Money-Judgments Recognition Act (UFMJRA). The background of *Hubei Gezhouba Sanlian Industrial Co. Ltd.* and *Hubei Pinghu Cruise Co. Ltd. v. Robinson Helicopter Co. Inc.* (*Hubei v. Robinson*) was the crash in China in 1994 of a helicopter made by Robinson (RHC) in the U.S., which resulted in claims of negligence, strict liability, and breach of implied warranty. Initially, the plaintiffs tried to bring the case in California, at the seat of Robinson. However, Robinson successfully argued *forum non conveniens*. In the process, it had to agree: (i) to submit to the jurisdiction of the appropriate court in China, (ii) suspension of the statute of limitation, and (iii) "to abide by any final judgment rendered in China."[149] The case was eventually brought to court in China in 2001 and on February 17, 2004, Robinson was served with process and told to appear in court in China for a hearing on March 25, 2004. At the trial, Robinson did not make an appearance and some US$6.5 million were awarded to the Chinese plaintiffs by default. Subsequently, Robinson neither tried to challenge the jurisdiction of the Chinese court nor appealed the judgment in China. Therefore, it became res judicata. Finally, in 2006, the Chinese parties filed a complaint in court in California seeking recognition and enforcement of the decision pursuant to the UFMRJA. Judge Cooper ruled as follows:[150]

19. A civil suit for recognition of a foreign judgment may be brought under the UFMJRA if the judgment is made by any governmental unit other than the United States, and the judgment grants or denies recovery of a sum of money. . . .

20. The UFMJRA recites several exceptions under which a court must deem a foreign judgment not conclusive or may choose not to recognize the foreign judgment. The Court may only deny recognition if one of the exceptions explicitly stated in the UFMJRA applies to the facts presented. . . .

---

148. The decision is unpublished. The facts were confirmed by Mark R. Waterfill and Jim Chapman, Indianapolis, who may well be the first U.S. attorneys to accomplish the recognition and enforcement of a Chinese default judgment in the U.S. in a state that has not implemented the Uniform Foreign Money-Judgments Recognition Act (UFMJRA).

149. 2009 WL 2190187 (C.D. Cal.), at para. 4.

150. Ibid., paras. 19 et seq., footnotes omitted.

21. The UFMJRA states a foreign judgment is not conclusive if it was rendered under a system which does not provide impartial tribunals or procedures compatible with the requirements of due process of law. . . .

22. RHC has not presented any evidence, nor does it contend, that the PRC court system is one which does not provide impartial tribunals or procedures compatible with the requirements of due process of law. RHC cannot avail itself of this particular exception based on a challenge to the judgment at issue. The Court comes to this conclusion based on the following:

a. The exception . . . applies when the "system" in which the foreign judgment was rendered does not provide impartial tribunals or procedures compatible with the requirements of due process of law.

b. The exception does not provide a means for challenging a particular judgment. To allow such a challenge would "convert[ ] every successful multinational suit for damages into two suits[,]" and allow parties "to object at the collection phase of the case to the procedures employed at the merits phase[.]" *Society of Lloyd's v. Ashenden*, 233 F.3d 473, 477-78 (7th Cir.2000) (Posner, J., interpreting Illinois' UFMJRA).

c. The exception also applies if the procedures of the foreign court system are not compatible with the requirements of due process of law. Because it is likely "that no foreign nation has decided to incorporate our due process doctrines into its own procedural law[,]" courts have interpreted due process in this UFMJRA exception to refer to "a concept of fair procedure simple and basic enough to describe the judicial processes of civilized nations, our peers." *Ashendon*, 233 F.3d at 476-77; *Shell Oil Co. v. Franco*, 2004 WL 5615657 (C.D.Cal.2004) (citing *Ashendon*).

d. In addition, the foreign procedures need only be "compatible" with the requirements of due process of law. Courts have interpreted this to mean that the foreign procedures are "'fundamentally fair' and do not offend against 'basic fairness.'" *Ashendon*, 233 F.3d at 477; *Society of Lloyd's v. Turner*, 303 F.3d 325, 330 (5th Cir.2002) (citing *Ashendon*).

e. The PRC court system's use of the procedures of the Hague Convention for service of process on foreign defendants does not offend notions of basic fairness. Use of the Hague Convention is compatible with the relaxed notion of due process of law under *Ashendon*. . . .

Conclusion:

28. Service of process was proper under Federal Rule 4, the 9th Circuit Direct Mail ruling, and the Hague Convention.

29. The PRC Judgment was final, conclusive, and enforceable under the laws of the PRC and involved the granting of recovery of a sum of money.

30. California's UFMJRA applies to this action seeking recognition of the PRC Judgment, and none of the stated exceptions to recognition in the UFMJRA are applicable on the facts presented.

31. Plaintiffs are entitled to the issuance of a domestic judgment in this action in the amount of the PRC Judgment, with interest calculated as set forth in the PRC Judgment, for purposes of enforcement.

The decision by Judge Cooper was appealed by Robinson, but the United States Court of Appeals for the Ninth Circuit merely ruled that "RHC is estopped from arguing that the judgment of the Higher People's Court of Hubei Province in the People's Republic of China (PRC) in favor of Hubei . . . is not 'enforceable where rendered' under California's Uniform Foreign-Money Judgments Recognition Act (UFMJRA) . . . . RHC's failure to pay the final PRC judgment was 'clearly inconsistent' with RHC's stipulation to the California court that it would 'abide by any final judgment rendered in the civil action commenced in China.' [A]ccepting RHC's argument that the PRC judgment is no longer enforceable would create the perception that the California court was 'misled' in granting RHC's *forum non conveniens* motion and would 'impose an unfair detriment' on Hubei."[151]

The UFMJRA does not contain a reciprocity requirement. Given its undertaking to abide by a Chinese decision, such a requirement would not have helped Robinson anyway. However, some U.S. jurisdictions do still apply the reciprocity requirement, either as part of common law or as an addition to their implementation of the UFMJRA.[152]

7. In conclusion, we may say that although the U.S. has not ratified any major conventions for the mutual recognition and enforcement of judgments, U.S. courts, on the basis of comity, will generally enforce foreign judgments unless one of the grounds mentioned above is present. Occasionally, enforcement has been refused because reciprocity was not guaranteed. The procedure to be followed when seeking enforcement of a foreign judgment is the procedure of the court where enforcement is sought, i.e., it is usually determined by state law (Restatement (Second) of Conflict of Laws (1971), §§ 99–102). Nevertheless, it has been said that "the current U.S. approach to recognition and enforcement of foreign judgments involves a great deal of cost, complexity, and uncertainty, which creates numerous problems for both U.S. and foreign parties."[153]

---

151. 425 Fed. App'x 580, Memorandum. For discussion, see Mark Moedritzer, Kay C. Whittaker & Ariel Ye, *Judgments "Made in China" But Enforceable in the United States?: Obtaining Recognition and Enforcement in the United States of Monetary Judgments Entered in China Against U.S. Companies Doing Business Abroad*, Int'l Law. 2010, Vol. 44, No. 2, pp. 817–835.

152. On this question, see Robert L. McFarland, *Federalism, Finality, and Foreign Judgments: Examining the ALI Judgments Project's Proposed Federal Foreign Judgments Statute*, 45 New Eng. L. Rev. 63 (2010), at p. 92.

153. S.I. Strong, *Recognition and Enforcement of Foreign Judgments in U.S. Courts: Problems and Possibilities*, 33 Rev. Litig. 45 (2014), at p. 50.

In the next section, we will examine how U.S. judicial decisions fare in China and certain other foreign countries.

3. Enforcement of U.S. Judgments Abroad

Just like the U.S. is looking at its own domestic law when deciding whether a foreign country judgment should be recognized and enforced or not, other countries apply their own rules about the recognition and enforcement of a judicial decision from the U.S. We have already pointed out that the U.S. has not entered into bilateral or multilateral agreements in this field. Thus, no other country is currently *obligated* under international law (treaty) to recognize and enforce an American judgment. However, there are quite a few bilateral and multilateral treaties between other countries. Thus, when it comes to the enforcement of one third-country judgment—such as a decision from England—in another third country—such as France or India—it is always worth checking whether the respective countries are bound by a treaty. We will elaborate on some EU rules to this effect below.

When it comes to the recognition and enforcement of a U.S. judgment in another country, however, we only have to look at the domestic laws and practices of the country concerned. The answer to the question will, therefore, vary from one country to another.

We have already pointed out that **China** is generally reluctant (to say it diplomatically) to recognize and enforce foreign judgments. The common understanding that China generally does not do so, however, is outdated. First, China has entered into almost 40 bilateral agreements that include provisions on the reciprocal recognition and enforcement of judgments in civil and commercial cases. Such agreements have been concluded, *inter alia*, with Argentina, Brazil, France, Italy, Russia, Spain, and Turkey. Separate agreements exist for judgments from Hong Kong and Macao. In the absence of an agreement, Chinese courts approached for the recognition and enforcement of a foreign judgment are entitled to do so under Articles 281 and 282 of the PRC Law of Civil Procedure, as last amended in 2017.[154] One of the conditions for recognition and enforcement is reciprocity. The first time such a procedure was successful in the absence of an agreement was on December 9, 2016, when the Nanjing Intermediate People's Court (Jiangsu Court) recognized and enforced a judgment from Singapore.[155] Thus, an American party seeking to enforce an American judgment against a Chinese party in China should provide multiple examples of the recognition and enforcement of Chinese judgments in the U.S. to make the case of reciprocity. However, it is too

154. A semi-official English version is available at http://cicc.court.gov.cn/html/1/219/199/200/644.html.

155. Seehttp://www.bakermckenzie.com/en/insight/publications/2017/01/first-time-prc-court-recognizes-a-foreign/.

early to say whether the Nanjing decision will be followed by other courts in China and whether those courts will consider that there is already enough evidence of reciprocity in the U.S.[156]

In contrast to China, **Canada** is very open to the recognition and enforcement of U.S. judgments. Like in the U.S., the applicable rules in Canada are not based on statute but on common law.[157] A much-cited precedent was provided by the Supreme Court of Canada in *Beals v. Saldanha*.[158] Two Canadians had done some real estate business in Florida and were sued for damages there in 1986. The Canadians, poorly advised by their lawyer, did not participate in the trial and, as a consequence, a jury awarded the American plaintiffs about US$210,000 in compensatory damages plus US$50,000 in punitive damages. The Canadians chose to ignore the judgment and by the time action was brought for enforcement in Canada in 1998, the amount, with interest, had grown to about C$800,000. Somewhat belatedly, the Canadians now tried a variety of defenses but to no avail. The Canadian Supreme Court ruled in 2003:

A. The "Real and Substantial Connection" Test and Foreign Judgments . . .

[28] International comity and the prevalence of international cross-border transactions and movement call for a modernization of private international law. . . . Subject to the legislatures adopting a different approach, the "real and substantial connection" test, which has until now only been applied to interprovincial judgments, should apply equally to the recognition and enforcement of foreign judgments. . . .

[31] The appellants submitted that the recognition of foreign judgments rendered by courts with a real and substantial connection to the action or parties is particularly troublesome in the case of foreign default judgments. If the real and substantial connection test is applied to the recognition of foreign judgments, they argue the test should be modified in the recognition and enforcement of default judgments. In the absence of unfairness or other equally compelling reasons which were not identified in this appeal, there is no logical reason to distinguish between a judgment after trial and a default judgment.

[32] The "real and substantial connection" test requires that a significant connection exist between the cause of action and the foreign court. Furthermore, a defendant can reasonably be brought within the embrace of a foreign jurisdiction's law where he or she has participated in something of significance or was actively involved in

---

156. An overview is provided by Wenliang Zhang, *Recognition of Foreign Judgments in China: The Essentials and Strategies*, in Petar Šarčević et al. (eds.), *Yearbook of Private International Law*, Vol. XV, 2013/2014, pp. 319–347. For details, see Wenliang Zhang, *Recognition and Enforcement of Foreign Judgments in China*, Wolters Kluwer 2014.

157. For discussion, see Geneviève Saumier, *Recognition and Enforcement of Foreign Judgments in the Canadian Common Law Provinces*, in Petar Šarčević et al. (eds), *Yearbook of Private International Law*, Vol. XV, 2013/2014, pp. 313–318.

158. *Beals v. Saldanha*, [2003] 3 S.C.R. 416, 2003 SCC 72.

that foreign jurisdiction. A fleeting or relatively unimportant connection will not be enough to give a foreign court jurisdiction. The connection to the foreign jurisdiction must be a substantial one.

[33] In the present case, the appellants purchased land in Florida, an act that represents a significant engagement with the foreign jurisdiction's legal order. Where a party takes such positive and important steps that bring him or her within the proper jurisdiction of a foreign court, the fear of unfairness related to the duty to defend oneself is lessened. If a Canadian enters into a contract to buy land in another country, it is not unreasonable to expect the individual to enter a defence when sued in that jurisdiction with respect to the transaction. . . .

[35] A Canadian defendant sued in a foreign jurisdiction has the ability to redress any real or apparent unfairness from the foreign proceedings and the judgment's subsequent enforcement in Canada. The defences applicable in Ontario are natural justice, public policy and fraud. In addition, defendants sued abroad can raise the doctrine of *forum non conveniens*. This would apply in the usual way where it is claimed that the proceedings are not, on the basis of convenience, expense and other considerations, in the proper forum. . . .

B. Defences to the Enforcement of Judgments

[39] Once the "real and substantial connection" test is found to apply to a foreign judgment, the court should then examine the scope of the defences available to a domestic defendant in contesting the recognition of such a judgment.

[40] The defences of fraud, public policy and lack of natural justice . . . still pertain. This Court has to consider whether those defences, when applied internationally, are able to strike the balance required by comity, the balance between order and fairness as well as the real and substantial connection, in respect of enforcing default judgments obtained in foreign courts.

[41] These defences were developed by the common law courts to guard against potential unfairness unforeseen in the drafting of the test for the recognition and enforcement of judgments. The existing defences are narrow in application. They are the most recognizable situations in which an injustice may arise but are not exhaustive.

[42] Unusual situations may arise that might require the creation of a new defence to the enforcement of a foreign judgment. However, the facts of this case do not justify speculating on that possibility. Should the evolution of private international law require the creation of a new defence, the courts will need to ensure that any new defences continue to be narrow in scope, address specific facts and raise issues not covered by the existing defences.

(1) The Defence of Fraud

[43] As a general but qualified statement, neither foreign nor domestic judgments will be enforced if obtained by fraud.

[44] Inherent to the defence of fraud is the concern that defendants may try to use this defence as a means of relitigating an action previously decided and so thwart the

finality sought in litigation. The desire to avoid the relitigation of issues previously tried and decided has led the courts to treat the defence of fraud narrowly. It limits the type of evidence of fraud which can be pleaded in response to a judgment. If this Court were to widen the scope of the fraud defence, domestic courts would be increasingly drawn into a re-examination of the merits of foreign judgments. That result would obviously be contrary to the quest for finality.

[45] Courts have drawn a distinction between "intrinsic fraud" and "extrinsic fraud" in an attempt to clarify the types of fraud that can vitiate the judgment of a foreign court. Extrinsic fraud is identified as fraud going to the jurisdiction of the issuing court or the kind of fraud that misleads the court, foreign or domestic, into believing that it has jurisdiction over the cause of action. Evidence of this kind of fraud, if accepted, will justify setting aside the judgment. On the other hand, intrinsic fraud is fraud which goes to the merits of the case and to the existence of a cause of action. The extent to which evidence of intrinsic fraud can act as a defence to the recognition of a judgment has not been as clear as that of extrinsic fraud. . . .

[51] The historic description of and the distinction between intrinsic and extrinsic fraud is of no apparent value and, because of its ability to both complicate and confuse, should be discontinued. It is simpler to say that fraud going to jurisdiction can always be raised before a domestic court to challenge the judgment. On the other hand, the merits of a foreign judgment can be challenged for fraud only where the allegations are new and not the subject of prior adjudication. Where material facts not previously discoverable arise that potentially challenge the evidence that was before the foreign court, the domestic court can decline recognition of the judgment.

[52] Where a foreign judgment was obtained by fraud that was undetectable by the foreign court, it will not be enforced domestically. "Evidence of fraud undetectable by the foreign court" and the mention of "new and material facts" . . . demand an element of reasonable diligence on the part of a defendant. . . . [i]n order to raise the defence of fraud, a defendant has the burden of demonstrating that the facts sought to be raised could not have been discovered by the exercise of due diligence prior to the obtaining of the foreign judgment.

Such an approach represents a fair balance between the countervailing goals of comity and fairness to the defendant. . . .

(2) The Defence of Natural Justice

[59] As previously stated, the denial of natural justice can be the basis of a challenge to a foreign judgment and, if proven, will allow the domestic court to refuse enforcement. A condition precedent to that defence is that the party seeking to impugn the judgment prove, to the civil standard, that the foreign proceedings were contrary to Canadian notions of fundamental justice.

[60] A domestic court enforcing a judgment has a heightened duty to protect the interests of defendants when the judgment to be enforced is a foreign one. The domestic

court must be satisfied that minimum standards of fairness have been applied to the [Canadian] defendants by the foreign court.

[61] The enforcing court must ensure that the defendant was granted a fair process. . . . [i]t is not the duty of the plaintiff in the foreign action to establish that the legal system from which the judgment originates is a fair one in order to seek enforcement. The burden of alleging unfairness in the foreign legal system rests with the [Canadian] defendant in the foreign action.

[62] Fair process is one that, in the system from which the judgment originates, reasonably guarantees basic procedural safeguards such as judicial independence and fair ethical rules governing the participants in the judicial system. This determination will need to be made for all foreign judgments. Obviously, it is simpler for domestic courts to assess the fairness afforded to a Canadian defendant in another province in Canada. In the case of judgments made by courts outside Canada, the review may be more difficult but is mandatory and the enforcing court must be satisfied that fair process was used in awarding the judgment. This assessment is easier when the foreign legal system is either similar to or familiar to Canadian courts. . . .

[64] The defence of natural justice is restricted to the form of the foreign procedure, to due process, and does not relate to the merits of the case. The defence is limited to the procedure by which the foreign court arrived at its judgment. However, if that procedure, while valid there, is not in accordance with Canada's concept of natural justice, the foreign judgment will be rejected. The defendant carries the burden of proof and, in this case, failed to raise any reasonable apprehension of unfairness. . . .

(3) The Defence of Public Policy

[71] The third and final defence is that of public policy. This defence prevents the enforcement of a foreign judgment which is contrary to the Canadian concept of justice. The public policy defence turns on whether the foreign law is contrary to our view of basic morality. As stated in Castel and Walker, . . . :

> . . . the traditional public policy defence appears to be directed at the concept of repugnant laws and not repugnant facts.

[72] How is this defence of assistance to a defendant seeking to block the enforcement of a foreign judgment? It would, for example, prohibit the enforcement of a foreign judgment that is founded on a law contrary to the fundamental morality of the Canadian legal system. Similarly, the public policy defence guards against the enforcement of a judgment rendered by a foreign court proven to be corrupt or biassed.

[73] The appellants submitted that the defence of public policy should be broadened to include the case where neither the defence of natural justice nor the current defence of public policy would apply but where the outcome is so egregious that it justifies a domestic court's refusal to enforce the foreign judgment. . . . The appellants claimed that the public policy defence provides a remedy where the judgment, by its amount alone, would shock the conscience of the reasonable Canadian. . . . I do not agree. . . .

⁷⁵ The use of the defence of public policy to challenge the enforcement of a foreign judgment involves impeachment of that judgment by condemning the foreign law on which the judgment is based. It is not a remedy to be used lightly. The expansion of this defence to include perceived injustices that do not offend our sense of morality is unwarranted. The defence of public policy should continue to have a narrow application.

⁷⁶ The award of damages by the Florida jury does not violate our principles of morality. The sums involved, although they have grown large, are not by themselves a basis to refuse enforcement of the foreign judgment in Canada. Even if it could be argued in another case that the arbitrariness of the award can properly fit into a public policy argument, the record here does not provide any basis allowing the Canadian court to re-evaluate the amount of the award. The public policy defence is not meant to bar enforcement of a judgment rendered by a foreign court with a real and substantial connection to the cause of action for the sole reason that the claim in that foreign jurisdiction would not yield comparable damages in Canada. . . .

Presumably, the Supreme Court of Canada was the last instance and the defendants had no further options of appeal. Did this leave them entirely without remedy?

The courts of many other countries—probably most other countries, in fact—are not so sympathetic to the recognition and enforcement of U.S. judgments if either punitive damages were awarded or if the amounts might otherwise be disproportionate to proven loss.[159] Another issue that frequently creates difficulties when it comes to the enforcement of U.S. judgments in other countries is the jurisdiction of the U.S. court. If the defendant was domiciled in the court district or otherwise voluntarily submitted to its jurisdiction, this problem does not arise. However, if the U.S. court relied on an extraordinary or long-arm jurisdiction, such as the transient jurisdiction based on service of process during a brief visit to the state, such judgments will rarely be enforceable abroad. In 2001, The Committee on Foreign and

---

159. For example, while German courts cannot refuse to serve an American lawsuit under Art. 13(1) of the Hague Service Convention, they can and will rely on the public policy exception in §328(1)(4) of the German Civil Procedure Code to refuse recognition and enforcement of an American judgment awarding punitive damages and/or statutory damages if the award is considered disproportionate to the actual damages or if it is not even entirely clear what specific harm is to be compensated by the statutory damages amount. For further analysis, see Martin Konstantin Thelen: *Are Statutory Damages the New Punitive Damages?—Haftungs- und Prozessrisiken durch pauschalierte Schadenersatzansprüche im U.S.-amerikanischen Recht*, Zeitschrift für Vergleichende Rechtswissenschaft 2018, pp. 156–188.

For further analysis see Norman T. Braslow, *The Recognition and Enforcement of Common Law Punitive Damages in a Civil Law System: Some Reflections on the Japanese Experience*, 16 Ariz. J. Int'l & Comp. L. 285 (1999); Charles Calleros: *Punitive Damages, Liquidated Damages, and Clauses Pénales in Contract Actions: a Comparative Analysis of the American Common Law and the French Civil Code*, Brook. J. Int'l L. 2006, Vol. 32, No. 1, pp. 67–119; John Y. Gotanda, *Punitive Damages: A Comparative Analysis*, 42 Colum. J. Transnat'l L. 391 (2003–2004); and John Y. Gotanda, *Charting Developments Concerning Punitive Damages: Is the Tide Changing?*, 45 Colum. J. Transnat'l L. 507 (2006–2007).

Comparative Law of the Association of the Bar of the City of New York compiled a *Survey on Foreign Recognition of U.S. Money Judgments* outlining typical problems related to jurisdiction, public policy, procedural defects, reciprocity, choice of law, time limits, and fraud, and where they are most likely to arise.[160] Unfortunately, a similarly comprehensive and more recent survey is currently not available.

Courts in **Mexico** follow two different approaches when asked to recognize and enforce a foreign judgment.[161] Judicial orders and decisions from Latin American countries that are signatories either to the 1979 Inter-American Convention on Extraterritorial Validity of Foreign Judgments and Arbitral Awards (the "Montevideo Convention"),[162] or to the 1984 Inter-American Convention on Jurisdiction in the International Sphere for the Extraterritorial Validity of Foreign Judgments (the "La Paz Convention"),[163] will be recognized and enforced pursuant to a simplified procedure. However, since the U.S. rarely ratifies any of the Inter-American conventions, for judgments from the U.S. and the rest of the world, the matter is more complicated and requires strict compliance with a highly formalized procedure called *homologación*. Romelio Hernández, in his excellent summary,[164] explains that the procedure, in principle, is conducted by state courts pursuant to state law, wherever the enforcement is sought. This could be quite different in Aguascalientes from Jalisco or Yucatán, etc. Fortunately, most of the 31 Mexican states provide that the procedure for the recognition and enforcement of *foreign* judgments will be conducted pursuant to the Federal Code of Civil Procedure (FCCP). The procedure needs to be initiated by a letter rogatory issued by the court that adopted the judgment. The letter rogatory requesting the execution of a judgment is different from a letter rogatory requesting gathering of evidence and the like. For the latter, the Hague Convention on Gathering of Evidence Abroad and certain other international conventions on mutual assistance in judicial proceedings provide somewhat standardized procedures. Unfortunately, no comparable convention has yet been widely adopted for the recognition and enforcement of foreign judgments. Article 571 of the FCCP, in combination with general guidelines for letters rogatory, allows us to make a list of 12 requirements for the successful execution of a U.S. judgment in Mexico:[165]

> 1. The letter has to be issued by the court or judicial authority that adopted the decision and now requests its recognition and enforcement.

---

160. Available at http://brownwelsh.com/Archive/ABCNY_Study_Enforcing_Judgments.pdf.

161. I am grateful to David Wemhoff for preparation of this section. David relied *inter alia* on Romelio Hernández: *Avoiding Pitfalls: Enforcement of US Judgments in Mexico*, available at http://www.hmhlegal.com/Pdfs/EnforcementofUSJudgmentsinMexico.pdf. Questions and comments can be sent to David Wemhoff, Attorney at Law, 922 E. Wayne Street, Ste 204, South Bend, Indiana 46617, www.wemhofflaw.com.

162. http://www.oas.org/juridico/english/treaties/b-41.html.

163. http://www.oas.org/juridico/english/treaties/b-50.html.

164. Available at http://www.hmhlegal.com/Pdfs/EnforcementofUSJudgmentsinMexico.pdf.

165. I am paraphrasing Romelio Hernández: *Avoiding Pitfalls: Enforcement of US Judgments in Mexico*, available at http://www.hmhlegal.com/Pdfs/EnforcementofUSJudgmentsinMexico.pdf.

2. The letter has to specify the identity and domicile of the parties to the dispute and provide an address in the state or states in Mexico where notice can be served on the defendant.

3. The letter has to explain the nature, purpose, and extent of the request.

4. The letter has to explain the factual background to the dispute and the history of the proceedings.

5. The letter has to include all judicial acts requested by the parties and/or adopted by the requesting court in the course of the proceedings.

6. The letter has to be signed in the original by the judge or clerk and attest that all included documents are true and correct copies of the originals.

7. The letter and accompanying documents must be *legalized* by the Secretary of State of the requesting authority. This usually involves obtaining an *Apostille* and having it attached to the authenticated documents. This confirms that the documents are real and have been properly issued by competent judicial authorities.

8. Article 553 FCCP provides that the letter and all accompanying documents have to be translated into Spanish. To be on the safe side, Romelio Hernández recommends that the translation be done by a certified translator appointed by the State Supreme Court of the Mexican state where the enforcement is sought.

9. The letter must include a statement to satisfy the comity or reciprocity requirement. Hernández reminds us in this context that under Article 571 FCCP, "Mexican courts will not enforce a foreign judgment when it is proven that the issuing [American] court would not enforce a [Mexican] judgment under similar circumstances." Thus, evidence should be provided that the requesting American court or the courts from that U.S. jurisdiction have in the past enforced Mexican judgments or at least have not refused requests for such recognition and enforcement.

10. The letter must include a statement that the requested judgment is final and has the force of res judicata.

11. The requesting court should transfer full and express powers for execution to the requested court, "including but not limited to a) power to seize debtor's property; b) to issue attachment or garnishment orders; c) to issue and make use of preventive or security measures; d) to impose fines; e) to decree the temporary arrest of any person rebel to comply with the court order; f) to order the entering into private property upon the use of public force; g) to carry out judicial auctions or bid sales for execution of seized property; to assigned moneys and funds out to the plaintiff, etc."[166]

---

166. Romelio Hernández, at pp. 3–4.

12. The letter has to provide the name and address of local counsel, i.e., an attorney admitted to the bar in the district of the requested court who has power of attorney to receive communications from the requested court and represent the plaintiff if, for example, assets to be seized have to be selected or partial executions have to be authorized.

Matters can be further complicated if a judicial decision concerns real estate or other matters where the Mexican courts may not recognize the original jurisdiction of the requesting U.S. court or courts and/or if the requested decision is a judgment in default and it is not proven beyond reasonable doubt that service of process was served on the Mexican defendant pursuant to the requirements under Mexican law.

If readers are thinking that any of the Mexican requirements are unreasonable, they should remember that the U.S. would impose the same or a very similar set of requirements on judgments from Mexico before agreeing to recognize and enforce them in the U.S. The easiest way for the U.S. to simplify matters would be to ratify one or both of the Inter-American conventions on the subject. As long as that does not happen, business entities and private parties on both sides will have to continue to spend more time and money on lawyers than necessary and still face defeat if any of the procedural minutiae could not be met in time.

In a market as highly integrated as the **European Union**, where tens of thousands of transactions are done across Member State borders every day, complicated procedures as described above would defeat the goal of developing an internal market where goods, services, and people can flow freely across all Member States. Thus, it has been a priority of the EU to develop alongside the free movement of factors of production also the free movement of judicial and other official decisions. To this end, the recognition and enforcement of judgments is governed by the EU Regulation 1215/2012 on Jurisdiction and the Recognition and Enforcement of Judgments in Civil and Commercial Matters ("the Brussels Ia or I bis Regulation").[167] This Regulation has replaced EU Regulation 44/2001 ("the Brussels I Regulation"), which itself had replaced a multilateral convention, the 1968 Brussels Convention on Jurisdiction and the Enforcement of Judgments in Civil and Commercial Matters. To the extent the provisions have remained the same across all three documents, the interpretations given to them in the case law of the European Court of Justice continue to apply. As has been mentioned before, the particular nature of an EU Regulation means that it is directly applicable law in all Member States and enjoys supremacy over potentially conflicting national norms. Within the scope of application of the Regulation, therefore, lawyers and their clients can safely ignore any remaining Member State laws (see also p. 713).

---

167. OJ 2012 L 351, 20 December 2012, p. 1, Documents, p. II-92. For family law disputes, see EU Regulation 2201/2003 Concerning Jurisdiction and the Recognition and Enforcement of Judgments in Matrimonial Matters and the Matters of Parental Responsibility ("the Brussels II Regulation"), OJ 2003 L 338.

Since it is a common requirement throughout the world for a foreign judgment to be recognized and enforced that the court of origin had jurisdiction over the defendant, the Brussels Ia or I bis Regulation first determines the acceptable bases of jurisdiction (Articles 4 to 35, see also above, p. 713). Articles 36 to 55 deal with the procedure for recognition and enforcement and the acceptable grounds for a refusal of recognition and enforcement. Article 52 stipulates that "[u]nder no circumstances may a judgment given in a Member State be reviewed as to its substance in the Member State addressed." The required documents and even the forms to be used are provided in the Annexes to the Regulation. Importantly, legalization is not one of the requirements. Finally, as with all official documents of the EU, the Regulation is available in all 24 official languages, including English. The case law of the European Court of Justice provides authoritative interpretations of its provisions where needed.

Per Article 36, the Regulation is applicable for the recognition and enforcement of a judgment from one Member State of the EU in another Member State of the EU. Judgments from Non-Member States, like the U.S., will be treated in accordance with the national law of the Member State where they are presented for recognition and enforcement. The national requirements vary, but are generally not much different from the Mexican list outlined above.

Section 3. Introduction to Alternative Dispute Resolution (ADR)

A. What Is ADR?

The freedom of commercial parties to an (international) business transaction to make a **choice of forum** for the settlement of any disputes is not limited to litigation vs. arbitration. ADR is broader than arbitration and "may be defined as *a range of procedures* that serve as *alternatives to litigation* through the courts for the resolution of disputes, generally involving the intercession and assistance of *a neutral and impartial third party*."[168]

Although the classifications vary, we may usefully distinguish the following forms of ADR:[169]

---

168. Henry Brown & Arthur Marriott, *ADR Principles and Practice*, Sweet & Maxwell 2nd ed. 1999, at p. 12 (emphasis added).

169. Brown & Marriott have no fewer than 18 methods for dispute settlement addressed in their book, see pp. 17–19 for the list. Klaus Peter Berger points out that in Europe, arbitration is sometimes *not* considered part of ADR but in some kind of third category in addition to litigation and the forms of ADR that ultimately do not provide a neutral with decision-making power. See Klaus Peter Berger: *Private Dispute Resolution in International Business—Negotiation, Mediation, Arbitration*, Wolters Kluwer, 3rd ed. 2015, Vol. II, p. 45. Like Berger, we are taking a different approach,

Negotiation and Good Offices: Negotiation seems to be the daily bread of business and parties will almost always negotiate before considering formalized dispute settlement procedures. However, negotiation as used in ADR is an enhanced form that follows certain principles and often relies on specially trained negotiators. One of the important starting points of good-faith negotiations is an establishment of undisputed facts. The law, by contrast, often plays a minor role. Instead of focusing on rights and obligations, negotiations focus on the parties' **interests** and contrast the best- and worst-case alternatives for each side to find a middle ground that may become a negotiated settlement.[170] In an ideal scenario, the negotiations will not just result in a compromise where both sides make some concessions compared to their preferred outcome, but it will "increase the pie" to be distributed, giving both sides more than they could have achieved on their own.

Conciliation, Facilitation, Mediation: The line between the good offices of a neutral negotiator and a facilitator or mediator in a conciliation procedure is not always clear or important. While negotiations take place in the presence of both parties, facilitation and mediation usually involve separate meetings where the neutral listens to partisan positions and looks for potential common ground. The term "shuttle diplomacy" has been used in this context.[171] Both facilitation and good offices can involve practical help with scheduling meetings, drawing up agendas, and the like. Unless specifically authorized by the parties, neither the neutral negotiator nor the neutral facilitator or mediator should evaluate the merits of the party positions, let alone make proposals for the resolution of the dispute. Instead, the facilitator or mediator should help the parties find their own solutions.

Expert Determination: By contrast to partisan negotiators or a neutral facilitator, a neutral expert can also be charged with drawing up a proposal how the dispute should be resolved if the negotiations or the facilitation do not achieve a settlement. The proposal should be based on a neutral evaluation of the facts and industry customs. In this sense, the expert is similar to an evaluative mediator. However, the expert is usually not a lawyer and does not evaluate the *legal* merit of the parties' positions. If so empowered by the parties, the expert may go beyond a proposal and adopt a final and binding decision. To be enforceable, the parties would have to agree beforehand that a judgment of the court can be entered upon the decision made by the expert.

Arbitration: Unlike the other forms of ADR, arbitration is generally adjudicative and will result in a final and binding decision unless otherwise agreed by the parties. Thus, the default settings are reversed: While other neutrals can only adopt a

---

namely that ADR includes all forms of dispute settlement that fall outside of the default public courts and, therefore, need an agreement between the parties.

170. The groundbreaking work has been and remains the book by Roger Fisher & William Ury, *Getting to Yes: Negotiating Agreement Without Giving In*, Houghton Mifflin 1981. For comprehensive analysis, see Chris Honeyman & Andrea Kupfer Schneider, *The Negotiator's Desk Reference*, Vols. 1 and 2, DRI Press 2017.

171. See, for example, David A. Hoffman, *Mediation and the Art of Shuttle Diplomacy*, Negot. J. 2011, Vol. 27, No. 3, pp. 263–309.

binding decision if specifically empowered by the parties, an arbitrator or an arbitration tribunal has to adopt a binding decision unless the parties specifically agree otherwise. Since arbitration is usually done by lawyers and is more formalized than expert determination, it takes longer and is more expensive. By contrast to the decision of an expert, an arbitral award can be enforced internationally with the help of the New York Convention.

Given the fact that negotiation is probably the beginning of any dispute settlement attempt, and given the fact that an adversarial procedure is the final escalation both in litigation and in arbitration, if an amicable settlement cannot be reached, it may not always be clear to the uninitiated what the point of ADR is, what the pros and cons are, and what kinds of disputes may benefit from going to ADR rather than litigation.

In a 2009 essay titled "Alternative Dispute Resolution — What Every Law Student Should Know," Professor Dunnewold wrote:

> The recent growth of ADR has been prompted primarily by the shortcomings of the adversarial litigation system. In a 1984 address to the ABA, then-Supreme Court Chief Justice Warren Burger acknowledged that while trials are the only way to resolve some disputes, overall, our adversarial legal system is too costly, painful, destructive, and inefficient. Indeed, ADR processes are designed to reduce both cost and trauma to the parties, and to ease the overwhelming dockets most courts have faced in the past several decades.
>
> Aside from the practical concerns of cost and crowded dockets, many ADR proponents envision a transformative approach to resolving disputes. In their view, traditional litigation focuses too much on winning and not enough on problem solving. Further, courts can impose only certain prescribed solutions, mostly involving money. So when a court or jury decides a dispute, the outcome may or may not resolve the underlying issues. In contrast, ADR processes like mediation focus on exploring the parties' "interests" and allow the parties themselves to craft solutions that advance those interests. Thus, ADR fosters flexible, individually tailored results that achieve joint gain for the parties, rather than a win-lose outcome.[172]

However, ADR and arbitration were not invented in the 1980s or even more recently. The concepts literally go back to early Jewish, Christian, and Islamic times and dispute settlement procedures involving elders or other trusted individuals as mediators, in the absence of functioning courts. Even as states constituted themselves and became increasingly organized, including the provision of courts for the settlement of disputes, certain educated and widely respected individuals were still called upon to sometimes intervene in disputes as mediators or arbitrators.[173]

---

172. Mary Donnewold, 38 STUDENT LAW. 14 (2009).

173. A short overview can be found in Frank D. Emerson, *History of Arbitration Practice and Law*, Cleve. St. L. Rev. 1970, Vol. 19, No. 1, pp. 155–164.

The origins of more modern and institutionalized forms of arbitration are probably to be found in medieval England, where merchants resorted to private dispute settlement by trusted peers as an alternative to the royal courts. In so doing, the merchants were looking simultaneously for expedited decisions, insider knowledge of the customs and exigencies of the trade, and confidentiality. Interestingly, from the beginning, there was also the question of enforcement. In general, decisions by the courts of one country—England in our example—were unenforceable anywhere outside of that country. By contrast, if a merchant agreed to arbitration but subsequently did not adhere to the decision of the tribunal, he or she would be shunned by the members of the guild or trade, which served as a powerful enforcement tool regardless of national borders or differences in legal systems.

Since the early days of arbitration, this form of private dispute settlement has evolved in remarkable ways, remaining relevant and becoming more widespread, in particular in cases with international dimensions. By contrast, the early limitations of court-based litigation are largely still in place and make this form of public dispute settlement relatively unattractive to international business, namely:

- inflexibility with regard to choice of language, law, and procedure;

- judges are unaccustomed to the specific nature and customs of the trade;

- long duration;

- lack of confidentiality; and

- difficulty or impossibility of enforcement in other jurisdictions.

Specifically for international commercial disputes, the International Smart Mediation and Arbitration Institute in Indianapolis lists the following advantages of modern-day ADR:[174]

• More friendly	—	ADR preserves business relationships
• Faster	—	ADR resolves disputes faster and has no appeals
• More professional	—	ADR relies on neutrals who understand your business
• Confidential	—	ADR preserves the confidentiality of business deals
• More Trustworthy	—	ADR does not put you at the mercy of foreign judges
• Cheaper	—	ADR, well designed, saves time and money
• More Accessible	—	ADR works with your own attorneys and can be all online
• Enforceable	—	Arbitration awards are enforced in more than 150 countries

---

174. www.SmartArb.org.

- More Successful   —   ADR is preferred by more than 90% of international lawyers.[175]

To be sure, to capture all or even just the majority of these benefits, ADR procedures have to be well designed and neutrals have to be carefully chosen. This will be the next focus of our analysis.

B. When and Why to Opt for ADR

Litigation does not require consent. Even if the parties to an IBT never agreed on anything related to dispute settlement, there are conflict rules, also referred to as the rules of private international law, that enable us to determine the applicable law and the forum or fora with jurisdiction over the parties and their business dealings. Under virtually any circumstances, there will be a court that can be called upon to hear a case and issue a decision that is binding on the parties, whether they like it or not. This means that litigation will always remain important for securing the rights of parties to an IBT, namely whenever they did not and cannot agree on ADR. Furthermore, as Golann and Folberg point out, the fact that litigation is always an option is a major reason why parties consider ADR in the first place; in other words, "[t]he wish to avoid the 'fire' of trial is a major factor in motivating parties to choose the 'frying pan' of settlement."[176]

We must never forget that, in contrast to litigation, ADR requires consent. At the very least, the parties have to agree once, when they enter into their business contract, to insert a valid arbitration clause. If that was done, further consent is not needed and a claim can be brought—at least in principle—without further cooperation of the defendant or respondent. Other forms of ADR require even more consent, namely after a dispute has arisen, to provide a resolution in the form of a settlement.

Against this background, we can provide some rules of thumb when it makes sense to opt for mandatory negotiation, conciliation, or mediation before allowing the parties to get a binding judgment or award. After a dispute has arisen, consent-based forms of ADR are more likely to succeed if:

- the parties have a long-standing business relationship and/or are interested in future business with each other, and/or
- all parties acted in good faith in the current situation and it is not clear that only one side is responsible for whatever went wrong and triggered the current dispute, and/or

---

175. To give but one example, the International Institute for Conflict Prevention & Resolution (CPR) managed to persuade thousands of companies to adopt one of several "corporate pledge" options pursuant to which negotiation and ADR will *always* be explored before litigation is initiated. See https://www.cpradr.org/resource-center/adr-pledges/corporate-policy-statement.

176. Dwight Golann & Jay Folberg, *Mediation—The Roles of Advocate and Neutral*, 3rd ed., Aspen 2016, at p. 4.

- all parties are interested in keeping the dispute and the underlying business transaction confidential and no party would benefit from exposing quality or financial problems of the other side, and/or

- the dispute is similarly important or unimportant to all parties so that everyone has a bit of room to maneuver and can make some concessions.

In contrast, consent-based ADR is not as likely to succeed if:

- at least one party does not have a significant interest in preserving the business relationship, and/or

- it is fairly clear that one side is not acting in good faith and/or is probably alone at fault, and is therefore not really interested in a swift and fair resolution that is bound to come out against it, and/or

- at least one party can gain leverage by exposing quality problems with the goods or services of the other party and/or financial or other problems of the other party, and/or

- at least one party has little or no room to make concessions because a successful resolution of the dispute is potentially a matter of survival for them.

As legal counsel, ask yourself the following questions, which will impact the willingness of the parties to negotiate and/or settle versus dragging the dispute through arbitration or the courts, regardless of time and cost:

- What happens if there is no settlement? Confidential and relatively quick arbitration? Or public and potentially protracted litigation? What are the best and worst alternatives to a negotiated agreement for each side?

- What are the financial and economic implications of the dispute? E.g., is this potentially threatening the survival of a business?

- Are there questions of principle involved for one or both parties, which make it hard to agree in spite of relatively small financial stakes?

- Are there differences in the perception of fairness and justice?

- Are there cultural differences that make it difficult to reconcile?

- Are claims or defenses being made for strategic purposes, for example, to persuade someone with a stronger position to enter into a settlement? To delay payments due? To go on a fishing expedition for documents of or about a potential competitor?

- Does a party want or should we get a binding public precedent instead of a private *inter partes* settlement?

- How and where does media publicity come into play? Who wants it? Who wants to avoid it?

- Does the dispute have symbolic value to one of the parties? Would a public victory have a special symbolic value?

- What about time factors? Which party has time on her side? Will there be a need for an injunction on behalf of the other party?

- What about emotional factors such as humiliation or revenge? Draw a line from totally rational to totally emotional and try to determine where the parties stand on this continuum. Emotion is poor counsel in negotiations.

- Are personality factors involved? How inclined are the parties to accept a mutually compromising settlement versus combative litigation?

- What are the practical considerations, such as cost, fee shifting, and risk? How much can and will a party spend in ADR? In litigation?

In the end, your default assumption should be that ADR is better than litigation unless there are specific reasons to think otherwise. You may want to write down all the pros and cons of ADR versus litigation and discuss them with your client before sleepwalking carelessly into litigation. In almost all cases, your focus as legal counsel should be on *how* to design the best possible ADR procedure for an IBT or a dispute, rather than *whether* to do ADR in the first place.

Virtually all forms of ADR can be self-administered by the parties (ad hoc) or administered by an ADR institution. Relying on an institution for support has many advantages, in particular for less experienced parties, but it comes at a cost. In particular, if the amounts at issue may not justify the cost, a compromise can be to rely on the rules of an institution and an experienced neutral, without relying on the actual services of the institution.

> Every dispute resolution process must be economical, fast, fair and risk-minimizing. In choosing between the different dispute resolution processes, a party will take into account the outcome of the process (recommendation, settlement or binding decision), the level of risk which it is willing to run, the costs involved, the time factor, the focus of the process on interests or legal positions, and the importance that it attaches to the future of the business relationship with the other side.
>
> Klaus Peter Berger: *Private Dispute Resolution in International Business—Negotiation, Mediation, Arbitration,* Wolters Kluwer 3rd ed. 2015, Vol. II, p. 43

Section 4. Negotiations After a Dispute Has Arisen

"Negotiation can be metaphorically compared to making a pie and then dividing it up. The process of conflict resolution affects both the size of the pie, and who gets what slice . . ."

Golann & Folberg, *Mediation*, p. 53

The negotiation experts at www.negotiations.com distinguish five scenarios of how negotiations in general can work out (adapted from https://www.negotiations .com/articles/negotiation-conflict-profiles/):[177]

Chart 6-2 Scenarios for Negotiations

Obviously, the bottom two scenarios are undesirable for a negotiator. This suggests that certain negotiation tactics or styles are preferable over others. However, whether a particular style can be successfully employed depends not only on the skills, personality, and temperament of a negotiator but also on the specific situation — in particular whether the parties to the transaction are thinking beyond the current scenario because they want to sustain their business relationship, and whether one side has significant leverage over the other.

Leverage comes in many flavors, including how important a particular transaction is for the bottom line or even survival of the companies. If a large distributor with deep pockets — for example, Costco — negotiates whether or not to enter into a long-term supply contract with a relatively small manufacturer — say Feit Electric, a company making light bulbs — it is obvious that the deal is more important for the one side than the other. However, the single most important factor in the negotiations will be information. Where is the bottom line for Feit, the price below

---

which they will no longer make a profit? Who are potential alternative suppliers for Costco? What are the prices and the quality the competitors are willing to offer? In general, negotiators will apply a variety of strategies, including threats, bluffs, misleading clues, etc., to obtain as much information as possible from the other side while providing as little as possible about their own.

A *competitive approach* can be appropriate where the outcome is necessarily a zero-sum game, i.e., the gains of one side are necessarily the losses of the other. Golann and Folberg provide the example of a lawyer negotiating on behalf of a client with an insurance adjuster over the amount to be paid to compensate for a given property damage. The lawyer will try to get the maximum amount for her client while the adjuster will push toward a minimum amount to protect the interests of the insurance company. Neither side cares much about a past or future business relationship and both sides have an interest in swift agreement on a particular amount that will satisfy their client or employer.[178]

By contrast, a *collaborative approach* can be beneficial for both sides when the outcome is not a zero-sum game, i.e., by collaborating, the parties can increase the size of the pie to be distributed. Instead of viewing the other side as a competitor, the negotiators treat each other as potential partners and look out for each other's needs and interests.[179] Of course, this usually requires some level of trust between the parties,[180] as well as a vision for (potential) future business dealings. Golann and Folberg cite the example of two businesses seeking to develop a joint venture.[181]

In our case, when parties in different countries have contracted for an IBT and a dispute has already arisen, all options are potentially on the table. If both sides just walk away from each other (*avoid*), both sides lose. The transaction fails and future relations become impossible. If one side concedes or is made to concede (*compete, accommodate*), it loses while the other side wins. Future relations are also unlikely. By contrast, future relations will be possible if the parties *compromise* over a given size of pie or *collaborate* to increase the size of the pie they can share. In ADR, a collaborative approach aimed at increasing the size of the pie usually requires a look beyond the current dispute and a commitment to "make it up" to the other side in

178. Dwight Golann & Jay Folberg, *Mediation — The Roles of Advocate and Neutral*, Aspen 3rd ed. 2016, at p. 13.

179. See, in particular, Roger Fisher & William Ury, *Getting to Yes — Negotiating Agreement Without Giving In*, Penguin rev. ed. 2011. See also Michael Benoliel (ed.), *Negotiation Excellence — Successful Deal Making*, World Scientific Publ. 2nd ed. 2015; Melanie Billings-Yun, *Beyond Dealmaking — Five Steps to Negotiating Profitable Relationships*, Jossey-Bass 2010; Adam Galinsky & Maurice Schweitzer, *Friend & Foe: When to Cooperate, When to Compete, and How to Succeed at Both*, Crown Business 2015; Leigh Thompson, *The Mind and Heart of the Negotiator*, Prentice Hall 6th ed. 2014; and Michael Wheeler, *Negotiation*, Harvard Business Essentials 2003.

180. On the subject of trust, see, in particular, Keld Jensen, *Trust Factor — Negotiating in Smartnership*, Palgrave Macmilan 2013; as well as Dejun Tony Kong, Kurt T. Dirks & Donald L. Ferrin, *Interpersonal Trust Within Negotiations: Metaanalytic Evidence, Critical Contingencies, and Directions for Future Research*, Acad. Mgmt J. 2014, Vol. 57, No. 5, pp. 1235–1255.

181. *Golann & Folberg*, above, at p. 14.

future dealings. This is often best accomplished by bringing in higher-level executives from both companies and specially trained outside facilitators.[182] By contrast, in litigation, lawyers are usually expected by their clients—and sometimes even required by their professional ethics—to pursue maximal positions via adversarial strategies, with little or no consideration given to future business between the parties.

Golann and Folberg identify seven stages of negotiations and the different approaches taken at each stage by competitive versus collaborative negotiators:[183]

Chart 6-3
Stages of Negotiations

Stage	Competitive/Adversarial Approach	Cooperative/Problem-Solving Approach
1. Preparation	• Plan and research • Identify alternatives to agreement for each party and other power factors • Set goals and bottom line • Decide what information to request and provide • Counsel client	• Plan and research • Assess the interests of each party • Identify potential options that satisfy both sides' interests • Identify information needed • Identify alternatives to agreement and bottom line • Counsel client
2. Initial Interactions	• Set tone • Establish credentials • Seek to impose agenda	• Set tone • Establish rapport and trust • Work out agenda
3. Exchanging and Refining Information	• Ask questions and bargain for information • Exaggerate value of one's alternative, denigrate opponent's • Present extreme positions	• Ask questions and share information • Explain needs and interests • Share data regarding options
4. Bargaining	• Argue legal case • Demand and trade concessions • Mislead opponent about intentions and test their resolve	• Discuss relative importance of interests • Consult about potential solutions that may satisfy both sides' goals
5. Moving Toward Closure	• Evaluate offers • Stress power and threaten impasse • Create time constraints	• Identify valuable options • Create alternative outcomes

---

182. www.negotiations.com offers specialized training for prospective negotiators.

183. Dwight Golann & Jay Folberg, *Mediation — The Roles of Advocate and Neutral*, Aspen 3rd ed. 2016, at pp. 27–28, with further explanations. Reprinted by permission.

Stage	Competitive/Adversarial Approach	Cooperative/Problem-Solving Approach
6. Reaching Impasse or Agreement	• Propose self-serving principles • Suggest favorable impasse-breaking methods • Dig in; compromise only if necessary • Accept impasse if goal is not reached	• Select most valuable terms • Propose fair principles to allocate value • Show openness to compromise • Reassess needs, options, and goals as necessary
7. Finalizing and Writing Agreements	• Attempt to avoid implementation risks • Prepare opposing drafts • Get or manipulate approval	• Consult about implementation issues • Memorialize terms • Get approval and buy-in

Whichever approach is taken—and skillful negotiators will often switch from one style to another depending on how a dispute evolves—if a settlement is reached at the end, it should be memorialized in the form of a contract, including a clause providing that a judgment of the court shall be entered upon the contract for enforcement, if necessary.

Q: What should we be willing to accept in order to settle this dispute?

A: *Anything* as good as or better than what you can reasonably expect from arbitration or litigation, after considering *all* of the associated costs and likely impact on the business.[184]

In the next section we turn to mediation as a more formalized method of ADR with the help of a qualified mediator.

Section 5. Moving from Negotiation to Mediation of IBT Disputes

"Mediation is overwhelmingly the most popular and most frequently used ADR process across jurisdictions."[185]

As we are designing contracts, or strategies for resolution of a dispute that has already arisen, we should generally think of different forms of dispute settlement as parts of a process; pieces that complement rather than replace each other. Since negotiation, conciliation, and mediation cannot resolve a dispute unless both parties agree to a settlement, we usually need to have at least *the option* of following up with litigation or arbitration, if a settlement cannot be reached.

184. Michael McIlwrath & John Savage, *International Arbitration and Mediation—A Practical Guide*, Wolters Kluwer 2010, p. 173 (emphasis added).

185. https://sites-herbertsmithfreehills.vuturevx.com/31/7491/landing-pages/0883a-adr-practical-guides-no1-d5.pdf.

At this point, we are going beyond the question dealt with in Section 3, namely *when* it makes sense to require certain forms of negotiations, facilitation or mediation before litigation or arbitration, to the question of *how* a mediation procedure should be structured for maximum chances of success. As always, our focus is on settlement of *commercial* disputes.

Similar to the other ADR procedures, mediation can be accomplished in the framework of an ADR or mediation institution, with the institutional support, rules, and guidelines, or it can be accomplished ad hoc or self-administered by the parties. In the latter case, the parties can save the money that would go to institutional fees, but they have to design their own rules and procedures, preferably with the help of an experienced mediator.

While many organizations today offer mediation services and model rules for mediation, the International Mediation Institute (IMI) stands out because it brings together many of the most prestigious and experienced institutions for the development of "global professional standards" for mediators and mediation procedures, rather than providing its own mediation services.[186] The IMI is a charity under Dutch law and based in The Hague. The Board is composed of directors of the following ADR organizations, all of which are first-rate providers of mediation services:

- American Arbitration Association/International Center for Dispute Resolution (ICDR)
- Centre for Effective Dispute Resolution (CEDR)
- International Chamber of Commerce (ICC)
- JAMS
- Singapore Mediation Centre and Singapore International Arbitration Centre
- Bahrain Chamber for Dispute Resolution
- Netherlands Mediation Institute
- Corporate Counsel International Arbitration Group (CCIAG)

Many other ADR organizations cooperate with the IMI and on its website it provides links to these organizations and their rules and model clauses. Importantly, it also provides a certification for mediators, so that those considering mediation

---

186. See www.imimediation.org. For further analysis, see Neil Carmichael, *Certifying International Competency Standards for Mediators: A Look at IMI's Initiative*, World Arb. & Med. Rev. 2009, pp. 83–89; Judith P. Meyer & Michael Leathes, *How Mediators Can Obtain Professional Certification and Thereby Elevate Their Profession: A Look at IMI's Voluntary Credentialing Program*, Disp. Res. J. 2008, Vol. 63, No. 1, pp. 22–27.

The European Union has been formally supporting cross-border mediation at least since the adoption of Directive 2008/52 of May 21, 2008, on Certain Aspects of Mediation in Civil and Commercial Matters (OJ 2008 L 136, pp. 3–8). However, this does not mean that it has been able to agree on common standards or minimum qualifications. For discussion, see Ashley Feasley: *Regulating Mediator Qualifications in the 2008 EU Mediation Directive: The Need for a Supranational Standard*, J. Disp. Res. Vol. 2011, No. 2, pp. 333–350.

services know who are the most qualified professionals to provide them. Finally, the IMI has a "decision tree" on its website to help parties prepare for successful mediation. If done right, the IMI claims that "mediation has at least an 80% chance of successfully leading the parties to an agreement, including situations where the parties are deadlocked. Few other processes have a success rate that high."[187]

Mediate.com in Eugene, Oregon, lists the following "Roles of the Mediator":[188]

"The mediator's ultimate role is to do anything and everything necessary to assist parties to reach agreement. In serving this ultimate end, the mediator may take on any or all of the following roles:

Convener: The mediator may assist in contacting the other party(ies) to arrange for an introductory meeting.

Educator: The mediator educates the parties about the mediation process, other conflict resolution alternatives, issues that are typically addressed, options and principles that may be considered, research, court standards, etc.

Communication Facilitator: The mediator seeks to ensure that each party is fully heard in the mediation process.

Translator: When necessary, the mediator can help by rephrasing or reframing communications so that they are better understood and received.

Questioner and Clarifier: The mediator probes issues and confirms understandings to ensure that the participants and the mediator have a full understanding.

Process Advisor: The mediator comes to be trusted to suggest procedures for making progress in mediation discussions, which may include caucus meetings, consultation with outside legal counsel and consultation with substantive experts.

Angel of Realities: The mediator may exercise his or her discretion to play devil's advocate with one or both parties as to the practicality of solutions they are considering or the extent to which certain options are consistent with participants' stated goals, interests and positive intentions.

Catalyst: By offering options for considerations, stimulating new perspectives and offering reference points for consideration, mediator serves as a stimulant for the parties reaching agreement.

---

187. See https://www.imimediation.org/tools-and-resources/online-tools/decision-tree/. For critical analysis, see Jacqueline Nolan-Haley, *Mediation: The Best and Worst of Times*, Cardozo J. Confl. Res. 2015, Vol. 16, No. 3, pp. 731–740.

188. James Melamed, "Roles of the Mediator." Originally published by www.mediate.com. Reprinted by permission. See https://www.mediate.com/divorce/pg31.cfm. The organization also provides training programs and certifies mediators. While focused more on family and workplace mediation than on commercial disputes, the basic principles apply to all areas of mediation.

Responsible Detail Person: The mediator manages and keeps track of all necessary information, writes up the parties' agreement, and may assist the parties to implement their agreement."

What is *not* among the roles of the mediator on this list is an evaluation of the facts and the law on behalf of the parties. Some have argued that it is fundamentally incompatible with the role of a mediator to do an evaluation and come up with proposals how the dispute can or should be resolved.[189] Others take the position that the role of the mediator can evolve from being a mere facilitator in a conciliation procedure to taking on an evaluative function, if the parties so desire. As outlined above, we shall define conciliation as a procedure where the neutral does not have an evaluative function and does not make any proposals, but merely facilitates settlement along party-developed compromises. By contrast, we shall define mediation as a procedure where the neutral may go further and evaluate the merits of the party positions and — unless a settlement can be reached — may come up with one or more nonbinding proposals for the resolution of the dispute, if the parties so agree.[190] Given the different approaches taken in the U.S. and internationally in this regard, it is important for the parties to make it clear in their dispute settlement clauses and agreements which kind of procedure and involvement of the neutral they prefer.

The International Institute for Conflict Prevention and Resolution (CPR) outlines the mediation procedure as follows:[191]

1. **Agreement to mediate** (either in the form or a pre-dispute clause (ex ante) or in form of an ex post submission agreement);

2. **Selection of the mediator** (since agreement between the parties is not always forthcoming, mediation institutions like CPR offer assistance in selecting a mediator and parties can agree to pick one of several suggested candidates to get the procedure started);

3. **Selection or drafting of the rules of procedure** (in institutional mediation, the parties normally choose the standard institutional rules, although they can modify them to some extent; in ad hoc mediation, the parties can either chose the rules offered by an institution and adapt them or completely draw up their own);

---

189. See, in particular, Lela Love, *Top Ten Reasons Why Mediators Should Not Evaluate*, Fla. St. Univ. L. Rev. 1997, Vol. 24, pp. 937–948.

190. This approach is consistent with Art. 7(4) of the 2018 UNCITRAL Model Law on International Commercial Mediation and Settlement Agreements Resulting from Mediation (Documents, p. II-120), Rules 7(4) and 10(3) of the 2014 AAA-ICDR International Mediation Rules (Documents, p. II-151), Rule 9 of the 2011 JAMS International Mediation Rules & Procedures (Documents, p. II-156), as well as Rule 6, para. 3, of the 2017 CPR International Mediation Procedure (Documents, p. II-159). Most other institutional mediation rules are silent on the matter and, therefore, do not prevent a mediator from making proposals, unless otherwise agreed by the parties.

191. See https://www.cpradr.org/resource-center/rules/mediation/cpr-mediation-procedure.

4. Exchange of information (this may include a simplified and non-compulsory discovery procedure);

5. Presentations by the parties of their positions and claims;

6. Negotiations (with a focus on underlying interests and concerns);

7. Settlement (if a settlement is reached, it will be drawn up in writing by the parties or the mediator and formally executed as a contract; if litigation is pending, the settlement should provide that the parties will request dismissal of the case; to make a settlement directly enforceable, it should be submitted as a request to the court at the seat of the mediation or to the court with jurisdiction over the obligated party or parties to obtain a consent judgment;

if a settlement is not reached, the parties can agree to give the mediator authority to draw up a settlement proposal, which may or may not include an evaluation of the facts and the law;

if a resolution still cannot be reached, the parties can agree to move on to binding arbitration; in this case the parties can engage one or three new arbitrators or agree to rely on their mediator to take on the role of arbitrator;

at all times, the confidentiality of the mediation procedure should be preserved to the extent possible under the law; if mediation evolves into arbitration, the parties can largely maintain the confidentiality; by contrast, if litigation becomes necessary, it will be a question of the applicable rules of procedure whether at least some of the information exchanged during the mediation can remain confidential).

The Centre for Effective Dispute Resolution (CEDR) provides a range of resources on its website, including model clauses for contracts in more than 20 languages, model mediation procedures, and a code of conduct for third-party neutrals.[192]

An important step for the strengthening of international commercial mediation was taken on August 7, 2019, when some 50 countries signed the UN Convention on International Settlement Agreements Resulting from Mediation. This so-called "Singapore Convention" is aimed at doing for mediation what the New York

---

192. See https://www.cedr.com/commercial/resources/. For further information, see also Peter Binder, *International Commercial Arbitration and Mediation in UNCITRAL Model Law Jurisdictions*, Wolters Kluwer 4th ed. 2019; Nick Carr, *Commercial Mediation: A Practical Guide*, Law Brief Publishing 2018; Carlos Esplugues & Louis Marquis (eds.), *New Developments in Civil and Commercial Mediation—Global Comparative Perspectives*, Springer 2015; Carlos Esplugues Mota et al. (eds.), Civil and Commercial Mediation in Europe, Vols. I and II, intersentia 2014; Dwight Golann & Jay Folberg, *Mediation—The Roles of Advocate and Neutral*, Wolters Kluwer 2016; Dilyara Nigmatullina, *Combining Mediation and Arbitration in International Commercial Dispute Resolution*, Routledge 2018; David Richbell, How to Master Commercial Mediation, Bloomsbury Professional 2014; Omer Shapira, *A Theory of Mediators' Ethics: Foundations, Rationale, and Application*, Cambridge Univ. Press 2018; Catherine Titi & Katia Fach Gomez (eds.), *Mediation in International Commercial and Investment Disputes*, Oxford Univ. Press 2019.

Convention has done for international arbitration (Documents. p. II-127). Articles 3 to 5 of the Singapore Convention require the enforcement of a settlement agreement if a number of preconditions are met. What remains to be seen is whether the Convention will be ratified swiftly by a sufficiently large number of countries to give it global importance.

The following sample clauses can be inserted in contracts to provide for mandatory mediation attempts before parties can resort to arbitration or litigation:

1. Institutional Mediation and Negotiation-Mediation-Arbitration Step Clauses

International Centre for Dispute Resolution (ICDR) of the American Arbitration Association:

"In the event of any controversy or claim arising out of or relating to this contract, or a breach thereof, the parties hereto agree first to try and settle the dispute by mediation, administered by the International Centre for Dispute Resolution under its Mediation Rules, before resorting to arbitration, litigation, or some other dispute resolution procedure. The place of mediation shall be [city, (province or state), country]; the language(s) of the mediation shall be _____."

Centre for Effective Dispute Resolution (CEDR):

"If any dispute arises in connection with this agreement, the parties will attempt to settle it by mediation in accordance with the CEDR Model Mediation Procedure and the mediation will start, unless otherwise agreed by the parties, within 28 days of one party issuing a request to mediate to the other. Unless otherwise agreed between the parties, the mediator will be nominated by CEDR.

The mediation will take place in [named city/country; city/country of either/none of the parties] and the language of the mediation will be [English]. The Mediation Agreement referred to in the Model Procedure shall be governed by, and construed and take effect in accordance with the substantive law of [England and Wales].

If the dispute is not settled by mediation within [14] days of commencement of the mediation or within such further period as the parties may agree in writing, the dispute shall be referred to and finally resolved by arbitration. CEDR shall be the appointing body and administer the arbitration.

CEDR shall apply the UNCITRAL rules in force at the time arbitration is initiated. In any arbitration commenced pursuant to this clause, the number of arbitrators shall be [1–3] and the seat or legal place of arbitration shall be [London, England]."

International Smart Mediation and Arbitration Institute (SmartArb):

Ex Ante Option 1: Stand-Alone SmartArb Assisted Mediation Services: This option provides for mediation as a discreet process and leaves it to the parties to select arbitration or litigation with different neutrals or judges if the mediation should not render a satisfactory solution to the dispute.

Highly qualified mediators are able to settle a remarkable percentage of all (commercial) disputes, as long as the parties are acting in good faith and have an interest in continuing their business relationship.

"In case of a disagreement arising out of the present contract or the underlying business transaction, the parties shall attempt in good faith to settle their dispute by mediation administered by the International Smart Mediation and Arbitration Institute (SmartArb) before resorting to litigation, arbitration, or some other method of dispute resolution."

Ex Ante Option 2: Separate Institutional Mediation and Arbitration Using SmartArb Services: Parties should consider this option, if they want a traditional mediation like in option 1 but also want the assurance that they can go to arbitration in case the mediation fails and will not have to litigate abroad. The mediation and arbitration procedures will be conducted independently and with different neutrals to preserve maximum confidentiality of the mediation attempts.

"In case of a disagreement arising out of the present contract or the underlying business transaction, the parties shall attempt in good faith to settle their dispute by mediation administered by the International Smart Mediation and Arbitration Institute (SmartArb). If a settlement to the full satisfaction of all sides is not accomplished within 60 days of initiation of mediation procedures, either party is free to demand arbitration administered by SmartArb regarding any unresolved controversies. Except to pursue a provisional remedy that is authorized by law and unavailable from the arbitrator, neither side shall resort to litigation."

Ex Ante Option 3: Connected Institutional MedArb Using SmartArb Services: By contrast to options 1 and 2, the following clause allows a mediator to change roles and take on the decision-making powers of an arbitrator if the parties should not be able to settle their dispute via mediation. There are efficiencies in using the same person, who already became familiar with the case during mediation, as the final arbiter. However, the fact that a mediator may obtain decision-making powers later in the procedure can also change the dynamics of the mediation.

"In case of a disagreement arising out of the present contract or the underlying business transaction, the parties shall attempt in good faith to settle their dispute by mediation administered by the International Smart Mediation and Arbitration Institute (SmartArb). If a settlement to the full satisfaction of all sides is not accomplished within 60 days of initiation of mediation procedures, either party is free to demand arbitration administered by SmartArb regarding any unresolved controversies. Except to pursue a provisional remedy that is authorized by law and unavailable from the arbitrator, neither side shall resort to litigation. To the extent the parties do not agree otherwise, the mediator shall take on the role of arbitrator."

International Institute for Conflict Prevention & Resolution (CPR):

Option 1: Mediation Clause

"The parties shall attempt in good faith to resolve any dispute arising out of or relating to this Agreement promptly by confidential mediation under the [then current] CPR Mediation Procedure [in effect on the date of this Agreement], before resorting to arbitration or litigation."

Option 2: Negotiation-Mediation Clause with Designated Mediator Option

"a. Negotiation Between Executives: The parties shall attempt in good faith to resolve any dispute arising out of or relating to this [Agreement] [Contract] promptly by negotiation between executives who have authority to settle the controversy and who are at a higher level of management than the persons with direct responsibility for administration of this contract. To initiate a negotiation, a party shall give the other party written notice of any dispute not resolved in the normal course of business. Within [30] days after delivery of the notice, the executives of both parties shall meet at a mutually acceptable time and place, and thereafter as often as they reasonably deem necessary, to attempt to resolve the dispute. All negotiations pursuant to this clause are confidential and shall be treated as compromise and settlement negotiations for purposes of applicable rules of evidence.

b. [Mediation]: If the dispute has not been resolved by negotiation as provided herein within [45] days after delivery of the initial notice of negotiation, [or if the parties failed to meet within] 20 [days,] the parties shall endeavor to settle the dispute by mediation under the CPR Mediation Procedure [currently in effect OR in effect on the date of this Agreement], [provided, however, that if one party fails to participate as provided herein, the other party can initiate mediation prior to the expiration of the] 45 [days.] The parties have selected [insert name] as the mediator in any such dispute, and [he][she] has agreed to serve in that capacity and to be available on reasonable notice. In the event that [insert named mediator] becomes unwilling or unable to serve, the parties have selected [insert name] as the alternate mediator. In the event that neither person is willing or able to serve, the parties will agree on a substitute with the assistance of CPR. Unless otherwise agreed, the parties will select a mediator from the CPR Panels of Distinguished Neutrals."

2. Ad Hoc Mediation and Negotiation-Mediation-Arbitration Step Clauses

International Smart Mediation and Arbitration Institute (SmartArb):

Ex Ante Option 6: Ad Hoc MedArb Using SmartArb Rules: Ad hoc procedures are administered by the parties themselves without the systematic involvement of an ADR institution. In principle, the parties to a commercial dispute can not only select the place, the language, and any neutrals they want, they can also design their own procedural and substantive rules, as long as they agree between themselves. Ad hoc ADR is usually cheaper and more flexible than institutional ADR. However, since party agreement may not always be forthcoming, once a dispute has arisen, it is wise to include a back-up plan in a dispute settlement clause:

"In case of a disagreement arising out of the present contract or the underlying business transaction, the parties shall attempt in good faith to settle their dispute by party-administered mediation. If the parties cannot agree on a mediator within 30 days of the initiation of proceedings, either side may call upon the Secretary General of the International Smart Mediation and Arbitration Institute (SmartArb) for the appointment of a qualified mediator. To the extent the parties do not agree otherwise, the mediation shall be conducted pursuant to the mediation rules of SmartArb.

If a settlement to the full satisfaction of all sides is not accomplished within 60 days of initiation of mediation procedures, either party is free to initiate party-administered arbitration regarding any unresolved controversies. Except to pursue a provisional remedy that is authorized by law and unavailable from the arbitrator, neither side shall resort to litigation. To the extent the parties do not agree otherwise, the mediator shall take on the role of arbitrator and the arbitration shall be conducted pursuant to the arbitration rules of SmartArb in whatever form is current at the time of the initiation of arbitration proceedings."

In many cases, parties may not wish to include lengthy and detailed clauses in their commercial contracts because they fear that it may spook the other party. For parties or contract drafters wishing to insert a clause that provides for tiered mediation-arbitration in a cost-effective ad hoc format, the SmartArb has a model clause and proven rules:

"Any disputes related to this business transaction shall be settled in a cost-efficient MedArb procedure pursuant to the Ad Hoc Rules of the International Smart Mediation and Arbitration Institute in Indianapolis."

Notes and Questions

1. Remember that mediation requires consent. Although the statistics are in favor of trying mediation before adversarial procedures like arbitration or litigation, the statistics are also skewed because in many cases where consent-based solutions are unlikely, the parties will not even try mediation. Thus, we must assume that about 50% of all commercial disputes cannot or would not be successfully resolved with mediation alone. Does this make trying mediation worthwhile if certain basic parameters are met? Absolutely. Does it mean that providing for mediation is good enough and we don't need to worry about "what if"? Absolutely not. Thus, a good dispute resolution clause can never only provide for mediation and leave the rest to chance or to conflict rules/the rules of private international law.

2. Review the strengths and weaknesses of the sample mediation and step clauses provided above.

Section 6. International Commercial Arbitration[193]

A. Introduction

As a general rule, dispute settlement clauses should provide for mechanisms that actually work and provide timely, fair, cost-efficient, and enforceable solutions to the parties of an agreement. Very rarely should a party deliberately propose or accept a clause that it considers ineffective, on the assumption that this may be in her favor if she gets sued.

From the point of departure that dispute settlement clauses should actually work, there are good reasons why arbitration has become the method of choice for international business partners. This may seem a bit surprising, given the fact that parties to B2B transactions can theoretically choose any one of almost 200 national court systems for the settlement of their disputes. Every one of those is staffed with publicly appointed judges and backed by the police powers of the respective state to provide enforcement of the judgments, if necessary. So how can it be that private arbitration tribunals increasingly have the edge over public courts, in particular if we consider that most of the arbitration tribunals are not permanent courts and instead constituted ad hoc when a case is brought and staffed with just about anyone who the parties want to entrust their issue with, including arbitrators, who do not have to be trained as lawyers?

---

193. For further reading, see, in particular, American Arbitration Association, *Handbook on Arbitration Practice*, JurisNet 2016; American Arbitration Association, *Handbook on Commercial Arbitration*, JurisNet 2nd ed. 2016; Nigel Blackaby & Constantine Partasides, *Redfern and Hunter on International Arbitration*, Oxford Univ. Press 6th ed. 2015; Gary Born, *International Commercial Arbitration,* Vols. I, II, and III, Wolters Kluwer 2nd ed. 2014; W. Laurence Craig et al., *Craig, Park and Paulsson on International Chamber of Commerce Arbitration*, Oxford Univ. Press 4th ed. 2017; Martin Domke, Gabriel Wilner & Larry E. Edmonson, *Domke on Commercial Arbitration*, a hardcopy of the book was last published in 2014 by Thomson Reuters, but the entire book has been updated and made available on Westlaw and includes many useful forms and document samples in the appendices. Herbert Kronke et al. (eds.), *The New York Convention: Recognition and Enforcement of Foreign Arbitral Awards*, Wolters Kluwer 2010; Margaret Moses, *The Principles and Practice of International Commercial Arbitration*, Cambridge Univ. Press 3rd ed. 2017; Sundra Rajoo, *Law, Practice and Procedure of Arbitration*, Lexis/Nexis 2nd ed. 2017; Thomas Schultz & Federico Ortino (eds.), *The Oxford Handbook of International Arbitration*, Oxford Univ. Press 2020; S.I. Strong, *Research and Practice in International Commercial Arbitration*, Oxford Univ. Press 2009; Tibor Várady, John J. Barceló & Arthur T. von Mehren, *International Commercial Arbitration—A Transnational Perspective*, Westlaw 7th ed. 2018; Stephen Ware & Ariana Levinson, *Principles of Arbitration Law*, West Academic 2017; Frank-Bernd Weigand, *Practitioner's Handbook on International Commercial Arbitration*, Oxford Univ. Press, Oxford Univ. Press 3rd ed. 2019; Maureen Weston et al., *Arbitration—Law, Policy, and Practice*, Carolina Academic Press 2019.

The short answer—and a very sad answer indeed, given the huge amount of time and money that is spent around the world to educate our lawyers and judges and set up our courts—is that of about 200 countries in the world, based on many years of practical experience, the author would not recommend to clients to litigate in about 180 of them. In other words, about 90% of all national court systems in the world are not recommended for parties seeking timely, fair, cost-efficient, and enforceable solutions to their disputes. The problems vary from one country to another. Sometimes they are related primarily to the judges themselves, sometimes the problems are related primarily to the legal system and the general administration of justice.[194] Of course, generalizations are always dangerous and I do not want to be misunderstood. I am not saying that there are no judges in the countries of Central and Latin America, Africa, Asia, or Southern, Central and Eastern Europe that are competent, honest, and trustworthy. In some countries, problems are systemic and affect all procedures, for example the enormous delays in Italian or Indian courts.[195] In other countries—for example, China and Russia—problems are more random, such as when it becomes a question of hit and miss whether one gets a fair-minded, competent, and incorruptible judge, and/or whether the authorities will allow for rule of law or seek to influence the outcome of a case behind closed doors. Reliance on luck, however, should not be part of a well-designed dispute settlement strategy.

In contrast to dispute settlement via litigation in public courts in front of randomly selected judges, and subject to general laws and procedures, arbitration provides for dispute settlement in private tribunals, in front of specifically selected arbitrators, and subject to the rules and procedures chosen by the parties. And while judges are often underpaid, overworked, and have little incentive to take on extra cases or make extra efforts merely because a case raises complicated and/or international issues, arbitrators are engaged ad hoc and are very much interested in building a reputation of being qualified, impartial, efficient, and responsive to justified needs and interests of the parties. The confidentiality of arbitration proceedings is another benefit appreciated by many businesspeople.[196] The most important aspect of arbitration versus litigation, however, is often the length of the proceedings. In general, arbitration is a single-step procedure and does not provide for appeals. Typical business disputes will usually be settled in five to ten months. Rarely does an arbitration take longer than a year and a half. By contrast, litigation will often take a year or more and, if there is an appeal, a final result may easily take five to ten years to obtain. Finally, arbitral awards will be recognized and enforced in more than

---

194. See p. 707, note 19 above.

195. See Tushar Kumar Biswas, *Introduction to Arbitration in India: The Role of the Judiciary*, Wolters Kluwer 2014.

196. See Kyriaki Noussia, *Confidentiality in International Commercial Arbitration: A Comparative Analysis of the Position Under English, US, German and French Law*, Springer 2014; Elza Reymond-Eniaeva, *Towards a Uniform Approach to Confidentiality of International Commercial Arbitration*, Springer 2019; Ileana M. Smeareanu, *Confidentiality in International Commercial Arbitration*, Wolters Kluwer 2011.

160 countries on the basis of the 1958 New York Convention, whereas no similar convention exists for the mutual recognition and enforcement of court decisions.

Certain limitations are warranted for arbitration, however. First, while arbitration is often the best form of dispute settlement involving companies of comparable levels of expertise and bargaining power, it is far less suitable for disputes between vastly disparate parties. This is particularly noticeable in business-to-consumer transactions, so-called B2C contracts. In contrast to judges, who are paid by the government and do not benefit from additional cases being brought, arbitrators are free-lance and are paid only when they are selected to hear and decide a case. This creates an imbalance if, for example, General Motors ends up in a dispute with a buyer of one of its cars. For the arbitrator, the consumer will almost certainly be a one-time customer, while GM could become a profitable revenue stream if it selects the same arbitrator repeatedly for similar cases. The conflict of interest for the arbitrator and resulting difficulty of deciding the case objectively should be obvious. This is why many countries, in particular in Europe, do not allow arbitration clauses to be added to B2C contracts.[197]

Second, arbitration is not a good tool for settling relatively minor claims. In such cases, the court fees would be minor as well and the procedure would be effectively subsidized by the government. However, no such subsidization takes place in arbitration and the fees can easily become prohibitive. This is compounded by the fact that arbitration for the most part does not know and is not able to accommodate class action suits to aggregate many relatively small claims against a single defendant resulting from similar or identical problems.[198]

In recent years, a number of American companies, including many of the larger banks, have started to include arbitration clauses in the contracts with their private customers. As *The New York Times* reported on May 5, 2016, this resulted in, *inter alia*, only a tiny fraction of disputes valued at $2,500 or less going to arbitration and the vast majority of millions of claims about questionable fees and overcharges and the like were abandoned by the customers, including many where efforts to build

---

197. However, the EU has also created an Online Dispute Resolution (ODR) Platform specifically for B2C contracts formed online, which addresses these and other concerns and may well be the model to be considered also in the United States and other countries. For more information see below, Section 7.

Being aware of the issue, the Chartered Institute of Arbitrators has developed *Guidelines for Arbitrators Dealing with Cases Involving Consumers and Parties with Significant Differences of Resources*, see http://www.ciarb.org/docs/default-source/ciarbdocuments/international-arbitration -guidelines-2011/2011significantdifferencesofresources.pdf?sfvrsn=6.

198. This issue is discussed in detail in S.I. Strong, *Class, Mass, and Collective Arbitration in National and International Law*, Oxford Univ. Press 2013. See also S.I. Strong, *Class and Collective Relief in the Cross-Border Context: A Possible Role for the Permanent Court of Arbitration*, Hague Yearbook of Int'l Law 2010, pp. 113–140.

It is noteworthy in this context that Judicial Arbitration and Mediation Services (JAMS), the single largest provider of ADR services in the world, has introduced a set of rules intended for class action arbitration; see www.jamsadr.com/rules-class-action-procedures/.

a class action case were blocked on the basis of the arbitration clauses (pp. A1 and B3). To counter this trend, the Consumer Financial Protection Bureau has proposed a prohibition of arbitration clauses in B2C contracts for the financial companies subject to the Bureau's regulations. Even if adopted, however, this would not affect any such clauses in contracts by cell phone or car rental companies, etc., let alone individual employment contracts.

For our purposes, we will limit the analysis to the cases where arbitration is voluntarily agreed to in contracts between businesses that generally understand what they are doing and are able to negotiate their deals on a level playing field. Even in such contexts, however, it is usually not worthwhile to actually go to arbitration for claims much lower than $50,000 with a single arbitrator, or about $150,000 with a panel of three arbitrators.[199] Such relatively small cases should be settled amicably, allowing the parties to return to doing business together and thus recovering the shared losses from the earlier dispute. That being said, some arbitration service providers have recently introduced procedures and other measures to provide their services also in cases where only relatively small amounts of money are at stake.[200]

Case 6-9

Filanto, S.p.A. v. Chilewich International Corp.

789 F. Supp. 1229 (S.D.N.Y. 1992)
(Paragraph numbers added, footnotes and some details omitted.)
Charles L. Brieant, Chief Judge (starting on p. 1230):

[1] By motion fully submitted on December 11, 1991, defendant Chilewich International Corp. moves to stay this action pending arbitration in Moscow. Plaintiff Filanto has moved to enjoin arbitration or to order arbitration in this federal district.

[2] This case is a striking example of how a lawsuit involving a relatively straightforward international commercial transaction can raise an array of complex questions. Accordingly, the Court will recount the factual background of the case, derived from both parties, memoranda of law and supporting affidavits in some detail.

---

199. As part of its efforts to contain arbitration costs and make arbitration accessible for smaller claims, the International Chamber of Commerce (ICC) has created an expedited procedure aimed at resolving cases in a timeframe of about six months. This procedure is automatically applied for smaller claims—unless deemed inappropriate for a particular case. The threshold below which a claim is small for the ICC has been set at US$2 million, see Art. 30 ICC Rules with Art. 1(2) of Appendix VI to the ICC Rules.

200. For example, JAMS provides a consumer arbitration procedure where the filing fee for the consumer is only US$250 and all other procedural costs have to be borne by the company using the arbitration clause in its consumer contracts; see www.jamsadr.com/consumer-minimum -standards/. For smart contracts secured via the Blockchain, the International Smart Mediation and Arbitration Institute (SmartArb) in Indianapolis offers some low-cost ADR options, see www .SmartArb.org.

[3] Plaintiff Filanto is an Italian corporation engaged in the manufacture and sale of footwear. Defendant Chilewich is an export-import firm incorporated in the state of New York with its principal place of business in White Plains. On February 28, 1989, Chilewich's agent in the United Kingdom, Byerly Johnson, Ltd., signed a contract with Raznoexport, the Soviet Foreign Economic Association, which obligated Byerly Johnson to supply footwear to Raznoexport. Section 10 of this contract—the "Russian Contract"—is an arbitration clause, which reads in pertinent part as follows:

> "All disputes or differences which may arise out of or in connection with the present Contract are to be settled, jurisdiction of ordinary courts being excluded, by the Arbitration at the USSR Chamber of Commerce and Industry, Moscow, in accordance with the Regulations of the said Arbitration." [sic] . . .

> This contract was signed by Byerly Johnson and by Raznoexport, and is sometimes referred to as "Contract No. 32-03/93085".

[4] The first exchange of correspondence between the parties to this lawsuit is a letter dated July 27, 1989 from Mr. Melvin Chilewich of Chilewich International to Mr. Antonio Filograna, chief executive officer of Filanto. This letter refers to a recent visit by Chilewich and Byerly Johnson personnel to Filanto's factories in Italy, presumably to negotiate a purchase to fulfill the Russian Contract, and then states as follows:

> "Attached please find our contract to cover our purchase from you. Same is governed by the conditions which are enumerated in the standard contract in effect with the Soviet buyers [the Russian contract], copy of which is also enclosed." . . .

[5] The next item in the record is a letter from Filanto to Chilewich dated September 2, 1989. This letter refers to a letter from Chilewich to Filanto of August 11, 1989, which "you [Chilewich] sent me with the contracts n 10001-10002-10003." These numbers do not correspond to the contract sued on here, but refer instead to other, similar contracts between the parties. None of these contracts, or their terms, are in the record, both parties having been afforded ample opportunity to submit whatever they wished.

[6] The last paragraph of the September 2, 1989 letter from Filanto to Chilewich states as follows:

> "Returning back the enclosed contracts n 10001-10002-10003 signed for acceptance, we communicate, if we do not misunderstood, the Soviet's contract that you sent us together with your above mentioned contract, that of this contract we have to respect only the following points of it:
>
> — n 5 Packing and marking
>
> — n 6 Way of Shipment
>
> — n 7 Delivery—Acceptance of Goods
>
> We ask for your acceptance by return of post." [sic] . . .

[7] The intent of this paragraph, clearly, was to exclude from incorporation by reference *inter alia* section 10 of the Russian contract, which provides for arbitration. Chilewich, for its part, claims never to have received this September 2 letter. In any event, it relates only to prior course of conduct.

[8] It is apparent from the record that further negotiations occurred in early 1990, but the content of those negotiations is unclear; it is, however, clear that deliveries of boots from Filanto to Chilewich were occurring at this time, pursuant to other contracts, since there is a reference to a shipment occurring between April 23, 1990 and June 11, 1990.

[9] The next document in this case, and the focal point of the parties' dispute regarding whether an arbitration agreement exists, is a Memorandum Agreement dated March 13, 1990. This Memorandum Agreement, number 9003002, is a standard merchant's memo prepared by Chilewich for signature by both parties confirming that Filanto will deliver 100,000 pairs of boots to Chilewich at the Italian/Yugoslav border on September 15, 1990, with the balance of 150,000 pairs to be delivered on November 1, 1990. Chilewich's obligations were to open a Letter of Credit in Filanto's favor prior to the September 15 delivery, and another letter prior to the November delivery. This Memorandum includes the following provision:

> "It is understood between Buyer and Seller that USSR Contract No. 32-03/ 93085 [the Russian Contract] is hereby incorporated in this contract as far as practicable, and specifically that any arbitration shall be in accordance with that Contract." . . .

[10] Chilewich signed this Memorandum Agreement, and sent it to Filanto. Filanto at that time did not sign or return the document. Nevertheless, on May 7, 1990, Chilewich opened a Letter of Credit in Filanto's favor in the sum of $2,595,600.00. The Letter of Credit itself mentions the Russian Contract, but only insofar as concerns packing and labeling. . . .

[11] Again, on July 23, 1990, Filanto sent another letter to Chilewich, which reads in relevant parts as follows:

> "We refer to Point 3, Special Conditions, to point out that: returning back the above-mentioned contract, signed for acceptance, from Soviet Contract 32-03/93085 we have to respect only the following points of it:
>
> — No. 5—Packing and Marking
>
> — No. 6—Way of Shipment
>
> — No. 7—Delivery Acceptance of Goods".

It should be noted that the contract referred to in this letter is apparently another contract between the parties, as the letter refers to "Sub. Contract No. 32-03/03122", while the contract sued on in the present action is No. 32-03/03123.

[12] This letter caused some concern on the part of Chilewich and its agents: a July 30, 1990 fax from Byerly Johnson, Chilewich's agent, to Chilewich, mentions Filanto's July 23 letter, asserts that it "very neatly dodges" certain issues, other than arbitration, covered by the Russian Contract, and states that Johnson would "take it up" with Filanto during a visit to Filanto's offices the next week. . . .

[13] Then, on August 7, 1990, Filanto returned the Memorandum Agreement, sued on here, that Chilewich had signed and sent to it in March; though Filanto had signed the Memorandum Agreement, it once again appended a covering letter, purporting to exclude all but three sections of the Russian Contract. . . .

[14] There is also in the record an August 7, 1990 telex from Chilewich to Byerly Johnson, stating that Chilewich would not open the second Letter of Credit unless it received from Filanto a signed copy of the contract without any exclusions. In order to resolve this issue, Byerly Johnson on August 29, 1990 sent a fax to Italian Trading SRL, an intermediary, reading in relevant part:

> "We have checked back through our records for last year, and can find no exclusions by Filanto from the Soviet Master Contract and, in the event, we do not believe that this has caused any difficulties between us.

> We would, therefore, ask you to amend your letters of the 23rd July 1990 and the 7th August 1990, so that you accept all points of the Soviet Master Contract No. 32-03/93085 as far as practicable. You will note that this is specified in our Special Condition No. 3 of our contracts Nos. 9003001 and 9003 [illegible]". . . .

Filanto later confirmed to Italian Trading that it received this fax.

[15] As the date specified in the Memorandum Agreement for delivery of the first shipment of boots—September 15, 1990—was approaching, the parties evidently decided to make further efforts to resolve this issue: what actually happened, though, is a matter of some dispute. Mr. Filograna, the CEO of Filanto, asserts that the following occurred:

> "Moreover, when I was in Moscow from September 2 through September 5, 1990, to inspect Soviet factories on an unrelated business matter, I met with Simon Chilewich. Simon Chilewich, then and there, abandoned his request of August 29, 1990, and agreed with me that the Filanto-Chilewich Contract would incorporate only the packing, shipment and delivery terms of the Anglo-Soviet Contract. Also present at this meeting were Sergio Squilloni of Italian Trading (Chilewich's agent), Kathy Farley, and Max Flaxman of Chilewich and Antonio Sergio of Filanto". . . .

[16] Mr. Simon Chilewich, in his sworn affidavit, does not refer to this incident, but does state the following:

> "In fact, subsequent to the communications and correspondence described above, I met with Mr. Filograna face to face in Paris during the weekend

of September 14, 1990. During that meeting, I expressly stated to him that we would have no deal if Filanto now insisted on deleting provisions of the Russian Contract from our agreement. Mr. Filograna, on behalf of Filanto, stated that he would accede to our position, in order to keep Chilewich's business". . . .

[17] Plaintiff does not address or deny defendant's version of the Paris meeting. Filanto's Complaint in this action alleges that it delivered the first shipment of boots on September 15, and drew down on the Letter of Credit. . . .

[18] On September 27, 1990, Mr. Filograna faxed a letter to Chilewich. This letter refers to "assurances during our meeting in Paris", and complains that Chilewich had not yet opened the second Letter of Credit for the second delivery, which it had supposedly promised to do by September 25. Mr. Chilewich responded by fax on the same day; his fax states that he is "totally cognizant of the contractual obligations which exist", but goes on to say that Chilewich had encountered difficulties with the Russian buyers, that Chilewich needed to "reduce the rate of shipments", and denies that Chilewich promised to open the Letter of Credit by September 25. . . .

[19] According to the Complaint, what ultimately happened was that Chilewich bought and paid for 60,000 pairs of boots in January 1991, but never purchased the 90,000 pairs of boots that comprise the balance of Chilewich's original order. It is Chilewich's failure to do so that forms the basis of this lawsuit, commenced by Filanto on May 14, 1991.

[20] There is in the record, however, one document that post-dates the filing of the Complaint: a letter from Filanto to Chilewich dated June 21, 1991. This letter is in response to claims by Byerly Johnson that some of the boots that had been supplied by Filanto were defective. The letter expressly relies on a section of the Russian contract which Filanto had earlier purported to exclude — Section 9 regarding claims procedures — and states that "The April Shipment and the September Shipment are governed by the Master Purchase Contract of February 28, 1989, n 32-03/93085 (the "Master Purchase Contract")." . . .

[21] This letter must be regarded as an admission in law by Filanto, the party to be charged. A litigant may not blow hot and cold in a lawsuit. The letter of June 21, 1991 clearly shows that when Filanto thought it desirable to do so, it recognized that it was bound by the incorporation by reference of portions of the Russian Contract, which, prior to the Paris meeting, it had purported to exclude. This letter shows that Filanto regarded itself as the beneficiary of the claims adjustment provisions of the Russian Contract. This legal position is entirely inconsistent with the position which Filanto had professed prior to the Paris meeting, and is inconsistent with its present position. Consistent with the position of the defendant in this action, Filanto admits that the other relevant clauses of the Russian Contract were incorporated by agreement of the parties, and made a part of the bargain. Of necessity, this must include the agreement to arbitrate in Moscow. In the June 21, 1991 letter, Mr. Filograna writes:

"The April Shipment and the September Shipment are governed by the Master Purchase Contract of February 28, 1989 N. 32-03-93085 (the 'Master Purchase Contract') The Master Purchase Contract provides that claims for inferior quality must be made within six months of the arrival of the goods at the USSR port". . . .

[22] Against this background based almost entirely on documents, defendant Chilewich on July 24, 1991 moved to stay this action pending arbitration, while plaintiff Filanto on August 22, 1992 moved to enjoin arbitration, or, alternatively, for an order directing that arbitration be held in the Southern District of New York rather than Moscow, because of unsettled political conditions in Russia.

Jurisdiction/Applicable Law

[23] Plaintiff bases subject matter jurisdiction in this action on diversity of citizenship, as Filanto is an Italian corporation with its principal place of business in Italy, while Chilewich is a New York corporation with its principal place of business in New York, thereby invoking New York law and choice of law rules, under *Erie R. Co. v. Tompkins*, 304 U.S. 64 . . . (1938).

[24] This Court, however, finds another overriding basis for subject matter jurisdiction which will affect our choice of law: chapter 2 of the Federal Arbitration Act, which comprises the Convention on the Recognition and Enforcement of Foreign Arbitral Awards and its implementing legislation, *codified at* 9 U.S.C. § 201 *et seq.* . . . . The United States, Italy and the USSR are all signatories to this Convention, and its implementing legislation makes clear that the Arbitration Convention governs disputes regarding arbitration agreements between parties to international commercial transactions:

"An arbitration agreement or arbitral award arising out of a legal relationship, whether contractual or not, which is considered as commercial, including a transaction, contract, or agreement described in section 2 of this title, falls under the Convention. An agreement or award arising out of such a relationship which is entirely between citizens of the United States should be deemed not to fall under the Convention . . ." 9 U.S.C. § 202 . . . .

[25] The Arbitration Convention specifically requires courts to recognize any "agreement in writing under which the parties undertake to submit to arbitration . . ." Convention on the Recognition and Enforcement of Foreign Arbitral Awards Article II(1). The term "agreement in writing" is defined as "an arbitral clause in a contract or an arbitration agreement, signed by the parties or contained in an exchange of letters or telegrams". Convention on the Recognition and Enforcement of Foreign Arbitral Awards Article II(2).

[26] The Convention's implementing legislation also provides an independent basis of subject matter jurisdiction:

"An action or proceeding falling under the Convention shall be deemed to arise under the laws and treaties of the United States. The district courts of

> the United States. . . . . shall have original jurisdiction over such an action or proceeding, regardless of the amount in controversy." 9 U.S.C. § 203 . . . .

[27] Thus, although defendant has moved for a stay under Chapter 1 of the Arbitration Act, 9 U.S.C. § 3 (West 1970), this case actually falls under Chapter 2 of that title—the Convention and its implementing legislation.

[28] This independent jurisdictional basis is of some importance to this litigation. On a motion pursuant to the Arbitration Act, federal law governs issues relating to the arbitrability of a dispute. *Moses H. Cone Hospital v. Mercury Construction Corp.,* 460 U.S. 1, 24 . . . (1983) (Act "creates a body of federal substantive law of arbitrability, applicable to any arbitration agreement within the coverage of the Act"); *Prima Paint v. Flood & Conklin Mfg. Co.,* 388 U.S. 395, 404–05 . . . (1967) (application of federal arbitration law in diversity case permissible notwithstanding *Erie* since Arbitration Act was enacted pursuant to Congressional commerce power); *McPheeters v. McGinn, Smith & Co.,* 953 F.2d 771, 772 (2d Cir. 1992) ("Federal law . . . governs the current dispute as to the scope of the agreement") (citation omitted); *Genesco, Inc. v. T. Kakiuchi Co., Ltd.,* 815 F.2d 840, 845 (2d Cir. 1987) (same); *Coenen v. R.W. Pressprich & Co.,* 453 F.2d 1209, 1211 (2d Cir.) ("Once a dispute is covered by the Act, federal law applies to all questions of interpretation, construction, validity, revocability and enforceability"), cert. denied, 406 U.S. 949 . . . (1972).

[29] However, the focus of this dispute, apparent from the parties' submissions, is not on the scope of the arbitration provision included in the Russian contract; rather, the threshold question is whether these parties actually agreed to arbitrate their disputes at all. In such a situation, where the issue is whether there is any arbitration agreement between the parties, there is authority for the proposition that state, rather than federal law, should be applied. *Recold, S.A. de C.V. v. Monfort of Colorado, Inc.,* 893 F.2d 195, 197 n.6 (8th Cir. 1990) ("In addressing the issue of whether a party has entered into an agreement to arbitrate under the Arbitration Act, courts are to apply general state law principles . . .") (citation omitted); *Supak & Sons Mfg. Co., Inc. v. Pervel Industries, Inc.,* 593 F.2d 135, 137 (4th Cir. 1979) ("Section 2 [of the Act] dictates the effect of a contractually-agreed upon arbitration provision, but it does not displace state law on the general principles governing formation of the contract itself"); *Astor Chocolate Corp. v. Mikroverk, Ltd.,* 704 F. Supp. 30, 33 (E.D.N.Y. 1989) ("While federal law governs the issue of the scope of the arbitration clause, state law governs the issue of whether or not the clause is part of the contract"); *Cook Chocolate Co. v. Salomon, Inc.,* 684 F. Supp. 1177, 1182 (S.D.N.Y. 1988) ("At the same time, however, § 2 of the Act preserves general principles of state contract law as rules of decision on whether the parties have entered into an agreement to arbitrate"); *Duplan Corp. v. W.B. Davis Hosiery Mills, Inc.,* 442 F. Supp. 86, 87–88 (S.D.N.Y. 1977) (Congress in passing Arbitration Act did not intend "to create a federal law of contract formation"). Indeed, the Supreme Court has recently indicated that this analysis is correct, at least with respect to cases controlled by chapter 1 of the Arbitration Act:

"Thus, state law, whether of legislative or judicial origin, is applicable if that law arose to govern issues concerning the validity, revocability, and enforceability of contracts generally". *Perry v. Thomas,* 482 U.S. 483, 492 . . . (1987) (emphasis in original). See also *Volt Information Sciences v. Leland Stanford, Jr. University,* 489 U.S. 468, 475 . . . (1989) (same).

[30] Plaintiff at one point did contend that state law applied, for an understandable reason: New York law arguably imposes a heavier burden on a party seeking to compel arbitration than does its federal counterpart. Compare *Schubtex, Inc. v. Allen Snyder, Inc.,* 49 N.Y.2d 1 . . . (1979) (retention without objection by buyer of seller's printed forms containing arbitration clause insufficient basis to compel buyer to arbitrate) and *Matter of Marlene Industries Corp.,* 45 N.Y.2d 327, 333 . . . (1978) (parties "will not be held to have chosen arbitration as the forum for the resolution of their disputes in the absence of an express, unequivocal agreement to that effect") with *Pervel Industries, Inc. v. TM Wallcovering Inc.,* 675 F. Supp. 867, 869–70 (S.D.N.Y. 1987) (agreement to arbitrate may be inferred from parties' course of dealing), aff'd, 871 F.2d 7 (2d Cir. 1989). There is, however, some authority in this Circuit that federal law applies to contract formation issues when the existence of an agreement to arbitrate is in issue. *David L. Threlkeld & Co. v. Metallgesellschaft Ltd.,* 923 F.2d 245, 249 (2d Cir.) (applying federal law of contracts to dispute regarding existence of agreement to arbitrate), cert. dismissed, 112 S. Ct. 17, 115 L. Ed. 2d 1094 (1991); *Genesco, supra,* at 845 ("Hence whether Genesco is bound by the arbitration clause of the sales confirmation forms is determined under federal law, which comprises generally accepted principles of contract law") (footnote omitted); *Fisser v. International Bank,* 282 F.2d at 231, 233 (2d Cir. 1960) (same); *In re Midland Bright Drawn Steel Ltd.,* 1989 Westlaw 125788, 1989 U.S. Dist. Lexis 12368 (S.D.N.Y. 1989) (applying federal law to contract formation issue in case governed by Arbitration Convention). See also *Matter of Ferrara, S.p.A.,* 441 F. Supp. 778, 780–81 (S.D.N.Y. 1977), aff'd without opinion, 580 F.2d 1044 (2d Cir. 1978). Cf. *Fahnestock & Co., Inc. v. Waltman,* 935 F.2d 512, 517–19 (2d Cir.) (upholding under state law vacatur of punitive damages element of arbitrator's award), cert. denied, 116 L. Ed. 2d 331, 112 S. Ct. 380 (1991).

[31] This Court concludes that the question of whether these parties agreed to arbitrate their disputes is governed by the Arbitration Convention and its implementing legislation. That Convention, as a treaty, is the supreme law of the land, U.S. Const. art. VI cl. 2, and controls *any* case in any American court falling within its sphere of application. Thus, any dispute involving international commercial arbitration which meets the Convention's jurisdictional requirements, whether brought in state or federal court, must be resolved with reference to that instrument. See *Black & Pola v. The Manes Organization, Inc.,* 72 A.D.2d 514, 421 N.Y.S.2d 6 (1st Dep't 1979) (federal law determines whether parties have agreed to arbitrate if underlying dispute involves interstate commerce), aff'd, 50 N.Y.2d 821, 407 N.E.2d 1345, 430 N.Y.S.2d 49 (1980). See also *Threlkeld, supra, at* 250 (holding Convention and Arbitration Act preempt Vermont statute requiring *inter alia* that arbitration agreement be signed

by both parties). *But see McDermott International v. Lloyds Underwriters of London, 944 F.2d 1199, 1210–11* (5th Cir.) (noting conflicting authorities on whether state courts must apply Arbitration Act and stating that "state courts do not necessarily have to stay litigation or compel arbitration under the Convention either"), *reh'g en banc denied*, 947 F.2d 1489 (5th Cir. 1991). This Court believes that the Fifth Circuit is clearly wrong on this in light of Article VI of the Constitution, not therein mentioned; the Second Circuit also apparently disagrees with that court's conclusion. *Corcoran v. Ardra Insurance Co., Ltd.*, 842 F.2d 31, 35 (2d Cir. 1988).

[32] Accordingly, the Court will apply federal law to the issue of whether an "agreement in writing" to arbitrate disputes exists between these parties.

[33] Courts confronted by cases governed by the Arbitration Convention must conduct a limited, four-part inquiry:

> 1) Is there an agreement in writing to arbitrate the subject of the dispute. Convention, Articles II(l), II(2).
>
> 2) Does the agreement provide for arbitration in the territory of a signatory country? Convention, Articles I(1), I(3); 9 U.S.C. § 206; Declaration of the United States Upon Accession, reprinted at 9 U.S.C.A § 201, Note 43 (1990 Supp.)
>
> 3) Does the agreement arise out of a legal relationship, whether contractual or not, which is considered as commercial? Convention, Article I(3); 9 U.S.C. § 202.
>
> 4) Is a party to the contract not an American citizen, or does the commercial relationship have some reasonable relation with one or more foreign states? 9 U.S.C. § 202.
>
> *Ledee v. Ceramiche Ragno*, 684 F.2d 184, 186–87 (1st Cir. 1982); *Sedco v. Petroleos Mexicanos Mexican National Oil Co.*, 767 F.2d 1140, 1145 (5th Cir. 1985); *Tennessee Imports, Inc. v. Filippi*, 745 F. Supp. 1314, 1321 (M.D. Tenn. 1990); *Corcoran v. Ardra Insurance Co.*, Ltd., 657 F. Supp. 1223, 1227 (S.D.N.Y. 1987), aff'd, 842 F.2d 31 (2d Cir. 1988).

In this case, the second, third and fourth criteria are clearly satisfied, as the purported agreement provides for arbitration in Moscow, the Chilewich-Filanto relationship is a "commercial" relationship, and Filanto is an Italian corporation. The central disputed issue, therefore, is whether the correspondence between the parties, viewed in light of their business relationship, constitutes an "agreement in writing".

[34] Courts interpreting this "agreement in writing" requirement have generally started their analysis with the plain language of the Convention, which requires "an arbitral clause in a contract or an arbitration agreement, signed by the parties or contained in an exchange of letters or telegrams", Article I(1), and have then applied that language in light of federal law, which consists of generally accepted principles of contract law, including the Uniform Commercial Code. See, e.g., *Genesco, supra*, at 845–46 (holding under "general contract principles" that buyer agreed to

arbitrate disputes arising under unsigned sales confirmation forms due to parties'
course of dealing and buyer's signatures on related sales confirmation forms); *Sen
Mar, Inc. v. Tiger Petroleum Corp.* 774 F. Supp. 879, 883–84 (S.D.N.Y 1991) (denying
seller's motion to compel arbitration since arbitration clause not in signed writing
or in exchange of letters); *Midland Bright Drawn Steel, supra*, at 3–4 (holding seller
entitled to stay of arbitration since arbitration clause represented material alteration
of contract not accepted by seller); *Beromun Aktiengesellschaft v. Societa Industriale
Agricola, Inc.*, 471 F. Supp. 1163, 1171–72 (S.D.N.Y. 1979) (denying seller's motion
to compel arbitration since no contract ever formed between parties). But see *Astor
Chocolate, supra*, at 33–34 (applying state contract law in case governed by Convention). See also *Zambia Steel & Building Supplies Ltd. v. James Clark & Eaton Ltd.*, 2
Lloyd's Rep. 225 (1986) (United Kingdom) (seller's oral assent to sales note containing arbitration clause sufficient under Convention to compel arbitration).

[35] However, as plaintiff correctly notes, the "general principles of contract law"
relevant to this action, do not include the Uniform Commercial Code; rather, the
"federal law of contracts" to be applied in this case is found in the United Nations
Convention on Contracts for the International Sale of Goods (the "Sale of Goods
Convention"), *codified at* 15 U.S.C. Appendix (West Supp. 1991). This Convention, ratified by the Senate in 1986, is a self-executing agreement which entered
into force between the United States and other signatories, including Italy, on January 1, 1988. *See* Preface to Convention, *reprinted at* 15 U.S.C. Appendix (West Supp.
1991). Although there is as yet virtually no U.S. case law interpreting the Sale of
Goods Convention, see Taylor & Crisera, "U.N. Pact Has Wide Application", Nat.
L. J., Dec. 23, 1991 at 23, it may safely be predicted that this will change: absent
a choice-of-law provision, and with certain exclusions not here relevant, the Convention governs all contracts between parties with places of business in different
nations, so long as both nations are signatories to the Convention. Sale of Goods
Convention Article 1 (1)(a). Since the contract alleged in this case most certainly
was formed, if at all, after January 1, 1988, and since both the United States and
Italy are signatories to the Convention, the Court will interpret the "agreement in
writing" requirement of the Arbitration Convention in light of, and with reference
to, the substantive international law of contracts embodied in the Sale of Goods
Convention.

[36] Not surprisingly, the parties offer varying interpretations of the numerous letters and documents exchanged between them. The Court will briefly summarize
their respective contentions.

[37] Defendant Chilewich contends that the Memorandum Agreement dated March 13
which it signed and sent to Filanto was an offer. It then argues that Filanto's retention
of the letter, along with its subsequent acceptance of Chilewich's performance under
the Agreement—the furnishing of the May 11 letter of credit—estops it from denying its acceptance of the contract. Although phrased as an estoppel argument, this
contention is better viewed as an acceptance by conduct argument, e.g., that in light
of the parties' course of dealing, Filanto had a duty timely to inform Chilewich that

it objected to the incorporation by reference of all the terms of the Russian contract. Under this view, the return of the Memorandum Agreement, signed by Filanto, on August 7, 1990, along with the covering letter purporting to exclude parts of the Russian Contract, was ineffective as a matter of law as a rejection of the March 13 offer, because this occurred some five months after Filanto received the Memorandum Agreement and two months after Chilewich furnished the Letter of Credit. Instead, in Chilewich's view, this action was a proposal for modification of the March 13 Agreement. Chilewich rejected this proposal, by its letter of August 7 to Byerly Johnson, and the August 9 fax by Johnson to Italian Trading SRL, which communication Filanto acknowledges receiving. Accordingly, Filanto under this interpretation is bound by the written terms of the March 13 Memorandum Agreement; since that agreement incorporates by reference the Russian Contract containing the arbitration provision, Filanto is bound to arbitrate.

[38] Plaintiff Filanto's interpretation of the evidence is rather different. While Filanto apparently agrees that the March 13 Memorandum Agreement was indeed an offer, it characterizes its August 7 return of the signed Memorandum Agreement with the covering letter as a counteroffer. While defendant contends that under Uniform Commercial Code § 2-207 this action would be viewed as an acceptance with a proposal for a material modification, the Uniform Commercial Code, as previously noted does not apply to this case, because the State Department undertook to fix something that was not broken by helping to create the Sale of Goods Convention which varies from the Uniform Commercial Code in many significant ways. Instead, under this analysis, Article 19(1) of the Sale of Goods Convention would apply. That section, as the Commentary to the Sale of Goods Convention notes, reverses the rule of Uniform Commercial Code § 2-207, and reverts to the common law rule that "A reply to an offer which purports to be an acceptance but contains additions, limitations or other modifications is a rejection of the offer and constitutes a counter-offer". Sale of Goods Convention Article 19(1). Although the Convention, like the Uniform Commercial Code, does state that non-material terms do become part of the contract unless objected to, Sale of Goods Convention Article 19(2), the Convention treats inclusion (or deletion) of an arbitration provision as "material", Sale of Goods Convention Article 19(3). The August 7 letter, therefore, was a counteroffer which, according to Filanto, Chilewich accepted by its letter dated September 27, 1990. Though that letter refers to and acknowledges the "contractual obligations" between the parties, it is doubtful whether it can be characterized as an acceptance.

[39] More generally, both parties seem to have lost sight of the narrow scope of the inquiry required by the Arbitration Convention. *Ledee, supra,* at 186. All that this Court need do is to determine if a sufficient "agreement in writing" to arbitrate disputes exists between these parties. Cf. *United Steelworkers of America v. Warrior & Gulf Co.,* 363 U.S. 574, 582, 4 L. Ed. 2d 1409, 80 S. Ct. 1347 (1960) (party cannot be required to submit to arbitration absent agreement). Although that inquiry is informed by the

provisions of the Sale of Goods Convention, the Court lacks the authority on this motion to resolve all outstanding issues between the parties. Indeed, contracts and the arbitration clauses included therein are considered to be "severable", a rule that the Sale of Goods Convention itself adopts with respect to avoidance of contracts generally. Sale of Goods Convention Article 81(l). There is therefore authority for the proposition that issues relating to existence of the contract, as opposed to the existence of the arbitration clause, are issues for the arbitrators:

> "The district court reasoned that an arbitrator can derive his or her power only from a contract, so that when there is a challenge to the existence of the contract itself, the court must first decide whether there is a valid contract between the parties. Although this appears logical, it goes beyond the requirements of the statute and violates the clear directive of *Prima Paint*, 388 U.S. at 404, 87 S. Ct. at 1806 . . ." *Republic of Nicaragua v. Standard Fruit Co.*, 937 F.2d 469, 476 n.9 (9th Cir. 1991), cert. denied, 117 L. Ed. 2d 516, 60 U.S.L.W. 3615, 112 S. Ct. 1294 (1992).

[40] The *Standard Fruit* court is technically correct in its interpretation of the *Prima Paint* case, which drew a distinction between a challenge to the validity of the contract itself and a challenge to the validity of the arbitration clause; the former, in the Court's view, was a question for the arbitrators, while the latter was a question for the court. *Prima Paint, supra,* at 404, 87 S.Ct. at 1806.

[41] However, there are often limits to how many angels can dance on the head of a pin—even when the performance is choreographed by the distinguished courts just cited. There seems, for example, to be some confusion in the Ninth Circuit itself about the proper application of the *Prima Paint* rule, as a case decided six months prior to *Standard Fruit* shows. See *Three Valleys Municipal Water District v. E.F. Hutton & Co. Inc.*, 925 F.2d 1136, 1138–42 (9th Cir. 1991) (holding whether contract containing arbitration clause formed initially question for court). There are numerous cases in the Second Circuit where the court has—out of necessity—adjudicated relevant contract issues on motions to stay or compel arbitration. See, e.g., *McPheeters, supra,* at 773 (holding that defendant seeking arbitration not third-party beneficiary of underlying agreement); *Genesco, supra,* at 846 ("We focus not on whether there was subjective agreement as to each clause in the contract, but on whether there was objective agreement with respect to the entire contract") (citation omitted); *Maria Victoria Naviera, S.A. v. Cementos del Valle, S.A.*, 759 F.2d 1027, 1030 (2d Cir. 1985) (holding that contract containing arbitration clause was not modified by later agreement); *Midland Bright Drawn Steel,* 1989 Westlaw 125788 at 2-4, 1989 U.S. Dist. Lexis 12368 at 3 (resolving date when underlying contract formed and holding that contract did not include arbitration clause); *Beromun Aktiengesellschaft, supra,* at 1172 (denying motion to compel arbitration since "no contract ever existed between parties").

[42] Since the issue of whether and how a contract between these parties was formed is obviously related to the issue of whether Chilewich breached any contractual

obligations, the Court will direct its analysis to whether there was objective conduct evidencing an intent to be bound with respect to the arbitration provision. Cf. *Matterhorn v. NCR Corp.*, 763 F.2d 866, 871–73 (7th Cir. 1985) (Posner, J.) (discussing cases). See also *Teledyne, Inc. v. Kone Corp.*, 892 F.2d 1404, 1410 (9th Cir. 1990) (arbitration clause enforceable despite later finding by arbitrator that contract itself invalid).

[43] The Court is satisfied on this record that there *was* indeed an agreement to arbitrate between these parties.

[44] There is simply no satisfactory explanation as to why Filanto failed to object to the incorporation by reference of the Russian Contract in a timely fashion. As noted above, Chilewich had in the meantime commenced its performance under the Agreement, and the Letter of Credit it furnished Filanto on May 11 itself mentioned the Russian Contract. An offeree who, knowing that the offeror has commenced performance, fails to notify the offeror of its objection to the terms of the contract within a reasonable time will, under certain circumstances, be deemed to have assented to those terms. Restatement (Second) of Contracts § 69 (1981); *Graniteville v. Star Knits of California, Inc.*, 680 F. Supp. 587, 589–90 (S.D.N.Y. 1988) (compelling arbitration since party who failed timely to object to salesnote containing arbitration clause deemed to have accepted its terms); *Imptex International Corp. v. Lorprint, Inc.*, 625 F. Supp. 1572, 1572 (S.D.N.Y. 1986) (Weinfeld, J.) (party who failed to object to inclusion of arbitration clause in sales confirmation agreement bound to arbitrate). The Sale of Goods Convention itself recognizes this rule: Article 18(1), provides that "A statement made by or other conduct of the offeree indicating assent to an offer is an acceptance". Although mere "silence or inactivity" does not constitute acceptance, Sale of Goods Convention Article 18(1), the Court may consider previous relations between the parties in assessing whether a party's conduct constituted acceptance, Sale of Goods Convention Article 8(3). In this case, in light of the extensive course of prior dealing between these parties, Filanto was certainly under a duty to alert Chilewich in timely fashion to its objections to the terms of the March 13 Memorandum Agreement—particularly since Chilewich had repeatedly referred it to the Russian Contract and Filanto had had a copy of that document for some time.

[45] There are three other convincing manifestations of Filanto's true understanding of the terms of this agreement. First, Filanto's Complaint in this action, as well as affidavits subsequently submitted to the Court by Mr. Filograna, refer to the March 13 contract: the Complaint, for example, states that "On or about March 13, 1990, Filanto entered into a contract with Chilewich . . .". These statements clearly belie Filanto's post hoc assertion that the contract was actually formed at some point after that date. Indeed, Filanto finds itself in an awkward position: it has sued on a contract whose terms it must now question, in light of the defendant's assertion that the contract contains an arbitration provision. This situation is hardly unknown in the context of arbitration agreements. See *Tepper Realty Co. v. Mosaic Tile Co.*,

259 F. Supp. 688, 692 (S.D.N.Y. 1966) ("In short, the plaintiffs cannot have it both ways. They cannot relay [sic] on the contract, when it works to their advantage, and repudiate it when it works to their disadvantage").

[46] Second, Filanto *did* sign the March 13 Memorandum Agreement. That Agreement, as noted above, specifically referred to the incorporation by reference of the arbitration provision in the Russian Contract; although Filanto, in its August 7 letter, did purport to "have to respect" only a small part of the Russian Contract, Filanto in that very letter noted that it was returning the March 13 Memorandum Agreement *"signed for acceptance"*. . . . In light of Filanto's knowledge that Chilewich had already performed its part of the bargain by furnishing it the Letter of Credit, Filanto's characterization of this action as a rejection and a counteroffer is almost frivolous.

[47] Third, and most important, Filanto, in a letter to Byerly Johnson dated June 21, 1991, explicitly stated that "the April Shipment and the September shipment are governed by the Master Purchase Contract of February 28, 1989 [the Russian Contract]". Furthermore, the letter, which responds to claims by Johnson that some of the boots that were supplied were defective, expressly relies on section 9 of the Russian Contract — another section which Filanto had in its earlier correspondence purported to exclude. The Sale of Goods Convention specifically directs that "[i]n determining the intent of a party . . . due consideration is to be given to . . . any subsequent conduct of the parties", Sale of Goods Convention Article 8(3). In this case, as the letter post-dates the partial performance of the contract, it is particularly strong evidence that Filanto recognized itself to be bound by all the terms of the Russian Contract.

[48] In light of these factors, and heeding the presumption in favor of arbitration, *Moses H. Cone, supra,* at 24–26, which is even stronger in the context of international commercial transactions, *Mitsubishi Motors Corp. v. Soler Chrysler-Plymouth, Inc.,* 473 U.S. 614, 631 . . . (1985), the Court holds that Filanto is bound by the terms of the March 13 Memorandum Agreement, and so must arbitrate its dispute in Moscow.

Remedy

[49] Having determined that the parties should arbitrate their disputes in accordance with their agreement, the Court must address the question of remedy. As this action is governed by the Convention and its implementing legislation, the Court has specific authority to order the parties to proceed to arbitration in Moscow. 9 U.S.C. §206 (West Supp. 1991) ("A Court having jurisdiction under this Chapter may direct that arbitration be held in accordance with the agreement at any place therein provided for, whether the place is within or without the United States"). Defendant has not sought this remedy, since it would likewise be the defendant in the arbitration. However, it would be clearly inequitable to permit the party contending that there is an arbitration agreement to avoid arbitration. In the interests of justice, the Court will compel the parties to arbitrate in Moscow. Cf. *Tennessee*

Imports, supra, at 1322 n.4 (treating defendant's motion to dismiss as request to refer parties to arbitration). . . .

[54] Lastly, the plaintiff contends that if this Court does order arbitration, the Court should take judicial notice of the unsettled conditions in Moscow and order arbitration to proceed in this judicial district. The language of section 206 is concededly permissive: the Court "may direct that arbitration be held in accordance with the agreement at any place therein provided for". *9 U.S.C. § 206* (West Supp. 1991). These parties, though, did agree to arbitrate their disputes in Moscow. Compare *Oil Basins Ltd. v. Broken Hill Proprietary Co., Ltd.,* 613 F. Supp. 483, 486–87 (S.D.N.Y 1985) (section 206 furnishes sole authority for court to order arbitration outside its judicial district) with *Bauhinia Corp. v. China National Machinery & Equipment Import & Export Corp.,* 819 F.2d 247 (9th Cir. 1987) (ordering arbitration before American Arbitration Association when parties' agreements ambiguous as to arbitration site).

[55] Plaintiff relies on cases which have stated or held that forum-selection clauses may be invalidated when the chosen forum has become seriously inconvenient or dangerous. *The Bremen v. Zapata Off-Shore Co.,* 407 U.S. 1, 16 . . . (1972) (noting that invalidation of forum-selection clause appropriate when chosen forum "seriously inconvenient") (emphasis in original); *Rockwell International Systems, Inc. v. Citibank, N.A.,* 719 F.2d 583, 587–88 (2d Cir. 1983) (no adequate remedy in courts of post-revolutionary Iran). Whatever the applicability of these cases in the arbitration context, the chosen forum in this case does have a reasonable relation to the contract at issue, as the ultimate purchaser of the boots was a Russian concern and the Russian Contract was incorporated by reference into Filanto's Memorandum Agreement with Chilewich. Furthermore, though conditions in the Republic of Russia are unsettled, they continue to improve and there is no reason to believe that the Chamber of Commerce in Moscow cannot provide fair and impartial justice to these litigants. . . .

SO ORDERED.

Notes and Questions

1. This is a classic case where buyer and seller conducted extensive negotiations, sent many communications and contract drafts and clauses back and forth, and never arrived at one written, signed, and mutually accepted contract with clear and comprehensive terms. However, since neither side wanted to miss out on the business opportunity, they proceeded to implement their "agreement." As is so often the case in these scenarios, once a dispute arose between the parties, instead of proceeding immediately to an efficient and enforceable resolution method, the parties conducted a first round of litigation simply over the question of the applicable law and the appropriate forum for the dispute settlement. It should be easy to see how inefficient this is and, in extreme cases, can be detrimental to legitimate claims of one or both sides.

2. The main problem in *Filanto v. Chilewich* is whether a contract of sale was concluded that incorporated terms of "the Russian Contract." Under Article 19(3) CISG, if an acceptance provides for a different form of dispute settlement (arbitration versus litigation, in our example), it would be considered a rejection and a counteroffer and a contract would not yet be concluded. This can raise a tricky question: If the contract was concluded, it comes with a valid arbitration clause and any disputes, including questions of contract formation, would be determined by an arbitration tribunal. However, if the contract was not validly concluded, there is also no valid arbitration clause and any disputes, including questions of contract formation, would be determined in court. Does this mean that we will almost certainly get different outcomes if the first party to initiate dispute settlement proceedings chooses arbitration over litigation or vice versa? And does it mean that we are likely to see conflicting outcomes if one party initiates litigation while the other party initiates arbitration?

In effect, the District Court applies the CISG to the sales contract and U.S. contract law to the arbitration clause. This may seem strange, but is perfectly in line with the doctrine of separability (cf. para. 39). As Stefan Kröll has observed, "no one would apply the CISG to an arbitration agreement concluded as a separate agreement after a dispute has arisen or after the main contract has been concluded. That the arbitration agreement is incorporated into a contract in the form of an arbitration clause does not change its nature as a separate contract, as is evidenced by the doctrine of separability."[201]

Review the decision of the European Court of Justice in the *West Tankers* case above at p. 775 and compare it with the decision of the District Court in *Filanto v. Chilewich*. Are the two decisions contradictory or can they be reconciled? How could a universal rule be formulated for the appropriate forum and the applicable law if there is a dispute whether a contract with a choice of forum/arbitration clause and a choice of law clause has in fact been validly concluded?

3. In para 38, the court refers to U.S. participation in the United Nations Convention on the International Sale of Goods (CISG) as the State Department trying "to fix something that was not broken." What does the court mean with this statement and what does Chief Judge Brieant not understand?

———

Before we go into a step-by-step analysis of the arbitration process, we can summarize the pros and cons of international commercial arbitration versus transnational litigation:

201. See Stefan Kröll: *Selected Problems Concerning the CISG's Scope of Application*, 25 J.L. & Com. (2006), pp. 39–57, at p. 45.

Chart 6-4
Pros and Cons of Arbitration versus Litigation

Pro Arbitration (Con Litigation)	Con Arbitration (Pro Litigation)
Confidentiality versus Publicity Arbitration is confidential. Unless all parties agree, no records are published.	The confidentiality of arbitration means that there are few precedents available to predict how certain types of issues might be decided. A threat of public litigation can sometimes be used as leverage in settlement negotiations.
Location and Neutrality While the defendant court, as the default court with jurisdiction over a dispute, is often perceived as a home advantage or even blatantly biased toward its own corporate citizens, in arbitration, the parties can choose a neutral and mutually convenient location and a neutral tribunal.	
Expertise of Arbitrators Parties can choose arbitrators with intimate knowledge of the chosen legal system and even the respective business practices and customs. If technical expertise is important, parties can appoint arbitrators who don't have to be lawyers.	The onus of selecting the most suitable arbitrator(s) is on the parties.
Use of Counsel Parties can use their usual legal counsel in arbitration since there are no bar admission requirements, while they would need to hire local counsel for litigation in a foreign country.	
Rules of Procedure Parties can choose among various procedural rules or even draw up their own. This includes the choice of language for the proceedings.	Via forum selection, parties may have some influence over applicable rules of procedure, even in litigation.
Even though arbitral tribunals do not as such dispose of police powers, they can issue interim or partial awards that can be enforced via the public courts.	**Supportive Powers of the Courts** Public courts backed up by public enforcement powers can compel the production of evidence or secure assets while proceedings are pending or issue other types of injunctions.[202]

---

202. American lawyers need to remember, however, that the extensive discovery options available in the U.S. for the collection of pretrial evidence are not available anywhere else to a comparable extent. This is true for international commercial arbitration and for foreign courts. For further analysis, see Oliver Bolthausen & Peter H. Acker, *Obtaining Discovery in International Arbitral Proceedings: The European v. American Mentality*, 74 Arb. 3 (2008), pp. 225–236, and the discussion below, pp. 989–996.

Pro Arbitration (Con Litigation)	Con Arbitration (Pro Litigation)
Fairness and Efficiency Courts in many countries have a reputation of being biased against foreign litigants; judges can be incompetent and/or corrupt.	Via forum selection, parties may have some options to avoid unfair or inefficient courts.
Delays Courts in many countries are plagued by large backlogs of cases leading to long delays before a hearing can be scheduled, let alone a final decision.	Via forum selection, parties may have some options to avoid notoriously slow judicial systems.
	Scope Some disputes and claims cannot be subjected to arbitration, e.g., consumer disputes, class action suits, etc. Multiparty disputes also tend to raise more problems in arbitration; e.g., arbitrators cannot force third parties to join a procedure.
Outcome Arbitration is less formal and less adversarial than litigation and more often leads to compromise solutions rather than a winner-take-all result. This makes it easier for the parties to continue an ongoing business relationship.	In particular, if punitive damages may be an option and if there is a David versus Goliath constellation, a jury trial may result in much higher damage awards.
Enforcement The 1958 New York Convention has been ratified by 157 countries, virtually ensuring recognition and enforcement of foreign arbitral awards in most countries.	Recognition and enforcement of foreign judgments is a matter of national law, which makes enforcement unpredictable and difficult in most and impossible in many countries.
	Cost The base cost of arbitration is higher than the cost of litigation. The ratio is often reversed, however, if litigation is continued on appeal. Also, arbitrators are less likely to allow extensive discovery. Nevertheless, arbitration is usually too expensive for relatively minor claims.

Overall, the benefits of arbitration far outweigh the drawbacks when it comes to international B2B disputes. This is confirmed by studies conducted regularly by Queen Mary School of Law at the University of London in cooperation with White & Case LLP. Fifty-six percent of respondents confirmed that international arbitration was their preferred method of dispute settlement for IBT. Another 34% opted for international arbitration in combination with other forms of ADR, in particular mediation. Five percent named mediation alone as their preference. Finally, only two percent of attorneys voted for cross-border litigation alone and another two percent for cross-border litigation after mediation.[203] Against this background, it is not surprising that Professor Cuniberti recently made a highly persuasive argument that international arbitration rather than transnational litigation should be the default method of dispute settlement in commercial cases.[204]

B. 21-Step Guide to International Commercial Arbitration

1. Existence of an Arbitrable Dispute

A dispute is arbitrable if it can be settled by arbitration. If a dispute is not arbitrable, a party to an IBT can call on the courts in spite of an arbitration clause in the agreement and/or any arbitration awards obtained by the other party would not be enforceable. A dispute that is not arbitrable can still be settled by negotiation or mediation, or a party can simply stop pursuing its claims. However, a binding decision against the will of at least one of the parties can only be obtained from the courts.

Although parties are largely free to decide whether they want to arbitrate instead of litigate, there are some restrictions for subject matter or types of dispute that are not arbitrable. An example we have used before is the restriction placed by many countries on arbitration clauses in consumer contracts (see pp. 881–882 and 1011). The following case is a good illustration of the approach taken in the U.S. toward arbitrability in B2B transactions.

Case 6-10

Mitsubishi Motors Corporation v. Soler Chrysler-Plymouth, Inc.

473 U.S. 614 (1985)
(Paragraph numbers added, some footnotes omitted.)
Justice BLACKMUN delivered the opinion of the Court (from p. 3348).

[1] The principal question presented by these cases is the arbitrability, pursuant to the Federal Arbitration Act, 9 U.S.C. § 1 et seq., and the [New York] Convention on the Recognition and Enforcement of Foreign Arbitral Awards (Convention) . . . , of claims arising under the Sherman Act, 15 U.S.C. § 1 et seq., and encompassed within a valid arbitration clause in an agreement embodying an international commercial transaction.

---

203. See https://www.whitecase.com/publications/insight/2018-international-arbitration-survey-evolution-international-arbitration.

204. See Giles Cuniberti, *Rethinking International Commercial Arbitration — Towards Default Arbitration*, Edward Elgar 2017.

I

[2] Petitioner-cross-respondent Mitsubishi Motors Corporation (Mitsubishi) is a Japanese corporation which manufactures automobiles and has its principal place of business in Tokyo, Japan. Mitsubishi is the product of a joint venture between, on the one hand, Chrysler International, S.A. (CISA), a Swiss corporation registered in Geneva and wholly owned by Chrysler Corporation, and, on the other, Mitsubishi Heavy Industries, Inc., a Japanese corporation. The aim of the joint venture was the distribution through Chrysler dealers outside the continental United States of vehicles manufactured by Mitsubishi and bearing Chrysler and Mitsubishi trademarks. Respondent-cross-petitioner Soler Chrysler-Plymouth, Inc. (Soler), is a Puerto Rico corporation with its principal place of business in Pueblo Viejo, Guaynabo, Puerto Rico.

[3] On October 31, 1979, Soler entered into a Distributor Agreement with CISA which provided for the sale by Soler of Mitsubishi-manufactured vehicles within a designated area, including metropolitan San Juan. . . . On the same date, CISA, Soler, and Mitsubishi entered into a Sales Procedure Agreement (Sales Agreement) which, referring to the Distributor Agreement, provided for the direct sale of Mitsubishi products to Soler and governed the terms and conditions of such sales. . . . Paragraph VI of the Sales Agreement, labeled "Arbitration of Certain Matters," provides:

> "All disputes, controversies or differences which may arise between [Mitsubishi] and [Soler] out of or in relation to Articles I-B through V of this Agreement or for the breach thereof, shall be finally settled by arbitration in Japan in accordance with the rules and regulations of the Japan Commercial Arbitration Association."

[4] [Initially, Soler was very successful in selling cars under the agreement in its designated area, which caused Mitsubishi to increase the minimum sales target for Soler. In 1981, the market slowed down and Soler was no longer able to meet its target numbers. Soler requested that Mitsubishi should slow down or cancel some shipments and also asked for permission to sell some cars out of area, including the continental U.S., as well as Latin America. Mitsubishi and CISA refused permission for any out-of-area sales and started withholding deliveries to Soler. To preempt litigation by Soler,] Mitsubishi brought an action against Soler in the United States District Court for the District of Puerto Rico under the Federal Arbitration Act and the Convention. Mitsubishi sought an order, pursuant to 9 U.S.C. §§ 4 and 201,[3] to compel arbitration in accord with [Para.] VI of the Sales Agreement. . . . Shortly

---

3. Section 4 provides in pertinent part: "A party aggrieved by the alleged failure, neglect, or refusal of another to arbitrate under a written agreement for arbitration may petition any United States district court which, save for such agreement, would have jurisdiction under title 28, in a civil action or in admiralty of the subject matter of a suit arising out of the controversy between the parties, for an order directing that such arbitration proceed in the manner provided for in such agreement. . . . The court shall hear the parties, and upon being satisfied that the making of the agreement for arbitration or the failure to comply therewith is not in issue, the court shall

after filing the complaint, Mitsubishi filed a request for arbitration before the Japan Commercial Arbitration Association.

[6] [In its response before the District Court, Soler counterclaimed against Mitsubishi and CISA. . . .] In the counterclaim premised on the Sherman Act, Soler alleged that Mitsubishi and CISA had conspired to divide markets in restraint of trade. To effectuate the plan, according to Soler, Mitsubishi had refused to permit Soler to resell to buyers in North, Central, or South America vehicles it had obligated itself to purchase from Mitsubishi; had refused to ship ordered vehicles or the parts, such as heaters and defoggers, that would be necessary to permit Soler to make its vehicles suitable for resale outside Puerto Rico; and had coercively attempted to replace Soler and its other Puerto Rico distributors with a wholly owned subsidiary which would serve as the exclusive Mitsubishi distributor in Puerto Rico. . . .

[7] [The District Court ordered Mitsubishi and Soler to arbitrate the contractual elements of the dispute.] With regard to the federal antitrust issues, it recognized that the Courts of Appeals, following *American Safety Equipment Corp. v. J.P. Maguire & Co.*, 391 F.2d 821 (CA2 1968), uniformly had held that the rights conferred by the antitrust laws were "of a character inappropriate for enforcement by arbitration." App. to Pet. for Cert. in No. 83-1569, p. B9, quoting *Wilko v. Swan,* 201 F.2d 439, 444 (CA2 1953), rev'd, 346 U.S. 427 . . . (1953). The District Court held, however, that the international character of the Mitsubishi-Soler undertaking required enforcement of the agreement to arbitrate even as to the antitrust claims. It relied on *Scherk v. Alberto-Culver Co.,* 417 U.S. 506, 515–520 . . . (1974), in which this Court ordered arbitration, pursuant to a provision embodied in an international agreement, of a claim arising under the Securities Exchange Act of 1934 notwithstanding its assumption, arguendo, that *Wilko*, supra, which held nonarbitrable claims arising under the Securities Act of 1933, also would bar arbitration of a 1934 Act claim arising in a domestic context.

[8] The United States Court of Appeals for the First Circuit affirmed in part and reversed in part. 723 F.2d 155 (1983). It first rejected Soler's argument that Puerto

---

make an order directing the parties to proceed to arbitration in accordance with the terms of the agreement."

Section 201 provides: "The Convention on the Recognition and Enforcement of Foreign Arbitral Awards of June 10, 1958, shall be enforced in United States courts in accordance with this chapter." Article II of the Convention, in turn, provides:

"1. Each Contracting State shall recognize an agreement in writing under which the parties undertake to submit to arbitration all or any differences which have arisen or which may arise between them in respect of a defined legal relationship, whether contractual or not, concerning a subject matter capable of settlement by arbitration. . . .

"3. The court of a Contracting State, when seized of an action in a matter in respect of which the parties have made an agreement within the meaning of this article, shall, at the request of one of the parties, refer the parties to arbitration, unless it finds that the said agreement is null and void, inoperative or incapable of being performed." . . . Title 9 U.S.C. § 203 confers jurisdiction on the district courts of the United States over an action falling under the Convention.

Rico law precluded enforcement of an agreement obligating a local dealer to arbitrate controversies outside Puerto Rico. It also rejected Soler's suggestion that it could not have intended to arbitrate statutory claims not mentioned in the arbitration agreement. Assessing arbitrability "on an allegation-by-allegation basis," id., at 159, the court then read the arbitration clause to encompass virtually all the claims arising under the various statutes, including all those arising under the Sherman Act.[9]

[9] Finally, after endorsing the doctrine of *American Safety*, precluding arbitration of antitrust claims, the Court of Appeals concluded that neither this Court's decision in *Scherk* nor the Convention required abandonment of that doctrine in the face of an international transaction. 723 F.2d, at 164–168. Accordingly, it reversed

---

9. As the Court of Appeals saw it, "[t]he question . . . is not whether the arbitration clause mentions antitrust or any other particular cause of action, but whether the factual allegations underlying Soler's counterclaims — and Mitsubishi's bona fide defenses to those counterclaims — are within the scope of the arbitration clause, whatever the legal labels attached to those allegations." 723 F.2d, at 159. Because Soler's counterclaim under the Puerto Rico Dealers' Contracts Act focused on Mitsubishi's alleged failure to comply with the provisions of the Sales Agreement governing delivery of automobiles, and those provisions were found in that portion of Article I of the Agreement subject to arbitration, the Court of Appeals placed this first counterclaim within the arbitration clause. Id., at 159–160.

The court read the Sherman Act counterclaim to raise issues of wrongful termination of Soler's distributorship, wrongful failure to ship ordered parts and vehicles, and wrongful refusal to permit transshipment of stock to the United States and Latin America. Because the existence of just cause for termination turned on Mitsubishi's allegations that Soler had breached the Sales Agreement by, for example, failing to pay for ordered vehicles, the wrongful termination claim implicated at least three provisions within the arbitration clause: Article I-D(1), which rendered a dealer's orders "firm"; Article I-E, which provided for "distress unit penalties" where the dealer prevented timely shipment; and Article I-F, specifying payment obligations and procedures. The court therefore held the arbitration clause to cover this dispute. Because the nonshipment claim implicated Soler's obligation under Article I-F to proffer acceptable credit, the court found this dispute covered as well. And because the transshipment claim prompted Mitsubishi defenses concerning the suitability of vehicles manufactured to Soler's specifications for use in different locales and Soler's inability to provide warranty service to transshipped products, it implicated Soler's obligation under Article IV, another covered provision, to make use of Mitsubishi's trademarks in a manner that would not dilute Mitsubishi's reputation and goodwill or damage its name and reputation. The court therefore found the arbitration agreement also to include this dispute, noting that such trademark concerns "are relevant to the legality of territorially based restricted distribution arrangements of the sort at issue here." 723 F.2d, at 160–161, citing *Continental T.V., Inc. v. GTE Sylvania Inc.*, 433 U.S. 36 . . . (1977).

The Court of Appeals read the federal Automobile Dealers' Day in Court Act claim to raise issues as to Mitsubishi's good faith in establishing minimum-sales volumes and Mitsubishi's alleged attempt to coerce Soler into accepting replacement by a Mitsubishi subsidiary. It agreed with the District Court's conclusion, in which Mitsubishi acquiesced, that the arbitration clause did not reach the first issue; it found the second, arising from Soler's payment problems, to restate claims already found to be covered. 723 F.2d, at 161.

Finally, the Court of Appeals found the antitrust claims under Puerto Rico law entirely to reiterate claims elsewhere stated; accordingly, it held them arbitrable to the same extent as their counterparts. Ibid.

the judgment of the District Court insofar as it had ordered submission of "Soler's antitrust claims" to arbitration. Affirming the remainder of the judgment, the court directed the District Court to consider in the first instance how the parallel judicial and arbitral proceedings should go forward.[12]

[10] We granted certiorari primarily to consider whether an American court should enforce an agreement to resolve antitrust claims by arbitration when that agreement arises from an international transaction. 469 U.S. 916 . . . (1984).

II

[11] At the outset, we address the contention raised in Soler's cross-petition that the arbitration clause at issue may not be read to encompass the statutory counterclaims stated in its answer to the complaint. In making this argument, Soler does not question the Court of Appeals' application of ¶ VI of the Sales Agreement to the disputes involved here as a matter of standard contract interpretation. Instead, it argues that as a matter of law a court may not construe an arbitration agreement to encompass claims arising out of statutes designed to protect a class to which the party resisting arbitration belongs "unless [that party] has expressly agreed" to arbitrate those claims, . . . by which Soler presumably means that the arbitration clause must specifically mention the statute giving rise to the claims that a party to the clause seeks to arbitrate. . . . Soler reasons that, because it falls within the class for whose benefit the federal and local antitrust laws and dealers' Acts were passed, but the arbitration clause at issue does not mention these statutes or statutes in general, the clause cannot be read to contemplate arbitration of these statutory claims.

[12] We do not agree, for we find no warrant in the Arbitration Act for implying in every contract within its ken a presumption against arbitration of statutory claims. The Act's centerpiece provision makes a written agreement to arbitrate "in any maritime transaction or a contract evidencing a transaction involving commerce . . . valid, irrevocable, and enforceable, save upon such grounds as exist at law or in equity for the revocation of any contract." 9 U.S.C. § 2. The "liberal federal policy favoring arbitration agreements," *Moses H. Cone Memorial Hospital v. Mercury Construction Corp.*, 460 U.S. 1, 24 . . . (1983), manifested by this provision and the Act as a whole, is at bottom a policy guaranteeing the enforcement of private contractual arrangements: the Act simply "creates a body of federal substantive law establishing

---

12. Following entry of the District Court's judgment, both it and the Court of Appeals denied motions by Soler for a stay pending appeal. The parties accordingly commenced preparation for the arbitration in Japan. Upon remand from the Court of Appeals, however, Soler withdrew the antitrust claims from the arbitration tribunal and sought a stay of arbitration pending the completion of the judicial proceedings on the ground that the antitrust claims permeated the claims that remained before that tribunal. The District Court denied the motion, instead staying its own proceedings pending the arbitration in Japan. The arbitration recommenced, but apparently came to a halt once again in September 1984 upon the filing by Soler of a petition for reorganization under Chapter 11 of the Bankruptcy Code, 11 U.S.C. § 1101 et seq.

and regulating the duty to honor an agreement to arbitrate." Id., at 25, n. 32 .... [14] As this Court recently observed, "[t]he preeminent concern of Congress in passing the Act was to enforce private agreements into which parties had entered," a concern which "requires that we rigorously enforce agreements to arbitrate." *Dean Witter Reynolds Inc. v. Byrd*, 470 U.S. 213, 221 ... (1985).

[13] Accordingly, the first task of a court asked to compel arbitration of a dispute is to determine whether the parties agreed to arbitrate that dispute. The court is to make this determination by applying the "federal substantive law of arbitrability, applicable to any arbitration agreement within the coverage of the Act." *Moses H. Cone Memorial Hospital*, 460 U.S., at 24 .... See *Prima Paint Corp. v. Flood & Conklin Mfg. Co.*, 388 U.S. 395, 400–404 ... (1967); *Southland Corp. v. Keating*, 465 U.S. 1, 12 ... (1984). And that body of law counsels

> "that questions of arbitrability must be addressed with a healthy regard for the federal policy favoring arbitration. . . . The Arbitration Act establishes that, as a matter of federal law, any doubts concerning the scope of arbitrable issues should be resolved in favor of arbitration, whether the problem at hand is the construction of the contract language itself or an allegation of waiver, delay, or a like defense to arbitrability." *Moses H. Cone Memorial Hospital*, 460 U.S., at 24–25 ....

See, e.g., *Steelworkers v. Warrior & Gulf Navigation Co.*, 363 U.S. 574, 582–583 ... (1960). Thus, as with any other contract, the parties' intentions control, but those intentions are generously construed as to issues of arbitrability.

[14] There is no reason to depart from these guidelines where a party bound by an arbitration agreement raises claims founded on statutory rights. Some time ago this Court expressed "hope for [the Act's] usefulness both in controversies based on statutes or on standards otherwise created," *Wilko v. Swan*, 346 U.S. 427, 432 ... (1953) (footnote omitted); see *Merrill Lynch, Pierce, Fenner & Smith, Inc. v. Ware*, 414 U.S. 117, 135, n. 15 ... (1973), and we are well past the time when judicial suspicion of the desirability of arbitration and of the competence of arbitral tribunals inhibited the development of arbitration as an alternative means of dispute resolution. Just last Term in *Southland Corp.*, supra, where we held that § 2 of the Act declared a national policy applicable equally in state as well as federal courts, we construed an arbitration clause to encompass the disputes at issue without pausing at the source in a state statute of the rights asserted by the parties resisting arbitration. 465 U.S., at 15, and n. 7 .... [15] Of course, courts should remain attuned to well-supported claims

---

14. The Court previously has explained that the Act was designed to overcome an anachronistic judicial hostility to agreements to arbitrate, which American courts had borrowed from English common law. See *Dean Witter Reynolds Inc. v. Byrd*, 470 U.S. 219–221, and n. 6 ... (1985); *Scherk v. Alberto-Culver Co.*, 417 U.S. 506, 510, and n. 4 ... (1974).

15. The claims whose arbitrability was at issue in *Southland Corp.* arose under the disclosure requirements of the California Franchise Investment Law, Cal.Corp.Code Ann. § 31000 et seq. (West 1977). While the dissent in *Southland Corp.* disputed the applicability of the Act to

that the agreement to arbitrate resulted from the sort of fraud or overwhelming economic power that would provide grounds "for the revocation of any contract." 9 U.S.C. § 2; see *Southland Corp.*, 465 U.S., at 16, n. 11 . . . ; *The Bremen v. Zapata Off-Shore Co.*, [above, p. 763] (1972). But, absent such compelling considerations, the Act itself provides no basis for disfavoring agreements to arbitrate statutory claims by skewing the otherwise hospitable inquiry into arbitrability.

[15] That is not to say that all controversies implicating statutory rights are suitable for arbitration. There is no reason to distort the process of contract interpretation, however, in order to ferret out the inappropriate. Just as it is the congressional policy manifested in the Federal Arbitration Act that requires courts liberally to construe the scope of arbitration agreements covered by that Act, it is the congressional intention expressed in some other statute on which the courts must rely to identify any category of claims as to which agreements to arbitrate will be held unenforceable. *See Wilko v. Swan*, 346 U.S., at 434–435 . . . ; *Southland Corp.*, 465 U.S., at 16, n. 11 . . . ; *Dean Witter Reynolds Inc.*, 470 U.S., at 224–225 . . . (concurring opinion). For that reason, Soler's concern for statutorily protected classes provides no reason to color the lens through which the arbitration clause is read. By agreeing to arbitrate a statutory claim, a party does not forgo the substantive rights afforded by the statute; it only submits to their resolution in an arbitral, rather than a judicial, forum. It trades the procedures and opportunity for review of the courtroom for the simplicity, informality, and expedition of arbitration. We must assume that if Congress intended the substantive protection afforded by a given statute to include protection against waiver of the right to a judicial forum, that intention will be deducible from text or legislative history. *See Wilko v. Swan, supra.* Having made the bargain to arbitrate, the party should be held to it unless Congress itself has evinced an intention to preclude a waiver of judicial remedies for the statutory rights at issue. Nothing, in the meantime, prevents a party from excluding statutory claims from the scope of an agreement to arbitrate. *See Prima Paint Corp.*, 388 U.S., at 406 . . . .

[16] In sum, the Court of Appeals correctly conducted a two-step inquiry, first determining whether the parties' agreement to arbitrate reached the statutory issues, and then, upon finding it did, considering whether legal constraints external to the parties' agreement foreclosed the arbitration of those claims. We endorse its rejection of Soler's proposed rule of arbitration-clause construction.

III

[17] We now turn to consider whether Soler's antitrust claims are nonarbitrable even though it has agreed to arbitrate them. In holding that they are not, the Court of Appeals followed the decision of the Second Circuit in *American Safety Equipment Corp. v. J.P. Maguire & Co.*, 391 F.2d 821 (1968). Notwithstanding the absence of

---

proceedings in the state courts, it did not object to the Court's reading of the arbitration clause under examination.

any explicit support for such an exception in either the Sherman Act or the Federal Arbitration Act, the Second Circuit there reasoned that "the pervasive public interest in enforcement of the antitrust laws, and the nature of the claims that arise in such cases, combine to make . . . antitrust claims . . . inappropriate for arbitration." *Id.*, at 827–828. We find it unnecessary to assess the legitimacy of the *American Safety* doctrine as applied to agreements to arbitrate arising from domestic transactions. As in *Scherk v. Alberto-Culver Co.*, 417 U.S. 506 . . . (1974), we conclude that concerns of international comity, respect for the capacities of foreign and transnational tribunals, and sensitivity to the need of the international commercial system for predictability in the resolution of disputes require that we enforce the parties' agreement, even assuming that a contrary result would be forthcoming in a domestic context.

[18] Even before *Scherk*, this Court had recognized the utility of forum-selection clauses in international transactions. In *The Bremen*, supra, an American oil company, seeking to evade a contractual choice of an English forum and, by implication, English law, filed a suit in admiralty in a United States District Court against the German corporation which had contracted to tow its rig to a location in the Adriatic Sea. Notwithstanding the possibility that the English court would enforce provisions in the towage contract exculpating the German party which an American court would refuse to enforce, this Court gave effect to the choice-of-forum clause. It observed:

> "The expansion of American business and industry will hardly be encouraged if, notwithstanding solemn contracts, we insist on a parochial concept that all disputes must be resolved under our laws and in our courts. . . . We cannot have trade and commerce in world markets and international waters exclusively on our terms, governed by our laws, and resolved in our courts." 407 U.S., at 9 . . . .

[19] Recognizing that "agreeing in advance on a forum acceptable to both parties is an indispensable element in international trade, commerce, and contracting," *id.*, at 13–14 . . . the decision in *The Bremen* clearly eschewed a provincial solicitude for the jurisdiction of domestic forums.

[20] Identical considerations governed the Court's decision in *Scherk*, which categorized "[a]n agreement to arbitrate before a specified tribunal [as], in effect, a specialized kind of forum-selection clause that posits not only the situs of suit but also the procedure to be used in resolving the dispute." 417 U.S., at 519 . . . . In *Scherk*, the American company Alberto-Culver purchased several interrelated business enterprises, organized under the laws of Germany and Liechtenstein, as well as the rights held by those enterprises in certain trademarks, from a German citizen who at the time of trial resided in Switzerland. Although the contract of sale contained a clause providing for arbitration before the International Chamber of Commerce in Paris of "any controversy or claim [arising] out of this agreement or the breach thereof," Alberto-Culver subsequently brought suit against Scherk in a Federal District Court

in Illinois, alleging that Scherk had violated § 10(b) of the Securities Exchange Act of 1934 by fraudulently misrepresenting the status of the trademarks as unencumbered. The District Court denied a motion to stay the proceedings before it and enjoined the parties from going forward before the arbitral tribunal in Paris. The Court of Appeals for the Seventh Circuit affirmed, relying on this Court's holding in *Wilko v. Swan*, 346 U.S. 427 ... (1953), that agreements to arbitrate disputes arising under the Securities Act of 1933 are nonarbitrable. This Court reversed, enforcing the arbitration agreement even while assuming for purposes of the decision that the controversy would be nonarbitrable under the holding of *Wilko* had it arisen out of a domestic transaction. Again, the Court emphasized:

> "A contractual provision specifying in advance the forum in which disputes shall be litigated and the law to be applied is ... an almost indispensable precondition to achievement of the orderliness and predictability essential to any international business transaction. ...
>
> "A parochial refusal by the courts of one country to enforce an international arbitration agreement would not only frustrate these purposes, but would invite unseemly and mutually destructive jockeying by the parties to secure tactical litigation advantages. ... [It would] damage the fabric of international commerce and trade, and imperil the willingness and ability of businessmen to enter into international commercial agreements." 417 U.S., at 516–517. ...

Accordingly, the Court held Alberto-Culver to its bargain, sending it to the international arbitral tribunal before which it had agreed to seek its remedies.

[21] *The Bremen* and *Scherk* establish a strong presumption in favor of enforcement of freely negotiated contractual choice-of-forum provisions. Here, as in *Scherk*, that presumption is reinforced by the emphatic federal policy in favor of arbitral dispute resolution. And at least since this Nation's accession in 1970 to the Convention, see [1970] 21 U.S.T. 2517, T.I.A.S. 6997, and the implementation of the Convention in the same year by amendment of the Federal Arbitration Act, that federal policy applies with special force in the field of international commerce. ...

Notes and Questions

1. In effect, the Supreme Courts says, whatever the parties to an IBT have agreed to shall be enforced, even if it concerns an area subject to public policy mandates, such as antitrust legislation. The Court leaves open the question whether it would hold similarly for a domestic business transaction. Why would antitrust considerations (and other public policy) be less important in the context of *international* transactions? Or does the Court see other reasons for giving a higher priority to party autonomy in the case of IBTs?

2. Could this precedent be used to support arbitrability in all cases where the parties have inserted an arbitration clause in their agreement? How about employment

contracts? Consumer contracts? Prenuptial agreements about division of assets or even child custody in case of divorce? Why or why not?

3. Who is bound by the approach taken in *Mitsubishi v. Soler*? Who is not? What happens if antitrust concerns are not arbitrable in other countries, for example in Switzerland, where CISA is incorporated? What happens generally when the standards for arbitrability vary from one country to another?

4. The Supreme Court went on to examine the four part test developed by the First Circuit in *American Safety* (from p. 3356):

> First, private parties play a pivotal role in aiding governmental enforcement of the antitrust laws by means of the private action for treble damages. Second, 'the strong possibility that contracts which generate antitrust disputes may be contracts of adhesion militates against automatic forum determination by contract.' Third, antitrust issues, prone to complication, require sophisticated legal and economic analysis, and thus are 'ill-adapted to strengths of the arbitral process, i.e., expedition, minimal requirements of written rationale, simplicity, resort to basic concepts of common sense and simple equity.' Finally, just as 'issues of war and peace are too important to be vested in the generals, . . . decisions as to antitrust regulation of business are too important to be lodged in arbitrators chosen from the business community—particularly those from a foreign community that has had no experience with or exposure to our law and values.' See *American Safety*, 391 F.2d, at 826–827.

The Supreme Court ultimately disagrees with all four elements of the test and basically says that:

> [t]here is no reason to assume at the outset of the dispute that international arbitration will not provide an adequate mechanism. To be sure, the international arbitral tribunal owes no prior allegiance to the legal norms of particular states; hence, it has no direct obligation to vindicate their statutory dictates. The tribunal, however, is bound to effectuate the intentions of the parties. Where the parties have agreed that the arbitral body is to decide a defined set of claims which includes, as in these cases, those arising from the application of American antitrust law, the tribunal therefore should be bound to decide that dispute in accord with the national law giving rise to the claim. Cf. *Wilko v. Swan*, 346 U.S., at 433–434 . . . . [19] And so long as the

---

19. In addition to the clause providing for arbitration before the Japan Commercial Arbitration Association, the Sales Agreement includes a choice-of-law clause which reads: "This Agreement is made in, and will be governed by and construed in all respects according to the laws of the Swiss Confederation as if entirely performed therein." . . . The United States raises the possibility that the arbitral panel will read this provision not simply to govern interpretation of the contract terms, but wholly to displace American law even where it otherwise would apply. Brief for United States as Amicus Curiae 20. The International Chamber of Commerce opines that it is "[c]onceivabl[e],

prospective litigant effectively may vindicate its statutory cause of action in the arbitral forum, the statute will continue to serve both its remedial and deterrent function.

Isn't it a bit naive, to say it diplomatically, to assume that a foreign arbitral tribunal, in this case composed of three Japanese lawyers, would be able or even interested in enforcing American antitrust law (see note 19)? What do you think of the Supreme Court's idea that American courts would have sufficient opportunity to ensure respect of American public policy when a foreign award comes home for enforcement? Couldn't the parties simply seek enforcement in other countries if they are worried that the award would not be enforceable in the U.S.? Could you make an argument in defense of *American Safety*?

5. One of the important tools for the enforcement of American antitrust law is the ability of an injured party to claim treble damages from the party or parties in violation of U.S. law. However, punitive damages are frowned upon in most other countries and even explicitly prohibited in some.[205] Pursuant to *Mitsubishi v. Soler*,

---

although we believe it unlikely, [that] the arbitrators could consider Soler's affirmative claim of anticompetitive conduct by CISA and Mitsubishi to fall within the purview of this choice-of-law provision, with the result that it would be decided under Swiss law rather than the U.S. Sherman Act." Brief for International Chamber of Commerce as Amicus Curiae 25. At oral argument, however, counsel for Mitsubishi conceded that American law applied to the antitrust claims and represented that the claims had been submitted to the arbitration panel in Japan on that basis. . . . The record confirms that before the decision of the Court of Appeals the arbitral panel had taken these claims under submission. . . .

We therefore have no occasion to speculate on this matter at this stage in the proceedings, when Mitsubishi seeks to enforce the agreement to arbitrate, not to enforce an award. Nor need we consider now the effect of an arbitral tribunal's failure to take cognizance of the statutory cause of action on the claimant's capacity to reinitiate suit in federal court. We merely note that in the event the choice-of-forum and choice-of-law clauses operated in tandem as a prospective waiver of a party's right to pursue statutory remedies for antitrust violations, we would have little hesitation in condemning the agreement as against public policy. . . .

205. On the subject of punitive damages, see Voker Behr, *Myth and Reality of Punitive Damages in Germany*, J. L. & Com. 2005, Vol. 24, pp. 197–224; Jessica J. Berch, *The Need for Enforcement of U.S. Punitive Damages Awards by the European Union*, Minn. J. Int'l L. 2010, Vol. 19, No. 1, pp. 55–106; Ronald A. Brand, *Punitive Damages and the Recognition of Judgments*, Netherlands Int'l L. Rev. 1996, Vol. 43, No. 2, pp. 143–186; Norman T. Braslow, *The Recognition and Enforcement of Common Law Punitive Damages in a Civil Law System: Some Reflections on the Japanese Experience*, Ariz. J. Int'l & Comp. L. 1999, Vol. 16, No. 2, pp. 285–360; Theodore Eisenberg et al., *Juries, Judges, and Punitive Damages: An Empirical Study*, Cornell L. Rev. 2002, Vol. 87, No. 3, pp. 743–782; John Y. Gotanda, *Awarding Punitive Damages in International Commercial Arbitrations in the Wake of* Mastrobuono v. Shearson Lehman Hutton Inc., Harv. Int'l L.J. 1997, Vol. 38, No. 1, pp. 59–110; John Y. Gotanda, *Charting Developments Concerning Punitive Damages: Is the Tide Changing?*, Villanova University Working Paper Series 2006, available at https://digitalcommons.law.villanova .edu/wps/art65/; Scott R. Jablonski, *Translation and Comment: Enforcing U.S. Punitive Damages Awards in Foreign Courts—A Recent Case in the Supreme Court of Spain*, J. L. & Com. 2005, Vol. 24, pp. 225–243; Amy A. Kirby, *Punitive Damages in Contract Actions: The Tension between the United Nations Convention on Contracts for the International Sale of Goods and U.S. Law*, J. L. & Com. 1997, Vol. 16, No. 2, pp. 215–231; A. Mitchell Polinsky & Steven Shavell, *Punitive Damages:*

must we conclude that a party agreeing to arbitration outside of the U.S. effectively gives away its opportunity to claim treble damages if it should be the target or victim of an antitrust violation?

6. If you were to advise Soler in the negotiations of a distributorship agreement with General Motors and Isuzu, what kind of arbitration clause would you want, if any, after the experience with Mitsubishi and Chrysler?

7. The latest word by the U.S. Supreme Court on the arbitrability of alleged violations of federal and state antitrust law was rendered on January 8, 2019, in *Henry Schein v. Archer & White* (139 S. Ct. 524):

> Under the Federal Arbitration Act . . . and this Court's cases, the question of who decides arbitrability is itself a question of contract. The Act allows parties to agree by contract that an arbitrator, rather than a court, will resolve threshold arbitrability questions as well as underlying merits disputes. . . .
>
> Even when a contract delegates the arbitrability question to an arbitrator, some federal courts nonetheless will short-circuit the process and decide the arbitrability question themselves if the argument that the arbitration agreement applies to the particular dispute is "wholly groundless." The question presented in this case is whether the "wholly groundless" exception is consistent with the Federal Arbitration Act. We conclude that it is not. The Act does not contain a "wholly groundless" exception, and we are not at liberty to rewrite the statute passed by Congress and signed by the President. When the parties' contract delegates the arbitrability question to an arbitrator, the courts must respect the parties' decision as embodied in the contract. We vacate the contrary judgment of the Court of Appeals. . . .

II

> In 1925, Congress passed and President Coolidge signed the Federal Arbitration Act. As relevant here, the Act provides:
>
> "A written provision in . . . a contract evidencing a transaction involving commerce to settle by arbitration a controversy thereafter arising out of such contract . . . shall be valid, irrevocable, and enforceable, save upon such grounds as exist at law or in equity for the revocation of any contract." 9 U. S. C. § 2.
>
> Under the Act, arbitration is a matter of contract, and courts must enforce arbitration contracts according to their terms. *Rent-A-Center*, 561 U. S., at 67. Applying the Act, we have held that parties may agree to have an arbitrator decide not only the merits of a particular dispute but also "'gateway' questions of 'arbitrability,' such as whether the parties have agreed to

---

An Economic Analysis, Harv. L. Rev. 1998, Vol. 111, No. 4, pp. 869–962; Francesco Quarta, *Recognition and Enforcement of U.S. Punitive Damages Awards in Continental Europe: The Italian Supreme Court's Veto,* Hastings Int'l & Comp. L. Rev. 2008, Vol. 31, pp. 753–782. See also p. 856, note 157.

arbitrate or whether their agreement covers a particular controversy." *Id.*, at 68–69; . . . .

We must interpret the Act as written, and the Act in turn requires that we interpret the contract as written. When the parties' contract delegates the arbitrability question to an arbitrator, a court may not override the contract. In those circumstances, a court possesses no power to decide the arbitrability issue. That is true even if the court thinks that the argument that the arbitration agreement applies to a particular dispute is wholly groundless.

That conclusion follows not only from the text of the Act but also from precedent. We have held that a court may not "rule on the potential merits of the underlying" claim that is assigned by contract to an arbitrator, "even if it appears to the court to be frivolous." *AT&T Technologies, Inc. v. Communications Workers*, 475 U. S. 643, 649–650 (1986). A court has "'no business weighing the merits of the grievance'" because the "'agreement is to submit all grievances to arbitration, not merely those which the court will deem meritorious.'" *Id.*, at 650 (quoting *Steelworkers v. American Mfg. Co.*, 363 U. S. 564, 568 (1960)). . . .

We express no view about whether the contract at issue in this case in fact delegated the arbitrability question to an arbitrator. The Court of Appeals did not decide that issue. Under our cases, courts "should not assume that the parties agreed to arbitrate arbitrability unless there is clear and unmistakable evidence that they did so." *First Options*, 514 U. S., at 944 . . . .

8. Can you now formulate a basic rule for arbitrability in disputes resulting from international business transactions?

2. The Documents and Rules that Govern International Commercial Arbitration

When drafting or reviewing a contract with an arbitration clause and, in particular, when a dispute is evolving and arbitration may be initiated by either side, it is imperative for the lawyers to understand exactly—and comprehensively—which rules will govern the dispute. It is one thing for a lawyer to interpret a given rule in a way that is ultimately not supported by the tribunal or mainstream opinion. It is quite a different thing for the lawyer to overlook the applicability of the rule. Therefore, the following steps must be taken very seriously in order to compile a complete set of the applicable rules.

In general, there are "5 + 5" sets of rules that govern international commercial arbitration, namely:

Chart 6-5
The Rules Governing International Arbitration Procedures

The 5 + 5 Documents and Rules Governing Arbitration Procedures

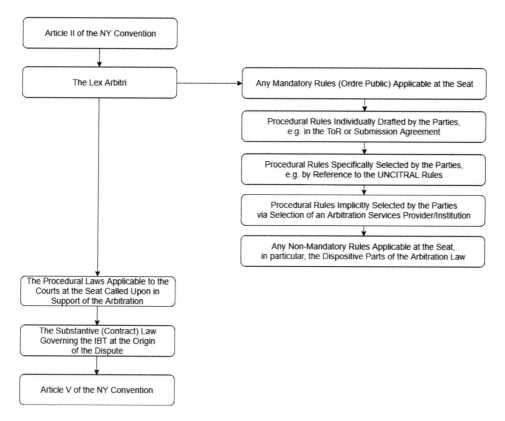

1. The law that governs the international recognition and enforcement of the agreement to arbitrate, Art. II of the United Nations Convention on the Recognition and Enforcement of Foreign Arbitral Awards, the so-called "New York Convention," Documents, p. II-500.

2. The law that governs the arbitration *procedures*, consisting of, in hierarchical order:

   i.   any mandatory rules (*ordre public*) applicable at the place or seat of the arbitration, and potentially at the place where an award needs to be enforced, for example, who can and cannot be an arbitrator in a given case; issues that are not arbitrable, etc;

   ii. the procedural rules individually drafted by the parties, typically as part of the "Terms of Reference," "Terms of Appointment," or "Submission Agreement" negotiated and agreed at the beginning of the arbitration;

   iii. any procedural *rules* specifically selected by the parties, for example by reference to the ICC Rules or the UNCITRAL Arbitration Rules in their contract or terms of reference, to the extent that these rules supplement and do not conflict with any mandatory provisions (i) and any individually agreed-upon rules (ii);

iv. any institutional rules applicable via selection of a particular arbitration *institution* by the parties, to the extent that they supplement and do not conflict with any mandatory provisions (i), any specifically agreed-upon rules (ii); and any other specifically selected procedural rules (iii);[206]

v. the arbitration law or laws applicable at the place of arbitration, to the extent that they supplement and do not conflict with any mandatory provisions (i), any individually agreed-upon rules (ii), any specifically selected procedural rules (iii), or any applicable institutional rules (iv);

The national arbitration laws are particularly important in ad hoc arbitration if specific procedural rules were not agreed upon, and in cases where the national courts have to be called upon to provide certain powers a tribunal might not have or might not be able to enforce, for example to impose certain interim measures, or to compel the production of certain evidence.

3. The procedural law of the *court* that may be called upon to help with evidence and/or interim relief.

4. The substantive law (contract law) that governs the dispute at issue; this is first and foremost the law chosen by the parties; in the absence of a valid choice of law, private int'l law or the rules on international conflict of laws determine the applicable substantive law.

5. The arbitral award of the tribunal plus the law that governs the international *recognition and enforcement* of the award, wherever such recognition and enforcement may be sought, including any mandatory rules (*ordre public*) about what may not be enforceable in the country where enforcement may be sought. See Arts. III–VI of the New York Convention.

If an award is to be enforced in the same country where it was rendered, this would have to be done pursuant to the domestic arbitration laws, e.g., §§ 9–13 FAA, because the New York Convention applies only to enforcement in other countries.

---

206. While it is uncommon for parties to select a particular arbitration institution — for example, the London Court of International Arbitration — but then select a set of rules *other* than the house rules of that organization — for example, the UNCITRAL Rules — it is perfectly possible to force a tribunal within an institutional arbitration to work under a different set of rules than those of the institution. It should be noted that the ICC has begun to resist such efforts (see below, p. 918). In any case, whether it makes sense is quite another question. Parties and their lawyers should at least have a good reason for a bifurcated selection; haphazard copy-pasting from earlier agreements would not qualify as a good reason.

Let's take a closer look:

1. Article II of the New York Convention — Respect for Arbitration Clauses and Agreements

The New York Convention of June 10, 1958, entered into force in 1959 and has been ratified by 159 states as of March 2019, including virtually all major trading nations. The status of ratifications, including any reservations or declarations made by some of the state parties, can be found at http://www.uncitral.org/uncitral/en/uncitral_texts/arbitration/NYConvention_status.html. In the U.S., the New York Convention was implemented via amendments to the 1925 Federal Arbitration Act, Documents, p. II-505.

Pursuant to Article I, the New York Convention applies to arbitral awards made in the territory of a state *other* than the state where the recognition and enforcement is sought. "State" in this context refers to country, not to one or more of the several states of the U.S. Thus, the New York Convention applies only to the recognition and enforcement of *foreign* arbitral awards. This means that an arbitral award made under the auspices of the American Arbitration Association in Washington, D.C., will be enforceable in the U.S. pursuant to the Federal Arbitration Act but without reference to or obligation under the New York Convention. It also means that it is usually better to select a place or seat for arbitration as neither the home country of the seller nor the buyer and certainly not the country where the majority of either side's assets are located.

Article II of the New York Convention imposes an obligation on the Contracting States and their courts to recognize an "agreement in writing" pursuant to which the parties have agreed to subject any disputes between them to arbitration, rather than litigation. The obligation is rather straightforward but not always respected. It entails two elements: First, if a party to an agreement with a valid arbitration clause approaches the courts of a Contracting State, and the other party to the agreement does not agree to the jurisdiction of these courts but invokes the arbitration clause, the courts should decline jurisdiction and refer both parties to arbitration instead. This obligation extends to preliminary remedies, for example if a party to an agreement with a valid arbitration clause requests an anti-suit injunction from the courts of a Contracting State to prevent the other party to that agreement from taking the dispute to court in violation of the arbitration clause. This could be called the ex ante obligation, to respect the arbitration clause at the beginning of a dispute.

Second, there is an ex post obligation on Contracting States to the New York Convention at the end of a commercial dispute, namely not to lend a hand in the enforcement of a judgment that was obtained in violation of an arbitration agreement. An example where this obligation becomes important is a case where one party to an agreement with a valid arbitration clause goes to court, the other party either does not participate at all or makes an appearance merely to dispute the jurisdiction of the court, yet the proceedings continue and the first party obtains a judgment by default or otherwise in its favor. Thus, the courts approached by the first party did not respect the arbitration agreement and asserted their jurisdiction anyway. In such a case, it becomes crucial for the other party and the functioning of the system as a whole that no other Contracting State agrees to the enforcement of the judgment, making the latter quite useless outside of the jurisdiction of the courts that disrespected the arbitration agreement and Article II of the New York Convention in the first place. With a bit of luck, the other party will be able to remove its assets from that jurisdiction before much harm can be done. The first party would then score a Pyrrhic victory with a judgment that is enforceable only in one single country in the world because it was obtained contrary to a valid mutual agreement that any disputes shall be settled by arbitration and not by litigation.

2. Procedural Rules

i. Mandatory Rules of Public Policy or Ordre Public

Certain rules are imposed by countries as a matter of public policy. They can usually not be contracted away by the parties to an IBT or to a dispute. Examples are rules on arbitrability of certain subject matter, such as real estate transactions, family matters, or antitrust law; but also certain minimum standards of procedure, such as rules on due process, including giving sufficient notice of proceedings or having impartial arbitrators without financial interests in the outcome of the dispute (see, for example, Section 4 of the English Arbitration Act).[207]

In an international arbitration, there may be several sets of mandatory rules that need to be taken into account. First, and most important, if a procedure does not conform to the mandatory rules of the country where it is *seated*, either party may be able to call upon the courts of that country or state and have the procedure stopped and/or any awards annulled. A court order of such kind would be a deadly blow to the arbitration or award.[208] It would leave only one option to the party or parties seeking to enforce their rights, namely to launch a completely new procedure in conformity with the mandatory rules, provided any statutes of limitation or other obstacles do not stand in the way.

Second, an award can also be challenged for incompatibility with mandatory rules of the country where *enforcement* is sought. We will come back to this under #5 below, when we discuss the provision of Article V(2)(b) of the New York Convention, pursuant to which a country can refuse the recognition and enforcement of a foreign award if such recognition or enforcement "would be contrary to the public policy of that country" (see also pp. 1014 et seq.). In such a case, however, the victorious party can still try to have the award enforced in other countries, as long as the other party has assets there.

---

207. For discussion see George A. Bermann & Loukas Mistelis, Mandatory Rules in International Arbitration, JurisNet 2011; as well as A.N. Zhilsov, *Mandatory and Public Policy Rules in International Commercial Arbitration*, Netherlands Int'l L. Rev. 1995, Vol. 42, No. 1, pp. 81–119.

208. For comprehensive analysis, see Alessandra Sardu, *The Fate of the Award Annulled in the Country of the Seat*, Global Jurist 2016, Vol. 17, Article No. 20160010, published online on October 29, 2016.

Since mandatory rules cannot be avoided by agreement of the parties or via the application of certain institutional rules, they have to be considered first. If there are no mandatory rules standing in the way of a procedure, we can proceed to the next level.

ii. Individually Negotiated Rules Agreed Between the Parties

The second most important set of rules governing an arbitration are any rules the parties have individually and specifically negotiated and agreed upon. It is not common for the parties to an IBT to include an expansive set of rules in the original agreement. However, an arbitration clause may well include such details as the seat of the arbitration, the language, and the number of arbitrators. More detailed rules — to the extent they are specifically negotiated by the parties — are more likely to be found in the Terms of Reference or an Agreement to Arbitrate that was drafted after the dispute arose (see below, p. 980). To the extent such individually negotiated rules are not incompatible with mandatory rules of the first category, they override any other procedural rules, such as those coming next.

iii. Procedural Rules Explicitly Selected by the Parties

To the extent the parties do not want to negotiate specific and individual rules or cannot agree on such rules, they may simply make a reference to a preexisting set of rules. For example, the parties could stipulate either in their arbitration clause (*ex ante*) or in Terms of Reference or an Agreement to Arbitrate (*ex post*), that they will apply the UNCITRAL Arbitration Rules[209] and/or the IBA Rules of Ethics in International Arbitration (Documents, p. II-265 and below, p. 988) and/or the IBA Rules on the Taking of Evidence in International Commercial Arbitration (Documents, p. II-239 and below, p. 989). The parties may even subject their arbitration to an institutional set of rules, such as the Arbitration Rules of the London Court of International Arbitration, without selecting the institution itself to administer the procedures. Finally, the parties could make reference to a national arbitration law to govern their proceedings, such as the English Arbitration Act of 1996. If the parties select a set of institutional rules or a national arbitration law, however, they should be aware that some provisions will not easily fit an ad hoc arbitration. For example, institutional rules regularly make reference to some administrative involvement or support provided by the institution (see, for example, Arts. 3, 4, 5, 6, 7, etc. of the ICC Rules, or Arts. 1, 2, 3, 5, 7, 9, 11, etc. of the LCIA Rules). By contrast, the UNCITRAL Rules were specifically crafted to be used in ad hoc arbitration without institutional support.[210]

---

209. For detailed analysis, see David D. Caron & Lee M. Caplan, *The UNCITRAL Arbitration Rules—A Commentary*, Oxford Univ. Press 2nd ed. 2013.

210. In fact, the first draft of the UNCITRAL Rules prepared by Prof. Pieter Sanders in 1974 was titled "A Preliminary Draft Set of Arbitration Rules for Optional Use in ad hoc Arbitrations Relating to International Trade." See Paolo Michele Patocchi & Tilman Niedermaier, *UNCITRAL Arbitration Rules*, in Rolf A. Schütze (ed.), *Institutional Arbitration—Article-by-Article Commentary*, Beck 2013, pp. 1007–1249, at p. 1013.

iv. Procedural Rules Implicitly Selected by the Parties

If the parties have opted for institutional arbitration, for example under the auspices of the Singapore International Arbitration Centre (SIAC), the rules of that institution will apply to any issues that are not otherwise regulated by mandatory public policy provisions at the seat of the arbitration, nor by individually negotiated rules, nor by specifically referenced rules. Some institutions will grant wide discretion to the parties to modify or deviate from the institutional rules, other institutions are a bit less welcoming with regard to modifications. For example, the SIAC Rules 2016 stipulate in Rule 1.1 "Where the parties have agreed to refer their disputes to SIAC for arbitration or to arbitration in accordance with the SIAC Rules, *the parties shall be deemed to have agreed that the arbitration shall be conducted pursuant to and administered by SIAC in accordance with these Rules.*" (emphasis added). The ICC Court even flat-out refused to administer an arbitration based on an agreement between the parties providing for significant modifications of the ICC Rules.[211] By contrast, the International Arbitration Rules of the International Centre for Dispute Resolution (ICDR) of the American Arbitration Association (AAA) provide in Article 1 a. "Where parties have agreed in writing to arbitrate disputes under these International Arbitration Rules or have provided for arbitration of an international dispute by the International Centre for Dispute Resolution of the American Arbitration Association without designating particular rules, the arbitration shall take place in accordance with these Rules, . . . *subject to whatever modifications the parties may adopt in writing*" (emphasis added).

Even if institutional rules seem to be hostile to modifications by the parties, the hierarchy of norms remains in effect and individually negotiated or specifically referenced rules based on party agreement—like the UNCITRAL Rules—will override implicitly selected institutional rules unless they are clearly incompatible with notions of due process, equality, and justice. This hierarchy is derived from party autonomy, namely to craft or choose whatever rules the parties want to govern their procedure.[212]

A more difficult question arises if parties explicitly select an institution to administer their dispute settlement procedure but also explicitly select the rules of a *different* institution. Such hybrid clauses have been accepted in some cases[213] and rejected

---

211. See *Samsung Electronics v. Mr. Jaffé (Qimonda)*, [2010] Rev. Arb. 571, at 575.

212. For example, the UNCITRAL Model Law, addressed at national legislatures, stipulates in Article 19 (1) the ". . . the parties are free to agree on the procedure to be followed by the arbitral tribunal in conducting the proceedings." See also the discussion in Nigel Blackaby & Constantine Partasides, *Redfern and Hunter on International Arbitration*, Oxford Univ. Press 6th ed. 2015, paras. 6.07 to 6.18.

213. In 2014, the Singapore High Court had to assess an arbitration agreement providing for arbitration before the Singapore International Arbitration Centre (SIAC) in accordance with the ICC Rules. The clause was upheld. See *Insigma Technology Co. Ltd v Alstom Technology Ltd* [2008] SGHC 134; similar also the decision by the Singapore High Court in *HKL Group Co Ltd v Rizq*

in others.[214] In reality, the majority of hybrid clauses occur from careless drafting or—more specifically—from copy/paste work done by careless lawyers. It is somewhat difficult to conceive good enough reasons why a party would want one arbitration institution to administer its case, yet refuse their rules and opt for another institution's rules. In practice, what sometimes happens is that the parties struggle to agree on the institution and finally settle for one side choosing the forum and the other side choosing the rules. Another motivation can be that parties want the ICC Rules but not the high cost of ICC arbitration. However, instead of getting what they want, the parties may first have to litigate over the validity of the entire agreement to arbitrate. Therefore, hybrid clauses rarely do make sense and are often considered to be pathological clauses. Indeed, Jae Hee Suh of Allen & Overy writes that "[s]uch clauses may be a source of strife for the whole duration of the dispute—from jurisdictional battles to challenges at the enforcement stage."[215] At the very least, parties and counsel should have a clear set of goals and should openly discuss and evaluate those goals before putting hybrid clauses into contracts or agreements to arbitrate.

v. Arbitration Rules Applicable by Default at the Seat of the Arbitration

If the parties did not negotiate specific rules or did not make a choice in favor of a set of rules or an arbitration institution, or if any of the rules negotiated or selected by the parties does not cover a particular question, we still need to find a fallback option, a set of rules that kicks in as a matter of last resort. The default law is the arbitration law applicable at the seat of the arbitration. Thus, if an arbitration is to take place in London, the English Arbitration Act of 1996 and the relevant case law interpreting its provisions will be the fallback option.

The need to have a good fallback law for unforseen issues, and the need to have good fallback court support discussed in the next paragraphs, are the main reasons why we should always think carefully about where the *seat* of an arbitration should be.

3. National Civil Procedure Law

Even though a valid choice of arbitration rather than litigation by the parties generally prevents recourse to state courts for settlement of the dispute, there are

International Holdings Pte Ltd [2013] SGHCR 5, declaring the hybrid clause operable on condition that SIAC would accept (the clause is reproduced below, at p. 953).

214. In response to the *Insigma* decision cited in the previous footnote, the ICC amended its Rules and inserted a provision in Article 1(2) that the International Court of Arbitration of the ICC "is the only body authorized to administer arbitrations under the [ICC] Rules." In spite of this, the Swedish Court of Appeal decided in 2015 that an arbitration clause was valid even though it provided for application of the ICC Rules before the Arbitration Institute of the Stockholm Chamber of Commerce (SCC Arbitration), see Svea Court of Appeal, Case No. T 2545-14 Russian Federation v. I.M. Badprim SRL, available at https://www.jpinfonet.se/Views/Pages/GetFile.ashx?portalId=89&cat=79572&docId=2281406&propId=1578. The ICC itself is highly unlikely to return the favor. For further discussion, see Nathalie Lendermann, *Procedure Shopping Through Hybrid Arbitration Agreements*, Nomos 2018, in particular pp. 126–208 and 271–401.

215. See http://arbitrationblog.practicallaw.com/interpretation-of-pathological-clauses-a-cautionary-tale/.

cases when state courts are needed in support of arbitration procedures. These cases can occur *before* arbitration procedures are properly initiated, for example if one party calls upon a state court in spite of the existence of a valid arbitration agreement and the other party needs an injunction to prevent this, or if one party—usually the respondent—refuses to nominate or accept an arbitrator to delay or prevent the proceedings. A need to call upon a state court for support can also arise *during* the arbitration procedures, for example if witnesses or other forms of evidence are not produced voluntarily for evaluation by the arbitrators. Furthermore, the need to call upon a court can arise in different states, depending on the location of evidence, assets, or parties. In general, the option to get court backup is more important in ad hoc arbitration, but it may also be needed in institutional arbitration.

Whether or not a national or state court will be willing and able to provide the requested support for an intended or ongoing arbitration procedure depends first on the national procedural law that must be applied by that court. Some states and some courts are more friendly than others toward arbitration, but in general the judges don't mind if certain types of high-stakes and complicated commercial cases, in particular those with international dimensions, are taken care of elsewhere. Nevertheless, the selection of a suitable seat for the arbitration in a country with an arbitration-friendly legal system can be critical for the successful settlement of the dispute.[216]

Based on personal experience and feedback from fellow arbitrators, I have a clear preference for just a handful of countries where I would want to seat an arbitration, because I like both the efficiency and arbitration friendliness of the courts and the national arbitration laws. Switzerland[217] and the UK[218] are my favorites in Europe and Singapore is my favorite in Asia. The U.S. courts are good but the codification of arbitration law is relatively rudimentary and everything else has to be cobbled together from case law.[219] Other places have good arbitration institutions but I have limited confidence when it comes to potential court support. Examples would be the Cairo Regional Center for International Commercial Arbitration in Egypt, the Asian International Arbitration Centre in Kuala Lumpur, Malaysia,[220] or the Conciliation and Arbitration Centre of the Chamber of Commerce in Panama.

---

216. Compare, for example, Gonzalo Vial, *Influence of the Arbitral Seat in the Outcome of an International Commercial Arbitration*, Int'l Law. 2017, Vol. 50, No. 2, pp. 329–346.

217. For more information, see Manuel Arroyo (ed.), *Arbitration in Switzerland—The Practitioner's Guide*, Wolters Kluwer 2013; Bernhard Berger & Franz Kellerhals, *International and Domestic Arbitration in Switzerland*, Stämpfli 3rd ed. 2015; Eliott Geisinger & Nathalie Voser, *International Arbitration in Switzerland*, Wolters Kluwer 2nd ed. 2013; Gabrielle Kaufmann-Kohler & Antonio Rigozzi, *International Arbitration Law and Practice in Switzerland*, Oxford Univ. Press 2015; Stefanie Pfisterer & Anton K. Schnyder, *International Arbitration in Switzerland*, Dike Publishers 2012.

218. For more information, see Andrew Tweeddale & Keren Tweeddale, *Arbitration of Commercial Disputes: International and English Law and Practice*, Oxford Univ. Press 2007.

219. More profound analysis is available in James H. Carter & John Fellas (eds.), *International Commercial Arbitration in New York*, Oxford Univ. Press 2nd ed. 2016.

220. The authoritative works on arbitration in Malaysia are Sundra Rajoo, *Law, Practice and Procedure of Arbitration*, LexisNexis 2nd ed. 2017, as well as Tun Arifin Zakaria, Sundra Rajoo & Philip Koh (eds.), *Arbitration in Malaysia—A Practical Guide*, Sweet & Maxwell 2016.

Obviously, these are subjective choices. What is important, however, is that legal counsel does not choose the seat of an arbitration based on geographic convenience or attractiveness as a travel destination, in particular if the parties may not be equally committed to a swift and consensual resolution of their dispute.[221]

Gary Born on the Meaning and Importance of the Seat of an International Arbitration

The location of the arbitral seat is a critical issue in any international arbitration. The location of the arbitral seat can have profound legal and practical consequences, and can materially alter the course of dispute resolution. . . .

The significance of the arbitral seat includes relatively mundane issues of convenience and cost. . . . factors such as visa requirements, availability of air or other transportation, hearing facilities, hotel accommodations, support staff (such as interpreters, stenographers, secretaries), and the like can bear heavily on the smooth progress of an arbitration.

Much more significant than the convenience and cost is the effect of the law of the arbitral seat . . . on the arbitration. . . .

The arbitration legislation of the arbitral seat governs a number of 'internal' and 'external' matters relating to arbitral proceedings. The 'internal' matters potentially governed . . . include: (a) the parties' autonomy to agree on substantive and procedural issues; (b) standards of procedural fairness in arbitral proceedings; (c) timetable of arbitral proceedings; (d) consolidation, joinder and intervention; (e) conduct of hearings, including the parties' opportunities to be heard and the examination of witnesses; (f) rights of lawyers to appear, and their ethical obligations, in the arbitral proceedings; (g) pleading and evidentiary rules; (h) permissibility and administration of oaths; (i) disclosure, 'discovery', and related issues; (j) confidentiality; (k) rights and duties of arbitrators; (l) arbitrators' remedial powers, including to grant provisional measures; (m) arbitrators' relations with the parties, including liability, ethical standards, appointment and removal; and (n) form, making and publication of the award. In addition, and less clearly, the law of the arbitral seat sometimes governs: (o) interpretation and enforceability of the parties' arbitration agreement (including issues of arbitrability); (p) conflict of laws rules applicable to the substance of the dispute; and (q) quasi-substantive issues, such as rules concerning interest and costs of legal representation.

The 'external' matters potentially governed by the law of the arbitral seat concern judicial supervision of the arbitral proceedings by the courts of the arbitral seat. Among other things, these include: (a) arbitrators'

---

221. See also Franco Ferrari (ed.), *Forum Shopping in the International Commercial Arbitration Context*, Sellier European Law Publishers 2013.

competence-competence and the allocation of competence to consider and decide jurisdictional challenges between arbitral tribunals and national courts; (b) annulment of arbitral awards; (c) selection of arbitrators; (d) removal and replacement of arbitrators: (e) evidence-taking in aid of the arbitration; and (f) provisional measures in support of the arbitration. . . .

See Gary B. Born: *International Arbitration—Cases and Materials*, Wolters Kluwer 2nd ed. 2015, pp. 599–600 (footnotes omitted).

4. The Substantive Law Governing the IBT

Under #2 and #3, we discussed the procedural laws that govern or may govern an arbitration, and potential court support. At this point, we turn to the substantive law that governs the business transaction and will be applied by the arbitral tribunal. In the case of an IBT, this will be, first and foremost, the contract law chosen by the parties or—in the absence of a valid choice or if the chosen legal system does not cover a particular issue—the contract law applicable by way of private international law or the rules on conflict of laws.[222] However, the substantive law could also be the rules governing the financing of the transaction (Part Three), the shipping of the goods (Part Four),[223] issues of insurance law (Part Five), or the rules on intellectual property protection. If the seller reserved title and the buyer did not pay in full, a claim may fall under property law. If fraud or gross negligence is involved, even tort law may play a role.

5. The Rules Governing the Recognition and Enforcement of the Arbitral Award

Recognition and enforcement of an award is generally governed by Articles III–VI of the New York Convention, provided the award was rendered abroad. This will be discussed in detail below, at pp. 1014 et seq. The national procedural law of the court called upon for enforcement also plays a role, in particular if it contains mandatory rules about enforcement or cases when enforcement should be refused as a matter of public policy or *ordre public*.

The following hypothetical demonstrates that the determination of the applicable law can be anything but easy:

---

222. For detailed discussion, see Part Two, pp. 113 et seq.; as well as Franco Ferrari & Stefan Kröll, *Conflict of Laws in International Commercial Arbitration*, JurisNet 2019;

223. Miriam Goldby & Loukas Mistelis, *The Role of Arbitration in Shipping Law*, Oxford Univ. Press 2016.

Hypothetical 6-1: Determination of the Applicable Law

Seller S in Indianapolis (Indiana, USA), and Buyer B in Sheffield (UK) enter into an agreement for the supply of several large and highly innovative 3D printing machines for the production of auto body parts. The machines have to be set up by S in Sheffield and S has to provide several weeks of training for the operators in the factory of B. The contract between S and B does not determine the applicable substantive law. Regarding dispute settlement, it provides for arbitration in Stockholm.

After the machines are set up, B's operators struggle to get the desired results. Eventually, B decides that the machines are not suitable for the purpose agreed upon in the contract with S, refuses to pay the second half of the purchase price, and wants a return of earlier payments plus damages. S maintains that the machines conform to the contractual terms and insists on full payment.

Following the advice of her lawyers, B files a claim for breach of contract in federal court in Indianapolis, *inter alia*, to benefit from the application of the UCC with its perfect tender rule and from the easy enforceability of the anticipated judgment against S.

S comes to you with the following questions:

1. In addition to arguing inadmissibility in the Indianapolis court, where can S file a case against B to compel B to pursue arbitration? Which law would the forum apply?

2. Would it make a difference for the answer to question 1 if S was incorporated in Delaware, with a head office in New York and merely doing business out of Indianapolis?

3. If S initiates arbitral proceedings in Stockholm and B does not participate, which legal rules would determine whether and under which conditions S could obtain a default award?

4. Which substantive law would have to be applied to the questions of performance versus non-performance and remedies?

5. Assuming that S can stop the litigation in Indianapolis and obtain a favorable award in Stockholm, how and under which legal rules could S enforce the award against B if B mainly or exclusively has assets in the UK?

6. Is it possible that the court in Indianapolis rules the arbitration clause to be invalid and proceeds with the litigation, while the arbitral tribunal in Stockholm rules the arbitration clause to be valid and proceeds with the arbitration? What would be the effect on the enforceability of the award? The judgment? Would a court in the UK have to make its own decision on the validity of the arbitration clause in the contract? Which rules would it apply? Would an appellate court in the U.S., called upon to review the Indianapolis judgment, become the fourth institution to determine whether or not the arbitration clause was valid?

7. If S should be able to find assets of B in another country, for example, France, could S present the Stockholm award there for recognition and enforcement? Would

a French court have to review the validity of the arbitration clause? Which law would the court apply? To what extent would it follow the earlier decisions of the U.S. courts? The Stockholm tribunal? A UK court that did or did not recognize the award?

Some of these questions are discussed in the following court decision:

Case 6-11

Ust-Kamenogorsk Hydropower Plant JSC v. AES Ust-Kamenogorsk Hydropower Plant LLP

The Supreme Court of the United Kingdom
Judgment Given on 12 June 2013, Trinity Term, [2013] UKSC 35

LORD MANCE (with whom Lord Neuberger, Lord Clarke, Lord Sumption and Lord Toulson agree)

Introduction

[1] An agreement to arbitrate disputes has positive and negative aspects. A party seeking relief within the scope of the arbitration agreement undertakes to do so in arbitration in whatever forum is prescribed. The (often silent) concomitant is that neither party will seek such relief in any other forum. If the other forum is the English court, the remedy for the party aggrieved is to apply for a stay under section 9 of the Arbitration Act 1996.

[2] The issue on this appeal is whether, if the other forum is a foreign jurisdiction outside the European régime of the Brussels Regulation (EC) No 44/2001 and the Lugano Convention, the English court has any and if so what power to declare that the claim can only properly be brought in arbitration and/or to injunct the continuation or commencement of the foreign proceedings. (It is clear that injunctive relief in relation to foreign proceedings within the Brussels/Lugano space is impermissible under the Regulation and Convention: *West Tankers Inc v Allianz SpA* [see above, p. 775].

[3] By order dated 16 April 2010, Burton J granted the respondent, Aes Ust-Kamenogorsk Hydropower Plant LLP ("AESUK"), such a declaration together with an injunction in relation to the bringing of proceedings against it by the appellant, Ust-Kamenogorsk Hydropower Plant JSC ("JSC"): [2010] 2 All ER (Comm) 1033. By order dated 1 July 2011 the Court of Appeal dismissed JSC's appeal against the judge's order: [2012] 1 WLR 920.

[4] The perhaps unusual feature is that AESUK has not commenced, and has no intention or wish to commence, any arbitration proceedings. Its contention is simply that JSC should not pursue or be free to pursue court proceedings against it. If JSC commences arbitration proceedings, then no doubt AESUK will defend them.

Background

[5] AESUK is the current grantee and lessee of a 25 year concession granted by agreement dated 23 July 1997 entitling it to operate an energy producing hydroelectric

plant in Kazakhstan. From 1997 to 2007, the concession was held by its parent or affiliate company, Tau Power BV. JSC is the current owner and grantor of the concession, having succeeded to the concession's original owner and grantor, the Republic of Kazakhstan.

⁶ The concession agreement is governed by Kazakh law (clause 31), but contains a London arbitration clause (clause 32). It was common ground below and it remains common ground, at least for the purposes of this appeal, that this clause is governed by and to be construed in accordance with English law. It is therefore unnecessary to consider authority in this area such as *C v D* [2007] EWCA Civ 1282, *Sulamérica Cia Nacional de Seguros SA v Enesa Engenharia SA* [2012] EWCA Civ 638 and *Arsanovia Ltd v Cruz City 1 Mauritius Holdings* [2012] EWHC 3702 (Comm).

⁷ The arbitration clause provides in summary that, subject to provisions contained in clauses 17.8 and 17.9, any dispute or difference arising out of or in connection with any matter or thing in relation to the provisions of the concession agreement and the transactions contemplated by the parties that cannot be resolved by negotiation should be settled by arbitration in accordance with the Rules of Conciliation and Arbitration of the International Chamber of Commerce (the "ICC") to be conducted in London.

⁸ Relations between the owners and holders of the concession have for some years been fraught. Burton J summarised the history in paras 5 to 10 of his judgment, and it is unnecessary to repeat it here. Some salient facts suffice.

⁹ First, during the period when it owned the concession, the Republic of Kazakhstan brought proceedings in Kazakhstan against AESUK's predecessors in title, Tau Power BV, and on 8 January 2004 obtained from the Kazakh Supreme Court a ruling that the arbitration clause was invalid. This was on two grounds: that the arbitration agreement included tariff disputes, which would put such disputes beyond the control of the Republic contrary to its public policy; and that the reference in clause 32 to the Rules of the ICC was not a reference to the ICC and left the arbitral body unspecified.

¹⁰ Burton J and the Court of Appeal held that they were not bound by the Kazakh court's conclusions in relation to an arbitration agreement subject to English law, and that neither ground was sustainable. Tariff disputes were in fact outside the arbitration agreement, by reason of the reference to clauses 17.8 and 17.9, under which they fell to be dealt with by an expert; and the reference in clause 32 to the ICC was plainly sufficient to mean that any arbitration was to be by the ICC. There is no appeal to this Court in relation to these matters.

¹¹ On 12 June 2009 JSC brought proceedings against AESUK in the Specialist Inter-District Economic Court of East Kazakhstan Oblast ("the Economic Court"), alleging that AESUK had failed to supply information concerning concession assets pursuant to a request duly made under the concession agreement. AESUK's application to stay these proceedings under the arbitration clause was dismissed on 28

July 2009 on the ground that the clause had been annulled by the Supreme Court's ruling of 8 January 2004.

[12] On 31 July 2009 AESUK issued proceedings before the English Commercial Court claiming declarations that the arbitration clause was valid and enforceable and a without notice interim anti-suit injunction restraining JSC from pursuit of the proceedings before the Economic Court. AESUK's attempt to rely on this injunction in the Kazakh courts was rejected by the Economic Court on 5 August 2009 and on an appeal to the East Kazakhstan Regional Court on 11 September 2009. Both the Economic Court and the Regional Court also held that JSC was entitled to the information which it had requested.

[13] Meanwhile on 21 August 2009 the interim injunction granted by the English Commercial Court was continued by consent pending a challenge by JSC to the jurisdiction of the English courts and amended to provide that JSC would withdraw its request for information the subject of the Kazakh proceedings. However, despite being requested, JSC did not undertake either that it would not resubmit a request for information or that it would not commence further proceedings in Kazakhstan. Hence, the continuation of the present proceedings, leading to Burton J's and the Court of Appeal's judgments and orders.

Burton J's order

[14] The order dated 16 April 2010 giving effect to Burton J's judgment declares in paragraph 2 that JSC "cannot bring", and orders in paragraph 3 that JSC "is restrained from bringing" "the claim, the subject matter of the [Kazakhstan proceedings], or any other claim arising out of or in connection with any matter or thing in relation to the provisions of the Concession Agreement. . . ., save only for [excepted matters], otherwise than by commencing arbitration proceedings in the International Chamber of Commerce in London and pursuant to its Rules." By its order dated 1 July 2011 giving effect to its judgment, the Court of Appeal simply dismissed the appeal against Burton J's order.

[15] In its terms and form, Burton J's order was and is a final order, as to both the declaration and the injunction which it granted. Indeed, in para 1 of his judgment, Burton J recorded that he was being asked to give "final relief" on AESUK's arbitration claim form, and in the final para 54 to 56 of his judgment, referring back to para 21, he concluded that AESUK was entitled to the grant of "(limited) final declaratory and injunctive relief". In these paragraphs, he made clear that he regarded an injunction in the wording of his later order as "limited" in a way which would avoid any concern about "usurpation or ouster" of the jurisdiction of the arbitrators, if any arbitration were to take place, and would give "the opportunity. . . . for any proper challenge to be made to the jurisdiction of the arbitrators or the applicability of the arbitration clause".

[16] Rix LJ, giving the main judgment in the Court of Appeal with which his colleagues agreed, addressed the nature of the order made by commenting (para 108) that it might possibly be said that a binding declaration as to the existence of the

arbitration agreement trespassed on the theoretical possibility that an arbitral tribunal might one day have to grapple with that very issue, that he did not himself think that it would do, but that he "need not decide that question here, for the judge has been cautious not to give such a declaration and the operator [AESUK] as respondent in this appeal has not sought to go further than the judge has gone".

[17] Before the Supreme Court, both sides have in their submissions treated the judge's order as a final order; and so in terms it is. Neither side has sought to have the order, if it stands, corrected or qualified. Appeals lie against orders, and parties are entitled and correct to take orders at their face value. Burton J's order was in terms a final order declaring that certain claims could only properly be pursued in arbitration, and restraining their pursuit in any other forum. If an arbitration were to be commenced, by either side, in the future, it would not, under Burton J's order, be open to the respondent to object to its commencement or to the jurisdiction of the arbitral tribunal by submissions which contradicted the terms of the declaration made and injunction ordered by Burton J. The Supreme Court can and should consider the order on that basis. Further, if the court has, consistently with the scheme of the Arbitration Act 1996, power to make any sort of declaration about arbitral jurisdiction, then Rix LJ was, in my view, right that there is no objection to its being a final and binding declaration.

The issue

[18] The issue is therefore whether the English court has power to declare that the claim can only properly be brought in arbitration and/or to injunct the continuation or commencement of proceedings brought in any other forum outside the Brussels/Lugano régime. Although Lord Goldsmith in his oral submissions laid some emphasis on the primacy of the declaratory relief claimed by AESUK and ordered by Burton J, in my opinion the claim and order for injunctive relief are more important. Before the court could order final injunctive relief, it had to conclude that there was a binding and applicable arbitration agreement—as JSC's own case in fact correctly stated at para 67. The order for injunctive relief carried by itself the basis of an issue estoppel in any future proceedings, precluding JSC from denying the existence or validity of such an agreement.

[19] The rival submissions regarding the court's power turn primarily on the scope and effect of the Arbitration Act 1996. Mr Toby Landau QC for AESUK advances a simple case. Independently of that Act, the court has a general inherent power to declare rights and further, under section 37 of the Senior Courts Act (formerly the Supreme Court Act) 1981:

> "The High Court may by order (whether interlocutory or final) grant an injunction or appoint a receiver in all cases in which it appears to the court to be just and convenient to do so".

[20] Despite its generality, there are statements limiting the application of section 37 to two situations: (a) where one party can show that the other party has invaded, or threatens to invade, a legal or equitable right of the former for the enforcement of

which the latter is amenable to the jurisdiction of the court, and (b) where one party to any action has behaved, or threatens to behave, in a manner which is unconscionable. . . . JSC has invaded or is threatening to invade AESUK's legal right not to be sued in Kazakhstan. Absent any contrary reason, there is, AESUK submits, no reason why the court should not exercise both its declaratory powers and its powers under section 37. To do so would support the commitment to arbitration contained in the arbitration clause. In contrast, JSC—although it invokes the supposed policy interests of international users of London arbitration—opposes the deployment of such powers in order to frustrate the arbitration clause.

The negative aspect of an arbitration agreement and exclusive choice of court clause

[21] At points in his submissions, Lord Goldsmith QC, representing JSC, suggested that any negative obligation inherent in an arbitration agreement is a mere ancillary to current or intended arbitral proceedings. As a matter of interpretation of a straightforward agreement to arbitrate disputes in a particular forum . . . , there is no basis for any such limitation. The negative aspect of an arbitration agreement is a feature shared with an exclusive choice of court clause. In each case, the negative aspect is as fundamental as the positive. There is no reason why a party to either should be free to engage the other party in a different forum merely because neither party wishes to bring proceedings in the agreed forum. Nor is there any basis for treating the Arbitration Act 1996 as affecting the *interpretation* of an arbitration agreement in this respect, although it is JSC's case that the effect of the Act is to preclude the court from granting *relief* to enforce the negative aspect of an arbitration agreement unless and until arbitral proceedings are on foot or proposed (see para 29 et seq below).

[22] The case-law also contains no support for JSC's argument that the negative aspect of an arbitration agreement is enforceable only when an arbitration is on foot or proposed. It is true that in most of the cases an arbitration was on foot, but none of the statements of principle identify this as relevant or critical. The case-law is worth considering more closely not only to make this good, but also as background to a consideration of JSC's submissions on the effect of the Arbitration Act.

[23] Both prior to the Arbitration Act 1996 and indeed subsequently—until the present case—the negative aspect was well recognised, and it was well established that the English courts would give effect to it, where necessary by injuncting foreign proceedings brought in breach of either an arbitration agreement or an exclusive choice of court clause. . . . A stay is not made conditional upon arbitration being on foot, proposed or brought. If there is power under section 37 to injunct the commencement or continuation of foreign proceedings, no reason is evident why the exercise of this power should depend upon such a condition. In each case it is, on the face of it, for either party to commence any arbitration it wishes at any time, or not to do so.

[24] In *Pena Copper Mines Ltd v Rio Tinto Co Ltd* (1911) 105 LT 846, an English law contract provided for any matter in difference to be referred to arbitration under the

Arbitration Act 1889 (and for an award to be a condition precedent to any liability in respect thereof), but Rio Tinto began Spanish court proceedings. No arbitration was on foot. The Pena company expressed itself "perfectly willing to refer" any dispute to arbitration, but that does not mean that it proposed to do so itself and no such condition was imposed upon it. After referring to the statutory power to stay which would have existed had Rio Tinto commenced English court proceedings, the Court of Appeal ordered Rio Tinto to desist from the Spanish proceedings. The arbitration clause involved, in Cozens Hardy MR's words, "probably an express negative, but. . . . certainly an implied negative", a contract "that they will not sue in a foreign court" (pages 850–851), and Rio Tinto's conduct in suing in Spain was, in Fletcher Moulton LJ's words, "certainly contrary to their contractual duties" (page 852). That an award was a condition precedent to any liability cannot have been decisive.

[25] By the 1990s it had come to be thought that the power to injunct foreign proceedings brought in breach of contract should be exercised "only with caution", because English courts "will not lightly interfere with the conduct of proceedings in a foreign court": see eg *Sokana Industries Inc v Freyre & Co Inc* [1994] 2 Lloyd's Rep 57, 66, per Colman J. But in *Aggeliki Charis Cia Maritime SA v Pagnan SpA (The "Angelic Grace")* [1995] 1 Lloyd's Rep 87, where the parties had agreed to arbitrate all disputes in London (an award not being a condition precedent to liability) and owners commenced such an arbitration while charterers sued in court in Venice, the Court of Appeal held, citing *Pena Copper* and other authority, that courts ought not to feel diffident about granting an anti-suit injunction, if sought promptly. Without it the claimant would be deprived of its contractual rights in a situation where damages would be manifestly an inadequate remedy. The time had come, in Millett LJ's words, "to lay aside the ritual incantation that this is a jurisdiction which should only be exercised sparingly and with great caution". An injunction should be granted to restrain foreign proceedings in breach of an arbitration agreement "on the simple and clear ground that the defendant has promised not to bring them". The principle was endorsed in the context of exclusive choice of court clauses by the House of Lords in *Donohue v Armco Inc* [2001] UKHL 64; [2002] 1 All ER 749, a decision recognising (para 24) that strong reasons are required to outweigh the prima facie entitlement to an injunction. In that case, a claim for fraud conspiracy was brought against Mr Donohue in New York in breach of an agreement providing for the exclusive jurisdiction of the English courts. Mr Donohue was refused an anti-suit injunction because strong reasons (in the form of alleged participation in the alleged fraud of other New York defendants not party to any exclusive jurisdiction agreement) existed why the New York proceedings should continue. But the consideration that Mr Donohue had not commenced English proceedings on the substance of the matter played no part in the reasoning. Indeed the House recognised that he would continue to have a prima facie right to recover any damage he suffered in consequence of the continuation of the New York proceedings against him contrary to the exclusive jurisdiction clause: paras 36 and 48 per Lord Bingham and Lord Hobhouse.

26 Lord Hobhouse also encapsulated the principle in *Turner v Grovit* [2001] UKHL 65; [2002] 1 WLR 107, when he said:

> "25 . . . . Under English law, a person has no right not to be sued in a particular forum, domestic or foreign, unless there is some specific factor which gives him that right. A contractual arbitration or exclusive jurisdiction clause will provide such a ground for seeking to invoke the right to enforce the clause. The applicant does not have to show that the contractual forum is more appropriate than any other; the parties' contractual agreement does that for him. . . . ..
>
> 27 The applicant for a restraining order must have a legitimate interest in making his application and the protection of that interest must make it necessary to make the order. Where the applicant is relying upon a contractual right not to be sued in the foreign country (say because of an exclusive jurisdiction clause or an arbitration clause), then, absent some special circumstance, he has by reason of his contract a legitimate interest in enforcing that right against the other party to the contract."

27 In the *West Tankers* case at first instance ([2005] EWHC 454 (Comm), paras 13, 59 and 72), Colman J referred to *The "Angelic Grace"* and *Donohue v Armco*, when granting a permanent injunction restraining the pursuit of the Italian legal proceedings which he had held to be in breach of a London arbitration agreement. That aspect of the decision was not questioned when the matter came before the Court of Appeal and the House of Lords, where Lord Hoffmann said, [2007] 1 Lloyd's Rep 391, para 10:

> "By section 37(1) of the Supreme Court Act 1981 the High Court has jurisdiction to grant an injunction (whether interlocutory or final) 'in all cases in which it appears to the court to be just and convenient to do so'. The English courts have regularly exercised this power to grant injunctions to restrain parties to an arbitration agreement from instituting or continuing proceedings in the courts of other countries: see *The Angelic Grace* [1995] 1 Lloyd's Rep 87."

He went on to refer to the court's power to grant an interim injunction under section 44, to which I revert below. The interpretation subsequently given to the Brussels Regulation by the Court of Justice in *West Tankers* (Case C-185/07) now means that an English court can no longer enforce contractual rights (or prevent oppression of the sort found to exist in *Turner v Grovit*) by injuncting a party within its jurisdiction from commencing or continuing proceedings in a foreign court within the Brussels/Lugano regime. But that limitation is irrelevant in this case.

28 Unless the Arbitration Act 1996 requires a different conclusion, the negative aspect of a London arbitration agreement is therefore a right enforceable independently of the existence or imminence of any arbitral proceedings.

The scheme of the Arbitration Act 1996

[29] JSC submits that it is contrary to the terms, scheme, philosophy and parliamentary intention of the Arbitration Act 1996 for an English court to determine that foreign proceedings involve a breach of an arbitration agreement or issue either declaratory or injunctive relief on that basis other than when arbitral proceedings are on foot or proposed and only then under the provisions of the Act. The Arbitration Act contains "a complete and workable set of rules for the determination of jurisdictional issues". The general rule is that the arbitral tribunal should consider jurisdictional issues in the first instance—with "the only exception to that general rule for a party *asserting* arbitral jurisdiction to be found in section 32". Unless and until one or other party commences an arbitration, the court should keep a distance. Any more general power contained in section 37 has been superseded by the Act, or should at least no longer be exercised. . . .

[31] JSC points out correctly that the 1996 Act embodies, (from Mustill and Boyd, Commercial Arbitration: (2001) Companion Volume to 2nd Ed, preface endorsed by Lord Steyn) "a new balancing of the relationships between parties, advocates, arbitrators and courts which is not only designed to achieve a policy proclaimed within Parliament and outside, but may also have changed their juristic nature": *Lesotho Highlands Development Authority v Impregilo SpA* [2005] UKHL 43, [2006] 1 AC 221, para 17. The Act was also a response to "international criticism that the Courts intervene more than they should in the arbitral process, thereby tending to frustrate the choice the parties have made to use arbitration rather than litigation as the means for resolving their disputes": Report on Arbitration of the Departmental Advisory Committee ("DAC") 1996 (with Lord Justice Saville as its chair), paragraphs 20–22. This criticism was addressed by the third of the general principles with which the Act, unusually, begins:

> "1. General principles.
>
> The provisions of this Part are founded on the following principles, and shall be construed accordingly—
>
> (a) the object of arbitration is to obtain the fair resolution of disputes by an impartial tribunal without unnecessary delay or expense;
>
> (b) the parties should be free to agree how their disputes are resolved, subject only to such safeguards as are necessary in the public interest;
>
> (c) in matters governed by this Part the court should not intervene except as provided by this Part."

[32] JSC's submissions in this area give rise to two questions. The first is the extent to which it is correct to regard the 1996 Act as a complete and workable set of rules for the determination of all jurisdictional issues in all situations. The other is what is meant by the word "should" in section 1(c). As to the first, section 1(c) is limited to "matters governed by this Part", and it is clear that the drafters of the Act were

not attempting a complete code of arbitration law. The DAC Report 1996 stated expressly that "The Bill does not purport to provide an exhaustive code on the subject of arbitration", but that they had "sought to include what we consider to be the more important common law principles, whilst preserving all others, in so far as they are consistent with the provisions of this Bill (see clause 81)". Clause 81 became section 81, reading

> "Nothing in this Part shall be construed as excluding the operation of any rule of law consistent with the provisions of this Part in particular, any rule of law as to—
>
> (a) matters which are not capable of settlement by arbitration;
>
> (b) the effect of an oral arbitration agreement; or
>
> (c) the refusal of recognition or enforcement of an arbitral award on grounds of public policy".

The DAC Report instances confidentiality as another subject deliberately left outside the scope of the Act.

[33] The use of the word "should" in section 1(c) was also a deliberate departure from the more prescriptive "shall" appearing in article 5 of the UNCITRAL Model Law. Article 5 reads that "In matters governed by this Law, no court shall intervene except where so provided in this Law". Article 5 had been the subject of forceful critique in *A New Arbitration Act?*, the 1989 report on the UNCITRAL Model Law by the DAC at a time when its chair was Lord Justice Mustill, who had also represented the United Kingdom at UNCITRAL. Even in matters which might be regarded as falling within Part 1, it is clear that section 1(c) implies a need for caution, rather than an absolute prohibition, before any court intervention.

[34] It is in these circumstances that the question now arises whether it is consistent with the 1996 Act for the English court to determine whether there is a valid and applicable arbitration agreement covering the subject matter of actual or threatened foreign proceedings and, if it holds that there is, to injunct the commencement or continuation of the foreign proceedings. JSC points to sections 32 and 72 of the Act as the means by which a challenge to the jurisdiction may, under certain conditions, be pursued during an arbitration and to section 67 as the means by which an award may be challenged for lack of jurisdiction. It submits, that, if AESUK convoked an arbitral tribunal, the arbitrators could rule on their jurisdiction under section 30, their ruling could be tested under sections 32, 67 and/or 72 and the court could in the meantime be asked to give interim relief under section 44.

Sections 30, 32 and 72 and Kompetenz-Kompetenz

[35] Section 30 provides that an arbitral tribunal may rule on its own substantive jurisdiction:

> "30 Competence of tribunal to rule on its own jurisdiction.
>
> (1) Unless otherwise agreed by the parties, the arbitral tribunal may rule on its own substantive jurisdiction, that is, as to—

(a) whether there is a valid arbitration agreement,

(b) whether the tribunal is properly constituted, and

(c) what matters have been submitted to arbitration in accordance with the arbitration agreement.

(2) Any such ruling may be challenged by any available arbitral process of appeal or review or in accordance with the provisions of this Part."

Section 30 reflects the principle of "Kompetenz-Kompetenz", discussed in *Dallah Real Estate and Tourism Holding Co v Ministry of Religious Affairs of the Government of Pakistan* [2010] UKSC 46, [2011] 1 AC 763. In short, any tribunal convoked to determine a dispute may, as a preliminary, consider and rule upon the question whether the dispute is within its substantive jurisdiction, without such ruling being binding on any subsequent review of its determination by the court under sections 32, 67 or 72 of the 1996 Act. However, a tribunal cannot by its preliminary ruling that it has substantive jurisdiction to determine a dispute confer upon itself a substantive jurisdiction which it does not have. Absent a submission specifically tailored to embrace them (as to which there is no suggestion here), jurisdictional issues stand necessarily on a different footing to the substantive issues on which an award made within the tribunal's jurisdiction will be binding.

[36] In *Dallah*, I put these points as follows (para 24):

".... Arbitrators (like many other decision-making bodies) may from time to time find themselves faced with challenges to their role or powers, and have in that event to consider the existence and extent of their authority to decide particular issues involving particular persons. But, absent specific authority to do this, they cannot by their own decision on such matters create or extend the authority conferred upon them."

Lord Collins said (para 84) that it does not follow, from the general principle that a tribunal has power to consider its own jurisdiction:

"that the tribunal has the exclusive power to determine its own jurisdiction, nor does it follow that the court of the seat may not determine whether the tribunal has jurisdiction before the tribunal has ruled on it. Nor does it follow that the question of jurisdiction may not be re-examined by the supervisory court of the seat in a challenge to the tribunal's ruling on jurisdiction. Still less does it mean that when the award comes to be enforced in another country, the foreign court may not re-examine the jurisdiction of the tribunal."

[37] Section 32 enables the court to determine any question as to the substantive jurisdiction of a tribunal "on the application of a party to arbitral proceedings", provided that the application is made by agreement of all the other parties or, subject to the court being satisfied of various matters, with the tribunal's permission. Section 44 provides for the court to have "for the purposes of and in relation to arbitral proceedings", and on the application of a party or proposed party to the proceedings,

the same power of making orders about certain listed matters as it has for purposes of and in relation to legal proceedings. The listed matters include the making of an interim injunction, but, save in case of urgency, the court is only to act on an application made under section 44 with the permission of the tribunal or the agreement of the other parties to the arbitral proceedings.

[38] Section 72 permits a party alleged to be a party to arbitral proceedings but who takes no part in them to take his jurisdictional challenge directly to the court without waiting for the tribunal to address the matter.

[39] In support of its submissions, JSC relies upon cases in which commercial judges have refused to permit the pursuit of court proceedings for a declaration as to the existence of a binding arbitration clause brought by a claimant in current or proposed arbitration proceedings: *ABB Lummus Global Ltd v Keppel Fels Ltd* [1999] 2 Lloyd's Rep 24; *Vale do Rio Doce Navegaceo SA v Shanghai Bao Steel Ocean Shipping Co Ltd* [2000] 2 All ER (Comm) 70. In *Vale do Rio*, Thomas J observed that it could not have been the intention that a party to a disputed arbitration agreement could obtain the decision of the courts on its existence without being subject to the restrictions contained in section 32 by the simple step of not appointing an arbitrator (para 53). Although he concluded (para 60) that the court had no "jurisdiction" to allow the application, earlier, in noting the change from "shall" to "should" in section 1(c), he had said that "it is clear that the general intention was that the court should usually not intervene outside the specific circumstances specified in Part 1 of the 1996 Act" (para 52).

[40] These cases have no direct bearing on the present situation. Here, no arbitration proceedings are on foot and AESUK does not intend or wish to institute any. Sections 30, 32, 44 and 72 of the Act are all in terms inapplicable. No arbitration tribunal exists to determine its own competence under section 30. The principle of Kompetenz-Kompetenz — or, in an anglicised version suggested by Lord Sumption, jurisdiction-competence — makes sense where a tribunal is asked to exercise a substantive jurisdiction and hears submissions at the outset as to whether it has such a jurisdiction. Even then, the court has the last word in establishing whether the substantive jurisdiction actually exists. But the principle has no application where no arbitration is on foot or contemplated. On JSC's case, a party wishing relief in relation to foreign proceedings brought or threatened contrary to an arbitration agreement, must however commence, or should be required to undertake to commence, an arbitration against the other party who is rejecting the existence or application of any arbitration agreement. Further, the only substantive relief that JSC could suggest might be sought in such an arbitration would be an order, within the power afforded by section 48(5)(a) of the 1996 Act, not to commence or continue any foreign proceedings; and the efficacy of any such order as arbitrators might make, in any such arbitration, if they held that they had jurisdiction, would depend upon the court determining for itself that the tribunal had jurisdiction, and then enforcing the tribunal's order under either section 44 or section 66 of the Act with the backing of the court's contempt jurisdiction.

[41] In these circumstances, there is, in my opinion, every reason why the court should be able to intervene directly, by an order enforceable by contempt, under section 37. To do so cannot be regarded, in the DAC's words, as "intervene[ing] in the arbitral process, thereby tending to frustrate the choice the parties have made to use arbitration rather than litigation as the means for resolving their disputes". On the contrary, JSC has complete freedom of choice in relation to the arbitration agreement. In denying that the court has any relevant jurisdiction, JSC is seeking to benefit by AESUK's reliance on an arbitration agreement, while itself denying its existence. A party is entitled to benefit by the existence of an arbitration agreement, but normally only by asserting it, e.g., by commencing an arbitration or applying for a stay under section 9. Those must however be the last things that JSC is willing to do.

[42] As to section 32, there is no party to arbitral proceedings who could apply to the court to determine any question of arbitral jurisdiction, and there are no other parties or tribunal with whose consent or permission any such application would have to be made and no tribunal whose substantive jurisdiction could be the subject of such an application.

Section 44

[43] Similarly, the court's powers listed in section 44 are exercisable only "for the purposes of and in relation to arbitral proceedings" and depend upon such proceedings being on foot or "proposed": see section 44(3). That alone is sufficient in my opinion to lead to a conclusion that section 44 has no bearing on the question whether section 37 empowers the court to restrain the commencement or continuation of foreign proceedings in the light of an arbitration agreement under which neither party wishes to commence an arbitration.

[44] I should however say something further about JSC's submission that section 44(2)(e) embraces the granting of an interim injunction to restrain the pursuit of foreign proceedings during a current or proposed arbitration. The careful limitation of the court's power to "the granting of an interim injunction" militates, he argues, against the existence of any general power to injunct foreign proceedings under section 37, even on an interim basis in relation to current or proposed arbitral proceedings, let alone on a permanent basis in their absence.

[45] It is helpful to set out section 44 in full:

"Court powers exercisable in support of arbitral proceedings.

(1) Unless otherwise agreed by the parties, the court has for the purposes of and in relation to arbitral proceedings the same power of making orders about the matters listed below as it has for the purposes of and in relation to legal proceedings.

(2) Those matters are—

(a) the taking of the evidence of witnesses;

(b) the preservation of evidence;

(c) making orders relating to property which is the subject of the proceedings or as to which any question arises in the proceedings—

(i) for the inspection, photographing, preservation, custody or detention of the property, or

(ii) ordering that samples be taken from, or any observation be made of or experiment conducted upon, the property;

and for that purpose authorising any person to enter any premises in the possession or control of a party to the arbitration;

(d) the sale of any goods the subject of the proceedings;

(e) the granting of an interim injunction or the appointment of a receiver.

(3) If the case is one of urgency, the court may, on the application of a party or proposed party to the arbitral proceedings, make such orders as it thinks necessary for the purpose of preserving evidence or assets.

(4) If the case is not one of urgency, the court shall act only on the application of a party to the arbitral proceedings (upon notice to the other parties and to the tribunal) made with the permission of the tribunal or the agreement in writing of the other parties.

(5) In any case the court shall act only if or to the extent that the arbitral tribunal, and any arbitral or other institution or person vested by the parties with power in that regard, has no power or is unable for the time being to act effectively.

(6) If the court so orders, an order made by it under this section shall cease to have effect in whole or in part on the order of the tribunal or of any such arbitral or other institution or person having power to act in relation to the subject-matter of the order.

(7) The leave of the court is required for any appeal from a decision of the court under this section."

[46] Section 44(2) is the modern successor to the First Schedule to the Arbitration Act 1934 and section 12(6) of the Arbitration Act 1950—section 44(2)(e) corresponds with paragraph 8 of the First Schedule and section 12(6)(h) of the 1950 Act. The matters listed in section 44 are all matters which could require the court's intervention during actual or proposed arbitral proceedings. The power to grant an interim injunction is expressed in general terms, but is limited, save in cases of urgency, to circumstances in which either the tribunal permits an application to the court or all the other parties agree to this in writing. There is no power to grant a final injunction, even after an award. There is authority (not requiring review on this appeal) that section 44(3) can include orders urgently required pending a proposed arbitration to preserve or enforce parties' substantive rights—eg an order to allow inspection of an agent's underwriting records or to submit a proposed transfer to a central bank: see *Hiscox Underwriting Ltd v Dickson Manchester & Co Ltd* [2004]

2 Lloyd's Rep 438; *Cetelem SA v Roust Holdings Ltd* [2005] EWCA Civ 618; [2005] 1 WLR 3555. Such orders can be said to be "for the purposes of and in relation to arbitral proceedings". But orders restraining the actual or threatened breach of the negative aspect of an arbitration agreement may be required both where no arbitration proceedings are on foot or proposed, and where the case is not one of urgency (and so not within section 44(3)). They enforce the negative right not to be vexed by foreign proceedings. This is a right of a different character both to the procedural rights with which section 44 is mainly, at least, concerned, and to the substantive rights to which the *Hiscox* and *Cetelem* cases hold that it extends.

[47] In *Starlight Shipping Co v Tai Ping Insurance Co Ltd (The "Alexandros T")* [2007] EWHC 1893 (Comm); [2008] 1 All ER (Comm) 593, Cooke J addressed the interrelationship of section 44 of the 1996 Act and section 37 of the Senior Courts Act 1981 in a context where proceedings were being pursued in China in apparent breach of an arbitration agreement and where arbitral proceedings were also current. He treated both sections as potentially available, adding that the matters relevant under section 44 could also bear on, though not govern in the same way, the exercise of the general discretion under section 37 (para 29). He considered that "the contractual right to have disputes referred to arbitration" must be an "asset" falling within section 44(3). In the upshot, he gave interim relief under section 44, on the basis that the matter was urgent under section 44(3) because the arbitral tribunal would not be able to issue an award restraining the claimants in the Chinese proceedings from pursuing such proceedings speedily enough or, therefore, effectively under section 44(5). At the same time, he also made an interim order under section 37, pointing out inter alia that "The difference between an order of this court and that of the arbitrators is that remedies for contempt are available if an order of this court should be breached" . . . .

[48] The better view, in my opinion, is that the reference in section 44(2)(e) to the granting of an interim injunction was not intended either to exclude the Court's general power to act under section 37 of the 1981 Act in circumstances outside the scope of section 44 of the 1996 Act or to duplicate part of the general power contained in section 37 of the 1981 Act. Where an injunction is sought to restrain foreign proceedings in breach of an arbitration agreement—whether on an interim or a final basis and whether at a time when arbitral proceedings are or are not on foot or proposed—the source of the power to grant such an injunction is to be found not in section 44 of the 1996 Act, but in section 37 of the 1981 Act. Such an injunction is not "for the purposes of and in relation to arbitral proceedings", but for the purposes of and in relation to the negative promise contained in the arbitration agreement not to bring foreign proceedings, which applies and is enforceable regardless of whether or not arbitral proceedings are on foot or proposed. . . .

[49] . . . [Civil Procedure Rules] CPR62.2 provides:

  "(1) In this Section of this Part 'arbitration claim' means—

    (a) any application to the court under the 1996 Act;

(b) a claim to determine —

(i) whether there is a valid arbitration agreement;

(ii) whether an arbitration tribunal is properly constituted; or

(iii) what matters have been submitted to arbitration in accordance with an arbitration agreement;

(c) a claim to declare that an award by an arbitral tribunal is not binding on a party; and

(d) any other application affecting —

(i) arbitration proceedings (whether started or not); or

(ii) an arbitration agreement." . . .

[50] I regard these provisions as wide enough to embrace a claim under section 37 to restrain foreign proceedings in breach of the negative aspect of an arbitration agreement. In circumstances where an arbitration claim includes under CPR62.2(d) "any other application affecting (i) arbitration proceedings (whether started or not); or (ii) an arbitration agreement", the requirement in CPR62.5(c)(ii) that "the seat of the arbitration is or will be within the jurisdiction" must be read as satisfied if the seat of any arbitration, if any were to be commenced or proposed under the arbitration agreement, would be within the jurisdiction. . . .

Section 37 of the Senior Courts Act 1981

[55] More generally, JSC's case depends upon a conclusion that the Arbitration Act 1996 either limits the scope, or as a matter of general principle qualifies the use, of the general power contained in section 37, so that it is no longer permissible to deploy section 37 to injunct foreign proceedings begun or threatened in breach of an arbitration agreement. Again, I cannot accept JSC's case.

[56] Section 37 is a general power, not specifically tailored to situations where there is either an arbitration agreement or an exclusive choice of court clause. To adopt words of Lord Mustill in the *Channel Tunnel* case, [1993] AC 334, 360E-F, with reference to the relationship between section 37 and the previous arbitration legislation (the Arbitration Act 1950):

"Under section 37(1) by contrast the arbitration clause is not the source of the power to grant an injunction but is merely a part of the facts in the light of which the court decides whether or not to exercise a power which exists independently of it."

The court may as a result need to be very cautious:

"in the exercise of its general powers under section 37 so as not to conflict with any restraint which the legislature may have imposed on the exercise of the new and specialised powers." (p 364B-C).

However, it is, in my opinion, entirely understandable that Parliament should not have thought to carve out from section 37 of the Senior Courts Act or to reproduce in the 1996 Act one aspect of a general power conferred by section 37. It cannot be deduced from the fact that it did not do so that it intended that the general power should never be exercised in any context associated with arbitration.

[57] On the contrary, it would be astonishing if Parliament should, silently and without warning, have abrogated or precluded the use by the English court of its previous well-established jurisdiction under section 37 in respect of foreign proceedings commenced or threatened in breach of the negative aspect of an arbitration agreement. One would have expected the intended inapplicability of section 37 to have been made very clear in both the DAC Report and the Act. The 1996 Act does in Schedule 3 or 4 provide for other presently immaterial amendments or repeals in respect of provisions in what was the Supreme Court Act and is now the Senior Courts Act 1981.

[58] *The "Angelic Grace"* [1994] 1 Lloyd's Rep 168 in particular was a highly prominent decision, expressed in emphatic terms during the very period when the DAC was preparing the Bill for the Act and its own report. Nothing in the DAC report of 1996 addresses either it or the long-standing and well recognised jurisdiction which was its subject-matter. Yet a regime under which the English court could no longer enforce the negative rights of a party to a London arbitration agreement by injunctive relief restraining foreign proceedings would have been, and would have been seen, as a radical diminution of the protection afforded by English law to parties to such an arbitration agreement. It would have aroused considerable interest and, no doubt, concern. The only sensible inference is that the drafters of the Act never contemplated that it could or would undermine the established jurisprudence on anti-suit injunctions.

[59] It was only later that the Court of Justice in Luxembourg restricted the use of such injunctions; and then only in relation to foreign proceedings in the area covered by the Brussels/Lugano régime and on the basis of the mutual trust affirmed to exist between courts within that regime. The interest and concern that this aroused witnesses to the interest that would have been aroused had the Bill or 1996 Act been seen as having any such radical intention or effect in relation to courts worldwide. The *West Tankers* case [2009] AC 1138 suggests that it did not occur to anyone until this case that it did.

Conclusion

[60] The power to stay domestic legal proceedings under section 9 and the power to determine that foreign proceedings are in breach of an arbitration agreement and to injunct their commencement or continuation are in truth opposite and complementary sides of a coin. Subject to the recent European inroad, that remains the position. The general power provided by section 37 of the 1981 Act must be exercised sensitively and, in particular, with due regard for the scheme and terms of the 1996 Act when any arbitration is on foot or proposed. It is also open to a court under section 37, if it thinks fit, to grant any injunction on an interim basis, pending the outcome of current or proposed arbitration proceedings, rather than a final

basis. But, for the reasons I have given, it is inconceivable that the 1996 Act intended or should be treated sub silentio as effectively abrogating the protection enjoyed under section 37 in respect of their negative rights under an arbitration agreement by those who stipulate for an arbitration with an English seat.

[61] In some cases where foreign proceedings are brought in breach of an arbitration clause or exclusive choice of court agreement, the appropriate course will be to leave it to the foreign court to recognise and enforce the parties' agreement on forum. But in the present case the foreign court has refused to do so, and done this on a basis which the English courts are not bound to recognise and on grounds which are unsustainable under English law which is accepted to govern the arbitration agreement. In these circumstances, there was every reason for the English courts to intervene to protect the prima facie right of AESUK to enforce the negative aspect of its arbitration agreement with JSC.

[62] It follows that Burton J had jurisdiction under section 37 of the Senior Courts Act 1981 to make the order that he did, and that there was nothing wrong in principle with his exercise of his power to do so. The Court of Appeal was right so to conclude, and the appeal should be dismissed.

Notes and Questions

1. The outcome of the case is consistent with earlier case law from the UK and various other jurisdictions, but it contradicts the judgment of the European Court of Justice in the *West Tankers Case*, above p. 740. One explanation for *West Tankers* is the applicability of the EU Regulation 44/2001 on Jurisdiction and the Recognition and Enforcement of Judgments in Civil and Commercial Matters,[224] to jurisdictional conflicts between courts of the Member States of the EU. However, the New York Convention precedes the founding of the EU and the adoption of the Brussels and Lugano Conventions, as well as Regulation 44/2001. Can Contracting States to the New York Convention create rules that conflict with their obligations under the New York Convention in the framework of the EU? Should they?

2. Further to question 1 and more specifically, should a court of one country be able to enjoin the courts of another country from examining an arbitration clause and accepting litigation after finding it limited or defective? What are arguments in favor of and against such a power? How and where can the decisions of the British

---

224. Regulation 44/2001 replaced an earlier convention between the EU Member States, the 1968 Brussels Convention on Jurisdiction and the Enforcement of Judgments in Civil and Commercial Matters. This is why the Regulation is commonly referred to as "the Brussels Regulation." A parallel convention extended—and continues to extend—the main features of the Brussels Convention to a number of European states that are not members of the EU, the 1988 Lugano Convention on Jurisdiction and the Enforcement of Judgments in Civil and Commercial Matters.

More recently, Regulation 44/2001 has itself been updated and replaced by Regulation 1215/2012 of 12 December 2012 on Jurisdiction and the Recognition and Enforcement of Judgments in Civil and Commercial Matters, OJ 2012 L 351, pp. 1–32. The updated and current Regulation is reproduced in the Documents at p. II-92.

courts be enforced? What do they mean for the proceedings in Kazakhstan? Could one say, therefore, that the European Court of Justice, in *West Tankers*, was wrong? Or that the UK Supreme Court in the present case is wrong? Or can the judgments coexist meaningfully?

3. What do you make of the fact that in the present case, there was not yet a case of actual arbitration proceedings competing with the litigation in Kazakhstan? It seems that one side of the dispute wanted to litigate in Kazakhstan but under no circumstances wanted to participate in arbitration in London, while the other side would be open to arbitration in London but under no circumstances wanted to be drawn in litigation in Kazakhstan. What, if anything, does this tell us about the trust placed by either party into the preferred dispute settlement mechanism of the other party? And — potentially — about the merits of their respective claims?

4. Can you explain the doctrine of Kompetenz-Kompetenz in paragraph 35 et seq.? When does it apply? When does it not? Is it fair to say that the doctrine always favors the first-seized forum because they get to decide whether they have competence or jurisdiction, while others cannot be seized until the first-seized forum declines jurisdiction?

5. What does the court mean by "[t]he difference between an order of this court and that of the arbitrators is that remedies for contempt are available if an order of this court should be breached"?

6. In *Kamenogorsk*, the issue was that one party to an arbitration agreement initiated litigation instead of arbitration. Another problem with an agreement to arbitrate can be the refusal of one party to participate in arbitration by not showing up and/or not appointing an arbitrator. We will examine below, at p. 1000, whether the other party can obtain an award in default.

3. *The Specific Situation in the U.S. — the Applicable Law for International Commercial Arbitration*

The legal rules governing B2B arbitration in the U.S. are complicated. On the one hand, there is the Federal Arbitration Act (FAA), which incorporates the New York Convention on Recognition and Enforcement of Foreign Awards and the Inter-American Convention on International Commercial Arbitration. However, the FAA itself does not establish jurisdiction of the federal courts. This has to be supplied by the Interstate Commerce Clause and will only apply to interstate and international cases. Moreover, the FAA is very short and quite outdated, compared, for example, to the English Arbitration Act, and in particular the various sets of rules provided by the major arbitration institutions. As a consequence, when the FAA applies, lawyers have to fill in many of the blanks and provide many updates by reference to case law. The reporters of the Restatement of the Law, The U.S. Law of International Commercial and Investor-State Arbitration[225] provide a summary of the problems:

---

225. See Documents, p. II-512.

George Bermann, Jack J. Coe, Jr., Christopher R. Drahozal, and Catherine A. Rogers

Restating the U.S. Law of International Commercial Arbitration [226]

2009 Penn State Law Review, Vol. 113, No. 4, pp. 1333–1342

[1334] II. The need for and purpose of the restatement

The United States occupies a unique place in the modern international arbitration system and in its historic evolution. On the one hand, in the early decades of the Republic the United States was one of the leading proponents of state-to-state arbitration as a means for resolving international disputes. More recently, American lawyers, arbitrators and arbitration specialists have been important contributors to the growth and development of the international commercial arbitration system, from its very inception and within its most venerable institutions. Over the years, a number of U.S. judicial decisions have become seminal reference points for international tribunals, commentators and even foreign courts in the development of international arbitration precedents.[1]

On the other hand, U.S. parties and lawyers have sometimes taken atypical approaches towards arbitral procedures, particularly when contrasted to some European counterparts, on matters as diverse as arbitrator independence, discovery and the role of lawyers. In this latter respect, some suggest that international arbitration has become "Americanized," meaning that it has transformed from a flexible and informal procedural mechanism into a more adversarial and complex process.[2]

In addition, the legal regime governing international arbitration in the United States is complex and difficult for newcomers to navigate. The United States has ratified the Convention on the Recognition and Enforcement of Foreign Arbitral Awards (the "New York Convention"), as well as the Inter-American Convention on International Commercial Arbitration (the "Panama Convention," collectively the "Conventions"). U.S. law has a now long-established history of providing strong support to both party autonomy in arbitration and the enforceability of arbitral agreements and awards. Despite these clear commitments to the Conventions, the American law on international arbitration is not always fully accessible to those who consult it. Foreign lawyers and foreign parties, as well as many U.S. judges

---

226. Reprinted by permission.

1. The most obvious example of a case cited abroad is the U.S. Supreme Court's decision in *Mitsubishi Motors Corp. v. Soler Chrysler Plymouth, Inc.*, [above, p. 900] (1985). Many foreign courts have cited it and other U.S. cases. See, e.g., *Fiona Trust & Holding Corp. v. Privalov* [2007] 1 All E.R. (Comm.) 891 (English Court of Appeal), afftd, [2007] UKHL 40 (House of Lords); *Hebei Imp. & Exp. Corp. v. Polytek Eng'g Co.*, XXIVa Y.B. Comm. Arb. 652, 668 (H.K. Court of Final Appeal, High Court 1999) (1999); *Gas Auth. of India, Ltd v. SPIE-CAPAG SA*, XXIII Y.B. Comm. Arb. 688, 694 (Delhi High Court 1993) (1998).

2. See, e.g., Lucy Reed & Jonathan Sutcliffe, *The "Americanization" of International Arbitration?*, Mealey's Int'l Arb. Rep., April 2001, at 11; Elena V. Helmer, *International Commercial Arbitration: Americanized, "Civilized," or Harmonized?*, 19 Ohio St. J. Disp. Resol. 35 (2003).

and lawyers, understandably find it challenging to assess the sometimes intricate relationships between international and domestic arbitration. As a result, the choice among potentially applicable laws and precedents is not always clear.

To some extent, this confusion finds its source in the federal statute governing inter-state and international arbitration, the Federal Arbitration Act of 1925 (the "FAA"). The FAA was enacted well before the New York Convention, and indeed well before the modern growth of arbitration as a viable and popular means of resolving commercial disputes. It is, accordingly, more skeletal than many other national arbitration laws that govern international arbitration, which were enacted much later. Chapters 2 and 3 of the FAA include the implementing legislation for the Conventions, though the interrelationship between the three Chapters is not always clear. Adding to the complexity, there are numerous different forms of state legislation, including the Uniform Arbitration Act, the Revised Uniform Arbitration Act ("RUAA") and other statutes that pertain directly to international arbitration and are often based on the Model Law on International Commercial Arbitration adopted by the United Nations Commission on International Trade Law ("UNCITRAL"). The direct application of these multiple state and federal laws can be difficult to understand, but this mix is rendered even more complex by the uncertainties sur-rounding the preemptive effect of the FAA. The FAA has not been held to "occupy the field," and thus preclude all state law on the subject. The full extent of its pre-clusive effect, however, remains uncertain in both the caselaw and the commentary.

In any particular arbitration, these various statutory sources can be supplemented further by the arbitral rules selected by the parties, as well as by the lex arbitri (the law of the place where the arbitral award is made for those awards made abroad) or the parties' choice of substantive law. The plethora, density and overlap among these different sources have created both ambiguities and gaps. The resulting complexity and incompleteness of the system has produced a great many questions that the Restatement will attempt to address with respect to United States arbitration law. . . .

———

As a consequence, lawyers should avoid heavy reliance on the default American arbitration law. Instead, they should opt for one of the following alternatives:

- By selecting a seat in a jurisdiction with clearer and more transparent laws, for example England, the parties can avoid the complexities of the American rules altogether.[227]

- Alternatively, the parties should opt for institutional arbitration and the application of well-developed and modern rules to the bulk of any issues that might appear. Examples are AAA-ICDR Rules and the Rules of JAMS. These are

---

227. Exceptions do happen. Resort to U.S. courts and laws may still become necessary if one party starts litigation (in the U.S.) in spite of an arbitration clause or when it comes to recognition and enforcement of an award.

modern and comprehensive codifications that will rarely require resort to the general arbitration laws.

- For ad hoc arbitration, the parties should explicitly provide for application of a comprehensive set of rules that does a similar job as the institutional rules mentioned in the preceding paragraph. The best of those options should be the Restatement itself. The UNCITRAL Rules are the most commonly selected (Documents, p. II-199). Some organizations, like The International Smart Mediation and Arbitration Institute, are also working on rule sets specifically for ad hoc arbitration that will be more modern and more easily updated than the UNCITRAL Rules.

4. Important Providers of (International) Arbitration Services

One of the most important choices to be made by the parties to an IBT is whether to conduct potential ADR procedures within an institutional setting or ad hoc. As a rule of thumb, reliance on a reputable institution makes things easier for the parties, which is of particular importance if they are less experienced, have significant interests at stake and/or cannot be sure of the cooperation of the other side. However, the services of the institutions are generally limited and still expensive. For example, the administrative and filing fees of the ICC will quickly exceed US$10,000 for a dispute of just a few hundred thousand dollars and do not include services such as meeting or conference rooms, secretarial or translation services, and the like. At the same time, parties can agree on using institutional rules or the UNCITRAL Rules without having to use an institution as such. The following chart provides some guidance on when to opt for institutional support.[228]

Chart 6-6
Some Guidelines for the Choice of Arbitration Format

	Relationship	Enforcement	Stakes	
↑ Level of **Seriousness** for the Party or Parties ↓	parties may not know or trust each other and/or have no specific interest in continuing their business relations	and there could be problems with enforcement of an award at the place or places where the assets are	and the amount of money potentially in dispute is very large and could be a matter of survival for either party	⇒ ICC
	parties may not know or trust each other and/or have no specific interest in continuing their business relations	and there are no particular problems expected with enforcement of an award at the place or places where the assets are	and the amount of money potentially in dispute is greater than US$1 million and could be a matter of survival for either party	⇒ quality regional arbitration institution

---

228. See also Rémy Gerbay: *The Functions of Arbitral Institutions*, Wolters Kluwer 2016.

	Relationship	Enforcement	Stakes	
↑ Level of **Seriousness** for the Party or Parties ↓	parties know & trust each other and/or have high level of interest in continuing their business relations	and there are no particular problems expected with enforcement of an award at the place or places where the assets are	and the amount of money potentially in dispute is higher than US$500,000; but not more than about US$10 million, and not a matter of survival for either party	⇒ ad hoc, panel of three
	parties know & trust each other and/or have high level of interest in continuing business relations	and there are no particular problems expected with enforcement of an award at the place or places where the assets are	and the amount of money potentially in dispute is relatively minor, maybe under US$2–3 million, and not a matter of survival for either party	⇒ ad hoc, sole arbitrator

The following are the most reputable institutional providers of arbitration services. While somewhat subjective, the list should provide a good starting point, in particular for less experienced parties.

Global

International Chamber of Commerce (ICC)[229]—www.iccwbo.org/

Permanent Court of Arbitration (PCA), the Hague (the PCA can only be called upon for disputes where at least one party is a state, a state-controlled entity, or an intergovernmental organization, in particular in investor-state arbitration cases)[230]—www.pca-cpa.org/

Regional

a. Americas

American Arbitration Association (AAA) and its International Center for Dispute Resolution (ICDR)[231]—www.icdr.org

---

229. For further reading, see W. Laurence Craig et al., *Craig, Park and Paulsson on International Chamber of Commerce Arbitration*, Oxford Univ. Press 4th ed. 2017; Yves Derain & Eric A. Schwartz, A *Guide to the ICC Rules of Arbitration*, Kluwer 2nd ed. 2005; Jacob Grierson & Annet Van Hooft, *Arbitrating Under the 2012 ICC Rules: An Introductory User's Guide*, Wolters Kluwer 2012; Erik Shafer, Herman Verbist & Christopher Imhoos, *ICC Arbitration in Practice*, Wolters Kluwer 2nd ed. 2015.

One of the few commentaries covering multiple institutional rules is Rolf A. Schütze (ed.), *Institutional Arbitration: Article by Article Commentary* (AAA, CIETAC, DIAC, DIS, HKTAC, ICC, ICSID, KLRCA, LCIA, MKAS, SCC, SIAC, Swiss Rules, UNCITRAL, VIAC), Beck/Hart/Nomos, 2nd ed. 2020.

230. See also Brooks Daly, Evgeniya Goriatcheva & Hugh Meighen: *A Guide to the PCA Arbitration Rules*, Oxford Univ. Press 2014.

231. See also Martin F. Gusy, James M. Hosking & Franz T. Schwarz: *A Guide to the ICDR International Arbitration Rules*, Oxford Univ. Press 2011.

Judicial Arbitration and Mediation Services (JAMS) is the largest ADR services provider in the U.S. and increasingly active also in international commercial arbitration—www.jamsadr.com/

The most widely used regional institution in Central and Latin America is the Centro de Arbitraje y Mediación de la Cámera de Comercio de Santiago (CAM Santiago), although it would be an exaggeration to think of it as the premier regional arbitration center for Central and Latin America.[232]

In Brazil, the leading arbitration institution is the Centro de Arbitragem e Mediação of the Câmera de Comércio Brasil-Canada (CAM-CCBC)—www.ccbc.org.br/Portal/Index

In Mexico, the Centro de Arbitraje de México (CAM) provides professional services for international commercial arbitration—www.camex.com.mx/

The Centro de Conciliación y Arbitraje de la Cámara de Comercio, Industrias y Agricultura de Panamá is also vying for the crown of the best and busiest center in the region—www.cecap.com.pa

b. Europe

There are many good arbitration centers in Europe. The centers that stand out are:

London Court of International Arbitration[233]—www.lcia.org/

Arbitration Institute of the Stockholm Chamber of Commerce—www.sccinstitute.com/

Swiss Chambers of Commerce[234]—www.swissarbitration.org/sa/en/

c. Asia and Pacific

Asia has also seen the development of quite a number of high-quality arbitration centers in the last 20 years. Any recommendations or preferences among them are largely subjective. Parties should always assume that an arbitration should not be seated in the country where either of the parties has a majority of her assets; at the same time we always want a seat where the arbitration can get qualified court support, if needed. Consider this when looking at the list, which is in alphabetical order:

---

232. https://www.cailaw.org/Institute-for-Transnational-Arbitration/Americas-Initiative/arbitral-institutions-guide.html. See also Jan Kleinheisterkamp: *International Commercial Arbitration in Latin America—Regulation and Practice in the MERCOSUR and the Associated Countries*, Oxford Univ. Press 2005.

233. See also Peter Turner & Reza Mohtashami: *A Guide to the LCIA Arbitration Rules*, Oxford Univ. Press 2009.

234. See, for example, Tobias Zuberbühler, Christoph M. Müller & Philipp A. Habegger, *Swiss Rules of International Arbitration—Commentary*, JurisNet, 2nd ed. 2013; as well as Daniel Girsberger & Nathalie Voser, *International Arbitration—Comparative and Swiss Concepts*, NOMOS 3rd ed. 2016.

Asian International Arbitration Center (AIAC), Kuala Lumpur[235]—www.aiac. world

Australian Centre for International Commercial Arbitration (ACICA)—www .acica.org.au/

Beijing Arbitration Commission (BAC)—www.bjac.org.cn/

China International Economic and Trade Arbitration Commission (CIETAC), Beijing[236]—www.cietac.org/

Hong Kong International Arbitration Center[237]—www.hkiac.org/en/

Japan Commercial Arbitration Association—www.jcaa.or.jp/e/

Singapore International Arbitration Center[238]—www.siac.org.sg/

d. Middle East

Cairo Regional Center for International Commercial Arbitration—crcica.org.eg/

Dubai International Arbitration Center—www.diac.ae/idias/

e. Africa[239]

Common Court of Justice and Arbitration (OHADA), Abidjan[240]—www.ohada .org/ccja.html

SUBJECT-MATTER SPECIFIC

a. Investor-State Arbitration

International Center for Settlement of Investment Disputes (ICSID), Washington, D.C.[241]—www.icsid.worldbank.org/apps/ICSIDWEB/Pages/default.aspx

NAFTA[242]—www.nafta-sec-alena.org/Home/Welcome

---

235. For comprehensive analysis see Sundra Rajoo & Philip Koh (eds), *Arbitration in Malaysia— a Practical Guide*, Sweet & Maxwell 2016.

236. See also Giovanni Pisacane, Lea Murphy & Calvin Zhang, *Arbitration in China: Rules & Perspectives*, Springer 2018; Jianlong Yu, Lijun Cao & Michael Moser, *A Guide to the CIETAC Arbitration Rules*, Oxford Univ. Press 2017; Sun Wei & Melanie Willems, *Arbitration in China: A Practitioner's Guide*, Wolters Kluwer 2015.

237. See also Michael J. Moser & Chiann Bao, *Guide to the HKIAC Arbitration Rules*, Oxford Univ. Press 2017.

238. See also Mark Mangan, Lucy Reed & John Choong, *A Guide to the SIAC Arbitration Rules*, Oxford Univ. Press 2014.

239. Lise Bosman (ed.), *Arbitration in Africa: A Practitioner's Guide*, Wolters Kluwer 2013.

240. Hygin Didace Amboulou, *Le Droit de L'arbitrage et des Institutions de Médiation dans L'espace OHADA*, Edition L'Harmattan 2015; Emilia Onyema, *Arbitration Under the OHADA Regime*, Int'l Arb. Rev. 2008, Vol. 11, No. 6, pp. 205–218; Fouchard Papaefstratiou, *OHADA Arbitration—A Critical Analysis*, Transnat'l Disp. Mgmt 2016, p. 4.

241. For detailed information and analysis, see Crina Baltag, *ICSID Convention After 50 Years: Unsettled Issues*, Wolters Kluwer 2017; Antonio R. Parra, *The History of ICSID*, Oxford Univ. Press 2nd ed. 2017; Jan Paulsson & Nigel Rawding, *Guide to ICSID Arbitration*, Wolters Kluwer 2nd ed. 2010; Roberto Pirozzi, *The ICSID Jurisdiction: An Issue Already Solved or a Question Still Open*, 17 Vindobona J. Int'l Com. L. & Arb. 33 (2013); as well as Christoph Schreuer & Loretta Malintoppi, *The ICSID Convention: A Commentary*, Cambridge Univ. Press 2009.

242. See, e.g., Frédéric Bachand & Emmanuel Gaillard (eds.), *Fifteen Years of NAFTA Chapter 11 Arbitration*, JurisNet 2011.

b. Intellectual Property[243]

WIPO Arbitration and Mediation Center, Geneva—www.wipo.int/amc/en/

c. IT and Internet/Blockchain-Based Transactions

Silicon Valley Arbitration & Mediation Center (SVAMC)—www.svamc.org/

International Smart Mediation and Arbitration Institute (SmartArb), Indianapolis—www.SmartArb.org

d. Trade in Agricultural Commodities

The Grain and Feed Trade Association (GAFTA), London[244]—www.gafta.com /Home

e. International Sport Disputes

Court of Arbitration for Sport, Lausanne, Switzerland[245]—www.tas-cas.org/en /index.html

5. *The Agreement to Arbitrate*

In general, any natural or legal person can be taken to court, with or without her consent. We have discussed above which courts may have jurisdiction for international cases. Some exceptions apply to states and certain other public entities, for example on the basis of foreign sovereign immunity.

By contrast, no natural or legal person can be forced into arbitration without her agreement. Therefore, an agreement to arbitrate between the parties to a dispute is a *conditio sine qua non* for the initiation of arbitration proceedings (cf. Article II(1) and Article IV(1)(b) of the New York Convention). However, the agreement to participate in arbitration—rather than litigation—does not need to be current at the time the dispute arises. Thus, two types of agreements to arbitrate can be usefully distinguished: The safest approach is to have a bullet-proof arbitration clause in the contract(s) underlying the IBT. At the time the parties enter into their agreements, they still want to deal with each other and generally anticipate a successful implementation of the transactions. This usually makes an *ex ante* agreement in favor of ADR more easy to obtain. Also, for the many reasons outlined in this book, almost every IBT should have an ADR clause, rather than leaving the parties no choice but transnational litigation. Thus, drafting quality clauses will be a frequent job for transactional lawyers and a major focus of this subsection.

---

243. Thomas D. Halket, *Arbitration of International Intellectual Property Disputes*, JurisNet 2012.

244. See, for example, Iryna Polovets, Matthew Smith & Bradley Terry, *GAFTA Arbitration as the Most Appropriate Forum for Disputes Resolution in Grain Trade*, 30 Ariz. J. Int'l & Comp. L. 559 (2013–2014).

245. Despina Mavromati & Matthieu Reeb, *The Code of the Court of Arbitration for Sport: Commentary, Cases and Materials*, Wolters Kluwer 2015.

Even if the parties did not include an arbitration clause or if the contract clause is flawed in some way, it is often possible to persuade the parties after a dispute has arisen to enter into a better agreement to arbitrate. However, such an *ex post* agreement can only be obtained if both parties are still committed to swift and fair resolution of their disagreement. As soon as one party sees advantages in having less efficient or even completely dysfunctional dispute settlement procedures—advantages such as gaining time or gaining leverage for a suboptimal settlement—she is unlikely to consent to an efficient arbitration alternative.

Ex ante agreements are usually short and included toward the end of the business contract. Parties shy away from long and complex arbitration clauses in their contracts because they may suggest that at least one side has been burned before and/or fears or expects problems in the implementation of the contract. Instead of spelling out the details of a dispute settlement procedure, *ex ante* agreements should point to rules or institutions that have those details if needed.

Ex post agreements, by contrast, are usually much more detailed since the parties already have a dispute and know what they need to get it settled. However, even *ex post* agreements can usefully refer to institutions and their rules or stand-alone rules to be more efficient and show neutrality.

Ex post agreements can be drawn up by the parties themselves and they may be called *Terms of Appointment*. They can also be suggested by a tribunal that has already been appointed. Then they may be called *Terms of Reference*. If the parties do not agree to a detailed set of rules in ad hoc arbitration or if details beyond any applicable (institutional) rules are needed, the tribunal can also adopt these in the form of Procedural Order #1. We will focus on *ex ante* agreements in this subsection and on *ex post* agreements in subsection 11.

As transactional lawyers, we are usually confronted with *ex ante* agreements in one of two ways. Either we are drafting or reviewing a contract that has not yet been finalized and we are advising the clients how to phrase a suitable arbitration clause. Alternatively, we are confronted with a contract that has been finalized but does not include a good arbitration clause because the parties did not get good advice when they drafted the contract, or they could not agree on good clauses suggested to them. If there is no arbitration clause, the only way to get to ADR is via an *ex post* agreement. However, if there is an arbitration clause but it is defective in some way, several responses are possible:

- First, as legal counsel reviewing the contract, we can urge parties to enter into a better dispute settlement agreement while they are still on good terms with each other and before a dispute actually arises.

- Second, we may leave a clause as is because it will be workable at least in some jurisdictions. For example, in the United States, after initial reservations, it has been the consistent policy of the Supreme Court to support arbitration and to uphold arbitration clauses and agreements even if they are less than perfectly formulated; this is based on the notion that the details may be unclear but at least it is clear that the parties wanted to arbitrate instead of litigate.[246] By contrast, in many European and other countries, the courts may declare an arbitration clause null and void if the institution, the seat, or the applicable procedural rules are not clearly identified.

- Third, we may need to advise the clients to adjust their business strategies in order to reduce the chances of having to resort to dispute settlement (for example, to seek payment in advance), to try harder to settle any disputes that may arise, knowing that rights may not be enforceable in practice, and/or to consider forum shopping options if transnational litigation becomes inevitable.

Obviously, having a suitable arbitration clause is much to be preferred. The internet abounds with suggestions for arbitration clauses, as well as case law where parties had to litigate over poorly crafted clauses. Almost every arbitral institution and many larger law firms also provides model clauses, albeit usually for arbitration or ADR involving their (expensive) services. There is certainly no shortage of advice, but not all of it is useful and not much of it is rendered without self-interest. A good starting point for neutral advice are the Guidelines for Drafting International Arbitration Clauses published in 2010 by the International Bar Association (IBA):[247]

Basic Drafting Guidelines

Guideline 1: The parties should decide between institutional and ad hoc arbitration.

Guideline 2: The parties should select a set of arbitration rules and use the model clause recommended for these arbitration rules as a starting point.

Guideline 3: Absent special circumstances, the parties should not attempt to limit the scope of disputes subject to arbitration and should define this scope broadly.

Guideline 4: The parties should select the place of arbitration. This selection should be based on both practical and juridical considerations.

Guideline 5: The parties should specify the number of arbitrators.

Guideline 6: The parties should specify the method of selection and replacement of arbitrators and, when ad hoc arbitration is chosen, should select an appointing authority.

Guideline 7: The parties should specify the language of arbitration.

Guideline 8: The parties should ordinarily specify the rules of law governing the contract and any subsequent disputes.

---

246. Hossein Fazilatfar, *Following the Supreme Court in Liberal Construction of Arbitration Agreements under the Federal Pro-Arbitration Policy*, 23 Willamette J. Int'l L. & Disp. Resol. 61 (2015).

247. The Guidelines, with Commentary, are available at https://www.ibanet.org/ENews _Archive/IBA_27October_2010_Arbitration_Clauses_Guidelines.aspx.

Based on these and many other recommendations, I have developed the following checklist for transactional lawyers looking to develop clear and unambiguous clauses in the shortest amount of time for virtually any type of IBT:

Checklist 6-2
Frank Emmert Rules on How to Draft a Bullet-Proof Arbitration Clause:
The "10½ Commandments" for a Successful Start of
the Arbitration Proceedings

1. Include the *written clause* in the main part (front) of the contract and have the parties *sign*. Do not rely on references to Standard Terms or websites in letters, let alone e-mails. Do not rely on General Terms, the small-print in the back of a contract. *Oral agreements do not count*

2. Make it clear that arbitration is *mandatory*, not optional, for both sides.

3. Include a broad statement that the parties have to submit *"all disputes"* that can possibly arise between them *"related to the contract or the underlying business transaction"* to arbitration, not just those about the rights and obligations under the contract or any other specific category of dispute (avoid narrow language such as "disputes . . . under this contract" but remember that duplication is useless and just inelegant, e.g., "arising out of, in connection with, or relating to this agreement").

4. Make it clear that arbitration shall be the *first and last instance* of dispute settlement, unless negotiation and/or mediation is required before arbitration; in case of multi-stage clauses, be sure to have sensible time limits.

5. Be perfectly clear and precise about the selected *tribunal*. When opting for institutional arbitration, look up the correct name every time. If large amounts of money are (potentially) at stake and/or the enforcement may have to be done in a country that might not be friendly to foreign business interests enforcing awards against local employers, avoid ad hoc arbitration unless parties know and trust each other *and* have strong interests in continuing collaboration.

6. Specify the *place* of arbitration even if identical to the *seat* of the tribunal.

7. Specify the *number of arbitrators and how they shall be selected*. Avoid unrealistic time limits. Do not name persons that may be unable to act.

8. Specify the *language* to be used for the arbitration.

9. Specify the procedural law/the arbitration rules to be used by the tribunal. For ad hoc, specify that the arbitrator(s) have to follow *well established rules* like the UNCITRAL Arbitration Rules, the LCIA Rules or the English Arbitration Act, or the Restatement, as well as various IBA Guidelines. When selecting institutional arbitration, use the house rules of the institution.

10. If the parties conclude more than one agreement, make sure that the arbitration clause is *exactly the same* in all agreements to avoid having to go to different courts or tribunals for different issues arising out of the same business relationship.

10½. Specify the *substantive law* to govern the contractual relationship and any claims arising between the parties.

Notes and Questions

1. While it is clear that there cannot be arbitration proceedings if there is no agreement to arbitrate, neither at the time when a contract between the parties was drafted and signed (*ex ante*), nor at the time when the dispute arose (*ex post*), it is far less clear what should happen when there was some kind of agreement, but it is unclear or incomplete. Typical problems in arbitration clauses include the following:

- arbitration may be optional, and not required, instead of litigation (example: "... in case of a dispute ... either party may call on the x court of arbitration ... ," see also examples below);

- the arbitration institution may be mislabeled (example: "London Arbitration Court" instead of "London Court of International Arbitration")

- the terms and conditions for the choice of arbitrators and/or the procedure may be difficult or impossible to meet (example: "Professor X as sole arbitrator" (she may not be available) or "Disputes rising in connection with this agreement shall be determined by a single arbitrator to be appointed by the Director General of the World Health Organization" (the WHO may not be willing or able to act as appointing authority) or "ICC arbitration under German law" (Is the reference to German law for the substance of the case? For procedure in case ICC Rules do not cover an issue? For procedure instead of ICC Rules?).)

From practical experience and conversations with other lawyers and arbitrators, we can safely say that more than 50% of all arbitration clauses used in international business transactions are less than ideal and likely, at a minimum, to cause headaches and uncertainty about the value of claims. In a worst-case scenario, a poorly drafted arbitration clause will first lead to litigation whether or not arbitration should be pursued, and then to further litigation on substance, instead of arbitration. A brief review of the pros and cons of arbitration versus litigation (above, Chart 6-4 on p. 898) should suffice to remind our readers how undesirable this outcome will be. Thus, businesspeople should always involve their lawyers when negotiating and drafting commercial contracts and lawyers should always spend more than a casual moment when reviewing arbitration clauses.

2. The IBA Guidelines for Drafting International Arbitration Clauses go into more detail, which may or may not be necessary or acceptable to the parties. They suggest to include provisions on:

- The authority of the arbitral tribunal and of the courts with respect to provisional and conservatory measures;

- Document production;

- Confidentiality issues;

- Allocation of costs and fees;

- Qualifications required of arbitrators;

- Time limits; and

- Finality of arbitration.

The view taken here is that the majority of these points are better taken care of *after* a dispute has arisen and the parties are drawing up the Arbitration Agreement, or the Terms of Reference. What would be arguments in favor of regulating these matters already in the contractual arbitration clause (*ex ante*)? What are the pros and cons of regulating them in the Arbitration Agreement or Terms of Reference (*ex post*)? What can and cannot be done in a Procedural Order by the tribunal?

3. Can you identify the strengths and weaknesses of the following Sample Arbitration Clauses?

Clauses Triggering Litigation

a. In the case of *HKL Group Co Ltd v. Rizq International Holdings Pte Ltd* ([2013] SGHCR 5), the Singapore High Court had to decide on the validity of the following arbitration clause (see also above, pp. 918–919):

> Any dispute shall be settled by amicable negotiation between two Parties. In case both Parties fail to reach amicable agreement, all disputes out of in connection with the contract shall be settled by the Arbitration Committee at Singapore under the rules of The International Chamber of Commerce of which awards shall be final and binding both parties. Arbitration fee and other related charge shall be borne by the losing Party unless otherwise agreed.

b. In a recent case in China, the Dalian Intermediate People's Court was confronted with a lawsuit brought by a Chinese party against an American company. The U.S. party objected to the lawsuit, claiming that there was a valid arbitration clause. The contract had been negotiated by e-mail and the relevant clause read "GOVERNING RULES: GAFTA89/23 COMBINED LONDON 125 ARBITRATION IF NECESSARY." The GAFTA references are to the rules of the Grain and Feed Trade Association. These rules are available online at http://www.gafta.com/. Pursuant to Pavani Reddy of Zaiwalla & Co Solicitors, "[t]oday, the majority of world trade in cereals and animal feed [is] carried out under GAFTA contracts and the institution has a range of about 80 standard form contracts . . . These contracts refer disputes to GAFTA administered arbitrations under forms 125 and 126. . . . GAFTA is a dominant international arbitration institution and is held in high respect around the world. . . . GAFTA contracts are governed by English law and provide for England to be the venue of the arbitration." (http://www.zaiwalla.co .uk/blog/2012/02/the-gafta-arbitration-process-explained/). In the end, the Chinese court held that Chinese law, specifically Article 18 of the Law of the People's Republic of China on Application of Laws to Foreign-Related Civil Relations (2010), allows parties to choose the law or rules applicable to an arbitration agreement. Whenever parties to an IBT have not made a choice, the laws or rules of the arbitration institution, or the law applicable at the seat of the arbitration shall apply. In the case at hand, London was determined to be the seat of the arbitration and the English Arbitration Act was held to be the applicable law. Under English law, the arbitration clause was considered valid. The Chinese court further pointed out that even if the parties had not mentioned London in the clause, GAFTA 125 Rules also point to London as the seat of the arbitration. Finally, the court held that the fact that the Chinese party was challenging the validity of the contract did not affect the effectiveness of the arbitration clause because of the principle of independence found in English law. (Case No. [2015] DMSCZ No. 24, decision of 13 July 2015.)

c. "Any dispute, controversy or claim arising out of or in connection with, or relating to this Agreement or any breach or alleged breach hereof shall, upon the request of any party involved, be submitted to, and settled by, arbitration."

d. "Arbitration. Any controversy, claim or dispute arising out of or relating to this Agreement, shall be settled solely and exclusively by binding arbitration in San Francisco, California. Such arbitration shall be conducted in accordance with the then prevailing commercial arbitration rules of JAMS/Endispute ("JAMS"), with the following exceptions if in conflict: (a) one arbitrator shall be chosen by JAMS; (b) each party to the arbitration will pay its pro rata share of the expenses and fees of the arbitrator, together with other expenses of the arbitration incurred or approved by the arbitrator; and (c) arbitration may proceed in the absence of any party if written notice (pursuant to the JAMS' rules and regulations) of the proceedings has been given to such party. Each party shall bear its own attorneys fees and expenses. The parties agree to abide by all decisions and awards rendered in such proceedings. Such decisions and awards rendered by the arbitrator shall be final and conclusive. All such controversies, claims or disputes shall be settled in this manner in lieu of any action at law or equity; provided however, that nothing in this subsection shall be construed as precluding the bringing an action for injunctive relief or other equitable relief. The arbitrator shall not have the right to award punitive damages or speculative damages to either party and shall not have the power to amend this Agreement. The arbitrator shall be required to follow applicable law. IF FOR ANY REASON THIS ARBITRATION CLAUSE BECOMES NOT

APPLICABLE, THEN EACH PARTY, TO THE FULLEST EXTENT PERMIT-
TED BY APPLICABLE LAW, HEREBY IRREVOCABLY WAIVES ALL RIGHT TO
TRIAL BY JURY AS TO ANY ISSUE RELATING HERETO IN ANY ACTION,
PROCEEDING, OR COUNTERCLAIM ARISING OUT OF OR RELATING TO
THIS AGREEMENT OR ANY OTHER MATTER INVOLVING THE PARTIES
HERETO."[248]

e. "English law-arbitration, if any, London according ICC Rules." (*Arab-African Energy Corp. v. Olieprodukten Nederland, B.V.2 Lloyd's Rep*)

f. "Disputes hereunder shall be referred to Arbitration to be carried out by Arbitrators named by the ICC in Geneva in accordance with the Arbitration Procedure set forth in the Civil Code of Venezuela and in the Civil Code of France with due regard for the law of the place of Arbitration." (Example provided in Craig, Park and Poulsson, *International Chamber of Commerce Arbitration*, Oceana 3rd ed. 2000, pp. 132–133)

g. "In the event of any unresolved dispute, the matter will be referred to the ICC."

h. "All disputes in connection with the present agreement shall be submitted in the first instance to arbitration. The arbitrator shall be a well known chamber of commerce (like the ICC) designated by mutual agreement between the parties." (quoted in Singapore International Arbitration Blog, Pathological Arbitration Clauses, https://singaporeinternationalarbitration.com/2013/03/08/pathological-arbitration -clauses/)

i. "Any and all disputes arising under the arrangements contemplated hereunder . . . will be referred to mutually agreed mechanisms or procedures of international arbitration, such as the rules of the London Arbitration Association." (Alan Redfern & Martin Hunter, *Law and Practice of International Commercial Arbitration*, Oxford Univ. Press 6th ed. 2015, para. 2-200, pp. 136–137.

j. "In case of a dispute, the parties undertake to submit to arbitration but in case of litigation, the tribunal de la seine shall have exclusive jurisdiction." (Example provided in Craig, Park and Poulsson, *International Chamber of Commerce Arbitration*, Oceana, 3rd ed. 2000, p. 128)

k. ". . . arbitration before the New York Commercial Arbitration Association." (*Warnes SA v. Harvic Int'l Ltd.*, SDNY, 1993 WL 228028.)

l. "[Parties undertake] to have the dispute submitted to binding arbitration through The American Arbitration Association [hereafter: AAA] or to any other US court. (. . .) The arbitration shall be conducted based upon the Rules and Regulations of the International Chamber of Commerce (ICC 500)." (quoted in Singapore International Arbitration Blog, Pathological Arbitration Clauses, https://singaporeinternationalarbitration.com/2013/03/08/pathological-arbitration-clauses/)

---

248. An updated recommendation is provided by JAMS here: https://www.jamsadr.com/files/Uploads/Documents/JAMS-Rules/JAMS-International-Clause-Workbook.pdf.

Clauses Recommended by Arbitral Institutions

m. The Chartered Institute of Arbitrators

"Any dispute or difference arising out of or in connection with this contract shall be determined by the appointment of a single arbitrator to be agreed between the parties, or failing agreement within fourteen days, after either party has given to the other a written request to concur in the appointment of an arbitrator, by an arbitrator to be appointed by the President or a Vice President of the Chartered Institute of Arbitrators."

n. The London Court of International Arbitration

"Any dispute arising out of or in connection with this contract, including any question regarding its existence, validity or termination, shall be referred to and finally resolved by arbitration under the LCIA Rules, which Rules are deemed to be incorporated by reference into this clause.

The number of arbitrators shall be [one/three].

The seat, or legal place, of arbitration shall be [insert city or country].

The language to be used in the arbitral proceedings shall be [insert language].

The governing law of the contract shall be the substantive law of [insert governing law]."

o. The International Court of Arbitration of the ICC

"All disputes arising out of or in connection with the present contract shall be finally settled under the Rules of Arbitration of the International Chamber of Commerce by one or more arbitrators appointed in accordance with the said Rules."

p. The American Arbitration Association/International Centre for Dispute Resolution: The website of the ICDR provides a sophisticated "Clause Builder Tool" that allows parties to an IBT and/or their lawyers to develop custom-made dispute settlement clauses. The most basic result may look something like this:

Any controversy or claim arising out of or relating to this contract, or the breach thereof, shall be determined by arbitration administered by the International Centre for Dispute Resolution in accordance with its International Arbitration Rules.

However, parties are explicitly invited to make additional choices, such as with or without expedited procedures, the number of arbitrators, the method of selecting the arbitrators, their qualifications, the place of arbitration, the language, etc.

q. UNCITRAL Model Clause

Any dispute, controversy or claim arising out of or relating to this contract, or the breach, termination or invalidity thereof shall be settled by arbitration in accordance with the UNCITRAL Arbitration Rules as at present in force.

Sample Multi-Stage Dispute Settlement Clauses

r. IBA Drafting Guidelines for Multi-Tier Dispute Resolution Clauses

Multi-Tier Guideline 1: The clause should specify a period of time for negotiation or mediation, triggered by a defined and undisputable event (i.e., a written request), after which either party can resort to arbitration.

Multi-Tier Guideline 2: The clause should avoid the trap of rendering arbitration permissive, not mandatory.

Multi-Tier Guideline 3: The clause should define the disputes to be submitted to negotiation or mediation and to arbitration in identical terms.

All disputes arising out of or in connection with this agreement, including any question regarding its existence, validity or termination ('Dispute'), shall be resolved in accordance with the procedures specified below, which shall be the sole and exclusive procedures for the resolution of any such Dispute.

(A) Negotiation

The parties shall endeavor to resolve any Dispute amicably by negotiation between executives who have authority to settle the Dispute [and who are at a higher level of management than the persons with direct responsibility for administration or performance of this agreement].

(B) Mediation

Any Dispute not resolved by negotiation in accordance with paragraph (A) within [30] days after either party requested in writing negotiation under paragraph (A), or within such other period as the parties may agree in writing, shall be settled amicably by mediation under the [designated set of mediation rules].

(C) Arbitration

Any Dispute not resolved by mediation in accordance with paragraph (B) within [45] days after appointment of the mediator, or within such other period as the parties may agree in writing, shall be finally settled under the [designated set of arbitration rules] by [one or three] arbitrator[s] appointed in accordance with the said Rules. The place of arbitration shall be [. . .]. The language of arbitration shall be [. . .].

[All communications during the negotiation and mediation pursuant to paragraphs (A) and (B) are confidential and shall be treated as made in the course of compromise and settlement negotiations for purposes of applicable rules of evidence and any additional confidentiality and professional secrecy protections provided by applicable law.]

s. American Arbitration Association

Neg1   In the event of any dispute, claim, question, or disagreement arising from or relating to this agreement or the breach thereof, the parties hereto shall use their best efforts to settle the dispute, claim, question, or disagreement. To this effect, they shall consult and negotiate with each other in good faith and, recognizing their mutual interests, attempt to reach a just and equitable solution satisfactory to both parties. If they do not reach such solution within a period of 60 days, then, upon notice by either party to the other, all disputes, claims, questions, or differences shall be finally settled by arbitration administered by the American Arbitration Association in accordance with the provisions of its Commercial Arbitration Rules.

Med 1   If a dispute arises out of or relates to this contract, or the breach thereof, and if the dispute cannot be settled through negotiation, the parties agree first to try in good faith to settle the dispute by mediation administered by the American Arbitration Association under its Commercial Mediation Procedures before resorting to arbitration, litigation, or some other dispute resolution procedure.

Int'l 5   In the event of any controversy or claim arising out of or relating to this contract, the parties hereto shall consult and negotiate with each other and, recognizing their mutual interests, attempt to reach a solution satisfactory to both parties. If they do not reach settlement within a period of 60 days, then either party may, by notice to the other party and the International Centre for Dispute Resolution, demand mediation under the International Mediation Procedures of the International Centre for Dispute Resolution. If settlement is not reached within 60 days after service of a written demand for mediation, any unresolved controversy or claim arising out of or relating to this contract shall be settled by arbitration in accordance with the International Arbitration Rules of the International Centre for Dispute Resolution.

Int'l 6   In the event of any controversy or claim arising out of or relating to this contract, the parties hereto agree first to try and settle the dispute by mediation administered by the International Centre for Dispute Resolution under its rules before resorting to arbitration, litigation, or some other dispute resolution technique.

t. Judicial Arbitration and Mediation Services (JAMS)

1. The parties agree that any and all disputes, claims or controversies arising out of or relating to this Agreement shall be submitted to JAMS, or its successor, for mediation, and if the matter is not resolved through mediation, then it shall be submitted to JAMS, or its successor, for final and binding arbitration pursuant to the clause set forth in Paragraph 5 below.

2. Either party may commence mediation by providing to JAMS and the other party a written request for mediation, setting forth the subject of the dispute and the relief requested.

3. The parties will cooperate with JAMS and with one another in selecting a mediator from the JAMS panel of neutrals and in scheduling the mediation proceedings. The parties agree that they will participate in the mediation in good faith and that they will share equally in its costs.

4. All offers, promises, conduct and statements, whether oral or written, made in the course of the mediation by any of the parties, their agents, employees, experts and attorneys, and by the mediator or any JAMS employees, are confidential, privileged and inadmissible for any purpose, including impeachment, in any arbitration or other proceeding involving the parties, provided that evidence that is otherwise admissible or discoverable shall not be rendered inadmissible or nondiscoverable as a result of its use in the mediation.

5. Either party may initiate arbitration with respect to the matters submitted to mediation by filing a written demand for arbitration at any time following the initial mediation session or at any time following 45 days from the date of filing the written request for mediation, whichever occurs first ("Earliest Initiation Date"). The mediation may continue after the commencement of arbitration if the parties so desire.

6. At no time prior to the Earliest Initiation Date shall either side initiate an arbitration or litigation related to this Agreement except to pursue a provisional remedy that is authorized by law or by JAMS Rules or by agreement of the parties. However, this limitation is inapplicable to a party if the other party refuses to comply with the requirements of Paragraph 3 above.

u. United States Arbitration & Mediation (USA&M)

Dispute Resolution. Any controversy or claim arising out of or relating to this contract, the relationship resulting in or from this contract or breach of any duties hereunder will be settled by Arbitration in accordance with the Commercial Arbitration Rules of the U. S. Arbitration & Mediation, Midwest ("USA&M") or the American Arbitration Association ("AAA"). All hearings will be held in St. Louis, Missouri before an Arbitrator who is a licensed attorney with at least 15 years of experience in commercial law. A judgment upon the award rendered by the Arbitrator shall be entered in a Court with competent jurisdiction. The Federal Arbitration Act (Title 9 U.S. Code Section 1 et. seq.) shall govern all arbitration and confirmation proceedings. As a condition precedent to the filing of an arbitration claim, the parties agree to first mediate any claims between them at USA&M or AAA. Any party refusing to mediate shall not prevent the other party or parties from pursuing their claims in arbitration. The parties will share the cost of mediation equally. Nothing herein will be construed to prevent any party's use of injunction, and/or any other prejudgment or provisional action or remedy. Any such action or remedy will not waive the moving party's right to compel arbitration of any dispute. The parties agree to also meet and negotiate in good faith in order to resolve any disputes which may arise between them.

v. Chartered Institute of Arbitrators

The parties shall attempt to resolve any dispute arising out of or relating to this contract through negotiations between senior executives of the parties, who have authority to settle the same.

If the matter is not resolved by negotiation within 30 days of receipt of a written 'invitation to negotiate', the parties will attempt to resolve the dispute in good faith through an agreed Alternative Dispute Resolution (ADR) procedure, or in default of agreement, through an ADR procedure as recommended to the parties by the President or the Vice President, for the time being, of the Chartered Institute of Arbitrators.

If the matter has not been resolved by an ADR procedure within 60 days of the initiation of that procedure, or if any party will not participate in an ADR procedure, the dispute may be referred to arbitration by any party. The seat of the arbitration shall be England and Wales. The arbitration shall be governed by both the Arbitration Act 1996 and Rules as agreed between the parties. Should the parties be unable to agree on an arbitrator or arbitrators, or be unable to agree on the Rules for Arbitration, any party may, upon giving written notice to other parties, apply to the President or the Vice President, for the time being, of the Chartered Institute of Arbitrators for the appointment of an Arbitrator or Arbitrators and for any decision on rules that may be necessary.

Nothing in this clause shall be construed as prohibiting a party or it's affiliate from applying to a court for interim injunctive relief.

w. The International Smart Mediation and Arbitration Institute (SmartArb)

See above, pp. 875–878.

6. *Initiation of Arbitration Proceedings*

Arbitral institutions often provide forms for the initiation of proceedings. For example, the web site of the International Centre for Dispute Resolution of the American Arbitration Association has a section "Rules, Forms & Fees" with a form ICDR Notice of Arbitration.[249] The claimant has to effect service of the form on the respondent (see above, p. pp. 750 et seq.) and submit copies, together with the filing fee, to the ICDR.

By contrast, the ICC does not have a specific form for their Request for Arbitration, but provides the following guidelines of what needs to be included:[250]

---

249. See https://www.icdr.org/sites/default/files/document_repository/ICDR_Notice_of_Arbitration.pdf.

250. See https://iccwbo.org/dispute-resolution-services/arbitration/filing-a-request/. Reprinted by permission.

"Requests" come in numerous styles and formats.

However, Article 4 (3) of the Rules provides that:

1. the name in full, description, address and other contact details of each of the parties;

2. the name in full, address and other contact details of any person(s) representing the Claimant in the arbitration;

3. a description of the nature and circumstances of the dispute giving rise to the claims and of the basis upon which the claims are made;

4. a statement of the relief sought, together with the amounts of any quantified claims and, to the extent possible, an estimate of the monetary value of any other claims;

5. any relevant agreements and, in particular, the arbitration agreement(s);

6. where claims are made under more than one arbitration agreement, an indication of the arbitration agreement under which each claim is made;

7. all relevant particulars and any observations or proposals concerning the number of arbitrators and their choice in accordance with the provisions of Articles 12 and 13, and any nomination of an arbitrator required thereby; and

8. all relevant particulars and any observations or proposals as to the place of the arbitration, the applicable rules of law and the language of the arbitration. The Claimant may submit such other documents or information with the "Request" as it considers appropriate or as may contribute to the efficient resolution of the dispute.

Under sub-paragraph "g," three possibilities should be anticipated:

1. Where the arbitration agreement provides for a sole arbitrator: The parties may, by agreement, jointly nominate an arbitrator for confirmation by the Court or Secretary General. In any case, the Claimant should submit in the "Request" any particulars concerning the choice of the arbitrator.

2. Where the agreement provides for three arbitrators: The Claimant should nominate an arbitrator in the "Request" for confirmation by the Court or Secretary General (unless the agreement provides for a different procedure).

3. Where the agreement provides for one or more arbitrators, or is silent or unclear as to the number of arbitrators: The Claimant should indicate a preference for either one or three arbitrators. If it opts for three, then the Claimant is encouraged at to nominate an arbitrator for confirmation together with its "Request". The financial consequences of three arbitrators should be borne in mind. Unless agreed upon by the parties, the Court will appoint a sole arbitrator save where it appears to the Court that the dispute is such as to warrant the appointment of three arbitrators (Article 12 (2)). Where there are multiple Claimants or multiple respondents, and where

the dispute is to be referred to three arbitrators, the multiple Claimants, jointly, and the multiple respondents, jointly, shall nominate an arbitrator (Article 12 (6)).

Under sub-paragraph "h," parties should be aware that:

1. The place of arbitration is fixed by the Court unless agreed upon by the parties (Article 18(1));

2. The applicable rules of law are those which the Arbitral Tribunal determines to be appropriate, unless otherwise agreed by the parties (Article 21(1));

3. The language of arbitration is determined by the Arbitral Tribunal in the absence of an agreement by the parties (Article 20);

4. The parties' positions and views regarding any of those issues should be included in the "Request" and the "Answer to the Request" respectively. The parties' comments will be considered by the Court or the Arbitral Tribunal when such issues are decided.

Filing Fee

Each "Request" must be accompanied by the non-refundable filing fee on the administrative expenses of US$5,000 (see Appendix III, Article 1 (1)).

One of the advantages of ICC arbitration is that the ICC will notify the respondents and the claimant does not have to worry about service in a foreign country.

All arbitration institutions require payment of a filing fee at the time of initiation of arbitration.

Ad hoc arbitration can be initiated by serving a "Notice of Arbitration" or a "Demand for Arbitration" on the respondent. The rules on how service has to be effected can be found in the 1965 Hague Convention on the Service Abroad of Judicial and Extrajudicial Documents in Civil and Commercial Matters, at least for the countries that have ratified it (see above, pp. 750 et seq.). Most jurisdictions have some rules about what needs to be included to make the initiation of an ad hoc arbitration valid, make the dispute "pending," and cause the statute of limitations to be tolled or paused. The details need to be determined by working through the 5 + 5 matrix introduced above, p. 913. In general, the parties have a choice of submitting more details about their case in the Notice or of keeping the Notice quite short and submitting the details of their claims and counterclaims only once the tribunal has been constituted.[251] As a general rule, the Notice of Arbitration or Demand for Arbitration does not have to be much longer than one page, as long as it has enough

---

251. The main reason why parties may want to keep the factual and legal claims in the Notice of Arbitration rather superficial and short is that the tribunal has not yet been constituted and it may not even be entirely clear that there is a valid arbitration clause and the case can and will be settled exclusively via arbitration. Thus, confidentiality is not fully secured at this point. Also, the claimant may be under some time pressure to bring her case in front of a particular tribunal before the expiration of the statute of limitations and/or before the respondent may bring a counterclaim

information for prospective arbitrators to check for any conflicts of interest, and for the respondent to know what will and what will not be pending.

Sample Document 6-1 contains general guidelines for a rather shorter version that may need to be supplemented in some jurisdictions. It is based in part on models provided by Aceris Law LLC.[252]

Sample Document 6-1
Demand for Ad Hoc Arbitration

IN THE MATTER OF AN ARBITRATION UNDER THE ARBITRATION RULES OF THE UNITED NATIONS COMMISSION ON INTERNATIONAL TRADE LAW (UNCITRAL)

BETWEEN:

[Claimant Name and Address]   (Claimant)

and

[Respondent Name and Address]   (Respondent)

NOTICE OF ARBITRATION

[Date]

[Claimant's attorney & law firm]
[Claimant's law firm address & contact info]
[Claimant's in-house representative & contact info]

1. This Notice of Arbitration is submitted on behalf of [Name of Claimant] (hereinafter "Claimant") pursuant to Article 3 of the Arbitration Rules of the United Nations Commission on International Trade Law in force as from 15 August 2010 (the "UNCITRAL Arbitration Rules") against [Name of Respondent] (hereinafter "Respondent"), (hereinafter collectively referred to as the "Parties").

2. Claimant is a company registered under the laws of [country or jurisdiction] and engaged, *inter alia*, in the business of [relevant commercial activity for the present case]. Respondent is a company registered under the laws of [country or jurisdiction] and engaged, *inter alia*, in the business of [relevant commercial activity for the present case].

3. Respondent entered into a contract with Claimant concerning [IBT x] on [date]. The contract provides for [brief description of the IBT]. Unfortunately, the implementation of the contract did not go as expected and [brief description of the factual events giving rise to the dispute].

4. As a consequence, Claimant is seeking [list primary claims, secondary claims (damages), costs (arbitration costs and attorney fees), and interest]. The total value of the claims is estimated at [x USD].

5. The contract is governed by the substantive laws of [jurisdiction or convention] pursuant to Article [specify Article of the contract where this is found], which provides as follows: [cite relevant provisions in full. Claimant should propose the governing law, unless parties have already agreed].

6. Pursuant to [Clause x] of the contract (copy included), if either party considers that a dispute cannot be settled amicably, it shall be submitted to arbitration by [a sole arbitrator/a panel of three arbitrators]. Attempts to settle the dispute amicably and arrive at a mutually satisfactory solution [describe briefly] were unsuccessful [if necessary, elaborate on required exhaustion of negotiation, conciliation and/or mediation options]. The contract provides that the arbitration shall have its legal seat in [place] and be conducted in [language].

7. In accordance with the arbitration clause, we hereby initiate arbitration for the final and conclusive settlement of all claims between the parties to the contract.

---

in a different forum. In any case, a comprehensive Statement of Claim has to be submitted once the matter is pending.

252. https://www.international-arbitration-attorney.com/model-answer-to-request-for-arbitration/. Reprinted by permission.

8. We nominate as our arbitrator [name, address, contact information] and request that you nominate an arbitrator as soon as possible and in any case no later than [x date]. The two arbitrators will then agree on the presiding arbitrator to complete the tribunal.

Alternatively: We suggest as sole arbitrator [name, address, contact information]. Please indicate by [x date] your agreement to the appointment of the sole arbitrator or, if you do not accept [name], please send three alternative nominations for the sole arbitrator by [x date].

9. Once established, the tribunal will communicate its requirements for the advancement of expenses and set deadlines for the exchange of the Statements of Claim and Response.

Sincerely Yours

Claimant Representative [Name of Law Firm, Name of Attorney, Signature]

[address, e-mail, fax, and phone number]

Once the Demand for Arbitration has been served on the respondent, the latter has only a relatively short period of time to file her initial response (typically 30 days, see Article 4 UNCITRAL or Article 5 ICC). Like the claimant, the respondent may be able to rely on institutional guidelines for the Answer. Article 5 ICC stipulates:

1) Within 30 days from the receipt of the Request from the Secretariat, the respondent shall submit an Answer (the "Answer") which shall contain the following information:

a) its name in full, description, address and other contact details;

b) the name in full, address and other contact details of any person(s) representing the respondent in the arbitration;

c) its comments as to the nature and circumstances of the dispute giving rise to the claims and the basis upon which the claims are made;

d) its response to the relief sought;

e) any observations or proposals concerning the number of arbitrators and their choice in light of the claimant's proposals and in accordance with the provisions of Articles 12 and 13, and any nomination of an arbitrator required thereby; and

f) any observations or proposals as to the place of the arbitration, the applicable rules of law and the language of the arbitration. . . .

5) Any counterclaims made by the respondent shall be submitted with the Answer and shall provide:

a) a description of the nature and circumstances of the dispute giving rise to the counterclaims and of the basis upon which the counterclaims are made;

b) a statement of the relief sought together with the amounts of any quantified counterclaims and, to the extent possible, an estimate of the monetary value of any other counterclaims; c) any relevant agreements and, in particular, the arbitration agreement(s); and

d) where counterclaims are made under more than one arbitration agreement, an indication of the arbitration agreement under which each counterclaim is made.

The Aceris International Arbitration Law Firm provides a number of model Answers to Requests for Arbitration and Responses to Notices of Arbitration under the ICC and other institutional rules. It also has a model for ad hoc arbitration under the UNCITRAL Rules, which is again relied on, in part, for the Sample Document 6-2.[253]

Sample Document 6-2
Response to Demand for Ad Hoc Arbitration

IN THE MATTER OF AN ARBITRATION UNDER THE ARBITRATION RULES OF THE UNITED NATIONS COMMISSION ON INTERNATIONAL TRADE LAW (UNCITRAL)

BETWEEN:

[Claimant Name and Address]   (Claimant)

and

[Respondent Name and Address]   (Respondent)

RESPONSE TO NOTICE OF ARBITRATION

[Date]

[Respondent's attorney & law firm]
[Respondent's law firm address & contact info]
[Respondent's in-house representative & contact info]

1. This Response to Claimant's Notice of Arbitration is submitted on behalf of [Name of Respondent] (hereinafter "Respondent") pursuant to Article 4 of the Arbitration Rules of the United Nations Commission on International Trade Law in force as from August 15, 2010 (the "UNCITRAL Arbitration Rules").

[If jurisdiction is contested: 2. On account of [arguments], there is no jurisdictional basis for an arbitral tribunal to hear any disputes between Claimant and Respondent or any claims which Claimant purports to have against Respondent in relation to [contract of x date and/or the underlying business transaction].

[Subsequent arguments on the merits are being presented only in the alternative that an arbitral tribunal should decide that it has jurisdiction and proceeds to hear arguments on the merits.]

3. Contrary to the factual background described by Claimant, the events giving rise to the current dispute developed as follows: [brief summary]

4. As a consequence and/or on account of the following legal reasons [brief summary], Claimant does not have [primary claims, secondary claims (damages), costs (arbitration costs and attorney fees), and interest] against Respondent. [Instead, Claimant conduct gives rise to the following counterclaims of Respondent: [list primary claims, secondary claims (damages), costs (arbitration costs and attorney fees), and interest].

5. [Comments on applicable substantive law, i.e., whether Respondent agrees with Claimant or presents an alternative.]

6. [Comments regarding alleged basis for arbitration, consistent with #1, and comments, if necessary, on required exhaustion of negotiation, conciliation, and/or mediation options, as well as seat/place and language. To the extent Respondent disagrees with Claimant's Notice of Arbitration on these matters, reasoned alternatives have to be presented.]

7. [Respondent contests [name] nominated as Arbitrator by Claimant on the grounds that [add arguments].]

Respondent nominates [name] to serve as [Co-Arbitrator/Sole Arbitrator] [address, contact information].

---

253. https://www.international-arbitration-attorney.com/model-answer-to-request-for-arbitration/. Reprinted by permission.

9. For all these reasons, Respondent respectfully requests the arbitral tribunal to

i) dismiss Claimant's claims in their entirety;

ii) declare that Claimant has violated its obligations under [contract/other basis for liability];

iii) order Claimant to compensate Respondent for damages and losses suffered as a result of Claimant's conduct, currently estimated in the amount of ...;

iv) order Claimant to pay all arbitration costs, including Respondent's attorney fees and expenses and the costs and expenses of Respondent's in-house counsel; and

v) order payment by Claimant of interest at a rate of [prime + +] on all of the above amounts as of the date these amounts were due and until the date of their effective payment.

Sincerely Yours

Respondent Representative [Name of Law Firm, Name of Attorney, Signature]

[address, e-mail, fax, and phone number]

Since the claimant will nominate her arbitrator with the Demand for Arbitration, and the respondent is at least invited to nominate his arbitrator in the Response, the tribunal should be well on its way to being established at this point. We still need to reflect on the choice of arbitrator, however.

7. Establishment of the Arbitration Tribunal

One of the biggest advantages of arbitration is the ability of the parties to select their arbitrators. This gives them the opportunity to select arbitrators they trust to be independent and impartial. They can also select individuals with specific qualifications and experience with regard to a particular industry, trade, or type of transaction. This may include not only legal knowledge, but also technical and commercial expertise. Other factors that will play a role in the selection of the arbitrators will be nationality (a sole or presiding arbitrator will usually be of a different nationality from either of the parties), language proficiency, availability, and cost. Among the substantive qualifications parties should be looking for is sufficient experience in arbitration, including the management of the proceedings, in particular if the case is complicated. This also means that individuals who are experienced litigators may not be the best arbitrators since they bring a different perspective to the procedure.

The first step toward establishment of the tribunal will be the decision whether to proceed with one or three arbitrators. Three factors should be taken into consideration:

First, selection of a sole arbitrator requires an agreement between the parties. If the parties to an IBT know and trust each other and have a strong interest in continuing their business relationship, such an agreement can usually be reached. If not, the parties have to resort to an outside authority for the appointment of the arbitrator. This is usually easy in institutional arbitration because the institution will step in to appoint the arbitrator (see, for example, Art. 12 ICC Rules). However, in ad hoc arbitration, the parties may have to call on a court at the seat of the arbitration to help out, which can be time-consuming and difficult, depending on the country at issue. Thus, in ad hoc arbitration, if the parties want to go with a sole arbitrator, they may want to nominate an appointing authority in their original arbitration clause, in case they cannot agree later when the dispute has arisen. An example of an appointing authority is the president of the local chamber of commerce.

By contrast, if the parties want to proceed with three arbitrators, the procedure is usually straightforward. Each party nominates one arbitrator and the two then agree on the presiding arbitrator. Nevertheless, even here it may be worthwhile having a backup plan in case agreement between the arbitrators is not forthcoming.

Second, cost is a major factor in deciding between one and three arbitrators (and even in the selection of the individuals). Different arbitrators, largely dependent on their level of experience and their reputation, charge different fees. For example, the ICC fee schedule (Documents, p. II-317–319) provides for minimum and maximum arbitrator fees. For a dispute over US$10 million, the minimum fees are US$40,492 and the maximum fees are US$154,964. Thus, an ICC arbitration with three well-known arbitrators will cost about US$500,000 for institutional and arbitrator fees alone, to which attorney fees, travel and accommodation expenses, and other administrative costs have to be added. By contrast, an ad hoc arbitration with a less well-known sole arbitrator over a comparable dispute does not have to cost more than US$30-40,000 in fees (see also below, pp. 1036 et seq.).

Third, the amount of work to be done should be taken into consideration. If a case is complicated and/or involves the evaluation of a large number of documents, potentially many witnesses or experts, etc., it may be better to have three arbitrators who can share the burden and ensure that nothing is overlooked. Efficient collaboration, however, is not necessarily automatic for three arbitrators who have never worked with each other. This makes the role of the presiding arbitrator even more important.

One way of managing the question of one or three arbitrators is to leave it open for subsequent decision. Thus, a clause might read something like this: "If the parties can agree on a sole arbitrator, the arbitration shall proceed accordingly. If agreement is not forthcoming within 30 days, each side nominates one arbitrator and the two shall then agree on the presiding arbitrator." Such a clause allows for the decision to be made at a later stage when the complexity of the issues and the amount in dispute are known. If the parties can still agree on a sole arbitrator, they can both save money. If at least one side thinks that it would be better to have three arbitrators, they can simply refuse to agree on a sole arbitrator.

Another consideration in this context is whether to appoint a Tribunal Secretary. Typically, this would be a junior lawyer or arbitrator who provides a range of administrative services to the tribunal without participating in the actual assessment of the claims. In complex arbitrations where a large amount of evidence needs to be taken into account, potentially involving multiple hearings to question multiple witnesses and experts, and in particular in multi-party arbitrations where just the timely communication of all notices and documents can be a major headache, a good administrative secretary may be essential for success. However, the parties should clearly delineate the powers and responsibilities of the administrative secretary in the Terms of Reference and ensure that everyone agrees on them. In particular, it should be made clear whether the administrative secretary can go beyond logistical and secretarial services and also conduct research for the tribunal, attend not only the hearings but also the deliberations, and potentially even draft procedural orders or the factual summary of the award on behalf of the tribunal.[254]

The next question is about the criteria to be taken into consideration when choosing individual arbitrators.[255] Again, several factors should be taken into consideration. The ideal arbitrator will be

- capable of meeting any *requirements stipulated in the arbitration clause* or agreement to arbitrate; a written or unwritten requirement may be that the sole or presiding arbitrator should be of a different *nationality* than both of the parties;
- knowledgeable in the respective *substantive area of law;*
- fluent in the chosen *language* of arbitration;
- experienced with the *procedure of arbitration* (in particular the sole arbitrator or the president of a tribunal of three);
- *independent and neutral* (this applies for all arbitrators, including a party-appointed arbitrator as a member of a panel of three);
- *willing to disclose* any facts that could become grounds for disqualification;
- *willing and available* to participate.

"Arbitrator" as a professional title is not protected and pretty much anyone, including individuals without legal education or even a modicum of experience, can call themselves arbitrators. The question is, therefore, how can a party to an IBT, her in-house legal counsel, and/or her external lawyer find a suitable arbitrator to be nominated as sole arbitrator or as member of a tribunal of three?

---

254. An excellent summary of the pertinent issues can be found in Michael Polkinghorne & Charles B. Rosenberg, *The Role of the Tribunal Secretary in International Arbitration: A Call for a Uniform Standard*, IBA 2014, available at https://www.ibanet.org/Article/NewDetail.aspx ?ArticleUid=987d1cfc-3bc2-48d3-959e-e18d7935f542. See also J. Ole Jensen, *Tribunal Secretaries in International Arbitration*, Oxford Univ. Press 2019.

255. Of course, finding the right arbitrators is not the only problem facing the claimant and respondent. Sometimes they have to first find the right lawyers to represent them in an arbitration. Although admission to a particular bar is not a requirement in arbitration, hence parties can simply rely on their usual counsel, and many law firms today have "dispute settlement," "ADR," or "arbitration" lawyers or groups, not all of them have the necessary experience to handle larger and more complex cases. If large amounts of money and/or the survival of a company may be at stake, The Global Arbitration Review (GAR) is one place where parties can find recommendations for the most experienced arbitration lawyers. ,See "GAR 100" at https://globalarbitrationreview.com /edition/1001477/gar-100-13th-edition.

Mauro Rubino-Sammartano, Chartered Arbitrator and President of the European Court of Arbitration in Strasbourg (France), wrote in 2017:

> Many users of international arbitration, particularly in-house counsel, have repeatedly expressed concern about the lack of adequate information on arbitrators, resulting in arbitrator selection based on vague and general reputation often informed by word of mouth or anecdotal information. Arbitral institutions and arbitration circles cannot remain indifferent to this need.[256]

To address the need for transparency, many arbitration institutions maintain rosters of neutrals that meet their institutional standards of knowledge and professionalism. A number of arbitration institutions also conduct training programs and issue certificates for successful participants. One of the most rigorous of these is the certification by the Chartered Institute of Arbitrators, and candidates have to show not only many years of experience in the field and a wide range of substantive knowledge but also pass a multi-step exam before they can become Fellows of the Chartered Institute of Arbitrators, let alone Chartered Arbitrators. Clients should always look for an arbitrator who is FCIArb or equivalent. Chambers and Partners maintain a number of rankings in their annual Global Guide. Among others, they list "most in demand arbitrators." While being listed here is certainly evidence of impeccable qualifications, it also means for a potential client that these arbitrators are the most expensive and the busiest, which often means that scheduling can be difficult. The same is often true for the arbitrators on the rosters of the largest arbitral institutions, like the ICC, and the arbitrators who may be nominated — in the absence of an agreement between the parties — by an Appointing Authority like the ICC.

For practical purposes, the following may be a good way to find an arbitrator who is not overly busy and expensive, yet qualified and professional: First, search for "FCIArb" or similar credentials on LinkedIn or go straight to the website of the Chartered Institute. There are approximately 1,300 Fellows of the Chartered Institute of Arbitrators in the system. Second, find about a dozen of them that list the required areas of experience or law — for example, construction law — as well as proficiency in the required language, and reside in the part of the world where the arbitration will be seated. Third, visit the personal websites of these arbitrators to see whether their recent activities fit your requirements and make them seem suitable for the dispute at hand. In this way, narrow the field to five or six candidates. Fourth, contact the candidates to ask whether they are potentially available for an arbitration proceedings in the field of construction law between a company in country x and another in country y during the months of z and willing to conduct an interview online for further information. Fifth, conduct two or three Skype interviews, more if necessary, to find the most suitable arbitrator for your case.

---

256. Mauro Rubino-Sammartano: *A Second (Quasi-Perfect?) Storm also in Arbitration?*, J. Int'l Arb. 2017, Vol. 34, No. 6, pp. 925–934, at p. 925.

In the interview, it is important that the neutrality of the arbitrator not be compromised. In other words, parties must not try to seek out how the arbitrator would decide their case in order to find one who is friendly to their side. The Chartered Institute of Arbitrators has developed Practice Guidelines for Interviews of Prospective Arbitrators that "[set] out the current best practice in international commercial arbitration" in this regard:[257]

Article 1 — General Principles

1. Subject to the caveats detailed in this Guideline, arbitrators may agree to be interviewed by a party prior to an appointment as part of the selection process. The mere fact that a prospective arbitrator had been interviewed by one of the parties only, prior to an appointment, should not, of itself, be a ground for challenge.

2. When considering a request for an interview, prospective arbitrators should enquire whether the arbitration agreement, including any arbitration rules and/or the law of the place of arbitration (lex arbitri) contain provisions prohibiting ex parte communications prior to appointment.

3. If minded to proceed with the interview, prospective arbitrators should request a copy of the arbitration agreement so that they are informed of the names of the parties and the general nature of the prospective appointment in order to check whether they have any conflict, any experience and qualifications required and any knowledge of the language in which the arbitration will be conducted.

4. After having cleared an initial conflicts check, prospective arbitrators should agree with the interviewing party, and confirm in writing, the basis upon which the interview is to be conducted.

5. Prospective arbitrators should not receive any remuneration or hospitality for agreeing to participate in an interview.

6. Prospective arbitrators should make contemporaneous notes of the matters discussed in the interview.

Article 2 — Matters to Discuss at an Interview
Prior to an Appointment

Matters to be discussed at an interview should be clearly defined and agreed with an agenda exchanged in advance. In any event, the content of an interview should be limited to the following:

   i. past experience in international arbitration and attitudes to the general conduct of arbitral proceedings;

  ii. expertise in the subject matter of the dispute;

---

257. Available, with Commentary, on the website of the CIArb at www.ciarb.org.

iii. availability, including the expected timetable of the proceedings and estimated timings and length of a hearing; and/or

iv. in ad hoc arbitrations, the prospective arbitrator's reasonable fees and other terms of appointment, to the extent permissible under the applicable rules and/or law(s).

Article 3—Matters That Should Not Be Discussed

The following matters should not be discussed either directly or indirectly:

i. the specific facts or circumstances giving rise to the dispute;

ii. the positions or arguments of the parties;

iii. the merits of the case; and/or

iv. the prospective arbitrator's views on the merits, parties' arguments and/or claims.

Article 4—Interviews for Prospective Sole or Presiding Arbitrators

If a prospective sole or presiding arbitrator is invited to an interview by one party, they should only agree to be interviewed by all parties jointly. If, however, a candidate is satisfied that a party who chooses not to attend such an interview was invited to attend and given reasonable notice of the interview, and does not object to the interview and/or the agenda, the interview may proceed in the absence of that party. In these circumstances, the prospective arbitrator should make a contemporaneous note of matters discussed in the interview and send it to all of the parties, any co-arbitrators and any institution, promptly after their appointment.

In institutional arbitration, the Terms of Appointment will be prescribed by the institution. Most institutions also fix the remuneration—which usually depends on the amount in dispute—or at least provide a range for the minimum and maximum honoraria the arbitrators can demand. Thus, if a party is looking for an arbitrator for an institutional procedure, it just has to ensure that the arbitrator accepts the institutional terms of appointment and remuneration schedule.

For ad hoc arbitration, the parties have to enter into a contract with the arbitrator to fix the Terms of Appointment. Again, the Chartered Institute of Arbitrators has developed Practice Guidelines to facilitate and professionalize the matter:[258]

Article 1—General Principles

1. Arbitrators should seek to agree with the parties the basis of their appointment before or immediately after accepting an appointment, bearing in mind the terms of the arbitration agreement, including any arbitration rules and the law of the place of arbitration (lex arbitri).

---

258. Available, with Commentary, on the website of the CIArb at www.ciarb.org. Copyright © Chartered Institute of Arbitrators. Reprinted with permission.

2. The terms of appointment should be recorded in writing and should address the nature of the appointment, arrangements for the arbitrators' remuneration and any other material terms agreed with the parties.

3. Once agreed, the terms of appointment may be amended only if all the parties and the arbitrators agree to the amendment.

Article 2 — Terms of Remuneration

The terms of remuneration should address the following:

    i.   method by which the arbitrators' fees will be calculated;

    ii. any commitment or cancellation fees;

    iii. reimbursement of expenses reasonably incurred;

    iv. value added or other taxes;

    v.   payment terms, including any arrangements for advance deposits on account;

    vi. final account for fees and expenses;

    vii. specific arrangements for remuneration and reimbursement of fees and expenses in the case of an early termination or settlement; and

    viii. any other relevant matters.

Once the required number of arbitrators has been agreed upon and appointed, the tribunal is constituted and ready to assume its charge. However, we still need to determine what is and what is not within the powers and obligations of the tribunal. To this end, we need to see what the parties want and what rules will govern the proceedings pursuant to the 5 + 5 matrix introduced above, in particular the hierarchy of norms under #2 (i) to #2 (v). The tribunal will typically ask for the Statement of Claim and Statement of Response of the parties, then schedule a Preliminary or Case Management Conference, and then draw up the Terms of Reference that determine the charge and the powers of the tribunal.

8. *Statement of Claim and Statement of Response*[259]

The Statement of Claim, sometimes also referred to as "Brief" or "Memorial," has to be addressed to the tribunal and the respondent. If less onerous rules for transmission of documents have not yet been agreed upon by the parties and are not included in institutional or other applicable rules, it should be served on the respondent according to the same rules and procedures that applied to the Notice of Arbitration.

The Statement of Claim follows a similar format as the Notice of Arbitration (above, p. 963). However, the claimant now needs to put together a comprehensive

---

259. For additional information, see, *inter alia*, Peter Ashford, *The IBA Guidelines on Party Representation in International Arbitration*, Cambridge Univ. Press 2018.

brief. It alerts the tribunal and the respondent what is at issue and—potentially—which facts and rules are or are not in dispute. The respondent will be given a certain amount of time to answer the claims with a Statement of Response, sometimes also referred to as "Counter-Brief" or "Counter-Memorial." Since the respondent may raise arguments unforeseen by the claimant or may even raise counterclaims, there will be a second round of briefs, usually referred to as Reply and Rejoinder or Rebuttal and Surrebuttal. By contrast to the Notice of Arbitration or Demand for Arbitration, which need not be longer than one page, the Statement of Claim and the Statement of Response have to be fully developed briefs. In fact, it is important for the parties to include every claim, every argument, and every reference to potential evidence supporting a claim or argument, because they may be preempted from raising a claim or presenting an argument or a piece of evidence at a later stage unless they can show that new facts or evidence only became available to them now.

Sample Document 6-3
Statement of Claim

1. Introductory Sentence: Something along the lines of: "this is a dispute between A, a manufacturer of X, and B, A's exclusive distributor in India, about _____ "

2. Roadmap: The basic claims and how they will be presented, for example, "B has been distributing but discontinued payments, therefore, B is in breach of the exclusive distributorship agreement and articles Y and Z of the CISG. We will first demonstrate that the tribunal was constituted in accordance with the agreement to arbitrate of _____ date and has jurisdiction over the dispute. Then we will show _____."

3. Legal Basis for the Arbitration, Establishment, and Jurisdiction of the Tribunal: Include verbatim copy of the arbitration agreement (clause or submission agreement); otherwise, summarize, as briefly as possible and as long as needed (four levels of analysis).

4. Procedural History: Recount any preliminary orders, injunctions etc.; if further preliminary or procedural orders are needed, provide reasoned requests.

5. Presentation of Facts: Favorable but truthful presentation of the story of what happened between the parties.

6. Presentation of Claims: List of primary claims, secondary claims (damages), costs, and interest.

7. Detailed Legal Analysis for Each Claim: (Four levels of analysis)

Primary or contractual claims
- Identification of applicable rules (statutory, case law, other)
- Statement as to correct interpretation of applicable rules for present case
- Distillation of relevant conditions to be met for claims to be supported by applicable rules
- Demonstration that the conditions are met by the facts in the present case (subsumption of facts under rules)
- Conclusion ("Therefore, _____ ")

Repeat for next claim, listing: damages, costs, interest.

8. Summary of Arguments: Circle back to Roadmap: "As we have shown, _____ "

9. Statement of Relief Sought: Formulate the tenor of the award (make it easy for you by making it easy for the arbitrators).

10. Appendices:

a. Calculation of Any Amounts Requested: Detailed calculations, justifying in particular any amounts that are not obvious. This should include calculation/justification of interest and cost.

b. Main Documentary Evidence

One of the important elements often underestimated is a persuasive calculation of any monetary claims, in particular for damages, costs, and interest. Claimants should always consider primary, i.e., contractual remedies such as specific performance; but the reality is that damages, including those for late and nonperformance, are often more important.[260] Moreover, claimants need to remember that tribunals cannot award what was not requested. If an attorney forgets to ask for costs and interest, the client will not get compensated for these losses. Finally, if claims are poorly substantiated, e.g., a claim for 10% interest is not persuasively presented, tribunals are more likely to refuse it altogether than to award a more reasonable level of, for example, five percent interest.

In most cases, the tribunal will set a deadline for the respondent to submit the Statement of Response and how it should be submitted. The respondent can make the work of the arbitrators easier and her brief more persuasive by following the same basic outline with her Statement of Response. This makes it very clear to what extent facts, law, and/or consequences/remedies are in dispute.

Sample Document 6-4
Statement of Response

1. Introductory Sentence: Something along the lines of: "In the dispute between A, a manufacturer of X, and B, A's exclusive distributor in India, we will present the following arguments and claims." Rather than agreeing with the Claimant ("As the Claimant has elaborated, the dispute is between _____ about _____," the introductory sentence can be very short and lead directly to the Roadmap.

2. Roadmap: First, Respondent should present any arguments that the arbitration was not properly initiated, the tribunal was not properly established, and/or the tribunal does not have jurisdiction. However, such a line of arguments should only be announced if the Respondent has serious claims and wants to block the arbitration from going ahead or at least lay the foundation for a claim against recognition and enforcement of any award. In the absence of serious problems with the procedure and/or tribunal, this part should be omitted.

Next, the Respondent needs to outline the basic counterarguments to Claimant's substantive claims and how they will be presented, for example, "Contrary to Claimant's allegations, B has been distributing but only discontinued payments after _____ therefore, B is not in breach of the exclusive distributorship agreement and articles Y and Z of the CISG."

Third, the Respondent needs to provide an overview of any substantive counterclaims she intends to present.

3. Legal Basis for the Arbitration, Establishment, and Jurisdiction of the Tribunal: Only if needed, i.e., if disputed.

4. Procedural History: Only to the extent Respondent needs to add missing information or wants to dispute the presentation in Claimant's brief; to the extent Respondent agrees with Claimant's presentation, no "response" should be included.

5. Presentation of Facts: Same as for procedural history: Respondent should present her version of the facts by adding missing information and by disputing factual allegations or interpretations of facts, such as the meaning of certain statements made by witnesses or language contained in documents, to shake arbitrator confidence in the completeness and truthfulness of the facts presented by Claimant. To the extent Respondent agrees with Claimant's presentation of facts, no "response" should be included. Language explicitly confirming Claimant statements such as "as Claimant has elaborated" should be avoided.

---

260. See, e.g., John Trevor (ed.), *Global Arbitration Review — The Guide to Damages in International Arbitration*, GAR 3rd ed. 2018.

6. Presentation of Claims: Primary claims (both negative and counterclaims), secondary claims/damages (both negative and counter), costs (arbitration proceedings, attorney fees, expenses), as well as interest.

7. Detailed Legal Analysis for Each Claim, first to Counter Claimant Claims, Second to Support Respondent Counterclaims: (Four levels of analysis)

a. Primary or Contractual Claimant claims:

- Identification of applicable rules (statutory, case law, other), pointing out, in particular, that Claimant has not identified applicable rules correctly and/or completely, and now Respondent is presenting the missing or alternative rules and why they need to be applied instead.

- Statement as to correct interpretation of applicable rules for present case (four levels of analysis), pointing out that Claimant's interpretation is incorrect because
    - ▸ the facts are different from Claimant's allegations; and/or
    - ▸ the applicable rules are not the one's suggested by Claimant, and/or
    - ▸ the applicable rules have to be interpreted differently from the way Claimant is suggesting, and/or
    - ▸ the applicable rules have to be applied differently to the facts of the case.

- Interim conclusion on rejection of primary or contractual Claimant claims

b. Secondary Claimant claims (damages):

repeat procedure under a)

c. Claimant claims to interest and cost:

repeat procedure under a)

d. Claimant calculation of any monies owed, in particular damages, interest and cost:

detailed rejection of Claimant's calculation of damage and other amounts, pointing out mistaken or unjustifiable Claimant claims

e. Presentation of Counterclaims:

Primary or contractual claims
- Identification of applicable rules (statutory, case law, other)
- Statement as to correct interpretation of applicable rules for present case
- Distillation of relevant conditions to be met for claims to be supported by applicable rules
- Demonstration that the conditions are met by the facts in the present case (subsumption of facts under rules)
- Conclusion ("Therefore, _____ ")

Repeat for next claims, listing: damages, costs, interest).

8. Summary of Arguments: Circle back to Roadmap: "As we have shown, _____ "

9. Statement of Relief Sought: Formulate the tenor of the award (make it easy for you by making it easy for the arbitrators).

10. Appendices:

a. Calculation of Any Amounts Requested: Detailed calculations justifying Respondent counterclaims, in particular any amounts that are not obvious ...

b. Main Documentary Evidence to support Respondent counterargument (not already presented by Claimant) and to support Respondent counterclaims

After the exchange of the Statement of Claim and the Statement of Response, the tribunal may give the parties an opportunity for Rebuttal and Surrebuttal, in particular if counterclaims and/or different facts and/or different rules were introduced in the Statement of Response.

Alternatively, the tribunal may directly proceed to scheduling the preliminary hearing or case management conference and provide an opportunity for discussion of the facts, rules, and arguments presented by the parties. The preliminary hearing is often conducted online these days to save time and money.

Either way, the tribunal will seek to establish exactly which facts are agreed upon and which are in dispute, to what extent the parties agree on the applicable law and rules and how they should be understood, and whether there are some claims that can be settled or removed from the procedure.

After the Preliminary Hearing or Case Management Conference, the parties will have an opportunity to submit revised pleadings accordingly.

However, before the tribunal can schedule the first meeting, it may have to deal with some emergency or preliminary measures of protection.

9. Emergency and Interim Measures of Protection

Emergency or interim measures or some form of interlocutory relief may be necessary for the protection of rights that may be lost before a final decision in a dispute over those rights can be obtained. With longer and longer delays before public courts, interim relief has become more important and is today frequently the primary battle ground. Until some years ago, emergency and interim measures were not as common in arbitration because of the shorter time lines. In addition, there was a perception that interim relief granted by an arbitral tribunal does not really work, unless it is endorsed and enforced by a court. Going to court, in turn, would often compromise the confidentiality of the proceedings and also bring all the problems of public litigation with non-specialized judges and potentially long delays into the arbitration process.

In recent years, things have changed. On the one hand, arbitral institutions have become more sophisticated when providing for emergency or interim relief, and public courts (in many countries) have become more supportive. On the other hand, parties to arbitral proceedings have also become more adept at removing assets and other measures designed to frustrate the outcome of an arbitration. This has created greater demand for and better supply of emergency or interim relief in arbitration.

Although any court or tribunal—once constituted—should be able to issue interim or emergency orders to safeguard justified interests of the parties to the case before it, the problem can be that it may take too long to do so. In arbitration, there may even be an incentive for a respondent hoping to remove assets or otherwise frustrate the dispute settlement procedure to obstruct the establishment of the tribunal to gain more time to do so. For this reason, the ICC has created an emergency arbitrator procedure in Appendix V of its Rules. This procedure allows the appointment of an emergency arbitrator separate from the establishment of the primary tribunal within as few as two days (Article 2). The emergency arbitrator will decide on the application before her within 15 days or less (Article 6(4)).

On its surface, the ICC emergency arbitrator procedure might seem like the solution to the problems outlined above. In practice, however, it solves only one problem, namely that an interim or emergency order cannot be obtained until a tribunal is established. Beyond that, the ICC Rules are surprisingly unclear. They neither stipulate the types of measures an emergency arbitrator can adopt, nor the conditions she should impose before doing so. Furthermore, the emergency arbitrator always has to provide an opportunity for the respondent to be heard (Articles 4 and 5(2)), even when alerting the respondent to the impending procedure may trigger the frustration of the claimant's rights. Finally, the emergency arbitrator can only issue her measures in the form of an "order" (Article 6(1)), which does not make them enforceable under the New York Convention. It is submitted that the ICC, given the fact that it will happily charge a minimum of US$40,000 for the procedure (Article 7), could have provided more clarity.[261]

To ensure a procedure that is not only quick and effective, but also safeguards the rights and interests of both parties, courts and tribunals should verify that the following conditions are met—and provide persuasive arguments to this end in the decision:

1. The principal claims have to be pending in ordinary procedures. Any request for interim or interlocutory relief needs to be ancillary to an ordinary procedure between the same parties over essentially the same claims. While a claimant should be able to combine a demand for arbitration with a request for emergency measures, any emergency measures should be terminated if the claimant at any time abandons the principal claims. This will prevent a claimant from seeking a final solution in a procedure that allows only a superficial analysis.

2. Based on a superficial or prima facie analysis, the principal claims have to be valid and supported in fact and law. This means that the arguments presented by the claimant in the main procedure, beginning with jurisdiction of the tribunal and extending to the merits of the claim, have to support a decision by the tribunal in favor of the claimant in the absence of actually presented or obvious counterarguments in favor of the respondent.

3. The interests of the applicant to obtain a temporary solution must outweigh the interests of the defendant in a continuation of the status quo until the final

---

261. Interestingly, the 2017 update of the ICC Rules did not provide any changes to the Emergency Arbitrator Rules in Appendix V.

For additional discussion, see, for example, Baruch Baigel, *The Emergency Arbitrator Procedure Under the 2012 ICC Rules: A Juridical Analysis*, J. Int'l Arb. 2014, Vol. 31, No. 1, pp. 1–18; Philippe Cavalieros & Janet Hyun Jeong Kim, *Emergency Arbitrators Versus the Courts: From Concurrent Jurisdiction to Practical Considerations*, J. Int'l Arb. 2018, Vol. 35, No. 3, pp. 275–306; Edgardo Muñoz, *How Urgent Shall an Emergency Be?—The Standards Required to Grant Urgent Relief by Emergency Arbitrators*, Yearbook on Int'l Arb. 2015, Vol. 4, pp. 43–68; Lawrence Newman & Colin Ong (eds.), *Interim Measures in International Arbitration*, JurisNet 2014; Fabio Santacroce, *The Emergency Arbitrator: A Full-Fledged Arbitrator Rendering an Enforceable Decision?*, Arb. Int'l 2015, Vol. 31, No. 2, pp. 283–312; Ank Santens & Jaroslav Kudrna, *The State of Play of Enforcement of Emergency Arbitrator Decisions*, J. Int'l Arb. 2017, Vol. 34, No. 1, pp. 1–15; and Dora Ziyaeva (ed.), *Interim and Emergency Relief in International Arbitration*, JurisNet 2015.

decision with full analysis of facts and law can be obtained. If the balance of interests is not clearly in favor of the claimant, or if the tribunal is otherwise concerned about the impact of the emergency measures on the rights and interests of the respondent, the tribunal should require a security deposit from the claimant to secure any subsequent damage claims by the respondent.

4. An interim or temporary solution is urgent because there is a real and imminent threat of frustration of claims or rights. The term "irreparable harm" may pose too high a bar, however. If necessary, the tribunal should be able to grant measures without hearing the respondent first. For example, if the respondent is domiciled and/or has most of his assets in a jurisdiction that is not exactly known for the consistent implementation of final foreign arbitral awards, the claimant has a significant financial claim that seems prima facie valid, and highly mobile assets of respondent like bank accounts, an airplane or a ship, appear in a place where they could be arrested to secure claimant claims, hearing the respondent before taking conservatory measures could frustrate those very measures. In such a case, the right of the respondent to be heard will need to be safeguarded *after* the measures have been put in place and, if the respondent presents persuasive arguments that the arrest measures should be terminated and/or should not have been imposed in the first place, the claimant will need to bear the consequences in the form of costs of the procedure and potential damage claims of the respondent. In the specific example of the arrest of an airplane or ship, the respondent can also be given the option of depositing security for the principal claims to have the ship or airplane released.

In practice, a number of different measures have been developed and need to be distinguished:[262]

Conservatory injunctions preserve the status quo with regard to the substantive or material rights and assets of the parties. An example would be an order prohibiting disposal or removal of certain assets.

Regulatory injunctions impose a change in the status quo of those same substantial or material rights and assets of the parties on a temporary basis until the final decision of the court or tribunal. An example would be an order requiring specific performance of a contract or granting of a (temporary) intellectual property license. In an extreme case, a regulatory injunction can impose an irreversible change, for example the sale of perishable goods, which can only be corrected later in the form

---

262. The categories in the UNCITRAL Model Law are a bit different. Article 17 suggests adoption of national rules empowering arbitral tribunals to "grant interim measures . . . to (a) Maintain or restore the status quo pending determination of the dispute; (b) Take action that would prevent, or refrain from taking action that is likely to cause, current or imminent harm or prejudice to the arbitral process itself; (c) Provide a means of preserving assets out of which a subsequent award may be satisfied; or (d) Preserve evidence that may be relevant and material to the resolution of the dispute."

of monetary compensation if the decision in the principal dispute does not confirm the interim relief measure. The appointment of an administrator of assets might be somewhere in the middle between conservatory and regulatory, depending on the powers of the administrator and the nature of the assets.

Procedural injunctions aim at safeguarding procedural rights of the parties and the integrity of the dispute settlement procedure as such. An important example are anti-suit injunctions. Other examples concern the preservation and production of evidence.

The greater the hardship imposed on the respondent and the less reversible the measures are going to be, the higher the standard to be applied for prima facie validity of the claims, urgency of the measures, and security deposit.

Finally, the tribunal should have the option of adopting the emergency measures in the form of a procedural order or in the form of an interim award. A procedural order is fine as long as enforcement can be achieved by procedural sanctions. For example, the IBA Rules on the Taking of Evidence in International Arbitration provide "[i]f a Party fails without satisfactory explanation to produce any Document . . . ordered to be produced by the Arbitral Tribunal, the Arbitral Tribunal may infer that such document would be adverse to the interests of that Party." (Article 9(5)). The situation is different, however, if a measure needs to be enforced outside of the arbitral proceedings. As we will see in our discussion of the different forms an award may take, an interim award is an "award" in the sense of the New York Convention and can be presented for recognition and enforcement by the public courts. At the same time, it does not terminate the main proceedings in the way a final award does.

10. *Preliminary Conference or Case Management Conference*

Once the arbitrators are selected and the tribunal is established, the next step is to determine the charge given to the tribunal, i.e., the questions and claims put before the tribunal, any questions or issues that may be related to the dispute but are not within the charge given by the parties to the tribunal, i.e., withheld from it, and the powers given to the tribunal to perform its obligations. The best way — and indeed a requirement in many rules — is a case management conference (cf. Article 24 ICC). Increasingly, this kind of meeting is done online, but in complex or multiparty cases the time and money spent on an in-person conference may be worthwhile. The points of departure are the Statement of Claim and the Statement of Response. However, rather than working from the documents, it is usually beneficial to have an open conversation beginning with claimant claims and the extent to which the respondent acknowledges them, as well as respondent counterclaims and claimant's position in this regard. The goal is to see whether at least some issues can be settled or excluded from the further proceedings. Then the conversation will turn to the facts that are mutually agreed versus facts that are in dispute, and the evidence that can and should be examined to determine disputed facts. Again, a major goal is to find out which facts are either not in dispute or not relevant. If an agreement or decision can be reached about the admissibility and production of documentary evidence, any experts to be involved, and the number and identity of witnesses to be heard, it may be possible to limit the amount of discovery and examination of evidence that will be needed. Next, the conversation will address the main legal arguments of the parties and the extent to which they are in dispute. If the applicability and interpretation of certain legal rules can be mutually agreed, this may make certain fact-finding exercises obsolete. Similarly, the amounts of the various financial claims and the justification of nonfinancial claims will be discussed to see whether some level of agreement can be reached. If the parties can pare down the issues and questions that need to be resolved, much time and money can be saved.

A second goal of the preliminary conference is to reach agreement about a variety of practical issues, such as deadlines for submission of briefs, methods of communication, time and place of future meetings, as well as financial matters (including deposits for expenses).[263]

The entire agreement reached at the preliminary conference will then be drawn up in the format of a contract called Terms of Reference or Submission Agreement, and signed by all parties, arbitrators, legal counsel, and any other participants in the arbitration proceedings.[264]

If an agreement between the parties about the Terms of Reference cannot be reached, the tribunal will establish a similar set of rules via a procedural decision commonly referred to as Procedural Order #1.

11. The Terms of Reference/Submission Agreement/Agreement to Arbitrate: Determining the Powers and Procedures of the Arbitration Tribunal

To determine the powers of an arbitration tribunal and the procedures it needs to follow, we first look to whether the parties have a specific agreement. Only to the extent that they do not, would we look for alternative sources that are part of the backup rules that govern the arbitration:

---

263. Guidelines for the Preliminary or Case Management Conference and the Terms of Reference can found in the *2012 UNCITRAL Notes on Organizing Arbitral Proceedings*.

264. The procedure outlined here is by no means prescribed or standardized. Different arbitrators have different approaches for organizing a dispute settlement procedure and there is no one right way of doing it (although there are many wrong ways). However, parties may want to compare what their arbitrators are doing with the steps outlined here and ensure that all essential elements are covered, in particular if they are dealing with less experienced arbitrators or a tribunal that does not work very well together.

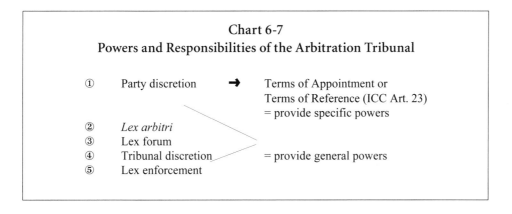

The ICC Rules require the drafting of "Terms of Reference (ToR)" (Art. 23, Documents, p. II-294). Under the 2015 CIETAC Rules, such Terms of Reference are optional (Art. 35(5)). Other arbitration rules refer only indirectly to something akin to Terms or Reference (see, for example, Art. 16(2) of the AAA Rules (Documents, p. II-364), Art. 15 of the 2012 Swiss Rules (Documents, p. II-449), or Arts. 14 and 22 of the LCIA Rules (Documents, p. II-336)).

Whether they are called "Terms of Reference," "Terms of Appointment," or "Submission Agreement," a carefully drafted agreement among all parties, their legal counsel, and all arbitrators, regarding the jurisdiction of the tribunal (the scope of its work and the rights and obligations of the arbitrators) and the ground rules for the arbitration procedure, is of paramount importance for the success of the arbitration itself and the enforceability of the resulting arbitral award. As a binding contract, it makes it hard for any of the participants to claim at a later stage that a certain act of the tribunal was illegal, unfair, or that a particular issue would allow a challenge of all or parts of the award. Such a contract is all the more important if the arbitration is conducted ad hoc and without the support and regulatory framework of a major arbitration organization.

The Terms of Reference are typically drawn up during or at the end of the preliminary conference, if it is combined with a meeting of all parties, or after the preliminary conference, if it is done online.

Checklist 6-3
Terms of Reference/Submission Agreement/Agreement to Arbitrate

Arbitration Institution

1. Header with information about the **arbitration institution**, address, case number, etc. if any

Parties

2. **Claimant** (information about legal personality, incorporation, ownership, main line of business, business activities relevant to present case, etc.)

Claimant formal name, address of registered office where communication should be sent,

Claimant representative(s) to be addressed, w/phone and fax numbers, e-mail

3. Respondent (information about legal personality, incorporation, ownership, main line of business, business activities relevant to present case, etc.)

Respondent formal name, address of registered office where communication should be sent,

Respondent representative(s) to be addressed, w/phone and fax numbers, e-mail

4. Reference to all arbitration clauses and/or submission agreements preceding the current agreement as the basis of the arbitration

Party Representatives

5. Claimant Representatives: "In this arbitration, C is represented by _____ under powers of attorney dated _____ and annexed"

Law firm name, address of the office where communication should be sent,

Claimant lawyer(s) to be addressed, w/phone and fax numbers, e-mail

6. Respondent Representatives: "In this arbitration, R is represented by _____ under powers of attorney dated _____ and annexed"

Law firm name, address of the office where communication should be sent,

Respondent lawyer(s) to be addressed, w/phone and fax numbers, e-mail

7. Statement about communications to the parties: traditional format: "All communications arising in the course of this arbitration should be made only to the legal representatives/both to the legal representatives and the corporate representatives by e-mail and/or by fax at the above names and numbers/and to be confirmed by receive receipt within 24 hours and/or hardcopy courier."

More modern format involving electronic data interchange (EDI): "All communications shall be transmitted electronically by PDF attachment sent by e-mail only to the legal representatives/both to the legal representatives and the corporate representatives at the above names and mailboxes and to be confirmed within 24 hours. Important documents and unconfirmed communications shall be retransmitted via DocuSign. The use of electronic document transmission via DocuSign shall satisfy any requirement that documents be provided in writing and/or served on the other party."

8. Statement that all communications shall be deemed timely if sent by e-mail/electronic data interchange by the due date at the place of sending, regardless of the corresponding time at the place of receipt, provided delivery is confirmed or a receipt is received on the next business day.

Arbitrators

9. Arbitrator nominated by claimant: name, address, position, address, phone, fax, e-mail

10. Arbitrator nominated by respondent: name, address, position, address, phone, fax, e-mail

11. Presiding arbitrator and the way (s)he was nominated: name, address, position, address, phone, fax, e-mail

12. Appointment of an Administrative Secretary, if desired, with name, address, position, address, phone, fax, e-mail, **powers and responsibilities** to be determined under #27

13. Declaration of independence and impartiality by each member of the tribunal, including the administrative secretary, if any: "The arbitrator . . . declares that he/she has no conflicts of interest as listed in sections 1 (non-waivable red list) and 2 (waivable red list) of the 2014 IBA Guidelines on Conflicts of Interest in International Arbitration. The arbitrator discloses any situations listed in section 3 (orange list) of the IBA Guidelines as follows . . . and requests an explicit waiver by the parties. The arbitrator discloses any situations listed in section 4 (green list) of the IBA Guidelines as follows . . . for informational purposes only. The arbitrator further commits to disclosing any change of circumstances that may arise during the arbitration proceedings with regard to any of the categories mentioned above."

14. Confirmation by the parties and the party representatives **that all members of the tribunal have been properly selected and appointed** and that neither the parties nor their representatives are currently aware of any grounds for challenges. Should an arbitrator, after the present agreement has been signed, notify a situation pursuant to #13 that could cause doubts about his or her continuing independence and impartiality, either party has to notify the tribunal within one week if it wants to challenge the arbitrator.

15. Statement about communications from the parties to the arbitrators: all communications to be sent simultaneously to all three arbitrators and/or the administrative secretary, if any, and copied to the legal representatives and the corporate representatives, if so required by the *lex arbitri*; by e-mail and/or by fax and/or by EDI, as per #7 above.

16. Copies of all communications from the parties to the arbitrators to be sent to the secretariat of the arbitration organization if so required by the *lex arbitri*.

17. Statement that all communications shall be deemed timely if sent by e-mail/electronic data interchange by the due date at the place of sending, regardless of the corresponding time at the place of receipt, provided delivery is confirmed or a receipt is received on the next business day.

Summary of the Parties' Claims and Relief Sought

18. Claimant summary

- jurisdiction of the arbitral tribunal
- claims (brief summary of facts, statement as to applicable law and its interpretation and application to the facts)
- relief sought (including contractual/primary claims, noncontractual or damage claims, interest, and cost)

19. Respondent summary

- jurisdiction of the arbitral tribunal
- defenses and any counterclaims (brief summary of facts, statement as to applicable law and its interpretation and application to the facts)
- relief sought (incl. contractual/primary claims, noncontractual or damage claims, interest, and cost)

20. Agreement on limitations regarding the length and number of written submissions to be exchanged, if so desired

21. Party statements / agreement as to amount in dispute (including claims and counterclaims), for the purpose of calculation of costs and fees

Powers and Responsibilities of the Arbitral Tribunal

22. List of principal issues to be determined by the arbitral tribunal

　　1.＿＿＿＿

　　2.＿＿＿＿

　　3.＿＿＿＿

23. List of issues *not* to be investigated or decided by the arbitral tribunal, if any

24. Agreement that the list of issues to be decided and/or not to be decided per #22 and #23 can be changed by agreement between the parties, in particular in case of a settlement, only on condition of simultaneous agreement on the distribution and payment of all costs and fees related to the arbitration.

25. Party agreement as to place/seat of arbitration

26. Party agreement as to time and place of hearings and whether any meetings will be held elsewhere and/or online; agreement on limitations and/or time limits for oral presentations, meetings, and hearings, if so desired

27. Party statements / agreement as to applicable law, procedural rules, and related matters

- Applicable procedural rules as per arbitration clause(s)

- Different or additional applicable substantive and procedural rules per this agreement: 5 + 5 elements of the *lex arbitri*

- Party statements/agreement as to the powers of the presiding arbitrator: in particular to issue procedural orders alone, if urgent, such as extending a deadline; possibly also to make certain decisions if one of the arbitrators is no longer willing or able to participate

- Party statements/agreement as to the powers and responsibilities of the Administrative Secretary, if one is appointed

- Agreement preventing the parties from resorting to ordinary courts for interim relief or any other issues within the jurisdiction of the tribunal

- Party statements/agreement as to the language of the proceedings

- Agreement that any party relying on documents or other evidence in other languages has to pay for translations and/or interpretation

- Party statements/agreement as to the applicability of the 2010 IBA Rules on the Taking of Evidence in International Arbitration and/ or additional or alternative provisions on hearing/compelling witnesses, appointing experts, etc.

- Party statement/agreement whether cross-examination of witnesses and experts shall be allowed

- Time limits on presentation of new evidence and/or new arguments, if so desired

28. Agreement how changes to the ToR can be made

Award(s)

29. Party statements / agreement that the tribunal is competent to issue **partial awards, interim awards, procedural orders** and other procedural directions or instructions as it may deem appropriate

30. Exclusion of decision-making by the tribunal as amiable compositeur or *ex aequo et bono*, if so desired

31. **Exclusion of punitive damages**, if so desired, and possibly other directions about remedies, e.g., currency

32. **Limitation of liability of the arbitrators** for any acts or omissions along the lines of Article 40 of the ICC Rules

33. Agreement on time limits, decision-making, notification, and deposit of the final award by the tribunal, if different from any institutional rules that may apply.

Signatures

Parties

Claimant   Respondent

Claimant Representatives   Respondent Representatives

Place and Date   Place and Date

Tribunal

Claimant Nominated Arbitrator   Respondent Nominated Arbitrator

Presiding Arbitrator

Tribunal Secretary (if any)

Place and Date

12. Exchange of Updated Briefs

If the preliminary or case management conference resulted in a modification of claims or any other changes that cannot be or were not memorialized in the Terms of Reference or Submission Agreement, the tribunal should give the parties an opportunity to update their briefs and arguments. It should be clear, however, that this opportunity cannot be used to expand claims or to introduce new legal arguments, unless otherwise agreed between the parties and accepted by the tribunal.

13. Procedural Decisions of an Arbitration Tribunal

To the extent that matters have not been settled in the Terms of Reference or Submission Agreement, the Tribunal may have to make decisions about a variety of matters during the proceedings. Subjects to be covered may include:[265]

- jurisdictional objections and admissibility of claims;
- separation or joinder of proceedings;
- admission of parties to a multiparty procedure, admission of *amici* submissions;
- decisions about the place and date of the main hearing and any other meetings;
- practical matters to be prepared for the main hearing, such as rental of facilities, contracting of secretarial and translation services;
- decisions about admissible evidence, such as:
- time and page limits for documentary evidence, requests for disclosure,

---

265. A good checklist is provided by the UNCITRAL Notes on Organizing Arbitral Proceedings, available at https://uncitral.un.org/en/texts/arbitration/explanatorytexts/organizing_arbitral_proceedings.

- selection of expert witnesses,
- identification of witnesses of fact and decisions about written statements, oral evidence, and cross-examination,
- decisions about physical inspection of places or things;
- practical matters like administrative support for the Tribunal, deposit of costs, as well as form, content, time line, and delivery of the final award.

The common format to be used for these decisions is the procedural order.

14. *Challenging an Arbitrator*

Another problem that may appear at this stage of the proceedings are doubts about the impartiality and independence of one of the arbitrators.[266] If one of the parties is unhappy with one of the arbitrators, the question of a challenge may arise. Several considerations will be necessary:

1. Once the Tribunal has been constituted and the Terms of Reference or Submission Agreement has been signed, a party cannot recall the arbitrator it has previously nominated just because it is no longer happy with the way the arbitrator is acting in the proceedings. A contract for works and services has been entered into and it can only be terminated prematurely if grounds for a challenge are identified.

2. An arbitrator can only be challenged if specific justifications can be identified or if there is a serious breach of the appointment agreement. The UNCITRAL Rules provide that "an arbitrator may be challenged if circumstances exist that give rise to justifiable doubts as to the arbitrator's impartiality or independence" (Article 12(1)). A secondary option is provided for cases in which "an arbitrator fails to act or in the event of the de jure or de facto impossibility of his or her performing his or her functions" (Article 12(3)). Similarly, the ICC Rules provide for the challenge of an arbitrator "for an alleged lack of impartiality or independence, or otherwise" (Article 14 (1)). Among the most comprehensive are the provisions in Sec. 24(1) of the English Arbitration Act of 1996 (Documents, p. II-540). The U.S. rule in Sec. 10(a) of the FAA (Documents, p. II-505) provides for "evident partiality or corruption." It has been strictly interpreted by the U.S. Supreme Court in *Commonwealth Coatings Corp. v. Continental Cas. Co.*[267]

On the one hand, the possibility of challenging an arbitrator is important to safeguard the integrity of the procedure and ensure that a tribunal can only proceed if both parties have confidence in its fairness and impartiality. This is particularly

---

266. For in-depth analysis, see Karel Daele, *Challenge and Disqualification of Arbitrators in International Arbitration*, Wolters Kluwer 2011; Chiara Giorgetti, *Between Legitimacy and Control: Challenges and Recusals of Judges and Arbitrators in International Courts and Tribunals*, Geo. Wash. Int'l Rev. 2016, Vol. 49, No. 2, pp. 205–258; Chiara Giorgetti: *Selecting and Removing Arbitrators in International Investment Arbitration*, Brill Research Persp. Int'l Inv. L. & Arb. 2018, Vol. 2, No. 4, pp. 1–93.

267. *Commonwealth Coatings Corp. v. Continental Cas. Co.*, 393 U.S. 145, at 147–149 (1968).

important given the fact that the award by the tribunal will usually be the first and final decision in the dispute, i.e., there is no appellate review for mistakes of fact or law. On the other hand, a challenge can be used for tactical purposes to delay the procedure or to build a case for a challenge to an award at the enforcement stage. The integrity of the procedure, therefore, has to be protected against an unsuitable arbitrator *and* against an unfounded challenge.

The standard for the required impartiality and independence of the arbitrators is found in the applicable laws per our 5 + 5 matrix (above, p. 913).[268] If nothing specific has been agreed between the parties, reference will usually be made to the 1987 IBA Rules of Ethics for International Arbitrators and/or the 2004 IBA Guidelines on Conflict of Interest in International Arbitration as the most widely accepted standards (Documents, pp. II-265 and II-269). The Guidelines provide a traffic light system with a nonwaivable red list, a waivable red list, an orange list with a duty to disclose, and a green list of items that do not require disclosure. It is recommended that the parties to an international arbitration stipulate in their Terms of Reference or Submission Agreement that the IBA traffic light system will be upgraded to turn both red lists into nonwaivable conflicts, require an explicit waiver for items on the orange list, and require disclosure for items on the green list (see also above, p. 983, #13).This is particularly important if procedures are being conducted in countries and/or with arbitrators from countries where the U.S. standards of due process or a similar level of safeguards are not necessarily understood and applied. However, such an enhanced standard can only be used to challenge an arbitrator if it was explicitly agreed upon in writing between the parties and the members of the tribunal.

3. Any challenge has to follow the procedure prescribed by the *lex arbitri*. In ad hoc arbitration, a challenge will normally have to be made before the tribunal itself (e.g., Article 13(2) UNCITRAL Rules). This gives an opportunity to the challenged arbitrator to explain to the parties and the other members of the tribunal the issues that are causing doubts about her independence or impartiality or to withdraw voluntarily. If the arbitrator is unable to dispel the doubts and refuses to withdraw, the tribunal itself or the appointing authority will need to make a decision. In most countries it may also be possible at this point for the party pursuing the challenge to call upon the public courts for help. Given the dual challenge of protecting the rights of the parties against an unsuitable arbitrator while also protecting the procedure against unjustified obstruction, it is again helpful if the arbitration is seated in a country that provides competent and efficient support in its courts.

In ICC procedures, a challenge is sent directly to the Secretariat, which will give "the arbitrator concerned, the other party or parties and any other member of the arbitral tribunal" an opportunity to comment. Subsequently, the matter is referred to a standing body of the ICC, the ICC Court of Arbitration, for final decision.

---

268. See also Nigel Blackaby & Constantine Partasides: *Redfern and Hunter on International Arbitration*, Oxford Univ. Press 6th ed. 2015, at pp. 268–278.

4. An important problem is the timing of an arbitrator challenge. Most procedural rules require that a challenge be made within a reasonably short time—usually two to four weeks—after the grounds for a potential challenge become known (for example, the ICC rules provide for 30 days in Art. 14(2)). Parties should not be able to hold back a challenge to see whether they like where a procedure is going. The reason is that the disruption to the procedure will be greater, the more the procedure has advanced. If a party does not make a challenge within the stipulated time, it is deemed to have waived the particular concern. The time bar should not only preclude later challenges within the same arbitration procedure but also challenges of the award itself at the enforcement stage for the same reasons.

5. The final question is: what happens with the procedure if an arbitrator challenge is successful? In principle, there are two options. First, the vacancy on the tribunal should be filled by the appointment of a new arbitrator pursuant to the same procedure as was applied at the outset. Second, the tribunal could continue as a truncated tribunal. As long as the procedure has not progressed to the main hearing, replacement of the arbitrator is usually to be preferred. The newly appointed arbitrator can be brought up to speed on the basis of the existing documents. However, if an arbitrator is challenged or otherwise no longer willing or able to participate in the proceedings after the main hearing, the truncated option may be preferable. Otherwise, the oral procedure, including the presentation of the main arguments by the parties and the hearing of experts and witnesses, may have to be repeated, which is time-consuming and expensive. As Redfern and Hunter have pointed out, a high-quality transcript of the oral proceedings may suffice to inform a replacement arbitrator and bring her up to date, as long as both parties and the other members of the tribunal so agree.[269]

This brings us to a more detailed discussion of evidence to be presented in writing and during the oral proceedings.

15. *Evidence*

As in civil or commercial litigation, five types of evidence can be considered in arbitration. They can be remembered via the acronym DEWIP, which is also a guideline on their importance in most cases:

- Documents
- Experts
- Witnesses
- Inspection of Things or Locales
- Parties

From a practical point of view, evidence comes in three "flavors." First, there is the evidence that the party making a particular claim has under its own control. Thus,

269. Ibid., at p. 284.

if the law prescribes certain conditions to be met in fact for the claim to succeed, the party can prove those facts and win. Second, there is the evidence that the opposing party controls or is presumed to control. This is trickier because the opposing party may not acknowledge that it has certain pieces of evidence, for example that a certain document existed or still exists. Alternatively, the opposing party may not want to surrender the evidence because it is not in their favor. We need to explore to what extent a claimant can force a respondent to hand over certain pieces of evidence to the tribunal. Third, there is the evidence that is under the control of third parties, which includes documents that exist but neither party has access to, and even witnesses that are independent from the parties and may not want to be dragged into a dispute. In the latter case, a tribunal may have no power at all to compel third parties to surrender any kind of evidence unless these third parties are either controlling or controlled by a party to the dispute[270] or have otherwise agreed to participate in the arbitration.

Like all questions about an arbitration, the questions about admissible evidence, requirements to produce evidence, and details of the assessment of evidence, have to be answered on the basis of the laws and rules applicable per our 5 + 5 matrix (above, p. 913). The most detailed rules are found in the 2010 IBA Rules on the Taking of Evidence in International Arbitration (Documents, p. II-239).[271] It is highly recommended that these rules be incorporated by agreement of the parties, usually as part of the Terms of Reference or the Submission Agreement. If this has not been done, tribunals may still resort to them as the most widely accepted standards for international arbitration procedures.

The IBA Rules provide for the production of documents[272] (Article 3), witnesses (of fact)[273] (Article 4), party-appointed experts (Article 5), tribunal-appointed experts (Article 6), and the inspection "of any site, property, machinery or any other goods, samples, systems, processes or documents" by the tribunal itself, a tribunal-appointed expert, or a party-appointed expert (Article 7).

---

270. On the doctrine pertaining to "groups of companies," see M.P. Bharucha, Sneha Jaisingh & Shreya Gupta, *The Extension of Arbitration Agreements to Non-Signatories—A Global Perspective*, Indian J. Arb. L. 2016, Vol. 5, No. 1, pp. 35–63; Christopher Drahozal, *Parties and Affected Others: Signatories and Nonsignatories to International Arbitration Agreements*, Cambridge Compendium on International Commercial and Investment Arbitration 2018, available at SSRN: https://papers.ssrn.com/sol3/papers.cfm?abstract_id=3125546.

271. For further analysis, see Peter Ashford, *The IBA Rules on the Taking of Evidence in International Arbitration: A Guide*, Cambridge Univ. Press 2013; Teresa Giovannini & Alexis Mourre (eds.), *Written Evidence and Discovery in International Arbitration: New Issues and Tendencies*, Wolters Kluwer 2009; Roman Khodykin & Carol Mulcahy, *A Guide to the IBA Rules on the Taking of Evidence in International Arbitration*, Oxford Univ. Press 2019; Nathan D. O'Malley, *Rules of Evidence in International Arbitration: An Annotated Guide*, Lloyd's Arbitration Law Library, Routledge 2nd ed. 2019.

272. See also Reto Marghitola: *Document Production in International Arbitration*, Wolters Kluwer 2015.

273. For further analysis, see Ragnar Harbst, *A Counsel's Guide to Examining and Preparing Witnesses in International Arbitration*, Wolters Kluwer 2015. See also Kaj Hobér & Howard S. Sussman, *Cross-Examination in International Arbitration*, Oxford Univ. Press 2015.

Documents are by far the most important form of evidence for arbitration proceedings. Pursuant to Article 3(1): "each Party shall submit to the Arbitral Tribunal and to the other Parties *all Documents available to it on which it relies . . .*" (emphasis added). Reliance is one of the notions understood quite differently in the U.S. and the rest of the world. The idea is that a party should submit the documents *necessary* to substantiate its claims. An American lawyer, to be on the safe side and avoid potential liability, will often cast a wide net and submit a large number of documents. By contrast, a European lawyer will be more likely to focus on a few crucial documents.

The second problem is the fact that documents (and other types of evidence) may not be available to the party that wants to rely on them because they are under the control of the opposing party. The IBA Rules provide in Article 3, paragraphs 2 to 13 the procedure for requests by one party and orders to produce addressed to the other party. A Request to Produce by one party addressed to another party "shall contain

(a) (i) a description of each requested Document sufficient to identify it, or

(ii) a description in sufficient detail (including subject matter) of a narrow and specific requested category of Documents that are reasonably believed to exist; in the case of Documents maintained in electronic form, the requesting Party may, or the Arbitral Tribunal may order that it shall be required to, identify specific files, search terms, individuals or other means of searching for such Documents in an efficient and economical manner;

(b) a statement as to how the Documents requested are relevant to the case and material to its outcome; and

(c) (i) a statement that the Documents requested are not in the possession, custody or control of the requesting Party or a statement of the reasons why it would be unreasonably burdensome for the requesting Party to produce such Documents, and

(ii) a statement of the reasons why the requesting Party assumes the Documents requested are in the possession, custody or control of another Party.

The formula in subparagraph (a) reflects the European tradition, namely the requirement in discovery to name exactly the document to be produced or at least to identify a "narrow and specific" category of documents to be produced. Broad "fishing expeditions" with demands for something like "every meeting record and internal communication related to the production or marketing of machines of type XYZ during calendar year 2019" will not be accepted in most international arbitration procedures.

Various American rules for international arbitration leave the extent of allowable discovery to the discretion of the tribunal. For example, Article 25.2 of the JAMS International Arbitration Rules & Procedures provides that "the Tribunal may order parties to exchange and produce documents, exhibits or other evidence *it deems necessary or appropriate*" (Documents, p. II-382, emphasis added).

In accepting or denying a request to produce by one party to another, the tribunal has to walk a fine line between protecting the efficiency of the procedure and the rights to privacy and confidentiality of the parties on the one hand, and the rights to a fair opportunity to prepare and present the case and to be heard on the other. If a tribunal is too restrictive in this regard, it may even jeopardize the enforcement of the final award, in particular in the U.S., if a persuasive argument can be made that the losing party did not have a fair chance at presenting her case.

The JAMS Arbitration Discovery Protocols provide factors to be considered, including

> "The amount in controversy.
>
> The complexity of the factual issues.
>
> The number of parties and diversity of their interests.
>
> Whether any or all of the claims appear, on the basis of the pleadings, to have sufficient merit to justify the time and expense associated with the requested discovery.
>
> Whether there are public policy or ethical issues that give rise to the need for an in-depth probe through relatively comprehensive discovery. . . .
>
> The parties' choice of substantive and procedural law and the expectations under that legal regime with respect to arbitration discovery. . . .
>
> Whether the requested discovery appears to be sought in an excess of caution, or is duplicative or redundant. . . . [and]
>
> Whether broad discovery is being sought as part of a litigation tactic to put the other side to great expense and thus coerce some sort of result on grounds other than the merits."

In light of the rights of both parties to be able to make their case, these considerations should not easily lead to a denial of a request to produce, in particular, as the JAMS Protocol continues, if

> the party seeking expansive discovery is willing to advance the other side's reasonable costs and attorneys' fees in connection with furnishing the requested materials and information.

To ensure transparency of the procedure and systematic review, in particular where a large number of documents is requested, Alan Redfern has created a "Schedule" for review of requests to produce:[274]

---

274. See Nigel Blackaby & Constantine Partasides QC, *Redfern and Hunter on International Arbitration*, Oxford Univ. Press 6th ed. 2015, at p. 68.

Chart 6-8
Sample Redfern Schedule for Document Production

Document or Category of Documents	Relevance and Materiality	Possession of Documents	Respondent's Objections	Tribunal Decision
1. Contract entered into in March or April 2017 between Respondent and Supplier S	Respondent claims that it was not aware of and not taking steps to contain potential quality issues with parts supplied by S. Contract should show performance standards promised, warranties given or declined, and similar indicators of potential quality issues.	Respondent has admitted that it sourced some parts in question from S. There must be a written contract for the transaction. This contract is not currently in Claimant's possession.	No contract was concluded in 2017 with S. The business relationship goes back to 2015. The contract of Jan 15, 2015, is not relevant to the present proceedings and contains confidential information, such as prices and profit targets. There never have been quality issues with parts supplied by S. Thus, Respondent objects on the following grounds: • lack of sufficient relevance (Art. 9(2)(a) IBA) • commercial confidentiality (Art. 9(2)(e) IBA)	
2. Minutes of Respondent's Board Meeting of May 8, 2017	Respondent claims that there were no quality issues or it was not aware of quality issues with parts supplied by S. The minutes of the Board Meeting taking place days after the accident should reveal whether R discussed problems with the parts, hence was already aware of the issues.	The meeting was referred to in a letter sent by R to S, which is in Claimant's possession. It is unlikely that no minutes were taken at the meeting. The minutes of the meeting are not currently in Claimant's possession.	The minutes of the Board Meeting of May 8, 2017, do not contain any reference to the relationship with S and/or the quality of parts supplied by S. Thus, the minutes are not relevant to the present proceedings. They do, however, contain commercially sensitive information and decisions on an unrelated corporate governance issue. Thus, Respondent objects on the following grounds: • lack of sufficient relevance (Art. 9(2)(a) IBA) • commercial confidentiality (Art. 9(2)(e) IBA)	

Document or Category of Documents	Relevance and Materiality	Possession of Documents	Respondent's Objections	Tribunal Decision
3. Communication between Respondent and its lawyers at Black and Coffin on or around May 8, 2017	Any communication between R and its regular legal counsel in the immediate aftermath of the accident and right before and after the Board Meeting of May 8, 2017, could show whether R was seeking help with a problem they were aware of before and that had finally materialized.	It is highly likely that R sought advice from its lawyers on how to handle the aftermath of the accident from a legal point of view. Any such communication is not currently in Claimant's possession.	In the aftermath of the accident, senior executives of R conducted several phone conversations with lawyers at B & C. These were not recorded, only some handwritten notes were taken that could no longer be found. In any case, the advice sought from and given by its lawyers benefits from legal privilege. Thus, Respondent objects on the following grounds: • loss or destruction of the documents (Art. 9(2)(d) IBA) • legal impediment (Art. 9(2)(b) IBA)	

Although the IBA Rules do not provide for fishing expeditions with open-ended demands, many European lawyers are still surprised by and opposed to the American approach taken by some tribunals. To provide a legal basis for significantly more restrictive discovery procedures, a working group of lawyers and arbitrators from civil law or continental European countries has developed the so-called 2018 Prague Rules on the Efficient Conduct of Proceedings in International Arbitration (Documents, p. II-251). While these Rules provide some useful details, for example on the procedure to be used for the appointment and hearing of experts (Article 6), the main difference from the IBA Rules is the approach taken on containment of evidence. First, the tribunal is given broader powers in line with the more inquisitorial traditions of continental European adjudication. Article 3 stipulates that "[t]he arbitral tribunal is entitled and encouraged to take a proactive role in establishing the facts of the case. . . ." To this end, the tribunal "may . . . at any stage of the arbitration and at its own initiative . . . request any of the parties to submit relevant documentary evidence or make fact witnesses available. . . ." Article 7 also clarifies that "the arbitral tribunal may apply legal provisions not pleaded by the parties. . . .".

Second, with regard to evidence, the tribunal is also encouraged to take an active role and to reduce the amount of evidence to be reviewed, if possible. Pursuant to Article 5, the tribunal "may decide that a certain [party-appointed] witness should not be called for examination . . . in particular if it considers the testimony . . . to be irrelevant, immaterial, unreasonably burdensome, duplicative or for any other reasons not necessary. . . ." Article 4 on documentary evidence is even more drastic. Pursuant to 4.2, "the arbitral tribunal and the parties *are encouraged to avoid any form of document production*, including e-discovery" (emphasis added). If document production by the other side is inevitable, "a party may request the arbitral tribunal to order another party to produce *a specific document* which is relevant and material to the outcome of the case . . ." (emphasis added). In contrast to the IBA Rules, there is no provision for requests for *a category* of documents or even a document that cannot be named but only described as reasonably believed to exist. Finally, pursuant to Article 8, "[i]n order to promote cost-efficiency . . . the arbitral tribunal and the parties should seek to resolve the dispute on a documents-only basis" and avoid a hearing altogether. Only if one of the parties so requests or "the tribunal itself finds it appropriate, the parties and the arbitral tribunal shall seek to organize" a hearing "in the most cost-efficient manner possible, including by limiting the duration of the hearing and using video, electronic or telephone communication to avoid unnecessary travel costs for arbitrators, parties and other participants."

Even to a continental European lawyer, the approach taken in the Prague Rules seems a bit extreme. One of the great benefits of arbitration versus litigation is the high degree of party control over the procedures. In my view, attorneys and parties agreeing to application of the Prague Rules sacrifice too much of that control in the name of cost efficiency. I would not only worry about the professional responsibility of an attorney who agrees to these Rules and unduly limits his discovery options. There is also a risk for the other side, during recognition and enforcement of the award, if a party did not get sufficient review of the evidence "or was otherwise unable to present his case" (Art. V(1)(b) New York Convention).

One of the features the Prague Rules and the IBA Rules have in common is the negative inference option if a party does not comply with orders to produce evidence. If a party is ordered by the tribunal to produce a specific document and fails to do so in a timely manner "without satisfactory explanation," Article 9(5) of the IBA Rules provides that "the Tribunal may infer that such document would be adverse to the interests of that Party." Article 10 of the Prague Rules stipulates much the same. In other words, the Tribunal will assume that the document would support the position or claim of the other party. Furthermore, according to Article 9(7) IBA, "[i]f the Arbitral Tribunal determines that a Party has failed to conduct itself in good faith in the taking of evidence, the Arbitral Tribunal may, in addition to any other measures available under these Rules, take such failure into account in its assignment of the costs of the arbitration, including costs arising out of or in connection with the taking of evidence." Again, the Prague Rules, in Article 11, contain parallel provisions.

In general, these provisions work quite well for documents and other evidence under the control of the parties. However, if and when important evidence is under the control of third parties, it may be necessary to fall back on the courts at the seat of the arbitration to obtain this evidence. This is yet another reminder of the importance of selecting a seat for the arbitration that has efficient and trustworthy courts to call upon. This explains why places like London, Stockholm,[275] or various towns in Switzerland[276] have become frequent destinations for arbitration proceedings and why we would discourage parties from selecting locations in countries or regions like Russia,[277] mainland China, East and Central Asia, and much of the Middle East, Africa, and Latin America as the seat of an arbitration.[278] However, if evidence and/or assets are exclusively located in one of the latter countries or regions, a procedural decision from a court in England, Sweden, or Switzerland may not easily be recognized and enforced there. This may provide a good enough reason for placing the seat of an arbitration in such a country in spite of reservations about its courts. In practice, it is advisable to look at recent cases involving the enforcement of institutional arbitration and/or court decisions requiring the production of documents or other evidence in the respective countries.[279] For example, China may more easily respect a decision on evidence by the Hong Kong International Arbitration Center (HKIAC) than by the Vienna International Arbitration Centre (VIAC).[280]

16. The Main Hearing[281]

Although a documents-only arbitration is possible if the parties so agree, it is still customary to organize at least one hearing during which the parties present the essential elements of their submissions and answer any questions the tribunal may have. If experts and/or witnesses of fact are submitting statements to the tribunal, the parties generally have the right to question or even cross-examine the witnesses.[282] This obviously requires a hearing and can hardly be done effectively online. However, if the amounts at stake are not particularly large and the facts and

---

275. See Ulf Franke & Annette Magnusson, *International Arbitration in Sweden: A Practitioner's Guide*, Wolters Kluwer 2013; Kaj Hober, *International Commercial Arbitration in Sweden*, Oxford Univ. Press 2011; Finn Madsen, *Commercial Arbitration in Sweden*, Oxford Univ. Press 3rd ed. 2007.

276. See also Gabrielle Kaufmann-Kohler & Antonio Rigozzi, *International Arbitration—Law and Practice in Switzerland*, Oxford Univ. Press 2015.

277. A good overview can be found in Kaj Hober & Yarik Kryvoi, *Law and Practice of International Arbitration in the CIS Region*, Wolters Kluwer 2017.

278. Although it has a complicated legal framework, New York City is also a popular place for arbitration. A good analysis of the applicable rules can be found in James H. Carter & John Fellas (eds.), *International Commercial Arbitration in New York*, Oxford Univ. Press 2nd ed. 2016.

279. For more general discussion, see also Michael Ostrove, Claudia Salomon & Bette Shifman, *Choice of Venue in International Arbitration*, Oxford Univ. Press 2014.

280. Which does not mean that the VIAC Rules are of inferior quality. For analysis, see Franz T. Schwarz & Christian W. Konrad, *The Vienna Rules: A Commentary on International Arbitration in Austria*, Wolters Kluwer 2009.

281. In general, see Alan L. Dworsky, *Little Book on Oral Argument*, Rothman 2nd ed. 2018.

282. See, for example, Article 26(2) UNCITRAL Model Law (Documents, p. II-185), Article 29(5) UNCITRAL Rules (Documents, p. II-199), Article 25(2) to (6) ICC (Documents, p. II-294), Article 20.4 and 20.8 LCIA (Documents, p. II-336).

evidentiary situation are more straightforward, hearings can be conducted by video conference or dispensed with altogether.

The goal of the oral hearing is to clarify any remaining misunderstandings and any issues that may not be clear in the written submissions, to eliminate from the contested matters any issues of fact or law that can still be agreed upon, and to examine evidence — in particular evidence not included in documents that can be reviewed anywhere and at any time. All of this needs to be accomplished in the shortest possible time since bringing together an entire tribunal and the party representatives, possibly the parties themselves, and any experts and witnesses that may need to be heard, in one place and for any amount of time is difficult and expensive. In most cases, tribunals will seek to limit the time for a hearing to a day or two, although in complicated cases or with multiple parties in an arbitration, the hearing may last a week or more.

While there are no fixed rules or requirements for the organization of the main hearing, there are some best practice suggestions:[283]

1. At an online pre-hearing conference, the schedule and other details of the hearing should be discussed. The tribunal should memorialize the agreed format and share it with the parties as a procedural order or for signature as a binding agreement.

2. The hearing begins with the opening statements of claimant and respondent. It is the responsibility of the tribunal to ensure that the representatives of the parties do not use their time to read the written submissions and instead focus on the main idea or theme of their submissions and/or any remaining contentious issues.

3. The next and most extended phase will be dedicated to the examination of evidence other than documentary evidence. The focus will be on experts and other witnesses. The parties themselves may also be heard. In this regard, Article 20.6 LCIA stipulates that officers, employees, owners, and shareholders of a party may be treated as witnesses. This may include administration of an oath and/or cross-examination.

If inspection of places or things is necessary, the tribunal is not likely to do such an inspection itself, let alone do it during the main hearing. Instead, the tribunal will charge an expert with the inspection, will have received and shared the expert report with the parties, and will then proceed to hear and question the expert about her findings at the main hearing.

Article 8 of the IBA Rules on the Taking of Evidence in International Arbitration provides further details, including the principle that the arbitral tribunal has control over the hearing and may limit or exclude witnesses or other evidence offered by the parties if it is "irrelevant, immaterial, unreasonably burdensome,

---

283. For details, see Nigel Blackaby & Constantine Partasides, *Redfern and Hunter on International Arbitration*, Oxford Univ. Press 6th ed. 2015, at pp. 404–409.

duplicative, otherwise [objectionable]" (Article 8(2)). Once again, the tribunal has to find the fine line between ensuring the rights of the parties to be heard and to present their case versus the need to protect the integrity and efficiency of the procedure.

4. If party- and/or tribunal-appointed experts disagree about important facts or findings, the tribunal may end up being more confused than informed. Various tribunals have applied a system of witness conferencing, or "hot-tubbing," with success. In essence, the experts are asked to check each other's findings in advance, highlight the areas of agreement and disagreement, and prepare their presentations accordingly. At the hearing, they are then jointly cross-examined about the open questions, hopefully giving the tribunal a better understanding of the issues and who may or may not have the more persuasive conclusions and why.

5. In their closing statements, the parties or their representatives are invited to update their key arguments in light of the review of evidence during the hearing. If more complex review is necessary, the tribunal may invite the parties to submit a set of post-hearing briefs within a relatively limited period.

17. Post-Hearing Briefs?

Any round of written submissions has to include a claimant brief, a respondent brief, and an opportunity for rebuttal and surrebuttal. This presents a real risk of significant delay and duplication of effort, unless the tribunal makes it clear that new evidence will not be admitted at this stage — unless there are good reasons otherwise — and that any arguments have to address questions left open at the oral hearing. Sensible page and time limits should also be imposed.

18. The Award by the Tribunal

"The award" is the main goal of the arbitration procedure. It is the equivalent of the judgment at the end of a litigation procedure. However, there are several important differences: First, the award is typically not subject to appeal. Some countries allow a challenge to an arbitration award before a court but only in extreme circumstances. For example, the English Arbitration Act of 1996 (as amended, Documents, p. II-540) allows a "challenge" to an award in two cases: lack of jurisdiction of the arbitral tribunal and/or a "serious irregularity" in the work of the tribunal (cf. Rules 67 and 68). For all other purposes, and unless the parties have specifically agreed on something different, an arbitration award is the final settlement of the dispute.

Second, the award also marks the end of the arbitration procedure. More specifically, it ends the mandate and all powers of the arbitral tribunal. When the final award is issued, the arbitrators return to being regular citizens with no special powers of decision-making that would be binding and enforceable under the New York Convention or any other arbitration law. Therefore, it is important that all open questions are settled in or before a final award is issued, including all claims and counterclaims, all matters related to honoraria, fees, and costs of the tribunal and who has to pay them, any claims for interest on monies due, as well as any other claims such as attorney fees and expenses of the parties.

The extent to which the tribunal has to provide reasons for its decisions on the merits differs from one set of rules to another. The New York Convention does not require reasons for an award to be eligible for recognition and enforcement. This is justified by the confidential nature of most arbitration proceedings. If persuasive reasons were required for enforcement, the confidentiality would often be compromised because enforcement may require resort to public courts. In case the *lex arbitri* requires reasons to be given, as it is the case for example under Article 32(2) ICC, 34(3) UNCITRAL Rules, and 26.2 LCIA, the tribunal should add a nonconfidential summary for recognition and enforcement.

Sometimes arbitral tribunals have to or want to make binding decisions during an arbitration procedure, for example about the jurisdiction of the tribunal, securing of assets, or compelling the production of evidence (documents, witnesses, etc.). In such cases, it is important that the tribunal distinguish these decisions from a final award and calls them partial award, interlocutory award, or procedural order. The differences are not universally recognized, but, in general, "procedural orders" are used internally to move matters forward, while "awards" settle issues with finality and external effect. Importantly, orders are not covered by the New York Convention and, therefore, are not enforceable pursuant to it (although they may be enforceable based on the national arbitration law (cf. Rule 42 of the English Arbitration Act)). By contrast, awards are covered by the New York Convention and can be enforced pursuant to it, even if they are not "final" awards but merely "partial," "preliminary," or "interlocutory" awards.

The effect of the final award to end the arbitration procedure *and also the existence of the arbitral tribunal* is different from a judgment, final or not, that does not also dissolve the court that issues it. Thus, the tribunal itself cannot provide clarifications of its own award or corrections of clerical errors because the tribunal ceases to exist when it renders the final award. For this reason, some arbitration institutions provide institutional remedies for clarification or correction of awards — see, for example, Art. 35 ICC and Art. 30 AAA. However, clarification and correction is not easily done in ad hoc arbitration, which makes careful drafting of the final award all the more important. Many arbitrators consider it good practice to share a draft of the award with the parties before finalizing the award to reduce the risk that something is overlooked, misstated, or miscalculated. National law may provide options for clarification and/or correction, as suggested in Art. 33 of the UNCITRAL Model Law (Documents, p. II-185).

Instead of settling their dispute informally or in the form of a contract, the parties may ask the tribunal to issue a consent award. In contrast to a contractual settlement, such an award has res judicata effect and can be enforced via the New York Convention, if necessary. If the parties also agree to dispense with reasons, the arbitrators will be able to finalize a rather short form — essentially equivalent to the nonconfidential summary of a regular award—much more quickly. This will not only save time but also money.

If a respondent refuses from the beginning to participate in an arbitration, or ceases to collaborate at any point in time during the arbitration, the tribunal can nevertheless proceed and in the end issue a default award. In contrast to litigation, however, the tribunal will not just accept the claimant's claims and issue an award simply stating that respondent was in default. Such an award would be too vulnerable at the recognition and enforcement stage if the respondent were to argue that she had not had a fair chance of presenting her case. Therefore, in case of respondent default, the tribunal will conduct the proceedings much as if the respondent was actually there, i.e., will take into account obvious arguments in favor of the respondent and obvious weaknesses in the arguments presented by the claimant (compare, for example, Article 25(b) of the UNCITRAL Model Law). In the final award, the tribunal will make great efforts to outline how and why the respondent was made aware of the proceedings and given every opportunity to present her case. The tribunal will also provide a critical examination of the claimant's claims in law and in fact and a carefully reasoned analysis of the merits of the case. In an extreme scenario, the claimant may lose the arbitration if she cannot make a persuasive case in support of her claims, even though the respondent never participated.

In general, all members of the tribunal have to sign the award, even if the decisions were taken by majority vote. If a member of the tribunal is unwilling or unable to sign the final award, the *lex arbitri* provides in most cases that the award can be signed by the presiding arbitrator alone, along with a statement that it was adopted by majority and that arbitrator x, for the following reasons, was unwilling or unable to sign (see, for example, Article 26.6 LCIA).

The following is an outline of a final award. It can be used by arbitrators with limited practical experience. More importantly, it should be used by party representatives who are reviewing a draft of a final award to make sure that it is complete and sensibly structured.

Sample Document 6-5

Elements of a Final Award

Institutional Case No. ...

In the Matter of an Arbitration

Under the ... Rules of Arbitration between

... [Claimant] and

... [Respondent]

Final Award

1.   Request for Arbitration and Constitution of the Tribunal

2.   The Parties and their Legal Counsel

3.   Summary of the Issues in Dispute

4.   Arbitration Agreement, Seat of the Arbitration, and Governing Law

5.   Terms of Reference

6.   Procedural History and Conduct of the Present Arbitration

7.   The Business Transactions between the Parties and the Issues in Dispute

8.   Claimant Submissions

9.   Respondent Submissions

10.   Evidence Presented to the Tribunal

11.   Findings of the Tribunal

  a.   Agreed upon, proven, and disputed facts

  b.   Applicable legal rules and their interpretation

  c.   Findings regarding primary claims of the parties (performance) [subsumption of facts under rules]

  d.   Findings regarding secondary claims of the parties (damages) [subsumption of facts under rules]

  e.   Interest

  f.   Cost

12.   Conclusions: Accordingly, the Tribunal renders the Final Award in the dispute between _____ _____ as follows:

(1)   [primary claims by claimant and respondent]

(2)   [secondary claims by claimant or respondent]

(3)   [pre-award and post-award interest]

(4)   [cost]

Date, Place, and Signatures of the Tribunal Members

Since arbitral awards are usually confidential, most of them are not published or at least not published in full. This makes it very hard to establish whether there is consistent case law on questions such as admissibility of evidence, preclusion of new arguments during or after the oral hearing, etc. One way of accessing information about arbitral awards is via court decisions enforcing them or otherwise supporting arbitration procedures, for example when an arbitrator is challenged. That being said, there are some sources for arbitral awards, although they cannot provide comprehensive coverage. The most comprehensive database is provided by Kluwer Arbitration (http://www.kluwerarbitration.com/), which contains more than 3,000 awards from a variety of sources. The ICC Dispute Resolution Library has more than 750 ICC awards in a redacted format, omitting the names of the parties and certain other information (http://library.iccwbo.org/dr.htm). Transnational Dispute Management (TDM) is another source for arbitral awards, with a focus on investor-state arbitration (https://www.transnational-dispute-management.com/). Finally, Westlaw lists some arbitral awards with reasonably good coverage of ICDR awards and somewhat less impressive coverage of a number of other arbitration institutions like the ICC and the LCIA.[284] However, all of these are subscription-based databases and quite expensive. The awards are generally redacted to prevent identification of the parties and industries. In many cases, they are further redacted and abbreviated, sometimes to the point of uselessness. In addition, the general subscription Westlaw offers to law schools largely excludes access to arbitral awards.

An open access database is provided by UNCITRAL, in cooperation with Shearman & Sterling and Columbia Law School, for court decisions and arbitral awards referencing provisions of the New York Convention (http://newyorkconvention1958 .org/?opac_view=-1). UNCITRAL also maintains CLOUT, a database of court decisions and arbitral awards relating to any of the UNCITRAL conventions and model laws (http://www.uncitral.org/uncitral/en/case_law.html). Finally, Pace Law School maintains a database of court decisions and arbitral awards discussing provisions of the CISG (http://cisgw3.law.pace.edu/). The latter is organized by CISG articles, providing easy access to case law on the interpretation of a particular provision or rule. Although many of the decisions are not available in English and/or not available in full text, the Pace database also includes a digest for each CISG article, a kind of article-by-article commentary.[285]

Finally, as already mentioned, arbitration awards are enforceable in most countries pursuant to the New York Convention, whereas no comparable international convention exists for the recognition and enforcement of foreign judgments. There is, however, an effort ongoing at the Hague Conference on Private International Law (HCCH) and a Convention on the Recognition and Enforcement of Foreign Judgments was opened for signature in 2019 (see above, p. 829). Whether this project can replicate the success of the New York Convention and secure ratifications by a large number of countries remains to be seen, however.

19. Challenges to an Award

Once an award is final and an arbitration is concluded, there are generally two ways, but limited reasons, for challenging the award:

1. An award can be challenged in court at the seat of the arbitration. If such a challenge is successful, and the award is annulled, it will be unenforceable anywhere

---

284. Https://1.next.westlaw.com/Search/Home.html?transitionType=Default&contextData =(sc.Default).

285. More information on print resources can be found here: http://guides.ll.georgetown.edu/c .php?g=363504&p=4181551.

in the world, unless the prevailing party can make a credible claim in some other jurisdiction that the annulment was obtained via fraudulent means or otherwise unjustified.

2. An award can be challenged in court in any country where enforcement is sought. If such a challenge is successful, the award will not be recognized and enforced in that jurisdiction. This, however, leaves the prevailing party with options to seek recognition and enforcement elsewhere.

If an award is either annulled in its entirety or its recognition and enforcement are refused in the place or places where the assets of the losing party are located, the prevailing party still has the option of relaunching the proceedings to obtain an enforceable decision. Obviously, the party or parties would want to avoid the problems that made the initial award unenforceable. For example, if an award was annulled because the arbitration clause was deemed invalid, an interested party may now want to resort to litigation instead. Alternatively, if recognition and enforcement were refused because an arbitrator was not sufficiently independent and impartial, a new round of arbitration with a different arbitrator should be able to fix the problem. However, in some cases the statute of limitations or other procedural hurdles may stand in the way of a second round of arbitration or litigation.

We will examine challenges at the seat in this section and the refusal of recognition and enforcement in other jurisdictions in the next section.

Case 6-12

Hall Street Associates, LLC. v. Mattel, Inc.

552 U.S. 576 (2008)
(Paragraph numbers added, most footnotes omitted.)
Justice SOUTER delivered the opinion of the Court (from p. 578).

[1] The Federal Arbitration Act (FAA or Act), 9 U.S.C. § 1 et seq., provides for expedited judicial review to confirm, vacate, or modify arbitration awards. §§ 9–11 (2006 ed.). The question here is whether statutory grounds for prompt vacatur and modification may be supplemented by contract. We hold that the statutory grounds are exclusive.

I

[2] This case began as a lease dispute between landlord, petitioner Hall Street Associates, L.L.C., and tenant, respondent Mattel, Inc. The property was used for many years as a manufacturing site, and the leases provided that the tenant would indemnify the landlord for any costs resulting from the failure of the tenant or its predecessor lessees to follow environmental laws while using the premises. . . .

[3] Tests of the property's well water in 1998 showed high levels of trichloroethylene (TCE), the apparent residue of manufacturing discharges by Mattel's predecessors between 1951 and 1980. After the Oregon Department of Environmental Quality (DEQ) discovered even more pollutants, Mattel stopped drawing from the well and,

along with one of its predecessors, signed a consent order with the DEQ providing for cleanup of the site.

[4] After Mattel gave notice of intent to terminate the lease in 2001, Hall Street filed this suit, contesting Mattel's right to vacate on the date it gave, and claiming that the lease obliged Mattel to indemnify Hall Street for costs of cleaning up the TCE, among other things. Following a bench trial before the United States District Court for the District of Oregon, Mattel won on the termination issue, and after an unsuccessful try at mediating the indemnification claim, the parties proposed to submit to arbitration. The District Court was amenable, and the parties drew up an arbitration agreement, which the court approved and entered as an order. One paragraph of the agreement provided that

> "[t]he United States District Court for the District of Oregon may enter judgment upon any award, either by confirming the award or by vacating, modifying or correcting the award. The Court shall vacate, modify or correct any award: (i) where the arbitrator's findings of facts are not supported by substantial evidence, or (ii) where the arbitrator's conclusions of law are erroneous." . . .

[Arbitration took place and the arbitrator decided that Mattel did not have to clean up or pay for the clean up of TCE because "the Oregon Drinking Water Quality Act" was not an environmental law, as contemplated by the parties in the lease agreement, but "dealing with human health as distinct from environmental contamination." Hall Street considered that the arbitrator's conclusions of law were erroneous and filed a "Motion for Order Vacating, Modifying And/Or Correcting Arbitration Accord." The case meandered between District Court and Court of Appeals for a while and eventually came before the Supreme Court on the limited question whether the parties to an arbitration agreement could add to the grounds for annulment/vacatur in the FAA.] . . .

II

[10] Congress enacted the FAA to replace judicial indisposition to arbitration with a "national policy favoring [it] and plac[ing] arbitration agreements on equal footing with all other contracts." *Buckeye Check Cashing, Inc. v. Cardegna*, 546 U.S. 440, 443 . . . (2006). As for jurisdiction over controversies touching arbitration, the Act does nothing, being "something of an anomaly in the field of federal-court jurisdiction" in bestowing no federal jurisdiction but rather requiring an independent jurisdictional basis. *Moses H. Cone Memorial Hospital v. Mercury Constr. Corp.*, 460 U.S. 1, 25, n. 32 . . . (1983); see, e.g., 9 U.S.C. §4 (providing for action by a federal district court "which, save for such [arbitration] agreement, would have jurisdiction under title 28").[2] But in cases falling within a court's jurisdiction, the Act makes

---

2. Because the FAA is not jurisdictional, there is no merit in the argument that enforcing the arbitration agreement's judicial review provision would create federal jurisdiction by private contract. The issue is entirely about the scope of judicial review permissible under the FAA.

contracts to arbitrate "valid, irrevocable, and enforceable," so long as their subject involves "commerce." § 2. And this is so whether an agreement has a broad reach or goes just to one dispute, and whether enforcement be sought in state court or federal. See ibid.; *Southland Corp. v. Keating*, 465 U.S. 1, 15–16 . . . (1984).

[11] The Act also supplies mechanisms for enforcing arbitration awards: a judicial decree confirming an award, an order vacating it, or an order modifying or correcting it. §§ 9–11. An application for any of these orders will get streamlined treatment as a motion, obviating the separate contract action that would usually be necessary to enforce or tinker with an arbitral award in court. § 6. Under the terms of § 9, a court "must" confirm an arbitration award "unless" it is vacated, modified, or corrected "as prescribed" in §§ 10 and 11. Section 10 lists grounds for vacating an award, while § 11 names those for modifying or correcting one.[4]

[12] The Courts of Appeals have split over the exclusiveness of these statutory grounds when parties take the FAA shortcut to confirm, vacate, or modify an award, with some saying the recitations are exclusive, and others regarding them as mere threshold provisions open to expansion by agreement. . . . We now hold that §§ 10 and 11 respectively provide the FAA's exclusive grounds for expedited vacatur and modification.

III

[13] Hall Street makes two main efforts to show that the grounds set out for vacating or modifying an award are not exclusive, taking the position, first, that expandable judicial review authority has been accepted as the law since *Wilko v. Swan*, 346 U.S.

---

4. Title 9 U.S.C. § 10(a) (2000 ed., Supp. V) provides in part: "In any of the following cases the United States court in and for the district wherein the award was made may make an order vacating the award upon the application of any party to the arbitration—

    (1) where the award was procured by corruption, fraud, or undue means;

    (2) where there was evident partiality or corruption in the arbitrators, or either of them;

    (3) where the arbitrators were guilty of misconduct in refusing to postpone the hearing, upon sufficient cause shown, or in refusing to hear evidence pertinent and material to the controversy; or of any other misbehavior by which the rights of any party have been prejudiced; or

    (4) where the arbitrators exceeded their powers, or so imperfectly executed them that a mutual, final, and definite award upon the subject matter submitted was not made."

Title 9 U.S.C. § 11 (2000 ed.) provides:

    "In either of the following cases the United States court in and for the district wherein the award was made may make an order modifying or correcting the award upon the application of any party to the arbitration—

    (a) Where there was an evident material miscalculation of figures or an evident material mistake in the description of any person, thing, or property referred to in the award.

    (b) Where the arbitrators have awarded upon a matter not submitted to them, unless it is a matter not affecting the merits of the decision upon the matter submitted.

    (c) Where the award is imperfect in matter of form not affecting the merits of the controversy.

    The order may modify and correct the award, so as to effect the intent thereof and promote justice between the parties."

427 . . . (1953). This, however, was not what *Wilko* decided, which was that § 14 of the Securities Act of 1933 voided any agreement to arbitrate claims of violations of that Act, see id., at 437–438, 74 S.Ct. 182, a holding since overruled by *Rodriguez de Quijas v. Shearson/American Express, Inc.*, 490 U.S. 477, 484 . . . (1989). Although it is true that the Court's discussion includes some language arguably favoring Hall Street's position, arguable is as far as it goes.

[14] The *Wilko* Court was explaining that arbitration would undercut the Securities Act's buyer protections when it remarked (citing FAA § 10) that "[p]ower to vacate an [arbitration] award is limited," 346 U.S., at 436 . . . , and went on to say that "the interpretations of the law by the arbitrators in contrast to manifest disregard [of the law] are not subject, in the federal courts, to judicial review for error in interpretation," id., at 436–437 . . . . Hall Street reads this statement as recognizing "manifest disregard of the law" as a further ground for vacatur on top of those listed in § 10, and some Circuits have read it the same way. . . . Hall Street sees this supposed addition to § 10 as the camel's nose: if judges can add grounds to vacate (or modify), so can contracting parties.

[15] But this is too much for *Wilko* to bear. Quite apart from its leap from a supposed judicial expansion by interpretation to a private expansion by contract, Hall Street overlooks the fact that the statement it relies on expressly rejects just what Hall Street asks for here, general review for an arbitrator's legal errors. Then there is the vagueness of *Wilko's* phrasing. Maybe the term "manifest disregard" was meant to name a new ground for review, but maybe it merely referred to the § 10 grounds collectively, rather than adding to them. See, e.g., *Mitsubishi Motors Corp. v. Soler Chrysler-Plymouth, Inc.*, [above, p. 900] ("Arbitration awards are only reviewable for manifest disregard of the law, 9 U.S.C. §§ 10, 207"); *I/S Stavborg v. National Metal Converters, Inc.*, 500 F.2d 424, 431 (C.A.2 1974). Or, as some courts have thought, "manifest disregard" may have been shorthand for § 10(a)(3) or § 10(a)(4), the paragraphs authorizing vacatur when the arbitrators were "guilty of misconduct" or "exceeded their powers." See, e.g., [*Kyocera Corp. v. Prudential-Bache Trade Servs., Inc.*, 341 F.3d 987,] at 997. We, when speaking as a Court, have merely taken the *Wilko* language as we found it, without embellishment, see *First Options of Chicago, Inc. v. Kaplan*, 514 U.S. 938, 942 . . . (1995), and now that its meaning is implicated, we see no reason to accord it the significance that Hall Street urges.

[16] Second, Hall Street says that the agreement to review for legal error ought to prevail simply because arbitration is a creature of contract, and the FAA is "motivated, first and foremost, by a congressional desire to enforce agreements into which parties ha[ve] entered." *Dean Witter Reynolds Inc. v. Byrd*, 470 U.S. 213, 220 . . . (1985). But, again, we think the argument comes up short. Hall Street is certainly right that the FAA lets parties tailor some, even many, . . . features of arbitration by contract, including the way arbitrators are chosen, what their qualifications should be, which issues are arbitrable, along with procedure and choice of substantive law. But to rest this case on the general policy of treating arbitration agreements as enforceable as such would be to beg the question, which is whether

the FAA has textual features at odds with enforcing a contract to expand judicial review following the arbitration.

[17] To that particular question we think the answer is yes, that the text compels a reading of the §§ 10 and 11 categories as exclusive. To begin with, even if we assumed §§ 10 and 11 could be supplemented to some extent, it would stretch basic interpretive principles to expand the stated grounds to the point of evidentiary and legal review generally. Sections 10 and 11, after all, address egregious departures from the parties' agreed-upon arbitration: "corruption," "fraud," "evident partiality," "misconduct," "misbehavior," "exceed[ing] . . . powers," "evident material miscalculation," "evident material mistake," "award[s] upon a matter not submitted"; the only ground with any softer focus is "imperfect[ions]," and a court may correct those only if they go to "[a] matter of form not affecting the merits." Given this emphasis on extreme arbitral conduct, the old rule of ejusdem generis has an implicit lesson to teach here. Under that rule, when a statute sets out a series of specific items ending with a general term, that general term is confined to covering subjects comparable to the specifics it follows. Since a general term included in the text is normally so limited, then surely a statute with no textual hook for expansion cannot authorize contracting parties to supplement review for specific instances of outrageous conduct with review for just any legal error. "Fraud" and a mistake of law are not cut from the same cloth.

[18] That aside, expanding the detailed categories would rub too much against the grain of the § 9 language, where provision for judicial confirmation carries no hint of flexibility. On application for an order confirming the arbitration award, the court "must grant" the order "unless the award is vacated, modified, or corrected as prescribed in sections 10 and 11 of this title." There is nothing malleable about "must grant," which unequivocally tells courts to grant confirmation in all cases, except when one of the "prescribed" exceptions applies. This does not sound remotely like a provision meant to tell a court what to do just in case the parties say nothing else.

[19] In fact, anyone who thinks Congress might have understood § 9 as a default provision should turn back to § 5 for an example of what Congress thought a default provision would look like:

> "[i]f in the agreement provision be made for a method of naming or appointing an arbitrator . . . such method shall be followed; but if no method be provided therein, or if a method be provided and any party thereto shall fail to avail himself of such method, . . . then upon the application of either party to the controversy the court shall designate and appoint an arbitrator. . . . ."

> "[I]f no method be provided" is a far cry from "must grant . . . unless" in § 9.

[20] Instead of fighting the text, it makes more sense to see the three provisions, §§ 9–11, as substantiating a national policy favoring arbitration with just the limited review needed to maintain arbitration's essential virtue of resolving disputes straightaway. Any other reading opens the door to the full-bore legal and

evidentiary appeals that can "rende[r] informal arbitration merely a prelude to a more cumbersome and time-consuming judicial review process," *Kyocera*, 341 F.3d, at 998; cf. *Ethyl Corp. v. United Steelworkers of America*, 768 F.2d 180, 184 (C.A.7 1985), and bring arbitration theory to grief in post arbitration process. . . .

[22] When all these arguments based on prior legal authority are done with, Hall Street and Mattel remain at odds over what happens next. Hall Street and its amici say parties will flee from arbitration if expanded review is not open to them. . . . One of Mattel's amici foresees flight from the courts if it is. . . . We do not know who, if anyone, is right, and so cannot say whether the exclusivity reading of the statute is more of a threat to the popularity of arbitrators or to that of courts. But whatever the consequences of our holding, the statutory text gives us no business to expand the statutory grounds. . . .

It is so ordered.

Justice STEVENS, with whom Justice KENNEDY joins, dissenting.

[29] May parties to an ongoing lawsuit agree to submit their dispute to arbitration subject to the caveat that the trial judge should refuse to enforce an award that rests on an erroneous conclusion of law? Prior to Congress' enactment of the Federal Arbitration Act (FAA or Act) in 1925, the answer to that question would surely have been "Yes." Today, however, the Court holds that the FAA does not merely authorize the vacation or enforcement of awards on specified grounds, but also forbids enforcement of perfectly reasonable judicial review provisions in arbitration agreements fairly negotiated by the parties and approved by the district court. Because this result conflicts with the primary purpose of the FAA and ignores the historical context in which the Act was passed, I respectfully dissent.

[30] Prior to the passage of the FAA, American courts were generally hostile to arbitration. They refused, with rare exceptions, to order specific enforcement of executory agreements to arbitrate. Section 2 of the FAA responded to this hostility by making written arbitration agreements "valid, irrevocable, and enforceable." 9 U.S.C. §2. This section, which is the centerpiece of the FAA, reflects Congress' main goal in passing the legislation: "to abrogate the general common-law rule against specific enforcement of arbitration agreements," *Southland Corp. v. Keating*, 465 U.S. 1, 18 . . . (1984) . . . and to "ensur[e] that private arbitration agreements are enforced according to their terms," *Volt Information Sciences, Inc. v. Board of Trustees of Leland Stanford Junior Univ.*, 489 U.S. 468, 478 . . . (1989). Given this settled understanding of the core purpose of the FAA, the interests favoring enforceability of parties' arbitration agreements are stronger today than before the FAA was enacted. As such, there is more—and certainly not less—reason to give effect to parties' fairly negotiated decisions to provide for judicial review of arbitration awards for errors of law.

[31] Petitioner filed this rather complex action in an Oregon state court. Based on the diverse citizenship of the parties, respondent removed the case to federal court. More than three years later, and after some issues had been resolved, the parties

sought and obtained the District Court's approval of their agreement to arbitrate the remaining issues subject to de novo judicial review. They neither requested, nor suggested that the FAA authorized, any "expedited" disposition of their case. Because the arbitrator made a rather glaring error of law, the judge refused to affirm his award until after that error was corrected. The Ninth Circuit reversed.

[32] This Court now agrees with the Ninth Circuit's (most recent) interpretation of the FAA as setting forth the exclusive grounds for modification or vacation of an arbitration award under the statute. As I read the Court's opinion, it identifies two possible reasons for reaching this result: (1) a supposed quid pro quo bargain between Congress and litigants that conditions expedited federal enforcement of arbitration awards on acceptance of a statutory limit on the scope of judicial review of such awards; and (2) an assumption that Congress intended to include the words "and no other" in the grounds specified in §§ 10 and 11 for the vacatur and modification of awards. Neither reason is persuasive.

[33] While § 9 of the FAA imposes a 1-year limit on the time in which any party to an arbitration may apply for confirmation of an award, the statute does not require that the application be given expedited treatment. Of course, the premise of the entire statute is an assumption that the arbitration process may be more expeditious and less costly than ordinary litigation, but that is a reason for interpreting the statute liberally to favor the parties' use of arbitration. An unnecessary refusal to enforce a perfectly reasonable category of arbitration agreements defeats the primary purpose of the statute.

[34] That purpose also provides a sufficient response to the Court's reliance on statutory text. It is true that a wooden application of "the old rule of ejusdem generis," . . . might support an inference that the categories listed in §§ 10 and 11 are exclusive, but the literal text does not compel that reading—a reading that is flatly inconsistent with the overriding interest in effectuating the clearly expressed intent of the contracting parties. A listing of grounds that must always be available to contracting parties simply does not speak to the question whether they may agree to additional grounds for judicial review.

[35] Moreover, in light of the historical context and the broader purpose of the FAA, §§ 10 and 11 are best understood as a shield meant to protect parties from hostile courts, not a sword with which to cut down parties' "valid, irrevocable and enforceable" agreements to arbitrate their disputes subject to judicial review for errors of law.[3] . . .

---

3. In the years before the passage of the FAA, arbitration awards were subject to thorough and broad judicial review. See Cohen & Dayton, *The New Federal Arbitration Law*, 12 Va. L. Rev. 265, 270–271 (1926); Cullinan, *Contracting for an Expanded Scope of Judicial Review in Arbitration Agreements*, 51 Vand. L. Rev. 395, 409 (1998). In §§ 10 and 11 of the FAA, Congress significantly limited the grounds for judicial vacatur or modification of such awards in order to protect arbitration awards from hostile and meddlesome courts.

Notes and Questions

1. In *Hall Street Associates v. Mattel,* one side argues that it would discourage parties from going to arbitration if awards could be set aside for reasons other than those stipulated in the FAA. The other side argues that parties would be discouraged from going to arbitration if they could *not* stipulate additional reasons, such as erroneous application of the law, for setting aside an award. The Supreme Court seems unsure which side is right. What do you think?

Consider the fact, on the one side, that pretty much anybody can call him- or herself an "arbitrator" and that many parties will sign contracts with arbitration clauses without much understanding of the consequences. Does this support a broad or a narrow interpretation of §§ 10 and 11 of the FAA?

Consider, on the other side, the goals of arbitration and the benefits over litigation. Would these be better served by a broad or a narrow interpretation of §§ 10 and 11 of the FAA?

Should there be a general emergency break against erroneous application of the law by an arbitrator? Why? Why not? What would be the consequences? (Compare also the discussion below, p. 1026, with regard to the public policy exception in Article V of the New York Convention.

Since the Supreme Court does not seem to allow such an emergency break, how can parties protect themselves from harm by an incompetent or biased arbitrator?

2. Remember that challenges to an award usually have to be made before the courts having jurisdiction over the seat of the arbitration and this means that the possible grounds for challenge may vary from one country to another. Recall the recommendation (above, pp. 919–922) to always seat an international (commercial) arbitration in a country that is generally friendly to arbitration to avoid problems with the courts.

England is certainly considered to be an arbitration-friendly country. What do you think of the following passages of the English Arbitration Act of 1996 (as amended)? Do they go farther or not as far as the FAA? For better or for worse?

§ 68 Challenging the Award: Serious Irregularity

(1) A party to arbitral proceedings may (upon notice to the other parties and to the tribunal) apply to the court challenging an award in the proceedings on the ground of serious irregularity affecting the tribunal, the proceedings or the award. . . .

(2) Serious irregularity means an irregularity of one or more of the following kinds which the court considers has caused or will cause substantial injustice to the applicant—

   (a) failure by the tribunal to comply with section 33 (general duty of tribunal);

(b) the tribunal exceeding its powers (otherwise than by exceeding its substantive jurisdiction: see section 67);

(c) failure by the tribunal to conduct the proceedings in accordance with the procedure agreed by the parties;

(d) failure by the tribunal to deal with all the issues that were put to it;

(e) any arbitral or other institution or person vested by the parties with powers in relation to the proceedings or the award exceeding its powers;

(f) uncertainty or ambiguity as to the effect of the award;

(g) the award being obtained by fraud or the award or the way in which it was procured being contrary to public policy;

(h) failure to comply with the requirements as to the form of the award; or

(i) any irregularity in the conduct of the proceedings or in the award which is admitted by the tribunal or by any arbitral or other institution or person vested by the parties with powers in relation to the proceedings or the award.

(3) If there is shown to be serious irregularity affecting the tribunal, the proceedings or the award, the court may—

(a) remit the award to the tribunal, in whole or in part, for reconsideration,

(b) set the award aside in whole or in part, or

(c) declare the award to be of no effect, in whole or in part.

The court shall not exercise its power to set aside or to declare an award to be of no effect, in whole or in part, unless it is satisfied that it would be inappropriate to remit the matters in question to the tribunal for reconsideration. . . .

3. Although the focus of our book is on business-to-business (B2B) transactions and business-to-consumer (B2C) contracts are largely excluded from the analysis, the subject of consumer arbitration is rapidly gaining in importance since more and more companies in industries such as mobile phone services, rental car services, banking, and other financial services include arbitration clauses in their consumer contracts. The following excerpt from the judgment of the European Court of Justice of October 26, 2006, in *Case C-168/05 Mostaza Claro*[286] shows the standard imposed by EU law on the Member States. These rules apply to any businesses offering goods or services to consumers based in the EU, including U.S. and other international companies to the extent they are active in the EU.

Ms. Mostaza Claro had entered into a mobile phone contract with Centro Móvil in May 2002. The contract included a dispute settlement clause providing for

---

286. [2006] ECJ I-10437.

arbitration in front of the Asociación Europea de Arbitraje de Derecho y Equidad (European Association of Arbitration in Law and in Equity) (AEADE). When Ms. Mostaza Claro wanted to terminate her phone contract prematurely, Móvil initiated arbitration proceedings. Ms. Mostaza Claro was given 10 days to refuse arbitration in favor of legal proceedings, but she presented arguments on the merits in front of AEADE instead. Eventually, the arbitrator ruled against her. After that, Ms. Mostaza Claro went to court to contest the arbitration decision "submitting that the unfair nature of the arbitration clause meant that the arbitration agreement was null and void."[287] The national court was unsure how the EU Directive 93/13 on Unfair Terms in Consumer Contracts[288] might impact the case and, pursuant to Article 267 TFEU, submitted the following question to the European Court of Justice:

> May the protection of consumers under Council Directive 93/13/EEC . . . require the court hearing an action for annulment of an arbitration award to determine whether the arbitration agreement is void and to annul the award if it finds that that arbitration agreement contains an unfair term to the consumer's detriment, when that issue is raised in the action for annulment but was not raised by the consumer in the arbitration proceedings?[289]

After reaffirming that it is for the national court to decide, on a case-by-case basis, whether a particular clause is indeed unfair, the European Court addressed the question whether a consumer is preempted from claiming the invalidity of an arbitration clause in court proceedings after an award has been rendered, if the

---

287. Ibid., para. 18.

288. OJ 1993 L 95, pp. 29–34. The Directive provides in Art. 3 "1. A contractual term which has not been individually negotiated shall be regarded as unfair if, contrary to the requirement of good faith, it causes a significant imbalance in the parties' rights and obligations arising under the contract, to the detriment of the consumer. 2. A term shall always be regarded as not individually negotiated where it has been drafted in advance and the consumer has therefore not been able to influence the substance of the term, particularly in the context of a pre-formulated standard contract. . . ." Annex 1 of the Directive provides a non-exhaustive list of terms which may be regarded as unfair and includes ". . . (q) excluding or hindering the consumer's right to take legal action or exercise any other legal remedy, particularly by requiring the consumer to take disputes exclusively to arbitration not covered by legal provisions. . . ." It seems clear from these provisions that EU law does not always prevent arbitration in consumer contracts (although the national law of a particular Member State may do so). First, a clause that is individually negotiated does not fall under Art. 3 of the Directive. Second, the list in Annex I is only indicative and a court may find that even a standard clause in a contract is not unfair because it does not actually cause a significant imbalance in the parties' rights and obligations. Third, this may be the case, in particular, if the chosen arbitration is regulated by the laws of the respective Member State; in such a case, the clause would not fall within the scope of Annex I (q) and should more easily qualify for the finding that it is not unfair.

On the subject of consumer protection in the EU, see also EU Directive 2011/83 on Consumer Rights, OJ 2011 L 304, pp. 64–88.

289. See para. 20 of the judgment.

consumer voluntarily participated in the arbitration proceedings without raising the invalidity of the clause.

[25] The system of protection introduced by the Directive is based on the idea that the consumer is in a weak position vis-à-vis the seller or supplier, as regards both his bargaining power and his level of knowledge. This leads to the consumer agreeing to terms drawn up in advance by the seller or supplier without being able to influence the content of those terms (Joined Cases C-240/98 to C-244/98 Océano Grupo Editorial and Salvat Editores [2000] ECR I-4941, paragraph 25).

[26] Such an imbalance between the consumer and the seller or supplier may only be corrected by positive action unconnected with the actual parties to the contract (Océano Grupo Editorial and Salvat Editores, paragraph 27).

[27] It is on the basis of those principles that the Court has ruled that the national court's power to determine of its own motion whether a term is unfair constitutes a means both of achieving the result sought by Article 6 of the Directive, namely preventing an individual consumer from being bound by an unfair term, and of contributing to achieving the aim of Article 7, since if the court undertakes such an examination, that may act as a deterrent and contribute to preventing unfair terms in contracts concluded between consumers and sellers or suppliers (Océano Grupo Editorial and Salvat Editores, paragraph 28, and Case C-473/00 Cofidis [2002] ECR I-10875, paragraph 32).

[28] That power of the national court has been regarded as necessary for ensuring that the consumer enjoys effective protection, in view in particular of the real risk that he is unaware of his rights or encounters difficulties in enforcing them (Océano Grupo Editorial and Salvat Editores, paragraph 26, and Cofidis, paragraph 33).

[29] The protection which the Directive confers on consumers thus extends to cases in which a consumer who has concluded with a seller or supplier a contract containing an unfair term fails to raise the unfair nature of the term, whether because he is unaware of his rights or because he is deterred from enforcing them on account of the costs which judicial proceedings would involve (Cofidis, paragraph 34).

[30] Under those circumstances, the result sought by Article 6 of the Directive which, as was recalled at paragraph 27 of this judgment, requires the Member States to ensure that consumers are not bound by unfair terms, could not be achieved if the court seised of an action for annulment of an arbitration award was unable to determine whether that award was void solely because the consumer did not plead the invalidity of the arbitration agreement in the course of the arbitration proceedings.

[31] Such an omission by the consumer could not then, under any circumstances, be compensated for by action on the part of persons not party to the contract. The regime of special protection established by the Directive would be definitively undermined. . . .

[33] Móvil and the German Government submit that, if the national court were allowed to determine whether an arbitration agreement is void where the consumer

did not raise such an objection during the arbitration proceedings, this would seriously undermine the effectiveness of arbitration awards.

[34] It follows from that argument that it is in the interest of efficient arbitration proceedings that review of arbitration awards should be limited in scope and that annulment of or refusal to recognise an award should be possible only in exceptional circumstances (Case C-126/97 Eco Swiss [1999] ECR I-3055, paragraph 35).

[35] However, the Court has already ruled that, where its domestic rules of procedure require a national court to grant an application for annulment of an arbitration award where such an application is founded on failure to observe national rules of public policy, it must also grant such an application where it is founded on failure to comply with Community rules of this type (see, to that effect, Eco Swiss, paragraph 37).

[36] The importance of consumer protection has in particular led the Community legislature to lay down, in Article 6(1) of the Directive, that unfair terms used in a contract concluded with a consumer by a seller or supplier 'shall . . . not be binding on the consumer'. This is a mandatory provision which, taking into account the weaker position of one of the parties to the contract, aims to replace the formal balance which the latter establishes between the rights and obligations of the parties with an effective balance which re-establishes equality between them.

[37] Moreover, as the aim of the Directive is to strengthen consumer protection, it constitutes, according to Article 3(1)(t) EC, a measure which is essential to the accomplishment of the tasks entrusted to the Community and, in particular, to raising the standard of living and the quality of life in its territory (see, by analogy, concerning Article 81 EC, Eco Swiss, paragraph 36).

[38] The nature and importance of the public interest underlying the protection which the Directive confers on consumers justify, moreover, the national court being required to assess of its own motion whether a contractual term is unfair, compensating in this way for the imbalance which exists between the consumer and the seller or supplier.

[39] Having regard to the foregoing, the answer to the question referred must be that the Directive must be interpreted as meaning that a national court seised of an action for annulment of an arbitration award must determine whether the arbitration agreement is void and annul that award where that agreement contains an unfair term, even though the consumer has not pleaded that invalidity in the course of the arbitration proceedings, but only in that of the action for annulment.

   What do you think of this decision of the European Court of Justice? Can you find relevant case law on how the matter is handled in the U.S.?

20. Recognition and Enforcement of the Award

   As we saw in the previous section, challenges to an award brought at the seat of the arbitration are subject to the law applicable in that country or jurisdiction. They may vary considerably from one country to another and may evolve over time.

By contrast, if the **recognition and enforcement** of an award is sought in any other country where assets may be found, the New York Convention comes into play.[290] Article V of the New York Convention stipulates that "[r]ecognition and enforcement . . . may be refused . . . only if [there is] proof that" one of the enumerated grounds for refusal is fulfilled.

Most of the grounds are relatively straightforward. Under Paragraph 1, recognition and enforcement can be refused if the parties did not validly enter into an arbitration agreement, if a party was not properly notified of the proceedings or otherwise unable to present her case, if the award goes beyond what was submitted to the tribunal by the parties, if the composition of the tribunal was not in conformity with the agreement of the parties, or if the award is not yet final and binding. These are grounds that may be interpreted slightly differently from one jurisdiction to another, but they are generally applicable everywhere.

Article V Paragraph 2, however, also allows for some grounds specific to the place where recognition and enforcement are sought to be invoked:

> Recognition and enforcement of an arbitral award may also be refused if the competent authority in the country where recognition and enforcement is sought finds that:
>
> (a) The subject matter of the difference is *not capable of settlement by arbitration* under the law of that country; or
>
> (b) The recognition or enforcement of the award would be *contrary to the public policy* of that country. (emphasis added)

The first of these country-specific exceptions caters to the fact that different countries consider different subjects to be unsuitable for arbitration (e.g., competition or antitrust matters) or seek to protect certain groups as the weaker parties in a contract (e.g., consumers, employees).

The second of the country-specific exceptions, the notorious "public policy" exception, is more problematic and has generated considerable amounts of case law and even more academic commentary. Since it is the only ground acceptable under Article V that allows for some level of substantive review, it is quite frequently invoked. However, it is universally accepted that the New York Convention does not allow review on the merits of an award. Thus, a claim that public policy is infringed simply because the law was applied incorrectly is not acceptable.[291] The

---

290. If the majority of parties to an arbitration agreement are domiciled in the Americas, the relevant treaty is the Inter-American Convention on International Commercial Arbitration (Panama Convention) of 1975. However, Article 5 of the Panama Convention provides verbatim the same grounds for refusal as Article V of the New York Convention.

291. See, for example, Reinmar Wolff, *Comments on Article V*, in Reinmar Wolff (ed.), *New York Convention on the Recognition and Enforcement of Foreign Arbitral Awards   Commentary*, C.II. Beck/Hart/Nomos 2012, at p. 430; as well as Anton G. Maurer, *Public Policy Exception Under the New York Convention: History, Interpretation, and Application*, JurisNet 2013.

following problems have been accepted in practice for a refusal of recognition and enforcement:[292]

- manifest disregard of the substantive law by the arbitrators;

- manifest disregard of the facts by the arbitrators;

- granting of unlawful relief—by the standards of the country where enforcement is sought—by the arbitrators;

- granting of punitive damages, if the country where enforcement is sought does not allow them;

- national security interests have been successfully invoked if an award seems to be aiding or abetting "globally recognized criminal offenses like piracy, terrorism, genocide, slavery, smuggling, drug trafficking and pedophilia";[293]

- awards obtained via or aiding or abetting bribery of public officials; and

- awards in violation of mandatory rules of antitrust or competition law, insolvency law, import/export restrictions, exchange controls, consumer protection, etc.[294]

---

292. *Wolff*, pp. 431–437, with case law references.

293. *Ibid.*, at p. 434.

294. For further analysis, see also George Bermann (ed.), *Recognition and Enforcement of Foreign Arbitral Awards: The Interpretation and Application of the New York Convention by National Courts*, Springer 2017; Emmanuel Gaillard & George Bermann (eds.), *Guide on the Convention on the Recognition and Enforcement of Foreign Arbitral Awards*, Brill/Nijhoff 2017; Herbert Kronke et al., *Recognition and Enforcement of Foreign Arbitral Awards: A Global Commentary on the New York Convention*, Kluwer Law International 2010; Marike Paulsson, *The 1958 New York Convention in Action*, Wolters Kluwer 2016.

For country- or region-specific analysis, see Ihab Amro, *Recognition and Enforcement of Foreign Arbitral Awards in Theory and in Practice, A Comparative Study in Common Law and Civil Law Countries*, Cambridge Scholars 2013; John K. Arthur, *Setting Aside or Non-Enforcement of Arbitral Awards in International Arbitration on the Public Policy Ground—A Regional Perspective*, in Vijay K. Bhatia et al. (eds.), *International Arbitration Discourse and Practices in Asia*, Routledge 2017, at pp. 21–26; Nicolas Bremer, *Seeking Recognition and Enforcement of Foreign Court Judgments and Arbitral Awards in Egypt and the Mashriq Countries*, J. Disp. Res. 2018, pp. 109–142; Ewan Brown, *Illegality and Public Policy—Enforcement of Arbitral Awards in England*, Int'l Arb. L. Rev. 2000, Vol. 3, p. 31; Helena Hsi-Chia Chen, *Predictability of 'Public Policy' in Article V of the New York Convention under Mainland China's Judicial Practice*, Wolters Kluwer 2017; Leonardo de Campos Melo, *Recognition and Enforcement of Foreign Arbitral Awards in Brazil: A Practitioner's Guide*, Wolters Kluwer 2015; Omar E. Garcia-Bolivar & Hernando Otero (eds.), *Recognition and Enforcement of International Commercial Arbitral Awards in Latin America: Law, Practice and Leading Cases*, Brill/Nijhoff 2014; Richard Garnett & Michael Pryles, *Recognition and Enforcement of Foreign Arbitral Awards under the New York Convention in Australia and New Zealand*, J. Int'l. Arb. 2008, Vol. 25, No. 6, pp. 899–912; Shubham Jain, *'Public Policy' as the Root Cause of Due Process Paranoia: An Examination of the Statute and Court Decisions in India*, Indian J. Arb. L. 2018, Vol. 6, No. 2, pp. 145–153; Reyadh Mohamed Seyadi, *The Effect of the 1958 New York Convention on Foreign Arbitral Awards in the Arab Gulf States*, Cambridge Scholars 2017; as well as Reyadh Mohamed Seyadi, *Understanding the Jurisprudence of the Arab Gulf States National Courts on the Implementation of the 1958 New York Convention on the Recognition and Enforcement of Foreign Arbitral Awards*, Int'l Rev. L. 2017, available at http://www.qscience.com/doi/pdf/10.5339/irl.2017.12; William R.

Unfortunately, not all courts in all countries stick to these rules in all cases when they are asked to recognize and enforce a foreign arbitral award. For example, courts in Saudi Arabia have occasionally refused to recognize and enforce foreign arbitral awards in their entirety because they included interest, in particular compound interest.[295] Central and South America currently presents a mixed picture. Brazil, Chile, Colombia, Mexico, and Peru are generally supportive of international commercial arbitration and usually do not present problems when it comes to the enforcement of foreign awards. This is in contrast to Argentina, Bolivia, Ecuador, Nicaragua, and Venezuela, where populist governments have a tendency toward opposition against enforcement of foreign awards, in particular in cases of investor-state arbitration, even including decisions by ICSID. The following case provides an example on point:

Case 6-13

Chevron Corporation and Texaco Petroleum Co. v. Republic of Ecuador

949 F. Supp. 2d 57 (D.D.C. 2013)
(Paragraph numbers added.)

Memorandum Opinion

[1] Petitioners Chevron Corporation and Texaco Petroleum Company filed this action to confirm an award issued by an international tribunal under 9 U.S.C. § 207 and the 1958 Convention on the Recognition and Enforcement of Foreign Arbitral Awards, better known as the New York Convention. Respondent Republic of Ecuador seeks to deny such confirmation on several bases. First, Ecuador argues that this Court lacks subject-matter jurisdiction because the case does not meet the requirements of the arbitration exception to the Foreign Sovereign Immunities Act. Second, it contends that confirmation must be denied under the New York Convention because the Award was beyond the scope of the submission to arbitration and is contrary to United States public policy. Finally, it maintains that this Court should, at a minimum, stay proceedings in this matter while Ecuador attempts to have the Award set aside by courts in the Netherlands, where the Award was rendered. Disagreeing on all fronts, the Court will deny Ecuador's request and grant Chevron's Petition to Confirm the Award.

I. Background

[2] According to the Petition, Chevron and Texaco (together "Chevron") entered into a contract with Ecuador in 1973, permitting Chevron to exploit oil reserves

Spiegelberger, *Russia Report: the Enforcement of Foreign Arbitral Awards in 2017*, Am. Rev. Int'l Arb. 2017, pp. 29–45.

295. See, e.g., Ahmed Altawyan, *International Commercial Arbitration in Saudi Arabia*, Council on Int'l Law and Politics 2018, at pp. 46 et seq., in particular p. 48; Excessive interest has been accepted as a potential ground for refusal even outside of Muslim countries. Instead of denying recognition and enforcement of the entire award, the courts, in such cases, should limit their interference to the interest part of the award.

in Ecuador's Amazon region, on the condition that Chevron provide a percentage of its crude-oil production at a reduced price to meet Ecuadorian domestic-consumption needs. . . . The agreement was amended in 1977 and expired in June 1992. . . . As Chevron began winding up its work in Ecuador in 1991, it filed seven breach-of-contract cases there against the Ecuadorian government, seeking over $553 million in damages for various breaches of the 1973 and 1977 agreements. . . . These disputes largely concerned allegations that Ecuador had overstated its domestic oil-consumption needs, and appropriated more crude oil than it was entitled to acquire at the reduced price. . . . The lawsuits remained pending in Ecuadorian courts until being incorporated into the arbitration at issue in this case in 2006. . . .

[3] Meanwhile, in 1997, the U.S.-Ecuador Bilateral Investment Treaty (BIT) entered into force. . . . ; Treaty Between the United States of America and the Republic of Ecuador Concerning the Encouragement and Reciprocal Protection of Investments, U.S.-Ecuador, Aug. 27, 1993, S. Treaty Doc. No. 103-15. The BIT generally provides certain legal protections to American and Ecuadorian investors when they engage in foreign direct investment in the reciprocal country. It specifically provides, *inter alia*, that disputes against one of the parties arising out of such investments may be resolved by resort to binding arbitration upon request of a company or national of the other party. . . . After more than a decade had elapsed without a determination of its claims pending in the Ecuadorian courts, Chevron filed a Notice of Arbitration in 2006 alleging that Ecuador had breached the BIT by allowing its claims to languish in those courts without a resolution. . . .

[4] A three-member arbitral Tribunal based at The Hague conducted several rounds of hearings concerning both its jurisdiction to hear the case and the merits of the dispute. . . . The Tribunal issued an Interim Award in December 2008 finding it had jurisdiction to hear the case, . . . a Partial Award on the Merits in March 2010 finding that the Ecuadorian courts' undue delay constituted a breach of the BIT, . . . and a Final Award in August 2011 concerning damages. . . . Ecuador petitioned the District Court of The Hague to set aside the Award in July 2010, but the court denied that request in May 2012. . . . Ecuador subsequently appealed the Dutch District Court's judgment, and its appeal remains pending. . . .

[5] Chevron now seeks an order confirming the Final Award under the New York Convention. Ecuador, not surprisingly, objects.

II. Analysis

[6] Ecuador raises three arguments in an effort to derail confirmation: the Court lacks subject-matter jurisdiction under the Foreign Sovereign Immunities Act, confirmation should be denied under the New York Convention, and a stay pending appeal in the Netherlands is appropriate. The Court addresses each in turn.

A. Foreign Sovereign Immunities Act

[7] Ecuador first argues that the Foreign Sovereign Immunities Act, 28 U.S.C. § 1604, deprives the Court of subject-matter jurisdiction. . . . The FSIA is "the sole basis for obtaining jurisdiction over a foreign state in our courts." *Argentine Republic*

v. Amerada Hess Shipping Corp., 488 U.S. 428, 434 (1989). Under the statute, "a foreign state is presumptively immune from the jurisdiction of the United States courts[ ] unless a specified exception applies." *Saudi Arabia v. Nelson*, 507 U.S. 349, 355 (1993). Because "subject matter jurisdiction in any such action depends on the existence of one of the specified exceptions . . . [a]t the threshold of every action in a District Court against a foreign state . . . the court must satisfy itself that one of the exceptions applies." *Verlinden B.V. v. Central Bank of Nigeria*, 461 U.S. 480, 493–94 (1983). Notably, "the defendant bears the burden of proving that the plaintiff's allegations do not bring its case within a statutory exception to immunity." *Phoenix Consulting, Inc. v. Republic of Angola*, 216 F.3d 36, 40 (D.C. Cir. 2000) (citing *Transamerican S.S. Corp. v. Somali Democratic Republic*, 767 F.2d 998, 1002 (D.C. Cir. 1985)).

[8] The FSIA provides an exception to foreign sovereign immunity for actions to confirm certain arbitration awards. See 28 U.S.C. § 1605(a)(6). Specifically, foreign sovereigns are not immune from suits

> in which the action is brought[ ] either to enforce an agreement made by the foreign state with or for the benefit of a private party to submit to arbitration all or any differences which have arisen or which may arise between the parties with respect to a defined legal relationship . . . or to confirm an award made pursuant to such an agreement to arbitrate, if . . . the agreement or award is or may be governed by a treaty or other international agreement in force for the United States calling for the recognition and enforcement of arbitral awards. Id. (emphasis added).

[9] Chevron asserts that its Petition falls under this exception because the Final Award was made pursuant to the BIT and is governed by the 1958 Convention on the Recognition and Enforcement of Foreign Arbitral Awards, also known as the New York Convention, implemented at 9 U.S.C. §§ 201 *et seq*. . . . This is correct.

[10] First, the Award's own language indicates it was rendered pursuant to the BIT, an agreement that provides for arbitration. . . .

[11] Second, the Award is clearly governed by the New York Convention, which controls "the recognition and enforcement of arbitral awards made in the territory of a State other than the State where the recognition and enforcement of such awards are sought." . . . Awards are enforceable in the courts of any signatory so long as "'the place of the award . . . is in the territory of a party to the Convention.'" *Creighton Ltd. v. Government of the State of Qatar*, 181 F.3d 118, 121 (D.C. Cir. 1999) (quoting Restatement (Third) of Foreign Relations Law § 471 cmt. b (1987)). Because the arbitration in this matter was conducted at The Hague and the Netherlands is a party to the New York Convention, the Final Award here is governed by the Convention. . . .

[12] Under the law of this Circuit, moreover, the arbitration exception in § 1605(a)(6) "by its terms" applies to actions to confirm arbitration awards under the New York Convention. *Creighton*, 181 F.3d at 123. "Indeed, it has been said with authority that the New York Convention 'is exactly the sort of treaty Congress intended to include

in the arbitration exception.'" *Id.* at 123–24 (quoting *Cargill Int'l S.A. v. M/T Pavel Dybenko*, 991 F.2d 1012, 1018 (2d Cir. 1993)). The Court thus finds that Chevron has satisfied the requirements of the FSIA's arbitration exception.

[13] Ecuador nonetheless raises a novel argument in contesting the applicability of the exception here. It contends that it never consented to arbitrate the underlying dispute in this matter, meaning the award was not rendered "pursuant to . . . an agreement to arbitrate," and that the Court must satisfy itself of the arbitrability of the underlying dispute before finding subject-matter jurisdiction over this enforcement proceeding. . . . Ecuador, however, points to no authority—nor can the Court identify any—suggesting that the Court must conduct such an independent, *de novo* determination of the arbitrability of a dispute to satisfy the FSIA's arbitration exception.

[14] Such an argument appears to be an attempt by Ecuador to get two bites at the apple of the merits of its dispute with Chevron, by seeking to have this Court separately determine the arbitrability of the underlying dispute under both the FSIA and the New York Convention. The inquiry Ecuador suggests runs counter to the clear teaching of this Circuit on the purpose and role of the FSIA. The FSIA is a jurisdictional statute that "'speak[s] to the power of the court rather than to the rights and obligations of the parties.'" *Creighton*, 181 F.3d at 124 (quoting *Landgraf v. USI Film Prods.*, 511 U.S. 244, 274 (1994)). Likewise, "§ 1605(a)(6) does not affect the contractual right of the parties to arbitration but only the tribunal that may hear a dispute concerning enforcement of an arbitral award." *Id.* (citing *McGee v. International Life Ins. Co.*, 355 U.S. 220, 224 (1957)). Inquiring into the merits of the enforcement dispute—that is, the arbitrability of the underlying claims—would involve an inquiry into the "contractual rights of the parties to arbitration" and would thus be beyond the reach of the FSIA's cabined jurisdictional inquiry.

[15] In contrast to the unprecedented merits-based review Ecuador seeks, the Court's approach here is consistent with those of numerous other federal courts, which have engaged in only these two jurisdictional inquiries—namely, whether the award was made pursuant to an appropriate arbitration agreement with a foreign state and whether the award "is or may be" governed by a relevant recognition treaty. See, e.g., *Blue Ridge Investments, LLC v. Republic of Argentina*, 902 F. Supp. 2d 367, 375 (S.D.N.Y. 2012) ("Here, Blue Ridge instituted the instant action 'to confirm an award made pursuant to [Argentina's] agreement to arbitrate.' The Award is governed by the ICSID Convention, 'a treaty or other international agreement in force for the United States calling for the recognition and enforcement of arbitral awards. Argentina and the United States are both signatories to the Convention. . . . Accordingly, this Court has subject matter jurisdiction under . . . Section 1605(a)(6).") (alterations in original); *Continental Casualty Co. v. Argentine Republic*, 893 F. Supp. 2d 747, 751 n.11 (E.D. Va. 2012) (collecting cases); *In the Matter of the Arbitration Between Monegasque de Reassurances S.A.M. v. Nak Naftogaz of Ukraine*, 311 F.3d 488, 494–95 (2d Cir. 2002) (finding jurisdiction under the FSIA in proceeding to confirm arbitration award under the New York Convention); *G.E. Transp. v. Republic of*

Albania, 693 F. Supp. 2d 132, 136 (D.D.C. 2010) (same); *Agrocomplect, AD v. Republic of Iraq*, 524 F. Supp. 2d 16, 33–34 (D.D.C. 2007) (denying jurisdiction because Iraq, where arbitration took place, "was not a signatory to the New York Convention or (to the best of the Court's knowledge) any other 'treaty or international agreement in force for the United States calling for the recognition and enforcement of arbitral awards' when it entered into the contract with the plaintiff") (quoting 28 U.S.C. § 1605(a)(6)).

[16] In any event, the Court's analysis in Section III.B, *infra*, affirms—albeit under a somewhat deferential standard of review—that Ecuador did consent to arbitration. Respondent's FSIA argument would thus be unlikely to prevail even if reviewed on its merits. Indeed, in any dispute where a respondent argues under the New York Convention that the award was beyond the arbitrator's power, such merits inquiry will always occur. See New York Convention, art. V(1)(c) (Court may deny confirmation where award beyond scope of submission to arbitration). There is thus no prejudice to either party that would be incurred by a Court's not engaging in the same analysis twice.

B. New York Convention

[17] The Federal Arbitration Act, 9 U.S.C. §§ 201–208, codifies the New York Convention. Pursuant to the Convention, a district court "shall confirm the [arbitral] award unless it finds one of the grounds for refusal or deferral of recognition or enforcement of the award specified in the said Convention." 9 U.S.C. § 207. "Consistent with the 'emphatic federal policy in favor of arbitral dispute resolution' recognized by the Supreme Court . . . the FAA affords the district court little discretion in refusing or deferring enforcement of foreign arbitral awards." *Belize Social Development Ltd. v. Government of Belize*, 668 F.3d 724, 727 (D.C. Cir. 2012) (quoting *Mitsubishi Motors Corp. v. Soler Chrysler-Plymouth, Inc.*, 473 U.S. 614, 631 (1985) [see above, p. 900]). Courts "may refuse to enforce the award only on the grounds explicitly set forth in Article V of the Convention." *TermoRio S.A. E.S.P. v. Electranta S.P.*, 487 F.3d 928, 935 (D.C. Cir. 2007) (quoting *Yusuf Ahmed Alghanim & Sons v. Toys "R" Us, Inc.*, 126 F.3d 15, 23 (2d Cir. 1997)) (quotation marks omitted); see also *Int'l Trading & Indus. Inv. Co. v. Dyncorp Aerospace Tech.*, 763 F. Supp. 2d 12, 19 (D.D.C. 2011) (collecting cases). Because "the New York Convention provides only several narrow circumstances when a court may deny confirmation of an arbitral award, confirmation proceedings are generally summary in nature." *Int'l Trading*, 763 F. Supp. 2d at 20 (citing *Zeiler v. Deitsch*, 500 F.3d 157, 167 (2d Cir. 2007)). The party resisting confirmation bears the heavy burden of establishing that one of the grounds for denying confirmation in Article V applies. See New York Convention, art. V; *Imperial Ethiopian Gov't v. Baruch-Foster Corp.*, 535 F.2d 334, 336 (5th Cir. 1976); see also *Ottley v. Schwartzberg*, 819 F.2d 373, 376 (2d Cir. 1987) ("[T]he showing required to avoid summary confirmation is high.").

[18] In contending that the Award here should not be enforced, Ecuador relies on two of the grounds for denying confirmation set forth in Article V. . . . First, it invokes Article V(1)(c), which allows a court to deny confirmation where "[t]he award deals

with a difference . . . not falling within the terms of the submission to arbitration, or it contains decisions on matters beyond the scope of the submission to arbitration." Second, Ecuador argues that confirmation may be denied under Article V(2)(b), which allows for denial of confirmation where "the recognition or enforcement of the award would be contrary to the public policy" of the country where confirmation is sought. Neither ground is availing.

1. Article V(1)(c): Arbitrability

[19] Ecuador first asserts that confirmation may be denied under Article V(1)(c) because it "never agreed—with the United States or with Chevron—to arbitrate the claims in the pending litigation or Chevron's Treaty claim of undue delay concerning that litigation." . . . It contends that since the Tribunal's decision on the arbitrability of the underlying dispute was incorrect, the Final Award was "beyond the scope of the submission to arbitration." See New York Convention, art. V(1)(c). To reach such a conclusion, Ecuador suggests that this Court must engage in an "independent determination" of the Tribunal's jurisdiction to resolve the underlying dispute. . . . Chevron disagrees, claiming instead that because the parties "clearly and unmistakably" agreed that the Tribunal should decide the arbitrability of the dispute, this Court's review of that decision should be highly deferential, a standard the Tribunal's reasoned decision entirely satisfies. . . . Chevron has the better of this debate.

[20] Ecuador maintains that this Court must conduct a *de novo* review of the Tribunal's decision on jurisdiction because, in the ordinary case, "the question of arbitrability . . . is undeniably an issue for judicial determination." *AT&T Tech., Inc. v. Commc'n Workers of Am.*, 475 U.S. 643, 649 (1986); . . . and *First Options of Chicago, Inc. v. Kaplan*, 514 U.S. 938, 943 (1995)). Ecuador, however, mischaracterizes the holdings of these cases, none of which provides that arbitrability is an issue for judicial determination in all circumstances. For example, while the AT&T Technologies court noted that, ordinarily, arbitrability is an issue for judicial determination, it held that where "the parties clearly and unmistakably provide otherwise"—*e.g.*, where they have submitted the arbitrability of the dispute to the arbitrators—the arbitrator determines the arbitrability of the dispute in the first instance. See 475 U.S. at 649; see also, e.g., *First Options*, 514 U.S. at 943 ("We agree with *First Options*, therefore, that a court must defer to an arbitrator's arbitrability decision when the parties submitted that matter to arbitration."). . . .

[21] In cases where the parties have clearly and unmistakably delegated the question of arbitrability to the arbitrator, a court may review that arbitrability decision, but it "should give considerable leeway to the arbitrator, setting aside his or her decision only in certain narrow circumstances." *First Options*, 514 U.S. at 943. Indeed, at least one federal circuit has explicitly rejected the position Ecuador takes here, holding that where the parties "clearly and unmistakably agreed to arbitrate issues of arbitrability," the party resisting confirmation of the award "is not entitled to an independent judicial redetermination of that same question." *Schneider v. Kingdom of Thailand*, 688 F.3d 68, 74 (2d Cir. 2012). To the extent that the parties here have "clearly and unmistakably" agreed to arbitrate arbitrability, then, this Court must

give substantial deference to that decision. In a confirmation proceeding where arbitrability has been clearly and unmistakably delegated to the arbitrator, "the [New York] Convention . . . does not sanction [a Court's] second-guessing the arbitrator's construction of the parties' agreement." *Parsons & Whittemore Overseas Co., Inc. v. Societe Generale de l'Industrie du Papier (RATKA)*, 508 F.2d 969, 977 (2d Cir. 1974).

[22] In deciding this question, the Court first considers whether an agreement to arbitrate exists at all, then analyzes whether such agreement intended the Tribunal to determine questions of arbitrability, and ends with a review of the Tribunal's decision on that issue in this case.

a. Existence of an Agreement to Arbitrate

[23] To begin, Chevron asserts that the "plain language" of the U.S.-Ecuador BIT demonstrates Ecuador's consent to arbitrate this dispute. . . . In its view, Article VI of the BIT constitutes "a standing offer to arbitrate any 'investment dispute' brought by a U.S. 'national or company.'" . . . This position is bolstered by two recent Second Circuit decisions interpreting bilateral investment treaties as creating written agreements to arbitrate for purposes of the New York Convention on facts similar to these. In a case involving both the U.S.-Ecuador BIT and a dispute between our same parties Chevron and Ecuador, the Second Circuit explained:

> The BIT provides that "an 'agreement in writing' for purposes of Article II of the . . . New York Convention" is created when a foreign company gives notice in writing to a BIT signatory and submits an investment dispute between the parties to binding arbitration in accordance with Article VI of the Treaty. All that is necessary to form an agreement to arbitrate is for one party to be a BIT signatory and the other to consent to arbitration of an investment dispute in accordance with the Treaty's terms. In effect, Ecuador's accession to the Treaty constitutes a standing offer to arbitrate disputes covered by the Treaty; a foreign investor's written demand for arbitration completes the "agreement in writing" to submit the dispute to arbitration. *Republic of Ecuador v. Chevron Corp.*, 638 F.3d 384, 392–93 (2d Cir. 2011) (emphasis added) (internal citations omitted).

[24] Likewise, when interpreting the Germany-Thailand BIT, the same court held that "[t]he existence of an arbitration agreement [between the investor and Thailand] is beyond dispute. Thailand, 'by signing the [treaty], and [the investor] by consenting to arbitration, have created a separate binding agreement to arbitrate.'" *Schneider*, 688 F.3d at 71–72 (quoting *Chevron*, 638 F.3d at 392). Although these decisions are not binding on this Court, given the Second Circuit's sound reasoning regarding directly comparable facts, the Court sees no reason to deviate from this approach here. This is, furthermore, a point Ecuador does not truly contest.

[25] Because the BIT constitutes Ecuador's "standing offer" to arbitrate, all Chevron must show is that it was a U.S. "company or national" that submitted an "investment dispute" in order for the Court to find it had a binding arbitration agreement with Ecuador. No one disputes that Chevron is a U.S. company or national. The BIT

defines an "investment dispute" to include "an alleged breach of any right conferred or created by this Treaty with respect to an investment." See U.S. Ecuador BIT, art. VI § 1. Because Chevron alleged that "Ecuador breached Article II(7) of the BIT through the undue delay of the Ecuadorian courts" in deciding Chevron's breach-of-contract cases regarding its initial investment in Ecuador, . . . it properly requested arbitration of an "alleged breach of [a] right conferred by [the BIT] with respect to an investment." See Section III.B.1.c, *infra* (discussing definition of investment). The Court thus finds it had a valid agreement to arbitrate under the BIT.

b. Who Determines Arbitrability?

[26] Having determined that the parties here entered into a valid agreement to arbitrate, the Court must now inquire whether that agreement "clearly and unmistakably" shows that they intended the Tribunal to decide questions of arbitrability. In this case, the U.S.-Ecuador BIT, which forms the basis of the agreement to arbitrate, provides that arbitration may be conducted "in accordance with the Arbitration Rules of the United Nations Commission on International Trade Law (UNCITRAL)." See U.S.-Ecuador BIT, art. VI § 3(a)(iii). Article 21 of the UNCITRAL rules requires that the arbitral tribunal "shall have the power to rule on objections that it has no jurisdiction, including any objections with respect to the existence or validity of the . . . arbitration agreement." UNCITRAL Arbitration Rules, art. 21, ¶ 1, G.A. Res. 31/98, U.N. Doc. A/RES/31/98 (Dec. 15, 1976). In this Circuit, clear and binding precedent dictates that in the context of a bilateral investment treaty, "incorporation of the UNCITRAL Rules provides clear[ ] and unmistakabl[e] evidence[ ] that the parties intended for the arbitrator to decide questions of arbitrability." *Republic of Argentina v. BG Group PLC*, 665 F.3d 1363, 1371 (D.C. Cir. 2012) (alterations in original) (internal quotation marks omitted). Indeed, the D.C. Circuit is not alone in this regard; the Second and Ninth Circuits have both reached the same conclusion. See *Chevron*, 638 F.3d at 394; *Wal-Mart Stores, Inc. v. PT Multipolar Corp.*, No. 98-16952, 1999 WL 1079625, at *2 (9th Cir. Nov. 30, 1999). And, indeed, Ecuador wisely yields to the unequivocal authority on this issue. . . . The Court, accordingly, finds that the parties here clearly and unmistakably agreed to have the arbitrator resolve issues of arbitrability.

c. Deferential Review of Tribunal's Decision

[27] Having so found, the Court may now engage in only deferential review of the Tribunal's decision, granting "considerable leeway to the arbitrator." *First Options*, 514 U.S. at 943. At the outset, it is worth noting that the "beyond the scope" defense to confirmation "should be construed narrowly" and that the party resisting confirmation on such basis "must . . . overcome a powerful presumption that the arbitral body acted within its powers." *Parsons*, 508 F.2d at 976. Indeed, such limited review is consistent with "the basic purposes of arbitration: to resolve disputes speedily and to avoid the expense and delay of extended court proceedings." *Fed. Commerce & Nav. Co. v. Kanematsu-Gosho, Ltd.*, 457 F.2d 387, 389 (2d Cir. 1972); see also *Rich v. Spartis*, 516 F.3d 75, 81 (2d Cir. 2008) (arbitration awards subject to very limited review "in order to avoid undermining the twin goals of arbitration").

[28] Unfortunately, the precise nature of the limited review contemplated by *First Options* is not clear from the cases that follow. See *Schneider*, 688 F.3d at 74 (expressing "no opinion on the precise standard for [deferential] review"). Ecuador, for example, contends that "the court should consider the arbitrators' reasoning [and i]f it does not hold up under scrutiny, it should be rejected," . . . but it offers no authority for this position.

[29] The Court need not determine exactly what standard of deference to employ, as even under a very mildly deferential standard, the Tribunal's decision appears well reasoned and comprehensive. In no way is it so erroneous, unjust, or unclear that this Court would be empowered to set it aside.

[30] The Tribunal here consisted of three learned arbitrators, one chosen by Chevron, one chosen by Ecuador, and one chosen by the first two arbitrators with the consent of the parties. . . . No one contends that the arbitrators were biased, inexperienced, or otherwise inadequate. The Tribunal held eleven days of hearings, four of which were solely devoted to jurisdiction. . . . It ultimately produced a 140-page opinion concerning arbitrability alone and addressing eight potential jurisdictional issues. . . . Ecuador thus cannot claim that the Award should be set aside for the Tribunal's failure to thoroughly engage with the issues or the parties' arguments.

[31] Looking beyond the comprehensiveness of the Tribunal's work to its reasoning, the Court again finds no reason for reversal. At arbitration, Ecuador contended that the underlying breach-of-contract and unreasonable-delay disputes were nonarbitrable because they were not covered by the U.S.-Ecuador BIT, arguing variously that the BIT did not cover investments that had "expired" prior to its entry into force and that, in any case, the surviving breach-of-contract claims could not constitute "investments" under the Treaty. . . . The Tribunal disagreed. It noted that the BIT defines "investments" to include "a claim to money or a claim to performance having economic value, and associated with an investment." . . . The Tribunal "agreed with [Chevron] that . . . [the underlying lawsuits] concern the liquidation and settlement of claims relating to [Chevron's initial investment in Ecuador] and, therefore, form part of that investment." . . . It further observed that treaty language "giv[ing] a further non-exhaustive list of forms that an investment may take" and "provid[ing] that '[a]ny alteration of the form in which assets are invested or reinvested shall not affect their character as [an] investment'" bolstered its conclusion that "once an investment is established, it continues to exist and be protected [by the BIT] until its ultimate 'disposal' has been completed—that is, until it has been wound up." . . . It then concluded that Chevron's "investments have not ceased to exist: their lawsuits continued their original investment through the entry into force of the BIT and to the date of commencement of this arbitration." . . .

[32] The Court can find nothing objectionable about this conclusion, which is based on the plain text of the BIT. . . .

2. Article V(2): Public Policy

[34] Ecuador also argues that confirmation must be denied because the award contravenes the public policy of the United States. . . . The public-policy exception under the New York Convention is construed extremely narrowly and applied "only where enforcement would violate the forum state's most basic notions of morality and justice." *Parsons*, 508 F.2d at 974 (citing Restatement (Second) of Conflict of Laws § 117, cmt. c (1971)); see also *Ministry of Def. & Support for the Armed Forces of the Islamic Republic of Iran v. Cubic Defense Systems, Inc.*, 665 F.3d 1091, 1097 (9th Cir. 2011); *TermoRio S.A. E.S.P.*, 487 F.3d at 938; *Admart AG v. Stephen & Mary Birch Found., Inc.*, 457 F.3d 302, 308 (3d Cir. 2006); *Karaha Bodas Co., L.L.C. v. Perusahaan Pertambangan Minyak Dan Gas Bumi Negara*, 364 F.3d 274, 306 (5th Cir. 2004); *Slaney v. Int'l Amateur Athletic Fed'n*, 244 F.3d 580, 593 (7th Cir. 2001); *M&C Corp. v. Erwin Behr GmbH & Co., KG*, 87 F.3d 844, 851 n.2 (6th Cir. 1996). The "provision was not meant to enshrine the vagaries of international politics under the rubric of 'public policy,'" and it does not provide that awards that might contravene U.S. interests may be resisted on such grounds. *Parsons*, 508 F.2d at 974. Likewise, "[a]lthough this defense is frequently raised, it 'has rarely been successful.'" *Cubic Defense Systems*, 665 F.3d at 1097 (quoting Andrew M. Campbell, Annotation, Refusal to Enforce Foreign Arbitration Awards on Public Policy Grounds, 144 A.L.R. Fed. 481 (1998 & supp.)).

[35] Ecuador points to no such "basic notion of morality and justice" that would be offended by the enforcement of the Award here; in fact, its public-policy argument is primarily a rehashing of its position that the Award was beyond the scope of the submission to arbitration. It also contends that enforcement would violate "strong public policies respecting foreign sovereignty and the autonomy of ongoing judicial proceedings." . . . Neither argument meets the extraordinarily high threshold required by the public-policy defense.

[36] As to Ecuador's first argument — that the Award was beyond the scope — both the Tribunal and this Court have separately found that Ecuador did consent to arbitrate this dispute. In fact, it could just as easily be argued that enforcing the Award here furthers the strong U.S. policy of "ensur[i]ng that private arbitration agreements are enforced according to their terms." *AT&T Mobility LLC v. Concepcion*, 131 S. Ct. 1740, 1748 (2011) (citation and quotation marks omitted); New York Convention, art. II. Indeed, analysis of a proposed public-policy defense "begins with the strong public policy favoring confirmation of foreign arbitration awards," *Cubic Defense Systems*, 665 F.3d at 1098, because "[t]he goal of the [New York] Convention, and the principal purpose underlying American adoption and implementation of it, was to encourage the recognition and enforcement of commercial arbitration agreements in international contracts and to unify the standards by which agreements to arbitrate are observed and arbitral awards are enforced in the signatory countries." *Scherk v. Alberto-Culver Co.*, 417 U.S. 506, 520 n.15 (1974).

[37] Ecuador's second contention — that enforcing the Award would flout its sovereignty — is similarly unavailing. Ecuador argues that enforcing the Award

would sanction the forcible removal of pending litigation from Ecuadorian courts, something it suggests the U.S. would never tolerate. Such a characterization is erroneous.

[38] Ecuador and the U.S. willingly entered into the BIT, in which they agreed to "provide effective means of asserting claims and enforcing rights with respect to investment, investment agreements, and investment authorizations." U.S.-Ecuador BIT, art. II(7). The present dispute found its way to arbitration because Chevron alleged a breach of this clause — namely, that Ecuador had failed to provide "effective means of . . . enforcing rights" in its court system by allowing Chevron's claims to languish there for fifteen years.

[39] In such an instance, the BIT explicitly states that disputes "arising out of . . . an alleged breach of any right conferred or created by this treaty" may be resolved through "courts or administrative tribunals" and through "binding arbitration." See *id.*, art. VI(1–3). The BIT leaves the choice of dispute-resolution method up to the national or company bringing the claim, and it provides that such awards shall be enforceable under the New York Convention. *Id.* In this sense, the BIT's provision for the arbitration of claims that a signatory has breached its treaty obligations operates as a backstop against the failure of the court systems of either of the signatory nations, and it has played that role appropriately here.

[40] Indeed, it strains credulity to argue that both these sovereign nations would have agreed to such a choice of dispute-resolution processes if they had anticipated it would lead to results that would "violate . . . [their] most basic notions of morality and justice." *Parsons*, 508 F.2d at 974. Given that the Court has found there was a valid agreement to arbitrate between the parties formed under the BIT, the Court cannot now say that enforcing it through the precise means contemplated by the treaty would contravene the strong public policy of the United States. As a result, confirmation may not be denied on this basis. . . .

[43] Finding that Ecuador has not carried its burden to show that any of the bases for denying confirmation in the New York Convention applies to the Award here, the Court must grant Chevron's Petition and confirm the Award.

C. Ecuador's Request for a Stay

[44] Finally, Ecuador argues that "the Court should defer a final decision on the merits of Chevron's petition pending resolution of the ongoing set-aside proceedings in the Hague," as permitted by Article VI of the New York Convention. . . . Under the Convention, district courts do have discretion to stay proceedings where "a parallel proceeding is ongoing in the originating country and there is a possibility that the award will be set aside." *Europcar Italia, S.p.A. v. Maiellano Tours, Inc.*, 156 F.3d 310, 317 (2d Cir. 1998). Noting that "the adjournment of enforcement proceedings impedes the goals of arbitration — the expeditious resolution of disputes and the avoidance of protracted and expensive litigation," the *Europcar* court found that "a stay of confirmation should not be lightly granted," and it identified a number of

factors district courts should consider in evaluating a request for a stay of proceedings. *Id.* at 317. These factors include:

(1) The general objectives of arbitration . . . ;

(2) The status of the foreign proceedings and the estimated time for those proceedings to be resolved;

(3) Whether the award sought to be enforced will receive greater scrutiny in the foreign proceedings under a less deferential standard of review;

(4) The characteristics of the foreign proceedings including (i) whether they were brought . . . to set the award aside (which would tend to weigh in favor of enforcement) . . . and (iv) whether they were initiated under circumstances indicating an intent to hinder or delay resolution of the dispute;

(5) A balance of the possible hardships to the parties . . . ; and

(6) Any other circumstance that could tend to shift the balance in favor of or against adjournment. . . . *Id.* at 317–318.

[45] "Because the primary goal of the Convention is to facilitate the recognition and enforcement of arbitral awards, the first and second factors on the list should weigh more heavily in the district court's determination." *Id.* at 318. Notably, Ecuador's initial request for a stay makes no mention of the *Europcar* factors, and its Second Opposition makes only passing reference to them. The Court, finding that the balance of factors weighs against staying the proceedings, will deny Ecuador's request.

[46] The first factor, the general objectives of arbitration, weighs strongly in favor of confirmation. The BIT, the UNCITRAL Rules, and the New York Convention all require immediate satisfaction of arbitral awards. Chevron submitted its Notice of Arbitration in this matter more than six years ago, a delay that surely does not constitute an "expeditious resolution" of the dispute, which originated in the early 1990s. See *G.E. Transport*, 693 F. Supp. 2d at 139 (finding that four-year delay "plainly weigh[ed] in favor of confirmation rather than adjournment").

[47] Likewise, the second factor, the status of the foreign proceedings, weighs in favor of immediate confirmation: although the Dutch proceeding is ongoing, the District Court of the Hague issued a decision denying Ecuador's petition to set the award aside more than a year ago, and the appeal will likely not be resolved until late 2013 or early 2014. . . .

[48] The third factor, whether the award will receive greater scrutiny in foreign proceedings, is a closer case. According to Chevron's expert, Jacob M.K.P. Cornegoor, who represents Chevron in the Dutch proceeding, "[T]he [Dutch] District Court reviewed the question whether a valid arbitration agreement was formed *de novo*," but reviewed the question of whether the dispute concerned an investment validly covered by the BIT as "one for arbitrators to consider and their answer should be reviewed under a more restrictive standard by the court." . . . This standard is not so much more exacting than the one applied here that it weighs strongly against

confirmation, and, indeed, the fact that the Dutch District Court has already denied the motion to set aside suggests that to the extent the standard is any more searching, it has not helped Ecuador in its attempt to resist confirmation.

[49] The fourth factor does not carry much force either way. Although the parties dispute whether the vacatur proceedings are an attempt to "hinder or delay resolution of the dispute," the Court cannot say that they are so obviously either legitimate or vexatious that this factor should sway its analysis here. The fact that the proceedings were initiated to vacate the Award, rather than confirm it, however, does weigh against a stay.

[50] The fifth factor, the balance of hardships, also counsels in favor of immediate confirmation. As Chevron notes, this dispute is more than twenty years old, and the arbitration itself began more than six years ago. Although Chevron will be entitled to prejudgment interest, which would continue to accrue in the event of a stay, that is not enough to offset its continued inability to obtain enforcement of its award. After such an extensive delay, the balance of hardships—and, indeed, the interests of justice—strongly favor immediate confirmation.

[51] Neither side presents any other significant circumstance that should be considered as an additional factor. Because the balance of the *Europcar* factors greatly supports immediate confirmation, the Court will deny Ecuador's request for a stay.

III. Conclusion

[52] For the aforementioned reasons, the Court will grant Chevron's Petition and order confirmation of the Award. A separate Order consistent with this Opinion will be issued this day.

JAMES E. BOASBERG, United States District Judge, June 6, 2013

Notes and Questions

1. Ecuador claims that the Foreign Sovereign Immunities Act (FSIA) stands in the way of recognition and enforcement of an arbitral award against a foreign country or government. What does FSIA say and what does it seek to accomplish? Paragraph 8 discusses an exception in FSIA. What does that say and what are the consequences in the present case and in general?

2. In paragraph 14, the court refuses to review the "arbitrability of the underlying dispute." In effect, it leaves the decision regarding the arbitrability to the original decision-makers, i.e., the arbitral tribunal (see also paras. 20 and 27). This approach is justified by the principle of Kompetenz-Kompetenz, i.e., the competence of the first seized court or tribunal to rule on its competence (see pp. 702, 780, and 932 et seq.).

3. In paragraphs 17 and 34–43, the court discusses the standard of review and the burden of proof for the grounds for refusal listed in Article V of the New York Convention. How can the U.S. approach be summarized?

4. Most provisions of Article V are quite narrow. The exception is, on its face, in the "public policy" exception. How could this provision be interpreted and how

does the present court interpret it? Do you agree with a more narrow interpretation or do you support a broader interpretation? Why?

5. Pursuant to the District Judge, the "basic purpose" of arbitration is "to resolve disputes speedily and to avoid the expense and delay of extended court proceedings"; subsequently, he cites another case where these were identified as "the twin goals of arbitration" and suggests that these goals require only limited review of arbitral awards in court (para. 27). Do you agree that these are the basic purposes of arbitration? Do you remember other, equally important purposes of choosing arbitration over litigation? Would those contradict or reinforce the conclusions of the present court regarding limited review?

6. The District Court judgment was appealed by Ecuador but affirmed en banc by the United States Court of Appeals for the District of Columbia; see 795 F.3d 200 (judgment of August 4, 2015).

7. For a critical review of investor-state dispute settlement (ISDS) via arbitration, as provided in many bilateral investment treaties (BITs), see, for example, Haley Sweetland Edwards, *Shadow Courts: The Tribunals That Rule Global Trade*, Columbia Global Reports 2016; as well as Frank Emmert & Begaiym Esenkulova, *Why Can't We Be Friends? Protecting Investors While Also Protecting Legitimate Public Interests and the Sustainable Development of Host Countries in Investor-State Arbitration*, 48 Tex. J. Bus. L. 2019, pp. 48–82; a more favorable analysis can be found in Meg Kinnear et al. (eds.), *Building International Investment Law — The First Fifty Years of ICSID*, Wolters Kluwer 2016.

Finally, our last example in this area is about the recognition and enforcement of an award that has been annulled at the seat of the arbitration:[296]

Case 6-14

Chromalloy Aeroservices v. Arab Republic of Egypt

939 F. Supp. 907 (D.D.C. 1996)
(Paragraph numbers added, most footnotes omitted.)
JUNE L. GREEN, District Judge

I. Introduction

[1] This matter is before the Court on the Petition of Chromalloy Aeroservices, Inc., ("CAS") to Confirm an Arbitral Award, and a Motion to Dismiss that Petition filed by the Arab Republic of Egypt ("Egypt"), the defendant in the arbitration. This is a case of first impression. The Court GRANTS Chromalloy Aeroservices' Petition

---

296. For further analysis see, *inter alia*, Claudia Alfons: *Recognition and Enforcement of Annulled Foreign Arbitral Awards: An Analysis of the Legal Framework and its Interpretation in Case Law*, Peter Lang Verlag 2010; Vesna Lazi-Smoljanič: *Enforcing Annulled Arbitral Awards: A Comparison of Approaches in the United States and in the Netherlands*, Zbornik Pravnog Fakulteta Sveucilista u Rijeci 2018, Vol. 39, No. 1, pp. 215–240.

to Recognize and Enforce the Arbitral Award, and DENIES Egypt's Motion to Dismiss, because the arbitral award in question is valid, and because Egypt's arguments against enforcement are insufficient to allow this Court to disturb the award.

II. Background

[2] This case involves a military procurement contract between a U.S. corporation, Chromalloy Aeroservices, Inc., and the Air Force of the Arab Republic of Egypt.

[3] On June 16, 1988, Egypt and CAS entered into a contract under which CAS agreed to provide parts, maintenance, and repair for helicopters belonging to the Egyptian Air Force. . . . On December 2, 1991, Egypt terminated the contract by notifying CAS representatives in Egypt. . . . On December 4, 1991, Egypt notified CAS headquarters in Texas of the termination. On December 15, 1991, CAS notified Egypt that it rejected the cancellation of the contract "and commenced arbitration proceedings on the basis of the arbitration clause contained in Article XII and Appendix E of the Contract." Egypt then drew down CAS' letters of guarantee in an amount totaling some $11,475,968.

[4] On February 23, 1992, the parties began appointing arbitrators, and shortly thereafter, commenced a lengthy arbitration. On August 24, 1994, the arbitral panel ordered Egypt to pay to CAS the sums of $272,900 plus 5 percent interest from July 15, 1991, (interest accruing until the date of payment), and $16,940,958 plus 5 percent interest from December 15, 1991, (interest accruing until the date of payment). The panel also ordered CAS to pay to Egypt the sum of 606,920 pounds sterling, plus 5 percent interest from December 15, 1991, (interest accruing until the date of payment).

[5] On October 28, 1994, CAS applied to this Court for enforcement of the award. On November 13, 1994, Egypt filed an appeal with the Egyptian Court of Appeal, seeking nullification of the award. . . . On December 5, 1995, Egypt's Court of Appeal at Cairo issued an order nullifying the award. . . .

[6] Egypt argues that this Court should deny CAS' Petition to Recognize and Enforce the Arbitral Award out of deference to its court. . . . CAS argues that this Court should confirm the award because Egypt "does not present any serious argument that its court's nullification decision is consistent with the New York Convention or United States arbitration law." . . .

III. Discussion

A. Jurisdiction . . .

1. The Standard under the Convention

[10] This Court *must* grant CAS's Petition to Recognize and Enforce the arbitral "award unless it finds one of the grounds for refusal . . . of recognition or enforcement of the award specified in the . . . Convention." 9 U.S.C. § 207. Under the Convention, "Recognition and enforcement of the award *may* be refused" if Egypt furnishes to this Court "proof that . . . [t]he award has . . . been set aside . . . by a competent authority of the country in which, or under the law of which, that award was made." Convention, Article V(1) & V(1) (e) (emphasis added), 9 U.S.C. § 201

note. In the present case, the award was made in Egypt, under the laws of Egypt, and has been nullified by the court designated by Egypt to review arbitral awards. Thus, the Court *may,* at its discretion, decline to enforce the award.[2]

[11] While Article V provides a discretionary standard, Article VII of the Convention *requires* that, "The provisions of the present Convention *shall not* . . . deprive any interested party of any right he may have to avail himself of an arbitral award in the manner and to the extent allowed by the law . . . of the count[r]y where such award is sought to be relied upon." 9 U.S.C. § 201 note (emphasis added). In other words, under the Convention, CAS maintains all rights to the enforcement of this Arbitral Award that it would have in the absence of the Convention. Accordingly, the Court finds that, if the Convention did not exist, the Federal Arbitration Act ("FAA") would provide CAS with a legitimate claim to enforcement of this arbitral award. *See* 9 U.S.C. §§ 1–14. Jurisdiction over Egypt in such a suit would be available under 28 U.S.C. §§ 1330 (granting jurisdiction over foreign states "as to any claim for relief in personam with respect to which the foreign state is not entitled to immunity . . . under sections 1605–1607 of this title") and 1605(a) (2) (withholding immunity of foreign states for "an act outside . . . the United States in connection with a commercial activity of the foreign state elsewhere and that act causes a direct effect in the United States"). *See Weltover,* 504 U.S. at 607 . . . . Venue for the action would lie with this Court under 28 U.S.C. § 1391(f) & (f) (4) (granting venue in civil cases against foreign governments to the United States District Court for the District of Columbia).

2. Examination of the Award under 9 U.S.C. § 10

[12] Under the laws of the United States, arbitration awards are presumed to be binding, and may only be vacated by a court under very limited circumstances:

> (a) In any of the following cases the United States court in and for the district wherein the award was made may make an order vacating the award upon the application of any party to the arbitration
>
> > (1) Where the award was procured by corruption, fraud, or undue means.
> >
> > (2) Where there was evident partiality or corruption in the arbitrators, or either of them.
> >
> > (3) Where the arbitrators were guilty of misconduct in refusing to postpone the hearing, upon sufficient cause shown, or in refusing to hear evidence pertinent and material to the controversy; or of any other misbehavior by which the rights of any party have been prejudiced.

---

2. The French language version of the Convention, (which the Court notes is *not* the version codified by Congress), emphasizes the extraordinary nature of a refusal to recognize an award: "Recognition and enforcement of the award *will not be refused* . . . unless. . . ." . . . (emphasis in the original).

(4) Where the arbitrators exceeded their powers, or so imperfectly executed them that a mutual, final, and definite award upon the subject matter submitted was not made. 9 U.S.C. § 10.[1]

[13] An arbitral award will also be set aside if the award was made in "'manifest disregard' of the law." *First Options of Chicago v. Kaplan,* 514 U.S. 938 [942] . . . (1995). "Manifest disregard of the law may be found if [the] arbitrator[s] understood and correctly stated the law but proceeded to ignore it." *Kanuth v. Prescott, Ball, & Turben, Inc.,* 949 F.2d 1175, 1179 (D.C.Cir.1991).

> Plainly, this non-statutory theory of vacatur cannot empower a District Court to conduct the same de novo review of questions of law that an appellate court exercises over lower court decisions. Indeed, we have in the past held that it is clear that [manifest disregard] means more than error or misunderstanding with respect to the law. *Al-Harbi v. Citibank,* 85 F.3d 680, 683 (D.C.Cir.1996) (internal citations omitted). . . .

[17] In the United States, "[W]e are well past the time when judicial suspicion of the desirability of arbitration and of the competence of arbitral tribunals inhibited the development of arbitration as an alternative means of dispute resolution." *Mitsubishi Motors Corp. v. Soler Chrysler-Plymouth, Inc.,* [above, p. 900] (1985). In Egypt, however, "[I]t is established that arbitration is an exceptional means for resolving disputes, requiring departure from the normal means of litigation before the courts, and the guarantees they afford." (Nullification Decision at 8.) Egypt's complaint that, "[T]he Arbitral Award is null under Arbitration Law, . . . because it is not properly 'grounded' under Egyptian law," reflects this suspicious view of arbitration, and is precisely the type of technical argument that U.S. courts are not to entertain when reviewing an arbitral award. *See Montana Power Company v. Federal Power Commission,* 445 F.2d 739, 755 (D.C.Cir.1970) (*cert. den.* 400 U.S. 1013 . . . (1971)) (holding that, "Arbitrators do not have to give reasons") (*citing United Steelworkers v. Enterprise Wheel & Car Corp.,* 363 U.S. 593, 598 . . . (1960)).

[18] The Court's analysis thus far has addressed the arbitral award, and, as a matter of U.S. law, the award is proper. *See Sanders v. Washington Metro. Area Transit Auth.,* 819 F.2d 1151, 1157 (D.C.Cir.1987) (holding that, "When the parties have had a full and fair opportunity to present their evidence, the decisions of the arbitrator should be viewed as conclusive as to subsequent proceedings, absent some abuse of discretion by the arbitrator") (*citing* the Restatement (Second) of Judgments § 84(3) (1982), *Greenblatt v. Drexel Burnham Lambert, Inc.,* 763 F.2d 1352 (11th Cir. 1985)). The Court now considers the question of whether the decision of the Egyptian court should be recognized as a valid foreign judgment.

---

1. The Court has reviewed the voluminous submissions of the parties and finds no evidence that corruption, fraud, or undue means was used in procuring the award, or that the arbitrators exceeded their powers in any way.

[19] As the Court stated earlier, this is a case of first impression. There are no reported cases in which a court of the United States has faced a situation, under the Convention, in which the court of a foreign nation has nullified an otherwise valid arbitral award. This does not mean, however, that the Court is without guidance in this case. To the contrary, more than twenty years ago, in a case involving the enforcement of an arbitration clause under the FAA, the Supreme Court held that:

> An agreement to arbitrate before a specified tribunal is, in effect, a specialized kind of forum-selection clause. . . . The invalidation of such an agreement . . . would not only allow the respondent to repudiate its solemn promise but would, as well, reflect a parochial concept that all disputes must be resolved under our laws and in our courts. *Scherk v. Alberto-Culver Co.,* 417 U.S. 506, 519 . . . (1974) (*reh. den.,* 419 U.S. 885 . . . (1974)) (citations omitted).

[20] In *Scherk,* the Court forced a U.S. corporation to arbitrate a dispute arising under an international contract containing an arbitration clause. *Id.* 417 U.S. at 518, 94 S. Ct. at 2456–57. In so doing, the Court relied upon the FAA, but took the opportunity to comment upon the purposes of the newly acceded-to Convention:

> The delegates to the Convention voiced frequent concern that courts of signatory countries in which an agreement to arbitrate is sought to be enforced should not be permitted to decline enforcement of such agreements on the basis of parochial views of their desirability or in a manner that would diminish the mutually binding nature of the agreements. . . . [W]e think that this country's adoption and ratification of the Convention and the passage of Chapter 2 of the United States Arbitration Act provide strongly persuasive evidence of congressional policy consistent with the decision we reach today. *Id.* at n. 15.

The Court finds this argument equally persuasive in the present case, where Egypt seeks to repudiate its solemn promise to abide by the results of the arbitration.[4] . . .

2. The Decision of the Egyptian Court of Appeal

[23] The Court has already found that the arbitral award is proper as a matter of U.S. law, and that the arbitration agreement between Egypt and CAS precluded an appeal in Egyptian courts. The Egyptian court has acted, however, and Egypt asks this Court to grant *res judicata* effect to that action.

[24] The "requirements for enforcement of a foreign judgment . . . are that there be 'due citation' [*i.e.,* proper service of process] and that the original claim not violate U.S. public policy." *Tahan v. Hodgson,* 662 F.2d 862, 864 (D.C.Cir.1981) (*citing*

---

4. The fact that this case concerns the enforcement of an arbitral *award,* rather than the enforcement of an agreement to arbitrate, makes no difference, because without the knowledge that judgment will be entered upon an award, the term "binding arbitration" becomes meaningless.

Hilton v. Guyot, [above, p. 834]. The Court uses the term 'public policy' advisedly, with a full understanding that, "[J]udges have no license to impose their own brand of justice in determining applicable public policy." *Northwest Airlines Inc. v. Air Line Pilots Association, Int'l*, 808 F.2d 76, 78 (D.C.Cir.1987). Correctly understood, "[P]ublic policy emanates [only] from clear statutory or case law, 'not from general considerations of supposed public interest.'" *Id.* (quoting *American Postal Workers Union v. United States Postal Service*, 789 F.2d 1 (D.C.Cir.1986)).

[25] The U.S. public policy in favor of final and binding arbitration of commercial disputes is unmistakable, and supported by treaty, by statute, and by case law. The Federal Arbitration Act "and the implementation of the Convention in the same year by amendment of the Federal Arbitration Act," demonstrate that there is an "emphatic federal policy in favor of arbitral dispute resolution," particularly "in the field of international commerce." *Mitsubishi v. Soler Chrysler-Plymouth*, [above, p. 900]; *cf. Revere Copper & Brass Inc., v. Overseas Private Investment Corporation*, 628 F.2d 81, 82 (D.C.Cir.1980) (holding that, "There is a strong public policy behind judicial enforcement of binding arbitration clauses"). A decision by this Court to recognize the decision of the Egyptian court would violate this clear U.S. public policy. . . .

IV. Conclusion

[31] The Court concludes that the award of the arbitral panel is valid as a matter of U.S. law. The Court further concludes that it need not grant *res judicata* effect to the decision of the Egyptian Court of Appeal at Cairo. Accordingly, the Court GRANTS Chromalloy Aeroservices' Petition to Recognize and Enforce the Arbitral Award, and DENIES Egypt's Motion to Dismiss that Petition.

Notes and Questions

1. What are the rules on foreign sovereign immunity in the U.S.? Explain the discussion in paragraph 11 of the decision. In which kind of cases would a foreign state be able to rely on sovereign immunity before a U.S. court and in which kind of cases would it not? Do some research, if necessary.

2. Can you enumerate all cases where a foreign arbitral award would not be recognized and enforced in the U.S.? To what extent are these scenarios giving discretionary powers to U.S. courts? To what extent may a U.S. court have to refuse recognition and enforcement? How do U.S. rules potentially differ from the rules on recognition and enforcement applicable in other countries? Consult paragraphs 13, 17, and 18 when formulating your answers.

3. Judge Green could not find a precedent for the question whether a foreign arbitral award could be recognized and enforced even if it had been annulled at the seat of the tribunal. She did find the *Scherk v. Alberto-Culver* decision, however, which discussed the invalidity of an arbitration clause (paras. 19–20). Do you agree that this is a persuasive precedent? Why? Why not?

4. After the Egyptian court annulled the arbitral award, the defendant requested that the U.S. court grant res judicata effect[297] to the Egyptian court decision (paras. 23 et seq.). In general, when does a court decision have res judicata effect? Is there a difference between purely domestic constellations and cases where the effect is invoked for a foreign court decision? What about res judicata of the earlier arbitral award? Can an arbitral award have res judicata effect? When? On what conditions?

5. In the end, the U.S. court decided to disregard the Egyptian annulment and recognize and enforce the original arbitral award. Can you summarize why the U.S. court came to this decision? Do you think it is a fair and correct decision? In what kind of cases would a U.S. court refuse the recognition and enforcement of a foreign arbitral award that has been annulled at its seat? When in doubt, should U.S. courts err on the side of recognizing or refusing to recognize a foreign arbitral award? Why?

6. Do you think that the fact that the respondent was the government of Egypt played a role in the annulment decision of the Egyptian court? The recognition and enforcement decision of the American court?

7. If the respondent does not pay voluntarily, the recognition and enforcement of the arbitral award in the U.S. is only useful for the claimant if the respondent has assets in the U.S. What kind of assets might a foreign state or government have in the U.S.? Could the claimant, for example, seize the building or the bank accounts of the Egyptian embassy in Washington, D.C.? Do some research into this question, if necessary.

8. Possibly because it could not find sufficient assets of the Egyptian state in the U.S., Chromalloy also pursued recognition and enforcement in France. Like the U.S. court, the French court granted recognition and enforcement in spite of the annulment in Egypt. See *The Arab Republic of Egypt v. Chromalloy Aeroservices Inc.*, Judgment of January 14, 1997, 22 Y.B. Comm. Arb. 691 (CA 1997).

21. *Cost and Duration of Arbitration Proceedings*

Conventional wisdom suggests that arbitration is generally faster than litigation, but also more expensive. In practice, the picture may be more differentiated. After having reviewed the material in this Part about international commercial litigation and international commercial arbitration, the reader should understand that the parties have many options for where to go for litigation — at least if they can agree at the time of entering into a contract or at the time a dispute arises — and there are even more options when it comes to choosing the format and location of arbitration proceedings. Naturally, these choices impact the cost and duration of the proceedings. Specifically, with regard to arbitration, the range of options goes from ad hoc arbitration with a single arbitrator, or ad hoc with a panel of three, to a great many

---

297. For further analysis, see, in particular, Silja Schaffstein, *The Doctrine of Res Judicata Before International Commercial Arbitration Tribunals*, Oxford Univ. Press 2016.

arbitration institutions with different rules, reputations, and remuneration scales. In Chart 6-6, above p. 944, we provided some guidelines for the choice of the arbitration format on the assumption that ad hoc is almost always cheaper than institutional arbitration and that the ICC is almost always more expensive than regional arbitration centers. These are generalizations that can serve as guidelines, but they are by no means always true. The following criteria should always be taken into consideration when estimating the cost and duration of arbitration proceedings:

- The duration of arbitration proceedings depends not only on the complexity of the dispute, but also on the availability of the chosen arbitrators. The duration is normally somewhere between 6 and 18 months. This does not always beat the speed of litigation in countries with efficient court systems. However, if there is an appeal, litigation will almost always take longer than arbitration.

- The cost of ad hoc arbitration is largely in the hands of the parties. The parties select the number of arbitrators, the place of arbitration, hence the travel expenses for the arbitrators, witnesses, attorneys, etc. The parties negotiate and accept the fees of the arbitrator or arbitrators, which can vary significantly.

- In institutional arbitration, many institutions fix not only their administrative fees, but also the honoraria for the arbitrators. These can be compared before a particular institution is selected. To some extent this also applies to travel expenses, hence the choice of place of arbitration. However, other expenses, in particular attorney fees and the expenses for witnesses, etc., will depend on the complexity of the case. Of course, the latter arise just the same in transnational litigation.

- Some institutions, like the ICC, allow their arbitrators a fee range. For example, the minimum fee per arbitrator for a dispute over US\$10 million under the 2017 ICC schedule is US\$39,167 while the maximum fee is US\$ 87,400. Thus, by choosing three well-known and expensive arbitrators, the parties can increase the cost of the arbitration very substantially. The cost calculator on the website of the ICC differentiates between minimum fees, average fees, and maximum fees. For a dispute over US\$10 million, the ICC will require an advance on costs in the amount of US\$170,799, based on the average cost of one arbitrator (US\$113,284) plus administrative expenses (US\$57,515). If three arbitrators are involved, the required advance on costs goes up to US\$397,367.[298]

---

298. The ICC Commission on Arbitration and ADR Task Force on Reducing Time and Cost in Arbitration published a first report on techniques for controlling time and cost in arbitration in 2007. An updated second edition taking into account rule changes in 2012 is available on the website of the ICC (https://iccwbo.org/content/uploads/sites/3/2018/03/icc-arbitration-commission -report-on-techniques-for-controlling-time-and-costs-in-arbitration-english-version.pdf). However, the techniques mostly address the options of organizing the proceedings in an efficient way and keeping various ancillary expenses under control. The report does not address the fee schedule of the ICC as such.

- The parties can agree on fee shifting in their submission or terms of reference, or they can agree that each side will bear its own cost and they will share the costs of the tribunal equally (the "American Rule," see above, pp. 786 and 790–793). With fee shifting, the losing party bears all expenses, including the costs of the tribunal and reasonable expenses for attorneys, travel, etc. of the winning party (the "English Rule"). If the parties have not agreed about distribution of cost, the institutional rules may provide for one model or the other. Finally, if neither the parties nor the institution provide clear rules, a party may ask the tribunal to impose all or most expenses on the other party for being in breach of its obligations and having caused the dispute, which the tribunal may or may not award, depending on its assessment of the case.

- While duration and cost are important, what matters most is to get a quality decision that can be enforced, if necessary. If a dispute requires court assistance, for example to force the appearance of a witness or the presentation of certain evidence, or to secure certain assets during the settlement procedure, the place of arbitration and choice of *lex arbitri* are much more important than relatively minor differences in cost or duration. Always remember that it makes no sense to save on the cost of the arbitration if the result is ultimately unenforceable or triggers further litigation or arbitration.

To provide some idea of the typical cost and duration of arbitration proceedings, the following data published by a number of regional institutions can be useful.

Chart 6-9
Average Cost and Duration in Certain Regional Arbitration Centers (2016)[299]

	London Court of Int'l Arbitration	Stockholm Chamber of Commerce	Hong Kong Int'l Arbitration Centre	Singapore Int'l Arbitration Centre
average duration overall	16 months	13.5 months	11.6 months	11.7 months
average duration sole arbitrator	15 months	10.3 months	N/A	11.3 months
average duration panel of three	19 months	15.8 months	N/A	11.7 months
average admin fees overall	N/A	N/A	US$9,281	US$5,853
average admin fees sole arbitrator	N/A	US$6,924	N/A	US$5,836

See also Vit Biolek, *Recent Trends in Increasing Efficiency in International Arbitration: How to Make Arbitration Cheap and Fast*, AkademikerVerlag 2019; Doug Jones, *Using Cost Orders to Control the Expense in International Commercial Arbitration*, Arb. 2016, Vol. 82, No. 3, pp. 291–301; as well as Sherlin Tung, Fabricio Fortese & Crina Baltag (eds.), *Finances in International Arbitration — Liber Amicorum Patricia Shaughnessy*, Wolters Kluwer 2019.

299. Data from Baker McKenzie, see http://www.bakermckenzie.com/en/insight/publications /2016/12/costs-and-duration-of-arbitration.

	London Court of Int'l Arbitration	Stockholm Chamber of Commerce	Hong Kong Int'l Arbitration Centre	Singapore Int'l Arbitration Centre
average admin fees panel of three	N/A	US$21,144	N/A	US$6,723
average arbitrator honoraria overall	N/A	N/A	US$ 19,588	US$26,852
average honorarium sole arbitrator	N/A	US$18,172	N/A	US$22,449
average total honoraria panel of three	N/A	US$133,350	N/A	US$70,904

The administrative fees and the scales for the arbitrator honoraria applicable in ICC arbitration are clearly disclosed in Appendix III of the 2017 ICC Arbitration Rules (Documents, p. II-314).

The Cairo Regional Centre for International Commercial Arbitration provides a very convenient fee calculator on its website. All the user has to enter is the amount in dispute and whether the arbitration is with a sole arbitrator or with a panel of three (see http://crcica.org/FeesCalc.aspx). A similar service is available on the website of the Singapore International Arbitration Centre, albeit in Singapore Dollars (in Spring 2020, 1 USD was about equal to 1.4 SGD), and on the website of the Stockholm Chamber of Commerce, albeit in Euros (http://www.sccinstitute .com/dispute-resolution/calculator/). The ICC also provides a cost calculator at https://iccwbo.org/dispute-resolution-services/arbitration/costs-and-payments /cost-calculator/. However, this leaves a wide range between minimum, average, and maximum arbitrator fees.

On the basis of their rules and regulations, we can compare the stipulated administrative fees and arbitrator honoraria in different arbitration centers as follows:

Chart 6-10
Comparison of Administrative Fees and Arbitrator Honoraria in Certain Arbitration Centers, Assuming a Dispute over US$10 million

	ICC (standard procedure)	Stockholm Chamber of Commerce*	Singapore Int'l Arbitration Centre	Cairo Regional Centre for Int'l Commercial Arbitration
admin fees	US$57,515	€38,200 plus estimated expenses of €19,905	average US$21,800 max US$28,650	US$39,200
min arbitrator honorarium	US$39,167	€50,000		US$27,375
average arbitrator honarium	US$113,284	€94,500	US$85,425	
max arbitrator honorarium	US$187,400	€139,000	US$113,670	US$132,027

	ICC (standard procedure)	Stockholm Chamber of Commerce*	Singapore Int'l Arbitration Centre	Cairo Regional Centre for Int'l Commercial Arbitration
estimated total sole arbitrator	min US$96,682 max US$244,915	€152,600	average US$105,675 max US$140,895	min US$66,757 max US$171,227
estimated total panel of three	min US$175,016 max US$619,715	€283,000 (incl. €36,915 for expenses other than SCC admin fees)	average US$276,183 max US$368,220	min US$121,325 max US$435,281

*For the SCC, the amount in dispute was stipulated at €10 million.

It should be noted that the cost estimates do not include the lawyer's fees and honoraria and they do not include expenses such as travel, interpretation and translation, conference rooms, etc. (except at the SCC).

These numbers do not compare unfavorably to litigation in the courts. For a comparable dispute over an amount of US$10 million or €10 million, Foris AG quotes court fees in Germany in the amount of €113,208.[300] This, however, covers only the first instance. If there should be an appeal, the court fees will be an additional €150,944. And if worse comes to worst, and there is a further appeal to the highest court, court fees of no less than €188,680 would have to be added, for a total of €452,800. As in arbitration, this does not include the lawyer's fees and honoraria, and it does not include expenses for travel and other logistics. More importantly, the average duration of the procedure at first instance is 10–12 months and, if there are appeals, the litigation may take five years or more. These numbers are probably comparable in most of the other EU Member States, except that some countries, like Italy, are notorious for exorbitant delays in proceedings.

In the U.S., the fee structure is less straightforward since the parties have to cobble together a variety of payments (filing fees, as well as fees for miscellaneous services such as evidence preparation, depositions, court reporter transcript fees, certification and photocopy fees for documents, and many more). However, in general, the court fees are much lower while the attorney fees may well be higher. The fact that court fees in the U.S. are less transparent and ultimately much lower than the fees or arbitral institutions, and the fact that each side normally has to pay its own attorney fees, are the main reasons why less experienced U.S. attorneys may perceive arbitration as necessarily more expensive. As we have seen, this is by no means inevitable since victory in arbitration, combined with fee shifting to the losing party, would

---

300. See https://www.foris.com/service-center/prozesskostenrechner.html#. Foris AG is in the business of litigation financing.

liberate the victorious side from any costs and fees. Such a result cannot normally be accomplished in litigation in the U.S.

Finally, third-party funding may also be available in arbitration.[301]

Section 7. Online Dispute Resolution (ODR)

Online ADR—or ODR—is different from traditional ADR because all elements are conducted online and the parties and tribunal members never meet in person. Conducting an entire procedure online has obvious advantages. First, it will be much easier to schedule meetings if people merely have to set aside a few hours of their time rather than having to travel half way around the world for an in-person meeting. Second, the cost savings can be significant. While the arbitrator honoraria do not necessarily change—unless they factor in not only the amounts in dispute but also the number of days spent on the case—travel and accommodation for the tribunal members, the party representatives, the parties themselves, experts and witnesses, as well as administrative, secretarial, and language support, can quickly cost US$100,000 or more for a single hearing.

While video conferences have become a standard part of almost all ADR procedures, an in-person hearing or meeting is still common for most procedures and remains valuable, in particular, if parties work in different languages, if the case is very complicated and requires a lot of back-and-forth for clarifications of facts and arguments, multiple parties are involved, emotions play a role, or the credibility of witnesses needs to be determined in cross-examination. These kinds of issues are still better resolved in face-to-face meetings compared to the rather impersonal online questionnaires and meeting rooms. In addition, online meetings tend to become inefficient if more than eight or ten persons have to participate and only work well if all parties have access to reliable high-speed internet. Attorneys and arbitrators who have doubts about any of these factors should be cautious before agreeing to an online-only procedure. Finally, the amounts at issue also play a role.

---

301. The International Council for Commercial Arbitration (ICCA), in collaboration with the Centre on Regulation, Ethics, and Rule of Law at Queen Mary College, University of London, has sponsored a Task Force on Third-Party Funding in International Arbitration since 2013. The most recent fourth report was published in 2018 and provides a state-of-the-art analysis of the status of third-party funding and potential challenges for disclosure, conflicts of interest, privileged communications and professional secrecy, and the impact on costs overall. It also contains "Best Practices in Third-Party Funding Arrangements" (pp. 185 et seq.). The report is available online at https://www.arbitration-icca.org/media/10/40280243154551/icca_reports_4_tpf_final_for_print _5_april.pdf.

See also James Clanchy, *Navigating the Waters of Third-Party Funding in Arbitration*, Arb. 2016, Vol. 82, No. 3, pp. 222–232; Khalil Mechantaf, *Third-Party Funding in International Arbitration: Active Funders as Parties in Arbitration Proceedings*, Arb. 2016, Vol. 82, No. 4, pp. 371–379; as well as Nikolaus Pitkowitz, *Handbook on Third-Party Funding in International Arbitration*, JurisNet 2018.

In an arbitration over a claim of US$500,000, the costs of an in-person meeting are more of an issue than in an arbitration over a claim of US$500 million.

One of the concerns in online-only ADR can be the security of the communication. The more individuals in more countries participate in an online dispute settlement procedure, the greater are the vulnerabilities, since one weak link can be enough to compromise the entire procedure. To address this problem and to bring the fast-growing opportunities provided by artificial intelligence (AI) to bear, a number of organizations are building cyber-mediation and cyber-arbitration platforms. These are not just websites or apps where video conferences with arbitrators and attorneys from different countries can be hosted. The platforms try to do much more. For example, some ODR providers experiment with software-based solutions for certain standard problems to eliminate the need for a human mediator or arbitrator altogether. These started out within certain e-commerce platforms; sanctions were initially focused on feedback and reputation, for example for untrustworthy sellers on eBay or Amazon. Meanwhile, we have a wide range of ODR procedures, from those involving human ombudsmen or mediators, to those where decisions are entirely taken by AI. An example of innovative but unproven approaches is provided by Kleros. Their system of "peer-to-peer justice" essentially relies on majority voting by submitting the basics of a dispute to a larger number of peers for an up or down vote.[302] CyberSettle, founded in 1996, is another such provider. It focuses on negotiation technology to facilitate settlement of monetary disputes. The parties submit confidential settlement offers and the computer system determines whether they are close enough to make a mutually acceptable settlement possible. If not, the parties are not bound and can undertake different forms of ADR using different baselines for their negotiations.[303] Modria Online Dispute Resolution by Tyler Technologies is another interesting solution for certain common types of disputes such as landlord/tenant, small claims, and divorce-related disputes.[304] The Internet Corporation for Assigned Names and Numbers (ICANN), which administers web addresses around the world, has developed Online Dispute Resolution Standards of Practice for ODR providers in the area of domain address disputes and the like. The ICANN standards, in turn, are based on best-practice standards drafted by a variety of other national and international organizations.[305] Professor Ethan Katsh's National Center for Technology & Dispute Resolution (NCTDR) is one of those organizations and has many useful links on its website, including a long list of ODR providers.[306]

---

302. https://kleros.io/en/. See also my review in https://www.researchgate.net/publication/335715800_A_Critical_Review_of_the_Kleros_Dispute_Revolution.

303. http://www.cybersettle.com/.

304. See https://www.tylertech.com/products/modria.

305. https://www.icann.org/resources/pages/odr-standards-of-practice-2012-02-25-en.

306. http://odr.info/provider-list/.

To provide some level of quality control and to support e-commerce providers and participants in different parts of the world, the United Nations Commission on International Trade Law (UNCITRAL) adopted the 2017 Technical Notes on Online Dispute Resolution.[307] They establish general principles for ODR, outline the stages of an ODR proceeding, define the roles and responsibilities of the participants, set standards for communications, and frame the different stages of the proceedings. Among the guiding principles is the requirement that ODR procedures should be based on the explicit and informed consent of all parties (Sec. II, para. 17).

For consumers shopping online, the EU Commission has created an online dispute resolution platform on the basis of EU Regulation 524/2013 on Online Dispute Resolution for Consumer Disputes.[308] In the area of B2B transactions, however, the EU has not been particularly active or innovative.

At the present time, for the kind of IBT transactions we are talking about in this book, the most important and most widely used online procedures are still hybrid procedures with some online and some offline elements.[309] It may be safely presumed, however, that the current stage of experimentation and the changes to be expected from Blockchain-based applications, will provide new and better opportunities for ODR in the not-too-distant future. These developments will only be accelerated by the Covid 19 pandemic of 2020.

307. See https://www.uncitral.org/pdf/english/texts/odr/V1700382_English_Technical_Notes_on_ODR.pdf.

308. OJ 2013 L 165, pp. 1–12. The Regulation is applicable from January 9, 2016, and has supremacy and direct effect in the EU Member States. For more information, see Ihab Amro, *The Resolution of Consumer Disputes Through Online Arbitration*, Arb., Vol. 83, No. 3, 2016, pp. 265–280.

309. Recommended further reading: Mohamed Abdel Wahab/Ethan Katsch/Daniel Rainey (eds.), *Online Dispute Resolution: Theory and Practice—A Treatise on Technology and Dispute Resolution*, The Hague 2012; Ihab Amro, *Online Arbitration in Theory and in Practice—A Comparative Study of Cross-Border Commercial Transactions in Common Law and Civil Law Countries*, Cambridge Scholars 2018; Julio C. Betancourt & Elina Zlatanska, *Online Dispute Resolution (ODR): What Is It, and Is It the Way Forward?* in Chartered Institute of Arbitrators: ADR, Arbitration, and Mediation—A Collection of Essays 2014, pp. 309–336; Naom Ebner & John Zeleznikow, *Fairness, Trust and Security in Online Dispute Resolution*, Hamline J. Pub. L. & Pol'y 2015, Vol. 36, No. 2, pp. 143–160; Martin Gramatikov (ed.), *Costs and Quality of Online Dispute Resolution*, Antwerp et al. 2012; Carolina Mania, *Online Dispute Resolution: The Future of Justice*, Int'l Comp. Juris. 2015, Vol. 1, No. 1, pp. 76–86; Ayelet Sela, *Can Computers Be Fair? How Automated and Human-Powered Online Dispute Resolution Affect Procedural Justice in Mediation and Arbitration*, Ohio St. J. Disp. Res. 2018, Vol. 33, No. 1, pp. 91–148; and Faye Fangfei Wang, *Online Arbitration*, Informa Law 2017.

Annex

Useful Resources, Tables, Index, and Glossary

Section 1.
Useful Resources Available Online

Part One: The General Framework for IBTs

Adams on Contract Drafting https://www.adamsdrafting.com/

ASIL Guide to Electronic Resources for International Law http://www.asil.org/resource/ie11.htm

Cornell University Law School Legal Information Institute [LII] https://www.law.cornell.edu/world

HG.org Legal Resources (formerly lex mundi) http://www.hg.org

Lex Mercatoria (international conventions, model laws, national laws, institutions, and institutional rules etc. on international commercial law) http://www.jus.uio.no/lm/index.html

United States Trade Representative (USTR) (information about current U.S. free trade agreements and federal laws regulating U.S. foreign trade) https://ustr.gov/

Part Two: Sales Contracts

International Chamber of Commerce http://www.iccwbo.org/

United Nations Commission on International Trade Law (UNCITRAL) http://www.uncitral.org/

Part Three: Payment and Financing Contracts

Institute of International Banking Law and Practice http://www.iiblp.org/

Part Four: Shipping Contracts

Admiralty and Maritime Law Guide http://www.admiraltylawguide.com/index.html

Part Five: Insurance Contracts

http://www.admiraltylawguide.com/insurance.html

Part Six: Dispute Settlement

Chartered Institute of Arbitrators Arbitrators https://www.ciarb.org/

Section 2.
Table of International Conventions, International Agreements, and National Statutory Materials

A. United States Statutory Materials

Federal Law

Constitution of the United States	T 35, 161
Federal Arbitration Act	T 293, 887, 911 + D II-505
Federal Electronic Signatures in Global and National Commerce Act (E-Sign) (2000)	T 357, 361–362, 385
Federal Railroad Safety Act (1970)	T 592
Federal Rules of Civil Procedure	T 200, 607, 753–754, 767, 816
Foreign Trade Antitrust Improvement Act of 1982	T 29
Marine Mammal Protection Act	T 31
Racketeer Influenced and Corrupt Organizations (RICO) Act	T 607
Sherman Act	T 26, 613, 900–910

State Law

California Code of Civil Procedure	T 767
Florida Deceptive and Unfair Trade Practices Act (FDUTPA)	T 267
New York Electronic Signatures and Records Act (ESRA) (1999)	T 385
New York General Obligations Law	T 380–387

Model Laws

Uniform Computer Information Transaction Act (UCITA) (2002)	T 357–359
Uniform Electronic Transactions Act (UETA) (1999)	T 357–361, 384, 399
Uniform Enforcement of Foreign Judgments Act (1948)	T 110
Uniform Foreign-Money Judgments Recognition Act (1962)	T 110, 763, 831
Uniform Foreign Country Money-Judgment Recognition Act (2005)	T 41, 110, 763, 831 + D II-68

B. International Conventions and Agreements

By Year of Adoption

1974	UN Convention on the Limitation Period in the International Sale of Goods	T 263 + D I-132
1978	Hague Convention on the Law Applicable to Agency	T 41
1978	Hague Convention on the Law Applicable to Matrimonial Property Regimes	T 41
1979	Inter-American Convention on Conflicts of Laws Concerning Commercial Companies	T 44
1980	UN Convention on International Multimodal Transport of Goods	T 593
1980	Vienna Convention on International Sale of Goods (CISG)	T 48, 185–228, 257–295 + D I-79
1986	Hague Convention on the Law Applicable to Contracts for the International Sale of Goods	T 41, 108 + D I-32
1988	Lugano Convention on Jurisdiction and the Recognition and Enforcement of Judgments in Civil and Commercial Matters	T 719 , 924, 940
1988	UN Convention on International Bills of Exchange and International Promissory Notes	T 1067
1988	UNIDROIT Convention on International Factoring ("Ottawa Convention")	T 423
1994	Inter-American Convention on the Law Applicable to International Contracts (Mexico Convention)	T 44
1994	WTO Agreements	T 31, 38
1995	UN Convention on Independent Guarantees and Stand-by Letters of Credit	D I-523
2001	UN Convention on the Assignment of Receivables in International Trade	T 423
2005	Hague Convention on Choice of Court Agreements (COCA)	T 41, 109 717– 718, 829 + D II-11
2005	UN Convention on the Use of Electronic Communications in International Contracts	T 365
2007	Lugano Convention on Jurisdiction and the Recognition and Enforcement of Judgments in Civil and Commercial Matters	T 43, 47, 719

2019	UN Convention on International Settlement Agreements Resulting from Mediation (Singapore Convention)	T 874 + D II-127
2019	Hague Convention on the Recognition and Enforcement of Judgments in Civil and Commercial Matters	T 41, 829 + D II-54

By Popular Name (in alphabetical order)

Hague Convention on Choice of Court Agreements (COCA) (2005)	T 717– 718, 764, 829 + D II-11
Hague Convention on the Recognition and Enforcement of Judgments in Civil and Commercial Matters (1971)	D II-43
Hague Convention on the Recognition and Enforcement of Judgments in Civil and Commercial Matters (2019)	T 829 + D II-54
Hague Convention on the Service Abroad of Judicial and Extrajudicial Documents in Civil and Commercial Matters (1965)	T 752, 818, 962 + D II-23
Hague Convention on the Taking of Evidence Abroad in Civil and Commercial Matters (1970)	T 41, 752, 818 + D II-32
Inter-American Convention on the Law Applicable to International Contracts (Mexico Convention)	T 44
Inter-American Convention on Letters Rogatory	T 752
Lugano Convention on Jurisdiction and the Recognition and Enforcement of Judgments in Civil and Commercial Matters	T 43, 47, 719
Mexico Convention on the Law Applicable to International Contracts	T 44 + D I-48
Montreal Convention for the Unification of Certain Rules Relating to International Carriage by Air (1929)	T 589, 593 + D I-729
Panama Convention on International Commercial Arbitration	T 942, 1015
New York Convention on the Recognition and Enforcement of Foreign Arbitral Awards	T 49, 764, 781, 887, 1015 + D II-500
Singapore Convention on International Settlement Agreements Resulting from Mediation (2019)	T 874 + D II-127
Vienna Convention on International Sale of Goods (CISG)	T 48, 185–228, 257–295 + D I-79
Warsaw Convention for the Unification of Certain Rules Relating to International Carriage by Air (1929)	T 589 + D I-721

Non-Binding Instruments

1985	UNCITRAL Model Law on International Commercial Arbitration	T 49 + D II-185
1987	UNCTAD Model Clauses for Marine Cargo Insurance	T 593 + D I-771
1996	UNCITRAL Model Law on Electronic Commerce	T 367–372
2001	UNCITRAL Model Law on Electronic Signatures	T 49, 367, 372–375
2005	Hague Principles on Choice of Law in International Commercial Contracts	T 109, 145 + D I-38
2010	UNCITRAL Arbitration Rules	T 917 + D II-199
2010	IBA Rules on the Taking of Evidence in International Arbitration	T 50, 989–996 + D II-239
2010	Uniform International Choice of Court Agreements Act (Draft)	T 765
2013	UNIDROIT Principles on the Operation of Close-Out Netting Provisions	T 418
2014	IBA Guidelines on Conflicts of Interest in International Arbitration	T 50, 983, 988 + D II-269
2018	UNCITRAL Model Law on Electronic Transferable Records (MLETR)	T 558
2018	Prague Rules on the Efficient Conduct of Proceedings in International Arbitration	T 994 + D II-251
2020	Asian Principles for the Recognition and Enforcement of Foreign Judgments	T 829

Industry Codes

CMI Uniform Rules for Sea Waybills	T 556
Uniform Rules for Collection URC 522 (ICC)	T 522 + D I-569

C. European Union Statutory Materials

D. National Statutory Materials of Countries Around the World

Section 3.
Table of Cases

A. United States Courts

B. International and Foreign Court Decisions

C. Arbitral Awards

Section 4.
Index and Glossary of International Trade and Business Terminology

5W Formula for claims: Who Wants What from Whom and Why?   T 60

10+2 Documentation required by U.S. Customs and Border Protection (CBP) at least 24 hours prior to the arrival of marine cargo, also referred to as "Importer Security Filing (ISF)."

Abandonment and Salvage A clause that may be included in marine insurance contracts. If a vessel or cargo owner prefers to abandon the insured assets, the insurance, in return for payment of the claim, obtains the right to salvage the vessel or goods.

Abd El Wahab, Mohamed International legal scholar and arbitrator,   T 1042
Cairo

Abnormal Spoilage When goods are stored or transported, a certain percentage may be considered as acceptable or normal spoilage. Abnormal spoilage exceeds this percentage and is considered avoidable and may, therefore, trigger damage claims against the warehouse or carrier.

Absolute Advantage/Disadvantage One of the reasons for trade.   T 9
See also *Relative Advantage/Disadvantage*, and *Comparative Advantage/Disadvantage*

Acceptance A *Draft* is a demand for payment, also called a *Bill of Exchange*; by adding his or her *Acceptance*, the *Drawee* indicates that she agrees to pay the amount at maturity.

Acceptance Credit A *Letter of Credit (L/C)* which includes a term *Bill of Exchange* in its required documentation. The bill will be accepted by the bank on which it is drawn, usually the *Issuing* or *Advising Bank*, and the proceeds paid to the *Beneficiary* at *Maturity*.

Accounts Payable Future payment obligations of a buyer toward her suppliers of goods or services.

Accounts Receivable Future claims of a seller against buyers of her   T 421–422
goods or services. See also *Receivables*

ACE or **Automated Commercial Environment** An internet-based filing system used by U.S. Customs and Border Protection for the processing of imported goods.

ACH Automatic Clearinghouse system   T 418

Act of God An event beyond human control, in particular a natural disaster such as an earthquake, flood, lightning, storm, or volcano eruption. See also *Force Majeure*

Acta Iure Imperii Acts or omissions by public authorities in the exercise of State authority; see, e.g., Art. 1 of EU Regulation 1215/2012.   T 713

Action Plan on a More Coherent European Contract Law   T 136

Actual Total Loss While a *Constructive Total Loss* may already be declared if the cost of repair of damaged property exceeds the value of the property, *Actual Total Loss* will be declared only if the property has been actually lost or at least abandoned by the owner. See also *Notice of Abandonment*   T 639, 647

AdobeSign Provider of *Digital Transaction Management (DTM)* services   T 356, 558

Ad Valorem Tariff Import duty calculated as a percentage of the value of the goods.

Advance Notice of Arrival (ANOA) Any ship approaching U.S. waters from abroad is required to give a 96-hour ANOA to the U.S. Coast Guard (vessels over 300 tons), respectively the port of destination (smaller vessels).

Advance Payment Guarantee A *Guarantee* issued by a bank, on behalf of a seller to a buyer, in relation to any advance payment that is made by the buyer to the seller to allow the contract to commence. If the contract is not completed, the buyer can claim reimbursement of the advance payment under the *Guarantee*.

Advice of Shipment A notice sent to the importer or buyer that the goods were shipped. Typically, the notice will include a copy of the *Invoice* to identify the goods and link them to the underlying contract, as well as a copy of the *Bill of Lading*.

Advising Bank A bank, normally located in the country of residence of an exporter/seller, used by an importer/buyer's *Issuing Bank* to validate the authenticity of a *Letter of Credit* before the L/C is passed on to the exporter/seller. If the bank is only an advising bank, it has no further obligations regarding the L/C and the exporter/seller usually has to present the required documents to the *Issuing Bank* in buyer's country. If the exporter/seller can present the L/C with the required documents to the advising bank to get paid, the bank also becomes a *Nominated Bank*. If the nominated bank has an obligation to pay upon complying presentation, regardless of approval by the issuing bank, the advising bank also becomes a *Confirming Bank*.

Affreightment A contract of affreightment is an agreement between the shipper and the carrier for a particular amount of cargo space on a particular vessel on a particular date. — T 563

Agency — T 601–603

Agent An agent represents the *Principal* in a business transaction. The agent has to have the consent of the principal, which may be implied if the principal was aware of the agent's actions and did not intervene. In such cases, the agent's acts are binding on the principal. If the agent acts without knowledge/consent of the principal or outside her authority but purportedly in the name of or on behalf of the principal, the acts are either not attributable to the principal or the principal is given the choice of ratifying the acts and accepting them as binding or rejecting them, in which case only the agent herself would be bound.

Air Waybill A contract for the shipment of certain goods by air, issued by the carrier upon receipt of the goods and given to the shipper/exporter/seller. Like other transport documents, in particular the *Bill of Lading* for maritime transport, it can be made out to be a document of title. In this case, the consignee/importer/buyer needs to get the original *Air Waybill* (AWB) from the seller to be able to collect the goods from the carrier. If the AWB is a document of title, it will usually be negotiable and can be transferred by the consignee to third parties who will then be entitled to receive the goods from the carrier. If the transaction involves *Letter of Credit* financing, it will be important for the shipper to receive a clean AWB from the carrier, confirming receipt of the goods in *Apparent Good Order*. — T 588–590

Alibaba.com Chinese online trading platform — T 7

Allocation of Resources See *Resource Allocation*

Allonge A slip of paper added to a *Financial Instrument*, in particular a *Bill of Exchange*, to create space for one or more additional *Endorsements*.

All Risks Clause See *Institute Cargo Clauses A*

Alongside If cargo has to be placed "alongside ship," it has to be on the dock or on a barge within reach of the ship's own rigging or tackle.

Alternative Dispute Resolution (ADR) Procedures to resolve disputes without recourse to public courts. — T 860 et seq.

American Arbitration Association (AAA) — T 694, 957, 963

American Institute Cargo Clauses | T 629–631 + D I-800

American Law Institute (ALI) Nonprofit organization promoting development of law in the U.S. and beyond with *Restatements* of the Law, Model Codes like the UCC, and guiding "Principles" for legislatures and administrative agencies. | T 48, 120

American Rule In litigation, each side has to pay its own attorney fees and the winning party, absent a specific rule that provides for reimbursement in a given area of law or for a specific claim, will not be able to demand her attorney fees from the losing party. The opposite is true under the *English Rule*. | T 573, 786, 791, 1038

Amendment A change in the terms to a *Letter of Credit (L/C)* that is already issued. Such changes can only be made with the agreement of all parties to the *L/C* (see Article 10 UCP600).

AML Procedures "Anti-Money Laundering" procedures required for financial institutions to combat tax evasion, money laundering, and organized crime. See also *KYC Procedures* | T 424–425

Annual Customs Bond or **Annual Import Bond** See *Customs Bond*

Anti-Dumping Duty A punitive tariff imposed by an importing country to offset unfairly low prices that are detrimental to domestic competitors.

Anti-Money Laundering (AML) Rules See *AML Procedures*, as well as *KYC Procedures*

Anti-Suit Injunction A preliminary remedy obtained from a court or arbitral tribunal prohibiting the other party in a dispute from pursuing certain court proceedings, either because they are generally considered incompatible with an arbitration clause or agreement, or because of lack of jurisdiction of the specific court. See also *Parasitic Litigation* | T 761, 775–785, 924–940

Antitrust See *Competition* | T 769

Anton Piller Order An *Interim Relief* order allowing searches of premises and taking of evidence without warning. | T 795

Apparent Authority Actions by an agent who does not have formal authority to bind a principal in a certain way can be binding on the principal based on apparent authority if the principal was aware and did not stop the actions or if the agent held titles or other credentials that created the impression of actual authority. See also *Signature Authority* | T 350

Apparent Good Order Confirmation by the carrier that freight was received free of obvious damage or irregularities, such as broken or leaking containers, torn packaging, or the like.

Applicant The importer or buyer who applies to an *Issuing Bank* for a T 438
Letter of Credit (L/C), or a *Guarantee/Bond* as the means to finance an international business transaction.

Appraisement Determination of the customs value of goods presented for importation. See also *Customs Valuation*, and/or *Valuation*

Arbitrage Buying commodities or other goods in one market and selling them right away in another market where the price is (slightly) higher.

Arbitration Method of *Alternative Dispute Resolution (ADR)*, instead of litigation, which relies on private agreement and privately selected experts as *Arbitrators*.

Advantages over litigation	T 863–864, 879–882, 898–899
Agreement to arbitrate (ex ante or ex post agreement)	T 948–960
Applicable laws and rules	T 912–924
Arbitrable dispute	T 900–912
Arbitration clause, separability	T 897
Arbitrator challenge	T 987–989
Arbitrator selection	T 966–972
Award	T 998–1002
Case management conference	T 979–980
Cost and duration	T 1036–1041
Default award	T 1000
Discovery	T 989–996
Evidence	T 989–996
Expedited procedures	T 882
Hearings	T 996–998
IBA Guidelines for Drafting International Arbitration Clauses	T 950
Interim measures	T 976–979
Online Dispute Resolution (ODR)	T 1041
Potential problems in consumer arbitration	T 881, 882
Recognition and enforcement of arbitral awards	T 1002–1036
Request for arbitration	T 960–964
Statement of claim and statement of response	T 972–976
Terms of reference	T 980–986

Arbitrator A neutral person selected by the parties to a dispute to analyze their factual and legal positions and give a final and binding *Award* in resolution of the dispute.

Arrest of a Ship Detainment of a vessel by the port authorities, in particular in a procedure of *Interim Relief*, to secure potential claims against the owners and prevent removal of the asset from the jurisdiction.

Arrival Notice A notice by the *Carrier* to the *Consignee* (the party to be notified as per the *Bill of Lading* and/or the *Letter of Credit*) of the arrival of the goods at the port of destination. The shipper/exporter/seller may be listed as an "also notify" party, in particular if he needs the arrival notice to get paid under the L/C.

ASEAN The Association of Southeast Asian Nations   T 39, 829

Asian Principles for the Recognition and Enforcement of Foreign Judgments   T 829

Assignment The transfer of rights embodied in a *Bill of Lading*, *Check*, *Bank Guarantee*, or *Letter of Credit* from the named *Beneficiary* to a third party. To confirm voluntary assignment, versus for example a theft of the document, assignment usually requires an *Endorsement* by the named *Beneficiary*. See also CFR III.-5.101 et seq.

Assured The *Beneficiary* under an insurance contract or policy.

ATA Carnet A guarantee issued by a chamber of commerce or similar agency for the benefit of customs authorities pursuant to which customs duties and taxes will be paid if goods that are admitted duty free on a temporary basis, for example as commercial samples for a trade fair, or as tools or equipment, are not re-exported or otherwise used in breach of the temporary importation permit.

ATDNSHINC "Any time day or night, Sundays and holidays included," an abbreviation used in shipping to indicate that a vessel will operate non-stop.

Attorney Fees See also *American Rule*, and *English Rule*, as well as *Fee Shifting*, and *Contingency Fee*   T 573–574, 663, 788–793

Attorney Fees in Different Countries See also *American Rule* and *English Rule*   T 790–793

Authority of Agents See *Signature Authority*, as well as *Apparent Authority*   T 350

Automatic Clearinghouse (ACH) system   T 418

Aut Punire Aut Dedere The principle that countries should prosecute or extradite foreign lawbreakers but not provide safe haven.   T 30

Aval A guarantee by a third party for a payment obligation; see *Avalize*, as well as Article 30 et seq. 1930 Geneva Convention on Providing a Uniform Law for Bills of Exchange and Promissory Notes (D I-485)   T 532

Avaliseur The person giving an *Aval*.

Avalize The process by which a third party, usually a bank, guarantees the obligations of the *Drawee* to pay under a *Bill of Exchange*, or the buyer under a purchase contract. The words "Per Aval" or "By Aval" and the signature of the avalizing (guarantor) must be written on the Bill or contract. The document then becomes an *avalized draft* or an *avalized contract*.   T 523

Average See *General Average*

Average Income vs. median income   T 25

Avoidance of a contract   T 319, 321

AWWL Always Within Institute Warranties Limits; an *Insurance Contract* term referring to the liability limits of the *Institute Cargo Clauses*.

Backhaul Returning goods to the shipper/exporter/seller, for example if the consignee/importer/buyer failed to make payment as previously agreed.

Back-to-Back Factoring See *Factoring*

Back-to-Back Letters of Credit A transaction where one *Letter of Credit (L/C)* is used as collateral to obtain another L/C. For example, a trader/seller/middleman obtains an L/C from his buyer and uses it as collateral to get an L/C from his own bank to pay the supplier or subcontractor who actually manufactures or supplies the goods for the buyer.

Step 1: Buyer → L/C → Seller → L/C → Supplier

Step 2: Buyer ← goods ← Seller ← goods ← Supplier

The seller's bank and the supplier/subcontractor have security because they know they will get paid if they fulfill the contract between the seller and the buyer.

Bad Faith in negotiations, contract performance   T 106, 302

Balloon Freight Bulky and lightweight goods where volume is more important than weight for the determination of shipping costs.

Banker's Acceptance A *Draft* with an *Acceptance* by a bank, i.e., the bank issues a contractual promise to honor the *Draft* at *Maturity*.

Banker's Draft or **Bank Draft** sometimes also referred to as a **Banker's Check.** A check drawn on the bank rather than the buyer; provides a high level of security for the seller, unless the draft is forged or the bank becomes insolvent.

Bank Guarantee A *Guarantee* is a third-party promise to indemnify   T 487–520
certain losses of one party to an IBT for the failure of another party to the IBT to honor its commitments and obligations. For example, if the buyer has paid an advance so that the seller can manufacture the goods, the buyer may ask for an *Advance Payment Guarantee* to make sure that she gets her money back if the seller does not deliver. *Guarantees* are more flexible than *Letters of Credit*. They do not have to rely on presentation of a set of documents. For example, a *Demand Guarantee* can allow the *Beneficiary* to simply demand payment, without providing evidence of non-performance. If the *Guarantee* is provided by an insurance company or similar institution, it is usually called a *Bond*. See also *Bid Bond/Guarantee*, *Performance Bond/Guarantee*, and *Standby Letter of Credit*

Bank Payment Obligation (BPO) An *SCF* mechanism similar to a *Letter of Credit* transaction. An Obligor Bank (comparable to the issuing bank of an L/C) gives an irrevocable and independent undertaking to make a specified payment at maturity to a Recipient Bank (comparable to the advising bank of an L/C), provided that a set of trade data is successfully matched. BPOs are usually governed by the Uniform Rules for Bank Payment Obligations (URBPO 750) of the ICC.

Bareboat Charter Chartering of a vessel without crew and supplies.

Barratry Fraudulent acts of the crew and/or master of a ship against the owners of the ship and/or cargo.

Barrel A measurement of volume used for oil trade. One barrel = 42 U.S. liquid gallons.

Battle of Forms See also *CISG* and *UCC*   T 210,
                                                                    230–237

Beam The width of a ship at its widest point.

Behavioral Economics T 26

Beneficial Cargo Owner (BCO) The consignee/importer/buyer to whom risk has passed and who will receive the goods at the port of destination.

Beneficiary The exporter or seller who gets paid in a *Letter of Credit (L/C)* financed transaction, or the party authorized to claim a sum of money from a bank under a *Guarantee/Bond*.
T 438

Berger, Klaus Peter International lawyer and arbitrator, Köln
T 127, 860, 866

Bermann, George International legal scholar and arbitrator, New York
T 769, 916, 942, 1016

BIC Business Identifier Code T 424

Bid Bond/Guarantee A guarantee issued by a bank on behalf of a seller to a buyer to support the seller's bid or tender for a contract. If the seller's bid is accepted, and they fail to sign a contract, the buyer can claim compensation under the guarantee.

Bilateral Investment Treaty (BIT) Treaty between two countries for the protection of investors from the one in the other country. Usually provides for arbitration of disputes rather than litigation in the national courts against the government of the country.

Bill Discounting See *Discounting*

Billing Practices of Lawyers in Different Countries See *Attorney Fees*

Bill of Exchange An unconditional order in writing drawn up by a seller or other *Beneficiary* asking the buyer or the *Advising Bank* or the *Issuing Bank* in a *Letter of Credit* transaction or in a *Documentary Collection* to pay a specific amount of money, often also referred to as a *Draft*. Unless otherwise stipulated, the order is for immediate payment, i.e., "at sight." An example would be the form filled in when a customer wants to withdraw cash from her own account at a bank teller. If the order is for payment at a future date, the Bill is called a *Term Bill of Exchange*. Payment can be ordered to the issuer, to the bearer, or to a specified third person. In the U.S., Article 3 UCC — or rather the respective implementations at the state level — provides the legal framework for negotiable instruments such as Bills of Exchange. Once it receives the 10 ratifications required for entry into force, the 1988 UN Convention on International Bills of Exchange and International Promissory Notes will also play an important role, in particular since it is generally well drafted and easily understandable. See also *Guaranteed Bill of Exchange*

Bill of Lading (BoL) A document that represents (1) a contract of car-   T 553–563
riage between a shipper/exporter/seller and a carrier, determin-
ing the terms for the transportation of specified goods, including
the point of departure, the destination, the shipping charges, and
who has to pay. (2) Issuing and handing over the BoL also confirms
receipt of the goods. If no *Notations* as to apparent damage or irregularities are included on the BoL, the BoL is called a *Clean Bill of
Lading* and confirms receipt of the goods in *Apparent Good Order*.
With notations, the BoL is called a *Soiled BoL* or a *Foul BoL* and will
not suffice to get paid under a *Letter of Credit*. Finally, (3) the BoL is
also a document of title that needs to be presented in the original by
the person receiving the goods at the destination — the consignee/
importer/buyer. See also *Combined Transport BoL*; *Straight BoL* versus *Negotiable BoL*; as well as *Long Form BoL* and *Short Form BoL*.

Bill of Material (BOM) A list of components of a larger device or
shipment.

Bill of Sale Confirmation of transfer of ownership in return for
money paid.

Bill Purchasing See *Bill Discounting*

Bitcoin A global digital currency allowing peer-to-peer (P2P) payments that avoid the banking fees for international wire transfers
and also avoid the bank's currency exchange fees. *Bitcoin* is not
yet widely used but could provide significant benefits for IBTs. See
also *Cryptocurrency*

Blanket Waybill A *Waybill* covering more than one shipment of
goods.

Blind Shipment A *Bill of Lading* where either the identity of the ship-
per/exporter/seller and/or the consignee/importer/buyer is withheld pursuant to instructions by the party who entered into the
contract for carriage and is paying the carrier.

Blockchain A system that maintains data in ledgers on many com-   T 356, 410,
puters. The records are safe because they cannot be hacked or cor-   417, 420,
rupted on all computers simultaneously.   558

Blocking Statute to prevent acts undertaken on behalf of foreign   T 753, 818
authorities, such as service of process, within the territory of a
country

Bls The abbreviation for "bales," for example bales of cotton.

Board Feet The unit of measurement used for lumber. One board
foot is a board of one inch thickness, twelve inches width, and one
foot length.

BoE *Bill of Exchange*

Bond A bond is an "I Owe You" issued by a borrower (usually a large corporation or a central or local government or municipality) in exchange for a loan. The issuer promises to repay the loan ("face value") after a fixed period of time ("maturity date") with a fixed or variable rate of interest. Since bonds are usually not made out to a specific lender, they can be traded privately ("over-the-counter"/ OTC) or publicly on exchanges. At the end of the specified period, the bondholder collects payment from the issuer. Longer-term bonds are often issued with annual or semi-annual coupons, entitling the holder to collect a certain amount of interest every year. The value of a bond is determined both by the credit rating/creditworthiness of the issuer, the rate of interest, and the time remaining until maturity. If the interest rate fixed in a bond is higher than the market rate, the value of the bond goes up. Conversely, if the market rate increases beyond the interest rate fixed in a bond, the value of the bond goes down. Thus, bonds move in opposite directions to market interest rates. See also *Call and Put Options for Loans*

Bonded Exchange A currency that cannot be freely converted into other currencies.

Bonded Freight Goods moving under the control of the customs authorities because they have not yet been processed and released into free circulation.

Bonded Warehouse A warehouse inside the customs controlled area where goods can be stored pending customs processing. Customs formalities will have to be completed and duties paid before the goods can be released from the Bonded Warehouse into free circulation. Conversely, if the goods are re-exported, no formalities and duties are required. See also *Inward Processing*

Bond Port The first port of entry where customs procedures have to be completed, sometimes also referred to as the *First Port of Call*.

Bonell, Michael International legal scholar, Rome   T 126

Born, Gary International arbitrator, London and Singapore   T 697, 833, 879, 921

Both-to-Blame Collision Clause A shipping contract clause pursuant to which the owners or shippers of cargo have to share the losses caused by a ship collision according to the monetary value of their share of the cargo if the collision was caused by negligence on both sides.

Bottomry A loan agreement where the hull of a ship, the "bottom," is used as *Collateral*. By contrast, *Respondentia* refers to loan agreements using the cargo of the ship as *Collateral*.   T 606

Break Bulk Cargo such as boxes, pallets, or bales, that is not in a container.   T 544

Bridge Point An inland place where goods are received by a maritime carrier for transport to port and loading on an oceangoing vessel.

Bridge Port A port where goods are received by a maritime carrier for transport to another port from where they are loaded on an oceangoing vessel.

Broker (1) a person who arranges a transaction between a seller and a buyer in exchange for a commission; (2) a person who takes care of customs clearance on behalf or an importer and charges either a flat fee or a percentage of the value of the imported goods.

Brokerage The amount paid to a *Broker* for his or her services.

Brussels I Regulation The *EU Regulation 1215/2012 on Jurisdiction and the Recognition and Enforcement of Judgments in Civil and Commercial Matters* determines which court in the EU has jurisdiction in disputes between individuals in different EU Member States, as well as disputes between an individual in a Member State and another in a third country. It also requires all Member States to recognize and enforce judgments rendered by a court with jurisdiction under the Regulation. Regulation 1215/2012 is successor to Regulation 44/2001, the original Brussels I Regulation. The new Regulation is therefore also called "Brussels Ia" or "Brussels I *bis*" Regulation.   T 744, D II-92

Budapest Convention on the Contract for the Carriage of Goods by Inland Waterway (CMNI)   T 593

Bulk Cargo shipped in loose form, usually in large quantities and on specialized vessels. Examples of cargo usually shipped in bulk are coal, coffee, crude oil, grain, scrap metal, etc.   T 543

Bulk Factoring See *Factoring*

Bulkhead A partition between different parts of a ship or other type of vessel.

Bunker Adjustment Factor Bunker oil is the lowest quality product obtained from crude oil. It is suitable only for large diesel engines, such as those used on ships. Since it is cheap, it is the most commonly used fuel in maritime transport, although it is also highly polluting. A bunker adjustment factor is a surcharge added to regular shipping rates in times of higher oil prices.   T 548

Cabotage Carriage of goods on water between ports within the same country. Many countries limit cabotage services to vessels flying the domestic flag. See, for example, the *Jones Act* of the U.S.

CAF or Currency Adjustment Factor A surcharge on maritime carriage or freight rates to compensate for currency fluctuations.

Call Option In sales transactions, the parties have to set the price in only one currency. This can be the seller's currency or the buyer's currency or, in particular if both parties are in countries with soft or non-convertible currencies, a third country currency. In particular, if there is a significant time between the formation of the contract and the time when payment is due, a fluctuation in exchange rates can have a major impact on the profitability and even desirability of the transaction for at least one of the parties. If the party who has to make payment in a foreign currency at a later point in time wants to hedge against unfavorable changes in value, she can agree with a potential seller on the right but not the obligation to purchase the currency at a given price at a future point in time or at any time before a given deadline. Thus, if the value of the foreign currency declines, she will buy on the open market. However, if the value of the foreign currency increases, she can call in her option and buy at a price that was previously determined and taken into account when the underlying IBT was negotiated. See also *Put Option*, *Forward Contract*, *Futures Contract*, and *Hedging*

Call and Put Options for Loans In securities transactions, for example *Bond* secured loans, interest rates may be fixed for long periods. This can bear a high risk for the borrower, if market rates decline significantly, or for the lender, if market rates increase significantly. *Call and Put Options* provide an escape clause for such cases. If a borrower has issued "callable" bonds, they can call these back from the bondholders/lenders before the maturity date if market rates drop significantly. Thus, the issuer can force an early repayment of a loan they can now obtain cheaper elsewhere. Naturally, the issuer/borrower will have to pay a higher interest rate for this option. Conversely, if a bond is "putable," the bondholder can put the bond back to the issuer before the maturity date and force an early repayment of the loan because they can now get a higher interest rate for their money elsewhere. Those bonds tend to command a lower interest rate.

Captain's Protest A document prepared by the captain of a ship to document damage or loss of cargo for presentation to the insurance.

CargoDocs Internet-based platform for the creation and transfer of   T 558
cargo and shipping documents.

Cargo Manifest A list of all cargo carried on a specific vessel at a
given time.

Cargo Tonnage In maritime shipping, cargo is either measured by
weight or by size (weight or measurement w/m). When "weight
tons" are used, they can refer to "short tons" (2000 pounds), "long
tons" (2240 pounds), or "metric tons" (1000 kilograms/2204.6
pounds). When the reference is to "measurement tons," it is either
calculated in units of 40 cubic feet (1.12 cubic meters) or in units
of cubic meters (1 cubic meter/35.3 cubic feet).

CARICOM The Caribbean Community is an international organization with 15 member states seeking to promote economic and
policy cooperation in the region.

Carmack Amendment The Carmack Amendment, 49 U.S.C. §   T 566, 592
10501(a)(2), was enacted in 1935 to provide uniform rules about
the rights and obligations of shippers and carriers in interstate
commerce. It holds carriers liable for damage to cargo unless they
can show that they were not negligent or that one of five exceptions
applies: (i) an Act of God; (ii) acts by public enemies; (iii) act or
default of the shipper; (iv) acts by public authorities; (v) inherent
vice or nature of the goods transported.

Carnet A customs document that allows duty-free importation on a
temporary basis, for example for a trade show. Duties only have to
be paid if the goods or vehicles are still in the country when the
Carnet expires. See also *Temporary Import Bonds (TIBs)* and *ATA
Carnet*

Carriage of Goods by Sea Act (U.S. 1936) See *COGSA*   D I-708

Carrier A natural person or corporate entity involved in the transportation of goods or persons by air, rail, road, or sea, or any combination of these modes of transportation.

Cartment A customs document that allows the transportation of
goods from one place to another while under customs bond, for
example during *Inward Processing.*

Case Management Conference Meeting between parties, attorneys,
and arbitrators to determine practical arrangements for an arbitration procedure.

Cash Against Documents (CAD) or D/P (Documents Against Payment) Payment term where the goods and/or the shipping charges have to be paid by the buyer before the bank hands over the *Bill of Lading (BoL)* or other title document required for release of the goods by the *Carrier*.

Cash in Advance (CIA) Payment term where the goods and/or the shipping charges have to be paid by the buyer before the goods are manufactured or sent.   T 418–428

Cash on Delivery (COD) Payment term where the goods and/or the shipping charges have to be paid by the buyer when she receives the goods.

Cash with Order (CWO) Payment term where the goods have to be paid by the buyer when the order is placed and before the goods are manufactured.

Caveat Emptor Buyer beware.   T 301

CCC Mark A mark attached by the manufacturer or importer on goods destined for sale in China to certify conformity with certain Chinese regulations and standards.

CE Mark A mark attached by the manufacturer or importer on goods destined for sale in the *European Economic Area (EEA)* to certify conformity with EU/EEA regulations and quality requirements.

Centre for Effective Dispute Resolution (CEDR) Provider of *Alternative Dispute Resolution (ADR)* resources and services.   T 874

Certificate of Acceptance Confirmation by the lessee that the goods or machines subject to a lease agreement have been delivered in conformity with the agreement.

Certificate of Inspection Confirmation by a third party that goods subject to an export/import agreement conform to certain contractual or regulatory requirements.

Certificate of Origin Confirmation by the authorities of the exporting country regarding the country of origin of the goods. The origin of wholly obtained goods is normally unproblematic. However, if goods are obtained from a third country and have been merely transshipped or modified in the exporting country, they may not qualify as originating goods from that country and may be treated differently by the customs authorities of the importing country.

Certificate of Service Official document confirming how and when a judicial or extrajudicial document was served on the addressee or defendant.

CFR ("C & F" or "cost and freight") An *INCOTERM*® pursuant to which the quoted price obligates the seller to perform (deliver the goods) at the stipulated destination *and* to organize and pay for *carriage* to this destination. The risk, however, passes to the buyer already when the goods pass the ship's rail, i.e., when they are handed over to the main *Carrier*, and the seller does not have to organize and pay for *insurance* beyond that point. Compare *CIF* and *CIP*. T 244

Chartered Institute of Arbitrators Provider of *Alternative Dispute Resolution (ADR)* resources and services. T 956, 969

Practice Guidelines for Interviews of Prospective Arbitrators T 970

Practice Guidelines Terms of Appointment Including Remuneration T 971–972

Charterparty A contract for "private carriage," i.e., a contract, usually written, between the owner of a vessel (ship or aircraft) and a client about the full and exclusive use of the vessel for the purposes of the client, usually the carriage of goods or persons from one place to another. The contract can be for a certain voyage (Voyage Charter), or for a certain time (Time Charter). Normally, the owner provides the vessel and crew, fully staffed and equipped, unless the contract is for a *Bareboat Charter*. See also UCP 600, Article 22 T 562–563

Check A simple *Financial Instrument* issued by a buyer and ordering his bank to make a payment immediately on demand to a named *Beneficiary*.

Choice of Forum Parties in B2B transactions have some discretion to choose the court or arbitral tribunal to decide any disputes that may arise between them. A public court may decline jurisdiction if it does not see a sufficient connection to the parties or the dispute (see also *Forum Non Conveniens*). T 145, 695, 759–767, 928

Choice of Law Parties in B2B transactions have wide discretion to choose the applicable substantive or contract law. However, they cannot avoid any applicable mandatory rules, e.g., on antitrust, consumer protection, or customs law. Furthermore, in litigation, a court will apply its own procedural rules and not allow a choice of law. Some element of choice may be achievable via a choice of forum. See also *Hierarchy of Norms* T 45–51, 113–149, 185, 211–214, 694

CIETAC China International Economic and Trade Arbitration Commission T 947

Claim A request or demand for specific monetary or non-monetary relief in litigation or ADR proceedings. See also *Statement of Claim, Counterclaim*, as well as *Cross-Claim*

Claimant See also *Respondent*. The claimant is natural or legal person that initiates litigation or ADR proceedings for monetary or non-monetary relief. In litigation, the terms "applicant" and "defendant" are more commonly used. In ADR, the terms "claimant" and "respondent" are usually preferred.

Claim Bases In IBT law, there are generally five potential *Claim Bases* to be considered: *Pre-Contractual*, contractual, torts, *Unjust Enrichment*, and property. Within these, *Primary Claims* are directed at *Performance* of the primary obligations of the parties under the IBT, i.e., delivery of the goods or services by the seller, and payment of the price by the buyer. If the primary performance is either no longer possible or insufficient to protect the other side, the primary claims can be replaced or supplemented by *Secondary Claims* for damages. In addition, parties may seek compensation for the *Costs of Dispute Settlement*, as well as *Interest*. T 60, 64

Claused Bill of Lading Same as a *Soiled BoL* or a *Foul BoL*

Clause Paramount A provision in a *Charterparty* or *Bill of Lading* incorporating a cargo liability regime, usually the *Hague Rules* or the *Hague-Visby Rules*, respectively the *COGSA*. A stand-alone *Bill of Lading* will usually have a direct reference to these rules. However, when there is a Charterparty, the BoL is no longer the contract of carriage and the addition of the Clause Paramount becomes necessary. Also, since the clause is "paramount," no other clause in the BoL, including individually negotiated clauses on the front of the contract, can overrule it and increase the carrier liability. See also *General Clause Paramount* and *United States Clause Paramount*, as well as *Himalaya Clause*   T 556–557, 566, 571

Clayton Act One of several U.S. anti-trust laws; the Clayton Act, *inter alia*, prohibits certain forms of price discrimination. See also *Sherman Act*

Clean Bill of Lading On a *Bill of Lading (BoL)*, the carrier will describe what she received for transportation to the point of destination. In most cases, the carrier has to rely on the specifications given by the shipper/exporter, for example if the goods are packaged in containers. However, if the carrier notices any irregularities, for example water or oil leaking from the packages or containers, she will make a note accordingly on the BoL. In this way, the carrier cannot be held liable for damage that had already occurred before the goods were handed over. A BoL with such notations is called a *Soiled* or *Foul Bill of Lading*, whereas a BoL without notations is called a Clean BoL confirming receipt "in apparent good order." In documentary sale transactions, the *Letter of Credit (L/C)* virtually always requires the presentation of a *Clean BoL* (see Article 27 UCP 600). Thus, if the shipper/exporter cannot get a *Clean BoL* from the carrier, she will not get paid under the L/C unless she can obtain a waiver from the consignee/importer/buyer before the L/C expires. For further discussion see, *inter alia*, Case 5-5.   T 656

Clearing Completion of a financial transaction involving exchange of goods for payment and/or exchange of documents for payment.

Clearing Systems See *Set-Off and Netting*

Closing Date Date when goods have to be handed over for shipment to avoid charges for delay.

CMI See *Comité Maritime International*

CMR Convention The 1956 UNECE Convention on the Contract for the International Carriage of Goods by Road, ratified by 55 countries in Europe, the Middle East, North Africa, the Caucasus, and Central Asia.   T 590, 593

CMR Road Consignment Note A *Road Transport Document* subject to the Convention on the Contract for the International Carriage of Goods by Road (*CMR Convention*). T 590

CMR Waybill See *CMR Road Consignment Note*

COD See *Cash on Delivery*

Code Civil The French civil code adopted in 1804, also called Code Napoléon. T 117–119

Codex Justinianus T 115

COGSA Carriage of Goods by Sea Act of the United States (1936). The *COGSA* is the U.S. implementation of the *Hague Rules*. T 563, 569–573, 575–583 + D I-708

Collateral Security for a loan or credit.

Collecting Bank Buyer's bank in a *Documentary Credit* or *Documentary Collection* transaction collecting cash payment or a *Time Draft* from the buyer in exchange for the *Bill of Lading* and other documents required by the buyer to receive the goods. T 520–523

Collection This is where a seller sends documents relating to a shipment through his or her bank, the *Remitting Bank*, to the buyer's bank, the *Collecting Bank*, asking that they are released when a payment is made (CAD or D/P) or a *Bill of Exchange* is accepted (D/A). See also *Documentary Collection* T 521

Collection Letter This is the cover form or letter sent by a bank or seller to a Presenting Bank, asking that the enclosed shipping documents are released to a buyer in exchange for payment or acceptance. See *Documentary Collection*

Combined Transport Bill of Lading A *Bill of Lading* used for *Multimodal Transport*.

COMECON The Council for Mutual Economic Assistance was the economic integration model forced by the Soviet Union upon its satellite states. T 13

Comité Maritime International (CMI) T 549, 556

Comity T 783, 824–827, 850

Comfort Letter A document making assurances about financial and professional qualities of another. For example, a parent company may issue a letter of introduction to potential business partners on behalf of a subsidiary, supplier, or customer. If a comfort letter is phrased as a unilateral promise to hold a third party harmless in case of problems, it can be legally enforceable as a contract, although in some jurisdictions questions of consideration may arise. In most cases, comfort letters create at best a moral obligation and are really just "comfort" letters.

Commercial Credit See *Letter of Credit (L/C)*

Commercial Invoice The bill sent by the seller to the buyer with the goods. It has to include a short description of the goods, including their quantity and price. If the seller is paid via *Letter of Credit*, complying presentation will require a Commercial Invoice with exactly conforming information about seller and buyer and the goods sold.. See UCP 600, Article 18.

Common Carrier A shipping company that operates or charters ships to carry goods, in particular containers, for multiple clients/shippers. Compare to *Private Carrier*	T 569
Common European Sales Law (CESL)	T 143
Common Frame of Refence (CFR) A draft civil code for the EU	T 132–143, 144 + D I-280
Contract formation	T 237–239
History	T 135–136
Performance and nonperformance	T 317–317
Purpose	T 137–139
Scope	T 136–137
Common Law	T 114
Communist Economic System	T 13, 15
Comparative Advantage/Disadvantage One of the reasons for trade. *Ricardo* showed for the first time that societies could benefit from specialization and trade even though they did not seem to have mutual absolute or relative advantages/disadvantages.	T 10–13

Competence-Competence See *Kompetenz-Kompetenz*

Competition

Cartel	T 23
Collusion by otherwise independent economic actors	T 23, 27

Complying Presentation Documents presented to a bank in compliance with a *Letter of Credit (L/C)*, giving the presenter a right to get paid.

Conciliation A method of *Alternative Dispute Resolution (ADR)* with the help of a neutral.

Confidentiality Agreement See *Nondisclosure Agreement (NDA)*

Confirmed Letter of Credit If there is a problem with a *Letter of Credit (L/C)*, the *Beneficiary* would normally have to bring claims against the *Issuing Bank*. If the *Issuing Bank* is in a country where claims by foreigners against financial institutions are not necessarily promising, the *Beneficiary* can ask for "confirmation" of the L/C by a bank in his own country. The *Confirming Bank* gives an independent promise to pay if a *Complying Presentation* is made by or on behalf of the *Beneficiary*. See also Article 8 UCP 600.

Confirming Bank A bank in seller's country used by buyer's bank, the *Issuing Bank*, to guarantee (confirm) a *Letter of Credit (L/C)*. By contrast an *Advising Bank* and a *Nominated Bank*, the *Confirming Bank* enters into an independent obligation to pay pursuant to the L/C even if it may not get reimbursed by the *Issuing Bank*.

Conflicts of Interest of arbitrators and other neutrals

Conflicts of Laws of different countries and how to resolve them

Consequential Damages

Consideration

Consignee Recipient of goods to be sold or transported.

Consignment A contract between the owner of goods, the *Consignor*, and a provider of services, the *Consignee*. The Consignment can be for transportation of the goods or for selling of the goods on behalf of the Consignor in exchange for a commission or fee.

Consignment Note Often used for road or rail transport instead of a *Bill of Lading*. Prepared either by the *Consignor* (sender) or the carrier, and signed by the carrier as proof of receipt of the goods to be transported for delivery to a given destination. By contrast to a *Bill of Lading*, a *Consignment Note* is usually not a contract of carriage and it is not negotiable.

Consignor Sender of a shipment by sea, road, rail, or air, also referred to as the shipper or exporter. Can also be the seller, charging a third party, the *Consignee*, to sell the goods on her behalf in exchange for a commission.

Constructive Service Notification of a defendant via service on a third party or publication in newspapers if the defendant cannot be located for personal *Service*.

Constructive Total Loss If property is damaged to the point that repair seems more expensive than justified by the remaining value of the property, a *Constructive Total Loss* may be declared. See s. 60, 1906 Marine Insurance Act (UK), as well as *Notice of Abandonment*

Consumer Arbitration See *Arbitration*

Container Freight Station (CFS) Facility where containers are inspected and weighed before rail, road, or sea transport.

Contingency Fee An arrangement with an attorney pursuant to which the client pays the attorney only if her case is successful and she gets paid by the other party. Typically, the attorney will take 30–40% of any monies awarded. Whether or not the attorney will cover filing fees and other costs if the case is unsuccessful depends on individual arrangements. See also *Attorney Fees*

Continuous Customs Bond or **Continuous Import Bond** See *Customs Bond*

Contract of Adhesion A standard form contract presented by one party, giving the other party little or no option to negotiate any of the terms, essentially forcing it to sign on the dotted line, to "take it or leave it."

Contract of Sale

Contra Proferentem Rule A general principle of contract law pursuant to which an ambiguous provision in a contract will be interpreted against the drafter and in favor of the other party.

Convention on Contracts for the International Sale of Goods (CISG) See *CISG*

Convention on the International Trade in Endangered Species (CITES) An example of *Mandatory Rules of (Public) Law or Policy* that could prevent an IBT from being lawfully executed and/or enforced.

Conversion An exercise of control over the property of another without the consent of the owner.

Corpus Iuris Civilis

Correspondent Bank A bank in a foreign country acting as an agent for a local bank that does not have a branch in that foreign country. The Correspondent Bank can be authorized to make or receive payments on behalf of the local bank or to represent it in other business transactions.

Cost of Dispute Settlement In IBT law, there are generally five potential *Claim Bases* to be considered: *Pre-Contractual*, contractual, torts, *Unjust Enrichment*, and property. Within these, *Primary Claims* are directed at *Performance* of the primary obligations of the parties under the IBT, i.e., delivery of the goods or services by the seller, and payment of the price by the buyer. If the primary performance is either no longer possible or insufficient to protect the other side, the primary claims can be replaced or supplemented by *Secondary Claims* for damages. In addition, parties may seek compensation for the *Costs of Dispute Settlement*, as well as *Interest*.

COTIF Convention Concerning International Carriage by Rail

Council for Mutual Economic Assistance See *COMECON*

Counter-Guarantee If buyer's bank wants to issue a *Payment Guarantee* to a seller in another country, it will need to involve a bank in seller's country since the seller would not want to present, let alone enforce, the *Guarantee* abroad. However, if seller's bank does not have a long-standing relationship with buyer's bank, it may ask for a *Counter-Guarantee* from buyer's bank before issuing the *Guarantee* letter to the seller. If a seller needs to provide a *Performance Guarantee* for a buyer in another country, the scenario would be the other way around. See also Article 5 URDG 758. — T 488–489, 512

Countertrade Sale of goods in exchange for other goods, rather than money; sometimes also called "barter trade."

Countervailing Duties While *Antidumping Duties* are imposed to offset unfairly low prices based on internal cross-subsidization by the manufacturer or exporter, countervailing duties are imposed to offset unfair subsidies by foreign governments.

Country Risk The likelihood that the political or economic situation in a country changes dramatically and negatively affects foreign investors and other international business partners.

Cover Transaction — T 183

CPT ("carriage paid to _____") An *INCOTERM®* pursuant to which the quoted price obligates the seller to perform (deliver the goods) at the stipulated seller's port of departure *and* to organize and pay for *carriage* to the stipulated destination, usually buyer's port. By contrast to *CFR*, this *INCOTERM®* is used for air, rail, or road transport, and in particular for multimodal transport. Like with *CFR*, the risk of damage to or loss of the goods passes to the buyer when the goods are handed over to the main carrier. Compare *CIF* and *CFR* — T 245

Credit Options for International Buyers — T 421–423

Credit Options for International Sellers — T 534–535

Credit Risk The likelihood that a buyer or seller cannot complete a transaction due to her inability to meet the contractual obligations after a deterioration in the financial position. See also *Default Risk*

Credit Risk Insurance Covers a percentage of the losses of a seller in case of default of her (foreign) buyer.

Cross-Claim If multiple parties are co-defendants because they may have "joint and several liability," one defendant can bring a *Cross-Claim* against another who is ultimately responsible. — T 570–573

Cryptocurrencies Digital-only currencies such as Bitcoin, Ether, Litecoin, or Ripple. These are not issued or controlled by any state authorities and exist only in digital wallets. *Cryptocurrencies* can be bought and sold and exchanged to and from *Fiat Currencies* on a number of online and physical exchanges or trading platforms such as Binance or Coinbase. They are typically secured on the *Blockchain*.

T 419

CTL *Constructive Total Loss*

Culpa in Contrahendo Literally "guilt in negotiations," the concept refers to a violation of the duty to negotiate in good faith and avoid harm to the other party during contract negotiations.

T 95–107

Cuniberti, Giles International legal scholar, Luxembourg

T 128

Currency Option A contract with a bank providing a right to a customer to purchase a certain amount of a foreign currency at a certain date and given price. In this way, a buyer can ensure that the price for a purchase does not increase due to currency fluctuations between conclusion of the contract and the time when payment is due. By contrast to a *Forward Transaction*, the customer is not obligated to exercise the option. However, if the customer does not exercise the option, for example because the exchange rate has declined and she can buy the currency cheaper elsewhere, the bank will usually collect an *option premium*. See also *Call Option*, *Put Option*, and *Hedging*

Currency Risk The possibility that the exchange rate between seller's and buyer's currencies changes significantly between conclusion of a contract and the time when payment is due.

Customary International Law One of the three main sources of international law, next to treaties and general principles of law. Customary international law is formed when countries consistently act in certain ways (custom) while under the impression of being obliged to do so (opinio iuris).

Customs Public authorities charged with the supervision of imports and the levying of import duties/tariffs.

Customs and Border Protection (CBP)

T 589

Customs Bond A kind of insurance or surety contract to guarantee compliance with customs procedures and requirements. On the basis of 19 U.S.C. §1623, U.S. Customs and Border Protection (CBP) requires a bond before processing international cargo, a so-called "International Carrier Bond." If any customs obligations or other legal requirements are not met by the importer or the carrier, CBP collects fees and fines from the surety provider rather than having to track down the carrier or importer. Customs bonds can be for single shipments ("single entry bonds") or for all shipments over a period of time ("annual" or "continuous bonds").

The amount required depends on the goods, the country of origin, and potentially other factors.

Customs Bonded Warehouse See *Bonded Warehouse*

Customs Broker A service provider helping exporters and importers with customs filings and procedures.

Customs Clearance Completion of customs formalities, including payment of any import duties/tariffs, and release of the goods into free circulation in the importing country.

Customs Cooperation Council (CCC) Former name of the *World Customs Organization.*

Customs Union Two or more countries having agreed on common import regulations and duties/tariffs towards third countries and the abolition of internal duties/tariffs between the members of the *Customs Union*. The *European Union* goes beyond a *Customs Union* with its harmonization of various trade rules across the internal market. By contrast, the *USMCA* is merely a *Free Trade Area* without common external tariffs and regulations.

D/A (Documents Against Acceptance) Mostly used in *Documentary Collection*, if the controlling documents (*Bill of Lading* etc.) are presented to the buyer in exchange for acceptance of the payment obligation via a *Time Draft*. Compare to *D/P* (Documents Against Payment), where the buyer has to pay at sight with cash or with a *Sight Draft* to get the controlling documents.

T 524

Damage Claims In IBT law, there are generally five potential *Claim Bases* to be considered: *Pre-Contractual*, contractual, torts, *Unjust Enrichment*, and property. Within these, *Primary Claims* are directed at *Performance* of the primary obligations of the parties under the IBT, i.e., delivery of the goods or services by the seller, and payment of the price by the buyer. If the primary performance is either no longer possible or insufficient to protect the other side, the primary claims can be replaced or supplemented by *Secondary Claims* for damages. In addition, parties may seek compensation for the *Costs of Dispute Settlement*, as well as *Interest*. See also *Proximate Cause, Force Majeure,* and *Mitigation of Damages*

T 60,
308–315

DAP ("delivered at place") An *INCOTERM®* pursuant to which the quoted price obligates the seller to perform (deliver the goods) at a specified place in buyer's country. Seller has to organize and pay for shipping and insurance to this point but buyer is responsible for unloading and customs clearance, if necessary, as well as final delivery. Selection of *DPU* accomplishes much the same thing, except that the seller would also have to organize and pay for unloading.

T 245

DAT ("delivered at terminal") An *INCOTERM*® pursuant to which the quoted price obligated the seller to perform (deliver the goods) at a terminal at buyer's port. Seller had to organize and pay for shipping and insurance to this point, as well as unloading, but buyer was responsible for customs clearance and final delivery. *DAT* was replaced with *DAP* and *DPU* with the 2020 update to the INCOTERMS®.

Data Protection See *General Data Protection Regulation (GDPR) of the European Union*

DDP ("delivered duty paid") An *INCOTERM*® pursuant to which the quoted price obligates the seller to perform (deliver the goods) at the quoted destination, usually the buyer's place of business. The seller is responsible for organizing and all expenses related to shipping and insurance all the way to the place of business of the buyer. — T 246

Debtor Insurance/Export Credit Insurance An insurance policy purchased by a seller to provide protection against non-payment by a buyer due to insolvency or political/economic turmoil in buyer's country.

Default Award Similar to a court, an arbitral tribunal may be able to issue a *Default Award* if the *Respondent* does not participate in the arbitration procedures. — T 1000

Default Judgment — T 750

Default Risk The probability of a state, corporation, bank, or individual defaulting on repayment of debt obligations. For states and corporations the risk is measured via credit ratings provided by Standard & Poor's, Moody's, or Fitch Ratings. For consumers, *FICO* scores provide a measure of the default risk. As a rule, obtaining credit becomes more expensive, or impossible, for higher-risk borrowers.

Defendant Court The public court(s) in the country and district where the defendant has her *Domicile*. — T 693

Deferred Payment Letter of Credit A *Letter of Credit* payable at a specified or determinable future date. At maturity, a *Bill of Exchange* or *Draft* is not required to evidence the maturity date and the exact amount, which was already provided in the Deferred Payment Credit. The purpose of a Deferred Payment L/C is for the *Beneficiary*, i.e., the seller, to give a grace period to the *Applicant*, i.e., the buyer. During this time, the merchandise can arrive and the buyer can use or re-sell it. Alternatively, buyer and seller can use a regular L/C and a *Term Bill of Exchange* or a *Time Draft*, in particular if the date when payment should be made or the exact amount to be paid under the L/C are not yet known. Also, a Deferred Payment L/C is not (easily) negotiable; if the Beneficiary may want to sell her right to payment, the involvement of a *Draft* is advisable. See also *Acceptance Credit*, and *Deferred Reimbursement Letter of Credit*

Deferred Reimbursement Letter of Credit From the perspective of the *Beneficiary*, this is a regular *Letter of Credit*, payable upon presentation of the required documents or at some point in time thereafter. However, the *Applicant* or buyer has an arrangement with the *Issuing Bank* pursuant to which the bank gives a grace period to the buyer before it seeks payment. During this time, the merchandise can arrive and the buyer can use or re-sell it. In effect, the Issuing Bank gives an unsecured loan to the Applicant. See also *Deferred Payment Letter of Credit*

Deferred Tax Principle according to which parent companies do not have to pay taxes on the income of their foreign subsidiaries until they actually receive some of that income.

Delay as nonperformance and/or cause for damage claims   T 313

Del Credere Clause Clause in a contract of sale whereby the sales agent acting on behalf of the principal/buyer also guarantees the payment obligations of the buyer. See CFR IV.E. – 3:313.

Delivery Charge Usually refers to cost of delivery from destination port to buyer facility.

Demand Guarantee If a bank has given a *Demand Guarantee* to back   T 488, up the payment obligation of a buyer, the seller can immediately   511–519 demand payment from the bank upon a breach by the buyer. If the seller sends a statement of breach and a written demand for payment to the bank, the guarantee is as good as cash and the seller does not need to provide further documents or evidence, as it would be the case with a *Suretyship Guarantee*. A demand guarantee is similar to a *Standby Letter of Credit*. It differs from a normal *Letter of Credit* (L/C) because the latter is intended as the primary form of payment, while the *Demand Guarantee* kicks in only after the intended primary form of payment has failed. See also URDG 758, D I-552.

Demurrage In shipping, this refers to a delay that is compensated   T 471
by payment of a fee. Typically, carriers will charge container
Demurrage if the consignee does not pick up the container with
the cargo within a couple of "free days" after arrival at the port
of destination. By contrast to *Demurrage*, the fee for late return
of the empty container is usually referred to as *Detention*. In bulk
or special cargo trading, ships are usually chartered for specific
dates and the freight rates for the voyage are calculated for those
dates. If the loading or off-loading takes longer, the shipowner will
demand *Demurrage* from the shipper/cargo owner/charterer who
is responsible for the loading/off-loading. By contrast, if the charterer gets the job done faster, she may be able to claim *Despatch* for
time saved in port. In currency trading, *Demurrage* is a fee charged
for holding on to currency and intended to push banks to circulate
money rather than hoarding it.

Department of Homeland Security (DHS)   T 589

Despatch In shipping, this is a financial bonus that can be claimed if
the loading or off-loading of a ship is done faster than agreed and
the time in port can be reduced.

Destination Delivery Charge (DDC) Covers handling of shipments
at destination port.

Detention In shipping, this refers to a fee charged by a carrier for extra
days during which a seller/exporter holds on to a container before
having it ready for pick-up or during which a buyer/importer holds
on to a container while unloading it. Typically, carriers will grant
a couple of "free days" for the exporter to load the container and
the importer to unload it. Detention is charged for days beyond
the free days.

Deviation (from a scheduled shipping contract) Under most legal   T 567
systems, the carrier has some freedom to re-route the goods or
change the vessels or mode of transport as needed. If delay or damage occurs in such cases, the question arises whether the *Deviation* was "unreasonable" and, therefore, any limitations on carrier
liability may no longer apply. See also *Liberty Clauses*

DEWIP Formula to remember the five forms of evidence in litiga-   T 989
tion and arbitration: documents, experts, witnesses, inspection of
things or places, parties.

DG Approver A person working for or on behalf of a carrier (shipping line) to handle the paperwork for shipment of dangerous goods. The *DG Approver* first checks whether the cargo specifications are in line with the rules in the current edition of the *IMDG Code* issues by the *International Maritime Organization (IMO)*. Then the *DG Approver* notifies the captain of the ship, any intended storage facilities, as well as the authorities at the ports of departure and arrival, and any transit or transshipment ports. After receiving approvals from all parties, the *DG Approver* notifies the cargo owner and the carrier confirms the booking. If any parties refuse to approve the shipment of the dangerous goods as intended, the *DG Approver* works with the cargo owner to modify the paperwork and/or intended route to see whether alternative arrangements will receive the necessary approvals.

Digital Transaction Management (DTM)   T 355

Direct Applicability of international norms in the national legal   T 35
order

Direct Effect of international norms in the national legal order   T 35

Discharge Unloading of the cargo at the port of destination; see *Port of Discharge*

Discounting The purchase of an accepted *Term Bill of Exchange* or   T 473, 484,
a *Letter of Credit* with a deferred payment *Maturity Date* at a dis-   522
count as a means of funding an advance from the discount date
until the maturity date of the bill or L/C.

Discounting Bank The bank that buys a *Term Bill of Exchange* or
another *Financial Instrument* at a discount before its *Maturity Date*, thus giving the *Beneficiary* or *Holder* earlier access to the
funds.

Discovery See *Pre-Trial Discovery*, as well as *Evidence*

Discrepancy An inconsistency of required and presented docu-   T 434–449
ments with the terms of a *Letter of Credit* (L/C) or an inconsistency between various presented documents required by a *Letter of
Credit* as condition of payment. The opposite would be a *Complying Presentation*.

Discriminatory Pricing Selling the same goods for different prices
in different markets, although the price difference is not justified
by differences in cost. This may be a violation of competition or
anti-trust rules.

Dishonor Refusal by a bank or other *Drawee* to accept a *Bill of*   T 450–484
Exchange or *Letter of Credit* and pay the stipulated sum of money.
Six grounds have been accepted in U.S. courts for the refusal to
honor a presentation: fraud, illegality, nullity, unconscionable
conduct, noncomplying documents, and expiration. See also UCC
§3-502, as well as Articles 14–16 UCP600.

Distributed Ledger Technology (DLT) See also *Blockchain*   T 356

Diversity Jurisdiction If an out-of-state person is sued in-state, she   T 721
can have the case removed to federal court based on diversity.

DocDex An abbreviation for the ICC's "Documentary Instruments
Dispute Resolution Expertise." Parties to a dispute over the interpretation of ICC rules regarding Documentary Credit (UCP 600),
Standby Letters of Credit (ISP98), bank-to-bank reimbursements
(URR 725), documentary collection (URC 522), demand guarantees and/or counter guarantees (URDG 758), forfaiting transactions (URF 800), bank payment obligations (URBPO 750), or
any other trade finance related rules or agreements, can request
a DocDex Decision from an ICC expert panel. Although technically not an arbitral award, thus not enforceable via the New York
Convention, the decisions are binding if all parties have agreed to
the procedure. Since they are obtainable within 2–3 months at
a relatively low cost (ca. 5,000–10,000$), DocDex can be a useful
tool enabling parties to avoid more time- and cost-intensive litigation or arbitration.

Dock Receipt Confirmation by a shipping company or *Carrier* that
goods have been received for shipment.

Dockside Damage to cargo and the question whether it is covered by   T 667–671
a marine cargo insurance contract

Documentary Collection When *Letters of Credit* are used, the buyer   T 520–533
and buyer's bank use the services of an *Advising Bank* and/or a
Nominated Bank and/or a *Confirming Bank* in seller's country
to "purchase" the controlling documents from the seller. When
Documentary Collection is used, the seller and seller's bank use the
services of a *Presenting Bank* in buyer's country to "sell" the controlling documents to the buyer. *Documentary Collection* is more
risky and less convenient for the seller. However, it may be cheaper,
since the banks carry no risk and provide no credit. See also *D/P*
and *D/A*

Documentary Credit A *Letter of Credit* that requires a number of
documents to be presented with a *Draft*. The opposite (and highly
unusual) is a clean credit that allows withdrawals without further
requirements.

Documentary Evidence   T 53–59

Documentary Sale A transaction, often international, involving mul-   T 71–82,
tiple legal documents, including a contract of sale, a financing or   429
payment contract, a shipping contract, and an insurance contract.
See also *Four Corners Model*

DocuSign Provider of *Digital Transaction Management (DTM)*   T 355, 403–
services   407, 558

Dodge, William International legal scholar, Davis   T 121

Domicile The residence of a natural person or seat of a company for   T 44, 704,
legal purposes.   715, 787

Domke, Martin International lawyer and arbitrator, New York   T 879

Domke on Commercial Arbitration Textbook available on Westlaw   T 879

Double Taxation Agreement (DTA)   T 30

D/P (Documents Against Payment) or **CAD** (Cash Against Docu-   T 524
ments) Mostly used in *Documentary Collection*, if the controlling documents (*Bill of Lading* etc.) are presented to the buyer in
exchange for payment at sight in cash or with a *Sight Draft*. Compare to D/A (Documents Against Acceptance) where payment is
made with a *Time Draft*.

DPU ("delivered at place unloaded") An *INCOTERM*® pursuant to   T 246
which the quoted price obligates the seller to perform (deliver the
goods) at a specified place in buyer's country. Seller has to organize and pay for shipping and insurance to this point, including
unloading, but buyer is responsible for customs clearance, if necessary, and final delivery.

Draft When submitting a *Letter of Credit* for "payment," "acceptance," or "negotiation," the beneficiary, i.e., the seller, will also
have to submit a "Draft" or *Bill of Exchange* demanding payment.
The Draft is made out in the name of the issuer or *Drawer*, i.e., the
seller, and addressed to the *Drawee*, i.e., the bank or person from
whom payment is demanded.

Draft Common Frame of Reference (DCFR) See *Common Frame of
Reference*

Drawback (of Customs Duties) A government program that refunds
import duties paid on raw materials or components if they are processed in country and then re-exported as part of (more) finished
products (manufacturing drawback). A refund may also be available if imported goods were rejected by the buyer or otherwise not
used (condition drawback).

Drawee The person to whom a *Bill of Exchange* is addressed for pay- T 524–527
ment or *Acceptance*. In most international transactions this is the
buyer. If the buyer has given a *Letter of Credit*, the *Drawee* may be
the *Issuing Bank* or the *Nominated Bank* or the *Confirming Bank*. If
the buyer is in default, the *Drawee* may be a bank having provided
a *Guarantee* or *Stand-by Letter of Credit*.

Drawer The person who issues a *Bill of Exchange*. In most international sales transactions this is the seller or another person who
has the right to get paid.

Drayage Local transport by truck; charge for local transport by truck.

Drop and Pull An agreement that a trucking company will drop off
a container for loading or unloading and pick it up again a few
hours later.

Dual Pricing See *Discriminatory Pricing*

Dualist State T 33–34

Dubai International Finance Center (DIFC) T 720

Due Process pursuant to Article 6 of the European Convention on T 772
Human Rights

Due Process Clause in U.S. Constitution T 755

Dumping Selling goods in a foreign market below cost or below the
prices charged in other markets. Since this may threaten domestic
competitors in that market, it may trigger anti-dumping duties.

Dunnage Inexpensive material used to fill up empty spaces between
goods or in containers to protect the goods from moving and getting damaged.

Duty A tax or charge imposed by an importing country to increase
the price of foreign goods and provide a measure of protection
for domestic competitors, as well as a source of revenue for the
government. Duties typically vary from one product to another,
depending on the existence and competitiveness of domestic manufacturers. They may also vary for different countries of origin of
the goods. Duties are often also referred to as *Tariffs*.

Duty Drawback A system where manufacturers can receive a refund
of the duties paid on imported components if they export the final
product.

e-Commerce See *Electronic Contracts*

Economic Risk See *Country Risk*

ECOWAS The Economic Community of West African States T 39

Effective Exchange Rate The rate actually applied in the market, including any taxes, fees, and commissions.

Electronic Data Interchange (EDI) is a system for the transfer of data in one of several electronic formats or standards. Companies adhering to the same standard (usually determined by the respective industry) can exchange approved documents like purchase orders, pro forma invoices, contracts, invoices, bills of lading, and various notices, via e-mail, cloud storage, web download, etc. EDI is not widely used for inter-bank communication, however. To that end, see *SWIFT*.

E-mail communication in contract formation See *Electronic Contracts*

Endorsement If a *Check* or *Letter of Credit (L/C)* is negotiable, the named *Beneficiary* can transfer the instrument by endorsing it and handing it to a third party. Endorsement means signing on the back of the instrument. Every recipient of a check does this when taking the check to her bank for deposit into her account. Since the recipient is the named *Beneficiary* of the check and not the bank, the bank requires the endorsement as proof that they have received the check with the consent of the named *Beneficiary* and are now entitled to present it to the *Issuing Bank*, who will then debit it from the account of the issuer and send the money. Article 3 of the UCC uses the term Indorsement instead of Endorsement, see, e.g., §3-204. See also *Negotiation*

Evergreen Clause An evergreen clause provides for the automatic renewal of a contract unless notice is given by one of the parties. For example, a contract may stipulate that it is concluded for one year and will automatically renew for another year at a time unless terminated by a certain date. Evergreen clauses are common in service, distribution, and supply contracts, and may also appear in lease agreements. Not all jurisdictions will enforce evergreen clauses in all B2B cases, in particular if the clauses were not disclosed at the time of conclusion of the original contract, are less than clear and unambiguous, renewal is for a full year or more at a time, and/or the notification deadline is very short. Additional limitations apply in consumer contracts.

Evidence in international arbitration   T 989–996

Evidence in transnational litigation   T 816–827

Exequatur An official decision or document allowing the enforcement of a judgment or similar judicial decision.

Exorbitant Jurisdictions The jurisdiction of a court over the parties   T 701, 706, to a dispute is generally based on voluntary submission by the par-   856 ties or domicile in the court district. Certain other grounds, such as nationality of the forum state or doing business in the forum state, are also accepted. Beyond those grounds, jurisdictional claims fall under *Exorbitant Jurisdictions* and are rarely recognized by other countries. See more generally *Jurisdiction*

Expert Determination A method of *Alternative Dispute Resolution*   T 861–879 *(ADR)* with the help of a neutral.

Export Controls Supervisory procedures to prevent exportation of goods for reasons of national security or trade sanctions. See https://www.trade.gov/us-export-controls

Export Credit Insurance Insurance provided by a public authority or private company to indemnify an exporter for nonpayment by foreign buyers.

Export Development Canada (EDC) A government agency provid-   T 535 ing export support and credit for Canadian companies similar to the *Export-Import Bank of the U.S.*

Export-Import Bank of the U.S.   T 422, 430,
                                                              489

Export License See *Export Controls*

Express Bill of Lading A BoL issued electronically, rather than in several originals. The pdf can be sent via e-mail instead of paper copies sent by courier. However, an electronic BoL can get into the wrong hands and, therefore, is not a document of title and not negotiable. It still serves as a receipt for the goods and a shipping contract but is usually referred to as a *Sea Waybill*, rather than a BoL. — T 554

Express Sea Waybill See also *Express Bill of Lading* and *Sea Waybill* — T 564

Externalities External cost and other factors, such as environmental pollution, an economic actor may choose to ignore in the absence of regulatory intervention. The leading author on "the protection of the commons" is *Ostrom*. — T 19

Extraterritorial Jurisdiction — T 29

EXW ("ex works") An *Incoterm*® pursuant to which the quoted price obligates the seller to perform (deliver the goods) at his own place of business. The buyer is responsible for organizing and all expenses related to shipping and insurance. — T 241

Factor A finance company engaged in *Factoring*

Factoring A form of *Supply Chain Financing (SCF)* in which a supplier sells her *Accounts Receivable* to a *Factor* at a discount to get paid before payment from her customers would normally be due. The *Factor* purchases the right to collect at a discount and takes it upon himself to get paid by the customers of the original supplier. Depending on the creditworthiness of the customers and the length of time until maturity, the Factor will pay about 75% of the invoice value up front and another 15–20% upon successful collection. *Factoring* is cheaper if it allows recourse, i.e., if a customer does not pay at maturity, the *Factor* can take recourse and get reimbursed from the supplier. If the customers have poor credit or had problems in the past, non-recourse Factoring may not be offered or may be too expensive. See also *Back-to-Back Factoring*, as well as *Bulk Factoring*, *Reverse Factoring*, and *Invoice Discounting* — T 421, 534

FAS ("free alongside ship") An *INCOTERM*® pursuant to which the quoted price obligates the seller to perform (deliver the goods) at the port. The seller is responsible for export clearance but the buyer is responsible for organizing and paying for the main carriage and insurance. — T 242

FCA ("free carrier") An *INCOTERM*® pursuant to which the quoted price obligates the seller to perform (deliver the goods) to the main carrier at a stipulated place. The seller is responsible for export clearance but the buyer is responsible for organizing and all expenses related to the main carriage and insurance. See also *FOB* — T 241

FCL Shipment "Full container load," see also *LCL Shipment* or "less than container load."

FCR A common abbreviation for *Forwarder's Cargo Receipt*. While a   T 201, 209
Bill of Lading (BoL) is issued by an actual carrier, an *FCR* is issued
by a *Freight Forwarder* taking temporary possession of the cargo
until carriage is organized and begins. By contrast to a *BoL*, an
FCR is not a transport document, it is not a document of title, and
it is not negotiable. As a substitute for a *BoL* in the list of documents required by a *Letter of Credit*, an FCR does not provide the
same level of security for the buyer.

FDUTPA Florida Deceptive and Unfair Trade Practices Act   T 267

Federal Aviation Authority (FAA)   T 589

Federal E-Sign Act   T 361, 388

Federal Maritime Commission   T 666

Federal Railroad Administration   T 592

Fee Shifting Under the *English Rule*, the cost of litigation, including   T 791–792
reasonable attorney fees of the prevailing party, will be shifted to
the unsuccessful party. By contrast, under the *American Rule*, each
side typically has to cover its own costs and honoraria regardless
of the outcome of the case. See also *Attorney Fees*, as well as *Contingency Fee*

Ferrari, Franco International lawyer and arbitrator, New York   T 217, 921

Fiat Currencies Regular national currencies, by contrast to   T 419
Cryptocurrencies

Fidelity Guarantee *All Risks* insurance normally excludes damage
or theft caused by employees of the assured party and other individuals authorized or contracted to handle the cargo (see *Institute
Cargo Clauses* A 4.1). A Fidelity Guarantee policy covers this kind
of loss or damage. However, it will include a significant deductible
to motivate the assured party to carefully select and supervise her
employees and agents.

Financial Instrument A document, including an electronic document, containing an unconditional promise of payment of a specified sum of money. Examples are checks and money orders. UCC
§3-104(b) defines an instrument as *Negotiable Instrument*, unless
otherwise specified.

Finding a Lawyer in a Foreign Jurisdiction   T 788–790

First Port of Call The first port of entry where customs procedures
have to be completed, sometimes also referred to as the *Bond Port*.

Fitzgerald, Peter International legal scholar, Gulfport · · · · · T 122, 186

Fixture An agreement between a cargo owner ("shipper") and a ship owner ("carrier"), often with the help of a broker, reserving the ship for a certain voyage and cargo (e.g., 25,000 tons of scrap metal from Livorno (Italy) to Guangzhou (China) with loading to begin on 1 October and off-loading to finish on or before 15 November).

Flags of Convenience Although merchant ships may be owned by companies in the U.S. or the EU, they are often sailing under the flag of a country like Liberia or Panama, where the health and safety standards are lower and modern Western labor laws and protections do not apply. One way of fighting this *Race to the Bottom* is the effort of establishing *Port State Control*. · · · · · T 548

FOB ("free on board") An *Incoterm*® pursuant to which the quoted price obligates the seller to perform (deliver the goods) at the port of departure. The seller is responsible for export clearance but the buyer is responsible for organizing and all expenses related to the main carriage and insurance. The risk passes to the buyer when the good cross the ship's rail. · · · · · T 243

Force Majeure · · · · · T 181, 216, 257, 280–295, 316–321, 335, 339, 353

Foreign Currency Drafts These are special foreign currency denominated bank cheques that customers can buy at any branch and send to their clients to pay off debts.

Foreign Direct Investment · · · · · T 16

Forfaiting A method of trade financing used for larger projects with longer payment horizons. In exchange for advancing the costs, for example for an infrastructure project, the seller obtains a bank or government guarantee from the buyer for 100% of accounts receivable. The receivables together with the guarantee are then sold to a financier at a discount. The *Forfaiter* assumes the risk of nonpayment "without recourse" and the seller obtains immediate cash. · · · · · T 422, 534

Formation of Contracts See *CISG* and *UCC*

Forum Choice See *Choice of Forum*

Free Trade Area An agreement between two or more countries pursuant to which the trade in (most) originating products between them is free from import/export duties. An example is the *USMCA* treaty, successor to *NAFTA*. By contrast, a *Customs Union* goes further and also harmonizes the external duties and trade rules of the participating countries. This enables the *Customs Union* to have open borders between its members since there is no need to check the origin of the goods.

Freezing Order An *Interim Relief* order securing assets of the defendant.   T 794

Freight Forwarder A freight forwarder makes shipping arrangements for the party to a contract of sale responsible for carriage. In addition to booking space with a *Carrier*, the freight forwarder may issue an *FCR* or forwarder's cargo receipt if she takes physical possession of the cargo before it is handed to the actual carrier. Sometimes freight forwarders even issue the *Bill of Lading* on behalf of the carrier when the goods are loaded onto the transport vessel. Some freight forwarders offer additional services such as arranging for pickup of the cargo from seller's premises and transportation to the port, inspection of the cargo, export clearance, and/or insurance.

Friedman, Milton International economist, Chicago   T 27–28

FTA See *Free Trade Area*

Full Faith and Credit Clause of the U.S. Constitution   T 110, 830–832, 838–847

Fully Integrated Contract or Agreement. A final written expression of the agreement between the parties that supersedes any earlier communications, drafts, and offers.   T 73, 350, 395–396

Fumigation Certificate Many countries require wood products or wooden packaging, including pallets, to be fumigated against unintended importation of insects or insect eggs or larvae.

Fundamental Breach (CISG)   T 142, 180, 183, 297, 301

FX Future Contract   T 410

Gabriel, Henry International legal scholar, Greensboro   T 120, 126, 144

GAFTA Grain and Feed Trade Association   T 953

Galanter, Marc International legal scholar, Madison   T 691

Garner, Bryan American legal scholar, Austin T 66, 69

GDPR General Data Protection Regulation of the *European Union* T 375–376

General Agreement on Tariffs and Trade (GATT) T 38

General Agreement on Trade in Services (GATS) T 38

General Average Average refers to the loss incurred when a ship and/ or its cargo is lost or damaged and full insurance is not available. *General Average* can be declared when some cargo is thrown overboard in order to save a ship during a storm. It means that the vessel owner/operator and all cargo owners share the loss of the party whose cargo was sacrificed. As a consequence, a cargo owner or her insurer can face claims even if her own cargo arrived undamaged. See s. 66 1906 Marine Insurance Act (UK) (D I-744), as well as *York Antwerp Rules* (D I-762), *Particular Average*, and *FPA Insurance Coverage*

General Clause Paramount A shipping contract clause typically used to incorporate the *Hague Rules* (D I-648) or the *Hague Visby Rules* (D I-655) into the contract. The most important effect is the limitation of liability via contractual acceptance by the cargo owner/ shipper. See also *United States Clause Paramount*

General Data Protection Regulation (GDPR) of the *European Union* T 375–376

Goode, Roy International lawyer and arbitrator, London T 127, 423

Good Faith Obligations T 302

Green Clause Letter of Credit See *Red Clause Letter of Credit*

Group of Companies Doctrine T 990

Gross Weight The total weight of the goods with packaging, pallets, container, etc. See also *Net Weight*

Guarantee A written promise (*Guarantee Letter*) by one party, the *Guarantor*, to pay if another party fails to pay its debts or perform its obligations. *Guarantees* are very flexible and can be used to secure a wide range of obligations, for examples, see *Advance Payment Guarantee, Bank Guarantee, Bid Bond/Guarantee, Bond, Counter-Guarantee, Demand Guarantee, Performance Bond/Guarantee*

Independence T 515, 519

Guaranteed Bill of Exchange To be protected against changes in the financial standing of a business partner, the *Drawer* of a *Term Bill of Exchange* (usually the seller) can ask the *Drawee* (usually the buyer) to add a *Guarantee* by her bank that the bill will be paid at maturity. The guarantee kicks in only if the drawee is in default.

particular with regard to "liability for loss or damage arising from negligence, fault, or failure in proper loading, stowage, custody, care, or proper delivery of any and all lawful merchandise or property." In practice, therefore, virtually all Bills of Lading drawn up in the U.S. include a choice of law clause in favor of *COGSA*. See *Carmack Amendment*

Hayek, Friedrich International economist, Vienna and London   T 27

Heckscher-Ohlin Theory of Trade   T 12

Hedging The practice of reducing the risk of adverse price developments in the market for foreign currency, commodities, interest rates, certain stocks, etc. by entering into contracts (*Futures Contracts*) that secure these assets at a known price at a given future date. See also *Call Option* and *Put Option*, as well as *Forward Contract*, *FX Future Contract*, and *Currency Option*

Hierarchy of Norms If more than one rule or set of rules is applicable   T 52, 63
to a particular question, and the different rules cannot be applied simultaneously because they are at least in some aspects incompatible or contradictory, the Hierarchy of Norms determines which rule or rules have priority.

Himalaya Clause A shipping contract clause that incorporates a limi-   T 557,
tation of liability regime, such as the *Hague Rules* or the *Hague*   595–600
Visby Rules, or the *COGSA*, into the shipping contract and extends the limitations beyond the parties to the contract to their servants, agents, subcontractors, downstream delivery carriers, and other persons acting on their behalf or in fulfillment of the obligations under the contract. The name originates from and English case involving a steamship called "Himalaya."

H & M Coverage Insurance contract for hull and machinery.   T 638, 647

Holder The person in physical possession of a *Financial Instrument* like a *Check* or *Bill of Exchange*.

Holder in Due Course See UCC §3-302.

Hot tubbing A discovery method where two or more experts are asked to get together and set out to what extent they agree and disagree on the facts or questions before an arbitral tribunal.

Howse, Robert International trade lawyer, New York   T 31

Hunter, Martin International lawyer and arbitrator, London   T 955, 989

IBA See *International Bar Association*

IBA Drafting Guidelines for Multi-Tier Dispute Resolution Clauses   T 957

IMDG Code The "International Maritime Dangerous Goods Code" is issued by the *International Maritime Organization* and updated every two years. It provides rules for the carriage of dangerous goods intended to protect both the marine and coastal environment and the individuals handling the goods, such as crew members, warehouse staff, etc. The Code includes rules on packaging, labeling, handling, storage, and emergency procedures in cases of accidents or spills. It covers, *inter alia*, explosives, flammable and toxic gases, flammable liquids, flammable solids, combustible substances, oxidizing substances, toxic substances, infectious substances, radioactive materials, corrosive substances, and various other dangerous substances.

IMO See *International Maritime Organization*

Inchmaree Clause A clause in marine hull insurance contracts protecting the owners against negligence by the master or crew, for example in navigation of the ship.

Interim Relief The possibility of getting a temporary decision from a court or arbitral tribunal to prevent harm that may occur before a final decision of the court or tribunal is made. See also *Prejudgment Attachment of Assets* (U.S.), *Freezing Order* (UK), *Negative Injunction, Quia Timet Injunction, Mareva Injunction, Anton Piller Order,* and *Writ ne exeat regno.* T 793–816, 976–979

Interline Waybill A *Waybill* issued for a shipment to be handled by more than one carrier.

Interlocutory Relief See *Interim Relief*

Intermodal Transport Bill of Lading A *Bill of Lading* used for *Multimodal Transport*

Internal Market of the EU T 133

International Bar Association (IBA) Professional organization representing bar associations, law societies, law firms, and individual lawyers from more than 170 countries in the promotion of law reform and professional standards. T 50

International Business Transaction See *IBT*

International Centre for Dispute Resolution (ICDR) of the *American Arbitration Association* Provider of ADR Services T 875

International Chamber at Paris Commercial Courts T 696

International Chamber of Commerce (ICC) Professional organization supporting more than 45 million companies in more than 100 countries in their cross-border transactions. T 49, 694

International Court of Arbitration (of the ICC) T 956

International Civil Aviation Organization (ICAO) T 589

International Commercial Arbitration See *Arbitration*

International Institute for Conflict Prevention & Resolution (CPR) Provider of Alternative Dispute Resolution (ADR) Services T 864, 873, 877

International Institute for the Unification of Private Law See *UNIDROIT*

International Law
Definition T 32
Remedies T 36
Sources T 32–44

International Maritime Organization (IMO) The IMO is a special-   T 548–549
ized agency of the United Nations "with responsibility for the
safety and security of shipping and the prevention of marine pollution by ships." To this end, the IMO develops conventions for
adoption by the UN member states, as well as guidelines and other
rules that can be adhered to on a voluntary basis or made mandatory by port authorities. The best-known convention is the 1973
International Convention for the Prevention of Pollution from
Ships (MARPOL Convention), and its various annexes, protocols,
and amendments. For more information, see http://www.imo.org/
en/About/Pages/Default.aspx.

International Mediation Institute (IMI)   T 871

International Trade

International Wire Transfer See *Payment*

Interstate Commerce Commission   T 592

Invoice Discounting A method of *Supply Chain Finance (SCF)* in
which a bank uses *Accounts Receivable* of a supplier as collateral to
give a loan to the supplier to bridge the time until the supplier gets
paid by her customers. By contrast to *Factoring*, *Invoice Discounting* is done without disclosure to the customers in many jurisdictions, i.e., the supplier herself collects payment from the customers
and then repays the loan.

Inward Processing A process whereby goods are temporarily
imported for processing and subsequent re-exportation. Instead of
presenting the goods for customs clearance, the processing takes
place inside the bonded customs area or under another regime of
customs oversight. Since 100% of the processed goods are subsequently exported, the procedure avoids import and export processing and payment of customs duties. In essence, the processing
is treated as if it was happening offshore. If the importer is unsure
whether all imported goods are re-exported after processing, she
may be entitled to *Drawback* of customs duties, i.e., import duties
are initially paid but subsequently refunded for those goods that
are re-exported. See also *Outward Processing*

IRAC Method for the analysis and presentation of a case   T 53

Irrevocable Letter of Credit (L/C) A *Letter of Credit (L/C)* that cannot be changed or withdrawn or revoked without everyone involved agreeing (buyer, seller, and banks). Under the UCP 600, the default for an *L/C* is to be irrevocable (Article 3).

ISIN or **International Securities Identification Number** A unique identifier for a commercial paper, bond, guarantee, stock, warrant, etc. The ISIN has 12 digits as per ISO 6166.

Islamic Law   T 37, 116

Israeli Law   T 116–117

Issuing Bank The bank that issues a Letter of Credit (L/C) on behalf of the buyer of goods, i.e., the buyer's bank. The issuing bank will charge the buyer for the amount in the L/C plus its fees.

Iura Novit Curia The principle that the court knows the law to be   T 217
applied, even if the parties do not plead it (correctly).

Ius Cogens   T 33

Ius Commune Casebook Series   T 136

Jackson, John International trade lawyer, Ann Arbor and Washing-   T 31
ton, D.C.

JAMS Judicial Arbitration and Mediation Services   T 881, 958

JAMS Arbitration Discovery Protocols   T 992

Jones Act Protectionist U.S. legislation regarding maritime com-   T 550
merce requiring that passengers and cargo transported between
U.S. cities must be carried on U.S. made ships, owned by U.S. citizens, and staffed with U.S. crews. The Jones Act is included in Section 27 of the 1920 Merchant Marine Act (as amended). Under the
current version "only" 75% of the crew of the vessel have to be U.S.
citizens.

Judgment NOV A judgment *non obstante veredicto* reverses the out-   T 298–301,
come of a jury verdict.   398

Judicial Arbitration and Mediation Services (JAMS) Provider of
Alternative Dispute Resolution (ADR) services

Jurisdiction The power of a court or public authority to make deci-   T 28–32,
sions affecting one or more persons, for example because of their   699 et seq.,
nationality or whereabouts, is called *jurisdiction in personam*; the   759–767
power over a thing (real estate, aircraft, ship, etc.) or a subject matter (someone's status as a citizen, refugee, or married spouse, etc.)
is called *jurisdiction in rem*. Jurisdiction in private law should be

distinguished, but is related to jurisdiction in criminal law. In the latter case, jurisdiction of a particular state can be based on the *territoriality principle*, i.e., to regulate anything done within its territory (including the aircraft and ships flying its flag), as well as the *active personality principle*, i.e., to regulate anything done by its nationals, and the *passive personality principle*, i.e., to regulate anything done to its nationals. More recently, public international law has evolved to accept jurisdiction based on the *protective principle*, i.e., to regulate certain activities done outside the territory and by non-nationals but against national security, as well as *universal jurisdiction,* to regulate certain activities of common interest of humankind, for example against pollution or piracy committed on the high seas.

Just-in-Time Delivery

Keynes, John Maynard International economist, Cambridge

KfW IPEX A government agency providing export support and credit for German companies similar to the *Export-Import Bank of the U.S.*

Kleinheisterkamp, Jan International lawyer and arbitrator, Hamburg

Knock-Out Rule in contract formation

Kompetenz-Kompetenz The power or competence of a court or tribunal to decide whether it has *Jurisdiction* over a case brought before it, i.e., whether it is competent to hear and decide the matter.

Kröll, Stefan International lawyer and arbitrator, Hamburg

Kronke, Herbert International legal scholar, Heidelberg

KYC Procedures "Know Your Customer" requirements for financial institutions to combat tax evasion, money laundering, and organized crime. See also *AML Procedures*   T 424–425

Lando, Ole International legal scholar, Copenhagen   T 135, 143

Last Shot Rule in contract formation   T 178, 217

LCIA See *London Court of International Arbitration*

LCL Shipment "Less than container load" refers to a shipment of small volume and weight that needs to be consolidated with other LCL shipments into an "FCL" or "full container load." Since many carriers no longer accept *Break Bulk* cargo, such small shipments are kept behind until several can be consolidated for shipment to the same port of destination. For the exporter or shipper, it means slower transport and higher cost per unit.

Leased Bank Guarantee Enterprises apply to larger international banks for a leased bank guarantee if their own bank is either too small to finance a particular large transaction or expansion or if their own bank is no longer willing to extend additional credit. The issuing bank of the leased guarantee, after checking the creditworthiness of the applicant, sends it to the applicant's main bank, which then provides the funding against the additional security of the leased guarantee. Leased guarantees are expensive because the applicant typically does not have a long-standing business relationship with the issuing bank and/or already has exhausted the normal credit lines.

Legalization The process of authenticating or certifying an official document by adding a stamp or seal of the secretary of state or ministry of foreign affairs; this confirms to foreign authorities that the document is genuine and that the issuing authority acted within the laws of the country of origin.   T 828

Legal Privilege Also called professional privilege, protects communication between client and lawyer from disclosure, including in litigation or arbitration. Cf. §3.5.(c) Restatement of Int'l Commercial and Investor-State Arbitration; as well as Art. 9(2)(b) IBA Rules on the Taking of Evidence in Int'l Arbitration.   T 817

Letter of Credit A contract between the buyer of goods, the *Applicant*, and his bank, the *Issuing Bank*, pursuant to which the bank will pay the seller of the goods, the *Beneficiary*, against presentation of certain documents, as specified in the L/C. If the L/C is for payment, it requires the issuing bank or the bank who is nominated in the L/C or who is advising or confirming the L/C to honor a *Draft* presented with the L/C "on sight," i.e., immediately when the documents are presented by the beneficiary. If the L/C is for *Acceptance* within a specified time, the issuing bank will make the payment at a later date, usually at maturity of the draft, as long as this happens within the specified time. If the L/C is for *Negotiation*, the issuing bank will make the payment to a third party who presents the L/C and the required documents. See also *Advising Bank*, *Nominated Bank*, *Confirming Bank*, and *Negotiating Bank* — T 428–485

Amount	T 440
Availability	T 439, 441
Cost	T 441, 448
Discounting	T 473
Electronic L/Cs	T 449
Expiration	T 440
Governing law	T 445
Honoring and dishonoring	T 450–484
Independence	T 432
Strict compliance	T 433
Terms	T 436–445

Letter of Indemnity A document promising that certain contractual obligations will be met and that otherwise financial reparations will be made to compensate for any damages or liabilities. — T 471, 553

Letters Rogatory Formal requests from the authorities of one country to the authorities in another country for some form of judicial assistance, for example, service of process on a person domiciled in the other country. — T 751–752

Lex Fori A concept in choice of law or conflict of laws analysis pursuant to which the applicable law is that of the state or country where the court/the forum for the settlement of the dispute is located. — T 47, 52

Lex Loci A concept in choice of law or conflict of laws analysis pursuant to which the applicable law is that of the state or country where a transaction or incident took place (where a contract was formed or a tort was committed) or where property is located.

Lex Mercatoria See *UNIDROIT Principles*

Liability Limitations (in shipping contracts) See also *Hague Rules*, *Hague-Visby Rules*, as well as *COGSA* — T 563–588, 591

Liability Limitations (in sales contracts) — T 184

Liberty (or Voyage) Clauses Provisions in shipping contracts granting certain "liberties" to the carrier, for example to change the vessel or the route of a shipment, often without a requirement to even notify the *Shipper* or the *Consignee*. — T 567

Market Power See *Competition*

MARPOL Convention The International Convention for the Prevention of Pollution from Ships

Maturity Date The date on which a *Bond, Bill of Exchange*, or *Letter of Credit* becomes due for payment. There are essentially four possibilities: (i) at sight, i.e., immediately when presented; (ii) at a fixed period after sight, e.g., 30 days after it is presented; (iii) at a fixed date; and (iv) at a fixed period after a fixed date, e.g., 90 days after arrival of the goods.

T 522

Median Income versus average income

T 25

Mediation A method of *Alternative Dispute Resolution (ADR)* with the help of a neutral. The *Mediator* helps the parties understand their situation in fact and in law and reach a compromise or settlement. If the *Mediator* — with the agreement of the parties — has the power to make proposals for the resolution of the dispute, we speak of "evaluative mediation," although the terminology is not consistently used.

T 861–866,
870–879

Advantages of *Mediation* over litigation	T 863
Pre-conditions for successful *Mediation*	T 864–866
Procedure	T 873–874
Roles of the *Mediator*	T 872

Mediator See *Mediation*

Merchandise Processing Fee (MPF) Processing fee charged by the U.S. Customs and Border Protection Service (CBP) per shipment of goods. Standard rate is 0.3464% of customs value, with a minimum of $25 and a maximum of $485.

Mercosur Mercado Común del Sur

T 39, 44

Merger Clause See *Fully Integrated Agreement*

Mexico Convention on the Law Applicable to International Contracts

T 44 + D
I-48

Mezzanine Instrument A financial security that is supposedly irrevocable but in fact depends on some action or omission by the applicant. For example, if the documents required under a *Letter of Credit* include a confirmation of arrival or conformity from the buyer/applicant, the L/C is technically not irrevocable because the buyer/applicant can simply refuse to issue the confirmation. This places the value of the security somewhere between a mere *Comfort Letter* and a genuine *Letter of Credit* or *Demand Guarantee*.

Negotiable Instrument An instrument or *Financial Instrument* is a document, including an electronic document, containing an unconditional promise of payment of a specified sum of money. Examples are checks and money orders. Instruments are negotiable if they can be transferred by the recipient to a third party. Transfer is usually done by physically handing over the original (paper) document or by transferring an electronic version. If the instrument is made out to a named person, it will need an *Endorsement* by the named person to indicate consent to the transfer. UCC §3-104(b) defines an instrument as *Negotiable Instrument*, unless otherwise specified.

Negotiable Letter of Credit If a *Letter of Credit* is negotiable, the beneficiary, i.e., the seller of the goods, can transfer the L/C, and thus the right to receive payment, to a third party. This can be of interest for the beneficiary if she wants to sell the L/C to her bank, for example because it is not mature yet but the beneficiary needs money now, or if she is just an intermediary between a manufacturer and a buyer and uses the L/C to pay for her purchase from the manufacturer that is then sold onward to the buyer (see also *Back-to-Back Letter of Credit*). If the beneficiary transfers the L/C, she normally needs to endorse it. See also *Endorsement, Transferable Letter of Credit* and *Assignment of Credit*

Negotiation §3-201 UCC defines "negotiation" as the transfer of possession, voluntary or involuntary, of a negotiable instrument such as a *Bill of Exchange, Promissory Note* or *Check*, from one person to another. If the instrument is made out to a named person, negotiation requires *Endorsement*. If it is made out to bearer or to holder, it can be negotiated by mere transfer of possession to the new *Holder*.

Negotiating Techniques See also *Alternative Dispute Resolution (ADR)*   T 866–870

Negotiorum Gestio See *Pre-Contractual Liability*

Net 30, 45, 60, 90, 180 A payment term in a sales contract giving a period of time (30 days, 45 days, etc.) for payment "same as cash," i.e., a free credit extended by the seller.   T 535

Netting A system used between banks to set off numerous individual payments between different banks that cancel each other out and reduce the number of physical money transfers needed at the end of a business day.   T 417

Net Weight The weight of the goods without any packaging, pallets, container, etc. See also *Gross Weight*, as well as *Tare*

New Jason Clause A shipping contract clause, typically found in a *Bill of Lading*, pursuant to which the cargo owner has to contribute in the *General Average* even if the relevant loss of cargo was caused by negligence of the master, crew, or ship owner. A typical formulation might be "In the event of accident, danger, damage or disaster before or after commencement of the voyage, resulting from any cause whatsoever, whether due to negligence or not ... the goods, shippers, consignees or owners of the goods shall contribute with the carrier in general average to the payment of any sacrifices, losses or expenses of a general average nature that may be made or incurred . . ."

New Trade Theory   T 12

**New York Convention on the Recognition and Enforcement of   T 1015 +
Foreign Arbitral Awards**   D II-500

New York Stock Exchange   T 608

Nominated Bank When an L/C is issued, the *Issuing Bank* can either give it directly to the *Beneficiary*, i.e., the seller, or it can use an intermediate bank, usually a bank in the country or even city of the seller. If the intermediate bank merely authenticates the L/C and passes it on to the seller, it is an *Advising Bank*. If the intermediate bank is also entitled to receive the documents from the seller and, after confirming with the *Issuing Bank*, proceed to pay the seller, it is a *Nominated Bank*. If the intermediate bank accepts an independent obligation to pay under the L/C, regardless of getting reimbursed by the *Issuing Bank*, it is a *Confirming Bank*. While the *Advising Bank* is typically selected by the *Issuing Bank*, the *Nominated Bank* is selected by the *Beneficiary* and may or may not be the same as the *Advising* or *Confirming Bank*. If the *Beneficiary* nominates a different bank, this *Nominated Bank* will either just receive the *Bill of Lading* and other required documents from the *Beneficiary* and then forward them to the *Advising* or to the *Issuing Bank* for payment or it may make payment right away to the *Beneficiary* in the form of a loan secured by the L/C. This can be done "against seller's indemnity," which means the beneficiary/seller has to indemnify the *Nominated Bank* if it turns out later that there is a problem with payment coming from the *Issuing Bank*. Alternatively, the *Nominated Bank* can purchase the L/C from the *Beneficiary* and pursue payment from the *Issuing Bank* at its own risk. In the first case, the cost of the loan can be very low if the *Beneficiary* has a good credit score with the *Nominated Bank*. In the second case, the Bank will discount the amount available under the credit to account for any risk and its own expenses. Sometimes the *Nominated Bank* is also referred to as the *Collecting Bank*.

Non-Disclosure Agreement (NDA) T 87–95

Non-Recourse Factoring See *Factoring*

Nostro Account An account held by a bank in a foreign currency in another bank for the purpose of Set-Off and Netting; see also *Vostro Account*

Notation A note or clause on a *Bill of Lading* or other transport document that the cargo was not received in apparent good order or otherwise in accordance with the original agreement. A *BoL* with a *Notation* is usually not accepted as a *Clean Bill of Lading*.

Notice of Abandonment If a ship, cargo, or other asset is seriously damaged, it may be declared a *Constructive Total Loss*, i.e., a repair, while possible, would cost more than the value would justify. The insured party can then issue a *Notice of Abandonment* to the insurers, i.e., a total surrender of all rights to the ship and/or cargo. The insured part thereby declares its intention to have the incident treated as an actual total loss and claim the insurance accordingly. T 639, 647

Noting (on a *Bill of Exchange*) If a *Bill of Exchange* is *Dishonored*, the *Drawer* may need evidence to that effect. Noting is the presentation of the *Bill of Exchange* by a notary public to the *Drawee* for acceptance or payment. The notary public then confirms that the bill was *Dishonored* and the reasons provided by the drawee. See also *Protesting* by a notary public.

N.O.V. A judgment *non obstante veredicto* reverses the outcome of a jury verdict. T 298–301

Novation Replacement of one obligation with another, where the replacement is deemed to have satisfied the former obligation, e.g., refinancing of a debt. See also Restatement 2nd of Contracts, §§115, 280. T 539

NVOCC Non-Vessel Operating Common Carrier, see also *Common Carrier*

Office of Foreign Assets Control (OFAC) at the Treasury Department, involved in combat against tax evasion, money laundering, and organized crime. See also *AML Procedures* and *KYC Procedures* T 424–425

Oligopoly A market dominated by a small number of large economic actors. See also *Competition* T 18–24

Onboard Bill of Lading A BoL issued at the time of loading of the goods onto the transport vessel, confirming that the goods were not just received for shipment but already loaded onto the vessel (see Article 20(a)(ii) UCP 600). T 554

On-Deck Carriage See Case 5-5

Online Contracting See *Electronic Contracts*

Online Dispute Resolution (ODR)

Open Account A trading term between buyer and seller where the seller agrees to deliver goods to a buyer before payment is made and without any form of guarantee of payment.

Open Cover A cargo insurance contract for multiple shipments, usually on a time basis, e.g., the year 2020. By contrast, a contract could be made out for a single voyage or shipment.

Opportunity Cost The fact that assets, such as time or money, can only be used in one way at a time. Thus, using them in one way creates the *Opportunity Cost* of not having them available for another type of use at that time. This justifies, *inter alia*, charging interest on late payments since the creditor incurs the *Opportunity Cost* of not having the money due to her.

Option See *Currency Option*

Ordre Public Another way of referring to *Mandatory Rules of (Public) Law or Policy*

Organization of American States (OAS)

Origin Receiving Charge (ORC) A fee charged at the port of origin or departure for the handling of a shipping container.

Ostrom, Elinor International economist, Bloomington

Outward Processing A process whereby goods are temporarily exported for processing and subsequent re-importation. Normally, when processed goods are imported, customs duties have to be paid. However, if the parts or raw materials for the processing originate from inside the same country or customs union where the final processed goods are destined, the manufacturer may be able to benefit from Outward Processing, i.e., relief from import duties on the share of the final processed goods that have previously been exported. In general, outward processing regimes have to be submitted for prior authorization to be eligible for customs relief. See also *Inward Processing*

Over-the-Counter or **OTC trading** See *Bond*

P&I Club Protection & Indemnity Club, a kind of mutual insurance

Pace Law School CISG Database

Pacta Sunt Servanda Contractual promises must be honored.

Performance of Contractual Obligations											T 60–61

Performance Risk The risk that the buyer or seller will not complete the contract in accordance with their contractual obligations.

Perils of the Sea and insurance cover, see, *inter alia*, Case 5-6											T 667

Period of Presentation The time period during which the seller or *Beneficiary* can present a *Letter of Credit (L/C)* to the *Advising Bank*, the *Nominated Bank*, or the *Confirming Bank*. Within the scope of application of the UCP 600, this period is normally 21 days from the date of issue of the *Bill of Lading* or other transport document (Article 14(c)) but it can be shorter, if so stipulated in the *L/C*.

Permanent Court of Arbitration (PCA)											T 945

Personal Jurisdiction Based on e-commerce transactions											T 363

Personality Principle See *Jurisdiction*

P & I Coverage Insurance contract for protection and indemnity.											T 637 et seq., 647

PICC Principles of International Commercial Contracts See *UNIDROIT Principles*

Piketty, Thomas International economist, Paris											T 27

Pilferage Theft of small amounts of merchandise.

Planned Economy See *Socialist Economy*

Polo, Marco International trader											T 6

Port of Discharge (POD) Port or airport where goods are unloaded after main carriage. If the carriage involves transshipment, there can be several PODs until the final POD.											T 555, 557

Port of Lading (POL) Port or airport where goods are loaded for main carriage.											T 557

Port State Control An effort by developed countries at imposing minimal standards of environmental protection, labor laws, as well as health and safety regulations, on ships calling into their ports that are otherwise running under *Flags of Convenience* where similar standards do not apply.											T 548

Positive Interest After a breach of contract, the other side may have a right to be placed in the position it would be in if the party in breach would have performed as promised, which usually includes lost profits. By contrast, if compensation is limited to the *Negative Interest*, the other side will only receive expenses.											T 63

Post-Judgment Interest Compensation for the *Time Value of Money*   T 62
from the time a payment is confirmed in a judgment (or arbitral
award) until the time the payment is actually made.

Prague Rules on the Efficient Conduct of Proceedings in Interna-   T 994
tional Arbitration

Pre-Contractual Liability See also *Culpa in Contrahendo*   T 95–107

Preferential Trade Agreement (PTA) An agreement between two or
more countries pursuant to which their mutual trade relations
are done on a preferential basis, i.e., on terms better than those
granted to other countries. This is incompatible with the WTO
Most Favored Nation requirement in Article I of the GATT and
generally only allowed for *Free Trade Areas*, *Customs Unions*, or
certain developing countries.

Pre-Hearing Conference See *Case Management Conference*

Prejudgment Attachment of Assets An *Interim Relief* order securing   T 794
assets of the defendant.

Pre-Judgment Interest Compensation for the *Time Value of Money*   T 62, 664
from the time a payment was due until the time it is confirmed in
a judgment and the debtor is ordered to pay.

Preliminary Relief See *Injunction*

Preliminary Ruling Procedure (Article 267 TFEU) See *European
Court of Justice*

Preservation Order See *Injunction*

Presenting Bank In a *Documentary Collection*, the seller ask his bank,   T 520–523
the *Remitting Bank*, to work with a bank in buyer's country to col-
lect the purchase price on his behalf. The *Remitting Bank* sends the
controlling documents (*Bill of Lading* etc.) to the *Collecting Bank*,
asking that they release them to the buyer or buyer's representative
in exchange for a payment in cash (*CAD* or *D/P*) or by acceptance
of a *Bill of Exchange* (*D/A*). If the *Collecting Bank* is conveniently
located for the buyer, it also serves as *Presenting Bank*. Otherwise,
two banks in buyer's country will be involved: The *Collecting Bank*
has the business relationship with the *Remitting Bank*, and the
Presenting Bank is handling the transfer of the documents to the
buyer in exchange for payment.

Presentment Presentation of a Financial Instrument like a *Check*, *Bill
of Exchange*, or *Letter of Credit* with a demand for *Payment* or for
Acceptance. See also UCC §3-501.

Pre-Trial Discovery   T 753, 817–
819, 898

Price Takers/Price Makers in a market economy — T 13–16

Primary Claims In IBT law, there are generally five potential *Claim Bases* to be considered: Pre-contractual, contractual, torts, *Unjust Enrichment*, and property. Within these, *Primary Claims* are directed at *Performance* or even *Specific Performance* of the primary obligations of the parties under the IBT, i.e., delivery of the goods or services by the seller, and payment of the price by the buyer. If the primary performance is either no longer possible or insufficient to protect the other side, the primary claims can be replaced or supplemented by *Secondary Claims* for damages. In addition, parties may seek compensation for the *Costs of Dispute Settlement*, as well as *Interest*. — T 60

Principles of European Contract Law (PECL) — T 135

Principles of European Tort Law (PETL) — T 136

Principles of International Commercial Contracts (PICC) See *UNIDROIT Principles*

Principles of Latin American Contract Law (PLACL) — T 121

Private Carrier While a *Common Carrier* transports cargo for multiple customers, a *Private Carrier* is only working for a single client or only carrying her own goods.

Private Carriage In maritime trade this refers to a ship being leased in its entirety by one client, also known as a *Charterparty*. Compare to *Common Carrier* and *Common Carriage*.

Private International Law The term used in many countries for international conflicts of law. — T 40–47, 52, 695

Process Server See *Service* — T 751

Pro Forma Invoice — T 77–82

Promissory Note A written promise by an issuer to a payee that a specified amount of money will be paid on demand or at a given maturity date. While an IOU only contains an acknowledgment of a debt, a Promissory Note adds a specific promise that payment will be made at a given time. While a *Bill of Exchange* is a trilateral instrument usually involving a seller, a buyer, and a bank, a *Promissory Note* is just bilateral. Since *Promissory Notes* are negotiable *Financial Instruments*, the payee can sell them (at a discount) before the *Maturity Date*. The 1930 Geneva Convention Providing a Uniform Law for Bills of Exchange and Promissory Notes (D I-485) has been ratified by some 25 mostly European countries and successors to the USSR. See also *Demand Guarantee* — T 523

Prorogation An agreement between the parties to a dispute and, in particular, an appearance of both parties before a court where neither of them challenges the jurisdiction of that court, can create jurisdiction where it did not exist before.

T 701, 759–760

Protection and Indemnity Club (P&I Club) Traditional for-profit insurance companies offer marine cargo insurance and hull insurance only with a variety of exclusions. To cover any remaining risks, for example, war risks, environmental damage, etc., ship owners often band together in P&I Clubs, providing mutual risk sharing on a not-for-profit basis.

Protesting (a *Bill of Exchange*) If a *Bill of Exchange* is *Dishonored*, the *Drawer* may need evidence to that effect. Protesting is the presentation of the *Bill of Exchange* by a notary public to the *Drawee* for acceptance or payment. The notary public then issues a formal deed of protest with the notary's seal to confirm that the bill was dishonored and the reasons provided by the drawee. The protest is generally accepted by courts around the world as evidence that the Bill of Exchange was dishonored. See also the less formal procedure of *Noting*.

Provisional Relief See *Injunction*

Proximate Cause Test for compensation of consequential damages

T 184, 274

PTA See *Preferential Trade Agreement (PTA)*

Public Policy See *Mandatory Rules of (Public) Law or Policy*, as well as *Ordre Public*

Punitive Damages Compensation beyond actual losses of the injured party

T 61, 184, 828, 852, 856, 889, 910–911, 917, 1016

Purchase Order

T 82–87

Put Option When the owner of currency or stocks wants to hedge against unfavorable changes in value, she can agree with a potential buyer on the right but not the obligation to sell the currency or stocks at a given price at a future point in time or at any time before a given deadline. Thus, if the value develops favorably, she will hold on to the currency or stocks, but if it develops unfavorably, she can sell at a known price. See also *Call Option* and *Hedging*

Quasi-Contractual Liability See *Pre-Contractual Liability*

Quia Timet Injunction An *Interim Relief* order preventing certain   T 795
actions by the opposing party.

Race to the Bottom Relocation of economic activity to the coun-   T 20,
try or region with the lowest level of wages and/or regulatory   26–27
intervention.

Rajoo, Sundra International lawyer and arbitrator, Kuala Lumpur   T 879, 920

Ratification of agent statements and actions by principal   T 403–407

Ratification of an international treaty or agreement International
treaties or agreements are negotiated by representatives of the
participating countries until a compromise is reached and a text
is signed. However, they generally do not become binding on the
participating countries unless they are approved domestically. The
Ratification procedure to be followed — for example, the required
majority in parliament — is usually fixed in the national constitution and varies from one country to another.

Receivables Seller's future claims to payment from her buyers. Can   T 421, 534
be used to obtain the funding needed to purchase or make the
goods from a bank or *Factor*.

Received for Shipment Bill of Lading A BoL issued at the time when
the goods are received by the carrier but before they are loaded
onto the vessel. See also *Onboard BoL*

Red-and-Green Method for analysis of documents   T 55–56

Red Clause Letter of Credit A special provision in an L/C pursuant
to which the *Beneficiary*, i.e., the seller, can get an advance — usually 20–30% — from the *Advising Bank* without additional security, and even before all documents required under the L/C, like a
Clean Bill of Lading, are submitted. This kind of provision on an
L/C is usually written in red ink. The liability for default of the
Beneficiary is borne by the *Applicant*, i.e., the buyer, via the *Issuing
Bank*. In this way, the buyer gives an unsecured loan to the seller
who uses the money to buy the material and proceed with production. Alternatively, a *Green Clause Letter of Credit* can provide
advance payment for 50–75% of the L/C value to cover all costs of
production and storage up to shipment. Such a clause is usually
written in green ink. In both cases, buyer and seller need to have
a relationship of trust. Otherwise, the buyer/applicant may ask for
an *Advance Payment Guarantee* as security.

Redfern and Hunter on International Arbitration Leading textbook
on international commercial arbitration

Redfern, Alan International lawyer and arbitrator, London · T 955, 989, 992–994

Redfern Schedule for document production in international arbitration · T 993

Red Letter Clause A limitation of liability extending to any kind of claim — contract, tort, etc. — and any reason — including negligence — sometimes formulated as "from any cause whatsoever." To make an unusually broad limitation of liability effective, courts have often required the clause to be clear and unequivocal, hence the highlighting in red.

Reefer Load A refrigerated truck or container. · T 568

Reich, Robert International economist, Berkeley · T 25, 27–28

Reimann, Mathias International legal scholar, Ann Arbor · T 210

Relative Advantage/Disadvantage One of the reasons for trade. See also *Comparative Advantage/Disadvantage* · T 9

Release Declaration by a creditor that a debt or payment obligation is no longer being pursued. · T 538–539

Reliance Liability See *Pre-Contractual Liability*

Remitting Bank Seller's bank in a *Documentary Collection* · T 522

Renvoi A phenomenon, largely theoretical, in the domain of private international law. If an international case comes before the courts of one state, its private international law rules might stipulate that the law of another state should be applied, for example that a German court should apply Egyptian law. However, in analyzing the Egyptian law, the German court might find that for the case before it, Egyptian private international law would stipulate the application of German law. If the German court merely refers to Egyptian substantive law, it ends up having to apply a foreign legal system in which it is not well versed. If the German court refers to the entire Egyptian legal system, including Egyptian private international law, the Renvoi would lead it back to applying its own legal system. · T 148–149

Replevin A claim for property that was unlawfully taken. · T 206

Res Judicata · T 516, 702, 768, 784–787, 828, 848, 858, 999, 1034–1036

Resource Allocation by economic actors   T 13–20

Respondent The term commonly used in arbitration for the
defendant.

Respondentia A loan agreement where the cargo of a ship is used as   T 606
Collateral. By contrast, *Bottomry* refers to loan agreements using
the hull of the ship, the "bottom," as *Collateral*.

Rescission of a contract See *Avoidance*

Restatement 3rd of Agency (2006)

Restatement 2nd of Contracts (1981)   T 295–307
                                                                          + D I-199

Restatement 2nd of Conflict of Laws (1971)   T 698, 723

Restatement 3rd of Foreign Relations Law (1987) §§481, 482 deal   T 844–846
with recognition and enforcement of foreign judgments

Restatement of International Commercial and Investor-State Arbi-   + D II-512
tration (2019)

Retention of Title   T 253, 344

Reverse Factoring A form of *Supply Chain Financing (SCF)* in which
a bank pays suppliers on behalf of a (large) manufacturer who still
has to make the goods and sell them to be able to pay for the supplies. In exchange for payment, the bank acquires the accounts
receivable of the suppliers and later collects from the manufacturer. The bank calculates its fees and interest rates based on the
credit rating of the (large) manufacturer, rather than the smaller
suppliers, but the latter pay (at least part of) the fees and interest.

Revocable Letter of Credit (L/C) A revocable *Letter of Credit* can
be terminated at any time by the applicant, i.e., the buyer of the
goods. Since this does not provide security for the seller, revocable
L/Cs are rarely used nowadays and, in fact, were dropped from the
UCP during the move from UCP500 to *UCP600*. Contrary to earlier rules, therefore, the default is the irrevocable L/C and an L/C is
never revocable unless it explicitly says so.

Revolut international money transfer services   T 420

Revolving Letter of Credit A single *Letter of Credit (L/C)* that is used to make multiple payments over a longer period, typically up to one year. For example, the *L/C* can stipulate that up to US$75,000 can be drawn on a monthly basis for 12 months. A revolving *L/C* is cheaper than a series of regular *L/C*s and does not require the full amount of collateral — 12 times US$75,000 = US$900,000 in the example — on the side of the applicant. The revolving *L/C* can be cumulative, which means that an unused portion rolls over and can be used later, for example if the beneficiary draws only US$25,000 during one month and wants to make up for it later. This would be an exception to Article 32 UCP 600. Securing multiple payments over an extended period can also be achieved by using wire transfers as the payment method and securing them with a *Standby Letter of Credit*. The standby will often be cheaper than the *Revolving L/C* and the terms of the standby are often more flexible, for example with regard to live shipping documents etc.

Road Transport Document A kind of *Waybill* specifically for road transport, sometimes also referred to as a Truck Consignment Note or a *CMR Road Consignment Note*. By contrast to a *Bill of Lading*, the Road Transport Document is not a document of title. It merely confirms receipt of the goods by the carrier by a given date and reflects the terms of the carriage contract, in particular the shipper/exporter/seller, the consignee/importer/buyer, the origin and destination and the goods to be carried with their respective weight and markings, as well as the freight charges paid or to be paid. Road Transport Documents are usually issued in three copies, one for the shipper, one for the carrier, and one traveling with the goods. See Article 24 of the UCP 600.

Rotterdam Rules The 2008 UN Convention on Contracts for the International Carriage of Goods Wholly or Partly by Sea.

Said to Contain (STC) When the cargo is handed over to the Ship's Mate or the Master of the Ship, the *Bill of Lading (BoL)* is issued, including information about the type and quantity of cargo. With containerized cargo, the Mate or Master does not have access since containers are usually sealed. A notion of "STC" on the BoL protects the carrier in case the customs officials or the consignee on arrival find a different type or quantity of cargo, although the seals are unbroken.   T 561, 672

Sales Contract See *Contract of Sale*

Sanhuri, Abd El-Razzak Egyptian scholar who translated and adapted the French *Code Civil* into Arabic and laid the foundations for the Egyptian civil code, which was then adopted with limited modifications by most other Arab countries.   T 119, 720

Saudi Arabia Courts   T 720–721

SCF See *Supply Chain Financing*

Schlechtriem, Peter International legal scholar, Freiburg   T 188, 234, 288

Schmidt-Kessel, Martin Consumer law scholar, Bayreuth   T 280

Schreuer, Christoph International legal scholar and arbitrator, Vienna   T 947

Schwenzer, Ingeborg International lawyer and arbitrator, Basel   T 105, 108, 121, 128, 257

SDR See *Special Drawing Rights*

Sea Waybill A transport document much like a *Bill of Lading*. However, while the BoL fulfills three functions (receipt for the goods, shipping contract, and document of title) and is by default negotiable, the Sea Waybill is not negotiable and not a document of title. It is still a receipt for the goods and a shipping contract and can be issued electronically and sent as a pdf attachment via e-mail rather than sending multiple originals of a BoL by courier. A Sea Waybill is essentially the same as a *Straight Bill of Lading* or an *Express Bill of Lading*.   T 555–556

Secondary Claims for Damages In IBT law, there are generally five   T 60
potential *Claim Bases* to be considered: *Pre-Contractual*, con-
tractual, torts, *Unjust Enrichment*, and property. Within these,
Primary Claims are directed at *Performance* of the primary obligations of the parties under the IBT, i.e., delivery of the goods or
services by the seller, and payment of the price by the buyer. If the
primary performance is either no longer possible or insufficient
to protect the other side, the *Primary Claims* can be replaced or
supplemented by *Secondary Claims* for damages. In addition, parties may seek compensation for the *Costs of Dispute Settlement*, as
well as *Interest*.

Self-Executing Norms of International Law   T 36

Service In the context of litigation or arbitration, service is the formal   T 750–759
delivery of notifications to the *Defendant* or *Respondent*. Unless
service is effected in accordance with the rules applicable at the
place where it is attempted, it has no legal effects and, for example, does not make court proceedings pending or enable a court
to issue a *Default Judgment* if the defendant does not show up. See
also *Hague Convention on the Service Abroad of Judicial and Extrajudicial Documents in Civil and Commercial Matters*

Set-Off If parties have payment obligations against each other, they   T 536–538
can rely on *Set-Off* to satisfy at least part of the obligations. For
example, if B owes S US$100,000 for a purchase but S also has a
debt to B for US$25,000 for delays and other problems with the
delivery, B can *Set-Off* and transfer only US$75,000. Both obliga-
tions will be satisfied. See also CFR III.-6.101 et seq.

Set-Off and Netting See *Netting*   T 537

Sherman Act   T 29, 613,
                                                                                        900–910

Shipbroker A person or company acting as an independent broker
between cargo owners and carriers for the arrangement of carriage
by sea. A *Shipbroker* can also be the agent between a seller and a
buyer of a ship.

Shipper's Load, Stow and Count (SLAC) When the cargo is handed   T 561, 672
over to the Ship's Mate or the Master of the Ship, the *Bill of Lading*
(BoL) is issued, including information about the type and quantity
of cargo. With containerized cargo, the Mate or Master does not
have access since containers are usually sealed. A notion of "SLAC"

on the BoL protects the carrier in case the customs officials or the consignee on arrival find a different type or quantity of cargo, or the cargo is damaged inside the container due to unsuitable packing, as long as the seals are unbroken. "Shipper's Load and Count" or "Shipper's Weight, Load and Count" (UCC §7-301) have the same effect.

Shore Clause Insurance contract clause seeking to extend maritime cargo insurance to on-shore storage. See also *Warehouse-to-Warehouse Clause*   T 668, 677

Short Form Bill of Lading A BoL that includes references to external terms and conditions, such as general terms on the website of the carrier. By contrast, a *Long Form BoL* includes all terms and conditions on the document itself.

Shuttle Diplomacy A technique employed in *Alternative Dispute Resolution (ADR)* with the help of a neutral.   T 861–879

Sight Draft A *Bill of Exchange* or similar *Financial Instrument* for payment "at sight," i.e., immediately upon presentation. The opposite would be a *Time Draft* that has is payable only at a future *Maturity Date*.   T 441, 522

Sight Payment Payment "at sight" requires payment at the time a complying presentation of the required documents is made. In a *Letter of Credit* transaction, this will require the additional submission of a *Sight Draft*. The alternative to sight payment is payment at a later time, which requires a complying presentation plus submission of a *Time Draft*. See also *Maturity Date*   T 441, 522

Signature Authority The authority of a particular individual to sign a contract with a certain level of financial and actual commitments on behalf of her employer or principal. See also *Apparent Authority*   T 350

Silence as Acceptance   T 175

Singapore Convention on International Settlement Agreements Resulting from Mediation (2019)   T 874 + D II-127

SINOSURE A government agency providing export support and credit for Chinese companies similar to the *Export-Import Bank of the U.S.*   T 535

SLAC See *Shipper's Load, Stow and Count*

Slack Business communication platform

Sliding Scale Test for determining whether a court has jurisdiction over a company because its goods or services can be accessed online from the respective country — T 363

Smart Contract A software application that executes certain instructions, for example the release of the purchase price, when certain conditions have been confirmed, for example the delivery of the goods to the shipping company. Smart Contracts are usually secured on the *Blockchain*. — T 356, 410, 417, 420

Socialist Economy The term "socialism" is widely used, yet widely misunderstood. The textbook definition suggests that socialism is a system where the means of production and exchange are no longer privately owned but owned and regulated by the community as a whole. This, however, is (also) the definition of a *Communist Economic System*. By contrast, when politicians like Bernie Sanders are advocating policies to reduce inequality, they are usually promoting a system better referred to as a market economy with social features (protection of consumers, the environment, progressive taxation, etc.), sometimes also called a social market economy. Although the advocates of a social market economy would tax wealthy people at higher rates, they generally do not seek the expropriation or socialization of the means of production and exchange. Capitalists have used the bogeyman of "socialism" or "communism" for decades to discredit politicians fighting for greater equality and social justice and have, unfortunately, found many followers among those who stand to gain the most from a more social market economic model. — T 15–18

Socialist Legal Systems — T 116

Soiled Bill of Lading Sometimes also called a *Foul Bill of Lading*, this is the opposite of a *Clean Bill of Lading*, i.e., the shipper declares *not* having received the merchandise in good condition, for example because the packaging was damaged. These kind of declarations on a *Bill of Lading* are also called *Notations* or *Clauses*. In most cases, an L/C will require the presentation of a *Clean Bill of Lading* and the bank will *Dishonor* the L/C if a *Soiled Bill of Lading* is presented.

Sooksripaisarnkit, Poomintr International lawyer and arbitrator, Launceston — T 678

Special Drawing Rights (SDRs) A basket currency maintained by the IMF. — T 551

Specific Performance of contractual obligations refers to the primary obligations of the parties, e.g., delivery of the goods or services by the seller and payment of the price by the buyer. In case of a breach, the other side may have a claim to specific performance, or it may only have a claim to damages, or both.

T 60–62, 206

Spoilage See *Abnormal Spoilage*

Stale Bill of Lading A *Bill of Lading* presented more than 21 days after it was issued, therefore not valid for getting paid under the L/C (Article 14(c) UCP 600).

T 554

Standby Letter of Credit A *Guarantee* issued by a bank, on behalf of a buyer that protects the seller against nonpayment for goods shipped to the buyer. The buyer pays the seller directly for the goods, usually by *Wire Transfer*. Only if the buyer fails to pay, does the seller claim under the *Standby L/C*.

T 486–487

Statement of Claim The *Claimant* brief initiating arbitration proceedings and/or the revised brief after the *Terms of Reference* of the *Arbitral Tribunal* have been agreed upon. The final version is important because the tribunal will have to address all claims in it and cannot award anything that was not claimed in it.

Statute of Frauds

T 204, 380–387, 392–394, 397–403

Statute of Limitations

T 701, 750

STC See *Said to Contain*

Stiglitz, Joseph International economist, New York

T 25–26

Straight Bill of Lading A non-negotiable *Bill of Lading*, i.e., a BoL that is made out to a named *Consignee* and cannot simply be transferred to another person via *Endorsement*. By contrast, the right to claim the goods covered by a *Negotiable Bill of Lading* can be transferred to another person by the named beneficiary or consignee simply by signing in the back. A *Straight Bill of Lading* is often called a *Sea Waybill*, if it is just a receipt for the goods and a shipping contract and not also a document of title.

T 555

Straight Letter of Credit (L/C) By contrast to a *Negotiable Letter of Credit*, a *Straight Letter of Credit* is only redeemable by the named *Beneficiary*. See also more generally *Letter of Credit*

T 439

Strong, Stacie International lawyer and arbitrator, Sydney   T 833, 850, 879, 881

Study Group on a European Civil Code   T 136

Subpoena An order for a witness to appear at a particular time and place to testify, or for specific documents or other evidence to be produced in court or ADR procedures.

Subrogation Subrogation occurs when one person steps into the position of another, taking over her rights and obligations. For example, if A is injured by B and receives compensation from insurer C, any rights of A against B are subrogated to C and the insurer can now proceed against the tortfeasor B.

Substantial Performance versus fundamental breach and perfect tender rule   T 303

Subsumption The technique of drawing the facts of a case under the applicable rules to show how the rules have to be applied to the facts and the outcome mandated by these rules.   T 66

Suing and Labouring Clause A provision in maritime insurance contracts allowing the insured party to claim expenses from the insurer for minimizing or preventing imminent losses that would otherwise have occurred and have to be covered by the insurer. The clause usually covers only preventive measures, and not corrective or remedial measures, such as legal actions against third parties after the damage was done. See s. 78 1906 Marine Insurance Act (UK).

Supply Chain Financing (SCF) Financial arrangements in a chain of suppliers, manufacturer(s) and customers that provide everyone with liquidity for their operations before the end user actually pays for the goods. See also *Reverse Factoring*.   T 409

Supranational Law   T 33

Supremacy Clause of the U.S. Constitution   T 161

Surety A bank, insurance company or other person who accepts responsibility for the performance of a contractual or other obligation by a principal and promises to indemnify a beneficiary for the consequences of the nonperformance.

Surety Bond A promise by a surety or guarantor to pay a given amount to a beneficiary, for example a developer, if the principal, for example a contractor, fails to fulfill her contractual obligations.

Surface Transportation Board   T 592

Surrender Bill of Lading See *Bill of Lading*

Swap See *Currency Swap*

Syndicate In the insurance markets, a syndicate is a group of individuals sharing the risk of one or more insurance contracts too large to be secured by any one of them alone. Syndicates have managers and underwriters much like insurance companies but they are not incorporated, do not have legal personality, and the individual members have no liability obligations for each other.

SWIFT Society for Worldwide Interbank Financial Telecommunications   T 416–417, 424, 439, 454, 496–497

Takaful An Islamic alternative to insurance. Under Islamic law, speculative business transactions with uncertain outcomes are prohibited. In some interpretations, this would include various forms of insurance since it is uncertain whether or not the loss will occur. Instead of buying insurance from a third party, under Takaful, the bearer of risk becomes a member in a kind of mutual fund and shares the loss or profit of the fund. When a loss occurs, the fund can reimburse the injured party via a kind of charitable donation, which diminishes the profits of the fund. The fund also takes a fee for the administration of the assets before disbursing its remaining profits to its members.

Temporary Import Bonds (TIBs) When vessels, machines, or other property is imported duty-free on a temporary basis, for example for a trade fair or construction project, some countries demand security that the property will be exported at the end of the project and will not be sold or discarded domestically. *TIBs* or *Carnets* may be obtained from customs brokers or trade associations against a fee plus a deposit of security. The deposit will be reimbursed when the property is re-exported.

Tare The weight of packaging material and equipment traveling with the actual goods. This may include the rail car or truck, for example if a truck with a container, or with the goods on pallets, is put on a train.

Tariff The customs tariff of a country is the classification of goods pursuant to the *Harmonized System (HS)*, with the respective import duties of the country.

Term Bill of Exchange A *Bill of Exchange* with a future *Maturity Date.*   T 522
See also *Time Draft*

Terminal Usually refers to an area in the port where containers are
prepared before being loaded on a ship or stored after unloading
from a ship.

Termination of a contract See *Avoidance*

Terms of Payment See *Payment*

Terms of Reference for an arbitration   T 980–986

Territoriality Principle See *Jurisdiction*

Thaler, Richard International economist, Chicago   T 26

Third-Party Liability Insurance that (only) covers what the insured
party may have to pay in legal liability to unrelated third parties.
The insurer is the first party and the insured is the second party,
while the injured person is a third party and not a signatory to the
insurance agreement.

Threshold Reporting Obligations on financial institutions to report   T 425
international transactions of more than US$10,000 to support the
fight against tax evasion, money laundering, and organized crime.

Through Bill of Lading A *Bill of Lading* for end-to-end carriage from   T 556, 597
seller/shipper to buyer/consignee. See also *Straight Bill of Lading*
and *Multimodal Bill of Lading* See also UCC §7-302.

Time Draft A *Check, Bill of Exchange,* or other *Financial Instrument*   T 441, 522
that is payable at a specified time after it is received and accepted,
for example "90 days after sight." The delayed maturity works like
a short-term credit provided by the recipient to the issuer. The
recipient of a *Time Draft* can wait until maturity and get paid in
full or she can sell the *Time Draft* before the *Maturity Date* at a discount to get the bulk of the money sooner. In that case, the short-
term credit is provided by the bank (*Discounting Bank*) or third
party who purchases the time draft from the first recipient and
holds it until maturity.

Time Value of Money Having a certain sum of money today rather   T 62
than at some time in the future is considered a value in and of
itself. On the one hand, the owner could get *Interest* if the money
is in a savings account. On the other hand, the owner could invest
the money in a way that generates profit or pleasure. To compensate for the *Time Value of Money,* creditors are entitled to interest
for late payment by their debtors. See also *Opportunity Cost, Pre-
Judgment Interest,* and *Post-Judgment Interest*

TIV Total Insured Value

Torpedo Action to preempt litigation in an unfriendly forum T 193, 774

Total Loss An unforeseen event leading to the loss or destruction of the cargo or other insured object beyond recovery or repair. As a consequence, the entire insured amount will be paid by the insurer to the insured party, and the ownership and any other rights in the insured object are transferred to the insurer, who may or may not seek to recover damages from third parties and/or some of the value remaining in the object.

Toth, Orsolya International lawyer and arbitrator, Nottingham T 127

Trade Financing T 409

Trade Secrets T 86, 207

Tramp Service One or more ships running on flexible routes and schedules and available for one-time or irregular shipping needs. This is different from *Liner Shipping*, where the schedule and routes are fixed.

Transaction Costs T 12

Transferable Letter of Credit See *Negotiable Letter of Credit*

Transfer of Purchase Price See *Payment*

Transformation of international law into the domestic legal order T 37–38

Transshipment Pursuant to UCP 600 Article 20(b) on *Bill of Lading*, *Transshipment* is defined as "unloading from one vessel and re-loading to another vessel during the carriage from the port of loading to the port of discharge." A parallel provision is included in UCP 600 Article 19(b) for multimodal or combined transport documents, in Article 21(b) for nonnegotiable *Sea Waybills*, in Article 23(b) for air transport documents, and in Article 24 (d) for road, rail, and inland waterway transport documents. Pursuant to the UCP 600, *Transshipment* is usually acceptable even if the L/C prohibits *Transshipment*.

Transient Jurisdiction Although a case against a foreign person generally has to be brought in defendant court (the court at defendant's *Domicile*), some countries allow additional contact points for the establishment of jurisdiction over a foreign person. One of the most far-reaching is *Transient Jurisdiction*, established by serving a court order on a defendant who is temporarily present in a jurisdiction, for example during a business- or holiday trip. T 719, 722, 856

Transportation Security Administration (TSA) T 589

Tripodi, Leandro International legal scholar, São Paolo   T 217

TRIPS WTO Agreement on Trade Related Intellectual Property Rights   T 39

Truck Consignment Note See *Road Transport Document*

Tuna Dolphin Dispute   T 31

Uberrimae Fidei The doctrine of *uberrimae fidei* — literally *Utmost Good Faith* — requires a party seeking marine (cargo) insurance to disclose to the insurance company at the time when the contract is to be signed all circumstances known to it that materially affect the risk (*Knight v. U.S. Fire Ins. Co.*, 804 F.2d 9, 13 (2d Cir. 1986))   T 622–628, 631, 678–689

UCC The Uniform Commercial Code is being developed by a joint committee of the American Law Institute and the Uniform Law Commission. Draft legislation is proposed to state legislatures for debate and adoption. Several Articles of the UCC are included in the Documents Collection.   D I-145 and I-581

Battle of forms	T 230–237
Formation of contracts	T 171–184 and 228–237
Funds transfers (Article 4A)	T 426–427
History	T 120
Implied warranties	T 229
Letters of credit (Article 5)	T 430
Parol Evidence	T 229
Perfect tender rule	T 296
Performance and nonperformance	T 295–316
Usages	T 229

UCP600 The Uniform Customs and Practice for Documentary Credits are rules for international letters of credit suggested by the *International Chamber of Commerce* and chosen by virtually all commercial banks around the world.   T 50, 429 + D I-500

Umbrella Coverage An insurance policy covering liabilities not otherwise covered by specific insurance. For example, cargo and hull insurance do not cover injury to third parties in a collision. Umbrella coverage does.

UN The United Nations, an intergovernmental organization and important producer of international conventions and international "soft law" based in New York.

situation is the delivery of goods and/or payment of the purchase price where the contract is either invalid from the start or successfully avoided later. The typical remedy is restitution of the unjust enrichment to the rightful holder or owner. — 191, 261–263, 432, 494

Usage of Trade — T 301

USMCA The United States-Mexico-Canada Free Trade Agreement, successor to *NAFTA* — T 39

Utmost Good Faith Sometimes also referred to by the Latin term *Ueberrima Fidei* (utmost good faith). Refers to the mutual obligation of the parties negotiating an insurance contract to give all relevant information and to disclose all elements of risk.

Vacatur of an arbitral award — T 292

Venue See *Jurisdiction*

Vienna Convention on International Sale of Goods See *CISG*

Vischer, Frank Private international lawyer and international arbitrator, Basel — T 46

Vis Major See *Force Majeure*

Vogenauer, Stefan International lawyer, Frankfurt — T 107, 121, 129

Vostro Account An account held by a bank on behalf of another bank for purposes of *Set-Off and Netting;* see also *Nostro Account*

Warehouse-to-Warehouse Clause Insurance contract clause seeking uninterrupted cover from seller's premises to buyer's premises, including multimodal transport and handling in between. — T 673, 677

Warsaw Convention for the Unification of Certain Rules Relating to International Carriage by Air — T 589 + D I-721

Waybill Generic term to cover different transport documents, for example an *Air Waybill*, a *Sea Waybill*, a *Road Transport Document*, or a *Rail Transport Document*. By contrast to a traditional maritime *Bill of Lading*, a waybill is neither a contract of carriage, nor a document of title. Thus, a waybill typically travels with the goods and identifies the shipper/exporter/seller, the consignee/importer/buyer, the goods themselves, their origin and destination, as well as weight and other identifiers, and the freight charges paid or to be paid. Since *Waybills* are not documents of title, they can also be issued electronically and sent as pdf attachments to e-mails from the seller/shipper to the buyer/consignee.